REFERENCE

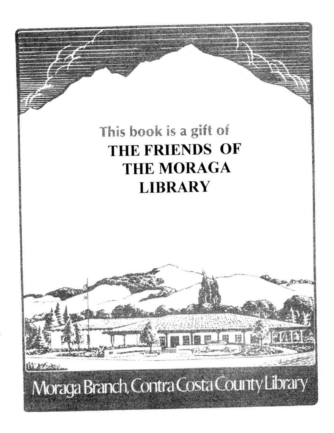

THE LIBRARY OF CONGRESS

CIVIL WAR
DESK REFERENCE

✶ ✶ ✶

Margaret E. Wagner, Gary W. Gallagher, and
Paul Finkelman, Editors

Foreword by James M. McPherson

A Grand Central Press Book
Simon & Schuster
NEW YORK   LONDON   TORONTO   SYDNEY   SINGAPORE

SIMON & SCHUSTER
Rockefeller Center
1230 Avenue of the Americas
New York, NY 10020

GRAND CENTRAL PRESS is a division of The Stonesong Press, Inc.

SIMON & SCHUSTER and colophon are registered trademarks
of Simon & Schuster, Inc.

For information regarding special discounts for bulk purchases,
please contact Simon & Schuster Special Sales:
1-800-456-6798 or business@simonandschuster.com

Designed by Helen Berinsky

Manufactured in the United States of America

10 9 8 7 6 5 4 3 2 1

Library of Congress Cataloging-in-Publication Data

The Library of Congress Civil War desk reference / Margaret E. Wagner, Gary
W. Gallagher, and Paul Finkelman, editors ; foreword by James M. McPherson.
      p. cm.
      "A Grand Central Press book."
      Includes bibliographical references and index.
      1. United States—History—Civil War, 1861–1865. 2. United States—History—Civil
War, 1861–1865—Chronology. I. Gallagher, Gary W. II. Finkelman, Paul. III. Title.
E468 .58 2002   973.7—dc21   2002075465

ISBN 0-684-86350-2

ACKNOWLEDGMENTS

A volume of this magnitude and complexity is, necessarily, a collegial effort. In addition to the editors, writers, advisers, and contributors to the book whose names are listed elsewhere, the Library of Congress thanks the following members of the Library's staff for their guidance and inspiration in the preparation of this volume: Harry Katz, Head Curator, Prints and Photographs Division, whose knowledge of the work of the Civil War's special artists and the popular art of the period guided development of "The Civil War in Literature and the Arts"; Mary Ison, Head of the Prints and Photographs Division Reference Section, who provided expert advice in the selection of illustrations for this volume; John Sellars of the Manuscript Division, compiler of the excellent written guide to that division's many Civil War collections; Clark Evans, Rare Book and Special Collections Division, ever-ready to answer questions on the division's extensive Lincolniana, Broadside, and Confederate Imprint collections; and John Hébert, Ronald Grim, Kathryn Engstrom, Ed Redmond, and the staff of the Geography and Map Division.

The assistance, via e-mail, of Bertil Haggman of Helsingborg, Sweden, who provided helpful information on Civil War guerrilla and partisan activity, is much appreciated. Edward Furgol, curator, the Navy Museum, the Naval Historical Center, provided detailed answers to questions about the war on the water. And the Library is deeply indebted to Publishing Office consultant Vincent Virga for his advice, support, and encouragement throughout the development of this volume.

Finally, the Library of Congress and Grand Central Press greatly appreciate the assistance of editor Bob Bender at Simon & Schuster, under whose guidance the text of this complex volume was honed and refined to its present shape. His assistant, Johanna Li, was always ready with answers to queries and with essential information that kept the editing and production process on track. This book would not have been possible without them.

For Sergeant Josiah Chaney of the Union Army,
and the many Civil War soldiers and civilians,
who, like him, endured the agonies of war,
as Sergeant Chaney wrote,
"for the sake of the country's millions
who are to come after us."

CONTENTS

FOREWORD: JAMES M. MCPHERSON   xvii

PREFACE: JAMES H. BILLINGTON, THE LIBRARIAN OF CONGRESS   xxi

ABOUT THE EDITORS   xxiii

CONTRIBUTORS   xxv

1. CIVIL WAR TIME LINE   1
    Time Line   3
    Sources   52

2. ANTEBELLUM AMERICA   53
    A Constitutional Problem   55
    Antebellum Time Line   57
    One Country, Two Cultures   69
        Demographics   69
        Immigration   72
        Economic Growth   73
        History of Slavery in America   77
        Religion and Reform   81
        Education and Culture   88
    The Rift Widens   90
        States' Rights   90
        Manifest Destiny   92
        Slavery Issues   93
    Compromise and Crisis   106
        The Missouri Compromise   106
        The Nullification Crisis   107
        The Mexican War (1846–1848)   108
        The Compromise of 1850   109
        The Kansas-Nebraska Act   111

Scott v. Sandford (The Dred Scott Case)	113
The Lincoln-Douglas Debates	115
John Brown and Harpers Ferry	118
Political Parties and Organizations	119
American Anti-Slavery Society	119
American Colonization Society (ACS)	120
American Party (Know-Nothings)	120
Constitutional Union Party	121
Democratic Party	121
Free Soil Party	122
Liberty Party	122
New England Emigrant Aid Company	122
Republican Party	123
Whig Party	124
The 1860 Election	124
Notable Antebellum Figures	127
Selected Resources	137
3. WARTIME POLITICS	**139**
Political Time Line, 1861–1866	143
Creation of the Confederate Government	160
The U.S. and Confederate Constitutions	162
Political Parties, Organizations, and Movements	164
Civil War Government Officials: United States of America	170
Civil War Government Officials: Confederate States of America	178
Other Notable Political Figures	186
Wartime Governors	191
United States of America Governors	196
Confederate States of America Governors	200
European Powers and the American Civil War	201
The Quest for Recognition	202
The Cotton Embargo	204
Erlanger Loan	204
Impressment of Foreign Citizens	205
Mexico	206
Confederate Recognition Denied	207
Suspension of the Writ of Habeas Corpus	207
Emancipation Proclamation	210
The Gettysburg Address	214
Black Emigration and Colonization	215
Securing Rights for Blacks in the Union	216
Voting Rights	217
Discrimination and Segregation	218
The Black Press	219
Service in the Union Army	219

Wartime Elections 220
    1862 U.S. Election 220
    1863 Confederate Election 220
    1864 U.S. Political Platforms 221
    1864 U.S. Election 223
Newspapers: The Politics of the Press 224
Abraham Lincoln's Second Inaugural Address 228
The Assassination of Abraham Lincoln 230
Selected Resources 232

4. BATTLES AND THE BATTLEFIELD **233**
The Theater of War 236
    The Eastern Theater 236
    The Western Theater 237
    Other Theaters of Operation 237
Significant Civil War Campaigns and Battles 239
    1861 242
    1862 249
    1863 274
    1864 293
    1865 320
Civil War Strategy 332
    National Objectives 332
    Military Strategy—United States 333
    Military Strategy—Confederate 337
Battle Tactics 339
    Typical Movement of Infantry 342
    Use of Cavalry 342
    Portents of Modern War 343
The Importance of Maps 345
    Union Mapping 345
    Confederate Mapping 346
    Mapping on the Move 347
Toward Modern War: Logistics and Communication 349
    Military Railroads 350
    Telegraph 353
    Signal Corps/Wig-Wag Signaling 358
    Military Aeronautics 362
Selected Resources 365

5. THE ARMIES **367**
Civil War Land Forces: General Organization 374
Civil War Armies: United States of America 376
    Army of Northeastern Virginia 379
    Army of the Potomac 379

Army of the Southwest (Army of Southwest Missouri)   380
Army of the Mississippi (1862 and 1863)   380
Army of Virginia   381
Army of the Frontier   382
Army of the Tennessee   382
Army of the Cumberland   383
Army of the Ohio (1861–1862 and 1863–1865)   384
Army of the James   385
Army of the Shenandoah   386
Army of Georgia   386
Civil War Armies: Confederate States of America   387
Army of Northern Virginia (Army of the Potomac)   390
Trans-Mississippi: District, Department, and Army   391
Army of Tennessee   392
Army of Vicksburg (Army of the Department of Mississippi and
East Louisiana)   393
Civil War Military Leadership   393
Civil War Generals—Union   393
Civil War Generals—Confederacy   398
Notable Civil War Officers   399
Commanders in Chief   399
Generals in Chief   401
Notable Officers   404
Fighting on Two Fronts: Black Soldiers in the Civil War   427
Early Struggles: 1861–1862   427
A Pivotal Year: 1863   430
Accomplishments and Tragedies: 1864   434
Peace and the Continuing Struggle for Recognition: 1865
and Beyond   437
Notable Special Units and Services   438
Aeronauts   438
Cavalry   438
Chaplains   438
Espionage/"Secret Service"   441
Invalid Corps/Veteran Reserve Corps   441
Marine Corps (Confederate and Union)   442
Mississippi Marine Brigade   442
Musicians   443
Sharpshooters   445
Signalmen/Telegraphers   445
Women Soldiers   445
Shadow Warriors: Partisan Rangers, Guerrillas, and Spies   447
Secret Service   452
Other Figures in the Secret Service   456

Army Life   461
  Decision   462
  Enlistment   463
  Conscientious Objection   464
  Training   465
  On the Move   466
  Pastimes—Sanctioned   468
  Pastimes—Unsanctioned   469
  Victuals   470
  Battle and Aftermath   472
  Visitors   474
  Mail Call   475
  Picket Duty: Eyeing the Enemy   476
  Desertion   477
  Perseverance   479
  Under God   480
  Courage and Sacrifice   481
Selected Reources   483

6. WEAPONRY   **485**
Repeating Rifles   494
Small Arms: Carbines and Musketoons   496
  How Soldiers Fired Rifle-Muskets and Repeaters   498
Small Arms: Pistols and Revolvers   498
Swords and Sabers   500
Making Gunpowder   501
War Rockets and Hand Grenades   502
Common Artillery Pieces   503
  Light Artillery   504
  Heavy Artillery   505
Artillery Projectiles   508
  How the Big Guns Were Fired   509
Some Notable Figures in Civil War Weaponry   510
Ordnance Glossary   512
Selected Resources   519

7. THE WAR ON THE WATER   **521**
Naval Events Time Line   524
Organization of Union and Confederate Navies   537
  United States Navy   537
  Confederate States Navy   540
Navy Yards and Stations   543
  Principal U.S. Navy Yards   543
  Principal C.S.A. Navy Yards and Stations   543

The Blockade   543
    The Operational Organization of the Blockade   548
    The British Presence in the Naval War   551
Ironclads   552
    A Telling Clash of Ironclads: The C.S.S. *Atlanta* versus
        the U.S.S. *Weehawken*   553
    Notable Ironclads   555
    Union Coastal Ironclads   555
    Union River Ironclads   558
    Confederate Ironclads   560
Commerce Raiders   563
The Evolution of the Submarine: The C.S.S. *Hunley*   565
Naval Mines or Torpedoes   567
Sailors   568
Marines in the Civil War   572
Notable Naval Figures   574
Selected Resources   581

8. PRISONS AND PRISONERS OF WAR   **583**
Principal United States and Confederate States Military Prisons   587
Time Line of Significant Events   596
Prisoner Exchange and the Dix-Hill Cartel   600
Major Prisoner-of-War Camps   604
    United States of America   604
    Confederate States of America   608
The Press, Published Reports, and Public Opinion   612
Prison Escapes   616
The *Sultana* Disaster   617
Selected Biographies   619
Selected Resources   622

9. MEDICAL CARE AND MEDICINE   **623**
Medical Care in the Nineteenth Century   625
General Hospitals   627
Field Hospitals and Hospital Trains and Ships   629
Federal Ambulance Corps   631
Amputation   634
Naval Medical Care   635
Medical Care for U.S. Colored Troops   637
Causes of Disease   638
Common Diseases and Infections   643
Medical Drug Supplies   651
Medical Officers   652

United States of America 652
Confederate States of America 653
Leaders in Civil War Medicine 654
United States of America 654
Confederate States of America 656
Female Nurses 657
Relief Organizations 661
United States of America 661
Confederate States of America 662
Selected Resources 664

10. THE HOME FRONT 665

Economic Conditions and Their Effects 668
The Southern Economy 668
The Northern Economy 672
Agriculture 673
Immigration, Homesteading, and Discrimination in the North 676
Education 679
The South 679
The North 683
The Bulwark of Religion 685
Religion in the Confederacy 687
Religion in the North 688
Recruitment of Soldiers 690
Conscientious Objectors 695
Volunteer Aid Societies 699
Women on the Home Front 701
Women in the Confederacy 701
Women in the Union 705
Postal Service 710
Patriotic Expressions and Home Front Celebrations 712
The Confederacy 712
Slave Celebrations and Emancipation 713
The Union 714
Civil War Flags: So Proudly Hailed 716
Riots 718
The South 718
The North 719
Refugees and Evacuations in the South 721
White Southerners 721
Contrabands/Freedmen 724
Notable Home Front Figures 726
Selected Resources 730

11. RECONSTRUCTION AND THE AFTERMATH OF THE WAR   731

Time Line of Notable Reconstruction Events   735
The South and North in the Aftermath of the War   743
Civil War Veterans and Pensions   745
African Americans during Reconstruction   747
Major Issues of Reconstruction   750
    Land   750
    Labor   753
    Education   754
    Black Civil Rights   756
    Black Suffrage   757
    Confederate Disenfranchisement and the Right to Hold Office   758
Wartime Reconstruction   759
    South Carolina Sea Islands   760
    Louisiana and the Mississippi Valley   761
    The Proclamation of Amnesty and Reconstruction, and
       the Wade-Davis Bill   762
    Coastal Georgia and South Carolina   763
Thirteenth Amendment   763
Presidential Reconstruction   764
Black Codes   766
Fourteenth Amendment   767
Congressional Reconstruction   770
The Impeachment of President Andrew Johnson   772
Bureau of Refugees, Freedmen, and Abandoned Lands   774
Fifteenth Amendment   778
Southern Governments under Republican Rule   779
Violence in the South   784
The North and West during Reconstruction   788
The End of Reconstruction   792
Notable Figures of the Reconstruction Era   797
Selected Resources   804

12. THE CIVIL WAR IN LITERATURE AND THE ARTS   805

Popular Art   806
    Some Outstanding Popular Art Publishers of the Civil War Era   808
Photography   811
    Some Notable Civil War Photographers   813
Civil War Artists and the Rise of Illustrated News   816
    Notable Illustrated Journals of the Civil War   819
    Some Notable Artist-Correspondents and Soldier-Artists
       of the Civil War   820
The War in Art: Civil War Paintings   826
    Some Notable Civil War-Era Artists   828

Civil War Sculpture 830
    Richmond, Virginia 832
    Washington, D.C. 834
Literature 836
    Some Notable Nineteenth-Century Civil War Novels 837
    Some Notable Twentieth-Century Civil War Novels 839
Civil War Poetry 843
    Some Notable Poets and Poems of the Civil War after 1865 845
Civil War Music 849
The Drama of the War, Revisited: On Stage, Screen, and Television 853
    On Screen 854
    Made for Television: Notable Movies, Series, and Documentaries 856
Selected Resources 857

13. STUDYING THE WAR: RESEARCH AND PRESERVATION **859**
Important Published Resources on the Civil War 860
    General Reference 860
    General Histories 862
    The Union 863
    The Confederacy 864
    The Military 865
    African Americans and the Civil War 867
    Women and the Civil War 869
    Abraham Lincoln 869
    Biographies, Autobiographies, and Personal Narratives 870
    Aftermath and Reconstruction 872
    Guides: Battlefields and Monuments 873
    University Presses and the Civil War 874
    Specialty Presses with Civil War Emphasis 875
    Commercial Presses that Publish Numerous Civil War Titles 875
    Civil War Periodicals 875
    Audio and CD-ROM Publications 876
Major Artifact and Archival Collections 877
National Historic Sites 887
Organizations: Battlefield Preservation 898
Civil War Soldiers and Sailors 900
Organizations: Descendants of Civil War Veterans 900
Living History: Civil War Reenactment 904
Organizations: Civil War Round Tables 905
Civil War Continuing Education Programs 905

INFORMATION ABOUT IMAGES **909**

INDEX **911**

FOREWORD

The Civil War was the most dramatic, violent, and fateful experience in American history. At least 620,000 soldiers lost their lives in that war—2 percent of the American population at the time. If 2 percent of the American people were to be killed in a war fought in the early twenty-first century, the number of American war dead would be 5.5 million. An unknown number of civilians also died in the Civil War—from disease or hunger or exposure brought on by the disruption and destruction of the war in the South. More Americans were killed or died in this war than in all of the other wars, combined, that the United States has fought. The number of casualties in one day at the battle of Antietam (September 17, 1862) was nearly four times the number of American casualties on D-Day, June 6, 1944. Twice as many people were killed and mortally wounded than were killed by the terrorist attacks on the United States on September 11, 2001. Indeed, the number of battle deaths in one day at Antietam exceeded the total battle deaths in all the other wars the United States fought in the nineteenth century: the War of 1812; the Mexican-American War; the Spanish-American War; and the Indian wars.

How did this happen? Why did Americans go to war against each other with a ferocity unmatched in the Western world between the end of the Napoleonic Wars in 1815 and the outbreak of World War I in 1914? From the beginning of the Republic, the institution of slavery in this boasted land of liberty had divided Americans. By the 1830s, militant abolitionists in the North and equally militant proslavery spokesmen in the South were engaged in a war of words that foreshadowed the war of bullets that would begin a generation later. The annexation of Texas in 1845 and the acquisition of one-half of Mexico in 1848 intensified the debate by layering the issue of the expansion of slavery on top of the argument about its morality where it already existed. Slavery, said Abraham Lincoln on numerous occasions, was an institution "founded on both injustice and bad policy.... There CAN be no MORAL RIGHT in the enslaving of one man by another.... The monstrous injustice of slavery deprives our republican example of its just influence in the world—enables the enemies of free institutions, with plausibility, to taunt us as hypocrites." Yet, like most Northerners, Lincoln recognized the constitutional legitimacy of slavery in the states where it existed. To prevent this evil from growing larger, however, and to place it on the road to "ultimate extinction" by the hoped-for eventual voluntary action of Southerners themselves, Lincoln—and the Republican party he helped found in the 1850s—pledged to prohibit slavery in all the territories before they became states.

In 1860, Lincoln won the presidency on a platform containing such a pledge. "A house divided against itself cannot stand," Lincoln had said two years earlier. "I believe this government cannot endure, permanently half *slave* and half *free*." Lincoln looked forward to the time, in what he hoped would be the not-distant future, when it would become all free. Now he was president-elect. For the first time in more than a generation, the South had lost effective control of the national government. Southerners saw the handwriting on the wall. The North had a substantial and growing majority of the American population. So long as slavery remained a divisive issue—so long as the United States remained a house divided—the antislavery Republican party would probably control the national government. And most Southerners believed that the "Black Republicans"—as they contemptuously labeled the party of Lincoln—would enact policies that would indeed place slavery on the road to "ultimate extinction."

Fearing such a consequence if they remained in the Union, the seven cotton states of the Deep South seceded, one after another, during the winter of 1860–1861. Several other slave states teetered on the edge of secession. Before Lincoln took office in March 1861, the seven seceded states formed the Confederate States of America. They took over almost all of the Federal property within their borders, with the conspicuous exception of Fort Sumter in Charleston Harbor. Confederate guns opened fire on the fort on April 12, 1861, and forced its capitulation a day later. Lincoln called out the militia to suppress an "insurrection." Four more slave states seceded.

These events transformed the principal issue of the sectional conflict from the future of slavery to the survival of the United States as one nation. Lincoln and most of the Northern people refused to accept the legitimacy of secession. "The central idea pervading this struggle," said Lincoln in May 1861, "is the necessity that is upon us, of proving that popular government is not an absurdity. We must settle this question now, whether in a free government the minority have the right to break up the government whenever they choose." Four years later, looking back over the bloody chasm of war, Lincoln said, in his Second Inaugural Address, that one side in the controversy of 1861 "would *make* war rather than let the nation survive; and the other would *accept* war rather than let it perish. And the war came."

What was accomplished by the terrible carnage and destruction of the Civil War? Northern victory in 1865 resolved two fundamental, festering problems left unresolved by the Revolution of 1776 and the Constitution of 1789. First was the question of whether the United States would survive as a republic and as a nation. Could this fragile experiment in republican government endure in a world bestrode by kings, queens, emperors, czars, and dictators? Americans were painfully aware that most republics throughout history had been overthrown from without or had collapsed from within. Some Americans still alive in 1861 had seen French republics succumb twice to emperors and once to the restoration of the Bourbon monarchy. Republican governments in Latin America seemed to come and go with bewildering frequency. Would the United States suffer the same fate? Many Americans feared so; many European monarchists and aristocrats hoped so; disunion in 1861 seemed to confirm these fears and fulfill these hopes. As Lincoln said at Gettysburg in 1863, the Civil War was the great test of whether a republic with a government of, by, and for the people would endure or would perish from the earth. The United States in 1865 passed the test. The Civil War preserved the Republic as one nation, indivisible. Since 1865, no state or region has seriously threatened to secede.

The other problem left unresolved by the Revolution and the Constitution was slavery. Founded on a declaration that all people are endowed with the unalienable right of liberty, the United States became the largest slaveholding country in the world, with 4 million slaves—one-eighth of the population—in 1861. Over the next four years, the war to preserve the Union from destruction by a rebellion undertaken to defend slavery became, inexorably, a war to destroy slavery in order to save the Union. The Emancipation Proclamation and the Thirteenth Amendment to the Constitution made the United States truly a land of the free.

Little wonder that the Civil War had a profound impact that has echoed down the generations and remains undiminished today. That impact helps explain why at least 50,000 books and pamphlets (some estimates go as high as 70,000) on the Civil War have been published since the 1860s. Most of these are in the Library of Congress, along with thousands of unpublished letters, diaries, and other documents that make this depository an unparalleled resource for studying the war. From these sources, the editors of *The Library of Congress Civil War Desk Reference* have compiled a volume that every library, every student of the Civil War—indeed, everyone with an interest in the American past—will find indispensable.

Several reference works on the Civil War are in print. But this one is unique in format and contains material unavailable in any other. Instead of alphabetical entries, *The Library of Congress Civil War Desk Reference* is organized topically by chapters. It can, therefore, be read as a narrative and thematic history of the war. At the same time, a reader interested in a specific item (a battle or information on a political activist) can go to the index or to the detailed subheadings in the table of contents, or to cross-references within the articles, to find, quickly and easily, the information he or she is seeking. The detailed time lines of important events in the opening chapter and in several other chapters are a unique feature of great value. Chapter 2 on the antebellum period and Chapter 11 on the Reconstruction era are also novel features that place the war in its broader context, without which the events of 1861–1865 cannot be fully understood.

Another characteristic makes this a special volume: the amount of attention given to important developments that are ignored or receive short shrift in other reference works. A few examples, among many that could be mentioned, are the contributions of topographical engineers and the advances in map-making; logistics and communications, especially via the telegraph and the initiation of military signal corps; developments in surgery and medical care; Civil War photography; and popular contemporary and later literature about the war. Numerous quotations from Civil War participants, both famous and obscure, enrich the text.

The reader should not merely accept my word about the quality of this book. Turn to the table of contents, or the index; look up something you are interested in, and then turn to the pages where it is discussed. You will be impressed. And soon you will be hooked. Your knowledge and understanding of this greatest of American wars will expand and deepen more than you thought possible from a single volume.

James M. McPherson

PREFACE

"The world has never had a good definition of the word liberty," Abraham Lincoln said early in 1864. "And the American people just now are much in want of one." Three years earlier, vast differences in regional development and varied interpretations of America's Revolutionary ideals had drawn the American people into the horrors of a long, fratricidal war. Sundering families, destroying friendships, and taking, eventually, more than 620,000 lives, the Civil War of 1861–1865 shook the very foundations of the Republic before the wounded, still troubled land reunited and began to rebuild: one nation, indivisible. Along with confirmation of Union, a new definition of liberty had emerged from this national anguish, one that excluded the possibility that any American could ever again claim ownership of another human being.

The Library of Congress Civil War Desk Reference is a guide through this defining chapter in American history, tracing its antecedents, providing telling glimpses of its armies in action and civilian activities on the home front, and outlining its complex and continuing reverberations. That this volume appears under the Library's aegis is particularly appropriate, for the Library of Congress has participated in, and preserved the records of American history for more than 200 years. Located within the U.S. Capitol during the Civil War era, the Library was then, as it is now, a vital resource for the national legislature as Congress considered questions crucial to the Union's prosecution of the war and the continuing development of the nation. President Lincoln borrowed books from the Library, schooling himself in military science, knowledge crucial for his role as commander in chief. Some Civil War figures *lost* the privilege of borrowing books from the

Library in 1861. An inventory of the 70,000-volume collection conducted that December revealed that 276 of the 856 books then absent from the shelves had been charged to "persons belonging to the so-called seceded states." Among the prominent Confederates who might have been included in this description was former Mississippi Senator Jefferson Davis, who had left the Senate in January, and soon thereafter became president of the Confederate States of America.

Now the largest library on earth—its collections available not only to members of the U.S. government but also to the American public and visitors from other lands as well—the Library of Congress holds more than 120 million items, most of them housed in three large buildings on Capitol Hill. Reflecting America's membership in the community of nations, and the diverse origins of its people, the Library's collections are drawn from around the globe. But the heart of this great institution is found in its vast collections of written, visual, recorded, and electronic materials that chronicle the origins and development of the United States of America. The Library has been called "the Nation's Memory." We preserve the memories and lessons of the Civil War not only in postwar books that examine the conflict, but also in millions of contemporary artifacts, ranging from letters of Civil War soldiers and nurses to the papers of President Lincoln; from Walt Whitman's poetry and the impassioned speeches of Frederick Douglass to the photographs of Mathew Brady and the drawings of Alfred Waud; from the copy of *Battle Hymn of the Republic* Julia Ward Howe deposited here for copyright to the maps Union and Confederate armies used as they struggled to determine the country's future.

Inspired by these testaments from an era of unprecedented challenges, the contributors to *The Library of Congress Civil War Desk Reference* have created a volume that is, itself, a testament to the ability of a great and democratic people to overcome rancor, to endure unspeakable tragedy, to find a common ground and move on.

JAMES H. BILLINGTON
The Librarian of Congress

ABOUT THE EDITORS

MARGARET E. WAGNER. Library of Congress writer/editor Margaret E. Wagner has contributed essays on military history to many of the Library's publications, including *Eyes of the Nation: A Visual History of the United States* (CD-ROM and DVD-ROM editions). She is the author/compiler of several multipanel educational exhibits for libraries and schools, including *Thomas Jefferson's Legacy, Reverberations of the Great War,* and *Scenes from the Civil War,* and is the author/compiler of the annual Library of Congress *Civil War* calendars. She was coeditor of *Mapping the Civil War* (Fulcrum/Library of Congress, 1992), *American Treasures in the Library of Congress* (Abrams/Library of Congress, 1997), and *The Nation's Library* (Scala/Library of Congress, 2000) and has edited numerous Library publications.

GARY W. GALLAGHER. John L. Nau III Professor of History at the University of Virginia, Gary W. Gallagher is editor of the *Civil War America* series at the University of North Carolina Press. He has published widely on the subject. His recent works include *The Confederate War* (1997), *The Myth of the Lost Cause and Civil War History* (2000, coedited with Alan T. Nolan), and *Lee and His Army in Confederate History* (2001). Active in the field of historic preservation, he is cofounder and past president (1987–1994) of the Association for the Preservation of Civil War Sites. He has received the Nevins-Freeman Award for distinguished contributions to the field of Civil War studies (1991), the William Woods Hassler Award for meritorious contributions to the field of Civil War studies (1998), the Laney Prize for the best book in Civil War history (1998), and the Fletcher Pratt Award for the best nonfiction book on the Civil War (1999).

PAUL FINKELMAN. Chapman Distinguished Professor of Law at the University of Tulsa College of Law, Paul Finkelman is the author of *An Imperfect Union* (1981, 2001), *Dred Scott v. Sanford: A Brief History* (1997), *Slavery and the Founders* (2nd ed., 2001), and coauthor of *A March of Liberty: A Constitutional History of the United States* (2001). He is the editor of the Scribners *Encyclopedia of the United States in the Nineteenth Century* and the coeditor of the Macmillan *Encyclopedia of World Slavery* (1998). His book *Slavery in the Courtroom* (1984) won the American Association of Law Libraries Joseph L. Andrews award. Professor Finkelman has lectured throughout the United States as well as in Canada, Great Britain, Germany, Colombia, and Japan, on subjects such as the Civil War, Lincoln, Emancipation, slavery, constitutional history, and Thomas Jefferson.

CONTRIBUTORS

Editors

Margaret E. Wagner
Gary W. Gallagher
Paul Finkelman

Principal Writers

Margaret E. Wagner
Linda Barrett Osborne
Susan Reyburn

Contributors

Alan Bisbort
Hannah Borgeson
Marisa Baldaccini
Sean Dolan
Sue Heinemann
Alex Hovan
Kevin Mahoney
Steve Merserve
Bill Miller
Catherine Osborne
Nicholas Osborne
Sean Price
Richard W. Stephenson
David Woodbury
R. Keith Young

Research

Harris Andrew
Athena Angelos
Heather Burke

Maps

David Woodbury
Ed Bearrs: Map Consultant
Richard J. Sommers: Map Consultant

The Library of Congress

W. Ralph Eubanks, Director of
  Publishing

Advisory Board

Irvin L. Jordan Jr., University of
  Virginia
Robert Schneller, Naval Historical
  Center
Jennifer L. Weber, Princeton
  University

Grand Central Press

Paul Fargis, President
Judy Pray, Executive Editor
Kerry Acker, Project Editor

CIVIL WAR TIME LINE

Unique in conception, permeated by a boundless optimism, and set apart by the unprecedented growth of its territory, economy, and population, the new United States of America was, by the 1830s, a nation of incalculable promise. Its energetic and egalitarian people, French traveler Alexis de Tocqueville wrote, were filled with a "strange unrest," perpetually in motion "for fear of missing the shortest cut to happiness." Where else but in America, de Tocqueville wondered, at a time when Europe was convulsed with troubles, "can we find greater cause of hope or more valuable lessons?" But he had also detected the possibility of a shadowed future for this promising land while traveling in the American South, where what Southerners called the "peculiar institution" of slavery was becoming ever more deeply ingrained in the social fabric:

> I can discover only two modes of action for the white inhabitants of these states; namely, either to emancipate the Negroes and to intermingle with them, or, remaining isolated from them, to keep them in slavery as long as possible. All intermediate measures seem to me likely to terminate, and that shortly, in the most horrible of civil wars.

The restless American energy de Tocqueville noted manifested itself very differently within the country's two major regions during the ensuing years. The shadow of the "peculiar institution" lengthened over the expanding land. And, slowly, the United States of America began to rend, North from South, along fault lines that marked differing interpretations of the Founding Fathers' philosophy; differing economic and concomitant social development; and inexorably diverging beliefs regarding the appropriateness of maintaining slavery in a country dedicated to the proposition that all men are created equal.

The first major temblor had actually occurred before de Tocqueville's visit. In 1818, the Territorial Assembly of the Missouri Territory petitioned the U.S. Congress for statehood. Slavery had existed there for many years; but at the time of its petition for statehood, the United States was evenly divided between slave and free states, and to admit a new slave state would have destroyed a delicate balance. The events and arguments that resulted in the Missouri Compromise of 1820 came, said Thomas Jefferson, "like a fire bell in the night," and constituted the first broad awareness that a potentially calamitous sectional rift was developing.

During the next forty years, the North became more industrialized and its population emerged more highly educated, mobile, and reform-minded. At the same time, the South relied increasingly on "King Cotton" and the slave labor that sustained its agrarian economy. Political crises revolving around the volatile questions of the retention of slavery in existing states and its expansion into newly acquired territory arose with alarming frequency and increasing rancor. In the North, the Abolition Movement—organizations of white and free black people who were passionately committed to ending slavery—gathered strength, adding to Southerners' fears of Northern interference with the South's way of life. Threats of secession by Southern politicians—who had long been a powerful force in national politics—accompanied the debates that yielded the Compromise of 1850. Such threats continued throughout the troubled, increasingly violent decade that followed (see Chapter 2, "Antebellum America" for more information on prewar events).

When Abraham Lincoln, who was personally opposed to slavery and politically opposed to its spread into new territory, became the leading candidate for president in 1860, secession threats were uttered with a new virulence. By then, however, many in the North had reached the end of their tolerance for what they viewed as Southern intractability and manipulation. Threats of secession had made the *right* of secession the central issue for many of these Northerners. "The question before the country . . . has become something more than an issue on the slavery question growing out of the construction of the Constitution," wrote Iowa Senator James W. Grimes shortly after the election. "The issue now before us is, whether we have a country, whether or not this is a nation. . . . I could agree to no compromise until the right to secede was fully renounced, because it would be a recognition of the right of one or more States to break up the Government at their will."

Many in the South perceived the fundamental issue to be something else entirely. "Fire-eater" and avid secessionist Edmund Ruffin of Virginia wrote, two days before Election Day, that the election would "serve to show whether these southern states are to remain free, or to be politically enslaved—whether the institution of negro slavery, on which the social & political existence of the south rests, is to be secured by our resistance, or to be abolished in a short time, as the certain result of our present submission to northern domination."

The people of the United States were now on the brink of demonstrating the terrible truth in another of Alexis de Tocqueville's cogent observations: "There are two things that a democratic people will always find very difficult—to begin a war, and to end it."

TIME LINE

1860

"[T]hree months back, so safe, so calm, so boastfully thriving, so proudly prosperous—& now with no foot of ground undisputed, no fireside safe, no interests protected, no law, no legislation. . . . North arrayed against South & South defending itself against the North is brother & sister attempting each other's life." Sallie Baxter Hampton of South Carolina, letter, mid-December, 1860.

November 6: Republican Abraham Lincoln is elected the sixteenth president of the United States. In this unique presidential contest, the winning candidate is not even on the ballot in ten Southern states.

December 4: In his final message to Congress, President James Buchanan, long a friend to Southern interests, condemns Northern "interference" in the slave policies of Southern states but also shocks some Southerners by denying that states have a right to secede.

December 10: South Carolina passes a state law calling for a secession convention on December 17. Both of its senators, James Chesnut and James H. Hammond, resign their seats in the U.S. Senate.

December 20: The South Carolina secession convention unanimously adopts a declaration that "the union now subsisting between South Carolina and other States, under the name of 'The United States of America' is hereby dissolved." By February 1, 1861, six other Southern states—Mississippi, Florida, Alabama, Georgia, Louisiana, and Texas—will have followed suit.

December 26: Because of certain assurances given to them earlier by President Buchanan, Southerners feel betrayed when U.S. Major Robert Anderson quietly transfers his small garrison from undefendable Fort Moultrie, in Charleston, South Carolina, to the just-completed and well-fortified Fort Sumter in Charleston Harbor. At this time, the United States Army comprises some 16,000 men, most of whom are on duty on the western frontier. Taken in toto, the militias of the seceding states exceed the U.S. force in strength.

1861

January 1861

"I cannot comprehend the madness of the times. Southern men are theoretically crazy. Extreme northern men are practical fools, the latter are really quite as bad as the former. Treason is in the air around us *every* where & goes by the name of Patriotism." Thomas Corwin to Abraham Lincoln, January 16, 1861.

1–6: Fort Pulaski, in Savannah, Georgia; two forts and an arsenal in Alabama; and the United States Arsenal at Apalachicola, Florida, are occupied by state militias.

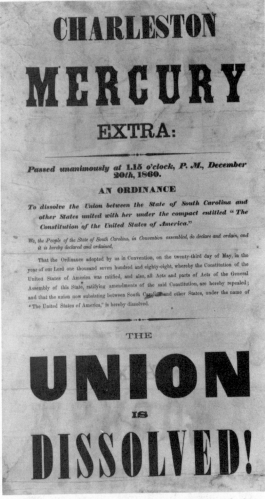

The Charleston Mercury *published this special edition announcing South Carolina's secession on December 20, 1860.*

5: U.S. senators from six Gulf states and Arkansas hold a caucus and conclude that further attempts at reconciliation are a waste of time. They urge the slave states to secede and form their own confederacy without delay.

9: The unarmed merchant vessel *Star of the West* arrives in Charleston Harbor carrying 200 troops to reinforce the Fort Sumter garrison. It is fired upon and retreats without landing the men. The next day, the *Charleston Mercury* will editorialize: "The first gun of the new struggle for independence (if struggle there is to be) has been fired, and Federal power has received its first repulse." *Also on this day:* Mississippi secedes from the Union.

10: In command of a small U.S. force at the installations protecting the harbor at Pensacola, Florida—as well as Pensacola Navy Yard, the best in the Deep South—Lieutenant Adam Slemmer orders guns spiked at a mainland fort and retires to Fort Pickens, on Santa Rosa Island, a few thousand yards offshore, as Florida and Alabama militia troops close in. The status of this fort and its garrison will worry the U.S. government fully as much as Fort Sumter and its personnel during the coming months; but Fort Pickens will remain in Union hands. *Also on this day:* Florida secedes from the Union.

11: Alabama secedes from the Union.

19: Georgia secedes from the Union.

26: Louisiana secedes from the Union.

29: Kansas is admitted to the Union as a free state. Including the seceding states, the Union now has four more free states than slave states.

February 1861

"Upon my weary heart was showered smiles, plaudits, and flowers, but beyond them, I saw troubles and thorns innumerable. We are without machinery, without means, and threatened by a powerful opposition; but I do not despond and will not shrink from the task imposed upon me." Jefferson Davis, provisional president of the Confederate States of America, letter to his wife, February 1861.

1: Texas secedes from the Union.

4: Representatives of six of the seven states that have seceded to date (no delegates from recently seceded Texas are present) meet at Montgomery, Alabama, to organize a new nation. *Also, on this day:* What will prove to be a spectacularly ineffective "peace convention" convenes in Washington, D.C.

8: The convention of seceding states unanimously adopts the Provisional Constitution of the Confederate States, which is largely based on the U.S. Constitution but has several significant differences. The permanent Constitution will be adopted March 11.

18: "Dixie" becomes the unofficial Confederate States anthem when it is played at a ceremony marking Jefferson Davis' inauguration as provisional president of the Confederate States of America. A Georgian, Alexander H. Stephens, who had initially opposed disunion, is chosen provisional vice president this same day.

March 1861

"The attempt to break up this Union is the most atrocious piece of political wickedness the world ever saw, and it is very, very bitter to have to accept the fact that that attempt has succeeded. . . . Surely no man ever assumed the reins of government beset by such complicated and oppressive difficulties as have surrounded you." Orville H. Browning, letter to Abraham Lincoln, March 26, 1861.

4: Abraham Lincoln is inaugurated. Though seven Southern states have by now seceded and formed a confederacy, Lincoln, in his inaugural address, seeks to keep avenues open to reconstruct the divided nation: "We are not enemies, but friends. We must not be enemies. Though passion may have strained, it must not break, our bonds of affection."

6: The new Confederate Congress authorizes an army of 100,000 volunteers for twelve months.

29: After much consultation with advisers, whose opinions are divided, President Lincoln determines that the United States shall not abandon Forts Sumter and Pickens. He orders preparations made for a relief expedition to Fort Sumter.

31: Lincoln orders an expedition prepared for Fort Pickens. Yet Southern commissioners, in Washington for talks, have, without Lincoln's knowledge, been led to believe that Fort Sumter's garrison will be withdrawn.

April 1861

"Our Southern brethren . . . have attacked their father's house and their loyal brothers. They must be punished and brought back, but this necessity breaks my heart." Major Robert Anderson, United States Army, commander of the Union garrison at Fort Sumter.

"The North is swollen with pride and drunk with insolence. . . . The North needs proof of the earnestness of our intentions and our manhood. Experience shall be their teacher. Let them learn." *Charleston Mercury*, April 11, 1861.

12–13: The Civil War begins when Confederate forces in Charleston fire on the U.S. garrison in Fort Sumter and the U.S. garrison returns fire.

15: President Lincoln calls for 75,000 U.S. militia to serve for ninety days. By this time, the South has already enrolled 60,000 men in its armed forces.

17: The crucial Upper South state of Virginia, home state of Robert E. Lee, secedes from the Union; a vote today by its state convention will be confirmed by referendum on May 23. Among the facilities taken over by the state are the U.S. armory at Harpers Ferry and the Gosport Naval Yard in Norfolk, Virginia, the largest shipbuilding and repair facility in the South.

19: In Baltimore—Maryland is a slaveholding state with deep sympathy toward the South, but it remains in the Union—rioters attack the Sixth Massachusetts Regiment, the first fully equipped unit to respond to Lincoln's April 15 call for troops. Some soldiers open fire; four soldiers and twelve Baltimore civilians are killed, and many people are wounded. Tension continues to build when other Marylanders tear down railroad bridges and telegraph lines leading to Washington.

21: The U.S.S. *Saratoga* captures a vessel with the romantic name *Nightingale*, which is carrying a cargo of 961 slaves. International trade in slaves has been against U.S. law since

*The Capitol, a barracks.
Captain Tate and the
District of Columbia Militia
respond to the national
emergency, May 1861.*

1808, but Africans have been brought into the Deep South illegally since well before the outbreak of the Civil War, and the domestic slave trade still thrives.

29: Under the primary leadership of Elizabeth Blackwell, America's first woman medical doctor, 3,000 women and several prominent men meet at the Cooper Institute in New York City and form the Women's Central Association for Relief, to coordinate the efforts of many small war-relief groups. This organization will be the nucleus of the United States Sanitary Commission. *Also on this day:* Because a Federal law prohibits black men from serving in state militias, and there are no black men in the U.S. Army, African American men organize their own drill company in Boston. Other black drill companies will be organized in the North, but their efforts are unwelcome. "This is a white man's war," they are told.

May 1861

"Is there a great deal of financial trouble at home? We cannot get any money out here, and we suppose the Department at Washington must be in great confusion. This news about our country is so absorbing we cannot think or talk of anything else. . . . No doubt many officers of our squadron will resign; but, as a Northern man, I, for one, hope that all the North will pull together and go in and win." Lieutenant George Hamilton Perkins, United States Navy, letter, May 1, 1861.

3: President Lincoln calls for 42,000 three-year army volunteers and 18,000 sailors and also expands the regular army to 22,714 men. *Also on this day:* U.S. General-in-Chief Winfield Scott proposes an envelopment strategy for fighting the South. Ridiculed as the "Anaconda Plan" by those who believe the war will end quickly after a decisive battle, Scott's plan will become an essential aspect of the overall strategy ultimately adopted by the Union.

6: Arkansas secedes from the Union.

8: Jefferson Davis signs a bill authorizing the enlistment of up to 400,000 additional volunteers for three years, or the duration of the war. The response is overwhelming.

9: In St. Louis, Missouri, civilians sympathetic to the South riot as U.S. Brigadier General Nathaniel Lyon and his troops march captured members of the pro-Southern militia through the city. Twenty-eight civilians and two soldiers are killed. Many Missourians who had not as yet taken sides tumble into the secessionist camp.

13: Martial law is declared in Baltimore. *Also on this day:* Britain, via an official proclamation by Queen Victoria, declares its intention to remain neutral in the American civil conflict and to accord to both sides the rights of belligerents, a recognition of the South's separate status that the United States had wished to avoid.

20: The Provisional Congress of the Confederacy votes to move the capital of the South from Montgomery, Alabama, to Richmond, Virginia. *Also on this day:* North Carolina secedes from the Union.

24: At Fort Monroe, Virginia, Union Major General Benjamin Butler refuses to return three runaway slaves to their master, a Confederate colonel. Butler calls the slaves "contraband of war." Hundreds of thousands of such "contrabands" will enter Union lines during the war. *Also on this day:* Grief sweeps through the North when dashing young Union Colonel Elmer Ellsworth, a friend and former law clerk of Abraham Lincoln, is shot dead while removing a secessionist flag from a hotel in Alexandria, Virginia. Ellsworth, whose Zouave Drill Team was renowned before the war, is the first well-known casualty of the Civil War.

June 1861

"Captain Whipple, U.S.A., visited camp [outside Washington, D.C.], and the regiment was sworn into the United States service by him, *to serve during the War, unless sooner discharged,* the men being confident of compelling the rebels to return to their allegiance to the United States Government, in a few months." Private John W. Jaques, Ninth New York State Militia, diary entry, June 8, 1861.

8: Tennessee voters approve secession from the Union.

10: Humanitarian and reformer Dorothea Lynde Dix is appointed Superintendent of Women Nurses for the U.S. Army. Over the next four years, as she works to organize hospitals, care for wounded, and establish the army's first professional nursing corps, her personality and problematical administrative techniques will earn her the name "Dragon Dix."

11: Delegates representing the pro-Union element in Virginia meet at Wheeling to organize a pro-Union government of what will eventually become a separate state: West Virginia.

13: President Lincoln signs an order creating the United States Sanitary Commission, a civilian organization established to assist the army in providing care for sick and wounded soldiers, and to respond to the needs of soldiers' dependents. It will grow to be the largest and most effective of many such organizations that operate during the war, and will become a power in national politics, with some 7,000 local chapters by 1863.

30: Deftly eluding the U.S.S. *Brooklyn,* a blockader, below New Orleans, Captain Raphael Semmes sails the C.S.S. *Sumter* into the Gulf of Mexico. His legendary career as a commerce raider has begun.

July 1861

"The Yankees in such a superiority of numbers . . . poured forth such a destructive fire into our ranks that our men were becoming confused and began to fall back. The gallant and noble General Barnard Bee dismounted his horse to rally the men, telling them as Carolinians they should never disgrace or dishonor their banner but die under its folds, and all of them rallied again, and, with a shout and yell that might have been heard for miles, they charged and repulsed the enemy, and drove them back from their position. It was not long before our brave General Bee fell mortally wounded." Lieutenant Richard Lewis, Fourth South Carolina Volunteers, C.S.A., letter, July 24, 1861, describing the first battle of Bull Run.

13: Robert S. Garnett becomes the first general killed in the Civil War when his Confederate forces are defeated by Union troops at Corrick's Ford in western Virginia.

21: The "Rebel Yell" makes its unnerving debut—and Thomas Jonathan Jackson is given the nickname "Stonewall" by Barnard Bee—at the first battle of Bull Run, where, after initial success, a Union force of 35,000 under Irvin McDowell is defeated by 30,000 Confederates under P. G. T. Beauregard and Joseph E. Johnston. Retreating Federals get tangled up with Washington civilians who had come out from the city to watch the contest, and the retreat becomes a rout. For many, this battle causes a rude awakening to the fact that the war will not be a short one. A large Confederate force is now situated close to the Union capital.

22: In the early morning hours, a telegram summons Major General George B. McClellan to Washington to take command of what will become the Army of the Potomac. *Later on this day:* Concerned over the effectiveness of militia officers hastily appointed by state politicians in the rush to expand the Union army, the U.S. Congress authorizes the creation of military boards to examine officers and remove those found to be unqualified.

22–23: President Lincoln signs two bills authorizing enlistments of a total of one million three-year volunteers.

25: A famed explorer and former presidential candidate, John C. Frémont, now a general, arrives in St. Louis to take command of Union forces in Missouri, beginning what will become a stormy and controversial early chapter of the war in the West.

Colonel (later brigadier general) Micah Jenkins led the Fifth South Carolina across Bull Run during the first battle there, July 21, 1861, threatening McDowell's left and forcing a general retreat.

August 1861

"Dear Soldier, If these socks had language they would tell you that many a kind wish for you has been knit into them, and many a tear of pity for you has bedewed them. We all think of you, and want to do everything we can for you; for we feel that we owe you unlimited love and gratitude, and that you deserve the very best at our hands." Letter from an unnamed civilian woman, quoted in *My Story of the War* by Mary A. Livermore, of the U.S. Sanitary Commission, 1888.

3: Congress passes legislation directing the U.S. Department of the Navy to construct three prototype ironclad vessels.

5: Congress levies the first Federal income tax in U.S. history.

6: Congress passes the First Confiscation Act, which states that contrabands who had been employed *directly by Confederate armed forces* are no longer slaves, but otherwise leaves their status uncertain.

10: Antisecessionists in Missouri are dealt a blow when Federal troops, engaged in the battle of Wilson's Creek, withdraw after their commander, Union Brigadier General Nathaniel Lyon, is killed.

28–29: Union forces capture two forts guarding Hatteras Inlet, North Carolina, an important Confederate access point to the Atlantic.

30: In Missouri, Major General John C. Frémont, assuming the administrative powers of the state, confiscates the property of all Missourians who favor the Confederacy and declares their slaves free—an action that threatens Lincoln's delicate maneuvering to keep the border state of Kentucky in the Union. In ordering Frémont to modify his emancipation proclamation (September 11), Lincoln will call it *"purely political,* and not within the range of *military* law, or necessity." With his confidence in Frémont eroding, Lincoln will relieve him of command on November 2.

September 1861

"We do not affirm that the North is fighting in behalf of the black man's rights, as such—if this was the single issue, we even doubt whether they would fight at all. But circumstances have been so arranged by the decrees of Providence, that in struggling for their own nationality they are forced to defend our rights. . . . Let us be awake, therefore, brethren; a generous emulation in a common patriotism, and a special call to defend our rights alike bid us to be on the alert to seize arms and drill as soon as the government shall be willing to accept our services." Editorial, *Anglo-African,* September 14, 1861.

1: The first school for contrabands (people who have escaped slavery) established in the South is started by Mary Chase, a freedwoman of Alexandria, Virginia.

3: Confederate forces enter Kentucky from Tennessee, an act that ends this border state's "neutrality," proclaimed by its governor and legislature on May 20. There is now one continuous front dividing South from North. It extends from the Atlantic Ocean to Kansas and the western frontier.

12–17: President Lincoln dispatches U.S. troops to arrest thirty-one secessionist members of the Maryland legislature as well as others suspected of collusion in a secessionist plot.

16–17: The Union occupies Ship Island, between New Orleans and Mobile, where the United States will develop a base for the Gulf Blockade Squadron as well as for the campaign against New Orleans.

October 1861

"We have been greatly interested since our last capture in examining a lot of newspapers found on board. They are as late as 8th October, and give us most cheering accounts of the war. We have gloriously whipped the enemy at all points, and have brought Missouri and Kentucky out of the Union. The tone of the European press is highly favourable to our cause, and indicates a prompt recognition of our independence. And all this cheering information we get from the enemy himself!" Captain Raphael Semmes, Confederate States Navy, journal entry, October 31, 1861, aboard C.S.S. *Sumter.*

21: What was intended as a "slight demonstration" to divert attention from a larger force moving against Confederates encamped near Leesburg, Virginia, becomes a humiliating and costly disaster for the Union when a brigade commanded by influential politician-soldier Colonel Edward Baker crosses the Potomac, climbs Ball's Bluff, and is pushed back over the steep bank and into the river. More than half the brigade, including Baker, are casualties. This defeat, hard on the heels of the bad Union showing at the first battle of Bull Run, prompts the establishment of a Joint Committee on the Conduct of the War (December 9, 1861), which will become an influential U.S. congressional body with broad power of investigation over the entire war effort.

November 1861

"The proscribed Americans (and there are many), attached to this regiment have, since their encampment here, formed themselves into a defensive association. They propose to cultivate a correct knowledge of the manual of arms and military evolutions, . . . actuated by the conviction that the time is not far distant when the black man of this country will be summoned to show his hand in this struggle for liberty." William H. Johnson, an African American who served with the 8th Connecticut Volunteers as an "independent man" (a status that was not clearly defined), reported to the Boston-based newspaper *Pine and Palm,* for which he was a correspondent, November 23, 1861.

1: Major General George B. McClellan replaces 75-year-old Winfield Scott as general in chief of U.S. armies. McClellan will forge the quickly raised and, in many cases, poorly led regiments from many states into an organized and formidable fighting force. But he will prove reluctant to employ his army aggressively in battle.

7: Navy Captain Samuel Du Pont leads U.S. forces to victory at Port Royal, in South Carolina's Sea Islands. These islands, home for some 10,000 contrabands abandoned by their retreating owners, will be the scene of major experimental work and education programs for freedmen.

8: A major international incident begins when the U.S. Navy stops the British vessel H.M.S. *Trent* and removes two Confederate ministers plenipotentiary en route to their posts in England and France. War with Britain will be averted when the emissaries are released early in January.

28: The Confederate Congress admits Missouri as the twelfth Confederate State. The Southern-leaning legislators of the state adopted a "secession ordinance" on November 3, at Neosho, Missouri, while retreating from Union forces. Although Missouri will, in fact, remain in the Union, its Confederate state officials will serve as a "government in exile," outside their state, for most of the war. The Confederacy will add a star to its flag, to represent Missouri.

December 1861

"We talk the irrepressible conflict, and practically give the lie to our talk. We wage war against slaveholding rebels, and yet protect and augment the motive which has moved the slaveholders to rebellion. . . . Fire will not burn it out of us—water cannot wash it out of us, that this war with the slaveholders can never be brought to a desirable termination until slavery, the guilty cause of all our national troubles, has been totally and forever abolished." Frederick Douglass, *Douglass Monthly*, August 1861.

3: In his message to Congress, President Lincoln recommends that "steps be taken" to colonize the slaves who had come into Union lines, along with any free blacks who wished to emigrate. Over the coming year, Congress will appropriate $600,000 to help finance the voluntary emigration of African Americans.

10: The Union state of Kentucky also becomes the thirteenth state claimed by the Confederacy when the Confederate Congress admits its "provisional government." (The Confederate flag will henceforth bear 13 stars.)

26: Martial law is proclaimed in St. Louis and around all railroads operating in Missouri.

1862

January 1862

"The field where our present encampment is was in cultivation in the summer, and also enclosed by a good fence, but it is a perfect plain now—all the rails burnt up and everything destroyed belonging to the farm. . . . The ground is still white with snow, and the wind which comes off the snow-clad hills and mountains is so cold and piercing that it almost chills the heart of every human." Lieutenant Richard Lewis, Fourth South Carolina Volunteers, letter to his mother from a camp near Centerville, Virginia, January 7, 1862.

15: Edwin M. Stanton is confirmed by the U.S. Senate as Secretary of War. He will prove to be energetic and efficient in the office, but debate on his character and value to the Union will continue long after the war.

27: Impatient with the inactivity of Union armies, President Lincoln takes the unprecedented step of issuing General War Order No. I, which "Ordered that the 22d of February 1862, be the day for a general movement of the Land and Naval forces of the United States against the insurgent forces." The president's Special War Order No. 1, issued January 31, will be specifically aimed at forcing Major General George B. McClellan to begin offensive operations in Virginia.

30: The ironclad U.S.S. *Monitor,* looking to some like "a cheesebox on a raft," is launched before a large crowd at Greenpoint, Long Island, New York.

31: With passage of the Railways and Telegraph Act, the U.S. Congress authorizes the president to take over any railroad "when in his judgment the public safety may require it." Rarely used in the Northern territory proper, the law will be the basis of major U.S. government railroad activity in the occupied South.

February 1862

"Why is it that the white people of this country desire to get rid of us? Does any one pretend to deny that this is our country? Or that much of the wealth and prosperity found here is the result of the labor of our hands? Or that our blood and bones have not crimsoned and whitened every battlefield from Maine to Louisiana? It is true, a great many simple-minded people have been induced to go to Liberia and to Hayti, but, be assured, the more intelligent portion of the colored people will remain here . . . where we have withstood almost everything." Lawyer, abolitionist, orator John Rock, speech, reported in the *Liberator,* February 14, 1862.

3: The Union government decides to treat captured Confederate privateer (nonmilitary raider) crews as prisoners of war, rather than pirates—thus averting an eye-for-an-eye hanging of Union prisoners of war. Confederate privateers will gradually be displaced, however, by commerce raiders who are military personnel.

6: Combined land/river forces under the command of Ulysses S. Grant and Andrew H. Foote take Fort Henry, Tennessee, a weak point in the Confederate lines. The fall of Fort Henry opens the Tennessee River to Union traffic into the Deep South.

11: U.S. Secretary of War Edwin M. Stanton establishes the United States Military Rail Roads (see also April 22, 1862). Former railway official Daniel McCallum, who becomes superintendent, is charged with ensuring the "safe and speedy transport" of men and supplies, a task that will become more challenging as the war and the military railroad system radically expand. In the Confederacy, control of railroads will not be as centralized or efficient.

16: Dealing a second blow to the Confederacy in the West, Brigadier General Ulysses S. Grant demands, and receives, the unconditional surrender of Fort Donelson, Tennessee, on the Cumberland River, from Brigadier General Simon B. Buckner. General Grant enters the limelight, lionized by the Northern press.

22: His appointment as provisional president having been confirmed by a general election, Jefferson Davis is inaugurated president of the Confederate States of America on this day. Morale in the Confederacy is low, due to Union triumphs in the West, but determination to succeed is high.

25: Nashville, Tennessee, becomes the first Confederate state capital and important industrial center to fall to the Union. *Also on this day:* Abraham Lincoln signs the Legal Tender Act, creating a national currency and altering the U.S. monetary structure.

27: The Confederate Congress authorizes President Davis to suspend the writ of habeas corpus in areas that are in "danger of attack by the enemy." Davis suspends the writ in several cities (including Richmond) that are not only in danger of attack from without but face collapse within, due to rising crime and violence among the increased wartime populations.

March 1862

"I have examined a number of persons, fugitives from Rockingham and Augusta Counties, who were arrested at Petersburg, . . . As all these persons are members in good standing in these [Dunker and Mennonite] churches and bear good characters as citizens and Christians, I cannot doubt the sincerity of their declaration that they left home to avoid the draft of the militia and under the belief that by the draft they would be placed in a situation in which they would be compelled to violate their consciences. . . . I recommend all the persons in the annexed list be discharged on taking the oath of allegiance and agreeing to submit to the laws of Virginia and the Confederate States in all things except taking arms in war." Sydney S. Baxter, War Department, C.S.A., report of March 31, 1862.

7–8: At the Battle of Pea Ridge (Elkhorn Tavern), Arkansas, the Confederates suffer a harsh blow, and outnumbered Union forces achieve a decided victory that helps to preserve Missouri as a Union state.

8: As preparations begin for the Union's major push toward Richmond via the Virginia peninsula (Peninsula Campaign, March–August), President Lincoln, frustrated by U.S. General in Chief George B. McClellan's extremely cautious approach to campaigning, demotes McClellan from general in chief to commanding general of only the Army of the Potomac.

8–9: The U.S. Navy suffers the worst day in its eighty-six-year history when the Confederate ironclad C.S.S. *Virginia* (formerly U.S.S. *Merrimack*) destroys two wooden Union vessels and runs others aground near Hampton Roads, Virginia. *Virginia*'s battle with the U.S. ironclad *Monitor* the next day (March 9), though a draw, will mark the eclipse of wooden warships and the beginning of a new era in naval warfare.

13: A new U.S. article of war forbids army officers, under penalty of court martial, to return fugitive slaves to their masters.

23: Ordered to conduct "diversionary" operations in Virginia's Shenandoah Valley, Confederate Major General Stonewall Jackson suffers a tactical defeat at the first battle of Kernstown.

Ironclad ships such as Monitor *and* Merrimack *were a hallmark of the Civil War on the water. These sailors aboard the Union ironclad* Lehigh *are engaged in a gun drill.*

But the encounter does prove a diversion; alarmed Union officials in Washington send troops slated for the Peninsula Campaign to deal with Jackson. This battle is the opening engagement of Jackson's Shenandoah Valley Campaign, which will become a milestone in American military history.

30: Vincent Colyer, an agent of the Brooklyn Y.M.C.A., is appointed superintendent of the poor for the Union's Department of North Carolina. He will shortly report: "Upwards of 50 [black] volunteers of the best and most courageous, were kept constantly employed on the perilous but important duty of spies, scouts, and guides. . . . They frequently went from 30 to 300 miles within the enemy's lines; visiting his principal camps and most important posts, and bringing us back important and reliable information."

April 1862
"We caught a rebel spy in our camp last week, disguised as a newspaper vender. Papers were found in his boots that convicted him beyond doubt, and he was hanged up by the neck, with very little ceremony." Sergeant Warren H. Freeman, Thirteenth Regiment Massachusetts Volunteers, U.S.A., letter to his parents, April 13, 1862.

3: Encouraged by Union successes to believe that current manpower would be enough to bring the war to a successful conclusion, U.S. Secretary of War Edwin M. Stanton orders all U.S. recruiting offices closed. They will not remain closed long.

5: Forces under Union Major General George B. McClellan begin the siege of Yorktown, Virginia, the first important action in the Peninsula Campaign.

6–7: The most devastating clash of the war thus far occurs at Shiloh Church, near Pittsburg Landing, Tennessee, when Albert Sidney Johnston's Confederates attack Ulysses S. Grant's unprepared forces. Reinforced, Grant recovers and achieves a victory on day two, but the cost in both Union and Confederate lives is great. Grant's recent lionization is superseded by criticism in the Northern press, and the North faces the fact that there will be no quick collapse of the Confederacy in the West. As Shiloh concludes, the Confederate bastion on Island Number 10 in the Mississippi River falls to Union troops commanded by Major General John Pope, who becomes a new Northern hero.

10: The U.S. Congress adopts a resolution, proposed by Abraham Lincoln and primarily aimed at the border states (which do not respond to it), offering "pecuniary aid" to "any state which may adopt gradual abolition of slavery."

11: Fort Pulaski, on the Savannah River, near the major Confederate port of Savannah, Georgia, falls to the Union after intense bombardment. Its capture strengthens the U.S. blockade of Southern ports.

16: As bad news continues to come in from the West, and with the Union army less than ten miles from Richmond, the Confederate Congress initiates the first general military draft in American history by passing the first of three Confederate conscription acts. *Also on this day:* President Lincoln signs a bill ending slavery in the District of Columbia. The only example of compensated emancipation in the United States, this law provides for a payment of up to $300 to loyal Unionist masters for each slave for whom they can prove a claim, and who is freed by this act.

18: The U.S. Congress passes a bill suspending seniority in the Army Medical Bureau, a measure that will increase the efficiency and effectiveness of medical care—especially after the young and progressive William Hammond is named surgeon general.

21: The Confederate government legitimizes the many guerrilla organizations fighting throughout the Confederacy by passing the Partisan Ranger Act. Though many partisan leaders, from former cavalry scout John Singleton Mosby to Missouri "bushwacker" William Quantrill, will officially enroll their men in the Confederate armed forces under this act, most Union officers will refuse to recognize partisans as anything other than outlaws. They direct their men to "Pursue, strike, and destroy the reptiles."

22: U.S. Secretary of War Edwin M. Stanton summons civil engineer, author, and inventor Herman Haupt to Washington and appoints him chief of construction and transportation of U.S. military railroads (see also February 11, 1862). Haupt will fulfill the role with admirable efficiency.

24: U.S. Navy Captain David G. Farragut leads his fleet through the gunfire from the two forts below New Orleans, beginning the campaign that will bring the largest city in the Confederacy into Union hands by May 1.

29: One of the most valuable members of Allan Pinkerton's Federal Secret Service network, Timothy Webster, is hanged by Confederate authorities in Richmond, Virginia. Other spies for both sides, including the South's Rose Greenhow, have been—and will be—imprisoned for their activities and then exchanged. But Webster's stunning success at winning the trust of Confederate officers and gaining access to sensitive material is an acute embarrassment to the Confederacy.

May 1862

"[M]y horse's head was blown off, and falling so suddenly as to catch my foot and leg under the horse. The regiment, seeing me fall, supposed I was killed or wounded, and began to falter and waver, when I, still penned to the earth by the weight of my horse, waved my sword and shouted forward! forward! Whereupon some of my men came to my assistance. . . . [S]eeing the flag upon the ground, the flag-bearer and all the color-guard being killed or wounded, I grasped it and called upon them to charge! Which they did, and together with others captured the fortifications." Lieutenant Colonel (later, Major General) Bryan Grimes, Fourth North Carolina, C.S.A., recollection of the battle of Seven Pines, May 31, 1862.

3: As Union Major General George B. McClellan begins to move the massive force he has assembled on the Virginia Peninsula, the Confederate army withdraws from Yorktown, Virginia, which has been under siege for a month. After the battle of Williamsburg (May 5), clashes on the Peninsula will increase, as Union forces aim toward the Confederate capital at Richmond.

8: At the battle of McDowell, Virginia, Stonewall Jackson wins the first victory of his Shenandoah Valley Campaign. Subsequent successes will allow Jackson to march to the Potomac River.

9: Union Major General David Hunter issues a declaration of martial law in the Department of the South (South Carolina, Georgia, Florida) that also declares slavery abolished in the department. That provision is quickly revoked by President Lincoln.

15: After rude behavior by a number of New Orleans ladies culminates in the dumping of a chamberpot's contents on naval hero David Farragut's head, Union Major General Benjamin

F. Butler, in command of occupying forces, issues an order that any woman who persists in insulting Northern soldiers "shall be regarded and held liable to be treated as a woman of the town plying her avocation." Outrage sweeps through the South—and erupts as far away as Britain, where the prime minister, Lord Palmerston, condemns the order in the House of Commons as "infamous."

20: The U.S. Congress passes the Homestead Act, granting 160 acres of land to a settler (man or woman) who stays on the land five years and makes certain improvements. A policy opposed before the war by Southern politicians fearful that homesteaders would bring antislavery sentiment with them into the territories, the act will make it possible for some 25,000 settlers to stake claims to more than three million acres before the war ends.

29–30: Under orders from General P. G. T. Beauregard, Southern troops evacuate disease-ridden Corinth, Mississippi, a crucial Confederate railroad junction, as Northern forces approach.

31: Confederate General Joseph E. Johnston is wounded at the battle of Fair Oaks (Seven Pines) on the Virginia Peninsula, and General Robert E. Lee assumes command of what will soon be known as the Army of Northern Virginia.

June 1862

"The most saddening sight was the wounded at the hospitals, which were in various places on the battlefield. Not only are the houses full, but even the yards are covered with them. There are so many that most of them are much neglected. The people of Richmond are hauling them away as fast as possible. At one place I saw the Yankee wounded and their own surgeon attending to them." Dr. Spencer Glasgow Welch, Surgeon, Thirteenth South Carolina Volunteers, C.S.A., letter to his wife, June 29, 1862.

6: After a naval battle in which the Union rams (boats equipped with devices for ramming and sinking other vessels) developed by Charles Ellet are supremely effective, Memphis, Tennessee, falls to the Union.

8–9: Thomas Jonathan (Stonewall) Jackson's legendary Shenandoah Valley Campaign, which kept Union troops occupied when they might have otherwise reinforced McClellan's army on the Virginia Peninsula, comes to a close with Confederate victories at Cross Keys and Port Republic.

12–16: James Ewell Brown (Jeb) Stuart leads 1,200 Confederate cavalrymen on a reconnaissance completely around Union lines on the Virginia Peninsula—winning skirmishes; capturing enemy soldiers, horses, and mules; destroying supplies; and marking a place for himself and his men in the history books.

17: Braxton Bragg replaces P. G. T. Beauregard as commander of the Confederacy's Western Department. *Also on this day:* The U.S. Congress passes the Land Grant College Act (First Morrill Act), one of the most important pieces of education legislation in United States history. President Lincoln will sign it into law July 2.

19: President Lincoln signs into law a measure prohibiting slavery in the territories of the United States.

25: A Union League is established in Pekin, Illinois. It is the first of many such leagues devoted to bolstering Northern morale and faith and counteracting the activities of such "Copperhead" organizations as the Knights of the Golden Circle, which are sympathetic to the South.

June 25–July 1: On the Virginia Peninsula, the costly Seven Days Campaign changes the course of the war in the East. Lee's Army of Northern Virginia relieves Richmond, and Lee seizes the initiative, which will take him, by September, across the Potomac River and into Northern territory.

July 1862

"Early this morning a detachment of cavalry, artillery, and infantry was sent back to recover the guns abandoned yesterday. No signs of the enemy were found until near the woods on the further side of the battle ground, where there was a picket line, which withdrew at their approach. They reported the enemy's dead as something astonishing, covering the fields, in many places piled up several deep." Josiah Marshall Favill, Fifty-Seventh New York Infantry, diary entry July 3, 1862, Harrison's Landing, Virginia.

1: At the battle of Malvern Hill, Virginia, which ends the Seven Days Campaign, fire from dueling Union and Confederate artillery causes a preponderance of the casualties and moves a correspondent to write: "The vast aerial auditorium seemed convulsed with the commotion of frightful sounds." McClellan continues his withdrawal, having failed to take Richmond; but Lee has failed to destroy or seriously cripple McClellan's army. *Also on this day:* The U.S. Internal Revenue Act of 1862 becomes law, establishing taxes on almost everything. Though most of these taxes will not live long past the war, the Bureau of Internal Revenue, also established under the act, will become a permanent fixture in American lives. *Also on this day:* President Lincoln signs the Pacific Railway Act, granting land and loans to corporations organized to build a railroad from Omaha, Nebraska, to Sacramento, California.

2: Abraham Lincoln calls for 300,000 new volunteers.

13: On the same day he receives a "manifesto" from border-state congressmen rejecting his proposed policy of financial compensation for slaveholders whose slaves are emancipated, Abraham Lincoln tells Secretary of State William Seward and Secretary of the Navy Gideon

Welles that he intends to issue an Emancipation Proclamation. His full cabinet will be informed on July 22.

17: After acrimonious debate, the U.S. Congress passes the Second Confiscation Act. Among its provisions are: freedom for the slaves of all those who support the Rebellion when those slaves come within Union control; an authorization for the president to "employ" blacks for suppression of the rebellion; and a further authorization for the president to provide for colonization "in some tropical country beyond the limits of the United States, of such persons of the African race, made free by the provisions of this Act, as may be willing to emigrate." Later in the war, this act will inspire a growing conflict between Congress and the president over which more properly should have authority over slavery and Reconstruction measures.

22: Officials from the Union and Confederate armies agree on an exchange cartel for prisoners of war. After more than one year of warfare, prisoners number in the thousands and present both governments with problems of proper housing and care. Under the system agreed upon this day, most prisoners will be returned with relative speed to their own side. The system will remain effective until late spring of 1863, when fundamental disagreements between the two sides, most particularly regarding the treatment of the North's black soldiers, will cause it to break down.

23: In the first phase of a planned invasion of Kentucky, Confederate General Braxton Bragg begins the largest Confederate railroad movement of the war. He sends 30,000 men, via a roundabout rail route of 776 miles, from Mississippi to Chattanooga, Tennessee.

August 1862

"I noticed a singular thing while waiting here. I was at the point where troops were thrown into [the] line of battle. I could see them when in column down the road run out of the ranks and hide something under the leaves in a fence corner. I found out later they were playing cards, being superstitious about taking them into battle. Here, too, I saw what I had never seen before: men pinning strips of paper with their names, company and regiment to their coats so they could be identified if killed." Captain Charles Minor Blackford, Second Virginia Cavalry, C.S.A., letter to his wife, Susan, August 11, 1862.

14: President Lincoln tells black leaders, whom he has invited to the White House, that slavery is "the greatest wrong inflicted on any people," but "There is an unwillingness on the part of our people, harsh as it may be, for you free colored people to remain among us." His advocacy of colonizing African Americans outside the continental United States draws violently negative reaction from many black leaders, particularly Frederick Douglass, who accuses Lincoln of "contempt for negroes."

21: Responding to rumors that the Union is enlisting black soldiers, Confederate army headquarters issues a general order that such "crimes and outrages" required "retaliation" in the form of "execution as a felon" of any officer of black troops who was captured.

22: Responding to Horace Greeley's potent pro-emancipation editorial, "The Prayer of Twenty Millions," Abraham Lincoln writes: "My paramount object in the struggle is to save the Union, . . . If I could save the Union without freeing any slave I would do it, and if I could save it by freeing all the slaves I would do it; and if I could save it by freeing some and leaving others alone, I would also do that."

24: The soon-to-be-renowned raider, C.S.S. *Alabama,* captained by Raphael Semmes, is commissioned as a cruiser in the Confederate navy, near the Azores in the Atlantic.

A thunderously eloquent advocate of African American rights, Frederick Douglass recruited black soldiers (his sons Lewis and Charles fought in the war), then fought to get them the equal pay they had originally been promised.

25: The U.S. War Department authorizes Brigadier General Rufus Saxton, military governor of the South Carolina Sea Islands, to raise five regiments of black troops on the islands, with white men as officers. The authorization states that these regiments are to receive "the same pay and rations as volunteers in the service"—but, in June 1863, the War Department will direct that black soldiers are to be paid less than whites.

30: As Union troops make a confused retreat to the Washington defenses after their humiliating defeat at the hands of General Robert E. Lee at the second battle of Bull Run (Manassas, August 28–30), U.S. Secretary of War Edwin M. Stanton calls for volunteer nurses to aid the wounded strewn along the troops' route. Many of the male volunteers behave abysmally; but the women, led by Clara Barton, perform admirably.

September 1862

[The rebels] were pouring a murderous current of shot and shell upon us, we returned the compliment; there [sic] uniform being of the color of the dirt, we could not see them very well, but we kept them at bay, the battle raged fearfully, men falling on both sides, now, the rebels advancing, and are driven back, then, our troops, advancing and meeting with the same fate, until it is doubtful, who would be the victors in the end. . . . The new organization—the Ambulance Corps, worked admirably . . . they could be seen with the green on their arm faithfully tending to their duties." Private

John W. Jacques, Ninth New York State Militia, U.S.A., diary entry, September 17, 1862, regarding the battle of Antietam.

17: Union forces under McClellan meet Lee's invading Army of Northern Virginia in the war's single bloodiest day of combat at the battle of Antietam (Sharpsburg), Maryland. Confederates bring to the field the hope that a victory will encourage the European powers to recognize the Confederacy as a nation and that it will result in victory for the "Peace Democrats" in the fall U.S. elections. President Lincoln must reverse the effect of recent Confederate victories and, further, needs a Union victory before he can issue the Preliminary Emancipation Proclamation that he has been prepared to release since July. The fierce battle results in Lee's withdrawal to Southern territory. *Also on this day:* British Foreign Minister Lord John Russell states that if the North refuses a planned British/French intercession to negotiate a peaceful settlement of the American Civil War, "[W]e ought ourselves to recognize the Southern States as an independent State."

22: Lincoln issues the Preliminary Emancipation Proclamation, declaring that on January 1, 1863, "all persons held as slaves, within any state, or designated part of a state, the people whereof shall then be in rebellion against the United States shall be then, thenceforward, and forever free." The proclamation causes waves of jubilation among some in the North, and heated protest among others.

24: In the wake of violent resistance to militia drafts under the recently passed U.S. Militia Law, President Lincoln issues a proclamation suspending the writ of habeas corpus and subjecting to martial law "all persons discouraging volunteer enlistments, resisting militia drafts, or guilty of any disloyal practice affording aid and comfort to the rebels." *On this same day:* The U.S. secretary of war creates the office of Provost Marshal General. In 1863, the Provost Marshal's Bureau of the War Department will help enroll eligible men under the first effective national conscription act (see March 3, 1863).

27: In the Confederate States, the Second Conscription Act goes into effect, allowing the call-up of men between ages thirty-five and forty-five. *On this same day:* The Confederate Congress enacts a law providing for civilian matrons and nurses in army general hospitals, "giving preference in all cases to females where their services may best subserve the purpose."

October 1862

"It is not for you and I, or us & our dear little ones, alone, that I was and am willing to risk the fortunes of the battle-field, but also for the sake of the country's millions who are to come after us." Sergeant Josiah Chaney, U.S.A., letter to his wife, October 3, 1862.

7: Though his first reaction to the Preliminary Emancipation Proclamation is to call it "infamous," Major General George B. McClellan issues a general order reminding his officers—

many of whom are equally disgruntled by the president's action—that the military is subordinate to civilian authority.

8: Confederate forces under General Braxton Bragg end their invasion of Kentucky after being defeated in the major Civil War battle fought on Kentucky soil, Perryville (Chaplin Hills).

10–12: Jeb Stuart leads his cavalry on another successful ride around the Army of the Potomac (see also June 12, 1862)—this time, raiding as far north as Chambersburg, Pennsylvania.

11: In the Confederacy, draft exemptions for various occupations are expanded. Among those added are owners or overseers of more than twenty slaves, a provision that creates considerable resentment among poorer white families and is objected to by some Confederate senators as legislation "in favour of slave labour against white labour."

13: As McClellan "reorganizes" the Army of the Potomac after Antietam—and fails to pursue Lee's army across the Potomac—the *Chicago Tribune* editorializes: "What malign influence palsies our army and wastes these glorious days for fighting? If it is McClellan, does not the President see that he is a traitor?"

14: Congressional elections in four Northern states result in gains for the Democratic Party, which opposes emancipation and favors a negotiated settlement with the Confederacy.

26: The Army of the Potomac finally begins to cross the Potomac River. But it moves so slowly that Lee is able to deploy his troops between McClellan's force and Richmond.

November 1862

"We have had a number of ladies from the country visiting the wounded; many of them have come twenty miles. They bring baskets full of all kinds of eatables. It does me good to see them come, as the very best we can give wounded men is not enough." Kate Cumming, nurse, Army of Tennessee, C.S.A., diary entry, November 13, 1862.

4: In the North, Democrats make further congressional and state office gains in several additional states—especially New York, where veteran politician Horatio Seymour is elected governor. No friend of emancipation, Seymour has said, "If it be true that slavery must be abolished to save this Union, then the people of the South should be allowed to withdraw themselves from the government which cannot give them the protection guaranteed by its terms."

7: President Lincoln removes Major General George B. McClellan from command of the Army of the Potomac, replacing him with Ambrose Burnside.

21: President Jefferson Davis appoints Virginian James A. Seddon secretary of war—the fifth man thus far to serve in the post under a president who tends to operate as his own war secretary. Seddon will serve the longest, not resigning until early 1865.

December 1862

"The great body of the aristocracy and the commercial classes are anxious to see the United States go to pieces . . . the middle and lower class sympathise [sic] with us [because they] see in the convulsion in America an era in the history of the world, out of which must come in the end a general recognition of the right of mankind to the produce of their labor and the pursuit of happiness." U.S. Minister to Britain Charles Francis Adams, letter to his son, December 25, 1862.

13: At the battle of Fredericksburg, the Army of the Potomac, fighting heroically but under poor leadership, suffers one of the worst Union defeats of the war. The people of the North, *Harper's Weekly* editorializes, "cannot be expected to suffer that such massacres as this at Fredericksburg shall be repeated."

20: The Union supply depot at Holly Springs, Mississippi, is demolished by Confederate cavalry under Earl Van Dorn. This raid, coupled with damage inflicted by cavalry led by Nathan Bedford Forrest, forces Major General Ulysses S. Grant to abandon his first campaign against Vicksburg—the Confederacy's last great bastion on the Mississippi River. This setback further depresses Northern morale.

December 31–January 2: After a combat-eve musical interlude, during which men of both sides joined in singing "Home Sweet Home," Braxton Bragg's Confederate army of Tennessee smashes into the right of William Rosecrans' Union army of the Cumberland to begin the battle of Murfreesboro (Stones River). It becomes the deadliest battle of the war in proportion to numbers (more than one-third of the Confederate force killed, wounded, or missing; 31 percent Union casualties). Regarded as a Union "win," this costly encounter raises spirits in the North. "I can never forget, whilst I remember anything," President Lincoln will write to Rosecrans, "you gave us a hard earned victory which, had there been a defeat instead, the nation could hardly have lived over."

1863

January 1863

"What we need is to feel that we are fighting for our lives and liberties; that is the way the rebels feel: they think that if they don't win, they will lose every liberty. Our people seem to be in an indifferent state, . . . ; they would like to see the South conquered, if it could be done by any moderate means; but when it comes to every man and woman making some great sacrifice, they don't think it worth while, and would rather have a disgraceful peace. . . . They don't seem to see that in case of such a peace, to be a native of the North would be sufficient to disgrace a man, and that we should always be considered a whipped nation." Major Charles Fessenden Morse, Second Massachusetts Infantry, letter, January 2, 1863.

1: Abraham Lincoln issues the Emancipation Proclamation. A stronger document than the Preliminary Emancipation Proclamation (September 22, 1862), it sanctions the enlistment of black soldiers and sailors in Union forces.

12: In his message to the Confederate Congress, Jefferson Davis calls Lincoln's Emancipation Proclamation "the most execrable measure in the history of guilty man" and vows to turn over captured Union officers to state governments for punishment as "criminals engaged in inciting servile insurrection"—a crime punishable by death.

20–22: Ambrose Burnside's plan to flank Lee's army by crossing the Rappahannock River above Fredericksburg, Virginia, devolves into the soon infamous "Mud March," when a dry January becomes very wet. Men, wagons, and horses sink into the muck, and the march is called off two days after it begins.

25: "Fighting Joe" Hooker replaces Ambrose Burnside as commander of the Army of the Potomac. A man whose character is problematical to some of his brother officers, Hooker will make administrative improvements that raise morale and lower the desertion rate.

February 1863

"In going to General Lee's headquarters I could see the Yankee camps distinctly, on the other side of the [Rappahannock] river. I could even see their forces drilling. Their camps are very extensive indeed, and the vast number of white tents which stretch across the plains give it the appearance of a great city." Dr. Spencer Glasgow Welch, Surgeon, Thirteenth South Carolina Volunteers, C.S.A., letter to his wife, February 15, 1863.

25: The National Currency Act becomes law in the North, providing a framework for greater investment in government bonds, by which the war is being financed, and laying the groundwork for the banking system that will prevail for more than fifty years. But the act fuels Democrats' suspicions that Republican wartime programs are attempting to build up a central moneyed despotism." (The act will be expanded and renamed the National Banking Act in 1864.)

26: The Cherokee Indian National Council repeals its ordinance of secession, abolishes slavery, and proclaims itself for the Union.

March 1863

"We halted on our way through Louisville and partook of a free dinner, prepared for us by the loyal ladies of that city. Soft bread, potatoes, boiled ham, cakes and hot coffee were served us till all were filled (and many a haversack was also filled), when we gave three cheers and a tiger for the generous donors. We found much excitement, as bands of guerillas came within six miles of the city the night before, conscripting men and confiscating horses and other supplies." David Lane, Seventeenth Michigan Volunteer Infantry, U.S.A., diary entry, March 27, 1863.

3: President Lincoln signs "An Act for enrolling and calling out the National Forces, and for other purposes"—the first effective Federal conscription law. Administration of the law will prove so inefficient and corrupt that the Act will be divisive during the war and a model of how *not* to frame a draft law thereafter. The war is not going well, and even such a fierce loyalist as *Chicago Tribune* editor Joseph Medill writes: "The Rebs can't be conquered by the present machinery." The influence of the Peace Democrats (Copperheads), led by Clement L. Vallandigham of Ohio, is on the rise. In the South, organizations in favor of peace and of rejoining the Union are forming at about this same time. They include the Peace and Constitution Society, in Arkansas; the Peace Society, in northern Alabama and northern Georgia; and the Heroes of America in western North Carolina and eastern Tennessee—though they will not be as influential as the North's Copperheads.

6: A mob of white men rampages through the black section of Detroit, destroying thirty-two houses, killing several black people, and leaving more than 200 homeless. A number of violent antiblack demonstrations occur in the North in 1863, fueled by job worries and inflammatory statements made by some leaders of the Democratic Party.

13: A friction primer accidentally ignites at the Confederate ordnance laboratory in Richmond causing an explosion that kills sixty-nine people (sixty-two of them are women ordnance workers). A similar horrific accident will take more than two dozen lives and wound many more—mostly women—at the North's Washington, D.C., Arsenal on June 17, 1864.

16: U.S. Secretary of War Edwin M. Stanton sends initial instructions to members of the newly formed American Freedmen's Inquiry Commission.

April 1863

"If we can baffle them in their various designs this year, next fall there will be a great change in public opinion at the North. The Republicans will be destroyed & I think the friends of peace will become so strong as that the next administration will go in on that basis. We have only therefore to resist manfully . . . [and] our success will be certain." General Robert E. Lee, C.S.A., letter to his wife, April 19, 1863.

2: At a time when the rations of the Army of Northern Virginia have been cut by 50 percent, one of the most serious of the South's food riots of 1863–1864 occurs in Richmond, when a mob of more than 1,000 people marches through the streets, sacking stores in the business district.

7: Eight Union ironclads commanded by Captain Samuel Du Pont attack Fort Sumter in Charleston Harbor and are repulsed, demonstrating that Charleston cannot be taken by naval forces alone.

The long struggle for Vicksburg culminated in a siege that drove many civilians into caves for safety—a predicament illustrated by Adalbert John Volck in this 1863 sketch titled "Cave Life in Vicksburg."

13: Major General Ambrose Burnside, now commanding the Union Department of the Ohio and concerned about the activities of Copperheads (Peace Democrats) in his command, issues a general order stating that any person committing "expressed or implied" treason would be subject to trial by a military court and punishment by death or banishment.

16: Vicksburg citizens celebrating the impregnability of their "Gibraltar of the West" at a gala ball are alarmed by the sound of artillery, as gunboats and transports bearing the first of General Grant's army pass on the river, on their way to establishing a base south of the city.

17: At the head of 1,700 Union cavalry, Colonel Benjamin Gierson embarks on a spectacular two-week, 600-mile raid through Mississippi during which the Federals tear up railroads, take captives, and divert attention and Confederate manpower from impeding Grant's operations around Vicksburg.

24: Struggling under runaway inflation, the Confederate government imposes a comprehensive tax law, including a progressive income tax, excise and license duties, and a 10 percent profits tax. A 10 percent "tax in kind" on agricultural produce is bitterly resented by farmers who are already subject to "impressment" of needed goods by Confederate commissary and quartermaster officers. *Also on this day:* President Lincoln issues General

Order, No. 100, "Instructions for the Government of Armies of the United States in the Field." Widely known as the Lieber Code—after its primary author, German-American political philosopher Francis Lieber (1789–1872)—these instructions represent the first attempt to codify the international law of war.

27: Leading the Army of the Potomac up the Rappahannock River to get beyond Robert E. Lee's left flank, Major General Joseph Hooker begins the Chancellorsville Campaign.

May 1863

"Our papers speak about the prisoners that we take as looking half-starved, ragged, etc. Now I could never see this. Those that I saw, and I should think there were 2,000 of them, were fully equal in looks and condition to the average of our men; they say we can never subdue them, that they will fight till there is not a man left. Their gray uniforms give them a kind of dirty appearance, and they nearly all wore felt hats, but some of them had on very neat and handsome uniforms. They lost heavily in the late battles, especially in officers, the most prominent of whom was Stonewall Jackson." Sergeant Warren H. Freeman, Thirteenth Regiment Massachusetts Volunteers, U.S.A., letter, May 18, 1863.

1: The Confederate Congress authorizes President Jefferson Davis to have captured officers of black regiments "put to death or be otherwise punished at the discretion" of a military tribunal. Black enlisted men are to "be delivered to the authorities of the State or States in which they shall be captured to be dealt with according to the present or future laws of such State or States." The prisoner exchange cartel established in July of 1862 begins to break down. *Also on this day:* Peace Democrat Clement Vallandigham gives a speech in Mount Vernon, Ohio, denouncing "this wicked, cruel and unnecessary war . . . for the freedom of the blacks and the enslavement of the whites." His subsequent arrest by soldiers who break down the door of his house in the middle of the night causes a riot during which the offices of a Republican newspaper are burned down.

1–5: Dividing his 60,000-man army, Robert E. Lee begins action on May 1 in what will be one of his most stunning victories, moving against Joseph Hooker's 130,000-man force at the battle of Chancellorsville, Virginia. This costly encounter (15 percent casualties for the Union, 22 percent for the Confederates, with the irreplaceable Stonewall Jackson mortally wounded) will send morale soaring in the South and plummeting in the North.

6: In Cincinnati, Ohio, a military commission convicts Clement Vallandigham "of having expressed sympathy for the enemy" and having uttered "disloyal sentiments and opinions," and orders him imprisoned for the duration of the war. The protests—and the troubling constitutional questions—aroused by this episode will cause Lincoln to commute the sentence. He will order Vallandigham escorted to the Confederacy, and on May 26, Vallandigham will be placed in Confederate hands at Murfreesboro, Tennessee.

15: At a strategy conference in Richmond, Robert E. Lee outlines a daring plan to invade Pennsylvania, drawing Union forces out of Virginia and dealing a blow to Northern morale and to the Republican party, while strengthening the hand of Northern Peace Democrats as well as Southern chances of European recognition. The invasion will also prove to be a giant raid for supplies.

18: After encounters with Confederates at Port Gibson (May 1) and Raymond (May 12); having occupied, and burned much of, Jackson, Mississippi (May 14); and then forced Confederates to retreat at Champion Hill (May 16) and Big Black River Bridge (May 17), Grant's army surrounds Vicksburg.

22: The second of two Union assaults of Vicksburg's formidable defenses (the first was on May 19) is repulsed, and Grant's army begins its siege of the city, whose defenders live in hope of rescue by forces under Joseph E. Johnston. *Also on this day:* The Bureau of Colored Troops is established in the U.S. War Department to coordinate and administer the raising of black regiments in every part of the country.

June 1863

"If you can't feed us, you had better surrender, horrible as the idea is, than suffer this noble army to disgrace themselves by desertion. . . . This army is now ripe for mutiny, unless it can be fed." Letter from "Many Soldiers" under siege—and down to quarter rations or less—within Vicksburg, to their commander, Confederate Lieutenant General John C. Pemberton, June 28, 1863.

7: At Milliken's Bend, on the Mississippi River above Vicksburg, two newly formed regiments of contrabands, as yet untrained, armed only with old muskets, and assisted by a Union gunboat, drive off a Confederate brigade attempting to disrupt Grant's supply line. Some captured black soldiers are reportedly murdered. The engagement changes some Union minds about the employment of black soldiers. "I heard prominent officers who formerly in private had sneered at the idea of negroes fighting," reported U.S. Assistant Secretary of War Charles A. Dana, "express themselves after that as heartily in favor of it."

9: The greatest cavalry battle of the war takes place at Brandy Station, Virginia, as Union forces under Alfred Pleasanton prove their mettle against Jeb Stuart's Confederates.

10: Robert E. Lee's army begins its march north toward Pennsylvania in the campaign that will reach its climax in the battle of Gettysburg.

20: West Virginia is admitted to the Union. Its constitution frees slaves born after July 4, 1863, and all others on their twenty-fifth birthday.

23: Union Major General William S. Rosecrans begins his Tullahoma campaign, which, by July 3, will compel Braxton Bragg's Confederate army to withdraw from Middle Tennessee to Chattanooga.

28: Fearing that Joseph Hooker has become "another McClellan," reluctant to be sufficiently aggressive in pursuit of Lee's invading Confederates, President Lincoln replaces him with George Gordon Meade as commander of the Army of the Potomac.

July 1863

"[W]e charged that terrible battery on Morris Island known as Fort Wagoner [sic], . . . A shell would explode and clear a space of twenty feet, our men would close up again, but it was no use we had to retreat, which was a very hazardous undertaking. How I got out of that fight alive I cannot tell, . . . Remember if I die I die in a good cause. I wish we had a hundred thousand colored troops we would put an end to this war." Sergeant Lewis Douglass, son of Frederick Douglass, Fifty-Fourth Massachusetts Infantry, letter to his future wife, July 20, 1863.

1–3: A limited engagement between a division of A. P. Hill's Confederates (marching toward the town in quest of shoes) and dismounted Union cavalry under John Buford blossoms into the three-day battle of Gettysburg, a decisive encounter of the war that turns Lee's invasion into a retreat. When news of this U.S. victory spreads through the North on July 4, the surge in morale is reflected in such newspaper headlines as the *Philadelphia Inquirer*'s "Victory! Waterloo Eclipsed!"

4: Vicksburg surrenders, a strategic victory of such importance that General Grant will later write in his memoirs, "[The] fate of the Confederacy was sealed when Vicksburg fell." With the fall of Port Hudson, 240 miles to the south, on July 9, the Confederacy is cut in two. "Grant is my man," President Lincoln will state on July 5, "and I am his the rest of the war."

11: Draft officers begin drawing names in a volatile New York City, where sentiment against "this war waged by Yankee Protestants for black freedom," already high among Irish workers, was exacerbated during a June longshoremen's walkout when black stevedores replaced striking Irishmen.

13–17: New York erupts into four of the bloodiest days of mob violence in the city's history.

18: The Union army's second assault (the first was on July 11) on formidable Fort Wagner, at Morris Island in Charleston Harbor, is led by the Fifty-Fourth Massachusetts, an African American infantry regiment commanded by Colonel Robert Gould Shaw. Widely publicized, this valiant but ill-fated assault—in which Colonel Shaw dies and casualties among the men are high—does much to convince Northerners heretofore skeptical that black regiments are effective combat units.

30: Grappling with the problem of how to ensure the safety of black soldiers and their white officers captured by Confederate forces, President Lincoln states an eye-for-an-eye policy: "For every soldier of the United States killed in violation of the laws of war, a rebel soldier shall be executed; and for every one enslaved by the enemy or sold into slavery, a rebel soldier shall be placed at hard labor on the public works." Unacceptable to many, and impractical to enforce, the policy will fade from view. The problem will remain.

August 1863

"Troops are daily passing, they say from Mississippi, to reinforce our army. We are expecting a battle every day. . . . General [Bragg] has a trying time, as there seems to be so many points from which the enemy can march their army right down on us; and they have so many more men than we have, that they can make any movement they please." Kate Cumming, nurse, Army of Tennessee, C.S.A., diary entry, August 28, 1863.

10: Meeting with President Lincoln, Frederick Douglass vehemently protests the disparity of pay between white soldiers ($13 per month, *plus* a clothing allowance of $3.50) and black soldiers ($10 per month, $3 of which could be *deducted* for clothing). This lower pay had been declared *after* many black soldiers had enlisted with the understanding that they would receive equal pay. Some black soldiers are refusing to accept the lower wages.

14: Missouri, from the 1850s, had been the scene of particularly vicious guerrilla warfare that sharply escalated after the declaration of war. Another tragic chapter begins today when a Kansas City building in which Union authorities have placed the wives and sisters of guerrillas collapses, killing five of the women. Enraged, scattered guerrilla bands begin to come together, plotting vengeance.

19: With 20,000 Federal troops now on hand, the draft—suspended after the July riots—resumes in New York City.

21–22: After issuing orders to "kill every male and burn every house," William Quantrill leads a force of 450 Confederate guerrillas in an attack on the prewar free-soil bastion of Lawrence, Kansas. The raid, during which they murder more than 180 men and burn 185 buildings, will so enrage the area's Union commander, Brigadier General Thomas Ewing, that he will issue General Orders, Number 11 (on August 25). Under this order, his troops will sweep four western Missouri counties clear of all but the most certainly loyal inhabitants. Thousands of refugees will be forced out on the roads, with the smoke from their own burning houses rising behind them.

September 1863

"[O]ne's heart grows sick of war, after all, when you see what it really is; every once in a while I feel so horrified and disgusted—it seems to me like a great slaughter-house and the men mutually butchering each other—then I feel how impossible it appears, again, to retire from this contest, until we have carried our points." Walt Whitman, U.S.A., letter, September 8, 1863.

2: As Union forces under Rosecrans move toward strategically important Chattanooga, Tennessee, the crossroads of the only rail lines still linking the eastern and western parts of the Confederacy, Ambrose Burnside's Union army of the Ohio occupies Knoxville, which has been evacuated by the Confederates.

5: Great Britain decides to detain the Laird Rams (vessels designed to sink other vessels) being built for the Confederacy in Birkenhead, England, thereby avoiding a diplomatic crisis with the United States.

9: Following the evacuation of Chattanooga by Braxton Bragg's Army of Tennessee the previous day, Union troops occupy the city—prompting Jefferson Davis to declare: "We are now in the darkest hour of our political existence."

10: Little Rock, Arkansas, falls to the Union, a loss that severely threatens the entire Confederate Trans-Mississippi Department, already cut off from the rest of the Confederacy by the fall of Vicksburg and Port Hudson. *Also on this day:* A brigade of Confederate soldiers plunders the offices, in Raleigh, of the *North Carolina Standard,* published by William H. Holden, who has been involved in organizing antiwar meetings and printed editorials advocating a negotiated peace with the North.

19–20: The bloodiest battle of the war in the Western Theater begins near Chickamauga Creek, in north Georgia. It concludes the next day, when retreating Union forces are saved from total disaster by the stubborn action of troops commanded by Major General George Thomas (known thereafter as "the Rock of Chickamauga") assisted by reserve units under Major General Gordon Granger. A major tactical victory for the Confederates, the Union retreat from Chickamauga ends in Chattanooga, Tennessee, which is placed under siege by Bragg's battered Confederates (who had suffered more than 30 percent casualties).

23: The longest and largest pre-twentieth-century movement of troops commences this day as U.S. Secretary of War Stanton moves bureaucratic mountains to dispatch more than 20,000 men, via rail, 1,233 miles to the relief of Chattanooga. They arrive near the city a mere eleven days after the plan is first proposed.

October 1863

"[T]he Yankees have been playing their same old game of destruction in our land, and what they have not laid waste to, our army have. Some of the poor women who ran off at the time of the last battle have come in and found their homes pillaged of everything, . . . they are in a state of starvation, and their husbands being in the army cannot provide for them in any way, nor can they expect anything from the country after being sacked by Yankeedom. This is one of the bitter fruits of the war." Lieutenant Richard Lewis, Fourth South Carolina Volunteers, C.S.A., letter, October 3, 1863.

13: Having run his campaign while in exile in Canada, Copperhead Clement Vallandigham is soundly defeated in the contest for governor of Ohio. Pro-Union candidates prevail in other state elections this day, as well, in part because of the Union triumphs at Gettysburg and Vicksburg. In the wake of sympathy stirred by the antiblack riots in New York City and elsewhere, and by public recognition of the valor of black regiments such as the 54th Massachusetts (see July 18), emancipation, roundly attacked by Democrats, has also become less controversial to many Northern whites. In the South, suffering from shortages, inflation, and the aftermath of Gettysburg and Vicksburg, 1863 congressional elections will change the nature of Confederate politics by bringing more conservative and negotiation-prone legislators (known as reconstructionists or tories) to Richmond and to the governorships of several Southern states. A faction that is prowar but anti-Jefferson Davis will also gather strength.

23: Grant arrives at Chattanooga, Tennessee, and cracks are soon apparent in the Confederate siege of the city, which has been going on for a month.

October 27–November 7: Chicago is the scene of the first "sanitary fair," an extravaganza featuring exhibits, food concessions, entertainment, and merchandise for sale to raise funds in support of the U.S. Sanitary Commission's services.

November 1863

"My company was examined and almost every one proved to be sound enough for soldiers.... some of them were scarred from head to foot where they had been whipped. One man's back was nearly all one scar, as if the skin had been chopped up and left to heal in ridges.... That beat all the anti-slavery sermons ever yet preached." Lieutenant Lawrence Van Alstyne, recruiting officer, Ninetieth U.S. Colored Infantry, letter, November 6, 1863.

Miss Mary J. Safford of Cairo, Illinois, was among the many women who organized and systematized hospital care for Union soldiers both as members of the Sanitary Commission and on their own.

4: Detaching some 15,000 men from Bragg's Army of Tennessee—and thus weakening the Confederate siege of Chattanooga—Lieutenant General James Longstreet leads his force toward the city of Knoxville, where they will engage in a siege of the occupying Federal troops. The siege will accomplish nothing and will end by December 4.

19: At the dedication of the military cemetery at Gettysburg, Pennsylvania, President Lincoln gives a short speech that proves to be one of the great orations in American history. The Gettysburg Address is a ringing declaration of the nation's "new birth of freedom" from the blood and agony of battlefields like Gettysburg, and a resolution that "government of the people, by the people, for the people, shall not perish from the earth."

25: Coming the day after the capture of Lookout Mountain, one of the bastions of the Confederate siege of Chattanooga, the "miracle of Missionary Ridge" occurs when men of George

Thomas' Union army of the Cumberland exceed their orders for a limited frontal assault and sweep Bragg's Confederates completely off the ridge. The siege of the city is lifted, and the door to Georgia is open to the Union army. Confederate official Hugh Lawson Clay reflects the general mood in the Confederacy at the news when he terms the defeat a "calamity . . . defeat . . . utter ruin. Unless something is done . . . we are irretrievably gone."

December 1863

"It is impossible not to rejoice over the misfortunes of such enemies as we are fighting, cruel and ruthless as they show themselves to be. . . . Homes, gardens, crops, mills, & all intended for the use & sustenance of the non-combatant population are relentlessly and systematically destroyed. They are going to starve & maltreat the inhabitants into submission. Short sighted people, & policy as misguided as it is wicked. They exasperate but do not subdue." Josiah Gorgas, chief of ordnance, C.S.A., journal entry, December 20, 1863.

8: Aware of unrest among some Confederates over Davis' policies and of the growing agitation for a negotiated peace, President Lincoln issues the Proclamation of Amnesty and Reconstruction. It offers pardon and amnesty to any secessionist—with some notable exceptions—who takes an oath of allegiance to the United States and all of its laws and proclamations, and outlines conditions for states to rejoin the Union. This is the first indication of Lincoln's moderate approach to Reconstruction, which will place him at odds with the more punitively minded Radical Republicans.

16: General Joseph E. Johnston assumes command of the Confederate army of Tennessee.

28: The Confederate Congress abolishes the practice of hiring substitutes for military service.

1864

January 1864

"I am forced to see enough of human misery. Would God I might never see more. Oh, this cruel, murderous war! Will it never end? Perhaps, when political intrigue can keep it going no longer." David Lane, Seventeenth Michigan Volunteer Infantry, U.S.A., journal entry, January 6, 1864.

2: Confederate Major General Patrick R. Cleburne proposes freeing slaves and recruiting them for service in the Confederate army, an idea that touches off a bitter debate among Southern military and political leaders but yields no result.

5: Black citizens of New Orleans draw up a petition for the franchise (the right to vote) bearing the signatures of more than 1,000 men, 27 of whom had fought under Andrew Jackson at the battle of New Orleans in 1815. It will be presented to President Lincoln on March 12 and to the U.S. Senate on March 15.

7: William Preston is named Confederate envoy to Mexico, where the French, long sympathetic to the Confederacy, are fighting to displace President Benito Juárez with a puppet emperor, Maximilian. The South, hoping for French recognition, supports the French action; the North opposes it. But neither side can do much to affect events, and the French will be dissuaded, by events in Europe, from recognizing the Confederacy.

February 1864

"A portion of the [Confederate] Congress came over this afternoon to take a look at us, among whom were [Jefferson] Davis, [Judah] Benjamin and Howell Cobb. . . . They are a proud, stern set of men, and look as if they would like to brush us out of existence. Still we are not going to be brushed out so easy." Sergeant John L. Ransom, Ninth Michigan Cavalry, U.S.A., diary entry while a prisoner of war, February 9, 1864.

15: In a secret session, the Confederate Congress appropriates $5 million for Canadian-based sabotage operations against the North. Former cavalryman Thomas C. Hines, who had proposed the espionage idea, will be dispatched to Canada to carry out "appropriate enterprises of war against our enemies." Rebel agents will have many meetings with Northern Peace Democrats in Canada in the coming summer, when Union home front morale is low and sentiments for peace are high.

17: When the Confederate Congress again authorizes President Davis to suspend the writ of habeas corpus (see also February 27, 1862) to suppress disloyalty and enforce the draft, Vice President Alexander H. Stephens is one of several powerful Georgians who protest the action with such vehemence that their response will create a backlash. The Georgia legislature will pass a resolution declaring the state's support for the war.

22: An underground movement to replace Abraham Lincoln with Secretary of the Treasury Salmon Chase as the Republican candidate for president in the 1864 election comes out in the open when the "Pomeroy Circular" is issued, decrying Lincoln's "manifest tendency toward temporary expedients." The ensuing backlash from Lincoln's supporters ends Chase's quest for the presidency.

27: The first Union prisoners of war arrive at Camp Sumter near Andersonville, Georgia. Soon filled to overflowing, "Andersonville" will become the most infamous prison camp of the Civil War.

March 1864

"It is very strange, as well as painful, to see how little is thought of death in the army; it is rarely alluded to. I remember one of our boys—he was in the same mess with me; he used to speak about some statistics of other wars, how many pounds of lead and iron it took to kill a man, and how few were killed in proportion to the number engaged, and what a good chance there was to get off whole—his name was Henry Holden, and he was the first man killed in my company at Bull Run." Sergeant Warren H. Freeman, Thirteenth Regiment Massachusetts Volunteers, U.S.A., letter to his parents, March 11, 1864.

9: At the White House, Ulysses S. Grant officially receives his commission as lieutenant general, a rank held by only George Washington before him, and is named general in chief of the U.S. armies.

13: A day after a delegation of free black Louisianans presents him with a petition for receiving the franchise, President Lincoln writes Michael Hahn, governor of (occupied) Louisiana, suggesting that the convention that is to meet in April to draw up a new state constitution consider "whether some of the colored people may not be let in [allowed to vote]." The constitution that emerges will not itself extend suffrage to black men but will include a clause allowing the legislature to enfranchise blacks in the future.

April 1864

"Went first to Gen. Lee's . . . he said he wanted every man to his post, that we had hard work to do this year, but by the blessing of Providence he hoped it would turn out well." Jedediah Hotchkiss, Topographical Engineer, C.S.A., journal entry, April 11, 1864.

12: While raiding important Federal communications facilities and posts in west Kentucky and Tennessee, Confederate cavalry commanded by Nathan Bedford Forrest attack and capture Fort Pillow, Tennessee, on the Mississippi River. Many of the United States Colored Troops defending the fort are murdered after they surrender, as are some white defenders and the fort's commander, Major William F. Bradford—"shot while trying to escape." News of this massacre will arouse Northerners, both civilians and soldiers.

17: "No distinction whatever will be made in the exchange between white and colored prisoners" is the most pressing of two conditions Union General-in-Chief Grant makes for prisoner exchanges to continue. Confederate authorities do not agree to the conditions, and the exchanges cease. But the taking of prisoners does not, putting a severe strain on prisoner-of-war facilities.

May 1864

"I propose to fight it out on this line if it takes all summer." Lieutenant General Ulysses S. Grant, May 11, 1864.

"We must destroy this army of Grant's before it gets to the James River. If he gets there it will become a siege, and then it will be a mere question of time." General Robert E. Lee speaking to Lieutenant General Jubal A. Early, spring 1864.

7: After a bruising but inconclusive two-day encounter with Lee's Confederates in Virginia's Wilderness (May 5–6), Grant withdraws his forces under cover of darkness. When it becomes apparent that this is not a retreat to the North—as has been the Union pattern after fierce battles on this front—but a move to the South, morale in the ranks surges. The men sing as they march. Unbeknownst to them, Grant has promised Lincoln that "whatever happens, there will be no turning back." When news of his advance is published in Northern papers, people become jubilant; their expectations are raised that final victory is at hand.

11: As Lee and Grant maneuver into position for their next clash, Jeb Stuart is mortally wounded during a helter-skelter encounter with Phil Sheridan's Union cavalry at Yellow Tavern, Virginia. Stuart will die the next day.

12: In the wake of clashes that began May 8–10, the Army of Northern Virginia and the Army of the Potomac engage in a bitter action in the "Mule Shoe" at Spotsylvania Court House, Virginia, before digging in. There will be two more all-out clashes (May 18 and 19) before Grant withdraws to try again to move around Lee's right flank—still pushing forward. Casualty reports will show that the Army of the Potomac suffered some 37,000 men killed, wounded, and missing since May 5—more than for all Union armies *combined* in any previous week of the war. Union civilians, recently so jubilant, will despair at the news. Confederate casualties are also high—at about 22,000 men out of a force roughly half the size of Grant's.

15: As Benjamin Butler's Union army of the James prepares for the second battle of Drewry's Bluff (May 16), a defeat that will leave it sealed off on the Virginia's Bermuda Hundred peninsula, Union Major General Franz Sigel is defeated at the battle of New Market, in the Shenandoah Valley—where Confederate forces include 247 Virginia Military Institute cadets whose courageous charge makes them instant Confederate heroes. Both Union groups thus fail in diverting resources from the main body of Lee's army, now locked in a running series of brutal encounters with the Army of the Potomac.

16: Union Major General Nathaniel Banks leads his dispirited troops back into southern Louisiana after a defeat at Sabine Crossroads (April 8) and a clash at Pleasant Hill (April 9), as well as difficulties with his gunboat support and logistics, force him to bring an end to the unsuccessful Red River Campaign. Intended as a detour on the way to Mobile, Alabama, where Banks was to keep troops tied down who would otherwise reinforce Joseph Johnston, the campaign winds up diverting Banks from Mobile altogether, allowing 15,000 Alabama troops to go to Johnston's aid as he faces Major General William T. Sherman's army approaching Atlanta.

June 1864

"The Kearsage [sic, U.S.S. *Kearsarge*] is still in the offing; Mailed a note yesterday afternoon for flag-officer Barrow, informing him of my intention to . . . engage the enemy as soon as I could make my preparations, and sent a written notice to the U.S. Consul . . . to the same effect. My crew seems to be in the right spirit, a quiet spirit of determination pervading both officers and men. The combat will no doubt be contested and obstinate; but . . . I do not feel at liberty to decline it. God defend the right, and have mercy upon the souls of those who fall, as many of us must!" Captain Raphael Semmes, Confederate States Navy, diary entry, June 15, 1864, aboard the commerce raider C.S.S. *Alabama*.

3: Protected by intricate trenchworks, Confederates pour a murderous fire into charging Union soldiers on the third and last day of the battle of Cold Harbor, Virginia, where Grant has gambled on a frontal assault against the Southerners Lee has been skillfully maneuvering to avoid open-field combat. Seven thousand Northerners are killed or wounded on this day. "I regret this assault more than any one I have ever ordered," Grant will say that evening. But he will continue to move forward.

8: In Chicago, a boisterous Republican Party (renamed, during the election, the National Union Party, to attract War Democrats) nominates Abraham Lincoln for a second term as president.

11–12: As Grant moves around Richmond toward Petersburg and the forces he dispatched to harass the enemy in the Shenandoah and around Lynchburg are themselves harassed by guerrillas and turned back, Phil Sheridan's cavalry, sent to destroy railroads, clashes for two days with Wade Hampton's Confederate cavalry at Trevilian Station, Virginia. With each side sustaining casualties of 20 percent, it is the bloodiest cavalry battle of the war.

12: The Army of the Potomac begins to cross the James River.

15: The Thirteenth Amendment to the U.S. Constitution (abolishing slavery), which has passed the Senate, falls thirteen votes short of passing the House of Representatives by the required two-thirds majority. *Also on this day:* Copperhead leader Clement Vallandigham returns to Ohio from his exile in Canada. Immediately enmeshed in Democratic meetings, and involved in leading a secretive society called the Sons of Liberty, he adds to the already considerable momentum of the Democratic movement for a negotiated peace—one that would probably leave the Union sundered and keep slavery in place. *Also on this day:* The U.S. Congress finally enacts legislation granting equal pay to black soldiers, some of whom have, for many months, been refusing to accept any pay until the inequity was rectified. But the legislation applies only to men who were free on April 19, 1861. A campaign to extend equal pay to men freed after that date will finally be successful in 1865.

18: The ten-month siege of Petersburg, Virginia, begins after Grant's forces, reluctant to make all-out assaults on the city's formidable defenses after their horrific experiences at Spotsylvania and Cold Harbor, fail to press their daunting numerical advantage. Since May 4, 65,000 Northern soldiers have been killed, wounded, or declared missing in Grant's Overland

Campaign. (Confederate casualties, some 35,000, constituted approximately the same percentage of their smaller force.) At home on sick leave, Union Brigadier General John H. Martindale writes to Major General Benjamin Butler that there is "great discouragement over the North, great reluctance to recruiting, strong disposition for peace." The price of gold rises, reflecting the pessimism of Northern financial markets. Democrats are denouncing Grant as a "butcher."

19: The U.S.S. *Kearsarge* sinks the Confederacy's most effective commerce raider, C.S.S. *Alabama,* in the waters off Cherbourg, France.

27: Having advanced to within thirty miles of Atlanta, but frustrated by Joseph E. Johnston's reluctance to commit his Confederates to battle, General Sherman assaults the entrenched center of Johnston's army at the battle of Kennesaw Mountain, Georgia. The battle, fought in 100-degree heat, gains Sherman nothing and provides civilians on the Union home front only increased frustration. In the South, morale soars. "Everyone feels unbounded confidence in General Johnston," writes Atlantan Mary Mallard, and an Atlanta paper predicts that Sherman's army will soon be "cut to pieces."

July 1864

"[President Davis] does not attempt to deceive us. He affords us no excuse to deceive ourselves. He cannot voluntarily reaccept the Union; we cannot voluntarily yield it. Between him and us the issue is distinct, simple, and inflexible. It is an issue which can only be tried by war, and decided by victory." Abraham Lincoln, message to Congress, December 6, 1864.

4: President Lincoln signs into law a repeal of certain exemption clauses of the Enrollment [Draft] Act of 1863, including the provision allowing payment of a commutation fee of $300 ("blood money" to its many opponents) instead of being drafted. *Also on this day:* The growing rift between congressional Republican radicals and President Lincoln over Reconstruction policy is reflected in the president's refusal to sign the Wade-Davis Bill, which includes conditions for seceded states' rejoining the Union that Lincoln views as retaliatory against the South and a refutation of his own more moderate approach.

9: Having driven on after his defeat at Kennesaw Mountain, Sherman has outflanked General Joseph E. Johnston and pushed the Confederates back to a position only four miles from downtown Atlanta. Civilians begin leaving the city. President Davis dispatches the caustic and unpopular Braxton Bragg to Georgia on a fact-finding mission. Bragg will recommend that Johnston be replaced by John Bell Hood.

11–12: Jubal Early and 15,000 Confederates he has led from Lynchburg, Virginia, down the Shenandoah Valley, and through the stubborn but unsuccessful resistance of Lew Wallace's 7,000 Federals at the Monocacy River, Maryland, arrive in front of Washington's fortifications, only

Dynamic General Philip H. Sheridan stands with his senior cavalry generals shortly before his assignment to the Shenandoah Valley in 1864. From left: Henry E. Davies, David M. Gregg, Sheridan, Wesley Merritt, A. T. A. Torbert, and James H. Wilson.

five miles from the White House. Their presence rivets the attention of Washingtonians—including a tall man in a stovepipe hat, who keeps popping up to look at them over the defenses. Before he realizes he's yelling at President Lincoln, Captain Oliver Wendell Holmes, Jr., shouts, "Get down, you damn fool, before you get shot!" Discouraged by the arrival of Union reinforcements, Early's troops will withdraw to the Shenandoah. The havoc they wreak on the way will aggravate General Grant into sending Phil Sheridan and a newly organized force to "follow [Early] to the death."

14: Under orders from General Sherman to "follow [Nathan Bedford] Forrest to the death, if it cost 10,000 lives and breaks the Treasury," 14,000 Federals fight Forrest's 7,000 cavalry at Tupelo, Mississippi, inflicting many casualties, including Forrest, who is wounded. Sherman is relieved of his fear that the formidable cavalryman—who had recently dealt the North its most humiliating defeat in the Western Theater (battle of Brice's Station, Mississippi, June 10)—would sever the railroad supplying his army.

17: Disturbed by Joseph E. Johnston's apparent intention to withdraw from Atlanta and leave its defense to the state militia, President Davis replaces the general with John Bell Hood. The action will stir controversy in the Confederacy but will please General Sherman, who believes that Hood will come out and fight in the open, something Johnston would not do.

18: President Lincoln issues a new call for 500,000 men. Coming just after Jubal Early's raid into Maryland, and in the midst of the costly stalemate in Virginia and Sherman's slow progress at Atlanta, it is an unpopular plea that sets his prospects for reelection in November even lower. *Also on this day:* Editor Horace Greeley and John Hay, President Lincoln's private secretary, meet in Niagara Falls, Canada, with Confederate agents Clement Clay and James Holcombe, to whom they hand a presidential safe conduct for travel to Washington to discuss "any proposition which embraces the restoration of peace, the integrity of the whole Union, and the abandonment of slavery." But the agents are not empowered to negotiate, and the Davis administration is only prepared to discuss a peace that would maintain Confederate independence and slavery. The failure of this Canadian encounter will become a potent piece of anti-Lincoln propaganda.

20: Confederate General John Bell Hood commences a series of unsuccessful offensives against William T. Sherman's army at Atlanta. Major clashes occur at Peachtree Creek (July 20), Atlanta (July 22), and Ezra Church (July 28).

30: An inspired plan precipitates tragedy at the Petersburg, Virginia, defenses. Four tons of gunpowder placed at the end of a 511-foot tunnel dug by Union soldiers blasts a huge hole in the Confederate defenses. But in the ensuing battle of the Crater, the Union attack becomes a misdirected muddle in which many of the attackers are trapped in murderous fire that Confederates pour down into the 30-foot-deep hole. Casualties are high; among them are some black troops who are killed as they try to surrender. Grant will call it "the saddest affair I have witnessed in the war."

August 1864

"It seems exceedingly probable that this Administration will not be re-elected. Then it will be my duty to so co-operate with the President elect, as to save the Union between the election and the inauguration; as he will have secured his election on such ground that he can not possibly save it afterwards." Abraham Lincoln, memorandum, August 23, 1864.

5: Shouting "Damn the torpedoes, full speed ahead," from his vantage point lashed to the mast of his flagship U.S.S. *Hartford,* Rear Admiral David Farragut leads his fleet past the guns and minefield protecting the largest of three forts guarding Mobile Bay, the last blockade-running port in the Gulf east of Texas. The three forts will fall in the following three weeks. Mobile, itself, will hold out until April 12, 1865.

11: After nearly a month of clashes and maneuvers between Hood's defending forces and Sherman's besiegers, a Wisconsin soldier writes, "We make but little progress toward Atlanta, and it may be some time before we take the place." Northern pessimism deepens. In the South, Atlanta remains a beacon for Southern hopes.

29–31: Democrats gather in Chicago for their national convention, which will nominate Major General George B. McClellan for president on a platform that is *pro* negotiated peace and *anti* emancipation. In the background, a plot to stir a Northern uprising from the excitement of the convention, hatched earlier between Copperheads and Confederates in Canada, fails to ignite when the seventy armed Confederate agents who show up in Chicago fail to find the anticipated number of eager Copperhead conspirators.

September 1864

"We cannot change the hearts of those people of the South, but we can make war so terrible . . . [and] make them so sick of war that generations would pass away before they would again appeal to it." General William T. Sherman, U.S.A.

2: Having cut the last railroad into the city and bested Hood's forces in two final encounters, Major General William T. Sherman wires Washington from within a long-disputed city: "Atlanta is ours, and fairly won." In the North, spirits soar; Sherman is dubbed the greatest general since Napoleon; and Lincoln's reelection, considered unlikely until the telegram arrives, suddenly looks possible. In the South, Mary Boykin Chesnut will reflect the gloom induced by the news when she confides to her diary: "Since Atlanta I have felt as if all were dead within me, forever. We are going to be wiped off the earth."

7: "I have deemed it to the interest of the United States that the citizens now residing in Atlanta should remove, those who prefer it to go South and the rest North." With those words, General Sherman precipitates the evacuation of Atlanta by civilians who had remained during the siege. Nearly 1,600 people leave behind their homes, most of their possessions, and terrible resentments. "War is cruelty and you cannot refine it," Sherman will say to Atlanta's mayor after giving the order. "When peace does come," he adds, "you may call on me for anything. Then will I share with you the last cracker."

8: Major General George B. McClellan, Democratic candidate for president of the United States, publishes a letter repudiating the crucial "peace plank" in the 1864 Democratic Platform: "I could not look in the faces of gallant comrades of the army and navy . . . and tell them that their labor and the sacrifice of our slain and wounded brethren had been in vain. . . . The Union is the one condition of peace—we ask no more."

27: At Fort Davidson, near Pilot Knob, Missouri, the invasion force Confederate General Sterling Price led into the state on September 19 is dealt its first major defeat by Brigadier General Thomas Ewing's Federals—even as infamous guerrilla "Bloody Bill" Anderson's men are massacring unarmed and wounded Union soldiers and militia men during an encounter at Centralia. Price had entered Missouri with the intent of bringing it, finally and actually, into the Confederacy. By the end of October, he will have been driven from the state, Bloody Bill Anderson will be dead, and organized Confederate resistance in Missouri will be at an end, though guerrilla war will continue.

October 1864

"Our disaster in the Valley—with Hood's at Atlanta makes me think the war party will triumph at the North. But tho' peace may be a long way off, I feel sure that Justice & Right will finally triumph. . . . surely all true Southrons would prefer *anything* to *submission*." Major General Stephen Dodson Ramseur, C.S.A., letter to his wife written shortly before his death at age twenty-seven at the battle of Cedar Creek, Virginia, October 1864.

4–7: One hundred forty-four blacks from eighteen states, including seven slave states, meet in Syracuse, New York, for a "National Convention of Colored Citizens of the United States," where they organize a National Equal Rights League, with John Mercer Langston of Ohio as president.

18–19: On his quest to crush Jubal Early in Virginia's Shenandoah Valley, where he is fighting a "hard war" (destroying all food and other supplies that can be of use to the Confederacy), Phil Sheridan rides into legend at the battle of Cedar Creek. After achieving victories at Winchester (September 19) and Fisher's Hill (September 22), Sheridan has departed his camp for a strategy conference in Washington when Early attacks so unexpectedly that the army Sheridan has left securely encamped begins a pell-mell retreat. Sheridan's return to the front on his warhorse Rienzi helps turn the morning's humiliating defeat into an afternoon of overwhelming victory—and generates a patriotic poem, "Sheridan's Ride," that becomes a preelection rouser in the North.

November 1864

"We shall know in a few days who is elected President of the United States. In my opinion Old Abraham will come in again, and I believe it would be best for us. McClellan might have the Union restored, if elected. I should prefer to remain at war for the rest of my life rather than to have any connection with the Yankees again." Dr. Spencer Glasgow Welch, Surgeon, Thirteenth South Carolina Volunteers, C.S.A., letter to his wife, November 3, 1864.

1: A new Maryland state constitution, abolishing slavery, takes effect.

7: A proposal by President Davis—that slaves purchased for war work as teamsters and laborers might be freed should they render faithful service—is castigated by the *Richmond Whig* as "a repudiation of the opinion held by the whole South . . . that servitude is a divinely appointed condition for the highest good of the slave."

8: Election Day in the North. Renewed confidence in Abraham Lincoln's war policies—instilled by Sherman's victories in Georgia and Sheridan's in the Shenandoah Valley—sweeps Lincoln into office for a second term. By election time, nineteen Northern states have enacted provisions for soldiers to vote in the field. Among these fighting men, Lincoln's margin is particularly high.

16: Organizing his 62,000-man army into two wings, Major General William T. Sherman embarks on a campaign in which he intends to "demonstrate the vulnerability of the South." Issuing orders that the men are to forage on the land and meet civilian resistance with "a devastation more or less relentless," Sherman leads them through Georgia toward the sea. By the time they arrive outside Savannah twenty-six days later, Sherman's "bummers" will have caused $100 million in damage.

30: Having led his Army of Tennessee out of Georgia and into Tennessee on a quest to secure reinforcements that will allow him to defeat George Thomas' Union army, then move on against Grant and Sherman, Confederate General John Bell Hood is dealt a severe blow at the battle of Franklin, Tennessee. Beginning in the afternoon and continuing far into the night, the battle involves some of the bloodiest fighting of the war. Six Confederate generals, including Patrick Cleburne and States Rights Gist are among the heavy Confederate casualties (Union casualties are comparatively light). Nevertheless, Hood leads his men on to Nashville, where his battered force entrenches four miles south of the city.

December 1864

"The past year has equaled any of its predecessors for carnage and bloodshed. Our land is drenched with the blood of martyrs! . . . Although woe and desolation stare at us every way we turn, the heart

This 1864 political cartoon accurately predicts "Slow and Steady" Lincoln's reelection victory over the Democratic candidate, former Union General in Chief George B. McClellan.

of the patriot is as firm as ever, and determined that, come what may, he will never yield." Kate Cumming, nurse, Army of Tennessee, C.S.A., journal entry, December 31, 1864.

15–16: Having prepared for battle so methodically and for so long that General Grant is chafing and Secretary of War Stanton is fuming, Union Major General George Thomas finally charges into Hood's Army of Tennessee at Nashville, breaks their lines, and pursues them as they make a disordered retreat—protected by Nathan Bedford Forrest's cavalry— through Alabama and into Mississippi. The gravity of this defeat sends shudders of distress through the Confederacy. General Hood will resign his command January 13.

22: A welcome telegram arrives at the White House from Major General Sherman: "I beg to present you, as a Christmas gift, the City of Savannah . . . ." Evacuated by Confederate troops on December 20, the city was occupied by the Federals the following day. Sherman has completed his March to the Sea (see also November 16, 1864).

1865

January 1865

"[Our] resources are unexhausted, and, as we believe, inexhaustible. . . . [we] have *more* men *now* than we had when the war *began*. . . . We are *gaining* strength, and may, if need be, maintain the contest indefinitely." Abraham Lincoln, Message to Congress, December 6, 1864.

"No positive news of Sherman's intentions. Indications are that Charleston, too, will be given up. Where is this to end? No money in the Treasury, no food to feed Gen. Lee's Army, no troops to oppose Gen. Sherman, what does it all mean. . . . Is the cause really hopeless? Is it to be abandoned and lost in this way?" Josiah Gorgas, Confederate chief of ordnance, diary entry, January 6, 1865.

11: The Missouri state constitutional convention abolishes slavery.

12: Moved by rumors of indifference and ill treatment of contrabands by Sherman's army, Secretary of War Stanton journeys to Savannah, where he and Sherman meet with several black leaders. One of the questions asked during this interview is how former slaves could best support themselves and their families in freedom. The answer: "We want to be placed on land until we are able to buy it, and make it our own."

15: After an abortive first effort, on Christmas Day, 1864, a second effort to capture Fort Fisher, North Carolina—a formidable bastion protecting the last major East-Coast blockade-runners' haven of Wilmington—is a success. General Lee's Army of Northern Virginia has lost its only avenue for receiving supplies by ship. As desertion rates from Lee's hungry and beleaguered army increase dramatically, Confederate Vice President Stephens will term the loss of the fort "one of the greatest disasters that had befallen our Cause from the beginning of the war."

16: Major General Willam T. Sherman issues Special Field Order No. 15, designating the coastline and riverbank thirty miles inland from Charleston to Jacksonville as an area for exclusive black settlement. Though more than 40,000 freedmen will have moved onto new farms carved out of this formerly Confederate land by June 1865, President Andrew Johnson will cause their eviction when, in August, he restores the land Sherman had set aside to its former Confederate owners.

23: With confidence in his leadership waning, President Jefferson Davis bolsters Confederate resolve by signing an act providing for the appointment of Robert E. Lee as general in chief of all Confederate Armies. (Lee will officially assume these responsibilities February 6.) It is with Lee and his Army of Northern Virginia that Confederate officials and civilians have placed their unreserved pride and greatest hopes since that army's first stunning victories in 1862.

24: Confederates send General in Chief Grant an offer to renewal of prisoner exchanges; he will agree.

31: After long delay, the U.S. House of Representatives passes the Thirteenth Amendment to the Constitution, abolishing slavery (it had been passed by the Senate April 8, 1864). When the 119 to 56 vote is announced, celebrations erupt in the House and in Washington's streets. "I have felt, ever since the vote," a Republican congressman will write in his diary, "as if I were in a new country." Ratification by two-thirds of the states will make the Thirteenth Amendment law on December 18, 1865.

February 1865

"The 'peace commissioners' returned on Sunday, & with the answer I expected—no terms save Submission will be listened to. It has had a good effect on the country. . . . The war feeling has blazed out afresh in Richmond, & the spirit will I hope spread thro' the land." Josiah Gorgas, Confederate chief of ordnance, diary entries, February 8, February 10, 1865.

1: "Why don't you go over to South Carolina and serve them this way," Georgians had reportedly asked General Sherman. "They started it." The idea had already occurred to the general (who had, on January 19, dispatched some troops in that direction), and today, Sherman leads 60,000 troops away from Savannah. His goal: to move north, through both Carolinas, destroying all war resources in his path, and come up on the rear of the Army of Northern Virginia, which would then be caught between two large Union forces. A much longer and more difficult campaign than Sherman's March to the Sea, this expedition will carve a corridor of destruction through the heart of South Carolina, against which, Sherman reports to Army Chief of Staff Henry W. Halleck, "the whole army is burning with an insatiable desire to wreak vengeance." But when the border of North Carolina is crossed, a Union officer will later note, "Not a house was burned, and the army gave to the people more than it took from them." *Also on this day:* Boston lawyer John Rock becomes the first African American admitted to practice before the U.S. Supreme Court—the same court that, in 1857, under Chief Justice Taney, had issued the Dred Scott decision, denying that any black person could be a citizen of the United States.

3: Aboard the Union steamer *River Queen* at Hampton Roads, off Fort Monroe, Virginia, President Abraham Lincoln and U.S. Secretary of State William H. Seward confer with Confederate Vice President Alexander H. Stephens; President *pro tem* of the Confederate Senate Robert Hunter; and C.S.A. Assistant Secretary of War John A. Campbell. A proposal for an armistice is among the subjects discussed, but President Lincoln makes it clear that the United States considers unconditional Confederate surrender the only acceptable means of ending the war.

18: As Sherman's army moves through the state capital of Columbia, now in flames, Union troops commanded by Alexander Schimmelfennig enter Charleston, South Carolina, the "fire-eater" stronghold where the war began. The previous night, Confederate troops had evacuated this city, heading out to join the forces being scraped together to oppose Sherman.

22: Confederate General Joseph E. Johnston, who had been relieved from command of the Army of Tennessee before the fall of Atlanta, is placed in command of the force being assembled to thwart Sherman. He is to be assisted by a number of able generals. But fighting manpower is scarce. *Also on this day:* An amendment to Tennessee's state constitution abolishes slavery.

March 1865

"The day you make soldiers of [slaves] is the beginning of the end of the revolution. If slaves will make good soldiers our whole theory of slavery is wrong." Politician and soldier Howell Cobb, C.S.A.

3: The U.S. Congress enacts legislation establishing a Bureau of Refugees, Freedmen, and Abandoned Lands. Assigned supervisory and management responsibilities for all abandoned lands in former Confederate territory, the Freedmen's Bureau is to have "control of all subjects relating to refugees and freedmen from rebel States." It is the first national social welfare agency. Another act passed this day establishes the Freedman's Savings and Trust Company, and a "Resolution to encourage Enlistments and to promote the Efficiency of the military Forces of the United States" declares that the wives and children of black soldiers will henceforth "be forever free."

4: Abraham Lincoln delivers his second inaugural address: "With malice toward none; with charity for all; with firmness in the right, as God gives us to see the right, let us strive on to finish the work we are in; . . . to do all which may achieve and cherish a just, and a lasting peace, among ourselves, and with all nations."

13: President Jefferson Davis signs a "Negro Soldier Law" authorizing the enlistment of slaves as soldiers. Such slave soldiers could not be emancipated "except by consent of the owners and of the states in which they may reside." This long-debated measure is enacted too late to have any significant impact.

14: A final attempt to secure European recognition for the Confederacy, predicated on the South's embracing its own policy of emancipation, fails when Britain's Lord Palmerston informs Confederate envoys James Mason and Duncan F. Kenner that Britain could not recognize the Confederate States as an independent nation "when the events of a few weeks might prove [the South's attempt at independence] a failure."

19–21: On its way to resupply and regroup at Goldsborough, North Carolina, before a final thrust into Virginia, Sherman's army—which has already clashed with Johnston's Confederates at Averasborough (March 16)—fights them again at the three-day battle of Bentonville. This proves to be the last significant Confederate effort to halt Sherman's advance.

24–25: With his beleaguered 55,000-man army facing Grant's 120,000, and expecting Sherman's 60,000 to arrive at his rear very soon, Robert E. Lee determines to break out of the siege at Petersburg and join up with Johnston—thus losing two important Virginia cities (Petersburg and Richmond) but preserving the Confederate army. The attempted breakout begins with an attack on Fort Stedman, east of Petersburg. Initially successful, it is broken when the Federals regroup and counterattack. The attempt costs Lee nearly 5,000 men and part of his own forward line. *Also on this day:* 32,000 Federals place Mobile, Alabama, defended by 2,800 Confederates, under siege.

April 1865

"Thank God I have lived to see this. It seems to me that I have been dreaming a horrid dream for four years, and now the nightmare is gone. I want to see Richmond." President Abraham Lincoln, after entering Petersburg with Grant, April 3, 1865.

"Relieved from the necessity of guarding cities . . . with our army free to move from point to point . . . and where the foe will be far removed from his own base . . . nothing is now needed to render our triumph certain, but . . . our own unquenchable resolve." President Jefferson Davis, April 4, 1865.

2: After Phil Sheridan's cavalry and a corps of Union infantry rout the Confederate force under George Pickett that was guarding Lee's line of retreat southwest of Petersburg (battle of Five Forks, Virginia, April 1), the Army of the Potomac attacks all along the Confederate lines around the city. Pushed hard, the Confederates hold on until they can withdraw under cover of darkness; meanwhile, Lee telegraphs Davis that Richmond must be given up. The evacuation of that city begins this night as well.

3: Grant enters Petersburg, accompanied by President Lincoln, who had traveled south to confer with his general in chief at nearby City Point, Virginia, a few days before.

4: President Lincoln arrives in Richmond, where fires the evacuating Confederates had set are still being extinguished. As he walks through the streets of what so recently had been the enemy capital, the president is surrounded by black people reaching out to touch him to make certain he is really in their midst. The only black correspondent to write for a major Northern newspaper during the war, Thomas Morris Chester, witnesses the scene. He will write: "What a wonderful change has come over the spirit of Southern dreams."

9: His force worn down to a hungry and weary 30,000 men constantly harassed by Union cavalry (who captured 8,000 Confederates at Sayler's Creek, April 6), and nearly surrounded by enemy forces that outnumber his by more than two-to-one, General Robert E. Lee surrenders the Army of Northern Virginia to Grant at Appomattox Court House, Virginia. (Formal ceremonies occur April 12.) The action does not formally end the war; many Southern fighting men elsewhere are still under arms. But this general and this army have long been the very heart of the Southern war effort. The impact of their surrender is reflected in a young Floridian's diary entry for April 10: "General Lee has surrendered the Army of Northern Virginia. . . . It is as if the very earth had crumbled beneath our feet." In the North, barely calmed down after the tumultuous celebrations of the fall of Richmond, crowds burst into song in city streets and cannons fire 500-gun salutes.

14–15: While attending a performance at Ford's Theatre, Abraham Lincoln is shot and mortally wounded by assassin John Wilkes Booth. He dies early the next morning. His death plunges the North into mourning—and stills the most powerful voice for moderate Reconstruction policies. Edgar Dinsmore, a black soldier from New York stationed in Charleston will write his fiancée: "Humanity has lost a firm advocate, our race its Patron Saint, and the good of all the world a fitting object to emulate." Andrew Johnson of Tennessee becomes the seventeenth president of the United States.

26: On the same day that John Wilkes Booth is tracked down and killed, Major General Sherman accepts the surrender of the Confederate troops commanded by Joseph E. Johnston, near Durham Station, North Carolina. Confederate forces in Alabama and Mississippi will surrender May 4, and other Confederate army and navy forces will continue to surrender through June.

Ruins of the Gallego Flour Mills in Richmond, Virginia, reveal the devastation that characterized many areas of the South after four years of war fought largely on Southern soil.

May 1865

"As we neared Atlanta, the scene was one of desolation and ruin. As far as the eye could reach, pile after pile of blackened brick could be seen, where once had stood stately mansions. I had no idea that Atlanta was so large a place as it is. There being few or no buildings, trees, or any thing else left standing, we had a full view of its extent." Kate Cumming, resident of Alabama, U.S.A., journal entry, May 5, 1865.

10: President Andrew Johnson proclaims armed resistance at an end—though one more small land engagement will be fought May 12 at Palmito Ranch, Texas. *Also on this day:* Jefferson Davis is captured near Irwinville, Georgia. He will be imprisoned. The Union blockade is partially lifted. In Kentucky, former Confederate guerrilla William Quantrill is mortally wounded. Other guerrillas will be pursued by Union army units for much of the year.

23–24: The Army of the Potomac (May 23) and the western army informally known as "Sherman's bummers" (May 24), march through the heart of Washington in a Grand Review. Though some contrabands walk with Sherman's troops, not one of the 166 regiments of United States Colored Troops marches in this celebration.

29: By proclamation, President Johnson grants amnesty and pardon to all persons who directly or indirectly participated in "the existing rebellion"—with some exceptions—upon the taking of an oath declaring their allegiance to the U.S. Constitution and laws. The proclamation indicates that Johnson will pursue a moderate Reconstruction policy; Radical Republican objections to some of its provisions indicate that troubled waters are ahead.

★   ★   ★

The United States, in 1865, was far different from the country of 1860. Whole areas of the South were in ruins, and fully one-quarter of its military-age white men were dead. The region was occupied by Union troops, its economy was shattered, and the potent political influence the South had wielded before the war was gone. North and South, the Civil War had taken more American lives than all other conflicts *combined*, through Vietnam. It had shaken assumptions, shattered illusions, and added fuel to the fires of social reform movements—from suffrage to labor unions—that had been kindled in the prewar North. In the South, it also gave birth to the gripping mythology encompassed in the term "Lost Cause."

Four million Americans who had been considered property in 1860 were now recognized as human beings and American citizens. But that fact had not erased prejudice; nor would measures taken to assist in the education and integration of these freedmen and women into the larger society, and to erase barriers faced by all people of color in most parts of the nation, be as persistent or effective as their advocates hoped. Rife with bitterness and recrimination, as well as efforts to ameliorate and rebuild, the Reconstruction era was to be one of the most volatile in American history (see Chapter 11, "Reconstruction and the Aftermath of the War").

Yet the Civil War did resolve the two primary issues that had sparked it. It eradicated slavery in the United States, and it answered the question Iowa Senator James W. Grimes had posed as the first Southern states were attempting to fulfill their threats to dismember the Union: "The question . . . is whether we have a country, whether or not this is a nation." The answer—inscribed in the blood and sacrifice of the people on both sides of this terrible conflict, and never thereafter challenged—was *Yes*.

SOURCES

Bailyn, Bernard, Robert Dallek, David Brion Davis, David Herbert Donald, John L. Thomas, and Gordon S. Wood. *The Great Republic: Nineteenth and Early Twentieth-Century America, 1820–1920*. Fourth ed. D. C. Heath and Co., 1993.

Current, Richard N., ed. in chief. *The Confederacy* [selections from the four-volume Simon & Schuster *Encyclopedia of the Confederacy*]. New York: Simon & Schuster, 1993.

Faust, Patricia L., ed. *Historical Times Illustrated Encyclopedia of the Civil War*. New York: Harper & Row Publishers, 1986.

Gallagher, Gary W. *The Confederate War*. Cambridge: Harvard University Press, 1997.

Klein, Maury. *Days of Defiance: Sumter, Secession, and the Coming of the Civil War*. New York: Alfred A. Knopf, 1997.

Long, Everette B., and Barbara Long. *The Civil War Day by Day*. Garden City, NY: Doubleday & Company, 1971.

McPherson, James M. *Battle Cry of Freedom*. New York: Oxford University Press, 1988.

_____ *For Cause and Comrades: Why Men Fought in the Civil War*. New York: Oxford University Press, 1997.

_____ *The Negro's Civil War: How American Blacks Felt and Acted during the War for the Union*. New York: Ballantine Books, 1991 (originally published 1965).

Diary and letter excerpts in the Time Line are from primary and secondary Civil War materials in the Library of Congress collections.

ANTEBELLUM AMERICA

Long before the Civil War, the terms "North" and "South" had acquired a fixed geographic and cultural certainty for Americans. In 1767, two English astronomers, Charles Mason and Jeremiah Dixon, completed a survey that marked what had been a disputed boundary between Pennsylvania and Maryland. By the early nineteenth century, the line of demarcation had become more significant; most free states were entirely north of the Mason-Dixon line (parts of Illinois, Indiana, New Jersey, and Ohio fell below it) and most slave states were entirely to the south of it. (Some sections of Delaware, Missouri, and Virginia were above it.) For the purposes of this chapter, the Mason-Dixon line defines the North and the South. (During the Civil War, however, four states entirely or primarily south of the line—Delaware, Kentucky, Maryland, and Missouri—remained in the Union. In the other chapters of this book, "the South" will refer to those states that joined the Confederacy.)

The two sections had much in common—the English language, a revolutionary heritage, and a population that was mostly Protestant. But the regional differences were striking and had become the subject of frequent comment. The ethnic diversity of New York and Pennsylvania contrasted with the ethnic homogeneity in most of the white South; the religious practices of the Puritans in New England differed greatly from those of the Anglicans in Virginia. Some 1,200 miles separated Maine in the North from Florida in the South, but slavery could make the two sections appear worlds apart. The slave system in the South and the free labor capitalism of the North produced two distinct economic philosophies that shaded Americans' views of those living on the opposite side of the Mason-Dixon line.

In 1858, two U.S. senators—William H. Seward of New York and James Hammond of South Carolina—bluntly expressed, for many, the way in which their own part of the country regarded the other. Seward held that valuing free labor had produced, in the North, a workforce that was educated, innovative, vibrant, industrious, and democratic. "We justly ascribe to its influences the strength, wealth, greatness, intelligence, and freedom, which the whole American people now enjoy. . . . [O]pening all the fields of industrial employment . . . to . . . all classes of men . . . brings into the highest possible activity all the physical, moral and social energies of the whole state. In states where the slave system prevails, the masters, directly or indirectly, secure all political power, and constitute a ruling aristocracy." Years before, Seward had criticized the effect slavery had produced. The South, he said, was left with "exhausted soil, old and decaying towns, wretchedly neglected roads."

In his hallmark "Cotton is King" speech to the Senate, Hammond dismissed the idea of the superiority of Northern society and the concept of free labor. "In all social systems there must be a class to do the menial duties, to perform the drudgery of life," he observed. ". . . Such a class you must have, or you would not have that other class which leads progress, civilization, and refinement. It constitutes the very mud-sill of society and of political government; and you might as well attempt to build a house in the air, as to build either the one or the other, except on this mud-sill. Fortunately for the South, she found a race adapted to that purpose to her hand . . . in short, your [the North's] whole hireling class of manual laborers and 'operatives,' as you call them, are essentially slaves. The difference between us is, that our slaves are hired for life and well compensated; there is no starvation, no begging, no want of employment among our people, and not too much employment either. Yours are hired by the day, not cared for, and scantily compensated, which may be proved in the most painful manner, at any hour in any street of your large towns. Why, you meet more beggars in one day, in any single street of the city of New York, than you would meet in a lifetime in the whole South."

In exalting the plantation system, many Southerners condemned the effects of urbanization on the North, asserting that its cities had become bastions of crime and discontent. In the North, remarked a Southern newspaper, "The prevailing class one meets with is that of mechanics struggling to be genteel, and small farmers who do their own drudgery, and yet are hardly fit for association with a Southern gentleman's body servant."

Northerners responded that the slave system had produced a region that was ignorant, backward, and cruel. Emily Burke, a Northern school teacher who had worked in the South, wrote, in her *Reminiscences of Georgia* (1850): "Those who have never lived in the Southern States can have but a faint conception of the evils that accrue to the master as well as slave, from their peculiar institutions. . . . [S]laveholders live in constant fear for the safety of their lives and property," and all are tainted by "the corrupting and demoralizing influence such a system has upon every thing that comes in contact with it."

Despite the fundamental differences between the regions, not until the antebellum period (from 1820 until 1861) did the growing sectional divide between North and South threaten to split the country. The years before the Civil War were marked by both a dramatic rift and heroic efforts to hold the Union together. But no matter what compromise was achieved or what crisis was temporarily averted, slavery continued to be a roadblock as the nation expanded into the western territories. Would the country embrace free labor nationwide, or would slavery continue as it had for centuries in America? It was, in the words of Senator Seward, "an irrepressible conflict between opposing and enduring forces." Until the United States came to a permanent national settlement on the status of slavery—and the attendant issues of Federal power and states' rights—the country would continue to be distracted from achieving its "manifest destiny."

A Constitutional Problem	The Civil War was the culmination of a political and social conflict that had its roots in the earliest days of America. This conflict was the emergence of slavery as the dominant social and economic institution in the South. As James Madison had shrewdly noted at the Constitutional Convention: ". . . the States were divided into different interests not by their difference of size, but by other circumstances; the most material of which resulted partly from climate, but principally from the effects of their having or not having slaves."

The nation's constitutional structure made it virtually impossible to imagine a national political solution to the matter of slavery. The Constitution did not give Congress the power to regulate slavery in the existing states. Amendment of the Constitution required the support of two-thirds of each house of Congress, and ratification by three-fourths of the states. Thus, as long as the South wanted to maintain the institution, the slave states had the power to prevent a constitutional amendment that could affect slavery. In numerous ways, the Constitution gave slavery special protection;

in the 1840s and 1850s, the Supreme Court expanded this protection even more with its decisions in *Prigg v. Pennsylvania* (1842) and *Dred Scott v. Sandford* (1857).

The U.S. Constitution, itself, reflected the importance of slavery in America. The five most significant clauses dealing with slavery were:

1. "Three-Fifths Clause" (Art. I, Sec. 2, Par. 3). Each slave was counted as three-fifths of a person for purposes of determining representation in Congress. This increased Southern power in the House of Representatives, where membership is based on the population of each state. The clause also provided that any "direct tax" levied on the states could be imposed only proportionately, and that only three-fifths of all slaves would be counted in assessing what each state's contribution would be. However, no one at the Constitutional Convention actually expected direct taxes to be imposed.

2. "Slave Trade Clause" (Art. I, Sec. 9, Par. 1). Congress was prohibited from banning the African slave trade before the year 1808.

3. "Capitation Tax Clause" (Art. I, Sec. 9, Par. 4). Any "capitation" or other "direct tax" had to take into account the Three-Fifths Clause. The "direct tax" portion of this clause was redundant; it was already provided for in the Three-Fifths Clause.

4. "Fugitive Slave Clause" (Art. IV, Sec. 2, Par. 3). States were prohibited from emancipating fugitive slaves, and runaways were to be returned to their owners "on demand."

5. "Amendment Provisions" (Art. V). Any amendment of the slave importation or capitation clauses before 1808 was prohibited.

Taken together, these five provisions gave the South a strong claim to special treatment for its peculiar institution. The Three-Fifths Clause also gave the South extra political muscle—in the House of Representatives and in the electoral college—to support that claim. Numerous other provisions of the Constitution supplemented the five clauses' direct protection of slavery. Some provisions that indirectly guarded slavery, such as the prohibition on taxing exports, were included primarily to protect the interests of slaveholders. Others—such as the guarantee of Federal support to "suppress Insurrections"; and the creation of the electoral college, which gave whites in slave states disproportionate influence in the election of a president—were written with slavery in mind, although delegates also supported them for reasons having nothing to do with slavery. With the Constitution explicit on some issues and vague or silent on others, Americans who held opposing positions on slavery and states' rights could all point to the document to support their views. They would do so with vigor during the antebellum period.

ANTEBELLUM TIME LINE

1777: Vermont (part of the former New Hampshire colony) proclaims itself an independent state. Its constitution prohibits slavery. This provision remains in effect when Vermont becomes the fourteenth state in the Union in 1791. Prior to this, all the colonies had allowed slavery.

1780: Pennsylvania passes a gradual emancipation law; this begins the process of ending slavery in the colonies. Rhode Island and Connecticut will follow this lead in 1784.

The Massachusetts Constitution bans slavery.

1783: The New Hampshire Constitution bans slavery.

1787: The Continental Congress, established under the Articles of Confederation, passes the Northwest Ordinance to facilitate the settlement of the northwestern territories—the area north of the Ohio River that will eventually become Ohio, Indiana, Illinois, Michigan, Wisconsin, and part of Minnesota. At the last minute, Congress amends the ordinance, declaring that "there shall be neither slavery nor involuntary servitude in the said territory." However, fugitive slaves in the territory must be returned to their owners. The ordinance will ultimately assume an almost mythical status for many Northerners. For Abraham Lincoln and other Republicans in the 1850s, it will become a fundamental touchstone.

The Constitutional Convention arrives at the three-fifths compromise, which allows slaves to be counted as three-fifths of a person in the apportioning of each state's representation in the lower house of Congress. The Convention also approves a clause that prohibits slaves from obtaining their freedom by fleeing to a state that has banned slavery.

1792: Kentucky joins the Union as a slave state.

1793: Eli Whitney's invention of the cotton gin greatly expands the area of the South in which cotton can be profitably grown, thereby increasing the demand for slaves.

Congress passes the first Fugitive Slave Act. It is now a Federal crime to assist fleeing slaves, and slaveholders are allowed to pursue runaways across state lines.

1796: Tennessee enters the Union as a slave state.

1800: Gabriel Prosser, a Virginia slave, plans an ambitious rebellion to capture the armories at Richmond and take over the city. The plot is quickly suppressed, and Prosser and more than 30 of his followers are executed. U.S. slaveholders' fears of such revolts have been augmented by the successful Haitian slave uprisings led by Toussaint L'Ouverture in the 1790s.

1803: The United States purchases the Louisiana Territory from France for $15 million. The territory, which extends about 828,000 square miles west from the Mississippi River to the Rocky Mountains, doubles the size of the nation. Slavery has been permitted by both France and Spain in this territory.

Ohio enters the Union as a free state.

1812: Louisiana joins the Union as a slave state.

1816: Indiana is admitted to the Union as a free state.

1817: The American Colonization Society, which advocates sending free blacks to new settlements in Africa, is founded in Washington. (See "Political Parties, Organizations, and Movements," in Chapter 3, "Wartime Politics.")

Mississippi joins the Union as a slave state.

1818: Illinois enters the Union as a free state.

The Territorial Assembly of the Missouri Territory petitions Congress for admission to the Union as a slave state. Because the Union is on the verge of being evenly divided between slave and free states, Missouri's petition initiates three years of sometimes rancorous political debate.

1819: Alabama is admitted to the Union as a slave state. Slave and free states now have equal representation in the Senate.

1820: In the continuing political debate on the admission of Missouri as a slave state, an argument erupts over whether Congress has the power to ban slavery in new states. Under the Missouri Compromise, Congress' agreement to admit Missouri as a slave state is counterbalanced by the admission of Maine as a free state. Congress then stipulates that, in the rest of the Louisiana Territory, all areas north of latitude 36°30′ shall be free. (See "Compromise and Crisis," page 106.)

Maine enters the Union.

1821: Missouri is granted statehood.

1822: After a slave revolt led by Denmark Vesey is thwarted in South Carolina, thirty-five rebels are hanged.

1824: Connecticut-born Charles G. Finney begins preaching and helps to initiate the Second Great Awakening, an evangelical Protestant movement that inspires many social reformers, including abolitionists.

1826: New Jersey passes the first personal liberty law, which requires a judicial hearing before any alleged fugitive slave can be removed from the state. Pennsylvania passes a similar law later in the year.

1829: David Walker, a free African American from North Carolina now living in Boston, pens his *Appeal,* which calls on slaves to rebel and overthrow the institution of slavery. Distribution of this pamphlet is forbidden in the South.

1830: David Walker dies mysteriously.

1831: In Southampton County, Virginia, Nat Turner leads a revolt by slaves in which about sixty whites are killed. The insurrection is soon quelled by white soldiers, who kill more than 100 slaves. (Turner himself is later caught and hanged.) Several Southern states then pass stricter slave codes.

In Boston, William Lloyd Garrison starts publishing *The Liberator,* an important abolitionist newspaper, which calls for an immediate end to slavery.

1832: In response to what they consider an unfairly high Federal tariff, South Carolinians hold a state convention and pass a nullification ordinance (see "Nullification Crisis," page 107). President Andrew Jackson acts quickly and decisively to counter South Carolina's threat of secession. After Congress passes a compromise tariff bill, South Carolina backs down.

1833: White and black abolitionists, including William Lloyd Garrison and Robert Purvis, come to Philadelphia from nine Northern states and form the American Anti-Slavery Society (see "Political Parties, Organizations, and Movements," in Chapter 3, "Wartime Politics"). Its goal is "the entire abolition of slavery in the United States."

Massachusetts author and abolitionist Lydia Maria Child publishes *An Appeal in Favor of That Class of Americans Called Africans,* which condemns slavery and helps to persuade Wendell Phillips, an attorney, Charles Sumner, a reformer and future U.S. senator, and others, to join the abolitionist movement.

1836: As the abolitionist movement grows and Congress is besieged with antislavery petitions, Southerners influence the House of Representatives to pass a series of "gag rules," which essentially smother any discussion by either automatically tabling the petitions or refusing to acknowledge them. Former president John Quincy Adams, now a representative from Massachusetts, leads the fight to repeal these rules, which he believes violate the First

Amendment right to petition government for the redress of grievances. The House will not fully repeal the gag rules until 1844.

The Mexican territory of Texas declares its independence, in part because U.S. settlers there want to use slave labor. Slavery is illegal in Mexico.

Arkansas enters the Union as a slave state.

1837: In Alton, Illinois, editor Elijah P. Lovejoy, who has been calling for the immediate end of slavery, is killed while trying to protect his press from repeated mob attacks. His murder generates an outcry in the Northern press and enrages many ordinary people, who see this as an attack on freedom of speech.

The Presbyterian Church splits into New School and Old School branches. The former, mostly in the North, opposes slavery; the latter, mainly in the South, does not.

Michigan enters the Union as a free state.

1839: Northern abolitionist Reverend Theodore Dwight Weld publishes *American Slavery as It Is*, primarily comprising excerpts from advertisements and articles in Southern newspapers. This condemnation of slavery, using slaveowners' own words, is one of the most powerful

In 1840, about 2.5 million blacks were enslaved in the United States; by the time the war broke out in 1861, there were four million. The slaves seen here are planting sweet potatoes.

antebellum attacks on the "peculiar institution." It is reprinted several times, and is an important source for Harriet Beecher Stowe in writing her best-selling antislavery novel, *Uncle Tom's Cabin* (1852).

1840: The first abolitionist political party, the Liberty Party, fields a presidential candidate, James G. Birney, who advocates banning slavery in the District of Columbia, ending the interstate slave trade, and not allowing any additional slave states into the Union. A number of abolitionists, including William Lloyd Garrison, object to the formation of an independent political party, and the ticket polls well below one percent of the vote.

1842: In *Prigg v. Pennsylvania,* the Supreme Court overturns the Pennsylvania personal liberty law (1826). The court rules that the Federal Fugitive Slave Law overrides state law but adds that enforcement of this law is a Federal responsibility.

1843: In response to the *Prigg* decision, Massachusetts passes a personal liberty law prohibiting state officials from assisting in the capture of fugitive slaves. Eight other states follow suit.

1844: At the Methodist General Conference, delegates are divided over whether one of the church's bishops, from Georgia, could remain a bishop while owning slaves (which he had recently acquired through marriage). Soon afterward, Southerners set up a separate branch: the Methodist Episcopal Church, South. Baptists will also split into Northern and Southern churches in 1845.

On May 29, in a speech in Boston, black abolitionist Charles Lenox Remond tells his listeners: "I speak after long thought. . . . if I can only sustain the Constitution by sustaining Slavery, then—'live or die—sink or swim—survive or perish,' I give my voice for the dissolution of the Union." This is also the position of William Lloyd Garrison, the nation's most prominent white abolitionist.

1845: Florida joins the Union as a slave state.

Having campaigned for election in 1844 on a platform calling for U.S. expansion into both Texas and Oregon, President James K. Polk readily signs congressional resolutions approving the annexation of Texas and its admission to the Union as a slave state.

Frederick Douglass details his experiences as a slave in his *Narrative,* one of a number of slave narratives that promote the abolitionist cause.

1846: The Mexican War breaks out after the United States annexes Texas. U.S. troops move to claim the Rio Grande as the southern border of Texas, and Mexico views this as an act of aggression. (Mexico claims that the boundary is farther to the north, along the Nueces River.) U.S. supporters of the war, including President Polk, see it as an opportunity to gain California and other Mexican territories in the Southwest. A significant minority of Americans who oppose the war view it as a land grab to benefit slave-owning interests.

In Congress, Representative David Wilmot of Pennsylvania introduces a proviso to a bill appropriating money for the purchase of territory from Mexico in an anticipated peace settlement. The "Wilmot Proviso" stipulates that slavery is to be barred from all such territory. Although it will be passed by the House and is provoking much debate, the proviso will be repeatedly rejected by the Senate.

Iowa enters the Union as a free state.

1848: Under the treaty of Guadalupe Hidalgo, which ended the Mexican War, the United States purchases the territories of California and New Mexico for $15 million (this area will become the future states of California, Utah, and Nevada, most of Arizona, as well as parts of New Mexico, Colorado, and Wyoming).

The Oregon Territory is created after a dispute over Canada's southern border is resolved with Great Britain. This acquisition will pave the way for admission of Oregon as a free state in 1859. (Washington, also part of this territory, does not become a state until 1889.)

Wisconsin joins the Union as a free state.

The Free Soil Party, founded by opponents of slavery in the territories, nominates former U.S. president Martin Van Buren and chooses Charles Francis Adams, a son and grandson of presidents, as his running mate. (See "Diplomats and Notable Figures in Foreign Affairs" in Chapter 3, "Wartime Politics.") The ticket garners only 10 percent of the vote but diverts enough Democratic votes to allow the Whig candidate, Zachary Taylor, to win. Free Soil candidates earn thirteen seats in the House and one Senate seat (in Ohio). Because the number of Whigs and Democrats is almost equal in the House, the Free Soilers gain the balance of power there. This emergence of a significant third party indicates the strength of the abolitionists and helps set the stage for the formation of the Republican Party.

1849: With the gold rush rapidly increasing its population, California drafts a constitution banning slavery and petitions Congress for admission as a free state.

1850: California's application for statehood and Texas' attempts to expand into the New Mexico territory increase the tensions surrounding slavery. Worried about a breakup of the Union, Senator Henry Clay of Kentucky develops the much-debated "Compromise of 1850." The Compromise is defeated in the Senate, but Senator Stephen A. Douglas of Illinois guides its passage through Congress as a series of individual laws. (see "Compromise and Crisis," page 106, and "Notable Antebellum Figures," page 127.)

Harriet Tubman, who escaped from slavery in 1849, makes the first of nearly twenty trips into the South to lead slaves to free soil via the "Underground Railroad" (see "Fugitive Slaves and the Underground Railroad," page 99, and "Notable Antebellum Figures," page 127). With the passage of the new fugitive slave law, the only safe refuge for runaways is outside the United States—primarily, in Canada.

1852: *Uncle Tom's Cabin,* Harriet Beecher Stowe's antislavery novel, is published. It rapidly becomes a huge best-seller and fans Northern abolitionist sentiment.

In a case involving eight slaves from Virginia, a judge upholds a New York law that grants freedom to slaves who are brought into a state by their owner while en route to another state. Most Northern states have similar laws rejecting any right of transit for slave owners. Virginia later contests the judge's decision, but New York's highest court will agree on the validity of the state law in *Lemmon v. The People* (1860).

1853: The Gadsden Purchase is negotiated with Mexico. It will add about 30,000 square miles to the area that will become the southern part of New Mexico and Arizona. Many Northerners see this as a ploy by Southerners to gain slave territory. In the following year, the deal will be only narrowly approved in the Senate. The amount of land acquired will be restricted to the amount that is essential for a southern rail route.

1854: Anthony Burns, a fugitive slave from Virginia, is arrested by Federal agents in Boston. In an effort to free him, radical abolitionists led by Reverend Thomas Wentworth Higginson attack the courthouse. A deputy marshal is killed. Although Bostonians offer to buy Burns' freedom, Federal officials, backed by U.S. troops, insist on returning Burns to his owner.

After much heated debate, Congress passes the Kansas-Nebraska Act (see "Compromise and Crisis," page 106), which repeals the part of the 1820 Missouri Compromise that called for free states in the plains area. Instead, the new law employs the doctrine of Popular Sovereignty. Residents of Kansas and Nebraska are allowed to determine, by majority vote, their state's slave or free status.

Eli Thayer starts the New England Emigrant Aid Society to recruit antislavery settlers for Kansas. (See "Political Parties, Organizations, and Movements," in Chapter 3, "Wartime Politics.")

The Republican Party, formed in July through a coalition of Free Soilers and antislavery Whigs and Democrats, demands the repeal of both the Kansas-Nebraska Act and the fugitive slave law. It also calls for an end to slavery in the District of Columbia. (See "Political Parties, Organizations, and Movements," in Chapter 3, "Wartime Politics.")

The American Party, better known as the "Know-Nothings," gains political clout and advocates a nativist platform in response to the recent large influx of immigrants, particularly Irish Catholics. (See "Political Parties, Organizations, and Movements" in Chapter 3, "Wartime Politics.")

1855: After passage of the Kansas-Nebraska Act, proslavery forces, mainly from neighboring Missouri, pour into the sparsely settled Kansas territory, as do many antislavery settlers recruited by Eastern emigrant aid societies. A proslavery legislature is elected in March after close to 5,000 armed proslavery men, dubbed "border ruffians," cross over from Missouri, vote illegally, and intimidate legitimate voters. Rejecting this legislature as fraudulent, antislavery residents establish the Free State Party, prepare a state constitution (the Topeka Constitution), and elect their own government in the fall.

1856: In May, civil strife escalates in Kansas when armed proslavery forces raid the town of Lawrence, the center of the Free State movement. They destroy printing presses, loot homes, and burn down the Free State Hotel. Enraged by the "sacking" of Lawrence, John Brown, an antislavery zealot, leads a counterattack and executes five proslavery settlers along Pottawatomie Creek. (See "John Brown and Harpers Ferry," page 118.) Soon a guerrilla war envelops the territory, earning it the epithet "bleeding Kansas."

Tempers flare in Congress during debates on whether to admit Kansas under the free-state Topeka constitution. On May 19 and 20, Senator Charles Sumner of Massachusetts gives an impassioned antislavery speech that includes insulting remarks about Senator Andrew P. Butler of South Carolina (who is not present). Sumner calls him a man who "has chosen a mistress to whom he has made his vows, and who, though ugly to others, is always lovely to him; though polluted in the sight of the world, is chaste in his sight—I mean the harlot, Slavery." On May 22, Butler's cousin, Representative Preston S. Brooks of South Carolina, attacks Sumner while he is sitting at his Senate desk and beats him into insensibility with a gold-headed cane. The House fails to expel Brooks, but he resigns, only to be reelected (he dies eight months after the assault). Northerners decry the attack as an attempt to stifle free speech, and some consider Brooks' unexpected death at age thirty-seven divine punishment. Sumner does not return to the Senate floor until December 1859.

The status of Kansas is a major issue in the presidential campaign. Democrat James Buchanan is elected, but the Republicans' first presidential ticket, headed by John C. Frémont, carries eleven of the sixteen free states.

1857: In the Dred Scott case (see *"Scott v. Sandford,"* page 113), the U.S. Supreme Court rules that blacks are not and cannot be U.S. citizens, thus Scott, a Missouri slave who in 1846 sued for his and his family's freedom, has no right to sue in U.S. courts. This decision, loudly condemned by many in the free states, destroys the Missouri Compromise, which had banned slavery north of 36° 30′ north latitude.

In Kansas, proslavery forces convene in the town of Lecompton and draft a constitution for statehood. The "Lecompton Constitution" includes a strong clause protecting slaveholders' "property" and specifically excludes free blacks from its bill of rights. When it is put up for ratification, antislavery advocates refuse to vote, so it "passes."

Commercial conventions in the South (meetings to stimulate industrial development) have become a forum for politicians who are defending slavery and are demanding that the

African slave trade be reopened. Many believe that access to a large supply of inexpensive slaves would ensure the spread of slavery into the western territories.

The Panic of 1857, spurred by overspeculation in railroad securities and real estate, shuts down banks and businesses—primarily in the North. The South escapes relatively unscathed.

1858: President James Buchanan (see "Notable Antebellum Figures," page 127) urges Congress to admit Kansas to the Union under the Lecompton Constitution, but Senator Stephen Douglas leads other Democrats in opposing it. This causes a rift in the party. The Senate approves statehood but the House does not. They compromise by calling for a new popular vote on the constitution in Kansas. When this occurs in August, Kansas voters reject the Lecompton constitution. Kansas does not join the Union until 1861, when it enters as a free state after Southern states begin to secede.

Senator James Hammond of South Carolina delivers his "Cotton is King" speech on March 4, expounding on the importance of the product to world industry and issuing a warning: "No, you dare not make war on cotton. No power on earth dares to make war upon it. Cotton is king." Citing the Panic of 1857, Hammond points out: "That cotton, but for the bursting of your speculation bubbles in the North, which produced the whole of this convulsion, would have brought us $100 million. We have sold it for $65 million and saved you. Thirty-five million dollars we, the slaveholders of the South, have put into the charity box for your magnificent financiers, your 'cotton lords,' your 'merchant princes.'"

In Illinois, Republican Abraham Lincoln gains national attention when he debates Democratic Senator Stephen Douglas in their race for a U.S. Senate seat. Although Douglas narrowly wins reelection, Lincoln emerges as a powerful orator and a potential presidential candidate for 1860.

In Charleston, South Carolina, a jury acquits the crew of *The Echo* of violating Federal laws banning the African slave trade; the slave ship had been seized with 320 Africans on board. The most famous episode in the illegal slave trade also occurs this year, after Charles Augustus Lafayette Lamar—godson of the Marquis de Lafayette—the enormously wealthy director of the Savannah, Albany and Gulf Railroad, and owner of a large cotton warehouse, purchases the racing schooner *The Wanderer*. The ship is outfitted for slave transport and returns to Jekyll Island, off Georgia's coast, with more than 400 Africans who are quickly sold for a tidy profit. Lamar and his colleagues are later prosecuted for violating the ban on the trade, but they escape punishment.

Minnesota enters the Union as a free state.

1859: On October 16, radical abolitionist John Brown and twenty-one of his followers seize the U.S. arsenal and several hostages in Harpers Ferry, Virginia (now West Virginia), in hopes of inciting a slave revolt. No slaves join them, however, and local troops soon trap them inside a fire engine house. On October 18, U.S. forces led by Colonel Robert E. Lee reclaim the building. Virginia quickly tries Brown for treason, murder, and inciting insurrection, and he is executed on December 2.

In December, Republicans nominate Representative John Sherman of Ohio (brother of William Tecumseh Sherman) as the new Speaker of the House, but Southerners, who hold the deciding votes, object. Sherman, along with sixty-seven other House Republicans, had recently signed a circular endorsing North Carolinian Hinton Helper's *Impending Crisis of the South* (1857), a book that depicts slavery as economically unsound and damaging to the South. A tense two-month stalemate ensues until Sherman withdraws and a compromise candidate is chosen.

1860: In February, Senator Jefferson Davis of Mississippi presents resolutions articulating the Southern position on slavery. Included is a call for a Federal slave code in the territories. Debate on these resolutions feeds tensions between Northern and Southern Democrats.

Disagreement over slavery in the territories splits the Democratic Party at its conventions in April and June. After Stephen Douglas is named the presidential nominee, the Southern states hold a separate convention and nominate John C. Breckinridge as their candidate (see "1860 Election," page 124).

In May, the new Constitutional Union Party (see "Political Parties, Organizations, and Movements," in Chapter 3, "Wartime Politics"), which includes former members of the Whig and American Parties as well as disaffected Democrats, nominates John Bell, a former U.S. senator from Tennessee, for president.

On November 6, the Republican candidate, Abraham Lincoln, is elected president with nearly 40 percent of the popular vote.

In December, in an effort to avoid secession, Senator John J. Crittenden of Kentucky (see "Notable Antebellum Figures," page 127) proposes his "Crittenden Compromise," which would extend the 36°30′ boundary line for slavery to the West Coast; protect existing slavery; and uphold fugitive slave laws as well as slavery in the nation's capital. The House and the Senate will reject the compromise in 1861.

After hearing of Lincoln's election, the South Carolina legislature calls a state convention. On December 20, the delegates unanimously vote to secede. Four days later, South Carolina issues its *Declaration of the Immediate Causes which Induce and Justify the Secession of South Carolina from the Federal Union*. Among the causes are: the Federal government's "encroachments upon the reserved rights of the States," "an increasing hostility on the part of the nonslaveholding States to the institution of slavery," the free states' assumption of "the right of deciding upon the propriety of our domestic institutions" and their denunciation of slavery as "sinful," "the election of a man to the high office of President of the United

States, whose opinions and purposes are hostile to slavery," and "the submersion of the Constitution." Other states will issue similar declarations after seceding from the Union.

On December 26, in Charleston, South Carolina, Major Robert Anderson covertly transfers the U.S. garrison from Fort Moultrie to the unfinished but much more defensible Fort Sumter.

1861: **January 3:** Delaware legislators reject secession. Georgia troops occupy Fort Pulaski. In the next month, Southern state forces take over a series of U.S. forts and arsenals.

January 9: Mississippi secedes. South Carolina forces in Charleston fire on the U.S.S. *Star of the West*, sent to reinforce and resupply Fort Sumter. The unarmed ship withdraws.

January 10: Florida secedes.

January 11: Alabama secedes.

January 19: Georgia secedes.

January 21: Senators from Alabama (Clement C. Clay and Benjamin Fitzpatrick), Florida (David Yulee and Stephen R. Mallory), and Mississippi (Jefferson Davis) withdraw from the U.S. Senate.

January 26: Louisiana secedes.

February 1: The Texas convention votes to secede (voters will ratify the secession on February 23), ending the first wave of secession.

February 4: Delegates from the seceding states convene in Montgomery, Alabama, to form a provisional Confederate government, until regular elections are held in November. In a last effort at reconciliation, a national "peace convention" is held in Washington. Eight Southern and five Northern states do not participate. The meeting proposes a slightly modified version of the Crittenden Compromise, but Congress rejects the recommendations.

February 8: The Montgomery convention adopts the Provisional Confederate Constitution.

February 18: Having been elected by the Montgomery convention (February 9), Jefferson Davis is inaugurated, in front of the Alabama state capitol building, as provisional president of the Confederate States of America. Alexander H. Stephens is provisional vice president.

February 27: The Washington peace convention ends without effect.

March 4: Abraham Lincoln is sworn in as the sixteenth president of the United States. In his inaugural address, he assures Southerners that he does not intend to interfere with slavery where it exists. Observing that "the Union of these States is perpetual," Lincoln asserts that states have no legal right to secede; thus, as president, he will carry out his oath of office to defend and preserve the Union.

March 11: The convention of seceded states in Montgomery unanimously adopts the Constitution of the Confederate States of America, portions of which are identical to the U.S. Constitution. Other sections significantly depart from the U.S. model, primarily in protecting slavery (see "The U.S. and Confederate Constitutions" in Chapter 3, "Wartime Politics").

March 21: Confederate Vice President Alexander H. Stephens delivers his "Cornerstone Speech" in Savannah, Georgia. In outlining the differences between the old and new American constitutions, he states that the U.S. Constitution regards the races as equal and slavery as a necessary evil, whereas the new Confederate government "is founded upon exactly the opposite idea; its foundations are laid, its corner-stone rests upon the great truth, that the negro is not equal to the white man; that slavery—subordination to the superior race—is his natural and normal condition." Davis takes exception to Stephens' emphatic assertion that slavery is the cornerstone of the Confederacy, believing that states' rights is the politically preferable position to take in promoting and defending the South's actions. Stephens' extemporaneous speech confirms for Northern abolitionists that slavery is indeed the central issue in the national crisis. It is also a milestone in the deteriorating relationship between Davis and Stephens.

March 22: The Missouri convention rejects secession, against Governor Claiborne F. Jackson's wishes.

April 12: On orders of the Confederate government, South Carolina forces in Charleston begin shelling Fort Sumter.

April 13: Fort Sumter surrenders. (The formal surrender ceremony occurs the next day.)

April 15: Lincoln issues a call for troops to put down the Southern insurrection.

Alexander H. Stephens, vice president of the Confederacy, observed in his March 21, 1861, "Cornerstone Speech" that "we are passing through one of the greatest revolutions in the annals of the world. Seven states have within the last three months thrown off an old government and formed a new. This revolution has been signally marked, up to this time, by the fact of its having been accomplished without the loss of a single drop of blood."

★　　★　　★

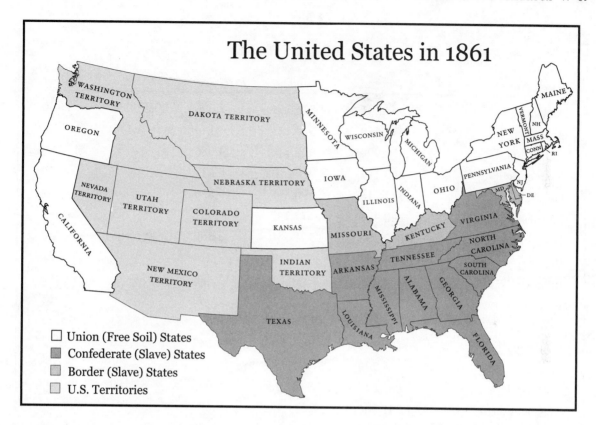

The United States in 1861

- ☐ Union (Free Soil) States
- ■ Confederate (Slave) States
- ▨ Border (Slave) States
- ▨ U.S. Territories

One Country, Two Cultures

Demographics

In 1860, the United States boasted a population of more than thirty-one million; about two-thirds of the population lived in the North. Blacks—both slave and free—constituted about 14 percent of the total U.S. population, but more than 95 percent of them lived in the South, mostly in slavery. In South Carolina, slaves made up 57 percent of the population; in Mississippi, they also exceeded 50 percent. Of the fifteen slave states, only Delaware had more free blacks than slaves, and Maryland had a free black population that nearly equaled the number of slaves. In Washington, D.C., free blacks also outnumbered slaves.

One striking demographic difference between the South and the North was the rate of urbanization in each region. In 1820, 10 percent of the Northern population and 5 percent of the Southern population lived in towns or

1860 CENSUS TABLE

State	Total	White	Free Blacks	Slaves	Indians[a]
Alabama	964,201	526,271	2,690	435,080	160
Arkansas	435,450	324,143	144	111,115	48
California	379,994	358,110[b]	4,086	—	17,798
Connecticut	460,147	451,504	8,627	—	16
Delaware	112,216	90,589	19,829	1,798	—
Florida	140,424	77,747	932	61,745	—
Georgia	1,057,286	591,550	3,500	462,198	38
Illinois	1,711,951	1,704,291	7,628	—	32
Indiana	1,350,428	1,338,710	11,428	—	290
Iowa	674,913	673,779	1,069	—	65
Kentucky	1,155,684	919,484	10,684	225,483	33
Louisiana	708,002	357,456	18,647	331,726	173
Maine	628,279	626,947	1,327	—	5
Maryland	687,049	515,918	83,942	87,189	—
Massachusetts	1,231,066	1,221,432	9,602	—	32
Michigan	749,113	736,142	6,799	—	6,172
Minnesota	172,023	169,395	259	—	2,369
Mississippi	791,305	353,899	773	436,631	2
Missouri	1,182,012	1,063,489	3,572	114,931	20
New Hampshire	326,073	325,579	494	—	—
New Jersey	672,035	646,699	25,318	18[c]	—
New York	3,880,735	3,831,590	49,005	—	140
North Carolina	992,622	629,942	30,463	331,059	1,158
Ohio	2,339,511	2,302,808	36,673	—	30
Oregon	52,465	52,160	128	—	177
Pennsylvania	2,906,215	2,849,259	56,949	—	7
Rhode Island	174,620	170,649	3,952	—	19
South Carolina	703,708	291,300	9,914	402,406	88
Tennessee	1,109,801	826,722	7,300	275,719	60

1860 CENSUS TABLE (CONTINUED)

State	Total	White	Free Blacks	Slaves	Indians[a]
Texas	604,215	420,891	355	182,566	403
Vermont	315,098	314,369	709	—	20
Virginia	1,596,318	1,047,299	58,042	490,865	112
Wisconsin	775,881	773,693	1,171	—	1,017
Territory					
Colorado	34,277	34,231	46	—	—
Dakota	4,837	2,576	—	—	2,261
Kansas	107,206	106,390	625	2	189
Nebraska	28,841	28,696	67	15	63
Nevada	6,857	6,812	45	—	—
New Mexico	93,516	82,924	85	—	10,507
Utah	40,273	40,125	30	29	89
Washington	11,594	11,138	30	—	426
District of Columbia[d]	75,080	60,763	11,131	3,185	1
Total	31,443,321	26,957,471	488,070	3,953,760	44,020

[a]Excludes 294,500 Indians who retained their tribal character.
[b]Includes 34,933 Asians.
[c]Indentured servants.
[d]Includes the populations of Georgetown City (8,733), Washington City (61,122), and the remainder of the District (5,225).

cities. By 1860, 26 percent of all Northerners but only 10 percent of Southerners lived in towns or cities. Urban development was concentrated primarily in the North. New York was by far the largest city in the United States, and its neighbor, Brooklyn (which remained a separate city until 1898), ranked third. In the Deep South, New Orleans, with a population of 168,675 (less than one-fourth the size of New York), was the largest city, and no other city surpassed even 50,000. Only three of the twenty-five largest cities— New Orleans, Charleston, and Richmond—would be in the Confederacy.

LARGEST U.S. CITIES, 1860

City	Population	City	Population
1. New York, NY	813,669	14. Washington, DC	61,122
2. Philadelphia, PA	565,529	15. San Francisco, CA	56,802
3. Brooklyn, NY	266,661	16. Providence, RI	50,666
4. Baltimore, MD	212,418	17. Pittsburgh, PA	49,221
5. Boston, MA	177,840	18. Rochester, NY	48,204
6. New Orleans, LA	168,675	19. Detroit, MI	45,619
7. Cincinnati, OH	161,044	20. Milwaukee, WI	45,246
8. St. Louis, MO	160,773	21. Cleveland, OH	43,417
9. Chicago, IL	112,172	22. Charleston, SC	40,522
10. Buffalo, NY	81,129	23. New Haven, CT	39,267
11. Newark, NJ	71,941	24. Troy, NY	39,235
12. Louisville, KY	68,033	25. Richmond, VA	37,910
13. Albany, NY	62,367		

Immigration

Immigration accounted for much of the growth in the U.S. population during the antebellum period. Increasing industrial opportunities, the opening of the American West, economic and political turmoil in Europe—including the Great Famine in Ireland (1845–1849) and the revolutions of 1848—all contributed to a surge in immigration. Before 1830, the largest numbers of immigrants were from Ireland and Great Britain. In the 1840s, Irish immigrants accounted for nearly half of all persons arriving from other nations. During the 1850s, German immigrants outnumbered Irish newcomers in the United States; in 1854, for example, 58,647 immigrants were from Great Britain, 101,606 were from Ireland, and 215,009 were from Germany. Most of those from Ireland, and more than half of those from Germany, were Roman Catholics. Most immigrants were from Western and Central Europe, but Chinese immigrants began coming to the United States, mostly to the Pacific Coast, in the late 1840s.

The immigrants could not compete with slave labor. Only one of eight European immigrants settled in the South. Others traveled west, but the majority clustered in Northern cities. They provided cheap labor for factories and contributed to a population that was increasingly diverse in its ethnic origins, its religious practices, and its cultural norms. The massive Catholic immigration, into what had previously been a mostly Protestant nation, led to a growth in nativist and anti-Catholic sentiments and to the moderate political success of the American Party ("Know-Nothings"; see "Political Parties, Organizations, and Movements" in Chapter 3, "Wartime Politics") in the 1850s. The following immigration figures do not include slaves illegally imported from Africa after 1808:

Years	Immigrants
1783–1820	260,000 (approx.)
1821–1830	143,439
1831–1840	599,125
1841–1850	1,713,251
1851–1860	2,598,214

Economic Growth

The period from 1800 to 1860 was one of rapid economic growth in the United States. The percentage of workers with nonagricultural jobs more than doubled, from 21 percent in 1810 to 45 percent in 1860. The gross national product was doubling every fifteen years; the annual per capita income growth was 1.7 percent.

Improvements in transportation—the building of roads and canals, the invention of the steamboat in 1807, and, especially, the development of the American railroad system in the 1830s—spurred this economic growth. In 1830, the United States had twenty-three miles of railroads; a decade later, there were 2,818 miles of track. By 1850, 9,021 miles of rail track had been laid; by 1860, the figure had tripled to 30,626 miles. But nearly two-thirds of the nation's trackage was in the North, which also had more rolling stock than the South. The railroad affected the South and the North in different ways. Atlanta and Chicago were minuscule settlements before 1840. Chicago had a population of only 4,470, and Atlanta's statistic was slightly less. In 1860, after the railroad had become central to their growth, Atlanta was still a small town of 9,554 people, with two rail lines intersecting it. Chicago, on the other hand, was a city of 112,172, the ninth largest in the nation, and had a half-dozen rail lines running through it.

The nature of agricultural production also changed during the antebellum period. However, most of this change took place in the North; only 40 percent of the workforce was in agriculture in 1860, compared with 68 percent in 1800. The decline in the number of agricultural workers in the North was a result of (a) innovations in farming techniques and equipment that allowed for more efficient farm production and (b) the rise of factories, complex business, steamboats, and railroads, which in turn provided attractive employment opportunities and drew Northerners and immigrants away from farms. In the South, however, agriculture continued to engage 80 percent of the workforce (including slaves), just as it had in 1800.

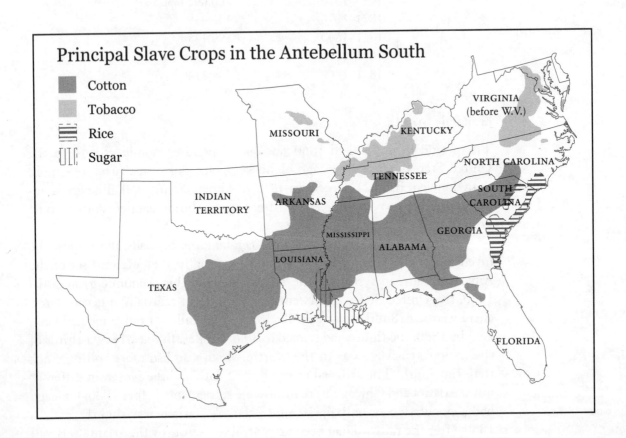

Southern agriculture was profitable for planters. When cotton prices soared during the 1850s, Southern planters devoted more and more acreage to this crop. They also increased their output of sugar and tobacco, but their per capita production of corn and other food staples decreased accordingly. Although Southern planters proclaimed "Cotton is King," their investment in this crop was increasingly costly because the prices of slaves also rose rapidly during the 1850s. However, the growth of cotton production did not increase the overall value of Southern farmland. Prime cotton land increased in value, but older lands, worn out by single-crop planting year after year, declined in value. Thus, in 1860, the average acre of farmland was worth $25.67 in the North, but only $10.40 in the South. Northern farmers, on average, owned $0.89 worth of farm machinery per acre; Southerners owned only $0.42 worth. The per-worker allocation of farm machinery was equally striking. Southerners owned only $38 worth of farm equipment for each worker; Northerners owned $66 worth. Southern planters continued to make a profit by relying on slave labor. Northern farmers reduced their reliance on labor and turned to more efficient and productive machinery.

Many Southerners invested in slaves to produce more cotton. Northerners invested in manufacturing companies, railroads, steamships, banks, insurance companies, and other aspects of modern economic development. In 1840, 80 percent of all American capital invested in manufacturing was in the North. In the twenty years before the Civil War, some Southerners, such as James D. B. De Bow (see "Notable Antebellum Figures," page 127), urged slaveowners to invest in manufacturing, mining, and other industrial enterprises. De Bow's argument for a South that was economically diversified and less dependent on the North or on Great Britain for its manufactured goods was ignored. By 1860, Northern investment in manufacturing had risen to 84 percent of the nation's total manufacturing; the slave states' investment had declined to only 16 percent. This was not just a function of the North's greater population. Between 1840 and 1860, Northern per capita industrial investment rose from $21.92 to $43.73. Southern industrial investment rose from $7.25 to $13.25 per capita.

The South's failure to invest in manufacturing was not the result of Southern poverty. On a per capita basis, Southern whites were nearly twice as rich as Northerners. The average Southern white adult was worth $3,978; the average Northern white adult was worth $2,040. Southern wealth was invested in slaves and was highly concentrated. Although nonslave Southerners constituted only 30 percent of the nation's free population, they included more than 60 percent of the wealthiest individuals. But wealth does not tell the whole story about the nation's economic well-being. Southern wealth was achieved not by greater production or innovations in business techniques, but by reallocating the wealth produced by nearly four million slaves to the one-third of all Southern white families that owned slaves. The result was a false prosperity based on agricultural commodities and slave ownership.

The skewed economic development of the South led to other discrepancies. Because the prewar South was geographically larger than the Northern states (by more than 300,000 square miles), other disparities were especially telling. By 1850, 86 percent of canal mileage was in the North, and by 1860, the South contained only 35 percent of the rail tracks. Despite the importance of cotton, the South manufactured only 10 percent of the country's cotton textiles, and much of this activity was in the border states.

Many explanations have been offered for the relatively slow industrialization of the South. Some historians blame the South's dependence on slave labor; they allege that it limited the demand for manufactured goods. Other scholars underline how much of Southern wealth was invested in land and slaves and thus was not available for industrial development. Still others point to the cultural value placed on agriculture in the South. Many white Southerners railed against the "wage slavery" they saw prevailing in the North. These defenders of the plantation slave system held up the ideal of the noble Southern gentleman farmer in the tradition of Thomas Jefferson.

All of these explanations make sense. They dovetail with two others: the potential for profit in different industries, and the South's need to subordinate its large black population. Throughout the prewar period, the demand for cotton, rice, and sugar remained high, and profits were strong. However, the concentration on commodity production clearly retarded the South's economic growth and prevented it from having an industrial infrastructure sufficient to fight a major war.

Equally important, almost all Southern whites accepted the idea of white supremacy and believed it was necessary. Most Southern whites also believed that plantation-based agriculture used slaves most productively and kept them subordinate to whites. In factories, especially in urban settings, they believed slaves would be corrupted and would be more likely to revolt or escape. Thus, racial subordination went hand-in-hand with plantation-based agriculture.

History of Slavery in America

The enslavement of Africans was a significant part of New World colonial societies by the middle of the sixteenth century. Most European nations were involved in slavery and the African slave trade when the British appeared on the American scene and established their first permanent settlement at Jamestown, in the Virginia colony, in 1607.

The British, however, were slow to become involved in slavery. Unlike Spain or Portugal, which had substantial numbers of slaves before 1492, Britain had no direct experience with slavery at this time. Initially, Virginia relied on indentured servants—people who worked for terms that usually ranged from three to seven years to pay for their passage to the New World. If they survived the indenture—many did not—they became free. Some blacks probably trickled into Virginia before 1619, but, in that year, authorities noted the arrival of a Dutch ship that sold the colony "20 and odd negroes," who were treated as indentured servants, as most blacks were before 1640, though some were treated as slaves. Between 1640 and about 1670, Virginia gradually established slavery through a combination of statutes, court decisions, and the day-to-day practices of the elite planters. From the 1660s to the 1690s, a series of statutes codified the emergence of slavery in Virginia by declaring, among other things, that the children of black women would follow the status of their mother; that conversion to Christianity would not affect the status of a slave; and that blacks and whites could no longer intermarry. In 1640, most Africans in Virginia were either indentured servants or free people; by 1700, the overwhelming majority of blacks were slaves. As the number of slaves grew, white colonists enacted stringent laws to govern them, and each colony gradually toughened its slave code, making it increasingly difficult for blacks to gain freedom.

This late eighteenth century newspaper advertisement announced a shipboard slave sale at Ashley Ferry, outside of Charleston, South Carolina. Bance Island, from which the slave ship took its name, was a major West African slave trading port.

What happened in Virginia happened in the other colonies as well, although slavery could differ markedly in many ways. Working conditions in South Carolina were especially horrific, and punishments in that colony were notoriously barbaric. Treatment of slaves was far milder in the Quaker colony of Pennsylvania and the Puritan colonies in New England. Yet, everywhere, slaves suffered the abomination of being regarded as property rather than human beings. Slaves could not legally marry, and families were often dissolved when masters had to sell them for cash or when executors had to settle estates. Slaves were also required to carry written permission from their owners whenever they left the plantation, and they could be whipped, branded, maimed, or executed for acts that whites could commit without criminal sanction. Some masters punished slaves by selling them to masters in the Deep South, away from their friends and families. Slaves could never complain to legal authorities about mistreatment, and—with the exception of the right not to be murdered—had no legal protections. Even that one supposed right was often meaningless; authorities did not interfere with even the most savage masters. Until the mid-nineteenth century, the punishment for murder of a slave was usually just a fine.

By the time of the Revolution, slavery was legal in all of the thirteen colonies. Slaves were not essential to production in the North; thus, their numbers were far fewer and they endured fewer restrictions than the slaves in the South. By 1760, of the 325,806 slaves in the British colonies, 285,773 (nearly 88 percent) lived in the South. Many slaves, especially in the North, gained their freedom by fighting in the patriot armies during the Revolutionary War. Others joined the British, who promised them freedom. Massachusetts (1780), New Hampshire (1783), and the fourteenth state, Vermont (1791), banned slavery in their constitutions. Pennsylvania (1780), Connecticut (1784), and Rhode Island (1784) passed gradual abolition statutes, which meant that as the existing slaves in those states died, no new ones would replace them. New York (1799) and New Jersey (1804) passed similar legislation. By the end of Thomas Jefferson's first term as president, there was a clear line between the North, where slavery was dead or dying, and the South, where it was vibrant. In the South, some masters freed their slaves in the wake of the Revolution. In 1782, Virginia passed new legislation that allowed masters to free some slaves within the state, and, for a few decades, the free black population grew dramatically in Virginia, Maryland, and Delaware. Ultimately, this movement for private manumission was limited and had little effect on slavery in the South.

In the 1780s and 1790s, some Northerners believed (erroneously) that the Southern states might soon follow their lead in ending slavery, but it became clear that the South had no intention or desire to do so. Furthermore, Eli Whitney's invention of the cotton gin in 1793 made slavery even more profitable by allowing large-scale, efficient processing of short-fiber cotton. The spread of the Industrial Revolution augmented the demand for cotton; textile manufacturing became a prime industry in the Northeast as well as in Britain. With the acquisition of the Louisiana Territory in 1803, the land available for cotton crops, as well as sugar, expanded, and so did slavery. The cotton kingdom expanded, and slaveholders migrated to Alabama, Mississippi, Louisiana, Florida, Arkansas, and Texas in search of profit. In South Carolina alone, cotton exports rose from 10,000 pounds in 1790 to more than 6,000,000 pounds in 1800. To cultivate this profitable crop, Southern planters began to increase their number of slaves. The slave population in the United States grew from nearly one million in 1800 to just under four million by 1860. South Carolina and Georgia imported between 80,000 and 100,000 slaves between 1783 and 1808, when the United States banned the African trade. Perhaps as many as 50,000 more slaves were illegally brought to the United States before 1861. Throughout the first half of the nineteenth century, the domestic slave trade grew and slaveowners in the East made great profits by selling slaves in the South and Southwest.

In general, nonslaveholding Southern whites were also committed to slavery. Many of them rented slaves or borrowed them on occasion from their relatives and neighbors. Furthermore, many Southerners who did not own slaves hoped and expected to be able to do so in the future, just as Americans have traditionally expected to accumulate property over time. The fact that slaveowners and their allies also held considerable political power in all three branches of government reinforced the social standing of masters and ensured that slavery would not be easily abolished. Between 1788 and 1850, nine slaveowners served as president of the United States and only three—John Adams, John Quincy Adams, and Martin Van Buren—had never owned a slave. In the House of Representatives, between 1788 and 1860, a slaveowner was the Speaker of the House for twenty-two sessions (forty-four years); in the Senate, Southerners served as president pro tempore for twenty-two of the thirty-six sessions and shared the office with a Northerner for thirteen more. A Northerner held the office by himself for only two sessions during this period. Southern dominance also prevailed on the Supreme Court. Between 1801 and 1861, Southerners made up the majority of justices for all but seven years (1830 through 1836).

Slaves constituted the most important privately held property in the South. As shown in the table below, there were nearly 400,000 slaveowners in 1860. This figure represents less than 5 percent of the free Southern population, but slaveowners were members of between 25 and 30 percent of all Southern white families. The head of a household was usually the actual *slaveowner*, but other family members had use of the slaves; thus, the slaveholding class was considerably larger than the U.S. census figures might suggest. Historian James McPherson has noted "a remarkably widespread distribution of ownership for such expensive property. By contrast, only 2 percent of American families in 1950 owned corporation stocks comparable in value to one slave a century earlier." This widespread ownership of slaves helps explain why Southern per capita wealth exceeded that of the North. Half of all slaveowners had five or fewer slaves, and although Virginia

State	Total Slave Owners	Percent of Free Families Owning Slaves (Approximate)
Alabama	33,730	35%
Arkansas	11,481	20
Delaware	587	3
Florida	5,152	34
Georgia	41,084	37
Kentucky	38,645	23
Louisiana	22,033	29
Maryland	13,783	12
Mississippi	30,943	49
Missouri	24,320	12
North Carolina	34,658	28
South Carolina	26,701	45
Tennessee	36,844	25
Texas	21,878	28
Virginia	52,128	26
Total	393,967	

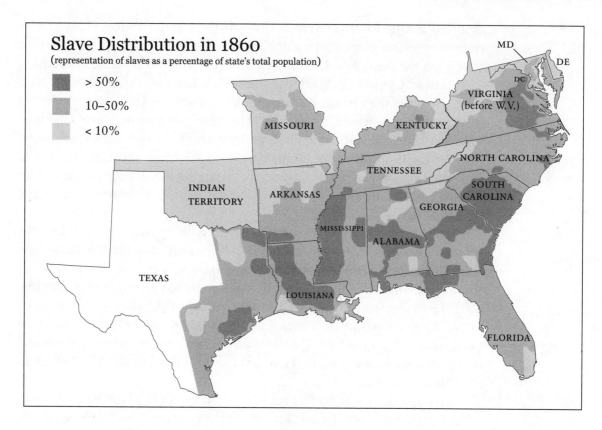

Slave Distribution in 1860
(representation of slaves as a percentage of state's total population)

- > 50%
- 10–50%
- < 10%

MD

DE

DC

VIRGINIA
(before W.V.)

MISSOURI

KENTUCKY

NORTH CAROLINA

INDIAN
TERRITORY

ARKANSAS

TENNESSEE

SOUTH
CAROLINA

GEORGIA

MISSISSIPPI

ALABAMA

TEXAS

LOUISIANA

FLORIDA

boasted that it had the most slaveholders, more than 70 percent of them had fewer than ten slaves. By contrast, South Carolina, with about half as many slaveholders, had almost twice as many plantations with fifty or more slaves. The main cotton-producing states—Alabama, Georgia, Louisiana, Mississippi, and South Carolina—contained a clear concentration of large slave plantations. Futhermore, as a fundamental part of Southern life for more than two centuries, slavery was not just a matter of economics; it was entrenched in the social culture; the distinction between the races was central to the order of Southern society.

Religion and Reform

"It's incredible to see the infinite number of subdivisions into which the [religious] sects in America have split," Frenchman Alexis de Tocqueville observed during his 1831 travels through the United States. "Like circles traced successively about the same point, each new one [is] a little farther away than the next. The Catholic faith is the immovable point from which each new sect separates a little further, while nearing pure Deism." These sects included the major Protestant denominations and their numerous smaller offshoots, which, along with other religious groups, made American religious life a complex mosaic. Although antebellum America was overwhelmingly Protestant, the Roman Catholic Church, whose members had accounted for only about 1 percent of the population during the American Revolution, was, by 1860, one of the largest Christian denominations in the United States.

America's religious devotion was especially apparent to outside observers. Tocqueville noted: "Sunday is rigorously observed. I have seen streets barred off before churches during divine services; the law commands these things imperiously, and public opinion, much stronger than the law, obliges everyone to show himself at church and to abstain from diversion." He went on to remark: "It's obvious there still remains a greater foundation of Christianity [in the United States] than in any other country in the world to my knowledge, and I don't doubt but that this disposition still influences the political regime."

Although there was greater religious diversity in the North, a variety of religious practices were found throughout the country. New England's Puritan heritage and its Calvinist principles continued in varied measure among Congregationalist and Unitarian churches, and the Dutch Reformed church was a strong presence in New York and New Jersey. The Episcopalian Church (part of England's Anglican Communion) flourished among the upper classes in Maryland, New York, Pennsylvania, South Carolina, and Virginia. The evangelical tenor of the Baptists and Methodists was heard throughout the country, particularly in the South. (By 1860, 80 percent of white Southern churchgoers belonged to a Baptist or Methodist denomination.) Lutherans had spread to the South from New York, New Jersey, and Delaware; in the early nineteenth century, they were steadily settling in the Midwest. Catholicism had spread nationwide but predominated in the North. There was also a prevailing Catholic presence in Louisiana, traceable to that state's French territorial days. In California and the southwestern territories, the Catholic Church remained a significant holdover from Spanish and Mexican rule. Numerous other religious sects—some influential, many shortlived, all comparatively small—dotted the American landscape:

Anabaptists, Adventists, the Amish, the Amana Society, Christadelphians, Dunkers (or Dunkards), Mennonites, Shakers, and the Society of Friends (Quakers). The Church of Jesus Christ of Latter-Day Saints (the Mormons) was the first home-grown religious tradition with a brand new canonical text. Their church originated in 1830 in New York, but the Mormons were the dominant presence in the Utah Territory by the late 1840s. The Jewish population, numbering perhaps no more than 2,000 in 1790, had grown to about 150,000 in 1860. Jews represented less than 1 percent of the American population, but established sizable communities in New York, Baltimore, Cincinnati, Louisville, and Philadelphia, and smaller, but notable communities in Charleston, St. Louis, and New Orleans.

Other groups with religious overtones added to the country's thick spiritual texture. The Freemasons (or Masons), a secretive fraternal organization with ceremonial rites, emphasized brotherhood and morality among its members. Freemasonry had been in America since 1730, and a number of the Founding Fathers, including Benjamin Franklin and George Washington, were Masons. Transcendentalism, a philosophical and literary movement centered in New England, grew out of the Unitarian Church and was especially influential in social reform. The movement stressed self-reliance, the divinity of man and nature, and the belief that intuition, rather than perception or reason, was the supreme source of knowledge. Like the Transcendentalists, many other groups established their own Utopian societies outside the mainstream of everyday American life. Whether religious or secular, these settlements were experiments in moral reform and the search for the ideal society.

For free blacks and slaves, maintaining traditional African religious practices in America proved exceedingly difficult. The mix of the various African religions (including Islam) the slaves had brought with them, the breakup of their families and tribal groups, and the influence of evangelical Christianity redefined their worship. Some common themes, such as belief in one supreme being as creator of the world, were shared by some African faiths and Christian religions. Over time, blacks merged African beliefs and folklore with Christianity and formed a distinct African American religious outlook. Many free blacks and slaves found particular comfort in the Christian belief that salvation and an afterlife in Paradise were available to *all* through Christ. Exodus themes and the figure of Moses were also prominent in black religious teachings.

Although free blacks were members of predominantly white Christian denominations, discrimination often kept them from fully participating in church services. Whites and blacks were generally seated separately, and black preachers were not always welcomed by white congregations. Thus, the establishment of black churches not only met spiritual needs but also offered relief from the hardships of living in a racist society. Among the earliest black churches was the African Baptist or "Bluestone" Church founded on a plantation in Mecklenburg, Virginia, in 1758. In 1816, the African Methodist Episcopal Church, comprising various independent black churches, was established in Philadelphia. It was the first black denomination in the United States. Four years later, a new denomination, the African Methodist Episcopal Zion Church, was formed in New York City. Many of the most prominent black abolitionists and workers on the Underground Railroad, including Frederick Douglass, Sojourner Truth, and Harriet Tubman, were members of this church (later known as "Freedom Church"). Other black churches— some independent and others affiliated with denominations—continued to form in the antebellum era. For most blacks, their church was the central institution in their community's life; independent from white control, these churches tended to their members in ways that racially integrated churches did not or could not.

For slaves, religious life was partially dictated by their owners. In the colonial era, slaveowners often paid little attention to their slaves' religion. But with the tightening of slave codes that kept slaves in bondage even if they were Christians, owners were more likely to favor religious instruction. Later, the evangelical movement promoted slave conversions, and the fear of slave rebellions and whatever else might come out of slave gatherings prompted many owners to require church attendance. Sitting in the same church but not the same section as their slaves, owners could keep an eye on them during their day of rest and could use the opportunity to instill God's teaching that servants must obey their masters—among other relevant lessons. However, slaves also created what became known as the "invisible institution." Secret nighttime services—held in slave quarters, the woods, or bayous—fostered the development of a distinct preaching and worship style and provided slave life with a crucial dimension that was outside the sphere of whites.

Despite a history of religious independence and tolerance in some quarters of the country, religious views inevitably clashed. Disagreements within Protestant sects led to further splintering. Protestants also felt threatened by the heavy Catholic immigration during the 1840s and 1850s. The history of mistrust and anger between Catholics and Protestants had been brought over from Europe. It manifested itself in a wave of anti-Catholic violence and discrimination. Protestants feared Catholics would put loyalty to the pope before their new country, and Catholic leadership called for the conversion of "all Protestant nations." Mormons also felt the sting of religious persecution. Their flight from Ohio, Illinois, and Missouri to Utah was marked by violence. Their practices, including polygamy, and their beliefs, such as Christ's appearance in the New World, generated considerable alarm. For the small Jewish population in America, anti-Semitism and religious hostility existed but was nowhere near the level of persecution and violence Jews suffered in Europe. Freemasonry, though not a religion, was also the subject of frequent criticism, particularly by the Catholic Church, which questioned its secretive and anticlerical ways. Such was the suspicion among many, including non-Catholics, after the disappearance of William Morgan, a former Mason who had threatened to publish a tell-all book on Freemasonry, that the Anti-Masonic political party formed and briefly thrived in the 1830s.

At the time of de Tocqueville's visit, the United States was in the midst of yet another spiritual upheaval: the Second Great Awakening. Church membership shot up accordingly. The Methodists, who had been a small sect in the late eighteenth century, became the largest Protestant denomination in the country. The Baptists witnessed tremendous growth as well. Congregations were formed quickly and easily—in part, because their individual churches operated independently, and ministers were not required to have formal training. In 1800, about 10 percent of the white population in the South belonged to an organized church; by 1860, the figure stood at 40 percent. The Christian message was also spread through organizations such as the American Bible Society (1816) and the American Tract Society (1825). Missionary work to black and Indian communities, particularly among Methodists and Baptists, took on new urgency and greater interest among the faithful.

The Second Great Awakening roused American Protestants of all stripes in the 1830s and 1840s and was marked by a greater emphasis on evangelicalism (meaning "pertaining to the Gospel"). Charles G. Finney (1792–1875), a Presbyterian and later a Congregationalist minister and the movement's greatest revivalist, explained revivalism as something that "always includes conviction of sin on the part of the church . . . [it's] a new beginning of obedience with God . . . a getting down into the dust before God, with deep humility, and a forsaking of sin . . . a new foretaste of heaven." Evangelicalism stressed the complete authority of the Bible, justification by God through faith alone (rather than faith and good works), and personal conversion and salvation. Just as they had in the colonial era, during the first Great Awakening, preachers accepted as fact humankind's basic sinful nature, but now added an important difference: people could reject sin and pursue moral action. This notion, and the need to be ready for Christ's impending return, was, in part, behind the social reform movement that shook antebellum America.

Religious revivalism, the sordid effects of the Industrial Revolution, greater leadership opportunities outside the home and classroom for educated upper- and middle-class women, and intellectual movements, such as Transcendentalism, all combined to inspire an age of reform. One of the largest reform efforts centered on eradicating drunkenness through abstinence and outlawing alcoholic beverages. Boston ministers and laymen founded the American Temperance Society in 1826 and made a great deal of progress: at its height ten years later, the society had more than 5,000 local chapters and 1.5 million members. Alcohol consumption plummeted. Prison and legal reform efforts led to the reduction of capital crimes and the abolishment of floggings and public hangings. Reformers also focused on ending prostitution, establishing orphanages, providing humane treatment for the insane, and garnering legislative support for common schools. Through a free public school system, reformers hoped to instill middle-class Protestant values in the nation's children, particularly those in poor families. More experimental reform endeavors focused on establishing utopian communities, such as New Harmony in Indiana, Brook Farm in Massachusetts, the Oneida Community in New York, and Shakertown at Pleasant Hill in Kentucky. Such communities, whether religious or philosophical, sought an ideal existence outside the corrupting forces of everyday life, and more than 600 were established in the nineteenth century. "We are all a little mad here with numberless projects of social reform," admitted Ralph Waldo Emerson, a visitor at the Transcendentalist community at Brook Farm. "Not a reading man but has the draft of a new community in his waistcoat pocket."

The women's rights movement, which had its first national convention in Seneca Falls, New York, in 1848, campaigned for legal and educational equality and the right to vote. Many of its leaders were also linked to the temperance and abolitionist movements, where they had gained organizational and leadership experience. Susan B. Anthony and other women's rights leaders would later focus on freeing the slaves and gaining citizenship for blacks as part of a larger bid for winning the franchise for themselves as well. Of all the reform movements, abolitionism (see "Resistance to Slavery, and the Abolitionist Movement," page 94) was perhaps the most incendiary. The American Anti-Slavery Society was modest in size, but its influence (and that of its allies) was so great that the South came to believe the North was teeming with abolitionists. (See "Political Parties, Organizations, and Movements," in Chapter 3, "Wartime Politics.")

As the abolition movement went forward and as the debate on slavery heated up, different opinions on slavery within many religious denominations became apparent. Increasingly, Northern Protestant ministers condemned slavery both in writings and from the pulpit, while their Southern counterparts sought to justify or condone it (see "Development of Proslavery Theory," page 105). Disagreements led to splits within several denominations. In 1837, the Presbyterian church divided into two groups: New School churches (mostly in the North) defined slavery as a sin, and Old School churches (whose stronghold was in the South) countered that it was not. In 1844, slavery issues ruptured the Methodist church. When Northern delegates to the Methodist General Conference objected to retaining James O. Andrew of Georgia as a bishop because he had become a slaveholder (through marriage), many of the Southern delegates withdrew and formed the Methodist Episcopal Church, South. (The Methodists did not reunite until 1939.) Similarly, in May 1845, after a Georgia slaveholder's application to serve as a missionary had been rejected by the American Baptist Home Missionary Society, Southern Baptists called their own convention and established a separate church.

Catholics varied in their opinions on slavery, and American bishops differed in their interpretations of Pope Gregory XVI's 1839 letter, *In Supremo Apostolatus*, which many read as a condemnation of the slave trade but not of slaveholding itself. Furthermore, many Catholics regarded abolitionism as part of a larger, nativist Protestant social movement that was strongly anti-Catholic and threatened conservative values. As a result, Catholics chose to remain outside the abolitionist crusade. National Jewish organizations did not issue particular positions on slavery, but there was great diversity of thought among rabbis. Some openly opposed it, like David Einhorn of Baltimore; others such as Dr. Morris J. Raphall of New York City viewed slavery as biblically sanctioned.

Education and Culture

Before the Civil War, the North was the center of education in the country. By 1850, New England was a world leader in educational facilities. Ninety-five percent of New England adults could read and write, and 75 percent of the children were in school. In the South, 80 percent of the white population was literate—a high rate compared with other countries at that time—but only 39.7 percent of the children were enrolled in school, which they attended, on average, eighty days a year, half that of the North. Every Northern state had some form of mandated public school system ("common schools"), but the South did little to support its own educational and cultural development. In 1860, no slave state had a statewide public school system, and literacy rates for poor whites were markedly low. Only 5 to 10 percent of slaves were literate and only two slave states, Missouri (15.3 percent) and Alabama (11.2 percent), had black school attendance rates in double figures. In the North, separate "colored schools" for blacks were the norm, though a precedent of integration had been set in Syracuse and Rochester (in New York State), Cleveland, Chicago, and throughout Massachusetts. In 1860, 66.8 percent of white children and 34.9 percent of black children in the North were in school, compared with 43.9 percent of white children and 3.2 percent of free black children in the South. (In three Northern states, more than half of all black children between ages six and twenty attended school; in four others, the rate exceeded 44 percent. Thus, in much of the antebellum North, an African American child had a greater chance of getting an education than a white child did in most of the antebellum South.)

In 1860, there were no consistent national educational standards and curricula. Rudimentary things like spelling were yet to be standardized. Various readers were available for arithmetic, history, geography, and grammar, and rote memorization was the preferred teaching method. Religious instruction, or Bible study, was held in nearly all schools in the North and the South. Public schools used the King James version of the Bible, which Catholics opposed; Protestant influence in education, frequent social discrimination against Catholics, and immigrants' need to stay connected to the Church led to the establishment of the Catholic parochial school system.

College enrollment was generally small and primarily consisted of wealthy and upper-middle-class white males. Beginning in the 1820s, growing numbers of women attended what were called female "seminaries" (the curricula usually focused on household management and "female accomplishments," but could also include classical coursework) and, later, "normal" schools (teacher training colleges). Only a handful of free blacks attended college before the Civil War; and just two black colleges—the Ashmun Institute (now Lincoln University), established in 1854 in Pennsylvania, and Wilberforce University in Ohio (1856)—were founded during the antebellum era. Another notable college, Oberlin, founded in 1833 in Ohio, was both coeducational and integrated. It was a prime training ground for evangelical preachers and abolitionists.

An educated and literate public created a huge and receptive market for the staggering increase in publications made possible by advances in printing during the antebellum period. At the turn of the nineteenth century, the United States had about 200 newspapers (twenty were dailies); by 1860, there were more than 3,700, and 387 were published daily. The practice of reprinting pieces from other newspapers exposed readers to events and opinions from around the country. Political pamphlets, religious tracts, society journals, and other publications flew off the nation's presses and added a critical component to political campaigns and social movements because they reached and influenced ever wider audiences. As a result, provocative and radical ideas received more play and carried more weight than they might have garnered a generation earlier. With its large urban population, the North had considerably more newspapers, journals, and cultural institutions (libraries, museums, lyceums, scientific and literary societies) than the South. New England's emphasis on education created a regional culture of innovation, enterprise, and experimentation. Perhaps this explains why it was the birthplace or home of more than half the nation's leading businessmen and more than 40 percent of those who developed the nation's most significant inventions in this period. The rest of the North produced 51 percent of the inventors and 34 percent of the business leaders.

Economic differences between the North and the South are easily quantifiable; the most important cultural differences between them are less so. By 1860, the South had become a closed society when it came to discussions of race, slavery, and public policy. Southern states banned the circulation of books, newspapers, or pamphlets that criticized slavery or questioned its morality. The most popular book of the 1850s, Harriet Beecher Stowe's *Uncle Tom's Cabin* (1852; see *"Uncle Tom's Cabin,"* page 110), was banned in most of the South. Similarly, it was dangerous and illegal to possess a copy of Hinton Rowan Helper's *The Impending Crisis* (1857). Helper, a white native of North Carolina, had no fondness for blacks. He hated slavery because he thought it was harmful to the nonslaveholding whites of the region. In his book, he advocated taxing slavery out of existence and sending blacks back to Africa. The South, he wrote, was "fast sinking into a state of comparative imbecility and obscurity" and was filled with "illiterate chevaliers of bowie-knives and pistols." After publishing his book, he was forced to flee the South. Similarly, the University of South Carolina forced out Francis Lieber, a legal and political scholar because he was seen as "soft" on slavery. (Lieber would have a substantial impact on the conduct of the Union army during the Civil War; see Chapter 1, "Time Line—April 1863," and "Shadow Warriors: Partisans, Guerrillas, and Spies," in Chapter 5, "The Armies.") Thus, Southerners grew up in a culture that defended slavery at every turn and, as early as the 1820s, shut off any contrary arguments. The intellectual and cultural chasm that developed between the two regions prevented any purposeful dialogue on what had emerged as the nation's most pressing problem. No meaningful discussion of slavery was possible, and Southerners were increasingly estranged from the North.

The Rift Widens

The sectional rift that slowly widened until secession and war split the country in two can be traced through a number of significant milestones dating back to the founding of the nation. Sectional and ideological tensions were readily apparent at the Constitutional Convention, and sectionalism affected various policy debates in the 1790s, including the first Bank of the United States and a Federal system of tariffs. In the nineteenth century, debates involving the increasingly intertwined issues of states' rights, westward expansion, and slavery became ever more heated and divisive.

States' Rights

The imperfect balancing act between constitutionally granted Federal powers and "states' rights" would dramatically manifest itself in the nineteenth century. To assert an individual state's sovereignty, states' rights advocates relied on the Tenth Amendment to the U.S. Constitution. ("The powers not delegated to the United States by the Constitution, nor prohibited by it to the States, are reserved to the States respectively, or to the people.") In times of crisis, individual states and regions would find states' rights a useful tool for protecting themselves from opposing views held by outside majorities. New Englanders would cite states' rights in opposing such Federal actions as the Louisiana Purchase (1803) and the War of 1812. (Northeastern states opposed the increasingly expensive war against Britain and kept their militias out of national service. At the Hartford Convention, held December 15, 1814–January 4, 1815, New Englanders met to air their grievances; they also discussed amendment of the U.S. Constitution, which they felt was advantageous to the South, and a proposal to secede from the United States.) Southerners would later embrace and promote the states' rights concept—brilliantly articulated by Senator John C. Calhoun (see "Notable Antebellum Figures," page 127)—and assert each state's right to protect its interests and political positions. The conflicting notions of constitutionally granted Federal powers and states' rights formed the crucial underpinning of the great antebellum issues: Could a state nullify Federal law (as South Carolina attempted to do in 1832)? Did Congress have the right to prohibit slavery in the territories? Did states have the right to secede from the Union?

Following the War of 1812, the nation's financial system was in disarray. In 1816, Congress chartered a new national bank, the Second Bank of the United States, to hold Federal funds and handle the Federal government's financial transactions. (The first bank, chartered in 1791, was a success, but its conservative policies angered Western and rural interests, and Congress did not renew its charter.) Many state and local politicians, particularly Westerners, despised the new bank, which they regarded as an aristocratic institution that favored Eastern commercial interests. Maryland challenged the bank's legality and attempted to tax it out of existence. In *McCulloch v. Maryland* (1819), the Supreme Court upheld the constitutionality of the bank in a sweeping decision that asserted great power for Congress. The court's decision worried the emerging states' rights Southerners; they saw it as a direct threat to the powers of the states.

Federal tariffs also provoked furious discussions of states' rights and, at the same time, illuminated the prominent differences between the North and the South. Tariffs (taxes on imported goods) protected Northern manufacturing interests by making foreign goods more expensive to purchase; domestic industries could then sell to the home market with less outside competition. Because the vast majority of industry was in the North and the South had few manufacturing businesses to protect, the South favored lower tariffs, which would enable it to purchase foreign goods at lower prices. In the 1830s, disagreement over tariffs, exacerbated by Southerners' perception that the North was trying to control the South's economy, led to the Nullification Crisis: South Carolina argued that it could nullify Federal tariffs to protect its economic interests. President Andrew Jackson's strong response to the crisis would serve as a model for Lincoln nearly thirty years later during the secession crisis. (See "Nullification Crisis," page 107.)

Manifest Destiny

Settlement in the Northwest Territory, the Louisiana Purchase, the annexation of Texas, and acquisition of territories following the Mexican War contributed to a notion of "Manifest Destiny" that flourished in the 1840s and 1850s. It was America's fate—its duty—to settle the land from the Atlantic Ocean to the Pacific, and millions of men and women, seeking better opportunities in as yet unexploited territory, gave life to this idea of destiny—and sounded a death knell for the free-roaming Indian nations in their way. The depth and scope of America were such that "I look in vain for the poet whom I describe," philosopher and author Ralph Waldo Emerson wrote in his 1844 essay, "The Poet." ". . . Our log-rolling, our stumps and their politics, our fisheries, our Negroes and Indians, our boasts and our repudiations, the wrath of rogues and the pusillanimity of honest men, the northern trade, the southern planting, the western clearing, Oregon and Texas, are yet unsung. Yet America is a poem in our eyes; its ample geography dazzles the imagination, and it will not wait long for metres."

As Western territories became organized for eventual admission to the Union, the issue of whether slavery should be permitted there became central to the growing rift between North and South. Plans to construct a transcontinental railroad (and whether to use a Northern or a Southern route) stalled as Congress and citizens wrestled with the matter. Antislavery advocates argued that allowing slavery in the territories would impede expansion and economic progress in the West, which was not suited for the plantation system; proslavery supporters insisted on access to Western lands. And as Southerners perceived that slavery and their own economic institutions might be halted in the West, they turned their attention even farther south, into Latin America. Manifest Destiny would come to encompass more than North American aspirations.

In 1859, Senator John Slidell of Louisiana (see "Diplomats and Notable Figures in Foreign Affairs" in Chapter 3, "Wartime Politics") introduced a bill to purchase Cuba from Spain, a long-time aspiration of President James Buchanan. Some Northern Democrats considered the acquisition of Cuba, which had some 400,000 slaves, to be the solution to the dilemma over Kansas' statehood. The South could stop wasting efforts to introduce slavery in the West. Instead, it could focus on expansion in the tropics, which seemed a natural fit for the plantation system.

Filibustering—launching expeditions to secure American proslavery interests on foreign soil—peaked in the 1850s. Private citizens formed their own armies of fellow adventurers and struck out for Mexico, Central and South America, and Cuba, where they hoped to take advantage of local unrest and overthrow existing governments. Manifest Destiny was invoked to justify these brazen undertakings into countries that were at peace with the United States. However, such actions violated American neutrality laws and led to diplomatic difficulties with the affected countries and with Great Britain, which also had interests in the region.

The most notable filibusterer was William Walker (see "Notable Antebellum Figures," page 127), who led several expeditions to Nicaragua and established a dictatorship there in 1856. As he repealed Nicaragua's ban on slavery and recruited Americans to settle on land confiscated from his political opponents, Walker stated that the success or failure of his Central American filibustering enterprise depended on "the re-establishment of African slavery" and "the permanent presence of the white race in that region." His plan to create an empire of Central American states folded when several nations in the region (Costa Rica, El Salvador, Guatemala, and Honduras) banded together and overthrew him. Walker returned to the United States and received an enthusiastic reception from many Democrats (and nearly all Southerners) for his glorious endeavors. He was condemned by others (mostly Republicans and Northerners) for his felonious actions. Southerners charged that abolitionists—and a British presence in the area—were to blame for Walker's failure. Northerners complained that Southern support for the bloody filibustering indicated a proslavery conspiracy to halt the growing power of the free states.

Slavery Issues

The greatest wedge between the North and the South was slavery. Southerners' emphasis on states' rights and on permitting slavery in the West was based on protecting slaveholding interests. Throughout the early nineteenth century and the antebellum period, a variety of slavery issues occupied the forefront of American politics and social movements.

THE AFRICAN SLAVE TRADE

Under the Constitution, Congress could not interfere with the African slave trade until 1808. In 1807, Congress passed legislation—enthusiastically endorsed and signed into law by President Thomas Jefferson—prohibiting the importation of African slaves into the United States after January 1, 1808. The law affected the slave states in different ways. By 1808, the upper South, especially Virginia and Maryland, had a large surplus of slaves. Slavery was still valuable and profitable in both states, but the rapid natural increase in the slave population meant that many slaveowners had more slaves than they could profitably use, especially in the tobacco growing regions, where poor farming techniques had worn out much of the available agricultural land. Thus, closing the slave trade was a great boon to slaveowners like Jefferson. They could now sell their slaves at higher prices in the Deep South.

For the Deep South, the end of the slave trade was painful. It raised the price of slaves, slowed the cotton boom, and made it more expensive for non-slaveholders to achieve the status of master. South Carolina, in the midst of a cotton expansion, was particularly hard hit as the price of slaves began to rise. Thus, throughout the antebellum period, there were persistent calls to reopen the African trade. Illegal African slave trade continued until the Civil War; perhaps 50,000 or more slaves were brought into the country. Although such trade was considered piracy under American law, few slave traders were punished because they were usually captured off the Southern coast, and sympathetic juries in that region refused to convict them (see Chapter 2, "Antebellum Time Line—1858," page 65). Efforts to stop the slave trade on the high seas generally failed because of Southern dominance of American politics, hostility toward Great Britain (which, after abolishing slavery itself, tried actively to suppress the international trade), and the United States' refusal to assist in policing the African coast. The U.S. Navy's priority was protecting American commerce, and its insufficiently equipped African Squadron was overmatched in chasing down slave ship traffic. Between 1843 and 1857, the navy seized only nineteen slave ships, and just six of these were condemned.

RESISTANCE TO SLAVERY, AND THE ABOLITIONIST MOVEMENT

As early as 1688, at a meeting in Germantown, near Philadelphia, Quakers were voicing opposition to slavery. During the nineteenth century, they were instrumental in organizing antislavery petitions to Congress and boycotts of produce from slaveholding farms. Many Quaker abolitionists, such as Levi Coffin, Isaac Hopper, and Thomas Garrett, served as conductors for the Underground Railroad (see "Fugitive Slaves and the Underground Railroad," page 99). Some of the first American women to give public speeches were Quakers who attacked slavery. Angelina and Sarah Grimké were two sisters who had converted from the Episcopalian church after leaving their slaveholding family in the South. Angelina, who later married the abolitionist Reverend Theodore D. Weld, specifically urged Christian women of the South to honor God's law by freeing their slaves.

Charles G. Finney, a leading revivalist preacher in the North, urged his converts to be "useful in the highest degree possible." Among those influenced by his teachings were a number of abolitionist leaders, including Reverend Weld, author of *The Bible Against Slavery* (1837), and Arthur and Lewis Tappan, two major financial supporters of the antislavery cause. Evangelical Protestantism also influenced African American abolitionists such as Sojourner Truth (see "Notable Antebellum Figures," page 127). Support for—and resistance to—slavery polarized religious denominations; the Presbyterian, Methodist, and Baptist churches all split into Northern and Southern branches in the 1830s and 1840s.

Two events in 1831—the publication of *The Liberator* and Nat Turner's rebellion—illustrated the rapid emergence of slavery as *the* central issue of American politics and culture. In January, William Lloyd Garrison began publishing the nation's most important antislavery paper, *The Liberator*. Garrison declared open war on slavery. He quoted the Declaration of Independence and demanded that America begin immediately to dismantle the institution:

> I *will be* as harsh as truth, and as uncompromising as justice. On this subject, I do not wish to think, or speak, or write, with moderation. No! No! Tell a man whose house is on fire, to give a moderate alarm; tell him to moderately rescue his wife from the hand of the ravisher; tell the mother to gradually extricate her babe from the fire into which it has fallen;—but urge me not to use moderation in a cause like the present. I am in earnest—I will not equivocate—I will not excuse—I will not retreat a single inch—AND I WILL BE HEARD.

Garrison soon organized the New England Anti-Slavery Society (1831) and the American Anti-Slavery Society (1833). The American Missionary Association, founded in 1846, organized antislavery churches in the American

William Lloyd Garrison was the uncompromising publisher of the antislavery newspaper The Liberator. *"My fanaticism," he explained in an 1854 speech, "is that I insist on the American people abolishing slavery or ceasing to prate the rights of man."*

North and West. Other abolitionist societies sprang up throughout the North, and abolitionists flooded the South with pamphlets and letters attacking slavery.

The movement launched campaigns that overwhelmed Congress with antislavery petitions calling for abolition in the District of Columbia, effective suppression of the African slave trade, and rejection of any new slave states. Southerners in the House of Representatives persuaded some Northerners to join them in passing a "gag rule" in 1836 that made it impossible to even read these petitions on the floor of the House. This strategy backfired when abolitionists equated slavery with a threat to all civil liberties. (In 1844, the "gag rule" was repealed.) In 1837, a proslavery mob from St. Louis, Missouri, crossed the Mississippi River into Alton, Illinois, and attacked and killed an antislavery editor, Reverend Elijah Lovejoy. The new movement now had its first martyr as well as concrete proof that slavery threatened the freedom of whites as well as blacks.

Initially, the main thrust of the abolitionist movement was moral. Garrisonians argued that slavery violated the spirit of Christianity and American democracy. By the late 1830s, other opponents of slavery, often called political abolitionists, made public policy and economics the thrust of their opposition. They organized the Liberty Party, which won no major elections but proved to be a thorn in the side of some mainstream politicians. In 1848, more moderate opponents of slavery organized the Free Soil Party, which simply opposed the spread of slavery into the territories. This party gained enough votes to tip the presidential election to Zachary Taylor that year. The most daring abolitionists were those who worked in the Underground Railroad. During the antebellum period, these abolitionists risked their lives and homes to help an estimated 1,000 fugitive slaves per year find freedom in the North and in Canada.

In the 1830s, agreement and common purpose developed among both black and white abolitionists, but, by 1840, their differences in philosophy and method were apparent. Most white abolitionists objected to slavery on religious and moral grounds but did not stress the need for racial equality or address the practical problems raised by emancipation. African Americans, and some significant white abolitionists, on the other hand, were as concerned with ending prejudice and discrimination as they were with ending slavery, and they looked to the vote as a way to achieve political—as well as economic and social—equality. Black abolitionists began operating independently from white organizations, although they still called on whites for resources and support. At the same time, white groups differed on whether to fight slavery primarily on moral grounds or to pursue political action. Despite these differences, there was, in the 1840s and 1850s, a growing urgency in the effort to end slavery. Some units within the women's suffrage movement connected their efforts to abolition and universal suffrage (see Chapter 11, "Reconstruction and the Aftermath of the War").

A further sign of opposition to slavery was the North's position on slaves traveling in the free states. The Constitution's fugitive slave clause and the Federal law only protected a master's right to claim a slave who had escaped into a free state. The Constitution did not deal with the rights of masters who passed through or visited free states with their slaves. From the 1780s to the 1830s, most free states allowed masters a right of limited visitation with their slaves. New York, for example, freed the slaves of masters who moved into the state, but visitors could keep their slaves in that state for up to nine months. (Meanwhile, most Southern states freed slaves who had been allowed to live or work in free states, although they did not free slaves who merely passed through a nonslave state. By 1824, courts in Missouri, Mississippi, Kentucky, and Louisiana had freed slaves who had lived in the North.)

In *Commonwealth v. Aves* (1836), the Massachusetts Supreme Judicial Court adopted a precedent from a 1772 British case, *Somerset v. Stewart*, in which the English Court of King's Bench ruled that any slave brought to England could claim freedom. In its decision, the Massachusetts court declared that slaves became free when they were brought into the state by their masters. By 1860, all but a few free states freed slaves whom masters had voluntarily brought into their jurisdiction. In 1852, a local New York court freed eight slaves owned by a Virginian who was in New York only long enough to transfer to a ship headed for New Orleans. The State of Virginia appealed this case to New York's highest court, which, in *Lemmon v. The People* (1860), upheld the freeing of the slaves.

When they left the Union, some Southern states cited the *Lemmon* case, and the lack of a right to travel with their property, as a reason for secession. Northern states, however, pointed out that Northern free blacks could not travel in the South and were arrested if they did. Northerners further complained that citizens of the free states were sometimes arrested or mistreated in the South on suspicion that they were abolitionists, and that Northerners could not carry with them, to the South, newspapers or books that were hostile to slavery. Thus, by 1860, slavery—among its other effects—had begun to undermine interstate travel and communication.

SLAVE REBELLIONS

Active opposition to slavery found its most potent expression in the resistance of slaves to their lot. Some reacted to oppression by escaping, temporarily running away, feigning illness, slowing down their rate of work, or refusing to perform certain tasks. Slaves also deliberately damaged machines, equipment, and tools, and they stole property from their masters, including livestock, food, and personal belongings. But the most dramatic form of resistance was open rebellion. In 1822, authorities in South Carolina uncovered a massive plot by slaves to seize Charleston and make war on slaveowners. A former slave, Denmark Vesey, had organized as many as 8,000 slaves around Charleston. South Carolina authorities found in Vesey's possession copies of antislavery speeches from the debates over Missouri statehood (see "The Missouri Compromise," page 106). They were seen as further proof of the danger in permitting public debate over slavery. Authorities arrested Vesey and 135 slaves. Vesey and thirty-five others were hanged, and forty-three slaves were transported out of the state. Following the arrests and executions, Charleston and various nearby towns suffered a rash of fires, which most whites in the area attributed to slaves.

In August 1831, Nat Turner, a Virginia slave, led the bloodiest slave rebellion in that state's history. With six other slaves, Turner killed his owner and the owner's family as well as others at nearby farms and plantations. His army eventually grew to about seventy-five slaves, and they killed about sixty whites. Militia units from Virginia and North Carolina, as well as the United States Navy, were involved in suppressing the rebellion. More than 100 blacks, including some who had not joined in the rebellion, were shot, lynched, or tried and hanged. Two months later, Turner, himself, was captured, tried, and hanged. Most troubling for Southerners was the fact that Turner had been well treated as a slave and had been allowed to conduct

FUGITIVE SLAVES AND THE UNDERGROUND RAILROAD

The problem of fugitive slaves was a constant source of irritation and friction between the North and the South. The Constitution gave Southerners the right to reclaim their runaway slaves through the Fugitive Slave Clause of Article IV, Section 2, which stated: "No Person held to Service or Labour in one State, under the Laws thereof, escaping into another, shall, in Consequence of any Law or Regulation therein, be discharged from such Service or Labour, but shall be delivered up on Claim of the Party to whom such Service or Labour may be due."

The vaguely worded clause did not indicate who should "deliver up" a runaway slave. In the Fugitive Slave Law of 1793, Congress provided some guidance, but the law's very loose standards of proof for the return of fugitives resulted in some free blacks being kidnapped and taken as slaves. A number of free states responded with the adoption of "personal liberty laws," which provided extra legal protections for blacks who were seized as fugitives. In 1837, Edward Prigg and three other Marylanders seized a black family in Pennsylvania. The family included one or two children who had been born in that state, and were thus clearly free, and their mother, Margaret Morgan, who was born in Maryland and had lived all her life as a free person. They were taken back to Maryland in violation of Pennsylvania law, and a Pennsylvania court subsequently convicted Prigg of kidnapping. In *Prigg v. Pennsylvania* (1842), the U.S. Supreme Court reversed this conviction, holding that all state personal liberty laws unconstitutionally interfered with the rights of a master to recover a fugitive slave. In a sweeping proslavery decision, Justice Joseph Story denied that fugitive slaves could claim any pro-

cedural rights or protections, and ruled that no state could interfere with the capture of a runaway slave. This decision left free blacks virtually unprotected from kidnappers. Story urged Northern officials to enforce the Federal law and to aid slavecatchers, but also asserted that the national government could not *require* them to do so because the states, and not the national government, paid their salaries.

Many slaves escaped on their own, simply by walking north ("following the North Star") or hiding on a boat leaving a Southern harbor. Others were aided by the Underground Railroad, which was neither subterranean nor a railroad. Rather, it was a secret, loosely organized system to help slaves flee from captivity in the South to the relative safety of the free states or the more secure freedom of Canada. The term itself came into currency after railroads gained prominence in the 1830s, but informal networks of whites and free blacks were helping slaves escape even before that. In line with the railroad imagery, the runaways came to be called "passengers," those who helped guide them to freedom were known as "conductors," and shelters along the way were referred to as "stations." But there was no set schedule, routes constantly changed, and reaching freedom often depended on chance and improvisation as much as planning. The term Underground Railroad came to encompass any form of assisted escape.

Danger was a constant on the Underground Railroad. Any form of assistance was illegal, and penalties for those caught were heavy. If recaptured, runaways risked torture, maiming, and being sold far away from family and friends. Those helping them might be sued, fined, or imprisoned; punishment was especially sever

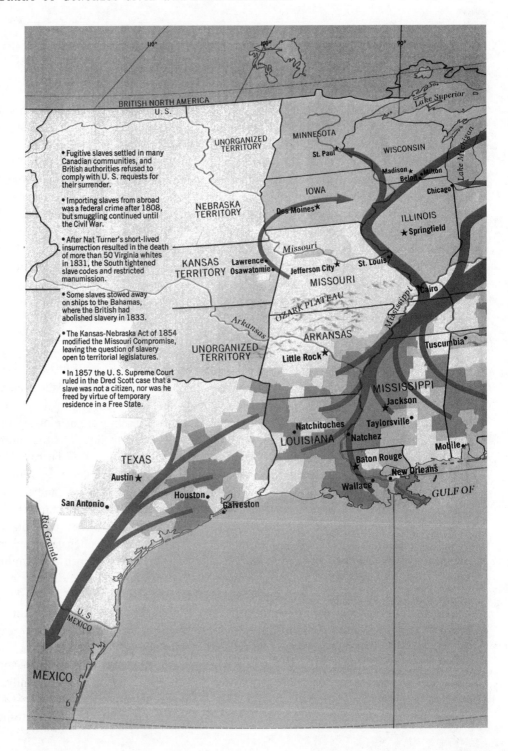

• Fugitive slaves settled in many Canadian communities, and British authorities refused to comply with U. S. requests for their surrender.

• Importing slaves from abroad was a federal crime after 1808, but smuggling continued until the Civil War.

• After Nat Turner's short-lived insurrection resulted in the death of more than 50 Virginia whites in 1831, the South tightened slave codes and restricted manumission.

• Some slaves stowed away on ships to the Bahamas, where the British had abolished slavery in 1833.

• The Kansas-Nebraska Act of 1854 modified the Missouri Compromise, leaving the question of slavery open to territorial legislatures.

• In 1857 the U. S. Supreme Court ruled in the Dred Scott case that a slave was not a citizen, nor was he freed by virtue of temporary residence in a Free State.

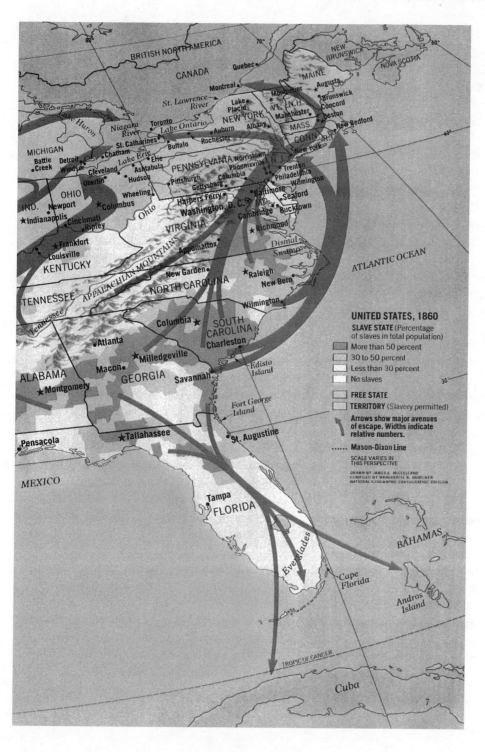

UNITED STATES, 1860
SLAVE STATE (Percentage of slaves in total population)
More than 50 percent
30 to 50 percent
Less than 30 percent
No slaves

FREE STATE
TERRITORY (Slavery permitted)

Arrows show major avenues of escape. Widths indicate relative numbers.

Mason-Dixon Line

SCALE VARIES IN THIS PERSPECTIVE

DRAWN BY JAMES E. McCLELLAND
COMPILED BY MARGUERITE B. HUNSIKER
NATIONAL GEOGRAPHIC CARTOGRAPHIC DIVISION

for people caught in the slave states. Most escapes were attempted at night. Passengers traveled from one station to the next primarily on foot or in wagons.

Because secrecy was essential to success, many of the activities and accomplishments of the Underground Railroad are difficult to document, especially the number of slaves who embarked on the journey and succeeded in finding freedom. Census records indicate that by the 1850s at least 1,000 slaves escaped annually. At some point, many of these would have either stopped at an Underground Railroad station or received some kind of assistance from abolitionists. The number of runaways probably far exceeded that annual statistic, given the secrecy and imprecise record keeping. Not every slave who escaped, however, attempted to reach free soil. Sometimes a slave ran away temporarily, perhaps because of ill treatment. Slaves who had been separated from family members by sale might try to hide near their loved ones. Still others, especially in the Deep South, escaped to cities like New Orleans and attempted to meld into those cities' significant free black populations.

More than 3,200 people have been identified as workers on the Underground Railroad. One of the most remarkable conductors was Harriet Tubman (see "Notable Antebellum Figures," page 127), who was born into slavery in Maryland. After she had fled to Philadelphia, she returned to the Eastern Shore of Maryland nearly twenty times and led to freedom more than 200 runaways, including her sister and her parents. A number of other successful runaways, such as Josiah Henson and John Mason, braved returning to the South to help lead others to freedom.

One of the boldest white conductors was John Fairfield, who had grown up in a slaveholding family in Virginia and had no trouble posing as a Southern entrepreneur or slave trader. Often, Fairfield brought his group of runaways to Levi Coffin, a white Quaker based in southern Indiana, who arranged the final leg of the journey to Canada. Coffin was dubbed "president" of the Underground Railroad by one frustrated Southern slave catcher, and the attribution stuck. It is thought that he assisted more than 3,000 runaways.

Equally important was William Still (see "Notable Antebellum Figures," page 127), an African American in Philadelphia who helped thousands of slaves escape and worked at the Pennsylvania Anti-Slavery Society. In 1849, Virginia slave Henry ("Box") Brown, with the assistance of a white friend, was packed into a customized box and mailed from Richmond to the society's office in Philadelphia—a journey that took twenty-seven hours. (His friend spent four and a half years in prison for trying to help others escape this way.)

The Underground Railroad, literally the route to freedom for many thousands of slaves, remains a powerful symbol of their desire for freedom and their willingness to take extreme risks to gain that freedom. The willingness of white and free black activists to disobey the law in the cause of freedom was equally heroic. Many fugitive slaves—Henson, Brown, Frederick Douglass, and others—wrote narratives of their lives, which added to the growing propaganda war against slavery. Some former slaves, like Douglass and "Box" Brown, became lecturers in the North and provided firsthand testimony of the horrors of slavery.

religious services as a lay preacher. Turner's master was not cruel but, for Turner and the slaves who joined him, that fact was irrelevant. Slavery itself was cruel.

Turner's rebellion, Vesey's plot, and countless smaller rebellions left Southern whites fearful. They blamed slave resistance on antislavery Northerners and free blacks. The emergence of a new and radical antislavery movement in 1831—only a decade after the Missouri Compromise debates— convinced Southerners that they were under assault from without, just as the rebellions convinced them that they were under siege from within.

FREE BLACKS

Free blacks had been in America since the seventeenth century; during the American Revolution, some black slaves were freed through military service, others escaped, and many were emancipated by laws passed in Northern states. In 1790, there were 59,000 free blacks living in the United States. The number of free blacks continued to increase throughout the first half of the nineteenth century. Most manumitted slaves had familial connections to slave owners or had performed some extraordinary service. They were also freed where slavery became unprofitable. The methods of manumission (formal emancipation) included court actions, instructions in owners' wills, and purchase of one's own or a family member's freedom with money earned when hired out. Black children born to free mothers also added to the population. By the start of the Civil War, the free black population had grown to 488,000 persons or about one-ninth of the total black population.

The presence of a free black population in the United States was perceived by Southerners as a threat to slavery. The influence of free blacks on slaves, particularly in urban areas, was especially disturbing to slaveowners, and educated and successful black professionals were at odds with predominating white views of white superiority. As a result, many slaveowners were supportive of colonization efforts to reduce the free black population by sending them to Africa. Some antislavery advocates thought that repatriating blacks to Africa might assuage whites' fears about the increasing number of free blacks living in the United States, and would lead to greater manumission. Others believed that blacks would never be fully accepted in American society and would be better off elsewhere (see "Political Parties, Organizations, and Movements," in Chapter 3, "Wartime Politics"). The first group of free blacks settled in Liberia in 1822; by 1865, some 10,000 blacks had emigrated there from the United States. The movement to emigrate received a boost when the Fugitive Slave Act was passed in 1850; in the next decade, colonization schemes focused on Nigeria, the Caribbean, and South America, rather than Liberia. But the great majority of free blacks opposed colonization. They pointed out that they were, in fact, American. "We are natives of this country; we only ask that we be treated as well as foreigners," declared Peter Williams, a black minister. "Not a few of our fathers suffered and bled to purchase its independence [in the Revolutionary War]; we ask only to be treated as well as those who fought against it." Many white abolitionists also opposed colonization.

Free blacks in the North faced numerous restrictions that limited their participation in daily American life (see "Securing Rights for Blacks in the Union" in Chapter 3, "Wartime Politics"). They were barred from most public places, including restaurants, hotels, and theaters—or they were relegated to separate areas at these establishments. Discrimination kept most blacks in unskilled, low-paying jobs (although some did own land, businesses, and other property) and made them targets of violent white mobs during times of crisis. Given the hardships imposed on the free black community, their own social institutions were critical to survival. Blacks established their own churches (see "Religion and Reform," page 81), Masonic lodges, newspapers (the first black-owned newspaper, *Freedom's Journal*, was begun in 1827), schools, abolitionist organizations, professional societies, and other organizations.

The situation was even more hostile in the South, where free blacks were often under curfew and had to carry proof of their status or risk enslavement. Most free blacks in the Upper South worked as rural laborers; further south, they were more likely to live in cities and work as artisans, tradesmen, and domestics. More than 3,000 free blacks owned slaves; many of these black owners had purchased relatives and loved ones, but strict manumission laws made it difficult to free them. Other black slaveholders were landowners themselves and regarded slaves as an important capital investment to generate more wealth. Some even had plantations in Louisiana, South Carolina, and Virginia. William Ellison, of South Carolina, a slave freed in 1816, became very wealthy as a cotton gin manufacturer, plantation owner, and slaveholder. At his death, he owned more than sixty slaves and 900 acres. Black slaveholders, though relatively few, ran counter to most Southern whites' definitions of "master" and "slave." In 1859, Arkansas passed legislation requiring free blacks to leave or be sold into slavery. Several other states considered similar legislation before the war broke out.

DEVELOPMENT OF PROSLAVERY THEORY

As the plantation economy boomed and the abolitionist and antislavery movement gained wide support, white Southerners became increasingly committed to preserving slavery and began to portray it as beneficial rather than as a necessary evil. Senator John C. Calhoun claimed it was "a positive good" and "the most safe and stable basis for free institutions in the world." By the 1840s, Southerners had developed an elaborate proslavery argument based on religion, science, history, and economics. Scientist-physicians, such as Dr. Josiah Nott of Mobile and Dr. Samuel Cartwright of New Orleans, created a huge body of literature to support the notion that blacks were genetically suited to slavery. Lawyers, like Thomas R. R. Cobb of Georgia and Chief Justice Thomas Ruffin of the North Carolina Supreme Court, developed legal doctrine, theory, and case law to support slavery. Economists argued for the centrality of slavery to the Southern and the entire American economy. Historians in the South pointed out that some of the greatest civilizations of the world, especially the Athenian Democracy and the Roman Republic, were based on slave labor.

Most important of all were the religious arguments. Southern ministers waxed eloquent on the duties of Christian masters to their slaves and the morality of enslaving Africans to introduce them to the gospel. They also noted that neither the Old nor the New Testament condemned slavery, nor did Jesus. Mosaic law provides for slavery, and all the early patriarchs had "servants." In the Bible story of Job, a great slaveholder, one of his trials was the loss of his slaves. His good character, which is tested in the story, was based in part on how he discharged his duty to his slaves, and his redemption included getting more slaves. While Northern ministers focused on the "Sermon on the Mount" to attack slavery, their Southern counterparts repeatedly cited a number of Biblical passages in support of slavery. Among them were Ephesians 6:5 ("Servants, be obedient to them that are your masters according to the flesh, with fear and trembling, in singleness of your heart, as unto Christ") and Leviticus 25:45–46 (". . . of the children of the strangers that do sojourn among you, of them shall ye

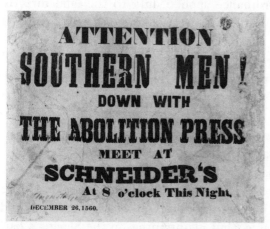

The small but vocal abolitionist movement infuriated Southerners, prompting meetings such as the one advertised here for December 26, 1860 (mistakenly printed as 1560).

buy, and of their families that are with you, which they begat in your land: and they shall be your possession. And ye shall take them as an inheritance for your children after you, to inherit them for a possession; they shall be your bondmen for ever: but over your brethren the children of Israel, ye shall not rule one over another with rigour").

Compromise and Crisis

In the forty years before the cannons were fired at Fort Sumter, as differences over slavery, states' rights, and the right of secession began seriously to pull the country apart, many in Congress made exhausting and monumental efforts to achieve some compromise that would preserve the Union—and the democratic ideals it was founded on.

The Missouri Compromise

In 1818, the Missouri Territory petitioned Congress for admission to the Union as a slave state. Representative James Tallmadge of New York amended the statehood bill to require a gradual emancipation scheme for the state. Tallmadge based his amendment on the Northwest Ordinance of 1787 (see "Antebellum Time Line," page 57), which had prohibited slavery north and west of the Ohio River. Almost all of Missouri was in fact directly west of the Ohio River and north of the river's most southern point. However, Southerners argued that the Ordinance applied only to the land directly above the river and not to territory that was west of where the river emptied into the Mississippi. Whatever the merits of Tallmadge's reliance on the Northwest Ordinance, his larger point was clear: it was time to take a stand against slavery, and this was the place to do it. The large Northern majority in the House accepted the amendment in February 1819, but the Senate rejected it. A few Northern senators, led by Jesse B. Thomas of Illinois, voted with the South.

In 1820, the House once again voted to admit Missouri as a free state; once again, this failed in the Senate. At this point, the Speaker of the House, Henry Clay of Kentucky, brokered a compromise. Missouri would enter the Union as a slave state and the northern counties of Massachusetts would enter as the new free state of Maine, thus maintaining, in the Senate, a balance of power between slave and free states. In addition, slavery would be forever prohibited north of 36°30' north latitude, which essentially was the southern boundary of Missouri. The compromise passed both houses, and

Maine was admitted to the Union as a free state on March 15, 1820. The slave state of Missouri entered on August 10, 1821.

For the next two decades, the Missouri Compromise enabled Congress to dodge the issue of slavery in the West, but in the end it proved unworkable. Although many Northerners came to see the Compromise as a central document of American politics, many Southerners opposed it, arguing that it was wrong to exclude slaveowners from so much of the western territories. Southerners were also deeply troubled by the debate over Missouri statehood, which had included tough criticism of their "peculiar institution." For the first time in American history, there had been a concerted congressional attack on the morality of slavery.

The Nullification Crisis

The main impetus for the nullification crisis was a Federal tariff, but the drama had deeper roots. The closing of the African slave trade, the creation of the Second Bank of the United States, the stinging debate over Missouri statehood, violent resistance to slavery by free blacks and slaves (particularly in South Carolina and Virginia), and the emergence of a fervent abolitionist movement—all of these contributed to an intense feeling, in South Carolina, that the state's institutions were under assault.

Beginning in 1816, South Carolinians had voiced increasing opposition to Federal tariff legislation. They interpreted it as an attempt by Northern industrialists to saddle Southerners with high taxes. In 1828, Congress passed a new tariff, which South Carolinians called the "tariff of abominations," that created unnecessarily high tariff rates. In response to the tariff, Vice President John C. Calhoun penned his *Exposition*, which argued that a state had the right to nullify Federal laws (such as the tariff) that imperiled its essential interests. In 1832, Congress passed a new tariff that pushed rates lower than they had been in 1824. Not satisfied with these lower rates, South Carolina's leaders called a state convention in November 1832. They enacted a nullification ordinance and threatened to secede if the United States attempted to use force to implement the law. In December, Calhoun, who fully supported the ordinance, resigned the vice presidency (after winning election to the Senate). President Andrew Jackson, a Southerner and a slaveowner, issued a proclamation in which he declared, "Our Federal Union, it must be preserved," and insisted that Federal laws must be observed. In March 1833, Congress, under the leadership of Senator Henry Clay, passed a new tariff that lowered rates, but also passed a "force bill" that authorized the president to call on the army or the navy, if necessary, to enforce Federal laws. South Carolina then rescinded its nullification ordinance, but petulantly passed another ordinance that nullified the force act. (With the force bill in hand, Jackson ignored this latest nullification as irrelevant.) Throughout this crisis, South Carolina was disappointed by the refusal of other slave states to support its opposition to the Federal law. However, as South Carolina State Representative James L. Petigru wrote, in a July 15, 1833, letter: "Nullification has done its work; it has prepared the minds of men for a separation of the States, and when the question is mooted again, it will be distinctly union or disunion."

The Mexican War (1846–1848)

In 1835, American settlers in Texas, which was then part of Mexico, rebelled against the government of Santa Anna. Texans defeated him at the battle of San Jacinto, and established the Republic of Texas. The independent nation was eager to join the United States (a move opposed by the North and favored by the South). In 1845, in his last significant act as president, John Tyler pushed through Congress a joint resolution annexing the Republic of Texas. Mexico immediately broke off diplomatic relations with the United States.

The annexation was completed at the end of 1845 and Texas was admitted to the Union as a slave state. When relations with Mexico deteriorated further, the new U.S. president, James K. Polk of Tennessee, a confirmed proponent of Manifest Destiny, seemed to welcome the possibility of war. In response to Mexico's complaints about the Texas annexation, he ordered U.S. troops, under General Zachary Taylor, to move south of Texas' generally accepted border and occupy an area that was traditionally considered part of Mexico. He also ordered American soldiers to "explore" in the vicinity of California, which Polk offered to buy from Mexico, thus exacerbating an already tense situation. A skirmish between American and Mexican troops served as a pretext for the United States to declare war on May 13, 1846. Sixteen months later, after a conflict in which many future Civil War officers gained valuable combat experience, Mexico City fell. Under the Treaty of Guadalupe Hidalgo, the United States acquired vast territories that would later become the states of California, Utah, and Nevada, most of Arizona, as well as parts of New Mexico, Colorado, and Wyoming.

Many Northerners considered the war to be part of a conspiracy to acquire new land for slavery, and a few Southerners, including John C. Calhoun and Alexander H. Stephens (the future Confederate vice president), opposed the war on either ethical grounds or because they realized it would undermine sectional relations. Northern Democrats who believed in Manifest Destiny faced a difficult dilemma: How could they support the war without appearing to support the spread of slavery? In 1846, Congressman David Wilmot of Pennsylvania offered a way out of this quandary. As an amendment to an appropriations bill, he offered what became known as the Wilmot Proviso; slavery would be prohibited in any territory acquired from Mexico. Although the Proviso died in the Senate (it passed in the House 115–106), its effect was explosive. Indeed, the whole matter of slavery in the territories would remain the most important political issue in the nation until the Civil War.

The Compromise of 1850

The most immediate issue facing the nation in 1850 was the admission of California into the Union. The Gold Rush of 1849 had brought hundreds of thousands of people into that territory; by 1850, California had a greater population than many states. But if it came in as a free state, it would shift the majority of Senate seats to the free states, which already had a majority in the House. In January 1850, an aging Senator Henry Clay proposed a compromise by addressing other issues as well, to accommodate various political interests. His plan would: (1) admit California as a free state; (2) forbid expansion of Texas at the expense of New Mexico, but the Federal government would settle Texas' debts; (3) permit citizens of New Mexico and Utah to decide for themselves whether to organize their territories as slave or free states; (4) ban the slave trade (but not slavery) in the District of Columbia; and (5) provide for a tougher fugitive slave law.

For nearly six months, the Senate debated the bill. Moderates supporting the bill included Clay, Thomas Hart Benton of Missouri, Sam Houston of Texas, Stephen A. Douglas of Illinois, and Daniel Webster of Massachusetts. Proslavery advocates, such as Jefferson Davis of Mississippi, John C. Calhoun of South Carolina, and James M. Mason of Virginia, opposed it, as did many younger Northerners, such as William H. Seward of New York, Salmon P. Chase of Ohio, and Hannibal Hamlin of Maine, who were against making any more concessions to the South. (These last three would all serve in

Abraham Lincoln's administration during the Civil War.) In a pointed speech that infuriated Southerners, Seward asserted that the Constitution gave Congress the power to prohibit slavery in the territories, but more importantly, he said, "There is a higher law than the Constitution."

Calling his proposal an "omnibus bill," Clay expected it to pass because there seemed to be something for everybody. His strategy backfired. The Northerners who opposed it objected to the fugitive slave law and to opening Utah and New Mexico to the possibility of slavery; Southerners voted against it because it made California a free state. In July, to Clay's shock, the bill failed. In August and September, Senator Douglas pushed the compromise through Congress by forging fragile majorities for each component of the bill. With a core of moderates, he got Southerners to support the bills they liked and Northerners to support the bills they liked. President Millard

UNCLE TOM'S CABIN

The publication of *Uncle Tom's Cabin, or Life Among the Lowly* by Harriet Beecher Stowe (1811–1896) placed a new stress on sectional relations. Stowe's book demonstrated the horrors of slavery and examined the conflicting attitudes of whites toward the South's peculiar institution. Initially serialized in the abolitionist paper *The National Era* in 1851–1852, it was published in book form in 1852, and 300,000 copies were sold in the United States alone during the first year of publication. It found a similar audience

Harriet Beecher Stowe, author of the bestselling antislavery novel Uncle Tom's Cabin, or Life Among the Lowly *(1852), which was banned in much of the South, noted that "I wrote what I did because as a woman, as a mother I was oppressed & broken-hearted, with the sorrows & injustices I saw, because as a Christian I felt the dishonor to Christianity—because as a lover of my country I trembled at the coming day of wrath."*

Fillmore, a Northerner with few scruples about slavery, signed each bill as it reached his desk.

The compromise halted a Southern disunion movement but in the end, the compromise was not the solution to a national problem. Some Northerners, like Daniel Webster, saw their careers and their reputations harmed for supporting the compromise. On the other hand, sectional opponents of the compromise, like Senators Davis, Mason, Chase, and Seward, thrived.

The Kansas-Nebraska Act

In 1854, Senator Stephen A. Douglas of Illinois steered the Kansas-Nebraska Act through Congress. Douglas' main goal was to secure congressional support for a transcontinental railroad that would link Chicago (his

---

in Great Britain, where the antislavery movement had originated. Eventually, the book was translated into most European languages. Two million copies were sold within a decade, making it the best-selling book—in proportion to population—of all time.

Stowe's story follows the struggles of Tom, an earnest and appealing old slave who is devoted to his kind but debt-ridden Kentucky master and sold to a slave trader, who in turn sells him to Augustine St. Clare. After St. Clare's death, Tom is eventually sold to a cruel plantation owner, Simon Legree. In making a slave the title character and a hero, and in creating vivid characters who did not fit standard stereotypes—the key villain (Legree) was a Northerner who had moved South, and some Southerners figured among the story's more sympathetic characters—Stowe humanized and individualized the face of slavery. In doing so, she presented a scathing indictment of the institution and the plight of slaves, both in bondage and as fugitives.

Stowe achieved her aim of jolting the conscience of the North, especially within the Christian community. For all its success, however, the book provoked bitter outrage in the South; it was denounced as propaganda, banned in most Southern states, and decried as a glaring example of Northern attacks against Southern honor and "domestic institutions." Southern writers quickly retaliated with their own proslavery novels, such as Mary Henderson Eastman's *Aunt Phillis' Cabin, or Southern Life As It Is* (1852).

In a widely repeated—and possibly fictional—anecdote, when President Lincoln met Stowe at the White House in late 1862, he greeted her with the words, "So you're the little woman who wrote the book that made this great war." What she had done was deliver her case to a large and receptive mainstream audience. Her book was a critically important contribution to the abolitionist movement and to the canon of American literature.

Senator Stephen A. Douglas of Illinois—"the Little Giant"—advocated "popular sovereignty" as a solution to the vexing issue of whether or not slavery should be permitted in the western territories.

home city) and San Francisco. To gain key Southern support for his plan, Douglas proposed organizing the Kansas and Nebraska territories for statehood without regard to slavery. The bill repealed part of the Missouri Compromise by allowing slavery north of the 36°30′ line through institution of a policy known as "popular sovereignty." Under this mode of territorial organization, the settlers would decide for themselves whether to allow slavery in the territory. Northern Democrats, hoping to finally get rid of the politically divisive issue of slavery, voted with Southerners to pass the bill. President Franklin Pierce, a Northern "doughface" Democrat (a Northerner with Southern principles), signed it into law.

The most immediate response to the act was the creation of a new political party, initially called the "Anti-Nebraska Party" but soon renamed the Republican Party. The Republicans won huge victories in the 1854 congressional elections. In 1856, with famed explorer-soldier John C. Frémont as their candidate, they captured eleven Northern states in the presidential election. For the first time, the nation had a viable and successful political party's pledge to stop the spread of slavery. Although Pennsylvania Democrat James Buchanan, also a doughface, won the election in 1856, he was clearly a sectional candidate. He swept the South but won only five free states.

Another significant response to the passage of the Kansas-Nebraska Act was a mobilization of resources in the North to send free-state settlers to the territories. At the same time, Southerners crossed into Kansas from Missouri to vote (illegally) in territorial elections or to participate in armed attacks on free-state settlers. Northern clergy were among the prime supporters of the New England Emigrant Aid Society, which Eli Thayer had begun organizing in 1854 to help free-soil supporters settle in Kansas and thus strengthen the antislavery vote there (see "Political Parties, Organizations, and Movements," in Chapter 3, "Wartime Politics"). By the end of 1855, Thayer's group had assisted more than 1,000 emigrants. As tensions mounted in Kansas, Northerners collected guns—dubbed "Beecher's Bibles" for abolitionist preacher Henry Ward Beecher—and sent them to antislavery settlers.

"Beecher's Bibles" were needed because of the third result of the Kansas-Nebraska Act. By 1856, a mini-civil war raged on the Kansas prairie, as free state and slave state settlers fought over the fate of the territory. A proslavery army sacked the free soil capital of Lawrence on May 21, 1856; partially in retaliation for this, on May 24, abolitionist John Brown captured and killed five proslavery settlers along Pottawatomie Creek (although the men in question had nothing to do with the sacking of Lawrence). In 1857–1858, President Buchanan tried to bring "Bleeding Kansas" into the Union under the Lecompton Constitution (named for the proslavery capital), which had been written by an unrepresentative convention and ratified in a fraudulent referendum. Senator Douglas organized a few Northern Democrats in the House who broke ranks to join the Republicans in defeating this constitution. Not until January 29, 1861, as Southern states were seceding, would Kansas join the Union as a free state.

Scott v. Sandford (The Dred Scott Case)

In his inaugural address on March 4, 1857, President James Buchanan noted that the issue of slavery in the territories had plagued the nation for nearly a decade. Indeed, as Buchanan soon discovered, it would plague his entire administration. But with the issue before the Supreme Court in *Dred Scott v. Sandford* (and with advance warning from at least one, and perhaps two, members of the Court as to what the decision would be), Buchanan urged the nation to accept the impending judgment. Most of the South would; much of the North would not.

The landmark case that would intensify the sectional divide and become one of the Supreme Court's most controversial decisions began eleven years earlier. In 1830, Dred Scott (1799?–1858), born a slave in Virginia, moved with his owner, Peter Blow, to Missouri, also a slave state. He was later sold to Dr. John Emerson, an army surgeon, and moved with him to military posts in Illinois and the Wisconsin Territory, both of which prohibited slavery. Scott and his wife, Harriet, returned to Missouri with the Emersons in 1842. The following year, Dr. Emerson died. With the help of friends, Scott sued Irene Emerson for his freedom—and that of his wife and children—by claiming that his residence in free territory had given him his freedom. As the case worked its way through the state judicial system, Scott lost it in 1847, won it in 1850, and lost it again in 1852. In 1854, in a Federal court, Scott sued John Sanford, Mrs. Emerson's brother (who by this time owned

Scott) for his freedom. Scott lost and appealed his case, which reached the U.S. Supreme Court in 1856. (The case would become known as *Scott v. Sandford* because of a clerical error.)

On March 6, 1857, just two days after President Buchanan addressed the nation, Chief Justice Roger B. Taney handed down a strongly worded proslavery opinion. By a seven to two vote, the justices ruled that Scott must remain a slave. Taney might have reached this result by relying on an earlier case, *Strader v. Graham* (1850). In that case, the Court refused to free a slave who had lived in a free jurisdiction but failed to sue for freedom while there, and instead returned to a slave jurisdiction.

However, rather than following the *Strader* precedent, Chief Justice Taney decided to settle all the issues surrounding slavery in the territories. He thus plunged headlong into controversial waters. In his written opinion, he denied that Scott had a right to sue for his freedom at all, since blacks could never be citizens of the United States:

> The question is simply this: Can a negro, whose ancestors were imported into this country, and sold as slaves, become a member of the political community formed and brought into existence by the Constitution of the United States, and as such become entitled to all the rights, and privileges, and immunities, guaranteed by that instrument to the citizen? One of which rights is the privilege of suing in a court of the United States in the cases specified in the Constitution.

For Taney, the answer was an emphatic *No.* Overlooking the fact that when the Constitution was being ratified, free black men in most of the Northern states, as well as in North Carolina, could vote, Taney declared that blacks:

> . . . are not included, and were not intended to be included, under the word 'citizens' in the Constitution, and can therefore claim none of the rights and privileges which the instrument provides and secures to citizens of the United States. On the contrary, they were at that time [1787–1788] considered as a subordinate and inferior class of beings who had been subjugated by the dominant race, and, whether emancipated or not, yet remained subject to their authority, and had no rights or privileges but such as those who held the power and Government might choose to grant them.

According to Taney, blacks were "so far inferior, that they had no rights which the white man was bound to respect."

Furthermore, Taney declared that Congress' ban on slavery in the western territories, the central provision of the 1820 Missouri Compromise—was unconstitutional because it violated the rights of slaveholders to their property, and that the Federal government had no right to restrict slavery in those areas. (This also subverted the concept of popular sovereignty, a key provision of the Kansas-Nebraska Act, since the court held that slavery was constitutionally permitted in the territories; territory residents could, of course, approve a state constitution that banned slavery and enter the Union as a free state.) The ruling shocked and outraged Northerners who had come to see the Missouri Compromise as a fundamental national agreement, nearly on a par with the Constitution itself. Politically, the opinion seemed to be a blatant attack on the Republican Party, which had made prohibiting slavery in the territories a major plank in its platform.

Taney had undoubtedly hoped to finally resolve the issue of slavery in the territories; instead, he only kept the matter alive. The decision led many Republicans to publicly support fundamental rights for blacks and black citizenship; some went further, calling for black equality and suffrage. In his debates with Stephen A. Douglas, Abraham Lincoln attacked the ruling and the contradiction between this decision and popular sovereignty, which Douglas advocated. The ruling also pushed some Northern Democrats into the Republican Party, which emerged victorious in the 1860 presidential election.

Dred Scott did not live long enough to witness the war that would ultimately resolve the nation's position on slavery, but he did die a free man. In May 1857, Peter Blow's children, who had helped Scott cover his legal fees, purchased Scott, his wife, and their daughters and freed them. On September 17, 1858, Dred Scott died of tuberculosis.

The Lincoln-Douglas Debates

In what would be an electrifying preview of the 1860 presidential election, the 1858 campaign to elect a senator from Illinois crystallized some of the issues that were dividing the nation. At this time, senators were elected by their state legislatures, rather than by popular vote, but Democratic incumbent Stephen A. Douglas and Republican challenger Abraham Lincoln took their campaigns on the road. From August 21 to October 15, in a series of seven historic debates around the state, the candidates focused on the Kansas-Nebraska Act, the Dred Scott decision, the Lecompton Constitution, and Popular Sovereignty. Most of the debates, held outdoors, drew audiences of 10,000 or more and were widely reported, transforming a local contest into a major event. Lincoln himself kept a scrapbook of the newspaper coverage and transcripts of the debates.

Lincoln began the campaign on June 16 at the Republican state convention in Springfield. In his now-famous "House Divided" speech, he declared: "A house divided against itself cannot stand. I believe this government cannot endure permanently half slave and half free. I do not expect the Union to be dissolved—I do not expect the house to fall—but I do expect it will cease to be divided. It will become all one thing, or all the other."

Douglas kicked off his campaign on July 9, in Chicago, with a speech that criticized Lincoln's "house divided" notion. "Mr. Lincoln asserts, as a fundamental principle of this government, that there must be uniformity in the local laws and domestic institutions of each and all the States of the Union," Douglas told his audience, which included Lincoln. "He therefore invites all the nonslaveholding states to band together, organize as one body, and make war upon slavery in Kentucky, upon slavery in Virginia, upon the Carolinas. . . . Mr. Lincoln advocates boldly and clearly a war of sections, a war of the North and the South, of free states against the slave states—a war of extermination—to be continued relentlessly until the one or the other shall be subdued."

Lincoln responded to Douglas by delivering his own speech the following evening, and a pattern developed as Lincoln trailed the senator around Illinois. "My recent experience shows that speaking at the same place the next day after [Douglas] is the very thing," Lincoln noted, "—it is, in fact, a concluding speech on him." Lincoln's advisers, however, felt they could gain a greater advantage by having their candidate appear with Douglas. The Lincoln camp then challenged the senator to a series of debates. As a national figure, Douglas was hesitant to share the stage with his lesser-known rival, but he accepted the challenge.

Lincoln particularly challenged Douglas, the primary author of the Kansas-Nebraska Act and a leading proponent of popular sovereignty, over what became known as the Freeport Doctrine. In the August 27 debate in Freeport, Lincoln asked: "Can the people of a United States Territory, in any way, against the wish of any citizen of the United States, exclude slavery from its limits prior to the formation of a state constitution?" Douglas replied: "I answer emphatically, as Mr. Lincoln has heard me answer a hundred times from every stump in Illinois, that in my opinion the people of a territory can by lawful means, exclude slavery from their limits prior to the formation of a state constitution. . . . It matters not what way the Supreme Court may here-after decide as to the abstract question of whether slavery may or may not go into a territory under the Constitution; the people have the lawful means to introduce it or exclude it as they please, for the reason that slavery cannot exist a day or an hour anywhere, unless it is supported by local police regulations."

From there Lincoln attacked Douglas for the inconsistency between popular sovereignty and the Dred Scott decision. Douglas could not back away from his cherished concept of popular sovereignty now, when so many voters favored it, yet the Supreme Court had undermined it in the Scott case by ruling that the right to slave labor in the territories was guaranteed in the Constitution (and was not a matter of popular vote). Although many agreed with Douglas that "slavery cannot exist a day in the midst of an unfriendly people with unfriendly laws," Lincoln continued to hammer away at the Freeport Doctrine and the apparent contradiction between popular sover-eignty and the Scott decision.

At the fourth debate, in Charleston, Lincoln brought home the point that slavery in the territories was a never ending issue that must end but his opponent had actually been keeping the issue alive. "Have we ever had any peace on this slavery question?" Lincoln asked.

> When are we to have peace upon it if it is kept in the position it now occu-pies? How are we ever to have peace upon it? That is an important question. To be sure, if we will all stop and allow Judge Douglas and his friends to march on in their present career until they plant the institution all over the nation, here and wherever else our flag waves, and we acquiesce in it, there will be peace. But let me ask Judge Douglas how is he going to get the people to do that? They have been wrangling over this question for at least forty years. . . . If Kansas should sink today, and leave a great vacant space in the earth's surface, this vexed question would still be among us. I say, then, there is no way of putting an end to slavery agitation amongst us but to put it back upon the basis where our fathers placed it, no way but to keep it out of our new territories—to restrict it forever to the old states where it now exists. *Then* the public mind will rest in the belief that it is in the course of ultimate extinction. That is one way of putting an end to the slavery agitation.

During the course of the campaign, Lincoln traveled more than 4,000 miles and gave more than sixty speeches. Douglas logged even more mileage and spoke fifty-nine times, with each speech running between two and three hours. In the end, Douglas won the legislative vote fifty-four to forty-six and was returned to the Senate. But the campaign and the debates had made Lincoln a contender for the 1860 Republican presidential nomination, and his scrapbook became the basis of the first book on the Lincoln-Douglas debates, which the Republicans distributed as campaign literature. In 1860, using many of the same arguments against the same opponent, and with the same issues in the hands of a national electorate, Lincoln would prevail.

John Brown and Harpers Ferry

One of the most dramatic acts against slavery took place on October 16, 1859, when abolitionist John Brown (1800–1859) and twenty-one followers seized the Federal arsenal at Harpers Ferry, Virginia (now in West Virginia). Funded by the Secret Six, a group of radical abolitionists, Brown and his men planned to arm themselves and start a guerrilla war against slavery in the Appalachian Mountains. Federal troops under the command of Colonel Robert E. Lee and Lieutenant J. E. B. Stuart soon arrived and attacked the armory engine house where Brown and his men were holed up. Brown was injured and captured, and ten of his men were killed.

Radical abolitionist John Brown, whose 1859 raid on the Federal arsenal at Harpers Ferry shocked both the North and the South, believed freedom for the slaves could only come about through armed conflict.

Word of the raid terrified Southerners, and Brown was quickly tried for a crime he had not committed: treason against the State of Virginia. As a citizen of New York, where he had moved following his guerrilla activities in support of the Kansas free soil movement, he could hardly have committed treason against Virginia. While in jail awaiting trial and, later, execution, Brown wrote hundreds of letters. He gathered a huge following in the North and even in Europe. A failed businessman, he had found his calling in the abolitionist movement and was seen by many as a Christlike figure who was sacrificing his own life to end slavery. But even though many people were sympathetic to Brown's goal of ending slavery and were impressed by his stoic resolve and bravery, most Northerners and almost all politicians (including virtually every Republican leader) denounced him. Southerners saw Brown as the embodiment of the Northern threat to Southern security and the South's life. In 1860, they referred to Lincoln and his party as "John Brown Republicans."

At his trial, Brown told the court: "I believe that to have interfered as I have done . . . I did no wrong, but right. Now, if it is deemed necessary that I should forfeit my life for the furtherance of the ends of justice, and mingle my blood with the blood of my children and with the blood of millions in this slave country whose rights are disregarded by wicked, cruel, and unjust enactments, I say, let it be done." He was convicted of treason, murder, and insurrection and, on December 2, 1859, was hanged in Charlestown, Virginia. Other captured raiders were executed after the new year.

The raid and executions exacerbated the divide between North and South, but they also delineated, for abolitionists, a critical moment in their decades-long struggle. Abolitionist Wendell Phillips (see "Notable Antebellum Figures," page 127) noted that Brown "has abolished slavery in Virginia. History will date Virginia Emancipation from Harper's Ferry." Poet Henry Wadsworth Longfellow observed in his journal: "This will be a great day in our history; the date of a new Revolution—quite as much needed as the old one. Even now as I write, they are leading Old John Brown to execution in Virginia for attempting to rescue slaves! This is sowing the wind to reap the whirlwind, which will come soon."

Political Parties and Organizations

American Anti-Slavery Society

In 1833, representatives from three leading abolition organizations gathered in Philadelphia to form the American Anti-Slavery Society, the first national organization of its kind. Founders included Bostonian William Lloyd Garrison (see "Notable Antebellum Figures," page 127), editor of *The Liberator*, and New York businessmen Arthur and Lewis Tappan. Within five years, the society had more than 200,000 members and more than 1,350 local units. Their massive mail campaigns distributed abolitionist literature around the country, and they overwhelmed Congress with petitions. In 1839, Garrison and the Tappans split over the direction of the society. Garrison's more radical supporters were attacking the Constitution (which upheld slavery), encouraging women to hold leadership positions in the organization, and pushing for wider social reforms, beyond abolition. During the Civil War, the society focused on obtaining a constitutional guarantee of freedom through the Thirteenth Amendment. The society functioned until 1870, following passage of the Fourteenth and Fifteenth Amendments, which provided blacks with citizenship and the right to vote.

American Colonization Society (ACS)

Founded in Washington, D.C., in 1817, the society raised funds to send free blacks to Africa and establish settlements there. The Reverend Robert Finley, a Presbyterian minister and the society's principal founder, believed that emancipated slaves would never find equality in the United States and would be better off creating their own communities in Africa. ACS members included prominent Americans such as James Monroe, Daniel Webster, Henry Clay, Andrew Jackson, and Francis Scott Key. In 1821, ACS leaders purchased land and founded Liberia on Africa's west coast at Cape Mesurado. The first group of free blacks was settled there in 1822. Liberia's capital city, Monrovia, was named for President James Monroe, who was in office at the time. The colony became the independent Republic of Liberia in 1847; by 1860, more than 10,000 free American blacks had emigrated. Many slaveowners favored colonization; they believed it would lessen the likelihood that free blacks in America would instigate slave rebellions. Most blacks were opposed to colonization, regarding it as a movement to rid the nation of free African Americans; most also preferred to remain in the country where they were born. Abolitionists criticized the scheme as well; they feared it would only benefit slavery by reducing the influence of free blacks.

American Party (Know-Nothings)

The short but spectacular rise of the American Party was a nativist reaction to the millions of immigrants pouring into the United States in the 1840s and 1850s. The Order of United Americans and the Order of the Star Spangled Banner espoused antiforeign and anti-Catholic views, and these and other secretive organizations fostered the Know-Nothing movement (members responded "I know nothing" when asked about their organization's activities or other members). The movement advocated allowing only native-born Americans to hold public office, toughening the requirements for citizenship, and ensuring the dominance of an Anglo-Saxon Protestant culture. In 1854, the Know-Nothings became the American Party and won big victories at the polls, particularly in Massachusetts but also in Delaware, New York, and Pennsylvania. The following year, the party split over slavery, and most of its Northern followers joined the new Republican Party. Millard Fillmore, a former Whig leader and U.S. president (1850–1853), ran as the American Party's presidential candidate in 1856 but won only Maryland. The party dissolved soon after.

Constitutional Union Party

The short-lived Constitutional Union Party attracted members as the growing sectional crisis dissolved or splintered other political parties. It drew moderates from the Upper South who feared the radicalism of John C. Breckinridge (of the Southern Democratic faction) and were unsatisfied with Stephen Douglas (of the Northern Democratic faction), and it appealed to remnants of the Whig and American parties. The party platform was not ideologically based; instead, it recognized "no political principle other than the Constitution of the country, the union of the states, and the enforcement of the laws . . ." and it characterized the platforms of partisan parties as misleading and deceptive. In May 1860, the party nominated John Bell, a former U.S. senator from Tennessee, for president. The Constitutional Unionists won Kentucky, Tennessee, and Virginia, but this loose, temporary coalition party did not survive long after the election.

Democratic Party

As the oldest continuous party in the United States, the Democrats (see also "Political Parties," in Chapter 3, "Wartime Politics,") had achieved a national membership by 1800 and, under President Andrew Jackson, became a dominant political force. The party favored limited government, and its trust in the common man was manifested in the "Jacksonian Democracy" of the 1830s, when more states extended the franchise to all white males and a greater sense of equality among Americans took shape. During the antebellum period, the debate over slavery in the territories divided the party; it split in two at the 1860 convention in Charleston. Southern delegates stormed out, insisting that slavery in the territories should be protected; most Northern delegates favored a party platform based on popular sovereignty. The convention reconvened in Baltimore, Maryland, but the factions met in separate buildings. The Northern-dominated faction nominated

Senator Stephen A. Douglas of Illinois for president; the Southern faction chose Vice President John C. Breckinridge of Kentucky as its nominee.

Free Soil Party

The Free Soil Party, officially organized in Buffalo, New York, in 1848, developed as a result of the Mexican War and the failed Wilmot Proviso. The party opposed extending slavery into the western territories gained in the war, and it promoted a homesteading law and support for internal improvements. Its members were a mix of radical New York Democrats ("Barnburners"), antislavery Whigs, and former members of the Liberty party, and its motto was "Free Soil, Free Labor, Free Men." In the 1848 election, former U.S. president Martin Van Buren was the Free Soilers' unsuccessful presidential nominee, but the party won one Senate seat and thirteen House seats. More significantly, its success in New York hurt the Democrats and propelled Zachary Taylor, the Whig candidate, to the White House. After the Compromise of 1850, the Free Soil Party declined (although it did send Charles Sumner of Massachusetts to the U.S. Senate in 1851). The Barnburners won political concessions in New York and returned to the Democratic fold; most other Free Soilers found refuge in the new Republican Party in 1854.

Liberty Party

James G. Birney and Gerrit Smith founded the abolitionist Liberty Party in 1840, over the objections of William Lloyd Garrison, a leader of the American Anti-Slavery Society, who opposed politicizing the cause. Party members understood that the South would not abolish slavery, but they were hopeful that their political presence would discourage congressional approval of laws supporting and protecting slavery. As the party's presidential nominee in 1840, Birney did poorly, but in 1844 he ran well enough to hurt Henry Clay (Whig) in New York, which may have tipped the election to James K. Polk (Democrat). The party had some successes at the local level but, in 1848, it joined the antislavery coalition that became the Free Soil Party.

New England Emigrant Aid Company

Originally known as the Massachusetts Emigrant Aid Company, this organization was formed in 1854 to support sending settlers opposed to slavery to Kansas to help ensure that the territory would enter the Union as a free state. Following the Kansas-Nebraska Act, the South was certain that the Kansas Territory would be proslavery, but an influx of primarily Western settlers—as well as the work of the Emigrant Aid Company and the efforts of other aid societies—prompted Southerners to establish their own immigration organizations to counter the free-state movement. The Emigrant Aid Company's aims were both philanthropic and entrepreneurial: it would found and help settle towns in Kansas (including Lawrence, Topeka, and Manhattan), and stockholders would receive dividends when company holdings were sold following the admission of Kansas as a free state. All told, the company sent between 1,200 and 2,000 settlers to Kansas, and one of its agents, Charles Robinson became the state's first governor (see "Wartime Governors," in Chapter 3, "Wartime Politics,"). In 1861, the company sold its Kansas and Missouri assets and essentially broke even on the venture.

Republican Party

Born in the Midwest, the Republican Party was formed in 1854 as a coalition that included former Whigs, antislavery Democrats, Free Soilers, and Know-Nothings. A sectional party, with policies that favored business, high tariffs, internal improvements, and social reforms, the Republicans appealed almost exclusively to Northerners and border state residents opposed to slavery. Though they opposed slavery in the territories and considered it a hindrance to economic interests and free labor, most party members believed the national government had no power to touch slavery in the Southern states. Most Republicans in the 1850s were neither abolitionists nor supporters of black rights and equality, although many Republican activists and leaders fervently opposed slavery and supported racial equality. Most Republicans believed that slavery was constitutionally protected, but that the institution would eventually die out if it was not allowed to expand into the territories. In 1856, the party nominated John C. Frémont, an explorer and former U.S. senator from California, for president; he won most of the Northern states but lost the election to Democrat James Buchanan. Four years later, the Republicans nominated Abraham Lincoln, a moderate from Illinois who had come to national attention during his debates with Senator Stephen A. Douglas in 1858. Lincoln's election as president in 1860 triggered the exodus of Southern states.

Whig Party

Taking their name from the British political party that opposed undue royal privilege and authority, the Whigs formed, in 1834, as an opposition group to Democrats and President Andrew Jackson, or "King Andrew" as he was called by his enemies. The Whigs generally favored regulation of the economy and government support of internal improvements. They attracted former Anti-Masonic Party members, states' rights advocates, eastern banking interests, and nearly any other group that was at odds with the Democrats. Two prominent U.S. senators, Henry Clay and Daniel Webster, led the party, and both William Henry Harrison and Zachary Taylor were elected president as Whigs. The party's opposition to the Democrats was its sole unifying element, and the Whigs eventually split into the antislavery "Conscience Whigs" and the proslavery "Cotton Whigs." Some members defected to the Free Soil Party, and after Winfield Scott's lackluster showing in the 1852 presidential race, the party fell apart. Its members were dispersed among the American, Republican, and Democratic parties.

The 1860 Election

The election season began with the collapse of the Democratic Party, which had dominated national politics since the turn of the century. Southern Democrats now dominated the party, forcing Northern Democrats to accept compromises over slavery. At their 1860 convention, Northern and Southern Democrats could not agree on a platform or a presidential candidate.

When the convention opened in Charleston, South Carolina, in April 1860, Senator Stephen A. Douglas of Illinois was favored for the party's nomination. Douglas, however, had alienated proslavery Democrats by breaking with a Democratic president, James Buchanan, over the administration's support for admitting Kansas as a slave state. The convention also objected to Douglas' "Freeport Doctrine" (see "The Lincoln-Douglas Debates," page 115), which he articulated in a debate in Freeport, Illinois, during his 1858 senatorial race. Douglas indicated that slavery as an institution could not exist without supportive legislation, so territorial residents could exclude it by refusing to enact such legislation. That position infuriated Southerners.

At the convention, although Douglas had a majority of the delegates, he did not have the two-thirds needed for nomination. Disruption occurred when, in deciding its platform, the convention rejected the Southerners' proposal of a Federal slave code and favored the Douglas forces' recommendation to leave the matter to the Supreme Court. Shortly after this vote, all the delegates from Alabama, Mississippi, Louisiana, Florida, Texas, and South Carolina, plus one-third of the Delaware delegation and part of the Arkansas delegation, withdrew. The Georgia delegates and most of the other Arkansas delegates soon followed. (With the exception of Delaware, all the states that withdrew from this convention later seceded from the Union.) The remaining delegates were deadlocked. The Southerners set up their own convention and approved the slavery code plank, but refrained from selecting a candidate. The main convention adjourned, after scheduling a new meeting in Baltimore on June 18. Those who had walked out called for a separate convention a week earlier (June 11, in Richmond), but did not nominate a candidate at that meeting either.

In Baltimore, when the convention voted to seat alternate delegations formed by Douglas supporters, many anti-Douglas delegates withdrew. After the remaining delegates nominated Douglas, the delegates who had withdrawn met and nominated John C. Breckinridge (then the U.S. vice president) for president, on a platform that demanded a Federal slave code. Herschel Johnson of Georgia, Douglas' running mate, observed: "Under these circumstances, it is difficult to resist the conviction that their fixed purpose was to break up the Democratic Party, regardless of the consequences."

In their platform, the Northern Democrats avoided a strong position on slavery. They stated that they would abide by the Supreme Court's decisions on constitutional issues involving slavery in the territories, including the concept of Popular Sovereignty. They also supported construction of a transcontinental railroad and the acquisition of Cuba (where slavery was legal); affirmed the nation's duty to "provide complete protection to all its citizens, whether at home or abroad, and whether native or foreign born"; and condemned free states' personal liberty laws as subverting the fugitive slave law.

The Democrats' Southern faction issued a platform that matched the Northerners' planks on Cuba, personal liberty laws, and naturalized citizens. Significantly different, of course, were the slavery planks. The Southern faction stated that all U.S. citizens were entitled to settle in any territorial area without any change in their personal or property rights (so slaveholders could keep their slaves); any new state should have the right of popular sovereignty and its own citizens should determine its slave or free status; and the laws in the free states that obstructed enforcement of the fugitive slave law subverted the Constitution.

The leading candidates for the Republican nomination were William H. Seward of New York and Salmon P. Chase of Ohio. Both were considered too radical on the issue of slavery to win. After a number of ballots, the "dark horse" candidate, Abraham Lincoln, gained the nomination. As a Westerner and a moderate, Lincoln seemed the most likely candidate to win the states of the lower North, such as Illinois and Indiana, which Democrat James Buchanan had carried in 1856. At the same time, Lincoln clearly reflected the strong Republican position against the expansion of slavery, and his articulate attacks on the Dred Scott decision had made him a hero among many Republicans.

The Republican party platform:

1. Reiterated the Declaration of Independence's principle that "all men are created equal";
2. Attacked all schemes for disunion but supported each state's right to "control its own domestic institutions";
3. Deplored Buchanan's backing of Kansas' Lecompton Constitution and called for admission of Kansas as a free state;
4. Accused the Buchanan administration of corruption;
5. Countered the argument that the Constitution allowed slavery to be introduced into the territories, proclaiming that freedom was the natural state of any territory;
6. Condemned any reopening of the African slave trade;
7. Called for equal rights for naturalized citizens and a Federally funded transcontinental railroad;
8. Proposed a Homestead Act, giving land to settlers;
9. Suggested a tariff to spur industrial development.

The Constitutional Union Party, which only lasted through the 1860 election, did not adopt a traditional platform. It claimed that its position was simply to support the Constitution and the Union, and it took no position on slavery in the territories. John Bell, a former U.S. senator from Tennessee and a longtime Whig leader, was the party's presidential nominee. Although a slaveowner himself, he did not aggressively advocate the rights of slaveholders, and he had opposed admitting Kansas as a slave state under the Lecompton Constitution.

The 1860 Presidential Election Returns

The 1860 election turned out to be a four-way race, but only three candidates ran in each section: Lincoln, Douglas, and Bell in the North, and Breckinridge, Douglas, and Bell in the South. The Republicans, led by Lincoln, competed only in the North, where they carried every free state except New Jersey and won the election; Lincoln won nearly 40 percent of the popular vote and a decisive 180 electoral votes (twenty-seven more than he needed to win). The Southern Democrats, led by Breckinridge, competed only in the slave states and carried eleven states. Douglas, running on the official Democratic ticket, competed in all states and won 29 percent of the popular vote nationwide (second to Lincoln) but carried only Missouri. Bell and the new Constitutional Union Party ran nationwide and won three states.

Notable Antebellum Figures

THE BEECHER FAMILY—The Beechers, who traced their American heritage as far back as 1637, were among the most preeminent nineteenth-century families in the United States. Connecticut native LYMAN BEECHER (1775–1863), the patriarch, was a dedicated Presbyterian minister and a man of strong opinions. He raised his thirteen children to share his moral opposition to slavery. His sons were enjoined to become clergymen and his daughters were encouraged to become educated. CATHARINE ESTHER BEECHER (1800–1878), the eldest child, was a strong advocate for higher education for women, founded several schools, and published *An Essay on Slavery and Abolitionism, with Reference to the Duty of American Females* (1837). EDWARD BEECHER (1803–1895), a Congregational minister, and president of Illinois College, helped organize the first state antislavery society. After the murder of abolitionist newspaper editor Elijah P. Lovejoy in Alton, Illinois, Beecher campaigned for both abolition and the protection of free speech. He wrote an acclaimed account of the troubles in *Narrative of the Alton Riots*.

HARRIET ELIZABETH BEECHER STOWE (1811–1896) became perhaps the most famous of Lyman Beecher's children (see *"Uncle Tom's Cabin,"* page 110). A teacher, she also published several stories and novels. Her most notable book, *Uncle Tom's Cabin, or Life Among the Lowly* (1851–1852), an antislavery novel, became the most famous book of the 1850s and one of the great rallying points of the abolitionist movement. HENRY WARD BEECHER (1813–1887) was pastor of the Congregational Plymouth Church of Brooklyn and one of the foremost pundits of American life. A leading clerical voice in the abolitionist movement, he helped send guns—"Beecher's Bibles"—to free soilers in Kansas, and he traveled to England to defend the Union's actions during the Civil War. CHARLES BEECHER (1815–1900), pastor of the Free Presbyterian Church in Newark, New Jersey, made clear his fierce antislavery views in *The Duty of Disobedience to Wicked Laws, A Sermon on the Fugitive Slave Law* (1851). THOMAS KINNICUT BEECHER (1824–1900), a Congregational minister, served as a chaplain in the Union's Army of the Potomac.

JAMES BUCHANAN (1791–1868). U.S. president (1857–1861), U.S. minister to Britain (1852–1857), U.S. secretary of state (1845–1849), U.S. senator (1834–1845), U.S. representative (1821–1831). A moderate Democrat from Pennsylvania, Buchanan unsuccessfully tried to straddle the splintered national fence and enjoyed the confidence of neither the North nor the South. He maintained that slavery was protected under the Constitution (he encouraged acceptance of the Dred Scott decision and admission of Kansas as a slave state), and he believed that states did not have a right to secede but that the Federal government was powerless to bring them back into the Union. The growing sectional crisis, the economic Panic of 1857, and financial scandals in his administration severely weakened his presidency. After leaving office, he supported the Union, but, to the end, he maintained that Northern extremists had pushed the country into war.

JOHN C. CALHOUN (1782–1850). U.S. senator (1832–1843 and 1845–1850), U.S. secretary of state (1844–1845), U.S. vice president (1825–1829, under John Quincy Adams, and 1829–1832, under Andrew Jackson), U.S. secretary of war (1817–1825), U.S. representative (1811–1817). A leading Southern statesman from South Carolina and a vocal proponent of slavery, Calhoun abandoned his early nationalist positions to advocate an extreme states' rights philosophy, and his opposition to high protective tariffs exacerbated the Nullification Crisis. As secretary of state, he helped bring Texas into the Union as a slave state, but as a senator he sought to keep California and Oregon out as free states. He worked to unify the South against abolitionist incursions, and although his positions would eventually fuel secession, Calhoun believed himself to be "a friend of the Union." Shortly before his death, he predicted the demise of the Union "within twelve years." His books—*Disquisition on Government* and *Discourse on the Constitution and Government of the United States,* published posthumously—show Calhoun to have been an original political thinker.

HENRY CLAY (1777–1852). U.S. senator (1806–1807, 1810–1811, 1831–1842, 1849–1852), U.S. representative (1811–1821, 1823–1825). A leader of the Whig party (and its presidential nominee in 1844), Clay earned his appellation as "the Great Compromiser" for his central role in resolving three major crises during the antebellum era. The Kentuckian guided passage of the Missouri Compromise, helped produce a compromise tariff to end the Nullification Crisis, and developed the Compromise of 1850 (which failed as an omnibus bill but later passed as a series of separate laws) and made it palatable to some Southerners by including a tough new fugitive slave law. A slave-owner himself, Clay favored gradual abolition (he served as president of the American Colonization Society from 1836 to 1849) and worried that ongoing debate over slavery was preventing the nation from pursuing territorial and economic expansion.

JOHN JORDAN CRITTENDEN (1787–1863). U.S. senator (1817–1819, 1835–1848, 1855–1861). Crittenden spent more than a half-century in politics, first as a Whig and later as a supporter of the Know-Nothing and Constitutional Union parties. Kentucky sent him to the U.S. Senate in 1835, and he later served as U.S. attorney general (1841 and 1850–1853) and governor of Kentucky (1848–1850). He is best known for his "Crittenden Compromise" (see "Antebellum Time Line—1860", page 66), an unsuccessful eleventh-hour attempt to preserve the Union. After its failure, Crittenden left the Senate and returned to Kentucky, where he worked successfully to keep his state in the Union. In May 1861, he chaired a border slave state convention, urging seceded states to reconsider their positions. The following month, he was elected to the U.S. House of Representatives, and though he remained a staunch Unionist, he opposed emancipation and confiscation of Confederate property. He died midway through the war, having seen his son George become a general in the Confederate army and his son Thomas a general in the Union army.

JOHN BROWN (see "John Brown and Harpers Ferry," page 118).

JAMES DUNWOODY BROWNSON DE BOW (1820–1867). A native of Charleston, South Carolina, De Bow gave up an unfulfilling law practice and focused on a career as an author of essays on economics and politics for the *Southern Quarterly Review*. As a representative to the Southern commercial convention in 1845, De Bow found his calling; within a year, he had started a business journal that became *De Bow's Review*. Respected and influential, but never financially sound, the *Review* ran pieces on business, economics, and agriculture, aimed at Southerners and Westerners. De Bow believed the South needed a balanced economy—a mix of manufacturing, banking, and agriculture—if it was to avoid succumbing to the economic might of the North. From 1853 to 1859, he published the *Review* in Washington, where he was working as the superintendent of the 1850 U.S. Census. Firmly proslavery and later strongly secessionist, De Bow stopped publishing in 1862, and during the war he served as the Confederate government's chief cotton agent. After the war, he resumed the *Review* and continued to promote Southern economic diversity and agricultural improvements, putting his own advice to work as president of the Tennessee Pacific Railroad Company.

MARTIN R. DELANY (1812–1885). A black physician whose medical training at Harvard ended early when a protest by white students forced him to leave, Martin Delany was an advocate for abolition and for colonization of blacks outside the United States. From 1843 to 1847, Delany published *Mystery*, an abolitionist newspaper in Pittsburgh, and he later coedited *The North Star* with Frederick Douglass. More radical than the antislavery movement in general, he even advocated a knowledge of "military science" so blacks could protect themselves from whites. He recommended colonization not in Liberia, but in Latin America, the Caribbean, or Nigeria, which he visited in 1859. That same year, Delany published *Blake, or the Huts of America*, a novel about a large-scale slave rebellion, which became popular with the free African American community in the North. He later recruited black soldiers for the Union and was commissioned a major in the army. After the war he served in the Freedmen's Bureau in South Carolina.

STEPHEN A. DOUGLAS (1813–1861). U.S. senator (1847–1861), U.S. representative (1843–1847). Dubbed "the Little Giant," five-foot-four-inch Douglas arrived in Illinois from New York at age twenty and within ten years had served as a state legislator, a secretary of state, and a justice on the state supreme court. In the U.S. Senate, Douglas worked to expand and preserve the Union; he did not favor slavery but did not seek to abolish it, noting that he dealt with it "as a political question involving questions of political policy." In crafting the Kansas-Nebraska Act (1854), he believed the only way to resolve the debate over allowing slavery in that territory and others was through Popular Sovereignty—allowing those in the territories to decide among themselves whether to permit or prohibit slavery. His debates with Abraham Lincoln during the 1858 Senate race brought his rival to national prominence. Douglas again faced off against Lincoln as the Northern Democrats' presidential nominee in 1860. He broke with prevailing tradition and campaigned personally for the presidency—a decision that weakened him physically. When war broke out, he strongly backed Lincoln. He died following a speaking tour of the border states, where he had gone to champion the Union cause.

FREDERICK DOUGLASS (1817?–1895). One of the leading orators and abolitionists of the nineteenth century, Frederick Douglass was born into slavery in Maryland. Always resourceful (he taught himself to read and write), Douglass escaped during the 1830s and eventually settled in New Bedford, Massachusetts. He attended his first convention of the Massachusetts Anti-Slavery Society in 1841. His eloquent speeches and intimate knowledge of life as a slave drew large audiences; he became a leading member of the New England Anti-Slavery Society and a promoter of women's rights. In 1845, he published his autobiography, *Narrative of the Life of Frederick Douglass, an American Slave, Written By Himself.* Fearful of capture— he admitted in the book to being a fugitive slave—Douglass moved to Great Britain, where he gave lectures until 1847. When he returned to the United States, friends purchased his freedom and helped him to start an abolitionist newspaper, *The North Star* (slaves followed the celestial body north, to freedom). Douglass continued his involvement in a variety of reform movements and supported the new Republican Party. During the war, he advised President Lincoln, worked ardently to recruit black soldiers, and protested their unequal treatment. In the Reconstruction era, he promoted civil rights for freedmen and worked for a variety of government agencies. An active civil rights advocate all his life, Douglass attended a suffrage convention the day he died.

HENRY HIGHLAND GARNET (1815–1882). Garnet was born a slave in Maryland but escaped at the age of nine with his family. In 1826, he attended a school in Canaan, New Hampshire, which was forced to close because it accepted black students. Garnet then moved to the Oneida Institute in Whitestown, New York, where he trained to become a Presbyterian minister. A prominent member of the American Anti-Slavery Society, he called for a violent uprising to combat slavery in 1843. This proved to be too radical a declaration, and Garnet fell out of favor with many abolitionists, but he later gave an impassioned speech on the floor of the House of Representatives in support of the Thirteenth Amendment to the Constitution. Earlier in his career, Garnet had been opposed to colonization, but he later saw emigration as a viable option along with integration. He was appointed minister to Liberia in 1881.

WILLIAM LLOYD GARRISON (1805–1879). After working on Benjamin Lundy's antislavery paper *Genius of Universal Emancipation* in Baltimore, Garrison moved to Boston and, in 1831, started his own journal, *The Liberator*, which would become the country's most prominent antislavery publication. In 1833, he helped found the American Anti-Slavery Society, which he continued to guide until 1865. A pacifist but also an uncompromising abolitionist, Garrison sought to end slavery through "moral suasion." In his speeches, he attacked both organized religion and the U.S. Constitution for abetting slavery, and he even suggested that Northern states should secede and form a new nation without slavery. Following the adoption of the Thirteenth Amendment (prohibiting slavery) in 1865, Garrison shut down *The Liberator*.

HORACE GREELEY (1811–1872). Influential, idealistic, and eccentric, Greeley was a tireless moral and social crusader who revolutionized journalism and spent thirty years as a dominant cultural figure. He was born to a poor New Hampshire family, apprenticed to a newspaper printer in Vermont, and, in 1841, when he was just thirty, founded the New York *Tribune*. He attracted top writing talent, including Charles A. Dana and Margaret Fuller, and he avoided sensationalism; instead, his paper emphasized good taste, solid reporting, and a wide range of intellectual subject matter. By the 1850s, the *Tribune* had the largest circulation in the nation. The paper originally backed the Whigs and later the Republicans, but it always bore Greeley's imprint and trumpeted his causes: emancipation of the slaves; opposition to capital punishment, the Mexican War, the Kansas-Nebraska Act, the Dred Scott decision; and support for westward expansion, trade unions, and restrictions on liquor sales. A popular and well-traveled speaker, Greeley had political ambitions that never equaled his journalistic success. He briefly served in Congress (1848–1849), and in 1872 he was nominated for president by a coalition of liberal Republicans and Democrats. Soundly defeated, he died several weeks after the election.

SARAH M. GRIMKÉ (1792–1873) and ANGELINA E. GRIMKÉ WELD (1805–1879). Born of a wealthy family in Charleston, South Carolina, Sarah and Angelina Grimké embraced the Quaker faith and moved to Philadelphia, where they quickly became involved in the abolition movement. In 1836, Angelina published an *Appeal to the Christian Women of the South*, inviting them to "overthrow this horrible system of oppression and cruelty, licentiousness and wrong." Her pamphlet was burned in South Carolina, but it led to her speaking before groups of women, in private homes, for the American Anti-Slavery Society. Sarah began speaking as well, and wrote an *Epistle to the Clergy of the Southern States* that was comparable to Angelina's work. Both sisters soon gave public lectures on abolition, at first for women only, and then for audiences of both sexes. They were criticized so heatedly for speaking in public that they became champions of women's rights.

WENDELL PHILLIPS (1811–1884). From a prominent Boston family, Phillips earned undergraduate and law degrees from Harvard University. Outraged at the murder of abolitionist editor Elijah P. Lovejoy, Phillips turned his career from the law to lecturing. He quickly became one of the most acclaimed speakers on the lyceum circuit and one of the leading champions of the abolitionist cause. A follower of William Lloyd Garrison, Phillips contributed often to *The Liberator* and served as a Massachusetts representative at the 1840 World Anti-Slavery Convention in London. During the Civil War, he criticized President Lincoln for his failure to push the issue of emancipation. In 1865, Phillips fought Garrison's decision to dissolve the American Anti-Slavery Society, and replaced him as the organization's president.

ROBERT BARNWELL RHETT SR. (1800–1876). U.S. senator (1850–1852), U.S. representative (1837–1849). Rhett was the most prominent among the South's "fire-eaters." He began fanning the flames of secession as early as the 1830s. On the House floor and in the Charleston *Mercury*, which his son edited, he vigorously attacked abolitionism, the Federal tariff, and anyone who was in opposition to him. In 1844, he broke with Calhoun, and in Bluffton,

South Carolina, under a tree later known as "Secession Oak," he delivered an impassioned speech against the unfairness of Federal tariffs and the states' right to act independently against the tariff. When Lincoln was elected president in 1860, Rhett espoused immediate secession lest the passage of time cause the South to waver in its demands. Hailed as "the father of secession," Rhett chaired the committee that wrote the permanent Confederate Constitution, but was disappointed when he did not achieve a prominent position in the new government. He spent the war years criticizing Jefferson Davis in scorching *Mercury* articles.

EDMUND RUFFIN (1794–1865). A Virginia native and ardent fire-eater, Ruffin first made a name for himself as an agricultural expert. His scientific approach to replenishing worn-out, single-crop farmland focused on the use of "marl" (calcareous soils), which, combined with other techniques—such as crop rotation and improvements to drainage, plowing, and fertilizers—produced dramatic results on his own depleted land. He published his theories in an influential piece called *An Essay on Calcareous Manures*, founded a distinguished monthly journal, *Farmer's Register*, served in the Virginia state senate (1823–1826), passionately defended slavery as a necessary institution, and wrote extensively on Southern issues for other publications, including leading newspapers, *De Bow's Review*, and the *Southern Literary Messenger*. Severely disappointed when Virginia did not immediately secede after South Carolina, Ruffin moved to Charleston in 1861 and became a member of the Palmetto Guard. Often credited with firing the first shot on Fort Sumter, the aging Ruffin returned to Virginia after its secession. Devastated by the Confederacy's defeat, he shot and killed himself two months after Lee's surrender at Appomattox.

WILLIAM STILL (1821–1902). Raised in rural New Jersey, the son of a runaway slave mother and a father who had purchased his freedom, Still worked on his family's farm until 1841. In 1844, he moved to Philadelphia, where he later became a clerk for the Pennsylvania Society for the Abolition of Slavery, chairman of the Philadelphia Vigilance Committee, and a leader of the Underground Railroad. Still was instrumental in ferrying thousands of slaves to freedom in the northern United States and in Canada. It is thought that approximately 95 percent of all runaway slaves who passed through Philadelphia stayed in Still's house. His copious notes and profiles of those he helped became the basis of a book, *The Underground Railroad* (1872), one of the best contemporary accounts of the system. In 1859, Still started a campaign to end segregation on Philadelphia streetcars; the practice, with his help, was stopped by 1867. In 1861, he started an organization to collect social and statistical information on African Americans. After the war, Still served on the Freedmen's Aid Commission. In 1880, he founded the first colored unit of the Young Men's Christian Association (YMCA).

ROGER TANEY (1777–1864). Chief Justice of the United States (1836–1864); U.S. secretary of the treasury (1833–1834); U.S. attorney general (1831–1833). Born in southern Maryland and raised on a tobacco plantation, Taney came from a wealthy family that had been in the area since the 1660s. As Andrew Jackson's attorney general and then his treasury secretary, Taney was a leading figure in the president's war on the second Bank of the United States. He then became a target for Whigs and other bank supporters who blocked his nomination to the U.S. Supreme Court. But following the death of Chief Justice John Marshall, President Jackson named Taney the new chief justice, and he was confirmed in 1836. Many of his opinions—particularly on banking, contracts, and commerce—have come to be highly regarded, yet he is inextricably associated with one of the Court's most controversial cases, the Dred Scott ruling which exacerbated sectional tensions. A former slaveowner himself, Taney had freed his own slaves and supported colonization, but he was vilified in the North for his ruling in the Scott case. During the war, Taney also drew ire from Union supporters for his defense of civilians' rights in *Ex parte Merryman* and his opposition to war politics.

SOJOURNER TRUTH (c.1799–1883). Born Isabella Bomefree in a Dutch-settled area of New York State, Sojourner Truth was emancipated under New York law in 1827. When her son was sold into slavery in Alabama—also illegal under New York law—Truth sued her former owner and won the boy's return. In 1843, she adopted the name by which she is known and became an itinerant preacher. Soon after, she began giving antislavery lectures and recounted her own experiences to support her arguments for abolition. A powerful and witty speaker, Truth was also an ardent advocate of women's rights and a committed evangelist. In 1863, she moved to Washington where she aided black refugees and, in 1865, tested the enforcement of a local statute prohibiting discrimination on streetcars. After the Civil War, she started a job placement service for black refugees and sought signatures to petition Congress to give western American lands to African Americans.

Harriet Tubman, herself an escaped slave, led hundreds of slaves to freedom on the Underground Railroad. Her reminder that "a live runaway could do great harm by going back, but that a dead one could tell no secrets" prompted cooperation by her charges during the dangerous trip north.

HARRIET TUBMAN (c.1821–1913). The most renowned conductor of the Underground Railroad, Harriet Tubman escaped from slavery to Philadelphia in 1849, but returned south nearly twenty times to rescue over 200 slaves, including members of her family. She was so successful that the State of Maryland offered a $40,000 reward for her capture. Tubman gave speeches against slavery, and, in 1858, she helped John Brown to plan his raid on Harpers Ferry. William Still, another leader of the Underground Railroad, declared that "in point of courage, shrewdness, and disinterested exertions to rescue her fellowman, she was without equal." During the Civil War, Tubman served as a spy and scout for the Union army, as well as a nurse for soldiers and black refugees.

WILLIAM WALKER (1824–1860). Tennessee-born, Walker gave up his professions as a doctor, lawyer, and journalist to pursue adventures as a filibusterer in Central America throughout the 1850s (see "Manifest Destiny," page 92). In 1853, after a failed attempt to capture the Mexican province of Sonora, Walker led fifty-eight of his followers to Nicaragua at the request of local revolutionaries. With financial assistance from the Accessory Transit Company, an American transportation firm, he captured the city of Granada in October 1855. In May 1856, the United States recognized his regime and he became president of Nicaragua in July. His goal was to create a Central American empire by exploiting the area's rich mineral resources and its interoceanic trade route, and introducing African slave labor to the region. In 1857, a coalition of Central American states defeated Walker's army and he returned to the

United States, where he was hailed as a hero. Three more failed expeditions followed; during the last, in 1860, Walker was captured in Honduras by the British, who regarded his activities as a threat to their interests on the Mosquito Coast. They turned Walker over to the Hondurans, who executed him on September 12, 1860.

DANIEL WEBSTER (1782–1852). U.S. senator (1827–1841 and 1845–1850), U.S. representative (1813–1817 and 1823–1827), U.S. secretary of state (1841–1843 and 1850–1852). A renowned orator, constitutional lawyer, and nationalist, Webster began his congressional career as a representative from New Hampshire, where he opposed protective tariffs as detrimental to New England's commercial shipping industry. As a U.S. senator from Massachusetts, he changed his position on tariffs, which benefited the region's manufacturing industries. In an 1830 debate with states' rights proponent Senator Robert Y. Haynes of South Carolina, Webster triumphantly expressed his view on the higher powers of the Federal government with one of his most famous lines: "Liberty *and* Union, now and forever, one and inseparable!" As a leader of the Whig party and harboring presidential ambitions, Webster backed the Compromise of 1850, speaking, he said, "not as a Massachusetts man, nor as a Northern man, but as an American." He upset antislavery groups, and many members of his own party, by suggesting that disunion was a greater evil than slavery, that the North had not fully cooperated in returning fugitive slaves, and that prohibiting slavery in the territories was pointless because the plantation system would not prosper in the West. His presidential aspirations unfulfilled—and unforgiven by many in his party because he supported the 1850 Compromise—Webster died having put preservation of the Union above his own political career.

SELECTED RESOURCES

These titles are representative of published works pertaining to the antebellum period. For additional information on published sources, see the annotated book list in Chapter 13, "Studying the War: Research and Preservation."

Davis, David Brion. *The Problem of Slavery in the Age of Revolution, 1770–1823.* New York: Oxford Press, 1999. Originally published by Cornell University Press, Ithaca, New York, 1975.

Finkelman, Paul. *An Imperfect Union: Slavery, Federalism, and Comity.* Chapel Hill: University of North Carolina Press, 1981.

Foner, Eric. *Free Soil, Free Labor, Free Men: The Ideology of the Republican Party.* Oxford and New York: Oxford University Press, 1995, 1970.

Freehling, William W. *The Road to Disunion: Secessionists at Bay, 1776–1854.* New York: Oxford University Press, 1990.

Kolchin, Peter. *American Slavery: 1619–1877.* New York: Hill and Wang, 1993.

McCardell, John. *The Idea of a Southern Nation: Southern Nationalists and Southern Nationalism, 1830–1860.* New York: Norton, 1979.

Oakes, James. *Slavery and Freedom: An Interpretation of the Old South.* New York: Knopf, 1990.

Potter, David M. *The Impending Crisis, 1848–1861.* New York: Harper & Row, 1976.

Stampp, Kenneth M. *And the War Came: The North and the Secession Crisis, 1860–1861.* Baton Rouge: Louisiana State University Press, 1970.

Stewart, James B. *Holy Warriors: The Abolitionists and American Slavery.* New York: Hill and Wang, 1996, 1976.

WARTIME POLITICS

In the first months after the firing on Fort Sumter, when the Union and the Confederate governments mobilized for war, it appeared as if the North faced the greater political challenge. Powerful—and very vocal—political factions argued about what the aims of the country should be in the coming conflict. Some called for a limited war followed by restoration of the Union to its presecession form; some argued for a full-scale war to restore the Union and achieve universal abolition; still others maintained that the South should be allowed to go in peace. By contrast, Confederate leadership faced the coming storm with a single objective and a unanimity of purpose: independence through military resistance aided by diplomatic recognition and foreign trade.

In time, the political leadership in the North overcame its fractured start and, despite some continuing dissent, settled into a relentless and effective pursuit of Abraham Lincoln's evolving vision of a new nation. Conversely, Confederate political leadership, despite scattered successes, suffered from near-paralyzing infighting, incompetence, and failed diplomatic efforts, and could never marshal a sustained and orchestrated response to the North's Unionist resolve. Meanwhile, the politics of running the war inevitably led to confronting the issue that was at the root of the conflict: slavery.

Throughout the war, free blacks in the North and in pockets of the South—as well as the growing number of freedmen—exerted continual pressure for emancipation and civil rights for all African Americans. At first, Lincoln and his Republican party approached the matter gingerly. Later, they incorporated emancipation and revolutionary social legislation into their program to defeat the South. The departure of Southern lawmakers from the U.S. Congress during the secession crisis of 1860–1861 seemed to signal disaster for the United States, but it proved to be a boon for Northern legislators. Bills that had once been snagged over sectional conflicts like slavery and states' rights now swiftly became law. During the war, Congress produced some of the most far-reaching legislation in U.S. history—and planted the seeds for a mushrooming bureaucracy. The laws created by that Congress resulted in land-grant colleges, a transcontinental railroad, the country's first income tax, a new national banking system, the first successful paper dollars ("greenbacks"), and land for homesteaders. Much of this legislation greatly accelerated the settlement of the West after the war. Congress also raised African American hopes for greater inclusion in American society when it banned slavery in the District of Columbia, approved equal pay for black soldiers, recognized the black governments of Liberia and Haiti, and repealed the fugitive slave laws.

Out of necessity, the Confederate Congress focused more on survival. Perhaps its best known act was its creation of the first military draft in American history (1862). By March 1865, this Congress, now desperate, had approved the enlistmeant of black soldiers. More than any other Confederate congressional legislation, these actions trace the downward arc of the Southern cause and its collision with the very principles on which the Confederacy was founded. As the war progressed, old ideas and alliances resurfaced among politicians (the Confederacy did not have formal political parties). The unity needed to form a new government and establish independence gave way in the face of advancing Union armies. Sharp conflicts also emerged as congressional representatives from "exterior" districts (those under Union control) clashed with those still in the Confederate domain ("interior" districts) over legislative priorities and the use of resources.

Although the Confederacy held a national election in November 1861, Jefferson Davis—a provisional president until then—ran unopposed in what was effectively a single-party election. By contrast, Federal war policy hinged very directly on the 1862 congressional elections and the 1864 presidential race between Lincoln, a Unionist Republican, and his former general-in-chief, George B. McClellan, a Peace Democrat. War weariness in the North had taken its toll by the summer of 1864, and with the main Union armies bogged down in sieges—Ulysses S. Grant at Petersburg, Virginia, and William T. Sherman at Atlanta, Georgia—Lincoln contemplated the prospect of losing the presidency. Three years of bloody warfare and untold thousands of casualties would go for naught if his opponent won and, as expected, pursued a negotiated settlement with the Confederacy. The fall of Atlanta in September 1864, coupled with subsequent Union victories in the

Shenandoah Valley, raised flagging spirits in the North and recharged Lincoln's reelection bid. In an unprecedented wartime election, the president and the Republican Party won major victories at the polls (see "1864 United States Election", page 223).

Relations with Europe (see "European Powers and the American Civil War," page 201) engaged the talents of Northern and Southern diplomats throughout the war. Faced with the Union blockade of Southern ports, Britain recognized the Confederacy's status as a belligerent but never granted the breakaway states full diplomatic recognition. Lincoln's issuance of the

March 4, 1861, Abraham Lincoln is inaugurated as the sixteenth president of the United States at the U.S. Capitol. Construction of the Capitol's new cast-iron dome stopped in May 1861 but resumed in 1862. "If people see the Capitol going on," said Lincoln, "it is a sign we intend the Union shall go on." The dome was completed in 1863.

Preliminary Emancipation Proclamation effectively made the war a war to end slavery, and it was a powerful deterrent against European recognition of or assistance to the Confederacy. No major European nation was willing to endorse slavery.

Presidents Abraham Lincoln and Jefferson Davis (see "Civil War Government Officials," page 170) relied on and struggled with their respective congresses and state governors to maintain the political and financial support needed to carry out the war. These relationships became ever more challenging as the war lengthened and expanded. For example, state governors, in the North and the South, had little difficulty recruiting troops in 1861, but, by 1863, the U.S. and Confederate congresses had stepped in to meet soldier shortages through the draft. Confederate policy never wavered from its goal of independence, but implementation of that policy ironically pitted the Confederate government against some state governors and legislators who insisted on their own state's sovereignty. And with the war's devastation came opposing demands, in both the North and the South: End the war with a negotiated peace settlement, or end the war only with the enemy's military surrender.

When the smoke cleared from the great Civil War battlefields, it became apparent that the superiority of Union political leaders over their Southern counterparts played a pivotal role in winning the war and restoring the Union. As Mary Chesnut, the wife of a Confederate congressman and the author of a remarkable wartime diary noted, "The Confederacy has been done to death by the politicians." But this was more than a military victory for Union arms. In restructuring the country's financial systems, opening up the West, and changing the very face of society through the emancipation of 4,000,000 slaves, Abraham Lincoln and the U.S. Congress redefined the relationship between the Federal government and individual citizens. The subsequent adoption of the Thirteenth, Fourteenth, and Fifteenth Amendments to the Constitution secured freedom for the slaves, made them citizens, granted them access to the ballot on the same basis as whites, and moved the nation one step closer to realizing its promise as a nation founded on liberty and equality. The Civil War was a key turning point in nearly every aspect of American life, including politics. The country was shedding its identity as a community of states and growing into a new entity—one united nation.

For the purposes of this chapter, the North refers to those states that were loyal to the Union (including the slaveholding states of Delaware, Kentucky, Maryland, and Missouri); the South refers to those states that formed the Confederacy.

POLITICAL TIME LINE, 1861–1866

1861

"If all do not join now to save the good old ship of the Union this voyage, nobody will have a chance to pilot her on another voyage."—Abraham Lincoln, February 15, 1861.

"There is not one true son of the South who is not ready to shoulder his musket to bleed, to die or to conquer in the cause of liberty here."—Jefferson Davis, June 1, 1861.

April 1861

12: Confederates fire on Fort Sumter. Major Robert Anderson, the U.S. garrison commander, formally surrenders on April 14.

15: Lincoln declares that an insurrection exists and calls for 75,000 troops.

17: The Virginia State Convention votes 88 to 55 to accept an ordinance of secession, which calls for a public referendum on the matter but essentially serves as an act of secession. On May 23, Virginians vote three to one to join the seven states (Alabama, Florida, Georgia, Louisiana, Mississippi, South Carolina, and Texas) that have already left the Union.

19: Lincoln announces the Union naval blockade of Confederate ports in Alabama, Florida, Georgia, Louisiana, Mississippi, and Texas.

23: So that they may fight against the Confederacy, free blacks in Boston call for the repeal of a Federal law banning blacks from the state militia.

27: Lincoln extends the naval blockade to include Virginia and North Carolina. In another proclamation, he suspends the writ of habeas corpus (see "Suspension of the Writ of Habeas Corpus," page 207) from Philadelphia to Washington, an area encompassing the volatile, slave-holding state of Maryland.

29: In a message to the Confederate Congress, Davis reiterates the South's right to secede and calls Lincoln's April 15 proclamation a declaration of war. When he asks for authority to prosecute the war, the Congress responds by granting Davis power to use all land and naval forces and to raise volunteers.

In his message to the Confederate Congress on April 29, 1861, President Jefferson Davis justified secession, noting that "We feel that our cause is just and holy . . . we seek no conquest . . . all we ask is to be let alone."

May 1861

6: The Arkansas legislature votes 69 to 1 to secede from the Union, and the Tennessee legislature approves holding a public referendum on secession, an action that is tantamount to secession. (The Tennessee voters will formally approve secession on June 8.)

13: Britain proclaims its neutrality in the American Civil War. It recognizes the Confederacy as a belligerent, but not as an independent, sovereign nation.

20: North Carolina's secession convention votes unanimously to leave the Union. The delegates also vote to ratify the Confederate Constitution. This is the last of the eleven states that form the Confederate States of America, although the Confederacy will also claim the deeply divided Union states of Missouri and Kentucky, including thirteen, rather than eleven, stars on the Confederate flag.

The Confederate Congress votes to move the Confederate capital from Montgomery, Alabama, to Richmond, Virginia.

23: Union Major General Benjamin Butler declares that three fugitive slaves who have crossed into Union lines at Fort Monroe, Virginia, are "contrabands of war." (The status of slaves who take refuge with the Union army will be debated during the first two years of the war.)

25: John Merryman, a farmer and Southern sympathizer, is arrested outside of Baltimore, Maryland, for recruiting Confederate troops and sabotaging bridges and railroad lines. Roger Taney, Chief Justice of the United States, acting as a Federal circuit court judge, issues a writ of habeas corpus on May 27 for Merryman's release. General George Cadwalader, commander of Fort McHenry, where Merryman is incarcerated, refuses to comply, citing Lincoln's suspension of habeas corpus. In a written opinion, Taney argues that the president's suspension of the writ is unconstitutional and that such power belongs to Congress. Lincoln ignores the opinion. He claims that the president has power to suspend habeas corpus in certain cases. Suspensions will occur throughout the war. Merryman is later released and is never tried for treason.

June 1861

13: Unionists from Virginia's western counties convening in Wheeling issue *The Declaration of the People of Virginia,* condemning the state's unlawful secession and traitorous activities. The delegates "imperatively demand the reorganization of the government of the Commonwealth." Eventually comprising fifty western counties, the new state of West Virginia is officially admitted to the Union on June 20, 1863.

July 1861

4: The U.S. Congress, which had adjourned in March and normally would not convene until December, opens a special session that lasts thirty-four days. In his message to Congress, read on July 5, Lincoln summarizes the events that have occurred since he took office and justifies his executive actions, including the suspension of habeas corpus. He asks for $400 million and 400,000 men as a means for "making this contest a short, and a decisive one."

11: The U.S. Congress formally expels the senators from Arkansas, North Carolina, Texas, and Virginia, and one senator from Tennessee, all of whom had already withdrawn. Andrew Johnson of Tennessee (see "Civil War Government Officials: United States of America," page 170), a loyal Unionist, is the only Southern senator who keeps his seat.

22: The U.S. House of Representatives overwhelmingly passes the Crittenden Resolution (named for Representative John Crittenden of Kentucky), which stresses the need to preserve the Union and to maintain noninterference with slavery where it exists. Senator Andrew Johnson of Tennessee introduces a similarly worded resolution that passes the Senate three days later.

August 1861

6: Lincoln signs the First Confiscation Act, which authorizes seizure of property—including slaves—that is being used for purposes of insurrection. The president also signs an act freeing slaves who are employed by Confederates against the United States. Congress gives its approval to all acts, orders, and proclamations issued by Lincoln since his inauguration, and then adjourns its special session.

16: Lincoln issues a proclamation that people in the states that have joined the Confederacy "are in a state of insurrection against the United States." With some exceptions, the proclamation bars commercial relations between Union and Confederate states.

17: In the *Anglo-African* newspaper, Dr. James W. C. Pennington, a black minister, petitions Congress for the abolition of slavery. The petition is widely circulated among blacks who urge emancipation as both a moral imperative and a strategy against the South.

30: Union Major General John C. Frémont, military commander of Missouri, orders the death penalty for all Confederate guerrillas found behind Union lines, and freedom for all slaves of Confederate sympathizers. Border-state Unionists are infuriated by any talk of freeing slaves, and Lincoln orders Frémont to rescind his proclamation.

September 1861

12–17: To prevent Maryland from joining the Confederacy, the U.S. government arrests and imprisons state legislators favoring secession.

November 1861

6: Voters in the Confederacy elect Jefferson Davis president (thereby changing his status from provisional president to president). Members of the first "regular" (not provisional) Congress are also elected.

8: Captain Charles Wilkes of the U.S.S. *San Jacinto* intercepts the British mail packet *Trent* and takes into custody Confederate diplomats James M. Mason and John Slidell, who are en route to Europe. The *Trent* affair outrages the Confederate and the British governments, and London regards the incident as an act of war against Great Britain.

December 1861

1: U.S. Secretary of War Simon Cameron presents a report on what is to be done with "those slaves who were abandoned by their owners on the advance of our troops into southern territory." Lincoln orders Cameron to delete passages supporting emancipation and employment of former slaves in the military. The greatly shortened final version, as in the original draft, relies on Congress, in its "wisdom and patriotism," to decide the matter after the war.

9: In the wake of stinging military failures at Bull Run and Ball's Bluff, Virginia (see Chapter 4, "Battles and the Battlefield"), the U.S. Congress creates the powerful Joint Committee on the Conduct of the War (known as the War Committee) to investigate the armed forces. Chairman Senator Benjamin F. Wade of Ohio, a leading Radical Republican, and Michigan's Senator Zachariah Chandler (see "Other Notable Political Figures," page 186) direct the Republican-dominated committee in examining almost every aspect of military business. The committee uncovers cases of fraud, waste, and bureaucratic bungling in military contracting and purchasing. Information that emerges from its investigations into massacres (see "Battle of Fort Pillow" in Chapter 4, "Battles and the Battlefield") and into the treatment of Union soldiers in Confederate prison camps outrages the public and prompts some reform measures and heightened support for the war. The committee also studies military department operations, and, most frequently, searches for the causes of military defeats.

Partisan in the extreme, and nearly bereft of critical military knowledge and experience, the committee plots the removal of Major General George B. McClellan and, later, General George Gordon Meade for not prosecuting the war aggressively enough; it also criticizes and praises generals—not necessarily for their military performance, but for their politics. The committee favors antislavery Republican-minded generals (especially John C. Frémont) and promotes support for its chosen military commanders by leaking to newspapers information gathered in its closed-door hearings. Generals Joseph Hooker and Benjamin Butler, who had troublesome failures at Chancellorsville and Fort Fisher, respectively, are regarded more highly than Meade, a Democrat who is suspected of being a Copperhead.

For the most part, Lincoln stands up to the committee's attempts to manage the war, but, at times, he finds it politically expedient to give in to its demands. Although the committee produces some positive results in its investigations, its emphasis on politically acceptable military leadership creates, among high-ranking officers, a distrust that harms the war effort. The committee's strengths and weaknesses may have offset each other during the war, but its wide-ranging investigative activities further expand congressional interests and authority.

1862

"Let Congress now pass the bill for abolishing slavery in the District of Columbia, and we may, with a still better grace, be able to ask for the sympathy of civilized Europe in our war against the slaveowners." Philadelphia *Bulletin,* quoted in the *Semi-Weekly Dispatch,* April 8, 1862.

"There is no doubt that Jefferson Davis and other leaders of the South have made an army; they are making, it appears, a navy; and they have made what is more than either—they have made a nation. . . . We may anticipate with certainty the success of the Southern States so far as regards their separation from the North." William Gladstone, Great Britain's Chancellor of the Exchequer, October 7, 1862.

January 1862

31: Antislavery Republicans call on Major General George B. McClellan to vigorously attack the South, and they begin promoting an agenda to free runaway slaves, emancipate slaves, and allow blacks to become soldiers. McClellan opposes turning the war into a crusade to free slaves. He fears that it will alter the war—that the military conflict will become a social revolution.

February 1862

18: The permanent Confederate Congress convenes in Richmond, Virginia.

22: On George Washington's birthday, Jefferson Davis is inaugurated as the first elected president of the Confederate States of America. In his inaugural address, he refers to the American Revolution as a precedent for secession. He accuses the North of promoting a revolution against states' rights and slavery, thus perverting the goals of the Founding Fathers, and he blames Northern intransigence for forcing secession and causing war.

25: Lincoln signs the Legal Tender Act, creating the first successful government-sponsored paper money system in U.S. history. The notes, popularly called "greenbacks," are unsecured by specie (coin). A significant extension of Federal authority, the act is intended as a temporary wartime measure to generate revenue and allow the Treasury to pay its bills. More than $400 million will be put in circulation by the war's end. In 1871, the Supreme

Court will uphold the constitutionality of this and subsequent tender acts for the payment of debts.

27: The Confederate Congress grants Davis the power to suspend habeas corpus, a conditional power that is subsequently renewed, over public objections. (A third law that suspends habeas corpus will be passed in February 1864, but then allowed to expire.)

March 1862

6: In a message to Congress, Lincoln calls for cooperation with any state that will gradually abolish slavery and proposes offering compensation to slaveholders. He notes that the current cost of the war would quickly "purchase, at a fair valuation, all the slaves in any named state." The resolution is not accepted by the satates.

April 1862

16: Lincoln signs a bill abolishing slavery in the District of Columbia. The bill provides for compensation to owners ($300 per slave) and authorizes $100,000 for colonization of freedmen. The action further underscores the constitutional quandaries slavery presents to the North; even though slaves in the District of Columbia are freed, the Federal government continues to enforce the fugitive slave laws. Runaways from loyal slave states will be returned to their owners until Congress repeals the fugitive slave laws on June 28, 1864.

In Richmond, Davis approves the Conscription Act, creating the first military draft in American history. It applies to white men between ages eighteen and thirty-five who could be drafted for three-year terms. The Act allows men to avoid military service by hiring a substitute to take their place, but this provision, which exacerbates class tensions, will be repealed on December 28, 1863. Other exemptions are allowed for those whose occupations are deemed critical to the war effort: government officials, mail carriers, telegraph operators, railroad workers, medical personnel, and certain laborers. A highly unpopular clause, added in October, grants exemptions to one white owner or overseer for every twenty slaves on a plantation.

25: Union Major General David Hunter proclaims martial law in the Department of the South and will declare slaves in Florida, Georgia, and South Carolina free on May 9. Lincoln revokes Hunter's order on May 19, again angering free blacks and white opponents of slavery in his own party.

May 1862

15: Union Major General Benjamin Butler, military commander of recently captured New Orleans, announces that any Southern woman who insults a Union officer will face arrest as a prostitute. The order outrages Southerners and elicits negative comment in Europe, but it stops what has been frequent harassment of Federal soldiers. After the Union takeover of the city, the Native Guards, a military organization of free blacks who refused to evacuate with the rest of the Confederate army, offer Butler their services.

Lincoln approves the creation of the Department of Agriculture (he calls it "the people's Department"), "to acquire and diffuse among the people . . . useful information on subjects connected with agriculture in the most general and comprehensive sense of that word." The department will receive cabinet status in 1889.

20: The U.S. Congress approves the Homestead Act, providing settlers with 160 acres each of public land on the condition that the grantee settles there, occupying or improving it for five years. Since the early 1830s, farmers, reformers, and others had been pushing unsuccessfully for a Homestead Act to facilitate western settlement. Southern lawmakers consistently blocked such legislation, regarding homesteaders as antislavery. (It was also opposed by some eastern businesses and landowners, who feared that free land would cost them employees and decrease property values.)

July 1862

1: Lincoln signs the first operative Federal income tax into law (the first income tax law, passed the previous year, was never enforced). It levies a 3 percent tax on income from $600 to $10,000, and a 5 percent tax on income above $10,000. Treasury Secretary Salmon P. Chase (see "Civil War Government Officials: United States of America," page 170) had calculated that the government would need $320 million in war funding for the upcoming fiscal year. Income tax revenue amounts to only $2 million in the first year, but brings in $20 million the following year, when tax rates are raised. Lincoln also signs the Pacific Railway Act into law. This will create the much-discussed, long-awaited transcontinental railroad that Republicans had been urging.

2: Lincoln signs the Land-Grant College Act (also known as the First Morrill Act; its sponsor was Senator Justin Morrill of Vermont), which transfers public lands—mostly in the West—to all states loyal to the Union. Colleges devoted to "agriculture and the mechanic arts" are to be built with money accumulated from selling these lands. Morrill had feared his bill would fail amid more pressing war legislation, but the act is popular with the public and becomes Congress' most important Federal educational legislation until the twentieth century.

Lincoln also signs into law the "Ironclad Test Oath," a loyalty oath required of elected or appointed government officials. In the Ironclad Oath, a person swears both past and future loyalty: he or she has never "borne arms against the United States" and will "support and defend the Constitution." Former Confederates would later be barred from U.S. government or military service unless they received a presidential pardon. The president had already approved less stringent loyalty oaths for ship masters headed to foreign ports,

Federal government employees, and military personnel. In addition, Union military commanders require Southerners in occupied territory, or suspected Southern sympathizers in the border states, to take loyalty oaths. With his eye on cooperation and future reconstruction, Lincoln will later order that these oaths require only a promise of future loyalty. In 1867, the Supreme Court will declare the Ironclad Oath unconstitutional.

13: Lincoln informs Secretary of State Seward and Secretary of the Navy Gideon Welles of his intention to issue an Emancipation Proclamation.

14: Lincoln signs an act establishing the Federal pension system for men who become disabled as a direct result of military duty. The act also provides pension benefits to widows and families of military personnel killed in the war. (In the 1880s and 1890s, Southern state governments will begin providing pensions to disabled Confederate veterans or their widows, but at a lower rate than under the Federal system. Confederate veterans and their widows never receive pensions through the Federal program, as is occasionally proposed, and both unwieldy systems eventually are tainted by corruption.)

17: After furious debate, the U.S. Congress approves and Lincoln signs the Second Confiscation Act, a landmark piece of legislation that has many significant provisions. A forerunner to the Emancipation Proclamation, the act grants freedom to slaves in rebellious states whose owners support the Confederacy as those areas come under Union control. Slaves from Confederate states who seek refuge behind Union lines are also declared free, although the act does not grant freedmen any particular civil rights. To keep the border states from seceding in response to the act, Lincoln insists on a provision for returning their fugitive slaves to owners who can prove they are loyal to the Union. Provisions are also made for the colonization of willing former slaves "in some tropical country." In keeping with its name, the act further authorizes the confiscation of Confederate property, though little is actually taken.

22: Lincoln reads his draft of the Preliminary Emancipation Proclamation (see "Emancipation Proclamation," page 210) to his cabinet. Secretary of State Seward advises the president not to issue the proclamation until it can be backed up by a substantial Union military victory. Lincoln agrees to wait.

August 1862

14: At the White House, Lincoln meets with black leaders to discuss establishing a colony in Central America for "able-bodied [black] men, with their wives and children." The president stresses the advantages of a black Central American colony, where colonists could find immediate employment in the coal mines. Lincoln believes it is better for the races to be separated and notes that "without the institution of slavery and the colored race as a basis, the war could not have an existence."

19: Horace Greeley, the influential editor of the New York *Tribune*, writes an open letter ("The Prayer of Twenty Millions") calling on Lincoln to free the slaves as a way of weakening the Confederacy.

22: In response to Greeley's editorial, Lincoln states that his main purpose is to preserve the Union, and, to achieve that goal, he is prepared to free none, some, or all of the slaves, depending on the circumstances. He closes by noting: "I have here stated my purpose according to my view of *official* duty; and I intend no modification of my oft-expressed *personal* wish that all men everywhere could be free." Lincoln's letter prepares the public to accept the Emancipation Proclamation, which he has still not issued.

September 1862

22: Bolstered by the Union battlefield victory at Antietam, Maryland (September 17), Lincoln issues the Preliminary Emancipation Proclamation declaring that all slaves held in any state still in rebellion on January 1, 1863, "shall be then, thenceforward, and forever free," but it preserves slavery in the border states. In Great Britain and France, where the upper classes are at once pro-Confederate and antislavery, the proclamation makes intervention on behalf of the South highly unlikely.

24: Governor Andrew Curtin of Pennsylvania hosts a three-day conference in Altoona. Union governors are invited to reassert their support for the war and for Lincoln's policies.

27: In its second Conscription Act, the Confederate Congress extends the military draft to white males ages eighteen to forty-five. Unlike the first Conscription Act, which provided no exemptions for conscientious objectors, this act provides specific exemptions to Dunkards, Mennonites, Nazarenes, and Quakers. When members of these groups are drafted, they must provide a substitute or pay a $500 exemption tax.

November 1862

4: U.S. congressional (and some gubernatorial) elections mark the first opportunity for voters to indicate their support for—or opposition to—the war.

In his annual message to Congress, December 1, 1862, President Lincoln wrote that "In giving freedom to the slave, we assure freedom to the free—honorable alike in what we give, and what we preserve. We shall nobly save, or meanly lose, the last best, hope of earth." The following month he would issue the Emancipation Proclamation.

(Elections were held on October 14 in Indiana, Iowa, Ohio, and Pennsylvania; see "Wartime Elections," page 220). Despite some gains by Democrats, the U.S. Congress remains firmly under Republican control.

1863

"We feel curious to know what the deluded people of the North think of the present unprecedented high prices of slaves in the South. Just at the very time when Lincoln declares that they are to be emancipated, they command higher prices than ever before. Could anything demonstrate more satisfactorily the futility of his infamous proclamation? The people of the South never felt that the institution of slavery was ever safer than at the present time." *The Spectator* (Augusta County, Virginia), January 6, 1863.

January 1863

1: Lincoln signs the Emancipation Proclamation which declares freedom for slaves in rebellious states and permits former slaves to join the armed forces. With the proclamation in hand, Lincoln will abandon plans for black colonization.

7: The Democrat-controlled Illinois state legislature swiftly and angrily responds to the Emancipation Proclamation by passing a resolution that criticizes Lincoln for turning the war into a mission to free the slaves and calls the proclamation "as unwarranted in military as in civil law" and "a gigantic usurpation." Reaction throughout the country is intense. The *Valley Spirit,* in Franklin County, Pennsylvania, believes: "It is unwise, ill-timed, outside of the Constitution and full of mischief. Its effect will be more thoroughly to unite and exasperate the whites of the South in their resistance to the National Government, and to make the war still more prolonged, bloody and bitter." Jefferson Davis calls the proclamation a desperate move on Lincoln's part and brands it "the most execrable measure recorded in the history of guilty man." But the Washington *Morning Chronicle* notes that "President Lincoln now destroys the right arm of rebellion—African slavery" and the New York *Tribune* hails the proclamation as ". . . a great stride toward restoration of the Union."

The *Christian Recorder* publishes the resolutions of a meeting of free blacks in Pennsylvania in response to the Emancipation Proclamation. "Resolved, That we, the colored citizens of the city of Harrisburg, hail the 1st day of January, 1863, as a new era in our country's history. . . . Resolved, That if our wishes had been consulted we would have preferred that the proclamation should have been general instead of partial; but we can only say to our brethren of the 'Border States,' be of good cheer—the day of your deliverance draweth nigh. . . . "

February 1863

25: Lincoln signs the National Currency Act, which sets up national banking standards for the first time since the 1830s. (The act will be revised and renamed the National Banking Act in 1864.) The new system of Federally chartered banks is designed to facilitate long-term financing of the war, but it will continue in force for the next five decades.

March 1863

3: Lincoln signs "An Act for enrolling and calling out the national Forces, and for other Purposes," a conscription law launching the Federal military draft. Able-bodied males between twenty and forty-five are eligible for service, though a man can hire a substitute or buy his way out for $300. There are no special exemptions based on religious opposition to war and military service; some conscientious objectors choose to pay the fee to avoid service. Based on population, each congressional district is assigned a quota of troops; the draft is not held in those districts that recruit enough volunteers to meet the Federal requirements.

Congress authorizes Lincoln to suspend habeas corpus. The president had done so early on, but he now has congressional approval.

10: In a five to four ruling on the Prize Cases (with all three of Lincoln's appointees in the majority), the U.S. Supreme Court upholds the Lincoln administration's policy that denies the existence of the Confederate States of America even though the Union is implementing a blockade of those states as if they are, in fact, a foreign, sovereign power. After Lincoln declared the blockade in April 1861, the U.S. Navy seized Confederate and foreign ships (the seized vessels being deemed "prizes") that violated the blockade. The legal issue at hand was whether the president had exceeded his constitutional authority in ordering the blockade, when Congress had not declared a state of war. The Court rules that although only Congress can declare war, Lincoln did have the power to put down an insurrection.

18: New Jersey's Democrat-controlled legislature (voting along party lines) passes peace resolutions protesting almost every aspect of the war—the suspension of habeas corpus; emancipation; the creation of West Virginia—and calls for peace. These resolutions infuriate state regiments in the field and prompt the Eleventh New Jersey Volunteers to respond with their own resolutions: "That we consider the passage, or even the introduction of the so-called Peace Resolutions, as wicked, weak, and cowardly, tending to aid by their sympathy, the rebels seeking to destroy the Republic."

26: The Confederate Congress passes the Impressment Act, authorizing local impressment agents to seize black freedmen and private property (including food, clothing, slaves, railroads, horses, and cattle) to supply the army and navy. Impressment had been used earlier by state governments and military officials in emergency situations, but, under the new policy, property seizures are regulated by state boards under the War Department and become a matter of course in maintaining the war effort (military units still impress goods as needed). Impressment is fraught with inequities; owners are compensated well below market value amid rampant inflation, those living near battle areas and rail lines are imposed on most, and inefficient management of impressed goods leads to waste. By autumn, there is strong public opposition to the act, and legislatures in Alabama, Arkansas, Florida, Georgia, Mississippi, North Carolina, Texas, and Virginia lodge official complaints, deeming the act a violation of states' rights. (April 24, the Southern Congress will also pass a controversial tax law.) The better equipped North uses the power of impressment only in emergencies—and infrequently even then.

May 1863

Elections are under way in the Confederacy. They are held between May and November (see "Wartime Elections, page 220").

1: Fearing that the Emancipation Proclamation and the Union's use of black soldiers will incite slave revolts and mass escapes to the Union, the Confederate Congress passes a resolution calling for the execution or other harsh punishment of captured white officers who command black troops. The fate of black soldiers was to "be delivered to the authorities of the State or States in which they shall be captured to be dealt with according to the present or future laws of such State or States." Usually, this meant death or being sold into slavery.

22: The U.S. War Department establishes the Bureau of Colored Troops to raise black regiments.

27: The performance of black troops at the battle of Port Hudson (see Chapter 4, "Battles and the Battlefield") is one of many engagements that will turn public opinion in their favor.

August 1863

10: Lincoln meets with abolitionist and former slave Frederick Douglass to discuss treatment of black soldiers by Union officers and Confederate captors. (Douglass had halted his recruiting efforts when he learned that black soldiers were receiving less pay than whites.) Lincoln provides some hope that changes will be made and Douglass, although not entirely convinced, resumes his recruiting activities.

September 1863

10: Georgia troops passing through Raleigh, North Carolina, destroy the newspaper offices of the *North Carolina Standard.* Throughout the summer, W. W. Holden, editor of the *Standard,* had promoted peace rallies throughout the state, unsettling the Confederate government.

November 1863

19: Lincoln delivers his Gettysburg Address (see "The Gettysburg Address," page 214) during ceremonies dedicating a cemetery at the Gettysburg, Pennsylvania, battlefield. Lincoln emphasizes that the United States is a nation, not a mere union of states, and he redefines the war as a fight to affirm the principles on which the country was founded.

December 1863

7: The Thirty-Eighth U.S. Congress convenes. The following day, Lincoln issues his Proclamation of Amnesty and Reconstruction (see Chapter 11, "Reconstruction and the Aftermath of the War"), popularly known as the Ten Percent Plan, for restoring loyal governments to seceded states. When one-tenth of the voting population, as tabulated in the 1860 census, has taken a loyalty oath to the United States, the state may form a loyal government. Lincoln's plan assumes that Reconstruction is a presidential power and that the secessionist states have never really left the Union. The proclamation also underscores Lincoln's commitment to preserving the Union. There are lenient conditions for restoring the breakaway states, instead of the harsh measures favored by the Radical Republicans.

1864

"I have not permitted myself, gentlemen, to conclude that I am the best man in the country; but I am reminded, in this connection, of a story of an old Dutch farmer who remarked to a companion once that 'it was not best to swap horses while crossing streams.'" Abraham Lincoln, June 9, 1864, reflecting on receiving the Republican nomination for president.

January 1864

2: Confederate officers in the Army of Tennessee, led by Major General Patrick Cleburne, present a report proposing to use black soldiers in the Confederate army because of the Union's superiority in numbers and resources, and the fact that slavery—once one of the Confederacy's "chief sources of strength"—is now one of the "chief sources of weakness . . . [a]part from the assistance that home and foreign prejudice against slavery has given to the North." Davis refuses to consider the proposal.

February 1864

17: The Confederate Congress expands the draft to now cover white men between the ages of seventeen and fifty.

22: A covert attempt to make U.S. Secretary of the Treasury Salmon Chase the 1864 Republican nominee for president is uncovered with the release of the "Pomeroy Circular," written by Senator Samuel Pomeroy of Kansas. Pomeroy deems Lincoln unelectable and describes the radical Chase as "an advanced thinker." Uproar over the circular prompts Lincoln's supporters to rally to his defense and ends Chase's presidential ambitions.

24: The U.S. Congress responds to the vigorous petitions of the Quakers and other pacifist churches and passes legislation permitting exemptions from military service for conscientious objectors. (An estimated total of 1,200 to 1,500 men for both the North and South were conscientious objectors during the war.)

March 1864

12: Louisiana blacks present a petition signed by more than 1,000 men (27 of whom had fought under Andrew Jackson) to Lincoln, in Washington. It calls for state suffrage for black Americans before the state can be restored to the Union. They write that, as natives of Louisiana, and with many of them owning real estate, they "all are fitted to enjoy the privileges . . . of citizens of the United States." Lincoln writes to Louisiana's appointed governor, Michael Hahn, the following day: "I barely suggest for your private consideration whether some of the colored people may not be let in [to the suffrage]—as, for instance, the very intelligent, and especially those who have fought gallantly in our ranks."

May 1864

31: White radicals meeting in Cleveland, Ohio, nominate John C. Frémont for president on a platform advocating equal rights for blacks in the South. Several influential black leaders, including Frederick Douglass, initially support Frémont over Lincoln. They feel the president is too cautious and lenient in his terms for Reconstruction, although a majority of blacks support Lincoln. Frémont later drops out of the race.

June 1864

7: At its political convention in Baltimore, the Republican Party takes on the name National Union Party for the 1864 election. The following day, Lincoln is nominated for president and the platform predictably endorses the party's handling of the war.

15: The U.S. Congress passes a law granting black soldiers, who were free as of April 1861, the same pay as whites. Further legislation will be necessary before freedmen are also granted equal pay (March 1865).

July 1864

4: Lincoln refuses to sign the last-minute Wade-Davis Bill, an attempt by the Radical Republicans to put Reconstruction under congressional control, replace Lincoln's policies, and dictate the nature of Reconstruction, particularly through the protection of black rights. Efforts to reorganize governments in Arkansas and Louisiana are already under way. Senator Benjamin F. Wade and Congressman Henry W. Davis and their supporters view these efforts as being far too lenient (see Chapter 11, "Reconstruction and the Aftermath of the War").

26: Blacks in Philadelphia adopt resolutions calling for the commissioning and promotion of black officers.

August 1864

30: At their political convention in Chicago, the Democrats endorse a platform that includes a "peace plank," which calls for an immediate end to hostilities. The next day, the party nominates Major General George B. McClellan as its candidate for president.

September 1864

8: In formally accepting the Democratic Party nomination for president, McClellan rejects the "peace plank" in the party platform, recognizing the adverse effect this would have on Union soldiers. Instead, he announces support for the reestablishment of the Union as a condition of peace.

October 1864

4–7: The National Convention of Colored Citizens of the United States meets in Syracuse, New York, with representatives from eighteen states (seven of them are slave states). They adopt resolutions (written by Frederick Douglass) demanding "the elective franchise," and they form the National Equal Rights League (see "Political Parties, Organizations, and Movements," page 164).

31: Nevada enters the Union.

November 1864

8: Lincoln is reelected president after winning 55 percent of the vote and carrying all but three Union states (see "Wartime Elections," page 220).

1865

"Blackguard and buffoon as he is [Lincoln], has pursued his end with an energy as untiring as an Indian and a singleness of purpose that might almost be called patriotic." The Charleston *Mercury*, January 10, 1865.

"If the people of Virginia only knew and appreciated General Lee's solicitude on this subject [using black soldiers] they would not longer hold back their slaves. Their wives and daughters and the negroes are the only elements left us to recruit from, and it does seem that our people would rather send the former even to face death and danger than give up the latter." Th. P. Turner, C.S.A., in a letter to Lieutenant S. R. Shinn, April 2, 1865.

"[T]he Death of Lincoln is sorrowfull news to all the loyal people and has been the cause of some of the copperheads turning and say they dont want to be called Democrats any more for they dont want to belong to such a party any longer and some of them say that the best news they have heard was that Lincoln was killed. I dont want them to say that where I am or I would be tempted to strike them with any thing that I could get a holt of first if I was to hear them talk that way, for I think we have lost a great and noble man. . . . " Mary Strieby in a letter to her husband, William, of the 30th Indiana Regiment, April 23, 1865.

January 1865

23: Under pressure from the Confederate Congress, Davis signs the General-in-Chief Act, creating a position of supreme commander of all Confederate armies. Robert E. Lee is appointed to the post on February 6, in an attempt to prop up collapsing military forces.

31: By a 119 to 56 vote, the U.S. House of Representatives passes the Thirteenth Amendment to the Constitution abolishing slavery (the Senate had done so on April 8, 1864), setting off huge celebrations in Washington. Ratification by two-thirds of the states will make the amendment part of the Constitution on December 18, 1865.

February 1865

3: At the Hampton Roads Peace Conference in Virginia, Lincoln and Secretary of State Seward meet with Vice President Stephens, Senator R. M. T. Hunter, and Assistant Secretary of War John A. Campbell of the Confederacy, on board the Union ship *River Queen*. The Confederates reject Lincoln's requirements for peace, including unconditional surrender, an immediate cease-fire, and the breakup of military units.

March 1865

3: Congress establishes the Freedmen's Bureau (officially called the U.S. Bureau of Refugees, Freedmen, and Abandoned Lands) to deal with refugees and freedmen from Confederate states and to help the 4,000,000 former slaves adjust to freedom. It provides food, constructs hospitals and schools, and is also responsible for managing abandoned land in former Confederate territory. It is the first national social welfare agency.

4: With an eloquence rivaling the Gettysburg Address, Lincoln delivers his Second Inaugural Address (see "Abraham Lincoln's Second Inaugural Address," page 228). He urges the nation to move forward "with malice toward none; with charity for all. . . . "

13: Davis signs the Negro Soldier Act, approving the use of black troops in the Confederate army. Owners are called on to volunteer their slaves, and those who serve may later be granted freedom, with their owner's and their state's approval. The measure comes too late to be of any use.

April 1865

4: Arriving in Richmond two days after Davis and his cabinet flee, Lincoln tours the city and visits the White House of the Confederacy, where he takes a moment to sit at Davis' desk. John A. Campbell, a former U.S. Supreme Court justice and later the assistant secretary of war for the Confederacy, concedes that the war is over and asks the president to work with Virginia in restoring order. Meanwhile, in Danville, Virginia, Davis issues his last message to the people of the South. Admitting that the fall of Richmond is a serious defeat, he vows to continue the fight and urges others to do likewise.

9: At Appomattox Court House in Virginia, General Robert E. Lee surrenders the Army of Northern Virginia to General Ulysses S. Grant (see Chapter 4, "Battles and the Battle-field"). Formal surrender ceremonies take place April 12.

11: In his last public address, Lincoln speaks to an enthusiastic crowd gathered outside the White House. In keeping with the magnanimous tone and policy he had long maintained, Lincoln outlines some of his plans for a generous peace. He acknowledges that there will be difficulties during Reconstruction and that the seceded states are not in accord with the Union, but says that the matter of secession is irrelevant. What matters most—"the sole object of the government"—is putting those states back into "proper practical relation" with the rest of the nation. He also advocates giving the vote to "very intelligent" blacks.

14: John Wilkes Booth shoots Lincoln at Ford's Theatre in Washington. The president dies the following day, and Andrew Johnson is sworn in as president.

May 1865

10: President Johnson officially declares that armed resistance to the Federal government has virtually ended. Near Irwinville, Georgia, Davis is captured by Union troops and taken into custody. He will be imprisoned at Fort Monroe, Virginia, on May 22.

29: Johnson grants general amnesty and pardon (with a few exceptions) to all persons involved in the "existing rebellion."

August 1866

20: With new state governments now in place in all the former Confederate states, Johnson officially declares that the insurrection is at an end and that "peace, order, tranquility, and civil authority now exist in and throughout the whole of the United States of America."

★   ★   ★

Creation of the Confederate Government

The Confederate States of America was born in Alabama at the Montgomery Convention. Delegates chosen at the secession conventions of the first six states to secede (South Carolina, Georgia, Florida, Alabama, Mississippi, and Louisiana; the seventh state, Texas, arrived later) met from February 4 to May 21, 1861, to create a new government. The delegates selected a provisional president and vice president, created a Provisional Congress, and drafted and adopted a Provisional Constitution and then a permanent Constitution. As the potential for war grew, the Confederacy desired to be formally recognized by foreign nations. To give the fence-sitting slave states a viable alternative to the Union, the Montgomery delegates rapidly established the machinery of government.

The Provisional Constitution, identical in many ways to the U.S. Constitution, was unanimously adopted February 8, and a committee began crafting a permanent version. That document also borrowed heavily from the U.S. Constitution, but the permanent Confederate Constitution contained some significant differences: slavery was expressly protected—though the importation of slaves was forbidden—and presidents served one six-year term and had the power of a line-item veto (see "The U.S. and Confederate Constitutions," page 162). After much debate, the permanent constitution was unanimously accepted on March 11, 1861. All the Confederate states had accepted it by the end of June.

Ironically, because this new constitution was so similar to the U.S. Constitution, it undermined the states' rights theory of the Confederacy, the very foundation of the secessionist movement. The Confederate Constitution retained a supremacy clause and other aspects of a powerful national government. As the independent-minded Southern states tried to assert their rights, their difficulties with the Confederate government exceeded most of the disagreements that had plagued relations between the U.S. government and the Southern states before secession.

Its quick choice of a president and vice president who were acceptable to the widely disparate delegates in attendance was among the most remarkable achievements of the convention. Between "fire-eaters" (extreme Southern rights advocates) and the more conservative border states' representatives (slave states that had not yet seceded had dispatched observers to Montgomery), nearly all of the most prominent first-tier presidential candidates were unattractive to one group or another.

On February 9, just five days after the convention began, Jefferson Davis, a Democrat from Mississippi, was chosen president. Alexander H.

Stephens, a moderate Democrat and former Whig from Georgia, became vice president. (See "Civil War Government Officials: Confederate States of America," page 178.) Negotiations among the delegates were held in private, making it impossible for historians to fully understand how Davis was ultimately selected, but certainly his experience in the U.S. House and Senate, his Mexican War service, and his tenure as secretary of war under President Pierce all contributed to his appeal. Additionally, he was favored by the representatives from Virginia, and the new Confederacy was counting on that state's secession to solidify its bid for independence. In a popular election held on November 6, 1861, members of the first regular Confederate Congress were chosen, and Davis and Stephens were confirmed by the voters as the Confederacy's president and vice president.

Other important work completed in Montgomery included: providing for the development of regular and provisional (wartime) armies, issuing bonds to finance the government, enacting all U.S. laws that were consistent with the new Confederate Constitution, and establishing critical national departments. These departments mirrored the governmental organization of the United States, with some exceptions. Both the U.S. and Confederate governments had a State Department, Treasury Department, War Department, and Post Office (post offices in the South were simply switched to Confederate control). Unlike the Union, however, the Confederacy added a Justice Department (the United States, which had an attorney general, would create a Justice Department in 1870) and declined to create an interior department. The Confederate Constitution also provided for the creation of a supreme court, but that provision was never fulfilled.

The Montgomery Convention formally closed after the Provisional Congress voted to relocate the Confederacy's capital to Richmond, Virginia. The unicameral Provisional Congress continued until February 17, 1862. It was then superceded by the first of two regular Congresses, both bicameral, and both operating under rules mostly adopted from the corresponding U.S. bodies. The First Congress convened on February 18, 1862, and the Second Congress began on May 2, 1864. Between 1861 and 1865, 267 men served in either the House of Representatives or the Senate of the Confederacy. In the end, these Congresses comprised representatives from the eleven Confederate states as well as from the "governments-in-exile"—Kentucky and Missouri (Union states also claimed by the Confederacy). Nonvoting members were on hand from the Five Civilized Tribes of the Indian Territory (Cherokee, Choctaw, Creek, Chickasaw, and Seminole, in what is now Oklahoma) and from the Arizona Territory.

The U.S. and Confederate Constitutions

Although the Confederacy borrowed heavily from the U.S. Constitution in crafting its own constitution—and even used the same format and identical language in most sections—there were significant differences. After more than seventy years in use, the U.S. Constitution had demonstrated its considerable strengths, but had also revealed some weaknesses, which the Confederates addressed (as did the U.S. Congress in its post-Civil War amendments). The Confederate Constitution enhanced presidential powers, guaranteed the protection of slavery, strengthened states' rights, and streamlined some governmental procedures, including impeachment and amendment of the constitution. The Bill of Rights and other existing amendments to the U.S. Constitution were incorporated into the body of the Confederate Constitution. Interestingly, the Confederate framers

COMPARISON OF THE UNITED STATES' AND THE CONFEDERACY'S CONSTITUTIONS

	U.S. Constitution	Confederate Constitution
Preamble	"We the People of the United States, in Order to form a more perfect Union, establish Justice, insure domestic Tranquility, provide for the common defence, promote the general Welfare, and secure the Blessings of Liberty to ourselves and our Posterity, do ordain and establish this Constitution for the United States of America."	"We the people of the Confederate States, each State acting in its sovereign and independent character, in order to form a permanent federal government, establish justice, insure domestic tranquility and secure the blessings of liberty for ourselves and our posterity—invoking the favor and guidance of Almighty God—do ordain and establish this Constitution for the Confederate States of America."
Congress	Congress may appropriate funding with a simple majority vote from both houses. Congress may collect taxes and duties to pay debts and maintain the nation's general welfare. Congress may regulate commerce and is not prevented from funding projects to improve trade and business.	Appropriation bills need a two-thirds vote in both houses to pass. Bills must address a specific topic and be titled to reflect the subject. (This was done to prevent appropriations from being buried in cumbersome and unrelated bills.) Congress may collect taxes but it may not authorize protective tariffs—those duties and taxes on foreign imports meant to favor particular domestic industries.

	U.S. Constitution	*Confederate Constitution*
		Congress has the power to regulate commerce but it may not appropriate money for any "internal improvements intended to facilitate commerce." The only exceptions are for navigation, rivers, and harbors.
Presidential Powers	The president signs a bill (in its entirety) into law or vetoes it.	The president has line-item veto power and may delete individual items from a bill before signing it into law.
	The president may hold office for an unlimited number of four-year terms. (The Twenty-Second Amendment, ratified in 1951, set presidential term limits.)	The president is restricted to one six-year term.
		The president may dismiss at will cabinet members; he may not dismiss civil servants except for "when their services are unnecessary or for dishonesty, incapacity, inefficiency, misconduct or neglect of duty."
		Dismissals must be reported to the Senate.
Slavery	Slaves are referred to as "other persons," "such persons," and "persons owing service."	The terms "negro slaves," "slaves," "slavery," and "slaveholders" are used.
	The importation of slaves may not be prohibited until 1808. (Effective that year, Congress permanently banned the slave trade.)	The importation of slaves is prohibited.
	A fugitive slave clause requires that runaways be returned to their owners.	No laws may be passed "denying or impairing the right of property in negro slaves . . ."
		Slaves remain the property of their owners when traveling in other Confederate states, and runaway slaves or those "unlawfully carried" into another state are to be returned to their owners. (This was in keeping with the U.S. Supreme Court's ruling in the Dred Scott case and it expanded on the U.S. fugitive slave clause by allowing an owner to act on his own in recovering a slave.)
States' Rights	Federal courts have power to hear cases between citizens of different states.	There is no provision for courts to hear civil suits between citizens of different states.
	Two-thirds of the states are needed to call a convention to amend the Constitution.	Only three states are needed to call a constitutional convention.

retained a provision for suspending habeas corpus, and they kept the "Necessary and Proper Clause" in Article I, Section 8, which gives Congress the power to make all laws needed for carrying out its constitutionally authorized powers. This clause would have allowed the Confederate Congress to develop the same far-reaching—and nationalistic—legislative program that emerged in the United States and that was ultimately at odds with a hard-line states' rights philosophy. The table on pages 160–161 highlights the significant differences between the two documents.

Political Parties, Organizations, and Movements

Democratic Party

Before the Civil War, the Democratic party was characterized by its strong support of states' rights, strict interpretation of the Constitution, and support for slavery and its expansion into the West. These tenets were under attack by what the Democrats felt were the Republican party's radical positions on abolition and other social issues, and its catering to special sectional and business interests. When the war began, the Democrats ceased to exist as a political party in the Confederacy, but political factions later formed. The anti-Davis faction comprised extreme states' rights advocates who opposed the increasing centralization of the Confederate government, and others who were dissatisfied with the president's conduct of the war. The pro-Davis faction approved of the government's war management and was willing to temporarily put aside states' rights concerns and support a strong Confederate government until independence from the Union was achieved.

In the North, the Democrats divided into "War" and "Peace" factions. The War Democrats, by and large, supported Lincoln's initial war aim of keeping the Union together. However, they generally opposed emancipation, black enlistment, and equal treatment for black troops, as did most other Democrats. At the start of the war, two-thirds of the Democrats in Congress either voted with the Republicans on war issues or abstained. Typical of the War Democrats was Senator Stephen A. Douglas, one of Lincoln's opponents in the 1860 presidential election but an active supporter of the war effort after Lincoln's inauguration (Douglas died in June 1861). After the first shots were fired, Douglas had declared "[T]here can be no neutrals in this war, *only patriots—or traitors.*" But some Democrats opposed all war aims and the legislation that came with them, including unprecedented taxation and a resurrected national banking system. Others, such as Peace Democrats also called *Copperheads* (see "Other Political Organizations," below) passively or actively supported the Confederacy. In 1864, the Democrats nominated Major General George B. McClellan for president as a "peace" candidate. The Peace Democrats—with the slogan "The Constitution as it is, the Union as it was"—pushed for a negotiated restoration of the Union with all its prewar institutions—including slavery—intact, despite the slim possibility that the Confederate states would willingly return. Northern voters, particularly Union soldiers, overwhelmingly rejected McClellan.

Republican Party

The ascendancy of the Republicans precipitated the first wave of slave-state secession in the wake of Lincoln's election. Republican support for high tariffs and an activist national government also disturbed the Southern states. Over the course of the war, the party's antislavery faction acquired considerable power in Congress; it dominated the more numerous moderate Republicans and ultimately dictated the course of Reconstruction in the postwar years. Its free-labor philosophy and its support for national policies such as land grant colleges dovetailed with its demands for the immediate abolition of slavery. Moderate and conservative Republicans also were probusiness, and while they opposed slavery, they generally preferred gradual emancipation or colonization plans. In the 1864 election, the Republican Party temporarily renamed itself the National Union Party to include War Democrats, such as Lincoln's running mate, Andrew Johnson, a slave-owning Unionist Democrat from Tennessee. When Lincoln was reelected, the Republican party held large majorities in both houses of Congress, and controlled most Northern state legislatures and governorships as well. Most War Democrats would later leave the party, breaking with the Republican core on issues of black citizenship and suffrage, tariffs, currency policies, and treatment of former Confederates.

Other Political Organizations

COPPERHEADS

Republicans used the term "Copperhead" as a derogatory sobriquet for Northern antiwar Democrats. Like the venomous copperhead snake, it was suggested, these "disloyal" Democrats—or Peace Democrats—threatened to poison the Union by striking silently, unlike the rattlesnake, which makes its presence known. Eventually, the term was widely used to describe nearly any opponent of the Republican administration, but in ordinary dialogue it still referred to that part of the fractured Democratic party that advocated a peaceful resolution to the war.

Centered in the lower Midwest—particularly the conservative, agrarian southern counties of Illinois, Indiana, and Ohio—Copperheads (also called *Butternuts,* for the color of the homespun clothing commonly worn in the area) were more akin to Southerners in their political sensibilities. They were staunchly at odds with New England reformers and Republican abolitionists, and they resented what they viewed as the complete usurpation of Federal power by Yankee interests. Some Copperheads favored ending the war by

A powerful and much-reprinted illustration by Lincoln supporter Thomas Nast is the commanding feature of this Congressional Union Committee broadside. Text below the illustration (not shown) warns citizens that accepting Copperhead calls for peace would destroy the Union. The broadside reprints Southern peace conditions cited in the October 16, 1863, Richmond Enquirer.

simply letting the seceded states go; others talked openly of a "Northwest Confederacy" to restore the Union, minus the troublesome New Englanders, or a return to prewar days. In his campaign for the Ohio governorship, Clement L. Vallandigham, a one-time congressman and the best known of the Northern antiwar politicians, railed against Republicans for turning the war into a crusade against slavery, an institution he did not support but found hardly worthy of causing such a disastrous war and destroying the Union. At a rally in Mount Vernon, Ohio, on May 1, 1863, he attacked the administration of "King Lincoln" and its "war for the freedom of the blacks and the enslavement of the whites." Major General Ambrose E. Burnside, head of the Department of the Ohio, had Vallandigham arrested for violating Burnside's General Order, No. 38, which stated that "the habit of declaring sympathy for the enemy will not be allowed in this department." When a military tribunal convicted Vallandigham, Lincoln commuted his jail sentence and sent him to Confederate lines near Murfreesboro, Tennessee. In October, John Brough soundly defeated Vallandigham, who had continued his unsuccessful gubernatorial campaign from Canada. This ended any real threat Vallandigham had posed to the war effort.

In addition to the Copperheads, secret or semisecret organizations sympathetic to the South existed in the North but never in the numbers, or with the political power, described in the rhetoric of some Republicans. Perhaps the largest of these clandestine organizations was the Knights of the Golden Circle. This Southern group, originally formed in 1854, sought the annexation of Mexico to expand slavery. The knights, however, seem to have faded away during the second year of the war, after their overt connections to the Confederacy became widely known. They were succeeded by the Order of American Knights, a group centered in the southern regions of the Midwestern states. This group melded into the more notorious Sons of Liberty, formed in 1864 and later led by Vallandigham himself. Federal agents arrested some of the organization's leaders and took credit for foiling Confederate plots.

NATIONAL EQUAL RIGHTS LEAGUE

In October 1864, 144 African Americans attending the National Convention of Colored Citizens of the United States formed the National Equal Rights League to campaign for equal rights and opportunities for blacks throughout the United States. Ohio lawyer John Mercer Langston, named president, immediately called for the formation of state auxiliaries. These quickly organized in New York, Ohio, Michigan, North Carolina, Tennessee,

Louisiana, and Pennsylvania, and held state conventions to articulate their demands. Resolutions called for enfranchisement, an end to segregation in public accommodations, and, as the Ohio League put it, "the repeal of all laws and parts of laws, State and National, that make distinctions on account of color."

NATIONAL UNION LEAGUE

These bipartisan Northern loyalist organizations (also called Loyal Leagues) were formed to counter the perceived threat from Copperhead and Southern-sympathizing elements. Primarily Republican, these groups espoused a patriotic, prowar agenda and coordinated concerted, state-by-state challenges to candidates put forth by the Peace Democrats. The influential leagues grew out of secret antisecessionist groups in eastern Tennessee and Kentucky and, by 1862, had spread to major cities throughout the Union.

NATIONAL WOMAN'S LOYAL LEAGUE

The leading women's rights activists—Susan B. Anthony, Elizabeth Cady Stanton, and Lucy Stone Blackwell—were among the most prominent founders of the league. Politically savvy, they understood that women's suffrage would have to wait until the war ended, so they concentrated their efforts on a patriotic enterprise, but their support for the war was contingent on black freedom as a Union war aim. At a May 14, 1863, meeting in New York City, Anthony noted: "There is great fear expressed on all sides lest this war shall be made a war for the negro. I am willing that it shall be. It is a war to found an empire on the negro in slavery, and shame on us if we do not make it a war to establish the negro in freedom. . . . " The league drew thousands of members, and its petition drive collected more than 400,000 signatures in support of the proposed Thirteenth Amendment to abolish slavery. The league was also quick to link emancipation and black rights with women's causes. Among others, it passed this resolution: "There never can be a true peace in this Republic until the civil and political rights of all citizens of African descent and all women are practically established."

Leading women's rights advocate Susan B. Anthony, cofounder of the National Woman's Loyal League, told members that "Had the women of the North studied to know and to teach their sons the law of justice to the black man . . . they would not now be called upon to offer the loved of their households to the bloody Moloch of war."

PEACE SOCIETIES

Southern peace societies, and the growing peace movement they supported, did considerable damage to the Confederate effort. These secret groups, active throughout the South, initially comprised ardent Unionists, but as the war dragged on, they drew thousands of draft dodgers, deserters, and other war-weary citizens. The Peace Society, established in Alabama, prompted a government investigation after it managed to get six peace candidates elected to the Confederate Congress in 1863. The Peace and Constitutional Party, founded in Van Buren County, Arkansas, promoted desertion from the ranks and cooperation with the Union army. The underground Heroes of America (HOA; also known as *Red Strings*, which they wore on their lapels) operated in southwestern Virginia, eastern Tennessee, and North Carolina. Well organized and proficient, HOA ran an underground railroad that transported deserters and draft resisters to the North; gathered military intelligence for the Union army; formed anti-Confederate guerrilla groups; and undermined recruiting and morale by promising members a share of wealth from Confederate property and plantation estates after the war.

In 1863, the peace movement flourished in North Carolina, where speakers at frequent rallies criticized government policies and urged acceptance of various proposals to end the war. William W. Holden, editor of the *North Carolina Standard*, ran for governor (unsuccessfully) on a peace platform and his press was destroyed when government agents cracked down on the movement. The following year, in Georgia, Governor Joseph E. Brown headed up a peace effort and called on the Confederate government in Richmond to begin peace proceedings. Many in the Southern peace movement wanted to accept peace proposals from the Northern Democrats, who were calling for reunion and constitutional protection of slavery. Peace advocates also called for state conventions, or a convention of all Confederate states, to discuss these proposals with U.S. officials. (Richmond refused to negotiate any settlement that did not include Confederate independence.) The Southern peace societies and their supporters, which included about 100,000 organized members, weakened morale and disrupted the Confederate government's prosecution of the war.

UNITED STATES SANITARY COMMISSION

Northern civilians formed the United States Sanitary Commission in June 1861 to care for soldiers in ways that the Federal government could not.

The commission provided medical supplies, distributed food, and recruited nurses, ambulance drivers, and cooks. It also advised government officials on prisoners of war, disabled soldiers, and other related welfare issues. Politically, the commission aggressively lobbied national and state officials, demanding medical reforms and insisting on adherence to military regulations to prevent the spread of disease. It vigorously campaigned for the removal of Clement A. Finley, the U.S. surgeon general, whose antiquated medical views and hostility toward reform hindered crucial measures to improve soldiers' health. After Finley was removed from office, the commission successfully backed the appointment of Dr. William Alexander Hammond as surgeon general (see also Chapter 9, "Medical Care and Medicine," and Chapter 10, "The Home Front").

Civil War Government Officials: United States of America

President

ABRAHAM LINCOLN (1809–1865). March 4, 1861–April 15, 1865. His election prompted an exodus of slave states from the Union, and his call for troops following the attack on Fort Sumter set off another round of secession. His entire presidency included only six weeks when the nation was not at war.

Abraham Lincoln's storied birthplace was a one-room cabin in Hardin County, Kentucky. He grew up on farmland in Indiana and Illinois, and given less than a year of formal schooling, he supervised his own education. His résumé included experience as a storekeeper, a surveyor, and a state legislator. In 1832, he served as a captain in the Fourth Illinois Regiment during the Black Hawk War, but saw no combat, and in 1836, he earned a license to practice law. His reputation as a brilliant attorney with a folksy manner drew him a large clientele that included corporations, particularly railroads. His 1842 marriage to Mary Todd of Kentucky produced four sons.

Lincoln gained a national reputation during his unsuccessful bid for the U.S. Senate in 1858. In a series of celebrated debates throughout Illinois, Stephen A. Douglas, the Democratic incumbent, and Lincoln, the Republican nominee, addressed issues of national importance, from slavery to Popular Sovereignty (see "The Lincoln-Douglas Debates"in Chapter 2, "Antebellum America"). The debates received widespread coverage and added to Lincoln's formidable stature in the new Republican party, which he had helped to organize. In 1860, he was the Republican presidential nominee.

Lincoln's views on slavery would eventually have an impact throughout the country. During his one term in the U.S. House of Representatives (1847–1849), he proposed gradual compensated emancipation in Washington, D.C. A key component of his debates with Douglas had been his insistence that slavery was wrong. His famous February 27, 1860, speech at New York's Cooper Union galvanized Republicans when he articulated why slavery should not be extended into the territories and why the Federal government had the authority to prevent such an extension. Although Lincoln's record was moderate by Republican standards, his election as president impelled Southern states to hold secession conventions to protect the institution of slavery.

Before taking office as president—and in his First Inaugural Address—Lincoln aimed to assure Americans, particularly those in states that had seceded or were considering secession, that he had no intention of abolishing slavery where it already existed. His ultimate purpose was to preserve the

President Abraham Lincoln, center, next to General in Chief Winfield Scott (standing) and members of his cabinet; from left, Edward Bates, Gideon Welles, Montgomery Blair, William Seward, Salmon Chase, Caleb Smith, and Simon Cameron in the White House Council Chamber, depicted in an 1866 lithograph. (Note the unfinished Washington Monument, through the left window.)

Union, and after the attack on Fort Sumter, the president, for all his gentle manner, was relentless in prosecuting a war to do just that. It took all of Lincoln's political skill to keep his cabinet, the Congress, and the Union states' governors behind the war effort and to hold polarized border states in the Union. Through party patronage and his sensitivity to the political interests of officials and the needs of ordinary Americans, he developed a strong backing that withstood legal challenges to his actions and editorial criticisms of his efforts. In suspending habeas corpus, ordering a naval blockade, nationalizing state militias—and, later, issuing the Emancipation Proclamation—Lincoln expanded presidential authority to an unprecedented degree. He regarded these acts as constitutionally sanctioned wartime measures, but his opponents branded him a tyrant.

Over time, Lincoln came to the conclusion that the war to save the Union and the fight to end slavery were not two separate missions. The Union could only be saved, and could only continue to hold out the promise of life, liberty, and the pursuit of happiness, if all Americans were free. When emancipation became a war measure against the South and a legitimate war objective, Lincoln abandoned his plan for establishing a Central American colony for freed slaves and began contemplating the constitutional protections that would be needed to guarantee this hard-won freedom. Although he did not live to see the Thirteenth, Fourteenth, and Fifteenth Amendments to the Constitution enacted, Lincoln unleashed the momentum that eventually brought about these changes.

At first Lincoln's choice of generals to lead the Union army disappointed him and tested his reservoirs of patience. Through the difficult days of 1861 and 1862, he found his footing in selecting satisfactory military leadership and began working with Secretary of War Edwin Stanton in directing the war effort. He gradually supported stiffer measures against the South as the war went on and, in a message to Congress in 1864, he rejected any notions of a peace without an unconditional surrender and the emancipation of the slaves. But his initial plans for Reconstruction (see Chapter 11, "Reconstruction and the Aftermath of the War") were remarkably lenient and generous—too much so, in the eyes of the Radical Republicans.

Lincoln grasped the intricacies of military strategy by traveling to battlefields, studying maps, and digesting military texts. He also became more astute in foreign affairs. He gingerly stepped around such potential international crises as the *Trent* affair and the confiscation of foreign vessels. He shrewdly realized that the Emancipation Proclamation would make it nearly impossible for European powers that opposed slavery to intervene on behalf of the Confederacy. He also displayed dexterity in balancing civil rights and necessary war measures. Martial law was in effect in the border states and thousands of military arrests were made, yet, Lincoln and his administration showed more restraint than Jefferson Davis, president of the Confederacy.

After presiding over four years of war, Lincoln was assassinated at Ford's Theatre in Washington, D.C., five days after General Lee surrendered the Army of Northern Virginia. The president had lived long enough to see that the Union's monumental undertaking would be successful and that his oath of office—"to preserve, protect, and defend the Constitution of the United States"—had been upheld.

Vice Presidents

HANNIBAL HAMLIN (1809–1891). March 4, 1861–March 4, 1865. As a New Englander, a former Democrat, and a vigorous opponent of slavery, Hamlin was selected as Lincoln's running mate to bring balance to the 1860 Republican ticket. A former governor of Maine and U.S. senator, he was disappointed in the limited role of the vice presidency, but he helped Lincoln organize the cabinet, urged quick and strong action against seceding states, and pushed for emancipation. Lincoln never moved as quickly as Hamlin wanted, but, late in life, Hamlin acknowledged that the president's steady and methodical approach was the wiser course. Hamlin's unhappiness in his job and his move toward the Radical Republicans prompted Lincoln to drop him from the 1864 ticket in favor of Andrew Johnson, a Southern Democrat.

ANDREW JOHNSON (1808–1875). March 4, 1865–April 15, 1865. Johnson's aggressive record as military governor of Tennessee, his intense loyalty to the Lincoln administration, and the fact that he was a Southerner and a War Democrat earned him a place on the Union Party ticket in the 1864 election. He had served only six weeks as vice president when he was sworn in as the seventeenth U.S. president, following Lincoln's assassination. (See Chapter 11, "Reconstruction and the Aftermath of the War.")

Secretary of State

WILLIAM H. SEWARD (1801–1872). March 5, 1861–March 3, 1869. Ambitious, able, and effective, Seward served as a Whig governor of New York and as a U.S. senator, joining the new Republican party as a critic of slavery. At first, as secretary of state, he underestimated the president's leadership; later, he became a loyal and effective cabinet member. His restraint during the *Trent* affair, a diplomatic crisis that sprang from the U.S. Navy's seizure of Confederate envoys traveling on a British ship, helped bring it to a peaceful conclusion. Later, he persuaded the British government to seize warships being built for the Confederacy in Liverpool. Seward's acute political instincts, ever tuned to the rhythm of the Northern home front, proved invaluable in forming the National Union Party (a prowar coalition of Republicans, War Democrats, and others), which won huge victories in the 1864 elections. The night Lincoln was assassinated, Seward was stabbed and seriously wounded by Lewis Powell, one of John Wilkes Booth's coconspirators, but he recovered, stayed in the cabinet, and supported Johnson's Reconstruction program.

Secretaries of the Treasury

SALMON P. CHASE (1808–1873). March 5, 1861–June 29, 1864. Governor of Ohio (1856–1860), U.S. senator (1849–1855, 1861), and a lawyer who defended runaway slaves, Chase emerged as a leading member of the newly formed Republican party and an unsuccessful candidate for the 1860 presidential nomination. He settled for appointment as secretary of the treasury, which required overseeing the monumental task of funding the war: collecting the nation's first income tax, obtaining loans, and helping to write congressional fiscal legislation. He promoted a national banking system that provided Federal security to bank notes and helped stabilize currency. Impatient with the president, wary of Seward, and with his eye on the 1864 Republican presidential nomination, Chase became an awkward and difficult presence in the cabinet and eventually resigned. The president gracefully overlooked his secretary's maneuverings and named him Chief Justice of the United States.

WILLIAM P. FESSENDEN (1806–1869). July 1, 1864–March 3, 1865. A Republican from Maine, Fessenden spent most of the war years as chairman of the Senate Finance Committee. He agreed to serve at Treasury on a temporary basis in the wake of Chase's departure, and, in his nine months on the job, the frugal secretary worked to hold down war expenditures and combat inflation. He returned to the Senate and became chairman of the Joint Committee on Reconstruction.

HUGH MCCULLOCH (1808–1895). March 9, 1865–March 3, 1869. McCulloch's expert management of the Indiana state bank led to his appointment as U.S. comptroller, responsible for implementing and enforcing the new national banking system regulations. With his close ties to the banking industry, he made bankers' transition to the new system considerably less painful than it might otherwise have been. As secretary of the treasury, he advocated a quick reduction of the war debt and an end to the use of legal tender notes (greenbacks) in favor of specie (coin), to avoid overspeculation.

Secretaries of War

SIMON CAMERON (1799–1889). March 11, 1861–January 19, 1862. Negotiating with insiders at the 1860 Republican convention, Cameron was promised a cabinet post in exchange for ending his presidential candidacy and supporting Lincoln. Unaware of the deal, Lincoln later warily agreed to honor it. Cameron's mismanagement and corruption in awarding army contracts, his overt and excessive patronage, and his published recommendation to arm slaves embarrassed the president, who obtained his resignation and shipped him out of the country as minister to Russia. Cameron returned to the Senate in 1867 and built a powerful Republican machine in Pennsylvania that lasted for decades.

EDWIN M. STANTON (1814–1869). January 15, 1862–May 26, 1868. A former U.S. attorney general, Stanton served as legal adviser to Secretary of War Cameron and then replaced him and cleaned up much of the contracting mess he had left behind. Stanton then threw himself into his duties to ensure that military units were adequately equipped and fed. He enforced strict compliance with conscription laws, placed restrictions on what he considered a reckless press, encouraged Lincoln to remove the slow-moving George B. McClellan from command of all Union armies, pushed for the Emancipation Proclamation, and encouraged the employment of black troops. Although he differed with the president on many issues—and let it be known to others that he did—the two worked effectively together. Lincoln set policy and handled political matters, and Stanton managed overall military operations and day-to-day war business. Wrongly suspected by some as having had a hand in the president's assassination, the secretary was devastated by the event and used every means at his disposal to track down the conspirators. A leading Radical in the cabinet, Stanton opposed much of President Johnson's conservative postwar Reconstruction program, but he refused to resign. His firing led to the president's impeachment, and he resigned when Johnson was acquitted.

Postmasters General

MONTGOMERY BLAIR (1813–1883). March 5, 1861–September 23, 1864. An army veteran and former mayor of St. Louis, Blair argued Dred Scott's case before the Supreme Court. A proponent of supplying and defending Fort Sumter, Blair served successfully as postmaster general. He instituted several innovations, including return receipts, and he designed the money order system that allowed soldiers to send and receive funds. Radical Republicans viewed Blair as too conservative. They promised Lincoln the withdrawal of his rival, John C. Frémont, from the 1864 presidential race in exchange for the postmaster's resignation. Blair obligingly resigned and later rejoined the Democratic party.

WILLIAM DENNISON (1815–1882). September 24, 1864–July 11, 1866 (see "Wartime Governors," page 191). A former Republican governor of Ohio and an ardent opponent of slavery, Dennison was named postmaster general as a reward for his loyal service and vigorous recruitment of Union troops. He resigned his office because he disagreed with Johnson's postwar policies.

Secretary of the Navy

GIDEON WELLES (1802–1878). March 7, 1861–March 3, 1869. A former Connecticut state legislator and newspaper publisher and editor, Welles had served, under President Polk, as chief of the naval Bureau of Provisions and Clothing. As secretary of the navy (and with the able assistance of assistant secretary Gustavus Fox) he rebuilt the service by initiating the construction of ironclad ships, supervising the blockade of the

Southern coastline, recruiting black seamen, and creating the world's second largest navy, after Great Britain. He disdained Seward and Stanton and remained loyal to Johnson in his battles with the Radical Republicans. A political moderate, Welles had helped organize Connecticut's Democratic Party, left it over the slavery issue and became a Republican, then returned to the Democratic fold after the war.

Secretaries of the Interior

CALEB B. SMITH (1808–1864). March 5, 1861–January 1, 1863. A leading Indiana Republican, Smith was appointed secretary of the interior in return for supporting Lincoln's 1860 candidacy at the convention. Charged with supervising Indian agents and keeping Native Americans out of the war, Smith focused on protecting the frontier against Indian attack. He resigned his office because of poor health.

JOHN P. USHER (1816–1889). January 8, 1863–May 15, 1865. An assistant to Caleb Smith, Usher was a native New Yorker who later practiced law in Indiana. Lincoln appointed him to succeed Smith only to maintain the support of Indiana Republicans. Although Usher persistently warned Lincoln that Chase was aiming for the presidential nomination, Lincoln had little use for him or his schemes (housing former slaves on confiscated land in Texas, sending American Indians to reservations in the Southwest, making political decisions to benefit Union Pacific Railroad Company shareholders like himself). Usher left office after Lincoln's death and later served as Union Pacific's chief counsel.

Attorneys General

EDWARD BATES (1793–1869). March 5, 1861–November 30, 1864. Dedicated to his job but inconsistent in his views, Bates had been a prominent attorney in St. Louis, a central figure in Missouri state politics, and, in 1856, president of the Whigs' last convention. As attorney general, he opposed emancipation (though he favored banning slavery in the territories), but he supported the legal positions behind the suspension of habeas corpus and the blockade of Southern ports. Realizing that he was losing his influence with the president, especially over emancipation, he resigned.

JAMES SPEED (1812–1887). December 5, 1864–July 17, 1866. As leader of Kentucky's pro-Union faction, Speed worked closely with Lincoln—first to keep his state neutral, then to support the North when war came. He was strongly opposed to slavery and just as strongly favored confiscating Confederate property in his state and granting the vote to black males. As attorney general, he supported Lincoln's lenient Reconstruction plan for the South but eventually, his views hardened and he joined the Radical Republicans.

Civil War Government Officials: Confederate States of America

The Confederacy's provisional government lasted from February 4, 1861, to February 17, 1862. The permanent government, established following the presidential and congressional elections of November 6, 1861, existed from February 18, 1862, the opening day of the first Confederate Congress, to May 10, 1865, the day Union forces captured Jefferson Davis and other high Confederate officials.

President

JEFFERSON FINIS DAVIS (1808–1889), president of the Confederate States of America (provisional president February 18, 1861–February 17, 1862; president February 22, 1862–May 10, 1865). Davis never sought the Confederate presidency. When he learned of his election as the provisional head of state, he accepted the position with considerable anxiety, for he would be building a nation while guiding it through a likely war with a stronger opponent.

Born into a well-to-do family in Christian (now Todd) County, Kentucky, Davis left Transylvania College in Lexington to attend the U.S. Military Academy at West Point, graduating in 1828. After serving seven years in the army, including participation in the Black Hawk War, he resigned his commission to marry Sarah Knox Taylor (daughter of his former commanding officer and future president Zachary Taylor) and become a planter in Mississippi. Just three months after their marriage, Sarah died of malaria. In 1845, Davis married Varina Howell, with whom he had six children, and that same year, he was elected to Congress. He resigned from Congress in 1846 and served as colonel of the 1st Mississippi Rifles in the Mexican–American War during which the heroic action of his regiment garnered him much esteem in his state. After the war, he was appointed and later, elected, to the U.S. Senate. President Pierce named him secretary of war in 1853, and he led an aggressive effort to update and revitalize the

President Jefferson Davis, fourth from left, with General Robert E. Lee (standing) and members of his cabinet; from left, Stephen Mallory, Judah Benjamin, Leroy Walker, John Reagan, Christopher Memminger, Alexander H. Stephens, and Robert Toombs in the Council Chamber at Richmond, depicted in an 1866 lithograph.

military. He introduced advanced technology into the service, including rifled cannon and rifled muskets, repeating weapons, and the minié ball (see Chapter 6, "Weaponry"); made harbor improvements, and sent expeditions to explore and map possible routes for a transcontinental railroad. Because of these improvements in war-making capability, he also instigated the creation of a new manual on battle tactics—one used by both sides during the Civil War (see "Battle Tactics" in Chapter 4, "Battles and the Battlefield").

Returning to the Senate in 1857, Davis was a prominent states' rights spokesman and a leader of the proslavery forces. He tried to avert secession by proposing compromise. When that failed, he followed his state delegation out of Congress. His hopes for a high military post in the Confederacy were exceeded when the Confederate convention elected him their provisional leader. He brought many talents to his office—particularly, a vigorous work ethic—but his poor personal skills, stubbornness, and intolerance for opposing views made him difficult to work with. Although he argued with his generals (except, most notably, Robert E. Lee, whom he admired), they were given broad authority, and he did not meddle much with his executive departments—with the exception of the Department of War, which had six secretaries in four years. A former war secretary himself, Davis essentially ran the department.

Davis tried to balance his cabinet with appointees representing each state. He relied extensively on his friend Judah P. Benjamin—perhaps the most gifted statesman in the Confederacy—who held several cabinet posts. Most cabinet officers performed their duties without presidential interference because so much of Davis' energy (and 80 percent of the civil service) was dedicated to the War Department. His military philosophy—win by not losing the army—was defensive and it reflected his defensive political sentiment. The Confederacy did not want to wage an offensive war; it simply wanted to be left alone as an independent nation (see "Civil War Strategy" in Chapter 4, "Battles and the Battlefield").

As president, Davis tried to balance respect for individual states' rights with the national measures—such as conscription, impressment, and the suspension of habeas corpus—necessary to continue the war. His poor grasp of foreign relations and his concentration on the defense of Virginia illustrated his difficulty in seeing a wider view of the war. Yet, for four years, he led a government that was outmanned and outgunned but seemed, at times, within reach of victory.

On April 2, 1865, Davis and his cabinet fled Richmond and attempted to set up the Confederacy's government in Danville, Virginia. From there, he headed south as cabinet members left, one by one, to return home or to escape to Europe. On May 10, Davis was captured outside Irwinville, Georgia. Though charged with treason and imprisoned for two years at Fort Monroe, Virginia, Davis was never tried. The government dropped the case, and Davis refused to ask for a pardon, which prevented him from ever returning to politics. After years of foreign travel, rootlessness (Brierfield, his plantation, now belonged to his former slaves, though he eventually regained ownership), and failed employment as the president of the Carolina Life Insurance Company, Davis returned to Mississippi. At Beauvoir, an estate owned by an admirer, Davis spent four years writing a massive history entitled *The Rise and Fall of the Confederate Government* (1881). A self-serving and legalistic work, the book did poorly, but in his remaining years, Davis did enjoy his status among war veterans as the central symbol of what would be called the Lost Cause.

Vice President

ALEXANDER H. STEPHENS (1812–1883). February 11, 1861–February 17, 1862 (provisional); February 22, 1862–May 10, 1865. A former Whig congressman from Georgia, Stephens voted against his state's secession, yet subsequently served as a delegate to the February 1861 convention in Montgomery, Alabama, where the Confederacy was organized. Selected vice president, he was soon in open opposition to Davis, protesting conscription and the suspension of habeas corpus. His strained relations with the president resulted in Stephens spending most of the war outside the sphere of political high command. As a peace advocate, he served as a Confederate commissioner at the failed Hampton Roads Peace Conference in February 1865. Imprisoned for several months after the war, he wrote a two-volume work, *A Constitutional View of the Late War Between the States* (1868, 1870), and later returned to Congress. He was elected governor of Georgia in 1882 and died after serving only a few months in office.

Secretaries of State

ROBERT A. TOOMBS (1810–1885). February 21, 1861–July 24, 1861 (provisional). A wealthy planter, Toombs was instrumental in leading Georgia out of the Union and creating the Confederate Constitution; yet he argued against bombarding Fort Sumter. He ended his brief tenure as secretary of state to become a brigadier general and saw action in the Peninsula campaign, at Second Bull Run, and at Antietam, where he was wounded. After returning to the Confederate Congress, he joined Vice President Stephens and Governor Joseph E. Brown, two fellow Georgians, in opposing Davis' war policies. He fled to Europe after the war, but returned in 1867 and never took an oath of allegiance to the United States.

ROBERT M. T. HUNTER (1809–1887). July 25, 1861–February 17, 1862 (provisional). An experienced politician and states' rights Democrat, Hunter served as Speaker of the U.S. House of Representatives and was elected a U.S. senator from Virginia. Realizing that his efforts to effect compromise with the North were doomed, he resigned from Congress. As secretary of state, he tried to make an alliance with Spain. He spent the balance of the war in the Confederate Senate, and, early in 1865, was a Confederate commissioner at the Hampton Roads Peace Conference.

WILLIAM M. BROWNE (1823–1883). March 7, 1862–March 18, 1862. Browne served his brief term as secretary of state while also working as Jefferson Davis' aide-de-camp. A native of Ireland, he was a former British diplomat and political journal editor. His other capacities in the Confederacy included commandant of Georgia conscripts and infantry brigade leader.

JUDAH P. BENJAMIN (1811–1884). March 18, 1862–May 10, 1865 (see also "Secretaries of War" and "Attorneys General"). Born in Christiansted, the Virgin Islands, of English and Jewish parents, Benjamin became a prominent lawyer, a sugar planter, and a Democratic senator from Louisiana. He delivered a stirring defense of Southern policy on the Senate floor shortly before resigning his seat during the secession crisis. Generally regarded by contemporaries—and later, historians—as a brilliant statesman and the most gifted of the Confederacy's leaders, he was Davis' most trusted cabinet member. He was sharply criticized at home for a series of military defeats during his six months as secretary of war; his Jewish heritage made him the target of additional insults from critics in the press, the statehouse, and the military leadership. As secretary of state, Benjamin focused on winning European recognition of the Confederacy. Eventually, he lobbied Davis to mitigate the main sticking point—slavery—by offering emancipation to slaves in return for military service, but the war ended before the plan could go forward. When the South fell, he escaped to England and established a highly successful law practice. His wartime persona remains somewhat of an enigma. He refused to pen any articles or memoirs about that period, and he later destroyed his personal papers. He retired to Paris, where he died and is buried.

Secretaries of the Treasury

CHRISTOPHER G. MEMMINGER (1803–1888). February 21, 1861–July 18, 1864. After participating in the South Carolina secession convention, Memminger, a successful lawyer and former bank director, was chairman of the committee that drafted the Confederacy's Provisional Constitution. As treasury secretary, he faced monumental battles against inflation and the states rights' advocates who hindered his efforts to centralize financial measures. Anticipating a short war, Memminger planned to pay for it, in part, by issuing treasury notes funded by government bonds. Later, however, he asked Congress for taxes that, even when approved, never filled the treasury. With the economy collapsing, Memminger resigned and later returned to his law practice in Charleston.

GEORGE A. TRENHOLM (1807–1876). July 18, 1864–April 27, 1865. An adviser to Memminger before becoming treasury secretary himself, Trenholm brought to the job extensive banking and business experience that had made him perhaps the wealthiest man in the South. He oversaw the Confederacy's British financial agency, Fraser, Trenholm & Co., and owned blockade-running ships. Unable to obtain foreign loans or to adequately exchange cotton and other goods for hard cash, both he and the Confederacy were bankrupt at the war's end, but he soon made another personal fortune as a cotton broker.

Secretaries of War

LEROY P. WALKER (1817–1884). February 21, 1861–September 16, 1861 (provisional). A gifted lawyer but an inexperienced administrator, Walker was appointed secretary of war on the recommendation of Alabama officials. (Jefferson Davis wanted each state represented in the cabinet, and an attorney general had already been appointed.) Of immediate concern were the Federal troops stationed in U.S. forts located within the new Confederacy, particularly at Fort Sumter. Walker managed to organize the Southern army and mobilize 200,000 men early in the war, but Davis essentially handled military operations and policy. Uncooperative governors, many of whom resisted Confederate control over their states' troops, and difficulties in supplying the army made Walker's tenure short and difficult. After resigning as secretary, he served as a brigadier general and military court judge, and later returned to his law practice.

JUDAH P. BENJAMIN (1811–1884) September 17, 1861–March 23, 1862 (see also "Secretaries of State" and "Attorneys General"). Like Walker before him, Benjamin was a secretary of war who had no military experience. He was roundly criticized following the Confederate defeat at Roanoke Island (February 8, 1862), even though Union forces vastly outnumbered the Southern forces. His loyalty to Davis allowed the president to continue functioning as de facto secretary of war. A month after Secretary of State

Hunter resigned, Benjamin's unimpressive stint at the War Department ended and his State Department career began.

GEORGE W. RANDOLPH (1818–1867). March 23, 1862–November 17, 1862. Grandson of President Thomas Jefferson, Randolph, a Richmond lawyer with experience in both the army and the navy, chafed under Davis, who persistently meddled with his department. Still, Randolph was largely responsible for devising the Confederacy's first conscription law, and his re-organization of the War Department lasted throughout the war. With plans to retake New Orleans and attend to issues in the West, the independent-minded Randolph became exasperated with Davis' delays and what today would be called micromanagement. He resigned and later served as a Confederate agent in Europe.

GUSTAVUS W. SMITH (1821–1896). November 17, 1862–November 21, 1862. Served as acting secretary.

JAMES A. SEDDON (1815–1880). November 21, 1862–February 6, 1865. A former U.S. congressman from Virginia, the sickly Seddon tirelessly applied himself to supplying Confederate armies, monitoring conscription exemptions, catching deserters, commandeering railroads, and even covertly trading cotton with the North in exchange for food. He fared better than his predecessors in his dealings with Davis. By siding with the president on most issues, he became a key military adviser—a role he used to push for an aggressive, offensive strategy. Vilified in the press as Confederate fortunes waned, Seddon resigned in anger when the Confederate Congress called on Davis to reorganize his cabinet.

JOHN C. BRECKINRIDGE (1821–1875). February 6, 1865–May 10, 1865. U.S. vice president (1857–1861), U.S. House of Representatives (1851–1855). After three years as an army general, during which he saw action at Shiloh, Chickamauga, and in the 1864 Shenandoah Valley campaign, Breckinridge was named to the cabinet in the closing months of the war. He oversaw the evacuation of Richmond and advised Davis to surrender the Confederacy honorably, rather than direct it into a rending guerrilla war. Escaping to Cuba and then to Europe, Breckinridge returned to the United States in 1869 after receiving amnesty.

Secretary of the Navy

STEPHEN R. MALLORY (1813–1873). February 28, 1861–May 2, 1865. A native of Trinidad, the West Indies, Mallory served as a customs official in Key West before Florida sent him to the U.S. Senate, where he became committee chairman for naval affairs. As navy secretary, he worked, with mixed results, to purchase cruisers, rams (ships with iron rammers protruding beyond their prows), and ironclads, and he initiated ship, as well as, torpedo (mine) construction in the South. With scant resources at his disposal, Mallory understood that commerce raiding and breaking the Union blockade were the most efficient means for Confederate survival. He was highly criticized for the loss of New Orleans, Memphis, and Norfolk (all taken by Union forces in 1862). Nevertheless, he kept his post throughout the war. He later returned to his law practice in Florida.

Postmaster General

JOHN H. REAGAN (1818–1905). March 6, 1861–May 10, 1865. A lawyer and U.S. congressman from Texas, Reagan acquired samples of Federal postal supplies and hired former Federal postal employees to create the Confederate postal service. The new Constitution required the service to be self-supporting as of March 1, 1863, and Reagan, a skilled administrator, met the deadline by cutting routes, raising rates, and arranging for low railroad charges. The only cabinet member still traveling with Davis when the president was captured in Georgia on May 10, 1865, Reagan took a conciliatory view after the war and later served as a U.S. congressman and senator.

Attorneys General

JUDAH P. BENJAMIN (1811–1884). February 25, 1861–November 21, 1861 (see also "Secretaries of State" and "Secretaries of War"). Although Benjamin's responsibilities as attorney general covered only civilian matters, he advised regularly on military issues as well. His close working relationship with Davis made Benjamin the president's pick for secretary of war when Leroy Walker resigned.

THOMAS BRAGG (1810–1872). November 21, 1861–February 17, 1862. The older brother of Confederate General Braxton Bragg, Thomas Bragg had served as governor of North Carolina and as a U.S. senator. During his brief tenure as Confederate attorney general, he focused on protecting civilian rights and advising the War Department to compensate owners adequately for impressed property. Unhappy that Davis seldom sought his advice, Bragg resigned and returned to North Carolina. There, despite his doubts that the South would win, he promoted support for the cause and kept Governor Zebulon Vance tethered to the Confederacy.

THOMAS H. WATTS (1819–1892). March 18, 1862–October 1, 1863. (Also see "Wartime Governors," page 191.) A successful lawyer and wealthy Alabama planter, Attorney General Thomas Watts dealt primarily with claims against the government. In the absence of a Confederate Supreme Court, Watts and the state courts were the highest sources of legal opinions and constitutional interpretations. Watts urged Jefferson Davis to use martial law only in legitimate emergencies, and he held that the Conscription Act was legal. However, after resigning his post and becoming governor of Alabama, he viewed the act as a violation of states' rights.

WADE KEYES (1821–?). October 1, 1863–January 4, 1864. An assistant attorney general from Alabama, Keyes served briefly as acting attorney general.

GEORGE DAVIS (1820–1896). January 4, 1864–April 26, 1865. Highly regarded as a lawyer, George Davis served in the Confederate Congress as a senator from North Carolina. Later, he was tapped for the attorney general post, in part to improve relations with his home state, which had an active peace movement. He also worked to improve relations between President Davis and his critics, particularly Governor Zebulon Vance. George Davis returned to his law practice after the war.

Other Notable Political Figures

CHARLES FRANCIS ADAMS (1807–1886). U.S. minister to Great Britain 1861–1868. The son of President John Quincy Adams and grandson of President John Adams, Republican Charles Adams took his post in London in May 1861. Studious, thorough, and even-handed, Adams vigorously argued the U.S. position that the Confederacy did not constitute an independent nation and that recognition of and aid to the rebellious states would be a violation of Britain's own declarations of neutrality. He helped engineer the release of James Mason and John Slidell in the *Trent* affair (see page 202); was instrumental in curtailing British construction of naval

THE FIRST LADIES

VARINA HOWELL DAVIS (1826–1906) was the second wife of Jefferson Davis and eighteen years his junior. Born near Natchez, Mississippi, she was bright, well-educated, and of an independent mind, startling Richmond society with her unconventional manner. Mrs. Davis quietly confided to some her doubts that the South would win the war, but she resolutely supported her husband throughout his presidency. When the Confederacy fell, she expressed relief to friends that the war was over, and she spent the next two years working for Davis' release from prison. She ardently defended him from criticism, and in 1890 published Jefferson Davis, a Memoir *to help rehabilitate his reputation. After his death, Mrs. Davis, who outlived all but one of her six children, devoted herself to writing and moved to New York City, where she spent the rest of her life.*

MARY TODD LINCOLN (1818–1882), wife of President Abraham Lincoln, was from a well-to-do Kentucky family. She oversaw a major redecoration of the White House, was a frequent visitor to nearby Union hospitals and although well regarded as a cordial and charming hostess, she was wrongly suspected by many in Washington of being a Southern sympathizer (her brother-in-law Benjamin Helm was a Confederate general). Protective of the president and devoted to her family, Mrs. Lincoln, always sensitive and increasingly depressed and erratic, endured a tragic tenure in the White House. In 1862, the Lincoln's son Willie died, and three of Mrs. Lincoln's half brothers, who fought for the Confederacy, perished in the war. She lost her husband to an assassin's bullet in 1865. After a brief stay in a mental asylum in 1875, she spent most of her remaining years in France before returning to Springfield, Illinois.

vessels for the Confederacy; and, through his skillful diplomacy, helped keep Britain from extending full recognition to the Confederacy.

JOHN BIGELOW (1817–1911). U.S. consul-general at Paris, 1861–1865. An abolitionist and former newspaper editor, John Bigelow was instrumental in preventing France from recognizing the Confederacy, and he foiled Southern efforts to build a naval fleet in Europe. He monitored secret Confederate construction contracts, was pivotal in keeping the French government from intervening on behalf of the South, and managed to turn public opinion in support of the Union by overriding the Confederacy's own propaganda efforts. Following the *Trent* affair, Bigelow wrote an influential and frequently reprinted article explaining U.S. actions. Because signing the piece himself would have violated diplomatic protocol, the article was attributed to General Winfield Scott.

ZACHARIAH CHANDLER (1813–1879). U.S. senator from Michigan 1857–1875 and 1879. A former mayor of Detroit and a cofounder of Michigan's Republican party, Chandler was an outspoken leader of the Radical Republicans and a powerful member of the Committee on the Conduct of the War (see Chapter 3, "Time Line—December 1861"). He was instrumental in getting John C. Frémont, the radical third-party presidential candidate, to bow out of the 1864 race in exchange for dropping conservative Postmaster General Montgomery Blair from the cabinet, thus helping to preserve the Republicans' hold on power. A harsh critic of Major General George B. McClellan and other Democratic generals who were, in his opinion, not aggressive enough, Chandler led efforts to impeach President Andrew Johnson, whose lenient Reconstruction policies he opposed. He lost his Senate seat in 1874 but later served as secretary of the interior (1875–1877) under President Grant.

HOWELL COBB (1815–1868). U.S. congressman from Georgia, 1842–1851 (Speaker of the House, 1849–1851) and 1855–1857; governor of Georgia, 1851–1853; U.S. secretary of the treasury, 1857–1860; chairman of the Montgomery secession convention, 1861. In the U.S. House of Representatives, Cobb maintained a strong pro-Union position and helped guide passage of the Compromise of 1850. But a month after Lincoln's election as president, Cobb resigned as treasury secretary, returned to Georgia, and urged secession. Known for his diplomacy and negotiating skills, he was elected chairman of the Montgomery convention. (His brother Thomas, also a delegate, was the primary author of the Confederate Constitution.) He was considered for the Confederate presidency but instead administered the oath of office to Jefferson Davis. He served as speaker of the Provisional Congress but then embarked on a military career, formed the Sixteenth Georgia Infantry, and rose to the rank of major general.

ANNA DICKINSON (1842–1932). Public speaker. Anna Dickinson was only 18 when, in 1860, she gave a well received speech before a Philadelphia antislavery meeting. In 1862, she was chosen by leading abolitionist William Lloyd Garrison to lecture for the Massachusetts Anti-Slavery Society, and, in the following year, she campaigned eloquently and successfully for Republican candidates in New Hampshire and Connecticut. After a speech in New York City, in which she promoted abolition, one newspaper reporter proclaimed, "Never have I seen in New York any speaker achieve such a triumph." Dickinson also espoused her abolitionist beliefs before the House of Representatives in 1864. Although she generated criticism because she "dared" to talk about such nonfeminine issues as the military conduct of the war, her youth and her fervor on the subject of abolition made her one of the best known and most popular orators during the Civil War.

JAMES MASON (1798–1871). Confederate envoy to Great Britain 1861–1863; Confederate commissioner on the Continent 1863–1865. The son of a prominent Virginia family and grandson of the Revolutionary War figure George Mason, James Mason served in the U.S. House of Representatives and the Senate. He authored the Fugitive Slave Law that became part of the Compromise of 1850. His service on the Senate Foreign Relations Committee and his friendship with Jefferson Davis led to his appointment as envoy to Great Britain. A principal in the *Trent* affair, Mason was well received by British businessmen, sold war bonds to private parties, and helped Confederate agents such as James D. Bulloch purchase naval vessels. But the British government never officially recognized him as a diplomat. In late 1863, he became Confederate commissioner on the Continent and split his time between England and France in a futile pursuit of diplomatic recognition for the Confederacy. One of his last duties was to deny, in Henry Hotze's London *Index*, a Confederate newspaper, that Richmond was behind Lincoln's assassination. After a stay in Canada, he returned to Virginia in 1869 under amnesty from President Johnson.

GEORGE B. McCLELLAN (1826–1885). Union general in chief (1861–1862), Democratic presidential candidate (1864) (see also "Notable Civil War Officers," in Chapter 5, "The Armies"). After his dismissal as head of the Union army in November 1862, McClellan set his sights on a political career. His deteriorating relations with the president and with Secretary of War Stanton had bolstered his political ambitions, and in 1864, the Democrats nominated him for president. Although he publicly disavowed the party's peace platform, realizing the negative effect it would have on the army, Republicans genuinely feared that the war-weary public would send McClellan to the White House. That autumn, a series of Union victories, including the capture of Atlanta, spelled defeat for McClellan. He won just 21 of 233 electoral votes. His interest in politics continued, and in 1878, he was elected governor of New Jersey, one of the three states he had won in 1864.

JOHN ROCK (1825–1866). A teacher, dentist, doctor, and lawyer, John Rock was also a brilliant antislavery speaker. In 1860, he began to study law; the following year, he became one of the few blacks admitted to the bar. An early supporter of the Republican party (but not of Lincoln, until the Emancipation Proclamation), Rock advocated equal rights for blacks. Before a session of the Massachusetts House of Representatives, he requested that the qualification "white" be removed from the state militia law. He also recruited black troops for the Massachusetts Fifty-fourth and Fifty-fifth Regiments and took the lead in black soldiers' battle for equal pay and treatment. He was the first African American received on the floor of the U.S. House of Representatives, and on February 1, 1865—the day after the House passed the Thirteenth Amendment—Rock became the first black accepted to argue cases before the Supreme Court.

JOHN SLIDELL (1793–1871). Confederate envoy to France 1861–1865. A former U.S. senator from Louisiana, Slidell's mission to France was delayed during the *Trent* affair. He enjoyed good relations with Napoleon III but was never able to convert French sympathy for the Confederacy into diplomatic recognition. Slidell arranged for the construction of commerce raiders in French shipyards, but U.S. diplomatic efforts kept the ships out of the war. Through a French bank, he completed negotiations for a Confederate bond issue which, by 1865, had raised more than $8 million for the Confederacy. After the war, Slidell refused to apply for amnesty and died in England.

LOUIS TREZEVANT WIGFALL (1816–1874). U.S. senator from Texas 1859–1861; Confederate senator from Texas 1862–1865. Wigfall called for secession 16 years before South Carolina, his home state, was the first to leave the Union. He cowrote the Southern Manifesto, declaring that compromise with the North was impossible, and he helped prevent passage of the Crittenden Compromise to avert the war. Wigfall enthusiastically supported controversial measures—conscription, impressment, the suspension of habeas corpus—as necessary to the war effort but insisted that once independence was gained, states' rights were to take precedence over the central government. A Confederate colonel, then brigadier general, Wigfall strenuously opposed Davis' military strategies, and his close ties to Generals Lee and Longstreet made him the military leadership's favored advocate in Congress. In January 1865, Wigfall successfully led congressional efforts to make Lee the general in chief of Confederate armies. After the war, he fled to Britain but returned to the United States six years later.

Wartime Governors

President Lincoln and President Davis needed the unflinching support of their state governors—who controlled the state militias—if they were to effectively prosecute the war and promote loyalty on the home front. For the most part, the Northern governors stood behind Lincoln; unfortunately for Davis, too often the Southern governors stood on their own. Aside from the strong states' rights philosophy of the Southern states, much of the explanation for this stance lies in the importance of party affiliation and presidential political skill. Most of the Union governors were Republicans, bound by party and similar ideology, and even if their personal loyalty did not lie with the president, their political fortunes often did. In the Confederacy, which did not have political parties, the lack of a disciplined, unifying structure meant that alliances were constantly forming and dissolving from issue to issue. Generally, governors who supported Davis did so because of their devotion to the Confederate cause, not because of a personal or party attachment.

Lincoln rewarded loyal supporters with government positions, sent cabinet members to campaign rallies for party candidates, and effectively used the party machinery to keep statehouses and governors' chairs filled with Republicans. Throughout the war, a stream of governors flowed through Washington seeking political patronage, favors, and posts for their allies, and the president followed their political and military recommendations when he could. Davis, on the other hand, was loyal to his allies but had neither the personal touch nor as much political patronage to exploit for the good of the cause.

Both the United States and the Confederacy had to rely on governors to help raise the huge armies that took the field during the war. The call went first to the state militias and then to the volunteer regiments raised by each state. In addition to meeting the demand for well-equipped troops, all state governors were burdened with managing wartime economies, meeting unprecedented manufacturing and food production needs, and providing for wounded soldiers and soldiers' widows. For many governors, defending the home front was the most pressing concern, requiring allocation of scant resources.

IN THE NORTH, most governors were very active in recruiting. Of note was Governor William Buckingham of Connecticut, who raised 54,882 volunteers—an astounding figure for a state with about 461,000 citizens. Connecticut was among the states with the largest per capita percentages of volunteers. Massachusetts governor John Andrew went beyond the available white male population to answer Lincoln's call for troops; he was prominent among those who pressured the president and Secretary of War Stanton to permit black soldiers. In January 1863, after much political wrangling, the celebrated Fifty-fourth Massachusetts was formed. Among the governors who favored allowing African Americans to serve as soldiers were Samuel Kirkwood of Iowa and Richard Yates of Illinois (see "Fighting on Two Fronts: Black Soldiers in the Civil War" in Chapter 5, "The Armies").

But when conscription was enacted, some Union governors resisted Federal attempts to draft soldiers or argued over quota figures. Governors also expressed objections to other policies and criticized the suspension of habeas corpus, military arrests, and military tribunals as threats to civil liberties. The border slave states, with their politically and culturally divided populations, were more susceptible to military interference in civilian affairs than others in the Union, and the governors of those states were more likely to raise heated objections to the Lincoln administration's policies. Also vocal was Governor Horatio Seymour of New York, who believed, as many others did, that the Emancipation Proclamation and the suspension of habeas corpus were unconstitutional and represented a disturbing trend toward greater Federal power. After draft riots broke out in New York City in the summer of 1863 (see Chapter 10, "The Home Front"), Seymour further complained to the administration about the designated state quotas, the execution of the draft, and the haphazard information regarding the conscription timetable.

When black regiments were forming in early 1863, Seymour refused to enroll black soldiers under state authority; recruitment of black troops had to proceed under Federal authority granted by the War Department. Still, the governor worked to meet recruiting quotas and remained dedicated to preserving the Union.

Governors' contributions to the war effort did not end with raising troops. In September 1862, Governor Andrew Curtin of Pennsylvania organized and hosted a governors' conference in Altoona to reaffirm the states' commitment to the war (which had not been going well for the Union) and to support Lincoln's call for additional troops. When Democrats gained control of the Indiana state legislature in 1863 and sought to limit or nullify Governor Oliver Morton's powers, Republican lawmakers deserted Indianapolis. Without a quorum, the Democrats were unable to pass partisan bills or approve state expenditures. Morton, one of the Union's strongest and most successful war governors, kept the state operating by arranging for loans from the Federal government, Republican county officials, and private sources. In Illinois, war fatigue and the peace movement threatened Governor Richard Yates' administration; he responded by arresting war dissenters and supporting the secret Union Leagues—organizations that passed along to the War Department the names of peace advocates and suspected Southern sympathizers. In 1863, when the Illinois House of Representatives, under Democratic control, called for a national convention to negotiate with the Confederacy, Yates suspended the legislature and governed the state on his own for a year, until Republicans took back the House.

Even in the western states, which were not directly involved in the conflict, governors supported the war effort. California and Nevada supplied gold, food, and raw materials to help sustain the Union armies. Other governors reached deep into their own resources. When Thomas Carney, a wealthy businessman, became governor of Kansas in 1863, he found the state treasury empty and the state's eastern border besieged with Missouri guerrillas. He guided the legislature in issuing successful new bonds backed up by his own funds, and he personally financed military border patrols until Federal troops arrived. Governor Erastus Fairbanks of Vermont, owner of a substantial manufacturing business, declined his salary and offered his firm's credit to pay for war supplies.

Iowa's Samuel Kirkwood had to be especially vigilant. In the north, he organized the Northern Iowa Brigade in response to Indian raids, and in the south he instituted civilian defense measures to keep disruptive Missouri partisans from spilling over into the state. In Illinois, Indiana, and Ohio, the governors also dealt with a strong Copperhead presence (see "Other Political Organizations," page 165) and with organizations sympathetic to the South. Kentucky's continuing request for Ohio's assistance in its defense, as well as John Hunt Morgan's destructive cavalry raid into Ohio, added to Governor David Tod's problems. In Maine, far removed from the battlefields, Governor Israel Washburn paid close attention to the home front, fearing that Confederate support in Canada posed a threat. He was unable to get the War Department to build defenses along the border, but he did oversee the creation of a coast guard. In Minnesota, governors struggled with battles between settlers and Indians, and Governor Alexander Ramsey begged for Federal troops to help stamp out Sioux revolts. (In the Confederacy, Texas Governor Francis Lubbock faced a similar situation and oversaw formation of a frontier regiment to combat Indian attacks.)

Governing was even more difficult in the Union's border states, which, at times, were ungovernable. Martial law, guerrilla warfare, and internal civil wars fought amid the larger war made governing a herculean task, especially in Missouri. There, Governor Claiborne Jackson fled Jefferson City, taking the state treasury with him, and, siding with the Confederacy, proclaimed a government in exile in Arkansas. (A twelfth star, representing Missouri, was added to the Confederate flag.) The new governor, Hamilton Gamble, mastered a balancing act to keep his state in the Union (more than 40,000 Missouri men served with the Confederacy and more than 100,000 with the Union; some served both sides). The presence of Union military commanders, who had jurisdiction over the state, and the guerrilla warfare William Quantrill and other Confederate "bushwackers" waged on Missouri also presented the governor with enormous challenges. To defend Maryland (a prime Confederate target that was invaded by Southern troops several times), Governor Augustus Bradford had to ask the War Department for additional troops when there were not enough volunteers. As in the other border states, Kentucky's population was divided in its support for the Union. In May 1861, Governor Beriah Magoffin proclaimed Kentucky's neutrality, but it was nullified in September when Union and Confederate forces crossed the state's borders. Magoffin condemned the provisional state government the Confederates established in December, and though that government was never an authoritative body, it nevertheless prompted the Confederacy to add a thirteenth star to its flag, representing Kentucky.

IN THE CONFEDERACY, President Davis often suffered from the curse of uncooperative state leaders who believed fervently in the principle of states' rights, on which the Confederacy had been founded. Some Southern governors felt that soldiers should remain in their home states to provide defense; Davis believed that using troops where they were needed most offered the best overall defensive strategy. Other gubernatorial objections centered on conscription, impressment, and depriving the governors of their right to appoint commanding officers. By the time the war ended, the refusal of some governors, such as Georgia's Joseph E. Brown, to fully cooperate with the Confederate government had done great harm to the Southern cause. Brown loudly condemned the Davis administration for violating state sovereignty on nearly every issue, from conscription to the suspension of habeas corpus. He opposed the use of Georgia troops outside the state, arguing that they were needed at home for defense (though many Georgians did serve in the Army of Northern Virginia and the Army of Tennessee). Brown's bitter attacks hampered and infuriated Davis and fueled opposition to the Davis administration.

In North Carolina, Governor Zebulon Vance, a former Unionist who reluctantly followed his state into the Confederacy, strongly opposed impressment and the suspension of habeas corpus. A gifted and skilled administrator, he sought to maintain effective government functions by keeping thousands of state employees at their jobs and out of the military. (As it was, North Carolina gave to the Confederacy a disproportionately large amount of its resources, human and otherwise.) The governor also had to contend with a growing peace movement led by W. W. Holden, a newspaper editor and former supporter who ran against him for governor in 1864 (see "Newspapers: The Politics of the Press," page 224). Vance himself advocated a negotiated peace settlement between the Union and the Confederacy but rejected outright his opponent's plan for a separate peace between North Carolina and the U.S. government. He handily went on to victory, a powerful testament to the confidence North Carolinians had in him under the most trying of conditions.

Because most of the war's battles were fought in the South, Confederate governors grappled with huge challenges not matched to the same degree in the North: widespread destruction of property and infrastructure; collapsing economies; food and soldier shortages; homeland defense; and Union occupation. Especially strapped was Virginia's governor, John Letcher, who unsuccessfully pleaded with his western counties not to secede (their secession created the Union state of West Virginia in 1863). He gave the Confederate government full cooperation, even on issues such as conscription and impressment, which he believed violated states' rights. As the war progressed—with many battles fought on Virginia's ravaged soil—Letcher's submission to the Confederate government damaged his popularity and his political prospects, especially after he threatened to use state troops to restrain civilians during the 1863 bread riots in Richmond.

Desperate times called for desperate measures that were previously unthinkable. South Carolina's Francis Pickens impressed goods, ordered martial law in the coastal regions, and watched his popularity plummet. His successor, Milledge Bonham, impressed thousands of slaves to build coastal and harbor defenses, often over the objections of slaveholders. Arkansas governor Harris Flanigan moved the state capital from Little Rock to Washington in 1863, governing only part of the state while Isaac Murphy, elected governor by Unionists in the northern part of Arkansas, worked with the U.S. government toward reconstruction. In Louisiana, governor Thomas Moore transferred his capital from Baton Rouge to Opelousas and then to Shreveport (by June 1862, most of lower Louisiana was under Federal control). From Shreveport, he continued to govern (with decreasing success) the unoccupied portion of the state until his term ended in 1864. Sections of Tennessee were also under Federal rule for much of the war. Andrew Johnson, who had served as the state's governor (1853–1857), returned as a military governor (1862–1865) initially controlling the western and central sections of the state, which favored the Confederacy.

The situation became especially grim for governors in the Deep South as the war progressed. In Mississippi, Governor John Pettus squared off against the state legislature and the military board in his efforts to reinforce Vicksburg, the state's most important port city, which fell in July 1863, after a brutal siege. As Union invasions of northern Alabama devastated the state's economy, Governor John Shorter, a strong ally of Davis, lost political backing because of his support of conscription and impressment. Florida governor John Milton, a strong and cooperative supporter of the Confederate government, willingly directed volunteers to the Confederate army when it became impossible to adequately outfit state troops. This exodus left the state with little defense against Union incursions and slave revolts, and Florida's coastal areas and southern sections were under Federal control by the war's end. Disconsolate over the Confederacy's demise, Milton committed suicide on April 1, 1865.

United States of America Governors

Note: Beginning in 1863, some politicians defined their political status as "Union" rather than Republican or Democrat. Most of these Unionists were Republicans, but some Democrats adopted the label. At its 1864 convention, the Republican Party renamed itself the National Union Party as a coalition of war supporters. After the war, members returned to the Republican and Democratic parties.

California

John Downey (1827–1894), governor 1860–1862. Democrat.
Leland Stanford (1824–1893), governor 1862–1863. Republican.
Frederick Low (1828–1894), governor 1863–1867. Union.

Connecticut

William Alfred Buckingham (1804–1875), governor 1858–1866. Republican.

Delaware

William Burton (1789–1866), governor 1859–1863. Democrat.
William Cannon (1809–1865), governor 1863–1865. Union.

Illinois

Richard Yates (1815–1873), governor 1861–1865. Republican.
Richard Oglesby (1824–1889), governor 1865–1869. Republican.

Indiana

Henry Smith Lane (1811–1881), governor 1861. Republican.
Oliver Perry Morton (1823–1877), governor 1861–1867. Republican.

Iowa

Samuel Kirkwood (1813–1894), governor 1860–1864. Republican.
William Stone (1827–1893), governor 1864–1868. Republican.

Kansas

Charles Robinson (1818–1894), governor 1861–1863. Republican.
Thomas Carney (1824–1888), governor 1863–1865. Republican.

Kentucky

Beriah Magoffin (1815–1885), governor 1859–1862. Democrat.
James Robinson (1800–1882), governor 1862–1863. Democrat.
Thomas Bramlette (1817–1875), governor 1863–1867. Democrat.

Maine

Israel Washburn Jr. (1813–1883), governor 1861–1863. Republican.
Abner Coburn (1803–1885), governor 1863–1864. Republican.
Samuel Coney (1811–1870), governor 1864–1867. Republican.

Maryland

Thomas Hicks (1798–1865), governor 1858–1862.
American (Know-Nothing).
Augustus Bradford (1806–1881), governor 1862–1866. Union.

Massachusetts

John Albion Andrew (1818–1867), governor 1861–1866. Republican.

Michigan

Austin Blair (1818–1894), governor 1861–1865. Republican.
Henry Crapo (1804–1869), governor 1865–1868. Republican.

Minnesota

Alexander Ramsey (1815–1903), governor 1860–1863. Republican.
Henry Swift (1823–1869), governor 1863–1864. Republican.
Stephen Miller (1816–1881), governor 1864–1866. Republican.

Missouri

Claiborne Fox Jackson (1806–1862), governor 1861. Democrat.
Hamilton Gamble (1798–1864), governor 1861–1864. Union.
Willard Hall (1820–1882), governor 1864–1865. Union.
Thomas C. Fletcher (1827–1899), governor 1865–1869. Republican.

Nevada

Henry Goode Blasdel (1825–1900), governor (1864–1871). Republican.

New Hampshire

Ichabod Goodwin (1794–1882), governor 1859–1861. Republican.
Nathaniel Berry (1796–1894), governor 1861–1863. Republican.
Joseph Gilmore (1811–1867), governor 1863–1865. Republican.

New Jersey

Charles S. Olden (1799–1876), governor 1860–1863. Republican.
Joel Parker (1816–1888), governor 1863–1866. Democrat.

New York

Edwin Denison Morgan (1811–1833), governor 1859–1863. Republican.
Horatio Seymour (1810–1886), governor 1863–1865. Democrat.

Ohio

William Morgan Dennison (1815–1882), governor 1860–1862. Republican (see "Civil War Government Officials: United States of America—Postmasters General").
David Tod (1805–1868), governor 1862–1864. Democrat.
John Brough (1811–1865), governor 1864–1865. Republican.

Pennsylvania

Andrew G. Curtin (1817–1894), governor 1861–1867. Republican.

Rhode Island

William Sprague (1830–1915), governor 1860–1863. Republican.
William Cozzens (1811–1876), governor 1863. Democrat.
James Y. Smith (1809–1876), governor 1863–1866. Republican.

Vermont

Erastus Fairbanks (1792–1864), governor 1860–1861. Republican.
Frederick Holbrook (1813–1909), governor 1861–1863. Republican.
J. Gregory Smith (1818–1891), governor 1863–1865. Republican.

West Virginia

Francis H. Pierpont (1814–1899), governor of the "Reorganized Government of Virginia" (western counties that seceded from Virginia) 1861–1863; governor of the Restored Virginia Government 1863–1868. Republican.
Arthur Boreman (1823–1896), governor 1863–1869. Republican.

Wisconsin

Alexander Williams Randall (1819–1872), governor 1858–1862. Republican.
Louis Harvey (1820–1862), governor 1862. Republican.
Edward Salomon (1828–1909), governor 1862–1864. Republican.
James T. Lewis (1819–1904), governor 1864–1866. Republican.

Confederate States of America Governors

Alabama

Andrew Barry Moore (1807–1873), governor 1857–1861. Democrat.

John Gill Shorter (1818–1872), governor 1861–1863. Democrat.

Thomas Hill Watts (1819–1892), governor 1863–1865. Democrat (see also "Civil War Government Officials: Confederate States of America—Attorneys General").

Arkansas

Henry Rector (1816–1899), governor 1860–1862. Democrat.

Thomas Fletcher (1819–1900), acting governor for 11 days in 1862. Democrat.

Harris Flanagin (1817–1874), governor 1862–1864. Democrat. (Confederacy).

Isaac Murphy (1802–1882), governor 1864–1868. Union (United States).

Florida

Madison Perry (1814–1865), governor 1857–1861. Democrat.

John Milton (1807–1865), governor 1861–1865. Democrat.

Georgia

Joseph E. Brown (1821–1894), governor 1857–1865. Democrat.

Louisiana

Thomas O. Moore (1804–1876), governor 1860–1864. Democrat. (Federal military rule 1862–1864).

Henry Allen (1820–1866), governor 1864–1865. Democrat (Confederacy).

Michael Hahn (1830–1886), governor 1864–1865. Free State (United States).

Mississippi

John Pettus (1813–1867), governor 1859–1863. Democrat.

Charles Clark (1811–1877), governor 1863–1865. Democrat.

North Carolina

John Ellis (1820–1861), governor 1859–1861. Democrat.

Henry Toole Clark (1808–1874), governor 1861–1862. Democrat.

Zebulon B. Vance (1830–1894), governor 1862–1865. Democrat.

South Carolina

Francis Pickens (1805–1869), governor 1860–1862. Democrat.

Milledge Luke Bonham (1813–1890), governor 1862–1864. Democrat.

Andrew Magrath (1813–1893), governor 1864–1865. Democrat.

Tennessee

Isham Green Harris (1818–1897), governor 1857–1862. Democrat.

Andrew Johnson (1808–1875), military governor of occupied Tennessee 1862–1865. Democrat (see Chapter 3, "Civil War Government Officials: United States of America—Vice President").

William Brownlow (1805–1877), governor 1865–1869. Whig.

Texas

Sam Houston (1793–1863), governor 1859–1861. Democrat.

Edward Clark (1815–1880), governor 1861. Democrat.

Francis Lubbock (1815–1905), governor 1861–1863. Democrat.

Pendleton Murrah (c. 1828–1865), governor 1863–1865. Democrat.

Virginia

John Letcher (1813–1884), governor 1860–1864. Democrat.

William Smith (1797–1887), governor 1864–1865. Democrat.

European Powers and the American Civil War

From the start of the Civil War, European nations watched the conflict closely, trying to gauge the likelihood of success in the Confederate bid for independence. To the American governments of the North and the South, the stakes were extraordinarily high: recognition of the Confederacy as a sovereign nation by a major European power would grant the seceded states a form of legitimacy and would almost certainly play a large role in determining the outcome of the war. To some European interests, the American war was an opportunity to exert greater influence in the Western Hemisphere, to weaken the trading power of an increasingly expanding competitor in world markets, and to happily witness the ignoble end of a bold experiment in democracy. Great Britain, the premier industrial and seafaring power in the world, had the naval might to puncture the Union blockade of Southern ports (see Chapter 7, "The War on the Water") and to bring much needed supplies and armaments to Confederate forces. But to do so could provoke a war with the United States. Thus, exactly one month after hostilities began, Britain declared itself neutral in the conflict. France and Spain, which also had interests in the Americas, were inclined to follow Britain's lead; neither country wanted to antagonize the United States. Among the major European powers, only Russia voiced support for the Union, but it, too, remained on the sidelines.

The Quest for Recognition

Confederate attempts to obtain European recognition—and Union efforts to prevent it—were at the center of American and European wartime relations. The Union blockade made the matter of recognition an exercise in both diplomacy and double-talk. The United States held that the Confederacy did not exist as an independent nation but was, instead, a collection of states in rebellion. Therefore, European recognition of those states was meaningless. However, because a blockade was an act of war and an action used against a foreign rather than a domestic entity, it could be argued that, in ordering the blockade, the United States had effectively recognized the Confederacy as a sovereign power. President Lincoln and Secretary of State William H. Seward overlooked the contradiction and maintained that the United States could both legally impose the blockade and deny the existence of the Confederate States of America. Britain, remaining neutral, came to accept this view, a necessity in light of its own demands that neutral nations honor British blockades. After the British acknowledged the legality of the Union blockade, the Union went so far as to seize British merchant ships bound for Nassau, Havana, and Matamoras, Mexico. The Union invoked the concept of "continuous voyage": Even though the ships were bound for neutral ports, their final destination was the Confederacy, so their cargo was eligible for seizure. The seizures led to several important legal cases, including the Prize Cases (see "Time Line—March 10, 1863, page 153).

In the fall of 1861, a diplomatic crisis erupted that became known as the *Trent* affair. The British vessel *Trent*, was en route to Europe with Confederate envoys James Mason and John Slidell aboard (see "Other Notable Political Figures," page 186). The U.S.S. *San Jacinto* intercepted the *Trent* and took the diplomats into custody. The action was celebrated in the North and condemned in the South (at the time, many Southerners welcomed the incident, hoping it would prompt Great Britain to recognize the

Confederacy); the outraged British government prepared for military action should the United States refuse to apologize and to release the prisoners. To defuse the situation, the British allowed the United States a face-saving measure: a suggestion that perhaps Captain Wilkes of the *San Jacinto* had acted without authorization. On this point, the United States found room to gracefully concede the matter and avoid war with Great Britain. Secretary of State Seward explained that Captain Wilkes had not followed proper procedures in boarding the *Trent* and arresting the envoys. No formal apology was made, but Lincoln ordered the two men released, and, in January 1862, Mason and Slidell were again headed to Europe. Once there, their mission was to win diplomatic recognition and public support for the Confederacy and to make necessary purchases in support of the war effort.

Britain's May 13, 1861, proclamation of neutrality had granted belligerency status to the Confederate government, which meant acknowledging that the Southern states were in rebellion and thus distinguishing Confederate raiders and privateers from mere pirates on the high seas. The belligerency status also allowed Confederate agents to purchase supplies in neutral ports and to contract for loans in neutral markets. In time, these agents arranged for British shipbuilders to construct commerce raiders— vessels that appeared to be merchant ships but, once outside British waters, could be equipped with armaments. These ships, including the *Alabama*, the *Florida*, and the *Shenandoah*, inflicted considerable damage on U.S. shipping (see Chapter 7, "The War on the Water"); the *Alabama* alone was responsible for capturing, destroying, or releasing on bond more than $5 million in U.S. ships and goods. (Because the most successful Confederate raiders were built and purchased in Britain, the United States, in 1865, made claims on Britain for reparations. The Alabama Claims Commission was formed to investigate the matter but was unable to resolve it satisfactorily. Talks were revived in 1871, and, with several other nations mediating the case, Britain agreed to pay $15.5 million in damages. The fact that the United States and Britain were able to ultimately settle their difference through arbitration contributed to a great strengthening of Anglo-American ties in the years ahead.)

Although the United States was unable to prevent the raiders from being built, the constant efforts of its minister to Britain, Charles Francis Adams (see "Other Notable Political Figures," page 186), halted the delivery of an even more devastating vessel. The South had contracted with the Laird

Shipyard, in Liverpool, to build several of its ironclad Laird Rams—ships outfitted with an iron prong on their bow, intended to smash blockading ships. Determined to keep relations with the North on an even keel, the British government bought the rams in October 1863, and kept them out of the Confederacy's hands.

The Cotton Embargo

Belligerency status was one thing, but nothing short of full diplomatic recognition as a sovereign nation would allow for overt intervention of British naval vessels on behalf of the Confederacy. The Confederacy was quite confident that a cotton embargo could bring about this intervention. The South's faith in its signature export was summed up in a stirring speech South Carolina Senator James Hammond delivered in 1858. "Cotton is king," he declared. More than three-quarters of the cotton that supplied British textile mills came from the South, and Southerners presumed that when the supply dried up as a result of the Federal blockade, British warships would intervene on behalf of Britain's vital national interests. To accelerate the crisis, Southern states—after the 1860 harvest had been shipped—initiated an embargo on those portions of the 1861 cotton crop that would otherwise have been sold overseas and began sowing only a fraction of the amount of cotton produced in prewar years.

The cotton embargo, however, was a colossal failure. What Hammond and other Southern leaders could not have foreseen was that Britain and France would not begin to feel the shortages until late in 1862. The bumper yields in the years just before the war had glutted the market, and British mills were well stocked. And when surpluses began to shrink, the British imported lower-grade, but adequate, cotton from Egypt and India, as well as cotton from Union-occupied areas of the Confederacy and from Confederate blockade runners. King Cotton as a tool of diplomatic leverage was a bust.

Erlanger Loan

The misplaced faith in international dependence on Southern cotton contributed to a financial crisis in the Confederacy that could only be ameliorated by foreign credit. The South, still unable to obtain foreign recognition, even in the wake of a string of military victories in 1862, was suffering from rampant inflation fueled by overprinting of paper money and an increasingly effective Federal blockade. Access to foreign markets for shipbuilding and munitions was critical to the war effort, but Confederate currency held no value abroad. To obtain funds, John Slidell, the Confederate commissioner in France, negotiated a deal with the Paris banking house of Émile Erlanger and Company for a bond issue backed by Confederate cotton. The cotton was to be delivered within six months of the end of the war, though investors could, on demand, convert their bonds into cotton in the Confederacy, whereupon it would be made available within ten miles of a spot accessible by rail or by a navigable river. This option was an incentive to some investors because the price of cotton in Europe was rising (the Erlanger loan cotton cost six pence [twelve U.S. cents] per pound, versus twenty-four pence [fifty U.S. cents] per pound in the European market), but the war and the blockade obviously made receiving and exporting the cotton problematic.

The Confederate government agreed to a £3 million bond issue at 7 percent interest. The Confederacy would reap 77 percent of face value and pay Erlanger a 5 percent commission. The terms were beyond the pale of ordinary loans, but the cash-strapped Confederacy was desperate for European credit and accepted the deal. Slidell argued that connection with a prominent European banking concern would lend inestimable credibility to the struggling Southern nation. The Erlanger loan renewed, for a time, the South's ability to conduct business on the Continent. Issued on March 19, 1863, in London, Liverpool, Frankfurt, Amsterdam, and Paris, the bonds eventually raised £1,759,894 ($8,535,486 in gold value). After initial enthusiasm, the value of the bonds dropped and soon became a barometer of the expectation of Confederate success—an expectation considerably lowered by major setbacks at Vicksburg and Gettysburg in July 1863.

Impressment of Foreign Citizens

Union and Confederate diplomats and their state departments were also occupied with handling other thorny issues beyond foreign intervention in the war. Britain protested that, in both the North and the South, British subjects were being impressed into American armies. Britain's Foreign Enlistment Act of 1819 prohibited its citizens from participating in wars between other countries, and British nationals living in America cited the act to avoid military service. Because many of these nationals planned to become American citizens—in some states, they had even voted after a year's residency—Americans expected them to contribute to the war effort. Britain accepted Lincoln's proclamation that any British citizen who intended to become an American citizen but refused military service was to leave the United States within sixty-five days. However, this did not solve the continuing matter of impressment. Pressure on immigrants to join the military often crossed over into harassment or even kidnapping. In a number of cases, recently arrived foreign men awoke from a drunken stupor to find they had enlisted in the service with the "help" of their new American friends. Responding to complaints from the British embassy, the U.S. Congress eventually set penalties for those who forced or deceived men into enlisting; the Confederate State Department's response was to order British consuls out of the Confederacy.

Mexico

As the American Civil War began, Mexico was ending its own three-year civil war, which returned Benito Juárez and the liberals to power. Juárez halted payment of Mexico's debts to Europe, and, in January 1862, Britain, France, and Spain sent a joint military force to Vera Cruz. The plan to collect the debts soon became a French mission to overthrow Juárez and set up a puppet government. Britain and Spain withdrew, leaving Napoleon III of France to further his own designs, and in June 1863 French forces occupied Mexico City. Having allied themselves with the French emperor, Mexican conservatives offered the crown of Mexico to Ferdinand Maximilian, the younger brother of the Austrian emperor.

The Confederacy, which had bungled its first diplomatic foray into Mexico with an ill-considered emphasis on the merits of the South's conservative, slave-based society—which Juárez opposed—welcomed a new Mexican government. The South was willing to toss aside the long-held Monroe Doctrine (a policy President James Monroe had articulated in 1823; it prescribed an end to European intervention in the Western Hemisphere) if a Mexican alliance could also lead to French recognition of the Confederacy and greater trade along the Mexican border. The United States, having recognized the Juárez government—and in keeping with the Monroe Doctrine—had demanded the withdrawal of the joint European military force and was warning France against expanding its empire in Mexico.

In June 1864, Maximilian was crowned emperor; again the Confederacy attempted to make an alliance. The new emperor, who sought to have his government recognized by the United States, spurned the offer. The United

States in turn refused to recognize Maximilian's government, and there matters remained until the close of the war.

Confederate Recognition Denied

Following the Confederate invasion of Maryland in September 1862, and the ensuing battle of Antietam on September 17, Confederate diplomatic hopes suffered a decisive setback, first by the military defeat, but more importantly by President Lincoln's issuance of the Preliminary Emancipation Proclamation. This instantly broadened Northern war aims to include determination of the fate of slavery in America. In Great Britain, which had outlawed slavery in 1833, antislavery sentiment ran high. The transformation of the war to save the Union into a war that would also end slavery made the Confederate cause nearly impossible for Britain—and, by extension, France—to embrace. Although Confederate attempts to win European recognition would continue until 1865, President Davis realized that foreign support was likely lost and he was defiant in a December 26, 1862, speech. "Never before in the history of the world had a people for so long a time maintained their ground, and showed themselves capable of maintaining their national existence, without securing the recognition of commercial nations," he said. "I know not why this has been so, but this I say, 'Put not your trust in princes,' and rest not your hopes in foreign nations. This war is ours; we must fight it out ourselves, and I feel some pride in knowing that so far we have done it without the good will of anybody."

Suspension of the Writ of Habeas Corpus

One of the greatest challenges facing the presidents of the two warring sections was the need to vigorously prosecute a domestic war while continuing to respect the civil rights of the civilian populace. The issue of individual civil liberties was quickly brought to the fore with Lincoln's limited suspension of the writ of habeas corpus (along with the imposition of martial law in the border states) after the Confederates fired on Fort Sumter. The writ of habeas corpus (meaning "you have the body"), under Article 1, Section 9, paragraph 2 of the U.S. Constitution, states: "The privilege of the writ of habeas corpus shall not be suspended, unless when in cases of rebellion or invasion the public safety may require it." Any judge may issue a writ, which requires that a person held in custody must appear in court to be officially charged. By suspending the writ, a person regarded as a threat to the public good—or to those in power—may be held in custody without due process of law. The Constitution was vague, however, about whether the president or Congress held the authority to suspend the writ.

Lincoln boldly proclaimed it an executive power, and in *Ex parte Merryman*, one of the most celebrated legal challenges of the war, he ignored Supreme Court Justice Roger Taney's writ of habeas corpus to free John Merryman, a Southern-sympathizing Marylander who had been arrested for burning bridges and soliciting Confederate recruits. (Taney issued this writ while acting as a circuit court judge, but the full U.S. Supreme Court refused to support him.) During the course of the war, some 18,000 civilians were arrested in the North for matters related to alleged disloyalty. Most of these arrests took place in the border states, where hostilities were raging and where many residents not only sympathized with the Confederacy but actually gave aid and comfort to the enemy.

In spite of some public disdain for this heavy-handed tactic, Northern political leadership regarded the suspension as a necessary evil. In March 1863, Congress passed the Habeas Corpus Act, which lent full legal weight to Lincoln's suspension and provided authority for similar actions in the future. Significantly, the Lincoln administration did not use the suspension of the writ as a partisan tool to prevent Democrats from campaigning for office or opposing the war. What is perhaps most remarkable about the North's Civil War experience is the level of dissent that Lincoln tolerated. Indeed, compared with the suppression of dissidents in the South—some of whom were lynched or executed—the Lincoln administration's use of the suspension of habeas corpus seems restrained. Still, in some areas, particularly parts of the Midwest, military commissions tried civilians for treason—or even treasonous opinions—often on flimsy evidence, even when civilian courts were open. Major General Ambrose Burnside's General Order, No. 38 prohibited declaring sympathy for the enemy, and his subsequent arrest of Ohio gubernatorial candidate Clement L. Vallandigham unleashed a firestorm of criticism. In 1866, in *Ex parte Milligan*, the Supreme Court would rule that military trials were unconstitutional where civil courts remained open, that civil courts and the writ of habeas corpus could only be suspended where martial law was in force, and that martial law could only be used in places where there was ongoing combat.

In the South, too, the writ was suspended. Unlike the blanket authority granted to Lincoln in 1863, the Confederate Congress gave President Jefferson Davis only limited power to suspend the writ. On February 27, 1862, the Confederate Congress sanctioned temporary suspension of the writ, in part to stymie organized resistance to conscription. It was suspended again on September 20, 1862, but staunch civilian opposition soon reversed the decision. On February 5, 1864, Davis succeeded in getting authority to suspend the writ for treasonable offenses, but once again the power to revoke the writ was short-lived in response to public outrage. The Confederate Congress did not grant Davis' subsequent requests.

However, in the Confederacy, military arrests occurred even where the writ was in place. During the war, the Confederate military arrested and imprisoned thousands of civilians; more than 4,000 cases have been documented, and the total figure was likely much higher. Confederate authorities also arrested foreign journalists and observers who, they suspected (usually without any evidence), were opposing slavery. Indeed, one of the least understood aspects of Confederate life is that civil liberties virtually disappeared during the war, and this led to the suppression of many who questioned the legitimacy of slavery or disagreed with war policy or the war itself. In Richmond's Castle Thunder prison, an entire floor was reserved for civilian political prisoners.

Similar in purpose to the military commissions in the North were the virtually invisible habeas corpus commissioners in the South, who operated throughout the war under the auspices of the War Department and with congressional approval, even when the writ was not suspended. The commissioners investigated cases, recommended the release of prisoners or handed them over to civilian courts for trial; they could also make no decision on a case and detain a prisoner indefinitely. Even though commissioners, essentially acting as the equivalent of district court judges, often took pains to function within a framework of accepted judicial practices, prisoners had none of the legal protections that defendants in a regular court of law are entitled to. The commissions' reports were never made public, so commissioners were not held accountable for their actions—or inactions.

Of all the wartime measures passed or implemented by the two governments, the authority to detain citizens indefinitely, without charge, was one of the most offensive to American sensibilities. Without the writ, sacred civil liberties became tenuous or nonexistent. Lincoln went to great lengths to justify this and other harsh measures adopted throughout the war, but the constitutionality of his actions remains a point of controversy among legal scholars. The suspension of habeas corpus is undoubtedly constitutional; the question centers on whether Lincoln had the authority to do so or if only

Congress could do so. In any event, under both the "invasion" and "rebellion" definitions of the suspension of habeas corpus, Lincoln was acting within the framework of the Constitution.

Emancipation Proclamation

The emancipation of the slaves was the single most dramatic and far-reaching action taken by the Lincoln administration. The action evolved gradually; Lincoln was always mindful that preserving the Union was his highest priority. If he could win the war by freeing all the slaves, some of them, or none at all, he would take whatever route would lead to victory.

Throughout his public life, Abraham Lincoln had consistently opposed the institution of slavery and advocated policies to restrict it from spreading into the western territories. His views fit comfortably with the new Republican Party and its antislavery roots; thus, his election as president in 1860 set off the first wave of secession. Responding to the crisis in his first inaugural address, Lincoln assured Southerners that it was not the intention of the Federal government to interfere with slavery where it existed. He pointed out that, as president, he had no power to do so, asserting that under the Constitution, the national government could "never interfere with the domestic institutions of the States."

When war came—only weeks after Lincoln had assumed office—his stated objective was restoration of the Union, and he refused to take any action against slavery, not only because he had no constitutional authority to do so, but because he feared that doing so would push Kentucky, Missouri, and Maryland into the Confederacy. Thus, in August 1861, when General John C. Frémont attempted to emancipate all slaves owned by Confederate sympathizers in Missouri, Lincoln overruled him. He did the same in May 1862, when General David Hunter declared that all slaves under his area of control in Florida, Georgia, and South Carolina were free. But the president urged border-state governors to accept some form of gradual, compensated emancipation for their slaves (in 1862, Congress abolished slavery in the District of Columbia, and Maryland and Missouri would emancipate slaves before the war ended), and he explored the feasibility of colonization for freedmen, a plan almost universally resisted by free blacks (see "Black Immigration and Colonization," page 215).

By 1862, it was apparent that predictions of a brief war had been wrong. The Confederacy's resistance remained firm. What kept thousands of Southern soldiers on the battlefield were slaves working on plantations to feed the army, and, in some places, building defensive fortifications. Black and white abolitionists had been pointing this out from the start of the war and were even quoting Southern newspapers on the subject. For example, the November 6, 1861, edition of the Montgomery *Advertiser* noted: "The institution of slavery in the South alone enables her to place in the field a force much larger in proportion to her white population than the North. . . . The institution is a tower of strength to the South, particularly at the present crisis, and our enemies will be likely to find that the 'moral cancer' about which their orators are so fond of prating, is really one of the most effective weapons employed against the Union by the South."

Thus, freeing slaves in the Confederacy became part of Lincoln's war strategy. Emancipation was also a valid war aim because of its diplomatic ramifications. By transforming the war into a crusade against slavery, Lincoln could all but ensure that British and French diplomatic recognition of the Confederacy would not be forthcoming.

Despite the advantages that emancipation would bring to the Union, it remained a delicate issue in the North. There were fears that hordes of freedmen would overrun Northern states, take jobs from white workers, and strain local resources. Even Northerners who opposed slavery were not prepared to welcome an influx of black neighbors. The prevailing attitude among whites—even those who were antislavery—was one of racial superiority, and many soldiers in the Union army who were eager to fight for the Union were *not* eager to fight for emancipation. There were also concerns over the president's constitutional authority to emancipate the slaves. But as the war progressed—and as Congress passed confiscation acts aimed at Southern property, including slaves—Lincoln devised an approach based on his constitutional authority to exercise presidential war powers. He carefully crafted the Emancipation Proclamation as a narrowly focused, legalistic document designed to withstand legal challenge. The president later explained: "I felt the measures, otherwise unconstitutional, might become lawful, by becoming indispensable to the preservation of the Constitution, through the preservation of the nation."

In June 1862, Lincoln had completed drafting his Preliminary Emancipation Proclamation. He presented it to the cabinet the following month but, on the advice of Secretary of State Seward, he awaited a positive military development before releasing it. Issuing the document following battlefield defeats in the summer of 1862 would have cast the proclamation as a desperate and meaningless gesture. His opportunity came in the wake of the Union victory at Antietam on September 17, 1862 (see Chapter 4, "Battles and the Battlefield"). The battle ended the Confederate invasion of Maryland and forced Lee's army to retreat to Virginia. On September 22, Lincoln issued the Preliminary Emancipation Proclamation. In this document, the president gave the rebellious states 100 days to return to the Union and to adopt immediate or gradual abolition with the assurance that plans for voluntary colonization of former slaves would continue. Otherwise, Lincoln declared that slaves in any state still in rebellion would then be "forever free."

No Confederate state returned to the Union. On New Year's Day, 1863, Lincoln signed the final Emancipation Proclamation, which differed considerably from the first document. The final proclamation, "a fit and necessary war measure," declared freedom for slaves only in rebellious sections of the country, but not in the border states or in Tennessee and parts of Virginia and Louisiana, most of which were under Union control. The proclamation also included a provision for enlisting former slaves in the Union army.

Because Lincoln's authority extended only to the seizure of property of those in rebellion (no proclamation could invalidate the legal ownership of slaves by masters in the loyal slave states), tens of thousands of slaves would have to wait for the Thirteenth Amendment, passed in December 1865, to gain their freedom. "It will be seen that the President only makes provision for the emancipation of a *part* of an injured race, and that the Border States and certain parts of the rebel States are excepted from the relief offered to others by this most important document," stated the *Christian Recorder*, an African Methodist Episcopal church newspaper in Philadelphia. Nonetheless, the newspaper continued, "[W]e believe those who are not immediately liberated will be ultimately benefitted by this act, and that Congress will do something for those poor souls who will still remain in degradation. But we thank God and President Lincoln for what has been done, 'and take courage.'"

Although the proclamation had no instantaneous effect on slaves outside the reach of the Union armies, it did immediately transform the war. The war to preserve the Union also became a moral crusade to end slavery, and that purpose made it highly unlikely that Britain could ever be compelled to enter the war on the side of the South. The proclamation also resolved the legal status of slaves who had claimed their freedom behind the security of Union lines, and it undermined the Confederacy as slaves fled to the North in greater numbers and joined the Union army. Tens of thousands more worked for the army as civilian laborers—nurses, cooks, and teamsters.

Thomas Nast's "Emancipation" (1865) illustrated the hopeful possibilities of life after slavery following the Union's victory.

Beyond the military consequences of the Emancipation Proclamation, surely none appreciated the meaning of the document so much as African Americans. On January 1, 1863, free blacks held celebratory meetings in cities throughout the North. Henry Turner, pastor of the Israel Bethel (A.M.E.) Church in Washington, D.C., captured the excitement of the day: "Seeing such a multitude of people in and around my church, I hurriedly went up to the office of the first paper in which the proclamation of freedom could be printed . . . and squeezed myself through the dense crowd that was waiting for the paper. The first sheet run off with the proclamation in it was grabbed for by three of us, but some active young man got possession of it and fled. The next sheet was grabbed for by several, and was torn into tatters. The third sheet from the press was grabbed for by several, but I succeeded in procuring so much of it as contained the proclamation, and off I went for life and death.

Down Pennsylvania [Avenue] I ran as for my life, and when the people saw me coming with the paper in my hand they raised a shouting cheer that was almost deafening."

The Gettysburg Address

At the November 19, 1863, ceremony dedicating a soldiers' cemetery in Gettysburg, Pennsylvania, where more than 51,000 were killed, captured, or wounded in the war's costliest battle, Lincoln eloquently laid out the meaning of the war. That the brief address became one of history's most famous and praised speeches is due not only to its stirring language or the event that occasioned it. In defining the purpose of the war, Lincoln was calling on the nation to continue America's grand experiment of government by the people.

During the ceremony, the president's address was overshadowed by renowned speaker Edward Everett's two-hour oration, which preceded it. Lincoln initially believed his speech was a failure, but, within days, newspaper and popular reaction assured him of its success. Even Everett observed its effectiveness in a letter to the president: "I should be glad if I could flatter myself that I came as near to the central idea of the occasion in two hours as you did in two minutes."

Five manuscript copies of the Gettysburg Address, written in Lincoln's hand—with minor word and phrase differences among them—are known to exist. The copies Lincoln gave to his private secretaries, John Nicolay and John Hay, are in the Library of Congress. He later made out a copy for Everett; this manuscript is at the Illinois State Historical Library in Springfield. Historian George Bancroft requested a copy from Lincoln; it is now at Cornell University. The Bliss Copy, reproduced here, was penned by Lincoln for inclusion in Colonel Alexander Bliss' book *Autograph Leaves of Our Country's Authors* (1864). It is considered the "standard" version and is the one most often reprinted. The original Bliss document is displayed in the Lincoln Bedroom at the White House.

Fourscore and seven years ago our fathers brought forth on this continent a new nation, conceived in liberty and dedicated to the proposition that all men are created equal.

Now we are engaged in a great civil war, testing whether that nation or any nation so conceived and so dedicated can long endure. We are met on a great battlefield of that war. We have come to dedicate a portion of that field as a final resting-place for those who here gave their lives that that nation might live. It is altogether fitting and proper that we should do this.

But, in a larger sense, we cannot dedicate, we cannot consecrate, we cannot hallow this ground. The brave men, living and dead who struggled here have consecrated it far above our poor power to add or detract. The world will little note nor long remember what we say here, but it can never forget what they did here. It is for us the living rather to be dedicated here to the unfinished work which they who fought here have thus far so nobly advanced. It is rather for us to be here dedicated to the great task remaining before us—that from these honored dead we take increased devotion to that cause for which they gave the last full measure of devotion—that we here highly resolve that these dead shall not have died in vain, that this nation under God shall have a new birth of freedom, and that government of the people, by the people, for the people shall not perish from the earth.

Black Emigration and Colonization

The movement to encourage black emigration and colonization outside the United States began more than 40 years before the Civil War and was organized principally by the American Colonization Society, which settled American blacks in Liberia (see "Political Parties, Organizations, and Movements," page 164). Most free blacks opposed colonization and strongly objected to the notion that they were not, in fact, American. But, in the 1850s, the colonization movement revived, and although most free blacks were opposed to it, some African Americans—notably, Henry Highland Garnet, Martin Delany, and James Holly—favored colonization. They believed that blacks would never overcome the blatant discrimination they fought against daily in the United States.

The start of the Civil War brought a resurgence of enthusiasm for colonization among whites, as the country struggled with the future of slaves seeking refuge in Union lines. Thus, emigration was a political issue and, as Frederick Douglass feared, was becoming "a grand scheme of public policy." Lincoln entertained and sometimes endorsed a series of colonization proposals. On December 3, 1861, he asked Congress for funds to acquire territory outside the United States, where contrabands and any free blacks who wanted to emigrate could be resettled. The *Anglo-African* called it "a speech to stir the hearts of all Confederates." Congress subsequently appropriated $600,000 for colonization by slaves freed in the District of

Columbia and by the Second Confiscation Act. Dr. John Rock, a Massachusetts black, spoke out against emigration: "This being our country, we have made up our minds to remain in it, and to try to make it worth living in." On the other hand, a supporter of emigration wrote in the *Anglo-African*: "Listen! We want our rights. No one is going to *give* them to us, so perforce we must take them. . . . We can make of Hayti the nucleus of a power that shall be to the black, what England has been to the white races, the hope of progress and the guarantee of permanent civilization."

Between December 1860 and 1862, more than 2,000 American blacks emigrated to Haiti; but they struggled under difficult conditions to start a new life. Most died or returned disillusioned to the United States, and the Haiti initiative ended. But in August 1862, Lincoln stunned black Americans by telling five black leaders whom he had invited to the White House that living together put both blacks and whites at a disadvantage ("I think your race suffer very greatly, many of them by living among us, while ours suffer from your presence"). He proposed colonization in Central America and the promise of profitable work in coal mines. This prompted an angry response from A. P. Smith of New Jersey, in the *National Anti-Slavery Standard:* "But say, good Mr. President, why we, why anybody should swelter, digging coal, if there be any in Central America? . . . But, say you: 'Coal land is the best thing I know of to begin an enterprise.' Astounding discovery! . . . If you please, sir, give McClellan some, give Halleck some, and by all means, save a little strip for yourself. . . . Good sir, if you have any nearer friends than we are, let them have that coal-digging job."

Lincoln, however, showed interest in several other colonization schemes, including Ambrose Thompson's "Chiriqui Improvement Company" to develop coal mines in Panama, for which he appointed U.S. Senator Samuel C. Pomeroy as United States colonization agent. In May 1863, 453 blacks emigrated to Ile à Vache, South of Haiti, but that project, like others, ended in disaster. Lincoln sent a ship to rescue the surviving colonists and later abandoned the idea of colonization. In July 1864, Congress repealed the 1862 law that appropriated funds for colonization.

Securing Rights for Blacks in the Union

Even as they campaigned for the emancipation of slaves, free blacks in the North also focused their efforts on obtaining voting rights, ending discriminatory laws, and serving in the Union army. Together with white abolitionists, they challenged accepted practices at both the national and state levels.

Voting Rights

At the start of the war, only Massachusetts accorded its black citizens full civil rights. Massachusetts, Maine, New Hampshire, Vermont, and Rhode Island allowed African Americans—a total of 7 percent of the Northern black population—to vote on an equal basis with whites. In New York, black men who owned at least $250 worth of property could vote, a requirement not prescribed for white voters. In Ohio, African Americans could vote if their ancestry was more than half white.

For black Americans and their white allies, voting was the logical complement to emancipation. Only political power could secure for blacks a meaningful freedom. Among the efforts to secure suffrage in the North was an appeal made to the "Citizens of Kansas" by a black convention in 1863: "This nation has long turned a deaf ear to the cry of the black man. . . . Happily the nation's conscience, schooled by misfortune, is becoming aroused to the necessity of repairing the many wrongs which it has inflicted on the black man. In the progress of this war, destructive of so many prejudices and fruitful of so many new ideas, it will doubtless be discovered that it is as necessary to make the black man a voter, as it was to make him a soldier. He was made a soldier to RESTORE the Union. He must be made a voter to preserve it."

Suffrage was an issue not only for most Northern and all Southern free blacks; it became a matter of greater debate as the Union army pushed south and freed slaves in the Confederacy. Even some abolitionists expressed concern that these freedmen were not ready to become voters. Frederick Douglass spoke to the heart of the matter when he addressed a meeting of the American Anti-Slavery Society in 1863: "It is said that the colored man is ignorant, and therefore he shall not vote. In saying this, you lay down a rule for the black man that you apply to no other class of your citizens. . . . If he knows an honest man from a thief, he knows much more than some of our white voters. . . . If he knows enough to take up arms in defence of this Government, and bare his breast to the storm of rebel artillery, he knows enough to vote. . . ."

Southern blacks joined in campaigning for the right to vote even before the war ended. In May 1864, a delegation from North Carolina petitioned President Lincoln to enfranchise blacks when the state was reconstructed. New Orleans' large population of wealthy, educated, and influential blacks, many of whom had served in the military, called for voting rights as a condition of restoring Louisiana to the Union. Although blacks petitioned Lincoln himself, voting rights for African Americans were not granted in the new Louisiana state constitution.

Discrimination and Segregation

Throughout the Union, blacks were denied more than the right to vote. Indiana, Illinois, Iowa, California, and Oregon banned blacks from testifying in court against whites. African Americans could not attend public school in southern Illinois and Indiana (where they were exempt from the school tax), and many public schools in the North were segregated. Even in New England, where schools were generally integrated, several cities maintained segregated schools. Campaigns by African Americans against inequities flourished in a climate of hope and reform. As one man wrote in September 1862, in the *Pacific Appeal*, a black San Francisco newspaper: "Everything around us indicates a change in our condition, and the revolution of events, and the change in the public sentiment toward us, all go to prove the necessity for us to prepare to act in a different sphere from that in which we have heretofore acted. . . . The only place the American historian could find for the colored man was in the background of a cotton-field, or the foreground of a cane-brake or a rice swamp, to adorn the pages of geography. . . . But . . . old things are passing away, and eventually old prejudices must follow."

In 1863, blacks in California were successful in securing the repeal of the law that forbade them to testify in court against whites; in 1865, Illinois repealed a similar law as well as one that prohibited black immigration into the state. At war's end, Indiana was the only Northern state with such "black laws" still in effect, but these were repealed or struck down by the courts by 1866. In Washington, D.C., a law prohibiting segregation on the city's streetcars was passed in March 1865. Shortly thereafter, when a conductor tried to eject Sojourner Truth from a streetcar, dislocating her shoulder, she had him arrested for assault and battery, and he lost his job. In the thirty years following the war, Northern states prohibited almost all segregation in public schools and transportation.

But even where discriminatory laws no longer functioned, de facto segregation remained. As Dr. John Rock (see "Other Notable Political Figures," page 186), a black physician and attorney from Massachusetts—the state with the most progressive attitudes toward African Americans—wrote in 1862: "The masses seem to think that we are oppressed only in the South. This is a mistake; we are oppressed everywhere in this slavery-cursed land. Massachusetts has a great name, and deserves much credit for what she has done, but the position of the colored people in Massachusetts is far from being an enviable one. While colored men have many rights, they have few privileges here. To be sure, we are seldom insulted by passersby, we have the right of suffrage, the free schools and colleges are opened to our children, and from them have come forth young men capable of filling any post of profit or honor. But there is no field for these young men. Their education aggravates their suffering. . . . The educated colored man meets, on the one hand, the embittered prejudices of the whites, and on the other the jealousies of his own race . . ."

The Black Press

By the time the Civil War broke out, black newspapers had a history of advocacy for emancipation and civil rights dating back to the publication of *Freedom's Journal*, the first black newspaper, in 1827. During the war, the black press gave voice to the political perspectives and concerns of free blacks and, later, of freedmen, commenting on such issues as abolition, colonization, suffrage, discriminatory laws and segregated schooling in northern states, and the recruitment and treatment of black soldiers.

The most important contemporary black newspaper, the *Anglo-African* of New York, forcefully called for equality beyond emancipation. *Douglass' Monthly*, published by Frederick Douglass in magazine format until August 1863, was read by more whites than any other African American paper. The *Christian Recorder*, begun in 1856, was the newspaper of the African Methodist Episcopal (A.M.E.) church, but also featured broader stories of interest to the Philadelphia black community. Local and regional publications included the *Pacific Appeal* in San Francisco and Cincinnati's *Colored Citizen*. The *Union* (*L'Union*) and later the *Tribune* (*La Tribune de la Nouvelle Orléans*), were bilingual New Orleans newspapers that articulated the viewpoints of the affluent and influential free blacks living in the city and of the freedmen of Louisiana, as well as the general concerns of African Americans in the South.

Service in the Union Army

From the outset of the war, free blacks offered their services to the Union army, yet the idea of armed black units was so controversial that although a few regiments were formed in 1862, using black troops did not become policy until 1863, following the Emancipation Proclamation (see "Fighting on Two Fronts: Black Soldiers in the Civil War" in Chapter 5, "The Armies,"). Racism, the potential repercussions in the border states, and the implications for equal treatment if blacks were capable of fighting and dying for their country, made the decision a political as well as a military one. When offered the services of two black regiments, Lincoln told an Indiana delegation in August 1862: "To arm the negroes would turn 50,000 bayonets from the loyal Border States against us that were for us."

When the Union did begin to recruit black troops in 1863, there was less enthusiasm among African Americans for enlisting than there had been at the beginning of the war. Having been rejected initially by Northern states and the Federal government, and now enjoying the prosperity of the wartime economy, black men hesitated to enlist. But by the war's end, 186,000 blacks had served (they were allowed to serve in the navy from the beginning of the war). In the army, they again experienced discrimination. They were more likely to be assigned labor and fatigue duty than white soldiers (and were still expected to perform combat duty), were paid less than their white counterparts, and were denied promotions, commissions, and command positions.

Wartime Elections

1862 U.S. Election

The 1862 election gave voters in all of the North their first opportunity to register their views on the war. Although both houses of Congress remained in Republican hands, the Democrats gained thirty-four House seats and several Senate seats. They also took control of the Illinois, Indiana, and New Jersey legislatures, and New Jersey and New York each elected a Democratic governor. Major Confederate military victories that year—combined with the unexpected length of the war, the high casualty rates, and concern that Lincoln was dangerously exceeding his authority in suppressing civil liberties—benefited the Democrats politically. Their success was also attributed to the shift in Republican policy to a more aggressive antislavery agenda. Passage of the Second Confiscation Act and issuance of the Preliminary Emancipation Proclamation, which prompted Democrats' fears that newly freed blacks would pour into the North and undercut the cost of white labor, also translated into Democratic votes.

1863 Confederate Election

Confederate elections were strung out between May and November. Some states offered absentee voting for soldiers and civilian refugees from areas under Union occupation. The upbeat mood of 1861 had fizzled as military setbacks, economic hardships, and dwindling support for Davis' policies provoked intense political debate. Critics attacked Davis for trampling states' rights in the name of wartime measures (suspension of habeas corpus, conscription, income taxation, impressment, and martial law) but offered few war-winning recommendations of their own. In many congressional races, ardent secessionists and Davis supporters did poorly at the polls, and peace candidates prospered. Wartime conditions and the lengthy time frame produced limited interest in the election, and several other factors contributed to voter apathy: few candidates campaigned avidly (many ran unopposed); newspaper election coverage was scant in some areas (owing to emphasis on war news as well as the paper shortages that limited or shut down press operations); and general disgust with bickering factions dampened support for the whole process.

When the votes were counted, the soldier vote and ballots from occupied districts maintained Davis' congressional majority. But there was a large turnover as well; newcomers made up nearly 40 percent of the second Confederate Congress. The combination of peace advocates, cooperationists (those who had opposed individual states seceding on their own during the 1860–1861 secession crisis), moderates, fire-eaters, and those defying labels resulted in a politically splintered body with considerably less unity than its predecessor. Whereas most members of the First Congress were bound by their enthusiasm for secession, representatives in the Second Congress were guided by more individual concerns, such as Davis' infringement on their constitutional rights. Their views were often shaped by where the Union army happened to be in relation to their home district. Representatives from occupied areas were more likely to support extreme amendments to wartime measures (including suspension of habeas corpus, extension of conscription, and impressment); they had the most to gain from such actions, which would have virtually no impact on their constituents.

1864 U.S. Political Platforms

Democratic Party Platform:

- Reaffirms the party's "unswerving fidelity to the Union under the Constitution."
- Demands immediate efforts to end hostilities and restore peace.

- Condemns U.S. military interference with elections in Delaware, Kentucky, Maryland, and Missouri.
- Condemns the "administrative usurpation of the extraordinary and dangerous powers not granted by the Constitution," including subversion of civil law by military law; suppression of a free press; disregard of states' rights; and the use of "unusual" loyalty oaths.
- Criticizes the Lincoln administration for disregarding the plight of U.S. prisoners of war.
- Praises U.S. soldiers and sailors for their service.

Republican (Union) Party Platform:

- Pledges unconditional government support "in quelling by force of arms" the rebellion against the United States and punishing traitors.
- Approves the Lincoln administration's position not to compromise with the Confederacy or accept any peace agreement that does not include the Confederacy's unconditional surrender.
- Declares that slavery was "the cause and now constitutes the strength of this rebellion" and that it must be forever prohibited in the United States.
- Thanks soldiers and sailors for their heroic and patriotic service.
- Applauds Lincoln for his wisdom and devotion as president under "unparalleled difficulty" and reaffirms its confidence in him.
- Approves of the Emancipation Proclamation and employing former slaves as Union soldiers.
- Asserts that all soldiers, without regard to race, are entitled to "the full protection of the laws of war," and violations of such laws by the Confederacy demand "prompt and full redress."
- Encourages foreign immigration, which has added to the wealth and power of the United States.
- Favors the "speedy construction" of a transcontinental railroad.
- Calls for economic responsibility, including "a vigorous and just system of taxation" and the use of a national currency.
- Supports the U.S. government position to oppose European attempts to overthrow republican governments on the "Western Continent."

1864 U.S. Election

By the fall of 1864, the presidential race between incumbent Republican—or National Union Party—candidate Abraham Lincoln and his former general in chief, Democratic candidate George B. McClellan, had evolved into a referendum on the war. A vote for Lincoln was a vote to see the war through and a refusal to turn back on the question of emancipation. On the other hand, a vote for McClellan was a vote to begin negotiating a peace settlement with the Confederacy.

Although only the states in the Union participated, the 1864 election marked the first national election ever held—anywhere—during wartime. Just as remarkable was the fact that soldiers were voting on the country's war aims not with their feet (either by reenlisting or deserting) but with their ballots. Nineteen states made provisions for absentee balloting; in those that did not, soldiers who received furloughs could vote at home. The soldier vote would prove to be critical, particularly in the lower Midwest, where the Copperheads were strongest.

Even in 1864, the Army of the Potomac still bore the stamp of McClellan, its former leader. "The Young Napoleon" had taken command of a dispirited rabble in the wake of the disastrous defeat at First Bull Run, and had forged it into a disciplined army. An exceptional organizer and teacher, McClellan's concern for his men has inspired, in many, undying devotion. As a candidate, McClellan—and the Peace Democrats—promised a prompt end to the slaughter and the astronomical expenditures occasioned by the war. Although, in the wake of Sherman's victory at Atlanta, McClellan rejected the peace plank in the Democratic platform and insisted that peace must mean restoration of the Union—not recognition of the Confederacy— neither he nor the Democratic leadership fully grasped the depth of the enlisted men's patriotic temper.

"McClellan was our first commander, and, as such, he was worshiped by his soldiers," wrote Theodore Gerrish, a private in the Twentieth Maine Infantry and author of *Army Life: A Private's Reminiscences of the Civil War.* Yet, he continued, "It was cruel [of] General McClellan to ask us to vote that our campaigns had all been failures, and that our comrades had died in vain."

Lincoln's popularity with the soldiers was far from universal. Some fighting men, particularly from New Hampshire and New York, openly supported McClellan and complained that they had been told by their officers that they would not be allowed to vote if they were not voting for Lincoln. Attempts to influence the soldier vote were not uncommon. Captain William Hyndman, a Pennsylvania cavalryman, wrote of a "curious circumstance" during the campaign. "Two of our pickets were captured by . . . guerrillas, and on being asked who they would vote for, replying they were McClellan men, they were promptly released by the rebel scoundrels and allowed to poll their votes at liberty." Aside from their military purposes, Lee's second Northern invasion (which had ended at Gettysburg the year before), John Hunt Morgan's daring 1863 raid through Indiana and Ohio, and Sterling Price's Missouri raid in the fall of 1864 (see Chapter 4, "Battles and the Battlefield") were intended to have a political influence: encouraging threatened Northern voters to register their disapproval of the war at the polls.

Overall, however, McClellanism was the exception rather than the rule in the army's ranks. By a three to one margin, soldiers chose Lincoln and the Union. They chose to finish the war that they believed the South had started, and, with this resolve, the Union armies turned back to the task of subduing the Confederacy in what would be six more months of warfare. General Grant summed up the importance of the soldier vote when he wrote that ". . . the overwhelming majority received by Mr. Lincoln and the quiet with which the election went off will prove a terrible damper to the Rebels. It will be worth more than a victory in the field both in its effect on the Rebels and its influence abroad."

When the votes were tallied, Lincoln had won 55 percent of the popular vote and every Union state except Delaware, Kentucky, and New Jersey. Further cementing Lincoln's mandate were Republican gubernatorial victories in every free state except New Jersey, and overwhelming control of the House of Representatives (149 Republicans to 42 Democrats). With a 42 to 10 Republican majority in the Senate, the repudiation of the Democratic peace platform was complete.

Newspapers: The Politics of the Press

The war waged in the press was an extension of the war fought on the battlefield—in the passionate ideological rhetoric of the editorial pages, in the competitive scramble for news scoops, and in the circumstances that forced some papers to shut down because of censorship or paper-and-ink shortages. More than 200 full-time correspondents reported on the war, and the leading New York papers spent from $60,000 to $100,000 annually on their war coverage alone. Smaller papers, with their emphasis on local rather than national news, relied on Associated Press reports or other dispatches. Even in

Washington, D.C., the nation's capital, residents eagerly awaited the delivery of Baltimore, Boston, and Philadelphia newspapers to supplement their local war coverage. But no matter their budget, scope, or circulation, newspapers weighed in editorially on war issues. And although newspapers in major cities had the most influence on policy and political matters—and were most likely to be used by politicians and army generals for promoting their own views and interests—smaller papers had an influence on the huge population of voters that lived outside metropolitan areas.

The demand for war news dramatically increased overall newspaper circulation. To meet that demand, the industry, for the first time on a large scale, relied on the telegraph. Since the 1840s, the telegraph had been an important but limited source of news; during the war, it was vital in providing up-to-the-minute battle coverage that drew ever more readers. This wider audience was also served a steady diet of political commentary on the war and those who were running it. Partisanship had long been a regular component of news stories—and remained so in many newspapers of the day—but some papers, led by the *New York Times*, made a concerted effort to provide objective, evenhanded coverage and to tone down the flowery or bombastic language that characterized much of nineteenth-century news writing. The *New York Herald*, in particular, distinguished itself for its thorough, wide-ranging war coverage. Yet it was on the editorial pages and in the opinion columns that the politics of the press had its greatest impact on the war effort. On both sides of the conflict, editors endorsed or opposed conscription, the suspension of habeas corpus, the Emancipation Proclamation, military strategy, and political appointments and performance.

In the South, the Confederate cause and the Davis administration enjoyed early, widespread support. As the war lengthened and the sacrifices deepened, that initial enthusiasm eventually gave way. Editors broke into pro-Davis and anti-Davis camps, and a strong peace movement later emerged in print. Richmond's five daily newspapers reflected the diversity of thought. The *Richmond Dispatch* had the largest readership in the Confederate capital and deftly combined patriotism with moderation. The *Enquirer*, regarded as the mouthpiece of the Davis administration, and the *Sentinel*, which earnestly backed government policies, were countered by the openly hostile *Examiner*, which accused the president of everything from laziness to incompetence to cronyism. By early 1862, the once supportive *Whig and Public Advertiser* had developed a harsher line on the president and his policies.

In Charleston, where the war began, editorial commentary reached a fever pitch. An ardent states' rights advocate, Barnwell Rhett Jr., editor of the *Charleston Mercury*, was vicious in his relentless attacks on Davis and the government, charging the president with inefficiency, ineptitude, poor prosecution of the war, and even worse military and political appointments. This last charge was not too surprising given that the editor's father—fire-eater Rhett Sr. (see "Other Notable Antebellum Figures" in Chapter 2, "Antebellum America,") dubbed the "Father of Secession" and a frequent contributer to the *Mercury*—was passed over when Davis chose his cabinet. Aside from the spectacular fireworks that flew off the *Mercury's* pages, what was significant was the effect the paper had on local morale. Rhett Jr.'s daily reminder of how long the city remained under siege was a constant damper on public spirits and undermined the Confederate cause; Davis' wife, Varina, once bitterly noted that she hated the editor more than any Republican. On the other end of the spectrum was the *Charleston Courier*, the only South Carolina paper to consistently back the Davis administration (although it did join the *Mercury* in opposing the government's last-ditch plan to enlist black soldiers in 1865). More importantly, it warned readers of the damage the *Mercury* was inflicting on its faithful citizens and on the Confederacy.

Perhaps the most prominent paper pushing a peace message was William W. Holden's *North Carolina Standard*, which boasted the largest circulation in the state. While its rivals, the *Raleigh Register* and the *State Journal* lined up behind the Davis administration, Holden denounced Davis as a tyrant and, as early as mid-1863, was insisting on peace negotiations with the Union. Confederate agents spent five months quieting peace agitators who showed up at rallies around the state and supported Holden's proposals. Other papers branded Holden a traitor for encouraging defeatist attitudes.

In the North, Lincoln also enjoyed the support of major papers and endured the sting of others. The influential *New York Tribune* carried the social reform policies of its editor, Horace Greeley (see "Other Notable Political Figures," page 186), to almost 300,000 readers. (The *New York Times* would reach a similar circulation during the war.) Although the *Tribune* was a strong Republican paper, it did not always toe the party line; Greeley was pushing for emancipation long before Lincoln was prepared to grant it. His open letter to the president, on August 19, 1862, calling for abolition and the use of black soldiers, prompted Lincoln's equally famous response on August 22. The president declared that he would do whatever it took to win the war, whether it was freeing all, some, or none of the slaves.

Although the *New York Times*, which also supported Lincoln, had urged caution and restraint on emancipation, the city's pro-Lincoln papers, with their huge readership and national influence, helped prepare the public for the Emancipation Proclamation. The *Chicago Tribune*, which had backed Lincoln early on, remained loyal while its crosstown rival, the *Times*, responded to the Emancipation Proclamation with an incendiary attack on the president. Some papers called Lincoln a buffoon or worse. The *La Crosse* (Wisconsin) *Democrat* labeled Lincoln a murderer. Smaller papers in Midwestern Democratic strongholds were more likely than the larger Northeast papers to call for peace negotiations and the restoration of the Union with slavery and states' rights intact.

The polarizing views held by citizens of the border states made for lively newspaper copy. Missouri's complex status—a Union slave state with many Confederate sympathizers—was reflected in two of the St. Louis papers: the *Missouri Republican* was a Democratic paper, and the *Missouri Democrat* was a Republican publication. At the *Republican*, editorials from its secessionist editor and its Unionist editor ran next to each other, making the paper's position on the issues murky at best.

Throughout the war, censorship hung over newspapers like a tight deadline. On July 1, 1861, Confederate Secretary of War Leroy Walker asked editors not to print sensitive military information, such as troop strength and location. For the most part, the Southern press abided by the request; one glaring exception was Rhett at the *Charleston Mercury*. Declaring that the public had the right to know these details, he further suggested that such information would already be known in the North by the time it was printed in the South. Generally, the Confederate government respected editorial freedom, but there were exceptions—and, in some instances, destroyed press equipment—as in the case of rabid Unionist William "Parson" Brownlow in eastern Tennessee (see "Wartime Governors," page 191), who was shut down, arrested, and briefly imprisoned.

A month after Walker's request, the U.S. War Department took a similar but more aggressive step, issuing an antileak order that nothing was to be telegraphed from Washington, D.C., regarding the army's movements, until "after actual hostilities." Given the erratic nature of military censorship and the enterprising activities of some reporters, military plans still found their way into print. Confederate generals read the Union papers with as much interest as the Northern public, and the information provided on troop movements, casualties, and military strength probably cost a number of U.S.

soldiers their lives. Union censorship and suppression were also prevalent in the volatile border states—and occasionally elsewhere—as military commanders ordered some papers shut down for subversive activities. In Chicago, General Ambrose Burnside shut down the *Times* for "repeated expression of disloyal and incendiary statements." Three days later, Lincoln rescinded the order. All in all, the Lincoln administration refrained from shutting down newspapers for political purposes, and the president simply tolerated an unprecedented amount of editorial abuse.

Ultimately, the political nature of the press revealed itself not just in what was said on the opinion page but in who was saying it. Political and editorial lines blurred throughout the country as editors turned into politicians and politicians turned into publishers. Holden in North Carolina raised his *Standard* as a platform on which to advocate for the peace movement and from which to launch his own gubernatorial campaign. (Defeated in 1864, he became the provisional governor in 1865, under Reconstruction, and was elected in 1868.) In Georgia, obstreperous Governor Joseph E. Brown (see "Wartime Governors," page 191), a leading critic of the Davis administration, helped editor Nathaniel Morse purchase the *Augusta Chronicle*. Morse rivaled Rhett in his brutal treatment of Davis and promoted Brown's peace agenda. At the *New York Times*, editor Henry J. Raymond, who stood up, in print, to mobs that attacked the pro-Lincoln paper during the 1863 draft riots, served as chairman of the Republican National Committee in 1864, ran Lincoln's reelection campaign (securing Andrew Johnson as his running mate), and won himself a seat in the U.S. House of Representatives. *New York Tribune* managing editor Charles Dana, author of numerous antislavery editorials (his "Forward to Richmond!" slogan over his pieces had prodded the Union army in 1861), resigned to become an agent of the War Department. In 1864, became an assistant secretary of war. (See also in Chapter 12, "The Civil War in Literature and the Arts," "Civil War Artists and the Rise of Illustrated News.")

Abraham Lincoln's Second Inaugural Address

Over the years, Lincoln's Second Inaugural Address has taken a well-deserved place as not only one of the most inspired speeches ever given by an American president, but as one of the finest in history. As the Emancipation Proclamation established the moral basis for the Civil War, the Second Inaugural established high moral standards for the peace everyone knew was imminent by March 1865.

Fellow-Countrymen:

At this second appearing to take the oath of the Presidential office there is less occasion for an extended address than there was at the first. Then a statement somewhat in detail of a course to be pursued seemed fitting and proper. Now, at the expiration of four years, during which public declarations have been constantly called forth on every point and phase of the great contest which still absorbs the attention and engrosses the energies of the nation, little that is new could be presented. The progress of our arms, upon which all else chiefly depends, is as well known to the public as to myself, and it is, I trust, reasonably satisfactory and encouraging to all. With high hope for the future, no prediction in regard to it is ventured.

On the occasion corresponding to this four years ago all thoughts were anxiously directed to an impending civil war. All dreaded it, all sought to avert it. While the inaugural address was being delivered from this place, devoted altogether to saving the Union without war, urgent agents were in the city seeking to destroy it without war—seeking to dissolve the Union and divide effects by negotiation. Both parties deprecated war, but one of them would make war rather than let the nation survive, and the other would accept war rather than let it perish, and the war came.

One-eighth of the whole population were colored slaves, not distributed generally over the Union, but localized in the southern part of it. These slaves constituted a peculiar and powerful interest. All knew that this interest was somehow the cause of the war. To strengthen, perpetuate, and extend this interest was the object for which the insurgents would rend the Union even by war, while the Government claimed no right to do more than to restrict the territorial enlargement of it. Neither party expected for the war the magnitude or the duration which it has already attained. Neither anticipated that the cause of the conflict might cease with or even before the conflict itself should cease. Each looked for an easier triumph, and a result less fundamental and astounding. Both read the same Bible and pray to the same God, and each invokes His aid against the other. It may seem strange that any men should dare to ask a just God's assistance in wringing their bread from the sweat of other men's faces, but let us judge not, that we be not judged. The prayers of both could not be answered. That of neither has been answered fully. The Almighty has His own purposes. "Woe unto the world because of offenses; for it must needs be that offenses come, but woe to that man by whom the offense cometh." If we shall suppose that American slavery is one of those offenses which, in the providence of God, must needs come, but which, having continued through His appointed time, He now wills to remove, and that He gives to both North and South this terrible war as the woe due to those by whom the offense came, shall we discern therein any departure from those divine attributes which the believers in a living God always ascribe to Him? Fondly do we hope, fervently do we pray, that this mighty scourge of war may speedily pass away. Yet, if God wills that it continue until all the wealth piled by the bondsman's two hundred and fifty years of unrequited toil shall be sunk, and until every drop of blood drawn with the lash shall be paid by another drawn with the sword, as was said three thousand years ago, so still it must be said "the judgments of the Lord are true and righteous altogether."

With malice toward none, with charity for all, with firmness in the right as God gives us to see the right, let us strive on to finish the work we are in, to bind up the nation's wounds, to care for him who shall have borne the battle and for his widow and his orphan, to do all which may achieve and cherish a just and lasting peace among ourselves and with all nations.

The Assassination of Abraham Lincoln

When General Lee surrendered his Army of Northern Virginia to General Grant at Appomattox Courthouse on April 9, 1865, it was the most crucial—though not the last—Confederate domino to tumble. The surrender set in motion the collapse of other Southern armies and the capture of Confederate leaders. It also provoked a shocking climax to the war.

Two days after Lee's surrender, President Lincoln gave an address on Reconstruction from the White House balcony. He spoke of the need to "begin with, and mould from, disorganized and discordant elements" to build the states anew. In this, his last public speech, he also indicated support for enfranchising literate blacks and black Union veterans. His audience included John Wilkes Booth, a twenty-six-year-old stage actor from Maryland whose Southern sympathies had transformed into Confederate fanaticism. Earlier in the year, he attempted to kidnap Lincoln in hopes of exchanging the president for Confederate prisoners of war. Distraught over Lee's surrender and mortified as he stood listening to Lincoln's vision for the future, Booth told a companion, "Now, by God, I'll put him through. That is the last speech he will ever make."

Booth fulfilled his promise three days later. On the evening of April 14, Good Friday, the president and Mrs. Lincoln, accompanied by Major Henry Rathbone and Miss Clara Harris, attended a production of *Our American Cousin* at Ford's Theatre. The presidential party took their seats between 8:30

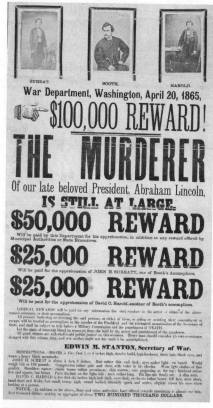

The War Department offered "liberal rewards" leading to the arrest of Lincoln's assassin and other conspirators. This broadside was one of the first "Wanted" posters to use suspects' photographs; the picture of John Wilkes Booth, center, was one of the actor's publicity shots.

and 9:00 P.M. Sometime between 10:15 and 10:30 P.M., with the president's guard momentarily absent, Booth entered Lincoln's box and shot the president in the back of the head with a .44 caliber derringer. After slashing Major Rathbone with a knife, Booth leapt to the stage (breaking his leg in the effort), shouted *Sic semper tyrannis* ("Thus always to tyrants"), and escaped into a rear alley. At the same time, Booth's associate Lewis Paine (sometimes spelled "Payne") assaulted Secretary of State William Seward in his home, but failed to kill him.

The president, alive but unconscious, was carried across the street to a boarding house owned by William Petersen. At 7:22 the following morning, Abraham Lincoln died, reportedly prompting Secretary of War Edwin Stanton to utter, "Now he belongs to the ages." Lincoln's assassination plunged the nation into mourning. Memorial services were held throughout the Union as the president's funeral train made a thirteen-day trip to Springfield, Illinois. Hundreds of thousands of people turned out, even in the middle of the night, to pay their respects as the Lincoln Special passed by. While some in the South celebrated Lincoln's assassination, coming as it did after four years of bitter war, many of the most prominent Confederates expressed sadness at the news, recognizing that Lincoln's death did not bode well for the future of the rebellious states. Perhaps none felt the loss of Lincoln more than former slaves, who likened the president's fate to that of Moses, who was taken by God after being allowed to gaze on the Promised Land but was unable to enter it with the people he had led from slavery.

Immediately after Lincoln was shot, the government worked swiftly to capture Booth and his coconspirators. Hundreds were arrested and interviewed, and Booth and David Herold—who also had been in on the earlier kidnapping plot and had directed Paine to Seward's home—were tracked down and found hiding in a barn outside of Port Royal, Virginia. In the early hours of April 26, Federal troops surrounded the barn and ordered the pair to surrender. Herold complied, Booth refused, and the barn was set afire. Sergeant Boston Corbett, acting against orders, fired a single shot into the barn, mortally wounding Booth.

A military tribunal convened on May 10 to try those charged as accomplices in the assassination: Herold, Paine, Samuel Arnold, George Atzerodt (Booth had assigned him to kill Vice President Johnson), Michael O'Laughlin, Dr. Samuel Mudd (who set Booth's broken leg the day after the assassination and did not inform authorities that he had treated him), Edmund Spangler, and Mary Surratt (owner of the boarding house where Booth's cohorts, including her son, John, plotted the assassination). Each was convicted and Atzerodt, Herold, Paine, and Mary Surratt were hanged on July 7 at the Washington Arsenal prison (now Fort McNair). Arnold and O'Laughlin (who also were part of the kidnapping plot), Mudd, and Spangler received prison sentences. O'Laughlin died of yellow fever in 1867, but the others were pardoned by President Johnson in 1869. John Surratt, who fled the country after the assassination, was captured in Egypt in 1866 and returned to the United States for trial. He was freed a year after the jury deadlocked eight to fur in favor of acquittal.

SELECTED RESOURCES

The following titles are representative of published works pertaining to wartime politics. For additional information on published sources, see the annotated book list in Chapter 13, "Studying the War: Research and Preservation."

Bogue, Allan G. *The Congressman's Civil War.* New York: Cambridge University Press, 1989.

Cooper, William J. *Jefferson Davis, American.* New York: Alfred A. Knopf, 2000. Illustrated, maps.

Davis, William C. *An Honorable Defeat: The Last Days of the Confederate Government.* New York: Harcourt, 2001. Illustrated.

Foner, Eric. *Politics and Ideology in the Age of the Civil War.* New York: Oxford University Press, 1980.

Franklin, John Hope. *The Emancipation Proclamation.* Garden City: Doubleday, 1963.

Neely, Mark E. Jr. *The Fate of Liberty: Abraham Lincoln and Civil Liberties.* New York: Oxford University Press, 1991.

_____. *Southern Rights: Political Prisoners and the Myth of Confederate Constitutionalism.* Charlottesville: University Press of Virginia, 1999.

Paludan, Philip S. *The Presidency of Abraham Lincoln.* Lawrence: University Press of Kansas, 1994.

Tap, Bruce. *Over Lincoln's Shoulder: The Committee on the Conduct of the War.* Lawrence: University Press of Kansas, 1998. Illustrated.

Yearns, Buck, ed. *The Confederate Governors.* Athens: University of Georgia Press, 1985.

BATTLES AND THE BATTLEFIELD

"The art of war is simple enough," wrote Ulysses S. Grant. "Find out where your enemy is. Get at him as soon as you can. Strike at him as hard as you can and as often as you can, and keep moving on." When Grant became the Union's general in chief in March 1864, he also became the premier practitioner of the art of war as he defined it, pursuing Robert E. Lee's Army of Northern Virginia unrelentingly across Virginia while directing Union armies on other fronts to push hard as well. By then, Union and Confederate armies had been battling one another, in clashes of increasing size and viciousness, for nearly three years. At war's end, many thousands of encounters had occurred. They ranged from skirmishes to full-scale battles larger and bloodier than any ever fought on the American continent.

The great majority of these encounters took place in Southern states. The first shots of the war were fired at Fort Sumter, in the harbor of Charleston, South Carolina; by 1865, most Confederate states had felt the hard hand of war. Vicksburg, Mississippi; Petersburg, Virginia; and Chattanooga, Tennessee, had been ravaged by sieges. Many other Southern cities and towns, including much of Atlanta, Georgia; Columbia, South Carolina; Napoleon, Arkansas; Winton, North Carolina; and large sections of Jackson, Mississippi, had been devastated by fire.

The most unremittingly contested ground was in the northernmost Confederate state, Virginia. The first major Civil War battle was fought near Manassas Junction, at a stream called Bull Run. The state capital, Richmond, located less than 100 miles from Washington, D.C., became the capital city of the Confederacy in mid-1861, and was, from the beginning, a prime target of Union military campaigns. It was protected primarily by Robert E. Lee's Army of Northern Virginia, which, from 1862 on, formed the most obvious expression of Southern military power and was the focal

Photographer Timothy O'Sullivan recorded this Union "Council of War" at Massaponax Church, Virginia, May 21, 1864, in the midst of the Overland Campaign. Lieutenant General Ulysses S. Grant, at left, is examining a map held by Major General George G. Meade.

point for the hopes of Confederate civilians, many of whom were never far away from battlefields, were turned into refugees by battles, or faced life under Union occupation.

The Union's own territory was rarely threatened and little damaged by the war, but the North faced the daunting task of invading and then holding key sections of Southern territory comprising some 750,000 square miles of often difficult terrain. As Union forces moved south, they were opposed by more than regular Confederate States of America (C.S.A.) troops. Bands of partisan rangers and guerrillas, often aided by angry and bitter civilians, ambushed Union army stragglers, wrecked encampments, sniped at Federal columns, and menaced civilians suspected of Union sympathies. (In several states, Union sympathizers formed guerrilla bands. See "Shadow Warriors: Partisan Rangers, Guerrillas, and Spies" in Chapter 5, "The Armies.")

As the war expanded, the conciliatory strategy with which the North had begun the conflict—a strategy based on the assumption that substantial pro-Union sentiment in the South would help end the war quickly—evolved first into pragmatism (taking whatever strict measures were deemed militarily necessary), and then into the "hard war" policy that was employed earlier but was most rigorously exercised during the final two years of the war. All the militarily useful resources of the South were regarded, in 1864–1865, as acceptable targets. Southern civilians—no strangers to hardship since the war began—watched crops, businesses, railroads, livestock, and often their homes, disappear as battle-hardened Union troops, sometimes living off the land and always determined that Confederate forces should not be able to do the same, moved through their territory.

Political and societal battles, many of them revolving around slavery and emancipation, were being fought in the midst of the war's battlefield clashes. These home-front conflicts and pressures often had a profound impact on the military conduct of the war, even as the outcome of battles often helped determine political and diplomatic moves and civilian conduct. *"Forward to Richmond! Forward to Richmond!"* thundered headlines in Horace Greeley's influential New York *Tribune* as the war entered its fourth month. *"The Rebel Congress Must Not be Allowed to Meet There on the 20th of July. BY THAT DATE THE PLACE MUST BE HELD BY THE NATIONAL ARMY!"* Under pressure from such strident sentiments—and abiding by President Lincoln's hope that the war could be settled by a decisive display of Northern military power—General in Chief Winfield Scott dispatched Brigadier General Irvin McDowell, and troops McDowell felt were unready, into battle with Confederates at First Bull Run. The Northern troops were routed. In 1862, the Preliminary Emancipation Proclamation stayed in President Lincoln's desk drawer from July to September—a period of Union setbacks and disappointments—until a dearly purchased victory at Antietam made it possible for Lincoln to release this controversial and crucially important document. Newspaper accounts, in 1863, of Union army actions at Milliken's Bend, Mississippi; Port Hudson, Louisiana; and Fort Wagner, South Carolina, highlighted the valor of black troops in these engagements, increased their acceptance among white military personnel, and moved the abolition of slavery a giant step closer to realization. In 1864, near the time when Southern fighting spirit was aroused to a new pitch by reports of a Northern plot to assassinate Jefferson Davis and his cabinet (see "Kilpatrick-Dahlgren Raid on Richmond," on page 296), photographs of recently released and terribly emaciated prisoners of war were circulated in the North and caused a hardening of anti-Southern sentiment that was echoed in the evolving "hard war" policy on the battlefield. In that same year, the conquest of Atlanta by Major General William T. Sherman's army, and victories won by forces under Major General Philip Sheridan in the Shenandoah Valley, were decisive factors in the reelection of Abraham Lincoln.

This chapter provides an overview of the clash of armed forces from 1861 to 1865 and highlights the most important encounters—their aims and their reverberations. For this was not a war of generals and armies alone. It was four years of combat between two populations of stubbornly determined American people; the most costly and terrible of all American wars—an intricate, multifront contest that decided the future course of the nation.

The Theater of War

A *theater of war* has been defined as "the entire land, sea, and air area that is or may become involved directly in war operations." The theater of the American Civil War comprised much of the nation—plus the areas in which U.S. naval vessels and Confederate blockade runners and commerce raiders maneuvered on the high seas.

Within this broad expanse, there were several *theaters of operation*— specific areas in which military operations were actually carried out. The two main theaters of operation during the Civil War were the Eastern Theater and the Western Theater.

The Eastern Theater

Roughly comprising the area east of the Appalachian Mountains, in the vicinity of the rival capitals of Washington and Richmond, the Eastern Theater was the area in which Robert E. Lee's Army of Northern Virginia confronted the powerful Union Army of the Potomac, commanded, in turn, by George B. McClellan, Ambrose E. Burnside, Joseph Hooker, and George Gordon Meade. When Ulysses S. Grant became general in chief of all Union armies (March 1864), he made his headquarters with the Army of the Potomac and determined its movements (as well as supervising the movements of all other Federal forces), but General Meade was in command of the Army of the Potomac itself until the Confederate surrender at Appomattox. The U.S. Navy conducted raids and enforced the Union blockade along the Atlantic coast. Partisan rangers and guerrilla bands were active in this theater throughout the war. Stonewall Jackson, James Longstreet, Jubal A. Early, Joseph E. Johnston, and P. G. T. Beauregard were among the Confederate generals who held commands in this theater. (Johnston and Beauregard also saw duty in the Western Theater.) Crucial Eastern Theater battles included First and Second Bull Run, Antietam, Chancellorsville, and Gettysburg.

The Western Theater

Primarily regarded as the area between the western slope of the Appalachian Mountains and the Mississippi River, the Western Theater was the site of battles that brought Ulysses S. Grant and his most trusted and capable subordinate, William Tecumseh Sherman, into prominence. Naval engagements, primarily in concert with land operations, occurred on major rivers, and there was much guerrilla and partisan ranger activity. Braxton Bragg, Albert Sidney Johnston, Joseph E. Johnston, Nathan Bedford Forrest, and John Bell Hood were among the Confederate generals who held important commands in this theater. Crucial Western Theater battles included Shiloh, Chickamauga, Vicksburg, Atlanta, and Nashville.

Other Theaters of Operation

The Trans-Mississippi Theater

Comprising the area west of the Mississippi River, the Trans-Mississippi Theater was the site of some of the most vicious guerrilla fighting in the war. This was especially true in the adjacent states of Missouri and Kansas, where pro-Confederacy Missouri "bushwackers" and pro-Union Kansas "jayhawkers" wrought havoc on each other, the U.S. Army, and the civilian population. Guerrillas were also active in Louisiana, which was a divided state after New Orleans and its surrounding areas were captured by the Union in the spring of 1862. Shreveport, Louisiana, housed the headquarters for the Confederate Trans-Mississippi Department; New Orleans served as the base for many Union operations in the area, as well as for wartime Reconstruction programs. Among the important battles in this theater were

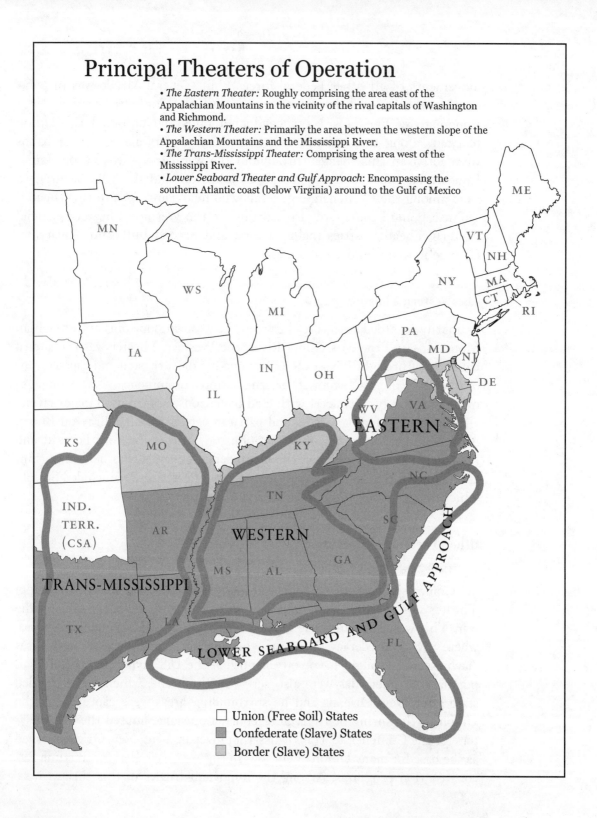

Principal Theaters of Operation

- *The Eastern Theater:* Roughly comprising the area east of the Appalachian Mountains in the vicinity of the rival capitals of Washington and Richmond.
- *The Western Theater:* Primarily the area between the western slope of the Appalachian Mountains and the Mississippi River.
- *The Trans-Mississippi Theater:* Comprising the area west of the Mississippi River.
- *Lower Seaboard Theater and Gulf Approach*: Encompassing the southern Atlantic coast (below Virginia) around to the Gulf of Mexico

EASTERN

WESTERN

TRANS-MISSISSIPPI

LOWER SEABOARD AND GULF APPROACH

IND. TERR. (CSA)

☐ Union (Free Soil) States
■ Confederate (Slave) States
■ Border (Slave) States

Wilson's Creek, Pea Ridge, and Mansfield. The last engagement of the Civil War took place at Palmito Ranch, near Brownsville, Texas.

THE LOWER SEABOARD AND GULF APPROACH

Encompassing the southern Atlantic coast (below Virginia) around to the Gulf of Mexico, this theater was the scene of the first volley of the war—at Fort Sumter, in Charleston Harbor—and of many other clashes aimed at controlling coastal defenses and Southern seaports. Important battles that occurred here included Fort Pulaski, New Orleans, Port Hudson, and Mobile Bay.

Every theater of operation encompassed *military departments*. For the Union, a military department was the basis of army organization in a geographical area, and a department name was usually applied to the military forces operating within each area. For example, the force operating within the Union's Department of the Tennessee was called the Army of the Tennessee—*not to be confused* with the Confederate Army of Tennessee, which operated in the same general area (see Chapter 5, "The Armies"). Union departments were changed and reorganized during the war. Territorial departments of the Confederacy were also created, discontinued, combined, and reformed according to the war's changing circumstances.

Significant Civil War Campaigns and Battles

Clashes between Union and Confederate forces ranged from skirmishes and limited bombardments to huge battles and months-long sieges. Most of these encounters took place in the course of *military campaigns*—a term defined by the present-day U.S. Department of Defense as "a series of related military operations aimed at accomplishing a strategic or operational objective within a given time and space." Significant campaigns and battles during each year of the Civil War are described here, in chronological order. The theater of operation in which each campaign or battle occurred is provided in *italic type*.

The "Battle Profiles" are adapted from Battle Summaries produced by the Civil War Sites Advisory Commission in its *Report on the Nation's Civil War Battlefields* (see Chapter 13, "Studying the War: Research and Preservation," for information on the Civil War Sites Advisory Commission and the American Battlefield Preservation Program). Often, battles were given different names by the opposing armies. When a battle is known by more than one name, the alternate name(s) is also provided.

Major Land Battles

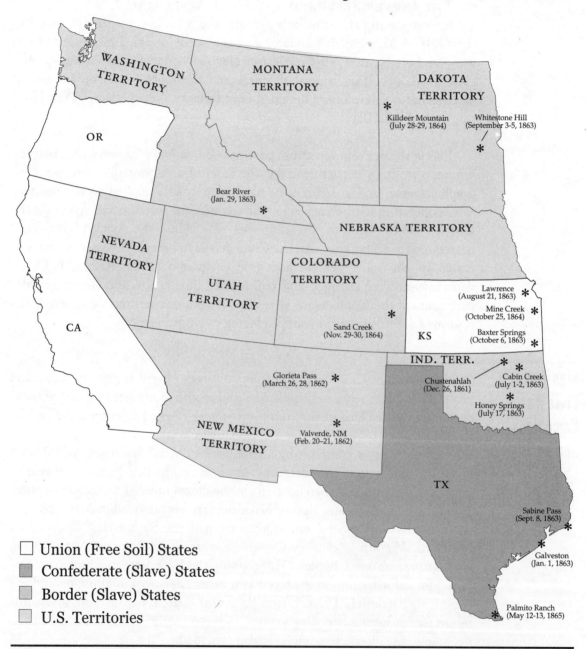

WASHINGTON TERRITORY

OR

MONTANA TERRITORY

DAKOTA TERRITORY

* Killdeer Mountain (July 28-29, 1864)

Whitestone Hill (September 3-5, 1863)
*

NEVADA TERRITORY

* Bear River (Jan. 29, 1863)

NEBRASKA TERRITORY

CA

UTAH TERRITORY

COLORADO TERRITORY

Lawrence (August 21, 1863) *

Mine Creek (October 25, 1864) *

* Sand Creek (Nov. 29-30, 1864)

KS

Baxter Springs (October 6, 1863) *

IND. TERR.

* *

NEW MEXICO TERRITORY

* Glorieta Pass (March 26, 28, 1862)

Chustenahlah (Dec. 26, 1861)

Cabin Creek (July 1-2, 1863)

* Honey Springs (July 17, 1863)

* Valverde, NM (Feb. 20–21, 1862)

TX

Sabine Pass (Sept. 8, 1863) *

* Galveston (Jan. 1, 1863)

□ Union (Free Soil) States
■ Confederate (Slave) States
■ Border (Slave) States
▨ U.S. Territories

* Palmito Ranch (May 12-13, 1865)

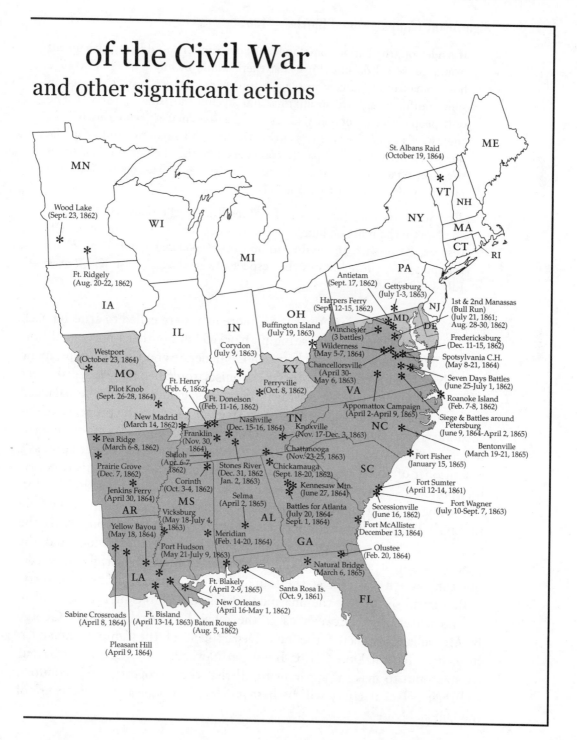

of the Civil War
and other significant actions

St. Albans Raid
(October 19, 1864)

ME

MN

VT

NH

Wood Lake
(Sept. 23, 1862)

WI

MI

NY

MA

CT

RI

IA

PA

Antietam
(Sept. 17, 1862)

Gettysburg
(July 1-3, 1863)

NJ

1st & 2nd Manassas
(Bull Run)
(July 21, 1861;
Aug. 28-30, 1862)

IL

IN

OH

Buffington Island
(July 19, 1863)

Harpers Ferry
(Sept. 12-15, 1862)

Winchester
(3 battles)

MD

DE

Fredericksburg
(Dec. 11-15, 1862)

Corydon
(July 9, 1863)

KY

Wilderness
(May 5-7, 1864)

Spotsylvania C.H.
(May 8-21, 1864)

Westport
(October 23, 1864)

MO

Ft. Henry
(Feb. 6, 1862)

Perryville
(Oct. 8, 1862)

Chancellorsville
(April 30-
May 6, 1863)

VA

Seven Days Battles
(June 25-July 1, 1862)

Pilot Knob
(Sept. 26-28, 1864)

Ft. Donelson
(Feb. 11-16, 1862)

Nashville
(Dec. 15-16, 1864)

TN

Knoxville
(Nov. 17-Dec. 3, 1863)

Appomattox Campaign
(April 2-April 9, 1865)

NC

Roanoke Island
(Feb. 7-8, 1862)

Siege & Battles around
Petersburg
(June 9, 1864-April 2, 1865)

New Madrid
(March 14, 1862)

Franklin
(Nov. 30,
1864)

Chattanooga
(Nov. 23-25, 1863)

Bentonville
(March 19-21, 1865)

Pea Ridge
(March 6-8, 1862)

Shiloh
(Apr. 6-7,
1862)

Stones River
(Dec. 31, 1862
Jan. 2, 1863)

Chickamauga
(Sept. 18-20, 1862)

SC

Fort Fisher
(January 15, 1865)

Prairie Grove
(Dec. 7, 1862)

Corinth
(Oct. 3-4, 1862)

Kennesaw Mtn.
(June 27, 1864)

Fort Sumter
(April 12-14, 1861)

Jenkins Ferry
(April 30, 1864)

AR

Selma
(April 2, 1865)

MS

Battles for Atlanta
(July 20, 1864-
Sept. 1, 1864)

AL

Secessionville
(June 16, 1862)

Fort Wagner
(July 10-Sept. 7, 1863)

Vicksburg
(May 18-July 4,
1863)

Fort McAllister
(December 13, 1864)

Yellow Bayou
(May 18, 1864)

Meridian
(Feb. 14-20, 1864)

GA

Olustee
(Feb. 20, 1864)

Port Hudson
(May 21-July 9, 1863)

Natural Bridge
(March 6, 1865)

LA

Ft. Blakely
(April 2-9, 1865)

Santa Rosa Is.
(Oct. 9, 1861)

FL

Sabine Crossroads
(April 8, 1864)

Ft. Bisland
(April 13-14, 1863)

New Orleans
(April 16-May 1, 1862)

Baton Rouge
(Aug. 5, 1862)

Pleasant Hill
(April 9, 1864)

Ft. Ridgely
(Aug. 20-22, 1862)

Significant Campaigns and Battles—1861

> If Anderson [the Union commander at Fort Sumter] would only give up, all would be well. I do not think that there would be any war. How strange how romantic life is now in Charleston! Almost every man is dressed in some uniform—all are so anxious and solemn, no balls or parties. The only people who as yet really suffer, are the dress makers, who usually have their hands full of ball dresses at this time. . . . The more I think of it, the more I feel the need of separate confederacies, and the north ought to let the south part in peace. . . . I wish the struggle was over!—Caroline Howard Gilman, letter to "Aunt Lala," January 11, 1861.

> The South must be made to feel *full* respect for the power and *honor* of the North: she must be humbled, but not debased by a forfeiture of self-respect, if we wish to retain our motto—*E pluribus unum*—and claim for the whole United States the respect of the world.—*New York Times*, July 1, 1861.

Even after war erupted in April 1861, more men were called to arms on each side, the Union began establishing its blockade of Southern ports, and limited engagements were fought between Confederate and Union troops, many in the North believed that Southern Unionists would bring the seceded states back into the Union if successful military engagements could be balanced with conciliatory policies. At this early stage of the war, the property of Secessionists and Southern sympathizers—including slaves—was often protected by Union troops. Even William T. Sherman, famous in later years as a practitioner of "total" or "hard war," adhered meticulously to this conciliatory policy, insisting that all property taken for Federal use must be paid for, and seeing to it that Union soldiers who stole or vandalized were punished. By the end of the year, hundreds of thousands of Americans were under arms, the Confederate States showed no inclination to rejoin the Union, and the Lincoln administration showed no inclination to admit their right to secede. But conciliation was still at the foundation of Northern military strategy: "[B]e careful so to treat the unarmed inhabitants as to contract, not widen, the breach existing between us & the rebels," General in Chief George B. McClellan instructed the new Department of the Ohio commander, Brigadier General Don Carlos Buell, on November 12. "It should be our constant aim to make it apparent to all that their property, their comfort, and their personal safety will be best preserved by adhering to the cause of the Union."

OPERATIONS IN THE CHARLESTON, SOUTH CAROLINA, HARBOR (JANUARY–APRIL 1861) *LOWER SEABOARD AND GULF APPROACH*

After the small Federal garrison at Charleston had moved from undefendable Fort Moultrie to the just completed and formidable Fort Sumter in Charleston Harbor, Southern forces, commanded by Brigadier General P. G. T. Beauregard, placed them under virtual siege, demanding they vacate the fort. Northern civilians came to regard the Federal soldiers as heroes, particularly their commander, Major Robert Anderson—who, in one of the ironies of the war, had been General Beauregard's much-respected artillery instructor. To the civilians and the military in the Confederacy, however, the Federal soldiers represented the Union's refusal to recognize the Southern states' right to secede. An unarmed merchant vessel, *Star of the West*, entering the harbor to bring reinforcements to Fort Sumter on January 9, was fired upon and forced to withdraw. In April, when the garrison was nearly out of provisions, President Lincoln's notice that he would resupply but not reinforce the fort incited the Confederate action that began the Civil War. The Charleston batteries opened fire on Fort Sumter April 12, and the fort returned fire on the Southern emplacements that were in range of their guns. No casualties resulted from this prolonged exchange of fire. After the fort's surrender, one Federal soldier was killed in an accidental explosion.

FORT PICKENS (JANUARY–OCTOBER 1861) *LOWER SEABOARD AND GULF APPROACH*

Located on Santa Rosa Island, off the Gulf Coast of Florida, Fort Pickens became a source of contention on January 10, the day Florida seceded from the Union. On that day, Lieutenant A. G. Slemmer moved the Federal garrison to the fort from Pensacola, which was threatened by approaching Confederate militia. Federal reinforcements arrived on April 12—the day Fort Sumter was fired upon. On October 9, a Confederate landing on Santa Rosa Island was unsuccessful. The fort stayed in Union hands throughout the war, and Pensacola was retaken May 10, 1862. The Union was thus able to keep Florida's coast and Confederate forts blockaded.

BLOCKADE OF THE CHESAPEAKE BAY (MAY–JUNE 1861) *EASTERN*

In this campaign, Union forces attempted to seize control of the vital waterways leading to the interior of Virginia, and the Confederacy sought to block access to Washington, D.C., via Chesapeake Bay and the Potomac River. Actions during this campaign included small engagements between Union gunboats and Confederate batteries at Sewell's Point, near Norfolk, Virginia (May 18–19, 1861) and at Aquia Creek, Virginia (May 29–June 1, 1861). The campaign culminated with what Union Colonel Joseph B. Carr later called "the disastrous *fight* at Big Bethel—battle we may scarcely term it" (Great Bethel, Bethel Church, Virginia; June 10, 1861). In this confused encounter, several Federal regiments—some dressed in gray uniforms that initially drew fire from other Union troops—were forced to withdraw after they had attacked Confederate positions. Though the clash had little lasting impact, it gave Southern confidence a boost and was an embarrassment to the Union. (Southern batteries were trained on the Potomac River in the fall of 1861, effectively inhibiting Union river traffic. These heavy guns were abandoned when Confederate General Joseph E. Johnston withdrew toward Richmond in March 1862, as McClellan was preparing to begin the Peninsula Campaign.)

OPERATIONS TO CONTROL MISSOURI (JUNE–OCTOBER 1861)
TRANS-MISSISSIPPI

With two proclaimed governments—one Unionist and one Secessionist—in Missouri, volunteers on both sides fought to gain military control of the state. Clashes during this campaign included:

- **Carthage (July 5, 1861):** Motley secessionist troops under Missouri governor Claiborne Jackson—a fiery proslavery Democrat who was deposed when he took his followers to the town of Neosho and formed a Confederate state "government"—met German-American troops under Union Brigadier General Franz Sigel and forced the Federals to retreat.

- **Wilson's Creek (Oak Hill, Springfield; August 10, 1861):** The major battle of the Civil War in Missouri, this fierce clash in which the Union commander, Brigadier General Nathaniel Lyon, was killed, pitted his 5,400 Federals against 11,000 Confederates under Brigadier General Ben McCulloch and Major General Sterling Price. The Union forces withstood repeated assaults, but after Lyon was killed, they retreated, leaving a huge section of Missouri under Confederate and prosecessionist sway. Coming less than a month after the Union defeat at First Bull Run (July 21; see page 246), this was another bitter setback for the North.

- **Lexington (September 12–20, 1861):** A nine-day siege of this northwestern Missouri town by Confederates under Major General Sterling Price, opposing greatly outnumbered Federals under Colonel James Mulligan (18,000 versus about 3,600), led to the surrender of the town when the Union department commander, Major General John C. Frémont, did not send the expected reinforcements. Although this was not a strategically important victory, it boosted Southern morale and was another blow to the North. The Confederates, however, soon withdrew from the town.

OPERATIONS IN WESTERN VIRGINIA (JUNE–DECEMBER 1861) *EASTERN*

While the Confederacy struggled to subdue Unionists in western Virginia—an area with relatively few slaves and substantial resistance to secession—Union forces sought to separate the area from the rest of the state and thus secure a protective buffer between Southern-held territory and vital east-west railroad lines in Maryland and Pennsylvania. Confederate failures in this campaign led to the formation of the state of West Virginia, which was admitted to the Union in 1863. The Union's successes, credited to Major General George B. McClellan, then headquartered in Cincinnati, Ohio, brought McClellan to national attention and paved the way for his subsequent appointment as Union general in chief. Actions in this campaign included:

- **Philippi, Western Virginia (June 3, 1861):** On one of two main routes through difficult mountainous terrain, Philippi was the scene of a minor skirmish when invading Federals, who had traveled through a rainy night, completely surprised and routed the Confederate garrison. The Confederates' speedy departure was headlined by the Northern press, which gleefully called the incident "the Philippi Races."

- **Rich Mountain, Western Virginia (July 11, 1861):** A Union force under Brigadier General William Rosecrans used an unguarded mountain path to cut off Confederates under Lieutenant Colonel John Pegram. More than 500 Confederate prisoners were taken, and the road was opened for a deeper Union incursion.

- **Cheat Mountain, Western Virginia (September 11–15, 1861):** On September 10, Federals under Rosecrans had forced Confederates to retreat south from Carnifix Ferry. The next day, General Robert E. Lee (not yet in command of the Army of Northern Virginia) split his troops into five columns and engaged in an unsuccessful five-day effort against the Union forces. His eventual withdrawal left the Union in firm control of the northern portion of Western Virginia and drew criticism from the Southern press, which dubbed the general "Granny Lee."

BULL RUN CAMPAIGN (MANASSAS, JULY 1861) *EASTERN*

Bowing to home-front pressures, Union General in Chief Winfield Scott sent Brigadier General Irvin McDowell and a poorly trained army into the war's first major battle. The intent was to push a sizable Confederate force, then in Virginia, within twenty-five miles of Washington, D.C., away from the Union capital. There was an assumption that a quick victory here—widely expected throughout the Union—would help bring the war to a speedy and favorable end. McDowell's troops, traveling very slowly, left Washington on July 16—a fact that Confederate President Davis learned quickly, by telegraph. Telegraph and railroads played key roles over the next four days—as they would throughout the war—as each side maneuvered its forces toward the battleground. In addition to the troops already converging

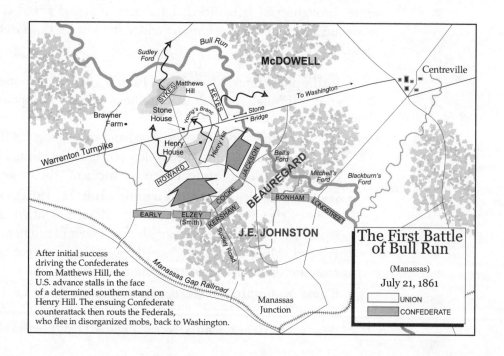

After initial success driving the Confederates from Matthews Hill, the U.S. advance stalls in the face of a determined southern stand on Henry Hill. The ensuing Confederate counterattack then routs the Federals, who flee in disorganized mobs, back to Washington.

The First Battle of Bull Run

(Manassas)

July 21, 1861

UNION
CONFEDERATE

on Manassas, these forces included 12,000 Confederates under General Joseph E. Johnston who were facing 18,000 Union troops under Major General Robert Patterson near Winchester, Virginia, some twenty-five miles to the northwest. Patterson proved a far less effective leader than Johnston, who was able to get his army to the battlefield in time to join with General P. G. T. Beauregard in defeating McDowell's Federals on July 21. Union troops first heard the unnerving "rebel yell" at First Bull Run, and Brigadier General Barnard Bee, who was later killed in the battle, bestowed the *nom de guerre* Stonewall on Brigadier General Thomas J. Jackson, whose troops were holding fast under a furious assault. Finally forced to retreat, the Union troops soon became mixed up with civilians who had come out from Washington to watch them gain victory, and an already confused situation turned into a rout. The humiliating loss at Bull Run sent shock waves through the Union, which, over the next few months, concentrated on organizing and training its armies. The failure by Johnston, Beauregard—and Jefferson Davis, who had traveled to Bull Run—to pursue the fleeing Union army and perhaps take Washington, incited criticism within the Confederacy at the time, and has remained a source of speculation. McDowell was relieved of command of the Union army and replaced by Major General George B. McClellan, who set about reorganizing and training troops—so successfully that in November, when seventy-five-year-old Winfield Scott retired, McClellan became general in chief of all Union armies.

BLOCKADE OF THE CAROLINA COAST (AUGUST–NOVEMBER 1861)
LOWER SEABOARD AND GULF APPROACH

Efforts to control the Southern coastline and close its numerous rivers and inlets to blockade runners began in August 1861, when the North began the long process of cutting off the Confederacy's access to foreign trade. These efforts included:

- **Hatteras Inlet Batteries (Forts Clark and Hatteras), South Carolina (August 28–29, 1861):** A Union amphibious expedition under Major General Benjamin Butler and Flag Officer Silas Stringham attacked and secured the batteries at this important haven for blockade runners. Some 670 Confederate prisoners were taken; one Union man was lost; and the Union had secured its first base of operations on the Carolina coast.

- **Battle of Port Royal Sound, South Carolina (November 7, 1861):**
A huge combined land-and-sea expedition under Union Brigadier General Thomas W. Sherman and navy Captain Samuel F. Du Pont attacked, captured, and began to secure the Hilton Head-Port Royal area, between Savannah, Georgia, and Charleston, South Carolina. Remaining in Union hands the rest of the war, this area became an important base for coaling and supplying blockaders. Port Royal also became a testing ground for educational and agricultural programs to assist freed slaves, some 10,000 of whom were left behind by their fleeing masters during this battle. The first Union regiment of freed slaves was recruited at Port Royal (see also Chapter 11, "Reconstruction and the Aftermath of the War"). An episode from this battle highlights the acutely rending nature of the Civil War. Commanding the leading U.S. warship, *Pocahontas*, which poured a determined and accurate fire into the forts protecting the Sound, was Commander Percival Drayton, a native of South Carolina. The troops his ship fired upon were under the command of his older brother, Confederate Brigadier General Thomas Fenwick Drayton.

BALL'S BLUFF (OCTOBER 21, 1861) *EASTERN*

Union forces under Colonel Edward D. Baker—an influential former Republican congressman and senator who was highly regarded by President Lincoln—engaged in what was to have been a diversionary maneuver while a larger Union force moved against Confederates encamped near Leesburg, Virginia. After climbing onto a high bluff overlooking the Potomac River, the Union soldiers met unexpectedly fierce opposition from Confederates under Brigadier General Nathan G. "Shanks" Evans, and were forced back over the edge of the bluff. More than half the brigade—including Baker—became casualties. Baker's death turned this encounter, which had limited military significance, into an event that had tremendous political repercussions. Coming just three months after the rout of Union troops at First Bull Run, it prompted the establishment of the Joint Committee on the Conduct of the War, which became a powerful U.S. congressional force throughout the conflict (see Chapter 3, "Wartime Politics").

BELMONT, MISSOURI (NOVEMBER 7, 1861) *TRANS-MISSISSIPPI*

Named for a town on the Mississippi River just opposite the bluffs of Columbus, Kentucky—a key Confederate stronghold—the large raid and reconnaissance of November 7 gave its leader, Brigadier General Ulysses S.

Grant, valuable operational and combat experience, though his force was repulsed with high casualties. A meeting between Grant and Confederate Brigadier General Benjamin F. Cheatham afterward, to discuss prisoner exchange, was characterized by the almost lighthearted cordiality that often marked such meetings during the early months of the war.

SIBLEY'S NEW MEXICO CAMPAIGN
(NOVEMBER 1861–MAY 1862) *TRANS-MISSISSIPPI*
Recently resigned from the U.S. Army, Confederate Brigadier General Henry Hopkins Sibley secured President Davis' approval for a grand plan to sweep the Federals from what is today New Mexico and Arizona and to open the door to California for the Confederates. Having raised a 3,700-man force of Texans, designated the Army of New Mexico, Sibley began the campaign in November. After some inconclusive fighting with Union troops under Colonel E. R. S. Canby at Fort Craig, and a successful engagement at Valverde (February 21, 1862), Sibley learned that the supplies he had anticipated securing at Albuquerque, and later at Santa Fe, had been destroyed by departing Union troops. About twenty miles from Santa Fe, Sibley's army was attacked by troops from nearby Fort Union. Although the Confederates initially considered the ensuing battle of Glorieta Pass (March 26–28, 1862) a victory, the destruction of their meager supplies by Union forces placed them in a difficult situation. When they were blocked by more troops as they approached Albuquerque, the Confederates retreated, reaching El Paso on May 4, their campaign a failure.

Significant Campaigns and Battles—1862

If I should tell you what our army has endured recently you could hardly believe it. Thousands of the men now have almost no clothes and no sign of a blanket nor any prospect of getting one, either. Thousands have had no shoes at all, and their feet are now entirely bare. Most of our marches were on graveled turnpike roads, which were very severe on the barefooted men and cut up their feet horribly. When the poor fellows could get rags they would tie them around their feet for protection. I have seen the men rob the dead of their shoes and clothing, but I cannot blame a man for doing a thing which is almost necessary in order to preserve his own life. I passed Goggans' body two days after he was killed at Manassas and there the poor fellow lay, robbed like all the others. (Do not say anything about this, for his family might hear of it.)—Dr. Spencer Glasgow Welch, Surgeon, Thirteenth South Carolina Volunteers, C.S.A.; letter, September 24, 1862.

When we arrived at Fredericksburg the sick were put in a barn near the river; here we found some cornstalks and made ourselves tolerably comfortable on them, with the addition of our blankets; but about midnight, after the battle, we were turned out of the barn into the field, as the barn was wanted for the badly wounded. We kept our cornstalks, however, and lay on the frozen ground two nights and one day. The field was covered all over with wounded men groaning and calling for water; some attempted to crawl on their bellies to the river side for a drop of water to relieve their thirst. In the course of two days these wounded men were carried away and we were put in the barn again; here we suffered terribly from the cold, as we had no way to warm ourselves.—Sergeant Warren H. Freeman, Thirteenth Regiment Massachusetts Volunteers, U.S.A.; letter, December 25, 1862.

The war exploded into full-scale combat in 1862. Union armies in the west made the earliest successful moves. Two forts crucial to the Confederate defensive line on the Tennessee and Cumberland Rivers were captured, thus opening those waterways for transport of troops and supplies deeper into the South. In the east, slower progress was made by Major General McClellan, who transported a huge force to the Virginia Peninsula in preparation for the first concerted Union movement against Richmond, the Confederate capital. In June, General Robert E. Lee replaced the wounded General Joseph E. Johnston as commander of the army that opposed McClellan's advance. Lee was soon leading the newly christened Army of Northern Virginia in campaigns that placed it at the center of the Confederate military endeavor. In the Gulf of Mexico region, New Orleans—the Confederacy's largest and most cosmopolitan city—fell to U.S. forces with relatively little resistance; but later in the year, farther north on the Mississippi River, the first Union campaign to take the strategically crucial riverside bastion of Vicksburg ended in failure. Battles grew larger, more ferocious, and bloodier—none more so than the clash, during Lee's first invasion of the North, at Antietam, Maryland, on September 17, the costliest single day of the war. The Union victory at Antietam made it possible for President Lincoln to issue the Preliminary Emancipation Proclamation (September 22). Coming after passage of the Militia Act and the Second Confiscation Act (both enacted on July 17; see Chapter 3, "Wartime Politics"), which empowered the president to employ African Americans to help suppress the rebellion, the proclamation heralded the widening of Union war aims to embrace the abolition of slavery as well as the restoration of the Union.

The battles of Fredericksburg, Virginia, and Stones River (Murfreesboro), Tennessee, ended the year—the first a Union disaster, the second a marginal Union victory. "The year closes less favorably than I had hoped and expected," wrote U.S. Secretary of the Navy Gideon Welles in December. "We have had some misfortunes, and a lurking malevolence exists toward us among nations, that could not have been anticipated. Worse than this, the envenomed, relentless, and unpatriotic spirit of party paralyzes and weakens the hand of the Government and country." In a camp on the Rappahannock River, in Virginia, Confederate surgeon Spencer Glasgow Welch wrote to his wife on December 28: "Our army was in better fighting trim at the battle of Fredericksburg than at any time since the war began, and it is still in the same condition. It does not seem possible to defeat this army now with General Lee at its head."

THE UNION OFFENSIVE IN EASTERN KENTUCKY (JANUARY 1862) *WESTERN*

Victories at Middle Creek (January 10; the Confederates also claimed this engagement as a victory) and Mill Springs (Logan's Cross Roads, January 19) cemented Union control of eastern Kentucky until Confederate Major General Braxton Bragg launched his offensive in the summer. Confederate Brigadier General Felix K. Zollicoffer was killed at Mill Springs.

UNION GENERAL AMBROSE BURNSIDE'S NORTH CAROLINA EXPEDITION (FEBRUARY–JUNE 1862) *LOWER SEABOARD AND GULF APPROACH*

Step by step, the Union extended its control of the Carolina coast inland, denying many vital waterways to blockade runners. The loss of Roanoke Island (February 8) was a severe blow to Southern morale, and the fall of New Bern, North Carolina (March 14), deprived the South of the second of its ten deep-water seaports with inland rail connections.

FEDERAL PENETRATION UP THE CUMBERLAND AND TENNESSEE RIVERS (FEBRUARY–JUNE 1862) *WESTERN*

In this campaign, under the overall direction of Department of the Missouri commander Major General Henry W. Halleck, two important victories—the capture of the Confederacy's Fort Henry (February 6) and Fort Donelson (February 16)—brought Major General Ulysses S. Grant a new nickname ("Unconditional Surrender") and public acclaim. But his reputation suffered a setback when his army was unprepared for the first day of the battle of Shiloh (April 6–7)—against combined Confederate forces that had been shifted to the area via railroad. (The Federals recovered and gained a victory on day two.) When the important railroad center of Corinth, Mississippi, was secured (May 30), the stage was set for Union campaigns against Vicksburg.

Battle Profile: Shiloh (Pittsburg Landing), Hardin County, Tennessee (April 6–7, 1862) *Western*

Campaign: Federal penetration up the Cumberland and Tennessee Rivers.

Principal commanders: Major General Ulysses S. Grant and Major General Don Carlos Buell (U.S.A.); General Albert Sidney Johnston and General P. G. T. Beauregard (C.S.A.).

Forces engaged: Army of the Tennessee and Army of the Ohio (U.S.A. 65,085); Army of the Mississippi (C.S.A. 44,968).

Estimated casualties: 23,746 total (U.S.A. 13,047; C.S.A. 10,699).

Description: After the fall of Forts Henry and Donelson, Confederate General Albert Sidney Johnston was forced to fall back, giving up Kentucky and much of West and Middle Tennessee. He chose Corinth, Mississippi, a major transportation center, as the staging area for an offensive against Major General Ulysses S. Grant and his Army of the Tennessee before the Army of the Ohio, under Major General Don Carlos Buell, could join it. It took Grant, with about 40,000 men, some time to mount a southern offensive along the Tennessee River. Having received orders to await Buell's Army of the Ohio at Pittsburg Landing, Grant failed to fortify his position; rather, he set about drilling his men, many of whom were raw recruits. When Johnston's Confederates attacked on the morning of April 6, many Union troops were routed, but some made determined stands. By afternoon, the Federals had established a battle line at a sunken road in a densely wooded thicket, a position that became known as the "Hornets' Nest" when repeated Southern attacks were repulsed by heavy Union fire. (Johnston, directing the attacks, was wounded in midafternoon and rapidly bled to death; Beauregard assumed command.) Eventually, massed artillery (sixty-two cannon) helped the Confederates to turn the tide. Although overcome, with heavy casualties, the Union defenders at the Hornets' Nest, under the command of Brigadier General Benjamin M. Prentiss, had bought

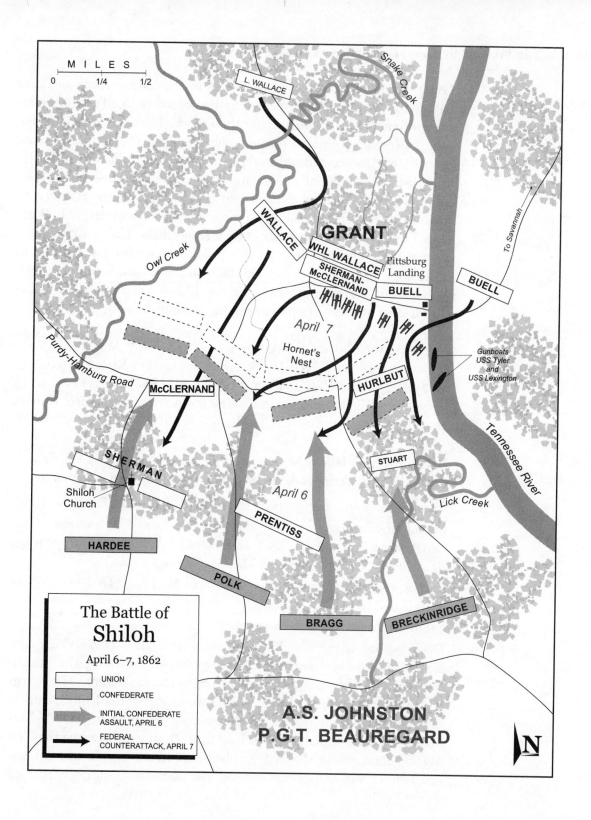

The Battle of
Shiloh

April 6–7, 1862

UNION

CONFEDERATE

INITIAL CONFEDERATE
ASSAULT, APRIL 6

FEDERAL
COUNTERATTACK, APRIL 7

MILES

0   1/4   1/2

Snake Creek

L. WALLACE

Owl Creek

WALLACE

GRANT

WHL WALLACE

SHERMAN-
McCLERNAND

Pittsburg
Landing

BUELL

To Savannah

BUELL

April 7

Hornet's
Nest

HURLBUT

Gunboats
USS Tyler
and
USS Lexington

Purdy-Hamburg Road

McCLERNAND

SHERMAN

Shiloh
Church

STUART

April 6

Lick Creek

Tennessee River

PRENTISS

HARDEE

POLK

BRAGG

BRECKINRIDGE

A.S. JOHNSTON
P.G.T. BEAUREGARD

N

Grant valuable time to bring his troops into a defensive line anchored with artillery and soon augmented by the arrival of Buell's men. Fighting continued until after dark, but the Federals held. By the next morning, the combined Federal forces numbered about 60,000, versus fewer than 40,000 Confederates. Beauregard, unaware of the arrival of Buell's army, launched an initially successful counterattack in response to a two-mile advance by William Nelson's division of Buell's army at 6:00 A.M. Union troops stiffened and began forcing the Confederates back. Beauregard ordered a counterattack, which stopped the Union advance but did not break its battle line. At this point, Beauregard realized that he could not win, and he retired from the field and headed back to Corinth. An ominous portent of things to come, Shiloh caused more casualties than had all of America's previous wars, combined.

Joint Army/Navy Operations against New Madrid, Missouri, Island No. 10 in the Mississippi River, and Memphis, Tennessee (February–June 1862) *Western*

Incremental Federal success in moving down river from Cairo, Illinois, increased the Union's control of the Mississippi River.

Battle Profile: Island No. 10, City of New Madrid, Missouri; Lake County, Tennessee (February 28–April 8, 1862) *Western*

Campaign: Joint operations on the Middle Mississippi River.

Principal commanders: Brigadier General John Pope and navy Captain Andrew H. Foote (U.S.A.); Brigadier General John P. McCown and Brigadier General William W. Mackall (C.S.A.).

Forces engaged: Army of the Mississippi (U.S.A.); Garrisons of New Madrid and Island No. 10 (C.S.A.).

Estimated casualties: Unknown.

Description: Island No. 10, about sixty river miles below Columbus, Kentucky, was the Confederate strongpoint for defending the Mississippi River. Nearby was New Madrid, one of the weak points. On February 28, Brigadier General John Pope, commander of the Union Army of the Mississippi, set out from Commerce, Missouri, to attack New Madrid. The force marched overland through swamps, reached the New Madrid outskirts on March 3, and laid siege to the city. Brigadier General John P. McCown, commander of the garrison defending both New

Madrid and Island No. 10, launched a sortie, under Brigadier General M. Jeff Thompson, Missouri State Guard, against the besiegers and brought up heavy artillery. On March 13, the Confederates bombarded the Yankees, to no avail. Because it did not appear possible to defend New Madrid, the Confederate gunboats and troops evacuated to Island No. 10 and Tiptonville. On March 14, Pope's army discovered that New Madrid was deserted and moved in to occupy it. On March 15, a U.S. Navy flotilla, under the command of Captain Andrew H. Foote, arrived upstream from Island No. 10. The ironclad *Carondelet*, on the night of April 4, passed the Island No. 10 batteries and anchored off New Madrid. The *Pittsburgh* followed on the night of April 6. The ironclads helped to overawe the Confederate batteries and guns, enabling Pope's men to cross the river and block the Confederates' escape route. Brigadier General William W. Mackall, who replaced McCown, surrendered Island No. 10 on April 8. The Mississippi was now open down to Fort Pillow, Tennessee.

BATTLE OF PEA RIDGE, ARKANSAS (MARCH 1862)
TRANS-MISSISSIPPI

A Union campaign, led by Major General Samuel R. Curtis, to drive Confederates, led by Major General Sterling Price, out of Missouri pushed Price into northwestern Arkansas, where he joined with forces under Brigadier General Ben McCulloch. Overall command was assumed by Major General Earl Van Dorn, then commander of the Confederate Trans-Mississippi Department, who determined to attack the Federals. Learning of the Confederate approach, Curtis set his army in defensive positions at Pea Ridge, Arkansas, near the town of Bentonville. The ensuing Confederate defeat (battle of Pea Ridge, or Elkhorn Tavern, March 7–8) left Missouri securely in Union hands for more than two years.

PENINSULA CAMPAIGN (MARCH–JULY 1862) *EASTERN*

Increasingly concerned by General in Chief George B. McClellan's reluctance to employ the now powerful and well-organized Army of the Potomac on the battlefield, President Lincoln issued War Order No. 3 on March 13, relieving McClellan as general in chief, but leaving him in command of the Department and Army of the Potomac—a move ostensibly taken to ease McClellan's burden of command as he prepared for the first major Union attempt to take the Confederate capital of Richmond, Virginia.

On March 17, McClellan began embarking his army on what would become known as the Peninsula Campaign. Rejecting the possible overland routes, he transported the Army of the Potomac—some 105,000 men, in all—by ship to Fort Monroe, Virginia. From there, they would move on Richmond via the James River Peninsula.

The campaign began with the siege of Yorktown, Virginia (April 5– May 3), which McClellan considered too strong to carry with a single assault. In fact, Confederate General John B. Magruder was holding the Southern defensive line with only 17,000 men. (He kept them in motion, so that they would seem more numerous.) After Magruder withdrew, McClellan proceeded, slowly, up the peninsula—which was muddy and difficult to maneuver in as a result of heavy spring rains. A battle at Williamsburg (May 5) resulted in a further Confederate withdrawal, which left the easternmost portion of Virginia in Union hands. Among the consequences of Norfolk's fall to the Union (May 9) was the destruction of the ironclad C.S.S. *Virginia* (better known as the *Merrimack*). In the first battle of Drewry's Bluff (May 15), Union naval vessels (including the celebrated U.S.S. *Monitor*) attempted a close approach to Richmond via the James River but were halted by river obstructions and shore battery fire. By May 31, however, the Army of the Potomac had pushed the Confederates, under Joseph E. Johnston, back to the Richmond suburbs. While leading an attack on two isolated Union corps at Seven Pines (Fair Oaks, Fair Oaks Station; May 31–June 1), Johnston was wounded, and Robert E. Lee assumed command. On June 12, Lee dispatched cavalry, under the command of Brigadier General Jeb Stuart, on a reconnaissance mission that became Stuart's famous ride completely around the Union army. Along the way, he destroyed supplies, took prisoners, and gained much information.

After formulating a bold plan—the hallmark of his Civil War leadership—Lee embarked on an offensive that initiated the series of battles now known as the Seven Days (June 25–July 1). After a brief engagement at Oak Grove (French's Field; King's School House; the Orchard; June 25), the Seven Days began in earnest with the battle of Mechanicsville (Beaver Dam Creek, Ellerson's Mill; June 26) and an encounter at Gaines' Mill (June 27), where McClellan, operating on the mistaken belief that his force was heavily outnumbered, determined to "save this army" and began a withdrawal. Clashes subsequently occurred at Savage's Station (Peach Orchard; June 29), White Oak Swamp (Charles City Cross Roads; Frayser's Farm; Glendale; Nelson's Cross Roads; New Market Road; Turkey Bridge; Willis' Church;

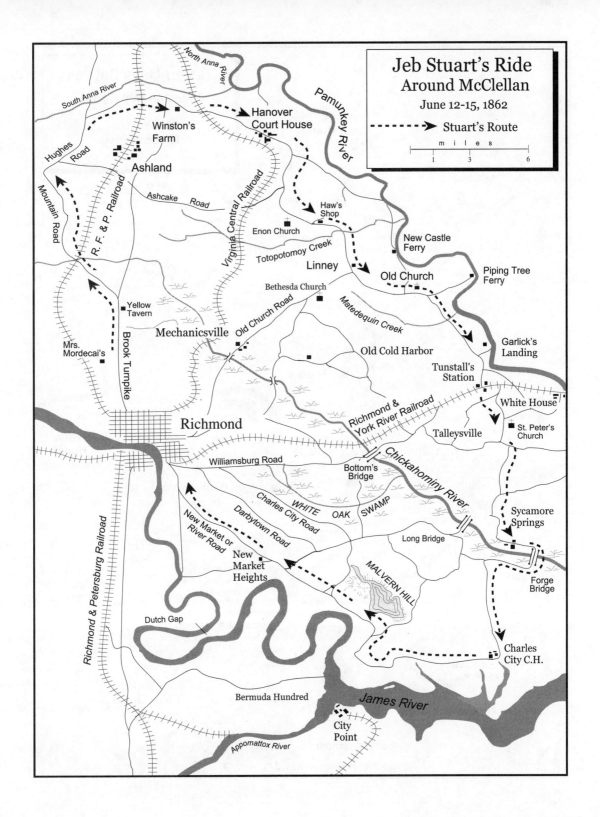

Jeb Stuart's Ride
Around McClellan
June 12–15, 1862

- - - → Stuart's Route

miles
1   3   6

North Anna River

South Anna River

Pamunkey River

Hughes Road

Winston's Farm

Hanover Court House

Ashland

Ashcake Road

Mountain Road

R. F. & P. Railroad

Virginia Central Railroad

Haw's Shop

Enon Church

New Castle Ferry

Totopotomoy Creek

Linney

Old Church

Piping Tree Ferry

Yellow Tavern

Bethesda Church

Old Church Road

Matedequin Creek

Garlick's Landing

Mrs. Mordecai's

Mechanicsville

Old Cold Harbor

Tunstall's Station

Brook Turnpike

Richmond & York River Railroad

White House

Talleysville

St. Peter's Church

Richmond

Williamsburg Road

Bottom's Bridge

Chickahominy River

Charles City Road

WHITE OAK SWAMP

Sycamore Springs

Darbytown Road

New Market or River Road

New Market Heights

Long Bridge

MALVERN HILL

Forge Bridge

Dutch Gap

Richmond & Petersburg Railroad

Charles City C.H.

Bermuda Hundred

James River

City Point

Appomattox River

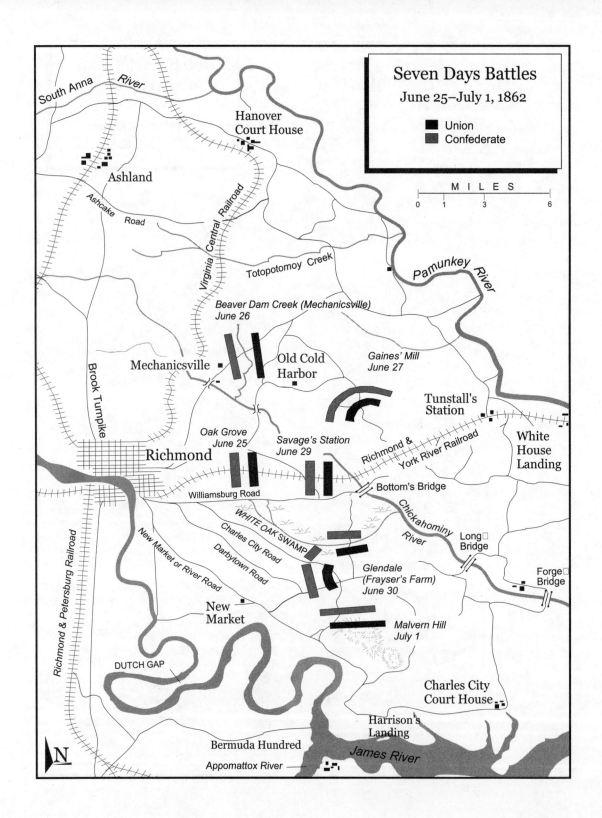

Seven Days Battles
June 25–July 1, 1862

■ Union
■ Confederate

MILES
0   1   3   6

South Anna River

Hanover Court House

Ashland

Ashcake Road

Virginia Central Railroad

Totopotomoy Creek

Pamunkey River

Beaver Dam Creek (Mechanicsville)
June 26

Brook Turnpike

Mechanicsville

Old Cold Harbor

Gaines' Mill
June 27

Tunstall's Station

White House Landing

Oak Grove
June 25

Richmond

Savage's Station
June 29

Richmond & York River Railroad

Williamsburg Road

Bottom's Bridge

WHITE OAK SWAMP

Chickahominy River

Long Bridge

Charles City Road

Darbytown Road

New Market or River Road

Glendale
(Frayser's Farm)
June 30

Forge Bridge

Richmond & Petersburg Railroad

New Market

Malvern Hill
July 1

DUTCH GAP

Charles City Court House

Harrison's Landing

Bermuda Hundred

Appomattox River

James River

N

June 30), and Malvern Hill (Crew's Farm; Poindexter's Farm; July 1), where Union artillery wrought terrible havoc on attacking Confederates, though McClellan continued his withdrawal. The Seven Days marked the effective end of the Peninsula Campaign, which had failed in its objective.

In the North, belief that the war would not last much longer faded, and President Lincoln's dissatisfaction with McClellan's cautious approach to battle increased. Lee had failed to destroy or severely damage the Army of the Potomac, but his aggressive tactics and his success in holding off a superior force formed the foundation of the faith the Southern people would have in him, and his army, throughout the war.

STONEWALL JACKSON'S SHENANDOAH VALLEY CAMPAIGN (MARCH–JUNE 1862) *EASTERN*

In this brilliant series of maneuvers and battles, Jackson diverted troops that had been designated to reinforce McClellan's army on the Virginia Peninsula and established, in the North, his reputation as a nearly invincible foe. Suggested by Robert E. Lee just before he assumed command of the Army of Northern Virginia, the Valley Campaign began with a tactical defeat at the battle of Kernstown (March 23), but it quickly developed into one of

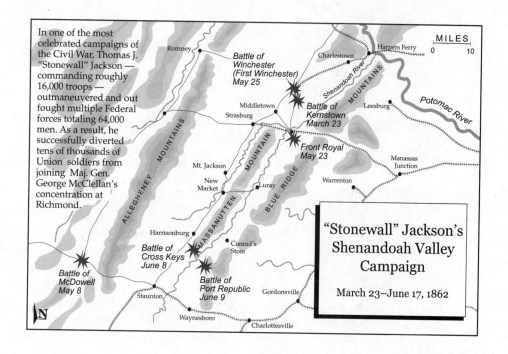

In one of the most celebrated campaigns of the Civil War, Thomas J. "Stonewall" Jackson — commanding roughly 16,000 troops — outmaneuvered and outfought multiple Federal forces totaling 64,000 men. As a result, he successfully diverted tens of thousands of Union soldiers from joining Maj. Gen. George McClellan's concentration at Richmond.

"Stonewall" Jackson's Shenandoah Valley Campaign

March 23–June 17, 1862

General Thomas J. (Stonewall) Jackson and his staff, photographed in Richmond by the firm of Vannerson & Jones, conducted the now-legendary Shenandoah Valley Campaign of 1862. Jackson's map maker, Jedediah Hotchkiss, is shown near the top on the left.

military history's greatest strategic campaigns. After engaging in a clever ruse (marching half his command *out* of the Valley, then rushing them back via railroad), Jackson defeated Union forces at the battle of McDowell (May 8), the action at Front Royal (May 23), the first battle of Winchester (May 25—a defeat that caused near panic in some parts of the North), Cross Keys (June 8), and Port Republic (June 9). His men marched so often and so far during this campaign, they became known as "Jackson's Foot Cavalry." And Jackson himself emerged from the Shenandoah Valley—eluding converging Union forces sent to defeat him—the foremost hero of the Confederacy.

Operations against Fort Pulaski, Georgia (April 1862)
Lower Seaboard and Gulf Approach

Located on an island at the mouth of the Savannah River, where it guarded Savannah, Georgia, from ocean attack, Fort Pulaski was occupied by Georgia troops in January 1861. Regarded as impregnable because of its thick brick walls and its island site, the fort nevertheless became an early Union target. In February 1862, a U.S. Army expedition led by Captain Quincy A. Gillmore established itself on nearby Tybee Island. By April 10, the Federals were prepared to begin their attempt to shatter the fort's formidable walls with rifled cannon (see Chapter 6, "Weaponry"). When the fort's defenders refused to surrender, the Union bombardment began. Five hours later, the cannons had cut a breach. On April 11, shells were getting through to the fort's magazine, and the Confederate commander, Colonel Charles H. Olmstead, surrendered. Without its defensive fortification, Savannah was no longer an effective port for Confederate blockade runners.

The Expedition to, and Capture of, New Orleans (April–May 1862)
Lower Seaboard and Gulf Approach

The Confederacy's first major defeat was the seizure of its largest city, the vital and cosmopolitan port city of New Orleans. The event was almost inevitable following the passage, on April 24, of the city's primary defensive forts, Jackson and St. Philip, near the mouth of the Mississippi River, by a naval squadron under the command of Union Captain David G. Farragut. This hair-raising nighttime adventure, at least as daunting as Farragut's 1864 conquest of Mobile Bay (see page 313), was described by Bradley Osbon, an officer on Farragut's flagship, U.S.S. *Hartford*, who was also a newspaper correspondent:

We were struck now on all sides. A shell entered our starboard beam, cut our cable, wrecked our armory and exploded at the main hatch, killing one man instantly and wounding several more. Another entered the muzzle of a gun, breaking the lip and killing the sponger who was in the act of "ramming home." A third entered the boatswain's room, destroying everything in its path and, exploding, killed a colored servant who was passing powder.

The squadron arrived at New Orleans on April 25 and received something less than a warm welcome from the residents. Beyond a voice protest, however, they could do little because all major Confederate armies were occupied elsewhere. "The crowds on the levee howled and screamed with rage," young citizen George Washington Cable would later write. "The swarming decks answered never a word; but one old tar on the *Hartford*, standing with lanyard in hand beside a great pivot-gun, so plain to view that you could see him smile, silently patted its big black breach and blandly grinned." After the mayor declined the honor of surrendering the city, Farragut sent marines in to raise the American flag on April 29. On May 1, Major General Benjamin F. Butler's army arrived to begin an eventful occupation. The easy fall of New Orleans was a severe blow to Southern morale.

OPERATIONS AT VICKSBURG, MISSISSIPPI, BATON ROUGE, LOUISIANA, AND FORTIFICATION OF PORT HUDSON (JUNE–AUGUST 1862) *WESTERN*

An unsuccessful sixty-seven-day attempt to take the Confederate Mississippi River bastion of Vicksburg by naval assault (May 18–July 24) convinced Admiral David Farragut, in command of the expedition, that Vicksburg would have to be taken by land. Moving back toward New Orleans, Farragut's Mississippi River flotilla landed a 3,200-man force at the former Louisiana capital of Baton Rouge. The city had been under Union control since the state government had evacuated it in late April, when New Orleans was about to fall (Baton Rouge officially surrendered to Union naval forces on May 9). But, even as Farragut landed the Union garrison troops, Confederate Major General Earl Van Dorn was moving to retake Baton Rouge, hoping thereby to break the Union blockade of the mouth of the Red River and perhaps even to recapture New Orleans. Major General John C. Breckinridge commanded the Confederate force (reduced in strength due to sickness) that, on August 5, assaulted the Federal troops (many of whom had also contracted fever) at Baton Rouge. Many of the city's citizens became refugees because of the battle; others, incensed by Union actions against their city—which had included a bombardment in late May, after guerrillas had fired on Union sailors—joined Southern soldiers in attacking the Union garrison. Though the Federals were hard pressed, the Confederates were forced to withdraw. (They scuttled their damaged ironclad ram C.S.S. *Arkansas*, which had been a thorn in Farragut's side at Vicksburg.) The Federals evacuated Baton Rouge on August 21 and returned to New Orleans. The Confederates, meanwhile, established themselves in Port Hudson, some twenty-five miles up the Mississippi, where they constructed such formidable defenses that, in the following year, two direct assaults against them by a vastly superior Union force would fail (see page 281). On December 17, 1862, another Federal force—8,000 men under Brigadier General Cuvier Grover—arrived in Baton Rouge, and the city remained firmly in Federal hands for the rest of the war.

CONFEDERATE HEARTLAND OFFENSIVE
(AUGUST–OCTOBER 1862) *WESTERN*

Deeply divided when the war began, the border state of Kentucky remained officially in the Union. (The Confederacy also claimed the state and added a star to its flag to represent it. About 25,000 Kentucky men fought for the South, and nearly 76,000 fought for the North.) In August, Confederate armies led by Major General Edmund Kirby Smith and, in overall command, General Braxton Bragg, moved into the state in an attempt to draw Union forces out of Tennessee; recruit Kentuckians for the Confederacy; and, if possible, encourage a popular uprising for the Confederacy. On August 29–30, Smith's army engaged Federals under Major General William Nelson at Richmond, Kentucky, and forced the Federals to retreat toward Louisville. On September 14–17, another Confederate success followed: the brief siege and capture of Munfordville. (Union forces reoccupied Munfordville on September 21.) Soon thereafter, Union and Confederate forces clashed at Perryville (battle of Perryville, Chaplin Hills, October 8)—a somewhat disjointed battle in which only portions of each force were engaged. Deemed at least a partial Union victory, this battle, the largest fought in Kentucky, precipitated what many in the South considered a premature Confederate withdrawal to Tennessee. Though some Union forces had been drawn out of Tennessee, Bragg's overall failure in this campaign caused waves of disappointment throughout the Confederacy. Despite criticism of the general from some in the government, President Davis left him in command of the Confederacy's Western Department. Union commander Don

Carlos Buell's failure to pursue Bragg aggressively, however, resulted in Buell's removal from command.

SECOND BULL RUN (MANASSAS) CAMPAIGN (AUGUST 9–SEPTEMBER 1, 1862) *EASTERN*

After defeating McClellan on the Virginia Peninsula, Robert E. Lee rapidly shifted his army north and west, to strike against the newly organized Federal Army of Virginia, commanded by John Pope. Smaller than the Army of the Potomac, Pope's force might more easily be pushed back, thus allowing the Confederates to recover lost territory and supplies and more effectively secure the area north of Richmond, with its vital railroads to the Shenandoah Valley. The first encounter of the campaign occurred when elements of the North's Army of Virginia, some 9,000 men under Nathaniel Banks, met 24,000 Confederates under Stonewall Jackson at Cedar Mountain (August 9) and were defeated after a hard-fought battle. Jackson's "foot cavalry" then made one of the great marches of the war (August 25–26) covering fifty miles around Pope's flank to seize the Federal supply depot at Manassas Junction. The campaign culminated in Pope's humiliating defeat at Second Bull Run (Second Manassas, August 29–30), which caused recriminations among Northern politicians and military officers. (Pope accused General McClellan of not reinforcing him promptly or adequately.) Meanwhile, Lee continued his march northward, toward Union territory.

Battle Profile: Second Bull Run (Second Manassas, Manassas Plains, Groveton, Gainesville, Brawner's Farm), Prince William County, Virginia (August 28–30, 1862) *Eastern*

Campaign: Second Bull Run (Manassas) Campaign.

Principal commanders: Major General John Pope (U.S.A.); General Robert E. Lee, Major General Thomas J. Jackson, and Major General James Longstreet (C.S.A.).

Forces engaged: Army of Northern Virginia (C.S.A.); Army of Virginia and units of the Army of the Potomac (U.S.A.).

Estimated casualties: 22,180 total (U.S.A. 13,830; C.S.A. 8,350).

Description: To draw Pope's army into battle, Jackson ordered an attack on a Federal column that was passing across his front on the Warrenton Turnpike on August 28. The fighting at Brawner's Farm lasted several hours and resulted in a stalemate. Pope, convinced that he had trapped Jackson, concentrated the bulk of his army against him. On

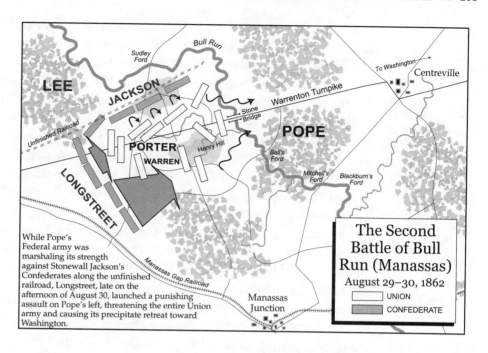

While Pope's Federal army was marshaling its strength against Stonewall Jackson's Confederates along the unfinished railroad, Longstreet, late on the afternoon of August 30, launched a punishing assault on Pope's left, threatening the entire Union army and causing its precipitate retreat toward Washington.

The Second Battle of Bull Run (Manassas)
August 29–30, 1862
☐ UNION
■ CONFEDERATE

August 29, Pope launched a series of assaults against Jackson's position along an unfinished railroad grade. The attacks were repulsed with heavy casualties on both sides. At noon, Confederate Major General James Longstreet and his troops arrived on the field from Thoroughfare Gap and took a position on Jackson's right flank. On August 30, Pope renewed his attacks, seemingly unaware that Longstreet was now on the field. When massed Confederate artillery devastated a Union assault by Fitz John Porter's command, Longstreet's wing of 28,000 men counterattacked in the largest simultaneous mass assault of the war. The Union left flank was crushed and the army was driven back to Bull Run. Only an effective Union rearguard action prevented a replay of the First Manassas disaster. Pope's retreat to Centreville was precipitous, nonetheless.

ANTIETAM CAMPAIGN (MARYLAND CAMPAIGN, SEPTEMBER 4–22, 1862) *EASTERN*

In Lee's first invasion of the North, he moved his army across the Potomac (September 4) hoping to secure supplies, acquire thousands of Maryland recruits (though it remained in the Union, Maryland was a slave state and had many Southern sympathizers), encourage European recognition of the

Confederacy, and demoralize the Union into suing for peace. As he moved into Maryland, Lee divided his force, sending two of his four columns to Harpers Ferry, to surround and capture the 12,000-man Union garrison there, which would otherwise threaten his rear. (Harpers Ferry fell to Stonewall Jackson's Confederates on September 15; 12,000 prisoners, and many weapons, were taken.) Major General George B. McClellan, whose Union force was pursuing Lee, became aware of the division of Lee's forces when a Union private, Barton W. Mitchell, came across a copy of Lee's orders, intended for Major General D. H. Hill. The document was wrapped around three cigars and left in a field recently occupied by Hill's division. This knowledge should have enabled McClellan to deal Lee a decisive defeat by moving against each element of Lee's divided forces in turn. But McClellan was characteristically overcautious in responding to this stroke of luck, and Lee was able to effectively block McClellan's slow response for a time sufficient to reconcentrate his forces (battles of South Mountain and Crampton's Gap, September 14). Lee's "Lost Order," therefore, had little effect on the outcome of what became the war's costliest one-day battle. Antietam (Sharpsburg; September 17) ended Lee's first invasion of the North and caused the Confederates to withdraw into Virginia. This dearly purchased Union victory also discouraged European recognition of the Confederacy—especially after President Lincoln issued the Preliminary Emancipation Proclamation in the aftermath of the victory (September 22). The European powers were uniformly opposed to slavery.

Battle Profile: Antietam (Sharpsburg), Washington County, Maryland (September 16–18, 1862) *Eastern*

Campaign: Maryland Campaign.

Principal commanders: Major General George B. McClellan (U.S.A.); General Robert E. Lee (C.S.A.).

Estimated casualties: 26,193 total (U.S.A. 12,469; C.S.A. 13,724).

Forces engaged: 115,000 total (U.S.A. 75,000; C.S.A. 35,000).

Description: On September 16, Major General George B. McClellan's Army of the Potomac confronted Lee's Army of Northern Virginia at Sharpsburg, Maryland. At dawn on September 17, Union Major General Joseph Hooker's corps mounted a powerful assault on Lee's left flank; the single bloodiest day in American military history had begun. Attacks and counterattacks swept across Miller's cornfield, and fighting swirled

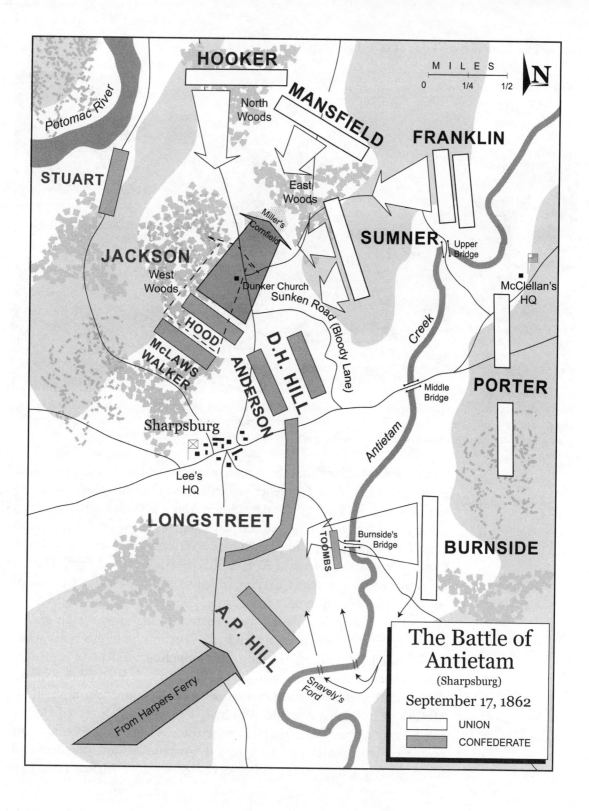

The Battle of
Antietam
(Sharpsburg)
September 17, 1862

UNION
CONFEDERATE

★ 267

Photographed by Alexander Gardner, President Lincoln's visit to the Antietam battlefield in October 1862 preceded his dismissal of McClellan the next month. The Union Army of the Potomac commander (sixth from the left), who had often disappointed his commander in chief, had failed to aggressively pursue Lee's retreating army.

around the Dunker Church. Union assaults against the Sunken Road eventually pierced the Confederate center, but the Federal advantage was not followed up. Late in the day, Union Major General Ambrose Burnside's corps finally got into action, crossing the stone bridge over Antietam Creek and rolling up the Confederate right. At a crucial moment, Confederate Major General A. P. Hill's division arrived from Harpers Ferry and counterattacked, driving back Burnside and saving the day. Although outnumbered nearly two to one, Lee committed his entire force; McClellan sent in less than three-quarters of his army which enabled Lee to fight the Federals to a standstill. During the night, both armies consolidated their lines. In spite of a crippling number of casualties, Lee continued to skirmish with McClellan through September 18, while removing the Confederate wounded south of the Potomac River. McClellan did not renew the assaults. After dark, Lee ordered the battered Army of Northern Virginia to withdraw across the Potomac into the Shenandoah Valley. McClellan did not pursue the Confederates in force. (A few Union units did give chase and were turned back.) His

PRAIRIE GROVE CAMPAIGN (NOVEMBER–DECEMBER 1862)
TRANS-MISSISSIPPI

Confederate efforts to regain control of northwest Arkansas and southwest Missouri met with failure when Southerners under Major General Thomas C. Hindman met Federals under Major General James G. Blunt and Major General Francis J. Herron at the battle of Prairie Grove (December 7). Fought in temperatures so cold that victorious Union troops found many unwounded Confederates frozen to death on the battlefield, Prairie Grove was also marked by the desertion of a newly recruited Confederate Arkansas regiment and the participation of Missouri "bushwackers" led by William C. Quantrill.

FREDERICKSBURG CAMPAIGN (NOVEMBER–DECEMBER 1862) *EASTERN*

Having succeeded George B. McClellan as commander of the Army of the Potomac, Major General Ambrose E. Burnside reorganized the army and secured President Lincoln's approval for a new campaign against Richmond. The effort disintegrated into failure along the Rappahannock River, at Fredericksburg, Virginia, midway between Washington and Richmond, when, on December 13, the Union suffered one of its worst defeats of the entire war. In this encounter, Burnside sent the 100,000-man Army of the Potomac—in formation and over open ground—against Lee's smaller force (72,000), which was well positioned on the high ground beyond the town. The names Prospect Hill and Mayre's Heights became synonymous with futile frontal assaults. "When within some three hundred yards of the rebel works, the men burst into a cheer and charged for the heights," wrote Union soldier Josiah Marshall Favill in his diary, after participating in the battle:

> Immediately the hill in front was hid from view by a continuous sheet of flame from base to summit. The rebel infantry poured in a murderous fire while their guns from every available point fired shot and shell and cannister. The losses were so tremendous, that before we knew it our momentum was gone, and the charge a failure. . . . I wondered while I lay there how it all came about that these thousands of men in broad daylight were trying their best to kill each other. Just then there was no romance, no glorious pomp, nothing but disgust for the genius who planned so frightful a slaughter.

London Times correspondent Francis Charles Lawley, viewing the battle from the Confederate lines, reported the victors' view of the terrible toll exacted

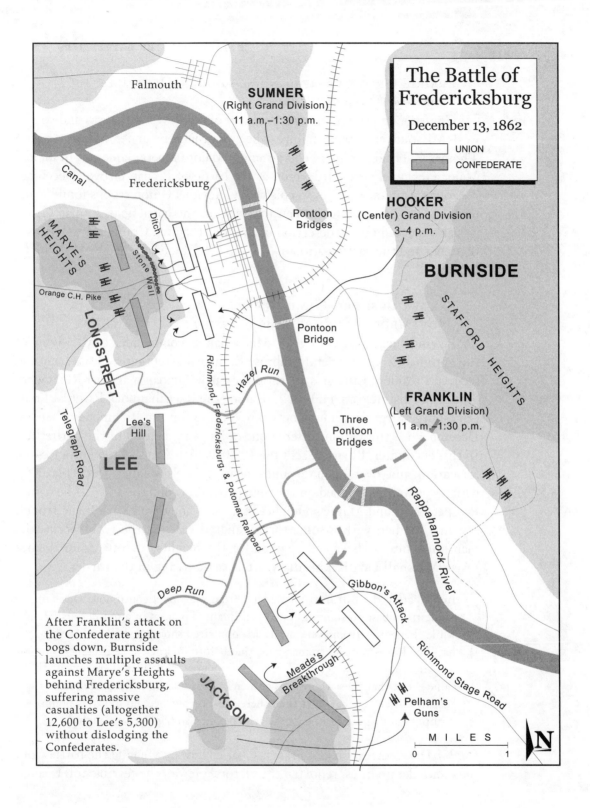

The Battle of Fredericksburg
December 13, 1862

UNION
CONFEDERATE

Falmouth

SUMNER
(Right Grand Division)
11 a.m.–1:30 p.m.

Canal

Fredericksburg

HOOKER
(Center) Grand Division
3–4 p.m.

Pontoon Bridges

BURNSIDE

MARYE'S HEIGHTS

Ditch

Stone Wall

Orange C.H. Pike

STAFFORD HEIGHTS

LONGSTREET

Pontoon Bridge

Telegraph Road

Lee's Hill

Richmond, Fredericksburg, & Potomac Railroad

Hazel Run

FRANKLIN
(Left Grand Division)
11 a.m.–1:30 p.m.

LEE

Three Pontoon Bridges

Rappahannock River

Deep Run

Gibbon's Attack

Richmond Stage Road

After Franklin's attack on the Confederate right bogs down, Burnside launches multiple assaults against Marye's Heights behind Fredericksburg, suffering massive casualties (altogether 12,600 to Lee's 5,300) without dislodging the Confederates.

JACKSON

Meade's Breakthrough

Pelham's Guns

MILES
0   1

N

on Union troops before their persistent attempts to break the Southerners' lines ended in full-scale retreat:

> Not for 50 years to come will that scene ever fade from the memory of those who saw it. There, in every attitude of death, lying so close to each other that you might step from body to body, lay acres of the Federal dead. . . . [in the town itself] layers of corpses stretched in the balconies of houses as though taking a *siesta*. In one yard a surgeon's block for operating was still standing, and, more appalling to look at than even the bodies of the dead, piles of arms and legs, amputated as soon as their owners had been carried off the field, were heaped in the corner.

Northern civilians were deeply shaken by this smashing defeat and its terrible cost (casualties on both sides—18,000 killed, wounded, and missing—amounted to three times the number of American men killed and wounded on D-Day in World War II; two-thirds of the casualties were Union). The

Still suffering the effects of their costly defeat at Fredericksburg, the Union Army of the Potomac moved doggedly into the new year. They were accompanied by artist Alfred Waud, who drew this scene, titled Winter Campaigning near Falmouth, Virginia, *on January 21, 1863.*

people of the North, *Harper's Weekly* editorialized, "cannot be expected to suffer that such massacres as this at Fredericksburg shall be repeated."

STONES RIVER, TENNESSEE, CAMPAIGN (DECEMBER 1862–JANUARY 1863) *WESTERN*

By Christmas, the Union Army of the Cumberland, some 47,000 men under William Rosecrans, was moving on Braxton Bragg's 38,000-man Army of Tennessee, dug in near Murfreesboro, Tennessee. On December 29, the Federals encamped within earshot of the Confederates (so close that, during the night, men of both armies joined in singing "Home Sweet Home"). At dawn on December 31, Bragg's men slammed into the Union's right flank. Initially driven back, the Federals were reinforced and were able to establish a new, strong line. On January 1, there was no fighting. On January 2, the fierce combat was renewed and Union forces eventually forced the Southerners back. Two days later, Bragg retreated to Shelbyville and Tullahoma, Tennessee. A close and hard-fought contest (Union and Confederate dead, wounded, and missing totaled 23,515), the battle of Stones River (Murfreesboro, December 31–January 2) was regarded as a Union "win." In the wake of the Federal loss at Fredericksburg, Virginia (December 13), this victory was badly needed to bolster the Lincoln administration and Northern morale.

Significant Campaigns and Battles—1863

I saw a gentleman, in the morning, Mr. Bell, just from the North. He says the people there are divided, disgusted, disheartened, and utterly sick of the war. . . . [He] says the North has no faith in Jo. Hooker [who had replaced Burnside as commander of the Army of the Potomac] and the question is 'Where have we been whipped today?' . . . Of course the chief topic of conversation is the war and everything connected with it, as that is everybody's business now.—Jedediah Hotchkiss, Topographical Engineer, C.S.A., journal entry, February 6, 1863.

*   *   *

We have been here so long that camp life seems a little stale to me; I want to be on the road; the excitement of marching, bivouacking, and battles I like, and would be perfectly contented to always live in this way, were it not for the anxiety I feel for Walter and Bob. The possession of Richmond, Vicksburg, and all their seaport towns would not atone for the death of one

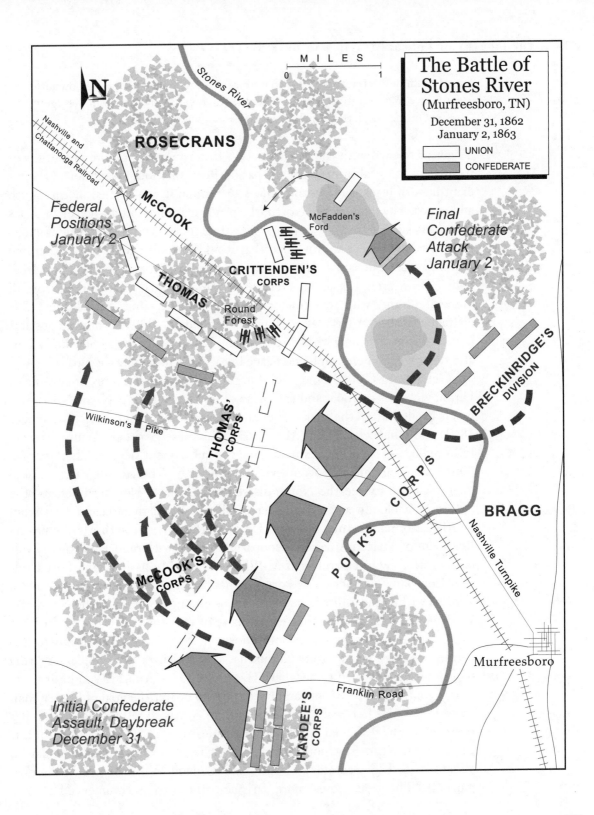

MILES

0   1

The Battle of
Stones River
(Murfreesboro, TN)

December 31, 1862
January 2, 1863

UNION

CONFEDERATE

N

Stones River

Nashville and
Chattanooga Railroad

ROSECRANS

McCOOK

*Federal
Positions
January 2*

McFadden's
Ford

*Final
Confederate
Attack
January 2*

THOMAS

CRITTENDEN'S CORPS

Round
Forest

BRECKINRIDGE'S DIVISION

Wilkinson's Pike

THOMAS' CORPS

POLK'S CORPS

BRAGG

Nashville Turnpike

McCOOK'S CORPS

Murfreesboro

Franklin Road

HARDEE'S CORPS

*Initial Confederate
Assault, Daybreak
December 31*

of them; my patriotism is not that great. I would willingly give my own life to save my country, but not the life of one of my brothers.—Eugene Carter, U.S.A., letter, April 27, 1863.

The year opened with the Emancipation Proclamation. A more potent document than the Preliminary Emancipation Proclamation, it sanctioned the recruitment of black soldiers and sailors. Although it was vilified by the South and opposed by many in the North, the proclamation incited wild celebrations among its supporters. It was also a milestone in the slow acceptance of abolition as a Northern war aim—one that would give all people of the reunited Union, as Lincoln said at Gettysburg on November 19, "a new birth of freedom." On March 31, Union General in Chief Henry W. Halleck wrote to General Grant, who was conducting operations against Vicksburg: "The character of the war has now very much changed. . . . There is now no possible hope of reconciliation with the rebels. The Union party in the South is virtually destroyed. There can be no peace but what is forced by the sword."

Gettysburg (July 3) and Vicksburg (July 4) were the sites of two major Union victories in 1863, and the surge of optimism they gave the North was much needed after the major Federal defeats at Fredericksburg (December 1862) and Chancellorsville (May 1863). But these Northern triumphs were followed by defeat at Chickamauga and the subsequent siege of Chattanooga, Tennessee (September–November). Major raids by Confederate partisans and guerrillas also caused the North distress this year. A Northern defeat—the failure of a bloody assault on Fort (or Battery) Wagner, near Charleston, South Carolina, on July 18—won fame for the Fifty-Fourth Massachusetts Regiment of African American troops. Combined with reports of equally valorous action by black troops at Milliken's Bend, Mississippi, and Port Hudson, Louisiana, the action at Fort Wagner widened the acceptance of black soldiers within the military itself as well as among civilians in the North. As 1863 ended, despair over the terrible cost of the war was growing on both sides, and no end was in sight. But in both the North and the South determination remained strong. Kate Cumming, a nurse with the Confederate Army of Tennessee, confided to her diary (December 31): "Another sun has run its yearly course, and to all appearances we are no nearer the goal of liberty than we were this day last year. No gleam of light comes to tell us that reason has returned to the darkened minds of our ruthless foe. . . . I have no fear for our cause; our martyrs have not offered up their lives in vain." That same day, in Washington, U.S. Secretary of the Navy Gideon Welles wrote in his own journal: "The year closes more satisfactorily than it commenced. . . . the heart of the nation is sounder and its hopes brighter. . . . The Rebels show discontent, distrust, and feebleness. They evidently begin to despair, and the loud declarations that they do not and will not yield confirm it."

BATTLE FOR GALVESTON, TEXAS (JANUARY 1, 1863)
TRANS-MISSISSIPPI

Even though the increasing Northern control of the Mississippi River made the movement of supplies from Texas to the rest of the Confederacy very difficult, efforts continued to close Texas ports to foreign trade. Federal forces had begun a blockade of Galveston on July 3, 1861, and captured the city itself in October 1862. But they retained possession for less than three months. On January 1, 1863, a combined land/sea assault by Confederates, under the command of Major General John B. Magruder, achieved a stunning victory over the defending Union forces and recaptured the city. Galveston was the only major Southern port still in Confederate hands at the war's end.

CHANCELLORSVILLE CAMPAIGN (APRIL–MAY 1863) *EASTERN*

The Union Army of the Potomac, now under the command of Major General Joseph Hooker, again attempted to outflank the strong Confederate position in Fredericksburg, Virginia. (A late January attempt had devolved into Ambrose Burnside's infamous "Mud March.") Begun in a promising fashion, this campaign resulted in disaster when General Robert E. Lee divided his smaller force and defeated Hooker at the battle of Chancellorsville (May 1–4), Lee's most brilliant victory of the war. Related battles included Fredericksburg II, (May 3) and Salem Church (May 3–4). Though a triumph for the South, this campaign resulted in the death of the irreplaceable Stonewall Jackson, wounded by his own men on May 2.

Battle Profile: Chancellorsville, Spotsylvania County (April 30–May 6, 1863)

Campaign: Chancellorsville Campaign.

Principal commanders: Major General Joseph Hooker (U.S.A.); General Robert E. Lee and Lieutenant General Thomas J. Jackson (C.S.A.).

Forces engaged: 191,220 total (U.S.A. 133,868; C.S.A. 57,352).

Estimated casualties: 30,051 total (U.S.A. 17,287; C.S.A. 12,764).

Description: Leaving a covering force under Major General Jubal Early in Fredericksburg, Robert E. Lee marched with the rest of his army to confront Joseph Hooker's Federals, moving toward Fredericksburg.

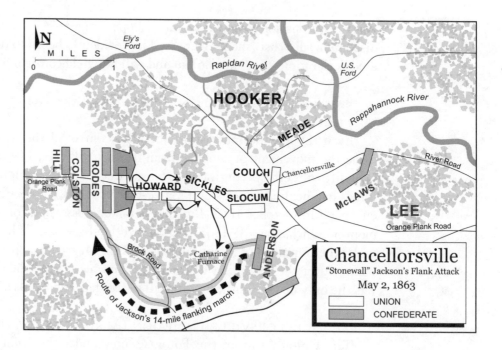

Hearing reports of a more formidable Confederate force than anticipated, Hooker ordered his army to concentrate at Chancellorsville. Pressed closely by Lee's advance, Hooker adopted a defensive posture, thus giving Lee the initiative. On the morning of May 2, Lieutenant General T. J. Jackson directed his corps on a march against the Federal left flank, which was reported to be "hanging in the air" (unanchored, and thus vulnerable to being turned). Fighting was sporadic on other portions of the field throughout the day, as Jackson's column reached its jump-off point. At 5:20 P.M., Jackson's line surged forward in an overwhelming attack that crushed the Union's Eleventh Corps. Federal troops rallied, resisted the advance, and counterattacked. Disorganization on both sides—and darkness—ended the fighting; later, while making a reconnaissance, Jackson was mortally wounded by his own men. Jeb Stuart took temporary command of Jackson's corps. On May 3, the Confederates attacked with both wings of the army and massed their artillery at Hazel Grove. This finally broke the Federal line at Chancellorsville. Hooker withdrew a mile and entrenched in a defensive "U" with his back to the river at United States Ford. Union generals Hiram G. Berry and Amiel W. Whipple and Confederate general Elisha F. Paxton were killed. On the night of May 5–6, after further Union reverses at Salem Church, Hooker recrossed to the north bank of the Rappahannock. Stonewall Jackson died from his wound, complicated by pneumonia, on May 10.

STREIGHT'S RAID IN NORTHERN ALABAMA (APRIL–MAY 1863) *WESTERN*

Union Colonel Abel D. Streight led what came to be called his "Mule Brigade" (his 2,000 infantrymen were mounted on mules to negotiate the mountainous terrain) on this seventeen-day raid to destroy Southern railroads. Ordered by Major General William Rosecrans, who believed that "This war must be conducted to annihilate the military power and exhaust the resources of the Rebels," the raid was a precursor of the 1864–1865 Union hard-war policy. It was also spectacularly unsuccessful. The mules proved more of a liability than an asset; and Streight came up against the resourceful Confederate cavalry commander Nathan Bedford Forrest, who clashed with the Federals at Day's Gap and Hog Mountain (April 30) and finally employed a ruse that made his force seem much larger than it was, to provoke Streight's Federals to surrender at Cedar Mountain (May 3).

SECOND VICKSBURG CAMPAIGN (APRIL–JULY, 1863) *WESTERN*

In the wake of his unsuccessful overland attempt to take Vicksburg (October–December 1862) and Sherman's defeat at Chickasaw Bluffs (December 27, 1862; see page 262), Major General Ulysses S. Grant kept pressure on the city with creative but less-than-successful endeavors. They included:

- **The Yazoo Pass Expedition (February–March 1863):** This attempt to establish a water route to Vicksburg that would not bring Union boats in range of the city's guns was under the command of Lieutenant Colonel of engineers James H. Wilson, who succeeded in cutting through a levee that blocked the proposed route. The Union plan had been anticipated by Confederate Lieutenant General John C. Pemberton, however, whose name was given to a small fort that stymied Union progress. The expedition failed after repeated Union artillery assaults and infantry probes failed to dislodge the Confederates in the fort.

- **Steele's Bayou Expedition (March 14–25, 1863):** As the Yazoo Pass Expedition was failing, U.S. Navy Captain David D. Porter attempted another water approach to Vicksburg via heavily overgrown bayous he suspected were linked. Unanticipated natural obstructions were compounded by obstructions put in place by Confederates. Slowed to a crawl, and beset by Confederate sniper fire, Porter was eventually rescued by troops led by Major General William T. Sherman. This expedition, too, ended in failure.

In April, Grant began the Second Vicksburg Campaign by sending Captain David D. Porter's fleet past the Vicksburg batteries to make possible the landing of Federal forces south of the city. While Brigadier General Benjamin H. Grierson's spectacular cavalry raid through central Mississippi to central Louisiana (April 17–May 2; see map on page 270) diverted some Confederate forces, Grant moved toward Vicksburg from the south, relying chiefly on the countryside to provide sustenance for his troops—a daring gamble inspired by the failure of his previous Vicksburg campaign, which had ended when Confederates ravaged his supplies and supply lines. Besting Lieutenant General John C. Pemberton's Confederates at Port Gibson (May 1), Jackson (May 14), and Champion Hill (May 16), Grant's Army of the Tennessee was repulsed in an assault on Vicksburg itself (May 19). A second assault (May 22) proved a near disaster. The Union army then placed the city under siege, while Pemberton's Army of Vicksburg—and the city's civilian

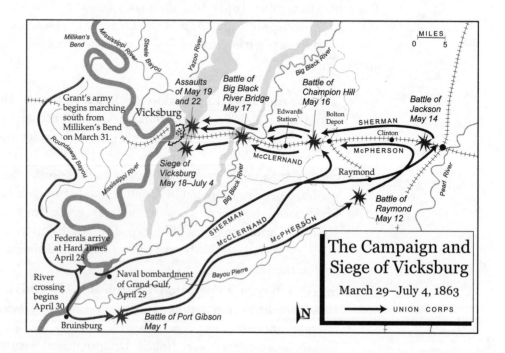

The Campaign and Siege of Vicksburg

March 29–July 4, 1863

→ UNION CORPS

population—waited in vain for help from Joseph E. Johnston's Confederate force. Food became scarce; Pemberton's men were eventually reduced to near-starvation rations. Dogs, cats, and rats were eaten by soldiers and civilians (many of whom had moved into caves to escape Union bombardments). The city fell on July 4, 1863, the day after the Union victory at Gettysburg. News of its fall reached Port Hudson, Louisiana, also under Union siege, and that city formally capitulated on July 9. The Union then controlled the entire Mississippi River; the Confederacy was cut in two.

OPERATIONS AGAINST THE DEFENSES OF CHARLESTON, SOUTH CAROLINA (APRIL–SEPTEMBER 1863)
LOWER SEABOARD AND GULF APPROACH

Renewed Federal efforts against Charleston Harbor and its defenses began with a naval assault by nine ironclads commanded by Union Rear Admiral Samuel Du Pont (April 7) and continued throughout the summer. One of the most memorable engagements of this campaign was the costly and unsuccessful Union assault, July 18, on Battery (Fort) Wagner on Morris Island, led by the Fifty-Fourth Massachusetts Regiment of African American infantry. Battery Wagner did not fall to the Union until September 7 (see "Fighting on Two Fronts: Black Soldiers in the Civil War," in Chapter 5, "The Armies").

SIEGE OF PORT HUDSON, LOUISIANA (MAY–JULY 1863) *WESTERN*

In conjunction with Grant's operations in Mississippi, Major General Nathaniel Banks laid siege to Port Hudson, south of Vicksburg on the Mississippi River—a bastion that protected the only segment of the Mississippi effectively under Confederate control (the 110-mile corridor between Vicksburg and Port Hudson). The Confederates held out for forty-eight days—withstanding two concerted Federal assaults, on May 27 and June 14. During the May 27 assault, two regiments of New Orleans free African Americans and Louisiana ex-slaves, part of the Union force, conducted themselves heroically—a fact that was well publicized by Northern newspapers. "The bravery displayed before Port Hudson by the colored troops was applaudingly received here by persons who have not been looked upon as friendly to the movement," wrote a Washington African American in the *Christian Recorder*, June 20, 1863. "There never was, nor there never will be, a better opportunity for colored men to get what they want, than now." Port Hudson surrendered July 9.

GETTYSBURG CAMPAIGN (JUNE–JULY 1863) *EASTERN*

Lee's second invasion of the North (which included the greatest cavalry battle ever fought on American soil—the battle of Brandy Station, Virginia, on June 9) filled the storehouses and stables of Virginia with captured supplies and livestock before ending in defeat in the monumental three-day battle of Gettysburg, Pennsylvania, a major turning point of the war.

Battle Profile: Gettysburg, Adams County (July 1–3, 1863)

Campaign: Gettysburg.

Principal commanders: Major General George G. Meade (U.S.A.); General Robert E. Lee (C.S.A.).

Forces engaged: 158,343 total (U.S.A. 83,289; C.S.A. 75,054).

Estimated casualties: 51,000 total (U.S.A. 23,000; C.S.A. 28,000).

Description: General Robert E. Lee concentrated his full strength against Major General George G. Meade's Army of the Potomac at the crossroads county seat of Gettysburg. On July 1, Confederate forces converged on the town from the west and the north, driving Union defenders back through the streets to Cemetery Hill. During the night, reinforcements arrived for both sides. On July 2, Lee attempted to envelop the Federals, first striking the Union left flank at the Peach Orchard, Wheatfield, Devil's Den, and Big and Little Round Tops with Longstreet's and Hill's divisions, and then attacking the Union right at Culp's Hill and East Cemetery Hill with Ewell's divisions. By evening, the Federals retained Little Round Top and had repulsed most of Ewell's men. During the morning of July 3, the Confederate infantry were driven from their last toehold on Culp's Hill. In the afternoon, after a preliminary artillery bombardment, Lee attacked the Union center on Cemetery Ridge. The Pickett-Pettigrew assault (more popularly called Pickett's Charge) momentarily pierced the Union line but was driven back with severe casualties. Stuart's cavalry attempted to gain the Union rear but was repulsed. On July 4, Lee began withdrawing his army toward Williamsport on the Potomac River. His train of wounded stretched more than fourteen miles.

Some forty Northern reporters covered the battle, and when their stories of Union victory were published, civilian morale, lowered by the recent and spectacular Federal defeat at Chancellorsville, rose sharply. "[T]he results of this victory are priceless," exulted New York diarist George Templeton Strong:

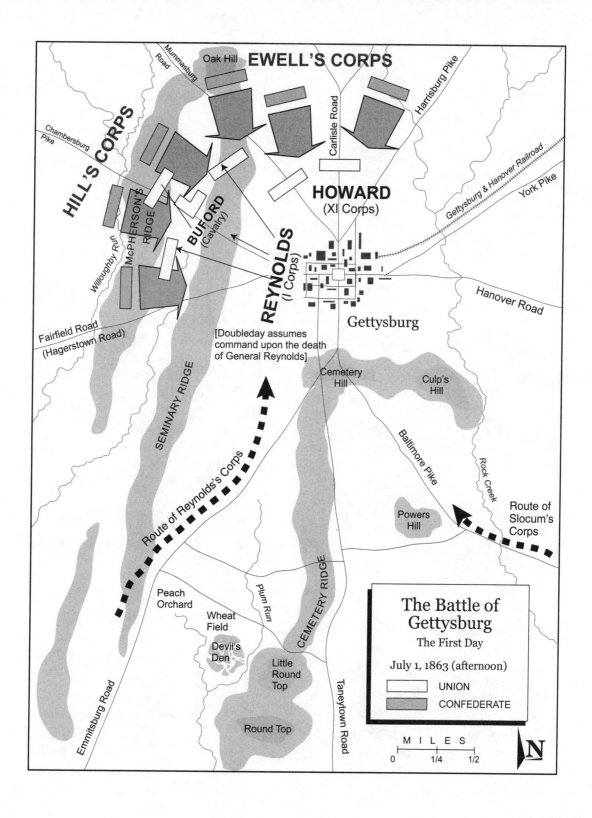

Oak Hill

EWELL'S CORPS

Mummasburg Road

Harrisburg Pike

Chambersburg Pike

HILL'S CORPS

Carlisle Road

Gettysburg & Hanover Railroad

York Pike

HOWARD
(XI Corps)

McPHERSON'S RIDGE

BUFORD
(Cavalry)

Willoughby Run

REYNOLDS
(I Corps)

Hanover Road

Fairfield Road
(Hagerstown Road)

Gettysburg

[Doubleday assumes command upon the death of General Reynolds]

SEMINARY RIDGE

Cemetery Hill

Culp's Hill

Baltimore Pike

Rock Creek

Route of Reynolds's Corps

Powers Hill

Route of Slocum's Corps

Peach Orchard

Plum Run

CEMETERY RIDGE

Wheat Field

Devil's Den

Little Round Top

Emmitsburg Road

Taneytown Road

Round Top

The Battle of Gettysburg
The First Day

July 1, 1863 (afternoon)

| | UNION |
| | CONFEDERATE |

MILES

0   1/4   1/2

N

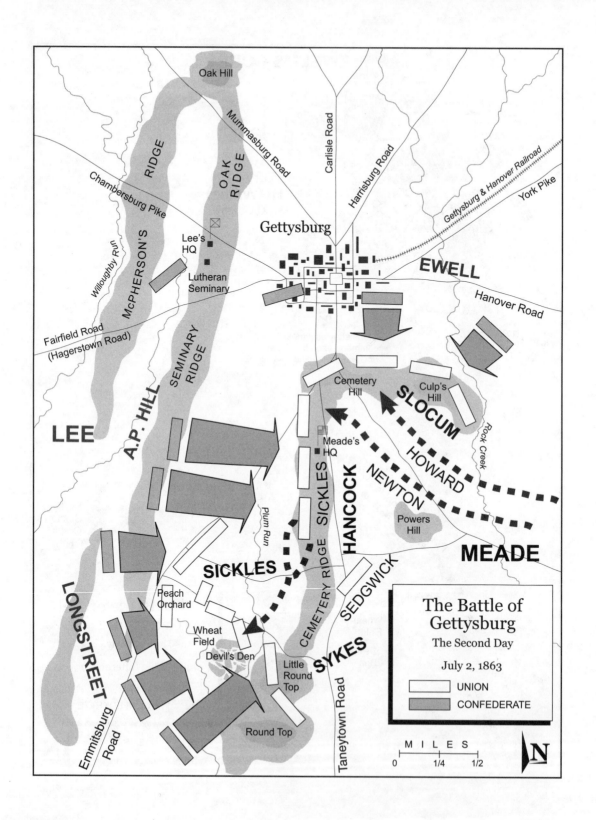

Oak Hill

RIDGE

Mummasburg Road

OAK RIDGE

Carlisle Road

Harrisburg Road

Chambersburg Pike

Gettysburg & Hanover Railroad

York Pike

McPHERSON'S RIDGE

Willoughby Run

Lee's HQ

Lutheran Seminary

Gettysburg

EWELL

Fairfield Road
(Hagerstown Road)

SEMINARY RIDGE

Hanover Road

LEE

A.P. HILL

Cemetery Hill

Culp's Hill

SLOCUM

Rock Creek

Meade's HQ

SICKLES

HANCOCK

NEWTON

HOWARD

Plum Run

Powers Hill

MEADE

SICKLES

CEMETERY RIDGE

LONGSTREET

Peach Orchard

SEDGWICK

Wheat Field

Devil's Den

Little Round Top

SYKES

Taneytown Road

Round Top

Emmitsburg Road

The Battle of Gettysburg

The Second Day

July 2, 1863

UNION

CONFEDERATE

M I L E S

0   1/4   1/2

N

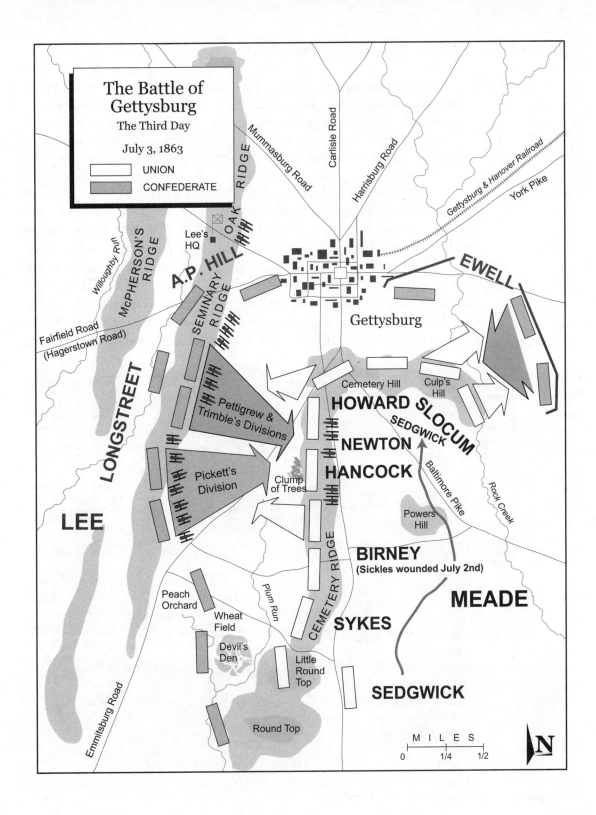

The Battle of Gettysburg
The Third Day

July 3, 1863

UNION
CONFEDERATE

Mummasburg Road

Carlisle Road

Harrisburg Road

Gettysburg & Hanover Railroad

York Pike

OAK RIDGE

A.P. HILL

Lee's HQ

McPHERSON'S RIDGE

Willoughby Run

SEMINARY RIDGE

Fairfield Road
(Hagerstown Road)

EWELL

Gettysburg

LONGSTREET

Pettigrew & Trimble's Divisions

Cemetery Hill

Culp's Hill

HOWARD SLOCUM

SEDGWICK

NEWTON

HANCOCK

Pickett's Division

Clump of Trees

Baltimore Pike

Rock Creek

LEE

CEMETERY RIDGE

Powers Hill

BIRNEY
(Sickles wounded July 2nd)

MEADE

Peach Orchard

Plum Run

SYKES

Wheat Field

Devil's Den

Little Round Top

SEDGWICK

Emmitsburg Road

Round Top

M I L E S
0   1/4   1/2

N

The charm of Robert Lee's invincibility is broken. The Army of the Potomac has at last found a general that can handle it, and has stood nobly up to its terrible work in spite of its long disheartening list of hard-fought failures. . . . Copperheads [Peace Democrats] are palsied and dumb for the moment at least. . . . Government is strengthened four-fold at home and abroad.

One Northern civilian observer, *New York Times* reporter Sam Wilkeson, wrote much more poignantly about the victory, for Wilkeson had just seen the dead body of his oldest son, "crushed by a shell in a position where a battery should never have been sent, in a building where surgeons dared not to stay."

Confederates had also been accompanied by reporters, notably Francis Charles Lawley of the *Times* of London, a member of a group of pro-Southern foreigners known as the "Jolly Congress." Lawley would later assign part of the blame for the Confederate defeat to the memories of all the South's earlier victories, which had "combined to inspire the leading

In a rare contemporary image of the battle, Alfred Waud sketched Colonel Normal Hall's Union brigade rushing to defend Cemetery Ridge against Pickett's Charge at Gettysburg.

Confederate generals with undue contempt for their enemy, although he was fighting on his own soil, with his back to the wall, and in a position which for strength and eligibility for defence [sic] had not been surpassed during twenty-seven months of warfare." But in the immediate aftermath of the battle, not all Confederates who participated saw the outcome as a dire defeat. Major Jedediah Hotchkiss wrote this journal entry for July 3:

> I met Pickett's Division, returning after the battle, that night, scattered all along the road; no officers and all protesting that they had been completely cut up. A general movement of wagons, wounded, prisoners, etc., took place to the rear, and the unmistakable signs of a retreat were plentiful. There was a general feeling of despondence in the army at our great losses, though the battle is regarded as a drawn one.

On July 4—as Vicksburg was capitulating and the Confederacy was split in two—Lee began leading his army south, pursued in due course by George Gordon Meade's Army of the Potomac. (Meade was roundly criticized for his slowness in this matter.)

TULLAHOMA, OR MIDDLE TENNESSEE CAMPAIGN (JUNE 23–JULY 3, 1863) *WESTERN*

Confederate General Braxton Bragg and his Army of Tennessee were repeatedly outmaneuvered by Union Major General William Rosecrans and his Army of the Cumberland in this Union campaign, which was intended to keep Bragg from dispatching a force to break the Union siege of Vicksburg, Mississippi. Bragg was forced to retreat eighty-five miles and to evacuate several strong positions. After moving across the Cumberland Plateau, his troops took up positions behind the Tennessee River.

JOHN HUNT MORGAN'S OHIO RAID (JULY 2–26, 1863) *WESTERN*

The longest cavalry raid of the war (more than 700 miles during twenty-five days of almost constant combat), Morgan's Ohio raid was undertaken in defiance of General Braxton Bragg's instructions to Morgan to stay south of the Ohio River. Morgan was convinced that only by bringing the war into the Northern homeland—and thus winning the support of Northern "Copperheads" or Peace Democrats—could pressure on the Confederacy be relieved. But during this destructive raid, Morgan and his "Terrible Men" made no distinction between enemies and potential allies as they held businesses for ransom; destroyed commercial buildings, railroads, and bridges; and looted

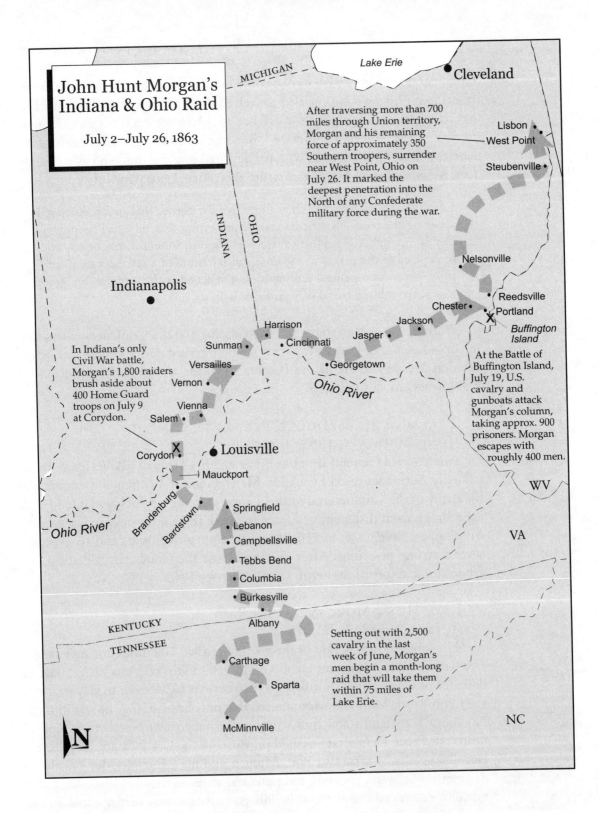

John Hunt Morgan's Indiana & Ohio Raid

July 2–July 26, 1863

After traversing more than 700 miles through Union territory, Morgan and his remaining force of approximately 350 Southern troopers, surrender near West Point, Ohio on July 26. It marked the deepest penetration into the North of any Confederate military force during the war.

In Indiana's only Civil War battle, Morgan's 1,800 raiders brush aside about 400 Home Guard troops on July 9 at Corydon.

At the Battle of Buffington Island, July 19, U.S. cavalry and gunboats attack Morgan's column, taking approx. 900 prisoners. Morgan escapes with roughly 400 men.

Setting out with 2,500 cavalry in the last week of June, Morgan's men begin a month-long raid that will take them within 75 miles of Lake Erie.

MICHIGAN

Lake Erie

Cleveland

Lisbon
West Point
Steubenville

Nelsonville

INDIANA
OHIO

Indianapolis

Reedsville
Chester
Portland
Buffington Island

Harrison
Cincinnati
Jasper
Jackson

Sunman
Georgetown

Versailles
Ohio River

Vernon

Vienna

Salem

Corydon
X
Louisville

Mauckport

WV

Ohio River
Brandenburg
Bardstown
Springfield
Lebanon
Campbellsville
Tebbs Bend
Columbia
Burkesville

VA

KENTUCKY
Albany

TENNESSEE

Carthage

Sparta

McMinnville

NC

N

local treasures. As a result, the Confederates won little but immediate panic and the undying enmity of the Northerners in their path. Some 14,000 Federal regulars were, however, diverted from other duty to pursue Morgan's cavalry, and 120,000 militia were mustered to duty in two Northern states before the Confederates were defeated by Union troops under Brigadier General Edward H. Hobson at Buffington Island. Morgan was subsequently captured (less than 100 miles from Cleveland) and sent to the Ohio Penitentiary as a common criminal. (He escaped on November 27.)

QUANTRILL'S RAID INTO KANSAS (AUGUST 1863)
TRANS-MISSISSIPPI

In the Kansas-Missouri corridor, the scene of exceptionally vicious guerrilla warfare since before war was officially declared, Confederate "bushwacker" William Quantrill led 450 guerrillas, from a number of separate bands, on a particularly bloody raid into Kansas. The raiders were unified by anger after five women who were related to guerrilla leaders died when a building in which they had been imprisoned by Union authorities collapsed. Attacking the prewar free-soil bastion of Lawrence (August 21–22), the bushwackers murdered more than 180 men and burned 185 buildings before moving back into Missouri. This raid so enraged the Union Army's area commander, Brigadier General Thomas Ewing, Jr., that he issued General Orders, No. 11 (August 25). Ruthlessly enforced by Federal troops, the order swept four western Missouri counties clear of all inhabitants except those who were proven Union loyalists. More than 10,000 people were forced out on the roads with only the goods they could carry, as troops burned their homes behind them. The bushwackers were not appreciably damaged by this forced removal of suspected collaborators; and the rancor caused by the Union action lasted for many years after the war.

CHICKAMAUGA CAMPAIGN
(AUGUST–SEPTEMBER 1863) WESTERN

Having regrouped after his successful Tullahoma Campaign (June–July 1863), Union Major General William Rosecrans led his Army of the Cumberland, divided into three columns, through difficult mountain terrain toward the Confederate stronghold of Chattanooga, Tennessee, held by Confederates under General Braxton Bragg. After he was reinforced with troops from Knoxville and Mississippi, Bragg evacuated Chattanooga (September 6) in order to meet the oncoming Federals. Squabbles with his subordinates disrupted his progress, but the main Confederate and Union forces

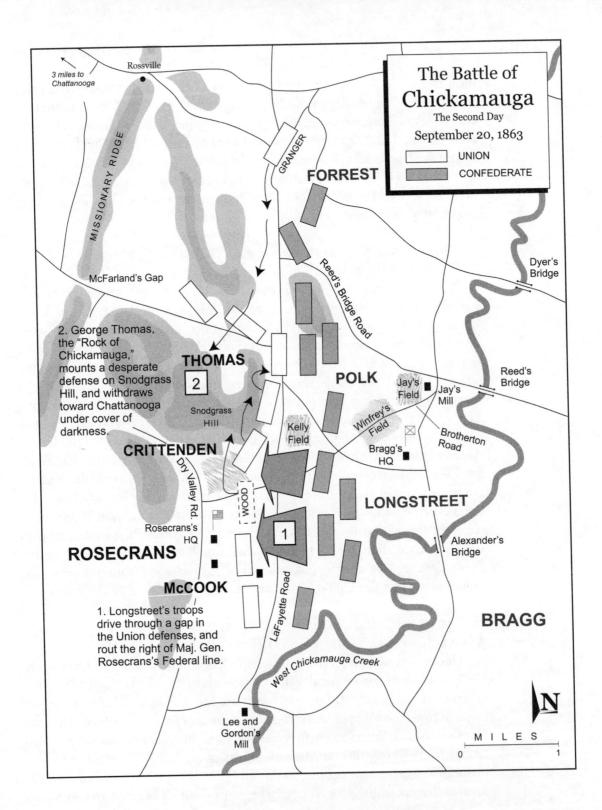

3 miles to Chattanooga

Rossville

MISSIONARY RIDGE

McFarland's Gap

GRANGER

FORREST

Reed's Bridge Road

Dyer's Bridge

Reed's Bridge

2. George Thomas, the "Rock of Chickamauga," mounts a desperate defense on Snodgrass Hill, and withdraws toward Chattanooga under cover of darkness.

THOMAS

2

Snodgrass Hill

POLK

Jay's Field

Jay's Mill

Winfrey's Field

Brotherton Road

Kelly Field

Bragg's HQ

CRITTENDEN

Dry Valley Rd.

WOOD

Rosecrans's HQ

LONGSTREET

1

Alexander's Bridge

ROSECRANS

McCOOK

LaFayette Road

BRAGG

1. Longstreet's troops drive through a gap in the Union defenses, and rout the right of Maj. Gen. Rosecrans's Federal line.

West Chickamauga Creek

The Battle of
Chickamauga
The Second Day
September 20, 1863

UNION

CONFEDERATE

Lee and Gordon's Mill

N

MILES

0   1

finally clashed at the battle of Chickamauga, Georgia (September 19–20), the bloodiest battle of the war in the Western Theater (estimated casualties: 16,170 Union troops, 18,454 Confederates killed, wounded, or missing). The Union forces broke when a gap in their line was exploited by troops under the command of Lieutenant General James Longstreet, and they were only saved from total destruction by the stubborn rearguard action of forces under Major General George Thomas (thereafter known as "the Rock of Chickamauga"), assisted by troops under Major General Gordon Granger. Rosecrans' troops retreated into Tennessee and joined Union forces that had occupied Chattanooga the day after the Confederate evacuation. They were placed under siege by Bragg's Confederates, who occupied the surrounding heights, including Lookout Mountain and Missionary Ridge. In Washington, Secretary of War Stanton initiated the longest and largest pre-twentieth-century movement of troops when he dispatched 20,000 men via railroad (September 23) on the 1,233-mile trip to relieve them. General Grant soon reached the city as well.

LITTLE ROCK, ARKANSAS, CAMPAIGN
(AUGUST–SEPTEMBER 1863) *TRANS-MISSISSIPPI*

Federal troops commanded by Major General Frederick Steele began to move toward the Arkansas capital of Little Rock on August 1. They skirmished with Confederate troops from time to time as they progressed. Southern forces withdrew from this important Confederate center on September 10, and the state government established itself in the city of Washington, to the southwest. Little Rock's occupation by the Union increased the Union threat against the entire Confederate Trans-Mississippi Department. It also gave Unionists in Arkansas a chance to establish their own civil government, which they did early in 1864. Two state governments—one loyal to the Union, the other loyal to the Confederacy—governed different sections of the state (divided roughly by the Arkansas River) for the remainder of the war. This division provoked an increase in guerrilla warfare within the state.

EAST TENNESSEE CAMPAIGN
(AUGUST–NOVEMBER, 1863) *WESTERN*

In August, responding to pleas for assistance from East Tennessee Unionists, Major General Ambrose E. Burnside led a Union force toward Knoxville and occupied the city on September 2. This effectively severed the

Confederates' most direct rail route between Chattanooga and Virginia. It also prompted an unsuccessful attempt—by 15,000 Confederates under Lieutenant General James Longstreet, who were detached from Bragg's force besieging Chattanooga—to dislodge Burnside's Federals (the Confederates' poorly executed Knoxville Campaign, in November–December 1863).

CHATTANOOGA-RINGGOLD CAMPAIGN
(OCTOBER–NOVEMBER 1863) *WESTERN*

With their back to the Tennessee River, and having fortified their front with trenches and rifle pits, Union forces that had retreated to Chattanooga, Tennessee, after the battle of Chickamauga, were besieged by General Braxton Bragg's Confederates. The Confederates were determined to starve the Federals out of this important city, which could be used as a Union gateway for movement into Georgia, but the Federals were just as determined to stay in possession and break the siege. Major General Ulysses S. Grant, who had been named head of the newly created Union Military Division of the Mississippi on October 16, arrived in Chattanooga on October 22. By November 1, the supply situation had been alleviated by the Cracker Line Operation (October 24–November 1), during which a new supply line was

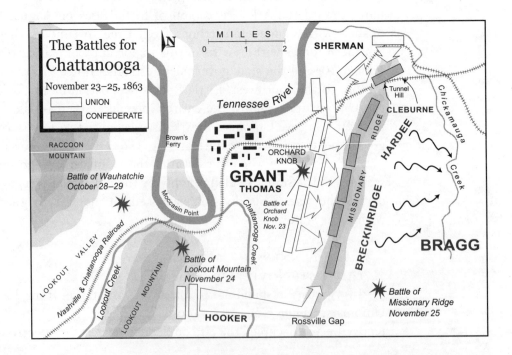

The Battles for **Chattanooga**

November 23–25, 1863

☐ UNION
■ CONFEDERATE

established, via the Tennessee River, from Bridgeport, Alabama. By November 14, Major General William T. Sherman and his reinforcing column of 17,000 men, gleaned from the Vicksburg and Memphis garrisons, had arrived as well. Plans were made to break the Confederates' hold on the heights surrounding the city. On November 23, Union troops knocked Confederates off Orchard Knob (their forward position on Missionary Ridge); on November 24, Lookout Mountain was taken; and on November 25, Major General George Thomas' troops precipitated "the miracle of Missionary Ridge," when they exceeded their orders for a limited frontal assault and pushed the Confederates into full retreat. The siege was broken, and Union troops would soon be heading into the heart of the Deep South. Chattanooga was to be the supply and logistics base for Sherman's 1864 Atlanta Campaign.

MINE RUN CAMPAIGN (NOVEMBER–DECEMBER 1863) *EASTERN*

In Virginia, Major General George Gordon Meade, commander of the Union Army of the Potomac, attempted to turn the exposed right flank of Lee's Confederate army, but his slow progress (due to harsh weather and the tentativeness of his lead corps, commanded by William H. French) enabled Lee to establish strong field fortifications along the west bank of Mine Run, just south of the Wilderness. Skirmishes (most notably at Locust Grove, on November 27) led to nearly 1,700 Union and some 600 Confederate casualties. But Meade's failure to surprise Lee, as well as the strength of the fortifications the Confederates had erected, led the Union commander to withdraw rather than engage Lee—who was, by December 2, eager to do battle. "I am too old to command this army," Lee said when he realized Meade's army had withdrawn. "I should never have permitted those people to get away."

Significant Campaigns and Battles—1864

Since leaving Richmond have scarcely rested any to invigorate our exhausted energies, and with it all a deficiency of rations. For the duration of forty-eight hours my Brigade did not have a mouthful of bread and but little flesh—very little straggling and very little complaining. Occasionally, when Gen. Rodes or Early passed the line, the cry was, 'Bread, bread, bread'; but through it all, we made a forced march for the last day, and arrived too late to inflict much damage on the enemy, which was very annoying, as we expected to get supplies from them, but instead found only empty wagons and worthless provisions.—Brigadier General Bryan Grimes, C.S.A., letter, June 22, 1864.

Near Ackworth's Station, [Georgia]. We now occupy a very strong position, with the enemy in our immediate front. Their pickets and ours are on
perfectly good terms; the men off duty meet each other between the lines,
exchange papers, and barter sugar and coffee for tobacco. We shall probably
make another grand movement in a day or two, which will carry us somewhere near Atlanta. The loss in our corps so far has been about four thousand killed and wounded,—a heavier loss, I think, than any other corps has
sustained in this army. We were about twenty-five thousand strong at the
beginning of this campaign. Life is cheap this year almost everywhere in
the army.—Major Charles F. Morse, U.S.A., letter, June 9, 1864.

A year of ferocious clashes in the Eastern Theater and crucially important
Union triumphs in the West, 1864 began quietly. Many in the South still har-
bored hopes for a Northern collapse and foreign intervention. Northern Peace
Democrats were still active, and there was to be a U.S. presidential election in
the fall. In March (just as the Kilpatrick-Dahlgren Raid was sparking Southern ire), President Lincoln appointed Ulysses S. Grant general in chief of all
Union armies. Believing that Union forces had pursued the war thus far "like
a balky team, no two pulling together," Grant quickly developed plans for offensives in all theaters of operation, so that outnumbered Confederates could
not shift their armies to meet isolated and uncoordinated Union assaults, as
they had done previously (e.g., before Shiloh and Chickamauga).

In May, Grant began his Overland Campaign in the Eastern Theater—
pushing Lee's Army of Northern Virginia back into siege lines around Petersburg through a series of brutal and costly clashes. In the West, and in
Virginia's Shenandoah Valley, the "hard war" policy—all supplies of potential use to Confederates were destroyed or confiscated—was brought home
in dedicated fashion by Major General Philip Sheridan's Army of the
Shenandoah and Major General William T. Sherman's western armies. Hard
pressed on all fronts, the Confederates still held Petersburg, Virginia, and
their capital of Richmond at year's end, but they had lost the key city of Atlanta (a September victory for the North that helped guarantee Abraham
Lincoln's reelection). In December, Savannah surrendered as well, and Fort
Fisher, North Carolina, guarding the last eastern seaboard port through
which supplies could reach Lee's beleaguered army, was severely threatened.
On December 16, the shattering of John Bell Hood's Army of Tennessee
at Nashville sent shudders through the South. "There is deep feeling in
Congress at the conduct of our military affairs," Confederate Chief of Ordnance Josiah Gorgas wrote in his diary on December 27. "They demand
[that] the Gen. Lee shall be made Generalissimo to command all our

Major General William T. Sherman (leaning on the breech of the gun) and his staff at Federal Fort No. 7, Atlanta, Georgia, 1864. Photograph by George N. Barnard.

armies . . . This Tenn. Campaign altho' the President can hardly be called responsible for it, except that he *suffered* it, has completely upset the little confidence left in the Presidents ability to conduct campaigns." In Washington, five days later, U.S. Secretary of the Navy Gideon Welles wrote in his own diary: "[P]rogress has been made during the year that has just terminated, and it seems to me the Rebellion is not far from its close. . . . "

MERIDIAN, MISSISSIPPI, CAMPAIGN (FEBRUARY 3–MARCH 4, 1864) *WESTERN*

From Vicksburg, Mississippi, Union General William T. Sherman launched a campaign to secure Mississippi's largest remaining railroad center. On February 1, he ordered 7,000 Memphis-based cavalry under Brigadier General William Sooy Smith to conduct a sweeping raid and meet up with the main force at Meridian. Two days later, with 20,000 men in two columns under his subordinates, Major General Stephen A. Hurlbut and Major General James B. McPherson, Sherman embarked on the campaign.

His progress toward his objective caused such consternation that Meridian was abandoned by the Confederates (on the orders of Lieutenant General Leonidas Polk) on February 14. For the next five days, Sherman's Union troops wrought destruction on some 115 miles of railroad track, sixty-one bridges, twenty locomotives, an arsenal, and assorted warehouses and other facilities of military value. Departing what was left of the city, Sherman's troops searched for Smith's errant cavalry on their way back to Vicksburg. (The cavalry had embarked late—much to Sherman's displeasure—and conducted a less than successful campaign before returning to Memphis.) In addition to confiscating or destroying supplies potentially useful to Confederate armies, Sherman's force escorted some 5,000 slaves and 1,000 white refugees back to Vicksburg.

KILPATRICK-DAHLGREN RAID ON RICHMOND, VIRGINIA (FEBRUARY 28–MARCH 3, 1864) *EASTERN*

Plotted by Union cavalry Brigadier General H. Judson Kilpatrick and employing some 4,000 troops under his command and that of Colonel Ulric Dahlgren, this daring raid was an unsuccessful attempt to enter Richmond, Virginia, and release the large number of Union prisoners of war held there. The raid itself, brought greater damage to the North than the South, however. Papers found on the body of Colonel Dahlgren, killed in an ambush by Major General Fitzhugh Lee's cavalry, outlined plans for the released prisoners to hold the city and wait for Union reinforcements; to burn Richmond thereafter; and to murder Jefferson Davis and his cabinet. Amid a firestorm of civilian and official outrage, General Robert E. Lee sent a letter of inquiry to Major General George Gordon Meade, commander of the Union Army of the Potomac. A subsequent investigation settled blame, by default, on the deceased Colonel Dahlgren; Brigadier General Kilpatrick denied responsibility for the content of the papers. The episode embittered and inflamed people throughout the Confederacy.

RED RIVER CAMPAIGN (MARCH–MAY 1864) *TRANS-MISSISSIPPI*

This joint army-navy expedition up the Red River in Louisiana, led by Major General Nathaniel Banks and Rear Admiral David D. Porter, sought to block the flow of supplies from Shreveport, Louisiana (headquarters of Confederate Trans-Mississippi Department commander Edmund Kirby Smith), into Texas. Approved directly by President Lincoln, the campaign interrupted General Grant's intended move against Mobile, Alabama, the

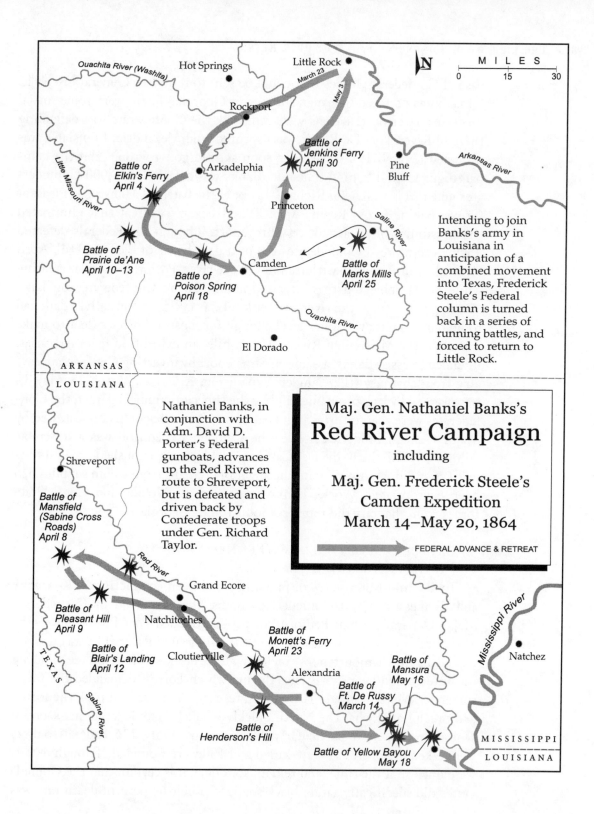

MILES
0   15   30

Ouachita River (Washita)

Hot Springs

Little Rock

March 23

May 3

Rockport

Arkadelphia

Battle of
Elkin's Ferry
April 4

Little Missouri River

Battle of
Prairie de'Ane
April 10–13

Battle of
Poison Spring
April 18

Camden

Battle of
Jenkins Ferry
April 30

Pine
Bluff

Arkansas River

Princeton

Saline River

Battle of
Marks Mills
April 25

Ouachita River

El Dorado

Intending to join
Banks's army in
Louisiana in
anticipation of a
combined movement
into Texas, Frederick
Steele's Federal
column is turned
back in a series of
running battles, and
forced to return to
Little Rock.

ARKANSAS

LOUISIANA

Nathaniel Banks, in
conjunction with
Adm. David D.
Porter's Federal
gunboats, advances
up the Red River en
route to Shreveport,
but is defeated and
driven back by
Confederate troops
under Gen. Richard
Taylor.

Shreveport

Battle of
Mansfield
(Sabine Cross
Roads)
April 8

Red River

Grand Ecore

Battle of
Pleasant Hill
April 9

Natchitoches

Battle of
Blair's Landing
April 12

Cloutierville

TEXAS

Sabine River

Battle of
Monett's Ferry
April 23

Alexandria

Battle of
Henderson's Hill

Battle of
Ft. De Russy
March 14

Battle of
Mansura
May 16

Mississippi River

Natchez

Battle of Yellow Bayou
May 18

MISSISSIPPI

LOUISIANA

Maj. Gen. Nathaniel Banks's
Red River Campaign
including
Maj. Gen. Frederick Steele's
Camden Expedition
March 14–May 20, 1864

FEDERAL ADVANCE & RETREAT

base of Confederate forces that could be sent to reinforce General Joseph E. Johnston as he faced Sherman's forces in Georgia. There were some initial successes: river obstructions were removed; the Confederate fort defending the Red River, Fort De Russy, was captured; and Alexandria, Louisiana, was occupied (March 19). But things soon started going wrong, and the campaign quickly fell behind schedule. Banks was defeated by 8,000 Confederates under Major General Richard Taylor at the battle of Mansfield (Pleasant Grove; Sabine Cross Roads; April 8) and began a retreat that eliminated the possibility of an assault on Shreveport. Though the Federals defeated Taylor's reinforced Confederates the next day (battle of Pleasant Hill, April 9), Banks continued his withdrawal. On the river, Porter, too, was retreating while being subjected to near continuous fire by Confederates on land. (During the retreat, the river's water level was falling; eventually, a dam had to be built to raise the water level enough for most of Porter's fleet to make it back to the Mississippi River.) Meanwhile, an expedition from Arkansas, intended to assist Banks' assault on Shreveport by diverting Confederate cavalry from that city (the Camden Expedition, Arkansas, March 23–May 3), was plagued by lack of supplies and by the superior numbers of men the Confederates were able to throw in its path after Banks began his retreat. Led by Major General Frederick Steele, the Camden Expedition was a miserable failure. Overall, the Red River Campaign had not accomplished any of its objectives; it did, however, incite the anger of civilians from whom supplies had been expropriated. Worse, Banks never went to Mobile, and Confederate forces from that city did reinforce Johnston in Georgia.

BATTLE OF FORT PILLOW, TENNESSEE
(APRIL 12, 1864) *WESTERN*

In the midst of a series of raids they had been conducting in Kentucky and Tennessee, 1,500 Confederates under the command of Confederate Major General Nathan Bedford Forrest surrounded Fort Pillow, an earthwork fortification on the east bank of the Mississippi River. The fort was defended by 580 Union troops, including 295 black soldiers. Fierce fighting was interrupted by a short truce during which Forrest demanded the fort's surrender. Major William F. Bradford refused. A last assault took the fort—and precipitated what the North quickly labeled a Confederate massacre of Union troops, most particularly, black troops. Only 226 Federal soldiers were taken prisoner; 231 were killed and 100 were wounded. Though details were unclear at the time (and remain so today), it is certain that the Confederates did specifically target black soldiers. Their 64 percent death rate was more than twice that of whites (31 percent). Many were reportedly killed after they had put down their weapons and surrendered. Fort Pillow resulted in an investigation by the U.S. Joint Committee on the Conduct of the War, and in waves of outrage among Northern soldiers and civilians, both white and black.

BERMUDA HUNDRED CAMPAIGN (MAY 1864) *EASTERN*

A large neck of land just fifteen miles south of Richmond, Bermuda Hundred's strategic importance during the Civil War centered on the Richmond & Petersburg Railroad, a vital connection between the Confederate capital and points south—particularly the important railroad center of Petersburg, only seven miles distant. On May 5, 1864 (as Grant's Overland Campaign was opening with the battle of the Wilderness; see page 304), Union Major General Benjamin F. Butler and his 39,000-man Army of the James were landed at Bermuda Hundred with orders to conduct operations against Richmond. They began pushing westward—but with ponderous slowness. Severely outnumbered Confederates under Major General George E. Pickett and General P. G. T. Beauregard clashed with Federals at Port Walthall Junction on May 7 (Butler's army destroyed tracks and cut the telegraph line) and at Swift Creek (Arrowfield Church) on May 9 (Butler rejected a plan from his corps commanders that might have resulted in the capture of Petersburg; instead, he withdrew behind his newly constructed defenses.) Deciding to move toward Richmond, Butler was engaged by reinforced Confederate forces at Drewry's Bluff (Fort Darling, second battle of Drewry's Bluff) on May 16 and was forced to withdraw. His troops were sealed up behind their own defenses on the Bermuda Hundred peninsula. The threat to Richmond was relieved and would not be renewed by "Bottled Up Butler."

ATLANTA CAMPAIGN (MAY 1–SEPTEMBER 2, 1864) *WESTERN*

Under orders from Ulysses S. Grant to "move against [Joseph] Johnston's army, to break it up, and to get into the interior of the enemy's country as far as you can, inflicting all the damage you can against their war resources," Major General William T. Sherman embarked on this campaign, comprising the most crucial series of operations in the West. Basically following the line of the Western and Atlantic Railroad from Chattanooga, Tennessee, to Atlanta, Georgia, Sherman dogged the Confederate Army of Tennessee through encounters at Snake Creek Gap (May 7–12; his forces encountered troops from Mobile, Alabama, who had recently reinforced

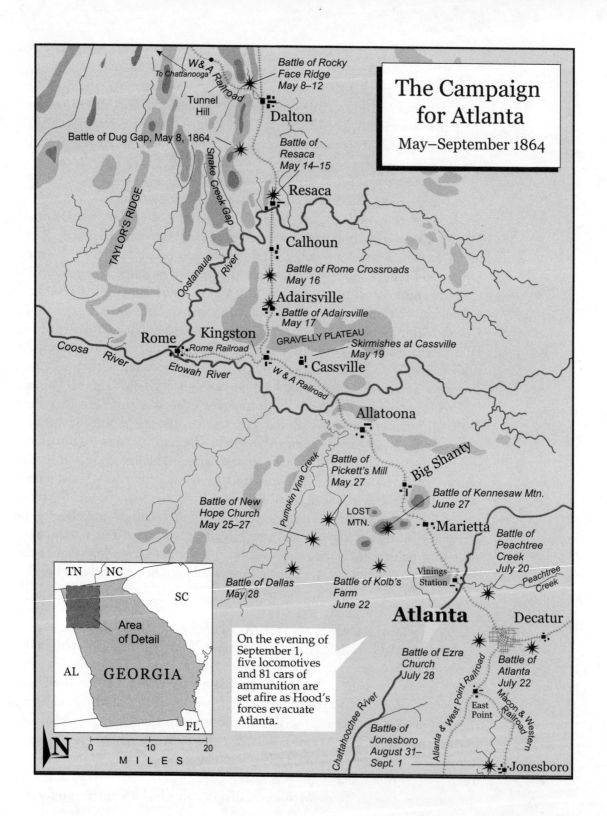

The Campaign for Atlanta
May–September 1864

Battle of Rocky Face Ridge May 8–12

To Chattanooga

W & A Railroad

Tunnel Hill

Dalton

Battle of Dug Gap, May 8, 1864

Snake Creek Gap

TAYLOR'S RIDGE

Battle of Resaca May 14–15

Resaca

Oostanaula River

Calhoun

Battle of Rome Crossroads May 16

Adairsville

Battle of Adairsville May 17

GRAVELLY PLATEAU

Skirmishes at Cassville May 19

Coosa River

Rome

Kingston

Rome Railroad

Etowah River

W & A Railroad

Cassville

Allatoona

Big Shanty

Battle of Pickett's Mill May 27

Battle of Kennesaw Mtn. June 27

Pumpkin Vine Creek

Battle of New Hope Church May 25–27

LOST MTN.

Marietta

Battle of Peachtree Creek July 20

Vinings Station

Peachtree Creek

Battle of Dallas May 28

Battle of Kolb's Farm June 22

Atlanta

Decatur

TN   NC

SC

Area of Detail

AL   GEORGIA

FL

N

0   10   20
M I L E S

On the evening of September 1, five locomotives and 81 cars of ammunition are set afire as Hood's forces evacuate Atlanta.

Battle of Ezra Church July 28

Chattahoochee River

Atlanta & West Point Railroad

East Point

Battle of Atlanta July 22

Macon & Western Railroad

Battle of Jonesboro August 31– Sept. 1

Jonesboro

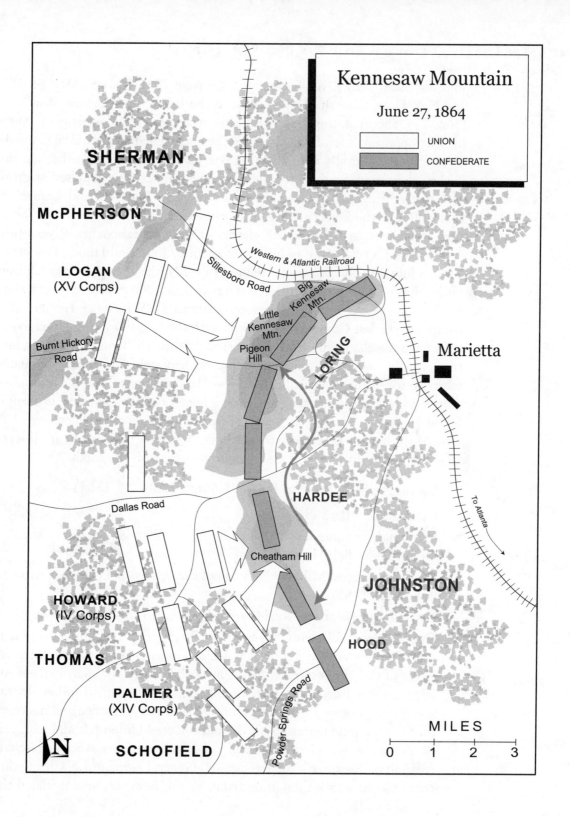

Kennesaw Mountain

June 27, 1864

UNION

CONFEDERATE

SHERMAN

McPHERSON

LOGAN
(XV Corps)

Stilesboro Road

Western & Atlantic Railroad

Big Kennesaw Mtn.

Little Kennesaw Mtn.

Pigeon Hill

LORING

Marietta

Burnt Hickory Road

Dallas Road

HARDEE

To Atlanta

Cheatham Hill

JOHNSTON

HOWARD
(IV Corps)

HOOD

THOMAS

Powder Springs Road

PALMER
(XIV Corps)

SCHOFIELD

N

MILES

0   1   2   3

Johnston; see "Red River Campaign," on page 296); Resaca (May 14–15); and New Hope Church (May 25–27). At the battle of Kennesaw Mountain (June 27), Sherman, impatient with repeated unsuccessful attempts to turn his wily opponent's left flank, attacked the entrenched center of the Confederate army in a literally uphill fight in one-hundred-degree heat that accomplished a surge in *Southern* morale when the attacks were repulsed at great cost to the Federals. But as Grant was doing in his Overland Campaign against Lee in the Eastern Theater, Sherman kept pushing. He forced Johnston ever closer to Atlanta with clashes at the Chattahoochee River (July 3–9; Johnston's retreat led to his replacement by John Bell Hood), Peachtree Creek (July 20), the battle of Atlanta (July 22), the battle of Ezra Church (July 28; the Confederates suffered an estimated 5,000 casualties to the Federals' 562), and the battle of Jonesboro (August 31–September 1; Sherman's troops cut the last Confederate rail link with the South, forcing Hood to retreat from the city). Union troops entered Atlanta, the Confederacy's industrial, supply, and communications hub, on September 2, 1862. Sherman's telegram to President Lincoln that day—"Atlanta is ours, and fairly won"—sent Northern spirits soaring and gave a huge boost to Lincoln's campaign for reelection in November. Southern spirits plunged at this new loss. Diarist Mary Boykin Chesnut wrote, "Since Atlanta I have felt as if all were dead within me, forever. We are going to be wiped off the earth."

Battle Profile: Atlanta, Fulton County (July 22, 1864)

Campaign: Atlanta.

Principal commanders: Major General William T. Sherman (U.S.A.); General John Bell Hood (C.S.A.).

Forces engaged: Military Division of the Mississippi (U.S.A.); Army of Tennessee (C.S.A.).

Estimated casualties: 12,140 total (U.S.A. 3,641; C.S.A. 8,499).

Description: Following the battle of Peachtree Creek (July 20), General Hood determined to attack Major General James B. McPherson's Army of the Tennessee. At night, he withdrew his main army from Atlanta's outer line to its inner line, enticing Sherman to follow. In the meantime, he sent Lieutenant General William J. Hardee and his corps on a fifteen-mile march to hit the unprotected Union left and rear, east of the city. Major General Joseph Wheeler's cavalry was to operate farther out on Sherman's supply line, and General Benjamin F. Cheatham's corps was to attack the Union front. Hood, however, miscalculated the

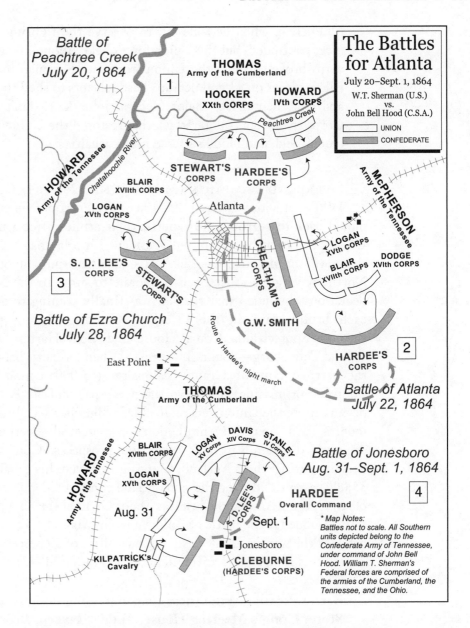

The Battles for Atlanta
July 20–Sept. 1, 1864
W.T. Sherman (U.S.)
vs.
John Bell Hood (C.S.A.)

Battle of Peachtree Creek
July 20, 1864

Battle of Ezra Church
July 28, 1864

Battle of Atlanta
July 22, 1864

Battle of Jonesboro
Aug. 31–Sept. 1, 1864

HARDEE
Overall Command

* Map Notes:
Battles not to scale. All Southern units depicted belong to the Confederate Army of Tennessee, under command of John Bell Hood. William T. Sherman's Federal forces are comprised of the armies of the Cumberland, the Tennessee, and the Ohio.

time necessary to make the march; Hardee was unable to attack until afternoon. Concerned about his left flank, McPherson sent his reserves— Grenville Dodge's Sixteenth Army Corps—to that location. Two of Hood's divisions ran into this reserve force and were repulsed. The Confederate attack stalled on the Union rear but began to roll up the left flank. Around the same time, a Confederate soldier shot and killed

McPherson when he rode out to observe the fighting. Determined attacks continued, but the Union forces held. About 4:00 P.M., Cheatham's corps broke through the Union front, but Sherman massed twenty artillery pieces on a knoll near his headquarters to shell these Confederates and halt their drive. Major General John A. Logan's Fifteenth Army Corps then led a counterattack that restored the Union line. The Union troops held, and Hood suffered high casualties.

OVERLAND CAMPAIGN (MAY 4–JUNE 12, 1864) *EASTERN*

While previous Federal Eastern Theater commanders had typically pulled back to regroup and reoutfit their armies after a major encounter, Ulysses S. Grant had promised President Lincoln that "whatever happens, there will be no turning back." His relentless pursuit of Lee's Army of Northern Virginia at first caused morale to surge in the North, where expectations abounded that the war was finally coming to an end. But with each brutal clash in the Overland Campaign—from the Wilderness, through Spotsylvania Court House and Cold Harbor, to the trenches around Petersburg—doubts increased. When casualty lists began showing the terrible cost of Grant's campaign (65,000 Union soldiers killed, wounded, or missing), some Northerners—particularly Peace Democrats—began calling the Union general in chief a "butcher." Transpiring during the months that preceded the Union's presidential election, these events dimmed Abraham Lincoln's reelection prospects. Confederates also lost heavily during the Overland Campaign. Given his smaller force, Lee's 35,000 casualties during the same period constituted a percentage comparable to Grant's. Among the lost was Major General J. E. B. (Jeb) Stuart, mortally wounded at the battle of Yellow Tavern (May 11). The bloodiest cavalry battle of the war (each side sustained casualties of 20 percent) also took place during this campaign—at Trevilian Station (June 11–12).

Battle Profile: Wilderness (encompassing combat at Parker's Store, Craig's Meeting House, Todd's Tavern, Brock Road, the Furnaces), Spotsylvania County (May 5–7, 1864)

Campaign: Grant's Overland Campaign (May–June 1864).

Principal commanders: Lieutenant General Ulysses S. Grant and Major General George G. Meade (U.S.A.); General Robert E. Lee (C.S.A.).

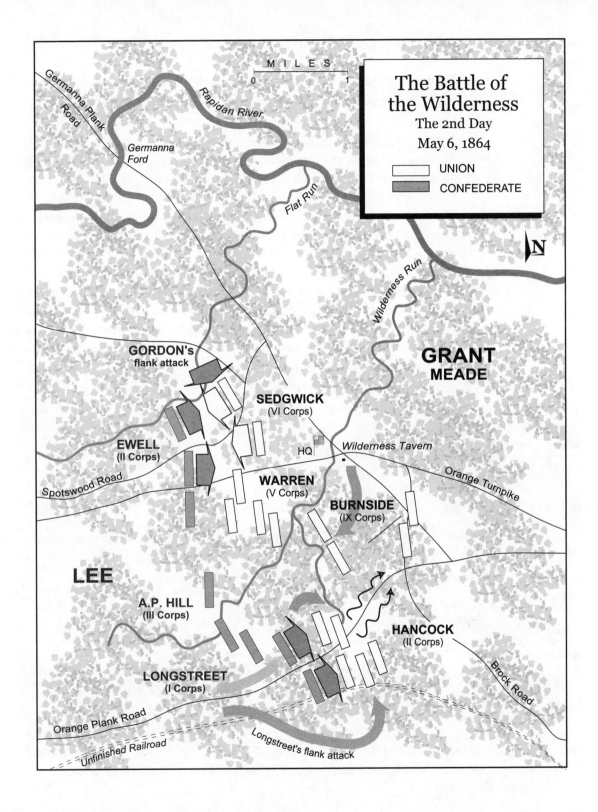

MILES

0   1

The Battle of
the Wilderness
The 2nd Day
May 6, 1864

UNION

CONFEDERATE

Germanna Plank Road

Rapidan River

Germanna Ford

Flat Run

Wilderness Run

GRANT
MEADE

N

GORDON's
flank attack

SEDGWICK
(VI Corps)

EWELL
(II Corps)

HQ

Wilderness Tavern

Orange Turnpike

Spotswood Road

WARREN
(V Corps)

BURNSIDE
(IX Corps)

LEE

A.P. HILL
(III Corps)

HANCOCK
(II Corps)

LONGSTREET
(I Corps)

Brock Road

Orange Plank Road

Unfinished Railroad

Longstreet's flank attack

★ **305**

Forces engaged: 162,920 total (U.S.A. 101,895; C.S.A. 61,025).

Estimated casualties: 29,800 total (U.S.A. 18,400; C.S.A. 11,400).

Description: On the morning of May 5, 1864, the Union Fifth Corps attacked Lieutenant General Richard S. Ewell's corps on the Orange Turnpike. During the afternoon, Confederate General A. P. Hill's corps encountered Brigadier General George W. Getty's Division (Sixth Corps) and Major General Whitfield S. Hancock's Second Corps on the Plank Road. Fighting was fierce but inconclusive; both sides were attempting to maneuver in dense woods. Darkness halted the fighting, and both sides rushed forward reinforcements. At dawn on May 6, Hancock attacked along the Plank Road and drove Hill's corps back in confusion. Lieutenant General James Longstreet's corps arrived in time to prevent the collapse of the Confederate right flank. At noon, a devastating Confederate flank attack in Hamilton's Thicket sputtered out when Longstreet was wounded by his own men. The Ninth Corps (Burnside) moved against the Confederate center but was repulsed. Union generals James S. Wadsworth and Alexander Hays were killed, as were Confederate

Wounded soldiers escape from the burning woods during the battle of the Wilderness. Drawing by Alfred Waud.

generals John M. Jones, Micah Jenkins, and Leroy A. Stafford. The battle was a tactical draw. On May 7, the Federals advanced by the left flank toward the crossroads of Spotsylvania Courthouse.

Battle Profile: Spotsylvania Court House (encompassing clashes at Laurel Hill and Corbin's Bridge, May 8; Ni River, May 9; Laurel Hill, Po River, and Bloody Angle, May 10; Salient or Bloody Angle, May 12; Piney Branch Church, May 15; Harrison House, May 18; Harris Farm, May 19), Spotsylvania County (May 8–21, 1864)

Campaign: Grant's Overland Campaign (May–June 1864).

Principal commanders: Lieutenant General Ulysses S. Grant and Major General George G. Meade (U.S.A.); General Robert E. Lee (C.S.A.).

Forces engaged: 152,000 total (U.S.A. 100,000; C.S.A. 52,000).

Estimated casualties: 30,000 total (U.S.A. 18,000; C.S.A. 12,000).

Description: After the Wilderness, Grant's and Meade's advance on Richmond by the left flank was stalled at Spotsylvania Court House on May 8. This two-week battle comprised a series of clashes along the

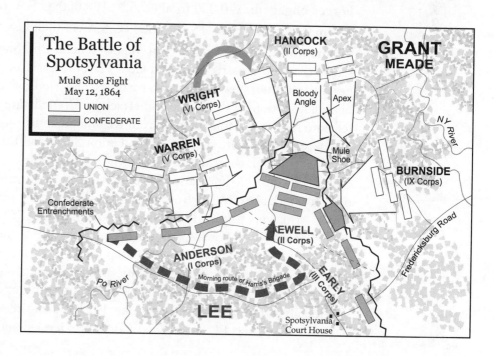

The Battle of Spotsylvania
Mule Shoe Fight
May 12, 1864
UNION
CONFEDERATE

HANCOCK (II Corps)
GRANT
MEADE
WRIGHT (VI Corps)
Bloody Angle
Apex
N Y River
WARREN (V Corps)
Mule Shoe
BURNSIDE (IX Corps)
Confederate Entrenchments
EWELL (II Corps)
Fredericksburg Road
ANDERSON (I Corps)
Morning route of Harris's Brigade
EARLY (III Corps)
Po River
LEE
Spotsylvania Court House

Spotsylvania front. The Union attack against the Bloody Angle (Mule Shoe), at dawn on May 12, captured nearly a division of Lee's army and came near to cutting the Confederate army in half. Confederate counterattacks plugged the gap, and fighting continued unabated for nearly twenty hours in what may well have been the most ferociously sustained combat of the Civil War. On May 19, a Confederate attempt to turn the Union right flank at Harris Farm was beaten back with severe casualties. Union generals John Sedgwick (Sixth Corps commander) and James C. Rice were killed. Confederate generals Edward Johnson and George H. Steuart were captured, and Junius Daniel and Abner M. Perrin were mortally wounded. On May 21, Grant disengaged and continued his advance on Richmond.

Battle Profile: Cold Harbor (Second Cold Harbor), Hanover County (May 31–June 12, 1864)

Campaign: Grant's Overland Campaign (May–June 1864).

Principal commanders: Lieutenant General Ulysses S. Grant and Major General George G. Meade (U.S.A.); General Robert E. Lee (C.S.A.).

Forces engaged: 170,000 total (U.S.A. 108,000; C.S.A. 62,000).

Estimated casualties: 15,500 total (U.S.A. 13,000; C.S.A. 2,500).

Description: On May 31, Union Major General Phil Sheridan's cavalry seized the vital crossroads of Old Cold Harbor. Early on June 1, relying heavily on their new repeating carbines and shallow entrenchments, Sheridan's troopers threw back an attack by Confederate infantry. Confederate reinforcements arrived from Richmond and from the Totopotomoy Creek lines. Late on June 1, the Union Sixth and Eighteenth Corps reached Cold Harbor and assaulted the Confederate works with some success. By June 2, both armies were on the field, forming on a seven-mile front that extended from Bethesda Church to the Chickahominy River. At dawn on June 3, the Second and Eighteenth Corps, followed later by the Ninth Corps, assaulted along the Bethesda Church-Cold Harbor line and were slaughtered at all points. An estimated 7,000 Union soldiers were killed or wounded in this action alone. "I regret this assault more than any one I have ever ordered," Grant said that evening. But he continued to move forward. On June 12, his army reached the James River, and on June 14, the Second Corps was ferried across the river at

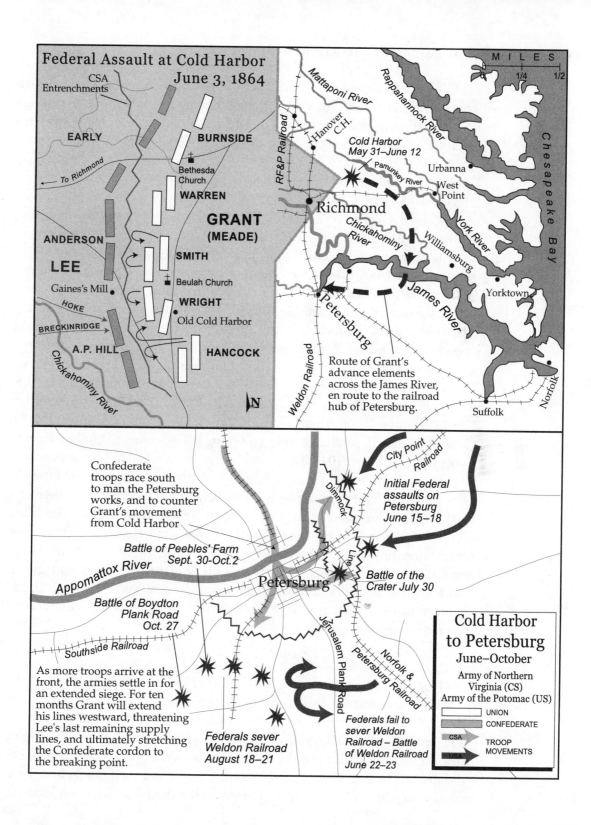

Federal Assault at Cold Harbor
June 3, 1864

CSA Entrenchments

EARLY

BURNSIDE

Bethesda Church

WARREN

GRANT (MEADE)

To Richmond

ANDERSON

LEE

SMITH

Beulah Church

Gaines's Mill

HOKE

WRIGHT

BRECKINRIDGE

Old Cold Harbor

A.P. HILL

HANCOCK

Chickahominy River

N

MILES

1/4   1/2

Mattaponi River

Rappahannock River

Hanover C.H.

Cold Harbor
May 31–June 12

Pamunkey River

Urbanna

RF&P Railroad

West Point

Richmond

Chickahominy River

Williamsburg

York River

Yorktown

Chesapeake Bay

Petersburg

James River

Weldon Railroad

Suffolk

Norfolk

Route of Grant's advance elements across the James River, en route to the railroad hub of Petersburg.

Confederate troops race south to man the Petersburg works, and to counter Grant's movement from Cold Harbor

City Point Railroad

Dimmock

Initial Federal assaults on Petersburg June 15–18

Battle of Peebles' Farm
Sept. 30-Oct.2

Appomattox River

Petersburg

Line

Battle of the Crater July 30

Battle of Boydton Plank Road
Oct. 27

Southside Railroad

Jerusalem Plank Road

Norfolk & Petersburg Railroad

As more troops arrive at the front, the armies settle in for an extended siege. For ten months Grant will extend his lines westward, threatening Lee's last remaining supply lines, and ultimately stretching the Confederate cordon to the breaking point.

Federals sever Weldon Railroad August 18–21

Federals fail to sever Weldon Railroad – Battle of Weldon Railroad June 22–23

Cold Harbor to Petersburg
June–October

Army of Northern Virginia (CS)
Army of the Potomac (US)

UNION	
CONFEDERATE	
CSA	TROOP MOVEMENTS
USA	

Wilcox's Landing by transports. On June 15, the rest of the army began crossing on a 2,200-foot-long pontoon bridge at Weyanoke. Bypassing the well-defended approaches to Richmond, Grant sought to shift his army quickly south of the river, to threaten Petersburg.

ACTIONS AGAINST NATHAN BEDFORD FORREST
(JUNE–AUGUST 1864) *WESTERN*

As Major General William T. Sherman moved deeper into the South during his Atlanta Campaign (see page 299), one of his foremost concerns was the security of his rail supply line from Chattanooga and Nashville, Tennessee. A chief reason for Sherman's concern was Confederate Major General Nathan Bedford Forrest, the South's most feared cavalry commander. Based in northeast Mississippi, Forrest had a long history of destructive raiding. To forestall such raids against his supply line, Sherman dispatched Brigadier General Samuel D. Sturgis, in Memphis, to seek out and destroy Forrest's corps. This first movement against Forrest began on June 2, 1864, and culminated in one of the most humiliating defeats in U.S. Army history—at Brice's Cross Roads, Mississippi (Guntown, Tishomingo Creek) on June 10. Sherman, furious, ordered a second try, telling Major General Andrew J. Smith, then in La Grange, Tennessee, to "follow Forrest to the death, if it cost 10,000 lives and breaks the Treasury. There never will be peace in Tennessee till Forrest is dead." Smith's attempt yielded better results for the Union. Engaging a Confederate force comprising Forrest's corps and 2,000 reinforcements—under the overall command of Lieutenant General Stephen D. Lee—near Tupelo, Mississippi (battle of Tupelo, or Harrisburg, July 14–15), Smith's Federals dealt with a series of uncoordinated Confederate charges and inflicted many casualties. Short on rations, Smith did not pursue and destroy the Confederates. But Forrest had been wounded in the battle, and Sherman's anxiety about his supply line was at least temporarily relieved.

PETERSBURG CAMPAIGN
(JUNE 15, 1864–APRIL 3, 1865) *EASTERN*

"We must destroy this army of Grant's before it gets to the James River," General Robert E. Lee said to Lieutenant General Jubal Early in June 1864, as Grant's Overland Campaign pushed the Army of Northern Virginia steadily back toward the Confederate cities of Richmond and Petersburg. "If he gets there it will become a siege, and then it will be a mere question of time." Grant's army began crossing the James River on June 12.

By June 15, 48,000 Federal troops, still suffering from the effects of the Union's bloody assaults at Spotsylvania Court House and Cold Harbor, were cautiously attacking some 5,400 Confederates, led by General P. G. T. Beauregard, defending the vital railroad center of Petersburg (assault on Petersburg, June 15–18). As Lee sent reinforcements to bolster Beauregard, the Union assaults failed, and Lee's prediction came true. Both sides dug in and erected elaborate trenchworks foreshadowing those that would stretch across World War I's stalemated Western Front. The ten-month siege of Petersburg had begun. In this longest sustained operation of the Civil War, Generals Grant and Meade gradually extended the Union lines around Petersburg, forcing Lee to stretch the Confederate lines, and his resources, to the breaking point. The Petersburg Campaign comprised long periods of deadly dull trench warfare, interspersed with clashes by which one side or the other attempted to gain advantage. In 1864, in addition to the initial assault on Petersburg, those clashes included:

- **Weldon Railroad Operations (June 22–August 21, 1864):** To tighten the siege on Petersburg, Grant determined to cut, as early as possible, the railroads that brought supplies into the city. The Weldon Railroad, closest to the Union lines in the summer of 1864, connected Petersburg to Weldon, North Carolina. The first Union attempt to cut it, in late June, failed. The second attempt, in mid-August, also met fierce resistance that culminated in the battle of Weldon Railroad (Globe Tavern; August 18–20), in which the Confederates did not succeed in shaking Federal forces loose from the position they had assumed astride the railroad line. Confederates in Petersburg were now forced to move supplies around the Union troops holding the severed rail line.

- **Battle of the Crater (Petersburg, Virginia; July 30, 1864):** In another operation that foreshadowed the Western Front operations during World War I, the commander of a regiment that included many coal miners—Lieutenant Colonel Henry Pleasants of the Forty-Eighth Pennsylvania—suggested tunneling under the Confederate lines at Petersburg and setting a huge powder charge that would blow a gap in the lines. In the face of much skepticism, the inventive plan was adopted and placed under the supervision of Major General Ambrose E. Burnside. The miners set to work on June 25. On July 23, the 511-foot tunnel was completed; four days later, 8,000 pounds of powder had been placed in two seventy-five-foot lateral galleries that ran under the Confederate lines. Preparations above the ground did not go as smoothly, however. When the explosion occurred—at 4:45 A.M. on July 30, killing some 300 Confederates and creating a crater some 170 feet long, seventy feet wide, and thirty feet deep—Union troops charged directly into the crater rather than advancing around it. Confederate forces rallied quickly and began firing down on the Federals—targeting, particularly, African American troops, even those attempting to surrender. There were 3,798 Union casualties and an estimated 1,500 Confederate casualties from the battle. Grant called it "the saddest affair I have witnessed in the war." The battle of the Crater became the subject of a military court of inquiry. Ambrose Burnside and two of his subordinates, Brigadier General Edward Ferrero and Brigadier General James H. Ledlie, were found chiefly responsible for this Union fiasco (see also "Significant Campaigns and Battles—1865" for information on further Petersburg engagements).

EARLY'S WASHINGTON RAID (JUNE 12–JULY 15, 1864) *EASTERN*
In May and June, 1864, Union troops under Major General David Hunter conducted a destructive raid into Virginia's Shenandoah Valley. The raid provoked fury in the South and negative editorial comment by some Northern papers. (Hunter's troops burned the Virginia Military Institute, the home of former Virginia governor John Letcher, and, in retaliation for guerrilla activity, numerous private homes.) The raid was brought to a halt by forces under Jubal Early, which had been detached from Lee's main army to meet Hunter at Lynchburg (June 16–18, 1864). Hunter's subsequent retreat into West Virginia left the Shenandoah Valley open to Early's force, which General Lee then dispatched on a mission into Northern territory, a successful effort to relieve the pressure on Southern troops defending Petersburg by menacing now-vulnerable Washington, D.C. As Early approached Washington, he exacted ransoms amounting to $220,000 from the Maryland cities of Hagerstown and Frederick before being met near the Monocacy River by some 7,000 Union troops (about half the number of Early's Confederates) commanded by Major General Lew Wallace. The one-day delay in Confederate progress won by the Federals at the battle of Monocacy (July 9) made it possible for reinforcements to reach Washington from Grant's army at Petersburg before Early could mount an all-out assault on the Union capital. The arrival of this Confederate force at the city, however, did create a sensation among the city's inhabitants and constituted the only major threat the city faced during the war. This was also the only time that

President Lincoln came under direct fire from Confederate forces. Visiting Fort Stevens, in the Washington defensive lines, he became so interested in seeing the invaders that a young captain, Oliver Wendell Holmes, Jr.—not realizing at first to whom he was talking—yelled out, "Get down, you damn fool, before you get shot!" (The president obeyed.) After these probing attacks revealed the increased strength of the Washington garrison, Early turned back toward the Shenandoah Valley, where he routed pursuing Northerners at the second battle of Kernstown (July 24). He also dispatched more than 2,600 cavalry on a raid into southern Pennsylvania. They burned much of the town of Chambersburg when its citizens refused to pay a $100,000 ransom. (The Confederates cited Hunter's earlier actions in the Shenandoah as justification for the action.) Early's raid and subsequent successes so angered General Grant that he formed a new Army of the Shenandoah, under the command of Phil Sheridan, and ordered it to "pursue Early to the death."

BATTLE OF MOBILE BAY, ALABAMA (AUGUST 5, 1864)
LOWER SEABOARD AND GULF APPROACH

A major entryway for supplies to the Confederacy from abroad, Mobile, Alabama, was accessed through Mobile Bay, which was guarded by the formidable Fort Morgan—as well as underwater mines (called *torpedoes* in the Civil War) and a small Confederate naval contingent of three gunboats and the ironclad *Tennessee*, under the command of Admiral Franklin Buchanan. U.S. Rear Admiral David Farragut had been planning for an assault on the Bay since January 1864. On August 5, he and his fleet of fourteen wooden ships and four monitors, began their attack. When one of the ironclads, U.S.S. *Tecumseh*, struck a mine and floundered, endangering the entire fleet, Farragut maneuvered his flagship, U.S.S. *Hartford*, through the minefield—while Farragut himself, lashed to a mast, shouted, "Damn the torpedoes, full speed ahead!" Despite valiant resistance from Fort Morgan, and particularly Buchanan's ironclad, which took on the entire Union fleet all by itself, the fort and the bay soon fell to the Union. The city of Mobile did not fall until 1865, but this battle closed its port to all shipping.

SHERIDAN'S SHENANDOAH VALLEY CAMPAIGN
(AUGUST 7, 1864–MARCH 2, 1865) *EASTERN*

Union Major General Philip Sheridan and his newly formed Army of the Shenandoah had two main objectives in what would prove to be one of the most decisive campaigns of the war: first, to destroy Confederate Lieutenant

General Jubal Early's army; and, second, to destroy the fertile Valley's capacity to be the "Breadbasket of the Confederacy." The hard war was to be brought home to the Valley's inhabitants under Grant's orders that nothing "should be left to invite the enemy to return. Take all provisions, forage and stock wanted for the use of your command. Such as cannot be consumed, destroy." Confederate invasion forces and guerrilla bands would find it much more difficult to operate in an area so deprived that, in Grant's words, "crows flying over it . . . will have to carry their provender with them." Pursuit of Early's army—tentative at first due to fear that a bad loss in the Valley would damage Lincoln's chances for reelection—became all-out after Sherman boosted Lincoln's chances by taking Atlanta on September 2. Major engagements in this campaign included:

- **Third Battle of Winchester, Virginia (Opequon Creek; September 19, 1864):** Outnumbered nearly three to one, Early's Confederates resisted stubbornly during this encounter, until a Union division got beyond their left flank and charged. The assault fragmented the Confederate ranks and led to a Confederate retreat. Although he had made some potentially disastrous tactical errors during the battle, Sheridan was able to report to Grant that he had sent Early's forces "Whirling through Winchester."

- **Battle of Fisher's Hill, Virginia (September 22, 1864):** Fisher's Hill, a high, steep bluff dominating the Valley at its narrowest point, was, when adequately manned, a nearly impregnable position. Early's Confederates settled into the hill's existing trenchworks on September 20. With their ranks reduced to approximately 9,000, their lines were spread too thin to defend against the Union attacks that were mounted, on September 22, against their front, flank, and rear. The Confederate lines broke, and Early's army was saved from complete disaster only by darkness and the failure of Union cavalry to cut off their retreat. The battle left the upper Valley clear of all but Union troops and—along with the victory at Winchester—provided another boost to Lincoln's reelection campaign.

- **Battle of Cedar Creek, Virginia (October 19, 1864):** With his campaign proceeding in good order, Sheridan was on his way to Washington for a strategy conference when Jubal Early put into action a bold plan proposed by Major General John Brown Gordon and Stonewall Jackson's former mapmaker, Major Jedediah Hotchkiss. In the early morning of October 19, Confederates surprised Union infantry forces and broke their lines, forcing them to retreat. The Confederates, however, did not press them hard enough to prevent their regrouping. General Sheridan, having heard of the battle, rode back on his warhorse, Rienzi, and inspired his men as they counterattacked. The event was memorialized in a poem, "Sheridan's Ride," and in many color lithograph depictions that became wildly popular in the North (see Chapter 12, "The Civil War in Literature and the Arts"). The counterattack smashed the Confederates and they retreated. Sheridan would meet and defeat the remnants of Early's army on March 2, 1865, at Waynesborough, Virginia.

PRICE'S MISSOURI RAID OF 1864 (SEPTEMBER–OCTOBER 1864) *TRANS-MISSISSIPPI*

Former Missouri governor Major General Sterling Price led a ragtag army (12,000 men, some one-third of whom were unarmed) on this last-ditch effort to recapture Missouri for the Confederacy. A secondary objective was to influence the approaching U.S. presidential election. Price believed that success in Missouri would help to ensure the victory of Peace Democrat George B. McClellan, who would then negotiate an end to the war that would recognize the Confederacy and leave it, and its institutions, intact. Fighting skirmishes all along the way, wrecking railroads, drawing sympathetic Missourians into his ranks (though many were guerrillas and bushwackers whose tendency to loot and pillage provoked protest), and confiscating so much loot and supplies that its march was slowed by its 500-wagon supply train, Price's force suffered severe casualties during frontal assaults at a Federal fort near Pilot Knob (September 28). The Confederates were finally forced to end their campaign and withdraw to Texas when they were defeated at the battle of Westport (October 23). This unsuccessful campaign proved to be the end of organized Confederate operations in the Trans-Mississippi Theater. In Missouri, however, guerrilla warfare continued.

FEDERAL RAID ON SALTVILLE, VIRGINIA (MASSACRE OF BLACK UNION SOLDIERS; OCTOBER 2, 1864) *EASTERN*

This Union foray, under Federal Brigadier General Stephen G. Burbridge, was directed at a railroad depot and supply center in southwestern Virginia, the only section of the state from which Lee could draw supplies for his entrenched army at Petersburg—particularly the vital commodity salt, without which beef could not be preserved for army rations. Some 3,600 Federals—including 400 black soldiers of the Fifth and Sixth U.S. Colored Cavalry—attacked 2,800 Confederate troops protected by stone and log barricades and were repeatedly repulsed. Some 350 dead and wounded were left on the field when they finally withdrew. The next morning, one of the more brutal events of the war took place: Confederates murdered a number of wounded black soldiers.

SHERMAN'S MARCH TO THE SEA (SAVANNAH CAMPAIGN; NOVEMBER–DECEMBER 1864) *WESTERN*

After pausing to rest and strategize in Atlanta and engaging in a brief pursuit of John Bell Hood's Confederate army, now heading toward Tennessee (see "Franklin-Nashville Campaign," on page 3), Major General William T. Sherman embarked (November 15) with his main force of 62,000 men (divided into two columns, to confuse the enemy as to his ultimate objective) on a march from Atlanta toward Savannah and the Atlantic Ocean, to "demonstrate the vulnerability of the South." Planning to travel without a supply train, Sherman issued orders that the men were to forage on the land. The orders also stated that his army was to abide by certain rules even as they attempted to destroy the area's militarily useful resources (rules that, in the event, were often broadly interpreted):

> In districts and neighborhoods where the army is unmolested, no destruction of such property [as houses, cotton gins, and grist mills] should be permitted; but should guerrillas or bushwhackers molest our march, or should the inhabitants burn bridges, obstruct roads, or otherwise manifest local hostility, then army commanders should order and enforce a devastation more or less relentless, according to the measure of such hostility.

In twenty-six days, Sherman's army marched 250 miles, with minimal opposition from Confederate militia, state troops, and a cavalry corps commanded by Major General Joseph Wheeler that was under-strength and could only harass, not assault, the Federals. The Georgia state capital of Milledgeville, on which both Union columns converged, was deprived of all military utility (November 22–24). Railroads in the surrounding area were destroyed, supply depots were wrecked, and government buildings in the city were sacked. As the columns continued toward Savannah, through a region that had been little touched by the war's devastation before, Sherman's "bummers" left a wide path of destruction in their wake; they caused some $100 million in damages before they arrived outside Savannah on December 10.

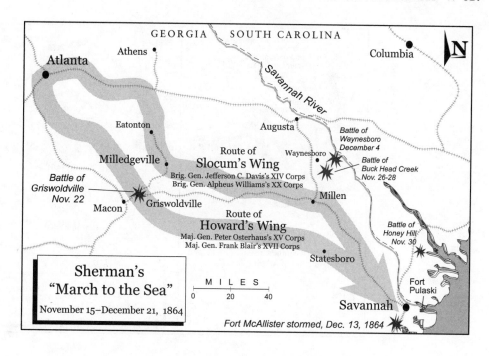

GEORGIA   SOUTH CAROLINA

Atlanta

Athens

Columbia

Savannah River

Eatonton

Augusta

Route of
Slocum's Wing
Brig. Gen. Jefferson C. Davis's XIV Corps
Brig. Gen. Alpheus Williams's XX Corps

Waynesboro

*Battle of
Waynesboro
December 4*

*Battle of
Buck Head Creek
Nov. 26-28*

Milledgeville

*Battle of
Griswoldville
Nov. 22*

Griswoldville

Macon

Millen

Route of
Howard's Wing
Maj. Gen. Peter Osterhaus's XV Corps
Maj. Gen. Frank Blair's XVII Corps

*Battle of
Honey Hill
Nov. 30*

Statesboro

Sherman's
"March to the Sea"

November 15–December 21, 1864

M I L E S
0   20   40

Fort
Pulaski

Savannah

Fort McAllister stormed, Dec. 13, 1864

FRANKLIN-NASHVILLE CAMPAIGN (HOOD'S TENNESSEE CAMPAIGN; NOVEMBER 29–DECEMBER 27, 1864) *WESTERN*

After retreating from Atlanta, Confederate General John B. Hood was pursued by Sherman to northwest Alabama. Sherman then withdrew to Atlanta and dispatched three of his corps to Nashville, Tennessee, where his former second in command, Major General George Thomas, had assumed command October 3, to help protect this area that provided vital support for Sherman's operations in Georgia. Reinforced by Nathan Bedford Forrest's cavalry, Hood did, in fact, invade Tennessee (November 21) with some 39,000 men who formed three columns, intending to defeat Thomas, crush Sherman's base of support, and, perhaps, move through Kentucky and toward Grant's rear at Petersburg. Instead, while Sherman marched toward the Atlantic coast at Savannah, Federal forces under Major General John M. Schofield met Hood's army head-on at Franklin, Tennessee (November 30), where Hood insisted on a disastrous frontal assault on entrenched positions that resulted in 6,200 casualties. Among the dead were six Confederate generals (Patrick R. Cleburne, States Rights Gist, H. B. Granbury, John Adams, O. F. Strahl, and John C. Carter). With five other generals wounded and one captured, the command structure of Hood's army was severely damaged.

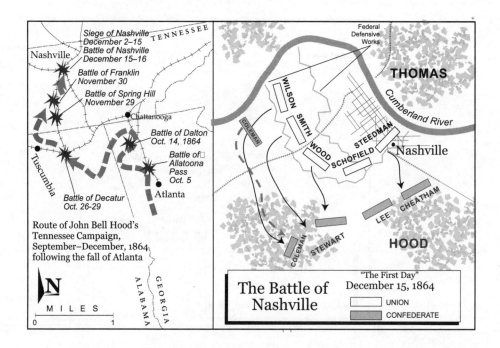

Federal forces withdrew to George Thomas' lines at Nashville (with their arrival, Federal strength in the city stood at about 70,000 men), and Hood immediately followed, forming lines around the city. After two weeks of preparation (during which Thomas was pressured by both Grant and Secretary of War Stanton to "attack Hood at once"), Thomas charged out of the city and all but destroyed the Confederate Army of Tennessee in the climactic battle of Nashville.

Battle Profile: Nashville, Davidson County (December 15–16, 1864)

Campaign: Franklin-Nashville Campaign (1864).

Principal commanders: Major General George H. Thomas (U.S.A.); General John Bell Hood (C.S.A.).

Forces engaged: Fourth Army Corps, Twenty-Third Army Corps, Detachment of Army of the Tennessee, provisional detachment, and cavalry corps (U.S.A.); Army of Tennessee (C.S.A.).

Estimated casualties: 9,061 total (U.S.A. 3,061; C.S.A. 4,500 captured, 1,500 killed and wounded).

Description: Before daylight on December 15, the first of the Union troops, led by Major General James Steedman, attacked the Confederate right and held down one Confederate corps there for the rest of the day. The Union attack on the Confederate left did not begin until the afternoon. A successful charge on Montgomery Hill, followed by attacks on other parts of the Southern left, were all eventually successful. When fighting stopped at dark, General Hood was able to establish a main line of resistance along the base of a ridge about two miles south of his original line. New battle works were thrown up, and Shy's Hill and Overton's Hill, on the Confederates' flanks, were fortified. In the morning, the Union Fourth Army Corps marched out to within 250 yards, in some places, of the Confederates' new line and began constructing fieldworks; other Union troops subsequently moved up as well. The Union attack began against Hood's strong right flank. After the Confederate positions on Shy's Hill and Overton's Hill were overrun by the Federals, Hood's army retreated to Tupelo, Mississippi. Hood resigned his command on January 13, 1865.

STONEMAN'S RAID INTO SOUTHWESTERN VIRGINIA (DECEMBER 1, 1864–JANUARY 1, 1865) *EASTERN*

Union Major General George Stoneman—a veteran, if undistinguished officer who had just returned to duty after being a prisoner of war—had one of his greatest wartime successes in this raid. After routing an understrength Confederate cavalry brigade at Kingsport, Tennessee (December 13), Stoneman's command of some 5,700 cavalry and horse artillery progressed toward Saltville, in southwestern Virginia, destroying every factory, train, bridge, supply depot, mill, mine, foundry, and warehouse (as well as what Stoneman called "four pestiferous secession printing-presses"). The Federals defeated Confederates under Major General John C. Breckinridge (December 18) and dispersed the 700 remaining Virginia home guards who were defending the crucial saltworks at Saltville, then destroyed the works along with 50,000 to 100,000 bushels of salt. These actions further strained the dwindling Confederate resources.

BUTLER'S NORTH CAROLINA EXPEDITION (DECEMBER 7–27, 1864) *EASTERN*

See "Operations against Fort Fisher and Wilmington, North Carolina, December 7, 1864–February 22, 1865" on page 321.

Significant Battles and Campaigns—1865

I have outlived my momentary depression, & feel my courage revive when I think of the brave army in front of us, sixty thousand strong. As long as Lee's army remains intact there is no cause for despondency. As long as it holds true we need not fear. The attacks of the enemy will now all be directed against that Army. Sherman from the South, Thomas from the West and Grant in front. We must sustain & strengthen this army—that is the business before us.—Josiah Gorgas, Chief of Ordnance, C.S.A., diary entry, January 25, 1865.

★   ★   ★

The news of Lee's surrender is true. Better than all my hopes was the prospect of the end of the war. . . . Joy on every face and tongue. I could not see or hear of a secession sympathizer. I went to bed happy . . . and came down this morning to be astounded by the news that President Lincoln was assassinated last night at Ford's Theater in Washington and Secretary Seward and his son were stabbed at almost the same hour. . . . It is too terrible to think of, and I cannot imagine the consequences. . . . What can we do with such a President as Andy Johnson? What effect will it have on the question of peace? Well, we can do nothing but wait. The nation's joy is changed to mourning and to mutterings of vengeance on the cowardly assassins and the infamous plotters who arranged the murders.—Lieutenant Oliver Willcox Norton, U.S.A., letter, April 15, 1865.

The year opened with expectations in the North for victory at last, and with despair in the South, accompanied by continuation of a fighting spirit. Hood's army had been broken at Nashville, but effective fighting forces still existed in the Western Theater, and Robert E. Lee's Army of Northern Virginia—low on rations, and experiencing a growing desertion rate—still stood fast at Petersburg and Richmond. But all the Union forces were now turning toward Lee, who, as the Union's Petersburg Campaign ended on April 2, was forced to relinquish Petersburg and Richmond. By April 9, pursued by forces that outnumbered his by nearly three to one, he was forced to surrender this army that had formed the heart of the South's military effort. The war continued for more than a month, through the assassination of Abraham Lincoln (April 14) and the accession of Andrew Johnson of Tennessee to the presidency. Mobile, Alabama, became the last major Confederate city to fall (April 12); troops under Joseph E. Johnston surrendered in North Carolina on April 26, the day presidential assassin John Wilkes Booth was killed; and President Johnson declared all armed resistance at an end on

May 10—two days before the last land fight of the war occurred, at Palmito Ranch near Brownsville, Texas.

OPERATIONS AGAINST FORT FISHER AND WILMINGTON, NORTH CAROLINA
(DECEMBER 7, 1864–FEBRUARY 22, 1865) *EASTERN*

The South's most important blockade-running port—and, in 1864, after Union Rear Admiral David Farragut's triumph at Mobile Bay, the only major Confederate seaport open to trade with the outside world—Wilmington, North Carolina, with its vital railroads and shipyards, was surrounded by fortifications and protected, by the width of a peninsula, from bombardment by Union vessels at sea. Its most formidable defense was Fort Fisher, which the fort's commander, Colonel William Lamb, had made such a bastion—it was protected by a minefield and many artillery emplacements—that it was known as the "Gibraltar of the South." In December 1864, Union General in Chief Ulysses S. Grant had dispatched a combined land-sea force under Major General Benjamin F. Butler and Rear Admiral David D. Porter to either take the fort or besiege it. Plagued by bad weather and Butler's inability to coordinate such a large combined-force operation, the December assault on Fort Fisher (battle of Fort Fisher, December 23–27, 1864) failed. Butler then disengaged entirely, instead of beginning a siege, as Grant had ordered. Infuriated, Grant relieved him of command and directed that a second attempt be made—this time under the joint command of Porter and Brigadier General Alfred H. Terry. With some 9,600 men and more than sixty ships—the largest army-navy operation of the Civil War—this expedition was a success. Beginning with a damaging bombardment (January 13–15), the expedition culminated in a land assault (January 15) that included some of the fiercest close-quarters fighting of the war. With the fort in Union hands and the subsequent arrival of reinforcements, the Union army, with river support from Porter's flotilla, moved against Confederate forces and fortifications defending Wilmington. The Confederates evacuated the city on February 22, and Union troops occupied it the same day. Depriving Lee of his most vital supply line, the fall of Wilmington was a devastating blow to the Confederacy.

PETERSBURG CAMPAIGN
(JUNE 15, 1864–APRIL 3, 1865) *EASTERN*

Still pressing to dislodge the Army of Northern Virginia from Petersburg and Richmond (see also "Petersburg Campaign" in "Significant

Campaigns and Battles—1864"), the Union's Army of the Potomac continued the trench warfare that characterized the siege. Before the two Virginia cities fell on April 2 and 3, clashes between the two forces included:

- **Battle of Hatcher's Run (Armstrong's Mill; Boydton Plank Road; Dabney's Mill; Vaughan Road; February 5–7):** Directed against Confederates guarding the Southside Railroad and the Boydton Plank Road, along which Confederate wagon supply trains reportedly moved, this encounter involved over 35,000 Union troops (1,512 of whom became casualties) and some 14,000 Confederates (casualty figures are uncertain) and forced the Confederates to stretch their already attenuated Petersburg lines, which, at the end of the encounter, extended thirty-seven miles. Confederate division commander Brigadier General John Pegram was killed during this battle.

- **Fort Stedman, Virginia (March 25):** Hearing of the rout of Jubal Early's remaining troops at Waynesborough, Virginia (March 2), General Robert E. Lee realized that Sheridan was now free to reinforce Grant at Petersburg. Before that happened, Lee determined to force enough of a break in Union lines to allow at least some of his men to escape and join General Joseph E. Johnston's Confederate army in North Carolina. Committing nearly half of his army, he chose Fort Stedman, at the right of the Union lines, as the target. Initially successful, the effort deteriorated, over the course of a long day, into a bloody fiasco that cost Lee more than 4,000 casualties. That evening, Lee wrote to Jefferson Davis: "I fear now it will be impossible to prevent a junction between Grant and Sherman, nor do I deem it prudent that this army should maintain its position until the latter shall approach too near." (Major General William T. Sherman's army, opposed by Johnston's Confederates, was moving up toward Lee's rear through North Carolina; see "Carolinas Campaign," on page 323.)

- **Battle of Five Forks, Virginia (April 1):** A key position on what was to be Lee's route of retreat from Petersburg, Five Forks was attacked by Union forces led by Major General Phil Sheridan and Major General Gouverneur Warren in the afternoon of April 1, after the Union forces had suffered a tactical defeat at Dinwiddie Court House (March 31). Though Lee had ordered Major General George Pickett to "hold Five Forks at all hazards," this proved impossible. The left flank of the outnumbered Confederates crumbled, and a division of Union cavalry charged the Confederate rear and captured over 1,000 prisoners. The victory at Five Forks allowed Grant to launch an all-out assault on April 2, that finally forced Lee's withdrawal from the Petersburg-Richmond area. Both cities were in Union hands by April 3.

CAROLINAS CAMPAIGN (JANUARY–APRIL 1865) *Western*

Major General William T. Sherman's western army began leaving Savannah, Georgia, on January 19. (Sherman and his main force embarked from the city on February 1.) Their route would take them through South and North Carolina and then into Virginia, where they could threaten the rear of Robert E. Lee's besieged Army of Northern Virginia. The marching orders for this campaign were the same as those for the March to the Sea in 1864, but the first leg of the Carolinas Campaign aroused the punitive instincts of the commanders and the troops, who believed that South Carolina, the "cockpit of secession," was still filled with virulent, dedicated disunionists. "The truth is," Sherman wrote Army Chief of Staff Henry W. Halleck on December 24, 1864, "the whole army is burning with an insatiable desire to wreak vengeance upon South Carolina. I almost tremble for her fate, but feel that she deserves all that seems in store for her." Sherman's army cut a wide and particularly destructive swath through the state. In some areas—

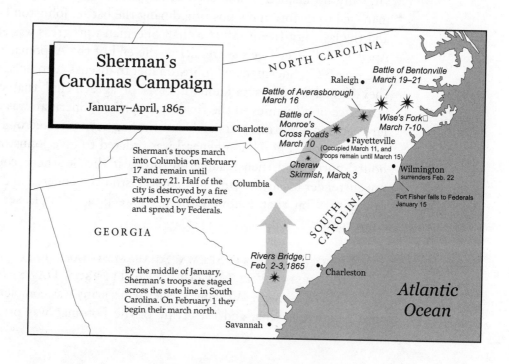

Sherman's Carolinas Campaign

January–April, 1865

Sherman's troops march into Columbia on February 17 and remain until February 21. Half of the city is destroyed by a fire started by Confederates and spread by Federals.

GEORGIA

By the middle of January, Sherman's troops are staged across the state line in South Carolina. On February 1 they begin their march north.

NORTH CAROLINA

Raleigh

Battle of Bentonville
March 19–21

Battle of Averasborough
March 16

Battle of Monroe's Cross Roads
March 10

Charlotte

Wise's Fork
March 7-10

Fayetteville
(Occupied March 11, and troops remain until March 15)

Cheraw
Skirmish, March 3

Columbia

Wilmington
surrenders Feb. 22

Fort Fisher falls to Federals
January 15

SOUTH CAROLINA

Rivers Bridge,
Feb. 2-3, 1865

Charleston

Savannah

Atlantic Ocean

for example, in Barnwell, renamed "Burnwell" by the troops—government buildings and the property of the wealthy suffered most. In others, there was no such discrimination. "The army burned everything it came near in the State of South Carolina," Major James A. Connolly wrote to his wife on March 12, "not under orders, but in spite of orders. . . . Our track through the State is a desert waste. Since entering North Carolina," he added, "the wanton destruction has stopped."

Moving, without significant opposition, between the relatively small Confederate forces in South Carolina, Sherman's army cut Charleston off from the interior, forcing the city's evacuation by Confederate troops on February 17. That same day, much of Columbia, the state capital, went up in flames. In North Carolina, as his force, divided into two columns, was moving to link up with two corps that had recently participated in the conquest of Wilmington (see "Operations against Fort Fisher and Wilmington," on page 321), Sherman was engaged by a Confederate army under General Joseph E. Johnston at Averasboro (March 16). The Confederates were unsuccessful in blocking Sherman's progress, but the action did put more distance between the two Union columns. By March 19, when Johnston's 20,000 Confederates engaged 30,000 Federals at Bentonville (battle of Bentonville, March 19–21), nearly 100,000 Federal troops were in the state and there was virtually no chance of any success for Johnston's force. Although he had managed to maintain his position during the battle, Johnston later fell back, and the last significant effort to halt Sherman's progress was at an end. On April 17–18, after Lee's surrender at the end of the Appomattox Campaign (see page 325), Sherman and Johnston met to discuss surrender. On April 18, they signed a "Memorandum or basis of agreement" that called for an armistice of *all* armies in the field. On April 24, Sherman was told that this far-reaching and controversial document had been rejected by President Andrew Johnson. The Union general was ordered to give Johnston forty-eight hours' notice and then resume hostilities if the Southern commander did not surrender his army. On April 26, Johnston surrendered and signed terms of capitulation that followed the less sweeping formula set by Grant at Appomattox.

WILSON'S RAID TO SELMA, ALABAMA (MARCH–APRIL 1865; AND THE SUBSEQUENT CAPTURE OF JEFFERSON DAVIS) *WESTERN*

As Major General William T. Sherman's army was completing its march into North Carolina, and the Army of the Potomac was preparing for its final moves against Petersburg and Richmond, the largest Union mounted force assembled during the war was gathering in Alabama for a strike at Selma, an important munitions and manufacturing center. Led by twenty-seven-year-old Brigadier General James H. Wilson, this 13,480-man force embarked on March 22 in three columns led by Wilson's division commanders: Brigadier General Edward M. McCook, Major General Eli Long, and Major General Emory Upton. Opposing them were scattered Confederate forces, some 8,000 to 9,000 strong, under Lieutenant General Nathan Bedford Forrest. On April 1, elements of two Union divisions clashed with some 2,000 men under Forrest's direct command at Ebenezer Church. After extensive hand-to-hand fighting, the Confederates retreated to Selma.

Well protected by defensive constructions, heavy guns, and an estimated 5,000 Confederate troops (plus civilians who had been pressed into service), the city was a forbidding target. It was forced to yield, however, after a three-pronged assault: Moving across swampy ground from the northwest, Long and his dismounted troops breached the Confederate left (Long was among those wounded); Upton led his men into gaps in the Confederate right; and Wilson led mounted cavalry, following Long's line of attack. By midevening of April 2 (the same day Petersburg and Richmond were evacuated by Confederates), Selma was in Union hands. (Forrest and many other defenders had managed to escape.) Wilson's men took 2,700 prisoners, 102 cannon, and an immense store of supplies. Over the next five weeks, as Wilson's men ranged through middle Georgia, continuing to demonstrate the intense vulnerability of the Southern interior, they captured five cities, hundreds of pieces of artillery, nearly 7,000 prisoners (including five generals), and either captured or destroyed small arms, iron works, foundries, locomotives, factories, and other valuable Confederate resources. On May 10, one of Wilson's units, the Fourth Michigan Volunteer Cavalry, captured Confederate President Jefferson Davis near Irwinville, Georgia.

APPOMATTOX CAMPAIGN (APRIL 2–12, 1865) *EASTERN*
After the battle of Five Forks (April 1) and the Union assault on Lee's Petersburg lines (April 2) finally broke the Confederate Petersburg-Richmond defenses (see page 321), the Army of Northern Virginia and the Confederate government evacuated those two cities. The Appomattox Campaign was Lee's last and ultimately futile attempt to lead his dwindling army to a rendezvous with the Confederates led by General Joseph E. Johnston, known to be falling back through North Carolina (see "Carolinas Campaign,"

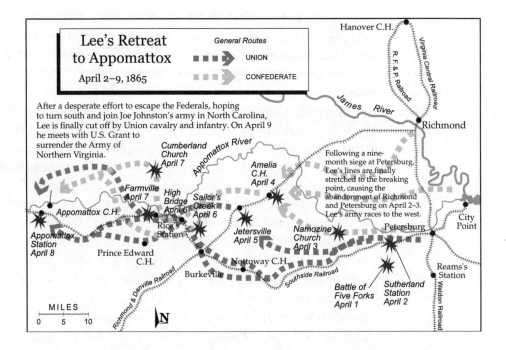

Lee's Retreat to Appomattox
April 2–9, 1865

General Routes
UNION
CONFEDERATE

After a desperate effort to escape the Federals, hoping to turn south and join Joe Johnston's army in North Carolina, Lee is finally cut off by Union cavalry and infantry. On April 9 he meets with U.S. Grant to surrender the Army of Northern Virginia.

Following a nine-month siege at Petersburg, Lee's lines are finally stretched to the breaking point, causing the abandonment of Richmond and Petersburg on April 2–3. Lee's army races to the west.

on page 323). Once unified, the Confederates would make a stand against the converging Union armies of Grant and Sherman. Moving along the Richmond & Danville Railroad (still operating as a Southern supply line), Lee shifted his march toward another possible supply base, Lynchburg, after the railroad was cut by closely pursuing Federals. On April 6, the valley of Sayler's Creek, a tributary of the Appomattox River, was the scene of three separate engagements between Lee's army and Union forces led by Major General Phil Sheridan and Major General George Gordon Meade. The day became known as "Black Thursday" among Southerners: some 8,000 men— at least one-fourth of Lee's remaining force—were overwhelmed and captured by Union troops. Outnumbered nearly three to one, Lee had few options left. When he received a message from Grant on April 7, calling for his surrender because of the "hopelessness of further resistance on the part of the Army of Northern Virginia in this struggle," Lee replied that he was not convinced the situation was hopeless—but he also asked for Grant's terms. Grant responded, in part:

> . . . *peace* being my great desire, there is but one condition I would insist upon—namely That the men and officers surrendered shall be disqualified

for taking up arms against the Government of the United States until properly exchanged.

A further exchange of messages led to the historic meeting between the two generals at the home of Wilbur McLean in the village of Appomattox Court House on April 9. (A last weak attempt to break out of Grant's pincers had been stopped dead in its tracks that morning.) At the McLean house, the terms of surrender were agreed upon:

Rolls of all the officers and men to be made in duplicate. One copy to be given to an officer designated by me [Grant], the other to be retained by such officer or officers as you may designate. The officers to give their individual paroles not to take up arms against the Government of the United States until properly exchanged, and each company or regimental

This 1867 lithograph by Major & Knapp Lithograph Company depicts Lee's surrender in the McLean house at Appomattox Court House, Virginia. Lee and Grant are seated at center.

commander sign a like parole for the men of their commands. The arms, artillery and public property to be parked and stacked, and turned over to the officer appointed by me to receive them. This will not embrace the sidearms of the officers, nor their private horses or baggage. This done, each officer and man will be allowed to return to their homes, not to be disturbed by United States authority so long as they observe their paroles and the laws in force where they may reside.

Later, aware that many of the surrendering soldiers were farmers and would not be able to put in crops without horses, Grant instructed his officers to "let any Confederate, officer or not, who claimed to own a horse or mule take the animal to his home." Grant also agreed to provide food for Lee's hungry troops. After the surrender ceremony took place on April 12 (four years to the day from the Confederate bombardment of Fort Sumter), the Civil War in Virginia was over; but other Confederate troops remained in the field. President Andrew Johnson would not proclaim hostilities at an end until May 10.

SIEGE OF MOBILE, ALABAMA (MARCH 25–APRIL 12, 1865)
LOWER SEABOARD AND GULF APPROACH

Though control of Mobile Bay had passed to the Union on August 5, 1864, the city itself remained in Confederate hands until this campaign. A joint endeavor involving about twenty U.S. Navy ships under the command of Rear Admiral Henry K. Thatcher (versus Confederate Admiral Franklin Buchanan's four-vessel flotilla) and U.S. Army troops led by Major General E. R. S. Canby, the campaign began on March 27 with a siege of Spanish Fort, the city's principal inner line of defense, that lasted until the installation was evacuated on April 8. The siege and capture of Fort Blakely, another key defensive fort held by Confederates under Brigadier General St. John R. Liddell, was one of the last large-scale Federal offensives of the war. African American forces played a significant role in its success. By April 12, all of Mobile's defensive installations had been abandoned. A formal demand was made for the city's surrender, and, by 12:30 P.M. that day, the United States flag was flying over Mobile's city hall. Nine U.S. vessels were sunk in the course of this campaign.

PALMITO RANCH, TEXAS (MAY 12–13, 1865) *TRANS-MISSISSIPPI*

Two days after President Andrew Johnson had declared hostilities at an end, inexperienced and ambitious Union Colonel Theodore H. Barrett violated his orders not to initiate any military action and attacked Confederates

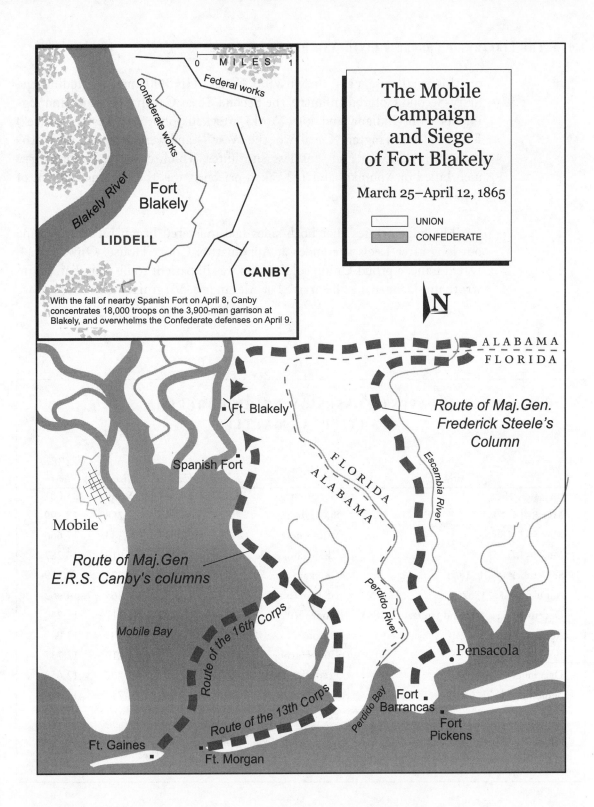

The Mobile Campaign and Siege of Fort Blakely

March 25–April 12, 1865

UNION
CONFEDERATE

With the fall of nearby Spanish Fort on April 8, Canby concentrates 18,000 troops on the 3,900-man garrison at Blakely, and overwhelms the Confederate defenses on April 9.

Federal works

Confederate works

Blakely River

Fort Blakely

LIDDELL

CANBY

N

ALABAMA
FLORIDA

Route of Maj. Gen. Frederick Steele's Column

Escambia River

Ft. Blakely

Spanish Fort

FLORIDA
ALABAMA

Mobile

Route of Maj. Gen E.R.S. Canby's columns

Perdido River

Route of the 16th Corps

Mobile Bay

Route of the 13th Corps

Pensacola

Perdido Bay

Fort Barrancas

Ft. Gaines

Ft. Morgan

Fort Pickens

on this small rise near Brownsville, Texas. His 800 men (including the Sixty-Second Colored Infantry, the Second Texas Cavalry [Union], and regiments from Indiana and New York) attacked John S. ("Rest in Peace") Ford's 350-man ragtag "Cavalry of the West"—and were defeated. This otherwise insignificant and senseless encounter, which cost the Union thirty men killed or wounded and 113 taken prisoner, was the last engagement of the U.S. Civil War.

The huge armies that both sides had mustered began returning home not long after Lee's surrender at Appomattox Court House. On April 24, David Lane, a proud Union soldier who was impatient to be a civilian again, wrote in his journal as he arrived at Alexandria, Virginia: "One year ago we

GREATEST LOSSES BY UNION FORCES IN PARTICULAR BATTLES

Date	Battle	Killed	Wounded	Missing	Aggregate Loss
July 1–3, 1863	Gettysburg	3,070	14,497	5,434	23,001
May 8–18, 1864	Spotsylvania	2,725	13,416	2,258	18,399
May 5–7, 1864	Wilderness	2,246	12,037	3,383	17,666
May 1–3, 1863	Chancellorsville	1,606	9,762	5,919	17,287
September 19–20, 1863	Chickamauga	1,656	9,749	4,774	16,179
August 28–30, 1862	2d Manassas[a]	1,747	8,452	4,263	14,462
December 31, 1862 and January 2, 1863	Stones River	1,730	7,802	3,717	13,249
April 6–7, 1862	Shiloh	1,754	8,408	2,885	13,047
June 1–4, 1864	Cold Harbor	1,844	9,077	1,816	12,737
December 11–14, 1862	Fredericksburg	1,284	9,600	1,769	12,653
September 17, 1862	Antietam[b]	2,108	9,549	753	12,410
June 15–19,1864	Petersburg	1,688	8,513	1,185	11,386

[a] Including Chantilly, Rappahannock, Bristoe Station, and Bull Run Bridge.
[b] Not including South Mountain or Crampton's Gap.

GREATEST LOSSES BY CONFEDERATE FORCES IN PARTICULAR BATTLES[a]

Date	Battle	Killed	Wounded	Missing	Aggregate Loss
June 25–July 1, 1862	Seven Days Battles	3,478	16,261	875	20,614
July 1–3, 1863	Gettysburg	2,592	12,706	5,150	20,448[b]
September19–20, 1863	Chickamauga	2,312	14,674	1,468	18,454
February 14–16, 1862	Fort Donelson	466	1,534	13,829	15,829
May 1–4, 1863	Chancellorsville	1,665	9,081	2,018	12,764
September 12–20, 1862	Maryland Campaign	1,886	9,348	1,367	12,601
December 31, 1862–January 1, 1863	Stones River	1,294	7,945	1,027	10,266
August 21–September 2, 1862	Manassas (Bull Run)	1,481	7,627	89	9,197
November 23–25, 1863	Missionary Ridge	361	2,160	4,146	6,667

[a] Because official Confederate casualty reports for battles late in the conflict were never submitted, or were lost, some of the war's costliest battles are not represented here.
[b] Most sources put Confederate casualties at Gettysburg closer to 28,000.

ESTIMATED TOTAL CASUALTIES AMONG CONFEDERATE FORCES IN LATER BATTLES*

Date	Battle	Estimated Killed
May 5–6, 1864	Wilderness	10,800
May 8–21, 1864	Spotsylvania	9,000–10,000
April 6, 1865	Sayler's Creek	7,700
November 30, 1864	Franklin	7,300
December 15–16, 1864	Nashville	6,500

*Official casualty lists are unavailable.

Source for tables on pages 330 and 331: William F. Fox, *Regimental Losses in the American Civil War, 1861–1865: A Treatise on the Extent and Nature of the Mortuary Losses in the Union Regiments, ...* Albany Publishing Company (Albany, NY, 1889). Also see Frances H. Kennedy, ed., *The Civil War Battlefield Guide.* Houghton Mifflin Co. (New York, 1990, 1998). See Chapter 9, "Medical Care and Medicine," for additional information on casualties.

passed through this city on our way to Richmond. Today we tread its streets with buoyant feet, . . . our work accomplished. I am filled with gratitude that I am permitted to see this day. 'Tis a long, weary road, the one we traveled, but what matter now? . . . We are going home." Men of the former Confederate States, now a devastated land, saw the end of the fighting through very different eyes: "The calamity which has fallen upon us in the total destruction of our government is of a character so overwhelming that I am as yet unable to comprehend it," Josiah Gorgas wrote in his diary on May 4. "I am as one walking in a dream, & expecting to awake. I cannot see its consequences, nor shape my own course, but am just moving along until I can see my way at some future day. It is marvelous that a people that a month ago had money, armies, and the attributes of a nation should to-day be no more, & that we live, breathe, move, talk as before." Fully a quarter of the South's military-age white men did *not* return home. North and South, some 620,000 people had perished in the war.

Civil War Strategy

Strategy: The art and science of developing and using political, economic, psychological, and military forces as necessary during peace and war, to afford the maximum support to policies, in order to increase the probabilities and favorable consequences of victory and to lessen the chances of defeat.

Military Strategy: The art and science of employing the armed forces of a nation to secure the objectives of national policy by the application of force or the threat of force.

U.S. DEPARTMENT OF DEFENSE

National Objectives

The overriding political objective, or national strategy, of the United States during the Civil War was restoration of the Union. Holding that secession was invalid, the United States sought to bring the seceded states back into the Union through military force that was tempered, during the first two years of the conflict, by conciliatory measures aimed at persuading Southern Unionists that the best course for the South was to rejoin the Union and restore the prewar status quo. The course of events, however, showed that Unionist sentiment in the South had been overestimated. The war expanded, casualties mounted, and the other question at the heart of the conflict merged with preservation of the Union to form a new Northern objective: to give the Union a new birth of freedom by reconstructing it *without* slavery. The Preliminary Emancipation Proclamation (September 22, 1862) and the stronger Emancipation Proclamation (January 1, 1863), as well as the enrollment of African Americans in the U.S. military service, also discouraged European powers, whose governments generally favored the Confederacy but were uniformly opposed to slavery, from intervening on behalf of the South.

The overriding objective of the Confederate States was to establish an independent slaveholding republic by successfully resisting Union attempts to negate secession. The South sought, initially, to protect its borders while attempting to bring the states of Missouri and Kentucky—each with valuable resources and substantial numbers of Confederate sympathizers pleading for assistance—firmly into the Confederacy. The generally defensive tenor of this national strategy was based on the belief that firm resistance would create war weariness among the Northern populace, and the United States Government would thus abandon its effort to reunify the nation, especially given the massive resources reunification by invasion would entail. As Confederate Secretary of War George W. Randolph noted in a letter, on October 10, 1861:

> They may overrun our frontier States and plunder our coast but, as for conquering us, the thing is an impossibility. There is no instance in history of a people as numerous as we are inhabiting a country so extensive as ours being subjected if true to themselves.

Before the issuance of the Emancipation Proclamation, the Confederacy also held out high hopes, and exerted both diplomatic and economic pressure (see Chapter 3, "Wartime Politics"), to secure recognition as a sovereign nation from the European powers. Although the likelihood of European recognition was considerably reduced after the proclamation's release, the South did not end its quest for recognition when it was issued. A Confederate delegation was in London petitioning the British government for recognition in March 1865, only three weeks before Lee's surrender at Appomattox Court House.

Military Strategy—United States

As Southern states began to secede and the probability of armed conflict grew stronger, United States General in Chief Winfield Scott, commanding U.S. forces that numbered only 16,000 men, advised the government to proceed prudently in the event of actual war with the breakaway states. A hero of the War of 1812 and the Mexican War (in which more than one-hundred future Civil War generals, North and South, had been under his command), Scott knew that a full-scale invasion of the South would prove to be terribly costly. Such an invasion, he estimated:

> might be done in two or three years . . . with 300,000 disciplined men, es-timating a third for garrisons, and the loss of yet a greater number by skir-mishes, sieges, battles and Southern fevers. The destruction of life and property on the other side would be frightful, however perfect the moral discipline of the invaders.

The "300,000 disciplined men" (which proved to be a drastic underestimate) would of course need to be recruited and trained.

In May 1861, when war was a fact, Scott proposed a strategy that would avoid such an invasion. Combining a naval blockade of seaports on the At-lantic and Gulf Coasts with moves to establish U.S. military control of the Mississippi River, this strategy, Scott said, would "envelop the insurgent states and bring them to terms with less bloodshed than by any other plan." Soon dubbed the "Anaconda Plan" in the press, after the snake that kills by constriction, Scott's scheme was rejected as too slow. Many in the North be-lieved that an immediate demonstration of military superiority—coupled with a conciliatory attitude—would end the rebellion quickly. The Union defeat at First Bull Run shook, but did not destroy, that belief.

George B. McClellan replaced Scott as general in chief in November 1861. A proponent of the firm-yet-conciliatory strategy to achieve recon-struction of the Union, McClellan developed plans for a massive thrust to-ward Richmond (the Peninsula Campaign) while urging field officers in all theaters to be careful in their treatment of Southern civilians. A few months later, McClellan's Peninsula Campaign had failed, more volunteers had been called up, and belief that Unionist sentiment in the South would result in reconciliation of the two sides had been seriously eroded. The conciliatory Union strategy began slowly to evolve into one in which military necessity dictated the actions of armies in the field. Nonhostile civilians and their property were still, for the most part, left unmolested; yet this, too, was be-ginning to change. On July 22, the War Department published an Executive Order authorizing Union field commanders to "seize and use any property, real or personal, which may be necessary or convenient . . . for supplies or other military purposes." And reprisals against Southern civilians who were

Published in 1861 by J. B. Elliott of Cincinnati, the cartoon-map, "Scott's Great Snake" derides Winfield Scott's encirclement strategy. As the war lengthened, Scott's plan did become an essential element of Union strategy.

proven to be or suspected of giving aid to Confederate raiders—particularly, to the guerrilla bands that were wreaking havoc with Union army operations—were increasing.

Also in July 1862, Congress passed the Second Confiscation Act, which provided for the liberation of slaves in Union-occupied areas of the rebelling states and allowed "employment" of black men in the war effort—opening the door for the recruitment of African American soldiers. Together with the Militia Act, passed the same day, which also made it possible for African Americans to serve in the army, this constituted a direct attack on slavery. That attack was reinforced in September, when President Lincoln issued the Preliminary Emancipation Proclamation. After January 1, 1863, when the final Emancipation Proclamation was issued, conciliation was no longer a real possibility.

In this era characterized by the increased range and accuracy of rifled weaponry and the organization of armies into units—from regiments to corps—that increased their maneuverability, it was nearly impossible for one great army to destroy a comparable opposing force by engaging in the kind of head-on clashes still envisioned in most civilian minds. Turning movements (sending a detached force around the flank of the opponent to sever lines of supply and communication), raids, control of seaports and rivers (particularly the Mississippi), and confiscation of Confederate resources had become the dominant aspects of Union military strategy by 1863. But coordination of Union movements in the various theaters of operation still left much to be desired. As early as the beginning of 1862, President Lincoln, who had proven to be an extremely adept student of the art of war, had been a firm proponent of simultaneous advances on the various fronts. Lincoln stated, as his "general view of the war":

> that we have the greater numbers, and the enemy has the greater facility of concentrating forces upon the points of collision; that we must fail unless we can find some way of making our advantage an overmatch for his; and that this can be done by menacing him with superior forces at different points, at the same time; so that we can safely attack one, or both, if he makes no change, and if he weakens one to strengthen the other, forebear to attack the strengthened one, but seize, and hold the weakened one, gaining so much.

Such simultaneous action was achieved on occasion. (In 1862, for example, Halleck and Grant pressed Beauregard's forces in the West, McClellan began the Peninsula Campaign in Virginia, and Federals took Fort Pulaski, in Savannah's harbor, as well as New Orleans.) But not until March 1864, when Ulysses S. Grant became general in chief of all Union forces, was this strategy employed consistently and effectively. By then, the blockade was severely restricting Confederate imports; large food-producing areas of the Confederacy were under Federal control; key transport and defense hubs—including Chattanooga, Memphis, Corinth, Vicksburg, and New Orleans—were occupied by Union forces; and the entire Mississippi River was under Union control. The Confederacy was being strangled, as envisioned by Winfield Scott's "Anaconda Plan." But it was being pierced, as well, by columns of Federal troops that continued destroying its resources and pressing toward its remaining strategically important cities. The capitulation of Atlanta,

Savannah, Petersburg, and Richmond; the Union's conquest of the South's vital East Coast seaport, Wilmington, North Carolina; and the Confederacy's increasing inability to cope with multiple threats finally ended the war.

Military Strategy—Confederate

Jefferson Davis eventually defined the South's general military strategy as "offensive-defensive," meaning that the main objective of Confederate forces was defense of Confederate territory. Where circumstances allowed, however, launching counteroffensives to Union moves would be an important means of providing an effective defense. Such offensives would display, in no uncertain terms, Confederate resistance to reconstruction of the Union, would damage the Union military, and would have a negative effect on Northern morale while bolstering the morale of the South. Robert E. Lee, whose Army of Northern Virginia protected the Confederate capital of Richmond, became the grand practitioner of the offensive-defensive strategy. He led his army on bold offensive strokes from the time he assumed its command on the Peninsula in 1862 to its last campaigns in 1864–1865.

In the earliest days of the war, the Confederacy sought to defend all of its massive territory. In the east and all along its extensive seaboard, this meant blocking Union incursions into Virginia and resisting the Federal blockade and assaults made on coastal cities. In the Western Theater—which was, in 1861–1862, one huge military department under the command of Albert Sidney Johnston—this meant establishing an attenuated line from the Cumberland Gap to the Mississippi River. The first major setbacks to the South occurred in this theater when that line was broken in February 1862 by Grant's victories at Forts Henry and Donelson, in Tennessee—two crucial links in the center of that defensive cordon. These Federal victories split Confederate forces in the region, caused the abandonment of the important Mississippi River fortification at Columbus, Kentucky and incited Johnston to withdraw from the vital rail and ordnance-manufacturing center of Nashville, which remained in Union hands for the rest of the war.

Before engaging in the subsequent battle of Shiloh, Tennessee (April 6–7, 1862), Johnston and P. G. T. Beauregard employed the telegraph and railroad to assemble forces from various points in the middle and western sections of the Confederacy. Their plan was to destroy Grant's pursuing army before it could be reinforced. Such use of the South's "interior lines" to concentrate troops where they were required most preceded the war's first major battle, First Bull Run, characterized preparations for the battle at

Chickamauga, Georgia, in 1863, and remained an important aspect of Southern strategy until constant Northern pressure on all fronts made shifting major forces all but impossible.

The Confederacy also relied heavily on limited raids, as well as more extensive offensive thrusts, to disrupt enemy communications and supply lines, replenish stores, and dampen Northern civilians' enthusiasm for the war. Even Robert E. Lee's two large-scale incursions into the North might be considered grand raids: Lee did not seek, in either case, to conquer and occupy land, as in an invasion. He did, however, hope to strike a blow that would, once and for all, induce the Union to negotiate a peace—and encourage foreign powers to recognize the Confederacy as a sovereign nation. The first of Lee's major raids ended at the battle of Antietam (Sharpsburg), Maryland, in September 1862, and the last ended at the battle of Gettysburg, Pennsylvania, in July 1863. Though nothing on the scale of these invasions occurred after Lee returned to Virginia from Gettysburg in 1863, Confederate incursions into Union-held territory continued well into 1864.

Partisan rangers and Confederate guerrilla bands, as well as regular Confederate cavalry, proved to be important elements of this raiding strategy from early in the war and were used most effectively against Union forces that were invading Southern and border states, or were based in the South as occupying troops (see "Shadow Warriors: Partisan Rangers, Guerrillas, and Spies," in Chapter 5, "The Armies"). In 1862, as Union Major General Don Carlos Buell was attempting to meet the threat posed by Confederates under Braxton Bragg and Edmund Kirby Smith in Tennessee and Kentucky (a movement that, itself, could be characterized as a large and partially successful raid), Buell reported that "formidable raids" were being made against his forces and that his "communications, 500 miles long, are swarming with an immense cavalry force of the enemy, regular and irregular, which renders it almost impossible to keep them open." Later in 1862, cavalry raids by forces under Earl Van Dorn and Nathan Bedford Forrest so thoroughly disrupted Grant's supply bases and lines of communication that the Union general was forced to end his first campaign to take Vicksburg. Continuing throughout the war, Confederate raids and guerrilla attacks compelled the Union to deploy many of its men to protect crucial rail and supply depots as the Federal armies moved South.

Gradually, offensive forays gave way to a primarily defensive Confederate posture in the final eighteen months of the war, under the pressure of dwindling resources (not only vital supplies, but also fighting men), decreased mobility (due to the capture or destruction of Confederate railroads and ports), increasing desertion rates, and ever-increasing Union pressure in all theaters of war—what has been termed a Union "strategy of exhaustion" against the South. These factors combined to defeat the Confederacy. The mortal blow came when Robert E. Lee was forced to surrender the trapped and outnumbered Army of Northern Virginia at Appomattox Court House, Virginia, April 9, 1865. (Lee rejected Confederate Brigadier General Edward Porter Alexander's suggestion that the Confederacy adopt a last, desperate strategy, to dissolve into small bands and carry on the struggle through guerrilla warfare.) All other major Confederate forces surrendered within the next two months.

Battle Tactics

Tactics: (1) The employment of units in combat. (2) The ordered arrangement and maneuver of units in relation to each other and/or to the enemy in order to use their full potentialities.

U.S. DEPARTMENT OF DEFENSE

The great similarity in battle tactics employed by both sides in the Civil War stemmed in part from the general nature of mid-nineteenth-century warfare and in great measure from the similar backgrounds of the war's core military leadership. A number of these men had been trained at the U.S. Military Academy at West Point, where they were greatly influenced by the instruction of Dennis Hart Mahan (1802–1871), who stressed the importance of defensive tactics and instructed his students in the art of entrenchment and fortification. Many also went on to fight against Native Americans in Florida and the West and, most influentially, to serve together in the Mexican War of 1846–1848. P. G. T. Beauregard and George B. McClellan were junior officers on Winfield Scott's staff during that war. Captain Robert E. Lee, also on Scott's staff and brevetted colonel for heroism in Mexico, commended a certain Lieutenant Ulysses S. Grant in a report. When Grant also received official thanks for his role in the attack on Mexico City, they were conveyed by Lieutenant John C. Pemberton, who would surrender Vicksburg to Grant in 1863. Future Confederates Jefferson Davis, James Longstreet, George Pickett, and Braxton Bragg fought alongside their future enemies Winfield Scott Hancock, George H. Thomas, and Joseph Hooker—all learning from the same combat experiences. (Offshore, Raphael Semmes, who would become the Confederacy's most feared commerce raider, shared quarters with Lieutenant John Winslow, future commander of the U.S.S.

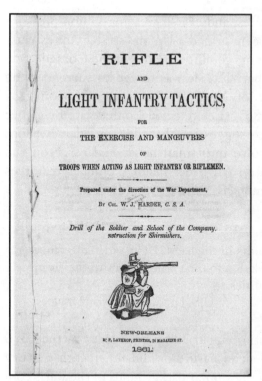

RIFLE

AND

LIGHT INFANTRY TACTICS,

FOR

THE EXERCISE AND MANŒUVRES

OF

TROOPS WHEN ACTING AS LIGHT INFANTRY OR RIFLEMEN.

Prepared under the direction of the War Department,

BY COL. W. J. HARDEE, C. S. A.

Drill of the Soldier and School of the Company.
Instruction for Skirmishers.

NEW-ORLEANS
M. F. LATHROP, PRINTER, 74 MAGAZINE ST.
1861.

Title page of an 1861 edition of William J. Hardee's Rifle and Light Infantry Tactics, *published in New Orleans. The influential tactical manual, used by the armies of both sides in the war, was first issued in 1855, when Hardee was in the United States Army. He later became a Confederate general.*

Kearsarge, which would bring Semmes' commerce raiding to a close by sinking his ship, the C.S.S. *Alabama*, in 1864.)

After its publication in 1855, future officers of the North and South were also extremely well-versed in the principles delineated in Major William J. Hardee's *Rifle and Light Infantry Tactics*, created at the behest of then U.S. Secretary of War Jefferson Davis. (Hardee would later serve under Commander in Chief Davis as a lieutenant general in the Confederate Army.) Hardee's *Tactics*—which emphasized more rapid deployment of infantry, an increased rate of advance (180 steps per minute at a stride of thirty-three inches—double that recommended in earlier manuals), and enhancement of the effectiveness of small-unit formations (and thus, the overall maneuverability of an army)—continued to be the standard text consulted by the military of both sides during the Civil War. Individual officers, of course, adapted the various tactical principles to circumstances in the field.

This was an era of change in battle strategy and tactics—due primarily to the introduction of rifled weaponry, though other technological innovations played their part as well (see "Toward Modern War: Logistics and Communication," on page 349). The increased range and accuracy of rifled weapons meant that the advantage in battle now typically rested with the defender armed with these longer-range weapons; artillery, its crews now more vulnerable to being shot by rifled muskets, became more of a defensive than an offensive weapon (see Chapter 6, "Weaponry"); and the cavalry charges and massed frontal assaults common at the beginning of the century were employed much less frequently, for they were far too costly (as demonstrated in the Union disaster at the battle of Fredericksburg in 1862, "Pickett's Charge" on the third day of Gettysburg, and the charge by Confederates against entrenched Federals at the battle of Franklin, Tennessee, in 1864). The widespread, routine use of breastworks and trenches—advocated by West Point instructor Mahan, but

While with the Union Army of the Potomac on the Virginia Peninsula, in May 1862, artist Alfred Waud sketched this unit Going to the Trenches *near Yorktown. The men's equipment indicates they would have to create the trenches before manning them.*

employed by many Civil War troops informally before many Civil War officers embraced their use officially—became a natural response to the improvements in weaponry. This, in turn, made traditional frontal assaults all the more deadly to attacking forces. Still, in this conflict where turning movements (moving beyond an enemy's flank and threatening some vital point in his rear) were used extensively to avoid head-on clashes, armies or elements of armies did often advance on one another across fields of battle. Not only did officers sometimes order frontal assaults, as at Fredericksburg, Gettysburg, Cold Harbor, and Kennesaw Mountain; but turning movements did not always succeed. Defenders might shift their lines to face the force attempting to turn them, or they might withdraw and regroup at a more advantageous position.

Typical Movement of Infantry

In battle, the Confederate and Union armies most typically relied on one or two lines of two ranks each, between 500 and 1,000 men long. This permitted the largest volume of fire to be delivered against the enemy. Unfortunately, unless the line was able to close very rapidly with the enemy's position, this method of advance also allowed the defending force to thin it with repeated salvos as it advanced. (Opening fire at 500 yards, defenders could get off eight to ten volleys in five minutes). So, in this area, too, tactics were evolving, distances between advancing ranks were increased, and some Civil War commanders were even experimenting with difficult-to-control scattered-order formations. On May 10, 1864, at Spotsylvania, 1861 West Point graduate Emory Upton—a courageous officer and a careful student of tactics—led twelve selected regiments in an attack *in columns* on entrenched and fortified Confederate positions at what was to become known as the "Bloody Angle." The force of Upton's columnar attack carried the position, though his regiments were later compelled to withdraw when troops failed to move up to support their flanks—in itself, a valuable lesson (see Upton's biography in the "Notable Officers" section of Chapter 5, "The Armies").

If a regiment was advancing in line of battle without exact knowledge of the enemy's location or strength, a thin line of soldiers, or skirmish line, was pushed up to 300 yards ahead and spaced to cover the regimental front. These skirmishers were to locate the enemy or find the weak points in the enemy line before the whole unit came under fire. Some skirmishers were drawn from the sharpshooters (snipers) that were effectively employed by both sides in the Civil War—in campaigns from the Peninsula, through Chattanooga and Gettysburg, to Grant's 1864 Overland Campaign and Petersburg. Zeroing in, particularly, on enemy officers, signalmen, and artillerymen, sharpshooters could be very effective in slowing an enemy attack and disrupting morale in the enemy force. In situations of extended trench warfare—such as at Vicksburg and Petersburg—they were a constant menace to enemy soldiers imprudent enough to show themselves above the trench line.

Use of Cavalry

Cavalry in the Civil War was used principally for reconnaissance, intelligence gathering, protecting the army's flanks from enemy approach, harassing the enemy's supply facilities and lines of communication, and presenting a screen against the reconnaissance of the enemy's cavalry. The cavalry's chief advantage lay in its ability to move rapidly over relatively long distances. Mounted cavalry proved largely ineffective against organized infantry, due to the disparity in firepower, but could be used to great effect against retreating or disorganized foot soldiers. When cavalry units encountered infantry, the troopers usually dismounted and fought as infantry themselves (a notable exception being Phil Sheridan's effective use of mounted cavalry against Jubal Early's infantry during the 1864 Shenandoah Valley Campaign). While dismounted in battle, every fourth man became a "horse-holder"; he took the mounts of the remaining three and held them ready behind the lines.

Portents of Modern War

The unprecedented size and complexity of the armed forces employed during the Civil War gave rise to innovations in army organization and command structure (see Chapter 5, "The Armies") as well as in the deployment of these huge armies. Railroads and steamboats were used extensively in troop deployments; military telegraph lines conveyed in minutes or hours reports and orders that previously would have taken much longer to reach their destinations (see "Toward Modern War: Logistics and Communication" on page 349); maps crucial to military operations were created in the field—occasionally with information gathered by Civil War "aeronauts" (see "Military Aeronautics," on page 362) and were sometimes reproduced for distribution to field units using new and creative methods dictated by necessity (see "The Importance of Maps," on page 345). Some officers, such as Ulysses S. Grant, demonstrated a special aptitude for the tactical use of combined forces. Specifically, he utilized river gunboats in conjunction with infantry assaults—foreshadowing the larger, more elaborate combined assaults of later wars.

As noted previously, entrenchment was a defensive tactic used by both sides. As McClellan's Peninsula Campaign began, John B. Magruder's Confederates were ensconced in trenches for a month during the siege of Yorktown (April 5–May 3, 1862). In the Western Theater, after the battle of Shiloh (April 6–7, 1862), Ulysses S. Grant was roundly criticized because his troops were *not* entrenched when the Confederates attacked on April 6, a factor that contributed heavily to the Union's losses on that day. In some instances, as in the siege of Vicksburg and, particularly, during the ten-month siege of Petersburg, Virginia, Civil War "trench warfare" portended the bloody four-year stalemate along 400 miles of World War I's Western Front. During these two Civil War stalemates, the opposing forces (like their

Western Front counterparts in the next century) lived in, and often fought from elaborate trench systems they had dug around the besieged cities. In *The Image of War: The Pictorial Reporting of the American Civil War*, William F. Thompson describes the Union trench system around Vicksburg in 1863:

> [T]renches slanted diagonally forward from the main system of fortifications and then branched out into a second inner ring. The network resembled a giant spider web with Vicksburg trapped at the center. . . . The trenches were also where many of the westerners lived and slept. Some of the main trenches were two levels deep, the upper step for the artillery and sharpshooters, the lower level for living quarters.

Confederate soldier Maurice K. Simons described in his diary on June 13, 1863, midway through the Vicksburg siege, the rhythm and sounds (land- and gunboat-based artillery, small arms fire, the occasional grenade) of this siege/battle:

> The fighting is now carried on quite systematically . . . in the morning there seems to be time allowed for breakfast, when all at once the work of destruction is renewed. There is about an hour at noon & about the same at sunset, taking these three intervals out the work goes on just as regularly as . . . on a well regulated farm & the noise is not unlike the clearing up of new ground when much heavy timber is cut down! Add to that the nailing on of shingles by several men & one has a pretty good idea of the noise. It might be supposed that a score of villages had sprung up all round him & that the inhabitants were vieing with each other to see who could be the most industrious.

A related tactic used by the Union during both these sieges—and employed much more systematically, but just as futilely, during World War I—was the attempt to tunnel under Confederate lines to place explosive charges that would create gaps Union forces could use to penetrate the Southern defenses. (Confederate forces sometimes "countermined"; at Petersburg, they tunneled in an attempt to intercept the Union diggers.) At both Vicksburg and Petersburg, mine explosions were achieved; in both instances, the outcome was more damaging for Union troops, trapped under enemy fire in the resulting crater, than for the defenders. The result at Petersburg is described on pages 311 and 312. A similar fate befell some Union soldiers after the mine explosion at Vicksburg, as Walter F. Thompson reports:

Late in June, the Federals exploded a mine under a sector of the enemy lines and pushed several regiments forward to rush through the gap in the defenses. To their horror, many of the men fell into their own mine crater. Schell [an artist for a Northern illustrated paper] sketched the Confederates rolling grenades down on the trapped men, who desperately tried to throw them back before they exploded.

Very much *un*like the conflict on the Western Front, however, the Civil War was primarily a war in which troops were in motion, playing cat-and-mouse with the enemy or meeting him head-on, learning from painful experience which tactics were best relied upon under the varying circumstances of this long, widespread, and bloody conflict.

The Importance of Maps

With huge armies maneuvering over vast areas, accurate topographical information was of crucial importance in the Civil War. Yet, of the few maps readily available in 1861, most were out of date or lacked vital information needed to prosecute the war. The situation had not improved much by 1862. During the Peninsula Campaign that year, Union Major General George B. McClellan reported: "Correct local maps were not to be found, and the country, though known in its general features, we found to be inaccurately described in essential particulars, in the only maps and geographical memoirs or papers to which access could be had; erroneous courses to streams and roads were frequently given, and no dependence could be placed on the information thus derived." Confederate officers—though operating near their own capital of Richmond—had no better information. Confederate general Richard Taylor noted that they "knew no more about the topography of the country than they did about Central Africa. Here was a limited district, the whole of it within a day's march of the city of Richmond . . . and yet we were profoundly ignorant of the country, were without maps, sketches, or proper guides, and nearly as helpless as if we had been suddenly transferred to the banks of the Lualaba (Congo River)."

Union Mapping

Keenly aware of the importance of good maps to military campaigning, Federal authorities gave full support to the mapping units that had been established before the war, such as the Army's Corps of Topographical Engineers and Corps of Engineers; the Treasury Department's Coast Survey; and the

Navy's Hydrographic Office. The fact that such units already existed in 1861 constituted a great advantage to the Union: they were able to build upon an existing organizational structure, which included equipment and trained personnel.

Occupancy of key positions in northern Virginia in 1861 enabled Federal officials to begin, in that region, the first major mapping project of the war. Compiled in the Topographical Engineers Office at the Division Headquarters of Brigadier General Irvin McDowell at Arlington, Virginia, the map of northern Virginia was a cooperative undertaking involving both U.S. Coast Survey and army personnel—and this was to be the pattern followed throughout the war. Coast Survey assistants provided valuable service to armies in the field as well as to the naval squadrons blockading Southern bays, harbors, and ports.

Federal authorities used every means at their disposal to gather accurate information on the location, number, movement, and intent of Confederate armed forces. Army cavalry parties were constantly probing the countryside in search of the enemy's picket lines; travelers and peddlers were interrogated; Southerners sympathetic to the Union were contacted and questioned; and spies were dispatched into the interior to obtain information. In the Eastern Theater, the army also turned to a new device for gathering information: the stationary observation balloon. Aeronaut John La Montain made one of the earliest sketches from the platform of a balloon. Dated August 10, 1861, the simple sketch shows the location of Confederate tents and batteries at Sewall's Point, Virginia.

Confederate Mapping

Throughout the war, the Confederate Army found it difficult to supply its field officers with adequate maps. The situation in the South was acute from the beginning of hostilities because of the lack of established government mapping agencies capable of preparing large-scale maps, and the inadequacy of printing facilities for producing them. The situation was further complicated by the almost total absence of surveying and drafting equipment, and the lack of trained military engineers and mapmakers to use the equipment that was available.

Robert E. Lee took prompt action to improve the Confederate mapping situation after he assumed command of the Army of Northern Virginia in June 1862. Five days after his appointment, Lee assigned Captain (later

Major) Albert H. Campbell to head the Topographical Department. Within a few days, two or three field parties were organized and dispatched into the countryside around Richmond to collect the data for an accurate map of the environs of the Confederate capital. As quickly as possible, other survey parties were formed and sent into Virginia counties in which fighting was likely to occur. Based on the new information, Confederate engineers under the direction of Campbell and Major General Jeremy F. Gilmer, Chief of Engineers, prepared detailed maps of most counties in eastern and central Virginia. The maps were drawn in ink on tracing linen and filed in the Topographical Department in Richmond.

Initially, when requests were received in the Topographical Department for maps of a particular area, a draftsman was assigned to make a tracing of the file copy. But, "So great was the demand for maps occasioned by frequent changes in the situation of the armies," Campbell noted, "that it became impossible by the usual method of tracings to supply them. I conceived the plan of doing this work by photography, though expert photographers pronounced it impracticable, in fact impossible. . . . Traced copies were prepared on common tracing-paper in very black India ink and from these sharp negatives by sun-printing were obtained, and from these negatives copies were multiplied by exposure to the sun in frames made for the purpose. The several sections, properly toned, were pasted together in their order, and formed the general map, or such portions of it as were desired; it being the policy, as a matter of prudence against capture to furnish no one but the commanding general and corps commanders with the entire map of a given region." By 1864, therefore, the Confederate Topographical Department was capable of supplying field officers with photo reproductions and was thereby able to avoid making time-consuming tracings or costly lithographic prints. The resulting photocopies, although crude by today's standards, were quite legible and were frequently cut and mounted in sections on cloth to fold to a convenient size to fit an officer's pocket or saddle bag. Because of the lack of printing presses and paper, maps remained in relatively short supply. The manuscript and photoreproduced copies that were available, however, were equal in quality to the more numerous maps by Federal authorities.

Mapping on the Move

Of course, not all the maps used by the Civil War forces were compiled and produced at headquarters in Washington or Richmond. On both sides, armies, corps, and divisions in the field had topographical engineers assigned to their staffs whose role was to gather information for the preparation of maps. Many significant reconnaissance maps were compiled in the field, detailed battlefield maps were prepared, and base maps supplied by headquarters were vastly improved as new information was collected.

One of the most accomplished Confederate topographical engineers traveling with armies in the field was a schoolmaster from Staunton, Virginia, Jedediah Hotchkiss, who joined Stonewall Jackson's staff in March 1862. He was immediately ordered by his commanding general to "make me a map of the [Shenandoah] Valley, from Harper's Ferry to Lexington, showing all the points of offense and defence [sic] in those places." The map Hotchkiss provided was of significant value to Jackson and his staff in planning and executing the celebrated Shenandoah Valley Campaign of 1862 (see page 259). Hotchkiss continued to produce valuable maps for Confederate forces throughout the war. (The Hotchkiss Collection of maps, and the personal papers of Jedediah Hotchkiss, are now at the Library of Congress.)

The tools, and results of, military map-making. Notebooks in this photograph were used by renowned Confederate cartographer Jedediah Hotchkiss. The folded linen map in the foreground was used by Sherman's field-grade officers. Photograph by Jim Higgins.

Among the foremost Union topographical engineers was Colonel William E. Merrill, who directed the Topographical Department of the Army of the Cumberland. This unit was chiefly responsible for providing the maps necessary for Major General William T. Sherman's Atlanta Campaign of 1864. Thomas B. Van Horne, in his *History of the Army of the Cumberland* (1875), noted: "The army was so far from Washington that it had to have a complete map establishment of its own. Accordingly, the office of the chief topographical engineer contained a printing press, two lithographic presses, one photographic establishment, arrangements for map-mounting, and a full corps of draughtsmen and assistants." The lithographic presses were invaluable for quickly providing multiple copies of a map. However, the weight of the presses and stones made transporting them difficult and necessitated that they remain in a central depot near the front lines.

In preparation for the Atlanta Campaign, the Topographical Department began the compilation of an accurate campaign map of northern Georgia, including information gained, said Van Horne, "by cross-questioning refugees, spies, prisoners, peddlers, and any and all persons familiar with the country in front of us." The Topographical Department was informed of the date of advance two days before it began, and the single copy of the map of northern Georgia over which it had been laboring "was immediately cut up into sixteen sections and divided among the draughtsmen, who were ordered to work night and day until all the sections had been traced on thin paper in autographic ink." Four sections at a time were then printed. Two hundred paper copies of the map were made. A special edition, printed directly on easily cleanable muslin, was issued to the cavalry. As a result of this, and comparable efforts, said Van Horne, "the army that General Sherman led to Atlanta was the best supplied with maps of any that fought in the Civil War." (The northern Georgia map is among 213 items in the Sherman Map Collection at the Library of Congress.)

Toward Modern War: Logistics and Communication

The unprecedented size of Civil War armies, and the vast areas through which they moved, created new challenges for those charged with keeping the armies mobile, supplied, and in touch with their own units and other commands. Existing resources, such as railroads, steamboats, and the telegraph, were pressed into military service. A recently developed signaling system became one of the most visible features of wartime military communication. And airborne observers provided field officers with intelligence on troop movements and the character of the land over which they were about to lead their troops. Considered in tandem with the improved weaponry employed by those troops, and the changes these were bringing about in battle strategy and tactics, these modes of logistical support constituted an important step toward the methods of warfare that became common in the twentieth century.

Military Railroads

The Civil War was the first conflict in which railroads were used extensively to transport and support armies, and they made a tremendous impact on the conduct of the war. Both the Union and the Confederacy depended on rail transport of troops, supplies, and the sick and wounded; both made extensive efforts to disrupt the enemy's rail systems; and both experimented with new military uses for railroads—in particular, "rolling" artillery batteries, mounted on railroad flatcars, were employed from the 1862 Peninsula Campaign (by Lee's Confederates) to the 1864–1865 siege of Petersburg, Virginia (by Grant's Federals). The Union confronted occasional problems securing adequate personnel and equipment, but, throughout the war, the United States was much richer in railroads, and much more organized in the administration of military railroads, than the Confederacy.

UNITED STATES

The Union began the war with a better developed and more extensive rail system than existed in the Confederacy (21,276 miles of track, as opposed to nearly 9,000 miles; during the war, the Union added 4,000 miles and the Confederacy added 400). In the first year of the conflict, the Federal government recognized that it was imperative to have a central authority coordinating the military use of railroad facilities. Accordingly, under the Railways and Telegraph Act, passed January 31, 1862, the president was given authority to impress any telegraph or railroad and all equipage, make regulations for the maintenance and security of these lines, and subject all railroad and telegraph company officers and employees to military authority. On February 11, 1862, the United States Military Railroads (U.S.M.R.R.) was established by the War Department and, by Executive Order, President Lincoln delegated the authority he had received from Congress to Daniel C. McCallum, an experienced railroad supervisor who had just been appointed military director and superintendent of railroads in the United States. Under this order, McCallum's authority was limited to railroads that were serving the military; on May 25, 1862, it was expanded to include all U.S. railroads. However, the U.S.M.R.R. directed its efforts almost totally to the privately owned railroads that operated in hostile or occupied Southern territory (though it did construct a line from Washington, D.C., to nearby Alexandria, Virginia, and the City Point & Army Line, which supplied troops engaged in the siege of Petersburg, Virginia).

From April 1862 through mid-September 1863, McCallum was assisted by civil engineer, author, and inventor Herman Haupt, who became the U.S.M.R.R.'s chief of construction and maintenance and a prime force in wresting organization out of chaos. Haupt personally supervised the building of fortifications as well as the construction or repair of track, bridges, and trestles. He and his crews—all civilians, including many "contrabands" (slaves who had escaped from the Confederacy)—also developed a method of ferrying loaded railroad cars across bodies of water that were not spanned by railroad bridges. During the slower, winter months, they worked on methods of destruction that could be used against Confederate railroads. Having become experts at extremely fast bridge-building, they experimented with methods of inciting equally fast bridge collapse, and they developed devices that could twist railroad ties so that they couldn't be straightened and reused by the Confederates. Ways of defending Union railroads, and railroad workers, against attacking Confederates and guerrilla bands were also explored. (Armoring railroad cars was one method but not much of this was done.)

Eventually, at a wartime cost of some $40 million, the U.S.M.R.R. maintained sixteen railways in the Eastern Theater and nineteen shorter lines in the West. It moved some 419 locomotives and 6,330 cars over 2,105 miles of track. The railroad's many significant achievements in logistical support included its backing of Major General William T. Sherman's army during the crucially important Atlanta Campaign of 1864. Supplies for 100,000 men and 35,000 animals were transported, from a supply base 360 miles distant, over a single-track railroad that was constantly subject to destructive raids by an energetic enemy. "To have delivered regularly that amount of food and forage by ordinary wagons," General Sherman later wrote in his memoirs, "would have required 36,800 wagons of six mules each, allowing each wagon to have hauled two tons twenty miles each day, a simple impossibility in roads such as then existed in that region of the country." But the emergency transport of 20,000 Union soldiers from the Army of the Potomac in Virginia to reinforce the army of William S. Rosecrans, recently defeated at Chickamauga and under siege at Chattanooga, was, perhaps, the railroad's most stunning achievement in the war. Organized under the press of potential disaster, the reinforcements—including equipment, horses, and artillery—were assembled, loaded, transported, and conveyed safely to a destination 1,200 miles away, within eleven days.

Confederate States

Military use of railroads in the Confederacy, though crucially important, was hampered by problems that grew in number and intensity throughout the war. Perhaps the most fundamental problem stemmed from the profound belief in states' rights—a basic tenet throughout the Confederate States. Most of the rail lines within the Confederacy represented a single state, and most state railroads resisted the few attempts at central control that were assayed by the Davis administration. In December 1862, when Secretary of War George W. Randolph appointed Colonel William M. Wadley to supervise "all the railroads in the Confederate States," the assignment, under extant circumstances, proved impossible for Wadley and for Frederick W. Sims, who replaced him in 1863. The variety of gauges (space between rails) used in the South also proved problematical, as did the fact that many railroad lines, even those servicing the same city, were not connected. The contents of railroad cars often had to be transported by wagon between different lines.

As the war progressed, labor and supplies became increasingly scarce. Railroad ties became so precious that, in January 1863, a Confederate Iron Commission was formed to determine which rail routes were indispensable. The ties of dispensable lines were then expropriated for use on lines deemed more important. (Fewer lines meant fewer routes for the supply and transport of troops.) Even wood became a problem when labor shortages made it difficult to cut sufficient quantities. For a period in 1863, for example, the North Carolina Railroad demanded that half of all wood brought to it for shipping had to be sold to the railroad, so that it could keep its trains moving. Spare parts became scarce, as did experienced personnel (especially after the Conscription Act of 1864 declared that a railroad could have no more employees than it had miles of road). Adequate maintenance became difficult or impossible. And as the war progressed, mile upon mile of railroad track was either being taken over or destroyed by invading Union forces.

Nevertheless, Confederate railroads' transport of essential supplies and men proved invaluable to military operations throughout the war. Before the battles of First Bull Run, Shiloh, and Chickamauga, for example, the Confederacy was able to shift thousands of troops quickly, by rail, from divergent locations and effect forceful concentrations against the enemy. In July 1862, General Braxton Bragg achieved the largest Confederate railroad movement of the war when he dispatched 30,000 men from Mississippi to Chattanooga, Tennessee, by a roundabout, 776-mile route that avoided Union forces. Traveling via the Mobile & Ohio line to Mobile, Alabama, and then northeast over five short Alabama and Georgia lines to Atlanta and Chattanooga, the troops arrived at their destination within two weeks.

Telegraph

The Civil War was the first conflict in which the electric telegraph played a major role. Private telegraph companies had been operating in the United States since the 1840s. When the war began, more than 50,000 miles of wire were in place, there were more than 1,400 stations, and nearly 10,000 people were at work as telegraph operators and clerks. A transcontinental line was completed in the fall of 1861. As with existing railroad mileage, the preponderance of existing telegraph service was in the North; only some 10 percent was located in the Confederate States. During the war, the Union constructed and then operated 15,000 miles of new telegraph lines, compared with about 1,000 constructed by the Confederates. Both sides, however, used the telegraph to great advantage during the war.

The telegraph changed the manner in which commanders exercised their authority. They could now be made almost instantly aware of developments along a wide front and issue orders accordingly. The two commanders in chief, Abraham Lincoln and Jefferson Davis, were able to keep in close touch with developments in the field, and their directives speedily reached field commanders. Each side tapped the other's telegraph lines, and each side combated the other's telegraphic intelligence-gathering by developing ciphers. (The Union armies apparently employed codes via telegraph more often than the Confederates.)

U.S. MILITARY TELEGRAPH SERVICE

Three components comprised the Union's extensive telegraphic net: private (commercial) telegraph companies, the Military Telegraph Service, and the Signal Corps Field Telegraph. The commercial companies, already in place, were relied on most heavily in the first months of the war. Pennsylvania Railroad executive Thomas S. Scott was designated general manager of all lines in and around Washington. (Because he was concerned primarily with Union railroad service at the time, Scott delegated the organization of the telegraph service to a young Pennsylvania Railroad superintendent, Andrew Carnegie.) In the Western Theater of Operations, Anson Stager, employed by the Western Union company, developed a military telegraph service, at the behest of Ohio governor William Dennison. This service helped Major General George B. McClellan, then headquartered in Cincinnati, to maintain contact with troops he was directing on operations in western Virginia. Stager suggested that the government should take control of all telegraphic services, and, in October 1861, the Union established the U.S. Military Telegraph Service and placed Stager in charge. Though it was attached to the Quartermaster's Department, the Telegraph Service was, in fact, a civilian bureau, and its operators were all civilians throughout the war (though their supervisors were granted commissions). These operators included a number of women (telegraphy being one of the first technical professions open to females), at least three of whom were cited in various publications for conducting themselves heroically under trying circumstances: Abbie Stubel, for her services with the Baltimore & Ohio Railroad throughout the war; Samantha French Brenisholtz of Pennsylvania, during the 1863 battle of Gettysburg; and Louisa E. Volker of Missouri, particularly during Confederate Major General Sterling Price's 1864 incursion into the state.

The office of Military Superintendent of Telegraph Lines, established in November 1861, reported directly to the army's quartermaster general; however, after Edwin Stanton replaced Simon Cameron as Secretary of War, Stanton assumed effective control of the service. Assistant superintendents were responsible for telegraphic operations in each of the country's military districts, and telegraph units accompanied all army and corps headquarters throughout the war. Because protection of information transmitted by telegraph was crucial, Stanton appointed Edward S. Sanford, president of the American Telegraph Company, as military supervisor of telegrams and instituted a rigid censorship. As was true of the administration of military railroads, however, there was sometimes friction between military commanders and civilian operators: "General [George Gordon] Meade desires to know under whose orders and authority the telegraph operators possessing the cipher are appointed and controlled," Major General Daniel Butterfield inquired irately at one point. "The operator, Mr. Caldwell, at these headquarters presumes to act in an independent manner and has left headquarters for Westminster, selecting his own location, without authority or permission. The commanding general is unable to send dispatches from the headquarters in cipher."

The third Union telegraphic component, the Field Telegraph Service, was formed as a unit of the Signal Corps, and its operators were trained army personnel. Unlike the civilian operators, Field Telegraph Service personnel used the Beardslee telegraphic device, which employed a dial instead of a key to transmit messages. Less reliable than the key device, the Beardslee was discarded after the Field Telegraph Service came under the supervision of the Military Telegraph Service in late 1863.

CONFEDERATE TELEGRAPH SERVICE

The two primary telegraph companies in the South at the outbreak of the war were the American Telegraph Company, operated by Edward S. Sanford (see page 354) and the Southwestern Telegraph Company, headed by Dr. Norvin Green and superintended by Nashville-based John Van Horne. The Civil War split these two companies. The Southern arm of the American Telegraph Company was reorganized in May 1861 as the Southern Telegraph Company (the name by which it was known throughout the war, though it was officially chartered, late in 1861, as the Confederated Telegraph Company). At its head was the only Southern director of the American Telegraph Company, Dr. William S. Morris of Lynchburg, Virginia. In August 1862, the Confederate States' Postmaster General John H. Reagan, who bore certain responsibilities pertaining to telegraph service, appointed Morris agent of the Confederate States for the management of all military lines within the Confederacy.

The Confederate military telegraph system was small. Most of the Confederacy's military telegraphing was handled by the civilian companies throughout the war, and most operators were civilians. As in the North, women worked in and sometimes took charge of telegraph offices—in Georgia, South Carolina, Louisiana, Florida, and Alabama—when male operators went off to war. This largely civilian network was a bulwark of the Confederacy's military efforts. Telegraph messages exchanged between Confederate forces at Manassas, Virginia, and Jefferson Davis in Richmond, were instrumental in getting Southern forces into position to win the first battle of Bull Run in 1861, and telegraphic communication continued to help field commanders concentrate their troops speedily to meet Union threats. Confederate operatives also became adept at tapping Union wires (by one account, Robert E. Lee's personal telegraph operator, C. A. Gaston, tapped General Grant's line for six weeks during the siege of Petersburg), and this eavesdropping often netted valuable intelligence. Tapped lines could also be used to transmit false information.

As with the operation of railroads, however, conflicts often erupted between civilian telegraph operators and military commanders in the Confederacy—especially when commanders took over lines or appointed operators without consulting Dr. Morris or Postmaster Reagan. Even officers who had a keen appreciation for the telegraph and its personnel could be the source of irritation. Morris complained when, in 1861, General P. G. T. Beauregard established a telegraph system around Charleston that paid its operators appreciably more than the chronically underpaid civilian operators elsewhere in the South. Military commanders also found Morris a source of irritation. On November 17, 1861, Major General John B. Magruder wrote to the Confederate Adjutant General:

> Dr. William S. Morris, president of telegraph company, has failed to send forward the materials and chemicals necessary to keep the telegraph lines in operation which I have constructed with so much labor . . . I have sent Mr. Conner, one of the telegraph operators, to Richmond for the purpose of getting the necessary chemicals and not having returned, so far as I have learned, I presume Dr. Morris has kept him also. For want of these articles the line is seldom in operation between Yorktown and Richmond even.

Other civilian/military disputes—particularly one involving General Braxton Bragg in 1862—became so serious that telegraph service was disrupted for appreciable periods of time. Civilians also complained about wartime service. The crucial role of the telegraph in dispersing war news was highlighted when newspaper editors, concerned about the high cost of telegraphic news, began forming a Confederate Associated Press in 1862.

Supply was another problem. When the war began, the South possessed no factories for the production of wire or glass (needed for insulation), and there was a desperate need for these and other materials. Morris started a wire factory at the Tredegar Iron Works in Richmond and managed to obtain sulphuric acid (for batteries) from throughout the Confederacy and from Mexico. But, increasingly, the South had to depend on blockade runners for the materials required to maintain the telegraph system. (They included fire clay and 13,000 pounds of bluestone [copper sulphate] for batteries each year.) As a result of shortages, complaints centering on faulty equipment increased. Competent telegraph operators were also in increasingly short supply. Though operators had been exempted from the draft in 1862, many enlisted in the army. As more lines were strung, and as military operations often made twenty-four-hour-a-day telegraph communications imperative, it became necessary to detail operators from the ranks of the Confederate army. But even this was not enough. In 1863, Morris wrote to the Secretary of War:

> [I]t not infrequently happens that the offices are *ordered open* from night to night for weeks consecutively and a man who had scarcely left his instrument during the day has to sleep with his ear on the Sounder, or not sleep at all.

Confederate telegraphers also encountered growing risks from invading Union troops. Sometimes, they escaped capture, or worse, by the skin of their teeth, as they struggled to keep the wires in service until the last possible moment. Particularly valorous were the efforts by Southern Telegraph Company operators to keep the lines humming during Major General William T. Sherman's March to the Sea. Low on all telegraph materials, unable to replace wire rapidly succumbing to rust, and with columns of blue-uniformed soldiers moving inexorably through their state, Georgia telegraph officials were nonetheless ordered by Superintendent Joseph B. Tree:

> Keep your offices open night and day. If you have to fall back, take it coolly and gather up the operators, instruments and material as you retire. If the enemy diverge from the Central or Georgia road, establish an office at the end of the break and send your business through by couriers.

The steadily increasing risks and impossibly long hours were not well compensated, however, especially as runaway inflation gripped the South. In October 1863, an operator in Kingville, South Carolina, wrote:

> I am now getting only a Salary of $83.33 per month, and I have myself wife & child to support and I pay the whole Salary & have to go in debt every month $41.67 for my board is $125.00 per month for Wife child & self. And it is cheap board at that.

That same month, a group of telegraph operators formed a union, the Southern Telegraph Association, and protested long duty hours and salaries "entirely inadequate to defray the expenses of living in the simplest manner." When their brief and unsuccessful strike ended less than two weeks after it began, the Southern Telegraph Association dissolved as well.

Despite these many problems, the telegraph was a crucially important element in the Confederate military effort throughout the war—though in the final months of the conflict, service was sporadic, as more and more territory fell to Union troops. After the war, the Southern Telegraph Company was reclaimed by its original parent, the American Telegraph Company. A number of its operating officers became prominent in the postwar telegraph industry.

Principal source: J. Cutler Andrews, "The Southern Telegraph Company, 1861–1865: A Chapter in the History of Wartime Communication," *The Journal of Southern History*, Vol. 30, No. 3 (August 1964).

Signal Corps/Wig-Wag Signaling

An essential supplement to telegraphic communication in supporting the movement of armies during the Civil War was a system of "wig-wag" signaling developed in 1856 by then-Lieutenant Albert J. Myer. As a medical student, Myer had written a thesis describing "A Sign Language for Deaf Mutes." His silent language for the deaf served as the basis for the military signaling system he established while serving as assistant surgeon with a regular U.S. Army regiment in Texas. (Further inspiration for the system was apparently derived from the hand and smoke signals of the various American Indian tribes that Myer observed in the course of his duties.) Patented by Myer in 1858, his system used a single flag—or, at night, a torch—which, when moved to the left or right, expressed a four-element code. In 1859, Myer formally presented the system to a military board

A photographer's portable darkroom sits in front of Butler's signaling tower at Cobb's Hill on the Appomattox River in 1864. Nearby, Grant's army had joined Butler's, and before them, Lee's veterans were making their last stand within the entrenchments at Petersburg.

chaired by Lieutenant Colonel Robert E. Lee, who thought it might be usefully employed in the field and ordered trials and further evaluation. One of the young officers ordered to assist Myer was Lieutenant Edward Porter Alexander, an 1857 graduate of West Point, who would, in 1861–1862, found the Confederate States Signal Service before moving on to compile a sterling record of achievement as a Southern artillery commander.

Myer was appointed Signal Officer of the U.S. Army on June 21, 1860, and with that appointment the Signal Corps of the United States was founded. (Formal authority for the Signal Corps was not passed by Congress until three years later.) At first, Myer himself was the only person on the corps' official roster. After further trials out west, he started, in the first days of the war, training a small contingent of officers and men from other army units who had been detailed to the Signal Corps. The first camp of instruction was established at Fort Monroe, Virginia; later, the camp was moved to Red Hill, near Georgetown in Washington, D.C. Trainee officers and enlisted men had to master complex flag movements that represented not only the twenty-six letters of the alphabet, but also a collection of more than 200 abbreviations and word substitutes Myer had devised to reduce the time required to relay information from point to point. When weather conditions kept them from signaling, the men served as scouts, couriers, or observers. Because their elevated signal stations were excellent vantage points for early detection of enemy troop movements, signalmen were often targeted by enemy sharpshooters. Myer also incorporated a system of field telegraphy into the Signal Corps activities (see "U.S. Military Telegraph Service," on page 353).

In 1862, Myer and his former assistant, Edward Porter Alexander, faced each other as enemies during the Peninsula Campaign, when both personally supervised signaling and observation activities—most particularly, the deployment of observation balloons. By the next year, however, Alexander had assumed a field artillery command, and Myer had relinquished his field duties with the Army of the Potomac to Captain Lemuel B. Norton. Myer then performed the necessary overall organizational and administrative Signal Corps duties as a staff officer in Washington. In November 1863, he was relieved of all his Signal Corps duties after a dispute with Secretary of War Stanton over control of the Military Telegraph Service, which Myer felt should have been placed entirely under Signal Corps jurisdiction. By then, however, the U.S. Signal Corps was firmly established; the value of its services and the valor and effectiveness of its men were well proven. In 1932, at the unveiling of a memorial to Albert Myer at the former Fort Whipple, Virginia, renamed Fort Myer in his honor, the Chief Signal Officer of the Army, Major General Irving J. Carr, outlined the Signal Corps' Civil War accomplishments:

> [I]n the field in every [Civil War] campaign, the men of the Signal Service were risking their lives in the forefront of battle, speeding orders of advance, warnings of impending danger or undismayed admissions of defeat. . . . That desperate moment at Allatoona Pass when Sherman's supplies were about to be captured on his advance to Atlanta, stands out as one of the most brilliant uses of signalling in the Civil War. The defenders were slowly driven into a small fort on the crest of a hill. At this moment, an officer caught sight of a white signal flag far away across the valley . . . upon the top of Kenesaw Mountain. The signal was answered and soon the message was waved across from mountain to mountain: "Hold the fort; I am coming. W. T. Sherman." Cheers went up. . . . they held until the advance guard of Sherman's army came up. This event had such national significance that the inspiration for the old hymn was taken from that event: "Hold the Fort, for I Am Coming."

It was the South, however, that first used wig-wag signaling in combat. At First Bull Run (Manassas, July 21, 1861), seeing the gleam of bayonets through the trees in the direction of Sudley Ford, Edward Porter Alexander's Confederate signalmen warned Colonel Nathan Evans, "Look to your left. You are turned." This timely warning, coupled with Evans' own speedy reaction to the threat, allowed the outnumbered Confederates to delay the Federal advance on their flank until the arrival of reinforcements under generals Barnard Bee and Thomas (Stonewall) Jackson, saved the day. This occurred nearly nine months before the Confederate Signal Service was an officially recognized entity; on April 19, 1862, it was authorized by the Confederate Congress and was implemented by a general order of May 29, 1862—nearly a year before formal recognition was extended to Myer's already functioning U.S. Signal Corps.

That same year, as Edward Porter Alexander was preparing to move to other duties, Major William Norris was placed at the head of the Confederate Signal Service. (This appointment engendered a dispute with James F. Milligan, a navy veteran who had established a network of signal stations in southeast Virginia and who believed he should have received the appointment. Milligan maintained his limited network, designated the Independent Signal Corps and Scouts, separately throughout the war, reporting directly to the Confederate adjutant and inspector general.) Eventually, the main Confederate Signal Service comprised one major, ten captains, twenty lieutenants, twenty sergeants, and about 1,500 men (quickly dubbed "flag floppers" by Southern soldiers). A three- to five-man squad was assigned to every division of infantry and brigade of cavalry. As was true for the Union signalmen, the chief mission of the Confederate Signal Service personnel was to maintain communications between units, especially those not connected by telegraph. And as was true for the North, most of these messages were sent using a cipher. Confederate signalmen also served as observers of enemy troop movements and signal activities—as did their Northern counterparts. But Southern signalmen had some additional duties not normally performed by U.S. signalmen. One duty was service on blockade-running steamers, as described by Confederate Signal Service veteran Dr. Charles E. Taylor in a 1903 article, "The Signal and Secret Service of the Confederate States":

> No steamer ventured to come into port, especially in the later days of blockade running, without at least one signal officer on board to communicate with the forts and batteries. Instead of flags or torches, each officer was provided with two large lanterns of different colors with sliding screens in front. Standing between these and using the same alphabet which was used in the army, he sent his message. In this case the two colors were used instead of the right and left waves of the flag.
>
> Stations were located for thirty or forty miles along the coast on both sides of the blockaded port. The blockade-runners came in close to shore after nightfall and from time to time flashed their lights toward the shore. These were soon answered. Information was then given as to the condition of things, the position and movements of the blockading fleet, and the chances of a safe home run. If it was decided to try to bring the steamer in, proper lights were shown for the pilot's guidance and a swift run was made for the port.

The observation activities of Confederate signalmen often merged with the Confederate secret service activities, particularly in the neighborhood of the Potomac River, where Confederate agents crossed between Northern and Southern territories or left messages at designated spots for pickup by signalmen-couriers. Indeed, Chief Signal Officer Norris became so involved in the running of what became known as the "Secret Line" (actually, a network of clandestine activities) out of the Signal Service's offices, that he was regarded by some as chief of military intelligence, rather than military communication (see "Shadow Warriors: Partisan Rangers, Guerrillas, and Spies," in Chapter 5, "The Armies"). But espionage activities remained in the background. (They were conducted with such secrecy that even the files pertaining to the Signal Service's clandestine activities were kept in cipher.) Most Confederate signalmen concentrated on communication and observation.

Military Aeronautics

In light of the prewar popularity of ballooning—and no doubt inspired by the balloon unit, *1er Compagnie d'Aerostiers*, organized during the French Revolution—a number of accomplished American "aeronauts" offered their services to the U.S. government when the war began. The men who served in what became the Balloon Corps remained civilians and worked, at first, under the auspices of the Corps of Topographical Engineers (where, in addition to observing troop movements, they assisted in compiling the information required for creating up-to-date maps; see "The Importance of Maps," on page 345). In March 1862, responsibility for the Union's balloon unit was transferred to the Quartermaster Department.

The best known of the U.S. Army's balloonists was Professor Thaddeus S. C. Lowe, a self-educated former magician's assistant who had built his first balloon in 1858. Preparing to attempt a transatlantic flight when the war broke out, Lowe was on a trial run out of Cincinnati on April 19, 1861, when the wind shifted and he was forced to land in South Carolina—where he was promptly jailed by suspicious Confederate authorities. Soon released—and having observed South Carolina's preparations for war during his unexpected visit there—he offered his services to the Union via a politically influential sponsor, Murat Halstead of the Cincinnati *Daily Commercial*. After meeting with President Lincoln on June 11, Lowe made an official trial flight. He ascended from the Columbia Armory in Washington in the balloon *Enterprise* on June 17, 1861, accompanied by officials of the American Telegraph Company. On this flight, the *Enterprise* was equipped with a telegraph key and wires that ran along one of the rigging wires to the ground. Lowe made history when he telegraphed President Lincoln:

> I have pleasure in sending you this first dispatch ever telegraphed from an aerial station, and in acknowledging indebtedness for your encouragement for the opportunity of demonstrating the availability of the science of aeronautics in the military service of the country.

It was not Lowe, however, but veteran Pennsylvania balloonist John Wise who was given the task of building the first balloon intended for

An officer ascends in Professor T. S. C. Lowe's observation balloon, Intrepid, *to observe the fighting at Fair Oaks, Virginia, in 1862. His climb is controlled by the soldiers anchoring the balloon.*

battlefield use. (Wise had submitted a lower construction estimate.) Lowe's independent attempt to get his own balloon to the scene of First Bull Run (Manassas) was unsuccessful because the available gas supply was reserved for Wise; but Chief Signal Officer Albert Myer's officially sanctioned attempt to get Wise's balloon to the battlefield also came to nothing when the balloon became snagged in trees during transport. With Wise's craft destroyed, Lowe did receive official sanction for going aloft *after* the battle, and he made significant observations of Southern troop movements in the wake of the Confederate victory. Lowe and his balloon unit also performed admirably during the Peninsula Campaign (March–August 1862).

Meanwhile, well-known aeronaut John La Montain, a somewhat contentious former sailor and one-time apprentice of John Wise, had also offered his services to the Union. When no one in Washington replied to his letters, La Montain went to Fort Monroe, Virginia, at the behest of Major General Benjamin F. Butler, who had heard of La Montain's offer of service. After some weeks of preparation, the aeronaut made a successful trial ascension on August 10, and a subsequent ascent from the Union ship *Fanny*, at Hampton Roads, to observe Confederate batteries on Sewell's Point, Virginia. Prone to self-promotion and, from the start, at odds with Lowe, La Montain's career as a "freelance" U.S. aeronaut ended in February 1862, when Union General in Chief McClellan ordered that his services no longer be used. Subsequently, Lowe constructed four balloons for Union use. The *Intrepid* and the *Union*, made of silk and coated with varnish, were large balloons intended for use in good weather. For them, Lowe was paid $1,500 apiece. The *Washington* and the *Constitution*, of similar construction, were smaller, filled with hydrogen, and intended for use in bad weather; Lowe was paid $1,200 for each of them.

The new Balloon Corps discomfited some Union officers who were firmly rooted in more traditional methods of reconnaissance. (Other officers were eager to ride in balloons and fully appreciated the advantages balloon observation offered.) The lack of military discipline among the civilian balloonists only exacerbated this unease. Nevertheless, the Balloon Corps provided valuable service until well into 1863—particularly at Fredericksburg and Chancellorsville. Shortly after the latter battle, however, on May 8, 1863, Lowe resigned after his pay was reduced from $10 per day to $6 per day by his new supervisor, Captain Cyrus E. Comstock. Though the military balloon unit continued to operate for a few months under the immediate direction of two brothers, Ezra and James Allen, things were not the same without Lowe's driving spirit. By August 1863, the unit had been quietly disbanded.

The Confederacy also experimented with balloon observation, though not as extensively. Information about the South's aeronautical efforts is spotty. In a 1996 *Civil War Times* article, "Air War over Virginia," Charles M. Evans, founding curator of the Hiller Aviation Museum, stated that the first Confederate attempt at ballooning was made by twenty-one-year-old Captain John R. Bryan, aide-de-camp to Brigadier General John B. Magruder. A totally inexperienced, but enthusiastic balloonist, Bryan launched his balloon on April 13, 1862, over Yorktown, Virginia, as Major General George B. McClellan's Army of the Potomac was engaged in its Peninsula Campaign. Despite Union ground fire and the jouncing of the rickety wicker basket in which he was riding, Bryan managed to sketch a rough map of Union positions that came into view as the balloon gained altitude. His second ascension was somewhat less successful—though he reached ground safely—and Bryan soon retired from ballooning.

As this was happening, the South was constructing at least one, and possibly two, "silk dress balloons"—made of bolts of colored silk originally intended to be made into ladies' dresses (but almost certainly not constructed, as legend has it, from actual dresses donated by Confederate women). Constructed by Captain Langdon Cheeves and Charles Cevor in Savannah, Georgia, and then transported to Richmond, the one silk dress balloon that certainly saw service first rose above the Virginia Peninsula June 27, 1862, tethered either to a boxcar on land or to the C.S.S. *Teaser* in the James River. Its tour of duty was relatively brief: it was aboard the *Teaser* when that vessel was captured by the U.S.S. *Maratanza* on July 4, 1862. Speculation that a second silk dress balloon was built and used for observation in either Richmond or Charleston, and then was destroyed, has not been confirmed.

Though used only sporadically, and only in the Eastern Theater, the Civil War's observation balloons did establish the value of airborne reconnaissance. In the next century, as the first motorized air forces came into their own over the battlefields of World War I, the skies were dotted with tethered observation balloons. Constantly under fire from enemy positions, the men stationed in these vulnerable craft performed duties similar to those performed by their Civil War precursors—observing troop movements and serving as artillery spotters. Improved twentieth-century weaponry, and the development, in the early years of the Great War, of a machine gun synchronized to fire between the blades of aircraft propellers, placed the lives of World War I balloon observers at maximum risk—and signaled the end of the era of manned stationary battlefield balloon observation.

SELECTED RESOURCES

These titles are a representative sampling of thousands of published works pertaining to Civil War battles. For additional information on published sources, see the annotated book list in Chapter 13, "Studying the War: Research and Preservation."

Bailey, Anne J. *The Chessboard of War: Sherman and Hood in the Autumn Campaigns of 1864.* Lincoln: University of Nebraska Press, 2000.

Bearss, Edwin C. *The Campaign for Vicksburg.* 3 vols: *Vicksburg Is the Key* (1985); *Grant Strikes a Fatal Blow* (1986); *Unvexed to the Sea* (1986). Dayton, Ohio: Morningside, 1985–1986.

Daniel, Larry J. *Shiloh: The Battle that Changed the Civil War.* New York: Simon & Schuster, 1997.

Eicher, David J. *The Longest Night: A Military History of the Civil War.* New York: Simon & Schuster, 2001.

Gallagher, Gary W., ed. *The First Day at Gettysburg: Essays on Confederate and Union Leadership.* Kent, Ohio: Kent State University Press, 1992.

_____. *The Second Day at Gettysburg: Essays on Confederate and Union Leadership.* Kent, Ohio: Kent State University Press, 1993.

_____. *The Third Day at Gettysburg and Beyond.* Chapel Hill: University of North Carolina Press, 1994.

Glatthaar, Joseph T. *The March to the Sea and Beyond: Sherman's Troops in the Savannah and Carolinas Campaigns.* New York: New York University Press, 1985.

Hennessy, John J. *Return to Bull Run: The Campaign and Battle of Second Manassas.* New York: Simon & Schuster, 1993.

Josephy, Alvin M. Jr. *The Civil War in the American West.* New York: Knopf, 1991.

Rhea, Gordon C. *The Battle of the Wilderness, May 5–6, 1864.* Baton Rouge: Louisiana State University Press, 1994.

_____. *The Battles for Spotsylvania Court House and the Road to Yellow Tavern, May 7–12, 1864.* Baton Rouge: Louisiana State University Press, 1997.

_____. *To the North Anna River: Grant and Lee, May 13–25, 1864.* Baton Rouge: Louisiana State University Press, 2000.

_____. *Cold Harbor: Grant and Lee, May 20–June 3, 1864.* Baton Rouge: Louisiana State University Press, 2002.

Sears, Stephen. *To the Gates of Richmond: The Peninsula Campaign.* New York: Ticknor and Fields, 1992.

_____. *Landscape Turned Red: The Battle of Antietam.* New Haven, CT: Ticknor and Fields, 1983. Collectors' ed., Norwalk, CT: Easton Press, [1988?].

Sommers, Richard J. *Richmond Redeemed: The Siege at Petersburg.* Garden City, NY: Doubleday, 1981.

Sutherland, Donald E. *Fredericksburg and Chancellorsville: The Dare Mark Campaign.* Lincoln: University of Nebraska Press, 1998.

Woodworth, Steven E. *Six Armies in Tennessee: The Chickamauga and Chattanooga Campaigns.* Lincoln: University of Nebraska Press, 1998.

THE ARMIES

It is rather tough, these cold and stormy nights, but a soldier is expected to stand it without flinching—that is duty. Visions of home, and the loved ones there reposing, during these solitary hours, of course spring up in the imagination, and if a tear comes unbidden to the eye, it only shows that in becoming soldiers we do not cease to be men.—Sergeant Warren H. Freeman, Thirteenth Regiment Massachusetts Volunteers, U.S.A., letter to his father, January 19, 1862.

From Fort Sumter, in 1861, through the last engagement at Palmito Ranch, Texas, in 1865, approximately three million men (and, clandestinely, an estimated 400 to 600 women) served in the armies of the Civil War. On the front lines of the struggle to determine whether the Union would endure, these soldiers were drawn from an overall population of 32 million Americans whose shared "national profile" included an inherent distrust of large professional armies. This characteristic—rooted in Colonial experiences with British armies during the Revolutionary era, and tenable because of the two oceans that protected America's flanks—meant that the huge armies assembled by each side were made up primarily of ordinary people. Drawn from all walks of life, these citizen soldiers were untrained in the prevailing methods of making war and unprepared for the grinding routine of army life and the tearing chaos of battle.

The tiny prewar United States Army provided the core of experienced soldiers who guided the development and direction of the armies in both the North and the South. These seasoned soldiers—many of whom had attended West Point together and had fought side-by-side in the Mexican War—now employed their talents to organize and train their less-experienced comrades and to lead them against each other in combat. The war waged by these huge new armies grew to be so intense and costly that, early in 1863, British

Civil War special artist Edwin Forbes captured this scene of an army Going into Bivouac at Night.

correspondent Francis Charles Lawley, an eyewitness to several of the blood-iest Civil War battles, published in his paper, the *London Times*, a heartfelt plea for European intervention:

> Will not England and France rush in to bring an end to this slaughter? ... if [the civilized Powers of Europe] could only witness the misery which is, from every acre of this once favoured continent, crying aloud to Heaven, it could scarcely be that they would risk some chance of failure rather than permit humanity to be outraged by a continuance of such ex-cess of anguish as had visited no nation since the sword first leaped from its scabbard, and the human heart was first sown with the bitter seed of vindicativeness [sic] and hate.

Written before Gettysburg and the brutal clashes comprising the Overland Campaign of 1864, this plea stirred sympathy but did not lead to European intervention—although the war continued to be of consuming interest throughout Europe, for both ideological and practical reasons. In addition to newspaper coverage, a number of European nations—including England, France, Prussia, and Switzerland—sent soldiers or knowledgeable civilians to observe the American conflict, examining everything from seacoast fortifications to deployment of forces in combat. Early assessments by these experts were not always favorable. One British observer, Captain Charles Cornwallis Chesney, characterized the Union army of 1861 as "an armed and dangerous mob." Later, his opinion of American forces improved, as both the Union and the Confederate volunteer armies became better trained and more practiced at large-scale warfare.

Both sides faced daunting problems when it became clear that the Civil War would be long and would require raising, training, and maintaining military forces of unprecedented size. The state militias, from Colonial times, had served as wells from which the United States drew armed forces in time of need. These part-time civilian soldiers were imperfectly trained, at best, and were viewed with a measure of contempt by the professional soldiers of the regular United States Army, particularly the officers trained at West Point. Especially in the North, which did not celebrate martial traditions as did many Southerners (ninety-six military schools were founded in the South, but only fifteen in the North, between 1827 and 1860), the professional soldiers' lack of respect for untrained citizen soldiers was reciprocated by politicians and civilians who had a deep-seated distrust of the professional military. General William T. Sherman's brother, Ohio senator John Sherman, stated that he "did not believe that a military education at West Point has infused into the Army the right spirit to carry on this war." Newspaper publisher Horace Greeley believed that "common sense is quite as competent as tactical profundity to decide questions of hastening or deferring operations against the rebels." Even Edwin Stanton, U.S. secretary of war from early 1862, seemed to belittle the value of formal military training. He omitted mention of it when he said, shortly after he joined the cabinet: "Patriotic spirit, with resolute courage in officers and men, is a military combination that never failed." This divide between professional soldiers and civilians would exist, to some degree, throughout the war.

In the North and, very particularly, in the South, state governments guarded their political and military prerogatives jealously. The regiments of volunteers that made up both Union and Confederate forces were raised by the states and were led, especially in the beginning, by political appointees or elected officers whose knowledge of military science was far from reliable. As these regiments were gathered into larger units, and as each side fielded armies larger than those ever before assembled on the American continent (most of which were responsible for vast geographic areas), centralization of command proved difficult for both sides.

The Confederate forces did not acquire a general in chief, Robert E. Lee, until February 1865—several weeks after the South's primary Western Theater army, the Army of Tennessee, had been shattered at the battle of Nashville (December 1864), and less than two months before Lee's own Army of Northern Virginia would be forced to surrender. This delay in appointing an overall commanding general may have stemmed, in part, from President Davis' experience as U.S. secretary of war under President Franklin Pierce (1853–1857), when his relationship with General in Chief Winfield Scott had been difficult. (The venerable soldier resisted the secretary's authority.) Yet, early in the war, President Davis had recognized the overwhelming character of his duties as Confederate commander in chief. On March 3, 1862, he summoned a general officer in whom he had utmost confidence—Robert E. Lee— to Richmond as his military adviser. In this capacity, Lee was given more than advisory duties; he was charged with "the conduct of military operations in the armies of the Confederacy" and given "control of military operations, the movement and discipline of the troops, and the distribution of supplies among the armies of the Confederate states"—the same responsibilities specified in early proposed legislation that would have established the office of Confederate commanding general, had Davis not vetoed it. Thus, acting as an ad hoc chief of staff, Lee was able to bring some centralized military planning and expertise to the Confederacy's high command—but only for three months. On May 31, 1862, when Joseph E. Johnston was wounded, Lee left Richmond to assume command of the Army of Northern Virginia, leaving Davis once more without an adviser/military chief of staff until he appointed the controversial Braxton Bragg to that position on February 24, 1864. This was a wise choice militarily, because of Bragg's strategic acumen and administrative capabilities, but the appointment was not applauded by many in the army and the government, whose opinions of the difficult general ranged from distrust to active hatred.

Throughout the war, Davis did have the assistance of a Confederate secretary of war. But due to occasional Confederate political upheavals, as well as the president's own military expertise and tendency to engage in what would today be called "micromanagement" of that department, the office was held by six different men between 1861 and 1865. (James A. Seddon served the longest; see Chapter 3, "Wartime Politics.") Differences between Davis and some of his commanding generals—most notably, Joseph E. Johnston, and most particularly *excepting* Robert E. Lee—interfered at times with the efficient movement of armies in the field, as did squabbles among Confederate officers, especially in the Western Theater.

The North had begun the war with the revered but aging Winfield Scott as general in chief. But the office soon passed to George B. McClellan; then, after a short period when the post was vacant, to Henry W. Halleck; and, finally, to Ulysses S. Grant. All three were seasoned professional soldiers. The North's commander in chief, Abraham Lincoln, had no experience comparable to that of Jefferson Davis (his short service in the Illinois militia during the Black Hawk War was chiefly behind the lines), but he proved to be a supremely apt student and quickly acquired as firm a grasp of military strategy and tactics as he had of political issues. His diplomatic skills were also considerable—and were often employed to keep the sometimes volatile members of his own cabinet focused on necessary action rather than superfluous debates. When Edwin Stanton replaced Simon Cameron as secretary of war in January 1862, Lincoln gained a sometimes controversial but essentially reliable ally in his prosecution of the war, a man upon whom he came to rely heavily.

During the period when there was no Union general in chief, Lincoln and Stanton established an advisory body known as the War Board, chiefly comprising the heads of the various army bureaus (adjutant general, quartermaster general, chief engineer, chief of ordnance, and commissary general). This embryonic version of an American general staff was headed, after its first three meetings, by Ethan Allen Hitchcock, a veteran of forty years' service in the army, whom Stanton had called back to active duty. Hitchcock functioned more ably as Stanton's personal military adviser (and commissioner for the exchange of prisoners) than as director of the War Board. But the board itself provided excellent operational advice and effected greater coordination among the different branches of the burgeoning U.S. armies. Items on its agenda ranged from seacoast defense and prisoner policies, through officer and enlisted personnel management matters and quartermaster functions, to field expeditions and the impact of the new ironclad vessels.

After December 1861, a U.S. congressional committee also became deeply involved in war matters. The Joint Committee on the Conduct of the War, established as an immediate result of the humiliating Union defeats at First Bull Run (Manassas, July 21, 1861) and Ball's Bluff, Virginia (October 21, 1861), gradually extended its interests and oversight until it had an impact on the selection of officers and on military strategy. This fact often adversely affected morale not only among staff and field officers, who resented being subjected to often heavy-handed political interference, but in the army's ranks as well. Many in the Army of the Potomac were convinced, for example, that the committee's activities, combined with Radical Republican rhetoric, were at least partially to blame for the Union's bloody defeat at the battle of Fredericksburg. Some members of the Joint Committee were equally convinced that certain officers, mostly those known to be Democrats, were not prosecuting the war aggressively enough (see "Time Line—December 9, 1861," in Chapter 3, "Wartime Politics").

Many on both sides had expected that the war would be "over by Christmas" of 1861. As it continued and grew in scope instead, both the South (in 1862) and the North (in 1863) instituted general conscription—the first time in American history that this step had been taken. Established, at least in part, as an added inducement to volunteer (volunteers were often rewarded with monetary payments, or bounties; draftees were not), the draft stirred protests among civilians on both sides. Protests were particularly vehement in the North, where violent draft riots occurred, the worst of them being in New York City (see Chapter 10, "The Home Front"). Draftees were allowed to furnish substitutes, and, in both the North and the South, this provision created resentment and engendered abuse (so much, in fact, that the Confederacy ended substitution in December 1863; it continued in the Union). Conscientious objection also inspired debate, in both regions, for the first time during the Civil War, and various legislative and informal arrangements were made to accommodate those whose religious beliefs prohibited them from engaging in combat. But few debates were more intense than those surrounding the incorporation of black soldiers into the Union's land forces (see "Fighting on Two Fronts: Black Soldiers in the Civil War," on page 427). A similar debate in the Confederacy resulted in passage of the "Negro Soldier" law in 1865—too late to make any difference in the South's war effort.

The huge Union and Confederate armies that were in the field by 1862 made it necessary to adjust army staff structure as well as the functioning and organization of the armies themselves. New weaponry and methods of transport led to experimentation in battle tactics (see "Civil War Strategy," "Battle Tactics," and "Toward Modern War" in Chapter 4, "Battles and the Battlefield"). Widespread partisan and guerrilla warfare led to the formation of both Unionist and pro-Confederate counterguerrilla units. Intelligence gathering, a haphazard enterprise on the part of the Union and Confederate governments when compared with the activities of European governments at the time, became a function of some field army organizations. "Secret service" was also a carefully concealed activity of the otherwise above-board Confederate Signal Service—only one of several avenues of intelligence gathering employed by the South (see "Shadow Warriors:

Partisan Rangers, Guerrillas, and Spies," on page 447). Much of this battle-ground intelligence gathering was devoted to locating enemy forces, determining who was in command and whether and in what direction they were about to move. Finding and defeating the enemy remained the main duty of the armies.

As this war of Americans versus Americans grew longer and more destructive, the sense of adventure and eagerness to "see the elephant" (experience combat) that initially prevailed among soldiers of both sides was slowly replaced by a tired determination to see the war through. Torn by the chaos of battle, the death of comrades, and the fight to control their own fears, Civil War soldiers were also buffeted by army routine, supply shortages, and home-front political battles that were reported in newspapers and letters and sometimes resulted in abrupt changes in command and alterations in strategy. Most soldiers were also torn between their belief in the importance of doing their duty for their country and their longing for, and concern about those at home. Confederate soldiers, particularly, worried about the well-being of their families as Union armies pressed ever more deeply into the South. In both armies, desertion rates waxed and waned according to home-front and battlefield events and the level of army morale. Yet, most men stayed at their posts. Many, on both sides, performed with extraordinary valor until their term of service expired, or they were debilitated by or died from disease, or they were severely wounded or killed in battle. Many soldiers explained their reasons for remaining at the front in eloquent letters to loved ones who feared for their safety.

"I came to the war because I felt it to be my duty," Private W. S. Shockley of the Eighteenth Georgia wrote to his wife Eliza in 1863. "I am not going to run away if I never come home I had rather di without seeing them [his two daughters] than for peple to tell them after I am dead that their father was a deserter. . . . It [is] every Southern mans duty to fight against abolition misrule and preserve his Liberty untarnished which was won by our fore Fathers. . . . I never yet regreted the step I have taken."

"I know if this war is not fought through and settled as it should be that our boys will have to be soldiers and pass through what I have," Massachusetts Captain Joseph W. Collingwood wrote to his wife in August 1862. "I had rather stay here for years than they should ever go on the battle field." (Captain Collingwood was killed four months later, at the battle of Fredericksburg.)

When the war finally was fought through and veterans returned home—absent 620,000 who had died in the conflict—most Northern soldiers, if not physically maimed in the conflict, settled back into a relatively normal civilian life. Many Southern veterans, however, faced ruined homes, a devastated economy, and a way of life that had been permanently altered. And the 186,000 African American men who had fought two wars while serving in the Union army—the war for acceptance by their white comrades and society at large, and the war against slavery and the Confederate States—faced further difficult decades as many hopes and expectations born of their service in the war and the abolition of slavery turned to disappointment in the face of postwar reversals (see Chapter 11, "Reconstruction and the Aftermath of the War").

This chapter provides basic information on the structure and organization of Civil War armies and on the people who served in them.

Civil War Land Forces: General Organization

The basic organizational structures of the Union and Confederate armies were virtually identical. On each side, the land forces comprised the following units (listed from smallest to largest numbers of combatants).

Company ("Battery" When Referring to Artillery Units)

Commanded by a captain. On paper, a company comprised 100 soldiers. By 1862, companies averaged between thirty and fifty soldiers, the result of attrition due to battle, disease, and other causes. Companies were often divided into smaller units commanded by a sergeant or a corporal. Official company designations were letters (or numbers), for example, B Company, Thirty-Fourth Alabama. Many were also known by unofficial designations—for example, the Clinch Rifles.

Regiment

Commanded by a colonel. The majority of Civil War soldiers most strongly identified with this organizational unit. Regiments were raised by state governments and usually comprised men from the same area. Often, at the outset of the war, friends, neighbors, and relatives would be in the same regiment. Officers were often elected by the men, particularly in the first years of the war. Regiments ideally comprised ten companies of 100 men each—though many did not achieve or maintain full strength. Union cavalry regiments often included twelve companies. A Civil War unit that failed to muster the ten companies required to be designated a regiment was often called a battalion.

Brigade

Commanded by a brigadier general. Brigades were the common tactical infantry and cavalry units of the Civil War. A brigade usually included from four to six regiments—though the number varied extensively as the war went on. Some brigades included as few as two regiments; others were made up of the remnants of as many as fifteen regiments. Confederate brigades were more likely than those of the Union to be made up of regiments from the same state.

Division

Commanded by a brigadier general or major general (U.S.A.); with rare exception, by a major general (C.S.A.). The second largest unit constituting an army. Divisions on both sides could include some 12,000 men organized in brigades (as few as two and as many as six). It was not unusual for Confederate divisions to include more brigades than Union divisions. A Confederate division was sometimes equal in strength to a single Union army corps.

Corps

Commanded by a brigadier general or major general (U.S.A.); a lieutenant general (C.S.A.). Derived from Napoleon's *corps d'armée*, the first Civil War corps were organized in the Union army in March 1862 by Abraham Lincoln and Major General George B. McClellan. The first Confederate corps were organized later in 1862 (September in the Eastern Theater, November in the Western). Before that time, however, Confederate divisions had occasionally been grouped, informally, into "wings" or "grand divisions." Composed of two or more divisions, each corps was given a number—though many were also known by the name of their commander. Corps became standard units of the United States Army in wartime after their first appearance in the Civil War.

Army

Commanded by a major general (U.S.A.); general (C.S.A.). The largest military field force, a Civil War army generally comprised multiple corps (the

Union Army of the Potomac included seven corps at Gettysburg) but might consist of two or, occasionally, only one. Union armies were generally named after rivers (e.g., Army of the Potomac). Confederate armies were usually named for the geographical area in which they were based (e.g., the Army of Northern Virginia)—though there were exceptions on each side.

Civil War Armies: United States of America

In April 1861, when the first shots of the Civil War were fired in Charleston Harbor, the United States Army stood at a total strength of 16,367 officers and men. (This number was slightly depleted when some 300 officers resigned, but few, if any, enlisted men left to join the Confederate service.) At that time, the Union Army was significantly smaller than the combined militias of the seven states that comprised the Confederate States of America. (Eventually, the Confederacy included eleven states.) Authorized in May 1861 to increase its strength to 22,714, the Regular Army remained a separate service throughout the war. Its units, which were assigned to various Union armies as needed, were distinguished by the designation "United States" (e.g., the Thirteenth United States Infantry).

The overwhelming majority of the 2.2 million men who served in Union armies during the Civil War served in the Volunteer Army, comprising regiments raised by the individual states. Thus, volunteer regiment designations included the name of the state in which the unit had been mustered (for example, the 105th Illinois Volunteer Infantry). The eventual size and complexity of this Volunteer Army created troubling problems for the North's leaders, particularly during the first year of the war. The president's call, on April 15, 1861, the day after Fort Sumter was taken, for 75,000 men to serve for ninety days was quickly followed by a call for 42,035 army volunteers to serve for three years, unless sooner discharged. After the Union defeat at First Bull Run (Manassas, July 21, 1861), Lincoln signed two bills authorizing the enlistment of one million additional men for three years. Some volunteers, however, were able to sign up for different periods. Logistical problems pertaining to the provision of adequate food, housing, medical care, and clothing attended the incorporation of hundreds of thousands of new soldiers into the national volunteer force. And these constituted only a portion of the challenge. Fundamental difficulties rested in the leadership and makeup of the new regiments themselves.

In the war's early stages, most Volunteer Army regimental officers were elected, and regimental commanders—as well as many higher officers in the

Volunteer Army—were often politically influential men who knew little or nothing of military practices and discipline. Many of the men felt no need to devote themselves to acquiring such knowledge, in part because they subscribed to the overwhelming assumption that the war would be short and the Union's might would easily prevail. Such leaders provided their men with little assistance in acquiring the skills that would make them effective soldiers and help save their lives on the battlefield. Most of these new soldiers were at least as inexperienced as their fledgling officers; further, they possessed a pronounced devotion to individual rights and often resisted the strictures of army routine when officers attempted to apply them. (Each regimental commander trained his men as he saw fit.)

These weaknesses in the Volunteer Army fast became glaringly obvious, particularly after the Union's defeat at First Bull Run (July 1861; see Chapter 4, "Battles and the Battlefield"). By 1862, examinations and other measures to ensure that officers had an acceptable amount of military knowledge were adopted by the Union. Earlier, while organizing the Army of the Potomac, veteran soldier George B. McClellan had instituted training programs to instill basic military skills in volunteers, and these programs became common practice in all U.S. armies after McClellan became general in chief (November 1861). This tougher training was often remarked upon in soldiers' correspondence: "The first thing in the morning is drill, then drill, then drill again," new soldier Oliver Willcox Norton wrote in a letter home, in October 1861. "Then drill, drill, a little more drill. Then drill, and lastly drill. Between drills, we drill and sometimes stop to eat a little and have a roll-call."

New officers and noncommissioned officers ("noncoms") who were conscientious often did double training—studying manuals at night so they were prepared to put their men through the requisite drills in the daytime. "Every night I recite with the other 1st Sergts and 2nd Lieutenants," George B. Turner of Ohio wrote to his father in December 1862. "We shall finish Hardee's Tactics and then study the 'Army Regulations.'" (William J. Hardee's *Rifle and Light Infantry Tactics* was a basic text used by the American military since its publication in 1855. A Georgian, Hardee became a lieutenant general in the Confederate Army; see "Notable Civil War Officers," on page 399.)

Experienced officers from Regular Army units also assisted in organizing the burgeoning Volunteer force and training its inexperienced officers and noncoms. Throughout the war, many Regular Army officers were

This Irvin lithograph published by the Sherman Publishing Company in 1874 depicts twenty of the Union's most influential Civil War military leaders. Top row, l to r: General George H. Thomas, General Philip Kearney, General Ambrose E. Burnside, General Joseph Hooker, General John A. Logan, General George G. Meade, General George B. McClellan; middle row, l to r: General Irvin McDowell, General Nathaniel P. Banks, General Philip H. Sheridan, General Ulysses S. Grant, General William T. Sherman, General William S. Rosecrans, General Daniel E. Sickles; bottom row, l to r: Admiral David G. Farragut, General John Pope, General Benjamin F. Butler, General Winfield S. Hancock, General John Sedgwick, Admiral David D. Porter.

granted leave to assume commands, usually at higher ranks, in Volunteer units. After the war, most of the surviving officers reverted to their Regular Army rank (see "Civil War Military Leadership," on page 393).

Once the fundamentals of combat were achieved, more complex drills involving brigades and divisions, and sometimes including mock battles, were engaged in. These provided both the officers and their troops with valuable experience in maneuvering. It also gave them a foretaste of the noise, smoke, and confusion they would encounter on the battlefield.

As the war expanded, the organization of U.S. land forces reflected the growing size and complexity of the conflict. The four Theaters of Operation in which the war's military campaigns occurred (see "The Theater of War," in Chapter 4, "Battles and the Battlefield") were divided into organizational units called "Military Divisions" or, more commonly, "Departments" (e.g., the Department of the Cumberland). A Union army usually bore a name derived from the department or geographical area in which it operated. Departments—and armies—were created, dissolved, merged, and renamed throughout the war, as circumstances dictated. The main Union armies that conducted significant campaigns during the war are listed in the following pages in the chronological order of their formation. Each army's primary theater of operation is also noted.

Army of Northeastern Virginia: Eastern

Commanding general (Department and Army of Northeastern Virginia): Irvin McDowell (July 8, 1861–August 15, 1861)

Just over a month after the war began, and three days after Federal troops crossed the Potomac River and seized Alexandria, Virginia (May 24, 1861), Brigadier General Irvin McDowell assumed command of this Union department—essentially comprising Virginia east of the Allegheny Mountains, south of the Potomac River, and north of the James River. He immediately began forging an army out of thousands of untried volunteers. Less than two months later, when that task was still woefully incomplete, he was ordered to push a large Confederate force, in position only twenty-five miles from Washington, away from the U.S. capital. His troops were trounced at First Bull Run (July 21). Four days later, the Department of Northeastern Virginia and its army were merged into the Military Division of the Potomac, which was then expanded into the Department of the Potomac on August 15 (see next).

Army of the Potomac: Eastern

Commanding generals (Department and Army of the Potomac): George B. McClellan (August 20, 1861–November 9, 1862); Ambrose E. Burnside (November 9, 1862–January 26, 1863); Joseph Hooker (January 26, 1863–June 28, 1863); George G. Meade (June 28, 1863–September 1, 1865)

The most powerful Union army and the principal Federal force in the Eastern Theater of Operations, the Army of the Potomac dueled primarily with Robert E. Lee's smaller, but equally formidable, Army of Northern Virginia throughout the war. Charged with the defense of Washington, D.C. and the conquest of the Confederate capital of Richmond, Virginia, the Army of the Potomac demonstrated resilience and persistence after costly defeats at Fredericksburg (December 1862) and Chancellorsville (May 1863) and in the bloody clashes at Antietam (September 1862), Gettysburg (July 1863), and the Overland Campaign (May–June 1864). Union General in Chief Ulysses S. Grant established his headquarters with the Army of the Potomac in March 1864 and stayed with it while directing all Union forces. He accepted Robert E. Lee's surrender at Appomattox Court House, Virginia, on April 9, 1865.

Army of the Southwest (Army of Southwest Missouri): Trans-Mississippi

Commanding generals: Samuel R. Curtis (December 25, 1861–August 29, 1862); Frederick Steele (August 29, 1862–October 7, 1862); Eugene A. Carr (October 7, 1862–November 12, 1862); Willis A. Gorman (temp., November 12, 1862–December 13, 1862)

In existence for only one year, the Army of the Southwest served basically as an army of territorial occupation. It concentrated on holding the southwestern portion of the state of Missouri—a state also claimed by the Confederacy—for the Union. In February 1862, the army pressed after an army of 8,000 Confederates under Major General Sterling Price. In northwestern Arkansas, Price was reinforced by troops under Major General Earl Van Dorn, but the combined force was defeated by the Army of the Southwest at the battle of Pea Ridge (Elkhorn Tavern), March 7–8, 1862. That victory secured Missouri for the Union for more than two years. After another offensive into Arkansas in the summer of 1862, the Army of the Southwest was assimilated into the Department of the Tennessee. Various units distinguished themselves during the campaigns for Vicksburg and Atlanta and during Sherman's March to the Sea.

Army of the Mississippi (1862) and (1863): Western

Commanding generals (1862 Army of the Mississippi): John Pope (February 23, 1862–June 26, 1862); William S. Rosecrans (June 26, 1862–October 24, 1862)

Commanding general (1863 Army of the Mississippi): John A. McClernand (January 4, 1863–January 12, 1863)

Established February 23, 1862, to bring the Mississippi River under Federal control, the 19,000-man Army of the Mississippi (with an accompanying river fleet) embarked on the successful New Madrid–Island No. 10 Campaign in March. These Confederate river bastions were taken in early April and the river was opened to the Union as far south as Fort Pillow, Tennessee. Following this success, Brigadier General John Pope was transferred to a command in the Eastern Theater (see "Army of Virginia," next). His successor, Major General William Rosecrans, led the army against Confederates under Major General Sterling Price at the battle of Iuka, Mississippi (September 9, 1862). The Confederates were forced from the field, but the Union did not score a decisive victory. Shortly thereafter, the Army of the Mississippi was absorbed into forces led by Major General William T. Sherman.

As the first Army of the Mississippi was disappearing, a second was being born. Formed, with President Lincoln's approval, by John A. McClernand, a "political general" and former U.S. representative from Lincoln's home district, this second Army of the Mississippi was to move against Vicksburg, Mississippi—where Ulysses S. Grant, who had little respect for McClernand, was already engaged in operations. A brief, laudable, and successful assault, made in concert with naval forces under David D. Porter, resulted in the capture of Fort Hindman at Arkansas Post, Arkansas, on January 10–11, 1863. McClernand's Army of the Mississippi accomplished little else as a discrete unit and was soon absorbed into the forces Grant commanded during his persistent attempts to take Vicksburg.

Army of Virginia: Eastern

Commanding general: John Pope (June 26, 1862–September 12, 1862)

This short-lived army—established to consolidate the hitherto fragmented Union force in northern Virginia—was chiefly distinguished by its lack of success—due, in large measure, to its commanding officer, John Pope. Though a courageous soldier, brevetted captain for gallantry in the Mexican War, Pope had an abrasive personality that inspired his Army of Virginia subordinates chiefly in the direction of animosity. Pope's small army was assigned to protect Washington, D.C., and to guard the Shenandoah Valley—while also relieving the pressure on McClellan's Army of the

Potomac on the Virginia Peninsula. Elements of the Army of Virginia—some 9,000 men under Nathaniel Banks—met 24,000 Confederates under Stonewall Jackson at Cedar Mountain, Virginia, on August 9 and were defeated after a hard-fought battle. At the end of the month, Pope's force clashed with Robert E. Lee's Army of Northern Virginia at the second battle of Bull Run (August 29–30), was soundly trounced, and withdrew into the defenses around Washington. Pope—who had accused his subordinate officers of "unsoldierly and dangerous conduct" at Second Bull Run—was relieved of command on August 5 and subsequently transferred to the western frontier, where he served until his retirement in 1886. By September 12, 1862, the Army of Virginia had been absorbed by the Army of the Potomac.

Army of the Frontier: Trans-Mississippi

Commanding generals: John M. Schofield (October 12, 1862–November 20, 1862); James G. Blunt (November 20, 1862–December 29, 1862); John M. Schofield (December 29, 1862–March 30, 1863); Francis J. Herron (March 30, 1863–August 7, 1863)

Established as the Army of the Southwest (see page 380), which had protected the same territory, was passing out of existence, the Army of the Frontier was dedicated to countering Confederate incursions into Missouri. In late fall of 1862, it pushed Confederate forces out of Missouri and into the Indian Territory and Arkansas. Pursuing the Confederates into Arkansas, and reinforced by troops dispatched from Springfield, Missouri, the Army of the Frontier engaged the Confederates in bitter cold weather at the battle of Prairie Grove (December 7, 1862). Its victory there, nine months after the Federal Army of the Southwest had defeated Confederates at Pea Ridge, reinforced the Union's hold on northwest Arkansas and western Missouri. The area was not seriously threatened again until the unsuccessful Sterling Price expedition in 1864. After Prairie Grove, the Army of the Frontier guarded Missouri against raiders and guerrillas until its units were dispersed to Vicksburg and to various garrisons in Missouri and Arkansas.

Army of the Tennessee: Western

Commanding generals: Ulysses S. Grant (October 16, 1862–October 24, 1863); William T. Sherman (October 24, 1863–March 26, 1864); James B.

McPherson (March 26, 1864–July 22, 1864); Oliver O. Howard (July 27, 1864–May 19, 1865); John A. Logan (May 19, 1865–August 1, 1865)

One of the greatest of the Union's western armies, the Army of the Tennessee was in the forefront of the most critical western campaigns during nearly three years of hard fighting, from the 1862 winter campaigns in Tennessee, through Vicksburg and Atlanta, to the Carolinas Campaign of 1865. It was present at Joseph E. Johnston's surrender near Greensborough, North Carolina, that April—a fitting conclusion because it had played a crucial role in the outcome of the war.

In October 1863, the Union reorganized its forces in the west and created a Military Division of the Mississippi, comprising the military departments of the Tennessee, the Cumberland, and the Ohio. Ulysses S. Grant was elevated to command of that Military Division, and William T. Sherman assumed command of the Army of the Tennessee, a subordinate position within Grant's new Military Division. This restructuring is particularly noteworthy because it allowed more coordinated action in the Western Theater—an important step toward ultimate Union victory. When Grant became general in chief of all U.S. armies in March 1864, Sherman was given command of the Military Division of the Mississippi, and the Army of the Tennessee was among the forces he oversaw. He retained that command until the Military Division was dissolved in June 1865.

Army of the Cumberland: Western

Commanding generals: William S. Rosecrans (October 24, 1862–October 19, 1863); George H. Thomas (October 19, 1863–August 1, 1865)

Established October 24, 1862, the Army of the Cumberland was the field force responsible for all of Tennessee east of the Tennessee River, as well as northern Alabama and northern Georgia. Its first major battle at Stones River (December 31, 1862–January 3, 1863) was a victory that was much needed by the Union, which had suffered a shattering defeat at Fredericksburg, Virginia, in the Eastern Theater, just two weeks previously. After occupying Chattanooga, Tennessee, in early September 1863, the Army of the Cumberland was defeated at Chickamauga, Georgia, later in the month, and was placed under siege in Chattanooga, to which it had retreated. After George Thomas replaced William Rosecrans as commander, the Army of the Cumberland was instrumental in breaking the Confederate siege of the city and subsequently—

with its strength at approximately 70,000 men—made up more than half of William T. Sherman's forces during the Atlanta Campaign of 1864. With Atlanta in Union hands (September 1864), the Army of the Cumberland was divided: two of its corps joined Sherman on his March to the Sea, and the remainder returned with George H. Thomas to Tennessee, where, at the battle of Nashville (December 15, 1864), they formed part of the force that shattered the Confederates' principal western army, the Army of Tennessee.

Army of the Ohio (1861–1862) and (1863–1865): Western

Commanding general (1861–1862): Don Carlos Buell (November 9, 1861–October 24, 1862)

Commanding generals (1863–1865): Ambrose E. Burnside (April 11, 1863–December 9, 1863); John G. Foster (December 9, 1863–February 9, 1864); John M. Schofield (February 9, 1864–August 1, 1865)

Two notable Union armies were designated Army of the Ohio. The first, organized early in the war, was led by Mexican War veteran Don Carlos Buell, a talented and well-connected officer of whom great things were expected. After accepting the surrender of Nashville, Tennessee (which had been evacuated by Confederate troops), in the wake of Grant's victories at Forts Henry and Donelson, Buell led the Army of the Ohio to a timely arrival on the second day of the battle of Shiloh (April 1862) and helped to prevent a catastrophic Union defeat. Later in the year, at Perryville, Kentucky (Chaplin Hills) on October 8, the Army of the Ohio fought Braxton Bragg's Confederates to a standoff that resulted in Bragg's withdrawal from Kentucky (a Union state) into Tennessee. Buell's failure to pursue Bragg aggressively (and his suspension of pursuit altogether after four days) resulted in public outrage in the North, and Buell was removed from command.

The second Union force to be designated the Army of the Ohio was a mobile force, initially commanded by Ambrose Burnside, formed to liberate East Tennessee Unionists. Firmly established in East Tennessee by early September 1863, the army was placed under siege in Knoxville, during November and December, by Confederates under James Longstreet, who had been detached from Braxton Bragg's forces besieging Chattanooga. The Knoxville siege was a failure. The Confederates withdrew, and the Army of the Ohio pursued and jousted with Longstreet's Confederates for a few months. Elements of the army were subsequently transferred to other areas, and a reduced-strength Army of the Ohio participated in the Atlanta Campaign. Afterward, augmented by a corps recently detached from the Army of the James (see the following), it took Wilmington, North Carolina, a crucial Confederate supply base, and then reunited with Sherman, who was moving north, toward the rear of Robert E. Lee's Army of Northern Virginia. Having formed the center of Sherman's force as it moved toward Raleigh, North Carolina, the Army of the Ohio was the occupation force in North Carolina after Joseph E. Johnston surrendered his western Confederate army (April 26, 1865). The unit was discontinued on August 1, 1865.

Army of the James: Eastern

Commanding generals: Benjamin F. Butler (commander, Department of Virginia and North Carolina, November 11, 1863–January 8, 1865; commander, Army of the James, April 28, 1864–January 8, 1865); Edward O. C. Ord (commander, Department of Virginia and North Carolina and Army of the James, January 8, 1865–June 14, 1865)

Comprising two corps and, at peak strength, 50,000 men, the Army of the James was the field force based in the Department of Virginia and North Carolina, which had been formed, in July 1863, from two previously separate Union departments. Under General Butler's direct command, the Army of the James embarked on the ultimately unsuccessful Bermuda Hundred Campaign in the spring of 1864. (At that same time, the Army of the Potomac was opening the Overland Campaign that forced Lee's Army of Northern Virginia back into siege lines near the crucial railroad center of Petersburg.) Moving toward Petersburg and Richmond from the seaward side, Butler's army received a drubbing at the second battle of Drewry's Bluff (May 16, 1864), got stuck, and was subsequently "bottled up" on the Bermuda Hundred peninsula. An important breakthrough at Chaffin's Farm (September 29–30)—in which African American troops in the Army of the James performed with conspicuous valor—endangered Richmond but did not result in its fall. Butler was relieved of command when he failed to besiege Fort Fisher, North Carolina, subsequent to a failed assault on the fort. Shortly thereafter, two divisions of the Army of the James, led by Major General Alfred H. Terry, successfully stormed that crucially important Confederate bastion (January 15, 1865). General Terry's Army of the James corps then became part of Major General John M. Schofield's Army of the

Ohio (see page 384), which joined the force that defeated Joseph E. Johnston and occupied North Carolina. The remaining Army of the James troops, under a new commander, Edward O. C. Ord, participated in the Appomattox Campaign that resulted in Lee's surrender. The Army of the James served as an occupying force in Virginia until the force was effectively discontinued August 1, 1865.

Army of the Shenandoah: Eastern

Commanding generals: Philip H. Sheridan (August 7, 1864–April 22, 1865); Alfred T. A. Torbert (April 22, 1865–June 27, 1865)

Although a Union force under Robert Patterson was briefly designated Army of the Shenandoah in the summer of 1861, the designation truly belongs to the army formed by Ulysses S. Grant in 1864 in response to Jubal Early's raid into Northern territory, during which Early's 15,000 troops posed the only serious Confederate threat to Washington, D.C. Placed under the command of cavalry general Philip H. Sheridan, the Army of the Shenandoah was directed to "pursue Early to the death." Its second objective was to destroy the fertile valley's capacity to be a source of resupply for Confederate Army regulars and for the guerrilla units that plagued Union troops in the area. Sheridan and his men accomplished both objectives. They smashed Early's Confederates in a series of engagements from late September to late October (and defeated the remnants in March 1865), and then confiscated or destroyed all militarily useful materials in the valley—including crops and livestock. They left only bare subsistence for most of the valley's inhabitants. Units of the army were subsequently detached. Sheridan joined Grant outside Petersburg, and another Army of the Shenandoah corps joined Sherman in Savannah, Georgia. The much depleted Army of the Shenandoah was an army of occupation in the valley until the force was abolished on June 27, 1865.

Army of Georgia: Western

Commanding general: Henry W. Slocum (November 7, 1864–June 17, 1865)

Comprising the two corps of the Army of the Cumberland that remained with the forces conducting Major General William T. Sherman's Georgia and Carolina campaigns (the rest of the Army of the Cumberland had been dispatched to Nashville with its commander, George Thomas, see page 383), this force was informally designated the Army of Georgia in November 1864. On March 28, 1865, the designation became official. The Army of Georgia comprised the left wing of Sherman's March to the Sea and participated in the short siege of Savannah and a subsequent campaign that left a wide swath of destruction in South Carolina. When Sherman's forces entered North Carolina, the Army of Georgia bore the brunt of Confederate resistance at the battles of Averasborough (March 16, 1865) and Bentonville (March 19, 1865), where its tenacious resistance countered the effects of repeated Confederate assaults. After helping to force Joseph E. Johnston's surrender in North Carolina (April 26), the Army of Georgia participated in the triumphant Grand Review in Washington (May 24) before being disbanded at the beginning of June.

Civil War Armies: Confederate States of America

Following the South's secession, hundreds of volunteer companies flocked to the Confederate banner and were, initially, simply sent where needed. At the same time, Jefferson Davis was developing a plan to establish a Confederate army that would emulate the organization of the United States Army as it had existed during the Mexican War (1846–1848). His intention was to establish a relatively small standing army—15,015 professional officers and enlisted men who, after the war, would serve as the Army of the Confederate States of America (A.C.S.A.). To meet the demands of the immediate crisis, however, the Provisional Army of the Confederate States (P.A.C.S.)—a force equivalent to the U.S Volunteer Army—was created by legislation passed on February 28, 1861 (a week before the authorizing legislation for the Regular Army was passed, March 6). Because the fledgling nation was at war almost from the start and troops had to be raised quickly, virtually all new Confederate soldiers were mustered into P.A.C.S. units.

In early March 1861, the Confederate Congress authorized President Davis to raise a maximum of 100,000 volunteers for twelve months' service. In May, raising 400,000 additional men was authorized, but the term of service was changed to three years or the duration of the war. Though the term of their service was greatly increased, volunteers and conscripts knew that their military status would end with the war. That would not be true of those serving in the Regular Army, however. Had the Confederacy still existed at war's end, they would have been required to serve their full term of service, however long past the war's end that might have extended.

Twenty of the Confederacy's most prominent generals are depicted by the Sherman Publishing Company in this lithograph published in 1874. Top row, l to r: General John B. Hood, General A. P. Hill, General Albert S. Johnston, General Richard S. Ewell, General James Longstreet, General William J. Hardee, General Sterling Price; middle row, l to r: General J. E. B. Stuart, General P. G. T. Beauregard, General T. J. (Stonewall) Jackson, General Robert E. Lee, General Joseph E. Johnston, General Fitzhugh Lee, General Braxton Bragg; bottom row, l to r: General Jubal A. Early, General John C. Breckinridge, General Leonidas Polk, General Wade Hampton, General E. Kirby Smith, Captain Raphael Semmes.

This fact considerably reduced the appeal of Regular Army service for many Southern men and is one of the major reasons that no more than 1,000 enlisted men and 750 officers and cadets were ever sworn in to the Confederate Regular Army.

Development of the large Confederate Provisional Army was plagued by many of the same problems that troubled the development of the Union

Volunteer Army. Chief among them was the presence of a large number of inexperienced regimental officers—often, influential or popular men elected by the men in their regiments. Preelection campaigns did not suit everyone's idea of proper military comportment. One disapproving soldier was Private C. C. Blacknall, of Georgia:

> Our election has not yet come off, and to one who like myself is not a candidate it is a time replete with feelings of disgust and contempt. The candidates of course are interested and busy. I could start out here now and eat myself dead on "election cake," be hugged into a perfect "sqush" by most particular, eternal, disinterested, affectionate friends. . . . I never dreamed before that I was half as popular, fine looking, and talented as I found out I am during the past few days.

The lack of experience and training that characterized many of the officers elected early in the war no doubt fed the resistance to military discipline that Southern enlisted men shared with many of their Northern counterparts. "Made my first detail for guard duty," Orderly Sergeant A. L. P. Vairin of the Second Mississippi noted in his diary on May 1, 1861, "to which most men objected because they said they did not enlist to do guard duty but to fight the Yankies—all fun and frolic."

Keeping army units adequately supplied—particularly with food, clothing, and medical necessities—was increasingly problematic as the conflict continued and the North tightened its blockade of Southern ports. But army hardships rarely bothered Confederate soldiers as deeply as did their awareness of hardships back home, particularly as the North's armies reached more deeply into the South. This was a primary reason that desertion—an increasing problem for both sides as the war progressed—particularly affected Confederate forces.

Between 750,000 and 900,000 men served in Confederate land forces through the four years of the war, and, as in the larger Union land military force, many Southern units that could be designated "armies" were created, merged, and disbanded over the course of the conflict. The main Confederate armies that conducted significant campaigns are listed in the following pages in the chronological order of their formation. Their primary theater of operation is noted after the colon.

Army of Northern Virginia (Army of the Potomac): Eastern

Commanded by: P. G. T. Beauregard (June 20, 1861–July 21,1861); Joseph E. Johnston (July 21, 1861–May 31, 1862); Robert E. Lee (June 1, 1862–April 12, 1865)

Originally designated the Army of the Potomac—its name when it fought at First Bull Run (Manassas) and into the second year of the war—this became the largest, most successful, and best known of all Confederate armies. It was organized around the first volunteers sent to the Department of Alexandria just after Virginia's secession, when a Union invasion of the South, via northern Virginia, was anticipated. On April 12, 1862, it absorbed the Army of the [Virginia] Peninsula, commanded by John B. Magruder—the first Confederate force to face McClellan's Federals when the Union's Peninsula Campaign began. The Army of the Potomac was formally redesignated the Army of Northern Virginia by Robert E. Lee (who had long referred to it by that name) when he assumed command after Joseph E. Johnston was wounded in the battle of Seven Pines, May 31, 1862.

With a new name, a new commander, and a substantial number of trained professional soldiers in leadership positions, the Army of Northern Virginia quickly began to forge a reputation for audacity, skill, and valor that placed it at the heart of the Confederacy's military effort. From the Seven Days' battles that brought McClellan's Peninsula Campaign to an unsuccessful conclusion, through its victory at Second Bull Run (Second Manassas, August 29–30, 1862) and its spectacular triumph against a vastly superior force at Chancellorsville (May 1–4, 1863), to its tenacious defense of Petersburg and Richmond, Virginia, after those two crucial cities were placed under siege by Grant's forces in the summer of 1864, the Army of Northern Virginia waged war so effectively—despite being consistently outnumbered by the forces it opposed—that it won the confidence of civilians throughout the South. Indeed, to many, Lee's surrender marked the end of the Civil War, even though other Confederate forces were still in the field.

The supreme practitioner of Jefferson Davis' "offensive-defensive" military strategy (see "Battle Strategy," in Chapter 4, "Battles and the Battlefield"), Lee twice led his army into Northern territory. The first expedition, in 1862, ended with the battle of Antietam (Sharpsburg, September 17), and an invasion in 1863 culminated in the three-day battle of Gettysburg (July 1–3)—a major turning point of the war. Normally, however, the Army of Northern Virginia operated in an extremely limited area—only sixty miles long and sixty miles wide—north of Richmond and between the Rappahannock River and Gordonsville, Virginia.

Trans-Mississippi: District, Department, and Army

District commanded by: Earl Van Dorn (January 10, 1862–May 23, 1862; assumed command January 29, 1862)

Department commanded by: Paul O. Hébert (temp; May 26, 1862–June 20, 1862); John B. Magruder (June 20, 1862, assigned but did not accept); Thomas C. Hindman (temp; June 20, 1862–July 16, 1862); Theophilus H. Holmes (July 16, 1862–February 9, 1863; assumed command July 30, 1862); Edmund Kirby Smith (February 9, 1863–April 19, 1865); Simon B. Buckner (temp; April 19, 1865–April 22, 1865); Edmund Kirby Smith (April 22, 1865–May 26, 1865)

Trans-Mississippi Army (Southwest Army) commanded by: Thomas C. Hindman (September 28, 1862–January 14, 1863); Edmund Kirby Smith (temp; January 14, 1863–February 9, 1863; assumed command January 17, 1863); Edmund Kirby Smith (February 9, 1863–April 19, 1865; assumed command March 7, 1863)

A widespread area constituting fully one-third of all Confederate territory, the Trans-Mississippi Department (which, when established, enfolded and superseded the Trans-Mississippi District) included Missouri, Arkansas, Texas, Indian Territory, and Louisiana west of the Mississippi River. This vast area became nearly autonomous after the fall of Vicksburg and Port Royal brought the entire Mississippi River under Union control (July 1863), thus splitting the Confederacy in two. The department was eventually dubbed "Kirby Smithdom," after Edmund Kirby Smith, who had assumed command of the department and its 40,000-man army earlier in the year.

The Trans-Mississippi Army—known as the Southwest Army before February 9, 1863, when it was reorganized to include all combat forces in the Trans-Mississippi Department—was the only principal army west of the Mississippi River. Its units were usually scattered, to protect the huge department, and were often plagued by lack of equipment. The vast area this army covered brought its cavalry to unusual prominence. (Cavalry drawn from this force became a part of the Army of Missouri, organized by Major General Sterling Price for his raid into that state in September and October 1864. The considerably reduced Army of Missouri merged with the Army of Trans-Mississippi in December, after the raid's unsuccessful conclusion.) The Trans-Mississippi Army engaged in relatively few major campaigns. Its most prominent achievement was the defeat of Union General Nathaniel Banks' Red River Campaign of 1864—primarily through Richard Taylor's victory at Mansfield, Louisiana, and a subsequent clash at Pleasant Hill. It also kept pressure on Union-held New Orleans and fought several battles in western Arkansas. It was the last major Confederate force to surrender (May 26, 1865).

Army of Tennessee: Western

Commanded by: Braxton Bragg (November 20, 1862–December 2, 1863); William J. Hardee (temp; December 2, 1863–December 16, 1863); Joseph E. Johnston (December 16, 1863–July 18, 1864); John Bell Hood (July 18, 1864–January 23, 1865); Richard Taylor (January 23, 1865–February 22, 1865); Daniel H. Hill (February 22, 1865–March 16, 1865); Joseph E. Johnston (March 16, 1865–April 26, 1865)

The South's primary western fighting force, the Army of Tennessee, was established late in 1862, when the small Army of Kentucky was merged with the army of what had once been Confederate Department Number 2 (forces originally designated as the Army of Mississippi). This new force, under the command of the contentious Braxton Bragg, embarked on an eventful—and troubled—course that took it, during the war, through Tennessee, northern Mississippi, Alabama, Georgia, and both of the Carolinas. Of the major battles in which it engaged—Murfreesboro, Chickamauga, Atlanta, and Nashville—only Chickamauga was a decisive victory. Otherwise, the Army of Tennessee was plagued by command squabbles (particularly under Bragg), logistical problems, and a dearth of trained professional soldiers in command positions, as well as inadequate manpower to cover effectively the huge territory over which it moved. Smashed by Federals under George H. Thomas at the battles of Franklin and Nashville, Tennessee, in November and December 1864, the Army of Tennessee remained in existence until the end of the war, though its effectiveness was greatly reduced in the last months of the conflict. Moving into North Carolina, with Joseph E. Johnston again in command, the remnants of the Army of Tennessee surrendered to William T. Sherman on April 26, 1865.

Army of Vicksburg (Army of the Department of Mississippi and East Louisiana): Eastern

Commanded by: John C. Pemberton (December 7, 1862–July 4, 1863)

This small army was charged with protecting the crucially important city of Vicksburg, Mississippi. Positioned on high bluffs overlooking the Mississippi River, the city and its formidable artillery prevented the Union from asserting control over the whole of the river. Ulysses S. Grant mounted two separate campaigns to take Vicksburg; the second campaign culminated in a three-month siege. Facing Grant's army of more than 70,000, the Army of Vicksburg, numbering 29,000 men gathered from Louisiana, Georgia, Alabama, Tennessee, Arkansas, Mississippi, and Missouri, was under the command of John C. Pemberton. A Pennsylvania-born West Point graduate who had served in the Mexican War with Grant, Pemberton was nonetheless a staunchly loyal Confederate who was caught, as the Union quest for Vicksburg pressed harder, between the conflicting plans of two superior officers— General Joseph E. Johnston and Commander in Chief Jefferson Davis. Under siege in the city, at near starvation rations, with half of his men suffering from debilitating illness, and with hope of reinforcement from Johnston's army fading to nothing, Pemberton surrendered the city and the Army of Vicksburg on July 4, 1863. He and his men were paroled by Grant, however, and most of them subsequently joined other Confederate forces and fought in later battles.

Civil War Military Leadership	Many political and military ranks constituted the "high commands" of the Union and Confederate military forces during the war. Listed in the chart on pages 394 and 395 are the individuals who filled those offices and directed the most crucial military operations.
Civil War Generals— Union	Originally, the Union Army had only two "grades" of general: brigadier general (one star) and major general (two stars). In 1864, Ulysses S. Grant became the first lieutenant general (three stars) since George Washington (though Winfield Scott had been brevetted to this rank in 1847).
	Borrowed from the British and first awarded during the Revolutionary War, a brevet rank, usually honorary and temporary, was granted extensively by the Union during the Civil War. A captain who showed gallantry

| *United States of America* | *Confederate States of America* |

Commander in Chief:
President Abraham Lincoln

Commander in Chief:
President Jefferson Davis

Commanded both the Army and the Navy, as well as the state militias, though these powers were tempered in many respects by congressional responsibilities with regard to the armed forces.

Secretary of War:
Simon Cameron (3/11/1861–1/19/1862)
Edwin M. Stanton (1/15/1862–5/26/1868)

Secretary of War:
Leroy P. Walker (2/21/1861–9/16/1861)
Judah P. Benjamin (9/17/1861–3/23/1862)
George W. Randolph (3/23/1862–11/17/1862)
Gustavus W. Smith (11/17/1862–11/21/1862)
James A. Seddon (11/21/1862–2/6/1865)
John C. Breckinridge (2/6/1865–5/10/1865)

The principal officer of the Executive Department of War, the administrative body of the military establishment. His authority did not include actual command of troops.

Secretary of the Navy:
Gideon Welles (3/7/1861–3/3/1869)

Secretary of the Navy:
Stephen R. Mallory (2/28/1861–5/2/1865)

Principal administrative officer of the Department of the Navy. Oversaw operation of all U.S. or Confederate Navy forces.

General in Chief:
Winfield Scott (7/5/1841–11/1/1861)
George B. McClellan (11/1/1861–3/11/1862)
Henry W. Halleck (7/23/1862–3/12/1864)
Ulysses S. Grant (3/12/1864–3/4/1869)

General in Chief:
Robert E. Lee (1/31/1865–5/10/1865)

Commanded all field armies.

Ordnance Department:
James W. Ripley (4/23/1861–9/15/1863)
George D. Ramsay (9/15/1863–9/12/1864)
Alexander B. Dyer (9/12/1864–5/20/1874)

Ordnance Bureau:
Josiah Gorgas (4/8/1861–5/12?/1865)

Responsible for providing armies with the necessary weapons, the means of transporting them, and the materials to build and repair them.

Subsistence/Commissary Department:
George Gibson (8/18/1818–9/29/1861)
Joseph T. Taylor (9/29/1861–6/29/1864)
Amos B. Eaton (6/29/1864–5/1/1874)

Commissary Bureau/Subsistence Department:
Lucius B. Northrop (3/27/1861–2/16/1865)
Isaac M. St. John (2/16/1865–5/12/1865)

Responsible for supplying the armed forces with food.

| *United States of America* | *Confederate States of America* |

Quartermaster Department:
Ebenezer Sibley (4/22/1861–5/15/1861)
Montgomery C. Meigs (5/15/1861–2/6/1882)

Quartermaster Bureau:
Abraham C. Myers (3/25/1861–8/10/1863)
Alexander R. Lawton (8/10/1863–5/12/1865)

Responsible for furnishing the armies with all their supplies—excluding those provided by the ordnance and subsistence departments. Transport, housing, clothing, horses, fuel, and stationery were among the materials supplied by this department.

Corps of Engineers:
Joseph G. Totten (12/7/1838–4/28/1864)
Richard Delafield (4/22/1864–8/8/1866)

Engineer Bureau:
Josiah Gorgas (acting, 4/8/1861–8/3/1861)
Daniel Leadbetter (8/3/1861–11/11/1861)
Alfred L. Rives [?](11/11/1861–9/24/1862)
Jeremy F. Gilmer (9/25/1862–8/17/1863)
Alfred L. Rives [?] (acting, 8/18/1863–3/9/1864)
Martin L. Smith (temp., 3/9/1864–4/2/1864)
Alfred L. Rives [?] (acting, 4/2/1864–June 1864)
Jeremy F. Gilmer (June 1864–April 1865)

Controlled the planning, building, and repairing of all fortifications and other defensive works; also created maps (topographical engineers). The engineers contributed to planning attacks and defensive maneuvers and were responsible for eliminating obstacles from the paths of their own armies and creating obstacles to deter opposing armies.

Signal Corps:
Albert J. Myer (6/27/1860–11/15/1863)
Benjamin F. Fisher (12/3/1864–11/15/1866)

Signal Service:
Edward Porter Alexander (5/1861–6/1862)
William Norris (6/1862–4/1865)

Created just before the Civil War, the Signal Corps was charged with establishing communication among army units. The Confederate Signal Service supervised the South's military telegraph operations (though most of the South's military telegraphy went over civilian-operated lines) and also engaged in intelligence activities. The U.S. Signal Corps also aided in intelligence gathering (chiefly, spotting and reporting troop movements), but was separate from the U.S. Military Telegraph office.

Provost Marshal General:
Simon Draper (10/1/1862–3/17/1863)
James B. Fry (3/17/1863–8/28/1866?)

Provost Marshal:
John H. Winder (acting, 3/1861–2/1865)
Daniel Ruggles (2/1865–5/1865)

Charged with securing prisoners charged of crimes of a general nature, preventing desertions, and pursuing deserters. In some Civil War armies, provost marshals also established intelligence-gathering networks.

in action, for example, might be made a brevet general—with the authority and pay accorded that higher rank (under Army regulations that applied during the Civil War) as long as the brevet promotion was in force. The heavy use of brevets by the Union allowed some officers to hold at least four ranks: an actual and a brevet rank in the Regular Army, and an actual and a brevet rank in the Volunteer Army. At least one Union enlisted man, Private Frederick W. Stowe, achieved officer status when he was brevetted a second lieutenant.

The North had 583 full ranking generals during the war; 1,367 other officers were brevetted as generals. The highest-ranking United States Civil War generals were:

U.S.A. GENERALS (REGULAR ARMY)

Line Rank	Name	Date of Rank	Termination
Lieutenant General			
1	Grant, Ulysses S.	March 2, 1864	Promoted to General U.S.A., July 25, 1866
Major Generals			
1	Scott, Winfield	June 25, 1841	Retired November 1, 1861
2	McClellan, George B.	May 14, 1861	Resigned November 8, 1864
3	Frémont, John C.	May 14, 1861	Resigned June 4, 1864
4	Halleck, Henry W.	August 19, 1861	Died January 9, 1872
5	Wool, John E.	May 16, 1862	Retired August 1, 1863
6	Grant, Ulysses S.	July 4, 1863	Lieutenant General March 2, 1864
7	Sherman, William T.	August 12, 1864	Lieutenant General July 25, 1866
8	Meade, George G.	August 18, 1864	Died November 6, 1872
9	Sheridan, Philip H.	November 8, 1864	Lieutenant General March 4, 1869
10	Thomas, George H.	December 15, 1864	Died March 28, 1870
11	Hancock, Winfield S.	July 26, 1866	Died February 9, 1888

U.S.V. MAJOR GENERALS (UNITED STATES VOLUNTEERS)

Line Rank	Name	Date of Rank	Termination
1	Dix, John A.	May 16, 1861	Resigned November 30, 1865
2	Banks, Nathaniel P.	May 16, 1861	Resigned August 24, 1865
3	Butler, Benjamin F.	May 16, 1861	Resigned November 30, 1865
4	Hunter, David	August 13, 1861	MOV January 15, 1866
5	Morgan, Edwin D.	September 28, 1861	Resigned January 1, 1863
6	Hitchcock, Ethan A.	February 10, 1862	MOV October 1, 1867
7	Grant, Ulysses S.	February 16, 1862	Major General U.S.A. July 4, 1863
8	McDowell, Irvin	March 14, 1862	MOV September 1, 1866
9	Burnside, Ambrose E.	March 18, 1862	Resigned April 15, 1865
10	Rosecrans, William S.	March 21, 1862	MOV January 15, 1866
11	Buell, Don C.	March 21, 1862	MOV May 23, 1864
12	Pope, John	March 21, 1862	MOV September 1, 1866
13	Curtis, Samuel R.	March 21, 1862	MOV April 30, 1866
14	Sigel, Franz	March 21, 1862	Resigned May 4, 1865
15	McClernand, John A.	March 21, 1862	Resigned November 30, 1864
16	Smith, Charles F.	March 21, 1862	Died April 25, 1862
17	Wallace, Lewis	March 21, 1862	Resigned November 30, 1865
18	Mitchel, Ormsby M.	April 11, 1862	Died October 30, 1862
19	Clay, Cassius M.	April 11, 1862	Resigned March 11, 1863 *(Did not serve)*
20	Thomas, George H.	April 25, 1862	Major General U.S.A. December 15, 1864

Source: John H. Eicher and David J. Eicher. *Civil War High Commands.* Stanford, CA: Stanford University Press, 2001.
Note: The abbreviation MOV indicates (honorably) *m*ustered *o*ut of *v*olunteers.

Civil War Generals—Confederacy

In the Confederacy there were four grades of general: brigadier general (lowest grade), major general, lieutenant general, and general (highest grade). All grades wore three stars within a wreath. At least 425 officers received appointments to one of these four grades. (Confederate Army regulations allowed brevet ranks, but there is no evidence that brevet appointments were made.) Men who served in the two highest ranks (lieutenant general and general) are shown in the following tables.

P.A.C.S. LIEUTENANT GENERALS
(PROVISIONAL ARMY OF THE CONFEDERATE STATES)

Line Rank	Name	Date of Rank	Termination
1	Longstreet, James	October 9, 1862	Paroled April 9, 1865
2	Smith, Edmund K.	October 9, 1862	General February 19, 1864
3	Polk, Leonidas	October 10, 1862	Killed June 14, 1864
4	Holmes, Theophilus H.	October 10, 1862	No record
5	Hardee, William J.	October 10, 1862	Paroled May 1, 1865
6	Jackson, Thomas J.	October 10, 1862	Died May 10, 1863
7	Pemberton, John C.	October 10, 1862	Resigned May 18, 1864
8	Ewell, Richard S.	May 23, 1863	Paroled July 19, 1865
9	Hill, Ambrose P.	May 24, 1863	Killed April 2, 1865
10	Hood, John Bell	September 20, 1863	Paroled May 31, 1865
11	Taylor, Richard	April 8, 1864	Paroled May 11, 1865
12	Early, Jubal A.	May 31, 1864	No record
13	Anderson, Richard H.	May 31, 1864	No record
14	Stewart, Alexander P.	June 23, 1864	Paroled May 1, 1865
15	Lee, Stephen D.	June 23, 1864	Paroled May 1, 1865
16	Buckner, Simon B.	September 20, 1864	Paroled June 9, 1865
17	Hampton, Wade, III	February 14, 1865	No record
18	Forrest, Nathan B.	February 28, 1865	Paroled May 10, 1865

C.S.A. GENERALS

Line Rank	Name	Date of Rank	Termination
1	Cooper, Samuel	May 16, 1861	Paroled May 3, 1865
2	Johnston, Albert S.	May 30, 1861	Died April 6, 1862
3	Lee,* Robert E.	June 14, 1861	Paroled April 9, 1865
4	Johnston, Joseph E.	July 4, 1861	Paroled May 2, 1865
5	Beauregard, P. G. T.	July 21, 1861	Paroled May 1, 1865
6	Bragg, Braxton	April 6, 1862	Paroled May 10, 1865
	Smith, Edmund K.	February 19, 1864	Paroled June 2, 1865
	Hood, John B.	July 18, 1864 (acting)	Reverted to lieutenant general, January 23, 1865

*Named General in Chief (special assignment) January 31, 1865.

Source for tables on pages 398 and 399: John H. Eicher and David J. Eicher, *Civil War High Commands*. Stanford, CA: Stanford University Press, 2001.

Notable Civil War Officers

Officers in each category are listed in the alphabetical order of their family names.

Commanders in Chief

JEFFERSON DAVIS, commander in chief, C.S.A. (1808–1889). A West Point graduate (1828), Jefferson Davis participated in the Black Hawk War (1832), served with distinction in the Mexican War (1846–1848), and was appointed secretary of war (1853–1857) in President Franklin Pierce's cabinet. As commander in chief of the armies of the Confederate States, he drew on this past experience in establishing a structure for the Southern armies (based on U.S. army organization). Not subject to as many attempts by vocal citizens, interest groups, and politicians to alter the objectives or influence the conduct of the war as was President Lincoln, Davis developed the South's primary "offensive-defensive" strategy. He guided the conduct of the war with such attention to detail that, at times, he encroached on the duties of his subordinates. His supreme self-confidence in his own grasp of military affairs often made him impatient of conflicting opinions. As the war neared its end, he reportedly said to his wife, Varina, "If I could take one wing and Lee the other, I think we could between us wrest a victory from those people." (See "Battlefield Strategy," in Chapter 4, "Battles and the Battlefield," and the biographical sketch in Chapter 3, "Wartime Politics"; and see photograph on page 143.)

ANDREW JOHNSON, commander in chief, U.S.A. (1808–1875). Staunch Unionist Andrew Johnson was a self-educated former tailor and longtime Tennessee politician whom President Lincoln appointed military governor of Union-occupied Tennessee in 1862. His skill and unwavering loyalty in this difficult position gained him the vice-presidential slot on the Republican (National Union) ticket in 1864. Tough, eloquent, and more sympathetic to his fellow Southerners than were the Radical Republicans of Congress, Johnson succeeded to the presidency on April 15. He immediately asked cabinet members to stay, and otherwise indicated that he would pursue President Lincoln's policies. Shortly thereafter, he disapproved the sweeping armistice Major General Sherman negotiated with General Joseph E. Johnston in North Carolina, insisting that Johnston's Confederate army be surrendered under terms similar to those extended by General in Chief Grant to General Lee. Johnson appointed the military commission that tried the Lincoln assassination conspirators, accused Confederate President Davis and other Southern leaders of inciting Lincoln's murder, and issued $100,000 reward for Davis' capture on May 2, 1865. Davis was captured by Federal troops on May 10—the same day President Johnson declared all Civil War hostilities at an end. (See photograph on page 766.)

ABRAHAM LINCOLN, commander in chief, U.S.A. (1809–1865). Like Jefferson Davis, Abraham Lincoln was born in Kentucky and served briefly, though mostly behind the lines, in the Black Hawk War of 1832 (the two men did not meet during that conflict). But, unlike Davis, that brief episode was Lincoln's only military experience before becoming commander in chief of United States forces. Immediately after his election, he was faced with the prospect of war. He relied on the advice of knowledgeable army professionals such as General in Chief Winfield Scott in developing military policy. But, largely self-educated in other fields, he also became an avid reader of strategy, tactics, and military history, and he quickly developed a firm grasp of the central tenets of military science. Though just as interested in the details of the war's conduct as Davis (he was regularly to be found in the War Department telegraph room, poring over dispatches), Lincoln was more suited temperamentally to delegating responsibility to subordinates. If they failed to live up to his expectations, he replaced them. His search for an appropriately aggressive general in chief went on for nearly three years. The appointment went at last to Ulysses S. Grant, a combative officer who shared Lincoln's belief that simultaneous advances by Union armies on all fronts would exhaust the Confederacy's capacity to wage war (see "Civil War Strategy," in Chapter 4, "Battles and the Battlefield" and the biographical sketch of Lincoln in Chapter 3, "Wartime Politics"; and see photograph on page 151).

Generals in Chief

ULYSSES S. GRANT, U.S.A. (1822–1885) general in chief, March 1864–March 1869. Born Hiram Ulysses Grant, the future commanding general of all U.S. armies was mistakenly enrolled at West Point as Ulysses S. Grant—and kept that name. Grant fought with distinction in the Mexican War, resigned from the army in 1854, after eleven years of service, and returned to service at the outbreak of the Civil War, first as colonel of the Twenty-First Illinois Volunteers, then as a brigadier general in the Western Department. Grant's first major victory—the capture of Forts Donelson and Henry—gained him a promotion to major general of volunteers. His lack of preparation on the first day of the battle of Shiloh was a blot on his record. But his recovery on the battle's second day, followed by bold maneuvering that led to the capture of Vicksburg, Mississippi, and his victories around Chattanooga reflected the capacities that caused President

This photograph, taken at Cold Harbor, Virginia, June 4, 1864—the day after the Union's costly assault in that battle—shows the resolute General in Chief Ulysses S. Grant with his war horse Cincinnati.

Lincoln to champion this rough-hewn, obstinately aggressive officer. As general in chief of the U.S. armies, Grant pursued a successful policy of hammering the South's armies, keeping them on the defensive, and destroying their ability to fight.

HENRY WAGER HALLECK, U.S.A. (1815–1872), general in chief, July 1862–March 1864. Dubbed "Old Brains" because of his intelligence and prewar intellectual pursuits, Henry W. Halleck graduated third in the West Point class of 1839. In 1846, he published *Elements of Military Art and Science*, which drew heavily from the principles of French military theorist Antoine-Henri Jomini, yet represented a distinctly American approach to the study of war (and also reflected the professional soldier's lack of regard for militias). Used as a text at West Point (Halleck had been an instructor there), the book influenced many of the Civil War's officers—including postwar military theorist Emory Upton (see his biographical sketch later in this section). Halleck's Civil War service commenced after a hiatus from the army during which he became a lawyer, made a fortune in business, and helped write the California constitution. Taking command of the Department of the Missouri in November 1861, he oversaw the successful campaign into Tennessee and the capture of Forts Henry and Donelson, that brought the field commander, Ulysses S. Grant, to prominence. But Halleck, himself, proved to be a better administrator and mentor of talented officers (such as Sherman and Grant) than a field commander. A less than stellar success as general in chief, he became army chief of staff when Grant succeeded him. He ended the war as commander of the Military Division of the James.

ROBERT EDWARD LEE, C.S.A. (1807–1870), general in chief, January 31–April 9, 1865. Robert E. Lee established such an impeccable record in the service of the United States—including distinguished service in the Mexican War—that he was offered command of the U.S. Army on April 18, 1861, two days before he resigned from the U.S. military to lead the forces of his native Virginia. After serving as military adviser to President Davis, he assumed command of the Army of Northern Virginia in 1862. Lee's strategic abilities and his capacity to inspire subordinates resulted in such stunning Confederate achievements as the Shenandoah Valley campaign, Second Bull Run, and Chancellorsville. In 1865, Lee was appointed general in chief of all

Robert E. Lee was appointed general in chief of Confederate armies January 31, 1865; assumed those wider duties February 9; and served as head of all Southern armies until his surrender, April 9, 1865. Photograph by Julian Vannerson, 1863.

the Confederate armies. Defeated at the battle of Gettysburg (July 1863), Lee spent the remainder of the war on Southern soil, skillfully fighting opposing forces that were greater in number and better supplied than his own. His graceful surrender at Appomattox Court House and his subsequent tenure as president of Washington College (renamed Washington and Lee University in his honor) won him increased respect and added luster to a life of dignity, forbearance, and devotion to duty.

GEORGE BRINTON MCCLELLAN, U.S.A. (1826–1885), general in chief, November 1861–March 1862. Having served in the Mexican War and as an official U.S. observer of the Crimean War (1853–1856), West Point graduate George McClellan resigned from the army in 1857 and became a railroad official. He returned to service in May 1861 and assumed command of the Department of the Ohio, where he oversaw successful operations in western Virginia that brought him to national attention. After the Union defeat at First Bull Run (July 1861), he was appointed commander of the U.S. forces protecting Washington. In November, he became general in chief of U.S. forces. Though he was an able administrator who was beloved by many of his men, McClellan proved to be an extremely cautious field commander, and his reluctance to move often set him at odds with President Lincoln. Relieved of supreme command in March 1862, but still in command of the Army of the Potomac, he initiated the daring Peninsula Campaign of 1862. His own cautious maneuvering is often blamed for its collapse. His failure to press Lee's retreating forces after the battle of Antietam in September 1862 led Lincoln to relieve him of command, permanently. McClellan resigned from the army on the day of the 1864 presidential election, in which he was decisively defeated by Lincoln.

WINFIELD SCOTT, U.S.A. (1786–1866), general in chief, July 1841–November 1861. A hero of the War of 1812, Winfield Scott was also the architect of the U.S. victory in the Mexican War. In that conflict, he commanded many American officers, including Ulysses S. Grant and Robert E. Lee, who would face each other on home soil less than twenty years later. Born in Virginia, but devoted to the Union, Scott was in his seventies when the Civil War began, and he was still characterized by the irascibility that had earned him the nickname "Old Fuss and Feathers." Knowing that it would take time to expand, train, and equip an efficient fighting force, in May 1861 he proposed a plan that would allow these vital activities to take place. This "Anaconda Plan" (see "Civil War Strategy" in Chapter 4, "Battles and the Battlefield") was ridiculed by a public convinced that the war would be short. Later that year, after Union defeats at First Bull Run and Ball's Bluff, Scott retired. As the war progressed, the plan he had outlined in 1861 essentially became the Union's winning strategy.

Notable Officers

NATHANIEL PRENTISS BANKS, U.S.A. (1816–1894). A lawyer, governor of Massachusetts, and U.S. congressman who has been considered by some historians to be one of the ablest Speakers of the U.S. House of Representatives (elected in 1856), Nathaniel Prentiss Banks volunteered for military service in 1861. Immediately commissioned a major general of volunteers, he served briefly in Maryland before becoming part of the force that opposed Stonewall Jackson during the Confederate general's brilliant Shenandoah Valley Campaign (May–June 1862). At the battle of Cedar Mountain, Virginia (August 9, 1862), Banks led his determined force in a smashing drive on Jackson's left that pushed it back—though Confederate reserves soon allowed Jackson to recover. Appointed head of the Department of the Gulf, headquartered in New Orleans, Banks led the campaign that resulted in the July 1863 surrender of Port Hudson, the last obstacle to the Union's free navigation of the Mississippi River. For this feat, he received official congressional thanks. He participated in the abortive Red River Expedition of 1864, left the army in August 1865, and was shortly reelected to Congress. (See also Chapter 11.)

P. G. T. (PIERRE GUSTAVE TOUTANT) BEAUREGARD, C.S.A. (1818–1893). A veteran of the Mexican War, P. G. T. Beauregard had just been appointed superintendent of the U.S. Military Academy at West Point when he resigned from the U.S. military and joined the Confederate cause. In April 1861, as commander of the forces at Charleston, South Carolina, he ordered the bombardment of Fort Sumter that began the Civil War. After serving as second in command under Joseph E. Johnston at First Bull Run, he was promoted to full general. Sometimes called "Napoleon in Gray," Beauregard had a flamboyant temperament and a tendency to aggravate his superiors that kept him from taking a place among the first-rank Confederate commanders. His stubbornness and tenacity, however, made him an excellent commander in difficult circumstances—for example, at the battle of Shiloh after the death of Confederate commander Albert Sidney Johnston, and during Grant's advance on Petersburg, Virginia, in 1864. Beauregard's books on the Civil War include *A Report on the Defence of Charleston* (1864) and *A Commentary on the Campaign and Battle of Manassas* (1891).

BRAXTON BRAGG, C.S.A. (1817–1876). A West Point graduate with combat experience against the Seminoles in Florida and in the Mexican War, Braxton Bragg was an energetic but quarrelsome officer who had trouble securing the loyalty of his subordinates. Retired from the U.S. Army in 1856, he was a Louisiana plantation owner and commissioner of public works until the secession movement began. He joined the Louisiana militia but was soon commissioned a brigadier general in the Confederate States Army and assigned to command the coast between Pensacola, Florida, and Mobile, Alabama. After promotion to major general, he became a corps commander and chief of staff under Albert Sidney Johnston, fought well at Shiloh, and eventually was given command of the Army of Tennessee. He won a notable victory at Chickamauga (September 1863), but did not follow through on his success. After his defeat at Chattanooga in November 1863, he surrendered his command to Joseph E. Johnston. Bragg finished the war as a military adviser to President Davis and in several minor commands. He fought his last battle on March 8, 1865, in North Carolina.

DON CARLOS BUELL, U.S.A. (1818–1898). Ohio native Don Carlos Buell graduated from West Point in 1841, saw action against the Seminoles, and was twice brevetted for gallant and meritorious conduct during the Mexican War. Appointed brigadier general of U.S. Volunteers on May 17, 1861, he employed his excellent organizational skills to help his friend and superior officer George B. McClellan organize the Army of the Potomac in 1861.

Shortly thereafter, Buell assumed command of the Army of the Ohio, which was charged with responsibility for invading and liberating the eastern part of the Confederate state of Tennessee, where Unionist sympathy was strong. As Grant achieved his first major victories at Forts Henry and Donelson, Buell led his army toward Nashville and occupied that city—recently evacuated by Confederate forces—on February 25, 1862. Promoted to major general, Buell arrived at the Shiloh battlefield with his men late on the first day of the battle (April 6, 1862) and helped Grant's severely pressed forces achieve a victory on day two. That proved to be the high point of Buell's Civil War career. After participating in the slow advance on Corinth, Mississippi, he led his force toward Chattanooga and was harassed all the way by Confederate cavalry and irregulars. They slowed his progress enough to allow Confederates under Braxton Bragg, moving toward Kentucky, to reach the Tennessee city before him. Buell's clash with Confederates under Bragg and Edmund Kirby Smith at Perryville, Kentucky, in October, though indecisive, led to a Confederate withdrawal from that Union state. But Buell did not press after the retreating Confederates, and he suspended his cautious pursuit of them after only four days. This inspired public outrage in the North and led to his being relieved of command on October 24. Though a military commission of inquiry did not condemn his conduct, Buell did not receive another command, and he resigned his commission in the regular army on May 23, 1864. Buell spent his postwar years in Kentucky, the state that had seen the eclipse of his career. He died in Rockport on November 19, 1898.

AMBROSE EVERETT BURNSIDE, U.S.A. (1824–1881). Ambrose Burnside—whose long side whiskers inspired the term "sideburns"—graduated from West Point in 1847 but left the army after six years and went into business. Active in local military organizations, Burnside organized the First Rhode Island Regiment and became its colonel upon the outbreak of the Civil War. After First Bull Run, he was commissioned brigadier general of volunteers. In early 1862, he won a promotion and much prestige for leading a successful expedition to the North Carolina coast. After the battle of Antietam and the dismissal of George B. McClellan, Burnside accepted command of the Army of the Potomac. He led it to a costly defeat at Fredericksburg (December 1862) and was himself relieved of command after a dispute with his subordinates. Transferred to the Department of the Ohio, Burnside proved an effective commander at Knoxville, Tennessee. But, in 1864, he was blamed for the bloody fiasco after the great mine explosion at

Petersburg, Virginia, an event that marked the close of his military career. He went on to important positions in railroading and politics: governor of Rhode Island, congressman, and U.S. senator.

BENJAMIN FRANKLIN BUTLER, U.S.A. (1818–1893). Among the first major generals of volunteers appointed by President Lincoln, "political general" Benjamin F. Butler also proved to be among the most problematical. A criminal lawyer and Massachusetts politician before the war, Butler was as adept at finding the limelight, as a general, as he was inept at effectively commanding troops. Relieved of command of Fort Monroe on the Virginia Peninsula (where he announced that runaway slaves would be regarded as "contraband of war") after his inexperienced troops endured a widely publicized defeat at Big Bethel, Butler redeemed his reputation with a successful army-navy operation against the blockade runners' haven of Hatteras Inlet, North Carolina (August 1861). In May 1862, he commanded the troops that occupied New Orleans. While there, he sanctioned the raising of the first officially recognized regiments of black Union troops (*with* black officers) and managed to offend civilians in the South, the North, and abroad by issuing the quickly infamous "Woman's Order" (May 15, 1862), which decreed that if any female New Orleans citizen exhibited "contempt for any officer or soldier of the United States, she shall be regarded and held liable to be treated as a woman of the town plying her avocation." Thereafter known as "Beast Butler," he assumed command of the Eastern Theater's Army of the James and, in that capacity, earned the new nickname "Bottled Up Butler," when the army became stuck during the Bermuda Hundred Campaign (1864). Butler was finally relieved of command by a furious Ulysses S. Grant after he failed to follow orders during the first expedition against Fort Fisher, North Carolina (December 1864). He resigned his commission on November 30, 1865. (See also page 619.)

ANDRÉ CAILLOUX, U.S.A. (1825–1863). The first African American hero of the Civil War, and a regimental officer at a time when black soldiers were just becoming accepted in the Union army and black officers were almost unheard of, André Cailloux, though born a slave, was, by the time New Orleans fell to the Union (April 1862), a prosperous free man of the city. Literate, fluent in both English and French, and of imposing physical presence, Cailloux had been a leader of one of the benevolent societies formed by free blacks in prewar New Orleans that—following long historical precedent—volunteered to serve the Confederate state government when war was declared. He served as first lieutenant of the "Order Company" of the Louisiana Native Guards until that unit was disbanded when the city fell under Union control. Fervently devoted to ending slavery as well as fighting discrimination against free black people, Cailloux quickly announced his support for the Union cause. He raised and trained a company of black soldiers and became a captain in the First Louisiana Native Guards, one of three black regiments mustered into the Union army in the fall of 1862. An exceptional leader, Cailloux also proved exceptionally courageous during the determined but unsuccessful assault on the Confederate bastion of Port Hudson (May 27, 1863). Continuing to fight after he was wounded, Cailloux was killed in the battle. The valor of the two black regiments that participated—some 20 percent became casualties—was widely reported in the North and was a major factor in the growing acceptance of black troops (see "Fighting on Two Fronts: Black Soldiers in the Civil War," on page 427).

Known as "the Stonewall of the West," Major General Patrick R. Cleburne was killed when Confederate forces charged Union lines at the battle of Franklin, Tennessee, in November 1864.

PATRICK RONAYNE CLEBURNE, C.S.A. (1828–1864). Born in Ireland and a veteran of the British army, Patrick Cleburne emigrated to the United States in 1849. He settled in Helena, Arkansas, became a druggist, and distinguished himself by remaining in the town and nursing the sick during a yellow fever epidemic. He practiced law from 1856 until the outbreak of the Civil War, when he became captain of the Yell Rifles, a company he had helped organize. Promoted eventually to major general, Cleburne proved to be a supremely effective commander in battles from Shiloh to Chickamauga, Perryville to Missionary Ridge. Dubbed "the Stonewall of the West" by admirers, he also stirred controversy by advocating freedom for Southern slaves so the freed men could be employed as soldiers. A tough disciplinarian, Cleburne was far from a dashing figure. He was usually dressed in a battered coat, and a minié-ball scar added to the often severe expression of his face. He held the respect of his men by demonstrating his concern for their welfare and his own unrelenting courage under fire. He was killed during a charge against Federal lines at Franklin, Tennessee.

Toward the end of the Civil War, Union Major General George Armstrong Custer (seated) posed for this photograph with his wife, Elizabeth Bacon Custer, and his brother, Thomas W. Custer. Tom Custer received two Medals of Honor for valor in Civil War combat.

GEORGE ARMSTRONG CUSTER, U.S.A. (1839–1876). Bright, aggressive, brave, and, at West Point, given to pranks and lapses in scholarship, George Armstrong Custer graduated at the bottom of his class in 1861 and plunged quickly into combat at the first battle of Bull Run. His service in the Peninsula Campaign of 1862 brought him to the attention of Major General George B. McClellan, who made him an aide. Further service, notably at a cavalry engagement at Aldie, Virginia (July 1863), brought him promotion to brigadier general of volunteers. At the time, he was the youngest general in the Union army. Custer soon became one of the Union's most celebrated front-line commanders. He served with distinction in 1864 at the battle of Yellow Tavern, Virginia (where Confederate cavalryman Jeb Stuart was mortally wounded), and in the Shenandoah Valley Campaign, having become one of Major General Phil Sheridan's most trusted subordinates. In the last weeks of the war, Custer's tenacity in pursuing Lee's retreating army won him plaudits—and brought him the distinction of being the officer who received the Confederate flag of truce when Lee sought to negotiate a surrender. Custer's brother, Second Lieutenant Thomas W. Custer, who served under the general during the war, had the distinction of being awarded two Medals of Honor for Civil War actions—at Namozine Church and Sayler's Creek, Virginia.

JUBAL ANDERSON EARLY, C.S.A. (1816–1894). West Point graduate Jubal Early served against the Seminoles in Florida before resigning from the army on July 31, 1838, to pursue a career in law. After interrupting his civilian pursuits in 1847–1848 for a year of volunteer service during the Mexican War, he returned to his native state of Virginia, where he was active in state politics. Although he was opposed to secession, he promptly joined the Confederate cause when the Civil War began and was attached to the Army of Northern Virginia. Early fought at Chancellorsville and in the Gettysburg and Wilderness campaigns, and by May 1864, he was a lieutenant general. Shortly thereafter, Lee dispatched him to the Shenandoah Valley (known as the "breadbasket of the Confederacy") to stop Union General David Hunter's destructive expedition into the region. When that mission was completed, Early was next dispatched down the Valley and into Maryland, on a raid that took him to the outskirts of Washington, D.C. (July 11). Because of the threat his presence represented, some of the troops arrayed against Lee at Petersburg, Virginia, were diverted to the capital's defense. Pursued relentlessly by Federals under Sheridan, Early suffered telling defeats at the battles of Third Winchester, Fisher's Hill, and Cedar Creek in the fall of 1864. After the remnant of his force was finally defeated at Waynesboro, Virginia, in March 1865, Early was relieved of command. He left the country after the war, but, in 1869, he returned to Virginia and the practice of law.

RICHARD STODDERT EWELL, C.S.A. (1817–1872). Richard Ewell graduated from West Point in 1840 and served with distinction in the Mexican War before resigning from the U.S. Army to enlist in Confederate service. As a major general under Stonewall Jackson in the Valley Campaign of 1862, Ewell defeated Union generals Nathaniel Banks, at Winchester, and John Frémont, at Cross Keys; provided invaluable assistance at Port Republic; and won Jackson's profound admiration. After participating in the Seven Days and Cedar Mountain battles, Ewell was so severely wounded in the leg during the Second Bull Run campaign (August 1862) that his leg required amputation. Though he had to be strapped to his horse when he rode, he returned to service in May 1863 as one of Lee's three corps commanders and held the Confederate left at the battle of Gettysburg. During the Wilderness campaign, he was injured so severely that he could no longer serve in the field. In command of Richmond's defenses until the city fell, Ewell was subsequently captured and inexplicably imprisoned for several months before being allowed to retire to his Tennessee farm.

NATHAN BEDFORD FORREST, C.S.A. (1821–1877). Born into near poverty, and having received barely six months of formal education, Nathan Bedford Forrest assumed responsibility for his family at age sixteen, after the death of his father. A native of Tennessee, he eventually established one of the largest slave-trading operations in the Memphis region, acquired plantation property and social status, and held various public offices. When the war broke out, Forrest enlisted as a private in the Confederate army, but was soon appointed a lieutenant colonel of a cavalry battalion he had raised at his own expense. He proceeded to prove himself one of the most skilled cavalry commanders on either side. He led his men through Union lines and away from besieged Fort Donelson before it capitulated to Federal forces (February 1862), fought at Shiloh, and participated in the Chickamauga campaign. Eventually raised to the rank of lieutenant general, Forrest specialized in daring raids, sometimes deep within Union lines. (One raid helped to bring Grant's first Vicksburg campaign to a halt.) He conducted those raids with a flair for maneuvering and the same aggressive spirit that at times brought him into conflict with his superior officers, notably Braxton Bragg. His last major engagement, the unsuccessful defense of Selma, Alabama, in April 1865, came a year after the one major blot on Forrest's wartime record. Forrest's cavalry had overrun the Union

The Confederacy's "Wizard of the Saddle," Lieutenant General Nathan Bedford Forrest, was defeated by only one Union general: James H. Wilson, in 1865.

garrison at Fort Pillow, Tennessee, and had killed or wounded well over half the defending soldiers. Subsequent testimony taken by Federal authorities characterized his action as a "massacre." Many of the soldiers killed by Forrest's men were African American.

WADE HAMPTON, C.S.A. (1818–1902). A Southern aristocrat and slaveholder, the son and grandson of veterans of the American Revolution and the War of 1812, and a lawyer and member of the South Carolina legislature, Wade Hampton had not favored secession. But when his state left the Union, and despite his lack of military training, he immediately raised a mixed command of infantry, cavalry, and artillery. Known as "Hampton's Legion," the unit won distinction at the first battle of Bull Run—where Hampton himself was wounded. In 1862, the legion was divided. Hampton led his cavalry, as a unit within Jeb Stuart's cavalry division, through the 1862 Peninsula Campaign, Antietam, and Gettysburg, where he was again wounded. After Stuart was killed (May 1864), Hampton succeeded to the command of the cavalry corps and participated in the Petersburg Campaign. On September 16, 1864, with the Union siege tightening and Confederate food supplies at a critical stage, Hampton led an audacious raid that captured 2,500 cattle from their Union guardians—one of the largest rustling operations in American history. Six weeks later, as Hampton's cavalry fought valorously at the battle of Burgess' Mill, Federal fire killed one of Hampton's sons, Frank Preston Hampton, and wounded another, Wade Hampton, Jr. Transferred to Joseph E. Johnston's command in 1865, Hampton delayed his own surrender. Even after Lee and Johnston had capitulated, he urged President Davis to continue the fight west of the Mississippi River. Though the war had left him financially ruined, Hampton continued to serve his state as governor and U.S. senator. (See also Chapter 11.)

WINFIELD SCOTT HANCOCK, U.S.A. (1824–1886). A West Point graduate and commended veteran of the Mexican and Seminole wars and the border war in Kansas, Winfield Scott Hancock was appointed brigadier general of volunteers in 1861 and set about helping to organize the newly assembled Army of the Potomac. Unflappable under fire, tenacious in battle, and fair in his treatment of subordinates and civilians who were under his jurisdiction, Hancock was respected by his fellow officers and held the absolute confidence of his men. Prominent in McClellan's 1862 Peninsula

Campaign, he also fought with distinction at Antietam, Fredericksburg, and Chancellorsville; and his actions during the battle of Gettysburg placed him among the great soldiers of the Civil War. After maneuvering skillfully to delay Confederate action until more Federal troops could arrive, Hancock led his corps in repelling an attempt to turn the Union flank, and his corps again held against the ferocious Confederate charge at the Union center. Severely wounded in the battle, Hancock recovered to fight at the Wilderness and Spotsylvania. After the war, he remained in the army; he was narrowly defeated by another Civil War veteran, James A. Garfield, in the 1880 presidential election.

WILLIAM JOSEPH HARDEE, C.S.A. (1815–1873). Author of *Rifle and Light Infantry Tactics* (1855), adopted as a textbook of the U.S. Army, West Point graduate William Joseph Hardee was twice promoted for meritorious service during the Mexican War. He resigned his U.S. commission when his native Georgia seceded from the Union in January 1861. Serving in the Confederacy's western army through most of the war, Hardee organized the original Arkansas Brigade ("Hardee's Brigade") and fought at Shiloh, Perryville, Murfreesboro, and Missionary Ridge. A leading figure in the contest with Sherman that preceded the fall of Atlanta (September 1864), Hardee was then placed in charge of the military department of South Carolina, Georgia, and Florida. He could not stop Sherman's relentless advance. Honored by his fellows and respected by his opponents, Hardee was described in E. A. Pollard's *Lee and His Lieutenants* (1867) as a man of "coolness that never failed; presence of mind never disturbed; and an intellect that rose, like his heart, in the tumult and dangers of battle."

JOHN BELL HOOD, C.S.A. (1831–1879). "Hood is a bold fighter," Robert E. Lee wrote to Jefferson Davis. "I am doubtful as to other qualities necessary." John Bell Hood's boldness was evident in the early days of the war, when the aggressiveness of his Texas Brigade during the Peninsula Campaign, at Second Bull Run, and at Antietam won him rapid promotion. Wounded at Gettysburg, and again at Chickamauga—after which his right leg was amputated—Hood recovered sufficiently to take command, in 1864, of a corps under Joseph E. Johnston. Accustomed to offensive campaigns, Hood proved far less successful in the defensive warfare Johnston was compelled to wage against General William T. Sherman's advancing forces. Impatient with Joseph E. Johnston, Jefferson Davis replaced him with Hood, but lack of supplies and low morale among his men forced Hood to abandon a plan he had hoped would split Sherman's force. After Atlanta fell, Hood moved against Sherman's supply line in Tennessee, intending to move on into Kentucky and toward the rear of Grant's army besieging Lee at Petersburg. But the smashing defeat of Hood's Army of Tennessee at the battles of Franklin, Tennessee (November 30, 1864) and Nashville (December 15, 1864), by Federals under George H. Thomas, led Hood to request to be relieved. He surrendered to Federal authorities in Mississippi on May 31, 1865.

JOSEPH HOOKER, U.S.A. (1814–1879). West Point graduate Joseph Hooker resigned from the peacetime army in 1853, returned to service in 1861, and was appointed brigadier general of volunteers. Nicknamed "Fighting Joe" for his display of bravery during the 1862 Peninsula Campaign, he was made a brigadier general in the regular army after he was wounded at Antietam (September 17, 1862). In 1863, Lincoln placed him in command of the Army of the Potomac. He reorganized it and greatly improved its morale, which had plummeted after its costly defeat at the battle of Fredericksburg (December 13, 1862). Hooker also established an effective Army of the Potomac intelligence-gathering unit, the Bureau of Military Information. "My plans are perfect," he told his staff as he prepared to move. "May God have mercy on General Lee, for I will have none." Shortly thereafter, at the battle of Chancellorsville (May 1863), Hooker, in command of an army of some 130,000 men, was roundly defeated by Lee, who was commanding a force less than half that size. Relieved of command at his own request, just before the battle of Gettysburg, Hooker was transferred and fought well in the push toward Atlanta. But when William T. Sherman did not choose him to command the Army of the Tennessee, he again asked to be relieved, and his field service came to an end.

THOMAS JONATHAN (STONEWALL) JACKSON, C.S.A. (1824–1863). (See illustrations on pages 210 and 388.) Skillful, tenacious, and a beloved, if demanding, leader of a force he trained to move so fast they were known as Jackson's "foot cavalry," West Point graduate and Mexican War veteran Thomas Jonathan Jackson conducted, during his relatively brief Civil War career, some of the most effective campaigns in American military history.

Dubbed Stonewall at the first battle of Bull Run, when his men stood fast under furious Union onslaught, Jackson performed with similar tenacity at Second Bull Run and Antietam. His Shenandoah Valley campaign of 1862 was a dazzling display of strategic science that kept Union forces from reinforcing McClellan's drive on the Confederate capital at Richmond. Jackson was devoutly religious, personally eccentric, and totally devoted to the well-being of the men under his command. When he died, as the result of fire from his own men during the confusion in the battle of Chancellorsville, Robert E. Lee, devastated by this loss, wrote: "I know not how to replace him."

ALBERT SIDNEY JOHNSTON, C.S.A. (1803–1862). A soldier noted for his integrity, 1826 West Point graduate Albert Sidney Johnston served in the Black Hawk War, resigned from the army in 1834, and drifted to the Republic of Texas, where he rose from private in the Texan army to its commander in less than a year. He resigned, farmed for a time, was colonel of the First Texas Rifles during the Mexican War, and later returned to duty as an officer in the U.S. Army. He served as paymaster general, commander of the Department of Texas, and commander of the Department of the Pacific before resigning at the outbreak of the Civil War. Assigned as commander of the Confederate Western Department, Johnston constantly faced forces superior in number to his own. In February 1862, he lost Fort Henry and Fort Donelson and was forced to withdraw from Nashville. When these reverses caused some in Richmond to demand that Johnston be replaced, President Davis refused, saying, "If Sidney Johnston is not a general, I have none." On April 6, 1862, the first day of the battle of Shiloh, Johnston led his Confederates in a sweeping rout of Union forces (though the Federals would regain the lost ground the next day). Wounded on that day, Johnston bled to death on the battlefield.

JOSEPH EGGLESTON JOHNSTON, C.S.A. (1807–1891). A disciplined career soldier and a veteran of combat in Florida in the 1830s and in the Mexican War, Joseph Johnston resigned from the U.S. Army in 1861 to become a brigadier general, and later a general, in the Confederate States Army. Though he displayed aggressive leadership at First Bull Run, Johnston's command behavior thereafter was cautious. Assigned in 1861 to command Confederate forces in northern Virginia, Johnston was wounded at Seven

Pines in 1862 and replaced by Robert E. Lee. Transferred to the West, he presided over the loss of Vicksburg, then proceeded to fight a defensive war, trying to keep Confederate forces intact for further use. Gradually falling back before William T. Sherman, Johnston was relieved of command in July 1864, but later was reassigned to the Army of Tennessee and fought several engagements in North Carolina. With the approval of President Davis, he approached Sherman with a bid for armistice but the sweeping provisions that were proposed were quickly disapproved by the U.S. government. Johnston surrendered to Sherman on April 26, 1865.

JAMES LONGSTREET, C.S.A. (1821–1904). A West Point graduate (1842) and a career soldier, James Longstreet served under Zachary Taylor and Winfield Scott in the Mexican War, during which he was wounded and brevetted major, before resigning from the U.S. Army on June 1, 1861. Though he sought a commission in the Confederate paymaster's department (he said he had abandoned his aspirations for military glory), his experience and reputation won him a commission as a Confederate brigadier general instead (June 17). Able service at First Bull Run and during the Seven Days battles around Richmond (1862) earned him Lee's confidence—and greater responsibility. He was promoted to lieutenant general in October 1862, after he participated in the battle of Antietam. Often blamed for the Confederates' loss of the battle of Gettysburg—because he disagreed with Lee's strategy, he delayed attacking on July 2—Longstreet fought well at Chickamauga, unsuccessfully at Knoxville, Tennessee, and with distinction during the Wilderness campaign. He was with Lee when he surrendered to Grant. After the war, Longstreet alienated many Southerners by becoming a Republican, accepting a number of Federal appointments, and criticizing Lee's conduct at Gettysburg. (See illustrations on pages 388 and 793.)

JAMES B. MCPHERSON, U.S.A. (1828–1864). Born in Ohio, James B. McPherson graduated at the top of his class at West Point in 1853 and taught practical engineering at the academy for a year before being assigned to field duty. Stationed in California when the war began, McPherson was ordered east and worked on fortifications near Boston before becoming an aide-de-camp to Major General Henry Halleck in the Department of the Missouri. A charming man and a talented and devoted officer, he was field engineer with Grant in the campaign against Fort Henry

Major General James B. McPherson was among the highest-ranking Union officers to be killed in Civil War combat.

and Fort Donelson in February 1862. Promoted to brigadier general of volunteers as the Union armies moved against Corinth, Mississippi, he was subsequently made military superintendent of railways in the district of Western Tennessee. A major general of volunteers by October 1862, McPherson commanded a division and then a corps; took part in Grant's 1863 campaign against Vicksburg; participated in Sherman's raid against Meridian; and remained in command of the District of Vicksburg until March 1864. Assuming command of the Army of the Tennessee when Sherman was promoted, McPherson proved an able and dedicated leader during the Atlanta campaign, when the Army of the Tennessee was repeatedly deployed to outflank Southern forces. Respected by his fellow officers and beloved by his men, McPherson was killed July 22, 1864, during the battle of Atlanta. The opposing Confederate forces were under the command of John Bell Hood, McPherson's West Point roommate.

GEORGE GORDON MEADE, U.S.A. (1815–1872). Sometimes called "a damned old goggle-eyed snapping turtle" by his men because of his hair-trigger temper and his spectacles, career soldier George Gordon Meade (West Point class of 1835) was also known as "Old Reliable" for his steadfastness in combat and his competence in command. Assigned at the beginning of the war to the defenses of Washington, D.C., Meade served under McClellan during the Peninsula Campaign and was severely wounded at Frayser's Farm during the Seven Days' battles. Only partially recovered, he fought at Second Bull Run, was commended for his action at South Mountain (September 1862), and showed such initiative and insight during the battle of Chancellorsville (May 1863) that two of his fellow officers recommended him as the next commander of the Army of the Potomac. He was, in fact, ordered to replace General Hooker only three days before the battle of Gettysburg. Successful in his decisive encounter—though criticized for failing to press Lee afterward—Meade remained in command of the Army of the Potomac for the rest of the war.

MONTGOMERY CUNNINGHAM MEIGS, U.S.A. (1816–1892). After graduating fifth out of forty-nine students in West Point's class of 1836, Montgomery Cunningham Meigs served briefly in the artillery. He then became an army engineer and worked on the Washington Aqueduct and the wings and dome of the U.S. Capitol building. The mixture of public works and private contracts to which he was exposed during this prewar period helped to prepare him for his appointment as U.S. quartermaster general, with the rank of brigadier general. Under his leadership, the department was expanded and reorganized, and a three-tiered supply depot system was created to ensure that the Union's resources could be spread efficiently across half a continent. Meigs' greatest organizational effort in that regard was put into effect to supply more than 100,000 men in the Army of the Potomac during the Peninsula Campaign of March—August 1862. On July 5, 1864, he was promoted to major general. In October of that year, his son, twenty-two-year-old John Rodgers Meigs, was shot and killed by Confederates in the Shenandoah Valley. (See photograph on page 482.) The questionable circumstances of the young Meigs' death continued to affect his father's attitude toward the South long after the war. Meigs served as quartermaster general until 1882.

JOHN HUNT MORGAN, C.S.A. (1825–1864). Commended by the Confederate Congress for his "varied, heroic and invaluable services," John Hunt Morgan was, for over two years, a celebrated raider and a thorn in the Union's side. A volunteer during the Mexican War, Alabama-born Morgan was a prosperous Kentucky businessman before the Civil War. He joined the Confederate army in September 1861 and immediately became a scout. In 1862, after receiving command of a squadron, he began his famous raids. His units captured men and trains, destroyed supplies, wrecked railroads—all with great energy and a tactical savvy that led to confusion among his pursuers. In December 1862, he took more than 1,700 Union prisoners at Hartsville, Tennessee, and was rewarded with command of a cavalry division. The next year, he was given leave to raid into Kentucky but he went even farther—to Indiana and Ohio. He was captured, escaped, returned to the Confederacy, and was given command of the Department of Southwest Virginia.

Confederate raider John Hunt Morgan was commended by the Confederate Congress for his "varied, heroic and invaluable services."

Morgan was killed while attempting to escape from Federals who surprised him at Greenville, Tennessee.

JOHN SINGLETON MOSBY, C.S.A. (1833–1916). A graduate of the University of Virginia, John Singleton Mosby practiced law before enlisting in the Confederate cavalry in 1861. After participating in the first Bull Run campaign, he was assigned to Major General J.E.B. Stuart's cavalry. He served on the Peninsula, at Second Bull Run, and at Antietam, and was briefly a prisoner of war. In January 1863, Mosby began the independent operations for which he became famous. Acting under the Partisan Ranger Act, which allowed the retention and division of captured property (see "Shadow Warriors: Partisan Rangers, Guerrillas, and Spies," on page 447), Mosby conducted increasingly daring raids on Federal posts. He began his operations with nine men, but his skill and the rangers' adventurous methods of operation soon attracted many others. By the end of the war, he commanded eight companies of well-equipped and efficient raiders—who, though generally well-disciplined, were regarded as outlaws by Federal authorities. After the war, Mosby returned to the law, served the United States government in several capacities, and published articles and books, including *Mosby's War Reminiscences* and *Stuart's Cavalry Campaigns* (1887).

GEORGE EDWARD PICKETT, C.S.A. (1825–1875). A graduate of West Point (1846), George Pickett served in Texas, Virginia, and Washington Territory before resigning his U.S. commission in 1861 and entering the Confederate army as a colonel. By October 1862, after fighting in the Seven Days' campaign, he had been promoted to major general and placed in command of a Virginia division that, two months later, participated in the battle of Fredericksburg. Not among the most distinguished of Civil War generals, Pickett's name will forever be chiefly associated with the massive Confederate charge against Union lines at Gettysburg on July 3, 1863. The costly failure of this frontal assault marked the end of that battle and of Lee's second invasion of Northern territory. Named commander of the Department of North Carolina (September 1863)—an area in which there was much Unionist sentiment—Pickett failed in a bid to retake New Bern and was shortly thereafter plunged into controversy. His order to court-martial some North Carolina men captured in Federal uniforms at a Union outpost and subsequently identified as former Confederate soldiers, led to the public execution of twenty-two of them, an event that caused outrage in the North.

After participating in the Bermuda Hundred Campaign (May 1864), Pickett suffered a mental and physical collapse but returned to duty before the final days of the Petersburg Campaign, where he led his men poorly at the battle of Five Forks (April 1, 1865). He was relieved of command shortly before Lee's surrender.

LEONIDAS POLK, C.S.A. (1806–1864). Leonidas Polk resigned his commission in the U.S. Army six months after graduation from West Point (1827) to enter the Virginia Theological Seminary. Eventually ordained a bishop of the Protestant Episcopal Church, he developed an interest in education and was instrumental in founding the University of the South (1860). In 1861, Polk accepted a commission (from Jefferson Davis, who had been a cadet with him at West Point) as a major general in the Confederate army. Assigned to defend the Mississippi River, Polk led his troops into strategically located Columbus, Kentucky, in violation of that state's declared neutrality. He defended the action as a military necessity. Forced to withdraw from Columbus after Grant's forces took Fort Henry and Fort Donelson (February 1862), Polk won the admiration of his men—though needlessly risking his own life—by leading four charges during the battle of Shiloh (April 1862). But his failure to attack the Union left when expected during the battle of Chickamauga (September 1863) aggravated his already contentious relationship with General Braxton Bragg. Polk was killed by artillery fire at Pine Mountain, Georgia, on June 14, 1864.

STERLING PRICE, C.S.A. (1809–1867). A Virginia native, Sterling Price moved to Missouri in 1830 and garnered valuable military experience when he led the Second Missouri Infantry during the Mexican War. (He was promoted from colonel to brigadier general and appointed as military governor of Chihuahua.) He then forged a career in politics that included service in the Missouri state legislature, a term in the U.S. House of Representatives, and four years as governor of the state (1852–1856). A moderate Unionist, Price was president of the 1861 state convention that decided against secession. But subsequent encounters with virulent Unionists—including Nathaniel Lyon, a Federal officer—drove him into the secessionist camp. Leading the Missouri state militia, he joined Confederates from Arkansas under Ben McCulloch in a victory against Lyons' Federals at Wilson's Creek (August 10, 1861). After a subsequent success at Lexington, Missouri, he moved into Arkansas, where his force became part of Earl Van Dorn's Confederate Army of the West.

Defeated at Pea Ridge, Arkansas (March 7–8, 1862), and unsuccessful at Iuka and Corinth, Mississippi, later that year, Price (by then a Confederate major general) returned to the Trans-Mississippi Department, where he helped defeat Frederick Steele's expedition in support of the Union Red River Campaign. In September 1864, Price led an expedition of his own: 12,000 Confederates, under his command, invaded Missouri in a last-ditch unsuccessful effort to bring the state into the Confederacy and, at the same time, influence the 1864 presidential election in the North. Well regarded by his men (they called him "Old Pap") but not well regarded by Jefferson Davis, who thought him the vainest man he had ever met, Price established a short-lived colony of ex-Confederates in Mexico after the war. He returned to Missouri in 1867, a few months before his death.

WILLIAM STARKE ROSECRANS, U.S.A. (1819–1898). A West Point graduate and, later, an instructor, William Starke Rosecrans resigned from the army in 1854 and became, in turn, an engineer, an architect, and the head of an oil-refining company. Reentering the army in 1861 as a volunteer aide-de-camp to Major General George B. McClellan, Rosecrans was soon commissioned a brigadier general. After a victorious engagement at Rich Mountain in western Virginia, where more than 500 Confederates were forced to surrender, he became commander of the Department of the Ohio and, later, the new Department of Western Virginia, where he took up the campaign that resulted in the expulsion of Confederate forces and the formation of the state of West Virginia. At Corinth, Mississippi, and Murfreesboro, Tennessee, Rosecrans proved his strategic abilities. But his defeat at the hard-fought battle of Chickamauga (September 1863) resulted in his being relieved of his front-line command. Temperamental, impatient with interference, and sometimes indiscreet, Rosecrans clashed more than once with superior officers. But he was well liked by his men, who called him "Old Rosy."

PHILIP HENRY SHERIDAN, U.S.A. (1831–1888). Feisty and indefatigable, Phil Sheridan was suspended from West Point for angrily chasing a fellow cadet with a fixed bayonet. He did graduate, however (1853), and served along the Rio Grande and in the Northwest before becoming quartermaster and commissary of Union troops in southwest Missouri at the beginning of the Civil War. Happier in his next assignment—colonel of the Second Michigan Cavalry—Sheridan embarked on years of aggressive campaigning that earned him the respect of his peers and the confidence of his men, who affectionately dubbed him "Little Phil." In actions from Perryville, Kentucky, to Chicka-mauga and to the magnificent charge that carried Missionary Ridge, Sheri-dan proved such a supremely effective fighter that Grant gave him command of all the cavalry of the Army of the Potomac. Placed in command of the Army of the Shenandoah in 1864, Sheridan pursued and defeated Jubal Early in the Shenandoah Valley—and angered resident civilians by destroying any-thing that could be of use to Confederate forces. He ended the war in hot pursuit of Lee's retreating army.

WILLIAM TECUMSEH SHERMAN, U.S.A. (1820–1891). West Point gradu-ate (1840) William Tecumseh Sherman left the army in 1853 to pursue, with-out much success, careers in business and law. Fond of the South and its people, he was superintendent of a Louisiana military college just prior to the outbreak of the Civil War. His passionate belief in preserving the Union led him to de-cline a post in the Confederate army and assume command of the Union's Thirteenth Infantry. After establishing a true rapport with Ulysses S. Grant, Sherman played a prominent role in the battle of Shiloh, the capitulation of Vicksburg, and the relief of Union forces at Chattanooga. As commander of the Army of the Tennessee and then of the Military Division of the Missis-sippi, he pushed Joseph E. Johnston's army to the gates of Atlanta. He then took the city from Johnston's replacement, John Bell Hood, and embarked on his March to the Sea and the subsequent Carolinas Campaign. His armies cut a swath of destruction through South Carolina, then moved into North Car-olina, where they defeated Confederate forces. Promoted to lieutenant general after the war, Sherman became general in chief of U.S. armies in 1869 under a newly elected commander in chief, President Ulysses S. Grant. Sherman's two-volume *Memoirs* were published in 1875.

EDMUND KIRBY SMITH, C.S.A. (1824–1893). West Point graduate Ed-mund Kirby Smith was twice brevetted for gallantry in the Mexican War. He commanded the military escort for the Mexican Boundary Commission (and served as botanist of the commission's expedition) and saw duty with the fa-mous Second U.S. Cavalry in operations against hostile Indians in the late 1850s. He resigned his commission in the U.S. Army on March 3, 1861, not long after his native state of Florida seceded from the Union. Promoted quickly from the rank of colonel of Confederate cavalry to brigadier general in the Army of the Shenandoah, he was wounded at the first battle of Bull Run, promoted to major general (October 1861), and, in 1862, given command of the Department of East Tennessee. Victorious at the battle of Richmond during the 1862 Confederate invasion of Kentucky, Smith received the thanks of the Confederate Congress and, in February 1863, was named commander of the Trans-Mississippi Department. Less than six months later, when Vicksburg and Port Hudson fell to the Union, Smith's command was cut off from the rest of the Confederacy. Left to his own devices, Smith used some creative methods to maintain his department—he sold cotton abroad, for example, to pay for necessary supplies. He oversaw the successful defense against the Union's Red River Campaign of 1864 (clashing with his subordinate, Richard Taylor, over strategy) and was the last Confederate commander to surrender his army (May 26, 1865). Smith traveled briefly to Mexico and Cuba before returning to the United States. He eventually became a distinguished professor of mathematics.

JAMES EWELL BROWN (Jeb) Stuart, C.S.A. (1833–1864). A flamboyant and beloved cavalryman, Jeb Stuart was dubbed "the eyes of the army" by Robert E. Lee, because of the invaluable intelligence he provided to Confederate commanders. A West Point graduate, Stuart was an aide to Lee when Lee commanded the U.S. force that dealt with John Brown's raid on Harpers Ferry in 1859. After being commissioned an officer in the Confederate cavalry in 1861, Stuart quickly established himself as a highly efficient commander who was capable of "seizing the moment"—as he did during his famous ride around McClellan's Federals during the Peninsula Campaign. A less successful foray—in Pennsylvania in 1863—resulted in the only controversial episode on Stuart's record: it caused him to arrive late at the Gettysburg battlefield. Stuart served brilliantly at Fredericksburg, protected Jackson's line of march at Chancellorsville, and, in 1864, pushed his ill-supplied men and weak horses hard in order to place his force between the Federals and Richmond. Engaging Union forces at Yellow Tavern, he received his first wound of the war—the one that cost him his life.

RICHARD TAYLOR, C.S.A. (1826–1879). Son of military hero and twelfth U.S. president Zachary Taylor, Richard Taylor was a graduate of Yale University, owner of a Louisiana sugar plantation, and a student of military and literary history. A member of the Louisiana Secession Convention, Taylor was appointed colonel of the Ninth Louisiana Infantry in July 1861 and was promoted to brigadier general just before serving under Stonewall Jackson during the Valley Campaign of 1862. In July of that year, he was given command of the District of West Louisiana and effectively used his smaller force against the opposing Union armies. In 1864, his victory over Nathaniel P. Banks at Mansfield, Louisiana, helped thwart the Union Red River Campaign, but a disagreement between Taylor and his commanding general, Edmund Kirby Smith, caused a rift that resulted in Taylor's transfer. Finally, as a lieutenant general, Taylor was given command of the remnants of John Bell Hood's defeated army. He dispatched some units to North Carolina to participate in Joseph E. Johnston's last battles with Sherman's Union forces. With the remaining troops, Taylor could do little but harass Federals in Alabama before being forced to surrender on May 4, 1865. Taylor's chronicle of the war and its aftermath, *Destruction and Reconstruction*, was published in 1879.

GEORGE HENRY THOMAS, U.S.A. (1816–1870). Stubborn, honorable, deliberate, and utterly reliable, George H. Thomas graduated from West Point in 1840 (his classmates included William T. Sherman and Richard S. Ewell), served with distinction in the Mexican War, and was attached to the famed Second Cavalry when the Civil War broke out. A native of southeastern Virginia, Thomas chose to continue serving the Union—a decision that alienated him from his relatives and friends. His Virginia origins also caused some in the U.S. army and government to doubt his loyalty—though it was amply proven throughout the war. A brigadier general as of August 1861, he was a major general in the regular army by the time the war ended, having fought in most major Western Theater campaigns. In 1863, he became known as "the Rock of Chickamauga," after he held his troops in place to cover the Union retreat into Chattanooga. Thomas' Army of the Cumberland broke the Confederate siege lines around the city, and Thomas later became Sherman's second in command during the Atlanta Campaign. Dispatched to protect Chattanooga and Nashville against John Bell Hood's Army of Tennessee, Thomas was so deliberate in his preparations before the battle of Nashville (December 1864) that his loyalty was questioned once more and he was almost removed from command. But his smashing victory against the Confederacy's main western army brought him the official thanks of Congress. Thomas remained in the army until his death in 1870.

EMORY UPTON, U.S.A. (1839–1881). Born into a devoutly religious and reform-oriented New York family, Emory Upton graduated from West

Major General Emory Upton's varied Civil War combat experience contributed to his development as the premier postwar military theorist in the United States.

Point in 1861 and was immediately enmeshed in training some of the volunteers flooding into the Union—militia and newly raised regiments that he later said were "so destitute . . . of instruction and training that . . . they did not merit the name of a military force." Courageous, intense, and ambitious, he was wounded at First Bull Run, proved himself a capable and imaginative commander during the Peninsula Campaign and at Antietam, and was appointed colonel of the 121st New York Volunteer Infantry in October 1862. On May 3, 1863, during the Chancellorsville campaign, Upton led his regiment in a daytime frontal assault on Confederate lines that left 278 of his 453 men dead or wounded. This was a seminal event in his development as the most influential military theorist in the postwar United States. A year later, his growing battlefield experience, courage, and inventiveness were again demonstrated at what became known as the "Bloody Angle" during the battle of Spotsylvania, when regiments that he had formed to attack in columns, rather than in the usual thin and vulnerable battle lines, breached the Confederates' formidable defensive lines. He further distinguished himself during Philip Sheridan's 1864 Shenandoah Valley Campaign, during which he was brevetted major general. In 1865, Upton commanded a division during James H. Wilson's cavalry expedition that took Selma, Alabama. After the war, Upton became commandant of cadets at West Point, toured Europe and the Far East as a military observer, and published the influential *Infantry Tactics* (1867) and *The Armies of Asia and Europe* (1878), an excellent description of the state of the military profession in the late nineteenth century. Passionately devoted to achieving organizational reform in the U.S. Army, Upton had completed a draft of a book outlining his theories when he committed suicide in 1881. Published posthumously, *The Military Policy of the United States* greatly influenced the development of the American army in the twentieth century.

STAND WATIE, C.S.A. (1806–1871). A controversial Cherokee whose signing of the treaty of New Echota, providing for surrender of Cherokee lands in Georgia, incited a number of Cherokee people to mark him for murder, Stand Watie remained an outspoken leader of the Southern Cherokee for much of his adult life. At the outbreak of the Civil War, after attempting to remain neutral, the Cherokee formed an alliance with the Confederate States, which, in 1863, the majority of the Cherokee nation repudiated. But Stand Watie remained loyal to the Confederacy throughout the war. He was the colonel of the "Cherokee Mounted Rifles," a regiment of volunteers he had raised. Later, he was promoted to brigadier general. Active as a raider and cavalry leader throughout the war, Stand Watie fought at Wilson's Creek and Pea Ridge. He was among the last Confederate officers to surrender, finally doing so on June 23, 1865.

JOSEPH WHEELER, C.S.A. (1836–1906). Born in Augusta, Georgia, Joseph Wheeler had barely two years' military experience after his 1859 graduation from West Point before resigning from the U.S. Army to fight for the South. He entered the Confederate army as a first lieutenant, but was soon promoted to colonel of the Nineteenth Alabama Infantry. He led the regiment through the Shiloh campaign, became a brigade commander, and, in 1862, was named commander of the cavalry of the Army of Mississippi. For the rest of the war, as he rose steadily in rank and in the estimation of his men and his commanding officers, "Fighting Joe" Wheeler led the cavalry in the Western Theater of operations. Shielding the infantry, conducting raids, participating in battles, contesting Sherman in his March to the Sea, Wheeler was a tenacious adversary to Union forces. He was twenty-eight years old when his capture ended his role in the war. When Wheeler returned to civilian life, he became a planter and a practicing lawyer, and then entered politics. He returned to the military to serve the United States during the Spanish-American War.

Confederate Major General Joseph Wheeler won the nickname "Fighting Joe" by his skillful use of limited cavalry resources.

Fighting on Two Fronts: Black Soldiers in the Civil War

For 186,000 Union soldiers, the Civil War was actually two wars. Because their skin was black, they had to fight for acceptance as men and soldiers in their own army, even as they were fighting Confederate armies and the institution of slavery. Their first battles were fought on the home front. Until late in 1862, black men of the Civil War era were prohibited, by Federal law, from serving in state militias, and there were no African Americans in the U.S. Army. Many black men, however, were eager to serve the Union cause—as African Americans had done from the Revolution through the War of 1812.

Early Struggles: 1861–1862

In the early months of the war, a few black men did manage to join otherwise all-white regiments—occasionally as regular soldiers, but more often as servants of white officers or as teamsters who drove supply wagons. On April 18, 1861, one enlistee, Pennsylvanian Nicholas Biddle, became the particular target of Southern sympathizers in Baltimore when he marched through the city with his unit, the "Washington Artillerists," on the way to Washington, D.C. Biddle was hit full in the face by a stone—and thus became one of the first Northern soldiers to shed his blood on behalf of the Union. Another man, William Henry Johnson, joined the Second Connecticut Volunteer Infantry as an "independent man"—a status with only the vaguest of definitions. After his ninety-day enlistment was up, he joined the Eighth Connecticut, fought at First Bull Run, and, early in 1862, participated in the Burnside Expedition that captured Roanoke Island and New Bern, North Carolina. Also a correspondent for the Boston-based *Pine and Palm*, an emigration society publication, Johnson reported to his paper that the "proscribed" (black) Americans attached to his regiment—"and there are many"—had formed a "defensive association" and were learning military science not only as a matter of self-protection but also due to their conviction "that the time is not far distant when the black man of this country will be summoned to show his hand in this struggle for liberty."

On the home front, many black men, unwilling to wait until the government decided they could serve, studied army manuals and sometimes organized drill companies. (One was established, for example, in Boston on April 29, 1861.) Meanwhile, spokesmen, both white and black, urged congressmen and the president to alter the policy that made the North's military campaign to reconstruct the Union a "white man's war." But the

These two African American soldiers were photographed while on picket duty at Dutch Gap Canal, Virginia, in 1864.

North's complex political currents, and prevailing assumptions about the suitability of African Americans for military service, made Union authorities reluctant to consider the proposition—especially when they believed that the war would be short (see Chapter 3, "Wartime Politics").

In May 1862, Major General David Hunter made a first—unauthorized and unsuccessful—attempt to form a black regiment, the First South Carolina Volunteer Infantry, at Hilton Head, South Carolina. (An authorized First Carolina was formed later in the year and placed under the command of noted abolitionist Colonel Thomas Wentworth Higginson.) Another unauthorized unit, the First Kansas Volunteer Colored Infantry, was successfully organized by politician-soldier James H. Lane in August and September; by the time the unit was officially mustered into U.S. service on January 13, 1863, it had already become the first black regiment to have a "baptism of fire." (On October 29, 1862, they engaged a unit of Confederate guerrillas at Island Mound, Missouri.)

On July 17, 1862, the United States Congress approved "An Act to amend the Act calling for the militia to execute the Laws of the Union." It stated, in part:

> the President . . . is hereby authorized to receive into the service of the United States, for the purpose of constructing intrenchments, or performing camp service or any other labor, or any military or naval service for which they may be found competent, persons of African descent. . . ."

That same day, Congress also approved the Second Confiscation Act, which states in its Section 11:

> That the President of the United States is authorized to employ as many persons of African descent as he may deem necessary and proper for the suppression of this rebellion, and for this purpose he may organize and use them in such manner as he may judge best for the public welfare.

These two congressional acts opened the door for black men to become Union soldiers, and the government quickly followed up. On August 25, 1862, the U.S. War Department authorized Brigadier General Rufus Saxton, military governor of the South Carolina Sea Islands, to raise five regiments of black troops on the islands, with white men as officers. An important provision of this order was the specification that these troops were to receive "the same pay and rations as are allowed by law to volunteers in the service." It was with this understanding that other black regiments, including the famed Fifty-Fourth Massachusetts, were recruited until the summer of 1863.

On September 27, 1862, the First Regiment of the Louisiana Native Guards, U.S. Army, comprising free black Louisianans and ex-slaves, was sworn into service in Union-occupied New Orleans. These were the first black soldiers to be *officially* mustered into United States military service. (The Second and Third Louisiana Native Guards were mustered in during October and November.) Organized under Major General Benjamin F. Butler, these black regiments included some seventy-five black captains and lieutenants and one major among their officers—a step that was reversed by Butler's successor (December 1862), Nathaniel Banks. Declaring that "the appointment of colored officers is detrimental to the service," Banks methodically drove the black officers out of the service, using charges of incompetence (an ineffective tactic; most charges proved to be unfounded) and a steady campaign of slights and humiliations. Because of similar opposition to black officers among many whites throughout the North, only thirty-two others were commissioned during the war: thirteen were chaplains, and at least eight were physicians (who had to meet far more stringent requirements than were demanded of white army doctors).

The Confederate government's reaction to the inclusion of blacks in Union armed forces was ominous. On December 24, 1862, President Jefferson Davis issued a proclamation directing that captured black U.S. soldiers and their white officers were to be turned over to state authorities and tried for insurrection or inciting insurrection—crimes punishable by death.

A Pivotal Year: 1863

On January 1, President Lincoln issued the Emancipation Proclamation (see Chapter 3, "Wartime Politics"). A stronger document than the Preliminary Emancipation Proclamation (issued on September 22, 1862, after the Union victory at Antietam), this document included a specific provision for black soldiers:

> And I further declare and make known that such persons [i.e., those held as slaves "within said designated States and parts of States"] of suitable condition will be received into the armed service of the United States to garrison forts, positions, stations, and other places, and to man vessels of all sorts in said service.

Called "the most execrable measure in the history of guilty man" by President Davis in his message to the Confederate Congress, January 12, 1863, the proclamation was received with emotions ranging from ecstasy to vilification in the North. This crucially important document marked the expansion of Northern war aims to include emancipation along with preservation of the Union, thus altering the nature of the war. It also proved an added stimulus to the aggressive recruitment of black soldiers, which was then under way in the North. Though enthusiasm for military service had lessened among some black men who had benefited from the heated wartime economy—or who had been subject to more blatant discrimination because of wartime pressures—tens of thousands of men quickly answered the call to service. One of the most eloquent recruiters was Frederick Douglass, who, on March 14, called "Men of Color to Arms!" in a statement published in the *National Anti-Slavery Standard:*

... By every consideration which binds you to your enslaved fellow-countrymen, and the peace and welfare of your country; by every aspiration which you cherish for the freedom and equality of yourselves and your children; by all the ties of blood and identity which makes us one with the brave black men now fighting our battles in Louisiana, in South Carolina, I beg you to fly to arms, and smite with death the power that would bury the government and your liberty in the same hopeless grave. . . . I am authorized to assure you that you will receive the same wages, the same rations, the same equipments, the same protection, the same treatment, and the same bounty, secured to white soldiers. . . . The iron gate of our prison stands half open. One gallant rush from the North will fling it wide open, while four millions of our brothers and sisters shall march out into liberty.

The fact that black soldiers would face special dangers from Confederate foes was reflected in the "Instructions for the Government of Armies of the United States in the Field," issued by the U.S. War Department on April 24:

The law of nations shows no distinction of color, and if an enemy of the United States should enslave and sell any captured persons of their Army, it would be a case for the severest retaliation, if not redress.

Concern deepened after the Confederate Congress passed a joint resolution, on May 1, 1863, authorizing President Jefferson Davis to have captured officers of black regiments "put to death or be otherwise punished at the discretion" of a military tribunal. Black enlisted men were to be ". . . delivered to the authorities of the State or States in which they shall be captured to be dealt with according to the present or future laws of such State or States."

Yet, recruitment of black troops continued unabated. On May 22, 1863, the U.S. War Department issued General Orders, No. 143, establishing the Bureau of Colored Troops. The order also established boards to examine candidates for commissions to command colored troops (Section III); the requirement that no recruiting of colored troops could be conducted by unauthorized persons (Section IV); and that noncommissioned officers of colored troops could be selected and appointed "from the best men of their number in the usual mode of appointing noncommissioned officers" (Section VIII). Major Charles F. Foster, Assistant Adjutant General of U.S. Volunteers, was appointed chief of the bureau, and served in that position until October 1867.

Less than a week after the Bureau was established, on May 27, 1863, the first of two all-out assaults was staged on the Confederate Mississippi River bastion of Port Hudson, Louisiana, which had been under Union siege since May 23. During this assault against heavily fortified positions, the First Louisiana Native Guards (later, the Seventy-Third U.S. Colored Infantry) and the Third Louisiana Native Guards (later, the Seventy-Fifth U.S. Colored Infantry) conducted themselves with extreme heroism. Some 20 percent of the two regiments were casualties, including Captain André Cailloux (see biographical sketch on page 407) and sixteen-year-old African American lieutenant John H. Crowder, both killed in action. A defeat for the Union (Port Hudson survived a second assault June 14 and did not capitulate until July 9), the May 27 assault, widely reported in the Northern press, marked a turning point in attitudes toward the use of black soldiers in combat. The *New York Times*, once lukewarm in its endorsement of black soldiers, stated, on June 11, "It is no longer possible to doubt the bravery and steadiness of the colored race, when rightly led."

Close on the heels of these favorable reports, on June 4, 1863, the U.S. War Department made an announcement that devastated the morale of black soldiers already in uniform and did little to entice others to join. Basing its decision on a provision of the Militia Act of July 17, 1862, which sanctioned the enlistment of black soldiers, it specified that black soldiers were thenceforth to be paid less than their white counterparts: $10 a month (as opposed to $13), out of which $3 was to be used for clothing (white soldiers received a clothing bonus). The act specified this pay for black government *laborers*. All black men who had been recruited as soldiers to date had entered the service with the understanding that they were to receive the same pay as white soldiers. The discriminatory pay itself, and the government's reneging on the earlier understanding of equal pay, expressed in its own War Department order of August 25, 1862, elicited a storm of protest from black soldiers, their white officers, and many civilians. Black soldiers were not, however, given the option of leaving the service if they found the new conditions unacceptable. Many determined that their only recourse was to refuse to accept any pay until the discriminatory policy was reversed—despite the hardship this caused them and the even greater hardship it caused their families, many of whom were turned away from white-run charities in the North as the pay strike continued.

But even as this controversy raged, black soldiers continued to fight with valor. On June 7, 1863, at Milliken's Bend, Louisiana, on the Mississippi River above Vicksburg, four newly formed, untrained and understrength regiments of contrabands, armed only with old muskets, and assisted by two understrength companies of white soldiers from the Twenty-Third Iowa Infantry and the gunboats *Choctaw* and *Lexington*, drove off a Confederate brigade that was attempting to disrupt Grant's supply line. The black soldiers—the Ninth Louisiana Infantry (Fifth U.S. Colored Heavy Artillery), the First Mississippi Infantry (Fifty-First U.S. Colored Infantry), the Thirteenth Louisiana Infantry (Sixty-Third U.S. Colored Infantry), and the Eleventh Louisiana Infantry (Forty-Ninth U.S. Colored Infantry)—performed valiantly in what one white officer later described as "a horrible fight, the worst I was ever engaged in, not even excepting Shiloh." The four black regiments sustained 35 percent casualties; one regiment, the Ninth Louisiana Infantry, had 45 percent of its men killed or mortally wounded, the highest proportion in a single battle throughout the entire war. Some captured black soldiers and at least two of their white officers were reportedly murdered by Confederates.

Like the action of the black troops at Port Hudson, the courageous performance of these fledgling black troops was widely reported and much celebrated in the North and throughout the Union army. Assistant Secretary of War Charles A. Dana declared, in a report to Secretary of War Edwin Stanton on June 22, 1863:

> . . . the sentiment in regard to the employment of negro troops has been revolutionized by the bravery of the blacks in the recent Battle of Milliken's Bend. Prominent officers, who used in private sneer at the idea, are now heartily in favor of it.

On July 18, 1863, a second Union assault on the formidable Battery (or Fort) Wagner at Morris Island in the Charleston, South Carolina, harbor (the first assault occurred on July 11), was led by the Fifty-Fourth Massachusetts (Colored) Infantry, a much-publicized unit commanded by Colonel Robert Gould Shaw. Arriving at the scene after a forced march from James Island—where three companies of the Fifty-Fourth had won plaudits from white soldiers when they held fast under fire, covering the retreat of a Connecticut regiment—the Fifty-Fourth undertook what proved to be an impossible task against a supremely well-engineered and well-fortified defensive position. Under a withering fire that included shells from nearby Southern batteries, and, as the Fifty-Fourth approached the wall of the fort, rifle fire that swept them at times from three sides, the Massachusetts regiment managed to gain a foothold at the fort before finally being pushed back at a cost of over 40 percent casualties—including, among the dead, Colonel Shaw. When Union men, under a flag of truce, later attempted to retrieve Shaw's body, they were reportedly told by a Confederate, "We have buried him with his niggers!" Intended as an insult, this became a rallying cry in the North.

On December 26, with the number of black soldiers growing, despite the discriminatory pay, and the end of the war nowhere in sight, the Free Military School for Applicants for the Command of Colored Troops opened its doors at 1210 Chestnut Street, Philadelphia. The brainchild of Thomas Webster, who had helped raise several black units in Pennsylvania, the school was established to help officer candidates—all white men at this time, many of them veterans of white regiments—pass the rigorous examination required for service as officers in black regiments; nearly 50 percent of those who had taken the exam to date had failed. Dubbed the "grandfather of the Officer Candidate School" by historian Dudley Cornish, the Free Military School, supervised by chief preceptor Colonel John H. Taggart, provided a rigorous thirty-day course (though many students stayed longer) that included both military subjects and such other courses as arithmetic, algebra, geography, and ancient history. Before it ceased operation September 15, 1864, 484 of its graduates passed their examinations. The stringent requirements for officer candidates in the United States Colored Troops (U.S.C.T.) made most of these men (some political appointees notably excepted) among the best-prepared officers in the United States.

Accomplishments and Tragedies: 1864

The year began with what many in the North regarded as a blatant miscarriage of justice. January 9–12, 1864, Sergeant William Walker of the Twenty-First U.S. Colored Infantry was tried before a court-martial for inciting a mutiny after he refused to perform military duties because the U.S. government was discriminating against black soldiers regarding pay. Convicted, he was executed before President Lincoln had a chance to review the case. "The Government which found no law to pay him except as a nondescript and a contraband," Massachusetts Governor John A. Andrew later stated, "nevertheless found law enough to shoot him as a soldier." But Walker's execution did not subdue the crusade for equal pay. On April 2, 1864, black soldier "E. D. W." wrote to the editor of the *Christian Recorder*, a prominent black newspaper:

Do we not fill the same ranks? Do we not cover the same space of ground? Do we not take up the same length of ground in the grave-yard that others do? The ball does not miss the black man and strike the white, nor the white and strike the black. But sir, at that time there is no distinction made, they strike one as much as another.

At times, in fact, minié balls were aimed *specifically* at black soldiers by Confederates fighting against them. The most infamous example occurred on April 12, 1864. While raiding important Federal communications facilities and posts in western Kentucky and Tennessee, Confederate cavalry commanded by Nathan Bedford Forrest attacked and captured Fort Pillow, Tennessee, on the Mississippi River. Many of the United States Colored Troops defending the fort were murdered after they surrendered, as were some white defenders. Quickly termed a "massacre" by Northerners, Fort Pillow engendered an investigation by the U.S. Congress' Joint Committee on the Conduct of the War. Many Northern soldiers, particularly black soldiers, adopted "Remember Fort Pillow" as a battle cry.

Six days later, April 18, at Poison Springs, Arkansas, 1,200 Union troops on a foraging expedition—438 of them black troopers from the First Kansas Colored Volunteers—were attacked by nearly 3,400 Confederates under Brigadier General John S. Marmaduke and badly defeated. Over half the Union casualties were black, and witnesses reported that some of them were murdered. Though Confederates denied the charge, evidence supported it. Almost immediately, black soldiers responded on the battlefield. At Jenkins Ferry, on the Sabine River in Arkansas, April 30, 1864—an overall Union defeat—a charge by the Second Kansas Colored Volunteers shouting "Remember Poison Springs!" overwhelmed a Confederate battery and resulted in numerous Southern casualties. Other black troops reciprocated Confederate brutality with ferocity, or "under the black flag" (i.e., giving no quarter). Confederate depredations against black Union soldiers on the battlefield also reinforced the Union's decision, April 17, 1864, to suspend

Christian Abraham Fleetwood, sergeant major of the Fifth United States Colored Troops, received the Medal of Honor for action at Chaffin's Farm near Richmond September 29, 1864. He is one of 23 African American Civil War soldiers awarded the nation's highest military decoration.

prisoner exchanges. The immediate cause of the suspension was the refusal by Confederate authorities to agree to the most pressing of two conditions Union General in Chief Grant made for prisoner exchanges to continue—that "No distinction whatever will be made in the exchange between white and colored prisoners."

On June 10, 1864, at the Battle of Brice's Crossroads, Mississippi, Confederates under Nathan Bedford Forrest dealt Union forces a severe defeat. With almost no assistance from white volunteers, three black regiments held back the Confederates, at times with hand-to-hand combat, and allowed the balance of the Union force to escape. Five days later, after U.S. Attorney General Edward Bates gave his opinion that black soldiers should receive equal pay, Congress finally authorized equal pay for all soldiers from January 1, 1864, and back pay to the level of white soldiers holding the same rank. But this was not a complete reversal of the discriminatory policy: the back pay applied *only* to those soldiers who were free on April 19, 1861. Tens of thousands of ex-slaves in the U.S. Army were thus excluded. It took many more months of protests before a law was passed on March 3, 1865, granting equal pay from their enlistment date for all black troops.

While the question of pay moved toward that final resolution, another battlefield tragedy occurred. On July 30, the explosion of a huge Union mine under the Confederate defenses outside Petersburg, Virginia, precipitated what is now known as the battle of the Crater. Union troops that charged into the crater left by the explosion were quickly trapped by Confederate troops, who fired on them from both front and flank. Officers and black troops were targeted, particularly. Some wounded black soldiers were reportedly bayoneted. Although white troops predominated in the attack, black units suffered more than 40 percent of the fatalities and 35 percent of the casualties. In 1894, Captain James A. Richard, who was with the Nineteenth U.S. Colored Troops at the Crater, recalled the battle—and its reverberations—in *Services with Colored Troops in Burnside's Corps:*

> The charge of Ferrero's division . . . through a broken and demoralized division of white troops, then forming line inside the enemy's works, and temporary capture of their interior works, with awful losses in killed, wounded and *murdered*, is a record to win back the previously prejudiced judgment of the president, cabinet, generals, and officers of the Army of the Potomac, who up to this time had thought negroes all right for service in a menial capacity, but from henceforth to take responsible places, like

the right flank of the army at Deep Bottom, Va., and the storming of strong works like Forts Alexander and Gregg.

As the year wound toward its close, with Union gains on the battlefield, black soldiers continued to make gains in the estimation of their white comrades. On August 17, 1864, U.S.C.T. officer Lewis Weld wrote his mother, from Virginia: "The colored troops are very highly valued here & there is no apparent difference in the way they are treated. White troops & Blacks mingle constantly together & I have seen no single Evidence of dislike on the part of the soldiers. The truth is they have fought their way into the respect of all the army." In the Western Theater, on December 9, Major General E. R. S. Canby issued General Orders, No. 81, Military Division of the West Mississippi, which declared the action of the Third U.S. Colored Cavalry in assaulting and destroying a heavily protected railroad bridge over the Big Black River that was a crucial Confederate supply line, "one of the most daring and heroic acts of the war."

Peace and the Continuing Struggle for Recognition: 1865 and Beyond

On February 18, 1865, the Twenty-First U.S. Colored Troops and two companies of the Fifty-Fourth Massachusetts were among the first Union troops that entered Charleston, South Carolina, the city where the war began. And on April 3, 1865, the Fifth Massachusetts Cavalry (colored) were in the vanguard of the Union troops that occupied the former Confederate capital of Richmond, Virginia. Fighting on two fronts, the Union's black soldiers had helped win signal victories on both: Southern armies were defeated and, with ratification of the Thirteenth Amendment in December 1865, slavery in the United States was at an end. Yet, when the Army of the Potomac and William T. Sherman's western armies marched through the heart of Washington, D.C., in a spectacular Grand Review (May 23–24), the only African Americans among the marchers were contrabands walking with Sherman's troops. Not one of the 166 regiments of U.S. Colored Troops was included in this celebration. The Reconstruction era would witness reverses to the progress black soldiers had helped African Americans achieve during the Civil War. America's black soldiers would be required to fight on two fronts in future wars well into the twentieth century, having to win, again and again, the recognition expressed in the inscription on Augustus St. Gaudens' sculpture memorial, dedicated in Boston May 31, 1897, to Colonel Robert Gould Shaw and the Fifty-Fourth Massachusetts Infantry:

The black rank and file volunteered when disaster clouded the Union cause, served without pay for eighteen months till given that of white troops, faced threatened enslavement if captured, were brave in action, patient under heavy and dangerous labors, and cheerful amid hardships and privations. Together they gave to the nation and the world undying proof that Americans of African descent possess the pride, courage, and devotion of the patriot soldier.

Notable Special Units and Services

Aeronauts

See "Toward Modern War" in Chapter 4, "Battles and the Battlefield."

Cavalry

See "Battle Tactics," "Use of Cavalry" in Chapter 4, "Battles and the Battlefield."

Chaplains

Chaplains had served with American armies since the Revolution, but the Civil War provoked new debates on their role and status in the armed forces. The debates, in large measure, arose because of the scope of the conflict. Just two years before Fort Sumter was fired upon, Congress had enacted a law allowing the appointment of only thirty chaplains for the nineteen regiments and 128 companies into which the 16,000-man U.S. regular army was then divided. Less than six months after Fort Sumter, Union land forces alone comprised 650 regiments, and thirty chaplains obviously could not serve them all. Southern armies in mid-1861 also comprised hundreds of regiments. But the prospect of incorporating large numbers of clergymen and other religious workers into the armed forces raised questions that many legislators in both regions—but especially those in the South—found troubling.

The Union addressed the question first, and most directly, by endorsing an increased number of chaplains. General Orders, Nos. 15 and 16, issued on May 4, 1861, directed regimental commanders to appoint chaplains. Their appointments were to be confirmed by regimental elections, but at least one appointment was countermanded by Secretary of War Stanton. He declined to recognize the unanimous election of Reverend Ella E. Gibson, a pastor of the Religio-Philosophical Society of Saint Charles, Illinois, by the men of

Men of the Ninth Massachusetts Infantry, an Irish-American regiment, pause to be photographed with their chaplain before celebrating Mass on a quiet Sunday morning at Camp Cass, Virginia, in 1861. Photograph by the Mathew Brady Studio.

the First Wisconsin Heavy Artillery, despite President Lincoln's declaration that he had "no objection to her appointment." Thus ended the short career of the only known woman chaplain in the Civil War.

At this early point, details regarding chaplains' uniforms, rank, and duties were somewhat vague. Their general responsibilities included maintaining "the social happiness and moral improvement of the troops" and reporting on their "moral and religious condition." More specific duties and privileges—including the appointment of chaplains for duty in regular and divisional hospitals (May 20, 1862) and the provision of military rank (the well-intended but still vague "chaplain without command," *assumed* to place chaplains at the rank of captain, April 9, 1864)—were included in subsequent congressional legislation. Without more specific official direction, most Union chaplains were chiefly guided by their own views of proper duty and by the officers under whom they served. But they could also consult *The Army Chaplain, His Office, Duties, and Responsibilities, and the Means of Aiding Him,* by Reverend William Young Brown. This earnest book stated, among other things, that chaplains should possess "ardent piety" as well as proficiency as teachers, resolution, energy, good health, and courage. Despite these admonitions, a number of ill-qualified men were accepted as chaplains during the first eighteen months of the war. They tarnished the reputations of chaplains in general, but their conduct focused more attention on the enlistment of chaplains with proper religious and personal credentials.

Through the first year of the war, U.S. law required that all chaplains be Christian—though Jewish soldiers were serving in the Union army. Ohio representative Clement L. Vallandigham proposed legislation, in July 1861, allowing non-Christian chaplains, but another full year passed before the words "religious denominations" replaced "Christian denominations" in the legislative authorization for chaplains. After the Emancipation Proclamation was issued, fourteen black chaplains joined the army—in most cases after waging an ardent campaign for acceptance. Henry McNeal Turner, pastor of the Israel African Methodist Episcopal Church in Washington, D.C., was the first appointee (September 10, 1863). Besides serving their regiments, most black chaplains were active recruiters for the U.S. Colored Troops—despite being subjected to the same racial discrimination as other African American soldiers. This included an initial determination that they would receive substantially lower pay than white chaplains. That decision was eventually reversed.

Throughout the war, some 2,300 chaplains served in Union armies, though no more than 600 were ever on active duty at the same time. Except for one Jewish chaplain, Rabbi Ferdinand L. Sarner of the Fifty-Fourth New York, all were Christian. Methodists were most numerous. The other major denominations represented were, in descending numerical order: Presbyterians, Episcopalians, Baptists, Congregationalists, Roman Catholics, and Unitarians.

Confederate States officials excluded chaplains entirely when the Southern army was first organized. They firmly believed that church and state should be strictly separated and that the churches themselves, rather than the government, should be responsible for supporting ministers in the army. Protests from Southern churches and civilians caused a reversal of that policy. Congress gave President Davis power to appoint as many chaplains as he deemed expedient to regiments and brigades. The president, in turn, delegated this responsibility to field commanders, who could appoint chaplains or allow their men to elect them. Duties and qualifications of Confederate chaplains were even more vague than those outlined for their Union counterparts, so Southern chaplains relied on the guidance published by a civilian: retired Methodist bishop James O. Andrews' *Letter to the Chaplains in the*

Army. Their pay was also significantly lower than that of U.S. chaplains: after starting at $85 per month, it was reduced almost immediately to $50, and was later raised to $80; Union chaplains generally received $120 per month (some of the Southern army chaplains received additional money from churches). Despite these difficulties, more than 600 men served as chaplains in the Confederate army. Though it was always possible in the South for Jewish chaplains to serve, all the South's chaplains were Christian.

Chaplains for both sides presided at prayer meetings and religious services, helped with the wounded (both on and behind the battlefield), comforted the dying, wrote letters for the wounded and to the families of soldiers who died, maintained camp libraries (containing both religious and secular material), served as postmasters, counseled the troubled, cautioned all in their charge against the encroachments of vice, and exhorted the faint of heart. In the Union armies, chaplains also served as teachers, both to illiterate soldiers—white and black—and to civilian contrabands. The U.S. War Department, after deciding in 1863 that chaplains were noncombatants, issued instructions that those who were captured in battle were to be immediately released, but chaplains were often treated as ordinary prisoners of war, and those who were taken prisoner performed their duties in prison camps. On both sides, chaplains inspired and guided the religious revivals that swept through the armies—chiefly in 1863 and 1864, the years when crucial turning points occurred in the war. A number of chaplains on both sides displayed remarkable courage, accompanying their regiments into battle and often saving the lives of wounded men under fire. Three Union chaplains who performed heroically—Francis B. Hall, Milton L. Haney, and John M. Whitehead—were awarded the Medal of Honor.

Espionage/"Secret Service"

See "Shadow Warriors: Partisan Rangers, Guerrillas, and Spies," on page 447.

Invalid Corps/Veteran Reserve Corps

The U.S. Invalid Corps, created by the War Department in April 1863, was an outgrowth of the unofficial practice of employing soldiers who were unfit for combat (due to injuries or illness) to assist in hospital work and other noncombat duties. Organized into two "battalions"—one fit to bear arms and serve on garrison duty, and the other capable only of hospital duty—the

Invalid Corps provided valuable wartime support services (including arresting and guarding deserters). Unfortunately, the sky-blue uniforms initially provided to the corps quickly became a source of derision (regular army blue was later adopted); and jokes were also generated by the fact that the Invalid Corps initials were the same as those stamped on unacceptable government equipment that had been declared "Inspected—Condemned." For those reasons—and to encourage veterans to reenlist—the War Department, on March 18, 1864, changed the name to Veteran Reserve Corps. Between 1863 and the summer of 1866, when it was disbanded, some 60,000 men served in the corps—mainly on noncombatant and garrison duty. In the summer of 1863, however, Veteran Reserve Corps men engaged in more active duty when they helped quell the 1863 draft riot in New York City (see Chapter 10, "The Home Front"). One year later, when Jubal Early led 15,000 Confederate troops to the outskirts of Washington, D.C., Veteran Reserve Corps men were among those who manned the city's defenses. Sixteen Invalid/Veteran Reserve Corps men were killed in action between 1863 and 1866.

In 1864, the Confederacy also organized an Invalid Corps, in which officers and men who were disabled in the line of duty were required to serve in order to receive pay. Less structured than the Union corps, the Confederate unit was often a place where Southern soldiers performed lighter duties while recovering sufficiently to return to their regular stations.

Marine Corps (Confederate and Union)

See Chapter 7, "The War on the Water."

Mississippi Marine Brigade

An excellent idea eventually defeated by leadership problems, the Mississippi Marine Brigade was a special United States combined army/navy force organized to combat Confederate guerrilla activity along the Mississippi River, especially in Arkansas and Louisiana (see "Shadow Warriors: Partisan Rangers, Guerrillas, and Spies," on page 447). It was approved in late summer, 1862, and deployed for duty in Louisiana by mid-March 1863, as Grant was preparing for his second campaign against Vicksburg. The brigade comprised the First Battalion Mississippi Marine Brigade Infantry, the First Battalion Mississippi Marine Brigade Cavalry, and Walling's Light Artillery Battery. Eight river transports allowed these land units to move swiftly and served as floating barracks, a mess hall, and a hospital. Five steamers, six coal barges, and three steam tugs provided logistical support, and gunboats gave the force an added punch. The brigade had been proposed by Brigadier General Alfred W. Ellet (former commander of the Union army's River Ram Fleet; see Chapter 7, "The War on the Water") and Rear Admiral David D. Porter, who commanded all naval forces on the Mississippi River. Confusion over who was in overall command was one of the problems that plagued the unit. Another was the method Ellet used to recruit volunteers for what promised to be arduous duty against particularly slippery foes. "Soldiering Made Easy!" his advertisements announced. "No long, hard marches, camping without tents or food, or carrying heavy knapsacks, but good comfortable quarters, and good facilities for cooking at all times." As a result, lazy, ill-disciplined, and generally unfit men preponderated in the 1,200 troops he assembled. Ellet's leadership, once they were under his command, didn't improve matters. He had chosen his nephew, Colonel Charles Ellet, to be his second in command, but the pair quarreled so bitterly in the summer of 1863 that the general had the colonel arrested. (Colonel Ellet subsequently resigned, for health reasons, and was replaced by his cousin, John R. Ellet.)

Discipline in the field was sadly lacking. When the Marine Brigade made its sweeps along the river, civilians who supported the Union often suffered equally with those who supported Confederate guerrillas. Having burned the towns of Austin, Mississippi, and Hopefield, Arkansas, in retribution for guerrilla activity—a retributive measure widely used by Union forces who were beset by Confederate irregulars—Marine Brigade members sank to unjustified pillaging after participating in the abortive Red River Campaign of 1864. Their behavior provoked one Union commander to report: "Marine Brigade has done more toward embittering [the people along the river] toward our cause than any movement yet made under the auspices of the Navy." Interservice rivalries and Admiral Porter's dislike for Brigadier General Ellet (who, he felt, was "adverse to harmonious action . . . [and] determined to assume authority and disregard my orders") also proved problematical. By late 1864, the Mississippi Marine Brigade had been disbanded.

Musicians

"I don't believe we can have an army without music," said Robert E. Lee—an indication of the important roles music and musicians played in the conduct of the Civil War. In battle, cavalry and artillery were directed according to bugle signals, and infantry drummers, such as the Fourth Virginia's Private

David Scantlon, became famous by risking their lives to "beat the rally," inspiring troops in the midst of combat. In camp, fifers and drummers (often, the youngest men in a company) memorized drum rolls and "calls" that got the men up ("Reveille"), assembled them ("second call" or the "long roll"), announced work details ("fatigue call" or "pioneer's call"), let the men know when the doctor was on duty ("surgeon's call"), and generally regulated daily life. Men who were convicted of crimes or who had exhibited cowardice in the face of the enemy were often drummed out of camp to the playing of the "Rogue's March."

The Civil War was the last major conflict in which bands played on the field of combat. At the beginning of the war, when no one realized how large the armies would become, the Confederate and U.S. army regulations stated that each regiment would have a regimental band, if its commanding officer so requested. Later, this was adjusted—formally, in the Union army, which

The band of the 107th United States Colored Infantry was photographed in Arlington, Virginia, in 1865 by William M. Smith.

established consolidated brigade-band organizations; informally, in the Confederate army. (It has been estimated that more than 400 Union army bands were organized during the war, and that the Confederate army had approximately 125.)

Some army bandsmen were professional musicians. At times, entire civilian bands enlisted as a group. The Staunton (Virginia) Saxhorn Band, for instance, became the Fifth Virginia Regiment Band, later known as the Stonewall Brigade Band. Other men were strictly army musicians; they learned to play only after they enlisted. Bands gave concerts in camp, serenaded honored officers and guests, played for special ceremonies and special events—and stirred the martial spirit as troops marched into battle. In both Union and Confederate forces, regulations decreed that musicians had to be trained as infantry. On both sides, bandsmen served during combat as stretcher bearers, couriers, and medical assistants, and many performed those duties heroically. A number of buglers, drummers, and musicians were cited for valor throughout the war. Twenty-two Union musicians were awarded the Medal of Honor. Among them were bugler Charles W. Reed and drummer Julian Scott, who later became noted for their Civil War art (see Chapter 12, "The Civil War in Literature and the Arts").

Sharpshooters

See "Battle Tactics," in Chapter 4, "Battles and the Battlefield" and "The Whitworth Sharpshooter" in Chapter 6, "Weaponry."

Signalmen/Telegraphers

See "Toward Modern War," in Chapter 4, "Battles and the Battlefield."

Women Soldiers

Civil War-era women were not allowed to be soldiers, but a small number, estimated at between 400 and 600, did campaign with the armies. Some disguised themselves as men and enlisted as regular soldiers. Others went into battle—but only to save lives. Several had accompanied their husbands or relatives to army camps and were moved by circumstance to bear arms—usually for extremely limited periods. Kady Brownell, for example, accompanied her husband, an orderly sergeant of the Fifth Rhode Island Infantry, to the front

A Woman in Battle—"Michigan Bridget" Carrying the Flag *from* My Story of the War: A Woman's Narrative *by U.S. Sanitary Commission worker Mary Livermore celebrates Bridget Devens, who traveled throughout the war with the First Michigan Cavalry, in which her husband was a private. Although she usually served behind the lines, Devens occasionally participated in combat.*

and became so much a part of the unit's camp life that she was dubbed a "daughter of the regiment." Adopting semimilitary dress, she joined a company of sharpshooters and, because of her prowess with a gun, was chosen company color-bearer—a rallying point for her own comrades as they marched into battle, and a target for enemy marksmen. At First Bull Run (July 1861), Brownell stood by her colors until the entire regiment had retreated. In a later engagement, near New Bern, North Carolina, Brownell's husband was severely wounded. She moved him to safety and then returned to the battlefield and rescued several other wounded men. Known thereafter as "the heroine of New Bern," Brownell left the army and returned to Rhode Island with her husband when his injuries rendered him unfit for further service. Annie

Etheridge served with the Third, and later the Fifth Michigan Volunteers, largely as a cook and nurse. But she was known to go into combat—to rescue wounded soldiers, a number of whom reportedly owed her their lives. Sarah Edmonds may have seen combat with the Second Michigan Infantry. She served with the regiment from First Bull Run to Fredericksburg (December 1862) and appeared on the rolls as "Private Franklin Thompson." Edmonds was the only female admitted to the postwar veterans' organization, the Grand Army of the Republic. Another woman, Sarah Roseta Wakeman, saw action in the Red River Campaign with the 153rd New York under the name "Edwin" or "Lyons" Wakeman. Only Wakeman's letters, discovered well into the twentieth century, revealed her gender. Though most women who have been identified as Civil War soldiers fought for the Union, there is evidence that some women served in the Confederate ranks. At least two women, for example, were reportedly discovered among Gettysburg's Southern dead.

One woman, Dr. Mary Edwards Walker—who served the North as a frontline nurse and doctor, and, almost certainly at one point, a spy—was subsequently awarded the Medal of Honor. She remains the only woman to have achieved that distinction (see Chapter 9, "Medical Care and Medicine").

Shadow Warriors: Partisan Rangers, Guerrillas, and Spies

I said to them that this bushwhacking must cease. The Federal troops had tolerated it already too long. Hereafter every time the telegraph wire was cut we would burn a house; every time a train was fired upon we should hang a man; and we would continue to do this until every house was burned and every man hanged between Decatur and Bridgeport. If they wanted to fight they should enter the army, meet us like honorable men, and not, assassin-like, fire at us from the woods and run. We proposed to hold the citizens responsible for these cowardly assaults, and if they did not drive these bushwhackers from amongst them, we should make them more uncomfortable than they would be in hell.—Colonel John Beatty, Third Ohio Volunteer Infantry, U.S.A., diary entry written at Paint Rock, Alabama, May 2, 1862.

As uniformed armies clashed on Civil War battlegrounds, a "shadow war" was also in progress. The most prominent warriors in this irregular conflict were the Confederate partisan rangers and the guerrilla and "counterguerrilla" bands, on both sides, that raided, looted, and generally harassed each other, army supply and communications facilities, and civilian settlements. Formed spontaneously, or under the Confederate Partisan Ranger Act (April 21,

1862), or the General Orders of various military department commanders, the bands ranged from military organizations with strict rules of conduct to murderous outlaw gangs. In *The Hard Hand of War*, historian Mark Grimsley divided Confederate guerrilla fighters into four categories, three of which could also be applied to the less numerous Northern irregulars who were active in the shadow war:

1. Regular organized cavalry units that happened, on occasion, to adopt irregular tactics.
2. Partisan rangers, such as John Singleton Mosby's Forty-Third Virginia Battalion ("Mosby's Rangers"). The term is applicable only to Confederates; the North passed no legislation comparable to the Partisan Ranger Act.
3. Politicized civilians who fought covertly, masquerading as noncombatants.
4. Simple outlaws who used the war as an excuse for crime.

Uniformed forces that conducted raids in support of military and political objectives (Union Colonel Able Streight's foray into northern Alabama, for instance, and Confederate Brigadier General John Hunt Morgan's raid into Indiana and Ohio, both in 1863) fall easily within the first category. But a wide variety of bands claimed legitimacy under the Confederacy's "Act to Organize Bands of Partisan Rangers." The relatively short and nonspecific piece of legislation stated, in essence:

> [T]he President . . . is hereby authorized to commission such officers as he may deem proper with authority to form bands of partisan rangers, in companies, battalions or regiments, . . . such partisan rangers, after being regularly received in the service, shall be entitled to the same pay, rations, and quarters during their term of service, and be subject to the same regulations as other soldiers. . . . for any arms and munitions of war captured from the enemy by any body of partisan rangers and delivered to any quartermaster at such place or places as may be designated by a commanding general, the rangers shall be paid their full value.

Though Mosby's Rangers and similar forces operating under this act were disciplined military units, other partisan ranger bands were not characterized by close attention to scruples, and their actions stirred complaints from

Premier Civil War special artist Alfred R. Waud made this portrait of an anonymous Confederate Guerrilla, *an embodiment of the ferocity that characterized many of the partisan groups, of both sides, that operated during the Civil War.*

Southern civilians and members of the government. As early as 1862, in Virginia—one of the first states to grant formal recognition to independent units—Confederate Brigadier General Henry Heth, commanding the district of Lewisburg (now in West Virginia), forwarded to the state governor a letter from the Commonwealth's attorney of Pocahontas County, William Skeen, complaining that "the rangers are a terror to the loyal and true everywhere, and cannot whilst engaged in the murder of our citizens and the stealing of their property be of any service to Virginia." On June 30 of the same year, Major General M. J. Thomson of the Missouri State Guard, on special service with the Confederate army in Mississippi, wrote President Davis about recruits who were eager to join the partisans because they had been "induced to believe that they are to be a band of licensed robbers, and are not the men to care whether it be friend or foe they rob." On January 3, 1863, Confederate Secretary of War James A. Seddon reported to President Davis regarding the irregulars:

> The permanency of their engagements and their consequent inability to disband and reassemble at call precludes their usefulness as mere guerrillas, while the comparative independence of their military relations and the peculiar awards allowed them for captures induce much license and many irregularities. They have not infrequently excited more odium and done more damage with friends than enemies.

Similar concerns continued to be expressed, and, on February 17, 1864, the Partisan Ranger Act was repealed. By then, however, numerous ranger/guerrilla bands were operating in Southern territory but well outside the scope of Confederate government or military control.

The activities of William C. Quantrill, who had registered under the Partisan Ranger Act, undoubtedly loomed large among the reasons the act was rescinded. Perhaps the most famous "bushwhacker" in the Kansas-Missouri corridor, Quantrill lives in history as the embodiment of the particularly vicious guerrilla warfare between pro- and antislavery factions that had plagued that long-contested area since well before the war. From the 1856 sacking of Lawrence, Kansas, by proslavery renegades, and John Brown's "retaliatory" murder of five proslavery men and boys who were innocent of involvement in the raid; to the wartime depredations of Charles Jennison's Union-affiliated Seventh Kansas Volunteer Cavalry ("Jennison's Jayhawkers"); through the massacre of unarmed Union soldiers by "bushwhackers" under "Bloody Bill" Anderson in the fall of 1864, the Kansas-Missouri corridor was the scene of the bloodiest guerrilla fighting of the Civil War era. Frank and Jesse James and Cole Younger were schooled in outlawry there, riding with Quantrill and others who sometimes proved to be pathological killers first, and Southern sympathizers second. Looting, terrorism, robbery, and particularly gruesome murders were visited upon the civilians of the two states by bushwhackers and jayhawkers—and sometimes by regular Union troops frustrated by the bushwhackers' ability to disappear into a countryside populated by friendly civilians.

The Kansas-Missouri corridor was not the only area where outlaw and guerrilla bands preyed on civilians and soldiers alike. In Tennessee and Kentucky, two states with severely divided loyalties, guerrilla bands not only harassed army columns and supply lines, they also attacked civilians suspected of sympathy for the other side. The behavior of Confederate irregulars in this area was particularly vicious toward African Americans who attempted to enlist in the Union army. They were killed or whipped and, in one instance in Kentucky, the left ears were cut off two black men who had been on their way to a recruitment station. In Tennessee, in July 1862, Major General Ulysses S. Grant declared: "Persons acting as guerrillas without organization and without uniform to distinguish them from private citizens are not entitled to the treatment of prisoners of war when caught and will not receive such treatment."

Partisans and guerrillas had become such a problem that, in August 1862, Union General in Chief Henry W. Halleck called upon legal scholar Francis Lieber (a devoted Unionist who had sons fighting on both sides) for an informed opinion regarding guerrilla warfare. The resulting essay, *Guerrilla Parties Considered with Reference to the Laws and Usages of War*, made a distinction between partisans (officially authorized troops who merely adopted irregular tactics and thus were entitled to due process under military law) and "self-constituted guerrillas" (who, as "freebooters," "brigands," and "assassins," were entitled to no more than summary execution). This essay, which Halleck ordered distributed throughout the Union army, proved to be the genesis of General Order, No. 100, issued on April 24, 1863. Also known as the Lieber Code, the order was the world's first formal guideline for the conduct of armies in the field.

In Arkansas—a divided state after Union soldiers took Little Rock in 1863—there were thousands of brutal encounters between regular and irregular forces, and between conflicting irregulars. These encounters had their beginnings in General Orders, No. 17, issued by the Confederate Trans-Mississippi Department commander, Major General Thomas C. Hindman, on July 17, 1862, four months after the South was defeated at Pea Ridge. The order stated, in part:

> For the more effectual annoyance of the enemy upon our rivers and in our mountains and woods all citizens of this district who are not subject to conscription are called upon to organize themselves into independent companies of mounted men or infantry, as they prefer, arming and equipping themselves, and to serve in that part of the district to which they belong. . . . Their duty will be to cut off federal pickets, scouts, foraging parties, and trains, and to kill pilots and others on gunboats and transports, attacking them day and night, and using the greatest vigor in their movements.

After another Southern defeat—at Prairie Grove, in December—Confederate government control of these guerrilla units was reduced to almost nothing. As in Missouri, some of the many bands that had formed devolved into little more than outlaws. To fight them, the Union army first used retributive measures; troops looted and burned the property of civilians suspected of aiding the irregulars, and cavalry were deployed to pursue the elusive and fast-moving guerrillas themselves. More effective measures included: the establishment of a provost marshal (a military police and intelligence-gathering organization), the recruitment of Arkansas Unionists for counterguerrilla units, and the development of fortified farm colonies that were able to resist guerrilla attacks. Captured irregulars were often executed in accordance with U.S. War Department instructions (General Orders, No. 30) and orders from U.S. Army general officers; but even before captured guerrillas could be executed under orders, many were summarily executed by the Union soldiers who caught them—just as Union soldiers were often murdered by guerrillas. As the support of the resident civilians became of greater importance to the Union army units occupying Arkansas, executions became less frequent. Many captured guerrillas were sent to the Little Rock Federal military penitentiary, where a new category of prisoner—"citizens arrested for violation of the laws of war"—was added to the rolls.

Louisiana, under partial Union occupation since the spring of 1862, was similarly plagued by outlaw and guerrilla bands during the war. With its long history of smuggling and other outlaw activities, as well as clashes among its several racial, ethnic, and economic groups, Louisiana became a fertile ground for irregular units when unpopular Union policies—particularly confiscation and conscription—created resentment and a will to retaliate. So troublesome did these irregular bands become, in both Louisiana and Arkansas, that, in addition to other countermeasures taken, a special combined land/naval force, the Mississippi Marine Brigade, was established to fight guerrillas along the Mississippi River in those two states (see "Notable Special Units and Services," on page 438).

As the war raged on and conscription, impressment, and invasion forces ravaged the South, guerrilla activity touched most parts of the Confederacy to some degree—from North Carolina and the mountains of North Georgia, to Alabama and Texas. Gathering information on these groups became one of the duties of another type of shadow warrior employed by both sides during the war: the people engaged in "secret service."

Secret Service

The United States, in 1860, was completely devoid of what is now called an "intelligence network." None had existed since the network developed by America's first "spymaster," George Washington, was disbanded after the Revolutionary War (Winfield Scott organized a group of Mexican nationals as spies during the Mexican War of 1846–1848, but they were active only during that conflict and only in Mexico.) Viewed as unsavory and ungentlemanly, spying and espionage were also regarded as unnecessary in a country not seriously threatened by other nations in the Americas and protected, by two oceans, from strong foreign powers. But in the aftermath of the 1860 presidential election, as it became clear that the United States would quite probably war with itself, the North and the South began to develop secret service organizations—an activity that bloomed, at times haphazardly, during the war.

Throughout the war, the Confederacy invested the amazing sum of $2 million in gold for secret service activities. Confederate agents were dispatched to Europe, to Washington, and to various areas in which Union armies were active. Some agents were already in place—among them were the "secession clerks," who remained in their U.S. government jobs in Washington after war was declared. Among its other operations, the Confederate Signal Service developed, between Richmond and Maryland, a "secret line" over which couriers carried information until the very last days of the war. In 1863, $1 million in gold was allocated to an ambitious program, based in Canada, that included a scheme to use the Knights of the Golden Circle, a secret U.S. political group sympathetic to the South, and other Northern Copperheads, to generate unrest and active revolt in the North. Focusing on the 1864 Democratic national presidential nominating convention in Chicago, armed Southern agents made plans with representatives of the Northern Copperheads to incite violence—and free the many Confederate prisoners held in the Chicago area. The effort was unsuccessful: Northern Copperheads proved insufficiently enthusiastic, and loyal Northern agents discovered the plot and arrested key leaders shortly after the convention. The well-funded Confederates in Canada remained active, however, even after the war was over, publishing tracts that defended prominent Southerners and denying Confederate complicity in the assassination of President Lincoln.

Intelligence gathering—and guarding against enemy spies—were also within the province of the field military units. Provost marshals guarded (imperfectly) against infiltration by Unionists; Union deserters were closely questioned; cavalry and partisan units, as well as civilians in occupied territories, gathered information (of varying degrees of reliability) about enemy strength, command changes, and events (such as a buildup of supplies, or unusual railroad activity) that might portend troop movements. Transmitted by couriers (who were often restricted to traveling at night, and via roundabout routes, to avoid capture) or, at times, by much speedier telegraph, this information often helped determine the Confederacy's own troop deployments. Northern newspapers—procured by spies, or during meetings between army pickets, or at Northern flag-of-truce parties—also provided valuable information. Before First Bull Run, Southern leaders were able to read detailed information on the composition of Union regiments in and around Washington that had been published in *The Washington National Republican*. (The informative accounts in Union newspapers led to greater caution in the Confederacy; Southern newspapers were much more circumspect and thus less useful to the

North.) Some Confederate army commanders—including Robert E. Lee, Jeb Stuart, and Stonewall Jackson—were also adept at spreading *dis*information— generating false stories about their movements and strength, to confuse Northern commanders.

In the North, a Chicago detective, Allan Pinkerton (1819–1884) became the Union's first spymaster when he helped foil a plot to assassinate Abraham Lincoln during the president-elect's train journey from Illinois to Washington. When George B. McClellan, a former client of Pinkerton, assumed command of the Army of the Potomac, Pinkerton became his intelligence chief. At first he was based in Washington; later, he stayed with McClellan in the field (but left several assistants in Washington to engage in counterespionage). Pinkerton's efforts, while uneven, did provide the Union with valuable information, primarily with regard to the composition of the opposing army. He gathered the information principally by interrogating prisoners, deserters (a particularly fruitful source), contrabands, and refugees, rather than through an actual spy network. He employed some two dozen agents, whose names he kept a closely guarded secret, but all these spies were transient. They performed short-term missions, mostly in Richmond, rather than going permanently undercover in the Confederacy. The fact that he and his operatives rarely attempted to infiltrate even nearby Confederate forces may partially account for Pinkerton's famous exaggerated estimates of Confederate strength, which were often blamed for General McClellan's cautious approach to combat. Other evidence suggests that McClellan himself was partly to blame. The general gathered intelligence from many sources besides Pinkerton's organization, and he always tended to believe the grossest estimates of the enemy's forces.

Pinkerton's self-proclaimed Federal Secret Service (not to be confused with today's Secret Service) disintegrated in 1862. The detective's close association with McClellan caused the Pinkerton spy organization to lose favor when the general was removed from command. Lafayette Baker (see his biographical sketch in the next section) then assumed chief responsibility for counterespionage activities in Washington and its environs. After a period of uncertainty, Pinkerton's role as the Army of the Potomac's intelligence officer was taken over by Colonel (later, General) George H. Sharpe, who headed the newly designated Bureau of Military Information. A lawyer and a Republican, Sharpe was a natural leader who also proved to be a talented spymaster. He gave Major General Hooker extremely accurate information on the movements and strength of Lee's Army of Northern Virginia before Chancellorsville, and

"Spymaster" Allan Pinkerton (alias, E. J. Allen; at left) stands with President Lincoln and Major General John A. McClernand at Antietam in October 1862—shortly before Pinkerton's secret service work for the Army of the Potomac ended with the dismissal of George B. McClellan.

provided Hooker, and then Meade, with excellent intelligence during the Gettysburg Campaign. Unlike Pinkerton, Sharpe sent out spies—soldiers and civilians—on scouting missions to penetrate the enemy's armies. He also established contact with sympathetic individuals in the South—most notably Elizabeth Van Lew and Samuel Ruth, both of whom supplied invaluable information during Grant's 1864 campaigns in the East.

In the West, Ulysses S. Grant appointed one of his division commanders, Grenville Dodge (1831–1916), to head the intelligence-gathering efforts (in addition to Dodge's regular command responsibilities). Dodge proved singularly adept at the assignment. He had garnered experience in running intelligence activities in 1862, when, serving in Missouri, he had picked men from the Twenty-Fourth and Twenty-Fifth Missouri regiments and formed a "Corps of Scouts" that gathered valuable intelligence for the Union's Army of the Southwest. Carefully trained by Dodge, these scouts largely avoided the miscalculations and exaggeration of Confederate troop strength that characterized Pinkerton's operations in the East. For Major General Grant, Dodge established a highly effective and widespread network of more than 100 spies whose identities were carefully concealed. (A number were discovered, however.) Extreme caution was his hallmark: He avoided using the telegraph and sent information, in code, only by messenger; written notes were destroyed, once the information inscribed on them had been noted on his own maps and in his single communications book. Many of his agents were sympathetic Southern whites and freedmen who lived in Union-occupied territories. He also employed at least two female agents: Jane Featherstone, in Jackson, Mississippi, and Mary Malone, who gathered intelligence in Mississippi and Alabama in 1863. Dodge and his people were able to keep Grant informed of Confederate movements and assisted immeasurably in the second campaign for Vicksburg, as well as subsequent Western Theater campaigns. Other U.S. armies established intelligence networks primarily to track irregular Confederate forces, whose activities were giving Union forces in the Western Theater particular difficulties. Unionists, contrabands, peddlers, and uncommitted civilians became sources of information in this shadow conflict that often resulted in the arrest, formal execution, or clandestine murder of its participants.

Other Figures in the Secret Service

JOHN C. BABCOCK, U.S.A. A former architect from Chicago, Babcock joined Pinkerton's organization to sketch enemy fortifications described by interrogated persons. Conscientious and curious, he was perhaps the only Pinkerton agent who ever did any scouting. As a result, the maps he drew were praised for their accuracy. When Ambrose E. Burnside assumed command of the Army of the Potomac, Babcock served as that army's intelligence chief, under the supervision of Provost Marshal Marsena R. Patrick, and proved exceptionally talented at procuring correct information from captured enemy soldiers and deserters. In February 1863, when command of the Army of the Potomac was assumed by Major General Joseph Hooker, Babcock wrote a description of duties for a proposed "secret service department" of that army. The document was a basis for the Bureau of Military Information, which became a reality under Colonel George Henry Sharpe.

LAFAYETTE C. BAKER (1826–1868), U.S.A. A former member of the infamous Vigilance Committee of San Francisco, Lafayette Baker had a natural proclivity for spying and informing, and he placed it at the disposal of the Union at the outbreak of hostilities. Captured during a mission into the South, he convinced Confederate authorities of his Southern sympathies and was returned to the North as a Southern spy. But his loyalties remained with the Union, and he delivered to Federal authorities such valuable information, garnered on his mission, that Secretary of War Stanton commissioned him a special agent with a "roving commission" (later, he was made special provost marshal of the War Department). A thorn in the side of the Army of the Potomac's Provost Marshal Marsena R. Patrick (who believed Baker to be "capable of making any statement however false, & of committing any act, however criminal, and of damaging the Public Service to gratify his own passions"), Baker was also a terror to Southern agents—and people he simply suspected of being agents. As the head of a secret police force, the National Detectives, which reported directly to Stanton, his spying gave way to largely unmonitored activities against corrupt contractors, counterfeiters, bounty jumpers, and other "vicious citizens." He also headed the pursuit of President Lincoln's assassins.

BELLE BOYD (1843–1900), C.S.A. Only seventeen when the Civil War broke out, Belle Boyd developed a flair for artful eavesdropping upon Union officers occupying the towns in which she lived that proved to be a boon to the Southern cause. Her most famous exploit was her warning, to Stonewall Jackson's forces, during the 1862 Shenandoah Valley Campaign, to advance rapidly so as to cross the bridges that Union soldiers were preparing to destroy. Boyd was captured and imprisoned briefly on two occasions, but she was freed both times. Captured again in 1864, as she sailed for England to deliver letters from President Davis, she was again freed (and later married her captor). That event marked the end of her career as a Civil War spy.

PAULINE CUSHMAN (1833–1893), U.S.A. Pauline Cushman's training as an actor prepared her well for her dramatic wartime role as "The Spy of the Cumberland." A native of New Orleans, she was the widow of an actor who had been in the Union army. Cushman rendered valuable services to Union intelligence even before the now-famous 1863 performance in Union-occupied Louisville, during which she toasted the Confederate cause. Banished by the Union provost marshal to the Southern lines, Cushman was able, by dint of the reputation she had gained from the Louisville scandal, to acquire information useful to Union authorities. Caught by Confederate authorities with compromising papers in her possession, she was court-martialed and sentenced to be hanged, but was reprieved when the Confederates were forced to retreat. Cushman was left behind—able, one last time, to provide useful information on Confederate strength and plans.

SAM DAVIS (1842–1863), C.S.A. As a private in the First Tennessee Infantry, Davis served in Western Virginia and the Shenandoah Valley before being wounded at Shiloh in April 1862. After recovering, he joined a company of scouts commanded by Captain H. B. Shaw ("Coleman's Scouts"). In November 1863, while carrying intelligence on Union troop movements, he was caught by Federal troops, jailed, questioned (at least once by Brigadier General Grenville Dodge), and threatened with being hanged as a spy if he did not provide information. Insisting he was a courier, not a spy, Davis quietly refused, his calm demeanor persisting through a subsequent trial, a swift conviction, and his last moments on the gallows. Davis' behavior during questioning and at his execution on November 27, 1863, was widely reported in newspapers and made him a Southern hero and martyr.

LOUIS PHILLIPPE D'ORLEANS, COMTE DE PARIS (1838–1894), and ROBERT D'ORLEANS, DUC DE CHARTRES (1840–1910), U.S.A. These two Frenchmen and brothers (Louis Phillippe was pretender to the French throne) served as unpaid captains and aides-de-camp in McClellan's Army of the Potomac. They were assigned to summarize (and thus, analyze, to some extent) the maze of intelligence reports flowing into the army's headquarters. This was the first time in the Civil War, and perhaps the first time in any American war, that this task was made an officer's principal duty.

Washington socialite Rose O'Neal Greenhow, one of the Confederacy's most successful spies, in Old Capitol Prison with her daughter, Rose.

ROSE O'NEAL GREENHOW (1815–1864), C.S.A. A fervent proponent of the Southern cause, Rose O'Neal Greenhow was raised in Washington, D.C., married Virginia gentleman Robert Greenhow (who died in 1854), and became a superb hostess and influence peddler. Presidents, congressmen, and military leaders visited the Greenhows' Washington home for sustenance and good conversation in the years preceding the Civil War. Shortly before the war began, she was recruited as a spy for the South, and she eagerly formed a network of messengers and contacts. In July 1861, she was able to warn the Confederate army of the Union's pending attack at Bull Run, an action that helped make that anticipated Confederate defeat into a rout of Union forces. Arrested later that year, Mrs. Greenhow, along with her youngest daughter, Rose, spent months in a Washington prison before being exchanged for other prisoners. Thereafter, she worked for the South mainly in France and England. Returning home, carrying gold for the Confederacy, she drowned off the coast of North Carolina, attempting to leave a ship that had grounded while running from a Union blockader.

WILLIAM NORRIS, C.S.A. See "Signal Corps/Wig-Wag Signaling" in Chapter 4, "Battles and the Battlefield."

WILLIAM J. PALMER (1836–1909), U.S.A. A cavalry captain, Palmer helped to gather accurate intelligence on the movements of Lee's army during its first invasion of Northern territory. The information was reduced in effectiveness when the civilian state officials to whom he reported directly left out some crucial facts in their telegraphed reports to Washington. Palmer's own scouting mission after the battle of Antietam, itself unusual for an army officer (officers generally *directed* intelligence activities and left the actual espionage to enlisted men and civilians), proved to be a heart-pounding adventure that included arrest and imprisonment in Richmond. Keeping his true identity and mission secret, he was treated as a prisoner of war and eventually paroled. Palmer returned to cavalry duty, saw much action in the Western Theater, and rose to the rank of brigadier general. He was awarded the Medal of Honor for action at Red Hill, Alabama, in January 1865.

SAMUEL RUTH (1818–1872), U.S.A. Superintendent of the Confederacy's Richmond, Fredericksburg, and Potomac Railroad, Ruth was sympathetic to the Union. Beginning in 1864, he supplied information on troop movements, supplies, and the condition of the South's rail network to Colonel George H. Sharpe, chief intelligence officer for the Army of the Potomac. Ruth also helped Union prisoners escape and communicated information on supply movements that resulted, at times, in the destruction of portions of his own rail line.

ELIZABETH VAN LEW (1818–1900), U.S.A. Behaving in such an eccentric fashion that she was discounted as a threat by her Richmond, Virginia, neighbors—despite her Northern origins and proclaimed sympathies—"Crazy Bet" Van Lew was one of the Union's most effective spies in the Confederacy. Schooled in Philadelphia in the 1830s, she had become an ardent abolitionist. She was also a proficient organizer, as was demonstrated by the elaborate system she devised for gathering and relaying information, particularly during 1864–1865. Her frequent visits to Union prisoners of war in Richmond's prisons yielded valuable intelligence; but perhaps her most valuable source of information was Mary Elizabeth Bowser, the former family slave Van Lew was able to place in the Confederate White House. Despite the hostility and resentment of many of her Richmond neighbors, Van Lew remained in Richmond after the war. She served as the city's postmaster during the Grant Administration.

TIMOTHY WEBSTER (1822–1862), U.S.A. Born in England, Timothy Webster came to the United States in 1830, became a New York City policeman in 1853, went to work for Chicago detective Allan Pinkerton a year later, and became one of his most effective investigators. After Pinkerton began his intelligence work for the Union, Webster joined him and served, briefly, as one of the Union's most effective spies. He traveled South, gathered some of the most accurate information provided to McClellan by

Pinkerton's network, and generally demonstrated, in the words of historian Edwin C. Fishel, "one of the few instances of professional competence in Pinkerton's bureau." Implicated by other Pinkerton agents who had been apprehended by Confederate authorities, Webster was arrested in Richmond, convicted of espionage, and sentenced to hang. Despite efforts by Pinkerton and others to have this unusually harsh sentence commuted, Webster was hanged on April 29, 1862.

JOHN C. WINDER (1800–1865), C.S.A. An 1820 West Point graduate, Winder resigned his U.S. army commission in 1861 and became a Confederate brigadier general. He was appointed provost marshal general and commander of military prisons in Richmond. There he enforced martial law, oversaw a "rowdy" civilian detective force, and managed counterespionage efforts. (He presided over the execution of Timothy Webster.) Winder also served as commissary general of prisons (see Chapter 9, "Prisons and Prisoners of War").

Army Life

The men who volunteered to fight for the North and the South joined the army for a variety of reasons: a quest for adventure, a desire to experience combat, a wish to see more of the world—or, for many, a sense of obligation to support the state and region in which they lived and the ideals in which they believed. Basically, these were ideals shared by the men of both sides. But Northerners and Southerners had come to view them in radically different lights. "We all declare for liberty," Abraham Lincoln said in 1864, "but in using the same word we do not mean the same thing."

Raised in a country that had proclaimed its independence, less than a century before, with a ringing declaration that all men are created equal and possess "certain unalienable rights," the citizen soldiers, on both sides, were characterized by a firm belief in their own worth and a stubborn individualism that did not surrender easily to the strictures of military discipline—until battlefield experience explained, as neither officers' words nor tactical manuals could, the purpose behind drills and procedures. On the battlefield, too, stubborn determination prevailed, as evidenced by four years of costly assaults and tenacious defenses. Yet battles, though crucial and rending and the most memorable events of their military service, were only a part of the life of Civil War soldiers. They endured the dust and mud of marches, supply shortages, bad food, the insults of civilians, sneak attacks by guerrillas, injuries, the loss of comrades, and uncertainties about what was happening at home. In camp, where so much of their time was spent, they were battered by disease and suffered through long periods of deadly boredom—which they sought to counteract with a wide variety of inventive pursuits.

Citizens of one of the most literate nations in the world, eloquent, opinionated, and largely uncensored, Civil War soldiers expressed their feelings and described their experiences in memoirs, broadsides, camp newspapers, diaries, and a veritable flood of letters. On the Union side alone, some 45,000 letters were dispatched *per day* in the Eastern Theater, and approximately 90,000 per day in the West. Many of these documents survive. The excerpts that follow, selected from letters and diaries of Union and Confederate soldiers, provide telling glimpses of Civil War army life.

Decision

The secession of seven states, punctuated by the shots fired at Fort Sumter, caused "Star-Spangled Fever" to rage through the North and inspired an equally strong surge of regional patriotism in the South. Flags waved; speeches, sermons, and editorials encouraged rallying to the cause; women applauded the gallant, and chastised men of insufficient patriotic fervor. Young boys, old men, and Northern African Americans formed drill companies. In men of military age, on both sides, this excitement encouraged a thirst for adventure and stimulated an eagerness to "see the elephant" (experience combat). For, in 1861, few Americans knew what war could be, and almost no one imagined what *this* war would become. Yet many young men chose to enlist only after long and sober reflection.

> I have delayed answering your letter in order that I might reflect on its contents. I have done so and come to the conclusion that if I do not participate in this war it will be the source of the deepest regret and disappointment in life. Like a bird of evil omen it will follow me and mar all my undertakings. You said that you would not except in case of the *direst necessity* consent to have my course [of study] interrupted. . . . What *direr* necessity can there be than the present, unless it be the very burnings of our own homes. . . . It is true hundreds of my age have fallen victims to disease and death while yet upon the threshold of the service. But why should not I die as well as they? Shall I sit ignobly here and suffer them to fight my battles & endure all for me? Never.—James Billingslea Mitchell

of Alabama, age seventeen, student at the University of Alabama; letter to his father, February 23, 1862.

★   ★   ★

I went to Cambridge and resumed my studies with what zeal I could. During that week we heard that the rebel forces were pushing forward and Northward. . . . I assure you, my dear father, I know of nothing in the course of my life which has caused me such deep and serious thought as this trying crisis in the history of our nation. What is the worth of this man's life or of that man's education if this great and glorious fabric of our Union . . . is to be shattered to pieces by traitorous hands. . . . If our country and our nationality is to perish, better that we should all perish with it.—Samuel Storrow, student at Harvard University; letter to his father, October 12, 1862.

Enlistment

In the early days of the war, so many men enlisted, in the North and the South, that government manpower quotas were quickly exceeded (see also Chapter 10, "The Home Front"). Signing up for terms of ninety days, one year, two years, or three years (in the Confederacy, the Conscription Act prolonged the service of one-year enlistees to three years, and the terms of soldiers already in service were extended to the duration of the conflict), the men were sent off to war with great ceremony. Entire towns turned out for speeches, for the presentation of national and regimental flags sewn by local women, and for concerts of stirring martial music. After major campaigns had resulted in thousands of casualties but no promise of an end to the conflict, voluntary enlistment and reenlistment flagged. Bounties (financial inducements for enlisting), offered by both sides almost from the beginning, were increased, though this fact had greater significance in the North, which had a sounder economy. Conscription—established in the South in 1862 and in the North in 1863, in part to encourage voluntary enlistment—created its own set of problems (even though conscripts amounted to only about 6 percent of Union soldiers, a somewhat higher percentage of Confederates). Draftees were more prone to become deserters. In the North, where bounties were richer and were offered by state, county, and city governments—and sometimes by individuals—as well as by the Federal government, "bounty-jumping" (signing up under a false name until the bounty was paid, deserting, and then repeating the process) became a going concern. Generally, draftees did not exhibit the same devotion to duty as did the majority of volunteers—who tended to look down on draftees until they proved themselves as soldiers.

> I have enlisted! Joined the Army of Uncle Sam for three years, or the war, whichever may end first. Thirteen dollars per month, board, clothes and travelling expenses thrown in. That's on the part of my Uncle. For my part, I am to do, I hardly know what, but in a general way understand I am to kill or capture such part of the Rebel Army as comes in my way.—Lawrence Van Alstyne, Company B, 128th New York State Volunteers; diary entry, August 19, 1862.

★ ★ ★

> That certainly is the only time we can remember when citizens walked along the lines offering their pocketbooks to men whom they did not know; that fair women bestowed their floral offerings and kisses ungrudgingly and with equal favor among all classes of friends and suitors; when the distinctions of society, wealth, and station were forgotten, and each departing soldier was equally honored as a hero.—Napier Bartlett, reminiscence about the departure of recently enlisted men, in *A Soldier's Story of the War, Including the Marches and Battles of the Washington Artillery*, 1874.

Conscientious Objection

The passage of draft laws by both sides made it necessary for authorities in each sector to confront an issue new to national debate (see also Chapter 10, "The Home Front"). Certain religious groups—most notably, the Society of Friends (Quakers), as well as the Mennonites, Dunkards, and Shakers—were opposed to making or supporting war. Yet no legal provision existed, at first, for exempting conscientious objectors from conscription. In October 1862, the Confederacy did pass an act specifically exempting Friends (Quakers), Nazarenes, Mennonites, and Dunkards from military service, *provided that* they furnish substitutes or pay a tax of $500. But, as conditions became more precarious for the Confederacy, exemptions on religious grounds were entirely eliminated in the South. In the North, no formal legislation pertaining to conscientious objectors was passed until the Conscription Act was amended on February 24, 1864. The amendment provided that persons whose conscientious scruples against bearing arms had been supported by satisfactory evidence would be assigned to hospital duty or to the care of freedmen, or would be required to pay $300—which would be "applied to the benefit of the sick and wounded soldiers." This was not a perfect solution; even after the amendment was passed, conscientious objectors were drafted into the Union army. While they awaited the determination of their appeals for exemption, they were subjected to punishments by their military commanders. As in the Confederate army, these punishments ranged from relatively benign to brutal.

> Two sergeants soon called for me, and taking me a little aside, bid me lie down on my back and stretching my limbs apart tied cords to my wrists and ankles and these to four stakes driven in the ground somewhat in the form of an X. I was very quiet in my mind as I lay there on the ground [soaked] with the rain of the previous day, exposed to the heat of the sun, and suffering keenly from the cords binding my wrists and straining my muscles. . . . I wept, not so much from my own suffering as from sorrow that such things should be in our own country, where Justice and Freedom and Liberty of Conscience have been the annual boast of Fourth-of-July orators so many years.—Cyrus Pringle, Vermont Quaker drafted into the Union army July 13, 1863; diary entry, October 6, 1863, after his refusal to drill or join in any martial activity.

⋆ ⋆ ⋆

> After reaching camp again, I was taken before a court of inquiry and courtmartialed, and sentenced to be drilled alone two hours a day for a certain number of days. I again refused to drill or learn the art of war. For this I was threatened to be punished severely; but I still refused to bear arms. Finally, I was asked if I would assist in cooking for the company. To this I consented, and I was not punished.—John A. Showalter, Mennonite, C.S.A.; account of his draft into Confederate military service, quoted in Edward N. Wright, *Conscientious Objectors in the Civil War.*

Training

"A collection of untrained men," wrote Confederate general Richard Taylor, "is neither more nor less than a mob, in which individual courage goes for nothing. In movement each person finds his liberty of action merged in a crowd, ignorant and incapable of direction. Every obstacle creates confusion, speedily converted into panic by opposition." Hordes of untrained men poured into Confederate and Union camps early in the war, and many served under inexperienced or irresponsible officers who were incapable of training them. Soon, however, both sides began weeding out unsuitable officers and instituting a wide variety of regular drills that occupied a great many hours of camp life. (Even late in the war, the amount of time devoted to drill varied with circumstances and the inclinations of officers.) These hours of drill, in turn, inspired a perpetual undercurrent of soldierly grumbling—even though the men in the ranks gradually gained a higher appreciation for the purposes and benefits of training. Men were schooled in the proper handling of arms— how to fire small arms from standing, kneeling, and prone positions, and how to parry and thrust with a bayonet. They learned to salute and to march in formation. They drilled as companies, regiments, and brigades. They engaged in sham skirmishes, and sometimes in more elaborate sham battles geared to preparing them for the noise, terror, and confusion of actual combat.

> We had our first Brigade drill day before yesterday. There were in one field four Regts of Infantry, a Battery of Artillery, and a Squadron of Cavalry. . . . The Cavalry charged down on us and for the first time I saw something that looked like fighting. The artillery blazed away, and we had a regular sham battle. It was a beautiful sight, and our officers expressed themselves well satisfied with the drill. We began to think we can whip twice our weight in Rebels.—George W. Landrum, unit unknown, U.S.A.; letter to his sister, January 1862.

★   ★   ★

> We are at present encamped in the woods in a very healthy locality. We are required to drill for hours each day and the strictest observance to duty is most rigidly exacted of both officers and men. No pains is [sic] spared to reduce the troops to a state of perfect discipline. Every officer, elected or appointed, in the reorganization had to undergo examination before a board of officers. Many were rejected on account of incompetency. All this is as it should be. The better drilled our army is, the more effective it will be.—Rufus W. Cater, Nineteenth Louisiana Volunteers, C.S.A.; letter to "Cousin Fanny," June 22, 1862.

On the Move

"The hardships of forced marches," said Stonewall Jackson, "are often more painful than the dangers of battle." An authority on the matter, General Jackson led his men on some of the most spectacular marches of the entire war,

A Stormy March–Artillery–Spotsylvania Court House *was captured for posterity in this pencil drawing by Edwin Forbes, created May 12, 1864.*

achieving feats of locomotion that earned them the name "Jackson's Foot Cavalry." They marched under the general's prescribed regimen: two miles in fifty minutes, followed by a ten-minute rest—preferably lying flat on the ground, in which position, Jackson noted, "a man rests all over." Throughout the opposing armies, mileage and regimens differed widely, but, in this mobile war, *everybody* moved—across plains, through swamps, up and down mountains, and into cities (both friendly and hostile), through dust and grasping muck. Marching was one of the great inspirations for what was known as "simmering down"—getting rid of unnecessary accoutrements that inexperienced soldiers took with them into the army. But it wasn't just the unnecessary items that sometimes went: coats and other clothing so heavy with rain that they became burdens, or not needed on a broiling hot day, were often discarded on the move, actions that were often regretted later.

[A]rrived in Baltimore, Md., about mid-day, expecting to meet there the "Eighth New York, volunteers," who having their arms with them, were to escort us through the city, but we were disappointed in not meeting them, so we pursued our march . . . passing through Pratt street, where the "Sixth Massachusetts, volunteers," were attacked by a mob, in April, while on their way to Washington; but our regiment was not molested, although many a black look was cast upon us, they freely offered us ice-water and other refreshments, but Colonel Stiles had ordered the men not to accept anything from them, as he was afraid they would try to poison us.—Private John W. Jacques, Ninth New York State Militia, U.S.A.; diary entry, May 28, 1861.

★　　★　　★

At TWO o'clk am; we are aroused by the "Long Roll" and to make matters worse the rain is falling in torrents, tents are soon struck and long before light we are slipping and splashing through the rain and mud, no one can understand why the "long roll" was beat; some say that Colonel Mills is mad because the men straggled so yesterday. The men are all worn out by yesterdays march and this addition of rain and mud completely uses us up. Let a soldiers clothing and blankets get thoroughly saturated with water and it will add thirty pounds to his burden; then take a step of twentyeight inches and slip back twenty of them, try it all day long and see how pleasant it is. (not to a soldier.)—W. W. Heartsill Lane Rangers, C.S.A.; journal entry, June 3, 1863.

Pastimes—Sanctioned

Dancing and theatrical entertainments—amateur and professional (occasionally, musicians or actors would stage performances at camps)—were among the ways soldiers found to amuse themselves. Reading was a favorite pastime; in many camps, literary societies and debating clubs were formed. Games, such as baseball, cards, and checkers were played. In the winter, it was not unusual for snowball fights to become elaborate sham battles, officers and men dividing into separate "armies" and letting each other have it, with vigor.

The boys are having a grand cotillion party on the green in front of my tent and appear to have entirely forgotten the privations, hardships, and dangers of soldiering. . . . The dance on the green is progressing with increased vigor. The music is excellent. At this moment the gentlemen are going to the right; now they promenade all; in a minute more the ladies will be in the center, and four hands round. That broth of an Irish boy, Conway, wears a rooster's feather in his cap and has for a partner a soldier twice as big as himself whom he calls Susan. As they swing, Conway yells at the top of his voice: "Come round, old gal!"—Colonel John Beatty, Third Ohio Volunteer Infantry, U.S.A.; diary entry written in Murfreesboro, Tennessee, March 26, 1862.

Officers of the 114th Pennsylvania Infantry while away some off-duty hours playing cards in their camp near Petersburg, Virginia, August 1864.

A fellow by the name of Vaughn is amusing the boys just now, he is a perfect curiosity—born in the city of New York, partly raised on the ocean, and having the advantage of general information, and personal observation gave him a decided advantage over us poor back woods fellows that was wonderful, he could sing funny Songs, dance clog, make funny speaches, play tricks, turn somer saults, and other things two numerous to mention.—D. P. Hopkins, Texas Ranger, C.S.A.; diary entry, April 12, 1862.

Pastimes—Unsanctioned

Intensely devoted to gambling—of any sort, at almost any time and anywhere, Civil War soldiers were also prone to a number of other pursuits frowned upon officially. Drinking was among the foremost of these unsanctioned activities. Even men who had been strict teetotalers when they entered the service often succumbed after some time in the army; and soldiers became adept at circumventing the restrictions officially placed on the distribution of liquor. Soldiers also went to nearby towns to seek the comforts of prostitutes, and venereal disease became a problem in some army camps. There was a definite line, however, between unsanctioned pastimes and crime. Soldiers caught crossing that line—stealing from their comrades, for example—were ostracized by their fellows and strictly punished.

> If you think soldiering cures anyone of wild habits it is a great mistake, it is like Sending a Boy in the Navy to learn him good manners. We have Drummer Boys with us that when they came at first could hardly look you in the face for diffidence but now could stare the Devil out of contenance [sic] and cant be beat at cursing, swearing and gambling.—Alfred Davenport, unit unknown, U.S.A.; letter to his family, March 9, 1863.

★　　★　　★

> All officers belonging to the Texas Frontier Regiment . . . are hereby required to prohibit gaiming by horse racing . . . whenever the same in any company or detachment shall become a nuisance to the service. If any member of the Regiment should so far lose sight of the interest and reputation of the service as to be caught horse racing or gaiming while on duty . . . the same shall be punished by court martial or otherwise.—Colonel McCord [first name unknown], Texas Frontier Regiment, C.S.A.; order of June 17, 1863.

Victuals

Even in the Union army, where, except for occasional commissary and quartermaster snafus, provisions were usually adequate (if often unappetizing), soldiers regularly looked outside official channels for edibles (see also "Causes of Disease," "Food" in Chapter 9, "Medical Care and Medicine"). Packages from home were often requested and always welcome. Men with a little extra pocket change (not spent on gaming) sought out the wagons or tents of sutlers (civilian merchants who were allowed to sell goods in army camps), though they often grumbled—and not without cause—about the sutlers' exorbitant prices. In both armies, foraging was rampant, not only for food but for other necessaries as well. In 1862, Major General William Rosecrans described, in a letter to Ulysses S. Grant, how some of his soldiers had "attacked the pigs of Danville," killing "eight of the hairy rascals" before officers could convey the information that "these natives were noncombatants, as loyal as possible considering their limited information." "We . . . today marched into Pennsylvania," Virginia Captain William N. Berkeley wrote his wife during Lee's second invasion of the North. "We are sitting by a fine rail fire. It seems to do the men good to burn Yankee rails as they have not left a fence in our part of the country. . . . In spite of orders, they step out at night and help themselves to milk, butter, poultry, and vegetables."

A year ago to-day I cradled rye for Theron Wilson, and I remember we had chicken pie for dinner with home-made beer to wash it down. To-day I have hard-tack. Have I ever described a hard-tack to you? . . . In size they are about like a common soda cracker, and in thickness about like two of them. . . . But . . . The cracker eats easy, almost melts in the mouth, while the hard-tack is harder and tougher than so much wood. I don't know what the word "tack" means, but the "hard" I have long understood. . . . . . Very often they are mouldy, and most always wormy. We knock them together and jar out the worms, and the mould we cut or scrape off. Sometimes we soak them until soft and then fry them in pork grease, but generally we smash them up in pieces and grind away until either the teeth or the hard-tack gives up. I know now why Dr. Cole examined our teeth so carefully when we passed through the medical mill at Hudson.—Sergeant Lawrence Van Alstyne, 128th New York Infantry U.S.A.; diary entry, August 1, 1863.

★　　★　　★

Did you ever see a "Confederate bread-tray"? It is the bark, girdled from the body of a stout hickory tree. Dough "made up" in this, I have often seen wrapped around a straight stick & held before the fire to bake. I have, myself, fried "Slapjacks" and not bad slapjacks either in a tin plate, having "made the batter" in a tin cup. I have often made Sassafras tea in a tin cup. We get good coffee now however, which is, I assure you, very acceptable. I have often prepared what I deemed a nice *dish* by boiling Green apples & even green plums, in Sugar or molasses in the aforesaid tin cup.—Rufus W. Cater, Nineteenth Louisiana Volunteers, C.S.A.

Every mess has and carries a *grater*—the boys call them *armstrong mills*—and as the corn in the fields we pass has not been gathered these *mills* keep us supplied with meal when the commissariat fails to give us our *three dodgers* per day.—Douglas J. Cater (Rufus' brother), Nineteenth Louisiana

Volunteers, C.S.A.; letters to their "Cousin Fanny," June 22, 1862. (Rufus was killed in 1863, at Chickamauga.)

Battle and Aftermath

Skirmishes, cat-and-mouse pursuits, sharp clashes between small units, and the danger of sudden death from sniper fire, hidden explosive devices, or guerrilla ambush—all these made life precarious for Civil War soldiers. But these experiences paled beside the ferocity of the war's great clashes. Never before had the American continent seen battles of the scope and brutality of Shiloh, Fredericksburg, Antietam, Chancellorsville, and Gettysburg, in which tens—and sometimes hundreds—of thousands of men did their level best to annihilate each other. Prebattle stillness gave way to the pop of musket and rifle fire, and the roar and crash of artillery. "You cannot imagine the noise made by a hundred-pound rifle shell whizzing through the air. . .," wrote Union lieutenant Eugene Carter in May 1862. "It seems like three or four engines going at the top of their speed, and when it bursts—thunder and zounds, what a noise!" Battling men shouted, wounded men screamed—particularly when, as at the Wilderness in 1864, they were caught in woods

As Colonel Ambrose Burnside's regiment fights the battle of First Bull Run, wounded men are cared for by their comrades. Drawing by Alfred R. Waud, July 21, 1861.

that had been set ablaze by exploding shells. Lines broke, were reformed, broke again. Men surged forward and penetrated enemy defenses, or died at their base from murderous fire. When the firing stopped, parched and shaken survivors were confronted by appalling scenes of carnage—and often, with the knowledge that the battle would resume on the following day. Such experiences formed a border between combat veterans and others—though many Civil War soldiers still sought to describe what they had been through. "I think mother must be about sick of these tales of blood," wrote Sergeant Warren H. Freeman of Massachusetts; "certainly I am; but what can I do? I say as little, and endeavor to describe in the least revolting manner the horrible scenes around me. I trust I may be spared the task of speaking of or participating in any more such conflicts."

Colonel Andrews gave the order "Commence firing!" . . . The effect was tremendous; we actually tore great gaps through their ranks, and their whole right was wavering; if we could have had any support at that time, we might have charged and driven their line like sheep, but that wasn't in [commanding general Nathaniel] Banks' programme. Meanwhile, the roar of musketry was perfectly deafening; the noise of the bullets through the air was like a gale of wind; our poor men were dropping on every side, yet not one of them flinched but kept steadily at his work. Sergeant Willis of my company . . . , who was acting first sergeant, stood directly in front of me; he received a ball in his head and fell back into my arms saying, "Lieutenant, I'm killed!" and almost instantly died; he was a very handsome young fellow, and as he expired his face had a beautifully calm expression. I laid him down gently on the ground beside me and had hardly done so, when one of my corporals named Pierson, who was touching me on the left, was shot almost in the same place, but not killed. . . . I received two bullets through my trousers, but wasn't scratched.—Lieutenant Charles F. Morse, Second Massachusetts Infantry, U.S.A.; diary entry, August 13, 1862, describing the battle of Cedar Mountain, Virginia, August 9.

★   ★   ★

I send you just for a curiosity some Yankee letters picked up by one of my men on the battlefield. . . . I do not know what else to do with them except throw them away. There was a great deal of pilfering performed on the dead bodies of the Yankees by our own men. Some of them were left as naked as they were born, everything in the world they had being taken from them. I ordered my men to take their fine guns & canteens if they wished, but nothing else. These letters had fallen out of the poor fellow's pack & were lying loose about the ground. The only thing I took was a fine canteen which I cut off a dead Yankee who was lying on his face in our path as we marched along. Just the sight of the battlefield after the fight was in itself horrible. For 7 or 8 days after the battle every man I saw asleep appeared to me like a dead man.—Lieutenant James Billingslea Mitchell, Thirty-Fourth Alabama C.S.A.; letter to his father, January 13, 1863, after he participated in the battle at Stones River (Murfreesboro).

Visitors

Army camps attracted a wide range of visitors and hangers-on. "Camp followers" (civilians who followed armies for profit and employment) included sutlers (traveling merchants), laundresses, illegal whiskey dealers, bakers, barbers, private servants or slaves, and contract laborers. "Vivandiéres"—women, sometimes wearing their own stylized uniforms—performed various camp and nursing duties, and Union camps attracted thousands of "contrabands" and other refugees. Politicians, religious workers, newspaper reporters and artists, photographers chronicling the war—as well as those simply seeking some profitable portrait-photo business—could often be found in camps. And soldiers were sometimes visited by friends or family members, who would stay for a few days, or longer, depending on circumstances.

Frances [the writer's wife] was here three weeks lacking two days, and made three round trips to City Point and back during that time, so she rode 1800 miles on the boat and some 450 on the cars; it gave her a chance to see something of the country and a little of what war is. She went within six miles of Petersburg and twenty miles of Richmond.—Eugene H. Freeman, Transport Service, U.S.A.; letter to his parents, written in Alexandria, Virginia, October 30, 1864.

★　★　★

Are you making preparations to come out here this winter? Colonel Hunt will have his wife to come out again, and a great many other officers are arranging for their wives to come on soon. Some of them are here already, but I think it best for you to wait until winter puts a stop to military operations. When we left the Rappahannock River last fall some of the officers carried their wives along by having them wrap up well and putting them in the ambulance; and if you were here and we had to move I could easily take you along that way. I want you to come just as soon as circumstances will permit, but this war has taught me to bear with patience those things which cannot be avoided and not to be upset when my wishes cannot be gratified.— Dr. Spencer Glasgow Welch, Surgeon, Thirteenth South Carolina Volunteers C.S.A.; letter to his wife written from Petersburg, Virginia, October 25, 1864.

Mail Call

Keeping in contact with home was vital to soldiers' morale. Letters bolstered courage and brought the reassurance of familiar "voices" to men fighting their way through dangerous and unfamiliar ground. The mails often brought not only spiritual, but also material sustenance to camps: in "care packages" containing foodstuffs or articles of clothing. (Mail *from* camps could contain material comforts for the people at home. Many Union soldiers, particularly, arranged for portions of their pay to be sent back to sustain their families.) But armies on the move often suffered without mail for too long— especially if they weren't near railroads or if rail lines had been disrupted. Sometimes mail was diverted by the enemy, and sometimes the enemy seemed to be the postal system itself: "Oh these vexatious postal delays," Union soldier David Lane moaned to his diary, August 30, 1863, after receiving a letter dated more than two weeks before. "They are the bane of my life. I wonder if postmasters are human beings, with live hearts inside their jackets, beating in sympathetic unison with other hearts." But Lane was luckier than many Southern soldiers, whose region suffered increasing shortages—including shortages of paper and ink—caused by the Union blockade and the war's destruction, and whose families often lived in areas under Union occupation. "The accursed invader has destroyed the ferry boats at Vicksburg and at Natchez," wrote Confederate soldier Rufus Cater in 1862, "and we must wait and wait in prolonged, painful suspense till accident, or till the termination of the war shall enable us to get any tidings from home."

> Sometimes our expeditions and reconnoissances take us away from camp for a month at a time, so that we neither receive nor send any letters until our return. The men always become rough and somewhat demoralized on these occasions. . . . By and by we get back to camp, and a big mail awaits us. All the men will have letters from mothers, wives, sisters, and friends; and there is a change immediately. A great quietness falls on the men; they become subdued and gentle in manner; there is a cessation of vulgarity and profanity, and an indescribable softening and tenderness is *felt* rather than perceived, among them. Those who were ready to shoot one another a few

hours before are seen talking with one another, and walking together, sometimes with their arms around one another. It is the letters from home that have changed the atmosphere of the camp. If the people at home only knew what "a means of grace" their letters are to the men, they would write frequently.—Letter written from Memphis, Tennessee, December 20, 1862, from Union soldier "G. T." to Mary Livermore of the U.S. Sanitary Commission and published by her in *My Story of the War*, 1888.

★　　★　　★

Why don't some one from home write to me? I have not received a line since I left Chattanooga. I am beginning to fear the Yankees have come up from Florida & there has been a battle at home, as there seems to be a perfect cessation of all communications. You must not forget that I am always as anxious to hear from home as you are to hear from me.—Lieutenant James Billingslea Mitchell, Thirty-Fourth Alabama C.S.A.; letter to his mother, October 4, 1863.

Picket Duty: Eyeing the Enemy

As the advance guard for larger forces, pickets and videttes (mounted sentries sometimes placed even farther out than the dismounted pickets) drew

This engraving of a sketch by "Oertel" depicting a Meeting of Union and Rebel Pickets in the Rappahannock *appeared in* Harper's Weekly *in 1863.*

duty that could be extremely dangerous. Pickets would be out front if the enemy attacked, and they were often prime targets for snipers. As a first line of defense, pickets occasionally served as a "reception committee" for refugees and deserters from the enemy army. At times, they also turned a blind eye to men deserting their own ranks—or became deserters themselves. In quieter times, however, picket duty could be extremely tedious. Often closer to enemy guards than they were to their own units, Confederate and Union pickets occasionally talked, met, and swapped goods and gossip. Because such conversations could be a source of intelligence for the enemy—if, for example, a picket let slip information about imminent troop movements—such fraternization was frowned upon officially.

> The rebel pickets are in plain sight on the other side of the river . . . and though no communication is allowed, there is some talking across the water. . . . There is a good understanding between [the two forces], and neither side will fire unless an attempt to cross is made. The rebs go in bathing on their side of the river, and our boys do the same on ours. Colonel Vincent and his staff rode along the lines in plain sight and I followed carrying the flag, but they did not fire. I thought it was a risky piece of business, but I think I can go where he can.—Private Oliver Willcox Norton, Eighty-Third Pennsylvania Volunteers, U.S.A.; letter to his cousin, June 1, 1863.

★ ★ ★

> Our company have been on picket duty for the last two days of the week, the lines being on the bank of the river. The enemy are disposed to be very friendly, and try frequently to exchange papers with us, but we are not allowed to hold any communication with them. The day that I was on picket, two men came down to the river, somewhat intoxicated, and invited some of the Yankees over without my being apprised of it, until they had nearly reached this side. I was a little afraid the General might find it out, as the orders were so strict in regard to their crossing, and I can tell you I made the Yankee boys get back to their own side in a hurry.—Lieutenant Richard Lewis, C.S.A.; January 18, 1863.

Desertion

Holding men in the army, Abraham Lincoln reportedly said, was like attempting to shovel fleas. Inspired by fear, resentment, anger at officers and politicians, disgust and depression over battle losses or lack of movement, worry about loved ones at home (especially among Southern soldiers), and greed (especially among the Union "bounty-jumpers"), desertion was a problem that waxed and waned in the armies of both sides throughout the war. Though statistics are incomplete, especially for the Confederacy, it is estimated that, at times, 5,000 to 6,000 men per month were absent without leave from the armies of each side. An estimated 300,000 soldiers, two-thirds of them Union men, are believed to have deserted during the course of the war. Many men deserted temporarily. They took extra-long sick leaves or returned home to bring in harvests, to help their families fight off out-laws, or simply to visit during times when their units weren't campaigning. Particularly in the South, some men deserted infantry units and enlisted in cavalry regiments or in units assigned closer to their homes. Other deserters had no intention of returning. They disappeared into the countryside, often aided by civilians. Living in forests, caves, and swamplands, some of these men—in states from Florida to Pennsylvania—banded together for protec-tion against the forces sent to retrieve them. Some men fled the country. In March 1864, the *Congressional Globe* reported one U.S. senator's statement that 10,000 to 15,000 Union deserters were then living in Canada.

Both sides attempted to induce enemy soldiers to desert and instituted increasingly strict measures to prevent their own soldiers from deserting. Each side, for example, passed laws imposing fines and prison sentences on civilians convicted of assisting in or inducing desertion. Within the armies, provost marshals and others were assigned to prevent straggling, check fur-lough passes, and arrest deserters. In addition to the contempt and ostracism they often faced from their comrades when they were returned to their old regiments, those convicted of desertion were subject to increasingly harsh punishments: shaving the head, being forced to wear barrel shirts, branding, and flogging (very rare in the Union army, which had outlawed flogging in 1861). Execution for desertion, unusual at the beginning of the war, became much more common in 1863 and 1864. (Still, Union records list only 147 ex-ecutions for desertion during the war. The number of executions for deser-tion in the Confederacy is unknown but is assumed to be comparably small.)

A soldier of the [Fortieth] Indiana, who, during the battle of Stone[s] River, abandoned his company and regiment and remained away until the fight ended, was shot this afternoon. Another will be shot on the 14th in-stant for deserting last fall. A man in our division who was sentenced to be shot, made his escape. . . . . Hitherto deserters have been seldom punished, and, as a rule, never as severely as the law allowed.—Brigadier General John Beatty, Third Ohio Volunteer Infantry, U.S.A.; diary entry, April 10, 1863.

★　★　★

A man was shot near our regiment last Sunday for desertion. It was a very solemn scene. The condemned man was seated on his coffin with his hands tied across his breast. A file of twelve soldiers was brought up to within six feet of him, and at the command a volley was fired right into his breast. He was hit by but one ball, because eleven of the guns were loaded with powder only. This was done so that no man can be certain that he killed him. If he was, the thought of it might always be painful to him.—Dr. Spencer Glasgow Welch, Surgeon, Thirteenth South Carolina Volunteers C.S.A.; letter March 6, 1863.

Perseverance

Instead of the short war that had been generally expected, the people of the North and South endured four years of conflict and destruction, and massive loss of human life. Soldiers who were early volunteers, and who survived privations, wounds, disease, boredom, and the multiple uncertainties of wartime, saw fewer and fewer familiar faces, as comrades died or were disabled. The terror of battle—and the horror of battlefields after firing ceased—contributed to a numbing fatigue, especially after months turned to years and no end was in sight. Disturbing news from home—a particular affliction of Southern soldiers—sometimes made it difficult to continue, as did pleas from loved ones who felt their soldiers had done enough and should come home. Despite these terrible pressures, hundreds of thousands of men in uniform remained determined to continue until their side prevailed.

Who would have dreamed in '61 that those of us who started out to finish the war in the course of a three months' service, would still be in the field three years afterwards, with the task still unaccomplished? . . . Over one half of our original number has disappeared from the muster rolls; killed in action; died of wounds, of disease, of fatigue and exposure, or perhaps resigned, unable to stand in the constant shock of arms. This old state of Virginia has become a vast cemetery, in which thousands of once bright and ambitious men belonging to the army of the Potomac now lie scattered in its shady nooks or somber woods. . . . amongst the survivors, the excitement and enthusiasm of early days has long since passed away, but the resolve still remains, and until the work is done this army will never lay down its arms.—Josiah Marshall Favill, Fifty-Seventh New York Infantry U.S.A.; diary entry, January 1, 1864.

★   ★   ★

Our regiment, after passing through the trying ordeal of many bloody campaigns, and consecrating the plains of many of our hardest and most sanguinary struggles with so many of her noblest veterans, still can boast of chivalry enough to add another crown to her never fading honors in all re-enlisting for the war, without any tempting bounty or the promise of home greeting them again soon. So you see the spirit and determination the Yankees will have to conquer in the ensuing spring before they can wield their sceptre with full sway in the land of liberty and freemen.— Lieutenant Richard Lewis, C.S.A.; letter to his mother, February 19, 1864.

Under God

Religion was a large factor in the lives of both the Union and the Confederate soldiers throughout the war, though the character of religious observance tended to grow more flexible with time and exposure to camp life and campaigning. To many, battlefield triumphs were reassurances that the Almighty approved of the actions and way of life of their army and government; defeats were a remonstrance for imperfections. Reverses inspired the religious revivals that swept through the armies of both sides—but so did victories. After the Union loss at the battle of Chickamauga and the subsequent victory over Confederates besieging Chattanooga (particularly the "miracle of Missionary Ridge"), a revival swept through Federal armies in the West. Other revivals occurred in the Union and the Confederate camps in 1863 and 1864. The following order from Major General George B. McClellan was issued early in the war, after he had undergone a religious conversion. Constraints against Sunday operations also lessened over time.

The major-general commanding desires and requests that in future there may be a more perfect respect for the Sabbath on the part of his command. We are fighting in a holy cause, and should endeavor to deserve the benign favor of the Creator. Unless in the case of an attack by the enemy, or some other extreme military necessity, it is commended to commanding officers that all work shall be suspended on the Sabbath; that no unnecessary movements shall be made on that day; that the men shall, as far as possible, be permitted to rest from their labors; that they shall attend divine service after the customary Sunday morning inspection, and that officers and men shall alike use their influence to insure the utmost decorum and quiet on that day. . . . the observance of the holy day of the God of Mercy and of Battles is our sacred duty.—Major General George B. McClellan, General Orders, No. 7, September 6, 1861.

★ ★ ★

[E]very evening, about sunset, whenever it was at all possible, we would keep up our custom, and such of us as could get together, *wherever we might be*, should gather for prayer. . . . I may remark, as a notable fact, that this resolution was carried out *almost literally*. Sometimes, a few of the fellows would gather in prayer, while the rest of us fought the guns. Several times . . . we met *under fire*. . . . we held that prayer hour every day, at sunset, during the entire campaign. And some of us thought, and *think* that the strange exemption our Battery experienced, our little loss, in the midst of unnumbered perils, and incessant service, during that awful campaign, was, that, in answer to our prayers, "the God of battles covered our heads in the day of battle" and was merciful to us, because we "called upon Him." If any think this a "fond fancy" *we don't*. [emphasis in original]—William M. Dame, Richmond Howitzers, C.S.A.; recollection of campaigning in 1864, published in *From the Rapidan to Richmond and the Spotsylvania Campaign*.

Courage and Sacrifice

From the quiet courage of soldiers who did their duty faithfully through years of routine and hardship to the stunning bravery demonstrated time and again by men of both sides in the heat of battle, the Civil War was a testament to the capacity of "common" people to exhibit uncommon valor. This war saw the birth of the highest decoration awarded to United States military personnel, the Medal of Honor, established as a permanent medal in 1863. Bestowed, at first, without adequate or uniform criteria (some medals were rescinded by a military board in 1916), the Medal of Honor was awarded to 1,519 men and one woman who acted with exceptional courage during the war. Among the recipients: Joshua Chamberlain, colonel of the Twentieth Maine during the battle at Gettysburg, where, his men out of ammunition, he led a bayonet charge that kept Little Round Top in Federal hands; Galusha Pennypacker, who became a general at age twenty-one, after he was severely wounded leading an assault on the Confederacy's formidable

After taking leave from West Point to fight at First Bull Run, John Rodgers Meigs, son of the Union's quartermaster general, graduated first in his class and immediately returned to combat duty. Cited several times for gallantry, he was killed in the Shenandoah Valley October 3, 1864, by Confederate guerrillas. This photograph of Cadet Meigs, at his desk, examining a laboratory specimen, was probably taken in 1861.

Fort Fisher; and Sergeant William Carney of the Fifty-Fourth Massachusetts, who rescued the Union flag during his regiment's legendary assault on Fort Wagner. He was the first black soldier to be awarded the medal. In addition to the 1,196 medals awarded to officers and men of the U.S. Army for Civil War action, seventeen were awarded to U.S. Marines, and 307 to sailors. (Naval officers could not receive the medal until early in the twentieth century.)

Confederates did not have an equivalent decoration during the war, even though legislation passed October 13, 1862, authorized the president "to bestow medals, with proper devices, upon such officers . . . as shall be conspicuous for courage and good conduct on the field of battle, and also to confer a badge of distinction upon one private or noncommissioned officer of each company after every signal victory it shall have assisted to achieve." Medals and badges were designed, but—with the exception of a few struck for specific units, and not by the Confederate government—none was manufactured or awarded because of problems surrounding the efforts of Julius Baumgarten, a civilian selected to oversee the task. In any event, designation of the soldiers to be honored with "badges of distinction," which was to be done by vote of the regiments themselves, was often difficult. Some regiments forwarded lists of hundreds of names, each honored for different engagements. Others refused to participate. Even General Lee was uncomfortable at singling men out. "We have an army of brave men," he wrote. Nevertheless, on October 3, 1863, General Orders, No. 131 established a Confederate Roll of Honor, to include "the names of all those who have been, or may hereafter be, reported as worthy of this distinction." The names were to be read out during regimental dress parades. Comprising more than 2,000 names when fighting stopped in 1865, the roll contains no descriptions of specific acts of heroism. But Civil War history is rich with accounts of the valor of individual Confederate soldiers, who, like their Union counterparts, faced the horrors of war and the possibility of violent death with courage and resolution.

> There is a reality in Religion. . . . I am able to look death in the face without fear. . . . Sometimes when I think how you will miss me at home it is hard to be entirely willing to never see you and the boys again, but . . . we will meet again in the better land. . . . Kiss the boys for me. Goodbye, my dearest, best earthly friend. God Bless you.—Captain Thaddeus J. Hyatt, unit unknown, U.S.A.; letters to his wife, Mary, August 4 and 31, 1864, discussing his premonition of death. He was killed less than three weeks later in the third battle of Winchester, Virginia.

★　★　★

> Now, after all, Love, I think it best to trouble myself little with fears of danger, and to find happiness in the hope that you and I and our dear children will one day live together again happily and in peace. It may be, dearest, this hope will never be realized, yet I will cherish it as my greatest source of happiness, to be abandoned only when my flowing blood and failing breath shall teach me that I have seen the last of earth. All may yet be well with us.—Major Elisha Franklin Paxton, Twenty-Seventh Virginia, C.S.A.; letter to his wife, January 19, 1862. Promoted brigadier general, Paxton was killed at Chancellorsville, May 3, 1863.

SELECTED RESOURCES

This list is a representative sampling of the thousands of titles published about Civil War armies. See also the annotated book list in Chapter 13, "Studying the War: Research and Preservation."

Billings, John Davis. *Hardtack and Coffee; or the Unwritten Story of Army Life.* Boston: G.M. Smith & Co., 1887. Reprint: Lincoln: University of Nebraska Press, 1993.

Burton, William L. *Melting Pot Soldiers: The Union's Ethnic Regiments.* Ames: Iowa State University Press, 1988. Reprint: Bronx (NY): Fordham University Press, 1998.

Eicher, David J., and John H. Eicher. *Civil War High Commands.* Stanford, CA: Stanford University Press, 2001.

Fishel, Edwin C. *The Secret War for the Union: The Untold Story of Military Intelligence in the Civil War.* Boston: Houghton Mifflin Company, 1996.

Geary, James W. *We Need Men: The Union Draft in the Civil War.* DeKalb: Northern Illinois University Press, 1991.

Grimsley, Mark. *The Hard Hand of War*. Cambridge, England: Cambridge University Press, 1995.

Hauptman, Laurence M. *Between Two Fires: American Indians in the Civil War*. New York: The Free Press, 1995. Illustrated; maps.

Linderman, Gerald F. *Embattled Courage: The Experience of Combat in the American Civil War*. New York: The Free Press, 1987. Illustrated.

McCarthy, Carlton. *Detailed Minutiae of Soldier Life in the Army of Northern Virginia, 1861–1865*. Illustrated by William L. Sheppard; introduction to the Bison Book edition by Brian S. Wills. Lincoln: University of Nebraska Press, 1993. (Originally published: Richmond: C. McCarthy, 1882.)

McMurry, Richard M. *Two Great Rebel Armies: An Essay in Confederate Military History*. Chapel Hill: University of North Carolina Press, 1989.

McPherson, James M. *For Cause and Comrades: Why Men Fought in the Civil War*. New York: Oxford University Press, 1997.

Mitchell, Reid. *Civil War Soldiers*. New York: Viking, 1988.

Moore, Albert Burton. *Conscription and Conflict in the Confederacy*. New York: Macmillan, 1924. Reprint: New York: Hillary House, 1963.

Robertson, James I., Jr. *Soldiers Blue and Gray*. New York: Warner Books, 1988; Columbia: University of South Carolina Press, 1988; New York: Warner Books, 1991. Illustrated.

Sifakis, Stewart. *Who Was Who in the Civil War*. New York: Facts on File, 1988. Illustrated. (Also available as two separate vols.: *Who Was Who in the Union*. New York: Facts on File, 1988; and *Who Was Who in the Confederacy*. New York: Facts on File, 1988.)

Trudeau, Noah Andre. *Like Men of War: Black Troops in the Civil War, 1862–1865*. Boston: Little, Brown and Company, 1998. Illustrated; maps.

Welcher, Frank Johnson. *The Union Army, 1861–1865; Organization and Operations*. Vol. 1: The Eastern Theater. Vol. 2: The Western Theater. Bloomington: Indiana University Press, 1989–1993.

Wiley, Bell Irvin. *The Life of Johnny Reb: The Common Soldier of the Confederacy*. Indianapolis: Bobbs-Merrill, 1943. *The Life of Billy Yank: The Common Soldier of the Union*. Indianapolis: Bobbs-Merrill, 1952. Illustrated.

Wright, Edward Needles. *Conscientious Objectors in the Civil War*. New York: Oxford University Press, 1931.

WEAPONRY

The best protection against the enemy's fire is a well directed fire from our own guns.—Admiral David G. Farragut, General Order for the attack on Port Hudson, Louisiana, March 14, 1863.

In the 1840s, as American soldiers—including many future Civil War generals—fought in Mexico, new types of ordnance were being developed. These weapons offered increased range, better accuracy, and heavier striking power than the weapons chiefly relied on in the Mexican War. Yet, in 1861, American arsenals were filled largely with outdated weapons. Soon, however, impelled by the secession crisis, both sides began to modernize and streamline their arms manufacturing, and to dramatically increase their acquisition of weapons from foreign markets.

Two related innovations altered the complexion of the Civil War: the infantryman's percussion rifle-musket, and the minié ball (see the "Ordnance Glossary" on page 512 for definitions of terms). The minié ball (more accurately, a minié *bullet*, since it was conical, i.e., bullet-shaped) was invented by Frenchman Claude Etienne Minié in 1848. Smaller than the diameter of the rifle barrel—and therefore easier to load than previous bullets—the minié ball was characterized by a hollow base that filled with gasses when the gun discharged, forcing it to expand into the rifling of the barrel. The spiraled rifling then gave a spin to the bullet. This innovation made using rifled weapons in combat more practical. It also vastly improved the weapon's accuracy, range, and rate of fire. The minié ball was adopted by the United States soon after its introduction. Immediately, James H. Burton, then Acting Master Armorer at the Harpers Ferry arsenal in what is now West Virginia, began experimenting with improved designs for the projectile. In 1855, Burton's improved minié ball design was adopted by the U.S. Army. The Burton minié balls were used by Union and Confederate troops throughout the war.

Civil War soldiers used a wide variety of small arms, primarily single-shot muzzle-loading smoothbore muskets (and including, in the first year of the war, flintlock weapons dating from early in the century). Gradually, however, the percussion rifle-musket supplanted these older weapons. The new shoulder-fired rifle-musket—most often a Springfield or an Enfield model—was used by both sides and accounted for 85 percent of all combat casualties in the Civil War. The reasons for the popularity of the rifle-musket are simple: "rifled" firearms (those with spiral grooves inside the barrel) had more than twice the range of the old smoothbore weapons, and they could be more reliably and accurately aimed. The rifle-musket (combined with advances in artillery) turned the Civil War into a conflict that favored a defensive position.

The most popular rifle-musket models were the caliber .58 Models 1861 and 1863 Springfields, made at the Federal arsenal in Springfield, Massachusetts and by many contractors. The .577 Models 1853 and 1856 Enfields, imported from Great Britain, were the second most commonly used rifle-muskets. Both were about four and a half feet in length (the Springfield was an inch longer and weighed slightly less than the Enfield) and used the same size minié bullet. In the North, the Springfield arsenal produced 800,000 of the caliber .58 Models 1861 and 1863; another 600,000 were supplied by private contractors. Exact figures for the South are more difficult to determine, but the Confederate ordnance chief, Josiah Gorgas, reported that the main rifle manufacturing plant in Richmond issued 322,231 infantry arms from July 1, 1861, to January 1, 1865, as well as another 34,067 cavalry arms and 44,877 swords and sabers. Combined, the North and South imported an estimated 800,000 Enfield rifles from Great Britain. (Another popular import was the Lorenz rifle-musket. Some 325,000 of them were purchased during the conflict.) Neither side enjoyed a huge advantage by having these main-line infantry weapons. All of the new rifle-muskets were muzzle-loading (that is, loaded from the front, by ramming the projectile down the barrel). Innovations in firearm technology, which continued as the war progressed, included breech-loading (loading from the back) and repeating and rapid-fire weapons.

Small arms (portable weapons) were used by several branches of the service. All officers could carry sabers and swords (although they often relied on revolvers). Carbines (shorter versions of rifles and muskets, designed for ease

Federal soldiers stacked their Model 1863 Springfield Rifle-Muskets in the streets of Petersburg, Virginia, while they attended church services the day after the city fell in April 1865.

of use on horseback) and pistols were carried by Civil War cavalrymen but also saw service aboard navy ships and Revenue Service cutters. Each branch of the service had its own standard weapons. The primary weapon of the infantryman was his muzzle-loading rifle-musket, to which an eighteen-inch (or longer) bayonet could be attached. Mounted troopers in the cavalry carried carbines, sabers, and revolvers. This specialization in weaponry was mostly brought about by the kind of fighting done by each branch of the service.

A trained infantryman could fire three times a minute, a rate that typically exhausted their forty to eighty rounds of ammunition in half an hour or less. Cavalry needed lightweight weapons that were operable with one hand—preferably, repeating firearms. Cavalry sabers, if carried, were rarely used. Revolvers were much more popular; cavalrymen often carried up to six of them to use in close combat. Such clashes were rare, however. In the Civil

Sharpshooters chose their targets carefully and fired from well-chosen vantage points. This depiction of an Army of the Potomac sharpshooter on picket duty, published in Harper's Weekly, *November 15, 1862, was based on a painting by Winslow Homer.*

War, the cavalry's most effective role was in intelligence gathering and sabotage (see "Use of Cavalry," on page 342).

After the early months of the war, enlisted artillerymen were issued revolvers. In close combat, however, artillerymen fought with sponge staffs or rammers more often than with swords or firearms. They used their revolvers to dispatch critically wounded horses as often as they used them to shoot at the enemy.

Though early versions of rapid-fire "machine guns" were first employed in combat during the Civil War, use of the Gatling gun (invented by Richard Jordan Gatling in 1862) and the so-called Coffee Mill guns was extremely rare. None were issued to troops by either government. The few that were used were privately purchased by officers who were willing to try new equipment and new tactics. Land mines and floating sea mines (both called "torpedoes"), initially condemned as barbaric and immoral, were used effectively by the outgunned Confederate military. Hand grenades were employed occasionally during the conflict.

Early in the war, as both sides began to form huge armies, the demand for arms so overtaxed the production capacity of American arms manufacturers that both governments went to private sources, at home and abroad, to satisfy their needs. The result was an array of weapons, ranging from very good modern arms to antiquated pieces. The variety of weapons required a variety of ammunition (the U.S. Ordnance Bureau issued five different calibers of minié ball and three of round ball).

The United States government had always relied on private sources for most arms—except muskets (both smoothbore and rifled), which were manufactured at Federal armories in Harpers Ferry, Virginia, and Springfield,

Massachusetts. When Virginia seceded, the new Confederate Ordnance Bureau moved the Harpers Ferry rifle-making machinery to North Carolina and the rifle-musket machinery to Richmond, Virginia. The Springfield Armory was incapable of supplying all the arms needed by Union armies—particularly after arms stored in Federal arsenals in the South were confiscated by the seceding states. The War Department then began issuing contracts to private companies that could manufacture the rifles according to the government's patterns—a practice that continued until late in the war.

Lacking the North's industrial base, the Confederacy was even harder pressed to arm its troops. Though approximately 200,000 small arms (mostly old-fashioned smoothbore weapons) were seized from Federal arsenals, the number was a fraction of what was needed. (Incredibly, several thousand modern small arms were shipped to the Confederacy from plants in the North before the U.S. government stopped sales to companies or agents in Confederate states.) The artillery situation was even more dire. According to David McIntosh, a Confederate artillery colonel and historian, "The Government had no equipment of field-artillery to start with. What was found in the arsenals in the Southern States which fell into the hands of the Confederate Government, consisted of old iron guns mounted on Gribeauval carriages, manufactured about 1812, but there was not a single serviceable field-battery in any arsenal. . . . Not a gun or gun-carriage, and, except during the Mexican War, not a round of ammunition had been prepared in any of the Confederate States for fifty years." In time, new factories in Southern cities began to turn out acceptable arms, but the supply of Southern-made weapons never approached a level that would satisfy the Confederacy's needs.

Confederate purchasing agents scoured the markets of Europe for usable ordnance. Caleb House, acting on behalf of the Confederate government, secured the entire production run of high-quality London Armoury Enfield Rifles for 1861 and 1862 before Northern agents arrived in Great Britain. A large number of these arms made it through the blockade and ended up in the hands of Confederate troops. Throughout the war, Europe was the Confederacy's best source of modern arms. Ironically, the Union army was also a principal supplier. In early Confederate victories, hundreds of thousands of small arms and cannon were captured, enabling the Ordnance Bureau to replace outdated or inferior weapons with better arms. Stonewall Jackson's troops captured so many arms and so much equipment from Union armies in the 1862 Shenandoah Valley campaign that they called the Union general, Nathaniel Banks, "Commissary Banks." (However, it is also true that, over the course of the war, Confederates lost as many weapons as they captured—leaving weapons behind, for example, after the Southern defeats at Fort Donelson and Vicksburg.)

Historians have generally placed more emphasis on Northern arms production and use because figures available for Northern production and issue of military goods are far more complete and accurate than are those of the Confederacy. In the summer of 1866, the War Department issued its final report on the material cost of the war to Congress. The figures regarding weapons and accoutrements purchased and manufactured by the government are both staggering and sobering: hundreds of millions of bullets, more than a billion percussion caps (the small metal tubes that created the spark needed to ignite the gunpowder), more than 10,000 artillery pieces, and enough complete sets of leather gear (accoutrements) to equip nearly 2.5 million men.

Of more than 4,000,000 rifles and muskets accounted for, nearly 2,000,000 were purchased from domestic and foreign markets, at an average price of $16.58 each. (Bayonets were included where appropriate.) The most expensive weapon in this group was the Colt Revolving Rifle, at an average price of $44.34 each. The least expensive ($4.50 each) was the Tower (Enfield) Rifle (some 4,000 Southern agents rejected Tower Rifles because of their various manufacturing flaws, but Northern agents bought them in the belief that even an inferior weapon was better than no weapon at all). The 1,869,453 rifles and muskets purchased between January 1, 1861, and June 30, 1866, cost $30,990,623.11, according to the War Department report.

Many of the South's records were destroyed in the last months of the war, and no accurate reports covering the manufacture and distribution of weaponry (and related accoutrements) exist for the Confederacy. However, one report, prepared for the Confederate War Department in November 1863 by Chief of Ordnance Josiah Gorgas, did survive. The report lists the transactions of the Bureau of Ordnance since January of that year.

The figures Gorgas provided in the report offer an indication of the magnitude of the war, particularly when one notes the issue, in the single year covered, of nearly forty-five million small arms cartridges, 318,000 field artillery rounds, and 267,000 pounds of horseshoes. The Union defeat at Chancellorsville in early May had garnered the Army of Northern Virginia enough captured equipment to arm all of its infantrymen with rifles for the first time since the war began. Gorgas does not record, however, how much Confederate equipment was lost in the Confederate defeat at Gettysburg or the surrenders of Vicksburg and Port Hudson in July.

After the war, at the request of officers assigned to prepare a full record of "The War of the Rebellion" for the United States government, Gorgas constructed a report on Confederate arms and equipment from memory (see the following table). It shows that the Confederacy, despite its lack of factories and its ordnance poverty at the time of secession, achieved remarkable success in supplying its troops. The South did not lose a single battle in the entire war because its armies lacked arms or ammunition. Even hard-to-make items—including friction primers required to fire artillery pieces, and the fuses needed to make shells explode—were distributed in sufficient quantity, although they were not always of sufficient quality.

WEAPONRY IN THE CONFEDERACY: THE GORGAS REPORT

Item	Quantity
Columbiads and siege guns	341
Field artillery pieces	1,306*
Gun carriages	1,375
Caissons	875
Traveling forges	152
Sets of artillery harness	6,852
Rounds of artillery ammunition	921,441
Friction primers	1,456,190
Fuses	1,110,966
Portfires	17,423
Infantry arms	323,231*
Cavalry arms	34,067*
Swords and sabers	44,877*
Small arms cartridges	72,413,854
Percussion caps	146,901,250

*Includes items captured, repaired, and reissued.

MOST COMMONLY USED CIVIL WAR RIFLES AND MUSKETS

U.S. Regulation Model Muskets and Rifles

U.S. Rifle, Model 1841	.54 caliber muzzle-loading percussion rifle, popularly known as "Mississippi" or "Jaeger" rifle; 25,296 manufactured at Harpers Ferry between 1841 and 1855; 68,000 by private contractors; many rerifled to .58 caliber and equipped with bayonets between 1855 and 1862.
U.S. Rifle-Musket, Model 1855	.58 caliber muzzle-loading percussion rifle; 47,115 manufactured at Springfield, 1857–1861; 12,158 manufactured at Harpers Ferry, 1859–1861.
U.S. Rifle-Musket, Model 1861 ("1861 Springfield")	.58 caliber muzzle-loading percussion rifle; 265,129 manufactured at Springfield, 1861–1863; 643,439 delivered by private contractors, 1861–1865. A variation, the "Special Model 1861," designed by Samuel Colt, was a hybrid of Enfield and Springfield patterns.
U.S. Rifle-Musket, Models 1863 and 1864	.58 caliber muzzle-loading percussion rifle; 255,040 of these models produced at Springfield, 1863–1865.

British-Manufactured Rifles and Muskets

Muskets, Patterns 1839 and 1842	.753 caliber, muzzle-loading smoothbore; 4,000 imported by Charles Bulkley for sale to the U.S. government; unknown quantities purchased by the U.S. and Confederate governments.
Rifled Musket, Pattern 1853	.577 caliber; manufactured by Royal Small Arms Factory at Enfield, England, and by Belgian and British contractors; nearly 16,000 manufactured by Robbins & Lawrence, Windsor, Vermont; issued to U.S. troops during the Civil War.
Enfield Sergeants Rifle and Naval Rifle, Patterns 1856, 1858, and 1860	.577 caliber, used same ammunition as rifle-musket; manufactured by private gun makers in London; approximately 8,000 imported during the Civil War.
Enfield Volunteer Rifle	.577 caliber; similar to rifle-musket.

Other European Rifles and Muskets

Converted Infantry Musket, Models 1798, 1807, and 1828 (Austrian)	.71 caliber, muzzle-loading smoothbores converted to percussion.
Lorenz Rifle Musket, Model 1854 (Austrian)	.54 caliber muzzle-loading percussion rifle.
Prussian Rifle Musket, Model 1839/55	.69 caliber.

MOST COMMONLY USED CIVIL WAR RIFLES AND MUSKETS (CONTINUED)

Prussian Jaeger Short Rifle, Model 1835/47

.58 caliber, muzzle-loading percussion rifle.

Converted Infantry Musket, Model 1822 (French)

.69 and .71 caliber muzzle-loading smoothbores converted to percussion.

Infantry Musket, Models 1842, 1853, and 1857 (French)

.70 and .71 caliber, muzzle-loading smoothbores converted to percussion.

Shot rifle (Carabine) Model 1842; Short rifle (Carabine a tige) Models 1846 and 1853; Short rifle (Carabine de Vincennes) Model 1859 (French)

.69 and .70 caliber muzzle-loading percussion rifles.

U.S. Navy Rifles

Jenks Rifle

.54 caliber breech-loading percussion rifle; stamped "USN" and issued only to naval personnel.

Whitney Navy Rifle ("Plymouth")

.69 caliber muzzle-loading percussion rifle.

Sharps & Hankins Navy Cartridge Rifle, Model 1861

.52 caliber breech-loading percussion rifle using No. 56 Sharps & Hankins rimfire cartridge.

Confederate Rifles and Muskets

Fayetteville Rifle

.58 caliber muzzle-loading percussion rifle; made at the Fayetteville, North Carolina, Armory & Arsenal with machinery from Harpers Ferry designed to manufacture the U.S. Rifle, Model 1855; approximately 20,000 manufactured.

Richmond Rifle-Musket ("C.S. Richmond")

.58 caliber muzzle-loading percussion rifle; manufactured at Richmond Armory & Arsenal (using machinery taken from Harpers Ferry); an almost exact copy of the U.S. Rifle-Musket, Model 1855; approximately 42,000 manufactured, 1862–1865.

Tyler, Texas, Enfield Rifle and Austrian Rifle

.577 caliber muzzle-loading percussion rifle (Enfield) and .54 caliber rifle (Austrian); made at Tyler, Texas, Armory for Confederate Ordnance Department, 1864–1865.

Cook Infantry Rifle

.577 caliber muzzle-loading percussion rifle; patterned after the Enfield Short Rifle; at least 20,000 manufactured by Cook & Brother, Athens, Georgia.

Many other manufacturers also made arms for the Confederacy.

THE WHITWORTH "SHARPSHOOTER"

Among the Civil War's most highly regarded weapons was the Whitworth "sharpshooter" rifle, which is generally rated as the most accurate small arm used in the conflict. Imported from Great Britain by the Confederacy, the muzzle-loading Whitworth became a particularly deadly weapon. In the hands of skilled Confederate snipers, these rifles recorded hits at ranges in excess of 1,000 yards. Weighing less than ten pounds, the Whitworth was far more portable than the heavy-barreled, bench-rested civilian target rifles Northern marksmen used in infrequent attempts to match the Whitworth's range.

Confederate officers (particularly Irish-born Patrick Cleburne) so valued the Whitworth's accuracy that they were willing to pay $1,000 apiece for the rifle (a price that included accessories, tools, and 1,000 cartridges). Most of the rifles that successfully survived the dangerous trip through the Union blockade arrived equipped with open sights graduated up to 1,200 yards as well as detachable Davidson telescopic sights. Sharpshooters armed with these deadly weapons often singled out Union signalmen, pickets, artillerymen—and soldiers who showed themselves above the trench lines. (These targets were favored by sharpshooters of both sides; but only the Southern snipers used Whitworths.

The preferred weapon of the North's famous "Berdan Sharpshooters" was the breech-loading Sharps rifle. The term "sharpshooter" did not evolve from the name of the weapon.)

A typical case of effective Confederate sharpshooting took place during the Federal assault on Fort Sumter in August 1863. Union troops were engaged in the excruciating labor of digging out sand emplacements on Morris Island, where their immense Parrott artillery guns (which they would name Battery Rosecrans and Battery Meade after two Union generals) could be set up. The work became exceedingly dangerous, as well as backbreaking, when Confederate sharpshooters, even from a distance estimated at 1,300 yards, picked off every man who stuck his head above the sandbag parapet. Thus, all work had to be done at night, which considerably delayed the process.

Officers were also targeted by sharpshooters. The best-known Union victim of a Confederate sniper wielding a Whitworth was Major General John Sedgwick, commander of the Sixth Corps of the Army of the Potomac, who was killed on May 9, 1864, near Spotsylvania Court House, Virginia. Just moments before, to encourage his men, he had said, "Don't worry, boys. They couldn't hit an elephant at this range."

Repeating Rifles

Repeating rifles gave the units carrying them a striking power never before known in warfare. The most common repeater of the Civil War, the Spencer (manufactured in rifle and carbine versions), held seven rounds that could be fired in well under a minute. The Henry Rifle (see page 516) held sixteen rounds—one in the chamber and fifteen in the tubular magazine beneath the barrel. Both designs astounded and dismayed Confederate soldiers, who called them "the damnyankee rifles you load on Sunday and fire all week."

This revolution in firearms technology almost did not happen. General James W. Ripley, U.S. Army chief of ordnance, opposed adopting magazine-fed arms because they were "too heavy" and the need for special ammunition created problems for field ordnance officers. The guns were also more complicated pieces of equipment and tended to break down more frequently than standard muzzle-loader single-shot muskets. Ripley, in concert with Quartermaster General Montgomery Miegs and others, also feared that the rapid-fire capabilities of these arms would encourage soldiers to waste ammunition—to allow the volume of fire they could produce to take the place of well-aimed shots at the enemy. Nevertheless, after voicing disapproval, Ripley obeyed without objection when instructed to place the War Department's first order for 10,000 Spencer Rifles (repeating carbines) in December 1861. This fact refutes the popular legend that Abraham Lincoln personally ordered the army to purchase Spencer Rifles after test-firing one on the White House lawn in August 1863. The first government testing of the new rifle had actually taken place at the Washington Navy Yard in June 1861, under the direction of Captain (later Admiral) John Dahlgren. On the basis of Dahlgren's positive report, the Department of the Navy ordered 700 Spencer Rifles with sword bayonets, and 70,000 cartridges, that same month—six months before Ripley's order.

U.S. General in Chief George McClellan ordered separate testing for the army to begin in November 1861, under the direction of Captain (later General) Alfred Pleasonton. Pleasonton concluded that ". . . the [Spencer] rifle is simple and compact in construction and less liable to get out of order than any other breech-loading arm now in use." Breech-loading was a time-saving improvement over muzzle-loading; a soldier could load his gun, with both the projectile and the gunpowder, from the rear of the barrel. Pleasonton recommended adopting the .56–56 Spencer Rifle for the infantry and the carbine of the same caliber for the cavalry. Although the War Department accepted his recommendation and issued its first order during the next month, the first Spencer Rifle used in combat was not a government-purchased weapon. Sergeant Francis O. Lombard, First Massachusetts Cavalry, fired his Spencer Rifle in a skirmish near Cumberland, Maryland, on October 16, 1862, two months before the government received the first of its Spencers. Lombard's rifle had been a gift from his personal friend, Christopher Spencer, the weapon's inventor.

The Spencer became a popular weapon. Colonel John T. Wilder arranged personal loans to purchase Spencers for the members of his "Lightning Brigade" when he was not able to get them from the government. General James H. Wilson had such faith in them he made sure every man riding on his 1865 Selma (Alabama) raid carried a Spencer. General George A. Custer attributed the Union cavalry's success at Gettysburg to the fact that the men of the Fifth Michigan Cavalry were armed with Spencer Rifles, which were, in his opinion, "the most effective firearm our cavalry can adopt." Perhaps the ultimate tribute came from the men who carried and used Spencers during the war. Sergeant James Larson, Fourth U.S. Cavalry, wrote, "[They] were to us our medals of honor, our Spencer carbines."

Small Arms: Carbines and Musketoons

The four- to five-foot-long rifles and muskets carried by Civil War infantrymen were difficult, if not impossible, to load and fire on horseback. For this reason, musketoons and carbines (short muskets and rifles) were issued to cavalrymen and, sometimes, to artillerymen.

In the Civil War era, American cavalry fought mostly as mounted infantry; they used their horses to transport them quickly from one place to another, but dismounted to fight. During the war, many cavalry leaders used a combination of mounted and dismounted tactics in battle. Confederate cavalry leaders such as J. E. B. Stuart and Wade Hampton used the saber, revolver, and carbine almost equally. John Mosby and John Hunt Morgan relied heavily on the revolver, and Nathan Bedford Forrest had his men do most of their fighting on foot, using the carbine or rifle. Some Union cavalry leaders, notably John Buford, successfully adhered to the prewar mounted infantry technique; he ordered his men to dismount in battle and fight with carbines and rifles. On the eve of the battle at Gettysburg, his dismounted men skirmished with the main Confederate force, delaying the enemy as the main Union army positioned itself for battle.

During the prewar search for the ideal cavalry weapon, inventors and innovators flocked to the War Department with a variety of breech-loading and, later, repeating firearms designed specifically for use by mounted men. When the war broke out, the arsenals of both the Union and the Confederacy devoted most of their production capacity to arming the infantry. As a result, private manufacturers supplied most cavalry arms.

Arming and equipping a cavalryman was more than three times more expensive than preparing an infantryman for battle. One reason was the cost of

MOST WIDELY USED CARBINES AND MUSKETOONS

U.S. Carbines and Musketoons

U.S. Musketoon, Model 1847 — .69 caliber muzzle-loading percussion smoothbore (some were rifled); designed for use by cavalry, artillery, and engineers.

U.S. Cavalry Rifled Carbine, Model 1855 — .54 caliber muzzle-loading percussion rifle.

Burnside Carbine, First through Fifth Models, 1861–1864 — .54 caliber breech-loading percussion rifle using a tapered brass cartridge; more than 55,000 Fourth and Fifth Models were purchased during the war.

Gallager Carbine, Model 1860 — .50 caliber breech-loading percussion rifle using "break open" action and brass or Poultney foil-and-paper cartridge and conical ball; 17,782 were purchased by the U.S. War Department.

Maynard "Second Model" — .50 caliber breech-loading percussion rifle, one of the earliest models using a separately primed metallic cartridge; more than 20,000 were purchased by the U.S. War Department.

Sharps Carbine, Models 1852, 1859, and 1863 — .52 caliber breech-loading percussion rifle using linen or nitred paper cartridge with pointed bullet; nearly 80,000 Sharps Carbines, in various models, were purchased during the war.

Smith Carbine — .50 caliber. Invented by a dentist, this breech-loading percussion rifle used India rubber cartridges (heavy paper and foil were also used) with pointed bullets; more than 30,000 were purchased during the war years, 1861–1865.

Metallic Cartridge (Rimfire) Carbines

Sharps & Hankins Cartridge Carbine, Model 1862 — .52 caliber single-shot using No. 56 Sharps & Hankins rimfire cartridge.

Spencer Repeating Carbine — .52 caliber seven-shot using .56-.52 Spencer cartridge; also made in 1865 by Burnside Rifle Co. in .50 caliber using .56-.50 Spencer cartridge.

Imported Carbines and Musketoons

Enfield Artillery Musketoon, Pattern 1856 — .577 caliber British muzzle-loading percussion rifle with a twenty-four-inch barrel that used the same cartridge as the Enfield rifle musket; 500 were imported by the North, significant numbers by the South.

Enfield Cavalry Carbine, Pattern 1858 — .577 caliber British muzzle-loading rifle that used the same cartridge as the Enfield rifle musket; fewer than 200 were purchased by the North, but significant numbers were imported by the South.

Confederate Carbines and Musketoons

Richmond Carbine — .577 caliber muzzle-loading percussion rifle; more than 2,500 were manufactured at the Richmond Armory and Arsenal by 1863.

Confederate (Richmond) Sharps Carbine — .52 caliber; a copy of the Sharps Carbine, Model 1859; approximately 3,000 were manufactured by the S. C. Robinson Arms Manufactory, Richmond, Virginia.

carbines compared with muskets. The average cost of a carbine used in Federal service was $23.51, compared with an average of $16.58 for a musket. Because so many of the cartridges for Northern carbines were made with metallic or India rubber cases rather than paper or linen, the average cost of a carbine bullet was 2.4 cents—nearly twice the cost of a round of musket ammunition.

The most common government and commercial carbines issued during the war were the Sharps, the Spencer, and the Burnside (designed by General Ambrose E. Burnside) in the North, which had an overwhelming advantage in numbers of carbines. In the South, the Richmond Armory and Arsenal had developed a .577 caliber carbine by 1863, and Robinson Arms Manufactory, a private firm in Richmond, Virginia, had devised a copy of the Sharps carbine used by the North, though the numbers manufactured were minute compared with those produced in the North or to the Enfield musketoons and carbines imported from Great Britain.

How Soldiers Fired Rifle-Muskets and Repeaters

A typical rifle-musket of the Civil War era was a single-shot muzzle-loader that required an intricate loading drill. The soldier first tore open a paper cartridge with his teeth, then poured the powder charge down the barrel, removed the paper from the bullet, set the bullet (nose upward) in the barrel, rammed it firmly against the powder charge with his ramrod, withdrew the ramrod from the barrel, cocked the rifle, placed a musket cap (also called a percussion cap) on the cone or nipple, aimed, fired, and started the entire procedure again. A well-trained soldier could fire his rifle-musket three times a minute.

Repeating rifles and carbines held multiple, self-contained cartridges; no percussion cap was needed to fire them. The soldier simply cycled one of the rimfire cartridges into the weapon's chamber, aimed, fired, and cycled the next round into position.

Small Arms: Pistols and Revolvers

Although the terms "pistol" and "revolver" are used synonymously in Civil War records, they actually designate two different types of weapons. "Pistols" were single-shot muzzle-loading arms; "revolvers" were repeating arms that held multiple charges in a revolving cylinder. With few exceptions, the revolvers used during the war were percussion arms loaded with linen- or paper-wrapped cartridges and separate percussion caps for each chamber of the cylinder.

SMALL ARMS: PISTOLS AND REVOLVERS

U.S. Revolvers

Beals (Remington-Beals) Navy Revolver, Model 1858	.36 caliber; percussion, six-shot, single action; this was the first of a long line of Remington Revolvers purchased by the U.S. War Department; 12,251 Beals Army and Navy models were purchased in 1860–1862.
Beals (Remington-Beals) Army Revolver, Model 1858	.44 caliber; similar to the Beals Navy model, with a slightly larger frame.
Colt Army Revolver, Model 1847	.44 caliber; percussion, six-shot, single action; used paper cartridges and round balls; initially manufactured at the Eli Whitney Armory, Whitneyville, Connecticut, later by Colt in Hartford, Connecticut.
Colt Model 1851 ("Navy")	.36 caliber; percussion, six-shot; approximately 17,000 purchased.
Colt Army Revolver, Model 1860 ("New Model Army")	.44 caliber; six-shot, single action. More than 100,000 purchased.
Colt Navy Revolver, Model 1861 ("New Model Navy")	.36 caliber; similar to the New Model Army; 2,056 were purchased by the U.S. War Department in 1862–1863.
Remington Navy Revolver, Model 1861	.36 caliber; similar to the Remington Army Revolver; approximately 5,000 were manufactured in 1862.
Remington "New Model" Army Revolver (1863)	.44 caliber; similar to the Model 1861; 125,314 Remington Revolvers were purchased by the U.S. War Department during the war.
Savage Navy Revolver	.36 caliber, six-shot, single action but fitted with a ring trigger that cocked the hammer and rotated the cylinder; 11,284 purchased by the U.S. War Department early in the war.
Starr Army Revolver, Model 1858	.44 caliber; six-shot, double action; 47,952, in various patterns, were purchased by the U.S. government.
Whitney Navy Revolver	.36 caliber; six-shot, single action; approximately 32,000 were manufactured in Whitneyville, Connecticut.

Imported Revolvers

Adams (Beaumont-Adams) Army Revolver, Model 1857	.44 caliber; five-shot, double action; Kerr (English) patent; some Adams revolvers were imported, others were manufactured in the United States under license.
Deane (Deane-Harding) Army Revolver, Model 1858	.44 caliber; five-shot, double action.
Lefaucheaux Revolver, Model 1855	.45 caliber; pinfire; six-shot, single action (this was the regulation French naval weapon).

Confederate Revolvers

Rigdon, Ansley & Co. Revolver	.36 caliber; six-shot, single action; copy of the Colt Navy Revolver, Model 1861.
Griswold & Gunnison Revolver	.36 caliber; six-shot, single action; copy of the Colt Navy Revolver, Model 1861; made in Griswoldville, Georgia, 1862–1864.
Spiller & Burr Revolver	.36 caliber; six-shot, single action; copy of the Whitney Revolver; manufactured under the supervision of James H. Burton (former Master Armorer at the Harpers Ferry Arsenal) in Richmond, Atlanta, Macon, and Augusta. Approximately 1,400 made on a contract for 15,000 pieces.

Imported Confederate Revolvers

The Confederacy imported many of the same models of revolvers as did the United States. In addition, they imported Devisme, Raphael, Perrin, and Houllier & Blanchard arms manufactured primarily in France—but in quantities too small to categorize them as "regulation" Confederate sidearms.

The most popular revolvers were those manufactured by Samuel Colt in his Hartford, Connecticut, factory. The vast majority of the Colt revolvers purchased for military use were either "Army" (.44 caliber) or "Navy" (.36 caliber) models. In the context of revolvers, these terms reflect only the caliber of the weapon—not their exclusive use by any particular branch of the service.

No U.S. government armory produced pistols or revolvers during the Civil War, and less than one percent of the arms manufactured by the government prior to the war were pistols. Largely because pistols and revolvers were officers' weapons, the government, as a rule, allowed individuals to purchase them from private sources. During the war, however, the revolver evolved into a primary weapon for the cavalry of both sides. To satisfy the demand for these arms, both the Union and the Confederacy placed contracts with private firms, an arrangement that led to an assortment of arms actually being used in battle. The models listed in the table on page 499 were purchased and issued in significant quantities by national or state governments during the war.

Swords and Sabers

With the exception of cavalrymen, few Civil War soldiers used swords (straight blade) and sabers (curved blade) as weapons. For officers and upper-level noncommissioned officers, they were badges of rank, used most often on formal occasions. Although sergeants, musicians, and medical staff were authorized to wear swords, few, if any, did so in the field. Artillerymen, too, were authorized to wear a slightly shorter saber than the model carried by the cavalry. By mid-1863, however, most enlisted men in the artillery branch had discarded sabers and replaced them with revolvers.

Scabbards worn by dismounted officers and noncommissioned officers most often were made of leather and had metal reinforcements at each end because of the scabbards' light weight. Cavalrymen and artillerymen used iron or steel scabbards, which were better able to withstand repeated contact with the horse and saddle. Unlike the ornamental swords of other branches of service, cavalry sabers often were used in charges, countercharges, and confusing melees in which firearms could harm friends as well as foes. Cavalry sabers also came equipped with a knotted cord, intended to be looped around the trooper's wrist to prevent his losing the weapon if it were knocked from his hand in battle.

Nearly all of the swords and sabers issued to troops in America were patterned after French models. The primary domestic manufacturer of swords and sabers was Ames Manufacturing Company of Chicopee Falls, Massachusetts. The more expensive swords carried by officers were, for the most part, imported from Belgium, Great Britain, France, and Germany. In addition, communities and military units often purchased engraved "presentation swords" for popular officers. These fancy, jeweled pieces—unsuitable for field use even as a badge of office—offered scores of different configurations.

Because Mexico, against which the United States fought in 1846–1848, had regiments of lancers in their cavalry, the U.S. War Department toyed with the idea of creating lancers in 1861. Only one regiment, the Sixth Pennsylvania Cavalry, ever carried lances in the field, however, and their lances were replaced with Sharps Carbines in May 1863. More than three-quarters of the lances purchased by the Ordnance Department were never issued. Cutlasses (short, curved swords) were designated for issue to the navy.

In this category of weaponry, the items purchased in the largest numbers by the U.S. Ordnance Department were light cavalry sabers (283,285) and cavalry sabers (189,114). A total of 524,209 swords, sabers, lances and cutlasses were purchased by the U.S. Ordnance Department during the war, at a cost of $3,079,414.60.

Making Gunpowder

In the 1860 census, only two gunpowder mills were noted in the South—one in Cheatham County, Tennessee, and the other in Pickens District, South Carolina. The same census noted many Northern gunpowder mills—sixty-seven in one Pennsylvania county alone. The mills needed three ingredients to operate: nitre (more commonly called saltpeter), charcoal, and sulphur. Charcoal (preferably made from willow, dogwood, or alder) and sulphur were in plentiful supply in the South, but nitre/saltpeter, the most important ingredient (comprising three-quarters of gunpowder), was not. Before the war, the United States had imported most of its saltpeter. After April 1861, the Union blockade made importation problematic for the South. In April 1862, the Confederate Congress created a Nitre Bureau, headed by Isaac M. St. John, a civil engineer from Georgia. The government announced that it would pay 75 cents a pound for nitre, and caves in northern Alabama, particularly in Jackson County, were reopened for nitre mining, as were some in Tennessee. By August 1862, gunpowder production in the South had reached an estimated 1,600 pounds a day. It has been estimated, based on existing records, that the Confederacy produced 1,735,531.75 pounds of saltpeter and imported 1,720,072 pounds between April 1861 and September 30, 1864.

The process of obtaining usable saltpeter began with the mining of nitre-bearing dirt, usually from an underground cave. (In the South, most of this labor was done by slaves.) After the dirt was hauled from the cave by tram, it was dumped into hoppers and then leached with water until it formed a "beer" of calcium nitrate. This "beer" was mixed with leachwater containing wood ashes or potash, causing a chemical reaction that formed potassium nitrate, which was then boiled until crystals of saltpeter formed. This crude saltpeter was boxed and shipped. In the South, most of it ended up in Augusta, Georgia, at the Confederacy's largest powder mill, run by George W. Rains.

War Rockets and Hand Grenades

When the Civil War started in 1861, a new weapon had superseded the noisy, inaccurate, and generally ineffective Congreve rocket used by the British in the Napoleonic wars and the War of 1812. Designed by British engineer William Hale in 1844, and improved by Captain (later Admiral) John A. Dahlgren in 1847, the "Hale Patent Rocket Launcher, 2.5 Inch" consisted of a metal tube, open at the breech and elevated by an adjustable bipod mount at the muzzle. The shooter placed the rocket in the breech, adjusted the elevation using a sight mounted on top of the launching tube, and launched the seven-inch or ten-inch-long rocket. Once launched, a vane in the exhaust nozzle stabilized the rocket by causing it to spin like a rifle bullet. Like the Congreve before it, the Hale was inaccurate and too small to be an effective substitute for artillery. Hale Rocket Launchers, in a number of different calibers, saw use, primarily, by the U.S. Navy.

Hand grenades were used mostly during siege or trench warfare, as at Vicksburg, Atlanta, and Petersburg. The most common Civil War hand grenades—"Ketcham" for the Union and "Rains" for the Confederacy—resembled fat metal cigars with arrowlike wooden tails and paper wings to stabilize them in flight. Both types carried an internal exploding charge and a detonator connected to a plunger in the grenade's nose. When the nose struck the ground, the plunger was forced upward, where it impacted

The Augusta [Georgia] Powder Works, designed by Colonel George Washington Rains, produced 2.75 million pounds of gunpowder for the Confederacy. In 1870, the U.S. Ordnance Bureau removed the machinery and razed the plant.

upon the detonator and exploded the main powder charge. The most common sizes were one-, three-, and seven-pounders.

The Adams and Confederate Spherical Grenades resembled miniature cannonballs. They were detonated by paper fuses that were lit before the device was thrown. The Haynes Excelsior patented grenade came in three pieces. A two-piece threaded outer shell surrounded an inner sphere that contained the powder charge and was studded with nipples for percussion caps. The grenade detonated when one of the percussion caps hit against the outer casing as the device struck the ground. Hand grenades were most useful in repelling assaults on fortified positions. In situations appropriate for hand grenades, it was not uncommon for soldiers to light the fuses on artillery shells and roll them down the parapets of their fort into the ranks of the attacking enemy below.

Common Artillery Pieces

Field-artillery is made up of three kinds—viz., the mounted batteries, whose cannoneers usually march on foot, but during the rapid movements ride upon the carriages and caissons, and which serve with the regiment, division, and army corps; the horse-batteries, whose cannoneers are provided with saddle-horses, and which are especially intended for service with the cavalry; and the batteries of position, consisting of the heaviest field-guns, intended especially for action against the enemy's material defences.—Major General George B. McClellan, *McClellan's Own Story*, 1887.

Light Artillery

The most widely used field artillery piece during the Civil War was the "Napoleon," officially designated the "Twelve-Pounder Field Guns, Model 1857." A twelve-pounder smoothbore with a range of 1,619 yards, the Napoleon derived its name from French emperor Louis Napoleon (Napoleon III), who underwrote its development in France. The term "twelve-pounder" (4.2-inch) referred to the weight of the projectile it could fire, and the term "smoothbore" indicated that, like smoothbore muskets, the barrels were not rifled. By 1863, Napoleons made up about 40 percent of the artillery used by both the Union Army of the Potomac and the Confederate Army of Northern Virginia. Bronze-barreled Napoleons were manufactured by both sides—more than 1,000 in the North, and between 500 and 600 in the South. Confederate Napoleons were readily identified by the absence of the characteristic muzzle swell on pieces made in the Union. Some Confederate Napoleons, products of Richmond's Tredegar Iron Works, were made of iron.

Often called the "workhorse" of Civil War artillery, the Napoleon was one of a number of smoothbore cannon used during the conflict. Like smoothbore small arms, Napoleons were not as accurate as rifled guns and did not have their range. However, Napoleons could be loaded faster than most artillery, and they were more efficient in defending against an infantry assault.

Of all American-made field artillery pieces, the Parrott Gun (also called the Parrott Rifle) was the most distinctive in appearance. Because cast-iron rifled guns were prone to burst when fired, Robert P. Parrott developed a system, patented in 1861, that strengthened them: a wrought iron reinforcing band was wrapped around the breech, thus giving the Parrott Rifle its distinctive look. These guns were cheaper to manufacture and more accurate than bronze smoothbores, but they continued to exhibit a disconcerting tendency to burst in action. Still, they were readily available and saw wide use in ten-pounder and twenty-pounder versions.

Among the best artillery pieces of the war was the three-inch Ordnance Rifle, patented by John Griffen in 1855. Made of wrought iron rather than cast iron, these guns had much stronger barrels than Parrotts. Of more than 1,000 Ordnance Rifles purchased by the U.S. government during the war, only one is known to have burst in action. That gun burst at the muzzle during the Wilderness fighting of 1864.

In addition to its reliability, the Ordnance Rifle was 100 pounds lighter than the Parrott and, therefore, more maneuverable. The fact that the gun rarely burst made up for its shorter range—1,835 yards at five degrees elevation, compared with the Parrot's 2,000-yard range. The U.S. War Department so prized the three-inch Ordnance Rifle that it continued to issue the model to the field artillery until well into the 1890s, when it was replaced by steel, breech-loading cannon. All open contracts for Parrott Rifles, by contrast, were canceled in June 1865.

These three weapons—the Napoleon, the Parrott Rifle, and the Ordnance Rifle—made up the bulk of Civil War field artillery, but other types of guns were also used. The Confederacy, hard-pressed to equip artillery units, used a number of outmoded bronze howitzers throughout the war. Both sides imported limited numbers of Whitworth Guns, breech-loading rifled cannons (chiefly six-pounder and twelve-pounder) that were extremely accurate, long-range weapons with a hexagonal bore that fired an elongated projectile, called a bolt. (Whitworth Guns imported after 1863 were muzzle-loaders.)

Heavy Artillery (Mortars; Siege and Seacoast Cannon)

Unlike field artillery pieces, siege and seacoast cannon and mortars were large, extremely heavy, and impossible to move quickly. As a result, their use was confined mostly to fortress defenses and long-term siege operations. The most common of the seacoast cannon was the Columbiad. First introduced into United States service in 1811, it was the country's primary defensive weapon for many years. The heavily reinforced breech of the Columbiad, necessary to keep the gun from bursting under the ignition pressure of several pounds of gunpowder, gave it a distinctive "bottle" shape. The Civil War Columbiads were:

- Model 1844 eight-inch and ten-inch (range, 1,800 yards).
- Model 1858 eight-inch and ten-inch.
- Model 1861 Rodman cast iron eight-inch, ten-inch, and fifteen-inch (range 4,680 yards at twenty-five degrees of elevation).
- Confederate copies of the Rodman in eight-inch and ten-inch versions.

The "Rodman" designation for Columbiads derived from U.S. ordnance engineer Captain (later General) Thomas J. Rodman, who perfected a method of casting the large guns, cooling them from the inside out—running

The First Connecticut Heavy Artillery fired this 17,000-pound, thirteen-inch seacoast mortar, known as the "Dictator," from a reinforced railroad car on the Petersburg & City Point Railroad.

a stream of water through the inside of the barrel while still keeping the outside hot. This regulated the crystallization of the metal so the guns could stand more internal pressure without breaking. Rodman also developed large-grain gunpowder for use with big guns.

The Cold Spring Foundry (across the Hudson River from the U.S. Military Academy and thus also known as the West Point Foundry) also produced Parrott Guns in 100-pounder (6.4-inch, range, 8,000 yards), 200-pounder (eight-inch), and 300-pounder (ten-inch) versions. All three of these guns had a distressing tendency to burst when fired and posed a greater danger to their own crews than to the enemy. The brittle cast iron used in manufacturing Parrotts simply could not handle the pressure generated by the ignition of a 100- to 250-pound powder charge.

The famous "Swamp Angel," used during the siege of Charleston, South Carolina, was an eight-inch 200-pounder Parrott Gun with such presumed power that Federal leaders authorized a grueling engineering job just to put this single gun in place in the marshy ground of Morris Island in Charleston

Harbor, where mud was twenty-feet deep. On August 22, 1863, the gun commenced firing on the city; sixteen shots were fired that day. The next day, firing resumed, but on the thirty-sixth shot, the gun's breech was blown out and the barrel was hurled atop the sandbag parapet, permanently disabled.

More common in Confederate than in Union use, Model 1829 thirty-two-pounder and Model 1831 forty-two-pounder seacoast guns saw action only in fortifications guarding major cities. These smoothbores employed a full range of artillery ammunition—shot, shell, case, canister, and grape—which they could throw more than a mile downrange.

An even more powerful weapon was the Model 1861 thirteen-inch seacoast mortar, used by Union troops in several locations throughout the war. The famous Petersburg "Dictator" mortar, mounted on a railroad flatcar, was the best known and most photographed of these guns. From its vantage point on a sharp curve in the rail tracks, it fired 200-pound shells more than two miles (3,600 yards); then, when moved only a few feet, it could change the direction from which it fired. This maneuverability had never been possible before with such a big gun. Still, the Dictator remained in use only a little more than two months of the ten-month siege. More maneuverable eight-inch and ten-inch seacoast mortars and twenty-four-pounder Coehorns proved more effective and easier to handle.

Mortars fired shells that contained either a time-fuse (bursting in midair) or a percussion-fuse (bursting on impact), and both were prone to defects, the most common being a lack of detonating. The time-fuse was used against troops; it exploded above the ground and showered them with a killing spray of metal. The percussion-fuse was used against fortifications, earthworks, magazines, and similar targets. Mortars were not nearly as accurate as rifled artillery, but they were loud and the potentially large area they were able to spray with their projectiles kept the enemy troops constantly on guard. "At Yorktown, the Confederates had an eight-inch mortar with which they did rather indifferent shooting," O. E. Hunt wrote in *The Photographic History of the Civil War*, "but the moral effect on the Federal soldiers of the screeching shells was great. Accordingly, the Federals thereafter paid close attention to the training of men for the use of a similar type of mortar, and at Petersburg there was a good opportunity to reply in kind. The Confederate gunners . . . were appalled by the sudden opening of the Federal mortars . . . and the moral effect was very depressing." Hunt estimated that both sides used close to 40,000 rounds of mortar ammunition at Petersburg.

Artillery Projectiles

Civil War field artillery generally fired four types of regulation projectiles:

1. *Solid shot:* As the name suggests, solid shot was a cast-iron ball for smoothbores, or an elongated shell, called a "bolt," for rifled guns. The weight of a solid shot gave the gun its designation as a "twelve-pounder," "twenty-pounder," and so on. [That designation, unfortunately, does not always accurately describe the size of a rifled gun projectile. The ten-pounder Parrott Rifle, Model 1861, for example, had a bore 2.9 inches in diameter, while the three-inch Ordnance Rifle and the ten-pounder Parrott Rifle, Model 1863, had bores three inches in diameter. In truth, rifled guns should be identified by "caliber" (bore diameter) rather than by the weight of a round ball they were said to shoot. All Civil War rifled artillery pieces except the Ordnance Rifle were assigned "pounder" designations only because that is how the army had always referred to its artillery.] Solid shot was designed to knock down the walls of fortifications or pierce the sides of ships. The other forms of artillery projectiles (shells, case shot, and canister) were used against troops.

2. *Shells:* Although shaped like solid shot, shells were hollow. A charge of gunpowder was packed inside to make them explode and scatter jagged pieces of iron shell fragments, known as shrapnel, over their targets. Slow-burning fuses, set inside wooden or metallic plugs and ignited by the cannon's discharge, exploded smoothbore shells after the passage of a predetermined length of time once they were in flight. Either the same sort of timed fuse or percussion impact fuses were used to explode rifle shells.

The most feared shell of all, according to many Civil War combatants, was the Hotchkiss projectile, which was used with three-inch rifled artillery guns. It was cast in two sections fused by a lead band. The band remained on the projectile as it left the gun, and it generated a terrifying screaming sound. "When the light was favorable," noted O. E. Hunt, "a peculiar phenomenon was often observed. The projectile seemed to gather the atmosphere as it sped along, just as our globe carries its atmosphere through space, and this apparently accounted for the statement that sometimes men were killed by the wind of a cannon-ball."

3. *Case shot:* Outwardly, this resembled the shell for each type of gun. The projectile had thinner walls, however, and it was filled with lead or iron balls packed in a sulfur mixture or in asphalt. A small bursting charge broke open the shell, scattering the shot through the air for a long-range shotgun

effect. In Confederate case shot, the inner projectiles generally were made of iron. The Union's inner projectiles were made of lead.

4. *Canister:* This dreaded ammunition consisted of a number of iron or lead balls packed in sawdust inside a tin (or tinned iron) cylinder. The cylinder was nailed to a large wooden plug at one end and crimped over an iron plate at the other. Most effective against massed infantry or cavalry at short range, canister turned a cannon into a gigantic shotgun. When the gun discharged, the tin cylinder virtually disintegrated and scattered the balls over a wide area, often killing or injuring dozens of enemy soldiers and animals at the same time.

Naval artillery used two distinctive projectiles rarely seen in the field artillery:

1. *Grape shot:* Although sometimes confused with canister, grape shot was a different type of ammunition. It consisted of iron top and bottom plates, and from nine to twenty-seven iron balls in layers, separated by more plates and held together by a long, threaded bolt passing through the center of the plates and secured by a large nut. When loading the cannon, the gunner removed the nut to allow the plates and balls to separate on firing. Grape shot was not used by field artillery because canister was easier to handle. The navy used it as an antipersonnel weapon and to destroy the rigging of enemy ships.

2. *Chain shot:* Chain shot consisted of two iron balls connected by a short length of heavy chain and fired from the same gun. The chain would cause the balls to spin in the air, thus entangling and bringing down the rope rigging of an enemy ship. There was little ship-to-ship combat in the Civil War, so chain shot was hardly a factor.

How the Big Guns Were Fired

An artillery battery comprised four to six guns and anywhere from eighty to 156 men. (Four-gun batteries made do, at times, with as few as forty-five men.) Most artillery pieces were fired in this way: one soldier dropped a bag of gunpowder of a predetermined weight into the front of the barrel. A second soldier rammed the projectile into the barrel, on top of the gunpowder charge. A third soldier, standing at the back of the gun, set a friction primer into the breech of the gun. A friction primer consisted of two small brass or copper tubes and a serrated wire. The larger of the two tubes was filled with gunpowder; the smaller tube, soldered onto it at a ninety-degree angle, contained fulminate of mercury. The wire was inserted into the smaller tube, attached to a lanyard. Another soldier pulled the lanyard, dragging it through the fulminate friction compound and causing the spark that set off the powder charge in the larger tube. This, in turn, sent a spark through the vent of the gun that ignited the bag of gunpowder, which then exploded and hurled the projectile out of the front of the gun. (If friction primers were not available, a "slow match" would be used. This was a length of saltpeter-soaked hemp fuse in a special holder designed to enter the breech vent of a cannon and ignite the powder. Slow matches were in greatest use during the first year of the war.) After the projectile was successfully fired (not always a certainty), another soldier cleaned the barrel out with water so the gun could be reloaded. Other soldiers assigned to the battery served as horse-holders and ammunition carriers and in other support capacities while the gun was being fired.

Some Notable Figures in Civil War Weaponry

JOHN M. BROOKE (1826–1906). A U.S. Navy officer noted for his invention of a sounding apparatus used to map the ocean floor, Brooke resigned on April 20, 1861, to enter the Confederate navy, and eventually became the chief of the Confederate Navy's Bureau of Ordnance and Hydrography. Though he is best known as chief designer of the ironclad C.S.S. *Virginia*, his artillery innovations were more vital to the Confederacy—particularly the Brooke rifle, a type of heavy artillery used on coastal fortifications and ironclads as well as in field batteries. The gun was cast in iron, had a strengthening wrought-iron band, or bands, around the breech, and was manufactured in different calibers (3-, 6.4-, 7-, 8-, and 11-inch). A three-inch "light" Brooke rifle used by the field artillery could fire a ten-pound projectile with a one-pound charge of gunpowder a maximum effective distance of 3,500 yards (two miles); time of flight was fifteen seconds. A ten-inch Brooke rifle, used on ironclads, was capable of shooting a 140-pound bolt 260 yards with a sixteen-pound powder charge, which could penetrate twelve inches of iron and eighteen inches of wood.

JAMES H. BURTON (1823–1894). Born in Virginia, Burton started work as a machinist at the Harpers Ferry Armory in April 1844. As foreman of the Rifle Factory Machine Shop at the armory, he learned techniques of mechanized arms production and interchangeable manufacture that had been developed there by James H. Hall. Promoted in 1849 to Acting Master Armorer, Burton began experimenting with improved designs for the minié ball recently developed by Captain Claude Etienne Minié of the French Army. The detailed drawings he made of his work survive and show that he experimented with several designs before settling on the improvement to Captain Minié's original design that was adopted by the U.S. Army in 1855. Burton's version of this more deadly accurate projectile was used by both sides throughout the Civil War. Burton left Harpers Ferry in 1854, worked briefly with the Ames Company of Chicopee, Massachusetts (builders of arms manufacturing equipment), then spent nearly five years as chief engineer of the Royal Small Arms Manufactory in Enfield, England. As the secession crisis deepened, he returned to Virginia. In June 1861, he was appointed superintendent of the Richmond Armory, where he put his invaluable knowledge to work for the Confederacy. Commissioned lieutenant colonel in the Confederate States Army in December 1861, he was placed in charge of all Southern armories and established a new armory in Macon, Georgia. Burton was taken prisoner in Macon in April 1865, subsequently signed the "Oath of Allegiance to the United States," and on October 4, 1865, was granted a presidential pardon by Andrew Johnson.

JOSIAH GORGAS (1818–1883). A West Point graduate (1846) from Pennsylvania, Gorgas married the daughter of a former governor of Alabama and came to sympathize with the South. When Alabama seceded from the Union in early 1861, Gorgas resigned his commission in the United States Army and returned to Alabama, where he had commanded the Mount Venice Arsenal in 1853. He was named the chief of the Confederate Bureau of Ordnance by Jefferson Davis and was later credited by General Joseph E. Johnston with "creating the ordnance department out of nothing." Starting virtually from scratch, Gorgas amassed weapons by capture, by purchases in Europe, by private donations, and via the mobilization of the Southern war production industry.

ROBERT PARKER PARROTT (1804–1877). A West Point graduate (class of 1824) and career artillery officer in the U.S. Army, Parrott was the superintendent of the Cold Spring, New York, Foundry (a private company) from 1836 until 1877. During that time, his experiments with artillery led to the design and manufacture of rifled cannons made of iron, commonly known as "Parrott Guns," and the projectiles they fired (the Parrott shell), a sight, and a fuse.

GEORGE WASHINGTON RAINS (1817–1898). A graduate of West Point (1842), trained as an engineer and chemist, and a hero of the Mexican War, Rains resigned from the U.S. Army in 1856 to become head of an iron works in Newburgh, New York. When the Civil War started, he moved to the South and was assigned to the Confederate Ordnance Bureau, where he helped to develop new methods of extracting nitre from limestone, in order to make gunpowder. By war's end, his Augusta Powder Works, a model of efficiency, had produced a total of 2.75 million pounds of gunpowder. He also collected 200,000 pounds of lead from window weights in Charleston, and the same amount from lead pipes in Mobile, and used this supply to make bullets. His brother, GABRIEL JAMES RAINS (1803–1881), also a U.S. Army war hero who joined the Confederacy, devised a means by which to construct land mines out of artillery shells. (Some officers questioned whether it was ethical to use land mines.) In June 1864, Gabriel Rains was named head of the Torpedo Bureau.

JAMES WOLFE RIPLEY (1794–1870). An 1814 graduate of West Point, Ripley fought as an artillery officer in the War of 1812, then against Creek and Seminole Indians under General Andrew Jackson. He headed the national armory at Springfield, Massachusetts, in the 1850s and, in 1861, was appointed U.S. chief of ordnance. Hard-headed, rigorous, and unswerving, Ripley brought immediate order to the vital task of amassing weaponry and ammunition for the Union military. He standardized the weaponry, increased output at all Northern armories and arsenals, and pushed for breech-loading carbines for the cavalry. But he resisted certain innovations (in particular, breech-loading rifles for the infantry, and repeating carbines) and his unrivaled ability to alienate colleagues generated pressure for him to resign. He was replaced by George D. Ramsay in September 1863. (Ramsay was replaced by A. B. Dyer in 1864.)

Ordnance Glossary

Action: The portion of a firearm consisting of the breech and the parts designed to fire and cycle cartridges.

Armory: Manufacturing or storage facility for arms and ordnance.

Siege guns, mortars, and piles of heavy artillery projectiles stockpiled by Union quartermasters for Major General George B. McClellan's 1862 Peninsula Campaign.

Arsenal: (1) Military installation for storing and upgrading small arms; (2) storage facility for ordnance and ordnance stores; also used for construction and repair of ordnance equipment.

Battery: (1) Two or more artillery pieces working together in the field; (2) the emplacement of artillery for offensive or defensive use; (3) a unit of artillery comprising, at full strength, six cannon (generally of similar caliber) in the Union army, and more often four in Confederate service.

Bayonet: Pointed metal weapon attached to the end of a rifle barrel; used for hand-to-hand fighting. Civil War bayonets were of two basic types: (1) socket bayonets, which slipped over the end of the barrel and used the front sight to lock them in place; and (2) sword bayonets, which were longer than socket bayonets, had a hand grip similar to that of a sword or saber, and attached to a bayonet lug welded onto the right side of the barrel. The sword bayonet was generally used on rifles that were shorter than rifle-muskets and muskets; the extra length of the bayonet made up for the rifle's shorter length.

Blakely Gun: A rifled, muzzle-loading, iron cannon designed by Alexander Blakely of Great Britain in a variety of configurations from 2.9-inch field pieces to 7.5-inch siege guns. Blakelys were distinguished by a wide wrought-iron reinforcing band, either between the trunions or enclosing the breech.

Bore: The inside of a gun barrel; also the diameter of the opening through which a projectile passes when the weapon is fired.

Breech: Rearmost portion of a gun barrel.

Breech-Loading: A firearms loading system that allows both the bullet and the powder charge to be loaded from the rear of the barrel, significantly decreasing reloading time.

Buck and Ball: A projectile consisting of one round ball and three pieces of buckshot, and designed for use in smoothbore infantry arms. When fired, the four pieces spread out to give the musket the effect of a small shotgun. (The buck and ball was often used by Confederate solders in .69 caliber muskets.)

Caisson: A two-wheeled cart for carrying two ammunition chests. The number of rounds in each chest depended on the caliber of the gun. A caisson for a six-pounder, for example, carried 100 rounds—fifty in each chest on the caisson.

Caliber: The bore diameter of a gun barrel, usually expressed in hundredths or thousandths of an inch and written as a decimal fraction. Caliber can also refer to the diameter of a projectile.

Canister: An artillery projectile consisting of a number of small iron or lead balls packed in a thin metal casing that had iron top and bottom plates.

Carbine: A short breech-loading or muzzle-loading shoulder arm designed primarily for use on horseback or by special troops (e.g., engineers).

Carriage (Gun): The three types of artillery carriages were: field, siege, and seacoast. Field carriages were the familiar two-wheeled variety. Light and easy to maneuver, they made it possible for artillery to accompany the armies in the field. Siege carriages were much heavier. Designed to hold heavy siege guns, their only movement was to traverse from side to side, allowing the gun to be aimed at different points from a fixed position. Seacoast carriages were divided into two classes: casemate carriages and barbette carriages. They were mounted behind walls and the gun was fired through an opening.

Casemate carriages allowed very little movement. Barbette carriages allowed the gun to be fired over the parapet of a fortification, and, on some of these carriages, the gun could be rotated a full 360 degrees.

Cartridge: A unit of ammunition consisting of a bullet and powder charge. During the Civil War, cartridges were of three types: externally primed, pinfire, and rimfire. Externally primed cartridges required a separate percussion cap for ignition. Rimfire cartridges had the primer built into the base of the metal cartridge case. Pinfire had a firing pin that struck a primer built into the cartridge (see "Pinfire" and "Rimfire").

Case Shot: A projectile with thin walls, containing lead or iron balls or pieces cast in a matrix of sulphur or pitch and having a small black powder bursting charge centrally located.

Chain Shot: A naval artillery projectile consisting of two iron balls joined by a short length of chain and fired from the same cannon. When fired, the balls separated and the chain stretching between them entangled and destroyed the rigging and masts of enemy ships.

Columbiad: A form of smoothbore seacoast cannon. Reinforced by heavy iron bands wrapped around the breech, these guns were capable of firing heavy projectiles long distances. They were used extensively in seacoast defenses.

Cylinder: On a revolver or revolving rifle, the rotating portion that contains the cartridges.

Dahlgren Gun: A smoothbore cannon with a distinctive "bottle" shape, invented by Admiral John A. Dahlgren of the U.S. Navy. The principal artillery piece of the Federal navy during the war, Dahlgrens were primarily nine- and eleven-inch guns, but some fifteen- and twenty-inch Dahlgrens were produced.

Deringer (or Derringer): A small, easily concealed, percussion pistol designed by Henry Deringer and copied extensively by other arms manufacturers. In the Civil War, neither War Department issued Deringers and other similar "pocket pistols," but some soldiers and officers purchased and carried their own. John Wilkes Booth used a .44 caliber Deringer to assassinate President Abraham Lincoln.

Double Action: In a self-cocking firearm, the act of pulling the trigger moves the next round into position for firing. The weapon can also be cocked by pulling back the hammer.

Enfield Rifle-Musket: Sometimes known as "The North's Second Rifle," the .577 caliber pattern 1853 Enfield Rifle-Musket was imported from England in great numbers by both the Union and the Confederate armies. (Both sides also imported Enfield "short rifles" and "musketoons" for use by cavalry and artillery troops, in smaller numbers.)

Flintlock: A muzzle-loading firearm that used a hammer holding a piece of flint. When the flint was struck against a spring-loaded steel plate (frizzen/pan cover), it produced a spark and ignited the main charge. Both armies issued flintlocks in the early days of the war. The U.S. musket Model 1816 was the flintlock most commonly issued.

Flying Battery: More often known as "Horse Artillery," a highly mobile artillery unit in which all battery members are mounted for use with cavalry or for sudden attacks on weak points in the enemy's lines.

Friction Primer: A device for firing a cannon. It consisted of two small brass or copper tubes and a serrated wire. The larger of the two tubes was filled with gunpowder. The smaller, soldered onto it at a ninety-degree angle, contained fulminate of mercury.

Fuse (Fuze): A device designed to cause an artillery shell or case shot to explode a predetermined length of time after leaving the barrel of a cannon, or upon impact with the target. Fuses are classified as timer-fuses, percussion fuses, and combination fuses.

Gatling Gun: Developed during the Civil War, but still problematic in design, Dr. Richard Jordan Gatling's six-barreled hand-cranked machine gun saw some limited action on the Petersburg front in 1864. An improved model was not officially adopted by the U.S. Army until 1866.

Grape Shot: A close-range, antipersonnel artillery round consisting of a number of iron balls arranged in layers between iron top and bottom plates that were held together by a heavy bolt. This "stand of grape" broke apart upon firing and produced a shotgun effect.

Gun: (1) An artillery weapon with a long barrel designed to throw solid shot, using a low elevation angle. The gun had no chamber and used a heavy charge of gunpowder. (2) A generic term for any artillery weapon or cannon. (3) A small arm such as a revolver, musket, rifle, or carbine.

Hammer: The part of a firearm mechanism that strikes a percussion cap or firing pin to discharge the arm.

Henry Rifle: One of the few real innovations in weaponry during the Civil War, the lever-action, .44 caliber Henry Rifle used a rimfire cartridge and a tubular magazine that allowed the user to fire sixteen shots before reloading. The rifle was invented and patented by B. Tyler Henry, plant supervisor for Oliver Winchester's New Haven (Connecticut) Arms Company in 1860. It has been estimated that 10,000 Henry Rifles were used during the war. They were particularly popular in the West.

Howitzer: A short cannon designed to fire explosive shells at medium velocity and with relatively high trajectories.

Internal Primed Cartridge: A self-contained cartridge; the ball, powder, and primer were all sealed in one cartridge (see also, "Rimfire" and "Pinfire").

Iron Sights: Open sights on a hand- or shoulder-held arm. They usually consisted of a rear sight adjustable for elevation and, sometimes, a front sight adjustable for windage.

Lance: A long wooden pole surmounted by a sharp metal tip. Only one Union cavalry regiment was issued lances during the Civil War—the Sixth Pennsylvania Cavalry, also known as Rush's Lancers.

Lead Base: Also known as a SABOT, this was a lead ring cast around the base of a rifled gun projectile. The lead expanded into the rifling grooves of the gun and provided a tight seal. This prevented the explosive gases from leaking out, so the full force of the exploding charge was used to send the projectile out of the barrel.

Lever Action: A repeating action with a reciprocating breechblock; used in Henry, Spencer, and other firearms of the Civil War period.

Limber: This two-wheeled cart, when linked to a field carriage, formed a maneuverable four-wheeled vehicle for moving a cannon. The limber carried a single ammunition chest to provide an immediate supply for the gun.

Lock: The part of a firearm's action containing the firing mechanism.

Magazine: A hollow tube to hold cartridges in a repeating arm.

Minié Bullet: Commonly called the minié *ball*, it was the standard infantry bullet of the Civil War. This hollow-base lead projectile, unlike the musket ball and smoothbore musket, expanded into a barrel's rifling grooves upon firing, vastly improving the distance and accuracy of the bullet.

Mortar: A short-barreled artillery piece designed to fire a projectile on a high trajectory to reach targets behind walls or fortifications. The typical mortar projectile exploded in the air, raining heavy fragments of the iron shell down on the enemy's soldiers.

Musket: A muzzle-loading shoulder arm with a smooth bore and a barrel length exceeding thirty-six inches.

Musketoon: A short muzzle-loading shoulder arm with either a rifled or a smooth bore. These shortened muskets were designed for use by cavalry and artillery soldiers. (Some musketoons were converted from muskets after the long musket barrel had been damaged.)

Muzzle: The forward end of a gun barrel.

Muzzle Loader: A weapon loaded by pouring a powder charge down the barrel and seating a bullet on top of it. These arms required a separate primer—either a charge of powder in the pan of a flintlock or a percussion cap.

Napoleon: Technically described as the "Twelve-Pounder Field Gun, Model 1857," this versatile smoothbore cannon was designed in France in the 1850s and named for Emperor Napoleon III. Manufactured by both sides, the Napoleon fired a 12.3-pound projectile and was easier to maneuver than the older Model 1841 twelve-pounder artillery.

Ordnance and **Ordnance Stores:** (1) Generic terms encompassing all military weaponry, along with the ammunition and equipment needed to keep them functioning; (2) artillery, including guns, howitzers, mortars, shot, shells, carriages, mortar beds, caissons, and traveling forges, together with the equipment and material needed for their construction, preservation, and repair.

Parrott Gun: Any one of a number of models of cast-iron cannon patented in 1861 by Robert P. Parrott. These guns are easily identified by the wrought-iron reinforcing band around the breech. Although the most common Parrotts were the ten- and twenty-pounders used by the field artillery, other widely used models included the thirty-pounder siege gun and 6.4-inch, eight-inch, and ten-inch seacoast guns.

Percussion Arm: A firearm using a percussion cap placed over a nipple (or cone) to ignite the powder charge.

Percussion Cap: A small metal tube containing a fulminating chemical to create a spark and ignite a powder charge when struck by the hammer.

Percussion Fuse: An artillery fuse containing a plunger and a percussion cap; designed to explode the bursting charge of a shell the instant it comes in contact with the target.

Percussion Shell: An artillery projectile equipped with a percussion fuse to burst the shell on impact.

Pinfire: A firearm ignition system that uses a metallic case cartridge with a protruding pin resting on a percussion cap inside the case. When the hammer hits the pin, pressure explodes the percussion cap and ignites the main powder charge. The United

States purchased and issued 10,000 pinfire revolvers from Lefaucheux of Paris in 1861 and 2,000 from other vendors.

Pistol: A nonrevolving handgun.

Quaker Gun: A fake cannon, generally made of wood; used to fool the enemy as to the strength of a fortified position.

Ramrod: A long metal or wooden rod used to push the bullet down the barrel of a muzzle-loading firearm.

Repeater (or **Repeating Rifle**): Among the new generation of weapons used during the Civil War, this one could fire multiple rounds without reloading.

Revolver: A handgun with a revolving cylinder and multiple chambers to hold more than one bullet and powder charge at a time.

Rifle: A shoulder arm with a rifled bore. The barrel was usually between thirty-two inches and thirty-six inches long, depending on the model.

Rifle-Musket: A muzzle-loading firearm manufactured with a rifled bore and a barrel length of approximately forty inches.

Rifled Musket: A muzzle-loading shoulder arm originally manufactured as a smoothbore and later modified by rifling the bore. Its barrel length was approximately forty-two inches.

Rifling: Grooves cut into the bore of a gun barrel to impart a spin to the bullet.

Rim Fire (or **Rimfire**): A firearm ignition system that uses a metallic case coated on the inside of the base with an explosive compound. When the firing pin strikes the edge of the case, the compound explodes and sets off the main powder charge.

Saber: A hand-held, pointed weapon with a curved blade; used primarily by cavalrymen.

Shell (Artillery): A hollow cast-iron projectile containing a bursting charge ignited by a fuse. Shells were designed to explode above enemy troops, raining iron fragments downward over a wide area, for maximum damage.

Shotgun: A smoothbore firearm designed to fire small pellets or single round balls. Shotguns were commonly used by Confederate cavalrymen, who sawed the barrels to twenty-two inches.

Shrapnel: Developed by British General Henry Shrapnel, this projectile consisted of a lead or iron shell containing lead or iron balls and a bursting charge and timed fuse. At the proper point in the projectile's flight, the bursting charge went off, scattering balls and pieces of the shell over a wide area. The American equivalent was properly known as "spherical case shot." During the American Civil War, the term "shrapnel" came to mean any fragment of an exploding artillery projectile.

Single Action: Revolver action that requires manual cocking of the hammer before each shot.

Singleshot: A firearm with no magazine or cylinder; capable of firing only one projectile with each loading cycle.

Small Arms: Weaponry—including firearms and edged weapons—small enough to be carried and used by an individual without assistance.

Smoothbore: A musket or artillery barrel manufactured without rifling (lands and grooves) inside the bore.

Solid Shot: Simple cannon balls—solid, nonexploding artillery rounds.

Spencer Rifles and **Carbines:** Considered by many soldiers to be the best infantry arm of the entire Civil War, Spencer rifles and carbines were seven-shot arms, made in several calibers, with a tubular magazine located in the butt of the stock. These lever-action arms were loaded by depressing the trigger guard, which opened the action, ejected the spent rimfire cartridge, and positioned a fresh cartridge from the magazine for firing. A quick-loading cartridge box—that held seven tubes containing seven cartridges each—was introduced during the war. This gave the soldier armed with a Spencer the capability of firing seventy rounds rapidly.

Springfield Rifle-Musket: Officially, the "U.S. Rifle Musket, Model 1855 (1861; 1863)." The Springfield was the regulation arm of the United States infantry during the Civil War. Characterized by interchangeable parts and conical ammunition, the Springfield was equipped with a ramrod and a twenty-one-inch socket bayonet. This rifle-musket was used in every major Civil War battle.

Time-Fuse: A detonating device designed to make an artillery shell or case shot explode at a predetermined length of time after leaving the barrel of the gun. The three most common varieties are wooden-case mortar fuses, metal-case (Bormann) fuses, and paper fuses, all cut to a specified length to make the projectile explode as planned.

Torpedo: Known today as land mines, or marine mines, the Civil War-era torpedo was an explosive device used principally against naval vessels. Either floating on the surface or suspended just below, torpedoes were designed to explode upon contact, or were detonated electrically from a wire. Torpedoes were also attached to the end of a spar, and rammed into a ship by an opposing vessel.

Trigger Guard: A band of metal encircling the trigger of a firearm, to prevent accidental discharge.

Vent: A hole in the breech of a cannon; designed to receive a friction primer and to permit ignition of the main powder charge in the gun's barrel.

SELECTED RESOURCES

See also the annotated book list in Chapter 13, "Studying the War: Research and Preservation."

Bilby, Joseph G. *Civil War Firearms: Their Historical Background and Tactical Use and Modern Collecting and Shooting.* Conshohocken, PA: Combined Publishing, 1996.

Bruce, Robert V. *Lincoln and the Tools of War.* Indianapolis: Bobbs-Merrill Co., 1956.

Coates, Earl J., and Dean S. Thomas. *An Introduction to Civil War Small Arms.* Gettysburg, PA: Thomas Publications, 1990.

Coggins, Jack. *Arms and Equipment of the Civil War.* New York: Fairfax Press; distributed by Crown Publishers, 1983 (originally published by Doubleday, 1962).

Davies, Paul J. *C.S. Richmond Armory: A History of the Confederate States Armory, Richmond, Virginia, and the Stock Shop at the C.S. Armory, Macon, Georgia.* Carlisle, PA: P.J. Davies, 2000.

Davis, Carl L. *Arming the Union: Small Arms in the Union Army.* Port Washington, NY: Kennikat Press, 1973.

Edwards, William Bennett. *Civil War Guns: The Complete Story of Federal and Confederate Small Arms, Design, Manufacture, Identification, Procurement, Issue, Employment, Effectiveness, and Postwar Disposal.* Harrisburg, PA: Stackpole, 1962.

Time-Life Books. *Echoes of Glory: Arms and Equipment of the Confederacy.* Alexandria, VA: Time-Life Books, 1991.

_____. *Arms and Equipment of the Union.* Alexandria, VA: Time-Life Books, 1991.

Thomas, Dean S. *Round Ball to Rimfire: A History of Civil War Small Arms Ammunition.* Gettysburg, PA: Thomas Publications, 1997.

Todd, Frederick P., et al. *American Military Equipage, 1851–1872: A Description by Word and Picture of What the American Soldier, Sailor, and Marine of These Years Wore and Carried, with Emphasis on the American Civil War.* New York: Scribner, 1980.

Vandiver, Frank E. *Ploughshares into Swords: Josiah Gorgas and Confederate Ordnance.* College Station: University of Texas Press, 1952.

Wiggins, Sarah Woolfolk, ed. *The Journals of Josiah Gorgas, 1857–1878.* Tuscaloosa: University of Alabama Press, 1995.

THE WAR ON THE WATER

I have been up all night, and have had a hard and lively time. Within two miles of Donaldsonville a rebel battery opened on us with artillery and sharpshooters. We were struck several times and had quite a spirited engagement. I got the *North America* by all right, with only four shots through her, and then leaving her at Donaldsonville I returned to the scene of action, and kept it up till they stopped firing. On my way down I trained my guns on everything I could see, as I was determined to make them pay dear for their whistle this time; but the levee is so high that one is not able to see everything behind it, and the rebels mass their sharpshooters at different points and fire into our gunboats when they pass; and although we blaze away back, we do not get a fair revenge.—Lieutenant George Hamilton Perkins, United States Navy; letter, July 4, 1863.

The rapid mobilization and extraordinary innovation of the Union and Confederate navies have often been downplayed in general accounts of the American Civil War. Yet, daring operations took place on rivers, along the Atlantic and Gulf coasts, and on the high seas. Ironclads, "tin-clads," submersibles, "double-enders," "ninety-day gunboats," "torpedo boats," "Davids" (small Confederate torpedo boats that attacked larger Goliath-like ships), and converted tugboats were among the many types of vessels that played an integral role in the strategies employed by the North and the South. Civil War clashes of American naval vessels also signaled the beginning of a new era in naval warfare.

At the outbreak of hostilities, the United States Navy was unprepared for the sort of naval operations that the Civil War came to demand, and the Confederate navy did not exist. In the ensuing four years, the Confederacy built a solid naval force from scratch, and the United States Navy was transformed from a skeletal force to one of the most powerful and battle-tested navies in the world.

Union naval strategy, at the start, was primarily focused on the blockade of Southern ports on the Atlantic and Gulf coasts and the need to hunt down Confederate commerce raiders and privateers. These efforts, combined with larger joint operations (with land forces) to control the Mississippi River from Cairo, Illinois, to the Gulf, were intended to isolate the South. Such a strategy demanded enormous numbers of men and ships. Fortunately for the Union, U.S. shipbuilding facilities and the flourishing merchant marine—an invaluable pool of vessels and experienced seamen—were predominantly

Twenty-one of the U.S.S Monitor's fifty-eight-man crew pose aboard the famed ironclad in the summer of 1862. At left is a portable cookstove; on the right, a visible dent remains on the turret, a third of the way up, where the ship was struck by heavy shot during its encounter with the C.S.S. Virginia on March 9, 1862.

associated with Northern ports. The Union also had the expertise of brilliant engineers such as John Ericsson, whose monitor-style ironclads (low-lying, armor-plated steam-powered vessels) turned the early tide of the war; James B. Eads, whose river-plying gunboats helped win the western campaign; and Benjamin Franklin Isherwood, whose steam-powered warships were built with such swiftness that they earned the nickname "ninety-day gunboats," and were used effectively on the blockade. As blockading U.S. warships slowly tightened their grip along the Atlantic and Gulf coasts, the Union's riverine force was penetrating the western waterways, venturing up rivers mined with torpedoes, and battling Confederate-held forts and the Confederate River Defense Fleet. By July 1863, the Union had complete control of the Mississippi River, thus choking off the Confederacy's western supply routes and achieving a primary military objective.

When the war began, the Confederacy, according to J. Thomas Scharf, a Confederate navy officer and historian, lacked adequate facilities and other resources to construct ships. Thus, the South endeavored to overcome the stark disadvantages in personnel, naval expenditures, and manufacturing capabilities by using an element of surprise to break the blockade. Under Confederate Secretary of the Navy Stephen R. Mallory's stewardship, the Southern navy procured sleek cruisers from British shipyards, used them with significant effect to prey on Union shipping, initiated a program of ironclad warship production, developed innovative devices like underwater explosives ("infernal machines") and torpedo boats (including the *David*), and created the first submersible to sink an enemy warship (the C.S.S. *Hunley*). The Confederacy also granted letters of marque and reprisal, which permitted privately owned vessels to act as "privateers" and attack Northern merchant ships. Unlike the commerce raiders, privateers were not part of the Confederate navy, but they operated under government license and profited by seizing "prizes" (captured ships and their cargo).

From the start, however, Union naval resources far outstripped those of the Confederacy. Beginning with forty-two active ships, the Union Navy expanded exponentially until, at war's end, 671 vessels plied the seas and rivers. Many were existing commercial vessels that were converted for use in the blockade. An odd assortment of ships was immediately pressed into service. Among them were fishing and whaling ships, tugboats, converted ferry boats, and some rickety clipper ships. Within three months from the start of the blockade, Union shipyards had built more than twenty steam-powered, 500-ton gunboats (the ninety-day gunboats). For the riverine warfare in the west, Union shipbuilders devised sidewheel-driven steamships of a shallow draft. With rudders and pilot houses at either end, they could move quickly in either direction in rivers or shallow waters (thus, their nickname: "double-enders"). Nearly sixty monitor-type ironclads, the state of the art in naval warfare, were also built. However, the Confederacy's high hopes for a large fleet of ironclads were diminished by the lack of critical resources and of the industrial capacity needed to turn them out quickly. Fewer than two dozen Confederate ironclads made it into service during the course of the war. The Confederate navy reached its peak in early 1864, with 753 officers, 4,460 enlisted men, and 539 Marine Corps personnel, as opposed to the U.S. Navy's 6,759 officers, 51,357 sailors, and 3,850 marines at about the same time.

The war on the water inevitably prompted technological developments and hastened other advancements already under way: steam engines would replace sail power, iron replace wood, and efficient screw propellers replace paddlewheels. Another revolutionary innovation born of battle was the revolving gun turret, which gave warships greater flexibility to engage the enemy and defend themselves. The practice of converting civilian merchant and commercial vessels into warships (as was done in the past) would come to an end, as these converted ships were not as useful as the armored steamships that were designed and built for war.

Ultimately, the U.S. Navy's overwhelming superiority stifled the fledgling Confederate navy, which proved a very resourceful foe. And, although Southern commerce raiding impacted Northern shipping and was a significant irritant, it never threatened to change the war's outcome; rather, the U.S. Navy's blockade and successful river operations that shut down Confederate ports were a key to Union victory.

NAVAL EVENTS TIME LINE

1861

January 9: The unarmed sidewheel steamer *Star of the West,* dispatched by President James Buchanan, is fired upon by South Carolina batteries in Charleston Harbor as it attempts to resupply Fort Sumter. The ship returns without discharging its cargo.

February 21: The Provisional Confederate Congress, meeting in Montgomery, Alabama, passes legislation creating the Navy Department, to be headed by Stephen R. Mallory, former U.S. senator from Florida, and one-time chairman of the Senate Naval Committee (see

"Civil War Government Officials: Confederate States of America," in Chapter 3, "Wartime Politics").

March 7: Under President Lincoln, Gideon Welles begins serving as Secretary of the Navy (see "Civil War Government Officials: United States of America" in Chapter 3, "Wartime Politics").

April 12: Confederate shore batteries open fire on Fort Sumter in Charleston Harbor, signaling the opening of hostilities.

April 19: President Lincoln proclaims a naval blockade of all ports in South Carolina, Georgia, Alabama, Florida, Mississippi, Louisiana, and Texas.

April 20: In anticipation of Confederate attack, the Union prematurely abandons the Gosport Navy Yard near Norfolk, Virginia, after destroying part of the facility and scuttling a number of vessels. Parts of four vessels are salvaged by the Southerners, including the remnants of the steam frigate U.S.S. *Merrimack,* destined to be rebuilt as an ironclad and rechristened the C.S.S. *Virginia.* Farther to the north, at Annapolis, the revered warship U.S.S. *Constitution* is moved away from shore as a precaution against Confederate capture. On April 24, the *Constitution,* under tow, with midshipmen on board, departs for Newport, Rhode Island, via New York. Newport remains the home of the U.S. Naval Academy until August 1865.

April 27: The Union blockade is extended to include Virginia and North Carolina.

August 3: An observation balloon ascends from the deck of the U.S.S. *Fanny,* in Hampton Roads, Virginia, and allows John La Montain to observe Confederate gun placements.

August 5: The U.S. Congress authorizes President Lincoln to enlist seamen for the length of the war.

August 28: Union warships attack Fort Hatteras, North Carolina; together with the surrender of Fort Clark, this action closes an important route to Southern blockade runners.

November 7: Union Flag Officer Samuel Francis Du Pont's naval squadron steams into Port Royal Sound, South Carolina, bombarding and forcing the evacuation of Fort Beauregard, as well as Fort Walker on Hilton Head Island. Union occupation of the sound establishes an important toehold on the Confederate coast for the balance of the war. Far to the west, in a battle at Belmont, Missouri, on the Mississippi River, General Ulysses S. Grant exhibits his early proclivity for combined army-navy expeditions—in this case, utilizing navy gunboats for troop transport and cover fire.

November 8: The U.S.S. *San Jacinto,* on station in the Old Bahama Channel, stops the British mail packet *Trent* and forcibly removes passengers James M. Mason and John Slidell, Confederate envoys to Europe.

November 11: Thaddeus Lowe, Lincoln's Chief of Army Aeronautics, launches an observation balloon from a navy "balloon-boat" in the Potomac River.

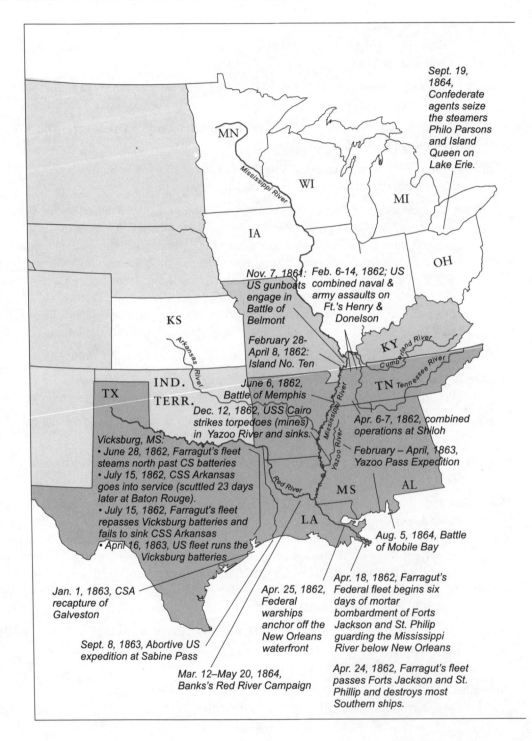

Sept. 19, 1864, Confederate agents seize the steamers Philo Parsons and Island Queen on Lake Erie.

MN

WI

MI

IA

OH

Mississippi River

Nov. 7, 1861: US gunboats engage in Battle of Belmont

Feb. 6-14, 1862; US combined naval & army assaults on Ft.'s Henry & Donelson

KS

Arkansas River

February 28-April 8, 1862: Island No. Ten

KY

Cumberland River

IND. TERR.

TX

June 6, 1862, Battle of Memphis

TN

Tennessee River

Dec. 12, 1862, USS Cairo strikes torpedoes (mines) in Yazoo River and sinks.

Apr. 6-7, 1862, combined operations at Shiloh

Vicksburg, MS:
• June 28, 1862, Farragut's fleet steams north past CS batteries
• July 15, 1862, CSS Arkansas goes into service (scuttled 23 days later at Baton Rouge).
• July 15, 1862, Farragut's fleet repasses Vicksburg batteries and fails to sink CSS Arkansas
• April 16, 1863, US fleet runs the Vicksburg batteries

Mississippi River

Yazoo River

February – April, 1863, Yazoo Pass Expedition

Red River

MS

AL

LA

Aug. 5, 1864, Battle of Mobile Bay

Jan. 1, 1863, CSA recapture of Galveston

Apr. 25, 1862, Federal warships anchor off the New Orleans waterfront

Apr. 18, 1862, Farragut's Federal fleet begins six days of mortar bombardment of Forts Jackson and St. Philip guarding the Mississippi River below New Orleans

Sept. 8, 1863, Abortive US expedition at Sabine Pass

Mar. 12–May 20, 1864, Banks's Red River Campaign

Apr. 24, 1862, Farragut's fleet passes Forts Jackson and St. Phillip and destroys most Southern ships.

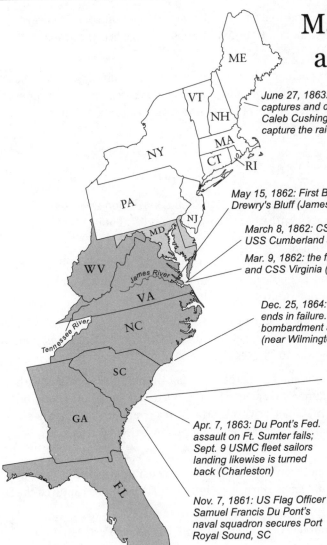

Major Naval Battles and notable events 1861–1865

June 27, 1863: CSS Archer captures and destroys the USS Caleb Cushing in Portland, Maine, but the Northerners capture the raiders of the CSS Archer later that day

May 15, 1862: First Battle of Drewry's Bluff (James River)

March 8, 1862: CSS Virginia and consorts destroy USS Cumberland and USS Congress

Mar. 9, 1862: the first battle of the ironclads, USS Monitor and CSS Virginia (Hampton Roads)

Dec. 25, 1864: first US fleet assault against Fort Fisher, NC ends in failure. Jan. 15, 1865, a second amphibious bombardment and invasion succeeds in capturing the fort (near Wilmington, NC)

Feb. 17, 1864: CSS Hunley sinks the USS Housatonic, and is the first submarine to destroy an enemy warship (Charleston)

Apr. 7, 1863: Du Pont's Fed. assault on Ft. Sumter fails; Sept. 9 USMC fleet sailors landing likewise is turned back (Charleston)

Nov. 7, 1861: US Flag Officer Samuel Francis Du Pont's naval squadron secures Port Royal Sound, SC

NOTABLE FOREIGN ENGAGEMENTS:
• July 16, 1863: In the Straits of Shimonoseki, Japan, the USS Wyoming — on patrol for Confederate commerce raiders — battles the makeshift fleet of a Japanese warlord, marking the first U.S. military engagement with Japanese forces
• June 19, 1864: the Confederate commerce raider CSS Alabama is sunk after dueling with the USS Kearsarge off the coast of Cherbourg, France
• Oct. 7, 1864: The Confederate raider CSS Florida is captured at Bahia, Brazil by the USS Wachusett in violation of Brazilian neutrality.
• June 22–28, 1865: The CSS Shenandoah destroys much of the American whaling fleet in the Bering Sea, a blow from which New England whalers never recover.

November 12: The blockade runner *Fingal,* acquired in Great Britain by the Confederate government, delivers military cargo to Savannah, Georgia. The *Fingal* later becomes the C.S.S. *Atlanta.*

December 8: A Union whaling ship, *Ebenezer Dodge,* is captured by Captain Raphael Semmes and the C.S.S. *Sumter* in the mid-Atlantic. It is one of eighteen American vessels that Semmes will take before moving on to an even more prolific raiding career as captain of the C.S.S. *Alabama.*

1862

January 9: Flag Officer David G. Farragut is ordered to command the Union's Western Gulf Blockading Squadron, which has been entrusted to carry out a critical objective: the capture of New Orleans, the largest city in the Confederacy.

January 11: A U.S. Navy squadron of nearly 100 ships, under the command of Flag Officer Louis M. Goldsborough, begins transporting 15,000 troops, commanded by Brigadier General Ambrose E. Burnside, from Hampton Roads, Virginia, to North Carolina.

January 16: The balance of naval power on the western rivers tilts further to the Union with the commissioning of seven armored river gunboats, including *Carondelet, St. Louis,* and *Cincinnati,* all of which prove essential to Ulysses Grant's combined operations.

February 6: In another of General Grant's combined operations, Flag Officer Andrew Foote, with four ironclads and three wooden gunboats, opens fire on Confederate-held Fort Henry on the Tennessee River, marking the first major riverine attack on a strategic Confederate position. Foote accepts the surrender of the fort even before Grant's 15,000 troops can get into position.

February 7: Flag Officer Goldsborough's naval squadron disperses Confederate naval resistance at Roanoke Island, North Carolina, and lands Burnside's infantry. The island is captured the next day.

February 14: In Tennessee, Flag Officer Andrew Foote's Federal gunboats attack Fort Donelson, as General Grant's infantry surrounds the fort from the inland side. The warships withdraw after suffering heavy damage from Fort Donelson's gunfire. Foote is wounded in the assault. The fort surrenders to Grant two days later. The capture of Forts Henry and Donelson opens the way for further operations on the Tennessee River, deep into Confederate territory.

February 25: The U.S.S. *Monitor* is commissioned. The ironclad has radically new features—a revolving turret housing two eleven-inch Dahlgren smoothbores, and forced draft ventilation that allows the crew to live in an artificial, "submarine" environment. The

Monitor is also uniquely ironclad—not simply converted from a preexisting vessel, as was the C.S.S. *Virginia.*

March 3: Forces under Flag Officer Samuel Francis Du Pont participate in the capture of Fernandina, Florida, creating another Union toehold on the southern Atlantic seaboard.

March 6: The U.S.S. *Monitor* sails from New York for Hampton Roads, Virginia.

March 8: C.S.S. *Virginia,* recently converted from the *Merrimack,* sails against the wooden ships of the Union blockading fleet at Hampton Roads. Under Flag Officer Franklin Buchanan, *Virginia* rams the U.S.S. *Cumberland,* causing it to go down, and forces the U.S.S. *Congress* and U.S.S. *Minnesota* aground. The *Congress* is set afire after surrender.

March 9: Under command of Lieutenant John L. Worden, the U.S.S. *Monitor,* which had arrived at Hampton Roads during the night, battles the C.S.S. *Virginia* for four hours. It is the first battle between ironclads, and one of the first in which both vessels maneuver strictly on steam power. Neither vessel is seriously damaged in the fight. The Hampton Roads battle signals the beginning of a new era in naval warfare. Wooden fighting ships will eventually be eclipsed by less vulnerable ironclad vessels.

March 17: A convoy of army transports and navy warships begins the monumental task of moving Major General George B. McClellan's 105,000-man Army of the Potomac, and its equipment, to the York and James Rivers for the start of the Peninsula Campaign of 1862.

April 4: The Union gunboat *Carondelet,* at night and in a terrific thunderstorm, fights its way past the batteries on Confederate-held Island No. 10 in the Mississippi River near New Madrid, Missouri. This is the first step toward cutting off and reducing the Southern stronghold. Island No. 10 will surrender on April 7.

April 16: Flag Officer David G. Farragut's massive fleet arrives at Ship Island, below New Orleans, in preparation for its assault on the seaport. Capturing New Orleans is critical to Union war strategy, which calls for complete control of the Mississippi River, thereby splitting the Confederacy.

April 18: Farragut's fleet begins five days of mortar bombardment of heavily armed Forts Jackson (seventy-four guns), on the west bank of the Mississippi River, and St. Philip (fifty-two guns), on the east bank, below New Orleans.

April 24: All but three vessels of Farragut's fleet successfully pass Forts Jackson and St. Philip on the lower Mississippi. Making its way upriver, the fleet engages a Confederate squadron before driving them off.

April 25: Farragut anchors eleven Union warships off the New Orleans waterfront and New Orleans surrenders. The retreating Confederates set the unfinished C.S.S. *Mississippi* afire.

Bradley Sillick Osbon, a naval officer and newspaper correspondent serving on board Farragut's flagship, the *Hartford*, will call the action the U.S. Navy's greatest single achievement in the war.

May 9: Norfolk, Virginia, and its valuable navy yard are evacuated by the Confederates as Federals solidify their hold on the Virginia peninsula. The C.S.S. *Virginia* is left without a port. Confederates will scuttle the ship on May 11 to prevent its capture.

May 10: In the battle of Plum Run Bend, Tennessee, the Confederate River Defense Fleet attacks a flotilla of seven Union ironclads. The fleet manages to sink two in shallow water. The battle is notable as one of the rare "fleet actions" of the Civil War. On the Gulf of Mexico, Pensacola, Florida, is occupied by Union forces. This port will become vital as a base for the U.S. Navy's blockade of other Gulf ports.

May 15: As part of the Peninsula Campaign to take the Confederate capital of Richmond, five Union warships, including the *Monitor*, ascend the James River. The ships are ordered to "push on to Richmond if possible, without any unnecessary delay, and shell the place into surrender." Even without army assistance, the small fleet is able to get within eight miles of the capital, but must turn back after a four-hour artillery duel with Fort Darling at Drewry's Bluff.

June 6: Captain Charles Davis leads his Union flotilla down the Mississippi River to Memphis, Tennessee, pitting five ironclads and four rams—ships with iron-reinforced prows—against a decidedly inferior fleet of Confederate defenders. While townspeople watch the battle of Memphis from the bluffs above the river, four of the eight Confederate vessels are captured and three are destroyed. Only the gunboat *Van Dorn* escapes, and Memphis surrenders to the Union.

June 28: Moving up the Mississippi River, Union Flag Officer David G. Farragut directs his fleet past the Vicksburg batteries, with fifteen killed and thirty wounded in the barrage hurled by the city's big guns.

July 1: Union Flag Officer Louis M. Goldsborough's fleet adds covering fire from the James River in the last of the Seven Days battles, the battle of Malvern Hill, which brings the Peninsula Campaign to a close. The fleet then accompanies army-operated transports that evacuate much of the Army of the Potomac downriver to Harrison's Landing.

July 15: The ironclad C.S.S. *Arkansas* travels down the Yazoo River and fights its way through the Union fleet before taking a position under the shore batteries at Vicksburg. Farragut, determined to destroy this new Confederate naval threat, moves his fleet past Vicksburg in a massive gun duel with the Vicksburg guns and the *Arkansas*. Though seriously damaged, the *Arkansas* survives. Three of Farragut's ships suffer heavy damage.

July 30: In honor of his decisive victory at New Orleans, David Farragut becomes the first U.S. flag officer to be commissioned rear admiral. His rank dates from July 16, the day Congress authorized the new grade.

August 6: The C.S.S. *Arkansas* battles four Union vessels at Baton Rouge and suffers heavy damage when its engines fail. The crew destroys the ship, ending a fearsome twenty-three-day career for the Southern warship, the last of its kind for the Confederates on the Mississippi River.

August 24: The C.S.S. *Alabama* is commissioned, and Raphael Semmes takes command of the new Confederate cruiser.

October 1: Union gunboats operating on western waters, previously administered by the War Department, are transferred to the Navy Department. The newly organized Mississippi Squadron is placed under the command of David Dixon Porter.

December 12: The Union gunboat U.S.S. *Cairo*, operating on Mississippi's Yazoo River above Vicksburg, strikes a mine (or "torpedo") and sinks.

December 31: While under tow off the coast of North Carolina near Cape Hatteras, the U.S.S. *Monitor* founders in a storm about 1 A.M. Four officers and twelve men are lost; forty-seven crewmen are rescued by the U.S.S. *Rhode Island*. (In 1973, the *Monitor* wreck was located, and, in 1975, the site was designated as the nation's first marine sanctuary. Artifacts recovered from the ship are on view at the Mariners' Museum in Newport News, Virginia.)

1863

January 1: Confederate forces under John B. Magruder attack the Union garrison and flotilla near Galveston, Texas, recapture the city, and temporarily drive off the blockading squadron. Confederates manage to seize the *Harriet Lane*, but the Union ship *Westfield* is destroyed by her crew to prevent its capture.

January 11: Commander David Dixon Porter's Union gunboats shell the defenses at Fort Hindman, Arkansas (Arkansas Post), fifty miles up the Arkansas River from its confluence with the Mississippi. Following a combined assault with Major General John McClernand's Union infantry, Porter receives the fort's surrender. Off Galveston, Texas, the C.S.S. *Alabama* under Raphael Semmes sinks the U.S.S. *Hatteras*.

January 14: Union gunboats and infantry at Bayou Teche, Louisiana, assault Confederate defenses and the gunboat C.S.S. *Cotton*. The *Cotton* is set afire by retreating Confederates the next day.

January 17: C.S.S. *Josiah Bell* and *Uncle Ben* capture the U.S.S. *Morning Light* and *Velocity*, temporarily disrupting the blockade of Sabine Pass, Texas.

January 31: Two Confederate ironclads, *Palmetto State* and *Chicora,* leave Charleston Harbor to break the Union blockade. Two Union vessels—the *Mercedita* and the *Keystone State*—are heavily damaged, but the blockade of the port remains intact. The Southern ironclads withdraw and return to port.

February 14: The U.S.S. *Queen of the West,* one of engineer Charles Ellet's original iron rams, runs aground on the Red River and is abandoned. The Confederates will soon make good use of it.

February 24: Lieutenant Commander George Brown's U.S.S. *Indianola,* which had earlier passed below the Vicksburg batteries, is rammed repeatedly in an encounter with four Confederate ships, including the recently captured *Queen of the West.* The partially submerged *Indianola* is surrendered to the Confederates.

February 28: The former commander of the U.S.S. *Monitor,* John. L. Worden, directs his new vessel, the monitor *Montauk,* up the Ogeechee River in Georgia and destroys the Confederate privateer *Rattlesnake,* the erstwhile C.S.S. *Nashville.*

March 11: Union warships traversing bayous to the Yalobusha River assault hastily built Fort Pemberton, Mississippi, for several days before later withdrawing. So ends the Yazoo Pass Expedition, another of Ulysses S. Grant's initial, ill-fated attempts to get an army in front of the Confederate fortress of Vicksburg, Mississippi. Grant's persistence will lead to Vicksburg's surrender on July 4, the day after the crucially important Union victory at Gettysburg, Pennsylvania.

March 14: Rear Admiral David G. Farragut's flagship, the *Hartford,* moves north past the Confederate batteries at Port Hudson, Louisiana, on the Mississippi River. One other warship, the *Albatross,* makes it through; two others are forced to fall back. The U.S.S. *Mississippi* is not so fortunate. After running aground, it has to be destroyed. Commander David D. Porter enters Steele's Bayou from the Yazoo River with five ironclads, four mortars, and four tugboats as part of an attempt to capture Vicksburg. General William T. Sherman's Union infantry march to the rescue of the gunboats a week later, when the expedition bogs down in the face of Confederate resistance.

March 25: Two Union rams, *Lancaster* and *Switzerland,* attempt to run the Confederate batteries at Vicksburg. The *Lancaster* sinks and the *Switzerland* is disabled.

March 31: Rear Admiral David G. Farragut, with the *Hartford, Albatross,* and a repaired *Switzerland,* passes the Confederate batteries below Vicksburg at Grand Gulf.

April 7: Rear Admiral Samuel F. Du Pont enters into Charleston Harbor with nine Union ironclads and attacks on Fort Sumter. Five of his ships are disabled under heavy fire from shore batteries, and the attack is called off as darkness descends.

April 16: A flotilla of twelve Union vessels under acting Rear Admiral David D. Porter pass the Vicksburg defenses under heavy fire, in anticipation of cooperating with Ulysses S. Grant's forthcoming Vicksburg overland campaign.

May 27: The Union gunboat *Cincinnati* is sunk in the Mississippi River by Confederate guns at Fort Hill. (The boat is later recovered.)

June 7: The gunboats U.S.S. *Lexington* and U.S.S. *Choctaw* help drive back Confederate attackers at Milliken's Bend, Louisiana, after Union infantry had been pinned against the Mississippi River.

June 17: In Georgia, the Confederate ironclad C.S.S. *Atlanta,* after a brief battle with the Union warships *Weehawken* and *Nahant* at the mouth of the Wilmington River, runs aground and surrenders to Captain John Rodgers of the *Weehawken.* The loss of the *Atlanta* is a blow to the Confederacy, which had considered the ship superior to its first ironclad, the *Virginia* (see also "A Telling Clash of Ironclads: The C.S.S. *Atlanta* versus the U.S.S. *Weehawken*" on page 553).

July 10: With wide-ranging naval involvement in what is a huge army operation intended to capture the "Cradle of the Confederacy," Union ironclads bombard Battery Wagner on Morris Island, one of the key defensive installations in Charleston Harbor.

July 16: In the Straits of Shimonoseki, Japan, the U.S.S. *Wyoming,* on patrol for Confederate commerce raiders, battles the makeshift fleet of a Japanese warlord who is intent on driving foreigners from those well-traveled waters. David Stockton McDougal, commanding the *Wyoming,* won the engagement at the cost of five dead and six wounded. This marks the first U.S. naval engagement with Japanese forces.

August 1: U.S. Rear Admiral David Dixon Porter takes Union naval command of the entire Mississippi River.

August 5: The U.S.S. *Commodore Barney* suffers damage from an electric torpedo in the James River. The ship survives but two crewmen are lost.

August 29: The Confederate submarine *H.L. Hunley* sinks, for the first of several times, in Charleston Harbor when it is swamped by the wake of a passing vessel as it maneuvers on the surface with an open hatch. Five crewmen are lost (see "The Evolution of the Submarine: The C.S.S. *Hunley*" on page 565).

September 6: Confederates vacate Battery Wagner on Morris Island in Charleston Harbor after intensive naval bombardment and in anticipation of an imminent infantry assault.

September 8: An expedition of Union gunboats and transports is forced to withdraw after heavy losses at Sabine Pass, Texas. Two gunboats, the U.S.S. *Clifton* and the U.S.S. *Sachem,* are disabled and compelled to surrender.

September 9: United States Marines and sailors attempt a night landing at Fort Sumter in Charleston Harbor and are turned back with heavy casualties. The attempt fails, in part, because Confederates, using a codebook recovered from a wrecked Union vessel (the *Keokuk*), are able to read flag signals between the Union commanders during the operation's planning.

October 5: The Confederate torpedo boat *David*, a cigar-shaped vessel with a spar torpedo, attacks the Union ironclad *New Ironsides*, which is blockading Charleston Harbor. The torpedo damages but does not destroy the warship, and the *David* returns to Charleston intact.

October 9: The British government seizes the *North Carolina* (built under the code name "El Tousson") and the *Mississippi* (built as "El Monassir"), twin-turreted oceangoing ironclads secretly being built for the Confederacy at the Laird shipyards. The British government will purchase the ships in February 1864.

October 15: For the second time, the Confederate submarine *H.L. Hunley* sinks in Charleston Harbor—this time, during a practice dive. The vessel's inventor, H. L. Hunley, and seven crewmen are killed.

1864

February 17: In Charleston Harbor, the C.S.S. *Hunley* submarine rams a torpedo into the U.S.S. *Housatonic,* which quickly sinks. The *Hunley* manages to disengage, but sinks en route to its base, with loss of all hands. This marks the first instance of a submarine's sinking an enemy ship.

March 12: Union gunboats and a Union force under Nathaniel Banks begin ascending the Red River in Louisiana, beginning the Red River Campaign. The gunboats arrive at Alexandria, Louisiana, three days later.

May 5: The C.S.S. *Albemarle* again engages Union ships near Plymouth, North Carolina, and severely damages the U.S.S. *Sassacus* before steaming back up the Roanoke River. In the engagement, the Union captures the warship C.S.S. *Bombshell*, which had, prior to its service in the Confederate navy, been the U.S.S. *Bombshell.*

May 8: Rear Admiral Porter's Mississippi Squadron, in danger of being trapped in the lowering water of the Red River, finds salvation in the construction of wing dams, which raise the water level. The last of his ships is able to pass over the rapids on May 13, after construction of a second dam—a rare bright spot in Nathaniel Banks' otherwise disastrous Red River Campaign.

June 19: Captain Raphael Semmes sails the *Alabama* out of Cherbourg, France, where it has been undergoing repairs, to do battle with the waiting U.S.S. *Kearsarge,* under the command of Captain John Winslow. After a dramatic open-seas exchange of broadsides, the damaged *Alabama* strikes her colors before going down. Thus ends the career of the raider responsible for capturing or destroying more than sixty vessels—predominantly Union merchantmen—valued at $6.5 million.

August 5: In the battle of Mobile Bay, Rear Admiral David Farragut wins one of the greatest naval engagements of the war. With a fleet of eighteen ships, Farragut fights past the forts flanking Mobile Bay, maneuvers amid mines, and defeats the Confederate warships in the bay.

This 1887 lithograph by L. Prang & Co. depicts the battle between the U.S.S. Kearsarge *and the C.S.S.* Alabama *(in background) off the coast of Cherbourg, France. Fifteen thousand spectators watched the battle from shore; less than ninety minutes after opening fire on the* Kearsarge, *the* Alabama *succumbed to its opponent's more accurate firepower and sank.*

August 6: The cruiser C.S.S. *Tallahassee,* captained by the resourceful John Taylor Wood, sails from Wilmington, North Carolina, to wreak havoc on Union shipping. In a three-week span, it will claim more than thirty enemy merchant ships.

October 7: The raider C.S.S. *Florida* is rammed and captured at Bahia, Brazil, by Commander Napoleon Collins and the Union sloop *Wachusett*. The *Florida*'s prize tally ends at thirty-seven ships.

October 19: The last of the Southern commerce raiders, the C.S.S. *Shenandoah,* enters Confederate service in the Madeira Islands.

October 27: Moving stealthily after dark up the Roanoke River to Plymouth, North Carolina, Union Lieutenant William B. Cushing, aboard *Picket Launch No. 1*, attacks the C.S.S. *Albemarle* with a torpedo fastened to a spar, and sinks the Confederate warship.

December 9: The U.S.S. *Otsego* falls victim to torpedoes in the Roanoke River, in North Carolina. The following day, the tug U.S.S. *Bazely* also explodes a mine and sinks alongside while attempting to rescue *Otsego* survivors.

December 24: A large Union fleet under the command of Rear Admiral Porter, cooperating with Major General Benjamin F. Butler to capture Fort Fisher at the mouth of the Cape Fear River near Wilmington, North Carolina, conducts a massive bombardment of the earthen works, with little effect. The infantry assault on the following day fails, and the entire expedition is withdrawn to Hampton Roads. (See also page 321.)

1865

January 12: Vice Admiral David D. Porter returns to Fort Fisher with a fleet of nearly sixty ships, including 8,000 infantry under Brigadier General Alfred Terry. Over three days of bombardment, the fleet will fire approximately 20,000 shells from over 600 naval guns. The fort will fall January 14, following assaults by Terry's infantry.

March 4: The Union transport *Thorn* sinks in the Cape Fear River after striking a torpedo.

March 24: The C.S.S. *Stonewall*, a European-built ironclad, leaves Spain for Havana, Cuba, but will not arrive before the war's end.

April 2–4: In the rapid evacuation of Richmond following Union breakthroughs at Petersburg, Confederate Secretary of the Navy Stephen R. Mallory orders the James River Squadron destroyed. Naval personnel will serve as infantry in the ensuing Appomattox Campaign.

April 4: President Lincoln, on a U.S. naval vessel, ascends the James River to Richmond and is escorted to the White House of the Confederacy by Rear Admiral David D. Porter, three other officers, and ten sailors.

May 3: In Washington, Georgia, President Jefferson Davis accepts the resignation of Secretary of the Navy Stephen R. Mallory.

June 28: On the final day of operations for the Confederate raider C.S.S. *Shenandoah,* and unaware of the collapse of the Confederacy, the raider takes eleven U.S. whaling ships in the Bering Sea. On August 2, the ship's commander, Lieutenant Waddell, learns from a British vessel that the Confederate armies have surrendered.

November 6: The C.S.S. *Shenandoah* docks at Liverpool, England, and is formally surrendered to British authorities after a 17,000-mile voyage. The second most effective Confederate raider, and the only Confederate vessel to circumnavigate the globe, the *Shenandoah* claimed thirty-eight prizes in its year of service.

★   ★   ★

Organization of Union and Confederate Navies

United States Navy

The U.S. Navy Department, established in 1798, went through a number of organizational changes in the intervening decades before the Civil War. In 1842, the Navy Department replaced its Board of Naval Commissioners with a structured bureau system. Department staff, headquartered in Washington, near the White House, consisted of about thirty-nine individuals at the outbreak of the war and grew to sixty-six by the war's end. The following list highlights some key bureaus and staff of the Civil War years. Some of the dates of duty are not available. (Flag officer was a temporary rank given to captains in command of squadrons. When a mission or voyage was over, the officer reverted to the rank of captain, the highest permanent rank in the U.S. Navy until July 1862. In August 1862, Rear Admiral was created as a permanent rank; in December 1864, Vice Admiral was created as a permanent rank.)

ORGANIZATION AND STAFF

Secretary of the Navy

Gideon Welles, March 7, 1861–March 3, 1869
Welles' administrative subordinates in 1861 included fourteen clerks and two messengers.

Assistant Secretary of the Navy

Gustavus Vasa Fox, August 1, 1861–May 22, 1866

Commander in Chief (Senior Flag Officer; Commodore commanding the Navy)

Charles Stewart, March 2, 1859–December 21, 1861

David G. Farragut, December 21, 1861–August 14, 1870

Chief Clerk

Gustavus V. Fox, May 9, 1861–July 31, 1861

William Faxon, August 31, 1861–August 1, 1866

Organization Office

Established in March 1861; renamed the Office of Detail in April 1861.

Silas H. Stringham, March 1861–April 1861

Office of Detail

Established in April 1861 and merged into the Bureau of Navigation on April 28, 1865. Responsible for the supply and control of personnel, including enlistments, personnel records and assignments, training, naval observatory, hydrographic office.

Charles H. Davis, April 1861–July 17, 1862

Bureau of Yards and Docks

Established August 31, 1842. Responsible for public works, public utilities, and government quarters on navy yards and naval stations; supervised their design, construction, repair, upkeep, and operation.

Joseph Smith, May 25, 1846–April 30, 1869

David Glasgow Farragut, commander of the West Gulf Blockading Squadron, gave the North its first great naval victory by capturing New Orleans in April 1862. He was promoted to rear admiral, and following his brilliant performance at Mobile Bay in August 1864, he was made a vice admiral. In 1866, he became the U.S. Navy's first full admiral.

Bureau of Construction, Equipment, and Repair

Established August 31, 1842; divided into Bureau of Construction and Repair, Bureau of Equipment and Recruiting, and Bureau of Steam

Engineering on July 5, 1862. Responsible for design, construction, and repair of propulsion and auxiliary machinery.

John Lenthal, November 17, 1853–July 5, 1862; commanded Bureau of Construction and Repair July 5, 1862–January 22, 1871

Bureau of Equipment and Recruiting

Organized from the Bureau of Construction, Equipment, and Repair, July 5, 1862.

Andrew H. Foote, July 17, 1862–June 3, 1863

Albert N. Smith, June 4, 1863–September 8, 1866

Bureau of Steam Engineering

Organized from the Bureau of Construction, Equipment, and Repair July 5, 1862.

Benjamin F. Isherwood, July 5, 1862–March 16, 1869

Bureau of Provisions and Clothing

Established August 31, 1842; included the Pay Office.

Horatio Bridge, October 1, 1854–July 11, 1869

Bureau of Ordnance and Hydrography

Established August 31, 1842; divided into Bureau of Ordnance (responsible for the offensive and defensive arms of the navy and shore stations where they are produced and tested), and Bureau of Navigation on July 5, 1862.

George A. Magruder, September 24, 1860–dismissed April 23, 1861

Andrew A. Harwood, April 24, 1861–July 5, 1862

Bureau of Ordnance

Organized from the Bureau of Ordnance and Hydrography, July 5, 1862.

Andrew A. Harwood, July 5, 1862–July 22, 1862

John A. Dahlgren, July 22, 1862–June 24, 1863

Henry A. Wise, June 25, 1863–June 1, 1868

Bureau of Navigation

Organized from the Bureau of Ordnance and Hydrography, July 5, 1862.

Charles H. Davis, July 17, 1862–April 27, 1865

Percival Drayton, April 28, 1865–August 4, 1865

Bureau of Medicine and Surgery

Established August 31, 1842. Responsible for operation of naval hospitals and medical activities, medical supplies, technical schools, and advising on hygiene and sanitation.

William Whelan, October 1, 1853–June 11, 1865

United States Marine Corps

Originally formed November 10, 1775, but lapsed after the American Revolution. Re-established July 11, 1798 (see "Marines in the Civil War," on page 573).

John Harris, commandant January 7, 1859–d. May 12, 1864

Jacob Zeilen, commandant June 10, 1864–November 1, 1876

United States Naval Academy (U.S.N.A.)

Founded August 15, 1845, as the U.S. Naval School, at Old Fort Severn, Annapolis, Maryland; became the United States Naval Academy on July 1, 1850. The Academy operated in Newport, Rhode Island, from April 1861 to August 1865. The Bureau of Ordnance and Hydrography oversaw the academy (October 10, 1845–July 5, 1862), followed by the Bureau of Navigation (July 5, 1862–March 1, 1867).

George S. Blake, September 15, 1857–September 9, 1865

Confederate States Navy

The Confederate Navy Department was established on February 21, 1861, by the provisional Confederate Congress, at Montgomery, Alabama. Modeled on its Northern counterpart, the Navy Department consisted of four bureaus and a Marine Corps. When the Confederate government moved from Montgomery to Richmond, Virginia, the Navy Department established its headquarters in the Mechanics Institute, Ninth Street, between Main and Franklin. Listed here are some key bureaus, offices, and staff of the Civil War years. Some of the dates of duty are not available.

ORGANIZATION AND STAFF

Secretary of the Navy

Stephen R. Mallory, February 28, 1861–May 2, 1865

Mallory's administrative subordinates included two chief clerks, three more clerks, and a messenger.

Ranking Officer of the Confederate States Navy

Franklin Buchanan, August 21, 1862–May 17, 1865

Naval Aide to the President

John Taylor Wood, 1863–May 1865

Register of the Navy

Established April 4, 1863.

James S. Jones

Engineer in Chief

Established April 21, 1862.

William P. Williamson, April 21, 1862–April 1865

Chief Constructor

Established April 30, 1863.

John L. Porter, April 30, 1863–April 1865

Office of Special Service

Responsible for construction of wooden gunboats.

Matthew F. Maury, January 1862

Thomas T. Rootes

John H. Parker

Bureau (Office) of Orders and Detail

Responsible for duties related to personnel, such as assigning crews and officers to ships; recruitment; and promotions. The bureau also procured and distributed coal for the navy.

Samuel Barron, June 11, 1861–July 20, 1861

Lawrence L. Rousseau, August 1, 1861–August 23, 1861

William F. Lynch, August 23, 1861–September 4, 1861

Franklin Buchanan, September 24, 1861–February 24, 1862

French Forrest, March 27, 1862–March 16, 1863

John K. Mitchell, March 16, 1863–May 6, 1864

Sidney S. Lee, May 6, 1864–April 1865

Bureau (Office) of Ordnance and Hydrography (Office)

Responsible for procurement and department-wide distribution of naval ordnance and munitions; dock and shipyard maintenance; navigational charts and equipment.

Duncan N. Ingraham, June 10, 1861–November 16, 1861

George B. Minor, December 1861–March 1863

John M. Brooke, March 1863–April 1865

Torpedo Bureau

Matthew F. Maury, 1861–

Gabriel J. Rains (Provisional Army of the Confederate States), June 1862–

Hunter Davidson, September 1862–

Bureau (Office) of Provisions and Clothing (included paymasters)

Responsible for supply of food and clothing to navy ships.

John DeBree, June 1861–April 1861

James A. Semple, August 1864–April 1865

Bureau (Office) of Medicine and Surgery

Administered naval medical facilities in several Southern ports, including a Richmond hospital.

William A. W. Spotswood, June 10, 1861–April 1865

Naval School (Drewry's Bluff, Virginia; James River; C.S.S. *Patrick Henry*)

Established May 15, 1862; schoolship scuttled April 2, 1865.

William H. Parker

Confederate States Marine Corps

Established March 16, 1861.

Lloyd J. Beall, commandant May 23, 1861–April 1865.

(*Source* for commanders and dates of service: John H. Eicher and David J. Eicher, Civil War High Commands (2001). Stanford, CA: Stanford University Press.)

Navy Yards and Stations

Principal U.S. Navy Yards

Navy yards are major facilities where naval ships can be dry-docked for repairs and extensive alterations. The table on pages 544–547 includes the most significant U.S. Navy yards of the Civil War era, along with their respective commanders and known dates of service.

U.S. Navy repair and supply stations—facilities where ships were supplied with fuel and necessary stores and sometimes underwent minor repairs—were established throughout the war to serve the expanding forces. Principal riverine installations included: Cairo, Illinois; Mound City, Illinois; and Memphis, Tennessee. The larger of the coastal stations were located at: Baltimore, Maryland; Beaufort, South Carolina; Port Royal, South Carolina; Ship Island, Louisiana; New Orleans, Louisiana; and Key West, Florida.

Principal C.S.A. Navy Yards and Stations

Navy yards in the Confederacy were captured from the Federal government. The Confederate naval stations were too modest to qualify as navy yards in the sense that the term was used in the prewar U.S. Navy. The official records of the Union and Confederate navies, however, contain Confederate references to "navy yard" which do not apply to the actual or former U.S. Navy yards.

The Official Records and correspondence are imprecise with respect to what constituted a naval station, as opposed to some lesser type of naval facility. As noted earlier, naval stations are facilities where ships can restock their fuel and stores, and undergo minor repairs. The locations of known naval stations and yards, and some known commanders and dates of service (when available), are listed in the table on pages 544–547.

The Blockade

On April 19, 1861, one week after the Confederates opened fire on Fort Sumter in Charleston Harbor, President Lincoln proclaimed a blockade of Southern ports. This was an ambitious objective; indeed, it was the largest blockade ever undertaken by any nation, covering 3,549 miles of coastline and 180 inlets (including bays, swamps, channels, rivers, lagoons, and harbors). The effort was made more difficult by the Union's paucity of ships. Of ninety commissioned warships in the U.S. Navy on that date, twenty-one were not seaworthy, twenty-seven were laid up for repairs, and twenty-eight were

PRINCIPAL U.S. NAVY YARDS

Navy Yard	*Commander, Known Dates of Service*
BostonYard (Charlestown Navy Yard), Massachusetts Established in 1800; built the U.S.S. *Merrimack, Cumberland, Hartford* (Farragut's flagship), and the monitor *Monadnock*.	William L. Hunson,1859– John B. Montgomery, 1862–1863 Silas H. Stringham, 1863–
New York (Brooklyn) Yard Established in 1801; during the war employed 6,000 workers; built the *Intelligent Whale* (1864), one of the U.S. navy's first submarines.	Samuel L. Breese, 1858–1861 Andrew H. Foote, February 1861–June 1861 Hiram Paulding, October 1861– Charles H. Bell, May 1865–
Norfolk (Gosport) Yard, Virginia Established in 1767; U.S.S. *Merrimack* converted to the C.S.S. *Virginia* here; yard damaged and abandoned by Union April 20, 1861; recaptured from Confederates May 10, 1862. Considered the premier navy installation.	Charles S. McCauley, August 1860–April 1861 John W. Livingston, May 1862–1864 John M. Berrien, November 1864– John J. Glasson, 1865
Pensacola (Warrington) Yard, Florida Established in 1826; Union surrendered yard to Southern militia forces January 12, 1861; evacuated and destroyed by Confederates May 9, 1862.	James L. Armstrong, October 1860–January 1861 William Smith, December 1862–1864 Theodore P. Greene, 1868–1869
Philadelphia Navy Yard, Pennsylvania Established in 1800; U.S.S. *New Ironsides*, an early experimental ironclad vessel (1862) commissioned here; during the war the yard built some vessels but primarily repaired and outfitted ships.	Samuel F. Du Pont, 1855–1861 James L. Lardner, June 1861– Thomas Turner, September 1861– Garrett J. Pendergast, October 1861 Cornelius K. Stribling, November 1862–1864 Joseph B. Hull Jr., November 1864– John P. Gillis, 1865–

PRINCIPAL U.S. NAVY YARDS (CONTINUED)

Navy Yard	*Commander, Known Dates of Service*
Portsmouth (Kittery) Yard, Maine Established in 1800; the U.S.S. *Kearsarge* (1861) built here.	George F. Pearson, October 1860– Theodorus Bailey, September 1864–1867
San Francisco Mare Island Naval Shipyard, California Established in 1854; built the first naval ship on the West Coast; during the war employed 300 workers.	David McDougal, March 1861– William H. Gardner, June 1861– Thomas O. Selfridge Sr., May 1862–1864 David McDougal, October 1864–
Washington Yard, District of Columbia Established in 1799 on a site selected by George Washington; President Lincoln frequently visited the yard; the U.S.S. *Monitor* repaired here after battle with the C.S.S. *Virginia*; Lincoln assassination suspects held here on board the U.S.S. *Montauk* and *Saugus*.	Franklin Buchanan, May 1859–April 1861 John A. B. Dahlgren, April 1861–July 1862 Andrew A. Harwood, July 1862– John B. Montgomery, December 1863–1865

PRINCIPAL C.S.A. NAVY YARDS AND STATIONS

Navy Yard	*Known Commander, Dates of Service*
Atlanta, Georgia	—
Charleston, South Carolina	Henry J. Hartstene, 1861 Duncan L. Ingraham, 1862–1865
Charlotte, North Carolina	Samuel Barron Richard L. Page, October 1862–1864 Henry A. Ramsay, 1864 George N. Hollins Catesby ap R. Jones
Columbus, Georgia	James H. Warner
Fort Jackson, Louisiana	William F. Lynch

PRINCIPAL C.S.A. NAVY YARDS AND STATIONS (CONTINUED)

Navy Yard	Known Commander, Dates of Service
Galveston, Texas	—
Halifax, North Carolina	James L. Johnson, 1863 James W. Cooke, 1864
Kingston, North Carolina	William Sharp, 1863 Benjamin P. Loyall, February 1864 Joseph Price, August 24, 1864–
Little Rock, Arkansas	John W. Dunnington
Marion Court House, South Carolina	—
Mobile, Alabama	Ebenezer Farrand, 1863–1865
New Orleans, Louisiana	Lawrence Rousseau, March 1861 George N. Hollins, August 1861 John K. Mitchell, January 1862 William C. Whittle, March 29, 1862–April 25, 1862
Norfolk (Gosport), Virginia	French Forrest, April 22, 1861–1862 Sidney S. Lee, March 27, 1862–May 1862
Oven Bluff Shipyard, Alabama	—
Pee Dee Navy Yard, South Carolina	Van Renssalaer Morgan, 1862 Edward J. Means, 1864
Pensacola, Florida	Victor M. Randolph, January 12, 1861– Duncan N. Ingraham, 1861 Thomas W. Brent, 1861–1862
Richmond Navy Yard (Rocketts), Virginia	Ebenezer Farrand, 1862 Robert G. Robb, 1862–1865
Saffold Navy Yard, Georgia	Catesby ap R. Jones, 1862
Savannah, Georgia	Josiah Tattnall, 1861–1862 Thomas W. Brent, 1862–1863
Selma, Alabama	Ebenezer Farrand Catesby ap R. Jones, May, 9, 1863–April 1865
Shreveport, Louisiana	Jonathan H. Carter

PRINCIPAL C.S.A. NAVY YARDS AND STATIONS (CONTINUED)

Navy Yard	*Known Commander, Dates of Service*
St. Marks Naval Station, Florida	Charles P. McGary, 1862
	Charles W. Hays, 1863
	Henry H. Lewis, 1864
Wilmington, North Carolina	William T. Muse, 1861–April 8, 1864
	James W. Cooke, 1864–1865
Yazoo City, Mississippi	Isaac N. Brown

Source for commanders and dates of service: John H. Eicher and David J. Eicher, *Civil War High Commands* (2001). Stanford, CA: Stanford University Press.

either in overseas ports or on their way home. Only fourteen were ready to put to sea to enforce the blockade. Nearly a quarter of U.S. naval officers resigned their commissions and offered their services to the Confederacy. In addition, the abandonment of the Gosport Navy Yard the day after Lincoln proclaimed the blockade cost the Union eleven ships, 3,000 pieces of ordnance, and millions of dollars worth of supplies and other property.

To overcome the seemingly insurmountable obstacles before him, Secretary of the Navy Gideon Welles immediately called for an additional 18,000 men and began purchasing or chartering ships. They were quickly armed and sent to sea, often with inexperienced crews who had to learn their new trade on the job. Within a year, purchases, coupled with a massive shipbuilding program, added 300 new warships to the fleet. By 1865, Welles and his capable assistant, Gustavus Fox, had purchased 418 ships (313 were steam-driven) and built another 208, of which more than sixty were ironclads. From a starting roster of 1,000 officers and 7,500 men, the navy had grown to nearly 7,000 officers and more than 51,000 men.

In the beginning, the blockade existed more on paper than in the waters of the Atlantic Ocean and the Gulf of Mexico. Its chief effect at that time was to serve notice to foreign nations that any attempt to trade with the Confederacy meant risking war with the United States (a risk that foreigners were unwilling to take). Within months of the surrender of Fort Sumter, however, the U.S. Navy scored its first success. In August 1861, the North Carolina port of Hatteras fell to a combined army-navy action that effectively closed two of the South's busiest shipping lanes and made the blockade a reality. From then until the fall of the South's last major port—Wilmington, North Carolina, in January 1865—the Union Navy extended its control of the Atlantic and Gulf coasts step by inexorable step.

The blockade created a new maritime industry: blockade running. Using fast, shallow-draft ships, enterprising captains attempted to elude the blockading fleet and deliver badly needed European munitions and supplies to the beleaguered South. According to figures compiled by historian Stephen R. Wise, approximately 1,300 attempts were made to break the blockade, of which 1,000 were successful. "The average lifetime of a blockade runner was just over four runs, or two round trips," writes Wise.

Even when it was more a dream than a reality, however, the blockade drove up prices in the South and encouraged blockade runners to devote more of their cargo space to highly profitable consumer goods than to military essentials such as medicine and munitions (e.g., coffee cost $249 a ton in Nassau, but was sold at Confederate ports for $5,500). The inflated pay scale also reflects the lure of blockade running. Ship captains would hope to make as much as $5,000 for a successful blockading run, as opposed to prewar pay of $150 per trip in the merchant trade.

Though it never succeeded in shutting down all foreign trade with the South, the Union navy managed to capture 1,149 Confederate ships and destroy 351 more, of which 136 captured and eighty-five destroyed were blockade runners. Shortages caused by the blockade, combined with a reduction of the South's internal transportation capacity (it was unable to import machinery and iron for railroads), were major factors in causing the runaway inflation that ruined the Confederacy's economy and crippled its war effort.

The Operational Organization of the Blockade

After Lincoln proclaimed a blockade of Confederate ports, the extensive—and geographically diverse—Southern coastline and the dearth of Union ships made it impossible for the existing Home Squadron to carry out the president's order. A Commission of Conference (also known as the Blockade Board, or Strategy Board) was established to determine the best methods for enforcing the blockade. The board, chaired by Captain Samuel Du Pont, studied the Southern topography, examined relevant maps and studies in government archives, and produced reports outlining and detailing procedures to execute the Anaconda Plan (see "Military Strategy—

United States" in Chapter 4, "Battles and Battlefields"). The plan relied on a naval blockade that would isolate and strangle the Confederacy, and an effective blockade required a huge investment in warships and other vessels.

In June 1861, two blockading squadrons were created. The Atlantic Blockading Squadron, operating out of Hampton Roads, Virginia, was responsible for the Atlantic seaboard, from Virginia to the tip of Florida. The Gulf Blockading Squadron, based at Key West, Florida, was assigned the entire gulf region, from the south of Florida to Brownsville, Texas. Throughout the spring and summer of 1861, the Union steadily acquired more ships for blockading duty, and the board recommended dividing the squadrons to better manage coastal operations.

In September 1861, the Atlantic Blockading Squadron was split into the North Atlantic Blockading Squadron (N.A.B.S) and the South Atlantic Blockading Squadron (S.A.B.S). Hampton Roads served as headquarters for the N.A.B.S, which covered the Chesapeake Bay down to Wilmington,

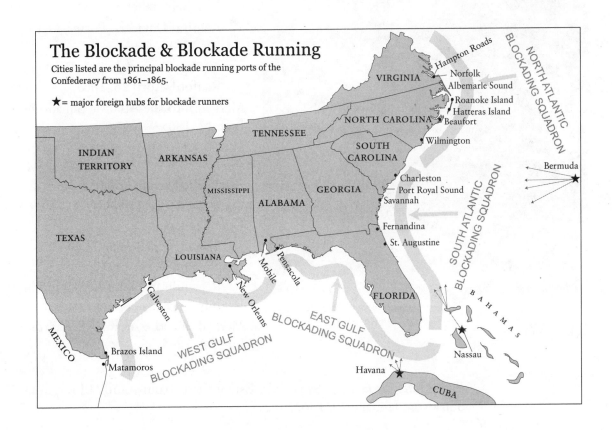

The Blockade & Blockade Running

Cities listed are the principal blockade running ports of the Confederacy from 1861–1865.

★ = major foreign hubs for blockade runners

North Carolina. Ships in the S.A.B.S. used Port Royal, South Carolina, as a main base, and operated from Wilmington to Cape Canaveral, Florida. On January 20, 1862, the Gulf Blockading Squadron was also divided. The West Gulf Blockading Squadron (W.G.B.S), at Pensacola, Florida, and Ship Island, Mississippi, patrolled the waters from Pensacola to the Rio Grande, while the East Gulf Blockading Squadron (E.G.B.S) remained based at Key West and covered the area from Pensacola to Cape Canaveral.

Blockade Squadron Commanders

North Atlantic Blockading Squadron: Established from Atlantic Blockading Squadron, September 18, 1861.

David Dixon Porter commanded the Mississippi River Fleet that helped capture Vicksburg and cut the Confederacy in two. He was rewarded for his remarkable service with promotion to rear admiral in May 1863.

Commanders:

Flag Officer Louis M. Goldsborough, September 18, 1861

Acting Rear Admiral Samuel P. Lee, September 5, 1862

Admiral David D. Porter, October 12, 1864

Acting Rear Admiral William Radford, April 28, 1865

Merged into the Atlantic Squadron, June 12, 1865.

South Atlantic Blockading Squadron: Established from Atlantic Blockading Squadron, September 18, 1861.

Commanders:

Flag Officer Samuel F. Du Pont, September 18, 1861

Rear Admiral John A. Dahlgren, July 6, 1863

Merged into the Atlantic Squadron, June 12, 1865.

East Gulf Blockading Squadron: Established from Gulf Blockading Squadron, January 20, 1862.

Commanders:

> Flag Officer William W. McKean, January 20, 1862
>
> Flag Officer James Lawrence Lardner, June 4, 1862
>
> Acting Rear Admiral Theodorus Bailey, December 9, 1862
>
> Captain Theodore P. Greene, August 7, 1864 (commander pro tem)
>
> Acting Rear Admiral Cornelius K. Stribling, October 12, 1864

Merged into the Gulf Squadron, June 12, 1865.

West Gulf Blockading Squadron: Established from Gulf Blockading Squadron, January 20, 1862.

Commanders:

> Flag Officer David G. Farragut, January 20, 1862
>
> Commodore James S. Palmer, November 30, 1864
>
> Acting Rear Admiral Henry K. Thatcher, February 23, 1865

Merged into Gulf Squadron, June 12, 1865.

The British Presence in the Naval War

Though the British government assumed a position of neutrality toward the American Civil War, many within the government, as well as significant numbers of civilians, particularly aristocrats, sympathized with the Confederacy. British shipbuilders constructed many of the South's finest ships, including feared commerce raiders like the *Alabama* and the *Shenandoah*. They were also commissioned to construct ironclad warships for the South, but through the intervention of Charles Adams, U.S. minister to Great Britain, the ironclads were never delivered.

The U.S. Navy's blockade of Southern ports along a 3,549-mile coastline, dotted with 180 openings, made it difficult for British merchant vessels to deliver goods in trade for cotton, tobacco, sugar, and rice. (It is perhaps not surprising, then, that British citizens were among those who sought to run the blockade. Some members of the Royal Navy even retired in order to take the helm of blockade-running vessels.) Because the Royal Navy was the preeminent maritime force in the world at the time, the United States government did not want to openly provoke British merchants. Nonetheless, British merchant ships were turned back when apprehended, and the specter of possible British retaliation loomed throughout the war.

One incident, early in the war, brought this issue to a crisis. Now dubbed the "*Trent* affair," it involved an unarmed British mail steamer (*Trent*) that left Havana, Cuba, on November 7, 1861. On board were James M. Mason and John Slidell, the Confederate commissioners to Great Britain and France, respectively, en route to London and Paris to plead for official recognition of the Southern cause. The *Trent* was overtaken by the *San Jacinto*, a Union warship commanded by Captain Charles Wilkes. Without U.S. government permission, Wilkes boarded the *Trent* and demanded, under the threat of force, the surrender of Mason and Slidell. The British captain reluctantly complied, and the *Trent* continued to Great Britain. The British government, incensed that one of their mail ships was commandeered on the high seas, gave President Lincoln an ultimatum: release the two Confederate officials or risk war with Great Britain. The tense situation was resolved when Mason and Slidell were released on January 1, 1862 (see "European Powers and the American Civil War," in Chapter 3, "Wartime Politics").

Ironclads

Ironclad warships were not an innovation of the U.S. Civil War. The British and the French navies had successfully used ironclads against Russian forts in the Crimean War. But when the Confederate ironclad C.S.S. *Virginia* (built upon the salvaged hull of the U.S.S. *Merrimack*) steamed out of Norfolk, Virginia, on March 8, 1862, to attack the wooden warships of the Union blockading squadron at Hampton Roads, naval warfare began to move into a new era. Ironically, the creation of the ironclad was partly due to the Confederacy's relative lack of funds. Cost estimates for the *Merrimack*'s restoration were $450,000, whereas covering the hull with three-inch iron plates would cost $172,523 and could be done sooner. News of the *Merrimack*'s conversion into an ironclad spawned a frenzied effort among Union authorities to produce an effective counterweapon. The U.S. government feared that the *Virginia* could destroy the blockade and threaten major Northern cities, perhaps even shell Washington, D.C., into submission. However, Swedish-born inventor John Ericsson's design for what became the U.S.S. *Monitor* was the answer. The entirely unique *Monitor* was well-suited to the challenge. Essentially an armored raft, the ship's most spectacular feature was its revolving turret with twin eleven-inch Dahlgren guns.

Built in New York in record time (a little over three months), the *Monitor* arrived at Hampton Roads, Virginia, on the night of the *Virginia*'s victory over the Union's wooden-hulled blockaders. On the following day, March 9, 1862, the two iron vessels squared off and pounded each other for four hours, often at close range. Neither ship suffered significant damage. When the *Virginia* retired, technological balance on the water had been restored, and the *Monitor* claimed a tactical victory for neutralizing the threat to the wooden fleet.

The clash of the ironclads at Hampton Roads led to "monitor fever" in the North; Union ship development evolved into dozens of variations of the original *Monitor* (sixty Union ironclads were built during the war). Yet, even before the Hampton Roads encounter, Union armored vessels had been operating successfully on the western rivers—principally in the Mississippi River basin below Cairo, Illinois. The "city-class" gunboats (built by James B. Eads and nicknamed "Pook's Turtles" for their designer, Samuel Pook) were the first Union ironclads. Pook's ships were 175 feet long by fifty feet wide, and boasted two and one-half inches of iron backed by two feet of oak forward, and one foot down the sides. Flat-bottomed, slow moving, designed with ominous profiles, and armed with fourteen guns each, they were formidable ships of war. They were not, however, invincible. Three of these city-class gunboats were sunk during the course of the war.

Production of ironclads remained a Confederate priority throughout the war, but, because of a lack of adequate shipyards and material, fewer than two dozen of the approximately fifty ironclads intended for the Confederacy became available for service. The exploits of a number of these vessels—particularly the *Arkansas*, the *Albemarle*, the *Tennessee*, and the original *Virginia*—are still celebrated in Civil War literature.

A Telling Clash of Ironclads: The C.S.S. Atlanta versus the U.S.S. Weehawken

The British-built *Fingal* was a maneuverable and successful blockade-running ship that made port at Savannah, Georgia. Realizing that the chances of getting out of Savannah were slim, *Fingal*'s owners sold the ship to the Confederacy, which converted it to an ironclad and renamed it *Atlanta*. With four guns, a crew of 145, and a speed of ten knots, the *Atlanta* was said to be the most formidable and fastest ironclad the South had built. The U.S. Navy's monitor *Weehawken*, backed by another monitor, the *Nahant*, confronted the

The ironclad warship U.S.S. Atlanta, *seen in the James River in 1865, existed under various identities. The ship was originally the blockade runner* Fingal, *then was converted to an ironclad as the C.S.S.* Atlanta *and closely resembled the first Confederate ironclad, the C.S.S.* Virginia. *Captured on June 17, 1863, in Wassaw Sound, Georgia, the* Atlanta *served as a Union warship on blockade duty. In May 1869 it was sold to Haiti, renamed* Triumph, *and lost at sea seven months later.*

Atlanta at the mouth of the Wilmington River in Wassau Sound, Georgia in the early morning hours of June 17, 1863. The *Weehawken* was able to get within 300 yards and fired five shots from fifteen-inch and eleven-inch guns. Four of the shots hit. None pierced the four-inch iron plate, but the residual damage of splintered wood wounded sixteen of the crew. Within fifteen minutes, the *Atlanta* surrendered. It was not a huge military victory for the Union, but it was a crushing psychological defeat for the Confederacy because the *Atlanta* had been considered "an improved *Merrimack*."

The battle was also perceived as a contest between American and British shipbuilding ideas. The U.S. Navy preferred the monitor style with the huge fifteen-inch guns; the British idea was to plate the sides of a faster ship with iron and outfit her with smaller rifled guns. "No persons were more interested in the result of the conflict than the Lords of the British Admiralty, ever alive to what might exercise an influence upon their navy," wrote Admiral David D. Porter. "The success of the *Weehawken* shattered their faith." In a way, this battle was a double victory for the U.S. Navy. It ended the career of a potentially formidable Confederate vessel before it even began, and it sent a message to Great Britain: the United States had a naval force that was not to be trifled with.

Notable Ironclads

(Vessels listed by their date of commission)

Union Coastal Ironclads

Monitor

Monitor; armed with two 11-inch smoothbore guns; revolving turret; crew of 58. Commissioned February 25, 1862. Fought the C.S.S. *Virginia* to a standstill at Hampton Roads, Virginia, March 9, 1862, in the first-ever battle of ironclads. Participated in shelling of Sewall's Point, Virginia, May 8, 1862, and Drewry's Bluff, Virginia, May 15, 1862. Went down in a storm off Cape Hatteras, North Carolina, December 31, 1862, en route to blockading duty.

Galena

Sloop; armed with two 100-pounder rifles, four 9-inch smoothbore guns; crew of 150. Commissioned April 21, 1862. Served in the N.A.B.S., W.G.B.S., and E.G.B.S. Struck 43 times and sustained major damage during shelling of Drewry's Bluff, Virginia, May 15, 1862. Its ineffective armor was removed in 1863; recommissioned as wooden screw sloop, February 15, 1864, and assigned to blockade duty as a gunboat. Participated in battle of Mobile Bay, August 5, 1864.

New Ironsides

Frigate; armed with fourteen 11-inch smoothbore guns, two 150-pounder rifles, iron ram on prow; crew of 460. Commissioned August 21, 1862. Served in the S.A.B.S.; flagship of Rear Admiral Samuel Du Pont. Participated in the bombardment of Charleston forts April 7, 1863 (hit more than 60 times) and summer 1863; served in the N.A.B.S. and led attacks on Fort Fisher December 24–25, 1864, and January 13–15, 1865. Damaged by torpedo from the C.S.S. *David*, October 5, 1863, but virtually invincible to gunfire with its high-quality, 4.5 inch-thick iron plate. Later served in the James River flotilla protecting the army base and General Ulysses S. Grant's headquarters at City Point, Virginia.

Roanoke

Monitor (originally a frigate); armed with two 15-inch and two 11-inch smoothbore guns, two 150-pounder rifles; crew of 350. In 1857, *Roanoke* brought filibusterer William Walker and 200 of his men back to the United States from Nicaragua (see pp. 92 and 134). Served on blockading duty early in the war. Later converted from a frigate to a three-turreted ironclad, the only monitor of its kind. Recommissioned June 29, 1863. Served in the N.A.B.S. at Hampton Roads, Virginia.

PASSAIC CLASS MONITORS

Designed by John Ericsson, these vessels were about 200-feet long—larger than the original *Monitor*—and featured improved boilers and ventilation. Each armed with one 15-inch and one 11-inch smoothbore gun; crew of 70 to 80. Ten ships were built in this class (*Camanche, Catskill, Lehigh, Montauk, Nahant, Nantucket, Passaic, Patapsco, Sangamon,* and *Weehawken*); all but *Camanche* saw service in the war. Ships commissioned between October 1862 and May 1865. Passaic monitors served in the N.A.B.S. and S.A.B.S. and participated in the bombardment of Charleston forts, April 7, 1863, and summer 1863.

Nahant: Challenged the C.S.S. *Atlanta* June 17, 1863, in Wassaw Sound, Georgia, and assisted the *Weehawken* in capturing the Confederate vessel without firing its guns.

Montauk: Shelled and destroyed the steamer C.S.S. *Nashville* February 28, 1863, in the Ogeechee River, near Ft. McAllister, Georgia; damaged by torpedo during battle. Served as a temporary prison ship for Lincoln assassination suspects; John Wilkes Booth's body was delivered to the ship April 27, 1865, and autopsied on board.

Weekhawken: Captured the C.S.S. *Atlanta* June 17, 1863 (see page 553); disabled and sank off Charleston, South Carolina, December 6, 1863, losing more than 30 men.

Onondaga

Monitor; armed with two 15-inch smoothbore guns, two 150-pounder rifles; double-turreted; equipped with locomotive headlight; crew of

130. Commissioned March 24, 1864. Served in the James River flotilla. Severely damaged the C.S.S. *Virginia II* and C.S.S. *Richmond* at Trent's Reach, Virginia, January 24, 1865. In April 1865 assisted in the confiscation of Confederate naval wares at Richmond.

CANONICUS CLASS MONITORS

Single-turret monitors, these warships marked further improvement to monitor-type vessels and were longer (235 feet in length) than the Passaic class. Each armed with two 15-inch smoothbore guns; crew of 85. Nine ships were built in this class (*Canonicus, Mahopac, Manhattan, Saugus,* and *Tecumseh*; the *Catawba, Manayunk, Oneota,* and *Tippecanoe* did not see service in the war). Commissioned April 1864 to February 1866. Primarily served in blockading squadrons; the *Canonicus* and the *Saugus* also served in the James River flotilla.

Canonicus: Participated in engagements at Trent's Reach, Virginia, June 21, 1864; Dutch Gap, Virginia, August 16–18, 1864; and Howlett's Farm, December 5–6, 1864. Participated in attacks on Fort Fisher, December 24–25, 1864 and January 13–15, 1865.

Manhattan: Participated in the battle of Mobile Bay, Alabama, August 5, 1864 (with a single shot, blew away five inches of iron armor and two-foot-thick wood backing on the C.S.S. *Tennessee* and helped force its surrender), and the bombardment of Fort Morgan, Mobile Bay, August 9–23, 1864.

Saugus: Participated in engagements at Trent's Reach, Dutch Gap, Howlett's Farm, Four Mile Creek (June 29–30, 1864) and Fort Fisher. Served briefly as a prison for Lincoln assassination suspects at Washington Navy Yard, April 1865.

Tecumseh: Struck a mine at battle of Mobile Bay as it attempted to cross a torpedo line; sank almost instantly, losing 93 of the 114 men on board.

MONADNOCK CLASS MONITORS

These vessels measured 260 feet long and could perform well at sea. Armed with four 15-inch smoothbore guns; crew of 167. Four ships were built in this class (*Agamenticus, Miantonomoh, Monadnock*, and *Tonawanda*) but only the *Monadnock* served in the war. Ships commissioned between October 1864 and October 1865.

Monadnock: Served in the N.A.B.S. and participated in the attack of Fort Fisher, North Carolina, December 24–25, 1864, and its capture, January 13–15, 1865. Participated in the advance on Richmond, April 1865.

CASCO CLASS MONITORS

Developed for operation in shallow waters, this class was a dismal failure. The class was originally designed by John Ericsson, but subsequent design changes (not by Ericsson) resulted in single-turret, light-draft vessels that were unable to bear heavy weight, suffered leakage, and were barely serviceable. Five of the vessels were completed as torpedo boats, 15 others were built as monitors; most did not serve in the war.

U.S.S. *Atlanta* and U.S.S. *Tennessee* (See Notable Confederate Ironclads.)

Union River Ironclads

Essex

Casemate gunboat (converted from a river ferry); armed with one 10-inch and two 9-inch smoothbore guns, one 32-pounder rifle; crew of 134. Commissioned October 1861. Served in the Western Gunboat Flotilla. First operated as a timberclad; twice reconfigured with addition of armor. Attacked the C.S.S. *Arkansas* at Vicksburg, Mississippi, July 22, 1862, and helped force its destruction at Baton Rouge, Louisiana, August 5, 1862. Attacked Natchez, Mississippi, September 3, 1862, and participated in the bombardment of Port Hudson, Louisiana, May 8–July 9, 1863. Remained active throughout the war.

CITY CLASS (OR "CAIRO" CLASS)

Gunboats with armored casemates; paddlewheel toward stern; armed with three 8-inch smoothbore guns, four 42-pounder rifles, six 32-pounder rifles, one 12- pounder rifle (armament of varying types was added and replaced on each vessel throughout the war); crew of 251. Seven were built (*Cairo, Carondelet, Cincinnati, Louisville, Mound City,*

Pittsburg, and *St. Louis* [renamed *Baron de Kalb*]); each had different-colored stacks to distinguish them from others in the class. Dubbed "Pook's Turtles" after their designer, Samuel Pook. Commissioned January 1862. Served in the Western Gunboat Flotilla.

Extensively active monitors, some or all were involved in operations at Forts Henry and Donelson, Tennessee, February 1862; Ft. Pillow, Tennessee April 13 and May 10, 1862; the battle of Memphis, June 6, 1862 (which saw the destruction of the Confederate River Defense Fleet); the White River expedition, June 1862; running past the Vicksburg, Mississippi, batteries, April 1863; the Red River expedition, March–May, 1864, and numerous other missions. The *Cairo* (December 12, 1862) and the *St. Louis* (July 13, 1863) both hit mines and sank in the Yazoo River. The *Cincinnati* received the surrender of the unfinished ironclad C.S.S. *Nashville* (May 10, 1865) in the Tombigbee River, Alabama.

Benton

Casemate gunboat (converted from a catamaran snagboat); armed with two 9-inch and seven 32-pounder smoothbore guns; seven 42-pounder rifles; center wheel; crew of 176. Commissioned February 24, 1862. One of the Union's strongest ironclads (though slow) and highly active throughout the war. Served in the Western Gunboat Flotilla; flagship of the Mississippi Squadron, 1862–1863. Participated in operations at Island No. 10, March 15, 1862; Fort Pillow, Tennessee, April 13 and May 10, 1862; the Battle of Memphis, June 6, 1862; several expeditions up the Red River, 1863–1865.

NEOSHO CLASS

The only monitors with sternwheels, which were encased in armor; single-turret, shallow-draft vessels; armed with two 11-inch smoothbore guns; crew of 100. Commissioned 1863. The two monitors in this class, the *Neosho* and the *Osage*, served in the Mississippi River Fleet and participated in the Red River expedition, March–May 1864. The *Neosho* also operated on the Cumberland and Tennessee Rivers; the Osage used a makeshift forerunner to the periscope, in combat (Blair's Landing, April 12, 1864); sank in the Blakely River, Alabama, March 29, 1865.

MILWAUKEE CLASS

Double-turreted monitors, design similar to Neosho class; armed with four 11-inch smoothbore guns; crew of 138. Commissioned May–August, 1864. All four vessels in this class (*Chickasaw, Kickapoo, Milwaukee,* and *Winnebago*) served in the W.G.B.S. The *Chickasaw* and the *Winnebago* both participated in the Battle of Mobile Bay, Alabama, August 5, 1864, and the attack on Fort Morgan, Mobile Bay, August 9–23, 1864; the *Milwaukee* sank in the Blakely River, Alabama, March 18, 1865, after hitting a mine.

Confederate Ironclads

Manassas

Casemate ram (converted from a towboat); armed with one 64-pounder smoothbore gun; crew of 35. Commissioned December 1861. Issued a letter of marque and reprisal to operate as a privateer. Taken into service by the Confederate navy (October 11, 1861) and assigned to the Lower Mississippi River. Run aground and burned after engaging the U.S.S. *Brooklyn, Mississippi,* and *Pensacola* at the battle of New Orleans, April 24, 1862.

Virginia

Casemate ram (converted from a frigate, the U.S.S. *Merrimack*); armed with two 7-inch rifles, six 9-inch smoothbore guns, two six-inch 32-pounder rifles; crew of 320. Commissioned March 1862. Flagship of the James River Squadron. Destroyed the U.S.S. *Cumberland* and U.S.S. *Congress,* March 8, 1862, at Hampton Roads, Virginia. The following day battled the U.S.S. *Monitor* in the first combat between ironclads. After Confederates abandoned Norfolk and the Gosport Navy Yard, its home base, the crew destroyed the ship to prevent capture May 11, 1862, off Craney Island in the James River.

Arkansas

Casemate ram; armed with two 9-inch, two 8-inch, and two 32-pounder smoothbore guns, two 6-inch rifles; crew of 200. Commissioned May

26, 1862. Powerful, but undermanned and not completely finished when put into service. Damaged the U.S.S. *Carondelet* and *Queen of the West* in the Yazoo River, July 15, 1862, and broke through the Union fleet to reach Vicksburg. There it fought off the U.S.S. *Essex* and *Queen of the West*, July 22, 1862. Suffered numerous engine failures and was attacked by the Essex near Baton Rouge, Louisiana, August 6, 1862; the crew burned the vessel to prevent its capture.

RICHMOND CLASS CASEMATE RAMS

Confederate Chief Naval Constructor John L. Porter developed a standard design for armored coastal and harbor defense vessels:150-foot-long, screw propelled flat-bottomed warships with six guns and 180-man crews. However, there was much variance in length, armament, and machinery among the six vessels generally categorized as the Richmond class.

Richmond: Armed with one 7-inch rifle, one 10-inch smoothbore gun, two 6.4-inch rifles. Commissioned July 1862. Served in the James River Squadron. Participated in engagements at Dutch Gap, Virginia, August 13, 1864; Fort Harrison, Virginia, September 29–31, 1864; and Chapin's Bluff, October 22, 1864. Crew sank ship near Drewry's Bluff, Virginia, April 3, 1865 to prevent capture as Richmond was evacuated.

Chicora (armed with two 9-inch smoothbores, four 6-inch 32-pounder rifles) and the *Palmetto State* (with ten 7-inch rifles) were both commissioned in November 1862, served in the defense of Charleston, attacked Union blockade ships January 31, 1863, and were sunk by their crews February 18, 1865, to prevent capture.

Savannah: Armed with two 7-inch rifles, two 6.4-inch rifles. Commissioned June 30, 1863. Served in the defense of Savannah, Georgia. Assisted in capture of a sidewheel sloop, the U.S.S. *Water Witch*, June 3, 1864. Destroyed to prevent capture December 21, 1864, just before its home base was captured.

North Carolina: Armed with two 7-inch and two 6.4-inch rifles. Commissioned December 1863. Served in the defense of Charleston, South Carolina; foundered off Smithville, North Carolina, September 27, 1864.

Raleigh: Armed with four 6-inch rifles. Commissioned April 30, 1864. Served in the defense of Wilmington, North Carolina, and challenged Union blockade ships. Grounded near New Inlet, North Carolina, May 7, 1864.

Atlanta

Casemate ram (converted from the blockade runner *Fingal*); armed with two 7-inch and two 6.4-inch rifles, spar torpedo; crew of 145. Commissioned November 22, 1862. Stationed at Savannah. Battled the U.S.S. *Weehawken* and U.S.S. *Nahant* in Wassaw Sound, Georgia, June 17, 1863, and was captured. Commissioned in the Union navy February 2, 1864, and served in the S.A.B.S., N.A.B.S., and James River.

Tennessee (II)

Casemate ram; armed with two 7-inch rifles, four 6.4-inch rifles; six inches of armor forward, five inches on the casemate; crew of 133. Commissioned February 16, 1864. Defended Mobile Bay, Alabama, and attempted to break the Union blockade. One of the South's finest and best built ironclads, the *Tennessee* was the Confederate flagship at the battle of Mobile Bay, August 5, 1864, where it was surrounded by Admiral Farragut's fleet and captured. Commissioned in the Union navy (August 19, 1864) as the U.S.S. *Tennessee*. Served in the W.G.B.S. and Mississippi Squadron and participated in the bombardment of Fort Morgan, Alabama, August 19–22, 1864.

Albemarle

Casemate ram; armed with two 6.4-inch rifles; crew of 150. Commissioned April 17, 1864. Operated out of North Carolina. The *Albemarle* sunk the U.S.S. *Southfield* at Plymouth, April 19, 1864 and the Confederates retook Plymouth the following day. On October 28, 1864, in an early morning attack, William B. Cushing, aboard the Union's *Picket Boat No. 1*, detonated a torpedo that sunk the *Albemarle*, leading to the Confederacy's loss of Plymouth and control of the Roanoke River area.

Commerce Raiders

Commerce raiding, which has a long record in the history of warfare, is principally conducted by weaker nations against an opponent that has an expansive merchant marine. By seizing and destroying merchant vessels, the raiders hope to accomplish a number of objectives, from luring enemy warships away from critical theaters of operation to simply causing economic chaos in the enemy's established trade patterns.

Raphael Semmes, famed captain of the Confederate commerce raider Alabama, *was eager to fight the awaiting U.S.S.* Kearsarge: *"I beg she will not depart before I am ready to go out." He was promoted to admiral February 10, 1865.*

The Confederacy made use of privateers, but the celebrated commerce raiding of the Civil War era was conducted by Confederate wooden naval cruisers. The largest and most successful of the various raiding programs initiated by the Confederacy was coordinated by Confederate agent James Dunwoody Bulloch, in England. Bulloch discreetly contracted for sleek cruisers to be built in British shipyards, and, when removed from England's neutral waters, to be outfitted with a crew and a warship's armament. Two of the most dreaded and successful Confederate raiders were built this way: the C.S.S. *Florida* and the C.S.S. *Alabama*. The *Florida*, under three separate captains, took thirty-seven Union vessels during its storied career. The *Alabama*, the most famous of the raiders, with the colorful Raphael Semmes in charge, seized sixty-seven Union merchant ships, of which fifty-one were destroyed (valued at more than $6,000,000). In what became the second most celebrated naval duel (behind the *Monitor* versus the *Virginia*), the 1,031-ton steamer U.S.S. *Kearsarge* tracked the C.S.S. *Alabama* to the coast of France. John A. Winslow, the captain of the *Kearsarge*, had learned that the *Alabama* had put into Cherbourg Harbor for repairs on June 11, 1864. On June 19, Semmes steamed out of port to confront the approaching *Kearsarge*. The hour-long battle ended with *Alabama*'s sinking.

Captain John Newland Maffitt, first captain of the C.S.S. Florida, *the Confederacy's first foreign-built warship. Early in Maffitt's command, he and his men rallied from a scourge of yellow fever that killed six of the crew. On February 12, 1863, the* Florida *captured and destroyed the* Jacob Bell, *valued at more than $1.5 million, one of 23 "prizes" the raider would claim under Maffitt.*

Commerce raiding was one of the most potent psychological weapons of the Confederate naval effort. The 200 merchant vessels destroyed in the raiding, and the millions of dollars of damage done, may have seemed devastating to commercial interests, but the campaign had only a negligible effect on the outcome of the war. The raiders' most significant accomplishment was to drive ships from the U.S. Merchant Marine to register under foreign flags, particularly via British agents. The extent of the monetary damage caused by the far-ranging Confederate cruisers can be gauged by the large size of the settlement for the "Alabama Claims" awarded by the Geneva Tribunal in 1872. The United States was awarded $15.5 million in compensation for the losses incurred among its merchant fleet by cruisers built in British yards. (In 1873, Great Britain paid the claims.) The total revenues of the United States for the entire period 1861–1865 were about $161 million, and the award was equivalent to 9.6 percent of that revenue.

CONFEDERATE STATES NAVY COMMERCE RAIDERS

Alabama	Bark-rigged, screw steam sloop-of-war; eight guns; took 67 prizes; traveled more than 75,000 miles in two years of service.
Archer	Civilian schooner captured by C.S.S. *Tacony*; one gun; destroyed revenue cutter U.S.S. *Caleb Cushing*.
Chickamauga	Schooner-rigged, screw steam cruiser; converted from the blockade runner *Edith*; five guns; captured seven prizes.
Clarence	Bark captured by C.S.S. *Florida*, converted into a raider; one gun; took six prizes.
Florida	Three-masted screw steam cruiser; nine guns; took 38 prizes.

CONFEDERATE STATES NAVY COMMERCE RAIDERS (CONTINUED)

Georgia	Brig-rigged screw steam cruiser; five guns; captured nine prizes.
Nashville	Brig-rigged sidewheel steamer; two guns; fired on by U.S.S. *Harriet Lane* at Ft. Sumter in the war's first gunfire at sea; took two prizes.
Shenandoah	Full-rigged clipper steam cruiser; eight guns; captured 37 prizes; only Confederate warship to circumnavigate the globe.
Sumter	Bark-rigged screw steamer; five guns; took 18 prizes.
Tacony	Bark; one gun; captured by C.S.S. *Clarence*; took 15 prizes.
Tallahassee	Schooner-rigged screw steam cruiser; originally the blockade runner *Atalanta*; three guns; captured 38 vessels.
Tuscaloosa	Originally the bark *Conrad*; three guns; took two prizes.

The Evolution of the Submarine: The C.S.S. Hunley

"Submarines" had begun to be developed as far back as the Revolutionary War, but it wasn't until the Civil War that so much previously theoretical work was moved from the drawing board and put into production. At this time, European powers were also developing submersible vessels. In November 1861, the U.S. Navy contracted with the French inventor Brutus de Villeroi, who was living in Philadelphia, to construct his proposed "submarine propeller." The navy acquired the submarine the following June and named it *Alligator*. Originally it was powered by a set of oars which were later replaced with a hand-cranked screw propeller. The submarine was lost in rough seas in April 1863 after being cut loose from its tow ship. There are reports, but little hard evidence, of the creation of several Confederate submarine vessels, and only a few can be adequately documented: the prototype *Pioneer*, now on display in New Orleans; the *American Diver*, lost in Mobile Bay; and the *H.L. Hunley*.

Named for inventor and businessman Horace Hunley, the C.S.S. *Hunley* was not the first submersible used in a combat situation. That distinction must go to David Bushnell's Revolutionary War-era *Turtle*. Robert Fulton's *Nautilus* also predated the *Hunley* as the first navigable submarine. But the *Hunley* will forever be remembered as the first submarine to sink an enemy warship in battle. The vessel that came to be called the *Hunley* was launched in July 1863, at Mobile, but it was referred to by various names, including "Fish Boat." In August 1863, the submersible was shipped via flatcar to Charleston, South Carolina, for operations against the Union blockading fleet.

The *Hunley* was a sophisticated, forty-foot-long vessel with an exterior hull of wrought-iron plates. The boat was equipped with two conning towers, dive planes, five sets of small portholes on top of the hull, and a bellows connected to a snorkel box that was used to pump fresh air into the submarine's compartment. (In one of its test runs, the *Hunley* and its crew stayed submerged for two hours and thirty-five minutes.) Seven seated crewmen propelled the boat by manually cranking a drive shaft that ran the length of the submarine. The commander controlled the submarine's depth with a dive plane control handle and steered the *Hunley* with a joystick-like lever that manipulated rods and cables, which turned the boat's rudder. A torpedo on a spar projected from its bow for the purpose of ramming the explosive into the hull of an enemy vessel. Once that was done, the submersible would back away and, at a safe distance, detonate the charge with a lanyard (a long cord with a hook attached to the torpedo).

During a test on August 29, 1863, five members of the first crew drowned and three escaped when the submersible was swamped. Convinced of the sub's reliable design, Horace Hunley himself subsequently came to Charleston and tested the vessel with a new crew of seven volunteers. On October 15, 1863, however, Hunley and the entire crew drowned in another accidental flooding of the ship.

The C.S.A. commander in the district, P. G. T. Beauregard, was determined to end the experiment, but Lieutenant George Dixon persuaded Beauregard to allow him to use it against the Union steam sloop-of-war *Housatonic*. Beauregard agreed, but stipulated that the *Hunley* must operate only partially submerged, in the manner of the "David" torpedo boats, for the safety of the crew. On February 17, 1864, following several successful trial runs in Charleston Harbor, Lieutenant Dixon slipped away from shore and steered the *Hunley* toward the *Housatonic*. Everything appears to have worked just as planned. The explosive was planted in the sloop's hull and detonated. The Union warship sank in minutes. Sailors aboard the *Housatonic* testified that the *Hunley* had pulled away, but it was never seen again. For over a century it was commonly believed that the submersible sank along with its victim, and was scrapped years later, when the wreckage of the *Housatonic* was salvaged.

However, *Housatonic* survivors' testimony, duly noted in U.S. Navy records as early as 1894, insisted that light signals were exchanged between the shore and an object in the water sometime after the attack. This, coupled with the report of a Confederate officer on shore who claimed to have answered a signal from the submersible on its return trip, had led investigators to map out possible routes the *Hunley* might have taken on its return to base. Finally, in August 1994, metal objects roughly matching the shape and length of the *Hunley* were identified in the historic channel. In May 1995, a diving expedition confirmed the discovery of the *Hunley*, completely intact, lying in twenty feet of water less than a mile from its destination. How it sank may remain a mystery, though it seems likely that it was swamped when hatches were opened to signal the shore crew, or when a porthole window was damaged. On August 8, 2000—136 years after the Confederate submersible and its eight-man crew were lost—salvagers raised the *Hunley* from the sea floor. The vessel was transported to a custom-built laboratory at the old Charleston Naval Shipyard in preparation for permanent exhibition.

Naval Mines or Torpedoes

In the mid-1860s, torpedo was the term used to denote explosive mines, on land or sea. Confederate disadvantages in men and material prompted widespread use of these so-called "infernal machines," which had been regarded, initially, as dishonorable or ungentlemanly weapons. First employed in the Potomac River in July 1861, they were mainly defensive weapons. They were set afloat in Southern harbors and rivers to keep the Union's naval presence at bay.

Several types of torpedoes were developed. Explosives were attached to wooden kegs or rafts, strung from driftwood, pronged to the river or harbor bottom, or attached to free-floating buoys. Most were detonated when they were struck by a ship, though a battery-detonated electric torpedo, activated by an observer, and a clock-work torpedo, set to a timer, were also used. A frame torpedo stuck in the Neuse River to impede General Burnside's advance in March 1862 is described below:

> Three heavy pieces of timber placed in the position, at the bottom of which was placed a box filled with old iron, stones, and other heavy materials, was sunk in the river, and then inclined forward at an angle of forty-five

degrees by means of ropes and weights. This heavy frame was capped by a cylinder of iron, about ten inches in diameter. Into this was fitted a shell, which was heavily loaded, resting on a set of springs, so arranged that the least pressure on the cylinder would instantly discharge the shell by means of a percussion cap ingeniously placed.

Adapted for offensive purposes, torpedoes could be attached to a spar at the front of a Confederate vessel and detonated by being rammed into the hull of a Union ship. The long narrow vessel that carried the spar came to be known as a "David," and it was among the oddest, but the most innovative and feared, naval weapons of the war.

Indeed, torpedoes came to be the Confederacy's most effective antiship weapons; they were responsible for destroying or seriously damaging forty-three Union vessels. The first Union vessel destroyed was the ironclad *Cairo*, on December 12, 1862, and the last was the army transport *R.B. Hamilton*, on May 12, 1865. The largest vessel sunk was the 1,240-ton sloop-of-war *Housatonic*, in Charleston Harbor, on February 17, 1864. The only recorded instance of a Union torpedo sinking a Confederate ship came on October 27, 1864, when the C.S.S. *Albemarle* was sunk in a daring raid (see Time Line, page 536).

Sailors

New England's long maritime tradition held the Union navy in good stead, providing the North with a strong base of experienced seamen. The South, which lacked this seafaring background, had more inexperienced sailors in its lower ranks, and most enlistees were drawn from Confederate armies.

In both navies, new sailors were sent to receiving ships (older ships docked at navy yards or ports) for training. These ships served as barracks and training facilities for the new recruits, who were taught the fundamentals of seamanship and navy life. Navigation, gunnery, handling sails, and other duties were covered quickly, and during the war sailors acquired most of their skills on the job in active duty.

In both navies, pay ranged from $12 a month for inexperienced men to $14 a month for ordinary seamen and $18 a month for seamen. Boys (minimum age thirteen in the North, fourteen in the South) were ranked according to their knowledge and physical ability and paid accordingly. Third-class boys received $7 a month; second class, $8; and first class, $9. In the Union navy, a bonus attached to blockade work was the prospect of prize money—a portion of the proceeds whenever a captured blockade runner was auctioned off. Likewise, crew members (many of them foreigners) on the Confederate commerce raiders signed on for a share of the spoils from captured ships.

Each sailor was assigned to a specific watch, battle station, and mess. From the moment he stepped on board, the sailor and his work were dictated by the ship's bell. Six four-hour watches beginning at 12 A.M. comprised the day (seven watches, if a captain used dog watches, dividing the 4 P.M. to 8 P.M. watch into two two-hour shifts). On some ships, sailors were on duty every other four hours; on others, they worked four hours then had eight hours off twice in a twenty-four-hour period. Discipline was strict. Drunkenness, disobedience, deficiencies at inspection, and fighting were punished with fines, loss of liberty, confinement in the brig, or being placed in irons. Sailors were also expected to carry out their work in silence so as to hear orders and maintain alertness on duty.

A typical day on board a warship began with reveille at 5 A.M. as crews scrambled to scrub down the ship, polish fittings, and clean the guns. Sailors then met with their mess (a group of eight to fourteen men) for breakfast. The meal usually consisted of biscuits or hard tack, salted beef, and coffee. Inspection followed, and the rest of the day could be spent on watch and in drilling: training with and repairing heavy and light artillery and small arms; practicing firefighting; and on ships with sails, maintaining the sails and rigging, masts, and spars. Coaling the ship could take anywhere from five to twelve hours, and when in port the crew also loaded firewood and supplies.

The main meal was served at noon and usually included meat (typically salted beef or pork, although fresh meat was often available several times a week), vegetables, bread, and coffee. Rice and beans were also on the menu, particularly in the Confederate navy. Sailors generally ate better than their counterparts in the army and could enhance their diets with seafood or items taken from other ships captured as prizes. Supper was served late in the afternoon or early evening. Both navies provided a daily ration of grog (rum or whiskey), which sailors could forgo and have the cost added to their pay (four cents a day in the Confederate navy, five cents daily in the Union navy. In 1862, the Union abolished the grog ration in an effort to instill temperance). In their free time, sailors read their mail and wrote letters, caught up on their sleep, played dice or dominoes, and entertained their shipmates with music and theatricals. In port, those with liberty (usually only about 15 percent of the ship's crew at a time) had four precious hours to do the town.

Despite the considerable danger crews faced when engaged in battle (sailors were also killed or wounded by snipers, tripped mines, and shipboard accidents), the hardest part of serving in the navies was boredom. This was particularly true for Union sailors on blockade duty. "Pretty stupid work this blockading. . . ." fumed Charles A. Post of the U.S.S. *Florida* in the North Atlantic Blockading Squadron. "If I had been in search of the millenium [sic] I could not have come to a better place! We never see an enemy, from morning to night."

The men also had to contend with long days and nights of routine drudgery and unhealthy shipboard conditions. Sharing crowded—and usually wet or damp—quarters, exposure to the elements, and poor diets at times, all contributed to ill health and the spread of disease. On vessels assigned to the rivers of the humid South, malaria, yellow fever, and typhus were especially serious threats to the crew. Each morning at sick call, the ship's surgeon assigned to the sick list those too ill to work, and they were relieved of their duties. Sailors appearing regularly on the sick list were usually sent home.

Throughout the war, both the Union and Confederate naval departments struggled to find adequate manpower to crew their ships. (Until late in the war, men enlisting in the navy were not paid the same enlistment bonus that men joining the army received.) Not only were warships perpetually undermanned, but also as fleets expanded, the crews that were enlisted were increasingly made up of inexperienced hands. The shortage of trained sailors was so acute in the South that Secretary of the Navy Stephen Mallory had to persuade the Confederate Congress to pass a law requiring the transfer of any man in the army who volunteered for service in the navy. He picked up few men, though. Army commanders, he claimed, would not allow the volunteers to leave their regiments.

The chronic shortage of men led Gideon Welles, U.S. secretary of the navy, to suggest recruiting former slaves ("contrabands") and abandoning the navy's prewar policy of limiting black seamen to no more than one-twentieth of a ship's crew. During the war, blacks made up about 15 percent

These engravings illustrate an account of Robert Smalls' escape to freedom, as published in the June 14, 1862, edition of Harper's Weekly. Smalls piloted the Planter, *a side-wheel steamer, out of Charleston Harbor and delivered the gunboat to U.S. authorities, reportedly with the words, "I thought Planter might be of use to Uncle Abe." Smalls later commanded the* Planter *for the Union Army.*

of the Navy's enlisted force. Like the Union's black soldiers, these sailors faced racial discrimination in their own service, at the same time they were facing the enemy. Unlike the army, whose units were segregated, black sailors served alongside white sailors.

Robert Smalls became one of the Union's most celebrated contraband sailors. In the early morning hours of May 13, 1862, Smalls commandeered the cotton steamer *Planter*, which had been converted into a Confederate dispatch boat based in Charleston. With sixteen other slaves, he expertly steered the *Planter*, fully laden with 200 pounds of ammunition and four guns, past the watches of the Confederate fortifications and made his way out to the Union blockade fleet. When he turned his contraband crew and supplies over to the Union flag officer, he became an instant hero to the abolitionist forces in the North and an inspiration to both slaves and free blacks in the South. After his break for freedom, Smalls joined the U.S. Navy as a pilot of the *Planter*. His intimate knowledge of the shallow inland waters of the South Carolina and Georgia coasts was indispensable to the Union campaign in and around Charleston, and one of his first orders of business was to help crews defuse the torpedoes he had helped the Confederate Navy deploy.

In the South, free blacks could enlist in the Confederate navy only with special permission from the Navy Department and the local squadron commander. Slaves, however, enlisted (with their owner's permission) to serve as officers' servants, stokers, or pilots—as Smalls had done in his torpedo runs for the Confederacy.

As Northern control of the Southern coast intensified, Confederate sailors had fewer opportunities to strike back against the enemy. Eventually, as their ships were destroyed to keep them from falling into Union hands, they shouldered muskets and marched into battle as infantrymen. One such group, known as "Tucker's Naval Brigade," fought and surrendered with a large portion of the Army of Northern Virginia at Sayler's Creek (at times mistakenly, but aptly, referred to as Sailor's Creek) only a few days before Lee's capitulation at Appomattox.

Marines in the Civil War

When the guns roared at Fort Sumter in April 1861, the U.S. Marine Corps, with fewer than 1,900 officers and enlisted men on the rolls, was the smallest branch in the military. Most of the marines were serving as ships' guards on scattered navy vessels, and the rest were grouped in small contingents at a handful of coastal barracks. The largest of these groups comprised approximately 338 marines at the Washington Barracks and Navy Yard.

The Corps suffered from a lack of trained leadership after nearly a third of its officers resigned to offer their services to the Confederacy. Although thirty-eight new officers were commissioned to replace them, the new men had little or no previous military experience. At the same time, the Corps' senior officers, many of whom had served since before the Mexican War, were too old for service at sea or in the field. Enlisted marines overwhelmingly remained with the Union during the secession crisis; still, numbers for the Corps remained low until recruiters were able to offer bounties approximating those paid to men joining the army. By the last year of the war, the Marine Corps claimed 3,850 men.

Marines were involved in the war from the beginning. In April 1861, three months after Florida and Alabama militia took control of the forts defending Pensacola, Florida, Fort Pickens, the lone holdout, was saved by Lieutenant John Cash, who led 110 U.S. marines and a contingent of soldiers

U.S. marines with fixed bayonets at the Washington, D.C. Navy Yard, April 1864. Marines primarily served on board ships as guards, sharpshooters, and gun crew members. Only on a few occasions did they fight on land during the war.

into the fort and occupied it until a larger garrison arrived. In July, Major John G. Reynolds commanded a marine detachment of twelve officers and more than 300 enlisted men in the first battle of Bull Run (Manassas).

For the most part, marines performed their traditional duties as detachments on board the ships of the U.S. Navy. With little ship-to-ship fighting and no need for boarding parties, they compiled an enviable record serving the big guns in countless actions. The marines who served ashore did so in small numbers—as part of landing forces or while directly assigned to assist the army. The amphibious assaults for which the marines were renowned in World War II were almost unknown in the Civil War (assaults on Fort Sumter and Fort Fisher are chief among the exceptions). During the war, the Marine Corps listed 148 officers and men killed, and 312 dead from other causes.

A Confederate "Corps of Marines" was established by an act of the Confederate Congress on March 16, 1861. Essentially, it adopted the laws and regulations of the U.S. Marine Corps—not surprising, since many of the officers were former U.S. Marines. Although the Confederate Congress authorized a corps of forty-six officers and 944 enlisted men, the numbers never passed 600 officers and men. The marines first saw action early in 1861, when they manned batteries and attempted to close the Potomac River to naval traffic. When Confederate General Joseph E. Johnston abandoned his lines along the Potomac in 1862, the marines took up a station in the Drewry's Bluff batteries guarding the southern approaches to Richmond. Throughout the war, they served there with superior efficiency. Not a single Union warship reached the city until it was evacuated shortly before the end of the war. Marine guard detachments were stationed at Charleston, South Carolina; Charlotte and Wilmington, North Carolina; Richmond, Virginia; Savannah, Georgia; and Mobile, Alabama. The latter two detachments earned commendations for their service as artillerymen.

Confederate Marines, serving as supplemental crew members of the C.S.S. *Virginia* and other vessels in the fledgling navy, saw only limited action afloat. They were increasingly assigned to inland commands as the Confederate naval bases fell to Union control. On both sides, marines were stretched thin and asked to do more than their manpower allowed.

Notable Naval Figures

FRANKLIN BUCHANAN (1800–1874). His distinguished career in the U.S. Navy included his appointment as the first superintendent of the Naval Academy (1845–1847) and commander of the Washington Navy Yard (1859–1861), so Captain Buchanan was torn in his loyalties when the Civil War began. Anticipating that his home state of Maryland would secede, he resigned from the U.S. Navy and then tried to withdraw his resignation when Maryland remained in the Union. When his request was refused, Buchanan joined the Confederate Navy and was made chief of the Bureau of Orders and Detail. He requested active duty and was put in command of the ironclad C.S.S. *Virginia* (formerly the U.S.S. *Merrimack*), which destroyed the U.S.S. *Congress* and U.S.S. *Cumberland*. Wounded in the attack, Buchanan was unable to command the *Virginia* the next day, March 9, 1862, when it dueled with the *Monitor*. In August 1862, he was made an admiral and began a two-year stint as commander of the Confederate naval forces in Mobile Bay. Seriously wounded during Rear Admiral Farragut's naval assault, Buchanan was taken prisoner while defending Mobile in August 1864. He was released, in an exchange for

Union prisoners, in February 1865, resumed his command at Mobile, and surrendered the city.

JAMES DUNWOODY BULLOCH (1823–1901). Bulloch began his career with the U.S. Navy at age sixteen. When his state (Georgia) seceded, he was captain of the commercial mail steamer *Bienville*, operating out of New York. Bulloch brought his ship back to New York, resigned, and offered his services to the Confederate navy. Secretary of the Navy Stephen Mallory dispatched Bulloch to Great Britain on May 5, 1861, as a civilian agent for the Confederate navy. He secured many important Confederate ships, including *Alabama*, *Florida*, *Shenandoah*, and *Stonewall*. Bulloch operated from Liverpool and settled there after the war. His nephew, Theodore Roosevelt, became president of the United States the year Bulloch died.

WILLIAM B. CUSHING (1842–1874). Forced to resign as a midshipman from the Naval Academy because of poor work habits, Cushing began the Civil War as an acting master's mate. Admired and praised by the secretary of the navy, admirals, and enlisted men alike for his bravery and resourcefulness, Cushing ended the war as a lieutenant commander. Among his daring exploits were: the capture of a blockade runner, which he brought to port in New York City; destruction of a Confederate salt works; raids on coastal North Carolina; night naval missions behind enemy lines; and the nearly suicidal mission of destroying the *Albemarle*, a Confederate ram vessel, with a torpedo in the Roanoke River. Prior to the assault on Fort Fisher in January 1865, Cushing spent six hours in a skiff, under enemy fire, as he marked the channel in preparation for the Union's sea-land offensive. Fort Fisher surrendered that same evening. His brother, ALONZO H. CUSHING, an artillery officer in the Eastern Theater, also fought heroically for the Union. Already wounded, he refused to abandon his gun during Pickett's Charge, and was killed at Gettysburg.

JOHN A. BERNARD DAHLGREN (1809–1870). "The father of American naval ordnance," Dahlgren invented and developed light bronze boat guns and heavy smoothbore shell guns—the U.S. Navy's standard shipboard armament in the Civil War—as well as rifled ordnance. Dahlgren's career with the U.S. Navy began as a midshipman in 1826, and he is credited with establishing the navy's ordnance department at the Washington Navy Yard,

Rear Admiral John A. Bernard Dahlgren and the naval gun he invented. (On the horizon behind him, barely seen, is the Confederate-held ruin of Ft. Sumter.) Dahlgren guns were dubbed "soda bottles" for their distinctive shape.

which he commanded on the eve of the Civil War. He created the first sustained weapons research and development program in American naval history and oversaw the most comprehensive quality-control ordnance program seen in the navy to that time. During the war, Dahlgren was Abraham Lincoln's choice for chief of the Bureau of Ordnance. The president visited Dahlgren often at the navy yard and regarded him as a sounding board and technical mentor. Dahlgren lobbied for sea duty and was given command of the South Atlantic Blockading Squadron.

PERCIVAL DRAYTON (1812–1865). Born into a prominent Southern family, but a longtime resident of Philadelphia and a career naval officer, Percival Drayton broke his family ties and remained with the Union navy. In one of the war's literal examples of "brother against brother," Drayton commanded the U.S.S. *Pocahontas* during the November 1861 Port Royal expedition, in which Confederate forces commanded by his brother, THOMAS FENWICK DRAYTON, were compelled to withdraw. In July 1862, Drayton was made a captain, and commanded the ironclad U.S.S. *Passaic*. In 1863, Rear Admiral David G. Farragut brought Drayton to the U.S.S. *Hartford* as fleet captain of the West Gulf Blockading Squadron. Drayton survived the war, but just barely. He was appointed head of the Bureau of Navigation in April 1865, and died after a brief illness four months later.

CHARLES ELLET JR. (1810–1862). Well known as an engineer and builder of suspension bridges before the Civil War began, Ellet had traveled to Sebastopol during the Crimean War and determined that the siege of that city could have ended with the use of "ram-boats." At the time, neither the Russians nor the U.S. Navy was interested in the innovative boats. However, after the debut of the ironclad C.S.S. *Virginia*, Ellet was commissioned a colonel by Secretary of War Stanton and charged to build a fleet of nine "ram-boats" from old steamers. Ellet commanded two of these rams and, along with five ironclads, fought in the battle of Memphis and destroyed the opposing Confederate river defense fleet on June 6, 1862. The capitulation of Memphis followed the Confederate defeat on the river. Ellet was the single casualty aboard the rams. Mortally wounded in the battle, he died on June 21, 1862.

DAVID GLASGOW FARRAGUT (1801–1870). Farragut began his remarkable naval career before the age of ten, when he received a midshipman's commission in 1810. He served under his guardian, Commander David Porter, in the War of 1812, and was a sixty-year-old captain by the time of the Civil War. Farragut's first command in the war was the West Gulf Blockading Squadron, and his victory at New Orleans, in April 1862, led to his promotion to rear admiral. The zenith of his military exploits came at Mobile Bay, August 5, 1864, when Farragut led his fleet through mined waters, shouting out "Damn the torpedoes!" and urging his ship forward. His victory there led to a vice-admiralship, and after the war Farragut was rewarded with promotion to full admiral. (The grades of vice admiral and admiral were created in 1864 and 1866, respectively, matching the equivalent army grades of lieutenant general and general.) Farragut's foster brother was Rear Admiral DAVID DIXON PORTER, who served under him in the war.

ANDREW HULL FOOTE (1806–1863). Foote began his naval career at age sixteen, when he left West Point and became a midshipman at Annapolis. Nearly forty years later, after distinguishing himself for his high moral character and battle experience off the China coast, he was given command of the upper Mississippi River flotilla by U.S. Secretary of the Navy Gideon Welles in August 1861. In conjunction with the land forces of General Ulysses S. Grant, he led the successful assault on Fort Henry, on the Tennessee River, and was wounded in the leg during the assault on Fort Donelson. For his heroics and success, Foote was promoted to rear admiral in July 1862. To allow him recuperative time, he was named head of the Bureau of Equipment and Recruiting. In June 1863, Foote was appointed head of the South Atlantic Blockading Squadron, off Charleston, but died before he could take the assignment.

GUSTAVUS VASA FOX (1821–1883). A consultant to President Lincoln during the Fort Sumter crisis, Gustavus Fox sailed with the Union fleet sent to resupply the fort, arriving on April 12, 1861, the day the Confederates fired on it. Fox returned to Washington with the evacuated Ft. Sumter force and became chief clerk of the Navy Department. In August Lincoln named Fox assistant secretary of the navy, a post created specifically for him. It was Fox who suggested that David Farragut lead the fleet against New Orleans. His competence, energy, and willingness to suggest and implement innovations (including production of monitor-style warships) were roundly praised, and he was instrumental in rebuilding the U.S. navy.

STEPHEN R. MALLORY (see "Civil War Government Officials: Confederate States of America" in Chapter 3, "Wartime Politics").

MATTHEW FONTAINE MAURY (1806–1873). Matthew Maury rose through the ranks of the U.S. Navy prior to the war, but a crippling leg injury in 1839 prevented him from going to sea again. Instead, he made his mark in the Navy Department's Depot of Charts and Instruments, performing brilliant work in the areas of meteorologic and oceanographic studies, as well as penning treatises on marine navigation. After his native state of Virginia joined the Confederacy, Maury took a post in Richmond in the Office of Orders and Detail, and quarreled with Secretary Mallory over Confederate naval strategy. Maury's idea that the Confederacy would be better served by large numbers of small, well-armed vessels in Southern waterways was beginning to win support when the success of the C.S.S. *Virginia* prompted an all-out call for ironclad production. In late 1862, Maury was dispatched to Great Britain where he purchased vessels (including the C.S.S. *Georgia*, an iron steamship) and supplies on behalf of the Confederacy.

DAVID DIXON PORTER (1813–1891). Even before becoming a U.S. Navy midshipman in 1829, Porter had logged junior service in the Mexican navy. The ambitious son of a naval officer, Porter was anxious to prove himself in the Union navy. For the first year, he commanded the Union gunboat *Powhatan* in the Gulf, and then joined the fleet of David Farragut for the expedition against New Orleans. In the fall of 1862, Porter assumed command of the Mississippi Squadron, charged with controlling the Mississippi River above Vicksburg; by late the following year, the newly promoted rear admiral's command expanded to include the entire Mississippi system above New Orleans. With the Mississippi secure, Porter took command of the North Atlantic Blockading Squadron. In the successful assault on North Carolina's Fort Fisher, in January 1865, Porter commanded the largest fleet of U.S. warships assembled during the war. In 1870, he was made admiral of the navy.

RAPHAEL SEMMES (1809–1877). As commander of the most feared of the Confederate commerce raiders, the C.S.S. *Alabama*, Semmes' name is identified more than any other with the Confederate navy. Appointed midshipman in the U.S. Navy in 1826, he saw service in the Mexican War and was promoted to commander in 1855. Having settled in Mobile, he followed Alabama out of the Union, and took eighteen U.S. merchantmen—commercial vessels flying the U.S. flag—while commanding the first of the Confederacy's commerce raiders, the C.S.S. *Sumter*. After the cruiser *Alabama* was assigned to Semmes, he embarked on a twenty-two-month career on the high seas. He evaded Union naval vessels (with a few exceptions) while capturing and destroying more than sixty vessels. The end came in June 1864, when the *Alabama* was destroyed in a duel with the U.S.S. *Kearsarge* off the coast of France. Semmes was rescued by a British yacht and made his way back to the Confederacy, where he became a rear admiral. In the waning days of the war, he commanded the James River Squadron, organized his sailors into ground troops when Richmond fell, and surrendered with Joseph E. Johnston's army in North Carolina.

JAMES IREDELL WADDELL (1824–1886). Beginning as a midshipman in the U.S. Navy in 1841, James Waddell served in the Mexican War and went on to teach navigation at the U.S. Naval Academy in the years preceding the Civil War. Commanding the commerce raider C.S.S. *Shenandoah* (the recommissioned British vessel *Sea King*), he targeted Union whalers in the Pacific Ocean until August 1865, when he was finally convinced, by a British captain, that the Confederacy had surrendered. Waddell then sailed the *Shenandoah* 17,000 miles without stopping and surrendered his ship to British authorities in Liverpool on November 6, 1865.

GIDEON WELLES (see "Civil War Government Officials: United States of America" in Chapter 3, "Wartime Politics").

JOHN LORIMER WORDEN (1818–1897). Best remembered as the commander of the U.S.S. *Monitor* in its historic battle with the Confederate ironclad *Virginia* at Hampton Roads, Virginia, John Worden began his naval career as a fifteen-year-old midshipman and concluded it as a rear admiral. In 1861, Worden was ordered to Pensacola, Florida, with secret orders for the U.S. naval forces stationed there, but he was taken prisoner during his return trip. Exchanged after seven months' imprisonment at Montgomery, Alabama, he took command of the *Monitor* in January 1862. During the *Monitor-Virginia* duel on March 9, Worden suffered partial blindness from a face wound, but later returned to command. In January 1863, Worden took command of the monitor *Montauk*, which destroyed the C.S.S. *Nashville* on February 28, 1863. He was then assigned to land duty, supervising construction of ironclads in New York. After the war, he was appointed superintendent of the U.S. Naval Academy, a position he held from 1869 to 1874.

SELECTED RESOURCES

See also the annotated book list in Chapter 13, "Studying the War: Research and Preservation."

Anderson, Bern. *By Sea and by River: The Naval History of the Civil War.* New York: Knopf, 1962.

Browning, Robert M., Jr. *From Cape Charles to Cape Fear: The North Atlantic Blockading Squadron during the Civil War.* Tuscaloosa: University of Alabama Press, 1993.

Canney, Donald L. *The Old Steam Navy,* 2 vols. (1. *Frigates, Sloops, and Gunboats, 1815–1885;* 2. *The Ironclads, 1842–1885*). Annapolis, MD: Naval Institute Press, 1993.

Luraghi, Raimondo. *A History of the Confederate Navy.* Translated by Paolo E. Coletta. Annapolis, MD: Naval Institute Press, 1996.

Musicant, Ivan. *Divided Waters: The Naval History of the Civil War.* New York: HarperCollins, 1995.

Reed, Rowena. *Combined Operations in the Civil War.* Annapolis, MD: Naval Institute Press, 1978.

Silverstone, Paul H. *Civil War Navies, 1855–1883.* Annapolis, MD: Naval Institute Press, 2001.

Surdam, David George. *Northern Naval Superiority and the Economics of the American Civil War.* Columbia: University of South Carolina Press, 2001.

Symonds, Craig L. *Historical Atlas of the U.S. Navy.* Annapolis, MD: Naval Institute Press, 1995.

Valuska, David L. *The African American in the Union Navy, 1861–1865.* New York: Garland, 1993.

Wise, Stephen R. *Lifeline of the Confederacy: Blockade Running during the Civil War.* Columbia: University of South Carolina Press, 1988.

PRISONS AND PRISONERS OF WAR

When war broke out between the United States and the Confederacy, neither side possessed the facilities or the wherewithal to house and care for vast numbers of prisoners over extended periods of time. Indeed, each side, confident that the war would be short-lived, failed to anticipate that such needs would arise. It was supposed that any prisoners of war could be detained at existing fortifications or jails, or—as happened later—simply "paroled" upon their oath that they would not take up arms again until properly exchanged for a like number of prisoners in enemy hands. Early in the war, this parole and exchange system, based on the traditional European model, was an informal arrangement practiced by a few Union and Confederate commanders on an ad hoc basis.

The scale of the suffering attendant to Civil War prisons, as with so many other aspects of the war, was not foreseen amid the patriotic fervor with which the warring sides went off to battle. Consequently, prison systems, in the North and the South, acted more or less provisionally until the problem became too unwieldy to resolve without massive loss of life. This short-sighted approach to the treatment of prisoners led to one of the war's great horrors: tens of thousands of men corralled into unsanitary pens, often exposed to the elements, without the food, exercise, shelter, or clean water needed to sustain them.

In the four years of the war, an estimated 409,608 Americans were held prisoner in one or more of the 150 military prisons. On the Union side, 211,411 men were taken prisoner. Of those, 16,668 were paroled without going to a prison camp and 30,218 died as prisoners of war. On the Confederate side, 462,634 men were captured, including those who surrendered at the end of the war; of those, 247,769 were paroled on the field and 25,976 died in Northern prisons. Mortality rates for Northerners in Confederate

On May 3, 1863, Civil War special artist Edwin Forbes made this drawing of Rebel Prisoners and Battle Flags Captured at Chancellorsville Being Taken to the Rear by Cavalry and Infantry Guards. *Despite this evidence of Northern success, Chancellorsville was a smashing defeat for the Union and perhaps Robert E. Lee's greatest battlefield triumph.*

prisons was 15.5 percent. Their Confederate counterparts in Northern prisons died at a rate just over 12 percent. The more than 56,000 dead, in the prisons of both sides, nearly equals the number of Americans killed during ten years of military conflict in Vietnam in the second half of the twentieth century. The death rate among all soldiers taken prisoner was approximately 13 percent—more than twice the death rate on the battlefield. Historians have no estimate of how many thousands more died in the months following their release, from diseases contracted while in captivity.

The first prisoners taken in the Civil War were U.S. Army regulars assigned to the Texas frontier. They were compelled to surrender when Texas seceded in February 1861. Initially, both sides scrambled to find usable facilities for prisoners—Texas, for example, employed the Alamo for some of the first Union prisoners. Later, military prisons took many forms, from existing jails and fortifications, to converted warehouses, to fenced-in areas containing tents or makeshift barracks.

In the early part of the war, most captors provided humane treatment, although the prisoners were usually underfed and confined in overcrowded buildings or pens. Their sufferings were generally from hunger, illness, and uncertainty about the future. Because paroles and exchanges were accepted practices in mid-nineteenth-century warfare, both sides expected a prisoner's tenure in custody to be short. Most troops received no training in how to endure or escape from captivity.

As the conflict progressed into its second year, both governments began to be pressured to relieve the overtaxed prison system and bring home soldiers who were in enemy hands. In July 1862, the Union and Confederate governments agreed to a cartel, or prisoner exchange, based on individual ranks. A Union private, for example, could be exchanged for a Confederate private, and a general for a general, but a commanding general was worth sixty privates.

By August 1862, the cartel had succeeded in effectively emptying the prisons. In time, however, the prisoner exchange began to fall apart. Questions were raised, on each side, about the enemy's good faith in complying with the cartel's terms. The Emancipation Proclamation and the advent of black troops in Union armies led to an impasse on the disposition of captured United States Colored Troops. Despite the fact that many of the North's black soldiers had been born free men, the South insisted they could be "returned" to slavery if captured. The North demanded that they be treated like white soldiers. Privately, Union officials questioned the military wisdom of continuing to allow Southern soldiers to return to the ranks in what had become a war of attrition. These issues led to the North's decision, in mid-1863, to end the prisoner exchange. Consequently, prison populations and mortality rates ballooned in camps in the North and the South.

Though terrible suffering was common at many Federal prisons—and perhaps with less justification, given Northern resources—Andersonville, or Camp Sumter, in Georgia, was the extreme example of the horrors of Civil War prisons. In a stockade originally designed for 10,000 men, and later expanded by ten (immediately overcrowded) acres, at one point nearly 33,000 men were crowded onto an unshaded plain. Some 13,000 men died there.

The Confederacy tried to recruit disaffected Union soldiers in eastern prison camps, focusing on those of foreign birth. Some 4,500 soldiers, not all of them born outside the United States, agreed to join Confederate units.

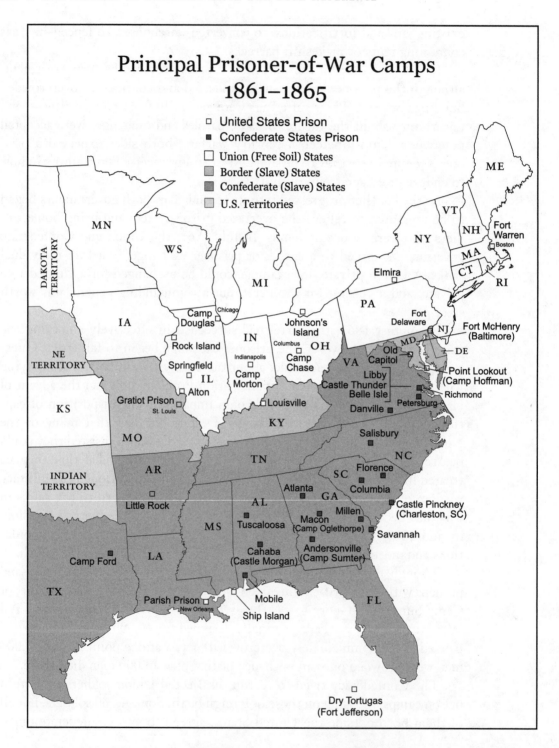

Principal Prisoner-of-War Camps 1861–1865

□ United States Prison
■ Confederate States Prison

☐ Union (Free Soil) States
▨ Border (Slave) States
▨ Confederate (Slave) States
☐ U.S. Territories

Some proved good engineers, but most were unreliable for military purposes. On the Union side, where labor was in less demand, Confederate prisoners were successfully recruited to fight against the Sioux and other Plains Indians. These so-called "Galvanized Yankees" were organized into six regiments of approximately 6,000 men, and many remained in service into 1866. The term "Galvanized Yankees" was sometimes also applied to Union soldiers who served the Confederacy.

Neither the Union nor the Confederacy subscribed to a uniform code of treatment for prisoners. (Later, nations were expected to conform to the Geneva Convention.) Bound only by ill-defined and flexible concepts such as "civilized warfare" and "the dictates of humanity," the captors on both sides routinely neglected their captives. Cut off from their comrades, chronically underfed and ill, and lacking basic provisions for physical and mental health, prisoners of war fought a daily battle to stay alive.

Principal United States and Confederate States Military Prisons

Many prisoner-of-war camps were short-lived facilities. Some opened and closed within a matter of months; others were in use for years. During the early days of the war, both governments utilized all manner of makeshift facilities—as well as established military structures, such as coastal fortifications—to temporarily hold prisoners until they could be exchanged. Over the course of the war, more than 150 facilities, North and South, were utilized to house prisoners of war. As the war progressed, and as the scale of the armies and the number of clashes continued to grow, so did the number of prisoners. When the formal arrangement for prisoner exchange broke down in 1863, prison populations soared in both the Union and the Confederacy. Consequently, some of the most notorious and overcrowded camps, including Andersonville (February 1864), did not become operational until late in the conflict.

PRINCIPAL U.S. MILITARY PRISONS

Arkansas	*Little Rock* (1864–1865); 718 peak population; 3 escapees; 217 deaths; converted buildings.
California	*Mare's Island* (1863, 1864?); 20 peak population; fenced-in barracks.

(continued)

PRINCIPAL U.S. MILITARY PRISONS (CONTINUED)

Delaware
Fort Delaware, Pea Patch Island (1861–1865); 12,600 peak population; 52 escapees; 2,460 deaths; coastal fortification.

District of Columbia
Arsenal Penitentiary (1861, 1862?); preexisting prison.
Carroll Prison (1862–1865); 1,000 capacity; 2,763 peak population; 16 escapees; 457 deaths; converted buildings.
Forest Hall (1861–1862, 1863?–1865?); converted building.
Old Capitol Prison (1861–1865); 500 maximum capacity; 2,763 peak population (combined totals of both Old Capitol and Carroll prisons); 16 escapees; 457+ deaths; converted building.
Washington County Jail (1861, 1862?); 240 peak population; preexisting jail.

Florida
Fort Jefferson, Dry Tortugas Islands (1864–1865); 900+ maximum capacity; 300? peak population; coastal fortification.

Fort Pickens (1862–1865); 146 peak population; 11 escapees; 2 deaths; coastal fortification.

Georgia
Fort Pulaski (1864–1865); 336? maximum capacity; 558 peak population; coastal fortification.

Illinois
Alton Prison, Alton (1862–1865); 800 maximum capacity; 1,891 peak population; 120 escapees; 1,508 deaths; preexisting prison.
Camp Butler, near Springfield (1862–1863); 2,100 maximum capacity; 2,186 peak population; 203 escapees; 866 deaths; fenced-in barracks.
Camp Douglas, Chicago (1862–1865); 6,000 maximum capacity; 12,082 peak population; 317 escapees; 4,454 deaths; fenced-in barracks.
Rock Island (1863–1865); 10,080 maximum capacity; 8,607 peak population; 41 escapees; 1,960 deaths; fenced-in barracks.

Indiana
Camp Morton, Indianapolis (1862–1865); 2,000 maximum capacity; 5,000 peak population; 150+ escapees; 1,763 deaths; converted buildings at fairground.
Evansville (1862, 1863?); 500 peak population; converted buildings.
Fort Wayne (1862, 1863?); 500 peak population; converted buildings.
Lafayette (1862, 1863?); 500 peak population; 28 deaths; converted buildings.

PRINCIPAL U.S. MILITARY PRISONS (CONTINUED)

	New Albany (1862, 1863?); 500 peak population; converted buildings.
	Richmond (1862, 1863?–1865?); 500 maximum capacity; 500? peak population; converted buildings.
	Terre Haute (1862, 1863?); 500 peak population; converted buildings.
Kansas	*Fort Riley* (1862); 17 peak population; 8 deaths; fortification.
Kentucky	*Columbus* (1862); preexisting jail.
	Lexington (1862–1863, 1864?–1865?); preexisting jail.
	Louisville (1863–1865); 6,737 peak population; 25 escapees; 343 deaths; preexisting prison and fenced-in barracks.
	Paducah (1862, 1863?–1865?); converted building.
Louisiana	*Louisiana State House*, Baton Rouge (1862–1863); converted building.
	Parish Prison, New Orleans (1863–1865); 1,856 peak population; 226 escapees; 213 deaths; preexisting prison.
Maryland	*Baltimore City Jail*, Baltimore (1861–1863, 1864?–1865?); 700? peak population; preexisting jail.
	Camp Hoffman, Point Lookout (1863–1865); 10,000 maximum capacity; 20,000 peak population; 50 escapees; 3,584 deaths; fenced-in tents.
	Castle Thunder (1862, 1863?–1865?); converted building.
	Fort McHenry, Baltimore (1861–1865); 600 maximum capacity; 6,957 peak population; 37 escapees, 33 deaths; coastal fortification.
	Hope Slater (1861–1863, 1864?–1865?); preexisting jail.
Massachusetts	*Fort Warren*, Boston Harbor (1861–1865); 175 maximum capacity; 394 peak population; 4 escapees; 12 deaths; coastal fortification.
Mississippi	*Ship Island* (1864–1865); 4,430 peak population; 5 escapees; 103 deaths; coastal fortification.
Missouri	*Benton Barracks*, St. Louis (1861–1862, 1863?–1865?); converted training camp.
	Gratiot Street, St. Louis (1861–1865); 500 maximum capacity; 1,800 peak population; 109+ escapees; 1,140 deaths; converted medical college.

(continued)

PRINCIPAL U.S. MILITARY PRISONS (CONTINUED)

Guerrilla Prison (Bingham Building), Kansas City (1863); 15 peak population; 5 deaths; converted building.

Missouri State Penitentiary, Jefferson City (1864); 15 peak population; no escapes; no deaths; preexisting prison.

Myrtle Street Prison (Lynch's Slave Pen), St. Louis (1861–1865); 100 maximum capacity; 150 peak population; converted buildings.

St. Charles (1861, 1862?); preexisting jail.

Schofield Barracks, St. Louis (1861, 1862?–1864?); converted training camp.

New Mexico Territory   *Fort Craig* (1861, 1862?); no deaths; preexisting fortification.

New York   *Albany Penitentiary*, Albany (1862–1863, 1864?–1865?); preexisting prison.

Castle Williams, Governor's Island, New York City (1861–1865); 250? maximum capacity; 713 peak population; island coastal fortification.

David's Island (1863–1865); 1,800 maximum capacity; 3,000 peak population; fenced-in barracks and tents.

Edward's Island (1863–1864, 1865?); fenced-in tents.

Elmira (1864–1865); 5,000 maximum capacity; 9,441 peak population; 17 escapees; 2,933 deaths; fenced-in barracks and tents.

Fort Columbus, Governor's Island, New York City (1861–1865); 250+ maximum capacity; coastal fortification.

Fort Lafayette, New York City (1861–1865); 50 maximum capacity; 163 peak population; 2 escapees; 2+ deaths; coastal fortification.

Fort Schuyler (1864–1865); 500 maximum capacity; 500 peak population; coastal fortification.

Fort Wood (Bedloe's Island) (1861, 1863–1864); 108 peak population; 3 deaths; coastal fortification.

Hart's Island (1865); 3,446 peak population; 4 escapees; 235 deaths; fenced-in barracks and tents.

Ludlow Street Jail, New York City (1861); preexisting jail.

Riker's Island, New York City (1864–1865); 1,000 maximum capacity; 1,000? peak population; fenced-in barracks.

Tombs Prison, New York City (1861–1862); 300 maximum capacity; 40 peak population; no escapes; no deaths; preexisting prison.

Ward's Island, New York City (1863?, 1864, 1865?); fenced-in baracks.

PRINCIPAL U.S. MILITARY PRISONS (CONTINUED)

Ohio
 Camp Chase, near Columbus (1861–1865); 4,000 maximum capacity; 9,423 peak population; 37 escapees; 2,260 deaths; fenced-in barracks.

 Camp Dennison (1862, 1863?–1865?); converted buildings.

 Johnson's Island, near Sandusky (1862–1865); 1,000 maximum capacity; 3,256 peak population; 12 escapees; 235 deaths; fenced-in barracks.

 McLean Barracks, Cincinnati (1863–1864); 179 peak population; 10 escapees; 4 deaths; converted buildings.

 Ohio Penitentiary (1863–1864); 68 peak population; 5 escapees; preexisting prison.

Pennsylvania
 Allegheny City Penitentiary, Pittsburgh (1863–1864); 118 peak population; no escapes; no deaths; preexisting prison.

 Chester (1863, 1864?–1865?); converted building.

 Fort Mifflin, near Philadelphia (1863–1864); 200 maximum capacity; 215 peak population; 42 escapees; 3 deaths; coastal fortification.

 Moyamensing Penitentiary, Philadelphia (1863, 1864?–1865?); preexisting prison.

South Carolina
 Hilton Head (1864–1865); 800? maximum capacity; 800 peak population; preexisting jail, fenced-in tents, converted building.

 Morris Island, Charleston (1864); 558? maximum capacity; 558 peak population; no escapes; 3 deaths; fenced-in tents.

Tennessee
 Irving Block, Memphis (1864–1865); 582 peak population; 1 escapee; 3 deaths; converted buildings.

 Knoxville (1863?–1865?); 4? deaths; preexisting jail.

 Tennessee State Penitentiary, and *Maxwell House*, Nashville (1863–1865); 7,460 peak population; 36 escapees; 359 deaths; preexisting prison and converted hotel.

Virginia
 Fort Monroe (1861–1865); 50? peak population; coastal fortification.

 Fort Norfolk, Norfolk (1864, 1865?); coastal fortification.

 Newport News (1865); 10,000 maximum capacity; 3,490 peak population; 17 escapees; 168 deaths; preexisting prison.

(continued)

PRINCIPAL U.S. MILITARY PRISONS (CONTINUED)

West Virginia
Atheneum Prison, Wheeling (1863–1865); 497 peak population; 12 escapees; 2 deaths; preexisting prison and converted building.
Charleston (1862–1863, 1864?–1865?); preexisting jail.

Wisconsin
Camp Randall, Madison (1862); 3,000? maximum capacity; 1,260 peak population; 142 deaths; converted fairgrounds.

Source: This U.S. prisons information has been adapted from Lonnie Speer, the "Prison Quick-Reference Guide" in *Portals to Hell: Military Prisons of the Civil War* (Mechanicsburg, PA: Stackpole Books, 1997), pp. 323–331.
Note: ? = unknown or best available figure.

PRINCIPAL C.S.A. MILITARY PRISONS

Alabama
Castle Morgan, Cahaba (1863?, 1864–1865); 500 maximum capacity; 3,000? peak population; 225? deaths; converted building.
Mobile (1863–1865).
Montgomery (1861, 1864?–1865?).
Selma (1864, 1865?); converted buildings.
Talladega (1861–1865?); converted buildings.
Tuscaloosa (1861–1863); converted buildings.

Florida
Castle San Marcos, St. Augustine (1861); coastal fortification.

Georgia
Americus (1861?, 1863, 1864?–1865?); preexisting jail.
Augusta (1861?, 1863, 1864?–1865?); preexisting jail.
Blackshear (1864); 5,000 maximum capacity; 5,000 peak population; unsheltered stockade.
Camp Davidson, Savannah (1864); 6,000? peak population; 2+ deaths; preexisting jail, fenced-in tents.
Camp Lawton, Millen (1864); 10,299 peak population; 488+ deaths; unsheltered stockade.

PRINCIPAL C.S.A. MILITARY PRISONS (CONTINUED)

Camp Oglethorpe, and *Davis Smith Negro Mart*, Macon (1861–1864); 600 maximum capacity; 1,900 peak population; converted fairgrounds.

Camp Sumter, Andersonville (1864–1865); 10,000 maximum capacity; 32,899 peak population; 329 escapees; 12, 919 deaths; unsheltered stockade.

Dalton (1864); guarded field?

East Point, near Atlanta (1861–1862, 1863?, 1864); guarded field.

Fulton County Jail, Atlanta (1861–1862, 1863?, 1864); preexisting jail.

Marietta (1861?–1862?, 1863, 1864?–1865?).

Thomasville (1861?–1864?, 1865).

Louisiana	*Baton Rouge* (1861–1862); converted buildings. *Shreveport* (1863, 1864?–1865?); converted buildings.

Louisiana
: *Baton Rouge* (1861–1862); converted buildings.
: *Shreveport* (1863, 1864?–1865?); converted buildings.

Mississippi
: *Bridge Prison*, Jackson (1863); converted covered bridge.
: *Meridian* (1863?, 1864–1865); 700 peak population; fenced-in barracks.

North Carolina
: *Charlotte* (1865); 1,800 maximum capacity; 1,200 peak population; 30+ escapees; guarded field.
: *Goldsboro* (1864–1865); 500+ peak population; converted buildings and guarded field.
: *Raleigh* (1861–1863, 1864?–1865?); 600 peak population; 600+ escapees; converted buildings and fairgrounds, fenced-in barracks.
: *Salisbury* (1861–1865); 2,000 maximum capacity; 10,321 peak population; 500+ escapees; 3,700 deaths; converted buildings and fenced-in tents.

South Carolina
: *Camp Asylum*, *Camp Sorghum*, et al., Columbia (1864–1865); 2,000 peak population; 373 escapees; preexisting jails, converted buildings, guarded field, and stockades.
: *Castle Pinckney*, Charleston (1861–1862); 150 maximum capacity; 300 peak population; no escapees; no deaths; coastal fortification.
: *Charleston* (1861–1865); 1,100 maximum capacity; 1,100 peak population; preexisting prisons, coastal fortifications, and converted buildings.
: *Charleston City Jail*, Charleston (1861–1865); 300 maximum capacity; 900 peak population; preexisting jail and fenced-in tents.
: *Charleston Guard House*, Charleston (1861–1865); 300 maximum capacity; 300? peak population; preexisting prison.
: *Florence* (1864–1865); 1,500+ peak population; unsheltered stockade.

(continued)

PRINCIPAL C.S.A. MILITARY PRISONS (CONTINUED)

	O'Connor House, Charleston (1864); 86 peak population; no escapees; no deaths; converted building.
	Richland County Jail, Columbia (1861?–1863?, 1864–1865); 500 peak population; preexisting jail.
	Roper Hospital, Charleston (1864); 200+? peak population; no escapees; no deaths; converted hospital.
Tennessee	*Botanico-Medical College*, Memphis (1861–1863?); converted buildings.
	Fort Misner, Columbia (1861?–1863?, 1864, 1865?); preexisting fortification.
	Knoxville (1861, 1862?); preexisting jail.
	Swim's Jail, Chattanooga (1862, 1863?); preexisting jail.
Texas	*Camp Ford*, Tyler (1863–1865); 4,900 peak population; 4+ escapees; 232+ deaths; unsheltered stockade.
	Camp Groce, or *Camp Liendo*, near Hempstead (1863); 500+ peak population; 20? deaths; converted buildings.
	Camp Van Dorn, or *Salado Camp* (1861); guarded field.
	Camp Verde (1861–1862); 350? peak population; guarded field.
	Galveston (1863); 100? peak population; converted buildings.
	Houston (1863); 100? peak population; converted building.
	Prison Town, Boerne (1862); 350 peak population; no escapes; no deaths; unsheltered stockade.
	San Antonio (1861); 360+ peak population; converted buildings.
	San Antonio Springs (1862); 350+ peak population; guarded field.
	San Pedro Springs (1862); 350 peak population; 12 escapees; guarded field.
	Texas State Penitentiary, Huntsville (1863); 232? peak population; preexisting prison.
Virginia	*Atkinson's Factory*, Richmond (1861–1862, 1863?–1865?); converted buildings.
	Barrett's Factory, Richmond (1862–1863, 1864?–1865?); 1,200 peak population; converted building.
	Belle Isle, near Richmond (1862–1864); 3,000 maximum capacity; 10,000 peak population; 300+? deaths; stockade.
	Castle Godwin, or *Lumpkin's Jail*, or *McDaniel's Jail*, Richmond (1861–1862); 75? maximum capacity; 600 peak population; preexisting jail.
	Castle Lightning, Richmond (1862, 1863?–1865?); converted building.

PRINCIPAL C.S.A. MILITARY PRISONS (CONTINUED)

Castle Thunder, including *Gleanor's Factory* and *Whitlock's Warehouse*, Richmond (1862–1865); 1,400 maximum capacity; 3,000+ peak population; converted buildings.

Crew and Pemberton Warehouse, Richmond (1861–1862); converted building.

Danville (1863–1865); 3,700 maximum capacity; 4,000 peak population; 70+ escapees; 1,297 deaths; converted buildings.

E.D.M. Prison (1862–1863, 1864?–1865?); converted buildings.

Edward's Prison (1862–1863, 1864?–1865?); converted buildings.

Frederick County Jail, Winchester (1862–1864, 1865?); preexisting jail.

Gordonsville (1862?–1865?); converted building.

Grant's Factory, Richmond (1863–1865); converted building.

Gwathmey Warehouse, Richmond (1861, 1862?–1865?); converted building.

Harwood's Factory, Richmond (1861–1863, 1864?–1865?); converted building.

Henrico County Jail, Richmond (1861–1863, 1864?–1865?); preexisting jail.

Howard's Factory, Richmond (1861–1863, 1864?–1865?); converted building.

Libby Prison, Richmond (1862–1865); 1,000 maximum capacity; 4,221 peak population; 60+ escapees; 20+? deaths; converted buildings.

Ligon's Warehouse, Richmond (1861–1862); 500+ maximum capacity; 600 peak population; converted building.

Lynchburg (1862–1863, 1864?–1865?); 500? maximum capacity; 500+ peak population; preexisting jail, converted buildings, and fairgrounds.

Mayo's Factory, Richmond (1861–1862, 1863?); 500? maximum capacity; 500 peak population; converted building.

McCurdy's Warehouse, Richmond (1862, 1863?–1865?); converted building.

Petersburg (1863?, 1864–1865); converted buildings and fairgrounds.

Prince Street Jail, Alexandria (1861); no deaths; preexisting jail.

Richmond City Jail (1861–1862); preexisting jail.

Richmond (15 lesser facilities and *Virginia State Penitentiary*) (1861–1865); 13,500 peak population; 200+ deaths; preexisting jails and converted buildings.

Ross's Factory, Richmond (1862, 1863?–1865?); 200? peak population; converted building.

(continued)

PRINCIPAL C.S.A. MILITARY PRISONS (CONTINUED)

Scott's Factory, Richmond (1862–1863, 1864?–1865?); converted building.

Smith's Factory, Richmond (1863–1865); converted building.

Taylor's Factory, Richmond (1861–1862); converted building.

Warwick & Barksdale Mill (1862–1863, 1864?–1865?); 4,000 maximum capacity; converted buildings.

Winchester (1862–1864, 1865?), preexisting jail and converted building.

Source: Confederate prisons information has been adapted from Lonnie Speer, the "Prison Quick-Reference Guide" in *Portals to Hell: Military Prisons of the Civil War* (Mechanicsburg, PA: Stackpole Books, 1997), pp. 332–340.

Note: ? = unknown or best available figure.

TIME LINE OF SIGNIFICANT EVENTS

1861

February: Federal troops in Texas surrender to state forces, effectively becoming the first prisoners of the Civil War. Most are subsequently paroled.

August 30: Union commander William Wallace agrees to the first formal (though unofficial) exchange of prisoners with Confederate Brigadier General Gideon Pillow. The exchange takes place on September 3. Unofficial exchanges of prisoners in the field take place in subsequent months.

1862

July 22: As representatives for their respective governments, Union General John Dix and Confederate General D. H. Hill create an exchange cartel. The cartel provides for the paroling and exchange of prisoners and bases the rate of exchange on a prisoner's rank. A parole, to be put in effect within ten days after capture, permits a prisoner to return to his own lines, provided that he does not take up arms until he is officially exchanged.

December 24: Confederate President Jefferson Davis declares Union General Benjamin Butler an outlaw because of his policies against the populace in occupied New Orleans. Davis orders that no Union commissioned officers will be paroled until Butler is punished, and he further decrees that white officers of black regiments, and the troops themselves, will be turned over to state governments "to be dealt with according to the laws of said States."

December 28: U.S. Secretary of War Edward Stanton suspends the exchange of commissioned officers. Three months later, the resume.

1863

February 28: The U.S. War Department issues General Orders, No. 49, which declares that paroles on the battlefield, in which prisoners are dismissed and declared paroled, are not valid and only commissioned officers can give paroles for themselves and those under their commands.

March 27: The U.S. War Department authorizes man-for-man exchanges of officers "without reference to the cartel."

April 24: The U.S. War Department publishes General Orders, No. 100—also known as the Lieber Code after its author, Dr. Francis Lieber—defining the laws of war. The code states that "if the government does not approve of the parole, the paroled officer must return into captivity, and should the enemy refuse to receive him, he is free of his parole."

May 1: In response to Davis' December 24, 1862, proclamation, the Confederate Congress declares that officers commanding black troops should not be turned over to the states, but "ought to be dealt with and disposed of by the Confederate government." Those officers "deemed as inciting servile insurrection . . . shall if captured be put to death or be otherwise punished at the decision of the court." Captured black soldiers, however, are still to be "delivered to the authorities of the State or States in which they shall be captured to be dealt with according to the present or future law of such State or States."

May 25: The U.S. War Department again halts exchanges and paroles of officers in response to the action of the Confederate Congress.

June 13: Confederate General E. Kirby Smith writes to his subordinate, General Richard Taylor: "I have been unofficially informed that some of your troops have captured negroes in arms. I hope this may not be so, and that your subordinates who may have been in command of capturing parties may have recognized the propriety of giving no quarter to armed negroes and their officers. In this way we may be relieved from a disagreeable dilemma."

July 3: The U.S. War Department issues General Orders, No. 207, reminding all field commanders that "all prisoners of war must be delivered at the places designated. . . . The only exception allowed is the case of commanders of two opposing armies, who are authorized to exchange prisoners or to release them on parole at other points mutually agreed upon. . . ." The order also declares: "It is the duty of the captor to guard his prisoners, and if through necessity or choice he fails to do this it is the duty of the prisoner to return to the service of his Government."

These Confederates were captured at Gettysburg in July 1863. Robert E. Lee proposed an exchange of prisoners with Union General George G. Meade as Gettysburg concluded; Meade replied, "It is not in my power to accede to the proposed arrangement."

August 24: The Confederates suggest that "the whole question of paroles be determined by the general orders of the United States, according to their dates, or that it be decided by former practice."

October: Confederate and Union exchange agents disagree about the balance of exchanged prisoners. Each side claims the other "owes" exchanges.

1864

January 12: General Benjamin Butler, outlawed by Jefferson Davis but now a Union agent of exchange, proposes to Confederates a resumption of man-for-man exchanges.

February 27: The first Union prisoners arrive at the still incomplete stockade at Andersonville, Georgia.

April 17: General in Chief Ulysses S. Grant orders that no exchanges may occur until the Confederates agree to treat black prisoners the same as white prisoners, and rectify the alleged imbalance in the number of exchanged prisoners (especially those from Vicksburg and Port Hudson).

May 7: The U.S. War Department again claims that the Confederates have violated the man-for-man exchange rate and asserts that the Southerners owe the Federals tens of thousands of exchanges. The Federals declare "all federal prisoners of war and all civilians on parole prior to May 7, 1864, . . . exchanged."

June 13: Confederate Secretary of War James Seddon writes to Confederate General Howell Cobb: "As to the white officers serving with negro troops, we ought never to be inconvenienced with such prisoners."

August 10: The Confederates agree to a man-for-man exchange, but not of black soldiers.

August 19: Grant expresses his views on exchange in a letter to Union Secretary of State William Seward: "We ought not to make a single exchange nor release a prisoner on any pretext whatever until the war closes. We have got to fight until the military power of the South is exhausted, and if we release or exchange prisoners captured it simply becomes a war of extermination."

August 27: Butler responds to the Confederates' August 10 proposal for a reinstatement of the man-for-man exchange by asking whether black troops are to be included.

September: Through special arrangements, a few thousand ill and invalid prisoners are exchanged.

September: As Sherman's army threatens Atlanta, Andersonville prisoners are moved to Charleston and Savannah, then to a newly established camp at Florence, South Carolina.

October 1: Lee proposes to Grant an exchange of prisoners of the armies in Virginia, but Grant again insists on the equal exchange of troops, regardless of color. Lee replies that "Deserters from our service and negroes belonging to our citizens are not considered subjects of exchange." Grant refers "the whole matter . . . to the proper authority for their decision."

October 15: Stanton gives Grant responsibility for all prisoner-of-war issues, charging him to "take any steps that you may deem proper to effect the release and exchange of our soldiers and all loyal persons held as prisoners by the rebel authorities."

December 31: General John Winder, commander of all Confederate prisons east of the Mississippi River, suggests unofficially, so he will not be "misunderstood," that since "there is no place that can be considered as safe from the operations of the enemy," officers and men whose terms of enlistment have expired be paroled.

1865

January 21: Grant informs Stanton that he has given instructions that negotiations are to be reopened with a view to resuming a general exchange.

April 3: Union troops occupy Richmond, confiscating those prison buildings not destroyed by fire. Libby Prison is subsequently used to house Confederate officials.

April 9: General Robert E. Lee surrenders the Army of Northern Virginia at Appomattox Court House.

April 26: Confederate General Joseph E. Johnston surrenders his army near Durham Station, North Carolina.

April–July: The Union gradually releases its Confederate prisoners after they have taken the Oath of Allegiance to the United States, most in June and July. The last Confederate prisoners are released from Fort Lafayette, New York, in November.

May 17: Camp Ford, Texas, is the last Confederate prison to be evacuated.

August 23: The trial by military commission of Henry Wirz, commander of Andersonville, begins. He is executed on November 10.

★　★　★

Prisoner Exchange and the Dix-Hill Cartel

During the first fifteen months of the war, the prisoner populations, in both the Union and the Confederacy, continued to grow, as did the public demand to release them. As the scale of the fighting increased, so did the burden of caring for captured enemy soldiers. In 1862, Union General Ulysses S. Grant's capture of Fort Henry and Fort Donelson in February, and the fighting at Shiloh, Tennessee, in April, produced thousands of prisoners in the Western Theater of operations. In the East, Major General George B. McClellan's campaign on the Virginia Peninsula, which culminated in Confederate victories for Robert E. Lee's forces in June, produced a steady flow of prisoners.

At this point, the major issue blocking prisoner exchange negotiations was the Union's refusal to acknowledge secession as legal. The Lincoln administration would not recognize the Confederacy as a sovereign nation. Instead, it held the Confederate states to be in rebellion, and regarded Confederate soldiers to be traitors. In effect, however, captured Southern troops were treated as prisoners of war even before the Dix-Hill cartel was agreed on.

After the first battle of Bull Run, public pressure was brought to bear on Lincoln to relax his position so that exchanges could be made. (Informal exchanges were in fact taking place on the battlefield.) On December 11, 1861, Congress passed a joint resolution stating that because informal exchanges had already taken place, and "such exchange does not involve a recognition of the rebels as a government," Lincoln should "inaugurate systematic measures for the exchange of prisoners in the present rebellion." By February 1862, Union General John Wool and Confederate General Howell Cobb were discussing the basis for a cartel. These men were replaced by General Daniel Hill for the South and General John Dix for the North (see "Selected Biographies" on page 619). On July 22, 1862, they agreed on a cartel patterned on a system the United States and British governments had used in the War of 1812. The Dix-Hill cartel provided for the parole and exchange of prisoners, using a rate of exchange based on rank. A parole, to be effected within ten days, allowed a prisoner passage back to his own lines. Once there, he would be precluded from taking up arms or performing other military duties until he was officially exchanged. Officers and enlisted men could be exchanged man for man with men of equal rank, or one-for-several, according to a rating system that placed a higher weight on men of higher rank (see "The Dix-Hill Cartel Prisoner Exchange System," page 603). Exchanges took place when equivalent numbers were assembled on both sides.

The cartel worked well enough to empty most prisons, but there were disagreements over interpretation and compliance almost from the start. The agents of exchange—Robert Ould for the Confederacy and Lorenzo Thomas, W. H. Ludlow, Ethan Hitchcock (designated Commissioner of Exchange), and Sam Meredith for the Union—continually argued about the validity of paroles and the return of paroled soldiers to battle before a proper exchange had been made. The Confederate government charged that the Union held noncombatants in prison and confiscated the property of Virginia citizens under an order by U.S. Secretary of War Edwin Stanton. In turn, Stanton's War Department issued several general orders clarifying the Union's position and pointing out Confederate breaches of the cartel. General Orders, No. 207 (July 3, 1863), for example, repudiated paroles in the field, pointing out that the cartel required delivery of paroled prisoners to specific sites. "It is the duty of the captor to guard his prisoners," the orders stated. "He cannot avoid this duty by giving an unauthorized military parole." Under these terms, the Confederacy would be forced to bear the burden of housing, feeding, and transporting prisoners.

The Preliminary Emancipation Proclamation, issued by President Lincoln in September 1862, raised the likelihood of black soldiers fighting against the Confederacy. Jefferson Davis issued his own proclamation declaring that captured black troops and their white officers would be turned over to the states to be dealt with according to state laws, rather than be considered prisoners of war. After the official Emancipation Proclamation in January 1863, the Confederate Congress modified Davis' statement. Although black troops would still be turned over to the states, white officers would be tried by the national government. In all cases, the punishment could be death. The Union declared it would retaliate by executing Confederate officers. Both sides backed down from their hard rhetoric about executions, but, unofficially, some Southern commanders and their troops adopted a policy of not taking black prisoners. There were instances—for example, at Fort Pillow, Tennessee and Saltville, Virginia—where Confederates killed surrendering blacks. When the Confederates did imprison some black soldiers, they received harsher treatment than whites and were put to hard labor far more often.

An impasse over technical matters and, particularly, irreconcilable differences about the status of black soldiers all but halted exchanges by the fall of 1863. Stanton wrote to Union General Benjamin Butler, soon to be appointed a special agent of exchange, in November 1863:

> It is known that the rebels will exchange man for man and officer for officer, except blacks and officers in command of black troops. These they absolutely refuse to exchange. This is the point on which the whole matter hinges. Exchanging man for man and officer for officer, with the exception the rebels make, is a substantial abandonment of the colored troops and their officers . . . and would be a shameful dishonor to the Government bound to protect them.

Although Butler negotiated some small exchanges in 1864, prisons on both sides continued to fill well past their capacities. Public pressure on the Lincoln administration to restore the exchange system increased. Lincoln stated in an April speech, "Having determined to use the negro as a soldier, there is no way but to give him all the protection given to any soldier." In an arrangement made by the U.S. and Confederate navies, black sailors were included in a prisoner exchange in October 1864.

There was a further reason for not resuming exchanges, however. General Ulysses S. Grant expressed the view that withholding manpower from the South would hasten the end of the war in a letter to Butler:

> It is hard on our men held in Southern prisons not to exchange them, but it is humanity to those left in the ranks to fight our battles. Every man we hold, when released on parole or otherwise, becomes an active soldier against us at once either directly or indirectly. If we commence a system of exchange which liberates all prisoners taken, we will have to fight on until the whole South is exterminated.

On October 15, 1864, Stanton conveyed to Grant the "authority to take such measures as he deems consistent with national honor and safety for the release of all soldiers and loyal persons held by the rebels in captivity." Arrangements were made for each government to provide food and supplies to its imprisoned soldiers, the Confederacy shipping cotton to New York to buy its supplies in the North. The first cotton arrived in late January 1865. By then Grant had assured Stanton that he had already authorized an agent to renew negotiations for exchange and that he had "no doubt but an arrangement will be entered into." In early February, man for man exchanges resumed. The Union made no mention of black soldiers, nor did the Confederacy. Several hundred black troops were included in the exchange. By then, Lincoln had won reelection, the Union was in a strong military position, and the crisis in the Confederacy was so great that even the once-rejected proposal of arming slaves and free blacks as Confederate soldiers was gaining acceptance.

Before the exchange could be completed, Confederate General Robert E. Lee surrendered the Army of Northern Virginia at Appomattox Court House. The last of the Confederate soldiers in battle—Lee's and those who surrendered later—were paroled in the field.

The Dix-Hill Cartel Prisoner Exchange System

The Dix-Hill cartel was signed on July 22, 1862. Under the agreement, private soldiers and common seamen were exchanged man for man. Officers were exchanged man for man with those of equal rank. The officers and crew of privateers and merchant vessels aiding the Confederacy were included in this military exchange. The Dix-Hill cartel stipulated the following scale of equivalents when exchanging officers for those of lesser rank:

Officers' Rank	Number of Privates or Common Seamen Needed for Exchange
General Commanding in Chief or Admiral	60
Flag Officer or Major General	40
Commodore or Brigadier-General	20
Captain in the Navy or Colonel	15
Lieutenant-Colonel or Commander in the Navy	10
Lieutenant Commander or Major	8
Lieutenant or Master in the Navy or Captain in the Army or Marines	6
Masters' Mates in the Navy or Lieutenants and Ensigns in the Army	4
Midshipmen and Warrant Officers in the Navy, Masters of Merchant Vessels and Commanders of Privateers	3
Second Captains, Lieutenants or Mates of Merchant Vessels or Privateers, Petty Officers in the Navy, Noncommissioned Officers in the Army or Marines	2

Source: United States Department of War. *The War of the Rebellion: A Compilation of the Official Records of the Union and Confederate Armies.* Series II. Vol. 4. Washington, DC: 1894–1899, pp. 266–268.

Major Prisoner-of-War Camps

United States of America

DELAWARE

FORT DELAWARE: Built in the 1850s on the site of a fort used in the War of 1812, this damp stone-and-masonry fortification gained a reputation, among Confederates, as one of the most dreadful of all Northern prisoner-of-war camps. The fort, near Wilmington and Delaware City, began receiving some of the first prisoners (including some naval personnel) captured by Union forces. Throughout the conflict, Fort Delaware held officers and enlisted men, civilian Southern sympathizers, informants, and spies. Scurvy, dysentery, measles, and diarrhea were prevalent, and a smallpox epidemic claimed many lives.

ILLINOIS

ALTON PRISON: Opened in 1833 as the Illinois State Penitentiary, Alton Prison was closed in 1860 and then reopened, in February 1862, as a Federal military prison. Built on the banks of the Mississippi River, the prison was exposed to harsh weather for much of the year, and its prisoners suffered from the exposure. In the winter of 1862, an outbreak of smallpox killed many inmates and forced authorities to open a quarantine hospital on a nearby island. In the three years of its existence, Alton housed 11,764 prisoners. Most were Confederate soldiers, but some, including several women, were political prisoners, guerrillas, or spies.

CAMP DOUGLAS: Camp Douglas, named for Senator Stephen A. Douglas, was established as a training camp in the city of Chicago. By February 1862, the first large group of Confederate prisoners had arrived. The facility also held political prisoners who had plotted to help imprisoned soldiers to escape. Bitter winters, rampant disease, and incompetent administration contributed to the death toll.

ROCK ISLAND: Situated on an island in the Mississippi River opposite Davenport, Iowa, the Rock Island Prison was renowned for hot, humid summers and bitterly cold winters. Between December 1863 and the close of the prison in the summer of 1865, some 12,400 Confederates were incarcerated

Originally a training camp for troops in the Chicago area, Camp Douglas, when it housed prisoners of war, had the highest death rate (10 percent) in a one-month period for any prison, including Andersonville. Andersonville, however, far exceeded this Union camp in the total number of prisoners who died.

there. Approximately 2,000 prisoners, or almost 16 percent, died. Most of the deaths were attributed to an 1864 smallpox epidemic, believed to have been started by prisoners transferred from Chicago's Camp Douglas.

INDIANA

CAMP MORTON: At the outbreak of hostilities, Indiana authorities converted animal barns and stockades at the Indiana State Fairgrounds, near Indianapolis, into a training camp for new recruits. Shortly after Grant's capture of Fort Donelson in Tennessee, on February 16, 1862, Camp Morton began to be used as a temporary staging facility for groups of prisoners destined for other Federal prisons. Poorly built or converted barracks provided inadequate shelter in the bitter northern winters. Intentionally limited rations—part of the harsh cost-saving programs devised by the U.S. Commissary General of Prisoners, Colonel William Hoffman and approved by Stanton (see page 614)—compounded the prisoners' misery.

MARYLAND

POINT LOOKOUT: The Federal government leased a resort on Point Lookout, Maryland, and used the site as a hospital complex and for military purposes, as well as to house prisoners. Two prison pens were constructed, one each for officers and enlisted men, and Confederate soldiers captured at Gettysburg were brought in to help finish construction. Point Lookout— officially called Camp Hoffman (for Colonel William Hoffman, U.S. Commissary General of Prisoners)—held some 22,000 prisoners at the war's end. From July 1863 until May 1865, approximately 52,000 men endured extended stays here. Unsanitary water and exposure to harsh weather off Chesapeake Bay took a severe toll because, unlike other Union prisoner-of-war camps, Point Lookout substituted often inadequate tents for wooden barracks. More than 3,500 prisoners died.

MASSACHUSETTS

FORT WARREN: Built on George Island in Boston Harbor, this pentagonal fort was named for Joseph Warren, who fell in battle at nearby Bunker Hill. Under the administration of Colonel Justin E. Dimick, Fort Warren was among the most livable of all Civil War prisons. It was renowned for decent food, visiting privileges, and permission to receive gifts from friends and family. When Dimick was compelled by health problems to leave in

1863, Fort Warren's legendary hospitality was curtailed. Nevertheless, the death of only twelve prisoners over the course of the war indicates far better than average conditions for prisoners. Fort Warren held political prisoners and blockade runners. In the immediate aftermath of the war, the Confederate vice president, Alexander H. Stephens, was confined there.

NEW YORK

ELMIRA: "Helmira," as it came to be called by many of the men imprisoned there, was among the most miserable of all Northern prisoner-of-war camps. With the main water supply polluted, and poor or nonexistent drainage of camp sewage, disease ran rampant through the camp. There was also a shortage of barracks to house all of the men during the freezing New York winters. These factors contributed to the highest mortality rate of any Union prison—over 24 percent. Elmira, at times, also served as something of a tourist attraction. Civilians paid a fee to climb on one of two observation decks overlooking the prison walls.

OHIO

CAMP CHASE: Initially a training camp for volunteers, Camp Chase was named for the one-time governor of Ohio, Salmon P. Chase, Lincoln's secretary of the treasury. The first inmates arrived in 1861. Under state control, rations were generous, and honor-bound Confederate officers were sometimes allowed to spend time in nearby Columbus. Once transferred to Federal control, however, many privileges were discontinued. Most of the officers were transferred north to Johnson's Island, leaving the enlisted men to cope with an enclosure that seasonal rains had transformed into an unhealthy swamp.

JOHNSON'S ISLAND: Established in October 1861 on an island in Lake Erie, offshore from Sandusky, Ohio, and eventually consisting of thirteen two-story buildings, Johnson's Island began to receive Confederate officers in April 1862. In 1863, the prisoner population rose to more than 3,200, and at war's end, there were more than 9,000 prisoners. Despite the most severe winters of any camp, the day-to-day life of the inmates was far better than that experienced by most of their counterparts. Prisoners formed their own government and maintained organized pastimes such as debating and theatricals. To supplement inadequate prison rations, a "rat club" facilitated the capture and distribution of rodents as food.

Confederate States of America

ALABAMA

CAHABA (CASTLE MORGAN): Castle Morgan, named for celebrated Confederate cavalry raider John Hunt Morgan, began operation in the spring of 1863. Small by most standards, the Cahaba prison consisted principally of an incomplete cotton shed. The stream that traversed the property served as the townspeople's source of water, and as their source of sewage removal upriver from the prison. In early 1865, Cahaba prisoners, along with many from Andersonville, were transferred to Camp Fisk, near Vicksburg, Mississippi, for release. Many were killed in the explosion of the steamship *Sultana* while en route home.

GEORGIA

ANDERSONVILLE: See "Andersonville" box on page 609.

This lithograph Map of Andersonville, Georgia, *depicts the most infamous prison camp of the Civil War.*

ANDERSONVILLE

In January 1864, near Andersonville in south central Georgia, slave labor began to erect a stockade fence of pine logs covering approximately sixteen acres. The site, chosen to accommodate overflow from the crowded prisoner facilities in Richmond, was fed by a stream, accessible by rail, and far from Union forces. Even before the prison was complete, the first trainload of Union prisoners was dispatched from Virginia.

Poor planning at Andersonville—officially designated Camp Sumter by the Confederates, after the county in which it was located—created an unhealthy morass well before overcrowding became a problem. No provisions were made to manage waste disposal; the stream passing through the prison brought waste downstream from guards' camps and the cooking station; and there were no shelters for inmates.

Designed to accommodate 10,000 prisoners, Andersonville held 26,367 men by the summer of 1864. Though enlarged by ten acres, the prison was still woefully crowded. By August 1864, Andersonville's population peaked at just short of 33,000. In the oppressive heat, men burrowed into the ground or rigged whatever shelters they could assemble from materials at hand, such as blankets and sticks, in a space averaging thirty-three square feet per man. During the worst days of August, more than 100 prisoners died per day. A multitude of diseases, from dysentery and diarrhea to scurvy and gangrene, facilitated by or in conjunction with malnutrition and exposure, decimated the camp's population. Thirteen thousand prisoners died, nearly 30 percent of the camp's population.

Historians generally agree that the enormous suffering at Andersonville resulted from an inept bureaucracy, limited resources, and a severely disrupted infrastructure, rather than deliberate cruelty. During the war, however, Northerners blamed what they perceived as the perfidy of the Southern slavocracy. The *New York Times,* on April 22, 1864, stated: "Diabolism will never abate as long as it is in their power to exercise it. The slaveholder is born to tyranny and reared to cruelty." Articles such as this, and mass-produced images of emaciated inmates, convinced many Northerners that the Confederates had deliberately run Andersonville as a death camp. Thus, the camp's commander, Captain Henry Wirz, was arrested, convicted of war crimes, and executed after the war. Other Southern prison officials were jailed for short periods, but none were executed. Prison memoirs kept alive, for decades, the anger and outrage over Andersonville, and Federal veterans' groups saw to the preservation of the prison site, in conjunction with the designation of the graveyard as a national cemetery.

Studies of Civil War prisons in general have since revealed harsh treatment and criminal neglect of captives on both sides of the conflict. In 1970, the U.S. Congress designated the Andersonville National Historic Site as a memorial to all prisoners of war in American history.

CAMP LAWTON: Just north of Millen, Georgia, Confederate authorities opened a newly built stockade prison. In October 1864, it began to receive some of the Andersonville population and prisoners from Savannah. Within a month, over 10,000 prisoners had been transferred there. As Sherman's troops approached, all the prisoners were evacuated to Blackshear and other prisons. In the short span of some six weeks, at least 488 Union prisoners died at Camp Lawton, though some accounts place the number of deaths at 700.

CAMP OGLETHORPE: The 800 Union troops captured at Shiloh in April 1862 were the first inmates at Macon's Camp Oglethorpe. The camp was later used to accommodate overflow officers from the population in Richmond's Libby Prison. Over 1,500 officers were transferred to Camp Oglethorpe in May 1864. In July, Union Major General George Stoneman, whose earlier attempt to liberate the prison had failed, was himself captured and briefly detained there with many of his men.

NORTH CAROLINA

SALISBURY: Established in 1861 in an unused cotton factory, Salisbury at first held a relatively small number of deserters and alleged spies. On December 12, the first 120 Federal prisoners of war arrived. Over the next three years, Salisbury's population numbered approximately 1,500 men at any given time. Mortality rates were low. In early 1864, over 8,000 prisoners from the crowded Richmond prisons were sent by rail to Salisbury. Whereas only 300 men died at Salisbury between November 1861 and the fall of 1864, over 3,400 (one in three) succumbed to the elements and unsanitary conditions during the five-month span from October 1864 to February 1865.

SOUTH CAROLINA

FLORENCE: Opening very late in the war, in response to the crisis unfolding at Andersonville, the prison camp at Florence, South Carolina, had a high death toll. From the fall of 1864 until February of the following year—a five-month span—at least 2,802 of the estimated 15,000 prisoners died. The short-lived Florence facility was a rectangular pen with a log stockade. A stream traversed the camp, but, as was the case at so many prisons, the running water quickly became an open sewer. Outside the perimeter of the stockade, a large mound of dirt served as a catwalk for prison guards, who also manned artillery pieces on platforms raised above the corners of the camp. Difficult conditions and Confederate scrutiny led more than 300 Union prisoners to enlist in the Confederate army rather than remain in the camp.

Texas

Camp Ford: Camp Ford, at Tyler, Texas, was the largest prisoner of war camp west of the Mississippi River. It had a relatively healthy environment for the estimated 6,000 prisoners who stayed there. A good supply of fresh water and steady rations of cornmeal and beef contributed to one of the lowest mortality rates of any camp.

Virginia

Belle Isle: Situated on an island in the James River at Richmond, with rocky rapids effectively serving to enclose the camp, Belle Isle prison contained the overflow of enlisted prisoners from the city. Prisoners lived mainly in tents and in a few shacks on one end of the eighty-acre island. The initial influx of prisoners began in 1862; as many as 5,000 men were eventually exchanged. In the fall of 1863, the reopened camp housed over 6,000 prisoners; the count rose to over 8,000 at the beginning of 1864. Prisoners were relocated to Andersonville; Salisbury, North Carolina; and Danville, Virginia.

Danville Prisons: Danville's large tobacco warehouses were expropriated by the Confederate government as quickly convertible military prisons. Situated in south central Virginia, with railroads connecting directly to the Confederate capital and points south, Danville soon became a central transfer point for prisoner-of-war and military hospital traffic. The warehouse prisons accommodated overflow prisoners from Richmond and groups of prisoners destined for camps in the Carolinas or Georgia.

Libby Prison: Libby Prison, in Richmond, was among the best known of any wartime prison facilities in the country. The proportionately higher incidence of literacy and social influence among the prison's population (primarily officers) ensured an enduring notoriety in published reminiscences. Its periodic use as a processing station for the Confederate prison system—the names and ranks of new Federal prisoners were recorded here, before their transfer to other facilities—meant that more prisoners passed through Libby than through any other Southern prison. Photographs and reproductions of sketches of Libby gave it a widely recognizable image even during wartime. The four-story building (a basement and three floors) took its name from the family firm that had leased it, Libby & Son, "Ship Chandlers and Grocers." When Confederate authorities expropriated the warehouse in March 1862—giving the Libby firm forty-eight hours to vacate—the sign remained and became its natural designation. Most prisoners were housed on the upper floors.

Libby Prison in Richmond, Virginia was the headquarters for the Confederate States Military Prisons. In 1864, a mine was placed beneath the prison with the threat that it would be blown up if there were an attempt to rescue prisoners during the Kilpatrick-Dahlgren raid on Richmond.

Prisoners considered uncontrollable—those caught attempting to escape; suspected spies; and slaves who had been sentenced to death—were detained in basement cells. More than 40,000 Federal prisoners were held in Libby for extended stays, and as many as 125,000 are believed to have passed through en route to other prisons. A large-scale transfer of Union officers from Libby to other camps was effected in May 1864. For the balance of the war, as Federal forces became further entrenched along the Richmond-Petersburg front, Libby was used predominantly as a staging pen for captives destined for prisons removed from the front. Throughout the life of the prison, mortality rates were low. With the fall of Richmond, Libby housed Confederate, rather than Union prisoners.

The Press, Published Reports, and Public Opinion

Newspapers in both the Union and the Confederacy played a significant role in shaping public opinion on the issue of prisoners of war. In the North, they placed continual pressure on the Lincoln administration to negotiate exchange. The heightened rhetoric and gruesome images in editorials and articles kept anxieties and emotions boiling. Official reports and pronouncements by key figures such as U.S. Secretary of War Edwin Stanton and the Confederate president, Jefferson Davis, also exaggerated both the amenities provided to prisoners on their own side and the treatment accorded by their adversaries.

Early in the war, when numbers were relatively small, the Northern press showed some appreciation of Lincoln's position in refusing to recognize the legitimacy of the Confederacy. "In a war of this kind words are things," wrote *Harper's Weekly* in November 1861. "If we must address Davis as the president of the Confederacy, we cannot exchange and the prisoners should not wish it." But *Harper's Weekly* had printed illustrations showing Confederate soldiers bayonetting wounded Union troops in August, and a description in the *New York Times* in July 1861 is perhaps more typical:

> Most shocking barbarities begin to be reported as practiced by the rebels upon the wounded and prisoners of the Union that fall into their hands. We are told of their slashing the throats of some from ear to ear; of their cutting off the heads of others and kicking them about as footballs; and of their setting up the wounded against trees and firing at them as targets or torturing them with plunges of bayonets into their bodies.

By December 1861, the *New York Times* was exhorting the government to abandon its insistence on making nonrecognition of the Confederacy an issue.

> The course pursued by our Government now is precisely that pursued by the British government [during the American Revolution]. Yet exchanges of prisoners were of constant occurrence [then]. Why may not the same course be pursued now? Why should any exchange of prisoners now involve a recognition of the South . . . any more than a similar change during the Revolution involved such a concession to the revolted colonies?

And on July 9, 1862, just days before the Dix-Hill cartel was concluded, the *Times* urged its readers:

> [Think] of the crowded and filthy tobacco warehouses, the brutal keepers, the sanguinary guards, the rotten food, the untended wounds, the unmedicined diseases, the miserable marches through the blazing South. . . . What horrors has death on the battlefield to this?

The Dix-Hill cartel and subsequent exchange of nearly all prisoners cooled the rhetoric, but the breakdown of exchanges and consequent difficulties of caring for the swelling number of captured soldiers renewed the furor over prison conditions. Along with press accounts, government investigations and statements stressed the depravity of the other side. Confederate Surgeon General Samuel Moore decried the "pestilential cells" housing prisoners at the Union's Fort Delaware and called it an "unworthy attempt to subdue or destroy our soldiers by pestilence and disease." Jefferson Davis, in his address to the Confederate Congress in December 1863, emphasized his notion of the disparity between attitudes toward prisoners in the North and the South. "By an indulgence, perhaps unprecedented, we have even allowed the prisoners in our hands to be supplied by their friends at home with comforts not enjoyed by the men who captured them in battle," he asserted. "In contrast to this treatment, the most revolting inhumanity has characterized the conduct of the United States toward prisoners held by them."

The Union Surgeon General, on the other hand, was informed that sick prisoners forming part of a special exchange showed "the visage of hunger, the expression of despair. . . . Their pinched features, ghastly cadaveric countenances, deep sephulcral eyes, and voices that could hardly be distinguished (some could not articulate) presented a picture which could not be looked upon without drawing out the strongest emotion of pity." Clamor for retaliation against Confederate prisoners, who were presumed to be well fed, clothed, and housed, grew in the North. "Retaliation is a terrible thing, but the miseries and pains and the slowly wasting life of our brethren and friends in those horrible prisons is a worse thing," declared the *New York Times* in March 1864. "No people or government ought to allow its soldiers to be treated for one day as our men have been treated for the last three years." Secretary of War Stanton approved a reduction of rations for Confederate prisoners in 1864. Prisoners in many camps were denied access to sutlers to buy goods, and few improvements were made to overcrowded and unhealthy environments.

In addition to newspapers, reports of investigations into prisons highlighted the most wretched cases of harshness and neglect. *Report No. 67*, issued in 1864 by the U.S. House of Representatives Committee on the Conduct of the War, stated that Union troops destined for Richmond, Virginia, prisons had their possessions stolen when they were captured, and later died miserably from lack of sustenance. Eight pictures of starved and depressed exchanged prisoners were included in the report. Several months later, the U.S. Sanitary Commission's *Narrative of the Privations and Sufferings of the United States Officers and Soldiers while Prisoners of War in the Hands of the Rebel Authorities* praised Northern prisons while concluding that the

Confederacy had "a predetermined plan, originating somewhere in the rebel counsels, for destroying and disabling the soldiers of their enemy, who had honorably surrendered in the field."

Such sentiments, continuously expressed, contributed to the growing conviction in the North that the Confederacy practiced a deliberate policy of oppression, torture, and extermination rather than acted, or failed to act, because it was overwhelmed by the volume of prisoners, given shortages and damage to its infrastructure. The Confederacy countered, as in the preliminary report of a joint committee of the Confederate congress in March 1865, by denying Union charges, attacking Union treatment of Confederate prisoners, and blaming the North for stopping the exchange.

An aggressive posture of defense could also be found in the Southern press. The *Richmond Dispatch*, in March 1864, replied to stories that mule meat had been fed to Libby prisoners:

> Well, what of it? It was vastly too good for men who have essayed to bring starvation on the people who captured them, and they would have no right to complain if they were forced to that fate they designed for us. . . . Better men have eaten mule meat, and thought it very good. . . . But the Yankees lied. The mule has not come to that fate yet. He is . . . too important to be fed to the Yankees.

An editorial in the *Richmond Examiner*, earlier in the year, deplored "the savage alertness with which [fearful Union soldiers] murder our unfortunate brethren upon the slightest exhibition of insubordination, and often without any ground at all except the dastardly nervousness of the sentinels in charge. . . . We observe nothing of the sort in the Confederacy."

In time, the Confederacy also came to believe that the Union deliberately mistreated and killed Confederate prisoners, while Southerners were the hapless victims of ruthless U.S. policies on all fronts. The war of words escalated, and positions became hardened. In the decades following the war, hundreds of book-length personal memoirs and articles were published detailing the horrific experience—mainly from the Union perspective—of soldiers who spent time in Civil War prisons. Memoirs, such as the *Andersonville Diary* of John Ransom, painted a partisan picture of monstrously cruel Confederate administrators and guards. In particular, in the 1880s, a host of Unionist prisoner-of-war memoirs were published, often calculated to gain Federal pensions for their authors.

Concurrent with these Union memoirs, and beginning at the end of the Reconstruction period in the late 1870s, Southern rebuttals and counter-charges were published through such outlets as the Southern Historical Society Papers. The subject of the treatment and mistreatment of prisoners evoked such rancor among veterans and civilians, North and South, that an objective study of the subject may well have been impossible in the climate of the times. Not until the War Department published *The War of the Rebellion: A Compilation of the Official Records of the Union and Confederate Armies* (1880–1901), were correspondence, reports, and other official documents related to the administration of Union and Confederate prisons widely available in an organized fashion.

Prison Escapes

Escapes from Civil War prisons were rare, and successful escapes were rarer still. Incomplete and lost records make it uncertain how many prisoners escaped during the first year of the war, but only 1,200 prisoners escaped between July 1862 and April 1865—a tiny number, considering that more than 400,000 men were incarcerated. Nonetheless, there were prisoners who made an attempt to win their freedom.

Some prisoners escaped while on work parties outside the prison walls; others disguised themselves, fell in with civilian contract laborers within the prison, and boldly walked out with them at quitting time. Some used bed-sheets to get over walls or built scaling ladders from planks lifted from their bunks. On at least one occasion, men in an island prison took apart hardtack crates to make dories. Confederates in western prisons sometimes set fires in one part of a prison to divert attention from an escape in another.

There were more than fifty escapes from Alton Prison, in Illinois. In many of them, the Confederates used the plainest of tactics: they simply charged the guards, braving their fire, and swarmed over the fences. The Southerners at Camp Morton, Indiana, refined this method by throwing stones at sentries to draw their fire. While the guards were reloading their muskets, the prisoners charged, seized the guns, scaled the stockade, and ran. Twenty men escaped from Camp Morton this way in September 1864, and thirty-one more used similar tactics two months later. Such tactics led administrators to increase security with cannon. Confederate guards used artillery to quell a mass escape attempt at Salisbury Prison in North Carolina, and Federal guards at Rock Island Prison, in Illinois, floated a barge in the Mississippi River mounted with two cannon.

Tunneling was by far the most common method of escape. The most famous exit was at Libby Prison, Virginia, but the Confederate Cavalry commander, General John Hunt Morgan, with six associates, also tunneled through a cement floor into an air shaft at the Ohio State Penitentiary in Columbus and made good their escape on November 27, 1863.

The escape at Libby Prison in early 1864 involved over 100 prisoners. Colonel Thomas E. Rose of the Seventy-Seventh Pennsylvania Infantry and Major Andrew G. Hamilton, of the Twelfth Kentucky Infantry, devised a plan calling for access to the basement. "Masonry was removed from the fireplace to admit a man to the storeroom below. . . . Falling through and dropping down ten feet would bring a person to the empty basement under the adjoining room" wrote Hamilton. For forty-seven days, as many as two dozen prisoners worked in shifts, digging the tunnel ten feet below the surface with makeshift tools, carefully scattering the dirt throughout the basement, and covering it with straw.

After digging a sixteen-inch-diameter shaft for a distance of approximately sixty feet, on February 9, 1864, 109 prisoners slipped through the tunnel and out of the prison. The first twenty-five men who exited had dug the tunnel; others were informed as the escape proceeded. The tunnel ended in a Richmond alley. A Unionist Virginia woman and regular visitor to the prisoners, Elizabeth Van Lew, aided those who managed to find her home. Fifty-nine men reached Union lines; forty-eight others, including Colonel Rose, were recaptured. Two escapees drowned.

Once out of prison, escapees were hunted—sometimes with dogs—and weakened by hunger and exposure. Those who evaded immediate recapture were fortunate if they could find assistance. In the South, Union men might hope to obtain help from slaves, and Confederate fugitives from Fort Delaware or Point Lookout might well find Southern sympathizers in Maryland. So strong was the antiwar feeling in the Midwest that Confederate escapees could find allies in Indiana, Illinois, and parts of Ohio. For all but a relatively few, however, extended journeys through enemy territory usually resulted in recapture.

The Sultana Disaster

On April 10, 1865, the day after Robert E. Lee surrendered the Confederate Army of Northern Virginia at Appomattox, Confederate authorities sent orders to Camp Fisk, near Vicksburg, Mississippi, to release the prisoners on parole. Nearly all of the Camp Fisk parolees were veterans of the prisons at

The steamship Sultana, *as photographed at Helena, Arkansas, April 26, 1865. The next morning, overloaded with recently released Union prisoners of war, the ship exploded and sank. An estimated 1,500 to 1,700 of her passengers and crew died—more lives than were lost in the April 1912* Titanic *disaster.*

Cahaba (Castle Morgan), near Selma, Alabama, and at Andersonville. To conduct the former prisoners upriver, toward Cairo, Illinois, the Federal government contracted with private steamboat lines. The *Sultana*—designed to carry 376 passengers—was loaded with 2,000 former prisoners of war, plus other passengers.

Such a load put too great a stress on the *Sultana's* already patched boilers. On April 27, 1865, some seven miles above Memphis, three of the steamboat's four boilers exploded. Much of the ship was destroyed by the blast, and large sections of the remnants burst into flames. Those of *Sultana's* passengers not killed outright were thrust into the water. Many of the men could not swim, and nearly all of them were weak from long months of debilitating captivity. They quickly drowned in the muddy current.

Between 783 and 786 people were ultimately pulled from the water and taken to Memphis hospitals, but over 200 of those rescued from the river did not survive. An estimated 1,500 to 1,700 people were killed. The destruction of the *Sultana* was the deadliest maritime disaster in the nation's history.

**Selected
Biographies**

BENJAMIN FRANKLIN BUTLER (1818–1893). Union general Benjamin Butler was declared an outlaw by Jefferson Davis in December 1862, after Butler ordered the execution of a Southern sympathizer who removed the U.S. flag from the government mint in New Orleans. Davis ordered that no U.S. officers would be paroled until "the said Butler shall have met with due punishment for his crime." In July 1863, when the Union halted the prisoner exchanges that had taken place under the Dix-Hill cartel, Butler offered to attempt to mediate the conflict. In early 1864, Grant appointed him commissioner of exchange, permitting him to negotiate with his Confederate counterparts. Although he had some initial success, exchanging two boatloads of prisoners, the negotiations ultimately failed. Butler (under orders from Grant and Lincoln) insisted that the Confederacy must treat African American troops the same as their white counterparts, and that the South exchange ex-slaves on an equal basis with other prisoners. Exchange resumed without these conditions near the war's end.

JOHN DIX (1798–1879). John Dix, a Union major general, was briefly secretary of the treasury during 1861. Although he served the Union in several diplomatic and military capacities, his greatest achievement lay in the prisoner-exchange pact to which he gave his name. The Dix-Hill cartel, initiated July 22, 1862, was the result of six months of negotiation with three separate Confederate officers. Dix himself aided the exchange of the first prisoners in the East.

DANIEL HARVEY HILL (1821–1889). D. H. Hill, a Confederate major general, shared authorship of the July 1862 Dix-Hill cartel. Hill, appointed by General Robert E. Lee, was the third Confederate to take part in the talks that led to the agreement. He met with Dix for the first time on July 18, 1862. Four days later, he signed the document authorizing the cartel.

ETHAN ALLEN HITCHCOCK (1798–1870). Ethan Hitchcock had spent almost two years serving in various positions in the Union army, when, in November 1862, he became the North's commissioner for the exchange of prisoners under the Dix-Hill cartel. Hitchcock traveled throughout the country to negotiate with prison camp officials and his Confederate counterparts. After the war, he stayed on as commissary general of prisoners, administering the claims of returning former prisoners who were either disabled or had financial difficulties with the government. He retired from this position in 1867.

WILLIAM HOFFMAN (1808–1884). William Hoffman was serving as a lieutenant colonel in Texas at the beginning of the Civil War; almost immediately, he became a prisoner of war when the Union command surrendered at San Antonio. Paroled and sent back to his own lines, he was formally exchanged (and thus permitted to return to duty). Named commissary general of prisoners for the Union in October 1861, he served in that assignment for the rest of the war. Hoffman had to build a system from the ground up. He leased Johnson's Island on Lake Erie, then acquired military training camps: Randall, Douglas, Butler, Morton, and Chase, among others. He continued to add properties to the prison system for the duration of the war, especially after the final breakdown of the Dix-Hill cartel. Like his Confederate counterpart, John Winder (see page 621), although with somewhat less urgency, he struggled under the twin pressures of increasing numbers of prisoners and diminishing resources. Hoffman helped to create a plan to release men from the camps (they could not be exchanged after the fall of 1863). Under this system, many deserters and some captured Confederate soldiers were permitted to take an oath of loyalty to the Union, promise to remain in Northern-controlled territories, and then released.

BENJAMIN HUGER (1805–1877). Benjamin Huger became a colonel in the Confederate army in 1861, and commanded parts of southern Virginia and North Carolina. While there, one of his major duties was the management of early prisoner exchanges. In 1862, the Confederates appointed Huger to negotiate a plan for a nationwide prisoner exchange with Union General John Wool; the initial talks proved unsuccessful, and Huger was relieved of his duties. He was replaced by Howell Cobb, who also failed. After another Confederate replacement (D. H. Hill) was brought in, the talks eventually led to the Dix-Hill cartel.

ROBERT OULD (1820–1882). In July 1862, Robert Ould became a Confederate agent of exchange under the Dix-Hill cartel. As the pact faltered, he was frequently embroiled in disputes with his Union counterparts. His responsibilities included negotiating with the Union; transferring money and goods from Northern families to their sons in Southern prisons; responding to complaints about prison conditions by Union officials; and protesting to Washington the treatment of occupied New Orleans in 1862. In 1864, Ould was called upon to negotiate prisoner exchanges with Union General Benjamin Butler. He tentatively agreed to treat blacks who had been free prior to their military service as prisoners of war, but he refused to grant such status to ex-slaves serving with the Union army. Early in 1865, Ould finally offered Ulysses S. Grant the return of every United States prisoner the Confederacy held, in exchange for an equal number of Confederate prisoners. At the war's end, he was tried on charges of having used funds sent to Northern prisoners for other purposes, but was acquitted.

LORENZO THOMAS (1804–1875). At the outbreak of the Civil War, Lorenzo Thomas was appointed acting adjutant general of the Union army; in August 1861, he filled the post permanently, with a promotion to brigadier general. In this capacity, he made the first exchange of prisoners in the East—3,000 Confederate soldiers for 3,021 Union soldiers—at Aiken's Landing on the James River. He then briefly directed the transfer of prisoners in the West.

JOHN WINDER (1800–1865). At the war's beginning, John Winder was appointed provost marshal of Richmond and assumed command of the area around the Confederate capital. He was responsible for the large number of Union captives held in the city, beginning with prisoners from the first battle of Bull Run (Manassas). Strict, uncompromising, and concerned about security and the prevention of escapes, Winder in time came to be blamed by Union prisoners for most of their suffering. In 1862, he acquired the building that became Libby Prison, and opened a camp on Belle Isle in the James River. His responsibility came to include prisoners in the Carolinas, Alabama, and New Orleans. In 1864, Winder was relieved of his Richmond command, in order to devote all his attention to the increasingly desperate prison system. Responsible for the Deep South prisons in Georgia and Alabama, he established headquarters in Andersonville, where he demonstrated some concern for the miserable conditions, but gave more attention to the possibilities of breakouts or rescue attempts. He opened new prisons in 1864, attempting to shift the bulk of the prisoners to remote locations where escape would be more difficult, as well as to ease the burden on overcrowded pens such as the one at Andersonville. In November, Winder officially became commissary general for all prisons east of the Mississippi, but his resources were rapidly dwindling. Early in 1865, he recommended—without success—that prisoners of war be paroled and sent across the lines, without waiting for exchanges.

HENRY WIRZ (1823–1865). Henry Wirz was born Heinrich Wirz in Switzerland in 1823. He joined General John Winder's staff after being wounded in battle, supervised military prisons, and took command of one in Tuscaloosa, Alabama, in 1862. He was recalled to Richmond and supervised prisons there until the inception of the Dix-Hill cartel. In September 1862, he began escorting Union prisoners to Richmond and Vicksburg, preparatory to their final release. After a medical furlough and, later, a diplomatic mission to France, he was given command of the already disastrously overcrowded and undersupplied stockade at Andersonville. Wirz seems to have tried to lessen some of the suffering, but quickly became irritated with the hopelessness of the situation and turned to an ever-stricter discipline. At the war's end, he was arrested and stood trial in Washington for war crimes: conspiracy to endanger the health of U.S. soldiers, and murder. In the fall of 1865, despite many irregularities at his trial, he was convicted and executed.

SELECTED RESOURCES

For additional published sources, see the annotated book list in Chapter 13, "Studying the War: Research and Preservation." There are also many studies of individual prisons both North and South.

Hesseltine, William B., ed. *Civil War History.* Volume 8, No. 2, June 1962.

_____. *Civil War Prisons: A Study in War Psychology.* Columbus: Ohio State University Press, 1930.

Hewett, Janet B. et al., eds. *The Supplement to the Official Records of the Union and Confederate Armies.* 81 Volumes. Wilmington, NC: Broadfoot Publishing Company, 1994–1998.

Speer, Lonnie R. *Portals to Hell: Military Prisons of the Civil War.* Mechanicsburg, PA: Stackpole Books, 1997. Illustrated.

The Trial of Henry Wirz. Washington: Government Printing Office, 1868.

United States Congress, House. *Report on the Treatment of Prisoners of War by the Rebel Authorities, during the War of the Rebellion.* House Report 45. 40th Congress, 3rd session. Washington: Government Printing Office, 1869.

MEDICAL CARE AND MEDICINE

Former Union Surgeon General William A. Hammond, reflecting in later years about his experience in the war, commented that "the Civil War was fought at the end of the medical Middle Ages." For the soldiers who went to war in 1861, the odds of succumbing to a disease were ten times greater than they would be for a subsequent generation of Americans in World War I. After being wounded, a Civil War soldier was eight times more likely to die of his wounds than his World War I counterpart. Although Louis Pasteur had discovered that microscopic organisms affected fermentation in the 1850s, and Joseph Lister was experimenting with antiseptics during surgery in 1865, Civil War medicine was unaware of the monumental advances born of research into bacteriology. The cause of disease was still attributed to mysterious miasma odors or to the increasingly outdated theory of an imbalance of humors.

Advancements in medical science lagged considerably behind the military's ability to inflict wounds on a massive scale. The U.S. Army Medical Department—and the Confederate Medical Department patterned after it—began the war understaffed and undertrained, and these problems were compounded by a general ignorance about how to prevent or contain communicable diseases and infections.

An estimated 620,000 men died during the Civil War. Of these, twice as many died as a result of disease contracted while in the army than died in battle (a problem exacerbated by the near complete lack of fitness or health screening among Civil War recruits). Considerably more men were rendered unfit for duty due to illness, so much so that a Civil War regiment virtually never went into battle at full strength, its numbers reduced even before catching sight of the enemy. So pervasive were illnesses among field armies that military operations were sometimes curtailed or altered as a result. When over one-third of his troops were incapacitated by illness, Confederate General P. G. T. Beauregard had added incentive to abandon the rail center of Corinth, Mississippi, to the approaching Federals in May of 1862. A third or more of the Union troops that occupied the city in June were also sick. Fearing further illness if the soldiers moved south in the summer, Union General Halleck discontinued his Mississippi invasion.

Initially, disease swept through military units as a result of bringing together individuals from disparate parts of the country into large groups. Epidemics of the so-called childhood diseases, mainly measles and mumps, as well as smallpox and other communicable diseases, incapacitated tens of thousands beginning with the earliest military encampments. Individuals from rural areas of the South and Midwest were particularly hard hit when brought into close contact with recruits from more populated eastern locales, whose immunities to common afflictions were already established. Midwesterners in the Federal service, having grown up immunologically removed from urban settings, died from disease at a rate 43 percent higher than their eastern counterparts. No soldiers, however, were immune to the camp diseases resulting from contaminated food and water, unsanitary living conditions, or mosquito bites. Diarrhea and dysentery accounted for at least 44,558 Union deaths, while the "camp fevers" of typhoid, typhus, malaria, and yellow fever struck down another 46,290. While most official medical records on the Confederate side were destroyed by fire upon the evacuation of Richmond in April of 1865, what partial records there are suggest nearly twice as many soldiers died from disease as from wounds, despite the heroic efforts of the Confederate Medical Department—this mainly due to shortages of necessary supplies and the destruction of resources and infrastructure. Under the circumstances, Southern medical care was well managed and innovative, but the same diseases and infections that swept through the camps and the front lines were pervasive in Confederate hospitals and prisons.

On the eve of the war, the U.S. Army Medical Department consisted of a surgeon general, thirty surgeons, and eighty-three assistant surgeons. Two dozen men resigned and joined Confederate service, and three assistant surgeons were dismissed for "disloyalty," leaving fewer than 100 staff members. Due to massive mobilization and massive casualties, some 12,000 doctors served in some capacity in the Union medical department during the ensuing four years, either in the army or as civilian contractors. Confederate records list 3,237 doctors; that number did not include civilians and volunteers. The

Confederate medical department also included a corps of dentists; they filled cavities, extracted teeth, and repaired fractured jawbones. (Union leaders failed to establish a similar body, although it was suggested.)

Eventually, most medical personnel received special consideration when captured. Following the battle of First Winchester in May 1862, Hunter Holmes McGuire, medical director under Thomas J. (Stonewall) Jackson, first proposed that all captured Union physicians be considered noncombatants and released, with the proviso that Confederate doctors would be similarly freed. This became the policy on both sides, except for an interval in the summer and fall of 1863. The U.S. government made this policy explicit in General Orders, No. 100 (the Lieber Code) of April 1863.

Most of these surgeons had limited experience, but they would gain it quickly in high-traffic hospitals. No dramatic medical advances came out of the Civil War, but the organization of an effective Ambulance Corps and hospital system was studied and built on in subsequent conflicts. The wounded were initially carried by litter, or by ambulance (a specially modified wagon), to a nearby field hospital, and later moved by wagon, train, or hospital boat to larger, permanent hospitals behind the lines. The wounded of a retreating army, if not left on the field, often suffered the agony of being transported along rutted roads in the back of an army wagon. So great was the discomfort, these men frequently begged to be left behind.

Volunteer groups, such as the U.S. Sanitary Commission, influenced and aided the administration of wartime medical departments, and accelerated the modernization of peacetime medical care. The large-scale involvement of women in nursing greatly facilitated the movement of women out of traditional societal roles.

The subject of medicine and medical care in the Civil War is rife with tragedy and almost unspeakable suffering. Yet, amidst it all are inspiring examples of heroic efforts, personal sacrifice, and deeply felt compassion. One also finds astounding examples of near-miraculous endurance and unwavering spirit.

Medical Care in the Nineteenth Century

In the first half of the nineteenth century, doctors mostly treated patients at home, where women household members assisted. Even surgery was performed in the patient's house, perhaps on the kitchen table. Although hospitals existed, they were primarily for the poor, especially those who had no one at home to care for them.

There were no firm licensing standards for doctors, and their medical training varied widely. Some medical practitioners simply attended several months of lectures before setting up their practice. In 1860, medical education in the United States did not equal the rigorous training available in Europe.

The very concept of illness was changing by the 1860s. Some doctors clung to the view that sickness arose from an imbalance in the body humors, or an "overexcitement" of internal systems. To curb bodily stimulation and flush out poisons, they administered purgatives like calomel; induced sweating with tartrate of antimony or Dover's powder (opium with ipecac); applied blister-provoking skin irritants such as Spanish fly, mustard, or oil of turpentine; and even used leeches to suck out blood (although bloodletting had fallen out of favor by the start of the Civil War). Early nineteenth-century doctors often used such therapies to the extreme, persisting aggressively with a treatment until they could see the desired change in the patient's condition. In the 1840s and 1850s, some physicians assailed this "heroic medicine." Oliver Wendell Holmes asserted that throwing all the medicines in America into the sea would be better for the people and worse for the fish, but others continued the practice of heroic medicine.

There were doctors, however, who recognized that there were distinct diseases, requiring disease-specific treatments. Yet even though they could identify such illnesses as typhoid, malaria, yellow fever, and typhus, they did not, for the most part, understand the causes of these diseases or know how to treat them. The role of microorganisms in disease had not yet been discovered; it was only in the 1850s that Louis Pasteur, in France, began to conduct the experiments that led to the germ theory of infection. One effective treatment that was known by 1861 was the use of quinine for malaria, although no one realized that the disease was spread by mosquitoes (which bred prolifically in the poor drainage conditions around army camps). Doctors also knew about the vaccine against smallpox, although it was not given consistently to all soldiers.

Surgery was one area of medicine that had seen major advances. In 1846, dentist William Morton, working with surgeon John Collins Warren at Massachusetts General Hospital, demonstrated how ether might be used as anesthesia. Surgeons began using chloroform in 1851, and, despite the danger of an overdose, this was the preferred anesthesia during the Civil War. It was used 76 percent of the time by Union doctors and almost universally by the Confederates.

Unfortunately, surgeons did not realize how important cleanliness was in preventing infection. (British surgeon Joseph Lister did not publish his findings on the effectiveness of antiseptics during surgery until 1867.) They failed to sterilize their instruments or "scrub in" before operating. As surgeon W. W. Keen described, "We operated in old blood-stained and often pus-stained coats [with] undisinfected hands. . . . We used undisinfected instruments from undisinfected plush-lined cases, and still worse used marine sponges which had been used in prior pus cases and had been only washed in tap water." Although antiseptics like carbolic acid, iodine, and bromine were available, surgeons often waited until "laudable pus" appeared as a supposed sign of healing before administering them.

General Hospitals

Relatively few hospitals existed at the outbreak of the Civil War, but several different kinds of hospitals were developed. For immediate care, field hospitals (described on page 629) were constructed with tents near the battlefield, and they were often backed up with more permanent facilities in quickly converted buildings nearby. For longer-term care, general hospitals were established, mostly in major cities. "Way hospitals," located near rail routes, helped care for soldiers en route from a battlefield to a general hospital. There were also several specialized hospitals, such as those reserved for smallpox patients or Turner's Lane Hospital in Philadelphia, which treated nervous system disorders.

During the first year of the war, both North and South scrambled to improvise general hospitals out of hotels, factories, warehouses, boarding schools, and even prisons. The army often commandeered any large building available. With an existing military organization, the North started with some facilities, but the first battle of Bull Run underlined the need for hospital expansion for both sides. The six existing Federal hospitals in Washington quickly filled, as did the twelve Confederate hospitals in Richmond. Edward Warren, a North Carolina surgeon, described the area "from Manassas Junction to Richmond . . . to Lynchburg," as "one vast hospital," as wounded soldiers were taken into private homes. By 1862, the North and the South began concerted efforts to construct new hospitals. Washington, D.C., became the main hospital center for the Union; Richmond, Virginia, was the Confederate center.

By 1865, there were 204 Federal general hospitals with 136,894 beds. Washington had sixteen hospitals; an additional seven were in nearby

Patients in a ward of Harewood Hospital, Washington, D.C., circa 1862–1865.

Alexandria, and two others in Georgetown and Point Lookout, Maryland. The Philadelphia area boasted twenty-seven hospitals. Throughout the war, Union hospitals treated more than 1,000,000 soldiers.

By the end of the war in the South, 154 hospitals had been created: fifty in Georgia, thirty-nine in Virginia, twenty-three in Alabama, twenty-one in North Carolina, twelve in South Carolina, four in Florida, three in Mississippi, and two in Tennessee. In Virginia alone, 293,165 soldiers were treated in general hospitals between September 1862 and December 1863.

In both the North and the South, many new hospitals followed the pavilion plan, developed by the British in the Crimean War and the French in Algeria. A number of long shedlike buildings (typically 150 feet long, 25 feet wide, and 12 to 14 feet high), each housing 60 to 100 beds, were connected by covered walkways. The wards often had ventilated roofs to promote good air circulation, imitating the airflow through tent hospitals. In a common design, the pavilions radiated out from a central hub, which contained the operating theaters, kitchens, and other general supply facilities. Toilets were usually located on the inside end of each pavilion. Among the largest hospitals were:

Union	Beds
Satterlee (opened June 1862 in Philadelphia)	3,500
Mower (opened December 1862 in Philadelphia)	3,500
Jefferson (opened in winter 1864 in Jeffersonville, Indiana, near Louisville)	2,600

Confederate	Beds
Chimborazo (opened October 1861 in Richmond)	8,000
Winder (opened April 1862 in Richmond)	5,000
Jackson (opened June 1863 in Richmond)	2,500

Chimborazo was like a small city. In addition to the hospital wards and operating rooms, it included five soup houses, five ice houses, a brewery, and a bakery producing 10,000 loaves of bread every day. It was also connected to a farm with 200 cows and several hundred goats.

Both the North and the South put convalescing soldiers to work as nurses, to greatly augment their staff. But, as soon as possible, recovering soldiers were sent back to fight. In June 1864, in just one week, Washington hospitals released more than 10,000 men to return to the battlefield.

Field Hospitals and Hospital Trains and Ships

Near the front line, doctors set up a dressing station for immediate emergency care. An assistant surgeon tended to soldiers with minor wounds (they then returned to battle) and ordered the severely injured to be transported to the regimental "hospital," usually located in a protected area, such as a gully, away from the immediate line of fire. Federal regulations allowed each regiment three hospital tents, one Sibley tent (a cone-shaped tent, like a tepee), and one common tent (in the shape of an inverted "V"). In contrast to the common tent, the hospital tent had side walls, allowing it to cover a larger area. Both Federal and Confederate hospital tents were fourteen by fifteen feet and could accommodate an average of eight to ten patients. Several tents could be joined together, or individual tents could be grouped. At Shiloh, the tent hospital grouping accommodated 2,500 beds.

When the war began, U.S. field hospitals were organized by regiment, an arrangement that scattered surgeons and resources and caused confusion as ambulance men and soldiers sought their own regimental facilities in the heat of battle. Jonathan W. Letterman, who became medical director of the Army of the Potomac on July 4, 1862, organized a new field hospital system in October. It centered on division (rather than regimental) hospitals, and specific jobs were assigned to each doctor. Letterman's division hospital system became the model for the Union armies. Confederate field infirmaries were often organized by brigade and sometimes by division. An infirmary corps serving wounded soldiers was made up of thirty detailed men and the assistant surgeons of each regiment.

Field hospitals generally consisted of a series of tents. Some doctors, including Charles S. Tripler, medical director of the Union Army of the Potomac, and Samuel P. Moore, the Confederate surgeon general (see "Leaders in Civil War Medicine," on page 654), preferred tents to buildings because of their better air circulation. However, when possible, a church, school, barn, or other large building might be hastily converted into a makeshift facility. Colonel C. C. Saunders of the Twenty-Fourth Georgia Infantry described one such converted facility during the battle of Chancellorsville:

> Here hundreds upon hundreds of the wounded of both armies were gathered up and brought for surgical attention. . . . After the house was filled the spacious churchyard was literally covered with wounded and dying. The sight inside the building, for horror, was, perhaps, never equaled within so limited a space, every available foot of space was crowded with wounded and bleeding soldiers. The floors, the benches, even the chancel and pulpit were all packed to suffocation with them. The amputated limbs were piled up in every corner almost as high as a man could reach; blood flowed in streams along the aisles and out at the doors. . . .

Many of the amputations took place at the field hospitals (see "Amputation," on page 634). The operating theater might have been a room or an open space under the sky; the table, improvised from a door. Most often, the operation was visible to a large number of waiting patients, many of whom described the surgery they saw as "sheer butchery." Once the leg or arm was amputated, or a bullet removed, the patient was taken to a nearby recuperation area and later sent to a depot hospital (near a rail line) and then a general hospital.

In 1862, the Union forces began converting rail cars into hospital trains. Twenty-four stretchers per rail car were suspended by rubber bands that attached to interior posts. There were also cook and dispensary cars and a car to transport surgeons. Although the Confederates also used rail transport, their system was less developed, and, as the war progressed, their rail lines were increasingly disrupted. Trains transported more than 250,000 wounded soldiers during the course of the war.

The U.S. government, with the help of the Sanitary Commission, as well as the Western Sanitary Commission (see "Relief Organizations," on page 661), also established hospital ships, converting several steamers into transport facilities. For example, the riverboat *D.A. January* was refurbished as a fully fitted 450-bed hospital. This ship carried 32,738 patients during the course of the war, with the low mortality rate of 2.3 percent.

Federal Ambulance Corps

Jonathan W. Letterman, the medical director of the Army of the Potomac and the organizer of the divisional field hospital system, also created a dedicated Ambulance Corps that became the model for the entire U.S. Army. His predecessor, Charles S. Tripler, had tried to initiate some improvements, such as calling on brigade surgeons to drill stretcher-bearers, and requesting an adequate number of ambulances from the Quartermaster Corps. However, Tripler's system was never successfully developed, partly because control of the ambulances and ambulance crews rested with the Quartermaster Corps, the volunteer surgeons were inexperienced, and cooperation from officers of the line was lacking.

The wagons designated as ambulances were often appropriated for other uses, and the civilian drivers hired to operate them were unreliable. Litter bearers—frequently regimental band members, as well as men detailed from the regiments—received little or no training in care for the wounded. Such was the case following the Union debacle at Second Bull Run (Manassas), in August 1862, where the lack of systematic ambulance teams meant many wounded lay on the field unattended for days after the battle. Letterman, not Tripler, was the medical director at the time, but he had not had enough time to train many ambulance men and was not present at the battle to take charge of the process.

However, the successful Ambulance Corps that Letterman ultimately developed had the advantage of being under the Medical Department. Instead of having ambulance crews selected by the Quartermaster Corps, teams of specially drilled military drivers and litter bearers were chosen by the Medical Department, and the ambulances were organized into corps and division, rather than regimental, units. These trained men moved quickly to transport the wounded to field dressing or "primary" stations, and, from there, to field hospitals. Those who could travel were then moved to general hospitals, relieving the crippling congestion in medical units closer to the front. Letterman also instituted a divisional supply system to eliminate waste and confusion, and assigned medical inspectors to provide administrative assistance to corps medical directors.

Under Letterman's organization of the Ambulance Corps, officers and men were permanently assigned and specifically trained for medical duty.

Zouaves and officers at an ambulance.

These assignments matched the army's organization. A captain was in charge of the ambulance service in an army corps with two or more divisions. A first lieutenant commanded an ambulance division, a second lieutenant a brigade, and a sergeant a regiment. Officers were also assigned specifically to care for the ambulances and for the horses that pulled them. The ambulances themselves were larger than the ones used previously and a spring suspension eased the ride for the wounded. Each carried a locked box with food and other supplies.

The September 17, 1862, battle of Antietam—a battle that produced more casualties than any other single day of the war—was the first full-scale test of Letterman's system. With help from the Sanitary Commission, which filled in gaps in supplies, improvement in transporting and caring for the wounded was dramatic. The absence of a comparable ambulance corps in resource-strapped Confederate armies—although Stonewall Jackson's medical director, Hunter Holmes McGuire, was credited with "perfecting" an "infirmary corps"—caused greater confusion and suffering for Confederate wounded. A shortage of ambulances plagued the Confederacy throughout the war.

In addition to Letterman, Henry Bowditch, a Boston physician whose son had lain on a battlefield without ambulance assistance before he died, campaigned for an army-wide ambulance corps. Bowditch and the Sanitary Commission proposed a plan in Congress early in 1863, but resistance from Secretary of War Edwin Stanton and Major General Henry Halleck killed it in committee.

A month later, Surgeon General Hammond sent a circular letter to medical officers urging them to adopt Letterman's system. The Army of the Tennessee did so promptly on March 30, 1863. In July, Letterman's Ambulance Corps faced the ultimate test of the war at the three-day battle of Gettysburg, where 3,000 attendants manned 1,000 ambulances and completed the removal of over 14,000 Union wounded by July 4, the day after the battle ended.

The effort of Bowditch and his fellow reformers, who aroused public indignation and secured the support of the press, led to passage of the Ambulance Corps Act on March 11, 1864. This legislation extended Letterman's system to all U.S. armies. Although the Quartermaster Corps still controlled the ambulances themselves, they were to be used only for medical purposes. Ambulance men were still detailed from the regiments, but the Medical Department could choose and train them. This organizational blueprint would be emulated by U.S. and foreign armies for decades to come. It was one of the few genuine advancements on the medical front that came out of the Civil War.

Amputation

Northern and Southern military forces' use of the .58-caliber minié ball—a large, conical lead bullet measuring over a half-inch in diameter—caused grievous wounds that would have challenged even modern doctors. In contrast to the modern bullet, which tends to create a neat hole, a minié ball often shattered several inches of bone, lodged in the tissue (rather than passing out of the body), and left a large wound area open to infection. The splintering of the bone led Civil War surgeons to rely heavily on amputation.

After a battle, field hospital surgeons—called "sawbones" because of their bone saws—worked around the clock in near-assemblyline fashion. To

STATISTICS ON AMPUTATIONS

Type of Amputation	Number of Cases	Number of Deaths	Percentage of Deaths
Hand or fingers	7,902	198	2.9%
At wrist joint	68	7	10.4
In forearm	1,761	245	14.0
At elbow joint	40	3	7.6
In upper arm	5,510	1,273	23.8
At shoulder joint	866	245	29.1
Foot or toes	1,519	81	5.7
At ankle joint	161	40	25.1
In leg	5,523	1,790	33.2
At knee joint	195	111	57.5
In thigh	6,369	3,411	54.2
At hip joint	66	55	83.3

Source: *The Medical and Surgical History of the War of the Rebellion*, Part III, Vol. II, p. 877 (see "Selected Resources on page 664").
Note: The figures are based on 29,980 cases reported by Federal surgeons.

ease their pain while awaiting the operation, wounded soldiers were given liquor, opium, or morphine. Just before the surgery, the patient was anesthetized, usually with a dab of chloroform on a cloth held under the nose. After probing with his fingers or another instrument, "the surgeon snatched his knife from between his teeth . . . wiped it rapidly once or twice across his bloodstained apron, and the cutting began" (to quote General Carl Schurz's description of an operation he witnessed at Gettysburg). Stacks of cut-off arms and legs piled up nearby, as surgeons hurried to treat as many patients as possible before the "irritative" period of infection began—usually, one to two days after the wound was received.

Naval Medical Care

The naval forces of both the North and the South operated their own medical services, separate from those of the army. William Whelan was the chief medical officer for the U.S. Navy, which had 120 medical officers at the war's beginning. Each Union ship usually had its own surgeon, with an assisting surgeon's steward, later called a nurse. One nurse was on hand for every 100 men. Four men detailed from the gun division transported the wounded. The Confederate Navy began with an estimated twenty-eight medical officers who resigned from the U.S. Navy at the beginning of the war. Among these was William A. W. Spotswood, who headed the Confederate Navy's Bureau of Medicine and Surgery. Spotswood was based in Richmond, Virginia.

Naval surgeons faced multiple challenges. The crews they served could be wounded during a battle at sea or by long-range projectiles and cannon balls fired from shore. On wooden ships, splinters from the ship's timbers caused more injuries than bullets and shells. Sailors on ironclads were wounded and killed by iron splinters, broken bolts, and sheared nuts. Doctors often operated on mess tables in the wardroom.

Steam propulsion increased the risk of illness from excessive heat (created by boilers) and bad ventilation, as well as accidents. Diseases including typhoid and malaria, generally called "ship fevers" (or "monitor fevers" on the ironclads) were prevalent; for example, an outbreak nearly sidelined the Union's South Atlantic Blockading Squadron in late 1862, while the West Gulf Blockading Squadron suffered from yellow fever and other diseases, with a mortality rate of nearly 12 percent in 1863 and 1864.

Patients could be moved to recuperate at onshore naval hospitals. Several of these had been built by the U.S. Navy in the 1830s, at sites including

The Naval Hospital "Red Rover."

"The Sister."

Convalescent Ward.

The Floating Hospital on the Mississippi, *drawn by Theodore Davis, published in* Harper's Weekly, *May 9, 1863, shows several views of the* Red Rover, *where nearly 2,500 Union sailors were cared for during the war.*

Philadelphia; Chelsea, Massachusetts; and Brooklyn, New York. The Confederate Navy operated hospitals at Richmond, Charleston, Wilmington, Savannah, and Mobile. The U.S. Navy created the first floating hospital in June 1862, after a Confederate steamer was captured by the Union gunboat *Mound City*. The steamer, renamed U.S.S. *Red Rover*, was refurbished and used to care for sailors of the Mississippi squadron. It featured bathrooms, windows covered with gauze blinds, an elevator between decks, and a 300-ton-capacity icebox. Among the staff were nurses from the order of Sisters of the Holy Cross, the first women to serve on a navy ship. The U.S.S. *Red Rover* also brought supplies to other navy ships on the western rivers.

Medical Care for U.S. Colored Troops

Over 29,000 black soldiers died from disease during the Civil War—nine times the number that died in battle. Those who became ill died at a rate two and a half times higher than their white counterparts. U.S. Colored Troops were often detailed to hot, unhealthy areas in the mistaken belief that they could not contract tropical diseases.

Just as discrimination marked the life of black troops in terms of pay, duty assignments, and overall treatment, prejudice permeated the attempt to provide adequate medical care for these men. It was difficult to find white doctors who would serve with black regiments, and where they did serve, a white physician himself remarked, "Very few surgeons will do precisely the same for blacks as they would for whites."

Although at least eight black doctors worked in the army during the war, only three were assigned to serve the U.S. Colored Troops. Many black physicians who sought to serve faced racial bias because they might be called upon to treat white soldiers or officers in battle. Alexander T. Augusta, a black surgeon assigned to treat blacks, was kept at a rendezvous camp for U.S. Colored Troops instead of with his regiment, to avoid just such a situation.

When medical boards established to screen and appoint doctors for black troops failed to provide an adequate number, some white officers secured physicians by making their own arrangements with medical schools, contract surgeons, and medical cadets. Where none were available, soldiers who appeared to have any medical knowledge at all—often, former patients who had served as medical stewards during their recovery—were appointed as acting assistant surgeons.

There were numerous instances of incompetence and outright brutality in treating more than 600,000 cases of illness and more than 10,000 battle wounds among black troops. Care was markedly better in regimental hospitals, where officers, surgeons, and men served together. But in general hospitals, where blacks and whites were segregated in separate buildings, black facilities were consistently understaffed and badly maintained, and the patients were neglected—facts that were reflected in the high mortality rates. In Vicksburg, for example, during the same period, 30.5 percent of the black patients died, but the white mortality rate was only 14 percent. Such disparity was typical of the care afforded black soldiers during the Civil War.

Causes of Disease

Although Civil War doctors may have been ignorant about the need for antiseptic conditions during surgery, they were aware of the role of good hygiene and sanitary conditions in the health of troops, as was clearly demonstrated by Florence Nightingale and the British Sanitary Commission during the Crimean War. South Carolina surgeon John Julian Chisolm complained that "bad and insufficient food, salt meat, indifferent clothing, want of cleanliness, poor shelter, . . . infected tents and camps, form a combination of causes which explains the fatality of an army in the field." Similarly, Union medical director Charles S. Tripler declared: "To bad cooking, bad [sanitation] polic[ing], bad ventilation of tents, inattention to personal cleanliness, and unnecessarily irregular habits we are to attribute the greater proportion of the diseases that actually occurred in the army."

There were, in fact, multiple causes for disease during the Civil War, and all were linked to the conditions endemic to fighting a war in the mid-nineteenth century. Poor sanitation and neglected hygiene, crowded living conditions (especially for men with no immunities), exposure to the elements, the presence of insects and vermin, contaminated water and food, poor diet, inadequate clothing and shoes, and poor ventilation contributed to illness. That many soldiers were not adequately screened for physical and mental fitness at the start of their service only added to the likelihood of a high rate of disease.

Sanitation and Hygiene

In the North, the U.S. Sanitary Commission both inspected camps for cleanliness and actively publicized the need for proper sanitation and hygiene. It issued eighteen pamphlets on this subject, including "Rules for

Nurses and officers of the U.S. Sanitary Commission photographed at Fredericksburg, Virginia, by James Gardner, May 1864. The Sanitary Commission stressed the need for cleanliness and proper hygiene in army camps.

Preserving the Health of the Soldier" by Dr. W. H. Van Buren. Union Surgeon General William Hammond penned his own *Treatise on Hygiene with Special Reference to the Military Service* (1863). Despite the fact that this knowledge was available, there were military surgeons who either failed to understand its importance, or, more likely, could not persuade their nonmedical commanders to put it into practice.

Both Northern and Southern recruits suffered from lack of discipline and ignorance about personal hygiene. Although one Union manual called for soldiers to "wash their hands and faces daily" and "bathe once a week," where "conveniences for bathing are to be had," this advice was often not followed. In the South, Dr. Chisolm reported that some soldiers who had served for six months had their first bath only when they were hospitalized. In the Confederacy, the problem was compounded by inadequate soap supplies.

Especially in the early years, camp hygiene was appalling. Food wastes, including offal, might be left lying around the camp rather than buried. Even when latrines were dug (regulations called for them to be eight feet deep), many soldiers failed to use them or neglected the daily task of shoveling six inches of fresh earth over the waste. As a result, the water supply was sometimes contaminated, and disease-carrying flies proliferated. At least in the Union army, inspections by the Sanitary Commission helped improve conditions, as did enforcement of published sanitation regulations.

However, following good sanitation and hygiene practices did not always eliminate or even diminish illness. Ideas of cleanliness were based on what one could see or smell, and cleansing was achieved by physical or chemical means. But these methods did not completely combat the larger problem: microscopic organisms, which were the actual cause of infection. These enemies were invisible, adaptable, and rapid-acting, and they remained unstoppable throughout the war because sufficient knowledge necessary to combat them did not exist.

Crowding and Ventilation

In an age in which doctors believed that "effluvias" and "miasms" caused disease—and in "crowd poisoning" that resulted when soldiers slept together in densely packed shelters—one area of hygiene that received consistent attention was ventilation. Overcrowded barracks were particularly a problem for new recruits, who were vulnerable to contagious illness. Tents, where air could circulate more freely, were thought to be healthier than huts. Hospitals and barracks were constructed with an eye to the free flow of air, which may have helped to keep tuberculosis and other airborne diseases in check.

Exposure

Exposure to cold, snow, ice, rain, mud, excessive heat, and unexpected weather changes also affected the likelihood of illness. Confederate troops, especially, lacked adequate clothing to protect them from the elements. A soldier under Stonewall Jackson remembered a march in Virginia where "icicles hung from [the men's] clothing, guns, and knapsacks; many were badly frost bitten, and I have heard of many freezing to death along the road side. My feet peeled off like a peeled onion on that march, and I have not recovered from its effects to this day."

Frostbite was a problem in the winter, sunstroke in the summer. Tents provided poor shelter against torrential rains such as those that drenched the troops at Vicksburg for most of five weeks. Many military doctors thought exposure to cold was a cause of the diarrhea that afflicted a majority of soldiers. They suggested wearing a "belly band," a flannel bandage, to protect against chill.

Insects and Vermin

Disease-carrying flies, mosquitoes, lice, fleas, and other insects proliferated in great numbers where sanitation and hygiene practices were poor. Lice carried rickettsia (microorganisms that caused typhus) and lived on unwashed bodies in dirty clothes. "Every soldier had a brigade of lice on him," a Confederate soldier commented. Another wrote of a different problem, "The nats [sic] are so bad here that we will have to smoke tobacco to keep them from eating us up." Scratching was a common response to insects, but was also a source of infection, which entered through tiny abrasions created in the skin. Although routine sanitation measures during the Civil War did not kill bacteria, they did cut down on the number of insects that carried disease.

Food

"The 'feeding' of an army is a matter of the most vital importance," wrote Union General William Tecumseh Sherman in his memoirs. "To be strong, healthy, and capable of the largest measure of physical effort, the soldier needs about three pounds gross of food per day." Whether a soldier in fact received this amount—or whether his meals were edible and nutritious—was, however, problematic. Although Union soldiers usually received an adequate amount of food, except on long campaigns where supply lines were extended, Confederate soldiers suffered from shortages that grew worse as the war progressed. In the winter of 1863–1864, for example, Confederate General Stephen Dodson Ramseur reported that soldiers in his North Carolina brigade received only one-eighth to one-fourth pound of uncooked meat and 1⅛ pounds of flour per day in December, and one-fourth to one-half pound of meat and one pint of cornmeal per day in January. Disruption of supply lines sometimes left Southern troops without food for days. Hunger led one North Carolina soldier to exclaim, "Had fried rat for breakfast & never ate better." Moreover, food too easily spoiled, or was tough, oversalted, or overrun by maggots, weevils, and other insects.

Troops deprived of food were susceptible to disease, but the larger problem was an unbalanced diet. In the standard ration, salt pork was the main meat source, hardtack was a common bread, and beans or peas provided the primary vegetable. The lack of fresh leafy green vegetables, or even potatoes, contributed to diseases such as scurvy. "Desiccated vegetables" (cubes of dried carrots, turnips, and the like) were offered to Union troops, who dubbed them "desecrated vegetables" and avoided them.

To supplement government rations, soldiers resorted to foraging, although, in the early years of the war, most Union generals forbade it. After 1863, however, it became an offensive tactic, particularly in the Western campaigns, and Sherman ordered his troops to confiscate food on their march from Atlanta to the sea, in order to deplete Southern resources. Some Confederate soldiers were authorized to demand food from civilians, and if refused, to forcefully appropriate it. On a milder note, in 1863, General Robert E. Lee had a contingent from each of his regiments "gather sassafras buds, wild onions, garlic, lamb's quarter, and poke sprouts" each day as vegetable supplements.

Poor cooking added to soldiers' food woes. Early in the war, these men (who had often never cooked before) took turns preparing meals. Most resorted to frying not only meat but also rice, beans, and a mixture of flour and water, creating greasy meals that doctors called "death from the frying pan." To improve the quality of food preparation, in 1863, the U.S. Congress mandated the use of specially detailed company cooks. Both Union and Confederate armies occasionally had African Americans do this work. The Christian Commission, a private Northern relief organization, developed a "kitchen on wheels," which had movable boilers capable of handling large quantities of boiled and baked food, but the device was introduced only in 1865.

Water

Water contaminated by excrement was a major source of dysentery, cholera, and typhoid. Soldiers drank from the same water in which people washed, laundered, and cooked; animals drank and bathed; and flies and mosquitoes proliferated. One Confederate soldier complained, "We drank more mud and wiggle tails than water."

Doctors on both sides advocated the boiling of drinking water, a preventive measure that, like sanitation practices, was often not followed. Filters were available but were rarely used. What saved many soldiers was their preference for coffee—made, of course, with boiled water. In the navy, or where troops were stationed near the coast, salt water was distilled for drinking, but troops did become ill from ingesting salt water.

Clothing and Shoes

Even the soldiers' clothing presented health problems. Bits of dirty clothing often became lodged in bullet wounds, increasing the likelihood of infection. Although after the first year Union soldiers were well supplied with clothing, their six-pound woolen uniforms were hot and heavy; marching in such garments, while carrying heavy packs, led to sunstroke and heatstroke. Confederate troops suffered from a lack of adequate clothing—especially shoes. In part, this resulted from the South's limited manufacturing capability and the disruption of its transportation network. In October 1862, one cavalry commander reported that of 2,319 men, fewer than half were fit for duty because many soldiers were "without a blanket, overcoat, shoes, or socks." In the winter, these deficiencies, which contributed to frostbite, pneumonia, and bronchitis, increased the problems of exposure.

Common Diseases and Infections

Despite staggering battle casualties, unprecedented on the American continent, the Civil War soldier remained at far greater risk of death by disease than by a minié ball. It is estimated that two-thirds of the war's fatalities were attributed to diseases such as diarrhea, dysentery, pneumonia, typhoid, and malaria. However high, this figure represented an improvement over the Mexican War, in which about seven times more soldiers died from disease than on the battlefield.

Described in the following pages are some of the leading causes of sickness or death among Civil War soldiers, along with some common treatments. By recording their results with different treatments, Civil War doctors helped lay the groundwork for drug research after the war.

Diarrhea and Dysentery

Although loose bowels may be symptomatic of a variety of illnesses, almost all cases were diagnosed as either diarrhea (frequently referred to as the "quick-step") or dysentery (if abdominal cramping and blood in the stools were present). Diarrhea accelerated dehydration, a problem compounded by the salivating effects of one commonly employed medicine: calomel. Diarrhea was thought to be caused by poor diet, and dysenteric infections were blamed on fecal contamination of water or food. The effect of a diet of green corn and apples on Confederate soldiers during the Antietam Campaign, for example, was graphically described by one witness who could trace the Confederate position "by the thickly strewn belt of green corn husks and cobs, and also, *sit venia loquendi,* by a ribbon of dysenteric stools just behind."

For both the Union and the Confederacy, diarrhea and dysentery played a significant role in depleting troops. Within the Union army, more than 1.7 million cases of diarrhea or dysentery were recorded, along with 44,558 deaths—more than for any other single illness—and these figures are considered low because deaths from related conditions may in fact have been from diarrhea. A similar frequency is assumed in the Confederacy, where close to a quarter million cases were reported east of the Mississippi River in the first two years of the war.

TREATMENT

Among the treatments used by Union doctors were Epsom salts or castor oil in the morning and a dose of opium at night; calomel (although it was banned by U.S. Surgeon General William Hammond in 1863); and ipecac. Confederate doctors might also have treated diarrhea with opium and calomel, a variety of natural astringents such as blackberry, marsh rosemary, knot grass, and sweet gum, as well as cathartics such as "blue mass" (a pill combining mercury and chalk). Only sometimes was the emphasis on improving the patient's diet.

Infection

Complications from infected wounds were common because surgical tools were not sterilized and doctors reused infected sponges, wiped surgical instruments off on dirty aprons, and probed wounds with unwashed, ungloved hands. These infections, or "surgical fevers," included tetanus, erysipelas (a streptococcal infection), and osteomyelitis (bone inflammation). Among the most deadly infections was pyemia (infection of the blood stream with abscesses), which killed nearly all of its victims. Much feared was the rank-smelling "hospital gangrene," where a small black spot of dead tissue appeared on the wound and quickly spread. The hospital gangrene that appeared during the Civil War was a disease that no longer exists.

TREATMENT

Among many different treatments for infection, hospital gangrene and erysipelas were similarly treated with fresh air, wholesome food, and stimulants such as brandy or wine. Nitric acid was applied topically to hospital gangrene, and Union surgeon Middleton Goldsmith successfully used applications of bromine as a remedy. Osteomyelitis patients might be given quinine, liquor, iodide of potassium, morphine, or opium. Sometimes mercurial drugs or cold compresses were used. There was no effective treatment for tetanus; there were, however, relatively few cases because the bacillus tetani was carried in horses' intestines, but most Civil War battles took place on unplowed, unmanured soil.

Efforts were made to keep hospitals clean to minimize infection. Antiseptics such as chlorine, carbolic acid, and charcoal were used to disinfect floors and chamber pots, and bromine vapor was sprayed in the air. In addition, antiseptics such as Labbaraque's solution (sodium hypochlorite); sulphuric, nitric, and other acids; and alcohol were, at times, applied directly to treat infections. These treatments showed a knowledge of antiseptics, but Civil War doctors did not understand how and when to apply them in order to avoid infection in the first place.

One unexpected effect of Confederate supply problems improved asepsis in some Southern hospitals. Sutures made of horsehair, because they had to be boiled, proved more aseptic than the silk threads utilized in both Northern and Confederate hospitals. Lack of supplies also led Confederate doctors to leave wounds unbandaged, allowing the proliferation of maggots, which actually assisted healing by devouring only diseased tissue.

Malaria

Signaled by chills and fever, malaria (also called "paroxysmal fever") results from the growth of an invading parasitic organism (Plasmodium) in red blood cells. Primarily a seasonal affliction, it is transmitted from person to person by the anopheles mosquito. Poor drainage in Civil War encampments, as well as canal construction projects, where stagnant water created ideal breeding grounds for mosquitoes, helped increase the spread of the disease. Among Confederate troops east of the Mississippi River, for example, one in seven diseased soldiers suffered from malaria in 1861 and 1862. There were 1.3 million malarial cases in the Union army during the war, yet fewer than 1 in 100 cases resulted in death. The prevailing strain was actually less lethal than the modern-day type.

Treatment

Malaria was widely treated with quinine, which was also taken as a preventive, usually with whiskey, to mute its bitter taste. When blockades restricted Confederate quinine supplies, Southern doctors resorted to external applications of turpentine as well as a concoction of whiskey and dogwood, poplar, and willow bark. Mercurial medications and salts were sometimes administered to Union troops to control diarrhea that accompanied the disease.

Measles

Measles reached epidemic proportions within the Civil War armies. The biggest outbreaks occurred when numerous new recruits (often without immunities) were mustered in—mainly at the start of the war, and again when black Union troops were organized, in 1863 and 1864. In the U.S. Army, more than 76,000 cases were reported during the war, and over 8,000 troops in the Confederate Army of the Potomac contracted the disease in July, August, and September 1861. Few soldiers died from measles, but those who contracted such illnesses as pneumonia, diarrhea, bronchitis, and typhoid during the weakened state of recovery had a higher rate of mortality.

Treatment

Doctors on both sides recognized that the disease often simply cured itself, and they recommended improved sanitation and ventilation to curtail outbreaks. A sassafras tea was one herbal remedy used in the South.

Pneumonia

Pneumonia killed many Civil War troops, but it usually appeared as a complication of other illnesses. Inadequate clothing (especially shoes), blankets, and tents, greater among Confederate soldiers, increased the risks of exposure to cold and damp and caused many colds to develop into pneumonia. The large Chimborazo hospital in Richmond reported 1,568 soldiers with pneumonia and pleurisy during the war; more than a third (583) died from the disease. In the Union army, about a quarter of the 77,000 or so cases were fatal.

TREATMENT

Although tartar emetic and other preparations of antimony, as well as bleeding, were the chosen antebellum remedies, Civil War doctors found these ineffective for the type of pneumonia they encountered. Confederate surgeons recommended a regulated diet, liquor, opium, and quinine, as well as various expectorants, including snakeroot. Counterirritants, such as mustard seed, were sometimes applied to produce "healing" blisters.

Smallpox

Civil War doctors were familiar with smallpox symptoms (although some reported cases may have actually been chicken pox), and they knew that soldiers could be vaccinated against it. Nevertheless, not everyone in a large grouping of soldiers—whether in a hospital, army camp, or prison—had been vaccinated, revaccinated where required, or vaccinated effectively, and small-scale epidemics were not uncommon in the North or the South. There were, for example, epidemics among the Confederate States Army of Northern Virginia in both the fall of 1862 and the winter of 1863–1864.

At the time of the Civil War, doctors used human vaccination scabs rather than animal virus for the vaccine. These scabs could carry other infections. The vaccine crusts were collected from vaccinated soldiers or from children, who were more desirable since they were presumed to be healthy. As supplies dwindled in the Confederacy, private doctors received five dollars for each uncontaminated scab they supplied. Both Union and Confederate troops sometimes broke out in ulcers, however, after being vaccinated. This was attributed by some to vaccine taken from carriers of syphilis, and by others to incipient scurvy. The cause was ultimately unknown.

TREATMENT

Smallpox patients were isolated and given fresh air. Some doctors used medication to treat symptoms like fever, tremors, and the pustules that

SELECTED SICKNESS AND MORTALITY STATISTICS FOR WHITE TROOPS IN THE UNION ARMY, 1861–1866

Disease	Number of Cases	Number of Deaths
Typhoid Fever	75,368	27,056
Typhus Fever	2,501	850
Diarrhea (acute and chronic)	1,325,714	30,481
Dysentery (acute and chronic)	259,482	7,313
Yellow Fever	49,871	4,059
Erysipelas	23,276	1,860
Smallpox and Varioloid	12,236	4,717
Measles	67,763	4,246
Scarlet Fever	578	70
Diphtheria	7,277	716
Mumps	48,128	72
Epidemic Catarrh	134,397	33
Syphilis	73,382	123
Gonorrhea	95,833	6
Scurvy	30,714	383
Rheumatism (acute and chronic)	254,738	475
Itch	32,080	0
Insanity	2,410	80
Inflammation of Brain	1,232	1,269[sic]
Inflammation of Membranes of Brain	805	741
Inflammation of Spinal Cord	1,479	235
Nostalgia	5,213	58
Neuralgia	58,774	18
Ophthalmia	8,904	1
Inflammation of Conjuctiva	65,739	1
Asthma	9,365	75
Bronchitis (acute and chronic)	195,627	1,179
Inflammation of Lungs	61,202	14,738
Cholera morbus	25,215	275
Dyspepsia	37,514	31
Inflammation of Liver (acute and chronic)	11,120	243
Jaundice	71,691	341
Inflammation of Kidneys	9,464	154

Source: Table C, "General Summary of the Sickness and Mortality of White Troops during the War," in *The Medical and Surgical History of the War of the Rebellion,* Vol. I, Part I, pp. 636–640. Just as white troops and black troops were segregated in the Union army, so were the statistics relating to their illnesses.

SELECTED SICKNESS AND MORTALITY STATISTICS FOR COLORED TROOPS IN THE UNION ARMY, 1864–1866

Disease	Number of Cases	Number of Deaths
Typhoid Fever	4,094	2,280
Typhus Fever	123	108
Diarrhea (acute and chronic)	125,899	4,646
Dysentery (acute and chronic)	28,040	2,118
Yellow Fever	190	27
Erysipelas	1,536	247
Smallpox and Varioloid	6,716	2,341
Measles	8,555	931
Scarlet Fever	118	2
Diphtheria	776	61
Mumps	12,186	12
Epidemic Catarrh	9,869	5
Syphilis	6,207	28
Gonorrhea	7,060	1
Scurvy	16,217	388
Rheumatism (acute and chronic)	32,125	235
Itch	3,156	0
Insanity	193	10
Inflammation of Brain	249	262[sic]
Inflammation of Membranes of Brain	166	108
Inflammation of Spinal Cord	68	45
Nostalgia	334	16
Neuralgia	6,018	5
Opthalmia	—	—
Inflammation of Conjuctiva	5,153	—
Asthma	762	18
Bronchitis (acute and chronic)	25,381	404
Inflammation of Lungs	16,133	5,233
Cholera morbus	1,151	30
Dyspepsia	2,607	5
Inflammation of Liver (acute and chronic)	1,949	135
Jaundice	15,545	73
Inflammation of Kidneys	778	24

Source: Table CXI, "General Summary of the Sickness and Mortality of Colored Troops during the War," in *The Medical and Surgical History of the War of the Rebellion,*" Vol. I, Part I, pp. 710–711. Just as white troops and black troops were segregated in the Union army, so were the statistics relating to their illnesses.

formed. The chief medical officer at Richmond's Louisiana Hospital wrote, "As to the prevention of the pitting . . . of the face, which was not so important in our class of patients, mercurial ointment [was] smeared from time to time. . . . "

Typhoid Fever

Also known as "continued fever," typhoid, which is caused by *Salmonella typhosa* bacteria, sprang from the same contaminated food and water that produced diarrhea. Sometimes identified by a distinctive rash, this bacterial infection grew from a gastrointestinal disturbance to include ongoing fever and, in more lethal cases, severe pulmonary complications. About one-quarter of all known typhoid fever cases resulted in death (there were more than 34,800 fatalities in the Union army). Some individuals who recovered from typhoid continued to "carry" the disease and spread it to others through their waste or by failing to wash their hands after relieving themselves.

TREATMENT

As with other fevers, purgatives were combined with opiates. More drastic remedies involved the use of turpentine, bleeding, and counterirritants like Spanish fly. It was recognized that improved sanitation might prevent the disease, although it was generally considered a miasmatic condition, caused by bad air.

Typhus

Similar in effect and symptoms to typhoid fever, typhus was characterized more by headaches and rashes. It was transmitted chiefly by body lice or fleas. Because of the restrictive manner in which typhus was transmitted—requiring the exchange of infected parasites—it was far less common than typhoid. In the Union army, compared with 148,631 reports of typhoid and typhoidlike fevers, only 2,624 cases of typhus were recorded, and some of these cases may have actually been typhoid.

TREATMENT

The remedies used for typhus were similar to those for typhoid.

Yellow Fever

This viral infection, like malaria, was spread from person to person by mosquitoes. Yellow fever was usually introduced by passengers arriving from tropical and subtropical climates. There was, for example, an outbreak among Union troops at Hilton Head, South Carolina, in late August 1861 after infected soldiers from Key West landed. Yellow fever's symptoms included jaundice and in the final stages of severe cases, internal hemorrhaging, with accompanying dark-colored vomit.

TREATMENT
Prescriptions for yellow fever were similar to those for other fevers. Attempts were made to quarantine the ill, but because the proper incubation period was unknown, these efforts were not always successful.

Medical Drug Supplies

As the war progressed, both armies set up regimental medicine wagons to supply surgeons in the field. At first, Union medical supplies included calomel and tartar emetic, which both carried the risk of mercury poisoning and could cause tooth loss. In May 1863, Surgeon General William Hammond ordered the removal of these from the available supplies table. Many doctors objected to Hammond's ban, and the order was largely disregarded.

Union and Confederate drug supplies commonly included anesthetics, antiseptics, narcotics, purgatives/cathartics (to clean out body poisons), diaphoretics (to increase perspiration), stimulants, and skin irritants.

Union blockades hindered Southern troops from acquiring drugs manufactured in the North, but some were smuggled in nonetheless. Two proprietors of Union drug firms were jailed for smuggling contraband. Memphis, Tennessee, was a thriving center of the black market; drugs might pass through in the stomachs of dead horses or under the hoop skirts of ladies.

Confederate Surgeon General Samuel P. Moore also encouraged doctors to substitute native plants as medicines, and directed Dr. Francis P. Porcher to research such remedies. Porcher's book, *Resources of Southern Fields and Forests, Medical, Economical, and Agricultural* (1863), listed more than 400 useful plants, and excerpts were published to foster collection of Georgia bark, skunk cabbage, white willow, cranesbill, pipsissewa, and other potential curatives. Among Porcher's suggestions were the use of flex opaca to increase sweating in smallpox patients, and horehound juice for coughs and colds.

The Confederacy set up several laboratories to manufacture medical supplies such as alcohol, silver chloride, ether, and blue mass, as well as native substitutes. Joseph LeConte, a South Carolina professor of chemistry and geology, and Alabama druggist Charles Theodor Mohr, a recent German immigrant, were two noted makers of pharmaceuticals. "There was no lack of materials for the construction of apparatus," Mohr wrote, "a drug grinding mill, a steam distillation apparatus and a contrivance for the production of high-grade alcohol from corn whiskey." These laboratories also examined smuggled medications and indigenous products to be sure they were safe for use.

Medical Officers

United States of America

Before the Civil War, the army Medical Department included a surgeon general, thirty surgeons, and eighty-three assistant surgeons. Three surgeons and twenty-one assistant surgeons resigned to join the Confederates, and three additional assistant surgeons were dismissed. During the war, this staff grew to include some 12,000 doctors, organized into seven categories:

1. Surgeons and assistant surgeons of the U.S. Army (the "Regulars," who had passed the Army's qualifying examinations).
2. Surgeons and assistant surgeons to the volunteers (offering supplementary support to the Regulars).
3. Regimental surgeons and assistant surgeons (supposedly commissioned by the state governor, but sometimes commissioned by the commanding officer).
4. Acting assistant surgeons, or "contract" surgeons, who were not commissioned and served mostly in general hospitals. (The aim was to have one hospital surgeon for every 100 patients.)
5. Medical officers of the Veterans Corps.
6. Acting staff surgeons.
7. Surgeons and assistant surgeons for black troops (established as a separate position).

In addition to the overall supervision of this organization of doctors, the surgeon general was responsible for setting up an effective hospital system and generally overseeing the medical care, including preventive measures, for all the soldiers. He was aided in this by the assistant surgeon general, who was transferred to Louisville, Kentucky, in October 1863, and subsequently given power to directly oversee the western sector. Although the number and type of medical personnel changed during the course of the war, a system evolved in which each army had a medical director; corps and divisions each had medical directors; and chief surgeons were responsible for brigades. After July 1862, each regiment was required to have a surgeon and two assistant surgeons. In addition, a medical inspector general was in charge of a team of medical inspectors. They checked up on sanitary conditions and determined which soldiers should be discharged for disability.

During the war, four men served as Union surgeons general: Colonel Thomas Lawson, Colonel Clement A. Finley, Brigadier General William Hammond, and Brigadier General Joseph Barnes. Colonel Robert C. Wood served as assistant surgeon general for most of the war. Colonels Lawson and Finley were considered members of the old guard (Lawson had held the office since 1836 and died in May 1861), not responsive to the needs of the war. When reformers on the Sanitary Commission pressed to have Finley removed, he was replaced by the progressive William Hammond. Hammond's conflict with Secretary of War Edwin Stanton and political maneuverings finally led to his replacement by Joseph Barnes.

Confederate States of America

The Confederate Medical Department was essentially organized along the same lines as the U.S. Army Medical Department, but it was much smaller, with an estimated 3,200 surgeons and assistant surgeons (excluding contract physicians and navy doctors), and it did not include an assistant surgeon general or medical inspector general. All doctors had to pass an examination given by an army medical board. Each regiment was expected to have a surgeon and an assistant surgeon. Following the line of command, senior surgeons had responsibility for brigades; chief surgeons, for divisions; and medical directors, for corps and armies. In addition to these field positions, there were surgeons in charge of individual general hospitals and the medical directors of all hospitals in a given area.

In May 1861, David C. DeLeon was asked to serve as acting Confederate surgeon general. He was followed by Charles Smith for two weeks. In July

1861, they were replaced by Samuel Preston Moore, who remained surgeon general throughout the war.

Leaders in Civil War Medicine

United States of America

DR. JOSEPH K. BARNES (1817–1883). After earning his medical degree at the University of Pennsylvania, Barnes joined the army in 1840. During the Civil War, he initially served in Missouri, but, in May 1862, he came to Washington as an attending surgeon. After an appointment as medical inspector general, he was named acting surgeon general in September 1863 and became surgeon general in August 1864, after William Hammond's court-martial. Barnes carried out many of the reforms begun by Hammond, and he actively recruited civilian doctors to provide adequate care for all the wounded. He helped to develop the Army Medical Library and to produce the *Medical and Surgical History of the War of the Rebellion.*

REV. HENRY WHITNEY BELLOWS (1814–1882). The Unitarian pastor of the Church of All Souls in New York City, Bellows helped Dr. Elizabeth Blackwell and others organize the Women's Central Association of Relief and, on its behalf, joined with other groups to establish the U.S. Sanitary Commission in June 1861 (see "Relief Organizations" on page 661). Bellows served as first president of the commission and brought in the organizational talents of Frederick Law Olmsted, the group's executive secretary, who was already known for his writings and his design of New York's Central Park.

DR. WILLIAM ALEXANDER HAMMOND (1828–1900). After earning a medical degree from the University of the City of New York, Hammond had served in the army, mostly in the West, from 1849 to 1859. He rejoined the army when the war broke out. With the backing of Major General George B. McClellan and the U.S. Sanitary Commission, Hammond was appointed surgeon general, with the rank of brigadier general, on April 25, 1862. He immediately set about reforming the medical services, implementing a medical inspection system, greatly expanding hospital facilities, building government pharmaceutical laboratories to ensure adequate supplies, and supporting the development of an ambulance corps to offer emergency treatment and remove wounded soldiers from the battlefield. He also established the Army Medical Museum and provided for the gathering of statistics to further medical understanding. His decisive leadership, however, brought him into conflict with army old-timers and Secretary of War Edwin M. Stanton. In 1864, he was court-martialed for "conduct to the prejudice of military discipline" and "unbecoming an officer and a gentleman." A presidential review exonerated him in 1878, and he was restored to the army's retired list. Following the war, Hammond had a distinguished medical career.

JANE HOGE (1811–1890) and MARY A. LIVERMORE (1820–1905). Hoge and Livermore became friends while doing charity work before the war. They joined forces in 1861 to advance the relief efforts of the northwestern branch of the Sanitary Commission (see "Relief Organizations," on page 661). Beginning in December 1862, they jointly directed the organization's Chicago office. Through speaking tours, they helped inspire the formation of 3,000 local aid societies. They also made investigative trips to the front and provided for the delivery of tons of fresh produce, clothing, and medical supplies to Union soldiers. One of their biggest successes was the October 1863 Chicago Sanitary Fair, which raised over $100,000. Both women later wrote books about their experiences: *The Boys in Blue* (1867) by Hoge, and *My Story of the War* (1887) by Livermore.

DR. JONATHAN W. LETTERMAN (1824–1872). A graduate of Jefferson Medical College, Letterman spent twelve years, before the war, as an army assistant surgeon on the western and southwestern frontiers. In June 1862, Surgeon General Hammond appointed him as medical director of the Army of the Potomac. Letterman soon restructured medical care in the field and instituted a much-needed ambulance system to rush the wounded to emergency "dressing stations" and then to field hospitals. He also standardized medical supplies in the field and clarified the chain of command. The success of his improvements led other Union armies to adopt his system, which was then officially established by Congress with the Ambulance Corps Act of March 11, 1864.

MARY EDWARDS WALKER (1832–1919). That female nurses became widely accepted during the Civil War marked a significant shift in the attitude toward women in the medical services, but Mary Walker's status as a surgeon was so radical that even other women found the notion unsettling. Born in Oswego, New York, Walker graduated from the Syracuse Medical

College and established a practice in Ohio. In her first three years of wartime service, she nursed the wounded in various campaigns before finally obtaining a surgeon's position with the Fifty-Second Ohio Infantry. She was the first female surgeon in the army medical services, and she held the post until June 1865. Her work was interrupted only by a four-month sojourn in a Confederate prisoner-of-war camp. In 1866, Walker became the first woman (and, to date, the only) awarded the Medal of Honor. She remained an outspoken advocate of women's rights, and died on February 21, 1919. Although her Medal of Honor was rescinded, Congress reinstated it in 1977.

Confederate States of America

DR. SAMUEL PRESTON MOORE (1813–1889). A graduate of the Medical College of South Carolina, Moore served for twenty-six years in the U.S. Army—as an assistant surgeon and then a surgeon—but resigned in February 1861. By July 1861, Jefferson Davis had selected Moore as the Confederate army's surgeon general, a position he held until the war's end. Starting with only twenty-four experienced surgeons, Moore essentially built the Confederate medical organization from scratch. He quickly formed medical boards to administer examinations for surgeons, and he ultimately increased the medical team to more than 3,000 doctors. Although the records of his administration and its achievements were mostly destroyed by fire, he is credited with vaccinating most of the army against smallpox, encouraging research into local herbal substitutes for blockaded medicines, and developing the "hospital hut," a thirty-two-bed ward designed to connect to other huts to form a modular hospital—the plan used for Richmond's huge general hospitals, Chimborazo and Winder. Moore also promoted publication of the *Confederate States Medical and Surgical Journal* (January 1864–February 1865).

JULIET OPIE HOPKINS (1818–1890). Hopkins, who had reportedly once helped run her father's Virginia plantation, moved from Alabama (where she was married to a judge) to Richmond in the summer of 1861, to help organize the hospital services for Alabama soldiers. She acquired facilities, hired and supervised nurses, made sure the wards were clean, and called on Alabama women to send supplies. During one foray to the front to bring back the wounded, she herself was injured. One Alabama neighbor wrote, "If you had been a man, you would have been a commanding general," and her picture was put on Alabaman war currency. When the state hospitals became part of the Confederate Medical Department in 1863, she returned to Alabama. Her enterprise was echoed in the similar efforts of other Southern women, such as MARY RUTLEDGE FOGG and LETITIA TYLER SEMPLE, who also established hospitals.

DR. JOSEPH JONES (1833–1896). A graduate of the University of Pennsylvania Medical Department, Jones joined a Confederate cavalry unit when the war started. Six months later, he moved to the medical branch, where he eventually became a surgeon major. During the war, Jones systematically studied wounds, disease, and treatments in army camps, hospitals, and prisons, and made many insightful observations on Civil War-era medical science. Using a microscope (unusual at the time), he noted the presence of bacteria in common camp diseases, although, in keeping with medical theory at that time, he failed to connect this with specific disorders. Following the war, Jones reported his observations in several publications, including a section of *Surgical Memoirs of the War of the Rebellion* (1871).

SAMUEL HOLLINGSWORTH STOUT (1822–1903). A civilian doctor with a medical degree from the University of Pennsylvania, Stout joined the army as a regimental surgeon, was assigned to Nashville, and later served as post surgeon and medical director in Chattanooga. In March 1863, he was given oversight of all the hospitals for the Army of Tennessee. This assignment encompassed much of Georgia, including Atlanta. He greatly expanded the number of hospital beds, encouraged the use of mobile hospitals, and maintained careful medical records. A medical inspector described the management of his department as "far superior to that of any other in the Confederacy."

Female Nurses The Civil War is often credited with opening the nursing profession to women. Despite Englishwoman Florence Nightingale's pioneering work in the Crimean War and the success of her 1860 book, *Notes on Nursing*, many people disapproved of women entering the male sphere of medical care, especially in a military setting filled with the horrors of war, death, and disease. Resistance to women nurses was voiced in both the North and the South, although somewhat less vociferously in the North, where more women were moving out of traditional roles. Increasing numbers of Northern women were employed outside the home (in factories or as teachers), and others engaged in political activity through such movements as abolition and women's rights. The demands of the Civil War, however, proved too great to preclude active help from the female half of the population.

As early as June 1861, Dorothea Dix was named superintendent of female nurses for the U.S. Army. Soon, two women doctors, the sisters Elizabeth and Emily Blackwell, began offering training for nurses through the Woman's Central Relief Association in New York. Other nursing "schools" followed. By July 1862, Union Surgeon General Hammond was calling for one-third of all army nurses in general hospitals to be women. (Women were not encouraged at the front.) In the South, African American women slaves were put to work in hospitals from the start. In September 1862, the Confederate Congress established positions for white women as hospital matrons, to tend to "the entire domestic economy of the hospital."

Eventually, some 3,200 women held paid nursing positions for the Union and the Confederacy, and many more offered their services for free. Catholic nuns—the only group of nurses who had received some past training in the profession—helped care for soldiers. Some sixty nursing nuns worked on hospital boats that were ferrying U.S. troops to the York Peninsula in 1862. The Sisters of Charity in Emmitsburg, Maryland, sent nuns to work as nurses in both Union and Confederate hospitals. Late in the war, at least one woman, Mary Edwards Walker, worked as a surgeon in a western Union army.

That male doctors downplayed women nurses' contribution is clear in the official text, *The Medical and Surgical History of the War of the Rebellion*, which notes: "According to the testimony of all the medical officers who have referred to this point, their [the women's] best service was rendered in connection with extra diet, the linen-room and the laundry. Male help was preferred [by surgeons] in the wards save in special cases of prostration and suffering. . . ." Wounded soldiers' memoirs suggest otherwise. For young soldiers unfortunate enough to require long-term medical attention, a female presence in hospital wards often meant a merciful tenderness of care that the other nurses—soldiers detailed to hospital duty, usually convalescent themselves—did not provide.

Although a few wartime female nurses, such as Louisa May Alcott and Jane Stuart Woolsey, wrote detailed accounts of their hospital service, the majority of those women are as anonymous as the multitude of rank-and-file soldiers they aided. The following group of women nurses are representatives of all those whose service was not recorded.

LOUISA MAY ALCOTT (1832–1888). In December–January, 1862–1863, Alcott worked as a nurse at Union Hospital in Washington, D.C. Although she had to leave because of a bout of typhoid fever, she recorded her observations. Her book, *Hospital Sketches* (1863), helped to establish her as a writer and gave her readers a vivid glimpse of the war effort.

CLARA BARTON (1821–1912). Working separately from the U.S. Sanitary Commission in 1862, Barton solicited food and medical supplies and carried them to the front in Virginia and Maryland. She became known as the "Angel of the Battlefield" as she set about warming up coffee and soup and tending the wounded. In June 1864, she began working in the field hospitals for General Benjamin Butler's Army of the James. Later, in February 1865, she set up an office to help reconnect missing soldiers with their relatives, and in July she oversaw the identification of unmarked graves at the Andersonville prison in Georgia. After the war, Barton helped organize the American Red Cross (in 1881) and served as its first president.

Clara Barton worked on her own to bring food and supplies to troops on the battlefield. She achieved lasting fame for her postwar efforts to create the American Red Cross.

MARY ANN BICKERDYKE (1817–1901). "Mother Bickerdyke," as she was called by grateful patients, started cleaning, feeding, and nursing Union soldiers at a field hospital in Illinois in June 1861. As a field agent for the Northwestern Sanitary Commission, she continued to help on the front lines, mostly in the Western Theater, throughout the war. She was known for her ability to find food and prepare nourishing soups, or to get dirty linen washed, and wounds cleaned, in the most primitive field conditions. At times, she left the field to solicit supplies, including some cows and chickens that she transported from Illinois to Memphis hospitals.

KATE CUMMING (c. 1828–1909). Beginning in April 1862, Cumming defied her family's notion of activities suitable for a "refined lady" and volunteered in Confederate hospitals. In September 1862, she became a hospital matron and managed the dietary and housekeeping operations of various Georgia hospitals. Her diary, recording her experiences, was later published as *A Journal of the Hospital Life in the Confederate Army of Tennessee* (1866).

DOROTHEA LYNDE DIX (1802–1887). When she was appointed Union superintendent of female nurses in 1861, Dix was already known for her work in reforming care for the mentally ill. At first, Dix accepted only plain-looking Protestant nurses over thirty. In part because of her rigidity, she encountered opposition on several fronts, but she got the nursing program started and continued to help run it even after her authority was limited in October 1863.

ELLA KING NEWSOM (later, Trader; 1838–1919). Called "the Florence Nightingale of the South," Newsom oversaw domestic operations for several hospitals on the front in Tennessee in 1861–1862. She became the matron of Academy Hospital in Chattanooga and later helped to set up hospitals in Marietta, Georgia.

PHOEBE YATES LÉVY PEMBER (1823–1913). In November 1862, Pember, a widow, took on the administrative duties of a matron at Richmond's Chimborazo, the Confederate army's largest hospital. In her memoir, *A Southern Woman's Story* (1879), Pember described the hostility she experienced from male doctors, as well as the "wars of the whiskey barrel," waged over the dispensation of medicinal spirits. However, she admitted that "antagonism was not always the rule."

SUSIE KING TAYLOR (1848–1912). The only African American woman to publish a memoir about her Civil War work, in *A Black Woman's Civil War Memoirs* (1902), Taylor served, mostly in South Carolina, as a nurse and laundress for the Thirty-Third U.S. Colored Troops. During 1863, she worked with Clara Barton, who was then in the Sea Islands.

SALLY LOUISA TOMPKINS (1833–1916). Soon after the war started, Tompkins set up a hospital for wounded Confederate soldiers in a private home in Richmond, using female nurses (including slaves). She soon established a reputation for cleanliness and healing (all but seventy-three of the 1,333 patients she treated during the war survived). When the Confederacy stopped using private hospitals, Tompkins was appointed as a captain in the Confederate cavalry just to keep her facility open.

GEORGEANNA (1833–1906) and JANE STUART WOOLSEY (1830–1891). These two sisters served as Union nurses, as did their sister, ELIZA WOOLSEY HOWLAND. Another sister, ABBY, spent the war collecting supplies for the U.S. Sanitary Commission. Georgeanna and Jane worked together at Fairfax Theological Seminary Hospital near Alexandria, Virginia, where they ran the nursing and dietary departments. Jane, who later helped found Presbyterian Hospital in New York City, described her war work in *Hospital Days* (1868); Georgeanna and Eliza told of their experiences in *Letters of a Family During the War for the Union* (1899).

Relief Organizations

During the war, various relief agencies in both the North and the South supplemented the government's efforts by gathering food and medical supplies and providing for nursing care and other assistance to the wounded. Most of these groups were started by women who were anxious to do what they could for the soldiers. Throughout the war, women were the main force behind these volunteer aid societies. (See also Chapter 10, "The Home Front.")

United States of America

U.S. SANITARY COMMISSION

In the North, the relief efforts of thousands of local groups were coordinated by this national organization, set up in June 1861 in conjunction with the Federal government. The commission was charged with inspecting and improving sanitary conditions in the camps and hospitals, as well as providing supplies, nursing care, and other services for the sick and wounded. Although headed by such men as Rev. Henry W. Bellows and Frederick Law Olmsted, the commission's work was carried out primarily by women, such as Jane Hoge and Mary Livermore. Indeed, the commission was, in part, an outgrowth of the Woman's Central Relief Association in New York. Headquartered in Washington, the Sanitary Commission ultimately established regional headquarters in ten Northern cities, which in turn facilitated the creation of thousands of local aid societies, or auxiliaries.

By collecting and distributing clothing, food, medicines, and other supplies to the army administration or directly to soldiers; by sending nurses and surgeons to field hospitals; by equipping hospital boats like the *Daniel Webster;* and even by evacuating the wounded from frontline areas when army ambulance services were inadequate, the Sanitary Commission operated essentially as a branch of the army's Medical Department. As the army organization became more efficient, the commission expanded its activities to include "rest stops" for soldiers traveling to and from the front, and agencies to help soldiers claim their pensions or back pay. All of these services were funded by donations and by lavish fund-raising events called "Sanitary Fairs." In cash and supplies, the Sanitary Commission contributed some $20 million to the war effort, along with the labor of its many unpaid volunteers (see Chapter 10, "The Home Front").

UNITED STATES CHRISTIAN COMMISSION
Started in 1861 by the Young Men's Christian Association in New York, this group raised some $6 million for the war effort. It sent food and coffee wagons to the front, as well as other supplies, including writing paper and postage stamps. At various permanent camps, it set up reading rooms stocked with Bibles, religious books, newspapers, and magazines.

WESTERN SANITARY COMMISSION
Formed in St. Louis in 1861, at the direction of General John C. Frémont, this group operated essentially independently of the U.S. Sanitary Commission. It set up hospital kitchens, provided medical supplies and other relief to soldiers in the St. Louis area, and outfitted the *City of Louisiana* as a hospital ship.

Confederate States of America

ASSOCIATION FOR THE RELIEF OF MAIMED SOLDIERS
The only relief society organized throughout the Confederacy, this association supplied artificial limbs to servicemen who had undergone amputations, thereby benefiting hundreds of soldiers and sailors. In March 1865, the Confederate Congress approved an act to facilitate the process of manufacturing, purchasing, and placing the artificial limbs.

RELIEF ORGANIZATIONS OF CONFEDERATE STATES

The Georgia Relief and Hospital Association was one of several statewide relief organizations. (Alabama, Louisiana, and South Carolina organizations were particularly active, and the Union states also had relief programs.) Among many services, the Georgia Association used state and private funds to supply doctors, medicines, and bandages to hospitals, and scarce medical supplies to surgeons in the field; equipped four Richmond hospitals; provided clothing for Georgia troops; and established wayside homes. In addition, all the Confederate state governments contributed to private relief efforts for their own troops.

Felicia Grundy Porter headed the Women's Relief Society of the Confederate States. Confederate medical director Samuel Stout called the benefits of these societies "incalculable . . . in convincing [the soldier] that he is not forgotten by the patriotic and generous citizens in the rear. . . . "

RICHMOND AMBULANCE COMMITTEE

Formed by men exempt from military duty, the Richmond Ambulance Committee helped to tend, feed, and transport wounded Confederate soldiers to hospitals in the interior. The members' contributions paid all expenses, and they were present at nearly every engagement of the Army of Northern Virginia, including Williamsburg, Chancellorsville, and Gettysburg.

WOMEN'S RELIEF SOCIETIES IN THE SOUTH

Although there was no single Confederate organization on the scale of the U.S. Sanitary Commission, Southern women set up hundreds of local relief societies, which collected clothing, food, and medical supplies for soldiers. Women's groups also set up wayside hospitals to provide nursing care and lodging for wounded soldiers traveling home from the front. A Women's Relief Society of the Confederate States was directed by Felicia Grundy Porter of Nashville, Tennessee.

SELECTED RESOURCES

For additional information on published sources, see the annotated book list in Chapter 13, "Studying the War: Research and Preservation." There are also numerous accounts written by doctors and nurses who served in the war.

Adams, George Worthington. *Doctors in Blue: The Medical History of the Union Army in the Civil War.* New York: Schuman, 1952. Illustrated.

Confederate States of America, Surgeon General's Office. *A Manual of Military Surgery Prepared for the Use of the Confederate States Army.* Richmond: Ayres & Wade, 1863.

Confederate States of America, War Department. *Regulations for the Medical Department of the C.S. Army.* Richmond: Ritchie & Dunnavant, 1863.

Cunningham, Horace Herndon. *Doctors in Gray: The Confederate Medical Service.* Baton Rouge: Louisiana State University Press, 1958.

Denney, Robert E. *Civil War Medicine: Care & Comfort of the Wounded.* New York: Sterling, 1994. Illustrated.

Freemon, Frank R. *Microbes and Minié Balls: An Annotated Bibliography of Civil War Medicine.* Rutherford, New Jersey: Fairleigh Dickinson University Press, 1993.

Steiner, Paul E. *Disease in the Civil War: Natural Biological Warfare in 1861–1865.* Springfield, Illinois: C.C. Thomas, 1968.

United States Sanitary Commission. *Surgical Memoirs of the War of the Rebellion* (2 volumes). New York: U.S. Sanitary Commission, 1870–1871.

U.S. Surgeon General's Office. *The Medical and Surgical History of the War of the Rebellion (1861–65)* (3 volumes in 6 parts). Washington: Government Printing Office, 1875–1885. Illustrated.

Wilbur, C. Keith. *Civil War Medicine, 1861–1865.* Old Saybrook, Connecticut: Globe Pequot Press, 1998. Illustrated.

THE HOME FRONT

The Civil War home fronts in the North and the South were so profoundly different that it is difficult to make statements that would apply to both of them. A "home front" generally means the civilian sector of a nation at war, but this nation was at war with itself. Although the Confederate States of America proclaimed itself a separate nation—and thus, theoretically, an alien power—few on either side thought of the others as "foreigners."

The meaning of home front was further blurred by the fact that almost all of the fighting took place in the South. With some exceptions, most notably Robert E. Lee's two incursions into Northern territory, ending at Antietam, Maryland (a slaveholding border state that remained in the Union) and Gettysburg, Pennsylvania; General Jubal Early's raid to Washington, D.C., and into Pennsylvania; and General John Hunt Morgan's cavalry raid into Indiana and Ohio, Civil War combat took place on Confederate soil. Thus, the war was much more intimately woven into the daily lives of Southern noncombatants. Distinct among Southern civilians were the 3.5 million slaves, who, unlike other civilian populations during wartime, secretly favored the other side; hundreds of thousands of Southern slaves fled to Union lines as the war progressed.

Conversely, portions of the Northern home front were almost completely untouched by the war. In the vast expanses of Minnesota, Utah Territory, and California, home front civilians were more concerned about Indian uprisings than Confederate incursions. This is not to minimize the effects of the war on the Northern home front; relatively "untouched" states like Illinois, with a population of 1.7 million, had 259,000 enlistees; Michigan, with 749,000, had 87,000 enlistees; and Connecticut contributed 55,000 soldiers out of a total population of 460,000.

The South

The Confederacy, as a political unit, comprised the eleven states listed in the following table, and the figures used for the South in this chapter refer only to that unit. They do not include the four slaveholding border states that did not secede from the United States: Delaware, Kentucky, Maryland, and Missouri. The most often cited figure for the number of slaves in the South at the start of the war is 4,000,000, but this figure includes the 429,401 slaves in the border states. The actual number of slaves in the Confederate States of America was 3,521,110. The following population counts of the states that later seceded from the United States were recorded in the 1860 census:

State	White Population	Slave Population*
Alabama	526,271	435,080
Arkansas	324,143	111,115
Florida	77,747	61,745
Georgia	591,550	462,198
Louisiana	357,456	331,726
Mississippi	353,899	436,631
North Carolina	629,942	331,059
South Carolina	291,300	402,406
Tennessee	826,722	275,719
Texas	420,891	182,566
Virginia	1,047,299	490,865

Source: U.S. Census Office, Eighth Census (1860).
*Not shown are the 132,760 free blacks who lived in the Confederate states, the highest number of whom lived in Virginia (58,042), North Carolina (30,463), and Louisiana (18,647).

Before the first shot was fired at Fort Sumter, the population of the Confederate states was 40.2 percent black (slave and free) and 59.8 percent white. The total population of the eleven Confederate states in 1860 was 9,101,090, the most populous being Virginia (1,596,206), Tennessee (1,109,741), and Georgia (1,057,248). South Carolina and Mississippi had more slave than free-born residents.

These figures were soon in flux, as many white, nonslaveholding males were conscripted into military service, slaves escaped to the Northern side in increasingly large numbers (especially in areas near Union troop encampments), and many white Southerners became refugees or emigrated to less embattled regions, including Mexico and Canada.

The dynamic of the Confederate home front was also profoundly shaped by the makeup of the white population. While 1.7 million whites were slaveholders (this number includes members of a slaveholder's family), most whites in the Confederate states did not own slaves. The largest single segment of the population, the 3.9 million nonslaveholding whites, constituted nearly half of the total population and two-thirds of the white population. These whites were not opposed to slavery per se; they simply did not own slaves. Though some of them were city laborers, generally, they were yeoman farmers and their families, for unlike the North, the Confederacy was primarily agrarian. On the eve of the war, the contrast between the two sides could not have been more stark in this regard. Massachusetts, for example, manufactured goods that were 60 percent more valuable than those produced in the eleven Confederate states combined.

The Confederate civilian home front dynamic was charged by another factor. After exemptions from the Confederate draft were expanded in October 1862, any able-bodied male who owned or was an overseer of twenty or more slaves was exempted from Confederate military service. Male heads of nonslaveholding households did much of the fighting in the war.

The North

The "North" is a somewhat misleading term. The geographical layout of the United States (other than the eleven Confederate states) at the outbreak of the war included twenty-three states scattered among New England, the mid-Atlantic region, the Midwest and West, plus seven territories (Nebraska, New Mexico, Utah, Washington, Colorado, Dakota, and Nevada) and the District of Columbia. The North covered about three million square miles; the Confederate states covered, roughly, 750,000 square miles.

The population of the North, according to the 1860 census, was 22,339,989, or two and one-half times that of the South. The population advantage was made more manifest by the fact that one-third of the South's people were slaves; thus, the pool from which soldiers were originally drawn, even before blacks were allowed to join the Union army, was close to four times greater. The Northern population also included 355,310 free blacks and, in the territories and the four "loyal" border states, 432,650 slaves.

The North had every conceivable economic advantage over the South: nearly five times the personal wealth; two and one-half times the number of rail miles; six times the real and personal property (not including slaves); and ten times the manufacturing capacity.

Economic Conditions and Their Effects

The Southern Economy

All monetary exchanges in the Confederate states were tendered by paper currency. The Confederacy's Secretary of the Treasury, Christopher Memminger, encouraged using these paper "treasury notes," and on March 9, 1861, the Confederate Congress authorized the printing of one million dollars in notes. By summer, standard denominations and visual cues had been established (Memminger's portrait was on the $5 bill), and firms in Columbia, South Carolina, and in Richmond, Virginia, printed the bills. Confusion set in early, however, as fractional currency (so-called "paper coins" or "shin-plasters") was also printed for amounts less than one dollar. The gold standard had been suspended; all bills were backed by little more than faith in the new government.

Memminger then tried to sell bonds and raise taxes to offset the cost of running a new national government, financing a war, and combating the inevitable inflation resulting from there being a greater demand for goods than

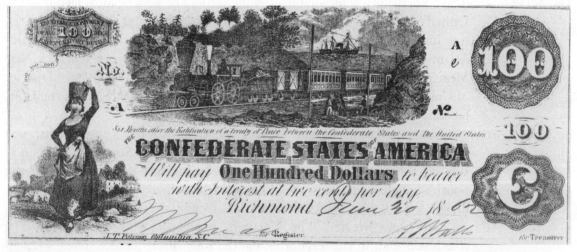

Confederate paper money, authorized by the Confederate Congress in March 1861, became increasingly worthless as inflation increased. This bill promises payment "to bearer" of $100, "with interest at two cents per day"–but only "six months after the Ratification of a Treaty of Peace between the Confederate States and the United States."

there was a supply. But the bonds did not sell well enough to raise the needed funds. Memminger resorted to printing more currency, and some individual states and counties (as well as counterfeiters) printed money as well, further eroding confidence in the Southern monetary system. All bills bore the message "will pay the bearer . . . six months . . . after the ratification of a treaty of peace between the Confederate States and the United States."

Direct taxes were only gradually imposed in the Confederacy. The first tax law was passed in August 1861. This comparatively slight tax (one-half of 1 percent of assessed property valuation, with heads of families holding under $500 in property exempted) eventually raised $17.4 million (35 percent of that amount came from taxes on slaves). The method of collection raised problems of its own, however. States that acted under a provision of the tax law that allowed them to pay the tax on behalf of their citizens (thus receiving a 10 percent discount) often borrowed money to do so—and then failed to tax their citizens to recover the borrowed amount. The Confederacy's 1861 national tax thereby helped to create individual state debts. A much more comprehensive tax law was passed in April 1863. It levied taxes on occupations, income, produce, and property on a graduated basis; again, people with taxable property valued below $500 were exempt. Overall, however, only 7 percent of all Confederate national revenue was secured via taxation.

The value of currency plummeted swiftly. The Confederate dollar was worth eighty cents in gold in late 1861; in 1863, it was worth twenty cents; in 1865, it was worth one and one-half cents. By the end of the war, $1,554,087,354.00 in Confederate bills were in circulation, and the people in the South had lost all confidence in the money, referring to it derisively as "shrunken cabbage" or "fodder." One diarist noted, in May 1864: "Never were debtors more eager to pay or creditors so loth to receive." Memminger was forced to resign two months later.

The policy of impressment also created economic hardship for the civilian population. The Confederate Congress passed a law, on March 26, 1863, requiring farmers and merchants to cede goods to government agents (for military use) in return for Confederate currency or a certificate that could be redeemed at a later time. Goods were assessed below market values, often by more than 50 percent. There was little consistency in applying the impressment law, and areas near where armies were stationed or transportation depots were located bore the greatest burden. Often, impressed food rotted because of inadequate transportation. Slaves were also impressed to work on fortifications or as teamsters, nurses, or cooks; a wage was paid to owners for their services. In March 1865, more than $500 million in redeemable

Confederate notes, and certificates for impressed goods and slaves, had not been paid; after the Confederacy collapsed, they were worthless. A tax in kind on agricultural produce, passed in April 1863, further added to farmers' woes.

Civilians resorted to black market exchanges for U.S. currency or simply bartered for desperately needed goods, including basic foodstuffs. Some women made clothing late into the evening and sold it to rich whites or traded it to available men in the community for farm chores they could not do themselves. Doctors routinely took food or clothing in exchange for services, and schools asked pupils to pay tuition in bacon, potatoes, and produce. Rather than sell their produce, farmers preferred to trade it for salt, sugar, tools, or clothing. The reverse was true for those in manufacturing. This notice was printed in a Savannah, Georgia, newspaper, in July 1864: "I will barter salt from my salt factory on the following terms: 4 bushels of salt for 5 bushels of corn and peas; 1 bushel of salt for 5 pounds of lard or bacon . . . 2 bushels of salt for 1 pr. of shoes."

Going without was not a choice in the Confederacy; it was an everyday reality. Rural areas were particularly hard hit by deprivations, but cities suffered too, including the Confederate capital of Richmond. In February 1863, master machinists at the city's Tredegar Iron Works earned $5 per day; carpenters were paid $2. Beef sold for $1 per pound; bacon, $1.25 per pound; butter, $3 per pound; cornmeal, $6 per bushel; flour, $30 per barrel; and shoes, $25 per pair. By January 1865, workers earned $10 per day, but the prices for goods were almost prohibitively expensive: $1,000 per barrel for flour; $100 per bushel for cornmeal; $8 per pound for beef; $15 per pound for butter.

The lack of basic goods was partly the result of an increasingly effective Northern blockade of Southern ports, but was also due to profiteers' hoarding of flour, corn, and other items produced in the South. Speculators tended to accumulate necessities such as cotton, salt, meat, shoes, and clothing, which they withheld from the market and then sold at increased prices. The Confederate government had fixed the price of food supplies for military purchasers, but—other than piecemeal efforts—not for the civilians on the home front.

Speculation by individuals, merchants, and traders produced public outrage. The *Daily Sun*, in Columbus, Georgia, railed in 1862: "We have in fact two wars upon our hands at once. Whilst our brave soldiers are off battling the Abolitionists a conscienceless set of vampires are at home warring upon their indigent families and threatening them with immediate starvation." Governors like Andrew Moore of Alabama and North Carolina's Zebulon Vance urged legislation but understood that laws against speculators were not effective. Georgia's governor, Joseph Brown, understood the difficulties, but nonetheless derided speculators as "a class . . . who remain at home preying upon the vitals of society, determined to make money at every hazard, who turn a deaf ear to the cries of soldiers' families and are prepared to immolate even our armies and sacrifice our liberties upon the altar of mammon." Yet the degree of actual speculation, as opposed to emotions surrounding it, is unknown.

All of these factors created a sense of desperation (see "Riots"). The Confederate states appropriated funds to help the families of soldiers who were on active duty or had been killed. Funding, in 1862, ranged from $62,000 in Arkansas to $2,000,000 in Georgia, and there were private charity efforts such as a free market in Mobile, Alabama, that fed 1,800 people. In 1863, the Confederate War Department began to supply essential foods, at cost, to citizens. But these efforts proved inadequate. Most civilians had to make do the best they could without government help. The enterprising spirit may have underscored some of the efforts at finding substitutes for staples, but a large number of people were seriously malnourished; many who survived the war had shorter lives because of tight wartime rations. Government clerk John Beauchamp Jones, raising a family on $6,000 per year—which ordinarily would have been considered a large income in the mid 1800s—wrote in his diary of July 17, 1863: "We are in a half-starving condition. I have lost twenty pounds and my wife and children are emaciated to some extent." In April 1864, he wrote "This is famine." In January 1865, he wrote, "What I fear is starvation." He survived the war, but died in February 1866, at age fifty-five, due in part to ruined health from his malnutrition during the war years.

In 1863, some creative solutions to food-shortage problems were published in the *Confederate Receipt Book*, thought to be the only cookbook published in the Confederacy. It contained recipes ("receipts") such as "Apple Pie without Apples": "To one small bowl of crackers, that have been soaked until no hard parts remain, add one teaspoon of tartaric acid, sweeten to your taste, add some butter, and very little nutmeg." The book also suggested what could be substituted for scarce items like coffee (acorns, chicory, peanuts, dandelion root, cotton seed, okra seeds); tea (raspberry leaves, holly leaves); and sugar (honey, molasses, sorghum). Among nonfood essentials, shoe polish, or blackening, was replaced by soot mixed with lard or cottonseed oil; tooth powder was made from pulverized charcoal; hair oil was made from lard scented with rose petals; soap was made from lye mixed with refuse grease.

The Northern Economy

Although the United States had a more robust economy, the North was plagued by a number of monetary and inflationary problems during the war. Secession provoked a financial panic that drained specie from the U.S. Treasury and lowered the government's credit ratings. The national debt, which had grown considerably in the wake of the Panic of 1857, was higher when Lincoln took office than it had been in forty years ($64,842,288). In 1861, war debts were mounting (by the war's end, the public debt totaled $2,680,647,870). Bankers wanted the government to levy more taxes, but politicians were wary of setting a precedent. (The first income tax ever levied by the U.S. government was the income tax law of August 5, 1861.)

The primary means by which the government proposed to pay for the war was by borrowing, in the form of bonds. U.S. Secretary of the Treasury Salmon P. Chase pushed for issuance of $50 million in bonds in July 1861, and another $514 million in February 1862. Because the bonds did not sell well, Chase hired Jay Cooke and Company, a private New York firm, to market them. Cooke pitched them to American "workingmen" as patriotic investments, foreshadowing the war bond drives of the next century, and sold them all, earning the nickname "financier of the Civil War." As it turned out, bankers and wealthy investors were the chief purchasers of the bonds, not "workingmen."

More significantly, Chase called for the "indispensably necessary" creation of "irredeemable and noninterest-bearing" U.S. notes, popularly known as "greenbacks" (they were printed with green ink). The Legal Tender Acts of 1862 and 1863 followed, and the greenbacks issued totaled $447,000,000 by the war's end. The notes also contained a disclaimer: "Legal tender in payment of all debts, public and private, within the United States, except duties on imports and interest." The paper currency, unlike the Confederacy's, was backed by the gold standard, though a $1 greenback was worth only ninety-one cents in gold by 1862. Gold peaked in value (i.e., the greenback dipped to its lowest value) on July 11, 1864, when $284 in greenbacks was required to purchase $100 in gold. On that day, Confederate General Jubal Early and 15,000 Confederate troops were "at the doors of Washington," initiating the "panic" in gold speculation (see "Early's Washington Raid" in Chapter 4, "Battles and the Battlefield"). Once Early's threat subsided, the price went back down. Regardless of the protests raised by bankers and financial experts, greenbacks were a huge success, even among Confederate citizens living in areas occupied by Union troops. In fact, after the war, greenbacks remained in circulation, because of their popularity.

Much of the Northern wealth produced during the war resulted from speculating on stocks. Lower Manhattan's Wall Street was the epicenter of American speculation, and the war fueled a frenzy of activity that made many people instantly wealthy—on paper. As *Harper's Weekly* stated in April 1865: "It is keeping within bounds to say that $250,000,000—in paper-money—was realized as profits by the operators in stocks between 1862 and 1864. . . . This profit was divided among many thousands of people . . . every body seemed to be speculating in stocks. Nothing else was talked of at clubs, in the streets, at the theatres, in drawing-rooms." Some of this instant wealth came from hoarding goods and speculating on essentials—at the expense of civilians on the home front.

In general, the Northern economy grew in all areas—agriculture, industry, mining, manufacturing, and railroad expansion. In an annual review through 1864, conducted by the country's first credit-rating agency, R. G. Dun (precursor of Dun & Bradstreet), the firm declared that all segments of the economy had prospered—an assessment based on the dwindling number of business failures. In the Northern states in 1860, for example, 2,733 failures were listed, with a total liability of $61,739,474. By 1864, the total failures were 510, with liabilities of $8,579,000. Many economists believe that this wartime economic expansion was responsible for the nation's continued prosperity for much of the rest of the nineteenth century (barring the Depression of 1873), even after the financially ruined Southern states had been brought back into the Union.

Agriculture

The North developed an agricultural advantage as the war progressed. Although the Confederate states had more agricultural acreage, the two sides' differing approaches to farming placed the North at an advantage. The cash crop in the South, following Northerner Eli Whitney's invention of the cotton gin in 1793, was "King Cotton." Crop diversification and modernization of techniques or machinery were practically nil; the main capital investment was in slave labor.

Slaves were the foundation of the South's "King Cotton" agrarian economy. This group of South Carolina contrabands was photographed by Timothy O'Sullivan in 1862, after the Union's successful expedition to Port Royal, South Carolina, in the fall of 1861.

In addition, prewar developments had created differences between the three main types of farmers in the South. As described in the MacMillan Information Now Encyclopedia, *The Confederacy*, those types were:

1. Large planters who produced a staple crop, mostly cotton, with slave labor, for sale in distant markets.
2. Large commercial farmers who employed tenants and day laborers to produce livestock, corn, and wheat, also for distant markets.
3. Smaller farmers and the women and children in their households who produced a subsistence for themselves and sometimes a surplus, usually for sale or for barter in the neighborhood.

Relations between the three groups deteriorated during the war, as the large commercial farmers lost their distant markets and the smaller farmers often lost nearly everything. Everyone suffered from the encroachments of invading Northern armies, the loss of acreage confiscated by the Confederate army to graze its own livestock, and natural disasters such as the drought that affected crops in Georgia and Alabama in 1863. Confederate national taxes also contributed to loss of Confederate farm yields (as well as to an increase in disaffection among Southern small farmers). Because the Confederate taxes had to be paid in cash, many small farmers, particularly, were forced to convert food crops—corn, rye, wheat, and barley—into something for which there was *always* an excellent (if often illegal) cash market: liquor. All these factors combined to destroy the South's prewar agricultural advantage.

In the North, wartime agriculture boomed as industrialized farms—particularly those in Iowa and Illinois—proved able not only to feed the population, but also to provide surplus for trade overseas (there were bumper crops in 1861 and 1862). Although the number of men engaged in farming decreased during the course of the war, farm production increased. Hogs were one example: the number of hogs butchered in Chicago rose from 270,000 per year when the war began to 900,000 per year in 1865. The disparity between the two sections, in agriculture and manufacturing, was revealed in the 1860 census (see the table below).

The push for higher farm production began quickly in the North. Less than a month after the bombardment of Fort Sumter, the *American Agriculturalist*, the leading farm journal in the United States, was exhorting Northern farmers to produce "one bushel more" for the war effort; in addition, the journal advised that "the foreign demand will alone greatly stimulate the

	North	South
Cash Value of Farms	$5,056,151,204	$1,579,349,508
Cash Value of Farm Implements, Machinery and Livestock	$930,413,926	$397,072,820
Capital Invested in Manufacturing	$892,512,979	$113,099,460
Percentage of Capital Invested in Manufacturing	17%	6%
Per Capita Investment in Manufacturing	$43.73	$13.25
Manufacturing Investments since 1840	+80%	−20%
Workers Living in Towns Pop. 2,500+ (1840)	10%	5%
Workers Living in Towns Pop. 2,500+ (1860)	26%	10%
Labor Force in Agriculture (1800)	68%	82%
Labor Force in Agriculture (1860)	40%	84%

Source: U.S. Bureau of the Census, 1860.

market for agricultural products, and enhance prices, thus affording means for liquidating debts incurred for land, and for implements, and other liabilities"—a prediction proven true by later events.

As early as September 1861, there was an increase in Northern wheat crops. As more Northern inventions—McCormick's reapers (manufactured in Cincinnati), Smalley's Corn Plow (made in New York City), and various other mowers, horse rakes, separators, sowers, cultivators, and drills—were purchased by confident Midwestern farmers, the harvests of wheat, oats, corn, and hay in the following years greatly improved. According to the Cincinnati *Gazette*, 100,000 Northern farmers had enlisted in the military by early 1862, but the new machines did the work of "three-fold the number of men" and were operable by the "volunteer's wife." The September 1863 *Merchant Magazine* wrote, "At the present time so perfect is machinery that men seem to be of less necessity. Of all the labors of the field, mowing was formerly deemed to be the most arduous, and the strongest men were required for it. We have seen, within the past few weeks, a stout matron whose sons are in the army, with her team cutting hay at seventy-five cents per acre, and she cut seven acres with ease in a day, riding leisurely upon her cutter."

Progressive farming reached its zenith in Iowa, where farmers no longer relied on only corn and wheat; they added acres of flax and sorghum and raised cattle for beef and sheep for wool. The *Davenport* (Iowa) *Daily Gazette* hailed "The dawn of Iowa's greatness." The U.S. Department of Agriculture, formed during the war, gave farmers information on such topics as improving livestock and grain production, seed supply, and the use of labor-saving devices.

Immigration, Homesteading, and Discrimination in the North

Immigration

The North had a large European immigrant population even before the start of the war. Between 1845 and 1860, 3,000,000 immigrants came to the United States; most were from Ireland and Germany. The potato famine, which began in 1845, brought the Irish to Eastern cities, such as New York, Boston, and Philadelphia. The failed revolutions of 1848 brought German-speaking Europeans to Cincinnati, Chicago, Milwaukee, St. Louis, and other Midwestern cities. Immigration slowed after 1860—partly because of the Civil War and because the economic and political problems that had precipitated Irish and German immigration were ameliorated—and increased again in 1863, as these figures indicate:

Number of Immigrants *to the United States*		*Major Countries of Immigrants'* *Origin, 1860–1864*	
1860	153,640	Germany	233,052
1861	91,918	Ireland	196,359
1862	91,985	England	85,116
1863	176,282	China	24,282
1864	193, 418	France	14,017
		Scotland	10,165
		Norway/Sweden	11,493

Some immigrants settled in the South, but the vast majority chose to live in the North. Many served in the Union army. The numbers of Germans (200,000) and Irish (150,000) who fought for the North allowed the formation of full regiments of German and Irish volunteers.

Many of the Irish who did not enter the army and who settled in New York lived in tenements, the conditions of which were so appalling that the city's Council of Hygiene and Public Health produced a report in 1865 delineating fifteen "nuisances" to public health:

> . . . filthy streets, neglected garbage and domestic refuse, obstructed sewers, neglected privies and stables, slaughter-houses . . . in close proximity to populous streets, droves of cattle and swine in crowded streets, bone-boiling and fat-melting.

The floors of "tenant-houses" were said to be "receptacles for street-mud, food, saliva, urine, faeces . . . the bed clothing is often little better." Irish immigrants who lived in these conditions played a major part in the violent New York City draft riot in 1863.

Homesteading

The Homestead Act of 1862 was intended to encourage a westward movement of thousands of hopeful settlers during the Civil War. Legislation to promote homesteading had been debated since the 1830s, but the resistance of Southern lawmakers, who opposed having the West inhabited primarily by small landowners without slaves, defeated all attempts. With the South no longer represented in Congress, the law was passed and went into effect on January 1, 1863.

Men or women who were citizens of the United States or "have filed his declaration of intention to become such" and were at least twenty-one years of age or the head of a household, could file for 160 acres of public land. By June 1864, 1,261,000 acres in states and territories west of the Mississippi River had been distributed. To earn title to the land, the homesteader had to live on it for five years and make improvements. This put more Midwestern land into agricultural production during the war—and expanded the North's advantage in farm production—but it did not inaugurate the egalitarian vision of Horace Greeley, who had hailed the act's goal to "give every man a home." Much of the best land was given in land grants to railroad companies or bought by speculators. By 1890, only 3.5 percent of the land west of the Mississippi had been earned by homesteaders.

Discrimination in the North

The ongoing reality of segregation, discrimination, and open racism against free blacks in the North was an important aspect of home-front life (see also Chapter 3, "Wartime Politics"). In 1860, Indiana, Illinois, and Iowa barred blacks from coming to the state (the restriction was rarely enforced, so there were some small populations). Some states segregated public accommodations, and Massachusetts was the only state that allowed blacks to serve on a jury. Many (not all) public schools were segregated, significantly in the cities and larger towns of New York, New Jersey, Pennsylvania, and southern Ohio. Blacks could not attend public school in southern Illinois and in Indiana (they were exempt from school tax there). Segregated schools for blacks were inferior and poorly maintained.

African Americans faced de facto segregation even where there were no discriminatory laws. Frederick Douglass spoke out against segregation in Philadelphia in 1862:

> There is not perhaps anywhere to be found a city in which prejudice against color is more rampant than in Philadelphia. Hence all the incidents of caste are to be seen there in perfection. It has its white schools and colored schools, its white churches and its colored churches, its white Christianity and its colored Christianity . . . and the line is everywhere tightly drawn between them. Colored persons, no matter how well dressed or how well behaved . . . are not even permitted to ride on any of the many railways

through that Christian city. Halls are rented with the express understanding that no person of color shall be allowed to enter. . . . The whole aspect of city usage at this point is mean, contemptible and barbarous.

Blacks could only ride on the front platform of most Philadelphia streetcars if permitted to ride at all. Reverend William Alston began campaigning against streetcar segregation in Philadelphia in 1859, but the policy continued until 1867, when it was ended by state law, not by city policy. A mass meeting called for continued agitation after Alston published a letter in the press, explaining how he had been denied boarding a streetcar with his seriously ill child. "Is it humane to exclude respectable colored citizens from your street cars, when so many of our brave and vigorous young men have been and are enlisting, to take part in this heaven-ordained slavery extermination . . . ?"

Most Washington, D.C., streetcars were also segregated. Beginning in 1863, Charles Sumner proposed amendments to the charter renewal grant of streetcar companies. When black army surgeon Major A. T. Augusta was late to court, where he was serving as a witness in a court-martial hearing in February 1864, he wrote an explanatory letter to the judge advocate:

Sir: I have the honor to report that I have been obstructed in getting to the court this morning by the conductor of car No. 32, of the Fourteenth Street line of the city railway. . . . When I attempted to enter the conductor pulled me back, and informed me that I must ride on the front with the driver . . . I told him I would not ride on the front, and he said I should not ride at all. He then ejected me. . . .

Sumner read this letter into the *Congressional Globe*. A law against streetcar segregation was passed in March 1865.

Education

See also "Education and Culture" in Chapter 2, "Antebellum America."

The South

During the Civil War, education suffered in the Confederate states much more than it did in the North, where the spiritual and cultural benefits of free schools were traditionally emphasized. A pattern of relative neglect of education had been established in the South prior to the war: there was no public school system; children of wealthy families were educated at home. After April

1861, education for Southern children became even more problematic because of shortages on the home front brought on by the Northern blockade of Confederate ports. The increasing presence of Northern armies on Southern soil was also disruptive, especially when those armies clashed with Confederate troops: most Civil War combat took place in Confederate territory.

Yet, education was offered and pursued in the South—generally, on a subscription basis. For whites who could not afford the tuition, an ad hoc barter system was employed; homespun goods or farm products could be traded for classroom instruction. Because so many white children had to help with planting and harvesting, the school year consisted of two three-month sessions—one in the summer and the other after the harvest. Nevertheless, many children of rural, nonslaveholding white families did not have time to attend classes; they were needed at home, to tend to the farm. They did not have money for books, slates, chalk, pencils, or shoes (the social stigma of sending children barefoot to school was a humiliation many whites could not face), and they lacked transportation.

Some Southern clergymen became teachers during the Civil War, but most teachers in the Confederacy were women. (This was a departure from prewar days, when work outside the home was generally considered unsuitable for women.) The pay was poor. In 1863, for example, a North Carolina teacher was paid $20 per month, plus board, to keep a schoolhouse open from 7:30 A.M. to 6 P.M. Though there was a shortage of qualified teachers, Southern white schools would not hire teachers born in the North. Many job postings specified that applicants must be "natives of the South, or some European country . . . at peace with the Southern Confederacy." When no teachers were available, children were taught at home by their mothers, if they were taught at all.

Most textbooks used in the Confederacy predated the war (McGuffey's "eclectic readers," Webster's spellers). Most of them had been published in the North, although a Confederate publishing industry did produce a number of cheaply bound books. Many Southerners felt that the predominant Northern perspective had warped schoolchildren in the decades prior to the war. There were, therefore, attempts to replace texts published in the North and written by Northerners with more acceptable Confederate texts, such as Marinda Branson Moore's *Dixie Primer* (1863). Her *Dixie Speller* (1864), pointedly left out "all Yankee phrases and allusions." Moore included the following in her geography primer: "Q. What is the present drawback to our trade? A. An unlawful Blockade by the miserable and hellish Yankee

58   CONFEDERATE SPELLING BOOK.

A soldier is a man who fights for his country.

It is the duty of every man to love his country, and to defend it bravely against its enemies.

———

Accent on the first syllable.

A mi a ble	Ab so lute ly	Fash ion a ble
fa vor a ble	ac cu ra cy	lam en ta ble
va ri a ble	ac ri mo ny	man age a ble
Me di a tor	ad mi ra ble	mat ri mo ny
rea son a ble	ad ver sa ry	pat ri mo ny
sea son a ble	al a bas ter	man da to ry
trea son a ble	al le go ry	nat u ral ly
Cu mu la tive	al li ga tor	nav i ga ble
cu li na ry	glad i a tor	pal at a ble
lu mi na ry	am i ca ble	prac ti ca ble
cu ri ous ly	ap pli ca ble	plan e ta ry
fu ri ous ly	an ti qua ry	sal u ta ry
du bi ous ly	cap il la ry	sanc tu a ry
du ti ful ly	an nu al ly	stat u a ry
ju di ca ture	car i ca ture	sal a man der
nu ga to ry	cat er pil lar	tab er na cle
nu mer a ble	char i ta ble	tran si to ry
su per a ble	hab it a ble	val u a ble

The Confederate Spelling Book, *published in Richmond, went through five editions during the war. Page fifty-eight, in the fifth edition (1865) provides a lesson in patriotism as well as spelling.*

Nation." Similarly, Professor L. Johnson's *Elementary Arithmetic* (1864) posed quiz questions such as: "If 1 Confederate soldier can whip 7 Yankees, how many soldiers can whip 49 Yankees?"

Before the war, the South was home to 260 institutions of higher learning and 3,000 private preparatory academies. Many of these were closed by the fall of 1861; most prospective (male) students had enlisted. A few of the largest institutions remained open, but male enrollment declined dramatically. Enrollment at women's colleges remained fairly steady. The largest school in the Confederacy, the University of Virginia, had 630 enrollees in 1860; sixty-six in 1861; forty-six in 1862; fifty in 1863; fifty-five in 1864. The University of North Carolina had 376 in 1860; and fifty by 1864. At all institutions of higher learning, the price of tuition, room, and board was increased, as were professors' salaries, but they could not keep pace with inflation. Many teachers doubled as custodians to make ends meet, and many students paid for tuition in unique ways. Augusta Female Seminary, in Staunton, Virginia (later, Mary Baldwin College), posted in its tuition package for September 1864: "Board $1400 or $67.50 if paid in produce at the market prices of 1860; viz, extra flour, $6; corn, 75 cents; molasses, 75 cents; wood, $2.50 per cord."

The Southerners who suffered most from lack of education were the slaves. In all Southern states except Tennessee, teaching slaves to read and write had been forbidden since well before the war. As a result, only 5 to 10 percent of the South's slave population was literate. As Union troops occupied parts of the South, education was brought to contrabands (who became known as freedmen after the Emancipation Proclamation) by the American Missionary Association (its teachers were called the Gideonites) and various "freedmen's aid" societies and black Northern churches (see Chapter 11, "Reconstruction and the Aftermath of the War"). African American Mary Chase founded the first school for contrabands in the South on September 1, 1861, in Alexandria, Virginia. Mary Peake, a free black woman, established the first school at Fortress Monroe, Virginia, two weeks later. By April 1864, the New England Freedmen's Aid Society reported 3,000 black students enrolled in Virginia. Similar efforts were made behind Federal lines in North Carolina, South Carolina, and Florida, although efforts in North Carolina were curtailed by a smallpox epidemic in 1864. An effort was also made to bring public education to black residents of New Orleans after the city fell to the Union, although wealthy blacks in the city were traditionally well educated. The New England Freedmen's Aid Society estimated that, by February 1865, 11,000 of 20,000 school-age black children were enrolled in New Orleans schools.

As the Union troops' efforts opened more of the Mississippi Valley, the freedmen's aid societies were allowed to set up schools for black pupils in Memphis, Vicksburg, Nashville, and outlying sections of Arkansas, Kentucky, Louisiana, and Tennessee. Classes were held in churches, many of which had been abandoned by the whites who fled from the Federal troops. Classes were sometimes relegated to cabins, sheds, and other "third-rate" buildings that were subject to the vicissitudes of weather, crowding, and a chronic lack of teaching materials.

Black adults also attended these schools. In 1863, a school in New Bern, North Carolina, had 160 pupils: fifty were between ages six and twelve years; ninety-five were between twelve and forty-five years; and fifteen were over forty-five years. Teachers throughout the South noted both children's and adults' eagerness to learn. Charlotte Forten, a black woman from a prominent Philadelphia abolitionist family, came to teach on the Sea Islands of South Carolina in 1862. She wrote in the *Atlantic Monthly*, in 1864:

> I never before saw children so eager to learn, although I had had several years' experience in New-England schools. Coming to school is a constant

delight and recreation to them. They come here as other children go to play. The older ones, during the summer, work in the fields from early morning until eleven or twelve o'clock, and then come into school, after their hard toil in the hot sun, so bright and as anxious to learn as ever. . . . Many of the grown people are desirous of learning to read. It is wonderful how a people who have been so long crushed to the earth, so imbruted as these have been,—and they are said to be among the most degraded negroes of the South,—can have so great a desire for knowledge, and such a capability for attaining it. One cannot believe that the haughty Anglo-Saxon race, after centuries of such an experience as these people have had, would be very much superior to them. . . .

The North

Despite logistical obstacles and the idealistic lure of the war among college-age young men, education progressed in the North during the Civil War. One of the most important educational developments in the North (and for the reunited nation after the war) was the Morrill Land Grant Act, passed by Congress in 1862. This act (also known as the Land Grant College Act), sponsored by Vermont Senator Justin Smith Morrill, set aside huge tracts of publicly owned forest, farm, and prairie land for each state, the profits from the sale of these lands were to be used to establish colleges with pragmatic curricula (scientific agriculture, mechanical arts) and affordable tuition. It was stipulated in the bill that this same benefit would accrue to any of the Confederate states that rejoined the Union. (A second Morrill Act, in 1890, set aside land to be used to establish colleges for black students.)

Before this act was passed, only a minority of Americans went to college (generally rich white males—although Oberlin College in Ohio was both coeducational and integrated). College curricula were usually based on the rarefied European system. According to the census of 1860, only 3 percent of the 397 colleges in the United States (North and South) had a department of agriculture and science. Not only did the Morrill acts expand educational opportunity, they advanced the cause of progressive agriculture and the Industrial Revolution.

Before the war, the North had traditionally been the center of lower education in the country. New England, by 1850, was a world leader in educational facilities; 95 percent of New England adults could read and write, 75 percent of the children ages five to nineteen were enrolled in school, and they attended classes six months a year. By contrast, 80 percent of the white population of the South was literate—actually, quite a high rate compared to other countries in the world at that time—but only one-third of the children were enrolled in school. As noted, slaves in the South were 90 to 95 percent illiterate because of laws forbidding them to be taught.

Free blacks in the North did have the opportunity for schooling throughout the nineteenth century, often supported by black churches, black aid and self help societies, and antislavery societies, with some public education also available. But both public and private schools were usually segregated. As early as 1793, schools were opened by African Americans in New York City and Pennsylvania. Education was considered as vital for girls as for boys, since all faced discrimination.

Education beyond primary school was not readily available to most black students. The Saint Francis Academy of Rome in Baltimore was an exception; run by black nuns educated in France, it boarded young black women from all over the country. By the end of the Civil War, it accepted young men as well. During the 1850s, several black high schools were founded, and black literary and educational societies provided supplementary education for adults.

Although Northern schools continued to use the texts they had used before the war, some propagandist texts began to appear, as they did in the Confederacy, such as the chapter titled "The Religious Character of Abraham Lincoln," in George Stillman Hillard's *Fifth Reader* (1863). More women began to teach when the men went to war. Teachers were generally paid better in the North than in the South, though there was a discrepancy based on gender. In a Pennsylvania school report for 1861, male teachers were listed as earning an average of $24.20 per month, while women received $18.11. Many of the women who taught during the Civil War were only in their mid-teens.

High schools, though not completely unknown, were uncommon. Of the 300 high schools in the United States at the outbreak of the war, one-third were in Massachusetts. In Northern areas with larger populations, a school might still be divided into different age groups, with older students receiving a broader array of subject matter. In Connecticut, for example, towns with more than 500 families established higher-level schools that offered geometry, surveying, algebra, and history for children who had completed the basics (grammar, reading, writing, arithmetic). Still larger communities brought other subjects into common schools, such as Greek or Latin, physical sciences, and natural, or "revealed," philosophy.

The Bulwark of Religion

In both the North and the South, religion was a strong factor in civilian life (see also "Religion" in Chapter 2, "Antebellum America"). Before the Civil War, differences in the social evolution of the North and the South (particularly, different views regarding slavery) had led to schisms in three major Protestant denominations: Presbyterian, Baptist, and Methodist. This was, in part, due to differing views of the church's overall responsibility in society. In the North, reform and the morals of society as a whole were considered a part of this responsibility. In the South, churches were generally considered, as Presbyterian minister James Henley Thornwell of South Carolina stated, "a spiritual body whose purposes are only the dispensation of eternal salvation, and not the creation of morality, decency and good order, which may . . . be secured without faith in the Redeemer." When war came, people of both sides called upon their churches, and the Almighty, to favor their cause and to help them defeat the enemy.

Illustrator (and dentist) Adalbert Volck lived in Union Maryland but had unreserved Confederate sympathies. Among his drawings celebrating the South is this 1863 depiction of a Southern clergyman offering the bells of his church to be melted down into ordnance.

Indeed, among the most ardent spokesmen for secession and defenders of the Confederate cause was Rev. Benjamin Palmer of New Orleans' First Presbyterian Church. Addressing departing troops, he said: "It is fitting that religion herself should with gentle voice whisper her benediction upon your flag and your cause. . . . It is a war of defense against wicked and cruel aggression, a war of civilization against a ruthless barbarism . . . a war of religion against a blind and bloody fanaticism. . . . May the Lord of Hosts be with you as a wall of fire, and shield your head in the day of battle."

The Puritan tradition, prominent in New England, influenced the way the war was presented to people in the North. In a sermon delivered at North Church, in Hartford, Connecticut, during the week after the "disaster of Bull Run," Horace Bushnell, one of the nation's most prominent pastors, depicted the North as embodying "political ideas shaped by religion . . . government was also conceived to be for the governed, just as the church was for the members; and both were God's institutes—ordinances of God . . . the only spring of authority." Bushnell then cast the South as "unreligious" and "abstract." To lift the people's morale, similar sermons, hailing the moral and religious authority of the Union cause, were delivered from the pulpits of churches all over the North.

Despite their belief that God looked with favor upon their respective causes, both sides, on the home front, grew concerned that the people would lapse, or were already lapsing, into moral degeneration and religious apathy. Soldiers away from home were subject to the evils of drink and wanton pleasures; those from rural areas were exposed for the first time to urban life. Six hundred Confederate clergymen and 2,300 in the Union were called away to minister as chaplains to the troops in the field. The various churches devoted much energy to ensuring that the troops were not without religious reading material. The U.S. Christian Commission distributed about 1.5 million Bibles, a million hymnals, and thirty-nine million tracts to Northern troops, and organized 300 portable libraries to circulate 30,000 volumes of uplifting reading matter. The Confederate Bible Society and the South Carolina Tract Society mobilized a similar, though smaller, effort for Southern troops. Periodic religious revivals were conducted among the troops of both sides, particularly in 1863 and 1864. The presence of ministers and religious reading created a buffer against the hours of tedium and loneliness and the sudden, often unpredictable, and chaotic moments of terror on the battlefield (see "Notable Special Units and Services—Chaplains" and "Army Life" in Chapter 5, "The Armies").

Religion in the Confederacy

Three-fourths of the South's white church members belonged to one of the evangelical denominations (Baptist or Methodist) that had split from its Northern counterpart in 1845 because of differing views on slavery. In almost all parts of the Confederacy, ministers favored secession and independence. (As the South faced increasing shortages, some churches even donated their bells to be recast as military hardware.) Churches suffered great losses in revenue as well as in staffing when clergy either fought in the armies or served as chaplains. (Robert E. Lee's chief of artillery and Stonewall Jackson's chief of staff were both ordained ministers, and Major General Leonidas Polk, who was killed in battle in 1864, was an Episcopal bishop.) In areas that were close to the front lines or under Union occupation, many churches curtailed their regular meetings. Some simply closed their doors as their congregations joined the growing number of refugees who left their communities as Union troops advanced. Many church buildings were damaged by their use as barracks, stables, and makeshift hospitals.

Before and during the Civil War, the repressive slave codes that covered all facets of slaves' lives extended to churchgoing as well. A sense of responsibility for slaves' moral welfare was among the reasons whites included slaves in their own congregations. The white preachers at these churches offered sermons that reinforced the slave system and the values inherent in being submissive to one's master. The slaves themselves sat, segregated, in the back or front pews, or in the balcony. Acceptable Bible texts included "Servants, obey your masters" and "Render unto Caesar the things that are Caesar's and unto God the things that are God's." Unacceptable texts included, "Ye shall know the truth and the truth shall make you free."

As the war progressed, slave codes forbidding blacks to be licensed as preachers were relaxed in areas where the shortage of white preachers was chronic. The blacks pressed into service were generally older, "respectable" gentlemen who dutifully urged all-black congregations to be meek and submissive. Where no preachers were available, planters' wives or other white women of prominence offered Bible study classes to black congregations. Sometimes, black gatherings, sanctioned by whites, were held at "praise houses" on the plantation. Black "exhorters" were allowed to preach at these sessions and, as white missionary Charles Jones wrote, were to "assist members in their Christian walk, by warnings, reproofs, and exhortations of a private nature. . . ."

When slaves were able to gather secretly for religious services—often at night, by candlelight, in slave cabins—prayers were offered for the victory of the Union, the continued health of President Lincoln, and the imminent arrival of freedom. Popular hymns included, "No Man Can Hinder Me" and "Way over in the Promised Land." Black lay preachers in the South were usually illiterate, but war correspondent George Hepworth described one slave who preached behind Union lines: "He was simply a genius—gifted far beyond most men, and needing only education to enable him to take position among those who make rather than follow public opinion. . . . I remember, too, some of his phrases: they were very beautiful, and were epic in grandeur."

President Jefferson Davis invoked God in his speeches (as did Lincoln) and, periodically during the war, he decreed days of fasting and of prayer for a Confederate victory. What the Confederate government failed to provide in the way of social aid was partially replaced by efforts of churches and affiliated religious charities. In Vicksburg, Montgomery, Augusta, and Richmond, Jewish congregations were among those that donated money to support families of departed soldiers.

Religion in the North

Northern civilians came to believe that they possessed the moral and spiritual high ground in the Civil War. In the early stages of the war, most Northern preachers stressed preservation of the Union. "It is not an antislavery war we wage," Reverend A. L. Stone of Boston's Park Street Church sermonized on April 21, 1861, "not a sectional war; not a war of conquest and subjugation; it is simply and solely a war for the maintenance of Government and the Constitution." By 1863, however, the gradual recasting of the war's aims had given the abolition of slavery a high priority and added to the conviction that the Union was right. (President Lincoln's Emancipation Proclamation, drafted in 1862, was implemented on January 1, 1863.) Much of the groundwork that made abolition a war aim was laid by Northern religious leaders, many of whom were involved in the abolitionist movement, and by principled commentators such as Frederick Douglass, whose eloquent speeches and widely read articles pricked the nation's conscience. The abolitionists were a distinct minority in the North and were barely tolerated by many Northerners, but the religious fervor of their message could not fail to color public discourse.

The stridency of abolitionist religious leaders was an undertone to the more moderating appeals of people like Ralph Waldo Emerson, who believed the war offered a chance to "redeem America for all its sinful years since the century began," and Henry James Sr., who saw the war as a redemptive moment and a "sacred responsibility," a "crisis to which that of our national birth or independence yields in dignity and importance, as much as body yields to soul, flesh to spirit, childhood to manhood."

Arguably, the most respected and influential religious leader in the North was Henry Ward Beecher (1813–1887), the "Great Preacher" whose sermons and lectures were syndicated in newspapers throughout the country. Beecher justified the war from his pulpit: "[W]hen the end is right, and when the inspiration is just and humane, then wars are just, provided they are the last resort."

The celebration of Thanksgiving as a national holiday of the United States began during the Civil War. A remarkable woman of the North, Sarah Josepha Hale, a writer and longtime editor of the popular magazine, *Godey's Lady's Book*, had been advocating a day of national thanksgiving—based on the Pilgrims' Thanksgiving celebration—for many years. The tumult of war and the deep belief, widespread in the United States, that progress on the battlefield did not stem from human offices alone, helped gain renewed support for the idea. On October 3, 1863, Abraham Lincoln issued a "Proclamation of Thanksgiving" that established Thanksgiving Day. It read, in part:

> ... In the midst of a civil war of unequaled magnitude and severity, which has sometimes seemed to foreign States to invite and to provoke their aggression, peace has been preserved with all nations, order has been maintained, the laws have been respected and obeyed, and harmony has prevailed everywhere except in the theatre of military conflict; while that theatre has been greatly contracted by the advancing armies and navies of the Union. ... No human counsel hath devised nor hath any mortal hand worked out these great things. They are the gracious gifts of the Most High God, who, while dealing with us in anger for our sins, hath nevertheless remembered mercy. ... I do therefore invite my fellow citizens in every part of the United States, and also those who are at sea and those who are sojourning in foreign lands, to set apart and observe the last Thursday of November next, as a day of Thanksgiving and Praise to our beneficent Father who dwelleth in the Heavens. And I recommend to them that ... they do also, with humble penitence for our national perverseness and disobedience,

commend to His tender care all those who have become widows, orphans, mourners or sufferers in the lamentable civil strife in which we are unavoidably engaged, and fervently implore the interposition of the Almighty Hand to heal the wounds of the nation and to restore it as soon as may be consistent with the Divine purposes to the full enjoyment of peace, harmony, tranquillity and Union.

Recruitment of Soldiers

Even though Southerners initially believed the North would offer little, if any, effective objection to secession, men began to arm and drill almost immediately after their states passed secession ordinances. At the same time, in the North, many believed that the South could not possibly stand up against the United States for long. At the outset of the conflict, then, recruitment for both sides was driven not only by the often-cited desire for honor and glory, but also by the thought that the cachet of military service could be obtained with minimal effort and personal risk.

At first, there was no formal system for recruiting; in Detroit, a newspaper reported that "everybody eagerly asks everybody else if he's going to enlist." Preachers, many of whom enlisted as either chaplains or common soldiers, drummed up support from their pulpits. One Minnesota teacher—a nineteen-year-old boy—shut down operations in his one-room schoolhouse and took his older students to enlist along with him. Although the faculty and administrators of many colleges were hesitant about the war effort, others urged their students to enlist. Some, such as President Charles Hovey of Illinois State Normal College, enlisted, themselves, and became officers. With such a vast enthusiasm for the cause in both the North and the South, there was little need for intensive recruiting; in fact, early in the war, there were *too many* volunteers. The governor of Ohio, for example, wrote to Lincoln to apologize for the fact that he was going to be forced to provide five more regiments than had been requested.

Most units, both North and South, were established in a similar manner. A community leader, usually a wealthy one, would be asked by the state government to raise a regiment in return for a colonelcy. These men would then recruit their friends, promising them that they would be made captains if they could raise their own companies. Then the prospective officers would travel the area, encouraging and persuading men until they had the full complement of a company. They used mass meetings, newspaper advertisements, broadsides, and pamphlets to spread the word. After a few men enlisted, they

THE
UNION
MUST BE PRESERVED!

The citizens of Reading are hereby invited to meet at

LYCEUM HALL
TO-MORROW, THURSDAY,

AT 6 O'CLOCK, P. M.,

To make such arrangements as may seem necessary to raise our proportion of Volunteers.

☞ We earnestly invite all who are in favor of preserving the Union to come.

☞ THE MEN ARE WANTED, AND THEY ARE WANTED NOW, AND IF THEY WILL NOT VOLUNTEER THEY MUST BE DRAFTED.

J. B. LEATHE, ⎞ Selectmen
J. S. CAMBELL, ⎬ of
S. A. PARKER, ⎠ Reading.

READING, JULY 9, 1862.

From F. A. Searle's Steam Job Printing Rooms, Journal Building, 118 Washington St, Boston.

In this 1862 Union recruiting poster, the men of Reading, Massachusetts, are warned that if sufficient forces don't volunteer now, they'll have to be drafted later.

began to recruit among their friends as well. At first, this was a simple matter; within a year of the war's start, however, volunteers became scarce and a system of inducements was put in place. These were both positive—in the form of monetary bounties—and negative—through government threats of a draft system.

Recruitment drives were competitive; towns vied against each other to see which could provide the most soldiers. Shame was a powerful weapon on the side of the recruiters. Pressure could be intense, especially when local papers ran sketches of those who had opted not to enlist and added symbols like white feathers, designating them as cowards. Women—wives, sweethearts, and mothers—also promoted enlistment. Kate Cumming, a nurse with the Confederate Army of Tennessee, wrote that "a man did not deserve the name of man if he did not fight for his country." Many women withheld their favors if their young men had not enlisted. In Richmond, a clerk noted in 1861, "Ladies are postponing all engagements until their lovers have fought the Yankees." Some older women simply refused to talk to their male friends who declined to enter the army. An able young man who did not sign up might expect to receive a package containing a bonnet, a petticoat, or other articles of female apparel.

As the war went on, anticipation of adventure and excitement faded before the reality of battle. There were still reasons to enlist, however. Soldiers in both the North and the South felt a patriotic pride in their respective causes. Those in blue fought to preserve the Union and, secondarily, to end slavery. Those in gray were intent on preserving the political independence and way of life of the South. A volunteer from Philadelphia wrote that "this contest is not the North against South. It is government against anarchy, law against disorder." A Michigan farmer who enlisted believed: "The Government must be sustained . . . if the union is split up the government is distroid and we will be a [ruined] nation." Fewer volunteers declared they were entering the war to achieve emancipation for the slaves, but some did. "Slavery has brought death into our own households already in its wicked rebellion," wrote a Massachusetts officer. "There is but one way [to win the war] and that is emancipation. . . . I want to sing 'John Brown' in the streets of Charleston, and ram red-hot abolitionism down their unwilling throats at the point of the bayonet."

White Southerners felt that they were fighting for their freedom from Northern domination. Edward Porter Alexander, a Georgian stationed with the U.S. Army in Washington Territory, wrote to his sister in 1860: "We suppose from the latest news we have that Lincoln is elected, and if so I *hope* and *expect* to be called in to help secede. . . . I believe the interests of humanity, civilization, and self-preservation call on the South to secede, and I'll go my arm, leg, or death on it." (Alexander became a Confederate brigadier general.) A Tennessee farmer felt that "any man in the South would rather die battling for civil and political liberty, than submit to the base usurpations of a northern tyrant." And a soldier in a Virginia regiment wrote to his wife, "If we should suffer ourselves to be subjugated by the tyrannical government of the North our property would all be confuscated . . . & our people reduced to the most abject bondage & utter degradation."

Volunteers were also called by honor to serve their country. A Confederate sergeant wrote to his wife in 1864, "I want this war to end and to be at home as bad as anybody can, but I do not believe I could enjoy myself at home in such times as these if I was able to do duty. Others would be fighting for their Country and My Country and home while I would be skulking my duty, and it would render me miserable." A Kentucky doctor who joined the Union forces told his sister, "I know no reason why I should not be as subject to duty as any man, as I have had the protection of government all my life. . . . My absence from home is, of course, a source of grief . . . but an all-absorbing, all-engrossing sense of duty, alike to country and family, impelled me."

For poorer men, and farmers fallen on hard times, joining the armed forces could also be the only way to make a living. "It seemed as if I were compelled to go in order to get out of debt," a Wisconsin man wrote his parents from the front. The need for money attracted some men to the U.S. Navy, which included, in some of its recruiting posters, promises of "chances for warrants, bounties and Medals of Honor," "$1.50 extra per month to all, Grog Money," and a share in prize money (from captured ships and contraband cargo). After conscription legislation was passed (April 1862, in the South; March 1863, in the North), there was also the fear of conscription. A draftee's life was harder than a volunteer's and was considered more shameful. A Northern recruit confided to his diary that "it is better by far to enlist voluntarily than to be dragged into the army as a conscript. Nothing to me would appear more degrading."

The recruitment of African American soldiers began in earnest after the Emancipation Proclamation (January 1, 1863). The governor of Massachusetts asked several prominent black leaders, including Frederick Douglass and Henry Highland Garnet, to lead the recruiting effort, and, in response, the men traveled across the North and even into Canada, making speeches and writing newspaper editorials which called upon free black men to enlist. Many African Americans did rush to defend their country, but because blacks were not permitted to be officers and their treatment if captured was known to be savage, finding men to enlist could be difficult. Many blacks also asked why they had not been welcomed into the army in 1861. The recruiters, however, motivated black men to join up by reminding them of the horrors of slavery and appealing to their racial pride. Henry Turner cried out to naysayers: "Those who have been taught by a God-blessed experience to abhor the monster slavery, and have felt its inhuman crushings, will look from a different standpoint . . . show us a chance to climb to distinction, and we will show the world by our bravery what the negro can do; and then as soon as we are invited to stand on such a basis as will develop these interior qualities, for us to deride the idea and scornfully turn away, would be to argue a self-consciousness of incapacity." In Philadelphia, men were encouraged by the newspapers: "Go with the view that you will return freemen. And if you should never return, you will die with the satisfaction of knowing that you . . . have assisted in giving liberty to our race in the land of our birth."

Although the Union had to employ enlistment bounties, conscription, and its formerly scorned black citizens, it never had the manpower problems that plagued the South. The Confederacy began the conflict with a smaller population, and, later in the war, as the likelihood of defeat increased, it was harder and harder to keep the ranks full. Some even proposed recruiting slaves into the fighting ranks, and legislation to that effect was finally passed in 1865—too late to have any effect on the war. Increasingly, too, women feared the loss of loved ones and spoke out against the war. One South Carolina woman stated, "I do not approve of this thing. What do I care for patriotism? My husband is my country. What is country to me if he be killed?" Some women worked assiduously to keep their husbands out of the service.

These women, far from pushing their men into the war, actively encouraged them *not* to enlist, or, if they were already in the army, to leave their posts. A North Carolina woman wrote her soldier husband as early as 1862: "I think you have done your share in this war." Other women begged their husbands to hire replacements, to find jobs that would keep them ineligible for the draft, or even to desert. Mary Chichester wrote to her son, a prisoner of war in the North, that she hoped, when he was finally exchanged and released, "that you will think, the time past has sufficed for *public* service, & that your own family require y[ou]r protection & help—as others are deciding." That last phrase was an ominous comment on the state of the Confederate army.

Increasing numbers of men deserted to bring some relief to wives incapable of doing all the work of a farm or plantation—and because they feared for their family's safety as Northern armies occupied more and more Southern land. Although a soldier's own desires also played a role, a Confederate official stated angrily that "desertion takes place because desertion is encouraged. And the ladies . . . are responsible . . . for the desertion in the army."

Many Southern women, however, actively supported military duty until the end. In 1864, the mother of William Mason Smith objected to his delight in receiving sick leave: "I am sure the Board was right not to send you back to the field, but you are wrong in the idea that their action makes you 'a free man.' You are *bound* by the duties of your position, & can only be 'free' when you conscientiously perform them. . .[Y]our time belongs to your Country & not to your pleasures . . . I hope you will not need the whole 60 days."

There were Northern wives, as well, who urged their husbands to come home. One wrote to her husband, serving in a New Jersey regiment, "Dear husband, come home. Get your discharge [for a sore foot]. . . . If you will give one of the doctors a couple of dollars you can be home here with us." Such sentiments caused the colonel of a Wisconsin regiment to protest that letters of "complaints, and whinings, asking him to 'come home,' etc., has more to do with creating discouragement and finally sickness and disease than the hardships he has to endure."

Despite the discouragements of a long war, growing pressures from home, and the attrition of their regiments from combat deaths, injuries, and illness, many Confederate and Union soldiers were determined to stay on duty until their cause was won. In 1864—a difficult year in which Union forces in the Eastern Theater lost 65,000 men killed, wounded, or missing during the six-week Overland Campaign, alone—more than half of all Union soldiers who had completed their term of service, some 136,000 men, reenlisted.

Conscientious Objectors

See also "Army Life" in Chapter 5, "The Armies."

As the early fervor in support of the war waned on both sides, there was increased pressure on young men of the North and the South to enlist in state militias and volunteer regiments. In April 1862—after major Confederate defeats in the Western Theater of Operations, and as Major General George B. McClellan and more than 100,000 Federal troops were beginning the Peninsula Campaign aimed at Richmond—the Confederacy instituted conscription. On March 3, 1863, the United States followed suit. Conscription was not a popular measure in the general population. For members of pacifist religious groups, it posed a particularly difficult dilemma.

There had been nonviolent religious groups in America from Colonial times; but the scope of the Civil War brought the question of conscientious objection to widespread debate for the first time. The tenets of the Quakers (or Society of Friends), Mennonites, Dunkards (or Tunkers), Shakers, Amana Society, Schwenkfelder Church, Christadelphians, Rogerines, and similar religious groups required that their adherents oppose war. During the Indiana Yearly Meeting, September 29 to October 2, 1862, for example (only two weeks after the war's costliest one-day battle, at Antietam, Maryland, September 17), Quakers advised all members of their meeting ". . . against giving countenance, or assistance, by our conversation, conduct, or property, to the shedding of human blood."

"Property" included money, and for many conscientious objectors even the payment of wartime taxes posed a moral dilemma—although within the pacifist sects, opinions on the matter were far from unanimous. When Quaker Joshua Maule refused to pay 8.5 percent of his assessed tax (the percentage designated for war expenditures) in 1861, other Quakers disagreed with his decision. Yet, many Quaker committees, formed to make recommendations about taxation, decided that people should pay normal taxes but without those specifically intended for war, as Maule had done. On occasion, when objectors withheld tax money or fines, their property was frozen or seized by the government.

Throughout the war, members of pacifist religious groups negotiated with state government officials and with Confederate and United States military and government figures, often emphasizing their support for their region, as well as their firm belief in nonviolence. As the war lengthened, and army manpower requirements grew larger, the pressure on pacifists, in both the North and the South, increased. An 1862 Quaker petition to the government of North Carolina protested the drafting of Quakers—and compared their own situation to that of Friends in the North:

> Your petitioners respectfully show that it is one of our fundamental religious principles to bear a faithful testimony against all wars and fightings, and that in consequence we cannot aid in carrying on any carnal war. We may further show that, according to the best information we can obtain,

until the present time, Friends of North-Carolina have not been called on to aid in the battle-field or military camp; but now our peaceful principles are in a measure disregarded, and many of our members are drafted to take part in the conflicting armies, while we understand our brethren in the United States are not.

The conscription laws passed in each region allowed exemptions from the draft for men in certain occupations, but no exemption specifically for conscientious objectors was initially included in either law. With the greater danger to their members presented by these comprehensive draft laws, pacifist groups more urgently petitioned government officials, requesting exemptions from military service based on their religious beliefs. In October 1862, the Confederate Congress passed an act specifically exempting Friends (Quakers), Nazarenes, Mennonites, and Dunkards from military service, *if* they supplied a substitute or paid a $500 tax. On February 24, 1864, the United States Congress amended the Union's conscription law to allow men who supplied satisfactory evidence of conscientious scruples against bearing arms to serve on hospital duty or care for freedmen rather than serve in combat units; alternatively, Northern conscientious objectors could pay a $300 tax that would be used for "the benefit of the sick and wounded soldiers." Northern draftees could also pay a substitute to serve for them. Substitution was no answer for most pacifists, however. Many believed that paying other people to fight was tantamount to fighting, themselves. (Substitution became so unpopular in the South that it was ended in December 1863; it continued in the North.)

Neither state exemption laws nor the exemption provisions enacted by the Confederate and United States Congresses provided perfect solutions to the dilemma faced by conscientious objectors. Members of nonviolent religious groups were still drafted (in the South, as war pressures increased, the granting of conscientious objector exemptions became very rare). To assist their drafted religious brethren, members of nonviolent religious groups who remained on the home front appealed, in writing and in person, to government and military officials. Members of the Society of Friends pooled money to pay exemption taxes on behalf of Quakers and other conscientious objectors who were unable to raise the money themselves. Quaker John B. Crenshaw, a member of the Baltimore Yearly Meeting, but a resident of Richmond, Virginia, throughout the war, recorded some of these activities in his diary:

10/20/62 . . . When we were at the War Office met some of the Va. Dunkards who have been brought on here as Conscripts, some of whom already paid Five hundred Dollars into the State Treasury under the State Exemption Law. When we went back to Camp Lee, at their request, I drew up a petition to the Sec. Of War asking that those who had so paid in might be excused and allowed to return home until the Legislature meets again, at which time they hope to be allowed to draw the amount from the State Treasury to pay the Confederate Treasury.

4/18/63 I was in Richmond today attending to some business. Got a release for Wm. Osborne, heard that C. H. Robinson's (Dunkard) application was refused but they offer a detail to Hospitals.

2/1/65 I went with David Moffit before the Secretary of the Navy and secured the release of his son from the Confederate States Navy.

Pacifist religious groups also published pamphlets (such as *Nonresistance, the Patience and the Faith of the Saints,* written by William Thurber, a conscript in the Confederate army from Charlottesville, Virginia) that explained their beliefs and petitioned for their accommodation. Journals published by the various groups reported on the status of conscientious objectors. They also published notices seeking information to help reunite families that had been torn apart because of conflicts between secular law and religious belief. This notice appeared in the *Friends Review* during the war:

Mitchel M. Rogers, who was a conscript in the rebel army, in North Carolina, and has escaped to Ohio, is anxious to find his wife, Amy Rogers, and their six children, who, he supposes, have come North, and are in one of the Western States. Information of them will be gratefully received if addressed to Jonathan Bailey, Wilmington, Clinton County, Ohio.

Quaker publications also included suggestions for how young Friends should act in the event of being drafted or arrested for refusal to submit, for example: "It is advised that some prudent and judicious Friend should accompany the person in his appearance before the Board of Enrollment," and "Should a Friend be arrested and sent to a Military post for trial by a court-martial, his case should be promptly attended to by Friends of the Meeting to which he belongs."

Some members of nonviolent religious groups did serve in combat units, by choice or under the duress of a large fine or their threatened arrest. "It is not correct that *many* Friends have thus acted in this time of trial," *The Friend* editorialized on February 6, 1864. "On the contrary such are comparatively few." The Quakers typically forgave those members who seemed to enter the war under duress, but those who fought actively and "felt justified on patriotic or other grounds were generally 'disowned' by their local Meeting."

Volunteer Aid Societies

Within two weeks of the outbreak of the Civil War, some 20,000 local aid societies formed to support the war effort in both the North and the South, although many did not last for the duration of the conflict. These societies were primarily organized and operated by women volunteers who sewed, cooked, knitted, and raised funds for soldiers and refugees.

In the Confederacy, relief and soldiers' aid societies rarely supplied troops who did not come from their own state or locality. This reflection of the states' rights viewpoint—and of the unease in surrendering to national authority—characterized the population of the Confederate states. Private funds and donations of supplies to supplement government efforts were especially necessary in the Southern states, which had neither the industrial base nor the war budget of the North. Many aid societies were forced to disband, however, as the war disrupted the population, and shortages plagued the resource-strapped South.

In the North, as early as April 29, 1861, 3,000 people met at Cooper Union, in New York City, to form the Women's Central Association for Relief, the precursor of the Sanitary Commission, to coordinate the efforts of many smaller groups. (After the Sanitary Commission itself was established, men ran the commission's national office and served as paid agents, but the vast majority of volunteers were women.) Seven thousand auxiliaries collected supplies and held Sanitary Fairs to raise funds to support the direct medical aid provided at battlefields and hospitals (see Chapter 9, "Medical Care and Medicine"). The Northwest Sanitary Commission Fair, held in Chicago in 1863, lasted two weeks and raised $100,000. Organized and led by Mary Livermore, Jane Hoge, and Eliza Porter, the fair drew thousands of contributions of items to sell and was a noted model for subsequent fairs in other Northern cities.

Sanitary Commission members and other Northern volunteers operated "refreshment saloons" that offered meals and accommodations to soldiers who were on leave or had been released from hospitals and were returning to camp. In the South, similar "wayside homes" were operated by volunteer aid societies. In both the Union and the Confederacy, local groups aided prisoners of war. Other activities included sewing and knitting. Groups usually worked together in private homes, churches, or public meeting places. Farm women raised and donated food. Thus, the society of Center Ridge, Alabama, in only one month of 1862, was able to supply "422 shirts, 551 pairs of drawers, 80 pairs of socks, 3 pairs of gloves, 6 boxes and a bale of hospital stores, 128 pounds of tapioca and $18 for hospital use."

When black men were finally accepted into the Union army, black soldiers' aid societies quickly formed. Organized by free blacks in the North and Southern blacks where the Union army occupied parts of the South, these societies helped soldiers and their families, provided nursing services, sent food and supplies to military units, wrote letters for those who could not write, sewed clothing, and engaged in fundraising. Black women also sewed or raised money to buy U.S. flags and regimental banners to present to black regiments. White women sewed flags as well—one Northern woman who thought an American flag should fly "on every inch of American soil" said she would make them all if the cloth was provided. The Confederate flag was new (three versions were used during the war), so there was a demand for volunteers to create these, as well as state and regimental flags, in the South. Women presented these flags in elaborate ceremonies to honor and support the troops.

The aid societies often focused on soldiers, but some were formed to help black refugees, contrabands, and, later, freedmen fleeing from the war. Elizabeth Keckley, a former slave who became Mary Todd Lincoln's seamstress, was a key figure in founding the Contraband Relief Association (later called the Ladies' Freedmen and Soldiers' Relief Association) in Washington, D.C., in August 1862. Keckley said the association "was formed for the purpose, not only of relieving the wants of those destitute people, but also to sympathize with, and advise them." In 1863, she appealed to free and wealthy blacks in the *Christian Recorder:* "If the white people can give festivals to raise funds for the relief of suffering soldiers, why should not the well-to-do colored people go to work to do something for the benefit of the suffering blacks." Many of these African American aid groups were independent of white organizations, but some blacks did form auxiliaries of national freedmen's relief organizations or joined integrated groups such as the American Freedmen's Aid Commission and the National Association for the Relief of Destitute Colored Women and Children.

Fundraising formed a significant part of volunteer aid activities. Fairs, bazaars, raffles, benefit performances, concerts given by well-known figures such as African American singer Elizabeth Taylor Greenfield (the "Black

Swan"), and other entertainments—including *tableaux vivantes* (in which women in costume posed in living "still-life scenes" based on historical or classical themes) and dramatic readings—proliferated in the North and the South. Fairs were held even in areas of the South that were beset by invasion. In Columbia, South Carolina, just weeks before it was conquered during Sherman's advance, a bazaar featured booths named for each Confederate state. As an observer wrote, "To go there one would scarce believe it was war times, the tables were loaded with fancy articles—brought through the blockade, or manufactured by the ladies."

Some fundraising drives had specific goals. For example, because the Confederacy began the war with no navy, some Southern port cities were particularly vulnerable. Concerned about their defense, women in those cities organized gunboat concerts, gunboat raffles, and gunboat fairs. (The *Charleston Mercury* called them "all the rage.") Through these activities, Southern women were able to pay for three ironclad gunboats. In the North, the Ladies' Union Bazaar Association focused on raising money to rebuild a black orphanage destroyed during the 1863 draft riots in New York.

Women on the Home Front

A struggle of the magnitude of the Civil War necessarily altered the traditional roles for all women on the home front. The sudden disappearance of thousands of men in uniform—and, for many women, the permanent loss or physical or mental debilitation of husbands, fathers, or brothers—required adjustments of varying magnitude. For many middle-class and upper-class white women in the North, the war had a liberating effect; their rewards were self-reliance and resourcefulness. Many formerly traditional housewives became zealously involved in organizations like the U.S. Sanitary Commission and the Freedmen's Aid Bureau. In both the North and the South, women were the main force behind efforts that involved voluntary aid. But the vast majority of women, black and white, in the North and the South, had little choice but to absorb the hardships caused by the war, struggle to raise their families, and, in many cases, simply survive the war.

Women in the Confederacy

In general, black and white women in the Confederate states had a much more difficult time than most Northern women. Most of the war was fought on Southern ground, the economy was devastated by the demands of war, and disruption and shortages plagued even the formerly wealthy. Class and race determined the severity of the impact.

Southern women, often using pen names, described their thoughts and experiences in publications.

- Constance Cary wrote a regular column, "Blockade Correspondence," for the *Southern Illustrated News*, in which the Confederate sympathizer "Secessia," living in Baltimore, and the Richmond refugee "Refugitta" discussed life in their respective communities. She also published stories, poems, and articles in other periodicals.
- Mary Webster Loughborough published *My Cave Life in Vicksburg* anonymously in 1864. A Northern reviewer said of this moving account that he had not "met a more interesting book on the war."
- Elizabeth Avery Meriwether, a refugee in Tuscaloosa, Alabama, won $500 in a contest sponsored by the Jackson *Mississippian*, for "The Refugee," a story based on her own experience.
- Marie Ravenel de la Coste wrote the lyrics to a well-known Confederate song, "Somebody's Darling," drawing on her observations in Confederate hospitals.

Through correspondence and diaries, like the ones kept by Confederate army nurse Kate Cumming and political hostess Mary Boykin Chesnut (see "Notable Home Front Figures," on page 726), often published after the war, other Southern women recorded their thoughts and feelings.

Many white women in the South were forced to work because of increasing inflation, the destruction of their homes and property, or the Confederacy's need for them in the workforce. On assembly lines at ordnance plants, they made minié balls, cartridges, fuses, percussion caps, and artillery shells. Wages at a Memphis plant in 1862 were $4.50 a week for adult women, $3 for girls. At an Augusta, Georgia, textile plant in 1863, the pay was $8 to $10 a week—less than men made, and worth little because of inflation. In 1863, women working in a Richmond arsenal were so desperate that they went on strike for more pay—an unusual occurrence in the South. Those who worked in arsenals were subject to the danger of explosions; for example, forty women died in an explosion at the Confederate States Laboratory in Richmond.

Women also worked as seamstresses in the South. By 1864, there were 4,000 women paid to sew clothing for Confederate soldiers. Some Southern women who needed an income but refused to work outside the home (they saw that as inappropriate behavior) took in sewing for other families, cooked meals, or made soap for sale. Some Southern women were spies, couriers, guides, and smugglers. Notable among them were Belle Boyd, who provided valuable information to Stonewall Jackson during his 1862 Valley Campaign, and prewar Washington hostess Rose O'Neal Greenhow. The outspoken Mrs. Eugenia Phillips of Alabama, who was living in Washington when the Civil War began, was suspected of being a spy. Twice imprisoned, she wrote, upon one arrest, "This day has ushered in a new era . . . one which marks the arrest and imprisonment of women for political opinions" (see also "Shadow Warriors: Partisan Rangers, Guerrillas, and Spies" in Chapter 5, "The Armies").

To support themselves and their families, some Southern women became teachers. Teaching was considered a respectable job for a woman. Before the war, however, affluent white women rarely worked outside the home. During the war, in addition to economic hardships, a shortage of male teachers and a desire to replace the Northern women teachers who had been working in the South drew even "well-bred" women into the profession. For example, in 1859, 7.5 percent of the public school teachers in North Carolina were women; by 1863, the number had jumped to 40 percent. Some women entered teaching with reluctance. One Louisiana woman felt she "would rather die" first, and proclaimed: "Teaching before dependence, death before teaching." She did begin teaching so that she would not be forced to accept charity.

Women served in government offices—primarily in the Post Office, the War Office, and the Confederate Treasury Department, where they numbered and signed paper currency. Sometimes, to get these jobs, they had to prove that they were impoverished. Judith McGuire, wife of a Confederate minister and civil servant, felt that simply applying proved that the need was obvious: "No lady would ever bind herself to keep accounts for six hours a day without dire necessity." Women filled positions as matrons and nurses in hospitals (see Chapter 9, "Medical Care and Medicine"). White women from middle- and upper-class families drew attention and created controversy by filling traditionally male roles, but many black (slave and free) and poor white women performed menial work in hospitals and attended to wounded soldiers without public recognition.

Away from the cities, women ran plantations and farms. Many plantation masters departed to help the war effort and left the white mistresses, who often felt vulnerable, to manage the land. Their degrees of success varied. But the majority of women who remained on plantations were slaves, and, unlike their white mistresses, they had always shouldered an equal share of the work. Some now had increased responsibilities and learned lessons in self-reliance and leadership that would carry over to the adjustment of emancipation. Other slaves, men and women, became what historians have called a "fifth column." They weakened the resolve of the Confederacy, disrupted work schedules, and organized stoppages and strikes in the fields. Some simply left the plantations and joined other contrabands behind Union lines.

The wives and daughters of white yeoman farmers were forced to eke out a living on the small plot of land left to them. The majority of Southern white women were in this situation, and life was usually much harder for them than for abandoned plantation mistresses or women who found work in the cities. They often had large families—including elderly members—to support, and they scarcely had a moment of leisure. After the household was asleep, many of these women stayed up late into the night, weaving, sewing, and knitting, to have something to trade for essential goods, because Confederate currency was increasingly worthless. The crops they raised were subject to impressment by the Confederate army, and the burden on them was proportionately greater than on the women of large landowning families.

The bitterness that had already begun to penetrate the Confederate home front by late 1862 spread, especially among poor white women whose breadwinners were fighting for a government that seemingly let its citizens suffer at the hands of profiteers. Accrued debts sometimes led to the profiteers taking a family's small plot of farmland, forcing farm women into even more desperate circumstances as refugees. A North Carolina mother of four, whose husband was at the front, wrote to Governor Zebulon B. Vance in 1863, after merchants had repeatedly refused to take her Confederate currency: "I have one nag and seven hed of hogs and I am nerly out of corn and I have bin walking the laste five dayes and have not got eny yet." A wife of a departed soldier wrote to the North Carolina governor, "I think that is to hard to take a poor man from his wife and children to leave her to perish to death when we go to these rich people but hear they wont let us have not one pound of meal for less than 50 cents."

Despite these hardships, devotion to the Confederate cause generally remained strong, even among women living in areas occupied by the Union army. "We are all loyal—we are very peculiarly situated and no people would do even as well as we do in the midst of the enemy," wrote Susan Emiline Jeffords Caldwell of Warrenton, Virginia. "We keep *true* to the South amid all our sore trials—and at times are to be pitied. To have the enemy around you and come in and take your horses, your meat, corn & wheat at their pleasure and compelled to submit quietly."

In 1864, Southerner Lucy Otey noted "the energetic and persevering efforts of *Southern Women* who can never faint or tire, in animating and sustaining the brave Soldiery of this Confederacy, while struggling for our Independence! . . . there are loving hearts and busy hands *at home*—praying and toiling, for their preservation and success."

As the war neared its end in 1865, many Southern women feared the consequences of a Union victory. "I want peace but I don't want to go back into the *union*," Susan Caldwell wrote in March. "I want *Independence* and nothing else—I could not consent to go back with a people who have been bent on exterminating us." Emma Holmes of South Carolina summed up her feelings in April: "To go back into the Union!!! No words can describe all the horrors contained in those few words. . . . We could not, we would not believe it. Our Southern blood rose in stronger rebellion than ever and we all determined that, if obliged to submit, never could they *subdue* us."

Women in the Union

For the vast majority of Northern women, the war was not literally at their doorstep, but their lives, too, were altered by the conflict. The impact varied from place to place and often depended on income and class. More women in the North than in the South had worked outside the home before the war. In 1860, 258,000 women were working in Northern factories—more than 135,000 of them in New England. In the Confederacy when the war began, only 12,000 women worked in manufacturing.

The Civil War created more than 100,000 new jobs for Northern women, who were called upon to replace men who had left for the army and to fill wartime needs. They worked in factories and as seamstresses in "sewing rooms," making uniforms, blankets, and tents for the troops. Like their Southern counterparts, they also worked in arsenals, and dozens died in explosions, including nineteen women at the Washington Arsenal (see "Civil War Sculpture" in Chapter 12, "The Civil War in Literature and the Arts"). Women in the North staged several protests and strikes about low wages and unhealthy conditions. Women who were sewing soldiers' uniforms at the Schuykill Arsenal in Philadelphia protested to Secretary of War Edwin Stanton when an order came down to fire any women who were not relatives of soldiers. Poorly paid seamstresses in New York who were often replaced by other desperate women when they were let go for striking, organized the Workingwomen's Protective Union to improve working conditions.

Women joined the burgeoning Federal bureaucracy as "government girls" in Washington, D.C. Clara Barton and others had worked in the Patent Office in the 1850s—the first women to breach this male domain—but they were let go before the war began. U.S. Treasurer Francis Spinner was the first government official to employ women in wartime; he hired women as clerks, copyists, and currency counters in 1861. By 1865, 447 women were working

Men and women volunteers—and some of the amputee veteran soldiers they are assisting—pose in front of the headquarters of the U.S. Christian Commission in Washington, D. C. Photograph by Mathew Brady studios, circa 1863.

in the Treasury Department. The U.S. Post Office employed postmistresses. (Abraham Lincoln particularly encouraged the hiring of war widows for the task.) Women also served in the War Department (in the Quartermaster General's Office), the Interior Department, and, later, the Freedmen's Bureau. Their jobs as civil servants caused controversy; although the attitude was less prevalent in the North than in the South, there was a perception that such work was inappropriate and unladylike, and government girls' morals were sometimes suspected. They were paid less than men, and it was thought that men would assume their jobs when the war ended. However, women continued to work in the government after 1865, while still earning only half the pay that men earned. Their salaries were not raised for twenty years.

The number of Northern women who became teachers increased markedly during the conflict. As men left for the battlefield, women became more accepted in the profession. A significant number of these new teachers were teenagers who had to work to help support their families. White and free black women in the North went south with the American Missionary Society and similar groups to teach contrabands and freedmen.

White women served as hospital matrons and nurses (see Chapter 9, "Medical Care and Medicine") and, after January 1864, by order of the U.S. War Department, black women were hired as hospital cooks and nurses. Black, as well as white, women also traveled with Union troops as laundresses or manual laborers; among them were contrabands who had escaped slavery and taken refuge behind Union lines. Among the Northern women who served the Union as spies and informers were: Elizabeth Van Lew, who lived in Richmond throughout the war, and Pauline Cushman, who was sentenced to be executed in the South but was rescued by Union troops. Alvira Smith, an Alabama Unionist, served as a scout and courier (see also "Shadow Warriors: Partisan Rangers, Guerrillas, and Spies" in Chapter 5, "The Armies").

Black and white Northern women ran farms and grew crops, as did women in the Confederacy. Some Northern women were impoverished by inflation, in cities and in rural areas (though many fewer than in the South), and by the loss of male support. Some soldiers' wives and widows lived without adequate income, and the promised government benefits were slow to arrive. The wives of black soldiers in the Union Army were particularly hard hit. Black soldiers were paid less than white troops (although most had enlisted with the understanding that they would receive the same pay), and they were often paid late, so the money they sent home was insufficient for their families. One U.S. soldier stationed in Florida wrote:

Women are prominently featured in this woodcut captioned Filling Cartridges at the United States Arsenal at Watertown, Massachusetts, *from* Harper's Weekly, *July 20, 1861. As the war progressed and more men joined the burgeoning armies, many more women took jobs outside the home.*

Our families at home are in a suffering condition, and send to their husbands for relief. Where is it to come from? The Government has never offered us a penny since we have been here [from October 1863 to March 1864]. . . . My wife and three little children at home are, in a manner, freezing and starving to death. She writes to me for aid, but I have nothing to send her.

Black troops of the Fifty-Fourth and Fifty-Fifth Massachusetts regiments refused to accept pay until accorded equal salaries with white troops. Their stand prompted this statement from an officer: "There is Sargeant Swatts, a man who has fairly won promotion on the field of battle. While he was doing the work of government in the field, his wife and children were placed in the poorhouse."

White women in the western states and territories of the Union had experiences similar to those of women in the South. They survived with fewer commodities and often found it necessary to improvise and "make do." As the war required more soldiers in the East and the South, Western men left home, and military garrisons were reassigned away from the frontier. White women in the West then became more vulnerable to Native American attacks and uprisings. The best known incident occurred in 1862 in Minnesota, where the Sioux Indians killed 800 white settlers and left many white families homeless. (Of the 2,000 Indians captured and tried for participating in the uprising, 303 were sentenced to hang. President Lincoln commuted the majority of the death sentences; but on December 26, 1862, thirty-eight Indians were hanged, in the nation's largest public mass execution.) Women who did not experience such upheaval often managed farms, in addition to their domestic duties. Some even homesteaded without the help of men to provide for their families.

Northern women wrote prolifically during the war:

- Mary Abigail Dodge (see page 727), writing under the pen name "Gail Hamilton," published patriotic articles such as "A Call to My Countrywomen" (1863). "Stitching does not crush rebellion or annihilate treason," she wrote to those putting their efforts into aid societies; rather, courage and sacrifice were required.
- Julia Ward Howe wrote the poem that became the lyrics of "Battle Hymn of the Republic." "The Flag," "Our Orders," and "The Jewelers' Shop in War-Time" were among her other poems.

- Louisa May Alcott wrote *Hospital Sketches* (1863; see "Female Nurses" in Chapter 9, "Medical Care and Medicine").

Northern women wrote novels, such as Caroline Kelly's *Andy Hall: The Mission Scholar in the Army* and Sarah Towne Smith Martyn's *Our Village in War-Time*, as well as pamphlets, books, and tracts for fund-raising. Sale of *The Diary of a Lady of Gettysburg*, published anonymously, benefited the Philadelphia Sanitary Commission Fair.

Women became dancers and actresses during the war, and established women entertainers often contributed their talents to raise funds for the war effort. The English Shakespearean actress, Frances Ann (Fanny) Kemble, who gave benefit dramatic readings in the North, also made another potent contribution to the Union war effort. In the 1830s, she had married wealthy Georgia plantation owner (and slaveholder) Pierce Butler. They were divorced in 1849. Kemble's abhorrence of slavery permeated her *Journal of a Residence on a Georgia Plantation*, which was published in the United States and England in 1863—primarily to influence public opinion in favor of emancipation (see "Notable Home Front Figures," on page 726). Another celebrated actress, Charlotte Cushman, traveled to the United States from Europe to give benefit performances for the Sanitary Commission. Her appearance in *Macbeth* in several Northern cities, including Washington, D.C. (where her performance was attended by the Lincolns) raised more than $8,000.

Postal Service

Both North and South viewed an uninterrupted postal service as a great morale booster for combatants and civilians alike. Gossip proliferated, rumors and propaganda were printed in newspapers, and telegraph lines were frequently cut. Thus, letters were often the only reliable means by which those on the home front could learn about their loved ones in uniform, and vice versa. Generally, the high illiteracy rate among slaves—reinforced by laws that forbade teaching slaves to read and write—negated any effect of postal service on their daily lives.

Given wartime conditions in the South, it is remarkable that a postal service even existed in the Confederacy. That it was generally regarded as successful is attributable to one man: Confederate Postmaster General John H. Reagan (1818–1905), one of only two of Jefferson Davis' cabinet to serve for the entire war. (Secretary of Navy Stephen Mallory was the other.) Although it was created by Davis in February 1861, the Confederate Post Office Department officially began service on June 1, 1861. Prior to secession, the U.S. Postal Service in the South was notoriously inefficient (it ran at a $2 million loss in 1860 alone). Reagan, determined to meet the Confederate Congress' mandate of a balanced operation by March 1, 1863, used the routes and offices established by the U.S. Postal Service, in place for seventy years prior to the war, as his foundation. He also raised basic postage from three cents to five cents, and then doubled it to ten cents on July 1, 1862. He cut jobs, eliminated some routes and franking privileges, cut the frequency of service, and enticed several U.S. postal employees to join the Confederate cause. He assigned the printing of postage stamps to two Richmond companies and a company in London.

Despite his tight rein and the high regard in which Davis held him, Reagan was not able to keep the system running efficiently once the war turned against the Confederacy. Rail lines were cut, shipments of mail and stamps were destroyed, and paper supplies dwindled to nothing. The cost of mailing a letter became prohibitively expensive for all but wealthy Southerners.

In the North, the U.S. postmaster general was Montgomery Blair (1813–1883). Blair had made a name for himself as one of Dred Scott's lawyers; eloquently, though unsuccessfully, he argued the slave's case for freedom before the Supreme Court in 1857. He was appointed postmaster general at the beginning of President Lincoln's first term. During the war, he devised an efficient mail service to and from the military and instituted compulsory payment of postage by the sender (in the South, troops were allowed to mail free of charge; the recipient paid the postage). He also created the postal draft system for the sending of money orders (the initial impetus was to allow soldiers to send and receive money).

Mail delivery in the North increased in volume and efficiency during the war—an improvement attributable to Blair's instituted practice of sorting mail into different classes (first class, second class, and so on) and his keeping the postage rate in the North at three cents during most of the war. This made writing letters a relative bargain; inflation increased the cost of everything else. Blair, originally a Democrat, was considered too moderate by the Radical Republicans in Congress. He was squeezed out as postmaster general in 1864. William Dennison, a short-term postmaster of little distinction, succeeded him.

Patriotic Expressions and Home Front Celebrations

The Confederacy

Early in the Civil War, when civilians were still in the first throes of enthusiasm, Southern communities gathered regularly at send-off parties for local enlisted men, or held feasts for companies of new soldiers who were passing through on their way to the war. One young man described being "pelted with fruit, flowers, cards & notes" by a large crowd of women. Public support, where communities were not devastated, continued throughout the war. In November 1864, a soldier in a Georgia regiment recorded his experience near Florence, Alabama: "Last Sabbath morning the citizens of Florence turned out en masse to witness the crossing of Stewart's and Cheatham's men over the Tennessee River . . . the grave and the gay . . . lined the sidewalks and thronged the streets, to see and welcome the grand old veterans of the Army of Tennessee." Victories also prompted celebrations; for example, crowds gathered in Richmond, Virginia, to hear a 100-gun salute marking the Confederate victory at First Bull Run (Manassas).

Civilians followed news accounts of battles and expressed support for and interest in the fortunes of the Confederacy. One letter to a Georgia newspaper in June 1863 proclaimed: "In breathless but hopeful anxiety, the public are awaiting the result of [Robert E.] Lee's movements at the North and [Joseph E.] Johnston's at the South. Upon their success hang momentous interests—no less to our mind than an early peace or the continuance of the war for an indefinite period." Troops wrote letters to newspapers to inspire courage and confidence on the home front by conveying what Brigadier General Clement Evans called "the soldier's spirit of cheerfulness." Lee's general orders, designed to evoke patriotic responses, were also published in newspapers. In response to Lee's reminder that the soldiers of the American Revolution "marched through suffering, privations, and blood, to independence" while maintaining "their high resolve to be free," the Richmond *Enquirer* implored: "Give the army subsistence and the army will give the country peace. . . . Rations is the great question. Will the people supply General Lee with meat!"

In the spirit of patriotic sacrifice, the Confederacy specified days of fasting and prayer. These were observed by the army and by civilians on the home front. A "ballad for the times, respectfully dedicated to the patriotic women of the South" exhorted: "Pray, maiden, pray!" Early soldiers' burials were ceremonies of dignity and honor. After First Manassas in 1861, the city of Charleston ceased business on the day its soldiers were buried. Three cavalry companies accompanied the bodies from the train to the city hall, and 1,000 soldiers escorted them to the cemetery. As the war progressed and such attention became impossible, troops were buried hastily in the aftermath of battle.

Slave Celebrations and Emancipation

Most Southern whites greeted invading Union soldiers with either hostility or indifference, but the region's slaves welcomed them and sometimes celebrated their approach with specially written songs. Some blacks burned or destroyed the property and goods of their former masters, creating what one white Southerner called a "perfect jubilee." In one county, the newly freed slaves held a procession around the countryside, with drums, flags, and chants of "Abe Lincoln and Freedom!" General Sherman wrote that, one day out of Atlanta, on his March to the Sea, his troops met "negroes . . . simply frantic with joy. Whenever they heard my name, they clustered about my horse, shouted and prayed in their peculiar style." Meanwhile, for slaves who were still beyond the reach of Union troops, celebrations were scant. Secret religious meetings, held in wooded areas, featured the ecstatic singing of freedom songs and prayers for the Northern cause.

When news of the Emancipation Proclamation reached blacks and sympathetic whites in the North and the South, festivity prevailed. Those in the North or in Union-occupied territories in the South had more freedom and resources for celebrations. Meetings and carnivals were held across the nation on January 1, 1863, when the proclamation went into effect. Henry Turner, pastor of an African Methodist Episcopal church in Washington, had to contend with many other celebrants to get one of the first copies of the newspaper that contained the proclamation. He finally succeeded in securing a copy and raced back to his church to read it aloud to his congregation. "Men squealed," he wrote later, "women fainted, dogs barked, white and colored people shook hands, songs were sung, cannons began to fire at the navy-yard, and follow in the wake of the roar that had for some time been going on behind the White House. . . . Great processions of colored and white men marched to and fro and congratulated President Lincoln on his proclamation. . . . Nothing like it will ever be seen again in this life." The night before the proclamation was made, George Payne, an ex-slave, addressed a contraband camp in Washington: "Haven't we a right to rejoice? You all know you couldn't have such a meetin' as dis down in Dixie! Dat you all knows. I have a right to rejoice, an' so have you; for we shall be free in jus' about five minutes."

In the occupied South, celebrations on New Year's Day were equally joyous. An enormous affair was held at Camp Saxton in the South Carolina Sea Islands, where the Union army sponsored a day of rejoicing for the soldiers and the freedmen of the islands. The program featured a band, the raising of the flag, speeches, prayers, songs, a dress parade by the black soldiers and their white officers, and a huge feast. A white teacher working on the Islands noted that "our hearts were filled with an exceeding great gladness; for . . . we knew that Freedom was surely born in our land that day."

The Union

Just as in the South, celebrations on the home front during the earliest months of the war tended to coincide with the presence of troops. Communities gathered to give their men an appropriate send-off, and these affairs generally included the presentation of flags (made by local women), speeches, patriotic and popular music, and a feast. On their way south, the First Vermont Regiment was met in a small town where "the town Band and the Fire Company . . . escorted us through the streets . . . to partake of refreshments prepared by the ladies."

Throughout the war years, parades, picnics, oratory, and fireworks continued to mark July 4 and other major holidays. Citizens' associations took on the responsibility for planning the programs and frequently assumed the costs so that the local governments could divert all of their financial resources to the war effort. Bunting and flags were hung, and towns and cities took on a festive look. However, in 1863, celebrations planned for Independence Day were canceled or muted in the wake of the casualties sustained at Gettysburg. The battle had ended on the previous day.

Home front celebrations were held for wounded or furloughed soldiers, and sometimes for troops on active duty if they were stationed close enough to a city or town. One of the most famous of these efforts took place in 1863, at Chicago's Northwestern Sanitary Fair, where "Soldiers' Day" featured a "grand dinner" for 800 wounded or paroled Union troops. The feast was made poignant by the battered condition of the men, many of whom were missing limbs, and could walk only with crutches. They had little or no appetite for the rich food set before them. Eventually, the soldiers were persuaded to give a demonstration of their battle cry, after which "excitement was at a white-heat, and there was no vent for it but in music." A dirge followed the playing of patriotic tunes, and finally "with swelling hearts and quivering voices, with tremulous clasping of the hands, and broken words of thanksgiving, the boys slowly returned to the hospital."

Washington, D.C., was the scene of some striking celebrations in the first months of 1865. On February 22, George Washington's birthday, President Lincoln ordered a nighttime illumination in the city to celebrate Sherman's successes in the Carolinas and the fall of the important Confederate port city of Wilmington, North Carolina. Singing crowds moved through the streets. On March 4, a traditional celebration was infused with extraordinary excitement by the increasing certainty that the North would be victorious and the Union would remain intact. The inauguration of Abraham Lincoln for a second term brought thousands of Union citizens to a muddy, storm-swept Washington. Amid rumors of Southern plots against the president and others, Secretary of War Stanton stationed sharpshooters on roofs surrounding the Capitol building where the inauguration ceremonies would take place. Watchful Union soldiers moved through huge crowds that included many black people dressed in their celebratory best. The Forty-Fifth Regiment United States Colored Troops made history as the first African American soldiers ever to march in an inaugural parade. Because of the weather, the inauguration ceremonies began in the Capitol's Senate chamber. But the rain stopped before President Lincoln was due to speak, and the ceremony continued outside. Noah Brooks, correspondent for the *Sacramento Daily Union*, described the crowd as a "sea of heads. As far as the eye could see, the throng looked like waves breaking at its outer edges." (A surviving photograph of the crowd shows John Wilkes Booth standing not far from the president.) The weather was still uncertain, the skies heavily overcast, when the presidential party assembled on the outside platform below the recently completed cast-iron Capitol dome, topped by the statue of *Armed Liberty*. The president came forward to speak. "Just at that moment," Brooks wrote of a phenomenon others reported, "the sun, which had been obscured all day, burst forth in its unclouded meridian splendor, and flooded the spectacle with glory and with light."

Northern citizens paid close attention to the newspapers. Printed "extras" quickly delivered battle news in the latter part of the war. The fall of Richmond on April 4, 1865, touched off major celebrations. In Washington, a 900-gun salute was fired. Chicago's celebration consisted of bonfires and

CIVIL WAR FLAGS: SO PROUDLY HAILED

I have a little flag; it belonged to one of our cavalry regt's; presented to me by one of the wounded. It was taken by the Secesh in a cavalry fight, and rescued by our men in a bloody little skirmish. It cost three men's lives, just to get one little flag, four by three. Our men rescued it, and tore it from the breast of a dead Rebel—all that just for the name of getting their little banner back again. The man that got it was very badly wounded, and they let him keep it. I was with him a good deal; he wanted to give me something, he said, he didn't expect to live, so he gave me the little banner as a keepsake. I mention this, mother, to show you a specimen of the feeling. There isn't a reg't, cavalry or infantry, that wouldn't do the same on occasion.—Walt Whitman, U.S.A.; letter to his mother, April 10, 1864.

Snapping in the winds that moved across the camps, battlefields, naval vessels, cities and towns of the Civil War, banners of the Union, the Confederacy, and hundreds of proud Civil War regiments symbolized ideals, pride, and unity. On the battlefront, they were rallying points for the units that displayed them—and targets for the opposing force. Civil War history abounds with the heroism of soldiers and sailors who died or risked death defending their flags, or charged forward to capture an enemy banner. These banners were sometimes supplied by the government, but were often sewn with care and pride by women on the home front and presented to regiments in elaborate patriotic ceremonies that deepened the soldiers' attachment to the banners their regiments displayed.

The Union banner, the "Stars and Stripes" became widely celebrated as "Old Glory" during the Civil War due to a retired shipmaster named Stephen Driver, who lived in Nashville, Tennessee—the capital of a Confederate state. Driver had coined the phrase in 1831, when a United States flag (then with twenty-four stars) was unfurled on his brig, the *Charles Doggett*. He carried that well-known flag with him to Nashville and kept it hidden until February 25, 1862, when Union forces took control of the city. Asked about the banner, he brought it out of hiding and, with a Union military escort, installed

singing in the streets, along with some firing of cannon. "Boston is gay," wrote Ellen Wright Garrison; people were "blowing soap bubbles . . . bells were pealing, cannon firing and pyrotechnic wonders being exhibited." When President Lincoln arrived in Richmond to inspect the city, shortly after its evacuation by the Confederate government, a crowd of black Southerners was waiting to greet him. Northern African American reporter T. Morris Chester wrote: "There is no describing the scene along the route. The colored population was wild with enthusiasm. . . . Everyone declares that Richmond never before presented such a spectacle of jubilee."

Less than a week later, Lee's surrender at Appomattox was the spur for a new round of ever-more-frantic revelry in the North and among Southern it himself in the tower of the state capitol. (This ceremony was cheered by the Sixth Ohio Regiment—which later adopted the nickname "Old Glory.") Captain Driver's flag was by that time, however, slightly out of date. When the Civil War began, the United States flag bore thirty-three stars. On July 4, 1861, a thirty-fourth was added, for Kansas; and on July 4, 1863, a thirty-fifth was added, for West Virginia. (Nevada, which entered the Union October 31, 1864, was not represented by a star until July 4, 1865.)

The Confederate States of America was represented by three official banners during the war. The first official Confederate States flag, the "Stars and Bars," was adopted March 14, 1861. Designed by Nichola Marshall of Marion, Alabama, the flag consisted of three equal horizontal bars (two red, a white bar in the middle), with a blue field in the upper left corner containing a circle of seven stars—representing the states that originally formed the Confederacy. As more states seceded, the number of stars increased to thirteen. (Two stars represented states that actually stayed in the Union but were also claimed by the Confederacy:

Missouri and Kentucky.) The design of this flag was deemed too similar to the Stars and Stripes, however, and in April 1862, the Flag Committee of the Confederate Congress began considering alternate designs. On May 1, 1863, the "Stainless Banner" became the new official design. The first flag of this new design—white, with a red field in the upper left containing crossed blue bars (the "Southern Cross") filled with stars—was used to enshroud the body of General Stonewall Jackson, who died May 10, 1863, after the battle of Chancellorsville.

The dominating white field made this second Confederate flag too closely resemble a flag of truce. On March 4, 1865, the Confederate Congress adopted an amended design that added a red vertical bar to the outer (fly) end of the white field. This was the Confederate States flag for the remaining two months of the Confederacy's existence.

The Union Stars and Stripes and the Confederate Stars and Bars are the flags seen at the beginning of each chapter of the *Civil War Desk Reference.*

---

blacks. A soldier from New Jersey who was stationed near Appomattox reported that when the news reached camp "greeting, congratulations and cheering beggars [sic] description. Shoes and hats flew high in the air. Speeches were made, called for loudly, but could not be heard for the cheering at every sentence. The Star Spangled Banner waved high in triumph—high and low, back and forth, over a sea of upturned faces." In Northern cities, events replayed the celebrations following the fall of Richmond. It is hard to say when and how these Union celebrations might have ended naturally, but after just a few days they were cut short abruptly by the assassination of Abraham Lincoln on the same evening that the United States flag was once again raised over Fort Sumter.

Riots

The South

Civilians in the Confederacy who faced hunger and starvation also had to deal with growing inflation, the selfishness of speculators and hoarders, and the relative indifference of the Richmond government to their plight. These factors sometimes provoked a desperate response, particularly among women whose husbands and brothers had gone off to war. Although the most famous "bread" riot—when a mob of hundreds demanded food and ransacked stores—occurred in Richmond in 1863, food riots took place in cities throughout the South, beginning as early as July 1861 in New Orleans. In 1862, raids on supplies were noted in two Georgia communities. By 1863, as the war continued to take its toll on civilians, the number of riots sparked by shortages of, and exorbitant prices set for, clothing and food increased.

On March 18, 1863, soldiers' wives rioted in Salisbury, North Carolina, and attacked the stores of merchants. On March 25, there was a disturbance in Mobile, Alabama. Also in March, women rioted in Raleigh, High Point, and Boon Hill, North Carolina, as well as in Atlanta, Macon, Columbus, and Augusta, Georgia. The Richmond press covered these events. On April 1, 1863, the same day a food riot took place in Petersburg, Virginia, women from Richmond met at the Belvedere Baptist Church to discuss a protest. The next morning, Mary Jackson, wife of a painter, led a crowd to the Governor's Mansion. The crowd soon became a mob estimated at 1,000 people. They ransacked some twenty stores in the city's business district. Mayor Joseph Mayo read the Riot Act, Governor John Letcher called out troops, and the crowd disbursed. Forty-four women and twenty-nine men were arrested, but only some were tried and convicted, mostly of misdemeanors (three were guilty of felonies). Although the Confederate government tried to suppress news of the riot, word spread, and John Moncure Daniel, in the Richmond *Examiner*, decried what he considered leniency toward the rioters. Crowds again formed on April 3, amid rumors of another riot, but none took place.

On April 17, 1864, when food supplies were diminished after the winter, women mobbed stores in Savannah, Georgia, and stole staples such as bacon, flour, and rice. Only three women were arrested, and no charges were pressed. Riots took place through 1865 in Georgia, Alabama, North Carolina, Virginia, and Texas. In February 1865, soldiers' wives used axes to break down the door of a government depot in Miller County, Georgia, and carried away fifty sacks of corn. This and other attacks by rural women on government storage facilities mirrored the desperation of their urban counterparts and their willingness to defy authority when starvation loomed.

Unionist areas of the South where slavery was limited—eastern Tennessee, northern Alabama, northwestern Arkansas, and western North Carolina—were marked by violence. Civilians were subject to attacks from Confederate loyalists and guerrillas, and those who did support the Confederacy were attacked by Unionist guerrillas or deserters from the Confederate army. The Confederate government executed Unionists who destroyed bridges to impede the war effort, displaying their bodies in public places. But even those Unionists who simply spoke out for peace put their lives in danger. In 1863, Confederates ransacked the offices of William Holden, editor of the Raleigh *North Carolina Standard* and a leader of the peace movement in his state, and he was forced to flee the city. The peace movement in North Carolina led to violence, in turn violently suppressed by Confederate troops over a five-month period.

The North

Riots in the North during the Civil War were not provoked by food shortages. In general, they were prompted by resistance to the draft, racial tension, and the Peace Democrats' (Copperhead) opposition to the conduct of the war and their charge of abridgment of rights and liberties in the North. The draft created resentment among immigrant workers who could not afford to pay for a substitute or a $300 commutation fee (a cash payment in lieu of military service). This same group suffered most from inflation and was vulnerable to the fear that freed blacks would take their jobs.

Some Democrats preyed on racial fears and prejudices, exhorting white laborers not to risk their lives for black freedom. A Democratic newspaper headline proclaimed "Shall the Working Classes be Equalized with Negroes?" and Ohio Congressman Samuel Cox declared that his state's troops would not do battle "if the result shall be the flight and movement of the black race by millions northward." In Cincinnati, Ohio, in 1862, when blacks were brought in to replace Irish dockworkers who had gone on strike, there was violence in black neighborhoods. Irish Americans attacked a tobacco factory that employed black women and children in Brooklyn, New York. In Illinois, contrabands imported to help harvest crops precipitated riots. On March 6, 1863, in Detroit, a rumor that a white orphaned girl had been raped by a black man resulted in a rampage in which several blacks were killed and damage was estimated at $20,000.

On July 17, 1862, Congress passed the Militia Act, which stipulated that white men between ages eighteen and forty-five could be drafted into state service and called by the Federal government to serve for up to nine months. Public unhappiness with the law soon found expression in the streets. On October 10, for example, crowds in Port Washington, Wisconsin, ejected the draft commissioner from the courthouse and destroyed his records and the homes of local officials. Six hundred troops were called in to stop the rioters. The national draft, instituted in March 1863, required enrollment of able-bodied white men between ages twenty and forty-five, and triggered even more disturbances. In Chicago, thousands of men protested the draft and attacked the police who were trying to disperse them. In Rutland, Vermont, miners battled U.S. troops; in Boston, three people were killed when an armory was attacked. Violence broke out in cities in Connecticut, New York, New Jersey, New Hampshire, Ohio, and Wisconsin.

A riot in New York City, begun on July 13, 1863 (peace was restored by July 17), reaped the most damage and notoriety. As in other Northern cities, workers had been told that blacks threatened their jobs. In June, black laborers replaced Irish strikers on the docks. Then, soon after the heavy casualties at Gettysburg were made known, the names of those chosen in the draft lottery were announced. This touched off a four-day rampage. At first, the rioters (who burned the draft office) included German as well as Irish immigrants, and some native-born artisans. By the second day, however, most of the mob was Irish and Catholic. They attacked the property of Republicans and abolitionists, burned police stations and the Colored Orphan Asylum, and murdered black people. Federal troops—some of them fresh from Gettysburg—were called in to suppress the riot. More than 100 people were killed. When New York City resumed the draft in August, more than $300,000 had been set aside, through bond sales, to pay for substitutes or commutations. Other cities followed this example. All commutation was banned the following year (March 1864).

The politics of Peace Democrats also touched off riots in the Midwest. Clement Vallandigham (see Chapter 3, "Wartime Politics"), who believed that secession was legal, gave a speech in Mount Vernon, Ohio, on May 1, 1863. The war, he said, was being fought "for the purpose of crushing our liberty and erecting a despotism . . . a war for the freedom of the blacks and the enslavement of the whites." When he was arrested by Union General

Ambrose Burnside for "expressed or implied" treason, rioters burned the Republican newspaper in Dayton, Ohio.

Vallandigham's arrest fueled the charge that Democrats were being persecuted for their opposition to Lincoln's policies, and raised questions about freedom of speech. In Illinois, where citizens came originally from the South as well as the North, Copperheads continued to criticize the administration and spoke out against fighting for emancipation, as opposed to preserving the Union. Democratic speeches, rallies, and newspaper articles in Coles and Edgar counties in favor of peace and civil liberties increased tension. In January and February 1864, Union soldiers on leave in the counties attacked Democrats, and two deaths resulted. On March 28, in Charleston, Illinois, a Democratic rally and a fatal fight between a Democrat and a soldier precipitated a riot that killed nine and wounded twelve men. Among those arrested, sixteen Democrats were held in a Federal prison for seven months, without trial, until ordered by Lincoln to be released. Excepting the New York City draft riot, the Charleston, Illinois, riot claimed more lives than any other in the North.

Refugees and Evacuations in the South

White Southerners

As Northern troops moved through the South, they caused tens of thousands of white Southern civilians to flee their homes out of fear of invasion, lack of food, the spread of disease, and forced military evacuation, or in the wake of the destruction of their homes, towns, and cities. An estimated 200,000 people within the Confederacy became refugees, often facing insecurity, poverty, and hunger. "Shew me a safe point and I'll go tomorrow, but no such happy valley exists in the Confederacy," wrote Jane Pringle of South Carolina, describing the situation faced by those who lived among strangers and amid the uncertainties of war.

Virginia attracted more refugees than any other state. Richmond's population had doubled by 1862. Raleigh, North Carolina, and Columbia, South Carolina, drew people from the coast. Those who lived west of the Mississippi took refuge in Texas. Refugees from Kentucky, Tennessee, and the states of the Deep South sought shelter in Georgia, particularly Atlanta, until Union General William T. Sherman demanded the evacuation of the civilians who remained when he captured the city in September 1864. "I have deemed it to the interest of the United States that the citizens now

Their belongings piled atop a wagon, a group of Southern refugees prepares to flee the path of advancing Northern armies.

residing in Atlanta should remove, those who prefer it to go South and the rest North," Sherman ordered. Nearly 1,600 people were removed.

Many of the refugees were women and children, who often tried to stay with their property until they had no choice but to move. A Georgia woman would not leave until the "bullets and shells were flying all around," and she was ordered from her home by the Confederate army. As early as 1862, the inhabitants of Charleston, South Carolina, were offered "refugee tickets" by the Confederate government, so that they could remove their families to places of safety, but most of the civilian population remained. The people of Vicksburg, Mississippi, trapped by the Union seige in May and June, 1863, took cover from bombardments in basements or in caves they dug into hillsides. By the time the Confederacy surrendered on July 4, water was difficult to find and the inhabitants were eating mule meat.

People often left their homes to avoid impending battle, or as battle raged—for example, when Baton Rouge, Louisiana, was shelled in 1862, when Jackson, Mississippi, burned in 1863, and when General James H. Wilson's Union cavalry was approaching Selma, Alabama, in 1865. After

Forts Henry and Donelson fell in 1862, refugees fled Nashville, Tennessee. Robert E. Lee described those fleeing Fredericksburg, Virginia, when it was bombarded by the Union army in December 1862:

> I have only seen the ladies in this vicinity when [they were] flying from the enemy, & it caused me acute grief to witness their exposure & suffering. But a more noble spirit was never displayed anywhere. The faces of old & young were wreathed with smiles & glowed with happiness at their sacrifices for the good of their country. Many have lost everything.

Disease forced others to leave. In Wilmington, North Carolina, civilians escaped a yellow fever epidemic in 1862.

Guerrilla activity caused some civilians to leave their homes. Mostly operating in the South, guerrillas also battled in the border states of Missouri and Kentucky, as well as in Kansas. Guerrilla warfare destroyed fields, homes, and livelihoods; burned bridges; cut rail and telegraph lines; and spread terror. In Missouri, the danger was so great that men willing to pilot a steamboat from St. Louis to Kansas earned $1,000. Some Confederate deserters, who hid in the countryside by day and plundered at night, also terrorized citizens (see also Chapter 5, "The Armies").

Refugees came from all classes and walks of life and faced innumerable difficulties in the new places they settled. Some state and local governments provided relief to soldiers' families, but, outside of one's home county, it was hard to prove eligibility for such aid. Pride kept many others from accepting charity. Those who could not find housing were reduced to living in churches, stables, tents, and caves. Price gouging for rent, food, and supplies was rampant. Refugees faced loneliness, anxiety, tension (even when they lived among distant family), suspicion, and hostility as strangers. One woman from Louisiana wrote of her exile in Texas: "The more we see of people, the less we like them, and every refugee we have seen feels the same way. They call us renegades in Tyler. It is strange the prejudice that exists all through the state against refugees."

Displaced Southerners also faced the decision of whether to seek help by moving behind Union lines where food, and sometimes jobs, were available. Bitterness and pride kept many from this choice. One plantation owner told his wife, when she suggested going to Union-occupied New Orleans: "Prepare for a divorce. . . . I will never associate with you again." Another Confederate woman, after months as a refugee from Baton Rouge, debated "whether 'tis nobler in the Confederacy to suffer the pangs of unappeasable hunger and never-ending trouble, or to take passage to a Yankee port, and there remaining, end them. Which is best? I am so near daft that I cannot pretend to say; I only know that I shudder at the thought of going to New Orleans." Yet desperation drove some secessionists to take a loyalty oath in order to receive aid from the Union army, although an article in an 1863 issue of *Leslie's* magazine described the women seeking food after Vicksburg fell as "full of hate to those from whom they asked favors."

Contrabands/Freedmen

Slaves did not hesitate to take refuge behind Union lines as the Federal army moved south. First dubbed "contraband of war" in May 1861 by General Benjamin Butler (see Chapter 11, "Reconstruction and the Aftermath of the War"), who refused to return them to their owners, and then called "freedmen" after the Emancipation Proclamation, former slaves crowded into makeshift shelters in cities or contraband camps that grew up near Union encampments. By 1865, hundreds of thousands of African American freedmen lived within Union lines and developed a way of life under the control of army commanders. By the end of 1862, most of the commanders had appointed general superintendents of contraband affairs to provide food, clothing, and shelter where necessary, and to employ the able-bodied on abandoned plantations or as laborers for the army.

The migration of black refugees caused disruption and confusion. J. G. McKee, an agent of the Western Freedmen's Aid Commission, in Nashville, Tennessee, noted in *The Colored Citizen* on November 7, 1863:

> I conjecture there cannot be less than four thousand contrabands who need help and instruction about this city. I find over 40 crowded into one small house. Sometimes 5 or 6 families in one room without fireplace or chimney, cooking their morsel on a few bricks, the smoke filling the apartment and steaming out at the door. . . . The colored citizens of Nashville deserve great credit. They organized a "Good Samaritan Society" during last winter. . . .

In the January 8, 1864, issue of the *Liberator*, Thomas Calahan, a United Presbyterian Church missionary in Louisiana, described the scenes he encountered:

... you have no idea of the state of things here. Go out in any direction and you meet negroes on horses, negroes on mules, negroes with oxen, negroes by the wagon, cart and buggy load, negroes on foot, men, women and children; negroes in uniform, negroes in rags, negroes in frame houses, negroes living in tents, negroes living in rail pens covered with brush, and negroes living under brush piles without any rails, negroes living on the bare ground with the sky for their covering; all hopeful, almost all cheerful, every one pleading to be taught, willing to do anything for learning. They are never out of our rooms, and their cry is for "Books! Books!" and "when will school begin?" Negro women come and offer to cook and wash for us, if we will only teach them to read the Bible. . . . And think of people living in brush tents gathering for prayer meetings that last far into the night. Every night hymns of praise to God and prayers for the Government that oppressed them so long, rise around on every side—prayers for the white teachers that have already come—prayers that God would send them more. These are our circumstances.

Unlike Southern white refugees, who often were unable to find employment in new locations, almost 200,000 contrabands and refugee freedmen contributed to the Union war effort. Some were impressed against their will—through the labor policies of military commanders—as civilian laborers, teamsters, cooks, carpenters, nurses, laundresses, and scouts (see "Major Issues of Reconstruction" in Chapter 11, "Reconstruction and the Aftermath of War"). Vincent Colyer, an agent of the Brooklyn YMCA and Superintendent of the Poor for the Department of North Carolina, reported in 1864:

In the four months that I had charge of them, the men built three first-class earth-work forts. . . . The negroes loaded and discharged cargoes. . . . A number of the men were good carpenters, blacksmiths, coopers, & co. . . . Upwards of fifty volunteers of the best and most courageous, were kept constantly employed on the perilous but important duty of spies, scouts, and guides.

Some contraband camps also became long-term homes for freed men and women. Mitchelville, established on South Carolina's Hilton Head Island in March 1863, was made up of simple cottages built by the ex-slaves themselves, with lumber supplied by the army. Women teachers from the North, paid for by the American Missionary Society, staffed the schools, and every child aged six to sixteen was required to attend classes. This was the first compulsory education law ever enacted in South Carolina.

Freedman's Village, located on the grounds of Robert E. Lee's former estate in Arlington, Virginia, opened on December 4, 1863. The original tent city was supplanted by 100 frame houses built by the army. Each one-and-a-half story structure was split down the middle to form a duplex. Rent for each unit was $3 per month. The village itself became a "model" freedman encampment, with parks, a home for the elderly, a hospital, and a school (with 900 students). Workshops were offered to provide the former slaves with new trades, such as blacksmithing and carpentry. The "temporary" village lasted nearly twenty years; in 1882, the U.S. Supreme Court ruled that it should be closed and the land used to expand Arlington National Cemetery.

Notable Home Front Figures

ANNA ELLA CARROLL (1815–1894). Anna Ella Carroll was one of the most influential women writers of the war period. During the 1850s, she served as a lobbyist and pamphlet writer for a number of groups, causes, and political campaigns, most notably the American Party (known commonly as the Know-Nothing Party). She earned fame for her 1861 justification of Lincoln's seemingly authoritarian actions (including his suspensions of the writ of habeas corpus). She won not only an audience with the president, but also the distribution of her pamphlets by Congress and the War Department. Carroll's second claim to fame, however, is still debated. To her deathbed, she and her supporters held that she had been responsible for the introduction of the "Tennessee Plan"—the use of the Tennessee and Cumberland Rivers by the Union to attack the South—which was successfully employed during the war. Her detractors maintained that, although Carroll did suggest a version of the plan, it had already been formulated—and, to an extent, executed—at the time of her proposal. Carroll fought fruitlessly for recognition and recompense from Congress and the War Department.

MARY BOYKIN CHESNUT (1823–1886). Mary Boykin Chesnut was born into a wealthy and influential South Carolina family. At the age of seventeen, she married James Chesnut, the heir to one of the largest plantations in South Carolina. In 1858, her husband was elected to the U.S. Senate, and, while in Washington, Mary began her famous career as a political hostess. In

1861, James resigned from Congress and the Chesnuts returned to the South. During the war, James served in several Confederate government positions. From her perspective as the wife of an official in Richmond, Mary wrote her diary, now considered to be among the finest first-person accounts of the war and its effects. Chesnut's diary has a pro-Southern slant and illustrates many of the typical prejudices of the time. She considered the idea of women working outside the home disgraceful: "We will not stand up all day and cut [Treasury] notes apart, ordered round by a department clerk. We will live at home with our families and starve as a body." Although against slavery, she described her belief as "narrowly self-interested," as she felt that slavery was degrading to white Southern women.

THOMAS MORRIS CHESTER (1834–1892). The only black American to report on the Civil War for a major daily newspaper, Thomas Morris Chester wrote for the Philadelphia *Press* from August 1864 through June 1865. Born in Harrisburg, Pennsylvania, Chester alternately lived in Liberia and the United States in the years leading up to the war. A supporter of colonization in Liberia, he nevertheless recruited black troops for the Massachusetts regiments and the Pennsylvania state militia, where he was designated a captain. In 1863, he lectured in England on behalf of the British and Foreign Anti-Slavery Society on the war's impact on American blacks. Hired as a war correspondent for the *Press*, he covered the activities of the Army of the James, reporting on the efforts of both black and white troops. He was one of the first reporters to enter Richmond when it was taken by the Union and wrote his first dispatch while sitting at what was once the desk of the Confederate Speaker of the House. In 1870, Chester became the first black American admitted to the English bar, and three years later, the first black admitted to the bar in Louisiana.

MARY ABIGAIL DODGE (1833–1896). Writing under the pen name "Gail Hamilton," Mary Abigail Dodge inspired Northern audiences with her patriotic articles. She began writing for newspapers while teaching in Hartford, Connecticut. In 1858, she moved to Washington, D.C., as governess to the children of Dr. Gamaliel Bailey, editor of the *National Era*. Dodge became a contributor to this antislavery newspaper. She lived in Hamilton, Massachusetts, during the war, where she published "A Call to My Country," in the *Atlantic Monthly* in 1863. "O women," she wrote, "the hour has need of you." She encouraged Northern women to be positive and confident about the war effort, self-reliant without complaint, brave, and sacrificing, in order to keep soldiers' morale strong and contribute to victory.

STEPHEN ELLIOTT (1806–1866). The first Episcopal bishop of Georgia, consecrated in 1841, Stephen Elliot was a leader in organizing a Confederate church separate from its Northern counterpart. His fiery sermons championed the Confederate cause. "We are engaged in one of the grandest struggles which ever nerved the hearts or strengthened the hands of a heroic race," he preached in 1861. "We are fighting for great principles, for sacred objects . . . to prevent ourselves from being transferred from American republicanism to French democracy . . . to rescue the fair name of our social life . . . from dishonor . . . to drive away the infidel and rationalistic principles which are sweeping the land and substituting a gospel of stars and stripes for the gospel of Jesus Christ." A slave holder himself, Elliott felt it was a Christian responsibility—what he called "this most interesting and necessary labor"—to instruct slaves in religion and make them part of the Episcopal community, and he called emancipation "the greatest calamity" for the freedmen because it left "unprotected [an] inferior race."

ELIZABETH KECKLEY (1818–1907). Born into slavery, Elizabeth Keckley became an accomplished seamstress who purchased her own and her son's freedom in 1855. After learning how to read and write, she moved to Washington, D.C., where her reputation as a seamstress brought her to the attention of Mary Todd Lincoln. Keckley became Mrs. Lincoln's employee and close confidant. In 1862, she helped found the Contraband Relief Association (later renamed the Ladies' Freedmen and Soldiers' Relief Association), an organization dedicated to the succor of freed blacks and run exclusively by African American women. In 1864, Keckley secured a visit for Sojourner Truth with President Lincoln. Keckley's friendship with Mary Todd Lincoln ended in 1868, with the publication of *Behind the Scenes, or Thirty Years a Slave and Four in the White House*, a book that shared Keckley's sometimes unflattering views about President and Mrs. Lincoln.

FANNY KEMBLE (1809–1893). Frances Ann Kemble, a celebrated English-born actress, championed abolition during the war with the publication of her *Journal of a Residence on a Georgian Plantation*, an account of the cruelty of slavery as she perceived it as the former wife of slave owner Pierce

Butler. Although Kemble lived on the plantation and wrote in 1838 and 1839, Butler had successfully prevented her from publishing the work at the time. She did so in 1863, five months after the Emancipation Proclamation, primarily to persuade Britain not to support the Confederacy. "Scorn, derision, insult, menace—the handcuff, the lash—the tearing away of children from parents, of husbands from wives . . . the labor of body, the despair of mind, the sickness of heart—these are the realities which belong to the system, and form the rule, rather than the exception, in the slave's experience," she wrote. Her words were read aloud in the House of Commons. The reception of the American edition was equally enthusiastic in the Northern United States. Kemble also wrote pro-Union articles for the British press and gave readings of Shakespeare in the United States and Britain to support the war effort.

FREDERICK LAW OLMSTED (1822–1903). Frederick Law Olmsted left his job as architect and superintendent of construction of New York City's Central Park to head the U.S. Sanitary Commission in 1861. At the time, he was preparing a condensation of three previously published accounts of his travels through the antebellum South. Olmsted's observations led him to criticize not only slavery, but also the inefficiency and static nature of the slave economy. He believed in planning, order, and organization to provide structure in a progressive society, and applied these principles to running the Sanitary Commission. Olmsted had overall responsibility for supervising the Commission's branch offices and for distributing food, clothing, and medical supplies to Union soldiers. He personally managed the equipping and staffing of hospital ships to transport wounded and ill troops during the Peninsula Campaign. He was also a founder of the Union League Club. Olmsted resigned from the commission in September 1863, pursuing a career in landscape architecture that brought him considerable fame.

GEORGE TEMPLETON STRONG (1820–1875). Treasurer of the U.S. Sanitary Commission, for which he raised and distributed nearly $5 million in donations, George Templeton Strong also founded New York City's Union League Club. He is famous for his diary, begun in 1835, which recorded events, personalities, ideas, and ideals of the Civil War in the North. Strong himself supported the war to preserve the Union, believing that slavery was wrong "on grounds of political economy, not of ethics." But by 1864, he wrote of slavery, "God pardon our blindness of three years ago! . . . [except] for our want of eyes to see and of courage to say what we saw, the South would never have ventured on rebellion." His movement toward emancipation as a goal of the war mirrored that of many Northerners, including Lincoln.

SELECTED RESOURCES

For additional information on published sources, see the annotated book list in Chapter 13, "Studying the War: Research and Preservation." Numerous diaries and letters also recorded experiences on the home front.

Chesnut, Mary Boykin Miller. *Mary Chesnut's Civil War*, edited by C. Vann Woodward. New Haven: Yale University Press, 1981. Illustrated.

Faust, Drew Gilpin. *Mothers of Invention: Women of the Slaveholding South in the American Civil War*. Chapel Hill: University of North Carolina Press, 1996. Illustrated.

Forbes, Ella. *African American Women during the Civil War*. New York: Garland Publishing, 1998. Illustrated.

Jimerson, Randall C. *The Private Civil War: Popular Thought during the Sectional Conflict*. Baton Rouge: Louisiana State University Press, 1988.

Massey, Mary Elizabeth. *Bonnet Brigades*. New York: Knopf, 1966. Illustrated.

_____. *Refugee Life in the Confederacy*. Baton Rouge: Louisiana State University Press, 1964.

Paludan, Phillip S. *A People's Contest: The Union and Civil War, 1861–1865*. New York: Harper & Row, 1988. Illustrated.

Stevenson, Louise L. *The Victorian Homefront: American Thought and Culture, 1860–1880*. New York: Twayne, 1991. Illustrated.

Volo, Dorothy Denneen and James M. Volo. *Daily Life in Civil War America*. Westport: Greenwood Press, 1998. Illustrated.

Wiley, Bell Irvin. *Plain People of the Confederacy*. Baton Rouge: Louisiana State University Press, 1943.

RECONSTRUCTION AND THE
AFTERMATH OF THE WAR

Reconstruction refers to the process by which the victorious North readmitted the rebellious states of the Confederacy into the Union. Historians often place the start of Reconstruction at the end of 1863, when Abraham Lincoln issued his Proclamation of Amnesty and Reconstruction, and the end in 1877, when the last Federal troops were removed from the South as part of the compromise that settled the disputed presidential election of 1876.

However, it might be more accurate to say that Reconstruction began with the start of the war itself and was a long-term process rather than a particular time period. From the moment the war began, Lincoln focused on the problem of reconstructing the Union. Equally important, from the start of the war, the Confederacy was constantly shrinking in size as United States soldiers occupied parts of the South. General Benjamin Butler's policy of refusing to return slaves who had escaped from their masters was an early implementation of a policy that would reconstruct the South. More important, Lincoln's Preliminary Emancipation Proclamation (September 22, 1862) and the final Emancipation Proclamation issued on January 1, 1863, were central aspects of Reconstruction. Similarly, the creation of West Virginia as an independent state, which began in 1862 and culminated with its admission to the Union on June 20, 1863, was an early example of how Congress would set about the reconstruction of the nation and the former slaveholding South.

Reconstruction encompassed a welter of conflicting attitudes and policies, but some general statements about the era are useful. The period was marked by conflict between Republicans (in the North and South), former

Richmond in ruins, as photographed by Alexander Gardner in April 1865. Large areas of the South were physically devastated by the Civil War.

slaves, and supporters of equality on one side; and Democrats, most white Southerners, and opponents of racial equality on the other. The supporters of racial equality were successful in providing former slaves with formal legal safeguards through three Constitutional Amendments—the Thirteenth, Fourteenth, and Fifteenth—and various statutes, including the Civil Rights Acts of 1866 and 1875. However, by the end of Reconstruction, white Southerners and their Northern Democratic allies had succeeded in undermining enforcement of these statutes and constitutional provisions, and were able to set the stage for the political marginalization of blacks, which led ultimately to their disenfranchisement by the end of the century. At the same time, despite valiant efforts by many Northern Republicans, attempts to provide land and economic opportunity for the former slaves were mostly failures. Indeed, most scholars generally agree that Reconstruction failed to accomplish its most pressing and difficult task: remaking the South into a democratic society in which people of all races had equal access to economic opportunity, political participation, and self-determination.

In his Second Inaugural Address, delivered on March 4, 1865, Lincoln characterized the tasks remaining before the nation: ". . . to finish the work we are in; to bind up the nation's wounds; to care for him who shall have borne the battle, and for his widow, and his orphan." These goals, Lincoln said, should be achieved with "malice toward none; with charity for all. . . ." But left unsaid—and unsettled—was exactly how this was to be accomplished. At issue, in determining the course of Reconstruction, were conflicting understandings, among supporters of the Union, of why the war had been fought. The conflict began as a war to preserve the Union but evolved into a crusade against slavery. By the end of the war, virtually all Republicans, and probably most Northern Democrats, understood the importance of both war aims and realized that the first, preserving the Union, could not have been accomplished without the second, ending slavery. Northerners differed, however, on two critical postwar issues: how to treat former Confederates and the Southern states in general, and how to treat former slaves. Most Northern Democrats wanted to quickly readmit the South into the Union but were reluctant to change the nature of race relations, North or South, beyond ending slavery. Most Republicans were opposed to immediate readmission of the former Confederate states.

Republicans were more divided on the future of the former slaves. The antislavery wing of the party, which would become known as Radical Republicans, was prepared to remake the American constitutional and legal order to protect the rights of free blacks and make them equal citizens. More moderate and conservative Republicans supported some, but not all, of these goals, and Democrats almost universally opposed all of them. Following the Second Inaugural, Lincoln had only the briefest time to pursue Reconstruction. Scholars once believed that Lincoln's intentions were to be "gentle" with the South and to be magnanimous toward former Confederates. At one level, this was clearly true. Lincoln did not envision harsh treatment of former Confederates or mass treason trials of former Confederate leaders. He wanted to reunify the nation. In that sense, his goals and partially formed plans for Reconstruction were strikingly different from what typically occurs in other nations in the wake of a civil war. Had he lived, perhaps his political skills and his stature as the victorious commander in chief would have enabled him to build a consensus as to the nation's approach toward Reconstruction.

But it is unlikely that Lincoln would have presented the South with a program that fully pleased Southern whites. Lincoln was surely not prepared to abandon the former slaves and the 175,000 or so surviving black Union veterans in the South. He was moving toward greater black rights at the end of his life, including advocating black suffrage for veterans and some other black males. Furthermore, it is unlikely that Lincoln would have tolerated the election of former Confederates to high office, as happened immediately after the war. Nor is there any likelihood that he would have accepted the oppressive Black Codes passed by most Southern states in 1865 and 1866.

Although Lincoln's brilliant political skills would have made Reconstruction smoother and easier, and doubtlessly more successful, great conflict would still have arisen in the postwar era. His death all but ensured bitter conflict between those who believed that Reconstruction should be limited to reestablishing the legal framework for reconstituted state governments in the South (and those states' representation in Congress), and those who believed that Reconstruction should encompass, at a minimum, the securing of blacks' political rights, economic security, and basic equality, or who saw this as an opportunity to initiate more complete social reform in the South.

The dispute between Lincoln's successor, President Andrew Johnson, and the Republican leadership in Congress would culminate in Johnson's being impeached by the House of Representatives and coming within one vote of conviction in the Senate. Johnson had a very limited idea of Reconstruction. He believed the focus should be on rebuilding the political framework of state governments in the South solely on the basis of white suffrage and white participation in those governments. He was opposed to any political rights and most civil rights for former slaves. In his mind, the postwar South would closely resemble the prewar South; blacks would no longer be slaves, but they would remain second-class citizens with few legal protections. Furthermore, Johnson believed that, as president, he held the primary if not the sole authority to implement these programs. Over Johnson's vetoes, Congress enacted civil rights legislation calling for Federal enforcement of measures designed to ensure blacks' right to vote and other hallmarks of full citizenship. In addition, Congress passed, and sent to the states for ratification, the Fourteenth Amendment, which made all persons born in the United States—including former slaves—citizens of the United States and of the state in which they resided. The amendment also prohibited the states from denying anyone in their jurisdiction equal protection of the laws, abridging the privileges and immunities of citizens of the United States, or denying anyone in their jurisdiction "life, liberty or property without due process of law" (see "The Fourteenth Amendment," on page 767).

At the same time, the white population of the South resented Federal military occupation and Federal institutions such as the Freedmen's Bureau, which was designed to aid and protect black progress. They resisted Reconstruction with all the tools at their disposal, including terrorism and murder. The Ku Klux Klan and similar organizations often directed their violence against schools set up for blacks, black voters, and whites who worked with blacks. Indeed, much of the white South, including people who rejected violence and terrorism, resisted anything that supported black freedom, independence, and political or economic power.

By the time Reconstruction ended (1877), the elements in Southern society that had controlled public life at the time of the Civil War had been restored to power. Blacks enjoyed legal freedom, but the legal protections Congress had created for them in the years immediately following the war were being circumvented in myriad ways, as segregation had become a way of life. The political disenfranchisement of blacks, through trickery, fraud, intimidation, violence, and statutes passed by white-dominated state legislatures, made it virtually impossible for the South's black population to defend its newly won rights. Southern state governments were reconstituted, and the South's legal representatives were readmitted to Congress, but the struggle over the meaning of the Constitution's and the Federal government's guarantees of equality under the law would persist until the present day.

TIME LINE OF NOTABLE
RECONSTRUCTION EVENTS

1861

May 24: Union General Benjamin Butler calls three slaves who escape behind Union lines at Fortress Monroe, Virginia, "contraband of war."

June 11: The Wheeling Convention opens in western Virginia. Unionists secede from the Confederate state of Virginia by the end of the convention, and the area will be admitted to the Union in 1863 as the state of West Virginia.

July 22: Congress passes the Crittendon-Johnson Resolution, which states that interfering in "established institutions" of the Confederacy, including slavery, is not a U.S. military objective.

August 6: Lincoln signs the First Confiscation Act into law.

September 1: Mary Chase, an Alexandria, Virginia, freedwoman, begins the first school for contrabands in the South. On September 17, Mary Peake, a free black from Hampton, Virginia, opens a school at Fortress Monroe.

November 7: The U.S. Navy occupies Port Royal on the Sea Islands off the coast of South Carolina.

1862

February 23: Lincoln appoints Andrew Johnson military governor of Tennessee.

March 13: Congress prohibits the U.S. Army from returning runaway slaves.

April 16: Congress abolishes slavery in the District of Columbia; compensation to owners averages $300 per slave. (This is the only instance of compensated emancipation.)

May 1: Union General Benjamin Butler officially takes control of New Orleans, beginning a process of wartime Reconstruction.

June 19: Congress prohibits slavery in U.S. territories.

July 17: Lincoln signs the Second Confiscation Act into law.

December 17: General Ulysses S. Grant appoints Ohio chaplain John Eaton as "General Superintendent of Contrabands for the Department [of the Tennessee]." Eaton sets up contraband camps and home farms in the Mississippi Valley.

1863

January 29: General Nathaniel Banks, U.S. military commander of Louisiana, issues regulations governing black laborers and planters in the state.

March 16: The War Department creates the American Freedmen's Inquiry Commission, which later becomes the Freedmen's Bureau.

December 8: Lincoln issues a Proclamation of Amnesty and Reconstruction, which offers a pardon and full rights to all those in the Confederacy who will take an oath of future loyalty and agree to accept all U.S. laws and proclamations pertaining to emancipation.

1864

February 22: Moderate Michael Hahn, who opposes voting rights for blacks, is elected governor of occupied Louisiana under Lincoln's Reconstruction plan, outlined in December. Only white men who took the loyalty oath are allowed to vote in this election.

March 13: Lincoln suggests, in a letter, that Governor Hahn should consider limited suffrage for blacks. Hahn does not follow his suggestion.

March 28: General Lorenzo Thomas issues an order setting aside property at Davis Bend for the use of freedmen. Grant had suggested to John Eaton that this land—once owned by Jefferson Davis' family—be used to create "a Negro paradise."

July 8: Congress passes (and Lincoln later refuses to sign) the Wade-Davis bill, authored by Ohio Senator Benjamin Wade and Maryland Congressman Henry Winter Davis, proposing terms for Reconstruction.

November 8: Abraham Lincoln is reelected president of the United States.

1865

1865: Northern investors in Southern land and businesses are initially welcomed by the economically depressed South. Later, they will be despised as "carpetbaggers."

1865: White voters in Connecticut, Minnesota, and Wisconsin reject referenda enfranchising blacks.

January 16: U.S. General William T. Sherman issues Special Field Orders, No. 15, which grants black families who apply forty acres of land on South Carolina's Sea Islands or the South Carolina and Georgia coast south of Charleston.

January 31: The U.S. House of Representatives passes the Thirteenth Amendment, ending slavery.

March 3: Congress establishes the Bureau of Refugees, Freedmen, and Abandoned Lands, and charters the Freedmen's Savings and Trust Company.

April 14: President Abraham Lincoln is shot at Ford's Theatre in Washington, D.C., and dies the following day.

April 15: Andrew Johnson is sworn in as president.

May 29: President Johnson announces his Reconstruction policy in two proclamations.

Spring–Summer: Some U.S. Army officers bar freedmen from entering Southern cities. This is one of several regulations devised, on a commander-by-commander basis, to control migration, including reinstating the pass system and instituting vagrancy laws.

Spring–Fall: "Negro conventions" held in several Southern cities protest the treatment of blacks.

Summer: Under Johnson's Reconstruction policy, Southern states elect delegates and convene constitutional conventions. Some candidates who maintained their loyalty to the Union are elected, but most delegates are former Whigs who served the Confederacy.

Summer–Fall: President Andrew Johnson pardons Confederates and restores to them confiscated and abandoned lands—including lands occupied by freedmen.

Summer–Fall: Southern states begin passing Black Codes to control the freedmen.

Fall: In the first state elections under Johnson's Reconstruction policy, the upper South chooses wartime Unionists. In the lower South, supporters of the Confederacy (both Whigs and Democrats) dominate.

December: Congress refuses to seat those Southern senators and representatives who were elected under Johnson's Reconstruction plan.

December 18: The Thirteenth Amendment, which bans slavery in the United States, becomes part of the Constitution.

1865–early 1866: Blacks hold state conventions to articulate their goals of civil and political equality.

Winter, 1865–1866: The Ku Klux Klan, a white supremacist organization that terrorizes blacks, is founded in Pulaski, Tennessee. In April 1866, the Klan holds its first national convention.

1866

1866: President Johnson sends generals James Steedman and Joseph Fullerton to report on the operations of the Freedmen's Bureau. Southern blacks overwhelmingly endorse its necessity.

February: Congress passes the Southern Homestead Act, which gives blacks and loyal whites first access to public land. This land is generally poor, and the majority of those posting claims are whites—frequently, lumber company agents. Only 4,000 blacks lay claims (75 percent of the claimants are in Florida), but many will later lose their land.

February 19: Johnson vetoes a bill extending the Freedmen's Bureau.

February 22: Johnson compares Radical Republicans Thaddeus Stevens and Charles Sumner, and abolitionist Wendell Philips, to Confederate leaders who are "opposed to the fundamental principles of this Government."

March 27: Johnson vetoes the Civil Rights bill, thereby denying government protection of freedmen's rights.

April 3: The Supreme Court, in *Ex parte Milligan,* rules that a U.S. citizen who was not a resident in a Confederate state or a prisoner of war, was not subject to trial and sentence in a military court for criminal offenses during a time of war.

April 9: Congress passes the Civil Rights bill over Johnson's veto. This is the first time in U.S. history that a presidential veto is overridden on major legislation.

May 1: Three days of racial rioting begin in Memphis, Tennessee. It is estimated that forty-six blacks and two whites are killed. Massive damage is done to black homes, schools, and churches.

June 13: Congress votes final approval of the Fourteenth Amendment.

Thaddeus Stevens of Pennsylvania was a leader of the Radical Republican faction and an adamant supporter of rights for black Americans.

July 16: Congress overrides Johnson's veto of a revised Freedmen's Bureau bill.

July 24: Tennessee is readmitted to the Union.

July 30: In a riot in New Orleans, sparked by an assembly of radical whites and blacks to overhaul the Louisiana constitution, thirty-four blacks and three whites are killed.

September: Five hundred delegates attend the Southern Loyalists Convention in Philadelphia and endorse the Fourteenth Amendment. Only one delegate, P. B. Randolph, is black. Most come from the upper South and Louisiana, where there is less opposition to their position than in the rest of the South.

Fall: A Republican landslide in the midterm elections raises the Republican majority in Congress to more than the two-thirds majority necessary to override a presidential veto.

December 3: In his annual address to Congress, Johnson claims that "the work of restoration" of the Southern states is complete, an opinion rejected by Congress.

1867

January: In *Cummings v. Missouri,* the Supreme Court declares that it is unconstitutional to require an officeholder to swear that he had always been loyal to the United States, since withholding office from someone who had once been but is not currently disloyal "imposes a punishment for an act which was not punishable at the time it was committed; or imposes additional punishment to that then prescribed."

January 7: Congress begins an investigation of President Johnson.

January 8: Congress grants the franchise to blacks in the District of Columbia, and later authorizes suffrage for black and white men in U.S. territories.

February 5: Congress passes the Habeas Corpus Act, which makes it easier for citizens to move cases to Federal courts.

March 2: Johnson vetoes the first Reconstruction Act, but his veto is overridden by Congress on the same day. *Also on this day:* Congress passes the Tenure of Office Act. The president is prohibited from removing from office any government official who had been approved by the

Senate until the Senate can confirm a new nominee for the position. *And:* Congress passes the Command of the Army Act, which calls for military orders from the president to be issued through the general of the army. It is a further restriction on Johnson's powers.

March 23: The second Reconstruction Act becomes law, over President Johnson's veto.

March 30: The United States buys Alaska from Russia.

Spring: The Union League, a political organization of local clubs that support Republican policy, begins to organize in the former Confederacy.

July 19: The third Reconstruction Act, passed over Johnson's veto, becomes law.

Fall: State constitutional conventions under Congressional Reconstruction begin to meet in the South.

1868

1868: Iowa and Minnesota give the franchise to black men.

February 21: President Johnson removes Edwin Stanton as secretary of war, allegedly violating the Tenure of Office Act.

February 24: Johnson is impeached by the House of Representatives.

March 4: Johnson's impeachment trial begins in the Senate.

March 11: The fourth Reconstruction Act becomes law, over Johnson's veto.

May 16: President Johnson is acquitted—by one vote.

June 22: Arkansas is readmitted to the Union.

June 25: Alabama, Florida, Louisiana, North Carolina, and South Carolina are readmitted to the Union.

July 28: The Fourteenth Amendment becomes part of the U.S. Constitution.

September 3: White Republicans allied with Democrats expel black members of the Georgia legislature.

1869

March 4: Ulysses S. Grant is inaugurated as president.

May 10: At the "wedding of the rails," the Union Pacific, the first transcontinental railroad, is completed, a sign of the industrial growth and the rapid development of the West that marks the Reconstruction period.

July 6: "True Republican" Gilbert Walker (who will become a Democrat in 1870) is elected governor of Virginia.

October 4: Conservative Democrats in Tennessee, who won a majority in the legislative elections, convene the legislature, effectively winning control of the state governments.

December 6: The National Labor Convention of Colored Men meets in Washington, D.C.

1870

January 26: Virginia is readmitted to the Union.

February 23: Mississippi is readmitted to the Union.

February 25: Hiram Revels, the first African American to be elected to the U.S. Senate, takes the Mississippi seat once held by Jefferson Davis.

March 30: The Fifteenth Amendment becomes part of the Constitution; on the same day, Texas is readmitted to the Union.

May 31: Congress passes the first act to enforce the Fifteenth Amendment.

July 15: Georgia is readmitted to the Union.

August 4: Conservative Democrats win a majority in the North Carolina legislature; they will impeach Republican governor William Holden in 1871.

December 12: Joseph H. Rainey of South Carolina, the first African American elected to the House of Representatives, is seated.

1871

February 28: Congress passes the second act to reinforce the Fifteenth Amendment.

April 20: Congress passes the third act to reinforce the Fifteenth Amendment, known as the Ku Klux Act.

November 1: A majority Democratic legislature convenes in Georgia. In 1872, the threat of impeachment will force Governor Rufus Bullock to resign.

1872

April 15: The Colored National Convention meets in New Orleans, with Frederick Douglass presiding.

November 5: Ulysses S. Grant is reelected President.

December 11: African American Pinckney B. S. Pinchback becomes acting governor of Louisiana.

1873

1873: Conservative Democrats, who won control of the Texas legislature in 1872, try to impeach Republican Edmund Davis; Davis is replaced by Democrat Richard Coke in 1874, when President Grant will not send troops to protect him.

1874

November 3: Conservative Democrats win the governorship and legislative majority in Alabama.
November 12: Conservative Democrat Augustus Garland is inaugurated as governor of Arkansas.

1875

March 1: President Grant signs into law the second Civil Rights Act, which requires that all citizens have equal access to public accommodations.

November 2: Conservative Democrats win control of the Mississippi legislature. Republican governor Adelbert Ames, facing impeachment, resigns in March 1876.

1876

November 7: Presidential election results between Republican Rutherford B. Hayes and Democrat Samuel Tilden are disputed. State elections for governor in Florida, South Carolina, and Louisiana are also in dispute.

1877

January 2: Democrat George Drew is inaugurated as governor of Florida.

March 2: Rutherford B. Hayes is declared president by a margin of one vote in the electoral college, after negotiations with Southern Democrats.

April 10: U.S. troops are withdrawn from the state houses in Louisiana and South Carolina, which was the first state to secede from the Union. Democratic governors Wade Hampton of South Carolina and Francis Nicholls of Louisiana begin their uncontested rule.

★　　★　　★

The South and North in the Aftermath of the War

When Carl Schurz toured the South on behalf of President Andrew Johnson in July through September of 1865, he reported that the landscape "looked for many miles like a broad black streak of ruin and desolation—the fences all gone; lonesome smoke stacks, surrounded by dark heaps of ashes and cinders, marking the spots where human habitations had stood; the fields along the road widely overgrown by weeds, with here and there a sickly patch of cotton or corn cultivated by Negro squatters."

The war, fought primarily on its territory, left the South physically devastated. Its economy was scarcely viable, and law and order were absent in many places where guerrillas and deserters roamed with impunity. Hunger and disease plagued the population, a significant number of whom were refugees. Most white Southerners initially felt exhaustion and despair, soon to be replaced by bitterness toward their conquerors, pride in themselves as people with distinct values and a way of life different from those in the North, and persistent racism and resentment toward former slaves. Some whites, notably yeoman farmers in the upcountry regions of several states, had remained Unionists and hoped to wrest political power from the planter class. Yet, most Southern Unionists were not supporters of black equality, and all whites in the South had to face the reality of the emancipation of the slaves. Among the majority of whites, there was a growing determination to preserve what they considered Southern identity and institutions, and the rise of the "Lost Cause"—the idealization of a society and culture perceived as noble and civilized but doomed by overwhelming forces—became an enduring myth to ameliorate defeat.

In contrast, the North ended the Civil War not only as the military victor, but with a boost to its morale and economy. Although hundreds of thousands had died in battle and from disease, or were disabled from wartime injuries, the percentage of losses among the Northern population was far smaller than the corresponding losses on the Southern side. The war's demands for industrial and agricultural goods had stimulated prosperity. Congress, free of dissent from Southern representatives, passed tariff and tax laws, supported railroad development and western expansion, and encouraged immigration—all to the benefit of businessmen and corporations. The role of the national government expanded; the budget in 1860 had been $63 million, but it had risen to $1 billion by 1865. Perhaps more significant was the perception of a national state; citizens identified themselves with the United States more than with the individual states where they lived. As the new magazine *The Nation* wrote in 1865: "The issue of the war marks an epoch by the consolidation of nationality under democratic forms. . . . This territorial, political, and historical oneness of the nation is now ratified by the blood of thousands of her sons. . . . The prime issue of the war was between nationality one and indivisible, and the loose and changeable federation of independent States."

Several, sometimes conflicting, attitudes colored the way the North shaped its postwar policies regarding the South. After Lincoln was assassinated, there was a call for vengeance, but this quickly subsided. Many had sympathy for the devastated population, and some proposed generous terms for including the ex-Confederate states in the Union. Others felt that winning the war would be meaningless without guarantees to protect the freedmen, and changes in the Southern economy and society. There were businessmen and industrialists ready to invest in rebuilding the South, and idealists ready to remold it into a vigorous, economically diverse, and efficient region based on free labor principles, as well as political principles of equality.

But while the future remained uncertain, the reality was that the Confederacy had lost the war. The eleven states that had fought the United States were placed under martial law and remained occupied by Federal troops when the war ended. Soldiers were enjoined to maintain the peace, and military and Freedmen's Bureau Courts dispensed justice. While the South complained vociferously at the time, and subsequently, that they were overrun by an occupying army, the fact was that there were too few troops in the South to adequately supervise the transition from slavery to freedom. By the end of July 1865, 641,000 troops of the one-million-men Union force had been released from duty. By autumn of 1866, only 38,000 troops remained, and many of these had been sent to the western frontier to combat Native Americans. The army mustered out many of its white soldiers, who had served longer than blacks. A disproportionate number of black troops then served in the occupying army, partly to provide them with food, shelter, and employment until the South could adjust to a free labor system. These blacks troops literally—and because of the symbolism of their presence as conquerors—bore the brunt of Southern resistance and hatred, suffering violence. But so too did white agents of the Freedmen's Bureau, Unionists, and those who dared to support Radical Reconstruction measures during the unsettling aftermath of the war.

Civil War Veterans and Pensions

When a Union soldier was discharged at the end of the war, he received an average of $250 in final and undrawn pay and bounties, and, if qualified, could receive a generous pension from the U.S. government. A Confederate soldier, in addition to returning to a devastated land, had no government to pay him nor any pension to look forward to. Southern state governments and volunteer groups did make an effort to provide artificial limbs, but not until Reconstruction ended could these governments offer pensions to Confederate veterans and soldiers homes to house those in need.

As early as 1861, Union volunteers were provided with the same benefits as soldiers in the regular army. On July 14, 1862, Lincoln signed into law a pension act that conveyed benefits for disabilities acquired directly during military service, or later, caused by injuries or disease resulting from service during the war. Secretary of the Interior J. P. Upshur called it "the wisest and most munificent enactment of the kind ever adapted by any nation." Benefits depended on rank—for example, a lieutenant colonel (and ranks above that level) received $30 per month for total disability; a private received $8 per month. Widows, orphans, and some other dependents, such as surviving mothers and sisters, were eligible to receive these amounts as well. In 1864, special benefits were designated for particular disabilities that caused severe impairment. For example, veterans could receive $25 per month for the loss of two eyes or two hands, $20 for the loss of both feet, and $20 for the loss of one hand and one foot. In 1872, the classifications became even more arcane; pension payments varied depending on how much of a limb was amputated. An 1873 law increased the amounts paid for a war widow's children.

The Civil War considerably increased the number of government beneficiaries. Before the war, 10,700 veterans and widows of earlier wars received pensions totaling a million dollars per year. By 1866, 126,722 beneficiaries were receiving a total of $15.5 million per year. Yet, between 1862 and 1875, the Pension Bureau declined 28 percent of applications, and many eligible veterans did not apply. Only 6.5 percent of all veterans (43 percent of those who were wounded), and only 25 percent of their eligible dependents, were receiving benefits by 1875.

Civil War pension figures seemed to peak in the mid-1870s, but the passage of the 1879 Arrears Act and the 1890 Dependent Pension Act vastly expanded the number of veterans on the rolls and the total amount paid to them. The Arrears Act allowed veterans who had not previously applied to receive a lump sum for back payments, upon acceptance of their applications. The Dependent Pension Act required only ninety days service in the Union army and evidence of disability from any cause to receive benefits. By 1906, the requirement had been reduced to simply old age.

By that time, Charles Eliot Howard, president of Harvard, had complained about abuses of the system:

> I hold it to be a hideous wrong inflicted upon the republic that the pension system instituted for the benefit of the soldiers and sailors of the United States has been prostituted and degraded. . . . As things are . . . one cannot tell whether a pensioner of the United States received an honorable wound in battle or contracted a chronic catarrh twenty years after the war. One cannot tell whether a pensioner of the United States is a disabled soldier or sailor, or a perjured pauper who has foisted himself upon the public treasury. I say that to put the pension system of the United States into this condition is a crime . . . against Republican Institutions.

Beyond Reconstruction, the pension system evolved into an adjunct of political patronage. Individual congressmen could be petitioned by applicants, and private pension bills were passed to award benefits in individual cases.

In addition to pensions, the Federal government built a system of National Homes for Disabled Volunteer Soldiers. Four branches were established from 1867 to 1870. The Sanitary Commission opposed the idea, preferring that disabled veterans be integrated into communities. In 1862, commission leader Henry Bellows had objected to "any general scheme for herding the invalids of the war into State or National institutions. . . . We don't want a vast net-work of soldiers' poor-houses scattered through the land, in which these brave fellows will languish away dull and wretched lives." However, the idea of veterans' homes received support in an 1864 petition from a variety of prominent Americans, including William Cullen Bryant, Henry Wadsworth Longfellow, Horace Greeley, Clara Barton, and P. T. Barnum. A total of fifteen homes were built; the last one in 1933.

The Civil War also created a need for orphanages and an outpouring of sympathy for the orphans' situation. Mother Mary Ann Bickerdyke, a battlefield nurse, was among those who urged soldiers' aid societies to continue their work so that "the same benevolence which led you to work for them [soldiers] would lead you to work for their children." In 1865, there were a dozen homes or schools for orphans of Union military personnel, and more were established by the states. Pennsylvania used a $50,000 grant from the

Pennsylvania Railroad to pay orphanages and boarding schools for the support of these children. When the program was in danger of being dropped, the orphans themselves presented songs, poems, and orations to the lawmakers, who then approved continued funding. New Jersey no longer needed to operate its home after 1876, but, in 1910, seven states were still operating orphanages for the children of Civil War soldiers. They were, in effect, boarding schools for the children of impoverished, living veterans.

African Americans during Reconstruction

While Union troops were occupying parts of the South during the war, and after the war ended, Southern blacks attempted to forge their own communities, free of the bonds of slavery. They moved to reaffirm family ties, to assert at least some economic independence, to set up their own churches, to establish schools and benevolent societies, and to voice their political concerns. In these efforts, they encountered considerable, often violent, resistance from white Southerners (see "Violence in the South," on page 784). Yet, they persisted; they rebuilt schools and churches burned by white terrorists, and later held political office and voted in large numbers.

Freed blacks legalized their marriages and searched for family members dispersed by slave owners. To show they were no longer slaves, some blacks adopted new names, and many insisted that whites call them "Mr." or "Mrs.," rather than using their first name, as when they were slaves. African Americans delighted in the freedom to travel, and some moved from rural areas to the cities, which they perceived as offering greater opportunities, greater access to schools and churches, and more protection against violence. From 1865 to 1870, the black population in the ten biggest Southern cities doubled, and some towns showed even greater growth. A few blacks moved out of the South altogether and settled in the North and the Midwest, including Kansas and what is present-day Oklahoma. The most important movement of former slaves, however, was within the South. Parents, children, and spouses, separated during slavery, searched for each other, hoping to recreate their families in freedom.

After the war, blacks were determined to have their own churches, rather than continue to be segregated in white-led churches. Even where the black population had been large enough to merit its own building in the antebellum South—and where blacks had provided the resources to construct them—these churches had been run, at least nominally, by white ministers. Blacks were able to assume control of some of these facilities and build others where they could be guided by black preachers. By the end of Reconstruction only a few Southern blacks remained in churches with whites—many of these in the Catholic church, which, in most cases, did not require segregated seating. More typical were black Methodists, who, by 1870, had formed their own Methodist churches. The greatest number of freedmen joined the black Southern Baptists, which operated without a clerical hierarchy such as that in the A.M.E. Church, and allowed individual ministers and congregations to practice in the manner they preferred. By 1877, the number of black Baptists was larger than the combined membership of all other black churches.

The church was an important training ground for African American leaders; many ministers were instrumental in spreading the "gospel" of political involvement. Through churches, fraternal organizations, and political groups, blacks expressed their goal of equal rights with white Americans. In the spring and summer of 1865, mass meetings and petitions flourished, and such organizations as the Equal Rights League in Wilmington, North Carolina, and the Union Monitor Club in Norfolk, Virginia, formed throughout the South. In 1865, and early 1866, statewide conventions called for political rights, suffrage, and education and protested widespread violence (see "Violence in the South," on page 784). Free blacks, ministers, artisans, and black veterans formed the majority of delegates, but as Reconstruction progressed, more and more freedmen became involved in politics.

Many Southern blacks joined the Union League, which grew out of a Unionist movement in Missouri, Kentucky, Tennessee, and Maryland. Its first Northern club had been formed in Pekin, Illinois, in 1862. An initially independent movement also developed in eastern cities such as Philadelphia and New York. Union League clubs, which supported both the war effort and the Republican Party, were attracting white Unionists, as well as some blacks, in the South even before the war ended. By 1867, black membership had mushroomed; some groups were integrated with whites, others were separate. In meetings held in churches, schools, and homes, or even in fields, local leagues offered political education and opportunities for debate and discussion. The leagues also helped to build schools and churches, provided aid, and supported better terms and wages for laborers. Some blacks rose to political leadership through the Union League, and more than eighty black lecturers traveled throughout the South in 1867 and 1868, supported by the Republican Congressional Committee. Southern blacks were almost uniformly Republican; in fact, they formed the majority of Republicans in the former Confederacy. Women were also politically active, attending mass meetings and parades, although they were denied the ballot. Black men, however, enthusiastically exercised the franchise. In some places, nearly 90 percent of the black voters filled in ballots. In others, threats from white Southerners stopped many black voters.

A significant number of African Americans served on the states' constitutional conventions and were elected to office, although they never controlled Southern governments, as whites in the South charged (see "Southern Governments under Republican Rule," on page 779). Political activism came at a price. Henry Johnson, a black South Carolina lawmaker, reported: "I always had plenty of work before I went into politics, but I have never got a job since. I suppose they do it merely because they think they will break me down and keep me from interfering with politics."

African Americans perceived education as a key to success and eagerly sought instruction during and after the war. Early schools were supported by the Freedmen's Bureau, religious groups, and philanthropists. Booker T. Washington later commented, "It was a whole race trying to go to school. Few were too young, and none too old, to make the attempt to learn. As fast as any kind of teachers could be secured, not only were day-schools filled, but night-schools as well."

The 1865 black state conventions called for schools for blacks, and, in 1866, Florida did levy a tax on black men to provide public education. The charge was fifty cents a month for each black student. Under Congressional Reconstruction, all the Southern states offered some public education. Higher education, especially teacher training, also expanded, with the establishment of a number of black colleges, including Fisk, Howard, Hampton, Tougaloo, and Atlanta. By 1869, more black teachers than white were working with the freedmen in the South.

In addition to obtaining an education, many Southern blacks strongly desired to own some land, but relatively few were actually able to achieve this goal. Most black Southerners worked as wage laborers or, over time, as sharecroppers for whites. Generally, freed blacks preferred the sharecropping system because it allowed them to work on their own rather than in gangs reminiscent of slavery. At first, blacks exercised some bargaining power as free laborers, but their leverage declined after a series of poor crops. Under a high-interest credit system, many sharecroppers soon found themselves heavily in debt to landowners. As one black man from Georgia pointed out: "No man can work another man's land . . . even for half [wages] and board and clothe himself and family and make any money. The consequence will be the freedmen will become poorer and poorer every year."

As opportunities for the freedmen dwindled and their rights were curtailed by violence, intimidation, and the maneuvers of restored Democratic governments in the South, the close of the Reconstruction period witnessed a revival of interest in emigration. In 1877, African American Henry Adams wrote from Shreveport, Louisiana, "This is a horrible part of the country and our race can not get money for our labor. . . . It is impossible for us to live with these slaveholders of the South and enjoy the right as they enjoy it." Although there was some interest in Liberia, few blacks emigrated there until after 1890. However, the idea of settlement in the West, particularly in Kansas, grew in popularity. Freedman Benjamin "Pap" Singleton, who published a circular, "The Advantage of Living in a Free State," in 1874, was among those who encouraged some 25,000 blacks to migrate to Kansas. The movement was known as *the Exodus*, and those who traveled there were Exodusters. They settled in established towns like Topeka and Dodge City, and founded all-black towns such as Nicodemus. Edward McCabe of Nicodemus promoted settlement in Oklahoma; by 1886, nearly 40,000 blacks had found homes there. By the turn of the century, more than 145,000 African Americans had settled in sixteen western states and territories—all but Texas, which had been part of the Confederacy.

Major Issues of Reconstruction

The Civil War created the need to integrate a large group of newly freed slaves into the economic and political life of the South, and to decide the terms by which the Confederate states could establish governments and be readmitted to the Union. From the time when Union troops first captured portions of the Confederacy to the final withdrawal of U.S. soldiers from the South in 1877, the same issues shaped the policies of Reconstruction: Who would own Southern land? What system of labor would replace slavery? How would the freedmen be educated? Were civil rights and suffrage necessary to secure the liberty and protection of blacks? What privileges of citizenship would ex-Confederates, particularly ex-Confederate leaders, lose or retain?

Land

During the war, particularly under the Second Confiscation Act, the United States confiscated some land from supporters of the Confederacy. Confiscation was not a frequent occurrence, however, since Lincoln did not want to alienate Southern loyalists. Moreover, Lincoln made Congress add to the act a

Timothy O'Sullivan took this photograph of five generations of African Americans who had labored as slaves on Smith's Plantation in Beaufort, South Carolina. Freed slaves desired their own land.

clause limiting confiscation to only the lifetime of the disloyal themselves. Most of the confiscated property was eventually returned to the families who had originally owned it. The United States acquired significantly more land forfeited by the failure to pay taxes or abandoned as Union troops advanced through the South.

The question of who should get this land—the freed slaves who had worked it, Southern Unionists, Northern investors, or Confederate planters—remained controversial through the early years of Reconstruction. Many blacks, and the Radical Republicans who supported them, felt that some land was owed to them for their years of enforced labor. Some white yeoman farmers who had remained loyal to the Union also favored redistribution of land at the expense of wealthy planters. There were some congressional efforts on behalf of major land redistribution, usually led by George Julian, chairman of the House Committee on Public Lands. Julian believed that, without land, the freedmen would be subject to "a system of wages slavery. . . more galling than slavery itself." Military commanders and Freedmen's Bureau agents, such as Rufus Saxton, the Bureau's director in South Carolina, Georgia, and Florida, also gave land to blacks or tried to negotiate its purchase at reasonable prices. But military decisions about land were made on an ad hoc basis, and no consistent policy evolved. In the case of Saxton, who had issued Circular 13 in July 1865, calling on his agents to set aside forty acres apiece for freedmen, President Andrew Johnson ordered the Bureau head, General Oliver Howard, to rescind the order. Howard was also directed to issue Circular 15 in September, ordering that pardoned Confederates were to be given back their land except for any small amount that had already been sold. Johnson's policy ended hopes of significant land reform.

The majority of white Federal military and government agents did not believe in large-scale land reform. Their objective was to restore the South's economy as quickly and efficiently as possible by allowing loyal Southerners to run large plantations, or leasing or selling them to white Northern investors. Most of these Northerners opposed slavery, but also intended to make a profit in cotton with blacks as wage laborers, not owners of land. After the war ended, almost all confiscated lands were returned to their original white owners—even the acres already occupied by the freedmen on the orders of military commanders. Forty thousand freedmen who had settled on land issued to them by Union General William T. Sherman, in his Special Order, Number 15, were evicted by the U.S. government in 1865. When the Freedmen's Bureau head, Oliver Howard, a Union general who had lost his arm at the battle of Fair Oaks, asked South Carolina blacks to devise a reasonable way for their former owners to reclaim this land, they issued a report that stated:

> General, we want Homesteads, we were promised Homesteads by the government. If it does not carry out the promises its agents made to all of us, if the government having concluded to befriend its late enemies and to neglect to observe the principles of common faith between its self and us its allies in the war you said was over, now takes away from them all right to the soil they stand upon save such as they can get by again working for *your* late and their *all time* enemies . . . we are left in a more unpleasant condition than our former. . . . You will see this is not the condition of really freemen.

You ask us to forgive the land owners of our island. *You* only lost your right arm in the war and might forgive them. The man who tied me to a tree and gave me 39 lashes and who stripped and flogged my mother and my sister and who will not let me stay in his empty hut except I will do his planting and be satisfied with his price and who combines with others to keep away land from me well knowing I would not have anything to do with him if I had land of my own—that man, I cannot well forgive. Does it look as if he has forgiven me, seeing how he tries to keep me in a condition of helplessness?

By the middle of 1866, half the land available to the Freedmen's Bureau had been returned to its original owners, and in the 1870s, despite delays while court cases were settled, the restoration was nearly complete.

Labor

As soon as the United States made emancipation a goal of the Civil War, it was accepted that a free labor economy would replace slavery. In the eyes of the Northern government and businessmen, negotiable contracts between owners and workers would replace forced labor, presumably giving the freedmen opportunities to move up the economic scale. They would, in this view, labor for wages but essentially preserve the plantation system as it otherwise had operated. The way to revive the South was to infuse it with Northern values of initiative and enterprise, not to remake it completely.

For most Southern whites, who also had no intention of dismantling the plantation system, the goal was to recreate, as closely as possible, the conditions that existed before the war: a large group of workers who were dependent on whites for their existence and therefore bound to submit to all restrictions and regulations. The future existence of families that had once dominated the South hinged, according to a Georgia newspaper, on "one single *condition—the ability of the planter to command labor.*" Early labor contracts, even those drawn up by U.S. military commanders during the war, often reinstated supervised gang labor. Freedmen were forbidden to leave plantations without the owners' permission or to hold meetings. These contracts were also common among Northern investors.

The terms of the other half of the contract—the owner's obligation to provide payment or shelter, education, and medical care—were often circumvented or ignored. Of this situation, James Yeatman, a Western Sanitary Commission inspector, wrote, in *A Report on the Condition of the Freedmen of the Mississippi* in 1864:

The poor negroes are everywhere greatly depressed at their condition. They all testify that if they were only paid their little wages as they earn them, so that they could purchase clothing, and were furnished with the provisions promised they could stand it; but to work and get poorly paid, poorly fed, and not doctored when sick, is more than they can endure. Among the thousands whom I questioned none showed the least unwillingness to work. If they could only be paid fair wages they would be content and happy. . . .

Black Codes passed by the Southern states shortly after the war's end reinforced white power to control labor. Among the stipulations, blacks could be fined for vagrancy, then forced to work for whites to pay off the fine. Apprenticeship laws required black youth to work without pay. Some laws banned whites from offering higher wages to lure workers away from other planters.

Most freedmen, on the other hand, defined freedom and free labor as working for themselves, as self-sufficient farmers on their own land. They sought autonomy to control the terms and conditions of their work. Labor and land issues were closely tied to each other because, with land, blacks had a chance of independent employment; without it, they were forced to work for wages or crop shares. By 1866, instead of creating individual contracts between freedmen and planters, most planters negotiated terms with large groups. But because it gave them more control over their workday, without white supervision, more and more freedmen preferred to sign labor contracts as a family. Their share would be one-third of the crop if the planter provided equipment and seeds, and half of the crop if they provided their own. Planters could minimize their costs this way, but they hesitated to give up their authority. Nonetheless, sharecropping evolved as the dominant labor arrangement in the postwar South.

Education

The freedmen—who, as slaves, had been denied instruction by law in all the states of the Confederacy except Tennessee—enthusiastically embraced the opportunities for education offered under Reconstruction. Even before the war ended, white and free black teachers traveled south under the auspices of freedmen's aid societies and the American Missionary Association to work with children and adults (see Chapter 10, "The Home Front"). The Freedmen's Bureau placed a high priority on education; it was considered the basis of all future economic and political success for blacks. But because the

Bureau was not well funded, it established no schools itself. Instead, it coordinated Northern philanthropic efforts and was working with nearly 3,000 schools (not including evening and private missionary schools, and schools run by blacks) by 1869. An increasing number of teachers were black. For African Americans, education was tied to citizenship. "In proportion to the education of the people so is their progress in civilization," declared A. J. Ransier, a black delegate to the South Carolina constitutional convention.

When the Southern states drew up new constitutions in 1867 and 1868, provisions for public education were included in all of them. (Unionist yeomen farmers and other less prosperous whites had sought such provisions before the war, putting them in conflict with planters who paid for private education for their own children.) Many Southern whites objected to the cost, often funded through taxes, but poor whites as well as blacks benefited from public education. There was also conflict over whether these new public school systems should be segregated. Southern whites tended to oppose integration, and Northern whites to be indifferent. Blacks preferred integration—as part of their equal rights under the Fourteenth Amendment, and because they feared underfunding of black schools—but they also accepted that school integration was not likely to happen. In 1866, the American Freedmen's Union Commission did state that integration was "inherently right" and refused to "shut out a child from our schools because of his color. . . . It took America three-quarters of a century of agitation and four years of war to learn the meaning of the word 'Liberty.' God grant to teach us by easier lessons the meaning of the words 'equal rights.'"

Although Tennessee passed a law for separate schools since it was already readmitted to the Union, most of the other Southern states did not specify one way or the other. Only two, Louisiana and South Carolina, provided for integrated schools, although they were rarely integrated in practice. At the college level, only South Carolina offered some measure of integration in public education. Starting in 1866, Berea College, founded by the American Missionary Association in Kentucky, accepted both white and black students until the state banned integration in 1904.

Black schools became a target of white supremacist organizations, such as the Ku Klux Klan. And as the Southern states amended their constitutions after Reconstruction ended, and instituted Jim Crow laws, separate—and inferior—schools for blacks were a cornerstone of segregation. Yet, education was the most successful aspect of Reconstruction. It set the stage for a dramatic rise in black literacy, from under 20 percent in 1870 to 55 percent by 1900.

Black Civil Rights

Although blacks recognized immediately that emancipation would be mean-ingless without a guarantee of equality under the law, when the Civil War ended only Radical Republicans in the North seemed to recognize the need for specifically conferring civil rights on African Americans. In 1865, the new governments forming in the South, under President Andrew Johnson's requirements for Reconstruction, were dominated by former supporters of the Confederacy. They considered the abolition of slavery intrusion enough, and had no intention of granting black rights. Even the poor yeomen farmers among Southern Unionists were concerned with securing rights for them-selves, not for the freedmen.

In 1864, the National Convention of Colored Citizens of the United States proclaimed:

> We believe that the highest welfare of this great country will be found in erasing from its statute-books all enactments discriminating in favor of or against any class of people, and by establishing one law for the white and colored people alike. . . . in the matter of government, the object of which is the protection and security of human rights, prejudice should be allowed no voice whatsoever.

In 1865, and early 1866, black conventions in the South politely demanded equal rights. But it was the advent of Black Codes in the Southern states, and reports of pervasive violence against freedmen, that convinced the majority of Republicans in Congress of the importance of legal protections. Although protection of civil rights had traditionally been the province of state govern-ments, moderate Republicans accepted that secession and defeat in war al-tered traditions. The stature and power of the national government had grown during the war, and the Republican majority in Congress proposed Federal safeguards if the Southern states did nothing to safeguard the freed-men themselves.

These intertwined issues—the granting of civil rights to blacks, and the power of the Federal government over the states to guarantee them—shaped the politics and policies of the Reconstruction era and beyond. In 1866, Con-gress overrode Johnson's veto of a civil rights bill that defined anyone born in the United States (except Indians) as a national citizen who had the right to make contracts, engage in lawsuits, and benefit from "all laws and proceed-ings for the security of persons and property." Congress then went on to pass the Fourteenth Amendment, the first section of which called for equality before the law. But, in its open language and its reliance on Federal courts for interpretation and enforcement, the Fourteenth Amendment left great latitude for defining what equality meant and for states to circumvent its intention under the guise of legality (see "Fourteenth Amendment," on page 767).

Black Suffrage

Political equality, centered in the right to vote, was the final cornerstone of Reconstruction. Even before the Civil War ended, free blacks pursued this right in the Northern states that did not allow them to vote (see Chapter 3, "Wartime Politics") and in Union-occupied areas of the Confederacy, particularly Louisiana. In December 1863, Frederick Douglass addressed a meeting of the American Anti-Slavery Society:

> [Our] work will not be done until the colored man is admitted as a full member in good and regular standing in the American body politic. . . . It is said that the colored man is ignorant, and therefore he shall not vote. In saying this, you lay down a rule for the black man that you apply to no other class of citizens. I will hear nothing of degradation or of ignorance against the black man. . . . If he knows an honest man from a thief, he knows much more than some of our white voters. . . . If he knows enough to take up arms in defence of this Government, and bare his breast to the storm of rebel artillery, he knows enough to vote. . . . All I ask, however, in regard to blacks, is that whatever rule you adopt, whether of intelligence or wealth, as the condition of voting, you shall apply it equally to the black man. . . .

When African American Henry Highland Garnet spoke before the House of Representatives in 1865, he pointed out:

> It is often asked when and where will the demands of reformers of this and coming ages end? . . . When all unjust and heavy burdens shall be removed from every man in the land. . . . When emancipation shall be followed by enfranchisement, and all men holding allegiance to the government shall enjoy every right of American citizenship. . . .

Voting rights for blacks was a controversial issue. Only five states in the North granted blacks the ballot on an equal basis with whites when the Civil War began, and initiatives to enfranchise blacks in other Northern states, voted on by whites in public referendums, failed. As Congress developed its

Reconstruction policies in 1866 and 1867, however, granting voting rights seemed not only simple justice, but a way for blacks to protect themselves without Federal intervention, since they would have the power to affect politics. Black voters were also expected to offset the power of former Confederate leaders and to maintain a Republican government in the adamantly Democratic South—a wish among Republican congressmen for political as well as idealistic reasons.

In 1867, Congress granted suffrage to blacks under its direct control, in the District of Columbia, and then in U.S. territories. But Republican congressmen were in conflict over whether the Southern states should be required to grant the vote to black men in their new constitutions before they could be readmitted to the Union. This requirement was finally embodied in the first Reconstruction Act of 1867. Even before the Fifteenth Amendment (1870) incorporated into the Constitution the right of black men to vote (see "Fifteenth Amendment," on page 778), they had eagerly entered politics in the reconstructed Southern state governments.

Confederate Disenfranchisement and the Right to Hold Office

The issues of whether to disenfranchise Confederates, and whether they should be allowed to hold office, were as controversial and hotly debated following the Civil War as issues of black equality and suffrage. Northern Radicals, white Southern Unionists, and, later, white Southern Republicans opposed immediate reinstatement of the right to vote, particularly to ex-Confederate leaders, because they wanted to replace the planter domination of government with a new group of lawmakers and governors who were sympathetic to reform. Concurrently, they wanted to keep the Republican Party in power. Radicals, and, later, moderate Republicans also feared that if Confederates held political power, they would never grant civil rights to blacks. Ex-Confederate leaders, of course, wanted to vote and hold office in order to return the South to their idea of "home rule."

Abraham Lincoln's Reconstruction plan restored voting rights to Confederates who took a loyalty oath to the U.S. government and agreed to accept abolition. Only a few classes of Confederates were denied this option. Andrew Johnson similarly called for a loyalty oath, but excluded fourteen groups of Confederates, including ex-leaders and men of property. These men could, however, apply to him personally for pardons (they were quickly granted). The Fourteenth Amendment passed by Congress denied some

Confederates the right to hold office, but not to vote, while the first Reconstruction Act kept this same group from serving as delegates to the constitutional conventions that would be called by the Southern states under the rules of Congressional Reconstruction.

When forming their new constitutions, Southern Republican delegates differed on whether to disenfranchise ex-Confederates in their states. Many believed disenfranchisement of any group was counter to the democratic spirit of the country. This view, held by the majority of black delegates, was expressed by freedman Thomas Lee of Alabama: "I have no desire to take away the rights of the white man. All I want is equal rights in the court house and equal rights when I go to vote." Upcountry white yeomen farmers who had resented planter power in the antebellum period tended to support Confederate disenfranchisement. Ultimately, Georgia, Florida, Texas, South Carolina, and North Carolina drew up constitutions with few or no voting restrictions for whites; Alabama, Arkansas, Louisiana, Mississippi, and Virginia had many restrictions. So unpopular were the Mississippi and Virginia provisions that, although their constitutions were finally ratified, the disenfranchisement clauses were defeated in separate votes.

Disenfranchisement was used as an issue to win white support by both Republicans and Democrats in the Reconstruction South. In 1869, Southern Democrats stressed removing voting limitations on ex-Confederates, rather than opposing black voting rights. Even Republican politicians quickly grew wary of the restrictions. In an attempt to win white voters to their party, all the Southern states but Arkansas had abolished Confederate voting restrictions by 1871.

Wartime Reconstruction

Wartime Reconstruction can be said to have begun as soon as Union troops captured portions of the Confederacy. The United States was then required to govern the occupied territory, formulate a plan to deal with abandoned and fugitive slaves, and, eventually, develop a process by which loyal governments could be established and states could be readmitted to the Union. At first, the United States had no policy on whether to return slaves who fled to Union camps to their owners. In May 1861, Union General Benjamin Butler called three escaped slaves, who had taken refuge behind Union lines at Fortress Monroe, Virginia, contraband of war. The term contraband came to refer to slaves who fled the Confederacy to take refuge with Union troops. After the issuance of the Emancipation Proclamation, they were called freedmen.

By August 1861, the first Confiscation Act was passed. It authorized the seizure of all property used to give military aid to the Confederacy, including slaves. The second Confiscation Act, in July 1862, further authorized seizure of property of anyone supporting the Confederacy, and declared that all slaves of these persons who came within Union lines "shall be deemed captives of war and shall be forever free." However, because confiscation was only permitted after a Federal court found a property owner guilty of disloyalty, the effectiveness of the act was limited. In addition, Lincoln insisted on a clause conforming to the Constitution that confiscation applied only to Confederate supporters themselves and not to their heirs. It was the Emancipation Proclamation of 1863, rather than the Confiscation Acts, which significantly affected the status of slaves in the Confederacy.

As the war continued, Reconstruction demanded policies that would recognize emancipation as an incontestable fact and would adjust the South's economic and political institutions to a system of labor based on freedom rather than slavery; challenge the traditional leadership of the planter class; and raise the issue of rights for blacks. Both Lincoln and Congress formulated such plans for wartime Reconstruction.

During the Civil War, military governments and governmental bodies formed by civilians who had stayed loyal to the Union ruled the occupied South. The occupied areas were testing grounds for models of Reconstruction. Local circumstances, the attitudes and outlook of individual military commanders, and the general political climate created varied approaches, but all emphasized the restoration of stability rather than the protection of blacks' rights.

South Carolina Sea Islands

In November 1861, the Union's capture of Port Royal, on the South Carolina Sea Islands, initiated the first of the early experiments in Reconstruction. The islands' white inhabitants fled to the mainland, leaving behind nearly 10,000 slaves who, being isolated from other communities, had developed a unique way of life. Few whites expected them to succeed on their own. Northern missionaries and teachers were successful in establishing schools (see Chapter 10, "The Home Front"), but failed to persuade the U.S. military officers and treasury agents, who sold land to collect unpaid taxes, to sell any more than a fraction of this land to the former slaves. Instead, the land was bought by Northern investors seeking to make a profit in cotton;

they hired reluctant blacks as plantation laborers. The freedmen continued to prefer growing subsistence crops instead of "the slave crop," cotton. Several Northerners abandoned the project, dividing their land into lots, which they sold to black workers. By 1870, it is estimated that Sea Islanders owned the most land, per capita, of blacks in the South.

Louisiana and the Mississippi Valley

Reconstruction on the Sea Islands took place without the presence of Southern whites or an influx of fugitive slaves. Louisiana, however, contained a significant number of white Unionists whom the United States tried to accommodate so that they would remain loyal. When the Union army, under General Benjamin Butler, occupied New Orleans and the sugar-growing parishes of southern Louisiana in April 1862, Butler, as commander of the Department of the Gulf, ordered blacks to continue working on the plantations of Unionists for wages, room, board, and medical care. They could not be physically punished by their former owners, but army provost marshals could take disciplinary measures against them. Butler rented abandoned plantations to investors from the North who also paid wages to black laborers. He was replaced by General Nathaniel Banks in December 1862, and Banks refined and extended his system throughout the areas that were later occupied by U.S. troops.

On January 29, 1863—four weeks after the Emancipation Proclamation took effect—Banks issued an order (followed by another on February 3) that allowed planters who took a U.S. loyalty oath to employ freedmen for three dollars a month or 5 percent of the year's crop, and to provide "just treatment, healthy rations, comfortable clothing, quarters, fuel, medical attendance, and instruction for children." Freedmen were forced by the army to sign yearly labor contracts. Banks instituted a pass system that limited the freedmen's ability to leave plantations, and, like Butler, called for provost marshals to enforce "continuous faithful service, respectful deportment, correct discipline and perfect subordination" on the part of black laborers. Frederick Douglass' reaction was typical of blacks and radical whites' responses to these rules. He declared: "[It] practically enslaves the negro, and makes the Proclamation of 1863 a mockery and delusion." The only order from Banks that Louisiana blacks favored was one that created a "Board of Education for the Department of the Gulf" in March 1864. By October, seventy-eight schools, with 7,900 students and 125 teachers, had been established.

After the fall of Vicksburg to the Union in July 1863, and the consequent flood of black refugees into Union lines, Banks' system was established in the entire Mississippi Valley. He defended his regulations as fair to blacks because they preserved their families, provided education, and abolished corporal punishment. In 1864, he increased wages, allowed the freedmen to choose their employers, and ordered planters to give their workers garden plots. He was, however, opposed to black suffrage, a right that the educated and prosperous free black community of New Orleans campaigned for. Black suffrage received no support from George Shepley, the military governor of occupied Louisiana, who had been originally appointed by Butler, or from Michael Hahn, elected governor, in February 1864, by those whites who had taken a loyalty oath, as prescribed in Lincoln's Proclamation of Amnesty and Reconstruction. Although Lincoln himself suggested that Hahn should consider a limited form of suffrage for blacks, black men did not receive the vote until a new state constitution was drawn up under Congressional Reconstruction and ratified in 1868 (see also Chapter 3, "Wartime Politics").

The Proclamation of Amnesty and Reconstruction, and the Wade-Davis Bill

Issued on December 8, 1863, Lincoln's Proclamation of Amnesty and Reconstruction offered a pardon and full rights to all those in the Confederacy who would take an oath of future loyalty and agree to accept emancipation. When the number equaled 10 percent of the votes cast in 1860, those who swore loyalty could form a new state government and create a constitution that abolished slavery. High-ranking Confederate military and civilian officeholders were excluded, as was anyone "treating colored persons, or white persons in charge of such, otherwise than lawfully as prisoners of war. . . . " Lincoln aimed at weakening support for the Confederacy and abolishing slavery. Because he maintained that states possessed no constitutional authority to secede, he did not believe that legally the Confederate states had ever left the Union. Therefore, he felt no need for a complicated process to reinstate them. Unlike the Radical Republicans in Congress, he did not plan to restructure the South politically and economically or convey rights to the freedmen.

Lincoln's Proclamation seemed excessively lenient to Congress, which passed the Wade-Davis bill in July 1864. Authored by Ohio Senator Benjamin Wade and Maryland Congressman Henry Winter Davis, the bill called for a *majority* of white men in a Southern state to pledge loyalty to the U.S. Constitution, followed by an election of delegates to a state constitutional convention. Delegates could be chosen only by those white men who could take an "Ironclad Oath" that they had not in any way supported the Confederacy—a provision that Lincoln objected to. Wade-Davis also guaranteed equality before the law for freedmen. Davis stated that any congressman who felt that secession and war "placed citizens of rebel states beyond the protection of the Constitution, and that Congress has supreme power over them as conquered enemies," should vote for his bill. The majority did, but Lincoln pocket-vetoed it.

These proposals for wartime Reconstruction on a national basis—from Lincoln and from Congress—highlighted the controversy over just how far the Federal government should go, beyond emancipation, to compel changes in the South. Under Lincoln's plan, for example, the new state constitution created by Louisiana delegates elected by the 10 percent of Unionists failed to grant not only black suffrage but also equality under the law. Congress refused to seat representatives from the "Lincoln-reconstructed" states of Louisiana, Arkansas, and Tennessee.

Coastal Georgia and South Carolina

As General William T. Sherman advanced through Georgia with the Union army, large numbers of freedmen followed but had no way to support themselves. In Savannah, Sherman and U.S. Secretary of War Edwin Stanton were told during a meeting with blacks: "The way we can best take care of ourselves is to have land, and turn in and till it by our labor. . . ." On January 16, 1865, four days after this meeting, Sherman issued Special Field Order, No. 15. This order set aside a strip from the coast thirty miles inland, stretching from Charleston to Jacksonville and including the Sea Islands, for the exclusive settlement of freedmen on plots of no more than forty acres per family. They would be granted "possessory titles" until Congress granted them full title. By June 1865, more than 40,000 blacks were living on these lands, but, in August 1865, Andrew Johnson restored the property to its Confederate owners and the freedmen were evicted.

Thirteenth Amendment

The first of the Reconstruction Amendments became part of the Constitution on December 18, 1865:

Neither slavery nor involuntary servitude, except as a punishment for crime whereof the party shall have been duly convicted, shall exist within the United States, or any place subject to their jurisdiction.

Congress shall have power to enforce this article by appropriate legislation.

Lincoln, addressing the lame-duck Congress in his annual message of December 6, 1864, called for passage of what would become the Thirteenth Amendment. An attempt to pass this amendment in April 1864, before the election, had cleared the Senate by a vote of thirty-eight to six, but was defeated in the House of Representatives by a vote of ninety-three to sixty-five, which failed to achieve the required two-thirds majority. The amendment was opposed by Democrats and conservative congressmen from the border states.

Lincoln could have waited for the Congress elected in 1864 (it was three quarters Republican) to pass the amendment, but he was anxious to have bipartisan approval and accordingly lobbied a group of lame-duck Democratic lawmakers. On January 31, 1865, the House passed the Thirteenth Amendment by a 119 to 56 vote. Sixteen Democrats voted in favor and eight more chose to be absent that day. Historians have reported that a scene of great jubilation followed, with cheering and weeping on the floor and in the galleries. The House adjourned in celebration after the vote.

The ratification of the Thirteenth Amendment was one requirement for Reconstruction on which both Lincoln's successor, Andrew Johnson, and the Radical Republicans agreed.

Presidential Reconstruction

Presidential Reconstruction refers to the plan formulated by Andrew Johnson for readmittance of the Southern states to the Union after the Civil War and to the governments those states formed in response. Republicans in Congress expected Johnson to demand strict terms of the Confederate states. "Treason is a crime and crime must be punished," he had said. "Treason must be made infamous and traitors must be impoverished." However, on May 29, 1865, Johnson announced a generous Reconstruction policy in two proclamations. The first offered pardon and the restoration of all property, except slaves, to any Southerner who would take a loyalty oath and support emancipation. Fourteen classes of people, including Confederate officials and those with taxable property worth more than $20,000, were excepted and would have to apply directly to the president for amnesty.

The second proclamation appointed William Holden as governor of North Carolina and empowered him to call an election for delegates to a new state constitutional convention. Voters and delegates were those who took the loyalty oath and were qualified to vote before secession—therefore, all white men. Johnson, an advocate of states' rights, left it to the constitutional convention delegates to define voters' and officeholders' eligibility for the future. The new constitution was also required to abolish slavery, repeal the ordinances of secession, and repudiate the Confederate debt (a condition added in October 1865). Johnson issued similar proclamations for Mississippi, Georgia, Texas, Alabama, South Carolina, and Florida.

Because Johnson considered secession illegal, the Confederate states, in his terms, had never actually left the Union. He wanted their full rights as states restored as quickly as possible. All the states embodied his lenient requirements in their new constitutions, and none gave any rights to the freedmen. In the fall elections following the writing of these constitutions, most of those elected in the Deep South, including governors, senators, and congressmen, had initially opposed secession but later served as Confederate officeholders. Since Johnson sometimes granted hundreds of pardons in one day (by 1866, he had issued more than 7,000 pardons), leading Confederates were only briefly disenfranchised and soon became eligible for office as well. Wartime Unionists did not take political control of the South, as many Northerners had hoped.

The new state governments made some attempts to economically modernize the South and to provide public education for whites only, but their emphasis on restoring the plantation model, with its controlled black labor supply, hindered any long-term substantive change. Black Codes (see page 766) passed by Southern legislatures defined land and labor policies, denied African Americans' rights, and prescribed behavior in ways that seemed to recreate slavery. Violence against blacks and Unionists was prevalent (see "Violence in the South," on page 784). Although Republicans in Congress were divided on the question of black suffrage, most had come to believe in the importance of equality before the law. And Charles Dana, editor of the *Chicago Republican*, wrote of developments under Presidential Reconstruction, "As for negro suffrage, the

Andrew Johnson of Tennessee became the seventeenth president of the United States on Abraham Lincoln's death.

mass of the Union men in the Northwest do not care a great deal. What scares them is the idea that the rebels are all to be let back . . . and made a power in the government again, just as though there had been no rebellion."

When the thirty-ninth U.S. Congress met in December 1865, Republicans refused to recognize the recently elected Southern senators and congressmen. They included Confederate vice president Alexander Stephens, nine former Confederate congressmen, seven former state officials, four Confederate generals, and four colonels. Congress formed a Joint Committee on Reconstruction "to inquire into the condition of the States which formed the so-called Confederate States of America," and began to legislate its own terms for reconstructing the Union.

Black Codes

In 1865 and 1866, Southern legislatures quickly enacted laws to curtail the newfound freedom of former slaves and to assert control over the labor of black people. Known as Black Codes, the new laws were designed to emulate many aspects of antebellum bondage, and to restore slavery at least in effect, if not in name. Although these codes usually guaranteed the rights of blacks to own property, sue, and marry, they spelled out restrictions on these rights, such as forbidding interracial marriage or allowing blacks to testify as witnesses only where either the plaintiff or the defendant, or both, were black.

To ensure that economic leverage remained with the predominantly white landowners, these codes specified various conditions for labor and included apprenticeship regulations that effectively compelled black children to work without pay. Black children whom white courts decided were not financially supported were apprenticed, and preference was given to former owners to decide where they would work. All-encompassing vagrancy laws subjected unemployed freedmen to arrest and a fine; if the fine could not be paid, they would be "hired out" until their employers paid the amount owed. In Virginia, vagrants included those who would not work for "the usual and common wages given to other laborers"; in South Carolina, these were "persons who lead idle or disorderly lives;" and in Alabama, "a stubborn or refractory servant; a laborer or servant who loiters away his time. . . ." Alabama, like the other states, also included provisions that "it shall not be lawful for any person to interfere with, hire, employ or entice away or induce to leave the service of another, any laborer or servant, who shall have stipulated or contracted in writing, to serve for any given number of days. . . ."

Mississippi and South Carolina passed the earliest and most severe codes. In Mississippi, African Americans had to show a written contract for employment each year. If they quit their jobs at any time during the year, they lost any money they had made to that point and could be arrested by any white person and returned to the planter for whom they worked. "Malicious mischief," "insulting" gestures or words, and "exercising the function of a minister of the Gospel" without a license were a few of the many other crimes for which blacks might be punished under the Mississippi code. South Carolina required blacks to pay, each year, a tax as high as $100 to be employed at anything other than farming or domestic work. It designated the rules that applied between "master" and "servant"—terms used in other states' Black Codes. For example, under South Carolina's Black Codes, blacks could not leave the plantation or have visitors there without permission of their "masters," or sell any produce without written permission.

The Mississippi and South Carolina Black Codes created such an uproar in the North that the other Southern states toned down the language they used and made no specific reference to race. However, these Black Codes still circumscribed behavior and prescribed the terms of work. Louisiana and Texas demanded that contracts "shall embrace the labor of all the members of the family able to work," to keep black women and children in the fields. In Florida, no "disrespect" was allowed; and, in North Carolina, even "the *intent* to steal" was a crime. In Alabama, the punishments allowed for those living in poorhouses or prisons included "the use of chain-gangs, putting in stocks, if necessary, to prevent escapes," and "such reasonable correction as a parent may inflict upon a stubborn, refractory child."

Black Codes that seemed to reinstitute de facto slavery so angered Congress that even moderate Republicans felt the need for a plan of Reconstruction that would protect the rights of blacks. Under the governments formed during Congressional Reconstruction, the last of these codes was dismantled.

Fourteenth Amendment

The Fourteenth Amendment became a part of the U.S. Constitution on July 28, 1868. The amendment was designed to protect the rights of black Americans, to prevent former Confederates from attaining political power, and to renounce responsibility for the Confederate debt. Its five sections were:

Section 1
All persons born or naturalized in the United States, and subject to the jurisdiction thereof, are citizens of the United States and of the State wherein they reside. No State shall make or enforce any law which shall abridge the privileges or immunities of citizens of the United States; nor

shall any State deprive any person of life, liberty, or property, without due process of law; nor deny to any person within its jurisdiction the equal protection of the laws.

Section 2

Representatives shall be apportioned among the several States according to their respective numbers, counting the whole number of persons in each State, excluding Indians not taxed. But when the right to vote at any election for the choice of electors for President and Vice President of the United States, Representatives in Congress, the Executive and Judicial officers of a State, or the members of the Legislature thereof, is denied to any of the male inhabitants of such State, being twenty-one years of age, and citizens of the United States, or in any way abridged, except for participation in rebellion, or other crime, the basis of representation therein shall be reduced in the proportion which the number of such male citizens shall bear to the whole number of male citizens twenty-one years of age in such State.

Section 3

No person shall be a Senator or Representative in Congress, or elector of President and Vice President, or hold any office, civil or military, under the United States, or under any State, who, having previously taken an oath, as a member of Congress, or as an officer of the United States, or as a member of any State legislature, or as an executive or judicial officer of any State, to support the Constitution of the United States, shall have engaged in insurrection or rebellion against the same, or given aid or comfort to the enemies thereof. But Congress may by a vote of two-thirds of each House, remove such disability.

Section 4

The validity of the public debt of the United States, authorized by law, including debts incurred for payment of pensions and bounties for services in suppressing insurrection or rebellion, shall not be questioned. But neither the United States nor any State shall assume or pay any debt or obligation incurred in aid of insurrection or rebellion against the United States, or any claim for the loss or emancipation of any slave; but all such debts, obligations and claims shall be held illegal and void.

Section 5

The Congress shall have power to enforce, by appropriate legislation, the provisions of this article.

Section 1 of the Fourteenth Amendment recognized citizenship at a national level as being beyond the power of the states to abridge, or of presidents or lawmakers to deny by passing or vetoing subsequent legislation. Although the Civil Rights Act of 1866 dealt with many of the amendment's concerns, and had been passed over Andrew Johnson's veto, some Republicans, such as moderate Senator John Bingham, thought it could be challenged on constitutional grounds. The Amendment placed these rights beyond such arguments.

Section 2 attempted to force the Southern states to accept black suffrage, or, if they did not, to limit the number of seats they could hold—and, therefore, their power—in Congress. Before emancipation, three-fifths of the slave population was counted in determining the number of congressmen and presidential electors a state would have. After emancipation, the entire population of freedmen would have been counted, increasing the number of representatives, if this section had not been added. Instead, if the South refused to give blacks the vote, they could not count them in determining representation. Northern states without black suffrage, however, would not be significantly affected because their black populations were relatively small.

Section 2 caused a furor among suffragists who had supported abolition and, putting aside their own efforts to win the vote, worked for emancipation during the war. Since congressional representation was reduced only for denying any group of "males" the ballot, gender was still a basis of exclusion. Even men who favored women's suffrage equivocated, deciding that while the country might be ready to endorse black rights, it was not ready to do this for women. Radical Republican Charles Sumner called the franchise for women "the great question of the future." But suffragist leaders such as Susan B. Anthony and Elizabeth Cady Stanton felt betrayed and angry. Stanton was incensed that uneducated men might be given the vote when educated women were not. The two broke away from the traditional reform movement to build an independent women's rights movement around their National Woman Suffrage Association and opposed the Fifteenth Amendment.

Although the third section of the Fourteenth Amendment did not disenfranchise every Confederate and applied only to those who had once sworn a loyalty oath to the United States and then served in the Confederacy, it did strike at the Confederacy's powerful leaders and military officers, with the hope that loyal Unionists would assume power. At the time of Reconstruction, Southerners and Democrats took less issue with Section 1 than with

Sections 2 and 3, which they felt to be extreme punishment for the South. The first section, however, calling for equality under the law, even though its terms are open to interpretation, has been a cornerstone for securing rights for people of color.

Congressional Reconstruction

"These are no times of ordinary politics," commented abolitionist Wendell Phillips in the early days of Reconstruction. "These are formative hours: the national purpose and thought grows and ripens in thirty days as much as ordinary years bring it forward."

In this spirit, the Republican-dominated Congress formulated its program for reconstructing the Southern states. For Radical Republicans, the central issues were providing both political equality and economic opportunity for the freedmen. But even moderate Republicans were alarmed by the resurgence of Confederate leadership in elections under presidential Reconstruction, and the prevalence of violence against blacks and Unionist and Northern whites. At a minimum, they sought to ensure equality under the law for black people, and as the South's intransigence grew, they accepted the need for black suffrage.

The Civil Rights Bill, passed over Johnson's veto on April 9, 1866, addressed the issue of equality before the law. It conveyed citizenship to all those born in the United States (except Native Americans), and granted blacks the rights of a citizen to make contracts, sue, hold property, and enjoy the "full and equal benefit of all laws and proceedings for the security of person and property, as is enjoyed by white citizens."

Four Reconstruction acts laid out Congress' requirements for readmitting the Southern states to the Union. The first, which became law on March 2, 1867, was intended "to provide for the more efficient Government of the Rebel States." It established five military districts in the South: (1) Virginia; (2) North Carolina and South Carolina; (3) Georgia, Alabama, and Florida; (4) Mississippi and Arkansas; and (5) Louisiana and Texas. Each district was to be governed by a commanding officer, and a military force would keep the peace and enforce the law. Military officers were expected to supervise the election of delegates to state constitutional conventions. The delegates were "to be elected by the male citizens of the state, twenty-one years old and upward, of whatever race, color, or previous condition, who have been resident in said state for one year . . . except such as may be disenfranchised for participation in the rebellion or for felony at common law."

Thus, the voters were Northern whites who had settled in the South, blacks, and those who had taken an ironclad oath of loyalty. The new constitutions were required to make provision for black suffrage. When the majority of those eligible to vote had ratified the new constitution and Congress had approved it, and the state had ratified the Fourteenth Amendment, it would be allowed back into the Union. President Johnson vetoed this, as he did every Reconstruction law. Congress overrode all the vetoes.

The other Reconstruction Acts evolved out of Southern and presidential responses to the first. The second Reconstruction Act, which became law three weeks after the first, provided details to carry out the Reconstruction process even when Southerners themselves took no action, preferring military rule to granting rights to blacks. The five military commanders were empowered to register voters, to set up the elections for delegates to the constitutional conventions, to assemble the conventions, and to oversee the adoption of state constitutions. Under this act, the army began to register voters, including freedmen, as the Republican Party organized in the South.

After Johnson criticized General Philip Sheridan, who oversaw Louisiana and Texas, for removing Southern officials from office, and Attorney General Henry Stanbery issued a legal opinion in Johnson's favor, narrowly interpreting the first two Reconstruction Acts, Congress passed the third Reconstruction Act over Johnson's veto on July 19. This act made clear that the congressionally mandated military governments took precedence over the civilian governments elected under Presidential Reconstruction so that commanders could remove civilian officeholders as they saw fit. It also gave registration boards the power to refuse to register any man they felt was not taking the ironclad oath in good faith, and broadly defined those who could be disenfranchised for serving the Confederacy.

Under Congressional Reconstruction, an estimated 635,000 whites registered to vote in 1867, but 10 to 15 percent of the white population were disenfranchised, and 25 to 30 percent of those eligible did not register. The blacks who registered in this period numbered 735,000. Although 80 percent of registered blacks voted in the fall elections, less than 50 percent of registered whites voted. The number of voters was high enough, however, to successfully call for constitutional conventions. Seventy-five percent of the elected delegates were Republicans—chiefly, Unionist whites, Northern whites, and blacks. The constitutions they produced enfranchised blacks, created public schools, and increased property taxes to pay for education and other public services; several also provided homestead exemptions from these taxes for small landowners. The Alabama, Arkansas, Louisiana, Mississippi, and Virginia constitutions disenfranchised some former Confederates, but the last of these clauses was repealed in 1872.

After the new constitutions had been written by elected delegates, the votes of a majority of registered voters were needed for ratification. To prevent ratification, some Southern whites terrorized black voters to keep them from voting for the constitution, and many more boycotted the polls themselves. In the Alabama elections on February 4, 1868, these tactics were successful. Congress subsequently passed the fourth Reconstruction Act on March 11, declaring that only a majority of the votes *actually cast* were necessary to ratify these constitutions. Within two months, six former Confederate states ratified their constitutions in this manner.

In June 1868, Congress readmitted Alabama, Arkansas, Florida, Louisiana, North Carolina, and South Carolina to the Union, with a provision (constitutionally debatable) that barred these states from amending their constitutions to disenfranchise blacks. In 1870, Mississippi, Texas, Georgia, and Virginia were also restored.

The Impeachment of President Andrew Johnson

The conflict between Andrew Johnson and the Republican-led Congress culminated in his impeachment by the House of Representatives and his trial in the Senate in 1868. Johnson's obstruction of congressional programs and policies, and his indiscreet speeches and public statements, provoked anger and frustration.

Johnson was adamantly opposed to black voting rights, which the Republicans in Congress had come to believe were necessary to protect the freedmen from legislation such as the Black Codes and to prevent the former Confederate leadership from regaining power. In his message to Congress in December 1867, Johnson declared that Southern African Americans were "utterly so ignorant of public affairs that their voting can consist in nothing more than carrying a ballot to the place where they are directed to deposit it. . . . Of all the dangers which our nation has yet encountered, none are equal to those which must result from the success of the effort now making to Africanize the half of our country."

The first attempt to impeach Johnson had actually begun almost a year earlier, when, on January 7, 1867, the House of Representatives passed a resolution calling for its Judiciary Committee to decide whether the president had been guilty of "high Crimes and Misdemeanors." This action alarmed the moderates but was pushed forward by the Radicals who believed—as the *New York Tribune* stated, in October 1866—that a president could be dismissed not only for criminal action but for "grave misuse of his powers, or any mischievous nonuse of them—for any conduct which harms the public or perils its welfare."

In June, the Judiciary Committee voted, five to four, that there were no grounds for impeachment, but the Radicals had them reopen the investigation and continue to receive testimony. When the committee finally decided that grounds for impeachment existed, the House of Representatives rejected this conclusion by a vote of 108 to 57 in December.

But Johnson continued to weaken the effects of Congressional Reconstruction by replacing those military officials who were most aggressive in remaking the South. For example, General Winfield Scott Hancock (a future Democratic candidate for president) who took over from Philip Sheridan, was far more conservative and conciliatory. When Johnson suspended Secretary of War Stanton, with whom he disagreed polically, and replaced him with Ulysses S. Grant, he explained his reasons to the Senate, as required by the Tenure of Office Act (see page 740). The Senate rejected his reasons and Grant returned the post to Stanton. In February 1868, Johnson dismissed Stanton outright, in favor of Lorenzo Thomas, but Stanton refused to vacate the office. (He literally barricaded himself behind the door.) Johnson then nominated Thomas Ewing as secretary of war, but, by then, the impeachment movement was actively under way.

Led by Thaddeus Stevens, the House of Representatives impeached Johnson by a vote of 126 to 47 on February 24, 1868. There were eleven charges, or articles of impeachment: eight concerning Stanton's dismissal and the violation of the Tenure of Office Act; one for violating the Command of the Army Act by putting pressure on the District of Columbia's commander to take orders directly from Johnson; one for attempting to "excite the odium and resentment of all the good people of the United States against Congress and the laws by it duly and constitutionally enacted"; and, finally, an omnibus article of general condemnation for the first ten charges.

At the Senate trial, which began on March 4, 1868, John Bingham, Benjamin Butler (as leading counsel), James Wilson, Thomas Williams, and John Logan prosecuted on behalf of the House. Johnson was defended by Attorney General Henry Stanbery, as well as Benjamin Curtis (whom *The Nation* described during the trial as "lucid and powerful"), William Evarts, and William Groesbeck.

Benjamin Butler articulated the main argument for the prosecution: an action warranting impeachment was "one in its nature or consequences subversive of some fundamental or essential principle of government, or highly prejudicial to the public interest, and this may consist of a violation of the Constitution, of law, of an official oath, or of duty . . . or, without violating a positive law, by the abuse of discretionary powers." The defense argued that Johnson had not violated the law and rather paradoxically stated that he had done nothing illegal because the Tenure of Office Act did not apply to Stanton (who had been appointed by Lincoln, not Johnson), but that he had violated the act to test its constitutionality in the Supreme Court.

Ultimately, factors other than the merits of the case seem to have determined the outcome, although Johnson's lawyers put up what was perceived as an excellent legal defense. Moderate Republicans were concerned that the precedent set by removing a president who differed from Congress along political lines was a violation of the separation of powers. Some feared that Benjamin Wade—who, as president pro tem of the Senate would replace Johnson as president—was too radical, not only in his views concerning Reconstruction but in his prolabor economic philosophy. Johnson himself was finally conciliatory; he promised to uphold the Reconstruction Acts and to appoint the widely respected General John Schofield as secretary of war. On May 16, seven Republicans and twelve Democrats voted to acquit Johnson on the eleventh article of impeachment. The total vote was thirty-five to nineteen, one vote short of the two-thirds majority necessary to convict him. After he was acquitted, by the same number, on two further articles on May 26, the case was dropped. Johnson continued to veto congressional legislation, but he never impeded Reconstruction during the remainder of his term.

Bureau of Refugees, Freedmen, and Abandoned Lands

The Civil War brought about an unprecedented need for the U.S. government to cope with a large refugee population, both black and white, and to assist former slaves in becoming part of a free economy and society. Although myriad freedmen's aid societies sprang up in the North, the largest and most comprehensive effort was made by the congressionally mandated Bureau of Refugees, Freedmen, and Abandoned Lands, known as the Freedmen's Bureau, which also provided assistance to white Southern refugees.

Operating under the War Department, the Freedmen's Bureau was established by Congress on March 3, 1865, and was expected to fund itself from the sale of confiscated land it controlled. In May, Major General Oliver O. Howard (see "Notable Figures of the Reconstruction Era," on page 797), nicknamed "the Christian general" because of his work with freedmen's aid societies, his well-known piety, and his strong religious beliefs, was appointed commissioner of the bureau. The assistant commissioners for each state were drawn from the army, and the staff eventually included subassistant commissioners, agents, surgeons, and education officials who worked at county and local levels. Even at its peak, the bureau employed only 901 people (more than one-third of them were clerks) to cover the entire South; there were, for example, never more than twenty agents at a time in the entire state of Alabama.

Although the life of the bureau was extended by congressional legislation in July 1866, when funds were appropriated for its use from its inception, the Bureau was seen as only a temporary solution for aiding refugees

This drawing of The Freedmen's Bureau *by Alfred Waud, published in* Harper's Weekly *on July 26, 1868, dramatizes the characteristic role played by bureau agents in resolving conflicts between blacks and whites in the South.*

and freedmen. Its main task was to establish the basis for a free labor society in which, it was believed, the market would take care of initial inequities and the freedmen would eventually prosper without government support. Bureau commissioners and agents, like most of those in the North, failed to understand the irreconcilable differences between planters and freedmen, arising from racism and class distinctions, which separated them in attitudes and aspirations. Even with bureau support, and certainly without it, blacks were not free to rise in the economic system of the nineteenth-century South.

In its efforts to help those displaced and impoverished by the war, the Freedmen's Bureau resettled 30,000 refugees, distributed twenty-one million rations (as well as clothing and fuel) in four years, and provided medical care for an estimated 500,000 freedmen, in addition to white Southerners. In many places, more whites received aid than blacks. Continuing concern about the debilitating effects of public relief, however, which Howard called "abnormal to our system of government," caused the bureau to quickly close camps set up for freedmen, but an attempt to discontinue food rations in 1866 was unsuccessful because crop failures heightened the South's economic distress. Another of the bureau's tasks was to assist black veterans in obtaining bounties for military service, as promised by the Federal government.

The bureau also managed land distribution in the former Confederacy; it controlled more than 850,000 acres in 1865. Some commissioners, particularly Rufus Saxton in South Carolina, actively supported giving, leasing, or cheaply selling land to the freedmen, and thousands of families were settled on confiscated and abandoned lands. In July 1865, Howard issued Circular 13, which provided forty-acre tracts for freedmen, but President Johnson ordered Howard to rescind the order. In September, Howard was forced to issue Circular 15, calling for the return of confiscated land to those owners who had received presidential pardons, except for a small amount that had already been sold by court decree. Even that land reverted to its original owners when crops were harvested. Johnson replaced Rufus Saxton in 1866, and, by the end of the year, the bureau no longer had any land to distribute.

Because white planters continued to own the majority of Southern property, and because many of them endeavored to enforce conditions as nearly approximating the gang-labor days of slavery as possible, agents of the Freedmen's Bureau advocated written contracts that stated the terms of the labor to be performed and the precise compensation to be paid in wages and/or crops. They helped the freedmen choose employers and secure fair wages, and they often negotiated contracts, monitored compliance, and adjudicated complaints over breach of contract. Although planters complained about their involvement, agents often, in effect, supported them, since bureau officials encouraged, and sometimes required, the unemployed to work, or enforced contracts more favorable to the planters than to their workers. Some also upheld the pass system and vagrancy laws, as the occupying Union army had done during the war. One bureau employee felt that contracts "succeeded in making the Freedman work and in rendering labor secure and stable—but it has failed to secure to the Freedman his just dues to compensation." Success in securing blacks' economic rights varied, but the bureau offered some protection to the newly freed labor force in a hostile environment.

The July 1866 Freedmen's Bureau bill also provided for Freedmen's United States Courts—with authority eclipsing that of the states—in an attempt to achieve equal justice for blacks and Unionist whites while the Southern governments formed under Presidential Reconstruction were in effect. The bureau courts arbitrated civil and criminal cases among blacks, but most cases were brought by blacks, against whites, for contract violations and violence against them. The courts also overrode or prevented the enforcement of the discriminatory provisions in the Black Codes passed by the states. Almost all Southern whites were adamantly opposed to the Freedmen's courts. As Colonel Samuel Thomas, head of the Mississippi bureau said in 1865, whites could not "conceive of the negro having any rights at all."

Nevertheless, the Freedmen's Bureau tried to persuade Southern courts to recognize equality before the law so that its own courts would be unnecessary. By the end of 1866, local courts had revised their proceedings sufficiently to regain jurisdiction, and this allowed blacks to testify. Agents remained advocates for the freedmen and prosecuted whites in these courts. Although they could overturn decisions that discriminated, some agents hesitated to override the civil courts. One bureau agent expressed what was, perhaps, the biggest weakness of the system: "It is of no consequence what the law may be, if the majority be not inclined to have it executed."

Finally, the Freedmen's Bureau was responsible for overseeing the creation of a school system for the former slaves that boasted some 250,000 students in 4,300 schools by 1870. In a unique cooperative arrangement, the bureau provided funds for bringing teachers from the North, owned many school buildings, and coordinated the effort. Church and private societies recruited teachers, paid their salaries, and decided what would be taught. From 1865 to 1870, the bureau invested nearly $5 million in the education of former slaves, in addition to $3 million contributed by Northern aid organizations, and $1 million by the freedmen themselves. Providing a foundation for black education in the South was considered by many to be its greatest success.

The effectiveness of the Freedmen's Bureau ultimately relied on the army of agents in the field and their individual loyalties, sympathies, and integrity. Even those who were conservative in introducing change met resistance from most white Southerners, for whom the bureau was a symbol of Northern intrusion. Bureau agents were subject to violence and attracted attacks by the Ku Klux Klan. In 1867, under Congressional Reconstruction, they were called upon to register voters and provide voter education for the freedmen, using literature supplied by the Republican Party's Union League when they had none of their own to distribute. Their association with the Republicans did little to endear them to the white South. By 1869, the bureau was only active in education and in helping veterans to collect their bounties. Those activities ceased in 1870 and 1872, respectively.

Fifteenth Amendment

The Fifteenth Amendment was officially incorporated into the Constitution on March 30, 1870. It stated:

> The right of citizens of the United States to vote shall not be denied or abridged by the United States or by any State on account of race, color, or previous condition of servitude.

> The Congress shall have power to enforce this article by appropriate legislation.

The Fifteenth Amendment was a relatively weak compromise in order to achieve ratification. Congress did not entirely reject the view that aspects of suffrage could be regulated by the states rather than the Federal government. With objections to unqualified manhood suffrage coming from many Northern states—for example, California and Oregon wished to keep Chinese immigrants from voting; Connecticut and Massachusetts had literacy requirements; and only those who paid state taxes could vote in Pennsylvania—it picked the narrowest possible grounds for protecting the right to vote and did not protect the right to hold office or bar devices, such as poll taxes, that effectively restricted the suffrage. However, it did represent a dramatic change in attitude, in a very short time. The once radical idea that any blacks were ready to have the vote yielded to a conviction that blacks needed to have the right to vote protected, in order to ensure their civil rights.

After Congress passed the amendment, on February 26, 1869, it was ratified by the seventeen Northern states that had Republican legislatures and
rejected by the four states controlled by Democrats. Congress then required
the Southern states still not readmitted to the Union—Virginia, Mississippi,
Texas, and Georgia—to ratify the Fifteenth Amendment, which guaranteed
its success.

Southern Governments under Republican Rule

The Republican governments that formed in the Southern states in 1868 were
elected by black and white voters under Congressional Reconstruction. They
began their rule weakened by the fact that, in the minds of many white Southerners, they were imposed by the North and were therefore illegitimate. Because many former white Southern politicians, as ex-Confederate leaders, were
at first banned from participation in the new government, the work of Reconstruction was largely left to three groups: white Southerners who supported
the plan of the Northern Republicans (contemptuously called scalawags); immigrants from the North (derogatorily referred to as carpetbaggers, for the receptacles in which they supposedly carried all that they owned); and African
Americans. Critics portrayed scalawags and carpetbaggers as out for personal
gain. Former Confederate Wade Hampton (see "Notable Figures of the Reconstruction Era," on page 797) called Southern white Republicans, "the
mean, lousy and filthy kind that are not fit for butchers and dogs." Later historians labeled scalawags as "vile, blatant, vindictive and unprincipled," and
considered carpetbaggers "too depraved, dissolute, dishonest and degraded to
get the lowest of places in the states they had just left."

Most of these men were actually competent and respectable and showed
some courage in standing up to their neighbors and trying to bring about
change. The scalawags included white Unionists, many of whom were upcountry yeomen farmers who had opposed secession and resented the old
system that had favored the planter class. There were also former Whigs,
some of whom had held office in the antebellum South, who wished to modernize their states by promoting business and industrialization. The Northerners were usually middle-class, educated men. Some came South as
teachers, agents of the Freedmen's Bureau, or investors in plantations, and
the majority were Union army veterans. Others, such as Governor Rufus B.
Bullock of Georgia, had lived in the South since before the war.

Many Northern blacks who came South and were active in the Republican Party had also served in the Union army, or worked as teachers or for the

Freedmen's Bureau. Some slaves who had escaped before the war returned, as did free blacks educated in the North. But a large number of freedmen who had never left home entered politics as well; many of them were teachers, ministers, or artisans who gained experience in the Union Leagues and went on to hold office.

This fragile coalition of Northern and Southern whites and African Americans suffered from factionalism; they disagreed over issues such as the extent to which blacks would take a leadership role in politics, whether land should be redistributed, or whether ex-Confederates should be allowed to vote and hold office. They shared and were guided by a belief in basic civil and political rights for blacks, a need for modernizing the economy, and a commitment to providing public services. "I do not hesitate to assert that the Southern Reconstruction Governments were the best governments those States ever had," African American John Lynch, a former Mississippi congressman, later wrote.

The Republican state legislatures tried to fulfill the promise of their progressive new constitutions. They abolished the Black Codes and corporal punishment; established public schools, hospitals, orphanages, mental institutions, and prisons; reduced the number of capital crimes; provided debt relief; gave workers the first lien on an employer's crop; and banned employers from firing workers for their political views. New laws increased married women's property rights, specified more grounds for divorce, mandated against child abuse, allowed interracial marriage, and required white fathers to support their mulatto children. South Carolina provided medical care for the poor, and Alabama offered free legal advice for its impoverished defendants.

Black legislators sought laws guaranteeing equal access to public transportation and accommodations, such as hotels and theaters, but although some were enacted—and some states charged their attorneys general with prosecuting violators—they were rarely enforced. Moreover, the vast majority of schools were segregated; only Louisiana tried to integrate its schools, and only New Orleans truly succeeded. The University of South Carolina was also integrated, and only South Carolina actively pursued land distribution, forming a commission to buy land and resell it on favorable credit terms. An estimated 14,000 black families had purchased land by 1876.

The 1883 chromolithograph on page 781, Distinguished Colored Men, *portrays several influential black leaders before the Civil War and during Reconstruction. Top left: Robert Brown Elliott; top right: Blanche K. Bruce; center: Frederick Douglass; clockwise from top of circle: William Wells Brown, R. T. Greener, Richard Allen, J. H. Rainey, E. D. Bassett, John Mercer Langston, P. B. S. Pinchback, Henry Highland Garnet.*

Although Southern whites bitterly complained of "Negro rule," blacks allowed whites to assume the prominent roles at the start of Congressional Reconstruction. Only three African Americans served in the Forty-First U.S. Congress, which met from 1869 to 1871: Hiram Revels, a senator from Mississippi; and Joseph Rainey of South Carolina and Jefferson Long of Georgia, in the House of Representatives. Even in state governments, blacks were underrepresented in proportion to their numbers. However, their influence increased during the course of Reconstruction, particularly in South Carolina, where four out of eight of the state's executive officers, three congressmen, and a state supreme court justice, Jonathan J. Wright, were black men.

In addition to the sixteen African Americans elected to the U.S. Congress during this period, eighteen blacks served as lieutenant governors, treasurers, superintendents of education, or secretaries of state. More than 600 won seats in the state legislatures, and many more served in local governments. South Carolina, Louisiana, and Mississippi led in the number of local African American officials; there were thirty-four black sheriffs in the plantation counties of Louisiana and Mississippi alone. High-ranking black officials in the states' Reconstruction governments included:

Governor

Louisiana: P. B. S. Pinchback

Lieutenant Governors

Louisiana: Oscar J. Dunn, P. B. S. Pinchback, Caesar C. Antoine
Mississippi: Alexander K. Davis
South Carolina: Alonzo J. Ransier, Richard H. Gleaves

Secretaries of State

Florida: Jonathan C. Gibbs
Mississippi: James R. Lynch, Hiram Revels, Hannibal C. Carter, M. M. McLeod, James Hill
South Carolina: Francis L. Cardozo, Henry E. Hayne

Treasurers

Louisiana: Antoine Dubuclet
South Carolina: Francis L. Cardozo

Superintendents of Education

Arkansas: Joseph C. Corbin
Florida: Jonathan C. Gibbs
Louisiana: William G. Brown
Mississippi: Thomas W. Cardozo

Despite their remarkable achievements, African Americans never dominated Southern politics. The only majority they ever attained was in South Carolina's House of Representatives, where the first black speaker was elected in 1872. In 1874, blacks also held a majority of the seats in the South Carolina Senate. Although no blacks were elected governor during Reconstruction—or, indeed, for more than a century after—P. B. S. Pinchback assumed the role in Louisiana from December 9, 1872, to January 13, 1873.

As part of the Republican governments' economic programs, the Southern states aggressively supported railroad development, either with direct grants or through laws endorsing railroad bonds. Even local communities invested. From 1868 to 1872, Southern track mileage increased by nearly 40 percent, but almost all of the new rails were laid in only four states: Georgia, Alabama, Arkansas, and Texas. Most other areas did not reap financial benefits. At the same time, state governments offered generous tax breaks to businesses, hoping to attract outside investment, yet were providing public education and services that required heavy expenditures. Property taxes increased, debts mounted, and credit ratings failed.

Republicans were blamed not only for the high taxes and states' indebtedness, but also for corruption. Competition for capital investors on the one hand, and state aid on the other, created a climate conducive to bribery and conflict of interest. Some government officials speculated in state bonds; authorized purchases by the state (at inflated prices) of property they owned; or bought shares at prices far under their market value. Critics pointed to corrupt or extravagant political figures such as South Carolina's governors, Robert K. Scott and Franklin J. Moses Jr., to discredit the work of the Reconstruction governments, but corruption was not unique to the South. It was also the time of the Whiskey Ring fraud in the Federal government and the Tweed Ring scandal in New York.

Republican government in the South was short-lived. Conservatives—who aligned themselves in the Democratic Party, the Conservative Union Party, or the Democratic and Conservative Party—vigorously worked to undermine Congressional Reconstruction. As early as 1868, they held a majority in Georgia's Senate and House of Representatives. Once the Southern states had been readmitted to the Union, conservatives were able to accelerate the process of "redeeming" the South as their own.

Violence in the South

Even before the Civil War ended, violence erupted against the freedmen and those who tried to help them. Educational facilities, white and black teachers, black Union soldiers, and white Unionists were among the frequent targets. Violence continued under Presidential Reconstruction. In Memphis, Tennessee, riots against blacks raged from April 30 to May 2, 1866; forty-six African Americans were killed and more than eighty were wounded. "Soon we shall have no more black troops among us," predicted a local newspaper. "Thank heaven the white race are once more rulers of Memphis." Three months later, on July 30, when New Orleans Radicals tried to reconvene the convention that had passed the constitution in 1864 in order to disenfranchise some Confederates and enfranchise some blacks, riots resulted in the deaths of thirty-four blacks and three whites, with more than 100 persons injured.

When, in 1867, the Radical Republicans enacted their vision of Reconstruction with a series of Federal laws, the violent resistance of white Southerners manifested a new resolve. Secret terrorist societies determined to overturn these reforms by creating a climate of fear. Most prominent among these groups was the Ku Klux Klan, but there were many similar organizations, such as the Knights of the White Camellia in Louisiana, the Knights of the Rising Sun in Texas, and Mississippi's White Line.

The Klan grew out of a social club started in late 1865 or 1866 by young whites in Pulaski, Tennessee. By 1867 it had spread to most Southern states, and Nathan Bedford Forrest, a former slave trader and cotton planter who had been a Confederate general during the war, was named as its Grand Wizard. Aimed at ending Republican rule and restoring Conservative domination of the South, "in effect, the Klan was a military force serving the interests of the Democratic party, the planter class, and all those who desired the restoration of white supremacy," wrote scholar Eric Foner in *Reconstruction: America's Unfinished Revolution*. "Its purposes were political in the broadest sense, for it sought to affect power relations, both public and private, throughout Southern society. It aimed to destroy the Republican Party's infrastructure, undermine the Reconstruction state, reestablish control of the black labor force, and restore racial subordination to every aspect of Southern life."

Methods included intimidation through scare tactics, arson, whippings, and outright murder.

During the 1868 presidential campaign, in which Republican candidate Ulysses S. Grant ran against Democrat Horatio Seymour, Conservative Democrats denied credit and threatened eviction to blacks who voted Republican. The Klan murdered Congressman James M. Hinds of Arkansas, three South Carolina state legislators and ex-delegates to the constitutional conventions. Some 200 blacks were killed in one Louisiana parish. Georgia and Louisiana went to the Democrats in the presidential election, since Republican voters had been so intimidated that they stayed away from the polls.

Violence continued, particularly against leading Republicans, freedmen who owned their own land, and educational efforts, which were seen as stepping stones to equality. After Republicans took control of the government in Laurens County, South Carolina, in October 1870, 150 blacks were forced from their homes, and thirteen black and white political leaders were killed. In Meridian, Mississippi, in March 1871, a judge and two black defendants were murdered during a court hearing, and, in a subsequent riot, thirty more people were killed. In Jackson County, Florida, "where," according to a black minister, "Satan has his seat," 150 people were slain, including a Jewish businessman who was considered too sympathetic to blacks.

Klan violence was usually generated locally, without direction from any identifiable centralized leadership. Membership in the Klan, or sympathy with its cause, permeated all strata of white society including poor farmers, local militia and law enforcement, and those in the governors' mansions of some Southern states. The Klan's terrorism was difficult to combat. Witnesses, even if found, were too frightened to testify, and white juries would not find white defendants guilty. Governors feared that engaging a black militia and supplying them with weapons would escalate the conflict. State anti-Klan laws, which subjected those contributing "to the disturbance of the peace" to fines and imprisonment, and offered financial rewards to informers, were ineffective.

Three Southern governors did, however, successfully slow down violence in their states by using some force themselves. Tennessee's William Brownlow, a Unionist during the war, recruited a militia from among Unionists in the eastern part of the state and declared martial law in nine counties. In Arkansas, governor Powell Clayton declared martial law in ten counties and employed black and white militia to arrest suspected Klansmen. In Texas, from 1870 to 1872, Edmund Davis had 6,000 suspects arrested.

However, in North Carolina, when governor William Holden attempted similar tactics, he was forced to release 100 people arrested by the militia when Federal courts upheld the Habeas Corpus Act. Its intent, ironically, was to protect blacks and loyal whites.

Despite small victories—and despite the fact that Grand Wizard Nathan Bedford Forrest ordered the end of the Klan in 1869—continued violence and instability aroused the U.S. Congress to action. Two Enforcement Acts aimed to protect the right of blacks to vote. The first, passed on May 31, 1870, levied fines and imprisonment on anyone convicted of preventing a qualified voter from casting his ballot; interfering with constitutional rights was named a felony. Although Federal marshals were enjoined to enforce the law, with trials to be held in Federal district and circuit courts, this law proved ineffective. When suspects were charged, witnesses often refused to testify and juries did not convict. The second Enforcement Act amended the first on February 28, 1871, appointing Federal election supervisors under the jurisdiction of Federal courts. Anyone hindering their work could be fined and imprisoned.

A third Enforcement Act—which became known as the Ku Klux Klan Act— was passed in April 1871, at President Grant's urging. This law made it a Federal crime to conspire to prevent citizens from exercising their voting rights or serving in office or on juries, or to deny them equal protection under the law. If states failed to uphold the law, Federal district attorneys could act to uphold it. The Ku Klux Klan Act also authorized the president to suspend the writ of habeas corpus and use military force if necessary. Giving the Federal government jurisdiction over the states' right to enforce criminal laws increased its powers and mapped out new, and controversial, constitutional and legal ground. African American Congressman Joseph Rainey gave one justification: "I desire that so broad and liberal a construction be placed upon its [the Constitution's] provisions as will insure protection to the humblest citizen. Tell me nothing of a constitution which fails to shelter beneath its rightful power the people of a country."

Attorney General Amos Akerman and Solicitor General Benjamin Bristow aggressively pursued enforcement of the law. Seven hundred men were indicted in Mississippi alone. In October 1871, Grant suspended habeas corpus in nine South Carolina counties. The arrests of some caused others to flee their homes. Those who confessed and named leaders were released with suspended sentences, and charges were dropped in nearly 2,000 cases, to clear the courts for trying those accused of the harshest crimes. Some 600 of the remaining group were convicted. Most were fined or given short terms in prison. Only sixty-five were sent to a Federal prison in New York.

Nonetheless, enforcement of the Ku Klux Klan Act severely diminished violent activity and brought a measure of peace to the Southern states and a boost of morale to Republican leadership. The presidential election of 1872, in which Grant was reelected, was the fairest in the South for some 100 years.

Violence against blacks, and against white Republicans, however, did not disappear. After both the Democratic and the Republican candidates claimed victory in Grant Parish, Louisiana, in 1873, blacks prepared to defend the county seat in Colfax. Armed whites laid seige for three weeks and finally massacred dozens of blacks, including fifty who had surrendered and laid down their weapons. In 1875, Democratic rifle clubs in Mississippi, their members undisguised, broke up meetings of Republicans and inflicted violence on political leaders. Several black leaders were killed in Yazoo County, and after attacking a Republican barbecue at Clinton, Mississippi, whites murdered an estimated thirty people, including teachers and churchmen. When Mississippi governor Adelbert Ames asked President Grant to send in troops to protect voters, Grant stated, "The whole public are tired out with these annual autumnal outbreaks in the South . . . [and] are ready now to condemn any interference on the part of the [national] Government."

In South Carolina, violence erupted in Hamburg, a town dominated by Republican blacks, after an altercation between the black militia and white farmers. On July 8, 1876, hundreds of whites killed fleeing militia men and broke into homes and shops. The Republican governor, Daniel Chamberlain, said of the massacre, "If you can find words to characterize [this] atrocity and barbarism . . . your power of language exceeds mine." Chamberlain ran in the fall against ex-Confederate Wade Hampton, who campaigned accompanied by armed "Red Shirts" that drew white crowds. Blacks were whipped and murdered, but, in this case, Republicans also attacked Democrats, and those blacks who supported the Democratic party were considered "deserters of their race." Although more South Carolinians voted Republican than ever before in the state, some were prevented from voting. The Democrats stuffed the ballot boxes, giving Hampton a narrow victory.

Even after the Democrats had resumed power in all the Southern states and had overturned the short-term rule of the governments which grew from Congressional Reconstruction, intimidation and violence remained as weapons to maintain white supremacy.

The North and West during Reconstruction

The period from 1865 to 1877 in the North was marked by contrasts: economic growth and depression; political corruption and reform; the development of wealthy and professional classes at odds with small farmers and laborers; efforts to end discrimination toward blacks and increasing indifference to their plight. As in the South, state governments expanded public services, public works, and education, and enlarged budgets and raised taxes to pay for them—a burden Northerners were much more able to bear.

From 1865 to 1873, industrial production increased by 75 percent in the North, and a significant portion of this increase was in heavy industry such as iron and steel manufacture. The completion of 35,000 miles of railroad routes opened up the West, which then absorbed some of the 3,000,000 immigrants who came to the United States during this period. By 1880, there were 2,000,000 people living in the area encompassing Minnesota, South Dakota, North Dakota, Nebraska, and Kansas—up from 300,000 in 1860. In addition to commercial farming, the West supported lumbering, mining, and ranching.

Although the ideal of a free-market economy—with laborers, both black and white, afforded the ability to rise through the system—had been a goal of Republicans in the aftermath of the war, the rise of industrialism and the consolidation of wealth created a new dynamic between capital and labor—and therefore in politics—in the North. The expansion of railroads exemplified the complexities and consequences of rapid growth. Initially, town, county, and state governments gave millions of dollars through land grants, direct grants, and bond issues to railroad development—as did the Federal government. At the same time, there was a consolidation of railroad ownership; fewer small independent companies operated, and businessmen such as Thomas Scott, Collis Huntington, James Hill, and Jay Gould acquired fortunes.

The railroad was a powerful transportation network that opened new markets, but in effect, it spawned monopolies that charged freight rates and warehouse fees that were too high for small farmers to pay. The Patrons of Husbandry, known as the Grange, formed in the Upper Mississippi Valley as a group of cooperatives designed to "*compel* the carriers to take our produce at a fair price." They pressed state governments to regulate railroads, but legislators were reluctant to intervene in any private industries. Illinois did create a commission with the ability to enforce its decisions in the courts. In 1877, the U.S. Supreme Court, in *Munn v. Illinois*, upheld a state's right to regulate businesses, such as railroads, that have an impact on the public.

In the West, partly to accommodate railroad construction, the Federal government pursued a policy to isolate Native Americans on reservations. Federal soldiers systematically destroyed the buffalo to force the adoption of farming and to end wide-ranging hunting on land that was coveted by railroads, ranchers, and farmers. In 1871, Congress decided that Indian nations would no longer be considered sovereign and abandoned the making of treaties. Although various Indian tribes resisted, and warfare with the United States continued until 1890, by the close of Reconstruction most Native Americans had been restricted to reservations.

Government concessions were also granted to other industries, besides railroads. Mining companies, for example, were granted millions of acres at no cost by the National Mineral Act in 1866. Business interests became increasingly identified with the Republican Party, although Democrats also supported industrial growth. Also during this period, the concept of what constituted a political party was changing. In 1865, differences in ideology had defined Republicans and Democrats; by the end of Reconstruction, parties had become more like business organizations centered on patronage, loyalty, and power. This kind of "party machine" organization, with its power to bestow thousands of jobs, coupled with the growing ties between business and politics and the high cost of campaigns, created opportunities for conflict of interest and outright corruption.

Congressmen and state legislators served on corporate boards, in paid positions, and as investors in companies receiving government aid. They received real estate, stock, and favors from business. In the case of the Credit Mobilier scandal, which broke in 1872, congressmen had been given shares in a dummy corporation, the Credit Mobilier, formed by Union Pacific stockholders; this corporation sold its services to Union Pacific—that is, to itself—at a large profit. Two congressmen lost their seats as a result of the scandal, and the Grant administration's reputation suffered from the involvement of Grant's vice presidents, Schuyler Colfax and Henry Wilson.

There were reactions against the growth of a wealthy industrial class and the questionable relationship of business to government. Labor began to organize; while only three unions had existed at the end of the Civil War, there were twenty-one in the early 1870s. Seemingly deprived of opportunities to move up the economic ladder, and locked into a lifetime of wage earning in factories, workers campaigned for better conditions. The eight-hour day became Federal law for government workers in 1868; it was passed by congressional Democrats and Radical Republicans who believed in reform. Battles for similar legislation raged on the state level, where business lobbyists fanned legislators' concern that government restraints on business would violate the principles of a free-market economy. Workers also called for paper money that would lower interest rates. But while the labor movement united workers from different European backgrounds, unions generally excluded women (an increasingly larger part of the workforce) and also prohibited blacks (who, at the Colored National Labor Convention of 1869, showed themselves to be adamant Republicans who supported the Grant administration's probusiness policies). In California, where a quarter of the workers were Chinese, they, too, were prohibited from joining unions.

A movement to reform corrupt government and to limit government intervention in the economy also achieved prominence in the Reconstruction period. Called Liberalism, it was propelled by the professional class and by intellectuals who believed that external or "scientific" laws should naturally regulate politics and economics, based on the principles of free trade, supply and demand, and the gold standard. Its proponents pressed for civil service reform, preferring exams and lifetime service to patronage. They opposed state intervention at both ends of the scale, whether favors to industrialists or meeting laborers' demands for an eight-hour day. Francis Parkman, a former Union officer of a black regiment, decried both "an ignorant proletariat and a half-taught plutocracy," yet the liberal reformers were more upset by Grange members and working men—and the political bosses they thought manipulated them—than by industrialists. They were among the forces behind the breakup of the Tweed Ring. Led by "Boss" William Tweed in New York, this political machine won the loyalty of the working class by doling out patronage jobs and city money to help Catholic schools and the poor.

Alarm at rule by the "masses" led some liberal reformers to advocate suffrage restrictions. "Universal suffrage can only mean in plain English the government of ignorance and vice," declared Charles Francis Adams Jr., in 1869. "It means a European, and especially Celtic, proletariat on the Atlantic coast, an African proletariat on the shores of the Gulf, and a Chinese proletariat on the Pacific." In the same year, however, 90 percent of New York Republicans voted for equal black suffrage, although the proposition failed. In the late 1860s, discriminatory laws in Northern states were dismantled, in accordance with the Civil Rights Act of 1866. In 1867, for example, Michigan banned school segregation and Pennsylvania ended segregation on streetcars. Most Northern blacks, however, continued to live in poverty and had few opportunities for advancement.

The liberal reformers saw Reconstruction in the South, including measures to protect the freedmen, as another form of dangerous government intercession. "The removal of white prejudice against the negro," wrote *The Nation* in 1867, "depends almost entirely upon the negro himself"—not, by implication, the efforts of government. Disgusted by examples of corruption in Republican Southern governments, these reformers increasingly called for the return of the South's "natural leaders," those ex-Confederates they considered had been unjustly treated, to restore order with their "intelligence and culture." *The Nation*, once a staunch supporter of abolition, wrote in 1871, "Reconstruction seems to be morally a more disastrous process than rebellion."

Democrats joined with liberal reformers to back Horace Greeley, the popular editor of the *New York Tribune*, for the presidential elections in 1872. A key element of his campaign focused on restoring home rule to the South. Grant's reelection victory indicated that support for Reconstruction still existed in the North. But, in Congress, while there remained a commitment to rights for blacks, there was little support for the actual Republican state governments in the South. They were considered corrupt and ineffective even by their fellow Republicans.

When the Panic of 1873 stunned the country—a financial collapse precipitated by the fall of banking giant Jay Cooke and Company, which was unable to sell bonds of the overextended Union Pacific Railroad—economic depression overwhelmed both the North and the South and persisted until 1878. Within a year, nearly 50 percent of iron manufacturers were no longer operating, and, within two years, 18,000 businesses had closed. More than 50 percent of railroads defaulted on their bonds between 1873 and 1876.

Unemployment skyrocketed—for example, one-third of the textile workers in Massachusetts lost their jobs. Wage reductions resulted in strikes, such as a strike of coal miners in Pennsylvania in 1875 that led to the trial of the Molly Maguires, a violent and radical labor group. Twenty of its members were hanged. By 1876, some railroads had cut wages by as much as 35 percent. In July 1877, workers for the Baltimore and Ohio Railroad struck, and the strike spread as far as Chicago and St. Louis.

Government forces were called out to stop this strike and some earlier ones. While the Federal government had been widely criticized for using troops to protect the Republican administration in Louisiana, President Grant pointed out that the Northern press and public had "no hesitation about exhausting the whole power of the government to suppress a strike." Wealthy Northern industrialists, as well as the middle class (both supporters of the Republican Party), increasingly equated Northern labor unrest with the needs and demands of freedmen in the South and the instability of weak Republican governments. They identified themselves more with Southern whites who could take control and maintain order. Preoccupied with its own economic concerns, and reluctant to champion government intervention to protect the rights of the freedmen (although willing to uphold business concerns and private property), the North retreated from Reconstruction.

The End of Reconstruction

In the South during Congressional Reconstruction, there were whites—many of them ex-Confederates, planters, men of influence and power—who saw their mission as "redeeming" their states from Republican and "Negro" rule (the latter was never a reality) with governments that would restore white supremacy, control black labor, and lower taxes, and a corresponding reduction in public education and services. Barely ten years after the elections for new constitutional conventions, these Democrats—or "Conservatives," as they were known—used fraud, intimidation, violence, and appeals to racial division, as well as legitimate economic grievances and charges of corruption, to discredit and destroy the Republican Party in the South, assert control over black voters, and regain power.

The table on page 793 shows, chronologically, the years when former Confederate states were readmitted to the Union under Congressional Reconstruction. It also lists the years when the Democratic party reasserted control over the Reconstruction-era Republican legislatures and/or governorships.

Although the length of time varied—in Virginia, Conservatives dominated the state even before Congress readmitted it to the Union, while in Florida and Louisiana, the process, after readmittance, took nine years—the paths these states followed were similar. After Congressional Reconstruction began, some Democrats pursued "the New Departure," a moderate strategy focused on economic rather than racial issues; restoration of the franchise to ex-Confederates rather than denial of it to blacks; and cooperation with Republicans who supported their philosophy. Taxpayers' Conventions, ostensibly concerned with lowering taxes, generally opposed public education and championed a government run by those who held property, excluding even poor whites. Lip service was paid to maintaining black civil and voting rights, in an effort to convince the North that there was no need for interference or protection.

However, where Democrats ruled in the border states and upper South, black rights diminished. In 1867, Maryland, which had not seceded and

State	Readmitted to the Union	Redeemed by Conservative Democrats
Tennessee	July 24, 1866	1869
Arkansas	June 22, 1868	1874
Alabama	June 25, 1868	1874
Florida	June 25, 1868	1877
Louisiana	June 25, 1868	1877
North Carolina	June 25, 1868	1870
South Carolina	June 25, 1868	1877
Virginia	January 26, 1870	1870
Mississippi	February 23, 1870	1876
Texas	March 30, 1870	1873
Georgia	July 15, 1870	1871

James Longstreet served as a Confederate general, but during Reconstruction he shocked Southerners by joining the Republican Party. Instead of working to restore conservative Democratic state government, he was appointed to several Federal offices.

was therefore never "reconstructed," shifted representational power in its constitution away from Baltimore and the areas of small farming to the plantation region in the southern part of the state, prompting the comment: "This they call a white man's Government. That is the right of a few white men, . . . to govern a great many white men. This is progress backwards." In 1873, Delaware, which had also remained in the Union during the war, initiated a poll tax. Delaware and Tennessee were among the first states to practice postwar segregation. In the Deep South, Georgia Democrats who controlled the legislature as early as 1870 and the governor's post in 1871, added a poll tax and new registration requirements, to prevent blacks from voting; replaced elective offices with appointments; and reinstated provisions similar to the Black Codes. These maneuvers were precursors to the curtailment of black rights and the consolidation of Democratic power throughout the South.

In 1873, the severe economic depression that struck the entire country, precipitated by the collapse of overextended railroads, weakened the Northern resolve to support Reconstruction and devastated the fragile economy of the South. In the North, the economic and cultural gap between laborers, the poor, and the middle class, and wealthy businessmen, professionals, and industrialists, widened, resulting in less sympathy for black workers in the South. Establishing a free labor system there was no longer a priority. The feeling grew that the South—in actuality, the elite—should decide what was best for itself. The disparity increased between the South's wealthy and its impoverished, including once self-sufficient white yeomen farmers, as cotton prices declined.

The elections of 1874 sent a Democratic majority to the U.S. Congress and restored Arkansas and Alabama to the Democrats. They also produced disputed results in the troubled state of Louisiana. In the election of 1872, Republican William Kellogg had defeated Conservative John McEnery in a contested election. McEnery formed his own militia, which in March 1873 tried to take over the New Orleans police station. The Colfax Massacre (described on page 787) followed in April. With under 2,000 Federal troops in Louisiana, whites were refusing to pay taxes or to follow the Kellogg government. In 1874, the White League was organized, and, on September 14, 3,500 of its members (many of them ex-Confederate soldiers) occupied the New Orleans city hall, statehouse, and arsenal, intending to install McEnery. President Grant was forced to send in additional Federal troops. Weeks later, after another contested election, Democrats tried to seat five of their party members in the state assembly; they also were removed by Federal troops. Many in the North actually sided with the Louisiana Democrats and considered armed Federal intervention in state matters extreme and dangerous.

Despite this, Congress did pass a Civil Rights Bill in 1875, but it was watered down from the original, which had prohibited discrimination in schools as well as public places. The burden of bringing discrimination suits rested with the individual, and few blacks were willing or able to initiate them. The Supreme Court declared the law unconstitutional in 1883. The Court also weakened other rights guaranteed by the Federal government. In the 1873 *Slaughterhouse* cases, where New Orleans butchers sued, under the Fourteenth Amendment, a city monopoly to regain their right to carry on their businesses, the Court drew its own distinction between national and state citizenship and declared that the states had power to decide what constituted the rights of citizens in state matters. In 1876, in *United States v. Cruikshank*, the Supreme Court overturned three Federal convictions of conspiracy to deprive blacks of their civil rights in the Colfax Massacre. The Court ruled that the Federal government could only enforce a *state's* violation of rights, not an individual's violation. The latter case was left to the state to prosecute.

By the mid-1870s, the North was no longer willing to support the Republican Reconstruction governments. In the South, even the Republican governments still in existence in Arkansas, Mississippi, Louisiana, and South Carolina concentrated on retrenching after the 1873 depression, limiting state debt, and cutting taxes. Blacks, who had continued to gain offices at the beginning of the decade, had little influence to stop the tide. Increasingly, the remaining Republican governments appealed to or allied with conservative whites to limit blacks' political role in government.

In the presidential election of 1876, the Republican nominee, Rutherford B. Hayes, was an Ohio governor who had once agreed with Congressional Reconstruction, but, in accepting his party's nomination, he promised to restore "the blessings of honest and capable local self-government" to the South. He ran against Democrat Samuel Tilden, the governor of New York, who had exposed corruption in his state and successfully destroyed the Tweed ring, and was campaigning on a platform of reform. The election results were uncertain. Victory depended on disputed returns in the three Republican Southern states—South Carolina, Louisiana, and Florida, which would determine the winner in the electoral college. When the Republican canvassing boards in the Southern states awarded their electoral votes to Hayes, Democrats threatened to inaugurate Tilden anyway. A bipartisan electoral commission, comprising of House, Senate, and Supreme Court members, also gave the victory to Hayes, and Democrats again protested. The Republicans in Louisiana and South Carolina invalidated Democratic ballots from counties torn by violence, infuriating Conservatives by naming Daniel Chamberlain governor instead of Wade Hampton in South Carolina, and Stephen Packard over Democrat Francis Nicholls in Louisiana.

The presidential election was finally settled by a series of negotiations between Southern Democrats and Northern Republicans. A meeting at Wormley House, a Washington hotel owned by a black man, James Wormley, on February 26, 1877, was said to clinch the bargain that gave the presidency to Hayes. Previous meetings and concessions, however, had already shaped the results. The agreement hinged on the fate of Reconstruction—although it had been virtually abandoned by this time—and on help for the South's devastated economy. Moderate businessmen on both sides perceived the advantage. Republicans offered support for Federal aid, particularly to Southern railroads, and for passage of the Texas and Pacific Railroad bill, as well as a cabinet post for Tennessee senator David Key. Southern Democrats, in turn, promised to support James A. Garfield as Speaker of the House—and, of course, Hayes as the president. Key did become postmaster general, but the Texas and Pacific bill did not pass, and Garfield was not championed by any Democrats.

President Hayes did not order the departure of the last Federal troops from the Southern states, as was popularly believed. He did order the troops that had been called out to preserve Republican government by surrounding the statehouses in Louisiana and South Carolina back to their barracks. He also recognized Democrats Hampton and Nicholls as the states' governors. The last Southern states were redeemed. Henry Adams, an African American from Louisiana, declared, "The whole South—every state in the South—had got into the hands of the very men that held us as slaves." In the North, *The Nation* predicted, "The negro will disappear from the field of national politics. Henceforth, the nation, as a nation, will have nothing more to do with him."

The process of blacks "disappearing" from politics happened over time. In the border states and the upper South, blacks continued to vote into the 1890s. Even in Arkansas and Texas, which had small black populations, they were not widely prevented from voting in the aftermath of Reconstruction. The last black representative in Congress, George H. White of North Carolina, served from 1897 to 1901. Some blacks remained as state legislators or on city councils, and there were also some "black districts" run by blacks where there was a large African American majority population.

In the Deep South, however, fraud and violence, as well as the gerrymandering of congressional districts, prevented blacks from effectively exercising the ballot even before the end of Reconstruction. Some Democratic legislatures made appointive those local offices likely to be won by blacks. Others required officeholders to post bonds, thus eliminating candidates without money. Blacks were gradually deprived of the right to serve on juries and removed from police forces and state militia. With the passage of segregation laws, beginning in the 1890s, the rights that black people had exercised during Reconstruction virtually came to an end.

Notable Figures of the Reconstruction Era

JOHN ARMOR BINGHAM (1815–1900). Trained as a lawyer, John Bingham was elected to the House of Representatives from his adopted state of Ohio in 1854. He served in Congress until 1873, with the exception of 1864–1865, when he held several court positions and won some fame as a special judge advocate in the trial of John Wilkes Booth and his accomplices in the assassination of President Lincoln. Bingham, though a moderate Republican, was also appointed chairman of the impeachment managers for President Johnson. As a congressman, he is noted for his work on the Fourteenth Amendment to the Constitution, particularly that part of the first section which declares that no state may abrogate the rights of any citizen of the United States without due process of law.

BLANCHE K. BRUCE (1841–1898). Born into slavery in Virginia, Bruce was thought to be the son of his owner. He was tutored as a child, and, after fleeing slavery during the Civil War, formed the first school for African American children in Kansas. He moved to Mississippi in 1868 and worked as a newspaper editor, tax assessor, and sheriff. As a U.S. senator from 1875 to 1881, he championed civil rights and opposed a law banning Chinese immigration to the United States in 1878.

FRANCIS L. CARDOZO (1837–1903). Francis Cardozo, the son of a white Charlestonian and a free black woman, was the first black to hold state office in South Carolina—as secretary of state (1868–1872) and then as treasurer (1872–1876). A graduate of the University of Glasgow in Scotland (1861) and a Congregationalist minister in Connecticut, Cardozo was sent back to Charleston in 1865 on behalf of the American Missionary Association. He helped to found the Avery Normal Institute, which trained black teachers, and he served as its first superintendent. Cardozo's political career ended when the Democrats reestablished control of South Carolina and turned out the Republicans of the Reconstruction era.

ROBERT B. ELLIOTT (1842–1884). Born of West Indian parents, Robert Elliott did not arrive in America from England until after the Civil War, but he quickly became one of the dedicated black architects of South Carolina's Reconstruction government. He participated in the state's constitutional convention and was elected to its legislature. He was elected twice to the U.S. House of Representatives, where he gave a noted speech on behalf of the pending Civil Rights Act, which was passed in 1875. Elliott left the U.S.

Congress in 1874. As South Carolina's Speaker of the House, he tried to end corruption in the state government.

NATHAN BEDFORD FORREST (1821–1877). Before the Civil War, Nathan Bedford Forrest owned several cotton plantations and was one of the largest and wealthiest slave traders in the South. During the war, he achieved the rank of lieutenant general. He became legendary for his command of the cavalry; Union General William T. Sherman proclaimed him "that devil Forrest." Forrest, however, also became infamous for his attack on Fort Pillow in 1864 and the subsequent massacre of black soldiers there. Questions remain as to the extent of Forrest's culpability, but he was still vilified for his role, and the Fort Pillow massacre became particularly important propaganda for the Radical Republican movement. When the war ended, Forrest tried to capitalize on the postwar railroad boom. He was also involved in politics and was intent on restoring the South to Democratic rule. He became Grand Wizard of the fledgling Ku Klux Klan in 1867. Two years later, he spoke out against lawless violence committed in the name of the Klan, and he dissolved the group. However, violence continued. In 1871, during four hours of testimony before a congressional committee investigating the treatment of freedmen, he described the Klan as an "organization . . . intended entirely as a protection to the people."

WADE HAMPTON (1818–1902). Born into a wealthy family in South Carolina, Hampton owned 900 slaves in the Mississippi Delta by 1860. He was noted for his skill as a Confederate cavalry commander during the war. Heavily in debt at the war's end, he avoided politics. He refused to run for the governorship of South Carolina in 1865, but nearly won in a write-in campaign. In 1876, however, he did run for governor, and although he promised to stem violence against blacks, he was supported by Red Shirts who effectively threatened black voters. The election results were disputed, and Hampton finally became governor as part of the settlement of the Hayes-Tilden election in 1877. The following year, he was elected to the U.S. Senate, where he served for thirteen years.

OLIVER OTIS HOWARD (1830–1909). Howard's Civil War career included a Medal of Honor for service at Seven Pines (awarded in 1893), division command at Antietam and Fredericksburg, and the Eleventh Corps at Chancellorsville. He commanded the Fourth Corps in the Campaign for Atlanta, and the Army of the Tennessee on Sherman's March to the Sea during the Carolinas Campaigns. One of his arms was amputated during the war. Intensely religious, and a longtime opponent of slavery, Howard was selected to oversee the Freedmen's Bureau. Although Howard was considered an honest and earnest administrator, the bureau experienced some corruption. In 1874, a court of inquiry cleared him of charges related to that corruption. Howard subsequently served as superintendent at West Point. Among his lasting legacies are the universities he helped to found: Howard University in Washington, D.C., in the late 1860s, and Lincoln Memorial University in Harrogate, Tennessee, chartered by the state in 1897.

ANDREW JOHNSON (1808–1875). Born to an impoverished family in North Carolina, Johnson became governor of Tennessee and owned five slaves before the Civil War. Although a champion of states' rights, Johnson was also a staunch supporter of the Union (see photo on page 766). He was the only senator from a seceded state who maintained his seat in Congress. Abraham Lincoln appointed him military governor of Tennessee, and, in 1864, Johnson replaced Hannibal Hamlin as Lincoln's running mate. He was sworn in as president upon Lincoln's assassination. At first, his plans won public and congressional favor in the North, but his generous terms for Reconstruction, his openly racist views in regard to civil rights, and his intransigence pitted him against Congress. He opposed the Fourteenth Amendment and vetoed Reconstruction bills. In 1868, he became the first president to be impeached, surviving conviction and removal by a single vote. Johnson was later elected to the U.S. Senate from Tennessee, but died soon after.

JOHN MERCER LANGSTON (1829–1897). The son of a former slave and the owner who freed her, Langston became one of the most prominent African Americans of the nineteenth century. He earned a master's degree in theology from Oberlin College, but, unable to gain entrance to a U.S. law school, he studied independently and successfully entered the bar in 1854. In 1855, he was elected town clerk in Brownhelm, Ohio; he is believed to have been the first black elected to public office in the United States. During the war, Langston was instrumental in recruiting the first black troops for the Union, including the famed Fifty-Fourth Massachusetts. He was appointed an inspector of the Freedmen's Bureau in 1868, and from 1869 to 1876, he was, variously, a professor of law, dean, vice president, and acting president of Howard University. He later served on the Board of Health for the District of Columbia, and served as a diplomat from 1877 to 1885. In 1888, Langston ran for Congress from Virginia in a disputed election. He held his seat for just three months in 1890 and was not reelected.

PINCKNEY B. S. PINCHBACK (1837–1921). A native of Georgia and the son of a white plantation owner and a free black woman, Pinchback went to school in Ohio, was a steamboat steward on the Mississippi, and settled in New Orleans in 1862. He enlisted in the Union army and recruited black troops during the Civil War, but resigned in 1863 after experiencing discrimination from white officers. That same year, he spoke publicly on behalf of black suffrage. Pinchback participated in Louisiana's constitutional convention in 1868, and was elected as Louisiana's lieutenant governor in 1871. When the governor, Henry Warmouth, was impeached, Pinchback served as governor for five weeks, the only African American to hold this position in any state until 1989, when C. Douglas Wilder began his term in Virginia. He grew rich during his tenure in office, in part from speculating in state bonds and by having the state purchase his property at inflated prices.

HIRAM REVELS (1822–1901). Hiram Revels, a free black from North Carolina, served as a clergyman for the African Methodist Episcopal Church in the Midwest and as a chaplain for a black regiment during the war. In 1865, he came to Mississippi to educate freedmen. He was elected to the state Senate in 1869. The following year, the Mississippi legislature chose him to fill an unexpired term in the U.S. Senate, where he took the seat once held by Jefferson Davis. He later served as president of Alcorn University, which was established, in part, so that Mississippi would not have to accept black students into its all-white university.

THADDEUS STEVENS (1792–1868). A believer in the "Equality of Man before his creator" (the inscription he wrote for his epitaph), Stevens was the most fervent member of the Radical Republican faction in Congress (see photo on page 739). As a Pennsylvania state legislator, he supported public education; as a convention delegate, he refused to sign the new state constitution in 1838 because it prevented blacks from voting. First elected to the U.S. House of Representatives from Pennsylvania in 1848, he spoke out for emancipation and for using black troops in the war. He opposed Andrew Johnson

This wood engraving, Time Works Wonders, *by Thomas Nast, appeared in* Harper's Weekly *on April 9, 1870. It shows Jefferson Davis as Iago in Shakespeare's* Othello, *gazing back at Hiram Revels (seated), who was elected to the Senate seat Davis once held.*

"TIME WORKS WONDERS."

IAGO. (JEFF DAVIS.) "FOR THAT I DO SUSPECT THE LUSTY MOOR HATH LEAP'D INTO MY SEAT: THE THOUGHT WHEREOF DOTH LIKE A POISONOUS MINERAL GNAW MY INWARDS". — OTHELLO.

and was a key figure in his impeachment. Stevens also championed radical legislation, including land reform. Although he "would have so remodeled all our institutions as to have freed them from every vestige of human oppression, of inequality of rights, of the recognized degradation of the poor, and the superior caste of the rich," he compromised when necessary—for example, on the Fourteenth Amendment—"because I live among men and not among angels."

CHARLES SUMNER (1811–1874). A Republican senator from Massachusetts, and an outspoken abolitionist, Sumner played an important role in the Reconstruction era. He was one of the acknowledged leaders of the Radical Republicans on Capitol Hill. At the Massachusetts Republican convention, he was the first delegate to urge emancipation and continually lobbied President Lincoln to free the slaves. For Sumner and his colleagues, both Lincoln's and Johnson's Reconstruction policies failed to go far enough to ensure the rights of freedmen. He characterized his own efforts as working for "absolute human equality, secured, assured, invulnerable." Sumner led the effort to remove Johnson from office, and authored the 1875 Civil Rights Act. He did not live to see its passage.

LAURA M. TOWNE (1825–1901). A native of Pennsylvania, Laura Towne grew up in a wealthy family and was an abolitionist. In 1862, on behalf of the Port Royal Relief Committee of Philadelphia, she traveled to the South Carolina Sea Islands, which were occupied by Union troops. She was one of hundreds of Northern teachers who went south to teach the contrabands (later known as freedmen). With a colleague, Ellen Murray, Towne founded the Penn School in September 1862 on St. Helena Island. She instructed former slaves in reading, writing, arithmetic, geography, and classical languages, mirroring her own education in Boston and Philadelphia. In 1870, the Penn School began to train African American teachers, and, for many years after, it offered the only secondary-school education for blacks on the Sea Islands. Although she had some of the paternalism toward blacks that was common in the period—"It is such a satisfaction to an abolitionist to see that [the black Sea Islanders] are proving conclusively that they can and will even *like* to work enough at least to support themselves and give something extra to Government," she wrote to a friend—Towne expressed her dedication and commitment by remaining in the community and running her school for nearly forty years.

LYMAN TRUMBULL (1813–1896). Originally from Connecticut, Trumbull first gained a reputation as a lawyer and politician at the state level in Illinois. In 1854, Trumbull was elected to the U.S. House of Representatives, but instead was seated in the Senate when Abraham Lincoln threw his support to Trumbull in the three-way contest (decided, at that time, by the state legislature). Originally a Democrat, Trumbull became a Radical Republican during the Civil War, although he once said that he was only "willing to be radical lawfully." Adherence to the law marked his entire career. He frequently censured the methods of Lincoln and of many Radical Republicans, while supporting their overall objectives. Perhaps his most notable achievement was the introduction of a bill that became the basis of the Thirteenth Amendment to the Constitution. He was also the architect of a bill to enlarge the Freedmen's Bureau and a civil rights bill; both were vetoed by President Johnson. Because he believed that the law took precedence over personal motives, Trumbull voted against conviction of Johnson during the impeachment proceedings. Disillusioned with the Radicals, Trumbull became a Liberal Republican. In 1876, when he was counsel to Samuel Tilden in the disputed presidential election, he again became a Democrat.

HENRY M. TURNER (1834–1915). Born a free black in South Carolina, and educated at Baltimore's Trinity College, Henry Turner was the minister for Washington, D.C.'s largest African Methodist Episcopal Church congregation. During the war, he was chaplain to a black regiment. In Georgia in 1865, he worked as an agent for the Freedmen's Bureau, and later participated in Georgia's constitutional convention and served in the state House of Representatives. Eventually he became an A.M.E. bishop and president of Atlanta's Morris Brown College. Disillusioned with the Federal government's overt retreat from the enforcement of civil rights for blacks in the 1870s, Turner was among the most outspoken proponents of black emigration. He traveled to Africa four times in the 1890s to encourage migration.

BENJAMIN FRANKLIN WADE (1800–1878). Benjamin Wade rose to prewar prominence in Ohio, as a lawyer, state senator, and judge. His time, both in office and on the bench, was marked by strong antislavery views. These beliefs followed Wade to the United States Senate in 1850. He was elected as a member of the Whig party, but, in 1854, he defected to the Republicans. During the next fourteen years, he was at the forefront of the Radical branch of the party. Convinced that President Lincoln was too lenient in his plans for reconciliation with the Confederate states after the war, he cosponsored the Wade-Davis Bill in 1864, which was passed by Congress and ultimately pocket-vetoed by Lincoln (see "Wartime Reconstruction," on page 759). In response to the tactics employed by the president, Wade published the Wade-Davis Manifesto, which, in addition to calling for strict standards of readmittance, expressed his conviction that, in decisions concerning Reconstruction, Congress was "paramount and must be respected." With Charles Sumner and Thaddeus Stevens, Wade was instrumental in championing a number of Radical plans, including the Civil Rights, Tenure of Office, and Military Reconstruction bills. In 1867, he was elected Senate President Pro Tempore. From this office (under the rules of the time), he would have succeeded to the presidency had Andrew Johnson been convicted in his impeachment trial.

SELECTED RESOURCES

For additional information on published sources, see the annotated book list in Chapter 13, "Studying the War: Research and Preservation."

Benedict, Michael Les. *A Compromise of Principle: Congressional Republicans and Reconstruction, 1863–1869.* New York: Norton, 1974. Illustrated.

———. *The Impeachment and Trial of Andrew Johnson.* New York: Norton, 1973.

Berlin, Ira, et al., eds. *Freedom: A Documentary History of Emancipation, 1861–1867.* Three Volumes. New York: Cambridge University Press, 1982.

Cox, LaWanda C., *Lincoln and Black Freedom: A Study in Presidential Leadership.* Columbia: University of South Carolina Press, 1994.

———, and John H., eds. *Reconstruction, the Negro, and the New South.* New York: Harper & Row, 1973.

Foner, Eric. *Freedom's Lawmakers: A Directory of Black Officeholders During Reconstruction.* Baton Rouge: Louisiana State University Press, 1996. Illustrated.

———. *Reconstruction: America's Unfinished Revolution, 1863–1877.* New York: Harper & Row, 1988. Illustrated.

Franklin, John Hope. *Reconstruction After the Civil War.* Chicago: University of Chicago Press, 1961. Illustrated.

McFeely, William S. *Grant: A Biography.* Newtown: American Political Biography Press, 1996.

Perman, Michael. *The Road to Redemption: Southern Politics, 1869–1879.* Chapel Hill: University of North Carolina Press, 1984.

Smith, John David. *Black Voices from Reconstruction, 1865–1877.* Gainesville: University of Florida Press, 1997.

Williams, Lou Faulkner. *The Great South Carolina Ku Klux Klan Trials, 1871–1872.* Athens: University of Georgia Press, 1996. Illustrated.

THE CIVIL WAR IN LITERATURE AND THE ARTS

When the Civil War began and patriotic ardor on both sides was at its peak, American civilians' ideas about what the war might bring sprang largely from the idealized battle scenes that were depicted in the painting and literature of the time, for the United States had endured no major war on its soil since the Revolution and the War of 1812. War, as depicted in those pre-Civil War arts, was noble, tidier than war ever is, and relatively untouched by chaos and horror. The brute face of war came home to Union civilians primarily through the work of the special artists who traveled with the armies on behalf of the nation's illustrated journals. People and scenes of the war were also recorded by Civil War photographers, such as Mathew Brady and his staff, who followed Northern armies, and Southerner Julian Vannerson, who photographed a number of prominent Confederate leaders. (In the Civil War era, photographs could not be published in magazines and newspapers as they are today, but they were widely exhibited and had great impact, nevertheless.)

In the South, many civilians became all too familiar with the actualities of war without visual aids. Large parts of the region became devastated battlegrounds, and tens of thousands of Southerners, their homes destroyed or conquered, became what Southern nurse Kate Cumming called a "floating population" of refugees. Yet, there too, artistic representations of the war and its leaders were important during the conflict. After 1865, the nostalgia for Southern gallantry and the prewar status quo engendered waves of what became known as "Lost Cause" images that were immensely popular among the South's white population. (*The Lost Cause* was the title of Edward A. Pollard's 1866 history of the Confederacy.) In the postwar years, Northern-based lithographers and publishers of illustrated newspapers also circulated images of new African American leaders, including those elected to Southern state governments and the U.S. Congress.

Throughout the conflict, men and women, in both the North and the South, wrote poems, novels, newspaper columns, and songs drawn from the war. Political cartoonists—such as the North's Frank Bellew, Henry Stephens, John McLenan, and Thomas Nast; Southern sympathizer Adalbert Volck; and famed London illustrator John Tenniel, who also favored the Confederacy—skewered those whose actions they did not favor and glowingly depicted those whose actions they did. Their work was widely circulated not only in illustrated journals but through the shops of Currier & Ives and other popular lithographers. Advertisers sold goods using Civil War images, and music publishers distributed hosts of Civil War songs—many with patriotic cover illustrations. Soldiers of both armies sketched war scenes on letters, and both soldiers and civilians, North and South, dispatched letters in envelopes decorated by stationers with war-related art—a popular means of artistic communication in the Civil War years.

All these visual records, combined with the depictions of the war's special artists and the many kinds of popular art that flourished during the war years, as well as the Civil War paintings of easel artists of the late nineteenth century, continue to bring the war home to Americans—and to many others, worldwide, who are intrigued by this painful chapter in American history. Along with the literature—ranging from histories and memoirs to war-related novels, poetry, and stage plays—that poured out during and immediately after the war, those contemporaneous visual depictions of the war feed the imaginations of modern painters, sculptors, movie and television producers, novelists, and poets who continue to examine the most terrible of American conflicts in their art.

Popular Art

As the Civil War began, photography was a relatively new and technically limited visual tool, and few people had access to, or the money to purchase, original paintings. The battle art that colored people's prewar conceptions was largely distributed by publishers of lithographic prints. Their products were sometimes based on famous paintings, but, more often, they were the work of commissioned artists and illustrators. In 1860, several hundred of these publishers were in business throughout the United States, but most of them were concentrated in Northern publishing centers: New York, Boston, Philadelphia, Hartford, Cincinnati, and Chicago. Their products were sold

This chromolithograph of Sheridan's Ride, *published in 1886 by Louis Prang, & Co., is one of numerous popular-art depictions of Major General Phil Sheridan's return to the battlefront to rally his troops during the battle of Cedar Creek, Virginia, October 19, 1864. Sheridan's ride, on his warhorse, Rienzi, was also the subject of an oft-recited wartime poem by Thomas Buchanan Read.*

in book shops, by street vendors, and in their own sales shops. Affordably priced, this popular art decorated homes, barns, warehouses, outhouses, bars, and hotels all over America.

Almost as soon as the Civil War started, the conflict became a central subject for these commercial image publishers. They produced battle scenes, group and individual portraits of leading soldiers, sentimental scenes—such as enlisted men taking leave of their wives, or nurses caring for wounded on the battlefield—and pictures commemorating the work of hospitals or the achievements of particular regiments. Commercial art publishers also waded into wartime political battles, reproducing and distributing political cartoons and other blatantly subjective art—some of which had originally been published in illustrated journals like *Harper's Weekly*.

Long dependent on Northern and European publishing houses for both visual materials and books, the South began the war with few publishing centers of its own—and only one-twentieth of America's paper mills. As the conflict continued, the region experienced ever-greater shortages of paper, ink, and other items necessary to produce popular art. With more and more men joining the army, there was also a severe shortage of artists and trained engravers. Yet, Southerners put as much value on popular pictorial art as did their Northern counterparts; despite shortages and other war-related problems, a few lithography houses and, briefly, two illustrated journals operated in the Confederacy during the war. The journal that made the briefest appearance, *Southern Punch* (August 1863–August 1864), was a humor magazine modeled after Britain's famous *Punch* magazine (which was sympathetic to the South). *Southern Punch* gave Confederate cartoonists an opportunity to ridicule Northern political and military figures—and to chastise their own compatriots who were not sufficiently engaged in the secessionist struggle.

The most commercial imagery appeared in advertising. Throughout the war, labels and other advertisements stirred the patriotism (and the inclination to purchase) of potential buyers of everything from soap to cigars—a practice that continued well after the conflict ended.

Immediately after the war, Northern lithography companies not only deluged Northern markets with commemorative Civil War art, they also catered to the Southern markets that had been closed to them during the war years. Many published lithographs of Southern war leaders, especially Robert E. Lee and Stonewall Jackson. And some produced sentimental prints, such as "The Burial of Latane," published by William Smith of New York, that rode the wave of the South's painful nostalgia for the "Lost Cause."

Today, the commercial art of all kinds that was produced during, and in the decades immediately following, the Civil War continues to provide telling glimpses of events and the popular responses to them. Popular art of the period is an essential component of major Civil War research collections, and some original popular prints, first offered for sale in the 1860s to 1890s, are being offered for sale—at considerably higher prices than when they first appeared—by galleries and auction houses.

Some Outstanding Popular Art Publishers of the Civil War Era

Currier & Ives, New York, New York

Established in the early 1830s by lithographer Nathaniel Currier (1813–1888), who was joined by partner James Merritt Ives (1824–1895) in 1857, Currier & Ives specialized in producing vivid prints of American scenes, customs, and events. Throughout the Civil War, Currier & Ives published sentimental and commemorative prints, battle scenes, portraits of prominent wartime figures, and other war-related images.

Kurz & Allison, Chicago, Illinois

Not established until 1885, when Austrian-born Louis Kurz (1835–1921) formed a partnership with fellow artist Alexander Allison, this firm became the midwestern counterpart to Currier & Ives. The Civil War images it produced in the 1880s and 1890s, when interest in the war was high, were beautifully rendered and are today highly prized by collectors.

Louis Prang & Company, New York, New York

A pioneer in color reproduction, German immigrant Louis Prang arrived in New York on April 5, 1850. Established on his own by 1860, Prang published his first Civil War image—an engineer's plan of Charleston Harbor, showing channels and forts—as soon as the conflict began. During the war, he published additional maps and plans of battles of the war; portraits of Civil War generals; two albums of war scenes by Winslow Homer (*Life in Camp*, twenty-four humorous scenes; and *Campaign Sketches*—both published in 1863); and war-related sheet music, with illustrated covers. After the war, in addition to commemorating the Union cause, Prang produced images that would appeal to Southerners—both those nostalgic for the Lost Cause and forward-looking freedmen. A Prang color lithograph of Hiram Revels, the first African American elected to the U.S. Senate (he occupied the seat once held by Jefferson Davis), received a generous endorsement from Frederick Douglass: "Every colored householder in the land should have one of these portraits in his parlor, and should explain it to his children, as the dividing line between the darkness and despair that overhung our past, and the light and hope that now beams upon our future as people."

Ayers and Wade, Richmond, Virginia

Publishers of *The Southern Illustrated News*, the South's attempt at a periodical comparable in quality to such Northern publications as *Frank Leslie's Illustrated News* and *Harper's Weekly*. In addition to its many other functions, *The Southern Illustrated News* was the only reliable Southern source of print portraits of leading Confederate military and political figures.

Blanton Duncan, Columbia, South Carolina

Publisher, circa 1862, of an unusual set of Confederate prints: four cartoons, *Dissolving Views of Richmond*, which made fun of Union General George B. McClellan's ultimately unsuccessful Peninsula Campaign of that year. The fourth cartoon, which shows McClellan unrealistically claiming victory, also shows him surrounded by Union soldiers "speaking" (in the word-balloon manner of cartoon characters) in foreign accents, an early visual depiction of the myth that the Confederacy was overpowered by immigrant hordes from the North.

Hoyer and Ludwig, Richmond, Virginia

This firm, started at the beginning of the Civil War by jeweler J. C. Hoyer and German-born printmaker Charles Ludwig, was dissolved in 1866. During its years of operation, it was responsible for creating some of the few examples of single-sheet Confederate graphics of which there are today some surviving copies, including: *Map of the Confederate States of America* (1861), published by A. Morris; *Map Showing the Battle Grounds of the Chickahominy* (ca. 1862), drawn by painter Edwin Sheppard; a facsimile of the Virginia Secession Ordinance (ca. 1861); and *President Jefferson Davis Arriving in the Field of Battle at Bull's Run*.

Pessou and Simon, New Orleans, Louisiana

Lithographers of some of the rare single-sheet war images that were published in the Confederacy, including two works by artist A. Persac: *Camp Moore (Tangipaha, Lna), 1861*, and *Camp Walker (Metary Ridge, Lna), 1861*—both depicting training camps brimming with early and eager volunteers.

Blelock and Company, New Orleans, Louisiana

This printmaking establishment moved to New York City after New Orleans fell to the Union in the spring of 1862, then returned to New Orleans immediately after the war. At some unspecified date before its New York relocation, the firm produced an imposing color lithograph of Confederate President Jefferson Davis, based on a Mathew Brady photo taken when Davis was a U.S. senator. While in New York, the firm responded to the marked Northern curiosity about Stonewall Jackson by producing, after Jackson's death, the sheet music for *Stonewall Jackson's*

Prayer. The lithographed portrait of Jackson by Henry C. Eno of New York on the song's cover was considerably more accurate than depictions of this outstanding general that had been circulated by Southern publishers earlier in the war.

Photography

Developed in the 1830s by Frenchmen Joseph Nicéphore Niepce and Louis Jacques Mandé Daguerre, the new art of photography had been sufficiently refined by 1860 to become a vivid means of documenting the Civil War. Though the necessary equipment was still large and clumsy to use, and "action" photographs were not yet possible, some breakthroughs in the 1850s had made photography a widely popular medium. Stereoscopic images (photographs that became three-dimensional when viewed through a handheld stereoscope), which became popular in the late 1850s, allowed people to peer at miniature black-and-white versions of such sights as the Egyptian pyramids and fabulous American landscapes in the comfort of their living rooms—thus creating the first real market for nonportrait photographs. At about the same time, *cartes de visite* (visiting cards) were introduced and caught on. These paper prints of individual portrait photographs, attached to 2.5-inch by 4-inch cards, were mass-produced during the Civil War years. Soldiers and their families exchanged these cherished mementos, and collectors eagerly acquired *carte de visite* images of famous people. These two new methods of distributing images considerably broadened the market for photography in the Civil War era.

Civil War photographers took an estimated 1,000,000 photographs between 1860 and 1865. The vast majority of these images were taken by Northern cameramen. A lack of supplies and operating capital made Southern photographers—who were much less numerous than those based in the North in the prewar years—all but nonexistent after the early years of the war. Consequently, there are very few battlefield photos in those places where victorious Confederates held the field.

Initially, Northern photographers concentrated on the Eastern Theater of operations. Thus, there are many more photographs of Gettysburg than of Vicksburg or Chattanooga. By the last year of the war, however, Northern photographers were systematically following Union offensives on both major fronts.

Photographers in the field had many challenges to overcome—particularly the problems involved in transporting cameras, tripods, lenses, chemicals, glass plates, distilled water, measuring cups, developing trays, portable darkrooms, and other assorted gear weighing between 100 and 150 pounds. The odd conveyances photographers generally used to carry their gear were soon dubbed *whatisit wagons* by the soldiers. Once these peculiar wagons halted, and the photographers set up to shoot, they had to take the time, and make sure their bulky cameras were stable enough, to ensure that they got a proper exposure for each shot. The required exposure time and the need for stability is what made "action photography" all but impossible.

As early as the summer of 1861, Mathew Brady began sending his assistants out to photograph armies in camps around Washington. Brady himself was apparently present at First Bull Run in July, and two of his assistants, George N. Barnard and James F. Gibson, chronicled the Bull Run battlefield and its environs soon after the Confederates withdrew from the Manassas line. Late in that year, one of Brady's most skilled photographers, Timothy O'Sullivan, was in South Carolina doing frontline work at the Union bases being established to support the naval blockade of Southern ports.

During General George B. McClellan's Peninsula Campaign of 1862, Gibson, assisted by John Wood, followed McClellan's army and took compelling photographs—particularly during the Seven Days engagements at the end of the campaign. Gibson's pictures of the Fair Oaks (Seven Pines) battlefield and of Union wounded at a soon-to-be-captured field hospital at Savage's Station gave an immediacy to the war and were vivid proof of the value of stationing photographers with or near the great armies.

Two days after the September 17, 1862, battle of Antietam, near Sharpsburg, Maryland, Alexander Gardner, with James F. Gibson assisting, began taking some of the most significant exposures of the entire war. Only a few hours after it was known that the Confederate Army of Northern Virginia had withdrawn, Gardner started documenting the northern end of the field, including scenes of Confederate dead around the Dunker Church. When Brady exhibited these photographs at his New York studio, the *New York Times* of October 20, 1862, noted: "Mr. Brady has done something to bring home to us the terrible reality and earnestness of war. If he has not brought bodies and laid them in our dooryards and along streets, he has done something very like it."

A second group of Gardner photos after Antietam, dated October 3 and 4, captured President Lincoln's famous visit to General McClellan's headquarters. Though Mathew Brady was accorded credit for the products of his studios, Gardner and Gibson retained copyrights to these works, and others.

Taking along his Antietam negatives, Gardner left Brady's employ sometime between November 1862 and the opening of his own Washington gallery in May 1863. James Gibson and Timothy O'Sullivan were among the first photographers to join Gardner's staff, now in competition with Brady. For the balance of the war, competing firms photographed soldiers in camp or raced to scenes of recent carnage. Among the more notable expeditions were: Brady's coverage of the Wilderness fighting of May 1864; Timothy O'Sullivan's work at Spotsylvania Court House, Virginia; Thomas C. Roche's photographs of Confederate dead at Petersburg on April 3, 1865; and the prodigious work of George Barnard, who followed William T. Sherman's armies on the campaign for Atlanta.

Some Notable Civil War Photographers

Biographical information on photographers who are credited with various Civil War pictures varies widely; in some cases, not even birth and death dates are known. Information is particularly scarce on Southern photographers.

GEORGE N. BARNARD (1819–1902). Connecticut-born, Barnard began his long career in photography at age twenty-three and became one of the most well-known and respected photographers in the United States. The photographs Barnard took throughout the war—particularly those published in his album *Photographic Views of Sherman's Campaign*—reflect his determination to record the destruction of battles. He believed that if such scenes were circulated widely enough, future wars might be avoided.

MATHEW B. BRADY (ca. 1823–1896). The most famous photographer whose name is associated with the Civil War, Brady was responsible for organizing a program to chronicle its progress comprehensively in photographic images. Details of his life and career appear on page 815.

GEORGE SMITH COOK (1819–1902). A native of Charleston, South Carolina, Cook was dubbed "Photographer of the Confederacy." In 1851, he joined Brady's gallery in New York, but he returned to the South at the outbreak of the war and became a practiced smuggler of photographic chemicals and similar essentials. He is credited with taking the first picture of ironclads in action, when the Union monitors *Weehawken*, *Montauk*, and *Passaic* bombarded the Confederate batteries at Fort Moultrie on September 8, 1863.

J. D. EDWARDS (b. circa 1860). Thirty years old when Southern states began to secede, New Hampshire-born Edwards, then living in New Orleans, may have begun taking pictures of local volunteers (including the colorful Washington Artillery) as early as January 1861. In April of that year, he took his camera to Pensacola, Florida, where he made at least sixty-nine images of Fort Pickens, Fort Barrancas, Fort McRee, the navy yard, and dozens of volunteer groups—the finest body of outdoor work by any wartime Southern photographer. Though many of these images were lost, a significant number survived.

ALEXANDER GARDNER (1821–1882). Scotsman Gardner had been a reporter and editor for the Glasgow *Sentinel* before coming to the United States in 1849. In New York City, he was employed by Mathew Brady in 1856 but parted company with Brady in 1863. Gardner is credited with three-fourths of the photographs of the Army of the Potomac, and his name is associated with some of the most famous Civil War photos, including Lincoln at Antietam, Lincoln's last photographic portrait, and the picture of the hanging of the Lincoln assassination conspirators. His *Photographic Sketch Book of the War* (1866), comprising 100 mounted photos, was the first published collection of Civil War photographs.

JAMES F. GIBSON (b. 1828). An employee of Mathew Brady when the war began, Gibson photographed the campaigns at Centerville and Bull Run in 1862. He joined Alexander Gardner's studio when the Scotsman broke with Brady in 1863. Thirteen of the images included in Gardner's *Photographic Sketch Book of the War* are credited to Gibson.

A. J. LYTLE. A Southerner, Lytle has the distinction of being the first known spy-photographer. He covered the war for three years while living and maintaining a photography studio in Baton Rouge, Louisiana—and working for the Confederate Secret Service. The *Photographic History of the Civil War* notes that Lytle "risked his life to obtain negatives of Federal batteries, cavalry regiments and camps, lookout towers, and the vessels of Farragut and Porter, in fact of everything that might be of the slightest use in informing the Confederate Secret Service of the strength of the Federal occupation of Baton Rouge."

JAMES M. OSBORN. With his business partner, F. W. DURBEC, Charlestonian Osborn took a camera and portable darkroom inside Fort

MATHEW BRADY (CA. 1823–1896)

Though it is unknown how many Civil War pictures pioneering photographer Mathew Brady actually took himself, the photographs taken by the staff he organized and dispatched to document the war provide invaluable views of the people and places involved in the conflict.

An early and enthusiastic student of photography, by 1844 Mathew Brady had opened his own daguerreotype studio at 207 Broadway in New York City. In the spring of that year, he won the first of many awards he was to receive in photographic exhibitions; and in 1850, he published his best-known antebellum work, a collection of portraits of famous citizens, titled the *Gallery of Illustrious Americans.*

Brady hired the brilliant Scottish portraitist Alexander Gardner in 1856 and, two years later, put him in charge of the new National Photographic Art Gallery at 350–352 Pennsylvania Avenue, N.W., in Washington, D.C. From then until 1863, when Gardner opened his own studio, the two men worked together to make an indelible mark on American history. Employing, in both studios, a staff of more than 100 photographers, technicians, and touch-up artists,

Brady, with Gardner's indispensable aid, made "Photo by Brady" one of the best-known bylines of the era. A photographic portrait of Abraham Lincoln, made in Brady's New York studio on February 27, 1860, the morning of Lincoln's seminal Cooper Union speech, became perhaps the earliest widely distributed image of the future president.

When the Civil War broke out, Brady organized a corps of photographers, assigned them to cover different armies and areas of operation, and secured permits from the Union authorities to make this possible. All expenses incurred in the enterprise were to be paid by Brady, not the government; but Brady's photographers did enjoy some marked cooperation, including use of army transports and railroads. To broaden the scope of his photographic record as much as possible, Brady also purchased the work of other cameramen in the field.

Though it is uncertain how many Civil War field photos Brady actually took himself—probably not many—he was indisputably a prime mover in creating a priceless photographic record of the war. Creation of this immeasurable legacy, however, cast him into such massive debt that he was forced to declare bankruptcy in 1872. Three years later, the Federal government provided some relief when it purchased his collection for $25,000.

Brady, whose reputation had remained secure even while his finances wavered, continued his photographic work in a succession of studios until his death in New York on January 16, 1896. He was buried in the Congressional Cemetery in Washington, D.C.

Sumter just after its 1861 surrender to the Confederacy. The more than forty images taken by this photographic team comprised a comprehensive record of the event that began the Civil War.

TIMOTHY H. O'SULLIVAN (1840–1882). Known now primarily for both his Civil War photographs and his postwar western landscapes, O'Sullivan learned photography under Mathew Brady, then joined Alexander Gardner's photographic team and made memorable photos of the Gettysburg battlefield (including his famous "The Harvest of Death"), among other images. In addition to his work in Pennsylvania, he traveled throughout Virginia and South Carolina. Forty-five of the photographs published by Alexander Gardner in his *Photographic Sketch Book of the War* were taken by O'Sullivan.

JULIAN VANNERSON (b. 1827). A native of Virginia, Vannerson made photographic portraits of some of the South's military leaders. Among them were an affecting photo of Joseph E. Johnston that was the model for an engraving published in the *Southern Illustrated News,* and several photographs of Robert E. Lee that served as models for many widely circulated engravings and lithographs after the war.

Civil War Artists and the Rise of Illustrated News

Not until 1880 did a photomechanical reproduction of a photograph first appear in an American newspaper, and photographs did not become standard fare until the debut of New York's *Illustrated Daily News* in 1919. But American editors, building on the examples provided by such European publications as Britain's *Illustrated London News* (founded 1842), France's *L'Illustration* (1843) and Germany's *Illustriete Zeitung* (1843), used a number of creative techniques to deliver to their readers depictions of important Civil War sites and portraits of wartime figures. By employing talented sketch artists in the field, and legions of engravers to "transcribe" the work of these artists (as well as the work of some photographers) onto the blocks used for printing, these American editors brought the war home visually to hundreds of thousands of eager subscribers.

In 1850, *Gleason's Pictorial Drawing-Room Companion,* published in Boston, became the first American illustrated weekly. This important first step was followed, in 1852, by American showman Phineas T. Barnum's ill-advised attempt at developing his own illustrated newspaper, the *Illustrated*

News, established with two partners. An unsuccessful enterprise (the paper went out of business in 1853), the *News* did provide added experience in American publishing for veteran engraver and English-born artist Frank Leslie, who would soon be a major force in U.S. publishing. An ex-employee of *Gleason's Pictorial*, Leslie supervised the engraving process used to produce illustrations in the *News*.

By 1861, the development of American illustrated periodicals was in full flower. The three most influential illustrated journals in the North were *Frank Leslie's Illustrated News*, established in 1855; *Harper's Weekly*, established in 1857; and veteran publisher John King's *New York Illustrated News*, established in 1859 and sold in 1861 to T. B. Leggett.

In the South, where the materials required for printing—as well as personnel, such as artists and engravers—became increasingly scarce as the war progressed, the European and Northern illustrated publications stimulated the creation of the always-struggling, but much appreciated *Southern Illustrated News*.

These top illustrated journals gained in popularity as the war progressed. Both soldiers and civilians were eager readers—though the illustrated papers were often so scarce in the field that newsboys arriving in camp with copies in their huge saddlebags were almost swept away by the chaos of soldiers attempting to buy one before they were gone (the scarcity once caused General William T. Sherman to order that newspapers were to be reserved for men who had seen combat). Soldiers were among the most unforgiving critics of inaccurate images reproduced in the journals' pages; they were also the most avid admirers of images that correctly depicted their wartime combat experiences.

Inaccuracy was often a problem, even in the depiction of war leaders. As late as 1864, for example, many papers were basing depictions of Union General Ulysses S. Grant either on a photo made early in the war, when his beard was very long, or on a photograph of a physically similar beef contractor named William Grant. A picture of Robert E. Lee, published in the January 17, 1863, edition of the *Southern Illustrated News* (his middle name was given incorrectly as Edmund rather than Edward), was actually a photograph of the Confederate general made some ten years before the war, when he had dark hair and was beardless. It was the only likeness the Southern engravers had to work with at the time, and the resulting out-of-date portrait was fixed in many Southerners' minds as a true representation of Lee's appearance until later in the war. (See photos on page 818.)

Depictions of war leaders in the illustrated press were often inaccurate, especially in the early years of the war: Grant (left) was shown with the longer beard he sported briefly when the war began; Lee (right) was shown with dark hair and no beard.

As the war grew longer and bloodier, more accurate depictions of people, events, and military life appeared in the papers. Much of this realism was due to the work of the special artists employed by these periodicals, who traveled with the military forces and sketched them in camp, in the midst of battle, and in the aftermath of combat. The sketches submitted by these artists—when reproduced faithfully by engravers (the best of whom were capable of polishing the hastily made "shorthand" illustrations occasionally sent in by artists caught in the heat of battle)—brought, to those on the home front, a deeper appreciation of the fearful toll of combat and the frightening brutality of the war. Occasionally, illustrations made by talented soldier-artists—such as Private Alfred E. Mathews of the Thirty-First Ohio, and Lieutenant George W. Bailey, who served under Grant in the West—appeared in these publications, as well, complementing the work of the professionals. Today, the original drawings and first-generation engravings of these wartime artists, housed in the Library of Congress and other institutions throughout the country, continue to reveal the Civil War experience in a unique and powerful fashion (see Chapter 13, "Studying the War: Research and Preservation").

Notable Illustrated Journals of the Civil War

Harper's Weekly

Founded in 1857 by Fletcher Harper (who had also established *Harper's New Monthly Magazine* in 1850), *Harper's Weekly* started out as a small sixteen-page folio, and quickly became a journal of prestige and influence. Subtitled "A Journal of Civilization," *Harper's* was backed by the considerable resources of Harper & Brothers publishers and was thus able to pay top salaries or commissions to its employees. By 1860, its circulation had reached 100,000 copies a week; by 1863, it was 120,000. Always noteworthy for its illustrations, the journal featured full- and double-page pictures of news events, as well as powerful political cartoons.

Frank Leslie's Illustrated News

Born Henry Carter in England, where he was an artist and engraver for the *Illustrated London News*, Frank Leslie (1821–1880) established *Frank Leslie's Ladies Gazette of Fashion and Fancy Needle Work* in 1854 and *Frank Leslie's Illustrated News* in 1855. An intelligent and ruthlessly ambitious man, Leslie developed a network of artists and photographers throughout the United States who joined his headquarters staff of sketch artists in providing him with the raw material for the sometimes lurid illustrations that quickly made his sixteen-page weekly popular and profitable. By 1860, *Leslie's* circulation was nearly 100,000; circulation surged to around 200,000 in the first year of the war; but by 1863 it had returned to just under 100,000 copies, placing *Leslie's* second, behind *Harper's Weekly* in popularity.

New York Illustrated News

Established in 1859 by publisher John King, the *New York Illustrated News* began with excellent prospects. It featured engravings of a quality that equaled the pictorial work in its rival publications. Compared to *Harper's* and *Leslie's*, however, its resources were limited. Discouraged by his inability to meet the expanding demand created by the war—the paper could never support more than a single full-time artist at the front—King sold the *News* to T. B. Leggett in 1861. That year, the circulation of the *News* rivaled that of *Leslie's*. But by 1863, the *News*, having lost its only full-time field sketch artist, was facing a financial crisis. W. Jennings Demorest bought the journal in 1864, but this proved only a temporary reprieve. Demorest's support of the most extreme faction of the Republican Party in the election campaign of that year probably contributed to the demise of the *News* after the election.

Southern Illustrated News

Established in September 1862 by Richmond publishers Ayers and Wade, this "News and Literary Journal for Southern Families" faced daunting obstacles—including shortages of sketch artists and cartoonists, engravers and die-makers, paper, ink, and presses. "Engravers Wanted," pleaded an ad in its pages in July 1863. "Desirous, if possible of illustrating the 'News' in a style not inferior to the 'London Illustrated News,' we offer the *highest salaries* ever paid in this country for good engravers." No one applied. Illustrations became relatively rare in the *Southern Illustrated News*, and, in November 1864, it ceased publication.

Some Notable Artist-Correspondents and Soldier-Artists of the Civil War

A distinctive band of artists/reporters/adventurers, the special artists of the Civil War provided home-front audiences with vivid combat and behind-the-lines scenes that captured the action and hardship of the war with an immediacy that was not possible with the ponderous photographic processes of the time. Braving sickness, the mud and dust of long marches, incoming fire—and the occasional agony of seeing their hard-won sketches unhappily altered either by inept engravers or to suit the inclinations of their editors—the artists followed (and, in some cases, served *with)* the armies in the field, from Fort Sumter to Reconstruction. Wearing sturdy clothes and wide-brimmed hats to shade their eyes; carrying large portfolios containing the paper, pencils, crayons, charcoal, ink, pens, brushes, and watercolors necessary to their jobs, the artists became experts at finding good vantage points (rooftops, hilltops, ships' masts, the higher reaches of trees, observation balloons) in the midst of chaos. They depicted valor, sacrifice, and the often-difficult "daily grind" of armies on the move. As the war progressed, they also depicted its uglier aspects: casualties, defeats, the destruction of cities, the execution of deserters, the terrible physical condition of many prisoners of war. Their drawings comprise a uniquely valuable contribution to the understanding of America's most devastating conflict. The most notable Civil War artist-correspondents include (in alphabetical order):

THEODORE DAVIS (1840–1894). Employed in 1861 by *Harper's Weekly*, Davis was probably the most traveled of the Civil War artist-correspondents. He sketched the war on the Potomac front and the Carolina coast, and he drew the battle of the *Monitor* and the *Merrimack*. Friendly with Ulysses S. Grant, whom he met in 1862, Davis was with him at Vicksburg and Chattanooga. Afterward, he marched through Georgia with William T. Sherman. Described as an "effervescent young man around whom many legends grew," he was wounded twice in the course of the war, and those injuries plagued him for the rest of his life. After the war, he was one of four veteran artists who prepared a complete set of Civil War illustrations for the Century Company. The collection was reprinted extensively throughout the late nineteenth and early twentieth centuries.

EDWIN FORBES (1839–1895). Trained in the fine arts at the National Academy of Design, Forbes took a job with Frank Leslie in 1862, in order to pay his bills. Intelligent, curious, and sensitive, he was dispatched to Virginia, the theater of operations in which he remained (with a few detours) for three years. Forbes covered the 1862 Shenandoah Valley Campaign, the second battle of Bull Run, the battle of Antietam, Burnside's 1863 "mud march," the Chancellorsville Campaign, the battle of Gettysburg, the Wilderness Campaign, the beginning of the siege of Petersburg, and Confederate General Jubal Early's 1864 move toward Washington, D.C. His favorite subjects were camp life and individual soldiers. After the war, Forbes published *Life Studies of the Great Army* (1876) and a two-volume memoir, *Thirty Years After: An Artist's Story of the Great War.*

WINSLOW HOMER (1836–1910). Best known now as a painter of seascapes and landscapes, Homer was also an engraver and a skilled commercial artist when *Harper's Weekly* hired him as a part-time artist and engraver. He covered Lincoln's 1861 inaugural in Washington, and McClellan's Peninsula Campaign, and was almost certainly with Grant in Virginia's Wilderness in 1864. Primarily interested in ordinary soldiers and scenes of camp life, Homer was far from the most prolific of the special artists. His Civil War work, reproduced in twenty-four engravings appearing in various editions of *Harper's*, included "The surgeon at work at the rear during an engagement," one of the first pictures to give attention to army doctors. (See page 822.)

HENRI LOVIE. Established in his own lithography business in Cincinnati before the war, Lovie supplemented his income by furnishing illustrations to

Winslow Homer drew fellow special-artist Alfred Waud hard at work sketching soldiers in a Maine regiment.

Leslie's. He was dispatched to sketch Abraham Lincoln in Springfield, Illinois, after the election of 1860, and to cover Lincoln's trip to Washington in 1861. He also covered General George B. McClellan's successful 1861 campaign against Confederates in western Virginia. Lovie made his most distinctive contributions in the Western Theater, first in Missouri and then with Grant's army when it captured Fort Henry and Fort Donelson. During the latter campaign, he produced some of the first graphic depictions of the war's wounded—a subject that artist-correspondents had previously avoided. Lovie was also the only artist who illustrated the full two days of fighting at Shiloh. He retired after covering the Vicksburg campaign.

ARTHUR LUMLEY (1837–1912). Age twenty-four when the war started, Dublin-born Arthur Lumley was hired by Frank Leslie in 1861 and assigned to sketch the army around Washington. He covered First Bull Run, portraying not only the combat prowess of the Union army but the subsequent break in morale and discipline and the panicked withdrawal from the battlefield. As the Union forces in the Eastern Theater regrouped in preparation for the Peninsula Campaign, he sketched camp and training scenes. In the midst of this assignment, he was hired away from *Leslie's* by the *New York Illustrated News*. During the siege of Yorktown, he made his first balloon ascension, with Union aeronaut Thaddeus Lowe (see "Military Aeronautics" in Chapter 4, "Battles and the Battlefield"). The resulting sketch was one of the most unusual illustrations of the war. Lumley covered Virginia for three years, depicting all aspects of the war. He resigned as a special artist more than a year before Appomattox.

THOMAS NAST (1840–1902). The only Civil War artist-correspondent who had previously sketched under fire (he covered Garibaldi's Italian campaign for three illustrated papers), Thomas Nast covered Lincoln's 1861 trip to Washington and the bitter violence of the 1863 New York conscription riots, and also depicted such war-front scenes as weary soldiers resting in the midst of a long march. But Nast evolved, during the war, primarily as a creator of sharp-edged editorial cartoons and sentimental and patriotic images that generated increased support for the war. "Christmas Eve, 1862," the first of Nast's sentimental wartime Christmas scenes, was a nostalgic depiction of a soldier and his wife, separated and thinking of each other. It became hugely popular. He also drew illustrations supporting many of the patriotic campaigns of *Harper's Weekly*, where he started thirty years of employment in 1862. Nast's ferocious cartoon barrage in favor of Lincoln and attacking George B. McClellan during the 1864 presidential campaign is particularly noteworthy.

ALLEN CHRISTIAN REDWOOD (1844–1922). A Virginian, Redwood was a Confederate soldier in the thick of action from early campaigns under Stonewall Jackson, through Chancellorsville and Gettysburg, to his capture just before Appomattox. He was wounded twice. After the war, he moved to Baltimore, opened an art studio, and began to work for lithographers. His only separate-sheet Confederate print, "Charge of Maryland Infantry (C.S.), Gettysburg July 3rd, 1863," was probably based on a postwar watercolor sketch executed as a model for an illustration in *Battles and Leaders* (1886). It is as a postwar illustrator of such war-related volumes, particularly the memoirs of former Confederates, that he is best known. Redwood also supplied the Confederate images in the complete set of Civil War images commissioned by the Century Company after the war.

CHARLES W. REED (1841–1926). A native of Boston, artistically talented Reed enlisted in the Ninth Massachusetts Light Artillery on August 2, 1862, and served until the end of the war. He participated in the battles of Gettysburg (for which he received the Medal of Honor), the Wilderness, Spotsylvania Courthouse, and Petersburg before being detailed as an assistant topographical engineer in November 1864. He was present at Appomattox when Lee surrendered. Throughout his service, Reed made many drawings, in sketchbooks and as illustrations on his many letters home, that constituted a particularly eloquent visual record of the war. After the war, Reed pursued a career as an artist and illustrator. His papers and sketches are now preserved in the Library of Congress.

FRANK H. SCHELL. One of Frank Leslie's sketch artists, Frank Schell covered the Federal occupation of Baltimore in 1861, after crowds there had attacked Union soldiers who were in transit to Washington. He was next assigned to Virginia, where he made a series of drawings of contraband African Americans who were working for the Union forces and gradually getting used to their newfound freedom. He also covered the abortive Union thrust at Little and Great Bethel in early June of 1861. In 1862, he was one of the artists with McClellan during the Peninsula Campaign. In September, he was at Antietam. The sketches he made of the aftermath of that bloody encounter—particularly of Union burial parties and the local "battlefield tourists," who often seemed callously indifferent to the carnage they were surveying—were graphic evidence that the Civil War artists were freeing themselves from portraying the war in the heroic imagery that had been prevalent when it began. After the war, Frank Schell was one of four artists employed by the Century Company to create a complete set of Civil War images.

FREDERICK B. SCHELL. Also employed by Frank Leslie, Fred Schell was assigned to Grant's army at Vicksburg in 1863. His drawings of this crucial campaign included some of the first field drawings of Ulysses S. Grant, as well as scenes of the initial and futile assault on Vicksburg's fortifications: the intricate web of trenches, Union and Confederate, that gradually surrounded the city; and Confederates dropping grenades on Union soldiers who had fallen into a crater made by the explosion of their own mine.

WILLIAM LUDWELL SHEPPARD (1833–1912). The artist son of the treasurer of the Richmond, Fredericksburg, and Potomac Railroad, Sheppard served during the war with the Confederate's elite Richmond Howitzers before being assigned to the topographical department of the Army of Northern Virginia. His reputation as a soldier-artist stems primarily from his postwar career as an artist and illustrator—particularly of Carlton McCarthy's *Detailed Minutiae of Soldier Life in the Army of Northern Virginia*. One of the primary creators of "Lost Cause" imagery, he created individual battle prints, including *The Charge of the First Maryland Regiment/at the Death of Ashby*, and *Virginia 1864*, which depicts a Confederate artillery unit under fire.

JAMES E. TAYLOR (1839–1901). Employed by *Leslie's*, Taylor had spent two years as a private in the Union army before becoming an artist-correspondent. Before joining Sherman in South Carolina, he covered General Phil Sheridan's 1864 campaign in Virginia's Shenandoah Valley. Many of the sketches he made of Sheridan's men, as they followed the Federal war policy of planned destruction of all resources useful to the enemy, were not published because Leslie and other editors were leery of their effect on the home front. Their reluctance was soon abandoned, however, particularly as photographs of emaciated Union soldiers released from Confederate prisons (reproduced as engravings in the papers) were circulated in the North.

FRANK VIZETELLY (1830–1883?). An Englishman dispatched in 1861 to cover the American Civil War for the *Illustrated London News*, Vizetelly created a body of Civil War imagery that spanned not only the course of the war but the experiences of both sides. Starting as a correspondent in the North—under which auspices he sketched Washington scenes, First Bull Run, the Union's Mississippi River gunboat fleet, and the battle of Memphis—he grew increasingly restive under Federal restrictions. Making his way South in late 1862, he sketched the remainder of the war from within Confederate lines and compiled a unique graphic record of the last days of the Confederacy.

ADALBERT JOHANN VOLCK (1828–1912). More of a Southern propagandist than a visual reporter, Baltimorian Volck had immigrated from Germany in 1848 and earned a degree in dentistry in 1851—thus becoming a man with two careers. A "Copperhead artist"—geographically a Northerner, he had heavily Southern sympathies—his cartoons, caricatures, and other acidic views of the North and its people, and his idealized images of the South, could not be widely circulated during the war. Not until the turn of the century was his work "rediscovered" by a wide audience. His postwar artwork includes illustrations for Emily V. Mason's 1872 biography of Robert E. Lee.

ALFRED R. WAUD (1828–1891). Among the most dedicated and talented, and undoubtedly the most prolific, of the Civil War special artists, "Alf" Waud (pronounced Wōde) was born in England, studied at London's Royal Academy, and, in 1850, emigrated to the United States, where he established himself as an illustrator for periodicals and books. In 1861, as an artist-correspondent for the *New York Illustrated News*, he made his first battle sketches at First Bull Run, then covered the Union fleet's attack on Hatteras Inlet. Moving to *Harper's* in 1862, Waud followed the Army of the Potomac in all its major campaigns, from Antietam to the siege of Petersburg. He was apparently present at Appomattox, where he sketched Lee leaving the McLean house after his surrender. Personable and canny, Waud was not shy about exposing himself to danger in quest of accurate images of the war (unlike most of the special artists, he carried a pistol). After the war, he was one of the four artists who compiled the Civil War images published by the Century Company. He also traveled through the postwar South and depicted the aftermath of the war in a series of historic images.

WILLIAM WAUD (1830–1878). Alfred Waud's younger brother, William Waud was dispatched to Charleston, South Carolina, by Frank Leslie in the winter of 1860–1861. He covered the excitement over South Carolina's secession, scenes of mobilization, and patriotic rallies. He sketched Jefferson Davis' inauguration in Montgomery, Alabama, and, back in Charleston, made sketches of all the Confederate installations around the harbor. On April 12–13, he had a thrilling pictorial "exclusive" as Confederate batteries shelled Fort Sumter. For the rest of the war, assignments—for *Leslie's* and, later, for *Harper's*—took him from Florida and New Orleans (where he covered Farragut's capture of the city, making some of his most thrilling pictures from a perch on the mainmast of the U.S.S. *Mississippi*) to the Virginia Peninsula during McClellan's 1862 campaign; to the siege at Petersburg, Virginia; and to Sherman's campaign through the Carolinas and Georgia. In 1865, he followed Lincoln's cortege from Washington to Springfield, Illinois.

The War in Art: Civil War Paintings

The story of Civil War "easel art"—paintings arising from an artist's own experience or imagination, or commissioned by a patron—is entwined with creation of the popular prints published by Currier & Ives, Kurz & Allen, and others. In the second half of the nineteenth century, there were very few art museums of the type we have today. Artists—if not already commissioned by popular lithographers—often created paintings with the hope that copies would be disseminated via the popular distributors—an arrangement from which they could derive some income. Memorial paintings were commissioned from some easel artists after the war—often, for state buildings, army regiments, or private collections. And a few artists, particularly those who were veterans of the war, executed Civil War paintings out of a sense of mission. Artists who earned their living primarily as special correspondents, cartoonists, or illustrators—such as Thomas Nast, William Ludwell Sheppard, James Taylor, and Allen Christian Redwood—also produced distinctive Civil War paintings during and immediately after the conflict. Winslow Homer's Civil War paintings were relatively few in number, but they are distinctive and occupy a niche all their own.

The Civil War was also a natural subject for painters who catered to the prefilm era's love affair with cycloramas and panoramic paintings. Introduced in Europe near the end of the eighteenth century, the huge circular cyloramas were the wide-angle-screen experiences of their day. Often completed by teams of painters working under a supervising artist—such as France's Paul Philippoteaux, creator of the two surviving Gettysburg cycloramas—these visual spectacles were generally displayed in specially erected buildings that surrounded viewers with details of the landscape of a battle. Together with the multipaneled panoramic battle paintings, and so-called "moving panoramas" (multiscene works pulled across a stage from huge spindle to huge spindle— very literally a "moving picture" show), these epic works, though not always epically artistic, inspired excitement from viewers and praise from critics. Only two are on permanent view today: the Gettysburg cylorama (at the battle site) and a depiction of *The Battle of Atlanta*, in Atlanta's Grant Park. (The latter work, by William Wehner's American Panorama Studio in Milwaukee, includes the type of three-dimensional foreground that nineteenth-century viewers would have seen.) Others survive only in murky photographs (Theophile Poilpot's *Battle of Shiloh* panorama) or in details (the single surviving panel of William Knight's panoramic depiction of "the Great Locomotive Chase," *Andrews' Raiders*). A panorama called *Army of the Cumberland* by William DeLaney Trimble Travis, a former special artist for the *New York Illustrated News* and *Harper's Weekly*, comprising thirty-two panels spanning 538 feet, is owned by the Smithsonian Institution.

The U.S. Civil War was a topic of much interest in Europe, and a number of European artists created Civil War paintings. A distinguished example is *Alabama and Kearsarge* (oil, 1864) by Edouard Manet, who may have been among the French spectators lining the shore as the legendary Confederate raider, captained by Raphael Semmes, was sunk by the U.S.S. *Kearsarge* off Cherbourg. Today, many artists—among them, Don Trioni and Mort Kunstler—continue to create Civil War paintings commemorating the lives of Civil War figures, land battles, the contributions of African American soldiers to the war, naval engagements, and women of the war. The work of Civil War-era artists can be seen in galleries and public buildings across the land.

Some Notable Civil War-Era Artists

CONRAD WISE CHAPMAN (1842–1910). The artistic son of an artist father—who was also a fervently patriotic Virginian—Chapman was living with his parents in Rome when the war broke out. He returned to the Confederate States and enlisted, serving first with the Third Kentucky Volunteers, then, after being wounded at Shiloh, with the Forty-Sixth Regular Virginia Volunteers. On an 1864 visit to his ill mother in Rome, he painted a series of richly detailed pictures based on the sketches he had made while on duty. They included a series of views of Charleston that are among the finest work produced by a Confederate artist during the war.

JOHN ADAMS ELDER (1833–1895). A Virginian, Elder studied art in New York but returned to the South after the outbreak of war and became one of the most effective portrayers of Southern heroism. His paintings include *General Stuart and His Staff* (oil, 1863), an oil portrait of Robert E. Lee, and the intense painting of *The Battle of the Crater* (oil, 1865). He also painted portraits of a number of Confederate leaders, including Stonewall Jackson.

GILBERT GAUL (1855–1919). A Northerner drawn to the "romance" of the Southern cause, Gaul began to paint military scenes in 1876. His award-winning *Holding the Line at All Hazzards* (oil, 1882) was notable for its depiction of battle from the perspective of common Confederate soldiers—ill clad and stoutly maintaining the defense of their line, despite intense fire and many casualties. *Union Troops at Cold Harbor (The Skirmish Line)* (oil, 1883), a powerful vignette of one of the war's most horrific battles, achieves startling immediacy from its depiction of soldiers firing directly at the viewer. *Charging the Battery* (oil, circa 1882)—a prize-winning depiction of a night battle—and *Taps* (oil, circa 1907–1909), a sentimental depiction of a dead Confederate soldier whose horse is standing guard beside him, are among Gaul's other Civil War works.

JAMES HOPE (1818–1892). Primarily a landscape artist, whose Civil War paintings sometimes suffer from that fact, Hope joined the Second Vermont Volunteers at the outbreak of the war. In 1862, at Antietam, he witnessed the carnage of "Bloody Lane"—the sunken road that became filled with the bodies of Confederate soldiers who had been caught in a Union crossfire. *After the Battle, The Bloody Lane—Battle of Antietam, Maryland, 1862* (oil, 1889), one of his most heartfelt Civil War paintings, was executed in the hope that it would help teach "coming generations of possible soldiers . . . how terrible a thing war is."

EASTMAN JOHNSON (1824–1906). One of the most important American painters of the nineteenth century, Johnson created a variety of paintings depicting American life in the latter 1800s—among them were images, primarily of the home front, during the Civil War. Paintings such as *Knitting for the Soldiers* (oil, 1861) and *The Field Hospital, or The Letter Home* (oil, 1867) reflected the war's impact on white Northern families whose men had gone to war. *The Pension Claim Agent* (oil, 1867) reveals an aspect of the war that became a part of everyday life for hundreds of thousands of soldiers, widows, and other dependents long after 1865: pension agents, both honest and dishonest, helped them to arbitrate claims. Among Johnson's most stirring Civil War images are those of African Americans, particularly the dynamic *A Ride for Liberty—The Fugitive Slaves* (oil, ca. 1862–1863).

JULIAN SCOTT (1846–1901). An artist who preferred to depict the common soldier, Scott lied about his age and enlisted in the Third Vermont Infantry at age fifteen. As a fifer/drummer, he should have been behind the front lines during combat; but at Lee's Mills, Virginia, in April 1862, he repeatedly, and under fire, rescued wounded men from a stream where, without his help, they would have drowned. For that action, he was awarded the Medal of Honor. Scott's wartime sketches became the bases for vivid postwar paintings, including *The Death of General Kearny* (oil, date unknown), *Surrender of a Confederate Soldier* (oil, 1873), *A Break, Playing Cards* (oil, 1891), and *Rear Guard at White Oak Swamp* (oil, 1869).

LILLY MARTIN SPENCER (1822–1902). One of the late nineteenth century's foremost American women artists, England-born Spencer was, by the 1850s, a celebrated artist and illustrator who specialized in portraits and domestic scenes. In 1866, she completed the oil painting *The War Spirit at*

Home—Celebrating the Victory at Vicksburg. Among other women artists of the period who executed Civil War paintings were Anna Mays (*Women's Sanitary Corps,* oil, ca. 1861–1865) and Currier & Ives artist Flora Bond (Fanny) Palmer (*Landing at Fort Fisher,* pencil with watercolor, 1865).

THURE DE THULSTRUP (1848–1930). A Swedish-born soldier of fortune, Thulstrup served in the French Foreign Legion before launching his American art career. Affiliated with *Harper's Weekly* for some twenty years, Thulstrup painted many Civil War battles and portraits of important Civil War figures—often under commission from popular lithographers, especially Louis Prang & Company. His war paintings include *Sheridan's Ride,* immediately issued as a chromolithograph, depicting one of the most famous episodes of the war (see page 843 and illustration on page 807).

WILLIAM B. T. TREGO (1859–1909). Creator of some 200 military paintings, many of which depicted the Civil War, Trego was the son of two painters who encouraged his ambition to pursue a career as an artist, though his legs had been crippled and his hands deformed by illness when he was a child. His evocative Civil War canvases include *Battery of Light Artillery En Route* (oil, 1882); *The Rescue of the Colors* (oil, 1899); *Horse Artillery Going into Battle, Petersburg, Virginia, 1865* (oil, date unknown); and *Mortar Battery Firing* (oil, ca. 1875). Trego committed suicide shortly after his parents died.

WILLIAM D. WASHINGTON (1834–1870). Though Richmond artist William Washington was primarily a landscape artist, he created several Civil War paintings, among them perhaps the most memorable Southern image to emerge from the war, *The Burial of Latane* (oil, 1864) (see "Civil War Poetry," on page 843). The quintessential "Lost Cause" image, it became wildly popular when reproduced as an affordable lithograph after the war.

Civil War Sculpture

Across the United States, many thousands of Civil War memorials, statues of Civil War heroes, and sculptured tributes to the hundreds of thousands of common soldiers who fought on both sides during the war stand as silent reminders of the most dangerously rending period in American history. Often, these sculptures dot former Civil War battlefields; 1,400 monuments, statues, and markers, for example, cover what is now Gettysburg National Military Park. At Stone Mountain, Georgia, the world's largest mass of exposed

Augustus St. Gaudens' sculpture memorial to Robert Gould Shaw and the Fifty-Fourth Massachusetts Regiment of African American troops is among the best known of the tens of thousands of sculptured Civil War memorials dotting the American landscape.

granite now bears the world's largest relief carving—comprising the likenesses of Jefferson Davis, Robert E. Lee, and Stonewall Jackson. Boston, Massachusetts, where members of the famed Fifty-Fourth Massachusetts Regiment of African American soldiers were mustered in, is home to Augustus St. Gaudens' powerful masterpiece devoted to that regiment and its commander, Colonel Robert Gould Shaw (see "National Historic Sites" in Chapter 13, "Studying the War: Research and Preservation"). Familiar, sometimes ignored by busy passersby, sculptural works commemorating the Civil War are, nevertheless, potent artistic reminders of a crucial period in the nation's history. The sculptural memorials in the war's two capital cities, Richmond, Virginia, and Washington, D.C., provide a sense of the meaning and impact of Civil War sculpture across the land.

Richmond, Virginia

First settled in 1637, Richmond was made the capital of Virginia in 1779, was raided by the British in 1781, and became the capital of the Confederate States of America in 1861. Filled with government offices, war-related industries, refugees, wounded soldiers, spies, and Union prisoners confined in various facilities, the city was also the target of Union campaigns throughout the war. Taken at last in early April 1865, Richmond was nearly in ruins from terrible fires that swept through the city when it fell. Today, the city is filled with reminders of the Civil War, including many sculpted memorials.

- **The A. P. Hill Monument and Grave:** Designed by William Ludwell Sheppard (1833–1912), and located at the intersection of Laburnum and Hermitage roads, the monument marks the grave of Ambrose Powell Hill, West Point graduate, Mexican War veteran, and Confederate general.

- **Hollywood Cemetery:** Dedicated in 1848, this hillside cemetery holds the graves of some 18,000 Confederate soldiers. They are memorialized by a stark, ninety-foot pyramid of granite blocks that stands in the midst of individual markers. J. E. B. Stuart, George Pickett, and Jefferson Davis are buried in this cemetery.

- **Richmond Howitzers Monument:** Located at Park Avenue and Harrison Street, this memorial to one of the South's elite units was dedicated in 1892.

- **Monument Avenue:** Established during the long campaign to erect a suitable statue to Robert E. Lee, Monument Avenue is now a graceful boulevard marked by sculptural tributes to five leaders of the Confederacy:

Robert E. Lee: Planning for a suitable statue began very shortly after Lee's death in 1870. There was debate over the best site, the selection of a sculptor, the statue's height, and the design of the monument itself. (About one design, ex-Confederate general Jubal A. Early fulminated: "If the statue of General Lee be erected after that model [I will] get together all the surviving members of the Second Corps and blow it up with dynamite.") Dedicated on May 31, 1890, French sculptor Jean Antoine Mercie's statue of General Lee, mounted on his beloved horse Traveler, faces toward the South, the region for which Lee had fought.

Jefferson Davis: The culmination of seventeen years of fund-raising, planning, and debate, this monument, a collaborative design by Richmond sculptors Edward V. Valentine and William C. Nolan, comprises three distinct parts: a statue of Davis, posed as if giving a speech; a statue of Vindicatrix, a robed female figure representing the spirit of the South (both by Valentine); and a semicircle colonnade composed of thirteen Doric columns representing the eleven Confederate states and two states that sent troops to the Confederate cause. The most symbolic monument on the avenue, commemorating not only a man, but the "Lost Cause" he represented, it was dedicated on June 3, 1907, at a ceremony attended by more than 80,000 people.

Stonewall Jackson: Executed by Richmond artist William F. Sievers, who was selected for the project by the Stonewall Jackson Monument Corporation on the strength of his work on the Virginia Memorial at Gettysburg, the bronze sculpture of Jackson mounted on his horse and facing North is on a pedestal that is relatively free of embellishments, bearing only the general's name and the legend, "Born 1824, Killed at Chancellorsville 1863."

J. E. B. Stuart: Though efforts to create a sculptural memorial to Stuart began in 1875, a design was not selected until May 1903. New York sculptor Frederick Moynihan created a statue that shows a dynamic Stuart, reins tight in one hand, drawn sword in the other, twisting around in his saddle.

Matthew Fontaine Maury: The only sculpture on Monument Avenue honoring a naval officer, this memorial, sculpted by William F. Sievers and dedicated November 11, 1929, shows Maury seated contemplatively in an armchair, holding a book representing his accomplishments in science and technology; behind him, on a pedestal, is a large world globe.

- **Soldiers and Sailors Monument:** Designed by artist and Civil War veteran William Ludwell Sheppard, the Soldiers and Sailors monument was dedicated in 1894. A tribute to all Confederate soldiers and sailors, it stands on Libby Hill, which affords one of the best views of the James River, including the site of the Confederate naval yard.

- **The Virginia State Capitol:** Dating from 1788, the Virginia State Capitol is the second oldest working capitol in the United States. Several sculptural works devoted to Confederate figures are located in its largest room, the old House of Delegates, which is now a museum. These include busts, in marble or bronze, of Confederate generals Stonewall Jackson, J. E. B. Stuart, Joseph E. Johnston, and Fitzhugh Lee, and of the Confederacy's president and vice president, Jefferson Davis and Alexander H. Stephens. The most striking sculpture in the room is the full-length bronze likeness of Robert E. Lee, placed where Lee stood, on April 23, 1861, when he accepted command of the Confederate forces in Virginia.

On the grounds of the capitol are statues representing three Civil War figures: Stonewall Jackson; his friend, doctor, and subordinate officer, surgeon Hunter McGuire; and Confederate governor William Smith.

Washington, D.C.

A city established specifically to be the capital of the new United States of America, on a site selected by George Washington, the Federal City was severely damaged during the War of 1812, when the British burned most of its public buildings, including the Capitol and the White House. During the Civil War, however, Washington was surrounded by a formidable latticework of fortifications and was never invaded or significantly damaged by Confederate fire. Forty-one sculptures in the nation's capital pertain directly to the Civil War. They include statues of Union officers: James A. Garfield, George Gordon Meade, Winfield Scott Hancock, David Farragut, John A. Logan, George H. Thomas, James B. McPherson, William T. Sherman, John A. Rawlins, George B. McClellan, Philip H. Sheridan, and Philip Kearny. Among other notable Civil War sculptures are:

- *The Arsenal Monument:* Sculpted by Lot Flannery and dedicated in 1865, this monument honors more than twenty-one young women who were killed in a horrific explosion at the Washington Arsenal on June 17, 1864, while making cartridges for Union weapons. The sculpture—a twenty-foot-high marble shaft topped by the statue of a weeping woman—is in the Congressional Cemetery, where the victims were buried at ceremonies attended by President Lincoln.

- *Emancipation:* Learning of Lincoln's assassination, Charlotte Scott, a former slave from Virginia, gave the first money she had earned in freedom—five dollars—toward establishing a suitable memorial. Soon freed men and women throughout the country were contributing to the cause: The Seventieth U.S. Colored Infantry alone sent in $3,000 donated by 683 enlisted men. In 1876, sculptor Thomas Ball's bronze representation of Lincoln with a freed slave (modeled on former slave Archer Alexander) was dedicated at elaborate ceremonies attended by more than 50,000 people, including President Ulysses S. Grant and Frederick Douglass, who delivered an eloquent dedicatory speech.

- *The Ulysses S. Grant Memorial:* Located at one end of the Mall, with the Capitol behind it, and facing toward the distant Lincoln Memorial, the Grant Memorial is the culmination of twenty years of intense endeavor by sculptor Henry Merwin Shrady. It comprises a broad plaza with an equestrian statue of General Grant at the center (the pedestal on which it is placed is decorated with inset sculptural panels of infantrymen, and flanked by four imposing lions). To each side are two of the most vivid sculptural representations of men in combat ever created by an American sculptor. The memorial was dedicated on April 27, 1922, two weeks after Shrady died.

- *The Lincoln Memorial:* A collaborative effort among artist Jules Guerin, architect Henry Bacon, and sculptors Ernest C. Bairstow (stonework) and Daniel Chester French (statue), the Lincoln Memorial faces the Grant Memorial at the other end of the Mall and is one of the most familiar and significant landmarks in Washington. Though the first efforts to establish a fitting national memorial to Lincoln were made in 1867, the Lincoln Memorial was not dedicated until May 30, 1922— and every aspect of its development was subject to intense debate.

- *Nuns of the Battlefield:* This bronze relief by Jerome Connor is located in the midst of one of Washington's busiest sectors (at Rhode Island Avenue and M Street, NW). The monument commemorates between 800 and 1,000 women religious, from twelve different orders, who nursed the wounded of both sides during the Civil War.

- *The African American Civil War Memorial: Spirit of Freedom:* In 1865, a reporter for the *Philadelphia Inquirer*, noting that none of the 166 regiments of United States Colored Troops were included among the 200,000 Union soldiers participating in the victory Grand Review in Washington, wrote: "Their time will come." One hundred and thirty-two years later, in 1997, the 186,000 African American soldiers and 18,000 black sailors who served the Union were officially recognized by this memorial. It comprises a central sculpture, a wall of honor (upon which the names of the soldiers and sailors, and 7,000 white officers who served with them, are inscribed), and a nearby museum. The bronze statue, *Spirit of Freedom* by sculptor Ed Hamilton, is the first major art piece by a black sculptor to be placed on Federal land anywhere in the District of Columbia.

- *Major John Rodgers Meigs:* A memorial to a young officer—the last surviving son of U.S. Quartermaster General Montgomery Meigs, killed by Confederate irregulars in 1864—this small bronze likeness of Brevet Major Meigs, lying exactly as he was found on the field, is one of several Civil War-related monuments in Arlington National Cemetery, and among the most poignant. (See photo on page 482.)

The cemetery, which is across the Potomac River from Washington, was established on land taken from Mary Ann Custis Lee, wife of Robert E. Lee, not long after the start of the war. The bodies of many Union and Confederate soldiers rest there today—as do those of more than 3,000 "contrabands"—African Americans who had escaped slavery. In 1914, a Confederate Monument created by Moses Jacob Ezekiel— one of the few sculptors of Civil War commemorative statuary who actually served in the war—was erected in the cemetery.

Literature

It has been estimated that more than 70,000 books have been written about the U.S. Civil War—and more join that body of work each year. Nonfiction works devoted to the war include histories, biographies, memoirs, diaries, Civil War-era oratory, and letters (see bibliographies in each chapter, and the annotated book list in Chapter 13, "Studying the War: Research and Preservation").

Fiction—most notably Harriet Beecher Stowe's *Uncle Tom's Cabin*— helped propel the dividing nation toward armed conflict. And fiction moved and sustained people on both sides during the war. War novels published during the conflict tended toward adventure stories and romance; for example, the short and ripping anonymously authored *The Lady Lieutenant: A wonderful, startling and thrilling narrative of the adventures of Miss Madeline Moore, who, in order to be near her lover, joined the Army, was elected lieutenant, and fought in western Virginia under the renowned General McClellan* (1862); and James Dabney McCabe's *The Aide-de-Camp*, a potboiler published in Richmond in 1863, in which the hero spies on an inebriated Abraham Lincoln from a secret passageway outside the president's office while seeking to steal Union plans. Since 1865, Civil War-related fiction—running the gamut from improbable yarns to thought-provoking literature—has continued to engage the attention and the emotions of readers of all ages and many nations.

Some Notable Nineteenth-Century Civil War Novels

Among the Pines, or, South in Secession-Time (1862)

By James R. Gilmore, a writer, Yankee businessman, and, in 1864, an unofficial peace emissary from Lincoln to Jefferson Davis, this novel, the first in a series of not particularly distinguished Civil War books by Gilmore, strove to give a true picture of life in the South.

The Carlyles: A Story of the Fall of the Confederacy (1905)

By Constance Cary Harrison, a Southerner who lived in Richmond throughout the Civil War and married Burton Harrison, Jefferson Davis' former chief of staff, after the South's surrender. She wrote lively wartime newspaper columns and became a popular novelist in the 1890s. Unlike *The Carlyles*, most of her novels did not deal directly with the war.

Corporal Si Klegg and His "Pard" (1887)

By Wilbur F. Hinman, this work is the first in a popular series of humor-laced Civil War books. The others in the series—including *Si Klegg, His Development from a Raw Recruit to a Veteran* (1897) and *Further Haps and Mishaps to Si Klegg and Shorty* (1898)—were written by soldier and editor John McElroy (1846–1929), a Civil War veteran who was captured in January 1864 and spent more than a year in Confederate prisons. His book *Andersonville* (1879) is a forceful recounting of his experiences as a prisoner.

The Days of Shoddy (1864)

By Henry Morford, one of two novels by this Civil War veteran to be based on his experiences during the war (the other being *Shoulder Straps*, 1863), this tale deals with military incompetence and war profiteering.

The Graysons (1887)

By Edward Eggleston, *The Graysons* is set before the Civil War and is one of the first novels to include Abraham Lincoln as a character.

Henry in the War, or The Model Volunteer (1899)

This is a tale written by and modeled on the career of Civil War General Oliver O. Howard, awarded the Medal of Honor for his leadership at the battle of Seven Pines. Postwar, he was head of the Freedmen's Bureau and a founder of Howard University in Washington, D.C.

How Private Geo. W. Peck Put Down the Rebellion (1887)

By George W. Peck, this is a book of humorous, fictionalized memoirs by a veteran of three years' service with the Fourth Wisconsin Cavalry. Though Peck was a newspaperman and also served as mayor of Milwaukee and governor of Wisconsin, he is best remembered as the author of humorous stories starring "Peck's Bad Boy."

Macaria; or Altars of Sacrifice (1864)

By Georgia-born Augusta Jane Evans. A well-known writer before the war, Evans was a devoted Confederate partisan who dedicated this novel to "the Brave Soldiers of the Southern Army." A fictional justification of the Southern cause—and a fervent denunciation of the North—this now-dated novel was banned in Federal camps.

Miss Ravenel's Conversion (1867)

By Civil War veteran John W. De Forest, this story of a New Orleans doctor who exiles himself to Boston because he favors the North contains some powerful Civil War battle scenes.

The Red Badge of Courage: An Episode of the Civil War (1895)

By Stephen Crane, this classic and influential story focuses on the mind of a young Union soldier, Henry Fleming, as he and his untried regiment undergo their first trials under fire.

Surry of Eagle's Nest (1866)

By Confederate veteran John Esten Cooke, *Surry of Eagle's Nest* is a novel in which the hero's life closely parallels that of Stonewall Jackson.

Tales of Soldiers and Civilians (1891)

By Ambrose Bierce, this is a collection of twenty-six short stories—including "An Occurrence at Owl Creek"—by a combat-hardened Union veteran who wielded a sharp-edged pen during a long and distinguished postwar literary career.

The Test of Loyalty (1864)

By James M. Hiatt, *The Test of Loyalty* is a tale that reflects an early obsession with Northern writers: the persecuted Unionists of the South. The story describes the plight of followers of "Parson" William G. Brownlow of Tennessee, the opinionated Unionist editor of the Knoxville *Whig*—which he renamed, after imprisonment and return from banishment to Federal territory, the Knoxville *Whig and Rebel Ventilator.*

Tiger-Lilies (1867)

By Sidney Lanier, *Tiger-Lilies* is a tale of a Confederate soldier, who, like the author himself, is captured by the Union army and whose parents are killed by a Confederate deserter while he's away.

Tobias Wilson, A Tale of the Great Rebellion (1865)

A Civil War epic by former United States senator Jeremiah Clemens, who despite his signature upon Alabama's ordinance of session (which he had fought against passing) and his subsequent designation as a major-general of the "Republic of Alabama," remained a Unionist and moved to Philadelphia in 1862.

Uncle Tom's Cabin (1852)

By Harriet Beecher Stowe, it is one of the most influential novels in American history (see Chapter 2, "Antebellum America," p. 108).

Some Notable Twentieth-Century Civil War Novels

Andersonville (1955)

By MacKinlay Kantor, *Andersonville* is a Pulitzer Prize-winning and grimly realistic novel depicting the horrors of the infamous military prison during the war. Kantor was also the author of *Long Remember* (1934, rev. 1956), about the battle of Gettysburg.

The Cavalier (1901)

By George Washington Cable, *The Cavalier* is a novel based on the Confederate army Civil War experience (1862–1865) of the author, who became an important figure in the "local color" movement in American fiction.

Cold Mountain (1997)

By Charles Frazier, this story of a wounded Confederate soldier and his epic journey homeward to North Carolina and the woman he left behind won the National Book Award.

Confederates (1979)

By Thomas Keneally, *Confederates* is an engaging portrayal of the rank-and-file fighting man under arms for the Confederacy.

The Crater (1980)

By Richard Slotkin, *The Crater* is a fictionalized account of operations surrounding the July 30, 1864, battle of the Crater at Petersburg, Virginia.

Faded Coat of Blue (1999)

This well-researched "novel of historical suspense" by Owen Parry is the first of a series of Civil War mysteries featuring recent Welsh immigrant and Union officer Abel Jones.

Forever Free (1927)

By Honoré Willsie Morrow, *Forever Free* is the first novel in a trilogy devoted to Abraham Lincoln (also including *With Malice Toward None*, 1928, and *The Last Full Measure*, 1930—all three collected as *Great Captain*, 1935).

The Friendly Persuasion (1945)

Jessamyn West's first book, this novel comprises a series of sketches of the life of a Quaker family in southern Indiana during the Civil War. Warmly received by reviewers, it was made into an equally popular movie.

Gone with the Wind (1936)

Arguably the best-known Civil War novel ever published, Margaret Mitchell's book about volatile Southerner Scarlett O'Hara differs in many respects from the film version released in 1939.

The History of Rome Hanks and Kindred Matters (1944)

Critically acclaimed upon its release, Joseph S. Pennell's novel does not shrink from the brutality of war as its protagonist investigates the lives of his hard-fighting Civil War ancestors.

House Divided (1947)

Ben Ames Williams' massive romance follows the fortunes of a Virginia family during the Civil War.

Jubilee (1966)

Based on the life of the author's great-grandmother and much additional historical research, Margaret Walker's novel tells the story of a slave family from the mid- to late nineteenth century.

Killer Angels: A Novel (1974)

By Michael Shaara, this is the acclaimed Pulitzer Prize-winning story of the battle of Gettysburg, told mainly from the viewpoints of Union Colonel Joshua Chamberlain and Confederate Lieutenant General James Longstreet. The book has been filmed for television.

Lone Star Preacher (1941)

Written by John W. Thomason Jr., the grandson of Thomas J. Goree, who served on James Longstreet's staff, this novel offers a compelling portrait of the Army of Northern Virginia through the eyes of Praxitiles Swan, a Methodist minister fighting with the Fifth Texas Infantry in Hood's Texas Brigade.

Long Remember (1934, rev. 1956)

By MacKinlay Kantor, this is a powerfully written account of how war descended upon the sleepy little town of Gettysburg, Pennsylvania, destroying life, property—and illusions—as seen through the eyes of a Gettysburg man lately returned from the Minnesota frontier.

The Long Roll (1911)

Mary Johnston's popular and meticulously researched story is set in the South and includes Stonewall Jackson as a main character, with the battle of Chancellorsville as its climax. The author, daughter of a Civil War officer, wrote a sequel, *Cease Firing* (1912), encompassing the period from Vicksburg to the end of the war.

Manassas, A Novel of the Civil War (1904, Civil War Classics edition 2000)

Filled with historical characters—including Underground Railroad "conductor" Levi Coffin and Frederick Douglass—Upton Sinclair's tale of a young man born and raised in Mississippi, whose convictions are shaken when his family moves North, culminates in the battle of Manassas.

The Oldest Living Confederate Widow Tells All (1989)

By Allan Gurganus, this is the tale of a young woman married to a Confederate veteran at age fifteen. The protagonist reflects on the Civil War and postbellum years on the eve of her 100th birthday.

The Perfect Tribute (1906)

Mary Raymond Shipman Andrews gives a fictional account of the circumstances of Lincoln's Gettysburg Address. This novel was popular for many years and many hundreds of thousands of copies were sold.

Rebel (1993)

By Bernard Cornwell, this is the first in a series of Civil War novels by the creator of the Napoleonic Wars adventures featuring rifleman Richard Sharpe. This book introduces readers to Nathaniel Starbuck, son of a Boston abolitionist minister, who elects to fight for the South.

Shiloh (1952)

By Shelby Foote, the author best known for his monumental three-volume, nonfiction history of the war, this is the story of the pivotal 1862 battle in western Tennessee.

Unto This Hour (1984)

A sprawling, well-researched fictional account of the campaign of Second Manassas (Bull Run) by Tom Wicker.

The Unvanquished (1938)

By William Faulkner, this is the story of "unreconstructed" Mississippians who continue to fight the war in the aftermath of Confederate defeat, as narrated by a young boy.

The Wave (1929)

This complex work by Evelyn Scott, comprising short-story-length vignettes, weaves letters, stream-of-consciousness fragments, newspaper accounts, army reports, and plantation and war songs into an episodic description of the Civil War's impact on many lives.

Civil War Poetry

The Civil War loosed a flood of poetry—including many poems of less than memorable quality—that appealed to and reflected the patriotism of soldiers and civilians of both sides. Many of these poems were published in newspapers and journals—often anonymously or under *noms de plume* such as "A Confederate Woman" or "E Pluribus Unum." Others were signed by their authors, and some proved memorable and inspiring long after the war.

The *Southern Literary Messenger* published, in its July–August 1862 edition, a poem by John Reuben Thompson (1823–1873) on the death and burial of William D. Latane, an officer under Jeb Stuart, killed on the Virginia Peninsula. "The Burial of Latane" became instantly popular. It inspired, among other things, a painting that became an icon of the Lost Cause after the war (see "The War in Art: Civil War Paintings," on page 826):

A little child strewed roses on his bier,
Pale roses, not more stainless than his soul.
Nor yet more fragrant than his life sincere
That blossomed with good actions, brief, but whole:
The aged matron and the faithful slave
Approached with reverent feet the hero's lowly grave. . . .

"Battle Hymn of the Republic," by Julia Ward Howe (1819–1910), is still a vital and stirring part of many American patriotic gatherings. Born in New York City, Howe had already published two collections of verse before the Civil War. In December 1861, she and her husband visited Washington, a city where morale had been considerably dampened by the Union defeat at Bull Run the previous July. One evening, after the group she was with sang *John Brown's Body*, someone suggested that she should write new words for the air, "good words for a stirring tune." "Battle Hymn of the Republic" was published in the February 1862 *Atlantic Monthly*. When set to the music of *John Brown's Body*, Howe's poem became the single most memorable song to emerge from the Civil War.

Sheridan's Ride, by Thomas Buchanan Read (1822–1872), one of the most popular poets of the day, commemorates General Philip Sheridan's gallop, astride his warhorse Rienzi, to rally faltering Union forces facing Jubal Early's Confederates at the battle of Cedar Creek, Virginia, October 19, 1864. Written quickly, and recited almost before the ink was dry by actor James Edward Murdoch to wartime Northern audiences that reportedly sprang to their feet applauding furiously, the poem quickly captured the North and remained popular until well after the war. Students were required to learn it by heart; it was one of the most oft-recited poems at school programs, though it is rarely heard or read in any venue today:

> With foam and with dust, the black charger was gray;
> By the flash of his eye, and the red nostril's play,
> He seemed to the whole great army to say,
> "I have brought you Sheridan all the way
> From Winchester, down to save the day!" . . .

Read, who was also an artist, made seventeen paintings depicting the ride. Some of these paintings (as well as those by other artists inspired by Read's poem or by Sheridan's ride itself) were made into popular color-lithographic prints, particularly in the 1880s.

Oliver Wendell Holmes published *A Voice of the Loyal North* as a broadside four months before the outbreak of the war. The author—who would later report on his search for his wounded son, Union officer and future Supreme Court Justice Oliver Wendell Holmes Jr., in "My Hunt after 'The Captain'" in the November 1862 *Atlantic Monthly*—wrote this poem for his Harvard class meeting of January 3, 1861. It was later carried by at least one newspaper and was also included in some of the inexpensive song books, or "songsters" that were published during the war.

Broadsides (single sheets meant for poster-like display) were a favorite method of circulating wartime poetry. A broadside of "The Stolen Stars" by Union General Lew Wallace (1827–1905)—who, after the war, would achieve lasting literary fame as the author of *Ben Hur*—was sold to raise funds for Union soldiers at the Great Western Sanitary Fair, December 1863. Other poetic broadsides celebrated the achievements of various Civil War armies or regiments. "The New Version of The Colored Volunteer" by Corporal Sam'l Nickless, for example, was "Composed and dedicated to the Twenty-Fourth Regiment, U.S.C.T" [United States Colored Troops]:

> It was said sometime ago, that the negro would not fight,
> But when they gave us arms, and all a soldier's right;
> And sent us to the field, how we made the Rebels stare,
> For they could not stand the charge of the Colored Volunteer.

Some Notable Poets and Poems of the Civil War after 1865

In the decades following the Civil War, poems and song lyrics were collected in commemorative volumes of widely varying quality as Civil War veterans' organizations were formed and became increasingly active. Throughout the twentieth century, and to the present day, poets have continued to contemplate the war and its universal themes of division, destruction, and reconciliation. Some notable poets who wrote on Civil War themes and examples of notable Civil War-related poems written after the war are listed below.

STEPHEN VINCENT BENÉT (1898–1943). Author of *John Brown's Body* (1928), an epic, Pulitzer Prize-winning poem. In this extensively researched 376-page verse treatment of Civil War matters—from John Brown's raid on Harpers Ferry and subsequent execution, to the war itself—Benét describes both the battleground and the home front. It includes verse "portraits" of many of the leading wartime figures, and describes the common soldiers of both sides:

. . .

So with these men and then. They were much like the men you know,
Under the beards and the strangeness of clothes with a different fit.
They wrote mush-notes to their girls and wondered how it would go,
Half-scared, half-fierce at the thought, but none yet ready to quit.

Other poems in which John Brown figures prominently include E. C. Stedman's "How Old Brown Took Harpers Ferry" and John Greenleaf Whittier's "Brown of Osawatomie."

PAUL HAMILTON HAYNE (1830–1886). A lifelong literary man who contributed to the *Southern Literary Messenger* and served on the staff of the *Southern Literary Gazette*, Hayne was a native of Charleston, South Carolina, and expressed his fervent patriotism through such poems as "The Battle of Charleston Harbor," and "Stonewall," in memory of General Jackson. His war poems were included in a book of his complete works, *Poems of Paul Hamilton Hayne* (Boston: 1882).

ROBERT LOWELL (1917–1977). A poet, playwright, autobiographer, and essayist, this native of Massachusetts penned *For the Union Dead* (1960), a

WALT WHITMAN

Poet—and Civil War nurse—Walt Whitman wrote many letters to his mother describing hospital and Washington scenes. His elegy for Abraham Lincoln, When Lilacs Last in the Dooryard Bloom'd, *is one of the great works in world literature.*

In 1862, poet and erstwhile "Free-Soil" news-paperman Walt Whitman traveled to Virginia to search for his brother, George Washington Whitman, a Union soldier wounded at the battle of Fredericksburg. Whitman located his brother and was thankful to discover that the younger man's wounds were not serious. The search, however, marked a turning point in Walt Whitman's life. Exposure to the casualties of Fredericksburg, and the misery attendant to understaffed military hospitals, inspired the forty-two-year-old Whitman to

volunteer as a nursing aid, in which role he served for over three years.

. . .

> Bearing the bandages, water and sponge,
> Straight and swift to my wounded I go,
> Where they lie on the ground after the
>   battle brought in,
> Where their priceless blood reddens the
>   grass the ground,
> Or to the rows of the hospital tent, or
>   under the roof'd hospital,
> To the long rows of cots up and down each
>   side I return,
> To each and all one after another I draw
>   near, not one do I miss, . . .
>   "The Wound-Dresser"

Whitman's abiding faith in the ideals of American democracy found expression in his poetry, even as the carnage of war tested that faith. Rather than interpret massive casualties and years of war as evidence of that democracy's failure, Whitman's experience with wounded soldiers—legions of men willing to sacrifice all for love of country—confirmed the poet's faith in the essential character of a brave and free people, as reflected in two volumes of Civil War poetry: *Drum-Taps* (1865) and *Sequel to Drum-Taps* (1866).

The first of Whitman's two elegies to Abraham Lincoln, "O Captain! My Captain!" takes its title from a line in Herman Melville's *Moby Dick*. First published in the New York *Saturday Press* in 1865, it proved to be the most popular of Whitman's poems during his lifetime:

O Captain! My Captain! Our fearful trip is
  done;
The ship has weather'd every rack, the
prize we sound is
    Won;
The port is near, the bells I hear, the people
  all exulting,
While follow eyes the steady keel, the vessel
  grim and daring:

But O heart! Heart! Heart!
O the bleeding drops of red,
  Where on the deck my Captain lies,
    Fallen cold and dead. . . .

The poet's second tribute to the fallen president was published in *Sequel to Drum-Taps*. "When Lilacs Last in the Dooryard Bloom'd," one of Whitman's finest poems and one of the great elegies of world literature, is filled with symbolism: the lilac, representing love and rebirth; the western star, Lincoln; the hermit thrush, the soul or the poet; coffins, representing death. The long work considers not only the death of Lincoln ("O powerful western fallen star") but also:

. . . battle-corpses, myriads of them,
And the white skeletons of young men, I
  saw them,
I saw the debris and debris of all the slain
  soldiers of the war,
But I saw they were not as was thought,
They themselves were fully at rest, they
  suffer'd not,
The living remain'd and suffer'd, . . .

It ends powerfully; the poet reconciled to the enduring mystery of death, resolving:

. . . their memory ever to keep,
  for the dead I loved so well,
For the sweetest, wisest soul of all my days
and lands—and this for his
    dear sake,
Lilac and star and bird twined with the
  chant of my soul,
There in the fragrant pines and the cedars
  dusk and dim.

sixty-eight-line poem that contemplates the legacy of Robert Gould Shaw and his fabled African American Civil War regiment, the Fifty-Fourth Massachusetts (who are portrayed on Augustus St. Gaudens' bronze memorial in Boston).

EDWIN MARKHAM (1852–1940). Author of *Lincoln, the Man of the People* (1901). Markham's *Man with the Hoe*, a spectacularly popular social protest poem, was published in 1899. *Lincoln* was also a great success; it spoke of "the Captain with the mighty heart" who:

Held on through blame and faltered not at praise.
And when he fell in whirlwind, he went down

As when a lordly cedar, green with boughs,
Goes down with a great shout upon the hills,
And leaves a lonesome place against the sky.

Lincoln and his assassination were the subjects of a great many postwar poems, among them R. H. Stoddard's "Abraham Lincoln," James Russell Lowell's "Ode Recited at the Harvard Commemoration," and Walt Whitman's "When Lilacs Last in the Dooryard Bloom'd" and "O Captain, My Captain!"

HERMAN MELVILLE (1819–1891). Born in New York City, novelist, short-story writer, essayist, lecturer, and book reviewer Melville had enjoyed days of literary popularity in the late 1840s and early 1850s, largely because of adventure novels like *Typee* (1846) that fictionalized his life as a seaman. But the increasing complexity and philosophical bent of his works had caused critics and public to turn away (one reviewer of *Moby Dick* said Melville should be served with "a writ *de lunatico*"). During the Civil War, in the midst of financial and family difficulties, he wrote many poems about the battles and central figures of the conflict. Seventy-two of them were collected in *Battle-Pieces and Aspects of the War*, including "Shiloh":

. . .
Foemen at morn, but friends at eve—
    Fame or country least their care:
(What like a bullet can undeceive?)
    But now they lie low,
While over them the swallows skim,
    And all is hushed at Shiloh.

Barely noticed at the time, the book is now considered among the best of the hundreds of volumes of poetry that emerged from the war.

ABRAM JOSEPH RYAN (1838–1886). Known as the "poet-priest of the Confederacy" and "the poet of the Lost Cause," Ryan was born in Maryland, the son of Irish immigrant parents. He was educated in Missouri and New York State, ordained in 1856, and served as a chaplain in the Confederate army from his enlistment September 1, 1862, to the end of the war. The suffering and loss he witnessed during the war—including the death of a younger brother in battle—was reflected in the poignancy of his war-related poems, many of which were published in *Father Ryan's Poems* (1879).

HENRY TIMROD (1828–1867). Poet, essayist, and war correspondent, Timrod was born in Charleston, South Carolina, and briefly reported on the war for the *Charleston Mercury*. Tuberculosis prevented him from spending more than a year in the Confederate army (1862). By 1864, he was editor of the Columbia *South Carolinian*. When Union forces burned the city, he was ruined. Paul Hamilton Haynes, a lifelong friend, edited the 1873 edition of *The Poems of Henry Timrod*. Among his war poems is "Ode," which was sung at the decorating of graves of the Confederate dead at Charleston's Magnolia Cemetery in 1867:

. . .
Stoop, angels, hither from the skies!
  There is no holier spot of ground
Than where defeated valor lies,
  By mourning beauty crowned!

WALT WHITMAN (1819–1892). One of the greatest American poets, Whitman's *Leaves of Grass* horrified many of his contemporaries but profoundly influenced American poetry. Whitman also created the most powerful and lasting poems to flow from the Civil War (see "Walt Whitman" box on pages 846 and 847).

Civil War Music

The Civil War left a particularly rich musical legacy for subsequent generations, starting with *The Battle Hymn of the Republic* (1862)—Julia Ward Howe's poem, sung to the popular tune *John Brown's Body* (1861)—and *Dixie* (published a year before the war broke out), and including such popular songs as *When Johnny Comes Marching Home*, *God Save the South*, *The Battle Cry of Freedom*, and *Tenting on the Old Camp Ground*.

During the war, as this legacy was being created, the most popular songs, in both the North and the South, were prewar ballads such as *The Last Rose of Summer* (1813), *Home Sweet Home* (1823), *Annie Laurie* (1835), and *Listen to*

Our National Confederate Anthem, *published in Richmond in 1863, has one of the rare illustrated music covers issued under the Confederacy.*

the Mockingbird (1853). But songs were being published and distributed at a furious pace—particularly in single-sheet broadsides and small, inexpensive books called "songsters" (which included both song lyrics and poems). Over 9,000 new songs were printed in the North during the war. Even in the South, where the materials necessary for publishing were much scarcer, 750 new songs appeared. (Some songs had two sets of lyrics—Northern and Southern—making music an artistic battlefield of sorts.) Notable Civil War songs include:

- *Battle Cry of Freedom*, by George Frederick Root (1820–1895), a musician, teacher, and partner in the Chicago-based music publishing firm of Root and Cady. Root, the most prolific of the wartime composer/songwriters, produced such other Civil War standards as *Tramp, Tramp, Tramp, The Vacant Chair*, and *Just Before the Battle, Mother*. The rousing *Battle Cry of Freedom* is his most memorable and lasting:

Yes, we'll rally round the flag, boys, we'll rally once again,
  Shouting the battle cry of Freedom,
We will rally from the hillside, we'll gather from the plain,
  Shouting the battle cry of Freedom.

- *The Bonnie Blue Flag*, lyrics by Harry Macarthy (c. 1880). This much-beloved Confederate song was written by British-born vaudevillian Harry Macarthy ("the Arkansas Comedian"). Set to the lively tune "The Irish Jaunting Car," it became one of the early song "hits" of the Civil War:

We are a band of brothers
    And native to the soil,
Fighting for the property
    We gained by honest toil;
And when our rights were threatened,
    The cry rose near and far—
"Hurrah for the Bonnie Blue Flag
    That bears a single star!"

- *Good Ol' Rebel Soldier*, lyrics by Major Innes Randolph, C.S.A. Stemming from the war, but published in the Reconstruction Era, this song, set to the old Irish tune "Joe Bowers," reflects the embitterment of many ex-Confederate soldiers. Randolph, despite the poor grammar and dialect he chose to use in his lyrics, was a well-educated man who achieved some postwar fame as a poet:

Oh, I'm a good old Rebel soldier, now that's just what I am;
For this "Fair Land of Freedom" I do not give a damn!
I'm glad I fit against it, I only wish we'd won,
And I don't want no pardon for anything I done. . . .

- *Lorena*, lyrics by Rev. H. D. L. Webster. Actually a prewar song, published in 1857, *Lorena* was almost certainly the single most popular sentimental ballad of the Confederate army. Lorena became a favorite wartime name—for babies, towns, and at least one steamship:

We loved each other then, Lorena.
    More than we ever dared to tell;
And what we might have been, Lorena,
    Had but our loving prospered well– . . .

- *Marching Through Georgia*, by Henry C. Work. A printer, inventor, and fervent abolitionist, Work composed a number of Civil War tunes, mostly for the Chicago music publishing house of Root and Cady, but none became as popular as *Marching Through Georgia*:

"Sherman's dashing Yankee boys will never reach the coast!"
So the saucy Rebels said, and 'twas a handsome boast'
Had they not forgot, alas! To reckon with the host,
    While we were marching through Georgia.

- *Maryland, My Maryland*, by James Ryder Randall (1839–1908). The lyrics to this song began as a poem written by Baltimore native Randall (then teaching English literature in Louisiana) after Union troops marching toward Washington clashed with Baltimore citizens in 1861. Its popularity blossomed, however, when it was set to the tune "Lauriger Horatius," better known as "O Tannenbaum" ("O Christmas Tree"). It was adopted as the state song of Maryland in 1939:

  The despot's heel is on thy shore,
  Maryland, my Maryland!
  His torch is at the temple door,
  Maryland, my Maryland!
  Avenge the patriotic gore
  That flecked the streets of Baltimore,
  And be the battle queen of yore,
  Maryland, my Maryland! . . .

- *Somebody's Darling*, music by John Hill Hewitt (1801–1890), words by Marie Ravenal de la Coste, whose fiancé, a captain in the Confederate army, was killed in the war, and who worked in Savannah's hospitals. A favorite, if melancholy, song of the Confederacy:

  . . .
  Tenderly bury the fair, unknown dead,
  Pausing to drop on his grave a tear;
  Carve on the wooden slab over his head,
  "Somebody's darling is slumbering here."

- *Taps*, not a song, but a poignant and dignified bugle call marking the end of a soldier's day. The version of *Taps* known today was adapted from an earlier call ("Tattoo") in 1862 by Union Major General Daniel Butterfield, with the assistance of bugler O. W. Norton of the Eighty-Third Pennsylvania Regiment.

- *When Johnny Comes Marching Home*, by "Louis Lambert," a pseudonym for Patrick S. Gilmore, who was bandmaster of Union General Benjamin Butler's army in New Orleans at the time he wrote the song.

There is speculation over the origin of the tune to which his lyrics were set. Some believe it was written by Gilmore; others contend it was either a Negro spiritual or a traditional Irish air Gilmore adapted in creating what rapidly became a hallmark American song:

When Johnny comes marching home again,
    Hurrah, hurrah,
We'll give him a hearty welcome then,
    Hurrah, hurrah!
The men will cheer, the boys will shout,
The ladies, they will all turn out,
And we'll all feel gay when Johnny comes marching home.

The Drama of the War, Revisited: On Stage, Screen, and Television

Well before the Charleston batteries fired on Fort Sumter, plays that centered on the growing divisions between North and South were being produced—including, in the North, the anonymously written *Our Union Saved* (January 1861) and several productions based on Harriet Beecher Stowe's novel *Uncle Tom's Cabin*. After war broke out, patriotic tableaux and plays—many of them of much less than memorable quality—were quickly written and staged for home-front audiences, sometimes with a speed that absolutely ensured poor quality. Less than a month after the first battle of Bull Run, the play *Bull Run*, by Charles Gayler (1820–1892), was on the boards at New York's Bowery Theater. Gayler's *Hatteras Inlet, or Our Naval Victories* was also quickly written and produced. It appeared some three months after the event it depicted. In the South, theater was also lively—as were the theater critics. On December 27, 1862, a new play, *The Guerrillas*, by James D. McCabe Jr., received a less than laudatory review in the *Southern Illustrated News*: "As a historical drama, the piece possesses no merit, as well known facts in connection with the Revolution [the Civil War] are totally overlooked or ignored. We consider this a very grave mistake. The Southern people are *making history* now, and our Southern play writers should be faithful chroniclers of the times in which we live. The rising generation demand this."

In the years immediately following the war, dramas such as *The Fall of Vicksburg: A Drama of the Great Rebellion* by John A. Parra (1866), *The*

Volunteer, "a military drama, in six acts, and accompanying tableaux: arranged from incidents of the late war, and respectfully dedicated to the Grand Army of the Republic" (1871), and *The Color Guard*; "a military drama in five acts, with accompanying tableaux" by Colonel A. R. Calhoun, were being presented—or at least published.

During the marked resurgence of interest in the Civil War that characterized the 1880s, a number of plays appeared. Among them were: *The Great Rebellion: Reminiscences of the Struggle that Cost a Million Lives* (1881), an ambitious five-act work by Cyrenus Osborne Ward; and *Loyal Mountaineers: or The Guerrilla's Doom* (1889), by J. Culver. After the turn of the century, Nobel Prize-winning novelist Sinclair Lewis made a foray into Civil War drama with *Jayhawker* (1935). Paul Green's *Wilderness Road* (1956), Saul Levitt's *The Andersonville Trial* (1959), and Robert D. Hock's *Borak* (1961) were also Civil War dramas. And in 1975, *Shenandoah*, based on an original screenplay, became a Broadway musical.

On Screen

From the earliest days of American cinema—not far removed from the 1860s—the Civil War has been a subject for filmmakers, though the earliest films, particularly, reflect the prejudices and attitudes not only of their creators but of the eras in which they were made. One of the great hallmarks of American film, for example, D. W. Griffith's epic *Birth of a Nation* (Epoch Producing Corp., 1915), is a masterwork marred by racial prejudice and celebration of the Ku Klux Klan. (It was based on Thomas Dixon's 1905 novel, *The Clansman*.)

Rapid and vast technical improvements in filmmaking—from the addition of sound and color to today's computer graphics—have improved the cinematic "canvas" upon which Civil War stories come to

T. J. Downs Mammoth Uncle Tom's Cabin, *of 1916, was one of many, sometimes very elaborate, stage versions of Harriet Beecher Stowe's influential novel that were produced during, and well after, the Civil War.*

life. Also, social progress has made possible the portrayal of aspects of the war that were long ignored, as reflected in the film *Glory* (Tri-Star, 1989), which brings to life, with great power and attention to historical detail, the story of one of the most celebrated of the 166 regiments of United States Colored Troops, the Fifty-Fourth Massachusetts. Other notable Civil War films are listed here, chronologically.

- *The General*, United Artists, 1927: In this silent comedy masterpiece, Buster Keaton plays a Confederate train engineer whose engine, the General, is stolen by Union raiders.
- *Abraham Lincoln*, United Artists, 1930: Episodic depiction of scenes from the sixteenth president's life.
- *Operator 13*, MGM, 1934: Drama about an actress and Union spy behind the lines.
- *So Red the Rose*, Paramount, 1935: A depiction of the war's emotional impact on a Southern family.
- *The Prisoner of Shark Island*, Twentieth-Century Fox, 1936: The travails of Dr. Samuel Mudd after he set the broken leg of Lincoln's assassin, John Wilkes Booth.
- *Gone with the Wind*, MGM, 1939: The epic film version of Margaret Mitchell's novel.
- *Santa Fe Trail*, Warner Bros., 1940: Raymond Massey portrays John Brown in this historically inaccurate but gripping film about the abolitionist's days in Kansas and his raid on Harpers Ferry.
- *The Red Badge of Courage*, MGM, 1951: A classic film version of Stephen Crane's classic novel.
- *Prince of Players*, Twentieth-Century Fox, 1955: Richard Burton plays Edwin Booth, the famous actor and brother of Lincoln's assassin, John Wilkes Booth.
- *Seven Angry Men*, Allied Artists, 1955: Raymond Massey again plays abolitionist John Brown in this tale of his abortive 1859 raid on the arsenal at Harpers Ferry.
- *Friendly Persuasion*, Allied Artists, 1956: Based on the Jessamyn West novel; the story of a Quaker family in southern Indiana facing questions of courage, faith, and the evil of violence when a son decides to join the army.

- *The Great Locomotive Chase*, Buena Vista, 1956: The story of Union raiders on a mission to commandeer a Confederate locomotive at Big Shanty, Georgia, and destroy Southern supplies.
- *Raintree County*, MGM, 1957: Based on the epic Ross Lockridge novel, the film centers on the life of an Indiana schoolteacher and his memories—including his Civil War experiences.
- *The Horse Soldiers*, United Artists, 1959: Based on Harold Sinclair's 1956 novel, the movie is a fictionalized account of Grierson's Raid, a Federal cavalry expedition through Mississippi during Grant's Vicksburg campaign.
- *Shenandoah*, Universal, 1965: Sentimental tale of a Virginia family whose patriarch, played by James Stewart, cannot keep them from being engulfed in the war.
- *Journey to Shiloh*, Universal, 1968: Enthusiastic volunteers from Texas learn the horror of war.

Made for Television: Notable Movies, Series, and Documentaries

- *The Americans*, NBC, 1961, seventeen episodes: Brother truly fights against brother in this series about a family whose loyalties are split by the war.
- *The Andersonville Trial:* A powerful 1970 adaptation of Saul Levitt's 1959 play (in which George C. Scott starred), this depicts one of America's most notorious trials—the prosecution of Henry Wirz, commandant of the Confederate camp for Union prisoners of war near Andersonville, Georgia.
- *The Blue and the Gray*, Columbia, 1982: A three-part miniseries based on a concept by Civil War historian Bruce Catton. The events are seen largely from the perspective of a war correspondent writing from the Deep South.
- *The Civil War*, PBS/Ken Burns, 1990: An eleven-hour exploration of the Civil War, featuring quotes from letters, period photographs and music, and creative camera techniques. One of the most influential and thorough film documentary treatments of the war to date.
- *The Divided Union*, Arts and Entertainment/Channel Four, 1987: Five-part British documentary that examines the developments of the

war from Fort Sumter to Lee's surrender at Appomattox and includes commentary on the war's impact on American life.

- *Gettysburg*, Turner Pictures/New Line Cinema, 1993: A sweeping portrayal of one of the principal battles of the Civil War, based on Michael Shaara's Pulitzer Prize-winning novel, *Killer Angels*.

- *The Gray Ghost*, CBS, 1957, thirty-nine episodes: Television's version of the exploits of Confederate raider John S. Mosby.

- *The North and the South* (Books 1 and 2), David L. Wolper Production/Warner Bros., 1985–1986: Based on the novels of John Jakes, these two miniseries follow the lives of a South Carolina family and a Pennsylvania family as their friendships are affected by the war.

- *Red Badge of Courage*, Twentieth-Century Fox, 1974: Remake of the 1951 film, based on Stephen Crane's novel.

- *Roots*, David L. Wolper Productions/ABC, 1977: Award-winning television adaptation of Alex Haley's novelized exploration of his family; includes episodes concentrating on the Civil War years.

SELECTED RESOURCES

Aaron, Daniel. *The Unwritten War: American Writers and the Civil War*. New York: Knopf, 1973.

Fahs, Alice. *The Imagined Civil War: Popular Literature of the North and South, 1861–1865*. Chapel Hill: University of North Carolina Press, 2000.

Garner, Stanton. *The Civil War World of Herman Melville*. Lawrence: University Press of Kansas, 1993.

Gelbert, Doug. *Civil War Sites, Memorials, Museums and Library Collections: A State-by-State Guidebook to Places Open to the Public*. Jefferson, NC: McFarland & Company, 1997.

Heaps, Willard Allison. *The Singing Sixties: The Spirit of Civil War Days Drawn from the Music of the Times*. Norman: University of Oklahoma Press, 1960.

Holzer, Harold, and Mark E. Neely Jr. *Mine Eyes Have Seen the Glory: The Civil War in Art*. New York: Orion Books, 1993.

Jacob, Kathryn Allamong. *Testament to Union: Civil War Monuments in Washington, D.C.*, with photographs by Edwin Harlan Remsberg. Baltimore: Johns Hopkins University Press, 1998.

Kinnard, Roy. *The Blue and the Gray on the Silver Screen: More than Eighty Years of Civil War Movies*. Secaucus: Carol Publishing Group, 1996.

Lively, Robert A. *Fiction Fights the Civil War: An Unfinished Chapter in the Literary History of the American People*. Chapel Hill: University of North Carolina Press, 1957.

Neely, Mark E. Jr., Harold Holzer, and Gabor S. Boritt. *The Confederate Image: Prints of the Lost Cause*. Chapel Hill: University of North Carolina Press, 1987.

Neely, Mark E. Jr. *The Union Image: Popular Prints of the Civil War North*. Chapel Hill: University of North Carolina Press, 2000.

Sears, Stephen W., ed. *The Civil War: A Treasury of Art and Literature*. New York: Hugh Lauter Levin Associates, 1992.

Smith, Kristen, M., ed. *The Lines Are Drawn: Political Cartoons of the Civil War*. Athens, GA: Hill Street Press, 1999.

Stern, Philip Van Doren. *They Were There: The Civil War in Action as Seen by Its Combat Artists*. New York: Crown, 1959.

Thompson, William F. *The Image of War: The Pictorial Reporting of the American Civil War*. New York: T. Yoseloff, 1960. Reprint, Baton Rouge: Louisiana State University Press, 1994 (original edition, 1959).

Whitman, Walt. *Walt Whitman's Civil War*. Walter Lowenfels, ed. New York: Knopf, 1960.

STUDYING THE WAR: RESEARCH AND PRESERVATION

66 I have been urged by many old friends and comrades to publish [my diary]," wrote Civil War veteran David Lane, "that our children and grandchildren may realize something of the hardships and trials their ancestors cheerfully endured for love of country." Several generations of Americans have read Lane's *A Soldier's Diary* (1905)—and the words of countless other participants, military and civilian, in the Civil War. These first-person accounts—preserved in libraries, museums, and private collections across the nation; repeated on videos and television programs; and accessible on audiotapes and CD-ROMS—tell the story of the war with an immediacy that is unmatched by any other resource. Each is a part in the mosaic that is the Civil War—its causes and consequences, and the lessons it teaches about the formation of the United States of today. But the mosaic is huge—comprising military, social, and personal histories. And the effects and meaning of wartime events, of the war as a whole, and of the roles its leaders played, continue to be debated and reexamined. Few other periods in American history have received such unremitting scrutiny in a quest for greater understanding. At the same time, the sites, symbols, and artifacts of the war are honored as compelling memorials to the years of struggle and sacrifice that resulted, as Abraham Lincoln said at Gettysburg, in "a new birth of freedom."

This chapter presents an overview of important resources for the study of the Civil War: basic reference books; major Civil War archival collections; representative organizations and activities devoted to the study and commemoration of the war; and major Civil War memorials—from former battlegrounds to monuments and museums—that may be consulted for a greater understanding of this crucial period in American history.

Important Published Resources on the Civil War

An estimated 70,000 books have been published on various aspects of the Civil War to date, and more are in the making. These have been joined, lately, by CD-ROM and Internet publications. The following list of nonfiction titles, therefore, cannot be comprehensive, but it includes essential reference works and many useful volumes on various aspects of the war.

General Reference

Boatner, Mark M., III. *The Civil War Dictionary.* David McKay Co., 1959. Vintage Civil War Library Edition, Random House, 1991. 974 pp. Comprising 4,186 short entries on subjects from A.A.D.C. ("One abbreviation for Additional Aide de Camp.") to Zulick, Samuel Morton ("Union officer . . .").

Boritt, Gabor S., ed. *Why the Confederacy Lost.* Oxford Univ. Press, 1992. 209 pp. Essays on the factors that led to the Civil War's outcome.

Current, Richard N., Paul D. Escott, Lawrence N. Powell, James I. Robertson, Jr., and Emory M. Thomas, eds. *Encyclopedia of the Confederacy.* Simon and Schuster, 1993. Four vol., 1,916 pp. This comprehensive reference work comprises short articles, by many experts in the field of Confederate history, on all elements of the Confederacy—military, political, social, and economic aspects, as well as biographies, bibliographic references, and special subjects.

Davis, William C., ed. *The Image of War, 1861–1865.* Six vol. Doubleday and Co., 1981–1984. 2,809 pp. Comprising 4,017 Civil War photographs—many of which do not appear in the Miller *Photographic History* (see below)—accompanied by many pointed and informative essays by Civil War experts. An outstanding photographic history of the war.

Dornbusch, Charles E., ed. *Military Bibliography of the Civil War.* New York Public Library, 1961–1972, 1987. Four vol. A listing of books and articles, divided into sections, by state, for unit histories and soldiers' memoirs. Also includes sections on campaign narratives, autobiographical and biographical accounts, and titles on general and specific subjects.

Dyer, Frederick H. *A Compendium of the War of the Rebellion: From Official Records of the Union and Confederate Armies, Reports of the Adjutant Generals of the Several States, the Army Registers, and Other Reliable Documents and Sources.* Dyer Publishing Co., 1908. Reprinted 1978. 1,796 pp. A three-part study compiled by a Union Civil War veteran. Part 1 provides statistics of Union army organizations; Part 2 lists 10,455 battle actions from campaigns to skirmishes and reconnaissances, with maps; Part 3 comprises capsule histories for 2,494 Union regiments. Almost all information in the compendium relates to Union forces.

Editors of Time-Life Books. *Echoes of Glory: Illustrated Atlas of the Civil War.* Time-Life Books, 1991. 320 pp. An overview of the war that includes paintings, photographs, drawings, and maps.

Eicher, David J. *The Civil War in Books*. Univ. of Illinois Press, 1997. 408 pp. An analytical bibliography of 1,100 important titles pertaining to the Civil War, arranged in categories. Each book included is evaluated in a short essay.

Faust, Patricia L., ed. *The Historical Times Illustrated Encyclopedia of the Civil War*. Harper and Row, 1986. 850 pp. A one-volume encyclopedia with 2,380 alphabetical entries, from short biographies of major Civil War figures to descriptions of major battles and campaigns, as well as short but generally informative entries on such topics as medicine and prisoners of war.

Heidler, David S., and Jeanne T. Heidler, eds. *Encyclopedia of the American Civil War: A Political, Social, and Military History*. ABC-CLIO, 2000. Five vol., 2,733 pp. Some 1,600 entries by various Civil War scholars on topics spanning the Civil War experience. Illustrated.

Long, E. B., and Barbara Long. *The Civil War Day by Day*: Doubleday and Co., 1971. 1,135 pp. An exceptionally useful resource, detailing events, on both battlefield and home front, that happened on each day, from November 1860 through 1865. Includes informative appendixes on casualties, the makeup of the armies, and other subjects.

McPherson, James M., ed. *The Atlas of the Civil War*. Macmillan Co., 1994. 223 pp. Deriving its information from the *Atlas to Accompany the Official Records* and other sources contemporary to the Civil War, this book presents detailed information on the disposition of units at crucial times during 98 battles or campaigns. The maps are accompanied by informative narrative.

————, and William J. Cooper, Jr., eds. *Writing the Civil War: The Quest to Understand*. Univ. of South Carolina Press, 1998. 354 pp. Fourteen historians, including Gary W. Gallagher, Joseph Glatthaar, Reid Mitchell, and Drew Gilpin Faust, examine the vast field of Civil War scholarship.

Miller, Francis Trevelyan, ed. *The Photographic History of the Civil War*. Ten vol. Review of Reviews Co., 1911, 3,497 pp. Reprinted by Blue and Grey Press, 1987. 3,497 pp. Originally published on the fiftieth anniversary of the beginning of the war, this definitive photographic history comprises 3,389 images and text by soldiers and historians on both sides. Each volume is devoted to a theme: Vol. 1, *The Opening Battles*; Vol. 2, *Two Years of Grim War*; Vol. 3, *The Decisive Battles*; Vol. 4, *The Cavalry*; Vol. 5, *Forts and Artillery*; Vol. 6, *The Navies*; Vol. 7, *Soldier Life and Secret Service*; Vol. 8, *Prisons and Hospitals*; Vol. 9, *The Armies and Leaders*; Vol. 10, *Poetry and Eloquence*.

Nevins, Allan, James I. Robertson, Jr., and Bell I. Wiley, eds. *Civil War Books: A Critical Bibliography*. Two vol. Louisiana State Univ. Press, 1967–1969. 604 pp.

Thomas, William G., and Alice E. Carter. *The Civil War on the Web: A Guide to the Very Best Sites*. SR Books, 2001. 199 pp., plus 1 computer optical disc. A handy guide through the maze of Civil War Web sites now on the Internet, providing detailed reviews of 95 sites noted as "the very best." Basic information is also listed for 300 other recommended sites, and the accompanying CD-ROM provides hotlinks to all the sites listed in the book. Foreword by Gary W. Gallagher.

United States War Department. *The War of the Rebellion: A Compilation of the Official Records of the Union and Confederate Armies.* Government Printing Office, 1880–1901. Several reprints (by National Historical Society, Broadfoot, and Morningside). Seventy vol. bound in 128 books. 138,579 pp. Perhaps the most important published resource on the Civil War, the Official Records [OR] comprise orders, dispatches, messages, and correspondence relating to the military operations of the war, as well as an atlas. In 1994, Broadfoot Publishing Company began a multivolume supplementary project, *Supplement to the Official Records of the Union and Confederate Armies,* comprising material that was not included in the original Official Records. Cornell University has put the complete text of the Official Records online at http://cdl.library.cornell.edu/moa/browse .monographs/waro.html.

Woodworth, Steven E., ed. *The American Civil War: A Handbook of Literature and Research.* Greenwood Press, 1995. Several thousand titles are covered in forty-seven narrative chapters written by Civil War experts. The chapters are clustered into eleven major subject headings; they include: general secondary sources, general primary sources, leaders, conduct of the war, the home front, and Reconstruction and beyond.

General Histories

Catton, Bruce. *The Centennial History of the Civil War.* Three vol. totaling 1,683 pp.: *The Coming Fury* (1961); *Terrible Swift Sword* (1963), and *Never Call Retreat* (1965). Doubleday and Co, 1961–1965. A sweeping contemplation of the war, from a largely Union perspective, concentrating on the Eastern Theater.

Donald, David Herbert, Jean H. Baker, and Michael F. Holt. *The Civil War and Reconstruction.* Norton, 2001. 781 pp.; reprint. An updated version of the original 1937 edition written by James G. Randall and revised in 1961 and 1969 by David Herbert Donald, this classic textbook on the war examines its causes, political considerations, the war itself, and Reconstruction through the Grant era.

Foote, Shelby. *The Civil War: A Narrative.* Three vol. totaling 2,934 pp. A panoramic view of the war that differs markedly from Catton's *Centennial History,* viewing it from a largely Confederate perspective and emphasizing the Western campaigns.

McPherson, James M. *Battle Cry of Freedom: The Civil War Era.* Oxford Univ. Press, 1988. 904 pp. This Pulitzer Prize-winning one-volume history of the war is characterized by a gripping narrative style and meticulous documentation.

———. *Ordeal by Fire: The Civil War and Reconstruction.* Alfred A. Knopf, 1982; latest edition 2000. 694 pp. A fact-packed, meticulously documented consideration of the growing national rift that resulted in the war, the war itself, and the difficult Reconstruction period.

Nevins, Allan. *Ordeal of the Union.* Eight vol., totaling 4,152 pp.: *Ordeal of the Union* [2 vol. totaling 1,183 pp.] (1947); *The Emergence of Lincoln* [2 vol. totaling 996 pp.] (1950); *The War for the Union* [4 vol. totaling 1,973 pp.] (1959–1971). Charles Scribner's Sons,

1947–1971. A massive history of the war and its causes, this epic, readable, and heavily documented work considers the entire scope of American life in the prewar and war years and demonstrates how American life was wholly transformed by the Civil War experience.

Weigley, Russell F. *A Great Civil War: A Military and Political History, 1861–1865*. Indiana Univ. Press, 2000. 612 pp. An intriguing account, not only of the war's battles, but also of the activities of Union and Confederate soldiers and government officials.

The Union

See also "Selected Resources" in all other chapters.

Bernstein, Iver. *The New York City Draft Riots: Their Significance for American Society and Politics in the Age of the Civil War*. Oxford Univ. Press, 1990. 363 pp. An extensive study of what has been called the North's greatest occasion of wartime unrest.

Curry, Leonard P. *Blueprint for Modern America: Nonmilitary Legislation of the First Civil War Congress*. Vanderbilt Univ. Press, 1968. 302 pp. In this analysis of wartime politics, Curry examines how the politics of the Civil War influenced the current political structure of the United States.

Geary, James W. *We Need Men: The Union Draft in the Civil War*. Northern Illinois Univ. Press, 1991. 264 pp. A fundamental contribution to the study of the Federal draft and its impact on the war effort, this work examines a variety of subjects, including the volunteer system, the bounty system, class discrimination, and alienation.

Hubbell, John T., and James W. Geary, eds. *Biographical Dictionary of the Union, Northern Leaders of the Civil War*. Greenwood, 1995. 683 pp. Includes 872 biographical sketches of men and women who have influenced the development of American policy, thought, and history—emphasizing their Civil War activities.

Klement, Frank L. *The Copperheads of the Middle West*. Univ. of Chicago Press, 1960. 341 pp. An excellent summary of Copperhead (Peace Democrat) activities, though the book's estimate of the movement's importance and influence may be exaggerated.

_____. *Dark Lanterns: Secret Political Societies, Conspiracies, and Treason Trials in the Civil War*. Louisiana State Univ. Press, 1984. 263 pp. An examination of major and minor antiwar organizations—and the pro-Lincoln Union Leagues—in the North. A valuable book filled with intriguing stories.

Paludan, Phillip S. *A People's Contest: The Union and Civil War, 1861–1865*. Harper & Row, 1988, 2d ed. Univ. of Kansas Press, 1996. 486 pp. Divided into three sections—"Learning War," "Making War," and "Finding War's Meanings"—this is a compelling examination of ways in which the Civil War transformed the North's people, as well as a chronological history of the war.

Rawley, James A. *The Politics of Union*. Dryden Press, 1974, 202 pp.; reprinted, Univ. of Nebraska Press, 1980, 202 pp. A valuable but brief and unannotated overview of Northern Civil War politics.

Silbey, Joel H. *A Respectable Minority: The Democratic Party in the Civil War Era, 1860–1868.* Norton, 1977. 267 pp. A comprehensive examination of the Democratic Party that focuses on notable Democrats, including Horatio Seymour and George B. McClellan.

The Confederacy

See also "Selected Resources" in all other chapters.

Ash, Stephen V. *When the Yankees Came: Conflict and Chaos in the Occupied South, 1861–1865.* Univ. of North Carolina Press, 1995. 309 pp. This comprehensive study of the occupied South explores guerrilla warfare and other forms of civilian resistance; the evolution of Union occupation policy from leniency to repression; the impact of occupation on families, churches, and local government; and conflicts between Southern aristocrats and poor whites.

Beringer, Richard E., Herman Hattaway, Archer Jones, and William N. Still Jr. *Why the South Lost the Civil War.* Univ. of Georgia Press, 1986. 582 pp. (Abridged ed., titled *The Elements of Confederate Defeat: Nationalism, War Aims, and Religion,* Univ. of Georgia Press, 1988). A thought-provoking examination of the Confederate war effort; considers Southern military maneuvers and officers, as well as Southern religion and psychology.

Curden, Robert F. *The Gray and the Black: The Confederate Debate on Emancipation.* Louisiana State Univ. Press, 1972. 305 pp. This documentary collection of newspaper accounts, official documents, correspondence between Confederate political and military leaders, and selections from the Official Records of the war, presents the Confederate emancipation debate in the participants' own words—without engaging in extensive analysis.

Early, Jubal A., J. William Jones, Robert A. Brock, James P. Smith, Hamilton J. Eckenrode, Douglas Southall Freeman, and Frank E. Vandiver, eds. *Southern Historical Society Papers.* Fifty-two vol., Southern Historical Society, 1876–1959, 20,382 pp. (vol. 1–38, 1876–1910; vol. 39–49, 1914–1943; vol. 50–52, 1953–1959). Reprinted, fifty-five vol., with a three-vol. index (1,460 pp.), Broadfoot Publishing Co., 1990–1992, 21,842 pp. A landmark compendium on Confederate history, containing official reports, wartime newspaper accounts, and articles by Civil War participants and specialists covering all aspects of the Confederate experience.

Gallagher, Gary W. *The Confederate War.* Harvard Univ. Press, 1997. 218 pp. An examination of the Confederate experience through the actions and words of the people who lived it, showing how the military and the home front responded to the war, endured great hardships, and assembled armies that fought with tremendous spirit and determination.

Goff, Richard D. *Confederate Supply.* Duke Univ. Press, 1969. 275 pp. Examines the arrangement, direction, strengths, and weaknesses of the Confederate supply department, the politics surrounding it, and the role supply problems played in the defeat of Confederate forces.

Parrish, T. Michael, and Robert M. Willingham. *Confederate Imprints: A Bibliography of Southern Publications from Secession to Surrender.* Jenkins Publishing Company and Gary A. Foster, 1987. 991 pp. A list of 9,500 books, pamphlets, broadsides, maps, sheet music, government and military reports, and circulars.

Rable, George C. *The Confederate Republic: A Revolution Against Politics.* Univ. of North Carolina Press, 1994. 416 pp. An original and well-researched consideration of the political culture of the Confederacy, focusing on Southern views that the Confederate states represented a revolution against sectional partisanship and party politics and an effort to return to the ideals of the American Revolution.

Thomas, Emory M. *The Confederate Nation, 1861–1865.* Harper and Row, 1979. 384 pp. An examination of the birth and evolution, both politically and militarily, of the Confederate States.

Wakelyn, Jon L. *Biographical Dictionary of the Confederacy.* Greenwood Press, 1977. 603 pp. Though marred by errors, this compendium of 651 biographical sketches provides useful information on military commanders, politicians, and various other notable figures in the Confederate States.

Warner, Ezra J., and W. Buck Yearns. *Biographical Register of the Confederate Congress.* Louisiana State Univ. Press, 1975. 352 pp. A collection of 267 biographical sketches of men who served in the Confederate Congress, including information on voting patterns, marriages, occupations, and education.

Wiley, Bell I. *The Road to Appomattox.* Memphis State Univ. Press, 1956. 121 pp. Presenting Confederate defeat not as inevitable, but as the result of Southern mistakes, the author includes discussions of Confederate undervaluation of Northern determination as well as Southern underestimation of antislavery feeling abroad.

The Military

See also "Selected Resources" in Chapter 4, "Battles and the Battlefield," Chapter 5, "The Armies," and Chapter 7, "The War on the Water."

Adams, Michael C. C. *Our Masters the Rebels: A Speculation on Union Military Defeat in the East, 1861–1865.* Harvard Univ. Press, 1978. 256 pp. Reprinted, 1992 as *Fighting for Defeat: Union Military Failure in the East, 1861–1865,* Univ. of Nebraska Press, 256 pp. An engaging, if unconvincing, work that argues—based on selective information— that what lay behind early Union military failures was the belief that Southerners were naturally superior soldiers.

Allardice, Bruce S. *More Generals in Gray.* Louisiana State Univ. Press, 1995, 301 pp. Includes information on 137 officers considered "other Confederate generals" who have been overlooked by previous historians. Though marred by errors, it provides valuable information on more obscure figures.

Catton, Bruce. "The Army of the Potomac Trilogy," *Mr. Lincoln's Army* presents information on the development of Lincoln's army, its early battles, and the president's loss of faith in General McClellan; *Glory Road* and *A Stillness at Appomattox* examine the army's difficulties and accomplishments under Burnside, Hooker, and Meade, and the leadership of Ulysses S. Grant. Doubleday, 1951–1953. 363 pp., 389 pp., 438 pp.

Connelly, Thomas L. *Army of the Heartland: The Army of Tennessee, 1861–1862* and *Autumn of Glory: The Army of Tennessee, 1862–1865*. Louisiana State Univ. Press, 1967, 1971. 305 pp., 558 pp. These two expertly researched volumes comprise an essential history of the South's greatest western army.

Eicher, John H., and David Eicher. *Civil War High Commands*. Stanford Univ. Press, 2001. 1,009 pp. A comprehensive biographical register and analysis of Civil War high commanders—including the presidents and their cabinet members, state governors, Union and Confederate general officers, and admirals and commodores of the two navies. Includes a geographical breakdown of Union and Confederate command structures and much additional information. An important resource for Civil War history.

Evans, Clement A., ed. *Confederate Military History: A Library of Confederate States History Written by Distinguished Men of the South, and Edited by General Clement A Evans*. Twelve vol. Confederate Publishing Co., 1899, 6,600 pp. Reprinted, nineteen vol., with an introduction by Lee A. Wallace, Jr., Broadfoot Publishing Co., 1987–1989, 12,585 pp. Comprising a volume on the Confederacy, a volume on each Confederate state and its involvement in the war effort (including registers of important officers attached to each state), a naval volume, and two index volumes, the reprint edition of *Confederate Military History* includes much more material than the original. 6,000 biographical sketches, 500 illustrations, and 156 maps are included in this valuable— though often biased and error-prone—resource.

Freeman, Douglas Southall. *Lee's Lieutenants: A Study in Command*. Three vols. Scribner's, 1942–1944. 773 pp., 760 pp., 862 pp. Divided into volumes that consider the periods (1) from Fort Sumter through the Peninsula Campaign, (2) Second Bull Run to Chancellorsville, and (3) the Gettysburg Campaign to the war's end, this study includes information on major figures as well as some photographs, maps, and helpful appendices.

Glatthaar, Joseph T. *Partners in Command: The Relationships between Leaders in the Civil War*. Free Press, 1994, 286 pp. An astute consideration of successful command relationships—including Lee and Jackson, and Lincoln and Grant—that compares such partnerships with unsuccessful associations, such as Lincoln and McClellan.

Grimsley, Mark. *The Hard Hand of War: Union Military Policy toward Southern Civilians, 1861–1865*. Cambridge Univ. Press, 1995. 244 pp. A carefully researched and well-written examination of the development of Union policy—from conciliatory, through a period of sterner measures dictated by military necessity, to the "hard war" policy prevalent in the last two years.

Hattaway, Herman, and Archer Jones. *How the North Won: A Military History of the Civil War*. Univ. of Illinois Press, 1983, 762 pp. One of the finest works on Union and Confederate strategy and tactics. In strong narrative style, it considers the essential factors that determined the outcome of the war—including the logistics of communications, transportation, and supply; the availability and allocation of resources; the organization and competence of the military and civilian supporting staffs; the influence of operations in different theaters on each other; and the manner in which commanders used, adapted, or ignored the "maxims of war."

Hunt, Roger D., and Jack R. Brown. *Brevet Brigadier Generals in Blue*. Olde Soldier Books, 1990. 700 pp. Includes information on 1,400 officers; some biographies are accompanied by photos.

Johnson, Robert Underwood, and Clarence Clough Buel, ed. *Battles and Leaders of the Civil War, Being for the Most Part Contributions by Union and Confederate Officers: Based upon "The Century" War Series*. Four vol. Century Co, 1887–1888, 3,091 pp. Reprinted, eight vol., Archive Society, Harrisburg, PA, 1991, 3, 091 pp. Comprising 388 articles by 226 authors—many of them leading participants in the Civil War—with illustrations by some of the war's leading "special artists." This important Civil War resource provides chronological coverage of the war's military events as well as articles on army life and descriptions of wartime life in major Southern cities.

McElfresh, Earl B., and Stephen W. Sears. *Maps and Mapmakers of the Civil War*. Harry N. Abrams, 1999. 272 pp. The crucial importance of having accurate maps in wartime is underlined in this well-illustrated and informative exploration of Civil War maps and their creators.

McMurry, Richard M. *Two Great Rebel Armies: An Essay in Confederate Military History*. Univ. of North Carolina Press, 1989, 204 pp. An insightful work that contrasts the Army of Northern Virginia with the Army of Tennessee.

Warner, Ezra J. *Generals in Blue: Lives of the Union Commanders*. Louisiana State Univ. Press, 1964. 680 pp. Comprising 583 capsule biographies and photographs of Union generals who received substantive commissions, with an appendix consisting of the names of 1,367 general officers by brevet.

_____. *Generals in Gray: Lives of the Confederate Commanders*. Louisiana State Univ. Press, 1959. 420 pp. Capsule biographies, with photographs, of 425 generals, plus nine "Trans-Mississippi" (far West) generals.

Williams, Kenneth P. *Lincoln Finds a General*. Five vols. Macmillan, 1949–1959. 902 pp. (vol. 1–2 paginated consecutively), 616 pp., 585 pp., 395 pp. A masterful view of the North's search for a successful wartime strategy and a military commander who could implement it. Intended as a seven-volume work, the study ends, because of the author's death, before the battles of Chattanooga and Grant's promotion to lieutenant general.

African Americans and the Civil War

See also "Selected Resources" in Chapter 2, "Antebellum America," Chapter 3, "Wartime Politics," Chapter 5, "The Armies," Chapter 10, "The Home Front," and Chapter 11, "Reconstruction and the Aftermath of the War."

Cornish, Dudley Taylor. *The Sable Arm: Negro Troops in the Union Army, 1861–1865*. Longmans, Green and Co., 1956; Modern War Studies edition, Univ. of Kansas Press, 1987, 342 pp. A thorough and scholarly account of African Americans in the Union army.

Foner, Eric. *Freedom's Lawmakers: A Directory of Black Officeholders during Reconstruction*. Louisiana State Univ. Press, 1996. 298 pp. Biographical dictionary, illustrated.

Freedmen and Southern Society Project. (Ira Berlin, Barbara J. Fields, Thavolia Glymph, Steven F. Miller, Joseph P. Reidy, Leslie S. Rowland, and Julie Saville, eds.) *Freedom: A Documentary History of Emancipation, 1861–1867*. A multivolume study of emancipation. Four volumes prepared for general readers and classroom use had been completed as of 2001: *Free at Last: A Documentary History of Slavery, Freedom, and the Civil War*; *Slaves No More: Three Essays on Emancipation and the Civil War*; *Families and Freedom: A Documentary History of African-American Kinship in the Civil War Era*; and *Freedom's Soldiers: The Black Military Experience in the Civil War*.

Glatthaar, Joseph T. *Forged in Battle: The Civil War Alliance of Black Soldiers and White Officers*. Free Press, 1990. 370 pp. A tightly researched examination of the relationships between black troops and their white officers, ranging from recruitment and wartime discipline to considerations of the postwar era.

Jordan, Ervin L., Jr. *Black Confederates and Afro-Yankees in Civil War Virginia*. Univ. Press of Virginia, 1995. 447 pp. The author examines the roles Virginia's half a million blacks played during the war—not only as slaves but also as factory workers, battlefield helpers, and in many other capacities. Examines the effects of the Emancipation Proclamation and of black Union soldiers and spies.

Litwack, Leon F. *Been in the Storm So Long: The Aftermath of Slavery*. Alfred A. Knopf, 1979; Vintage Books edition, 1980. 651 pp. A sweeping, well-researched history of blacks during the Reconstruction period. A follow-up volume, *Trouble in Mind: Black Southerners in the Age of Jim Crow*, was published by Knopf in 1998.

Moebs, Thomas Truxtun. *Black Soldiers-Black Sailors-Black Ink: A Research Guide on African-Americans in U.S. Military History, 1526–1900*. Moebs Publishing Co., 1994, 1,654 pp. An excellently indexed and thorough bibliography including both books and articles.

McPherson, James M. *The Negro's Civil War: How American Negroes Felt and Acted during the War for the Union*. Pantheon Books, 1965; paperback edition, 1991, Ballantine Books. 366 pp. Letters, newspaper editorials, speeches, and other material written and spoken by African Americans are woven together by the author's informing narrative in chapters ranging from "The Election of 1860 and the Coming of War" to reflections on postwar life in "The Negro Faces the Future."

———. *The Struggle for Equality: Abolitionists and the Negro in the Civil War and Reconstruction*. Princeton Univ. Press, 1964; paperback edition, with new preface, 1995. 474 pp. A meticulously researched study of the abolition movement and the African American Civil War experience.

Quarles, Benjamin. *The Negro in the Civil War*. Little, Brown, 1953. 379 pp. An older work that provides an overall view of the African American wartime experience.

Trudeau, Noah Andre. *Like Men of War: Black Troops in the Civil War, 1862–1865.* Little, Brown, 1998. 548 pp. Abundant in detail, this work examines the experiences and hardships of black Civil War soldiers both on and off the battlefield.

Women and the Civil War

See also "Selected Resources" in Chapter 2, "Antebellum America"; Chapter 3, "Wartime Politics"; Chapter 10, "The Home Front"; and Chapter 11, "Reconstruction and the Aftermath of the War."

Attie, Jeanie. *Patriotic Toil: Northern Women and the American Civil War.* Cornell Univ. Press, 1998. 294 pp. Focuses on the connection between the U.S. Sanitary Commission and the Women's Central Relief Association, women's roles in relation to the war, and the meaning of civic obligation in the wartime era.

Clinton, Catherine, and Nina Silber, eds. *Divided Houses: Gender and the Civil War.* Oxford Univ. Press, 1992. 418 pp. Eighteen essays, by historians, that examine the relationships between women and men during the Civil War Era—at home and in the new and grueling roles women assumed to support the war effort.

Culpepper, Marilyn Mayer. *Trials and Triumphs: The Women of the American Civil War.* Michigan State Univ. Press, 1992. 427 pp. This useful and readable work draws from a wide variety of sources to provide information on the experiences of both Union and Confederate women, on the home front and assisting in the war effort.

Edwards, Laura F. *Scarlett Doesn't Live Here Anymore: Southern Women in the Civil War Era.* Univ. of Illinois Press, 2000. 271 pp. Drawing on a multitude of sources, from government records and legal documents to newspapers and diaries, this work places the family as the central institution of Southern society, demonstrates the strong ties between domestic life and civil and political rights, and argues that women's home life greatly shaped their reactions and roles during the war.

Rable, George C. *Civil Wars: Women and the Crisis of Southern Nationalism.* Univ. of Illinois Press, 1989. 391 pp. Based on contemporary diaries and letters, this examination of Confederate women studies how wartime relationships, disruptions, and additional responsibilities reshaped their lives.

Sizer, Lyde Cullen. *The Political Work of Northern Women Writers and the Civil War, 1852–1872.* Univ. of North Carolina Press, 2000. 348 pp. Concentrates on nine Northern women who became involved in national wartime debates via their writing.

Abraham Lincoln

Bruce, Robert V. *Lincoln and the Tools of War.* Bobbs-Merrill Co., 1956. Reprinted, with a new preface, Univ. of Illinois Press, 1989. President Lincoln's interest in technology provides the foundation for this interesting study of various wartime innovations, and those instrumental in their development.

Cox, LaWanda. *Lincoln and Black Freedom: A Study in Presidential Leadership.* Univ. of South Carolina Press, 1981. 254 pp. An important and carefully considered work examining Abraham Lincoln's policies regarding emancipation.

Donald, David Herbert. *Lincoln.* Simon and Schuster, 1995. 660 pp. This richly documented biography focuses primarily on Lincoln as politician—both before and during the war—and as commander in chief.

Lincoln, Abraham. *The Collected Works of Abraham Lincoln* (Roy P. Basler, ed.). Eleven vol., 5,254 pp: vol. 1–8 and index volume, Rutgers Univ. Press, 1953–55; vol. 10, Greenwood Press, 1974; vol. 11, Rutgers Univ. Press, 1990.

McPherson, James M. *Abraham Lincoln and the Second American Revolution.* Oxford Univ. Press, 1990. 173 pp. A thought-provoking consideration of Lincoln as the central figure in the revolutionary transformation of the United States that occurred during the Civil War years.

Peterson, Merrill D. *Lincoln in American Memory.* Oxford Univ. Press, 1994. 482. Explores America's changing views of Abraham Lincoln from his death to the 1990s.

Biographies, Autobiographies, and Personal Narratives

Alexander, Edward Porter. *Fighting for the Confederacy: The Personal Recollections of General Edward Porter Alexander.* Ed. Gary W. Gallagher. Univ. of North Carolina Press, 1989. 664 pp. Originally intended solely for Alexander's family and friends, this memoir provides an intimate and exciting look at the general, his officers, and the Army of Northern Virginia.

Catton, Bruce. *Grant Moves South* and *Grant Takes Command.* Little, Brown, 1960, 1968. 564 pp., 556 pp. Two volumes that examine Grant's military career and provide telling glimpses of Grant as a leader.

Chambers, Lenoir. *Stonewall Jackson.* Two vol. William Morrow, 1959, 1,133 pp. Reprinted, Broadfoot, 1988, 1,133 pp. A careful and largely demythologized study of one of the Confederacy's greatest commanders.

Davis, Jefferson. *The Papers of Jefferson Davis.* (Haskell M. Monroe, James T. McIntosh, Lynda Lasswell Crist, Mary Seaton Dix, and Kenneth H. Williams, eds.). Eight vol., to date. Louisiana State Univ. Press, 1971–. 5,116 pp. A comprehensive compendium of Davis' papers, thus far covering the years from 1808 through 1862.

Davis, Varina Howell. *Jefferson Davis, Ex-President of the Confederate States of America: A Memoir by his Wife.* Two vol. Belford Co., 1890. 1,638 pp. Reprinted, with an introduction by Craig L. Symonds, Nautical and Aviation Publishing Co., 1990. 1,638 pp. Somewhat sentimental consideration of the Confederate president that offers interesting glimpses into his private life—as well as portraits of the people with whom he associated and the society in which they moved.

Edmondston, Catherine Ann Devereux. *"Journal of a Secesh Lady": The Diary of Catherine Ann Devereux Edmondston, 1860–1866.* Ed. Beth Crabtree Gilbert and James W. Patton. North Carolina Division of Archives and History, 1979. 850 pp. The wartime diary of the wife of a North Carolina plantation owner.

Freeman, Douglas Southall. *R. E. Lee: A Biography.* Four vol. Charles Scribner's Sons, 1934–1935; 1937. The classic biography of the Confederacy's leading general. Concentrates on the war years, but includes information on his family background and postwar years.

Grant, Ulysses S. *The Papers of Ulysses S. Grant.* Ed. John Y. Simon and others. Twenty-four vol. to date. Southern Illinois Univ. Press, 1967–. A thoroughly annotated presentation of Grant's letters and records.

_____. *Personal Memoirs of Ulysses S. Grant.* Two vol. Charles L. Webster and Co., 1885–1886. 1,231 pp. Reprinted, 1952, with an introduction by E. B. Long, World Publishing Co., 608 pp.; 1952 ed. reprinted 1982, with an introduction by William S. McFeely, Da Capo Press. 608 pp. One of the greatest memoirs ever written by a military commander.

Jackson, Mary Anna. *Life and Letters of General Thomas J. Jackson (Stonewall Jackson).* Harper and Bros., 1892, 479 pp. New edition, retitled *Memoirs of Stonewall Jackson by His Widow, Mary Anna Jackson,* includes additional material, Prentice Press, 1895, 647 pp.; 1895 ed. reprinted, with an introduction by Lowell Reidenbaugh, Morningside, 1993, 647 pp. Jackson's letters offer telling glimpses of this legendary figure. Includes his widow's reminiscences and seventeen essays composed by Confederate soldiers who served with Jackson.

Jones, John Beauchamp. *A Rebel War Clerk's Diary at the Confederate States Capital.* Two vol. Lippincott, 1866. 392 pp., 480 pp. (reprinted several times, including in an abridged edition edited by Earl Schenck Miers). A clerk in the Confederate War Office, Jones provides cogent descriptions of the inner working of the Confederate government and life in wartime Richmond. The diary covers the period from the beginning of the war until Lincoln's assassination.

Lee, Robert E. *The Wartime Papers of R. E. Lee.* Ed. Clifford Dowdy and Louis H. Manarin. Little, Brown, 1961. 994 pp. Though its lack of annotation presents a problem to researchers, this collection of 1,006 wartime papers of Robert E. Lee provides a vivid portrait of the Confederacy's most prominent general.

Marszalek, John F. *Sherman: A Soldier's Passion for Order.* Free Press, 1993. 635 pp. A biography of the Union's second greatest field commander; concentrates on the war years and on the subject's strong desire for order and control.

Shaw, Robert Gould. *Blue-Eyed Child of Fortune: The Civil War Letters of Colonel Robert Gould Shaw.* Ed. Russell Duncan, Univ. of Georgia Press, 1992. 421 pp. Letters of the commander of the legendary Fifty-Fourth Massachusetts Infantry.

Sheridan, Philip H. *Personal Memoirs of P. H. Sheridan.* Two vol. D. Appleton and Co., 1888, 986 pp. Reprinted 1992, 2 vol., Broadfoot, 986 pp. Reprinted 1992, with an introduction by Jeffry D. Wert, Da Capo Press, 535 pp. A classic military memoir that concentrates on "L'il Phil" Sheridan's Civil War experiences but includes material on his antebellum frontier duty and some postwar experiences.

Sherman, William Tecumseh. *Memoirs of General W. T. Sherman: Written by Himself.* Two vol., Appleton and Co., 1875, 814 pp. Reprinted 1957, with an introduction by B. H. Liddell Hart, Indiana Univ. Press, 814 pp. Library of America edition, two vol. in one, 1990; Penguin edition, ed. and with an introduction and notes by Michael Fellman, 2000, 855 pp. An engaging and detailed memoir by one of the Union's most effective generals, written with passion and intelligence.

_____. *Sherman's Civil War: Selected Correspondence of William T. Sherman, 1860–1865.* Ed. Brooks D. Simpson and Jean V. Berlin. Univ. of North Carolina Press, 1999. 948 pp. A collection of some 400 of William T. Sherman's wartime letters.

Simpson, Brooks D. *Let Us Have Peace: Ulysses S. Grant and the Politics of War and Reconstruction, 1861–1868.* An absorbing study demonstrating Grant's political acumen during and after the war.

_____. *Ulysses S. Grant: Triumph over Adversity, 1822–1865.* Houghton Mifflin, 2000. 533 pp. Covering Grant's prewar difficulties, his success as an army commander, army politics, and Grant's personal relationships.

Smith, Jean Edward. *Grant.* Simon & Schuster, 2001. 781 pp. Comprehensively researched and engagingly written, this full-scale biography integrates Grant's personal and public life and his military and political careers.

Sneden, Robert Knox. (Charles F. Bryan, Jr., and Nelson D. Lankford, eds.) *Eye of the Storm.* The Free Press, 2000. 330 pp. The recently discovered diaries of frontline Union private—and Confederate prisoner of war—Robert Sneden provide a compelling narrative that is interspersed with Sneden's equally compelling art, including depictions of life inside notorious Andersonville Prison, a "contraband" camp, and a plantation set afire by Union troops.

Strong, George Templeton. *The Diary of George Templeton Strong.* Ed. Allan Nevins. Four vol. Macmillan, 1952. Volume 3 reprinted in 1962 as *Diary of the Civil War, 1860–1865,* ed. Allan Nevens, Macmillan, 664 pp. A prominent New York lawyer and socialite, Strong filled his diary (particularly volume 3, covering the Civil War years) with forceful opinions and fascinating accounts of events.

Aftermath and Reconstruction

See also "Selected Resources" in Chapter 11, "Reconstruction and the Aftermath of the War."

Bentley, George R. *A History of the Freedmen's Bureau.* Octagon Books, 1970. 298 pp. Though brief and somewhat dated, this work remains a useful overview of the agency that played such a crucial role in Reconstruction.

Du Bois, W. E. B. *Black Reconstruction in America: An Essay toward a History of the Part Which Black Folk Played in the Attempt to Reconstruct Democracy in America, 1860–1880.* Harcourt, Brace, 1935. Reprinted, World Pub. Co, 1964, Cass (London), 1966, Atheneum, 1992. A classic study of the roles freedmen played in Reconstruction, Du Bois' work set the stage for future debate.

Foner, Eric. *Reconstruction: America's Unfinished Revolution, 1863–1877.* Harper & Row, 1988. 690 pp. This massive, meticulously documented study of the Reconstruction era begins with the Emancipation Proclamation and extends through a consideration of postwar legislation pertaining to African Americans. Foner also published the 297-page *A Short History of Reconstruction, 1863–1877* (Harper & Row, 1990).

Franklin, John Hope. *Reconstruction after the Civil War.* Univ. of Chicago Press, 1961. 258 pp. A well-crafted, fact-filled examination of the Reconstruction era.

Morris, Robert Charles. *Reading, 'Riting, and Reconstruction: The Education of Freedmen in the South 1861–1870.* Univ. of Chicago Press, 1981. An excellent overview of the Freedmen's Bureau's educational programs—but one that offers only brief considerations of policy, goals, resources, and opposition.

Rose, Willie Lee. *Rehearsal for Reconstruction: The Port Royal Experiment.* Bobbs Merrill, 1964. 442 pp. An examination of the educational, labor, and land-distribution experiments on the South Carolina Sea Islands that began after the islands fell to the Union in late 1861.

Sefton, James. *The United States Army and Reconstruction, 1865–1877.* Louisiana State Univ. Press, 1967, 284 pp. Reprinted by Greenwood Press, 1980, 284 pp. This scholarly overview of the army's role in the postwar South focuses on the military's role in enforcing civil policy from 1865 to 1868, while giving general coverage to the larger time span, and other topics (such as affairs in Washington).

Trelease, Allen W., *White Terror: The Ku Klux Klan Conspiracy and Southern Reconstruction.* Harper & Row, 1971. 557 pp.; paperback ed., Louisiana State Univ. Press, 1995. 557 pp. The best work on the Reconstruction Klan, providing an excellent description of the efforts of the army and state government to squash the movement.

Guides: Battlefields and Monuments

Civil War Advisory Commission. *Report on the Nation's Civil War Battlefields.* (See the *American Battlefield Protection Program* under Organizations: Battlefield Preservation, on page 898.)

Civil War Trust. *The Civil War Trust's Official Guidebook to the Civil War Discovery Trail.* 3d ed. 1996. A publication describing the discovery trail linking more than 500 Civil War sites in twenty-eight states.

Eicher, David J. *Civil War Battlefields: A Touring Guide.* Taylor Publishing Co., 1995, 228 pp. Presents forty-one maps covering some twenty-two campaigns and forty separate battles. Includes brief summaries of battle strategy and tactics and illustrated "tours" of each site. Foreword by James M. McPherson.

Greene, A. Wilson, and Gary W. Gallagher. *The National Geographic Guide to Civil War National Battlefield Parks.* National Geographic Society, 1992. 160 pp. This excellent pocket-size resource includes thirty-one battlefield maps accompanied by informative essays.

Kennedy, Frances H., ed. *The Civil War Battlefield Guide.* Conservation Fund, 1990; 2d ed. 1998. 495 pp. This guide to all the 384 principal battles designated in the Civil War Sites Advisory Commission Report includes battle maps and short essays by James M. McPherson, Stephen W. Sears, Edwin C. Bearss, and Gary W. Gallagher.

Thomas, Emory M. *Travels to Hallowed Ground: A Historian's Journey to the American Civil War.* Univ. of South Carolina Press, 1987. 155 pp. A reflective diary of this historian's battlefield journeys, this enjoyable reminiscence includes the author's reflections on what Civil War battlefields mean to Americans of today.

University Presses and the Civil War

SERIES DEVOTED TO THE CIVIL WAR

University of Arkansas Press: "The Civil War in the West"; "Portraits of Conflict"

Fordham University Press: "The North's Civil War"; "The Irish in the Civil War"

Johns Hopkins University Press: "War, Society and Culture"

University Press of Kansas: "Modern War Studies" (includes Civil War titles)

Louisiana State University Press: "Conflicting Worlds: New Perspectives on the American Civil War"

University of Missouri Press: "Shades of Blue and Gray"

University of Nebraska Press: "Great Campaigns of the Civil War"; "Key Issues of the Civil War Era"

Scholarly Resources: "The American Crisis Series: Books on the Civil War Era"

University of South Carolina Press: "American Civil War Classics"; "Women's Diaries and Letters of the Nineteenth Century South"

University of Tennessee Press: "Voices of the Civil War"

University Press of Virginia: "A Nation Divided: New Studies in Civil War History"

Specialty Presses with Civil War Emphasis

Broadfoot Publishing Company: "Army of Northern Virginia Series"; "Army of the Potomac Series"

H. E. Howard: "Confederate Regimental Series"; "Virginia Battles and Leaders Series"; "Virginia Regimental Series"

Longstreet House

McWhiney Foundation Press: "Civil War Campaigns and Commanders Series"

Morningside Press

Olde Soldier Books

Savas Publishing Company

Southern Heritage Press: "Journal of Confederate History Book Series"

Thomas Publications

Commercial Presses that Publish Numerous Civil War Titles

Burd Street Press

Edwin Mellen Press

Stackpole Books

White Mane Publishing Company

Civil War Periodicals

America's Civil War (http://www.thehistorynet.com/AmericasCivilWar)
e-mail: AmericasCivilWar@thehistorynet.com

Blue and Gray Magazine (http://www.bluegraymagazine.com)
e-mail: BGEDITORS@AOL.COM

Civil War Book Review (www.civilwarbookreview.com)

Civil War History (http://www3.la.psu.edu/histrlst/inst/journal.htm)
[The leading scholarly journal of the Civil War era; published quarterly]

Civil War Times Illustrated (http://historynet.com/CivilWarTimes/)
e-mail: cwt@cowles.com
See also Merideth, Lee W., comp. *Civil War Times and Civil War Times, Illustrated: 30 Year Comprehensive Index, April 1959-February 1989.* L. W. Merideth, 1990. 220 pp.

Gettysburg Magazine (http://www.morningsidebooks.com)
e-mail: msbooks@erinet.com

Journal of American History (http://www.indiana.edu/~jah)
[Leading scholarly journal, published by the Organization of American Historians]
oah@oah.org (Subscriptions, back issues)

Journal of Southern History (http://www.ruf.rice.edu/~jsh)
[Quarterly journal, devoted to the history of the American South, published by the Southern Historical Association, edited and sponsored by Rice University]
e-mail: jsh@rice.edu

Military Images (http://www.civilwar-photos.com)
[Periodical devoted to the photographic history of nineteenth-century U.S. soldiers and sailors]
e-mail: milimage@uplink.net

North and South Magazine (http://www.northandsouthmagazine.com)
e-mail: KPOULTER@aol.com

Virginia Magazine of History and Biography (See Virginia Historical Society, on page 886.)

Many state and local historical journals also publish Civil War-related articles.

Audio and CD-ROM Publications

See also Chapter 12, "The Civil War in Literature and the Arts," for a listing of Civil War videos.

Many of the titles previously listed are among the Civil War books now available through "audio book" dealers, such as Blackstone Audiobooks (http://www.blackstoneaudio.com) and Books on Tape (http://www .booksontape.com). Civil War music is available on cassettes, videotapes, and CDs in many stores and via the Internet. And much valuable Civil War research material is now on CD-ROMs and eBooks, published by companies such as:

Broadfoot Publishing Company (http://www.broadfoot.wilmington.net)

Digital Scanning and Publishing (http://www.digitalscanning.com) [eBooks]

Guild Press of Indiana (http://www.guildpress.com)

H-Bar Enterprises (http://www.hbar.com)

Major Artifact and Archival Collections

See also "National Historic Sites," on page 887. A number of battlefields and other Civil War historic sites have museums or research collections.

A few state archives are listed here. In general, *state vital statistics offices, historical societies, archives,* and *genealogical and historical societies* are excellent resources for tracing the history of individual Civil War soldiers as well as state units that served in the war.

California

The Huntington Library (http://www.huntington.org)
Fifty Civil War collections, including papers of military leaders; diaries of noncommissioned officers, privates, and private citizens; and materials focused on Civil War medicine.

Connecticut

The Connecticut Historical Society (http://www.chs.org)
Extensive Civil War holdings, including private letters of soldiers and their families, stationery, broadsides, edged weapons and firearms, costumes, prints, and lithographs.

District of Columbia

The Library of Congress (http://www.loc.gov)
America's oldest national cultural institution, the Library of Congress holds unparalleled collections of Civil War material, divided in eight Library divisions, plus a Web site that accommodates the National Digital Library:

1. *General Collections* (Thomas Jefferson Building, John Adams Building): Included in these vast collections are Civil War histories (from the Official Records of the war and regimental histories, to modern studies); biographies and autobiographies of Civil War figures; published reminiscences and diaries of Civil War participants; and some bound publications of the period.

2. *Geography and Map Division* (James Madison Memorial Building): Custodian of the largest cartographic collections in the world, the Geography and Map Division holds thousands of Civil War maps, from newspaper and lithograph maps prepared for a home-front audience to maps used by commanders in the field—including the sketchbooks and finished battle maps of Jedediah Hotchkiss, the Confederacy's peerless topographical engineer.

3. *Law Library* (James Madison Memorial Building): The world's largest law library, this Library division holds American statutes, including session laws of the Provisional and elected government of the Confederate States of America.

4. *Manuscript Division* (James Madison Memorial Building): Among the more than fifty million items held in this division are the papers of twenty-three American presidents, including Abraham Lincoln and Ulysses S. Grant. More than 1,000 discrete manuscript collections contain material pertaining to the Civil War. They include the papers of ordinary soldiers, sailors, U.S. Sanitary Commission workers (along with Sanitary Commission records and reports), freedmen's teachers, and interested citizens of both the North and the South, as well as prominent Civil War politicians, soldiers, and activists. These collections often include drawings, maps, photographs, and similar relevant items.

5. *Music Division* (James Madison Memorial Building): Holdings of this division include a large collection of original Civil War sheet music, as well as band scores of the era. Many of the sheet music covers are illustrated.

6. *Periodicals Reading Room* (James Madison Memorial Building): Civil War-era newspapers accessible here including the *New York Daily Tribune*, edited by Horace Greeley; the *Chicago Times*, the *Cincinnati Enquirer*, and the *Charleston Daily Courier*—as well as some of the more impromptu periodicals published by units of the Union army. Other

bound Civil War periodicals are housed in the Rare Book and Special Collections Division and the Prints and Photographs Division.

7. *Prints and Photographs Division* (James Madison Memorial Building): An especially rich resource for Civil War materials, this division houses thousands of Civil War photographs, including those taken by Mathew Brady and his staff; original drawings of special artist-correspondents, most notably Alfred R. Waud; popular color and black-and-white lithographs published during and immediately after the war; advertisements; sheet music covers; and bound volumes of illustrated periodicals such as *Harper's Weekly.*

8. *Rare Book and Special Collections Division* (Thomas Jefferson Building): This division's collections include the Alfred Whital Stern Collection of Lincolniana, consisting of contemporary newspapers, sheet music, broadsides, prints, stamps, coins, and autographed letters; a large body of publications concerned with slavery, the Civil War, Reconstruction, and related topics; and writings by and about Abraham Lincoln. The Confederate States of America Collection comprises some 2,000 publications of the South, including those issued by individual state governments and the Congress, departments, and offices of the Confederacy. The division also houses an extensive collection of Civil War broadsides, books, pamphlets, and other material published in the wartime Union.

9. *The National Digital Library—American Memory:* For those unable to visit the Library in person, a great deal of material is now available via the Library's Web site (http://www.loc.gov). The Library's Online Catalog, and more detailed information on each division and its holdings, are available via the Web site, as are digital copies of more than 7,000,000 items from the Library's collections. Many include detailed descriptions and commentary. Two major resources, accessible via the Library's main Web page, are particularly valuable for those interested in the Civil War:

- *THOMAS*, the Library's online legislative information service, provides access to current and proposed legislation, as well as historic documents—including the *Congressional Globe*, which reported congressional debates during the Civil War.

- *American Memory* Web pages are filled with browsable material on the Civil War era: selected photographs and daguerreotypes, maps, band music, sheet music, manuscripts (including items from the Abraham Lincoln papers), and the text of selected books (including bound speeches of such figures as "Copperhead" leader Clement Vallandigham) and periodicals.

Two print publications of use to those interested in exploring Civil War materials at the Library are:

> Sellers, John R., comp. *Civil War Manuscripts, A Guide to Collections in the Manuscript Division of the Library of Congress.* Washington, DC: Library of Congress, 1986. (Annotated, with illustrations.)

> Stephenson, Richard W., comp. *Civil War Maps, An Annotated List of Maps and Atlases in the Library of Congress.* (With illustrations.)

National Archives and Records Administration (http://www.nara.gov)
The National Archives, the repository for U.S. Federal Government records, is an unsurpassed source for records related to the Civil War and the soldiers and sailors who served either the Union or the Confederacy. Records housed at the main building (Archives I) include: regimental records, quartermaster documents, ordnance records, court of inquiry records, and muster rolls. Compiled Military Service Records (CMSR) of individual Union and Confederate servicemen are also housed here, as are pension records for Union servicemen, and card records of headstones provided for deceased Union Civil War veterans, ca. 1879–1915. Archives II, a building in College Park, Maryland, also offers much Civil War information: photographs (including images created by Mathew Brady and his staff, Alexander Gardner, and George N. Barnard), maps, plans and engineering drawings, diagrams, blueprints, and sketches of forts.

National Museum of Health and Medicine
(http://www.natmedmuse.afip.org)
Founded during the Civil War by U.S. Surgeon General William Hammond as the Army Medical Museum, what is now the National Museum of Health and Medicine houses the Otis Historical Archives comprising photographs of wounded soldiers, hospitals, and ambulances; medical material; and papers of Union medical officers.

Naval Historical Center (http://www.history.navy.mil)
Available to researchers *by appointment*, the Center's collections include photographs and printed archival material encompassing all of U.S. naval history. Much material is available online.

Smithsonian Institution (http://www.si.edu)
National Museum of American History (http://americanhistory.si.edu)
The Smithsonian's American History collections include many related to the Civil War: Mathew Brady photographs; a representation of General Sheridan's horse, Winchester; and portraits of many political and military figures of the time. The Smithsonian's *educational programs* focused on the Civil War include overnight study tours; battle-site seminars across the country; and lectures, seminars, and multisession courses in Washington. Online services include an e-mail Civil War newsletter and online programs such as "On the Road to Appomattox—Grant and Lee from War to Peace."

Georgia

Atlanta History Center (http://www.athist.org)

Augusta Museum of History (http://www.augustamuseum.org)

Port Columbus Civil War Naval Center (http://www.portcolumbus.org)

Illinois

Chicago Historical Society (http://www.chicagohs.org)
Houses an extensive collection of Civil War materials, particularly photographs and lithographs.

Chicago Public Library (http://www.chipublib.org)

Indiana

Colonel Eli Lilly Civil War Museum
(http://www.state.in.us/iwm/civiwar)

Kentucky

The Filson Club Historical Society (http://www.filsonclub.org)

Old Bardstown Village—Civil War Museum of the Western Theater/ Women in the Civil War (museum) (http://www.bardstown.com/~civilwar)

Louisiana

Louisiana State University (http://www.lsu.edu)
Civil War Center (http://www.cwc.lsu.edu/cwc)

The Special Collections department of the Hill Memorial Library at LSU (http://www.lib.lsu.edu) houses Civil War manuscript resources in the Louisiana and Lower Mississippi collections. The *Civil War Center* sponsors conferences, classes, and seminars, and maintains one of the great Internet resources for information on the Civil War. Among the many Civil War Web sites accessible via the center's main page is the *Civil War Book Review*.

Memorial Hall—Confederate Museum
(http://www.confederatemuseum.com)
Civil War materials include more than ninety manuscript collections, mostly the papers of soldiers and private citizens, but also including some papers of such noted Civil War figures as Albert Sidney Johnston, P. G. T. Beauregard, and Stonewall Jackson; the papers of the Louisiana Historical Society; and nine collections pertaining to the Mexican War, in which many Union and Confederate officers received combat training.

Maine

Maine State Archives
Civil War Collections
(http://www.state.me.us/sos/arc/archives/military/civilwar/civilwar.htm)
Voluminous archival records of Maine's participation in the Civil War, including regimental correspondence, municipal correspondence, and photographs. Some material is available online.

Maryland

National Museum of Civil War Medicine (http://www.civwarmed.org)
e-mail: Museum@civilwarmed.org
In addition to its educational displays and Civil War medicine artifacts, the museum conducts an annual conference on Civil War medicine.

Michigan

William L. Clements Library (http://www.clements.umich.edu)
This library holds the James S. Schoff Civil War Collection, comprising manuscript, photographic, and printed materials relating to all phases of the Civil War. The library's general collections include the Civil War-era newspapers of many eastern cities; examples of wallpaper newspapers from Vicksburg; and such influential Civil War publications as *Harper's Weekly* and *Frank Leslie's Illustrated Newspaper*.

New York

New York Public Library (http://www/nypl.org)
The extensive Civil War collections of the New York Public Library are found in several divisions. The Manuscripts and Archives division contains records and papers of the United States Sanitary Commission; a large number of diaries, personal memoirs, and letters, most belonging to soldiers in New York regiments; papers of U.S. Secretary of the Navy Gideon Welles and various naval officers; papers of the Army and Navy Claim Agency, the Army and Navy Pay Claim archives, and the Washington Hospital Directory archives; daybooks for the U.S. Navy Yard; and letter books, orderly books, and conscription records of the Confederate States. The Music Division maintains an important collection of broadsides and sheet music. Civil War items in the Prints Division include enlistment posters for the Union army, the register books of Mathew Brady's studio 1863–1865, and drawings by the staff artists of *Leslie's Weekly*. The Rare Book Division maintains a large collection of Confederate imprints, and the Schomburg Center contains original documents and other materials on slavery and emancipation in the Civil War period. Consult *Guide to the Research Collections of the New York Public Library*, compiled by Sam Williams (Chicago: American Library Association, 1975), for further information.

United States Military Academy
West Point Museum (http://www.usma.edu/Museum)
Library/U.S. Military Academy Archives (http://usmalibrary.usma.edu)
The West Point Museum houses what is considered to be the oldest and largest diversified public collection of militaria in the western hemisphere—including items pertaining to the Civil War and its officers, many of whom were West Point graduates. The United States Military Academy Archives, at the West Point Library, may also be a source of information.

North Carolina

Duke University
William R. Perkins Library (http://www.lib.duke.edu)
Rare Book, Manuscript, and Special Collections Library
(http://scriptorium.lib.duke.edu)

This library's collections relating to the history and culture of the American South are particularly strong, and include Confederate imprints, Civil War regimental histories, and Southern broadsides.

State Library of North Carolina
(http://statelibrary.dcr.state.nc.us/NCSLHOME.HTM)

The University of North Carolina at Chapel Hill
Wilson Library (http://www.lib.unc.edu/wilson)
The Library's Southern Historical Collection, including more than 2,000,000 items, contains much material on antebellum plantations, the Civil War, and Reconstruction. The North Carolina Collection includes Civil War-era woodcuts, engravings, lithographs, and photographs. Some material is browsable via the Web site.

Ohio

Bowling Green State University—Center for Archival Collections
(http://www.bgsu.edu/colleges/library/cac/cac.html)
The center has many manuscript collections that pertain to the Civil War, including records of the Twenty-First Ohio Volunteer Infantry, papers of individuals and families, and some records from the Johnson's Island Military Prison. Some documents are available online.

Pennsylvania

Civil War Library and Museum (http://www.netreach.net/~cwlm)
Many artifacts are exhibited in this three-floor Philadelphia museum and library, which also houses excellent research collections comprising more than 12,000 volumes, 100 linear feet of archival/manuscript material, over 100 reels of microfilm, and nearly 5,000 photographs. The museum offers programs and lectures, and it hosts meetings of a Civil War Round Table.

Grand Army of the Republic Civil War Museum and Library, Philadelphia (http://suvcw.org/garmus.htm)

Historical Society of Pennsylvania—Library
(http://www.hsp.org/library)
Located in Philadelphia, Historical Society collections pertaining to the Civil War include papers of the Pennsylvania Abolition Society; the

Underground Railroad records of William Still; letters of abolition zealot John Brown; some papers of the prewar president, James Buchanan, Civil War U.S. Secretary of the Treasury Salmon Chase, and General George Gordon Meade (including accounts of the battle of Gettysburg); Union army muster rolls, and papers of a number of Union regiments; and prints, drawings, cartoons, maps, and photographs.

The National Civil War Museum
(http://www.nationalcivilwarmuseum.org)
The 12,000 items in the Harrisburg, Pennsylvania, museum collections represent both the North and the South.

U.S. Army Military History Institute
(http://carlisle-www.army.mil/usamhi)
An Institute of the Army War College, the U.S. Army Military History Institute has an extensive library of books on U.S. Army history. Its Civil War collections contain many older, hard-to-find volumes pertaining to both Union and Confederate forces; a significant number of Civil War manuscripts; and many Civil War-era photographs (held by the Special Collections Branch).

South Carolina

The Charleston Museum (http://www.charlestonmuseum.com)
The oldest museum in the United States, the Charleston Museum has a fine collection of Civil War weapons and other period artifacts.

Texas

The Center for American History (http://www.cah.utexas.edu)
Located at the University of Texas at Austin, the center holds the George W. Littlefield Southern History Collection, one of the nation's principal resources for research on topics related to the history of the Confederate States of America.

Hill College
Harold B. Simpson History Complex
(http://www.hill-college.cc.tx.us/crc/crc.htm)
Comprising three divisions—the Texas Heritage Museum, the Research Center (dealing with research on the Civil War), and the Hill College Press—the History Complex includes a 5,000-volume Civil War library

and extensive archives. The collections focus on Confederate troops from Texas.

Virginia

University of Virginia—Alderman Memorial Library
(http://www.lib.virginia.edu)
Manuscript collections include papers of John D. Imboden, John S. Mosby, and Thomas L. Rosser. The collections also include nineteenth-century sheet music, maps of Civil War battlefields, broadsides, rare books, and Civil War-era newspapers.

The James G. Leyburn Library at Washington & Lee University
(http://www.w/u.edu/~library/leyburn/)

Lee Chapel and Museum, Washington & Lee Univeristy
(http://leechapel.wlu.edu/)

The Library of Virginia (http://www.lva.lib.va.us/)

Mariner's Museum (http://www.mariner.org)
Located in Newport News, the museum holds numerous Civil War exhibits, including artifacts recovered from the U.S.S. *Monitor*. The museum has an extensive research library.

The Museum of the Confederacy (http://www.moc.org)
The museum includes the White House of the Confederacy as well as excellent collections of Confederate artifacts—Confederate flags, government documents, personal papers, and photographs.

Pamplin Historical Park and the National Museum of the Civil War Soldier (http://www.pamplinpark.org)
This museum, in Petersburg, houses modern exhibits on the site of well-preserved remnants of the Confederate defensive lines during the siege at Petersburg. Pamplin Historical Park sponsors a number of Living History and thematic Civil War programs and a Civil War Symposium.

Virginia Historical Society (http://www.vahistory.org)
Houses an extensive collection of manuscripts, photographs, and artifacts from the Civil War, including the Maryland-Steuart collection of Confederate-manufactured ordnance and the uniforms of Confederate Generals Lee and Stuart. The famous "Seasons of the Confederacy" murals are featured at the museum. Located in Richmond, the Historical

Society publishes the quarterly *Virginia Magazine of History and Biography*, which is a membership benefit.

Virginia Military Institute
VMI Archives (http://www.vmi.edu/~archtml)
The VMI Civil War collections, housed in Lexington, Virginia, include papers of Confederate soldiers—from Stonewall Jackson and naval officer Matthew Fontaine Maury to VMI cadets and private citizens—as well as material on specific units and battles. Some material can be viewed via the archive's Web site.

Virginia Tech—Newman Library (http://www.lib.vt.edu)
Special Collections, Civil War Resources
(http://scholar2.lib.vt.edu/spec)
Holdings include letters and diaries of Union and Confederate soldiers, home-front letters, memoirs, contemporary research files, monographs, and books.

Wisconsin

Wisconsin Veterans Museum
(http://www.state.wi.us/agencies/dva/museum/wvmmain.html)
Located in Madison, the museum houses an interactive computer display through which the service records of the more than 91,000 Wisconsin Civil War veterans are available. A research library of 4,000 volumes, 2,000 pamphlets, and 200 periodicals is available to researchers—as are the personal papers of Wisconsin veterans.

National Historic Sites

One of the chief ways of honoring the past—and learning from it—is to preserve not only the written records left by participants, but also the places where events occurred that were significant to Americans' evolution as a people. Battlefields, homes of pivotal figures, depots along the Underground Railroad routes, forts, prisons, mustering-in sites for United States Colored Troops, and burial grounds are among the Civil War sites preserved by the National Park Service. As noted earlier, similar sites are preserved by the governments of the various states, counties, and cities. Web sites maintained by each state, public libraries, and state historical associations offer further information on Civil War historic sites. Artifacts and research collections are often affiliated with these sites, but the places themselves—the rise and fall of the terrain at Gettysburg, the cramped hiding places in an Underground Railroad depot, the haunting theater box where Abraham Lincoln received his mortal wound—give visitors the irreplaceable experience of walking in the pathways of history.

Following is a descriptive list of Civil War sites that are preserved and administered by the National Park Service (http://www.nps.gov).

Abraham Lincoln Birthplace, near Hodgenville, Kentucky
(http://www.nps.gov/abli)
A nineteenth-century one-room log cabin like the one in which Lincoln was born is now preserved in a memorial building near Hodgenville. This historic site also encompasses landmarks of the Thomas and Nancy Lincoln farm and includes a visitors' center.

Andersonville National Historic Site, Andersonville, Georgia
(http://www.nps.gov/ande)
A memorial to all American prisoners of war throughout the nation's history, the 495-acre Andersonville National Historic Site consists of the Civil War prison site and a national cemetery. On April 9, 1999, the National Prisoner of War Museum opened at Andersonville.

Andrew Johnson National Historic Site, Greenville, Tennessee
(http://www.nps.gov/anjo)
Encompasses the two homes, tailor shop, and gravesite of the man who became the seventeenth president of the United States upon the assassination of Abraham Lincoln.

Antietam National Battlefield, Sharpsburg, Maryland
(http://www.nps.gov/anti)
Site of the clash on September 17, 1862, that marked the bloodiest single day of the war and the end of Confederate General Robert E. Lee's first invasion of Northern territory.

Appomattox Court House National Historical Park, Appomattox, Virginia
(http://www.nps.gov/apco)
Constituting some 1,800 acres and twenty-seven original nineteenth-century buildings, the Appomattox Court House National Historical Park centers on the McLean home, where, on April 9, 1865, Confederate

General in Chief Robert E. Lee surrendered the Army of Northern Virginia to Union General in Chief Ulysses S. Grant.

Arkansas Post National Memorial, Gillett, Arkansas
(http://www.nps.gov/arpo)
In mid-1862, when the Union controlled most of the Mississippi River, Confederate General Thomas J. Churchill began construction of Fort Hindman, or the Post of Arkansas, on the Arkansas River, to protect the state capital of Little Rock. On January 10, 1863, however, Union forces under Sherman and McClernand captured the fort, the remains of which now rest under the Arkansas River. Remnants of Confederate trenches can still be viewed here, and in the *Arkansas Post Museum* are artifacts that further elucidate the Civil War era in Arkansas Post's long history.

Arlington House, the Robert E. Lee Memorial, Arlington, Virginia
(http://www.nps.gov/arho)
The site of Robert E. Lee's marriage, and the home where six of his seven children were born, Arlington House (once known as the Custis-Lee Mansion) is a fitting memorial for the Confederate general in chief and former U.S. Army officer, who won the respect of people in both the South and the North. Located in the hills of Arlington, Virginia, Arlington House overlooks the Potomac. Arlington National Cemetery was established on what were once the grounds of the house.

Battlefield National Cemetery, Washington, D.C.
(http://www.nps.gov/batt)
Battlefield National Cemetery, now part of Rock Creek Park in Washington, was established shortly after the battle of Fort Stevens during Jubal Early's raid to Washington in the summer of 1864. Forty-one Union soldiers who died defending Fort Stevens were interred in a specially created cemetery dedicated by Abraham Lincoln—who was under enemy fire himself during the battle. Monuments to the four Federal units that participated in the battle are also found at this cemetery.

Boston African American National Historic Site (http://www.nps.gov/boaf)
Comprising several historic sites located along the 1.6-mile Black Heritage Trail, the Boston African American National Historic Site includes the African Meeting House, where William Lloyd Garrison founded the New England Antislavery Society (1832), and where, years later, recruits

for the legendary Fifty-Fourth Massachusetts Infantry, United States Colored Troops, gathered to enlist. Also on this site is the Augustus Saint Gaudens memorial to Robert Gould Shaw and the Fifty-Fourth.

Brices Cross Roads National Battlefield Site, Baldwyn, Mississippi (http://www.nps.gov/brcr)
This one-acre site commemorates a cavalry battle at which Confederate troops under Nathan Bedford Forrest decisively defeated Union forces, under S. D. Sturgis, that were attempting to prevent Forrest from reaching a position from which he could disrupt General Sherman's lines of supply into Georgia.

Chickamauga and Chattanooga National Military Park, Fort Oglethorpe, Georgia (http://www.nps.gov/chch)
The first (and the largest) of four national military parks authorized by Congress (1890–1999), this 8,200-acre park commemorates some of the hardest fighting of the Civil War: the Union defeat at Chickamauga, which resulted in a retreat to Chattanooga; the Confederate siege of that city; and the actions by which the Union broke the siege.

Clara Barton National Historic Site, Glen Echo, Maryland (http://www.nps.gov/clba)
This site commemorates the life of the founder of the American Red Cross (established in 1882), who was a prime supporter of the Union forces during the Civil War. After the war, under the authority of the government, she superintended a search for missing soldiers. The Clara Barton National Historic Site is the house in which she lived after the war.

Colonial National Historical Park (Yorktown National Cemetery), Yorktown, Virginia (http://www.nps.gov/york)
The Yorktown National Cemetery is a Civil War site in the midst of a park that chiefly commemorates earlier American history—particularly the defeat of the British at Yorktown, which effectively ended the Revolutionary War. Interred here are 2,183 Civil War soldiers, all but ten of whom fought for the Union. Only 747 of the dead are identified.

Ford's Theatre National Historic Site, Washington, D.C. (http://www.nps.gov/foth)
Still an operating theater, as well as a historic site and a museum, Ford's Theatre is where President Lincoln was attending a performance of a

comedy, *Our American Cousin*, when he was shot by John Wilkes Booth. Lincoln died in the Petersen House, across the street from the theater, the next day; the house, also a part of this historic site, is much as it was on the day of his death. This historic site features talks by Park Service personnel, a museum in the theater's basement—and the presidential box, to one side of the stage, kept as it was on the night of the assassination.

Fort Donelson National Battlefield, Dover, Tennessee
(http://www.nps.gov/fodo)
Commemorating the Union victory that first brought Ulysses S. Grant to national attention, Fort Donelson National Battlefield comprises the fort and its associated earthen rifle pits and river batteries; the Dover Hotel (Surrender House), where Confederate General Simon B. Buckner surrendered to Grant; a visitor center; and the Fort Donelson National Cemetery, in which Union soldiers killed at Fort Donelson, and other American veterans representing seven wars, are interred.

Fort Moultrie National Monument, Sullivan's Island, South Carolina
(http://www.nps.gov/formo)
Fort Moultrie's history covers 171 years of seacoast defense—including the firing on Fort Sumter that began the Civil War.

Fort Pulaski National Monument, Savannah, Georgia
(http://www.nps.gov/fopu)
Encompassing 5,623 acres of scenic marsh and uplands, the Fort Pulaski National Monument centers on the brick fortress upon which Union forces, under David Hunter, demonstrated the superior destructive properties of rifled cannon in the barrages that prefaced the fort's capture by the North in early 1862. An ardent abolitionist, Hunter then ordered the release of the slaves in the area, and recruited many into the First South Carolina Colored Regiment. From October 1864 to March 1865, the fort also served as a prison for a group of Confederate prisoners of war who would become known as "The Immortal Six Hundred." Talks and demonstrations by Park Service rangers, and exhibits at the visitor center, provide information on the history and significance of this site.

Fort Scott National Historic Site, Fort Scott, Kansas
(http://www.nps.gov/fosc)
Comprising twenty historic structures, a parade ground, and five acres
of restored tall-grass prairie, the Fort Scott National Historic Site commemorates several aspects of American frontier history. In 1861, the
U.S. army returned to the fort, which had been abandoned for several
years, and built it into the largest and strongest Union point south of
Fort Leavenworth. Units mustered in at the fort included the First and
Second Kansas Colored Volunteer Infantry. A military prison built during the war housed some Confederate prisoners. The fort itself was a
haven for refugees from the fierce guerrilla warfare that marked the
Kansas-Missouri corridor. Eleven of the buildings at this historic site
contain rooms furnished in the style of the Civil War period. The site
also has three museum areas.

Fort Sumter National Monument, Sullivan's Island, South Carolina
(http://www.nps.gov/fosu)
Site of the first engagement of the Civil War, Fort Sumter became a national monument in 1948.

Frederick Douglass National Historic Site, Washington, D. C.
(http://www.nps.gov/frdo)
The nation's leading nineteenth-century African American spokesman,
Frederick Douglass spent the last years of his life in Washington, D.C.
The house he lived in, "Cedar Hill," is now the Frederick Douglass National Historic Site. A visitor center houses artifacts and exhibits providing information on his life and his many accomplishments.

Fredericksburg and Spotsylvania National Military Park, Fredericksburg,
Virginia (http://www.nps.gov/frsp)
Approximately 110,000 casualties occurred during the four major battles
fought in the vicinity of Fredericksburg, Virginia, making it the bloodiest ground on the North American continent. The Fredericksburg and
Spotsylvania County Memorial National Military Park commemorates
the heroism of soldiers of both sides in the battles of Fredericksburg (December 1862), Chancellorsville (May 1863), the Wilderness (May 1864),
and Spotsylvania Court House (May 1864). The park also includes:

> *Fredericksburg National Cemetery:* a cemetery for Union soldiers, on
> Marye's Heights, the formidable Confederate position that had

proven so impregnable to repeated Federal attacks during the battle of Fredericksburg. There are also two Confederate cemeteries in the Fredericksburg area.

Stonewall Jackson Shrine: The site where Confederate General Thomas Jonathan (Stonewall) Jackson died, several days after being wounded at the battle of Chancellorsville.

Old Salem Church: Used by both sides as a hospital during the war, the church was also an important civilian refugee center during the battle of Fredericksburg. Monuments to the Fifteenth New Jersey and the Twenty-Third New Jersey are located close by—farther east along Route 3 (the Old Plank Road).

Chatham Manor: This magnificent Georgian mansion served as a headquarters for several Union generals, including Irvin McDowell. President Lincoln visited the house, which was also a communications center and an artillery position during the battle of Fredericksburg. Clara Barton, Walt Whitman, Dr. Mary Walker, and Dorothea Dix are four of the prominent medical personnel who were associated with the house when it was used as a hospital.

General Grant National Memorial, New York City
(http://www.nps.gov/gegr)
Popularly known as "Grant's Tomb," the General Grant National Memorial is the final resting place of Ulysses S. Grant and his wife, Julia Dent Grant. Completed in 1897, and the largest mausoleum in North America, it houses a Visitor Center as well as a bookstore and exhibits providing information on Grant and his accomplishments.

Gettysburg National Military Park (http://www.nps.gov/gett)
Located fifty miles northwest of Baltimore, the small town of Gettysburg, Pennsylvania, was the site of the largest and bloodiest battle of the Civil War, fought on July 1–3, 1863. Considered a turning point of the war, the Union victory ended Robert E. Lee's second invasion of Northern territory. The military park commemorating this momentous battle occupies nearly 6,000 acres. The site has twenty-six miles of park roads and over 1,400 monuments, markers, and memorials, which makes it one of the world's largest collections of outdoor sculpture. The Gettysburg National Military Park also includes:

Gettysburg National Cemetery: Dedicated on November 19, 1863, when President Lincoln delivered the Gettysburg Address, this cemetery is the final resting place for American veterans from all United States wars—including 3,500 Civil War dead.

Gettysburg Civil War Collections: This military park holds the largest Civil War collection in the National Park Service: more than 40,000 cataloged objects, including weapons, uniforms, flags, military equipment, and battle relics. The William Gladstone Collection includes objects related to the U.S. Colored Troops and the involvement of African Americans in the Civil War. Gettysburg also has a major archival holding related to the battle and the creation of the National Military Park. These archives, comprising seventy significant collections, include original maps, drawings, blueprints, manuscripts, journals, and the Tipton photograph collection. Museum exhibits derived from the Gettysburg collections are housed in the park's visitor center and the cyclorama center, where the painting, *Cyclorama of the Battle of Gettysburg* is on display.

Harpers Ferry National Historical Park, Harpers Ferry, West Virginia
(http://www.nps.gov/hafe)
The scene of abolitionist and zealot John Brown's famous 1859 raid on the U.S. arsenal, the strategically located town of Harpers Ferry changed hands eight times during the Civil War, a fact that wrecked its economy and forced many residents to depart forever. By 1864, it had become Union General Philip Sheridan's base of operations during his campaign against Confederate troops in the Shenandoah Valley. The Harpers Ferry National Historical Park covers 2,300 acres in the states of West Virginia, Maryland, and Virginia. Many images from the park's photo archive are available online.

Kennesaw Mountain National Battlefield Park, Kennesaw, Georgia
(http://www.nps.gov/kemo)
Kennesaw Mountain Battlefield is a 2,884-acre park that preserves the Atlanta Campaign battleground on which Joseph E. Johnston's Confederate army repelled a determined assault by William T. Sherman's troops. The visitor center provides introductory information about the park and the battle. Each year, on Battle Anniversary Weekend (end of June), the park stages living history programs and artillery demonstrations.

Lincoln Boyhood National Memorial, Lincoln, Indiana
(http://www.nps.gov/libo)
On this southern Indiana farm, Abraham Lincoln grew from youth into manhood, as commemorated by exhibits in the visitor center. His mother, Nancy Hanks Lincoln, is buried here.

Lincoln Home National Historic Site, Springfield, Illinois
(http://www.nps.gov/liho)
The two-story home of Abraham Lincoln—the only home he ever owned—stands at the center of a four-block historic neighborhood that the National Park Service is restoring to its condition when the Lincolns lived there (1844–1860). The site's visitor center (which is also a visitor service facility for the City of Springfield) houses exhibits and displays.

Manassas National Battlefield Park, Manassas, Virginia
(http://www.nps.gov/mana)
Established in 1940 to preserve the scene of two major Civil War battles (First and Second Manassas, also known as First and Second Bull Run; both were defeats for the Union), this park comprises the more than 5,000 acres on which the two battles occurred, and visitor centers where introductory video programs and artifacts are shown.

Monocacy National Battlefield, Frederick, Maryland
(http://www.nps.gov/mono)
The battle of Monocacy, Maryland, July 9, 1864, between invading Confederate forces under Jubal Early and a much smaller force under Union General Lew Wallace, delayed Early's progress to the outskirts of Washington, D.C., and bought time for reinforcements to reach the capital. The visitor center at Monocacy National Battlefield houses an electric map orientation program, artifacts, and interpretive displays of the encounter some refer to as "the battle that saved Washington" (see also Battlefield National Cemetery, on page 889).

Pea Ridge National Military Park, Pea Ridge, Arkansas
(http://www.nps.gov/peri)
This 4,300-acre national military park preserves the site of a March 1862 Union victory that saved Missouri for the Union. The Pea Ridge site includes a National Park Service reconstruction of Elkhorn Tavern—the scene of bitter fighting on both days of this pivotal battle.

Pecos National Historical Park: Glorieta Pass, Pecos, New Mexico
(http://www.nps.gov/peco)
In its 6,600 acres, Pecos National Historical Park preserves 10,000 years of history, including the site of the Civil War battle of Glorieta Pass. Fought on March 28, 1862, the battle ended the attempted Confederate invasion of New Mexico.

Petersburg National Battlefield, Petersburg, Virginia
(http://www.nps.gov/pete)
The setting for the longest siege in American history (when General Ulysses S. Grant failed to capture Richmond in the spring of 1864 and settled into siege lines at Petersburg), this 2,460-acre national battlefield comprises six major units, including battlefields, earthen forts, and trenches. The *Poplar Grove National Cemetery* (http://www.nps.gov/pogr), in which 6,000 soldiers are buried, is also a part of the Petersburg National Battlefield.

Richmond National Battlefield Park, Richmond, Virginia
(http://www.nps.gov/rich)
Between 1861 and 1865, Union armies repeatedly set out to capture Richmond, the capital of the Confederacy. Three of those campaigns came within a few miles of the city. The park actually encompasses eleven different sites associated with those campaigns, including the battlefields at Gaines' Mill, Malvern Hill, and Cold Harbor. Established in 1936, the park protects approximately 1,400 acres of historic ground. Major museum and visitor center facilities include:

Chimborazo Medical Museum: Contains exhibits on medical equipment and hospital life, including information on the men and women who staffed the Chimborazo hospital—which, in the course of the war, grew to be the largest hospital complex in the world.

Civil War Visitor Center at Tredegar Iron Works: In addition to offering visitor center services, three floors of exhibits and artifacts are on display.

Cold Harbor Battlefield Visitor Center: Features visitor center services, exhibits and artifacts, and a five-minute electric map program describing the 1864 battle of Cold Harbor.

Fort Harrison Visitor Center: On September 29, 1864, a dawn assault by 3,000 Union infantry captured Fort Harrison. A self-guided historical walking trail begins at this center. Each year, on the anniversary of the battle of Fort Harrison, there is a living history demonstration.

Glendale/Malvern Hill Battlefields Visitor Center: Near the anniversary of the Seven Days' Battles at Malvern Hill, there is a living history encampment with artillery demonstrations and walking tours.

Shiloh National Military Park, Shiloh, Tennessee
(http://www.nps.gov/shil)
Established in 1894 to preserve the scene of the first major battle in the Western Theater of the Civil War, the park contains about 4,000 acres and includes the *Shiloh National Cemetery*, in which 3,500 Union soldiers are buried.

Stones River National Battlefield, Murfreesboro, Tennessee
(http://www.nps.gov/stri)
Site of a fierce battle December 31, 1862–January 2, 1863, the 570-acre National Battlefield includes *Stones River National Cemetery*, established in 1865, with more than 6,000 Union graves; and the Hazen Monument, believed to be the oldest Civil War monument. Portions of Fortress Rosecrans, a large earthen fort constructed after the battle, still stand and are preserved and interpreted by the National Park Service. Much of the nearly 4,000-acre battlefield is in private hands.

Tupelo National Battlefield, Tupelo, Mississippi
(http://www.nps.gov/tupe)
The battle of Tupelo, which was a part of a larger strategy by General William T. Sherman to protect the railroad that was his supply line, broke out on July 14, 1864, when Federal troops under General A. J. Smith battled Confederates under Nathan Bedford Forrest.

Ulysses S. Grant National Historic Site, St. Louis, Missouri
(http://www.nps.gov/ulsg)
This site commemorates the life, military career, and presidency of Ulysses S. Grant. Also known as White Haven, the site consists of 9.65

acres holding five historic structures: the main house (home of Grant and Julia Dent Grant), a stone building, a barn, a chicken house, and an ice house.

Vicksburg National Military Park, Vicksburg, Mississippi
(http://www.nps.gov/vick)
Established February 21, 1899, to commemorate one of the most decisive campaigns of the American Civil War—the months of battles and the final Union siege of the Confederacy's last great bastion on the Mississippi River—Vicksburg National Military Park is one of the more densely monumented battlefields in the world. The park contains 661 monuments, 594 cast-iron tablets and position markers, seventy bronze castings, 141 cannon and carriages, fifteen bridges, six buildings, and an ironclad river gunboat (city class), the U.S.S. *Cairo*. The U.S.S. *Cairo* Museum houses a variety of military and personal artifacts that were salvaged with the gunboat. Exhibits in the park's visitor center include material on what life was like for both sides during the siege, when many Vicksburg civilians lived in caves to escape the shelling. In the summer, there are Living History demonstrations. The *Vicksburg National Cemetery*, also in the park, embraces 116 acres and is the final resting place of 17,000 Union soldiers—more than in any other national cemetery; 75 percent of those interred are listed as unidentified.

Wilson's Creek National Battlefield, Republic, Missouri
(http://www.nps.gov/wicr)
Site of the first major Civil War engagement west of the Mississippi River, August 10, 1861, the 1,750-acre battlefield has changed little since the Civil War. In addition to battle-related exhibits, the Wilson's Creek visitor center houses the John K. and Ruth Hulston Civil War Research Library, comprising some 4,000 volumes concentrating on the Civil War period and the Civil War in the Trans-Mississippi Theater. The collection is noncirculating, but is available for use by serious scholars, by appointment.

Organizations: Battlefield Preservation

American Battlefield Protection Program (http://www2.cr.nps.gov/abpp)
e-mail: hps-info@nps.gov
The American Battlefield Protection Program (ABPP) promotes the preservation of significant historic battlefields associated with wars on

American soil. Focusing primarily on land use, cultural resource and site management planning, as well as public education, the ABPP encourages states, communities, nonprofit organizations, and individual citizens to become the stewards of significant historic battlefields. (In the year 2001, ABPP statistics showed that seventy-one of the nation's most significant Civil War battlefields had been lost; another fifty required urgent preservation.)

Included in the information available on the ABPP Web site is the full text of the *Civil War Sites Advisory Commission Report on the Nation's Civil War Battlefields*. Established in 1991, the commission was charged with identifying significant Civil War sites, determining their condition, assessing threats to their integrity, and offering alternatives for their preservation and interpretation.

The Civil War Preservation Trust (http://www.civilwar.org)
Formed in November 1999 by the merger of two of the nation's oldest and most successful historic preservation organizations, the Civil War Trust and the Association for the Preservation of Civil War Sites (APCWS), the Civil War Preservation Trust is now the largest battlefield preservation organization in the United States. The organization's 40,000 members promote preservation of Civil War battlefields. The Trust is committed to public education as an essential ingredient of preservation and is working with the National Park Service, the History Channel, and other organizations, in the development of educational programs. The Civil War Discovery Trail is a heritage tourism initiative that links more than 500 Civil War sites in twenty-eight states and promotes visits through themed itineraries. A traveling panel exhibit explores the experiences and memories of the Civil War through the words and images of those who experienced it.

The Conservation Fund (http://www.conservationfund.org)
Established to protect America's legacy of land and water resources, the Conservation Fund has established a Civil War Battlefield Campaign. Working in partnerships, the Campaign provides comprehensive and concise information on the 384 principal Civil War battlefields designated by the Civil War Sites Advisory Commission and promotes appreciation for Civil War history. Two Conservation Fund publications are devoted to the Civil War: *Dollar$ and Sense of Battlefield Preservation: the Economic Benefits of Protecting Civil War Battlefields*, a practical guide to

preservation initiatives (available from the National Trust for Historic Preservation at www.nthp.org); and *The Civil War Battlefield Guide* (1990, 1998), a guide to all the 384 principal battles designated in the Civil War Sites Advisory Commission Report. Proceeds from the sale of the guide are dedicated to battlefield preservation.

Civil War Soldiers and Sailors

Among the most personal links between Americans of today and the people of the Civil War era are the records of Civil War soldiers and sailors. Service and pension records housed in the National Archives and Records Administration in Washington—as well as in state archives, libraries, and historical societies—provide vital keys to the wartime experiences of the millions of people who served in the Union and Confederate forces.

The National Park Service, in cooperation with public and private partners, has established a computerized database that will provide easy access to basic information on Civil War military personnel. Still in its developmental stages as the twenty-first century began, the *Civil War Soldiers and Sailors System* (http://www.itd.nps.gov/cwss) focused initially on the Names Index Project, comprising names and other basic information from 5.4 million soldier records in the National Archives, with additional information on approximately 1,200 Union soldiers and sailors who received the Medal of Honor, and prisoner records of Union prisoners at Andersonville and Confederate prisoners at Fort McHenry. As the database develops, it will also include: histories of regiments in both the Union and the Confederacy; links to descriptions of 384 significant battles of the war; and other historical information, as well as links to selected Civil War Web sites.

Organizations: Descendants of Civil War Veterans

In the aftermath of the war, a number of Civil War veterans' organizations came into being. The most extensive and powerful of the Union's veterans' organizations was the Grand Army of the Republic (GAR), founded in 1866; in 1889, former Confederates formed the comparably influential United Confederate Veterans (UCV), which sponsored publication of the twelve-volume *Confederate Military History* (1899). Similar organizations, formed in the decades after the war, include, for Union veterans: the Military Order of the Loyal Legion of the United States (MOLLUS), Dames of the Loyal Legion, the Union Veterans' Union, and the Veteran Nurses of the Civil War (later, the National Association of Nurses of the Civil War). Additional organizations, honoring those who served the Confederacy, were the United Daughters of the Confederacy and the United Sons of Confederate Veterans. Civil War veterans and their organizations had profound effects on Reconstruction and on state and national politics in the postwar period.

Today, some of the veterans' organizations founded in the postwar period, as well as descendants of those organizations, remain active. Their members celebrate the valor and sacrifice of soldiers and civilians on both sides of the conflict, assist in genealogical research, maintain research facilities, and engage in educational and promotional activities. They include:

Dames of the Loyal Legion of the United States
(http://suvcw.org/mollus/dollus/home.htm)
Organized in 1899 as an auxiliary of the Military Order of the Loyal Legion of the United States (MOLLUS; see below), Dames of the Loyal Legion of the United States (DOLLUS) comprises six state societies and a National Membership-at-Large made up of lineal and collateral female descendants of commissioned Union officers. This commemorative organization fosters certain patriotic ideals.

Daughters of Union Veterans of the Civil War 1861–1865
(http://www.duvcw.org)
With a membership comprising direct descendants of Union veterans, this organization maintains a Civil War museum at its headquarters in Springfield, Illinois. Organizational projects include Civil War battle site preservation; keeping Civil War symbolism, music, art, and literature before the public; locating the graves of Union veterans and providing suitable markers for them; and engaging in volunteer activities at veterans' medical centers, state homes, hospitals, and nursing homes.

Military Order of the Loyal Legion of the United States (MOLLUS)
(http://suvcw.org/mollus)
Established in 1865, and restricted to Union officers and their eldest male child, MOLLUS, by 1899, had a membership of some 8,000 (compared with 409,000 members of the Grand Army of the Republic—open to all ranks—in 1890). Currently open to men who are descendants of

commissioned Union officers (with some nonhereditary memberships also available), present-day objectives of the organization are "to foster military and naval science, promote allegiance to the United States government, perpetuate the memory of those who fought to preserve the unity and indivisibility of the Republic and to honor the memory and promote the ideals of President Abraham Lincoln." MOLLUS publishes the *Loyal Legion Historical Journal* and maintains a War Library and Museum at its Philadelphia headquarters.

Military Order of the Stars & Bars (http://scv.org/mosb)
Membership in this organization is limited to male descendants, either lineal or collateral, of the Confederate Officer Corps; members of the Confederate Congress; or any elected or appointed member of the Executive Branch of the Confederate Government. They must be at least sixteen years old, and they must maintain active membership in the Sons of Confederate Veterans (see below). Dedicated to the preservation of Southern history, the organization sponsors literary activities and awards, including the annual Douglas Southall Freeman History Award, presented to the author of what is judged to be the "best book on a Southern theme."

Sons & Daughters of United States Colored Troops
(http://members.aol.com/sdusct)
The newest organization to honor Civil War veterans, this group is chartered by the African American Civil War Memorial Freedom Foundation (http://www.afroamcivilwar.org) and is devoted to honoring the historical legacy of those who served in the United States Colored Troops (USCT), and educating the public to the true role played by free blacks and slaves in the American Civil War. Membership is open to descendants of U.S. Colored Troops or those who "adopt" a USCT soldier. The African American Civil War Memorial (dedicated in 1997), with which the group is affiliated, maintains a museum and visitor center in northwest Washington, D.C. Visitors may view exhibits and receive assistance in searching for relatives who may have served with the USCT.

Sons of Confederate Veterans (http://scv.org/scvinfo.htm)
The direct heir of the United Confederate Veterans, and the oldest hereditary organization for male descendants of Confederate soldiers

(organized 1896), the Sons of Confederate Veterans is dedicated to preserving the history of the Southern experience in the Civil War period. Local, state, and national activities include preservation work, marking the graves of Confederate soldiers, historical reenactments, publications, and meetings devoted to the military and political history of the Civil War era. The SCV publishes a bimonthly magazine, *The Confederate Veteran.*

Sons of Union Veterans of the Civil War (http://suvcw.org)

Established in 1881 as the Sons of Veterans of the United States of America, a direct offshoot of the Grand Army of the Republic (GAR), the Sons of Union Veterans of the Civil War (SUVCW) includes over 6,000 men who are descendants of members of the GAR or of veterans eligible for membership in the GAR. Activities include graves' registration and marking, Civil War memorial registration and restoration, locating GAR and SUVCW records, and commemorative events "celebrating the deeds of the boys in blue." Sons of Veterans Reserve, the ceremonial uniformed military element of the SUVCW, participates in ceremonies, parades, living history programs, and reenactments.

United Daughters of the Confederacy (http://www.hqudc.org)

The outgrowth of many local memorial, monument, and Confederate Home Associations and auxiliaries to Camps of Confederate Veterans, the United Daughters of the Confederacy was organized in 1894 as the National Association of the Daughters of the Confederacy. Its name was changed in 1895. Its objectives include honoring the memory of Confederate veterans and those who served the Confederacy in other capacities—including the women of the South—and to preserve and mark historic Civil War sites. The Caroline Meriwether Goodlett Library, maintained by the UDC, is open to both members and nonmembers, by appointment. The *UDC Magazine* is published eleven times a year and is also available to nonmembers.

Woman's Relief Corps (http://suvcw.org/wrc.htm)

Established in 1883 as an auxiliary to the Grand Army of the Republic, the Woman's Relief Corps, which maintains headquarters and a museum in Springfield, Illinois, is a commemorative membership organization that promotes specific ideals and aims to perpetuate the memory of the Grand Army of the Republic (GAR).

Living History: Civil War Reenactment

One of the most vivid ways of preserving Civil War history and commemorating particular events is to stage reenactments. Military engagements, camp life, and civilian home life during the Civil War era are all portrayed by members of the many organizations devoted to Civil War reenactments. They are active across the country, and each has its own rules and scheduled activities. State associations and other alliances of Civil War reenactors have also been organized and facilitate coordinated living history presentations. Besides military drills, some organizations hold classes in such pursuits as Civil War cookery and nineteenth-century sewing methods. It has been estimated that some 45,000 people regularly give their time, resources, and energy to recreating a pivotal era in the nation's past. The presence of such a large cast of players has generated numerous publications and Web sites devoted to Civil War reenactments. Among them are:

Living the Memory (http://www.cw-reenactors.com)
Maintains a reenactors' mailing list and provides information on classes; Civil War-era clothing, etiquette, and cooking; and reenactment events—as well as reenactors' humor.

Civil War Shows (http://www.civilwarshows.com)
An easily searched site that maintains a large database of Civil War shows, events, and reenactments.

The Civil War Reenactors (http://www.cwreenactors.com)
Provides information on events, Civil War newspaper articles, uniforms and accoutrements, and other subjects, and provides links to related organizations.

Civil War Reenactment Organizations and Related Links
(http://suvcw.org/reenact.htm)
A page on the Sons of Union Veterans of the Civil War Web site; provides a host of links to sites listing reenactment events and organizations, as well as period sutlers (businesses that sell reenactor equipage).

Camp Chase Gazette (http://www.campchase.com)
A magazine; ten issues per year.

Civil War Courier (http://www.civilwarcourier.com); e-mail: csc1861@lcs.net
A tabloid newspaper and shopping guide.

The Civil War News (http://www.civilwarnews.com)
e-mail: mail@civilwarnews.com

A newspaper published every month but March. Provides coverage of preservation issues as well as information on reenactments, book reviews, features, and columns on collecting.

Organizations: Civil War Round Tables

In 1940, a group of men began gathering informally at the Abraham Lincoln Book Shop in downtown Chicago (still in operation today) to discuss their common interest in the American Civil War. Soon after, to formalize its activities, the group organized as the Civil War Round Table. It was the first of hundreds of Civil War Round Tables, located all around the United States (plus a few in other countries). The number of round tables—each was an autonomous organization—has ebbed and flowed over the years. After the Civil War Centennial, there were only sixty. Then, in 1968, Jerry L. Russell, a Civil War afficionado and public relations consultant from Little Rock, Arkansas, established the Civil War Round Table Associates (CWRTA) as a national umbrella group. Under Russell's leadership, the CWRTA began a national newsletter, encouraged the founding of new round tables, and, in 1975, inaugurated an annual National Congress of Civil War Round Tables. By the year 2000, Civil War Round Tables numbered more than 400. Most of these groups meet monthly for discussions, often led by Civil War scholars and historians. They organize battlefield tours and participate in preservation-related projects. Information on Civil War Round Tables can be secured by writing to: CWRTA, P.O. Box 7388, Little Rock, Arkansas, 72217.

Civil War Continuing Education Programs

A major aspect of every school's American History curriculum, the Civil War is also studied outside the general educational system by thousands of people who attend conferences and symposia, take battlefield tours, and register for courses at Civil War institutes. Many commercial tour businesses offer regular Civil War battlefield and historical-site tours, some of which are guided by Civil War experts. State historical societies, university summer schools, continuing education programs, and museums offer Civil War programs. Some examples of Civil War continuing education resources are listed here:

American Civil War Institute, Campbellsville University, Kentucky (http://www.campbellsvil.edu)
Established in 1996, the Institute is both an academic and a public relations arm of Campbellsville University. Its programs, chiefly symposia, emphasize the Western Theater of the Civil War.

American Military University, Manassas Park, Virginia
(http://www.amunet.edu)
An accredited private university specializing in military studies through distance learning, the American Military University offers a Master in Military Studies degree in Civil War Studies.

Blue and Gray Education Society
(http://www.blue-and-gray-education.org)
Offers seminars and battlefield visits conducted by historians, as well as a series of commissioned scholarly monographs.

The Civil War Institute at Carroll College, Waukesha, Wisconsin
(http://carroll1.cc.edu/civilwar/)
Established in 1995—to call attention to the college's 5,000-item W. Norman FitzGerald collection of Civil War materials—the Institute for Civil War Studies offers a Certificate of Civil War Studies educational and enrichment program. Some courses are offered online. Carroll College itself was chartered in 1846.

George Tyler Moore Center for the Study of the Civil War (Shepherd College)
(http://www.shepherd.wvnet.edu/gtmcweb/cwcenter.htm)
Growing out of Shepherd College's involvement as a "keeper of the standards" for the National Park Service's *Civil War Soldiers System* database, the George Tyler Moore Center for the Study of the Civil War, in Shepherdstown, West Virginia, was established to promote scholarly research of the war through the development of a comprehensive database on Civil War soldiers, through publications and educational programs. The center sponsors the Civil War & American Society Seminar Series.

Civil War Education Association, Winchester, Virginia
(http://www.winchesteronline.com/cwea.html)
e-mail: cwea@mnsinc.com
The association offers a comprehensive program of seminars, symposia, and tours featuring leading Civil War experts.

Civil War Era Center (The Pennsylvania State University)
(http://www3.la.psu.edu/histrlst/inst/welcome.html)
The center has both scholarly and public-education objectives. It stimulates work on the Civil War through editing the leading journal on the Civil War era, *Civil War Journal,* and sponsoring graduate work with

fellowships. For the public, the center offers a lecture series, two battle-field tours, and an institute for public school teachers.

Civil War Institute (Gettysburg College)
(http://www.gettysburg.edu/academics/cwi)
e-mail: civilwar@gettysburg.edu
Meeting annually during the week before the anniversary of the battle of Gettysburg, the institute's goal, as expressed by its director, Gabor Boritt, is "to bring to the literate general public history that many will find irresistible and do this without abandoning solid scholarly moorings." Participants come from all walks of life and range in age from sixteen to the eighties. Speakers include the finest Civil War scholars. Battlefield tours are part of the program.

Civil War Institute (The Ohio Historical Society, Columbus)
(http://www.ohiohistory.org/about/cwi)
Established to further understanding, interest in, and study of the American Civil War and the important events that led to and resulted from that conflict, the Ohio Historical Society Civil War Institute presents educational talks and other programs on Civil War topics.

Civil War Preservation Trust (see "Organizations: Battlefield Preservation," on page 898).

Louisiana State University, United States Civil War Center (see "Major Artifact and Archival Collections," on page 877).

National Museum of Civil War Medicine (see "Major Artifact and Archival Collections," on page 877).

Pamplin Historical Park (see "Major Artifact and Archival Collections," on page 877).

Smithsonian Institution (see "Major Artifact and Archival Collections," on page 877).

University of Virginia, Center for University Programs, Charlottesville, Virginia, e-mail: uvaseminars@virginia.edu
The center presents an annual Civil War Conference featuring leading Civil War scholars, as well as other programs on Civil War themes.

Virginia Center for Civil War Studies, Virginia Polytechnic Institute and State University, Blacksburg, Virginia (http://www.civilwar.vt.edu/)

Founded in 1999 and directed by noted Civil War historians James I. Robertson Jr. and William C. Davis, the center sponsors a popular Civil War Weekend in March; a week-long "Campaigning with Lee" study tour; an annual Civil War medical symposium; and other projects devoted to increasing knowledge about the Civil War and its continuing effects.

Women and the Civil War, Inc., Smithsburg, Maryland
(http://womenandthecivilwar.org)
This organization, devoted to recognizing women's efforts in the Civil War period, presents conferences and sponsors a discussion group.

Information about Images

To order reproductions of images in this book: Note the Library of Congress negative number provided. Where no negative number exists, note the Library division and the title of the item. Duplicates may be ordered from the Library of Congress, Photoduplication Service, Washington, D.C. 20540-4570; (202) 707-5640; fax (202) 707-1771. For further information, visit the Photoduplication Service page at the Library of Congress Web site: www.loc.gov.

Chapter 1

Charleston Mercury headline	LC-USZ62-11191
The Capitol, a barracks	LC-USZ62-86311
Colonel Micah Jenkins	LC-USZ62-62493
Ironclad *Lehigh*	LC-B8184-B686
Frederick Douglass	LC-USZ62-24165
Cave Life in Vicksburg	LC-USZ62-100070
Mary J. Safford	General Collections
General Philip H. Sheridan with his senior generals	LC-B816-8085
Slow and Steady	LC-USZ62-92036
Ruins of the Gallego Flour Mills	LC-B8184-144

Chapter 2

Slaves working in the field	(a)
Alexander Stevens	LC-BH8172-1430
Slave sale ad	LC-USZ62-10293
William Lloyd Garrison	LC-USZ62-46114
"Attention Southern Men . . ."	(b)
Harriet Beecher Stowe	LC-USZ62-11212
Stephen A. Douglas	LC-USZ62-110141
John Brown	(no # or division)
Harriet Tubman	LC-USZ62-7816

Chapter 3

Lincoln Inaugural	LC-USZ62-48564
Jefferson Davis	Manuscript Division
Abraham Lincoln	LC-USP6-2415A
"A Traitor's Peace"	(b)
Susan B. Anthony	LC-USZ61-84
President Lincoln and his cabinet	LC-USZ62-3559
Jefferson Davis and his cabinet	LC-USZC4-692
Varina Davis	LC-USZ62-94980
Mary Todd Lincoln	LC-USZ62-12458

Emancipation	LC-USZ62-2573
Wanted poster for Lincoln assassins	(b)

Chapter 4

General Ulysses S. Grant examining a map	LC-B8171-0703
Stonewall Jackson and staff	LC-USZ62-14015
President Lincoln with General George B. McClellan and other officers at Antietam	LC-B817-7951
Winter campaigning near Falmouth, Virginia	LC-USZC4-2392
Gettysburg drawing	LC-USZ62-7030
General William T. Sherman	LC-B8171-3626
Wounded soldiers escaping from the burning woods of the Wilderness	LC-USZC4-1308
Surrender at Appomattox	LC-USZC4-1321
Scott's Great Snake	(c)
Title page of *Rifle and Light Infantry Tactics*	(d)
Going to the trenches	LC-USZC4-8105
The tools, and results of, military map-making	(c)
A photographer's portable darkroom	LC-B8171-2500
Observation balloon *Intrepid*	LC-B8171-2348

Chapter 5

Going into Bivouac at Night	LC-USZC4-2058
Famous Union commanders of the Civil War	LC-USZC4-1729
Famous Confederate commanders of the Civil War	LC-USZC4-996
Ulysses S. Grant and his war horse, Cincinnati	LC-USZC4-4579
Robert E. Lee	LC-B8172-1

(a) Prints and Photographs Division, (b) Broadside Collection, Rare Book and Special Collections Division, (c) Geography and Map Division, (d) CSA Collection, Rare Book and Special Collections Division.

Major General Patrick R. Cleburne | LC-USZ62-107446

Major General George Armstrong
Custer, his wife, Elizabeth
Bacon Custer, and his brother
Thomas W. Custer | LC-USZ62-114798

Nathan Bedford Forrest | LC-B8171-2908x

Major General James B. McPherson | LC-B8172-6415

John Hunt Morgan | LC-USZ62-94183

Major General Emory Upton | LC-B8172-1835

Major General Joseph Wheeler | LC-B8172-1974

Negro picket at Dutch Gap Canal,
Virginia | LC-B8171-2553

Christian A. Fleetwood | LC-USZ62-44731

Ninth Massachusetts Infantry camp
near Washington, D.C. | LC-USZC4-4605

Band of the 107th U.S. Colored Infantry | LC-B8171-7861

Alan Pinkerton with President
Lincoln at Antietam, Maryland | LC-USZ6-61

Guerilla by Alfred Waud | LC-USZ61-1142

*A Woman in Battle—Michigan
Bridget—Carrying the Flag* | General Collections

Rose Greenhow and daughter | LC-USZ62-3131

*A Stormy March—Artillery—
Spotsylvania Court House* | LC-USZ62-7169

Officers of the 114th Pennsylvania
Infantry playing cards | LC-B8171-7145

Colonel Burnside's Brigade at Bull Run
by Alfred R. Waud | LC-USZC4-3129

*Meeting of Union and Rebel Pickets
in the Rappahannock* | LC-USZ62-100583

John Rodgers Meigs | LC-USZ62-120545

Chapter 6

Rows of stacked Federal rifles | LC-B8171-3229

*The Army of the Potomac—A
Sharpshooter on Picket Duty* | LC-USZ62-178

Augusta Powder Works | LC-B8184-5307

Railroad mortar at Petersburg,
Virginia | LC-B8184-10212

Supply depot at Yorktown, Virginia | LC-B8184-B82

Chapter 7

Sailors on deck of U.S.S. *Monitor* | LC-B8171-0660

Kearsarge and *Alabama* | LC-USZC4-3418

David Dixon Porter | LC-B8184-7945

John Newland Maffit | LC-USZ62-72757

David G. Farragut | LC-B813-1561

Robert Smalls and the *Planter* | LC-USZ62-117998

Atlanta | LC-B8184-5129

Raphael Semmes | LC-USZ62-23312

Six U.S. Marines at the Washington,
D.C. Navy Yard | LC-B8171-7697

John Dahlgren | LC-B8171-3417

Chapter 8

*Rebel Prisoners and Battle Flags
Captured at Chancellorsville Being
Taken to the Rear by Cavalry and
Infantry Guards* | LC-USZC4-4409

Three Confederate prisoners,
Gettysburg, Pennsylvania | LC-B8171-2288

Camp Douglas | LC-B8184-10180

Libby Prison, Richmond, Virginia | LC-B8171-7557

Map of Andersonville, Georgia | LC-USZC4-1332

Sultana | LC-USZ62-48778

Chapter 9

Patients in ward of Harewood Hospital | LC-B8171-1008

Zouaves and officers at an ambulance | LC-B8171-7636

The Floating Hospital of the Mississippi | LC-USZ62-97261

Nurses and officers of the
U.S. Sanitary Commission | LC-B8171-0741

Clara Barton | LC-USZ62-19319

Felicia Grundy Porter | LC-USZ6-1335

Chapter 10

Confederate States of America $100 bill | LC-USZ62-15585

Group of freed slaves in front of
buildings on Smith's Plantation,
Beaufort, South Carolina | LC-USZ62-67819

Page 58 from *The Confederate
Spelling Book* | PE1144.S67

*Offering of the Bells to be Cast into
Cannon* by Adalbert Volck | LC-USZ62-100062

"The Union Must be Preserved . . ." | (b)

Headquarters of the Christian
Commission in Washington, D.C. | LC-B8171-7720

*Filling Cartridges at the United States
Arsenal at Watertown, Massachusetts* | LC-USZ62-2581

Southern refugees preparing to flee
the path of advancing Northern
armies | LC-B8171-306

Chapter 11

The devastation of Richmond, Virginia | LC-B8171-7110

Thaddeus Stevens | LC-USZ62-15441

Five generations on Smith's Plantation,
Beaufort, South Carolina | LC-B8171-152-A

Andrew Johnson | LC-USZ62-67402

The Freedmen's Bureau | LC-USZ62-18090

Distinguished Colored Men | LC-USZC4-1561

James Longstreet | LC-B8172-2014

Time Works Wonders | LC-USZ62-108004

Chapter 12

Sheridan's Ride | LC-USZC2-500

Mathew B. Brady | LC-BH827-2102

Ulysses S. Grant | LC-USZ62-90934

Robert E. Lee | LC-USZ62-15588

Alfred R. Waud at work as
depicted by Winslow Homer | LC-USZ62-39448

Sculpture memorial to Robert Gould
Shaw and the Fifty-Fourth
Massachusetts Regiment of
African American troops | LC-D4-90156

Walt Whitman | LC-BH82-137

Our National Confederate Anthem | LC-USZ62-33407

Theater poster for *Uncle Tom's Cabin* | LC-USZC2-660

INDEX

Note: Bold page numbers refer to principal treatment of a subject; italic page numbers refer to illustrations.

Abolitionist movement, 2, 86–87, **94–98,** *105*

Ackworth's Station, Georgia, 294

Adams, Charles Francis, 25, 62, **186–87,** 203, 551, 790

Adams, Henry, 750, 796

Adams, John, 79, 186, 317

Adams, John Quincy, 59, 79, 186

Aeronautics/observation balloons, 346, **362–65,** *363,* 438, 525

African American Civil War Memorial: Spirit of Freedom, 835, 902

African American(s), 11, 12, 13, 26, 50, 412, 462; *see also* Contrabands; Freedmen; Slave(s); Slavery
  aid societies, 700
  in army, *see* African American soldiers
  Boston African American National Historic Site, **889**
  civil rights, pressure for, 139, 426
  colonization for freed slaves, 21, 58, 120, 129, 130, 148, 172, **215–16,** 727
  conventions, 44, 737, 741, 790
  demonstrations against, 27
  discrimination/segregation, 104, **218–19, 678–79**
  emancipation, pressure for, 139
  first Civil War military hero, 407–8
  first Medal of Honor recipient, 482
  first to argue before Supreme Court, 47–48, 190
  franchise, 35, 37, 87, 156, **217, 757–58,** 762
  free blacks, antebellum America, **103–4,** 143
  government laborers, 432
  in government positions, 190, 741, 782
  land and, 750–52
  leaders, 46, 150, *780*
  National Equal Rights League, **167–68**
  nuns, 684
  nurses, 660
  pay, 32, 39, 434
  press, **219**
  publications about, **867–69**
  racial rioting, 719–20, 738
  during Reconstruction, **747–50**
    civil rights, 756–57
    religion/churches, 747–48
  refugees, 724, 762
  religion/churches, 84
  replacing Irish dockworkers, 719
  schools/colleges, 88, 89, 682, 749
  securing rights in North, 139, **216–20,** 426
  segregation, *see* discrimination
  suffrage, 757–58
  women hired as hospital cooks/ nurses, 707
  YMCA unit for, 135

African American soldiers, 7, 30, 31, 34, 49, 175–76, 193, **219–20,** 281, 328, 372, **427–38,** *428, 435,* 602, 603, 700, 890
  aid societies, 700
  captured/prisoner exchange, 37, 154, 585, 597, 598, 599, 602
  chronological perspective:
    1861–1862 ("early struggles"), **427–30**
    1863 ("pivotal year"), **430–34**
    1864 ("accomplishments and tragedies), **434–37**
    1865– ("peace and continuing struggle for recognition"), **437–38**
  in Confederate army, 35, 49, 155, 158
  as cooks in army, 212, 642
  in inaugural parade, 715
  medical care, **637–38,** 660
  memorials, 831, **835,** 889
  pay, 156, 432, 709
  recruitment, 130, 335–36, **693–94**
  selected sickness/mortality statistics, 649
  success/acceptance of, 276
  targeted by Confederate forces, 37, 42, 298–99, 312, 315–16
  Union, 154
  veterans, 374
  wives of, 707

African Methodist Episcopal (A.M.E.) Church, 84, 748

African religions, 83

African Squadron (U.S. Navy), 94

Agamenticus, (U.S.S.) 558

Agriculture, 2, 28, 74–75, *74, 76,* 134, **673–76,** 707

Aid societies, *see* Volunteer aid societies

Aiken's Landing, 621
Akerman, Amos, 786
Alabama:
    during Reconstruction, 742
    population (1860), 666
    prisons/prison camps in, 592, 608,
        621
    readmitted, 740, 793
    secession, 3, 5, 67, 160
    Streight's raid in Northern, **279**
    wartime governors, 200
    see also Mobile, Alabama;
        Montgomery, Alabama;
        Selma, Alabama
Alabama (C.S.S.), 22, 39, 40, 203,
    340, 528, 531, *535*, 551, 563,
    564, 575, 579–80
Alabama Claims Commission, 203,
    564
Alamo, 584
Alaska (purchase from Russia), 740
Albany Penitentiary (New York)
    military prison, 590
Albatross (U.S.S.), 532
Albemarle (C.S.S.), 534, 536, 553,
    562–63, 568, 575
Alcohol/drinking, 469–70
Alcott, Louisa May, 658, **659,** 710
Alexander, Archer, 835
Alexander, Edward Porter, 339, 359,
    360, 395, 692–93
Alexandria, Louisiana, 298, 534
Alexandria, Virginia, 8, 350
Allatoona Pass, 360
Allegheny City Penitentiary
    (Pittsburgh) military prison,
    591
Allen, E. J. (alias), *see* Pinkerton,
    Allan
Allen, Ezra, 364
Allen, Henry, 200
Allen, James, 364
Alligator (U.S. submarine), 565
Allison, Alexander, 809
Alston, William, 679
Alton Prison (Illinois military
    prison), 588, **604,** 616
Amana Society, 83, 696
Ambulances, 22, 625, **631–34,** *632,*
    655, 663

Amendments, *see* United States
    Constitution
American Anti-Slavery Society, 59,
    87, **119–20,** 132, 133, 217,
    757
American Baptist Home Missionary
    Society, 87
American Battlefield Preservation/
    Protection Program, 239,
    898–99
American Bible Society, 85
American Civil War Institute, 905
American Colonization Society
    (ACS), 58, **120,** 129, 215
American Diver (C.S.S. submarine),
    565
American Freedmen's Aid
    Commission, 700
American Freedmen's Inquiry
    Commission, 27, 736
American Freedmen's Union
    Commission, 755
American Indians, 161, 177, 339,
    587, 665, 709, 744, 789
American Military University, 906
American Missionary Association,
    95, 682, 754, 755, 797
American Missionary Society, 725
American Party (Know-Nothings),
    63, 66, 73, **120–21,** 123, 726
American Red Cross, 659, 890
American Telegraph Company, 355,
    357
American Temperance Society, 86
American Tract Society, 85
Americus (Georgia) military prison,
    592
Ames, Adelbert, 742, 787
Ames Manufacturing Company, 501
Amnesty, 35, 51, 155, 159, 184, 189,
    190
Amputation, 630, **634–35**
Anaconda Plan, 8, 334, *335,* 336,
    404, 548
Anderson, "Bloody Bill," 43–44,
    450
Anderson, Richard H., 398
Anderson, Robert, 4, 6, 67, 143,
    242, 243
Andersonville (novel), 839

Andersonville Prison (Georgia), 36,
    585, **593,** 598, 599, 600, 605,
    608, **609,** 611, 615, 618, 659,
    888; *see also* Camp Sumter
Andrew, James O., 87, 440
Andrew, John Albion, 192, 198, 434
Andrews, Mary Raymond Shipman,
    842
Anesthesia, 626
"Angel of the Battlefield," *see*
    Barton, Clara
Anglo-African newspaper, 11, 145,
    215, 219
Antebellum America, **53–138**
    census table (1860), 70–71
    compromise and crisis, **106–19**
    Compromise of 1850, **109–11**
    constitutional problem, **55–57**
    demographics, **69–71**
    differences, North *vs.* South,
        69–90
    economic growth, **73–76**
    education and culture, **88–90**
    election of 1860, **124–27**
    Harpers Ferry and John Brown,
        118–19
    immigration, **72–73**
    Kansas-Nebraska Act, **111–13**
    largest U.S. cities (1860), **72**
    Lincoln-Douglas debates, **115–18**
    Manifest Destiny, **92–93**
    map of 1861 United States, *69*
    Mexican War (1846–1848),
        108–9
    Missouri Compromise, **106–7**
    notable figures, 127–37
    nullification crisis, **107–8**
    political parties and
        organizations, **119–24**
    religion and reform, **81–87**
    slavery, *see* Slave(s); Slavery
        history of, in America, **77–81**
        principal slave crops (map), *74*
        slave distribution in 1860
            (map), *81*
        slavery issues, **93–106**
    states' rights, **90–92**
    time line (1777–1861), 57–68
    widening rift, **90–106**
    see also Scott v. Sanford

Anthony, Susan B., 86, 168, *168*, 769

Antietam (Sharpsburg, Maryland) campaign, 23, 24, 181, 212, 237, **265–69**, *267*, *268*, 330, 633, 644, 665, 696, 812, 814, **888**

Anti-Masonic Party, 123

Anti-Nebraska Party, 112

Anti-Semitism, 85

Antoine, Caesar C., 782

Apalachicola, Florida, 4

"Apple Pie without Apples," 671

Appomattox campaign, 50, 159, 230, **325–28**, *326*, *327*, 339, 536, 600, 603, 617, 716

Appomattox Court House National Historical Park, **888–89**

Aquia Creek, Virginia, 244

Archer (C.S.S.), 564

Arizona/Arizona Territory, 161, 249

Arkansas, 156, 452, 742, 763
   Camden Expedition, 297, 298
   military prisons in, 587
   population (1860), 666
   readmittance to Union, 740, 772, 793
   secession, 8, 144
   wartime governors, 200

Arkansas (C.S.S.), 263, 530, 531, 553, **560–61**

Arkansas Post (Fort Hindman), 531, **889**

Arkansas River, 531

Arlington House (Robert E. Lee Memorial), **889**

Arlington National Cemetery, 836

Armies, **367–484**
   Army life, 461–83
   black soldiers in Civil War, **427–38**, *428*; *see also* African American soldiers
   communications in, *see* Logistics/ communications
   land forces: general organization, 336, **374–76**
      army, **375–76**
      brigade, **375**
      company, **374**
      corps, **375**
      division, **375**
      regiment, **374–75**
   leaders:
      commanders in chief, **399–401**
      generals (Confederate), **398–99**
      generals (Union), **393–97**
      generals in chief, **401–4**
      High command (Union and Confederate), **394–95**
      notable officers (profiles), **404–26**
   military strategy, *see* Strategy; Tactics, battle
   selected resources, 483–84
   shadow warriors: partisan rangers, guerrillas, and spies, **447–61**
   special units/services, **438–47**

Armies of the Confederacy, **387–93**
   Army of Northern Virginia, **390**
   Army of Tennessee, **392**
   Army of Vicksburg, **393**
   Trans-Mississippi: District, Department, and Army, **391–92**

Armies of the United States, **376–87**
   Army of Georgia, **386–87**
   Army of Northeastern Virginia, **379**
   Army of the Cumberland, **383–84**
   Army of the Frontier, **382**
   Army of the James, **385–86**
   Army of the Mississippi, **380–81**
   Army of the Ohio, **384–85**
   Army of the Potomac, **379–80**
   Army of the Shenandoah, **386**
   Army of the Southwest (Army of Southwest Missouri), **380**
   Army of the Tennessee, **382–83**
   Army of Virginia, **381–82**

Armstrong, James L., 544

"Armstrong mills" (grater), 471

Armstrong's Mill, 321

Army Medical Bureau, 17

Army Medical Museum, 655

Army organization, *see* Armies, land forces, general organization

Arnold, Samuel, 232

Arrears Act of 1879, 745

Arrowfield Church, 299

Arsenal(s):
   defined, 514
   women working in, 705
   see also Weaponry

Arsenal Monument, **834**

Arsenal Penitentiary (Washington, D.C.) military prison, 232, 588

Artifact/archival collections, **877–87**

Artillery, *see* Weaponry

Arts/literature, Civil War in, **805–58**
   artist-correspondents and soldier-artists, **820–26**
   artists of Civil War-era, **828–30**
   drama (stage/screen/television), **853–57**
   illustrated journals, **819–20**
   illustrated newspapers, **816–26**
   music, **849–53**
   novels about Civil War, **836–42**
      nineteenth-century, **837–39**
      twentieth-century, **839–42**
   paintings, **826–30**
   photographers of Civil War-era, **813–16**
   photography, **811–16**
   poetry, **843–49**
   popular art, **806–11**
   sculpture, **830–36**
      Richmond, Virginia, **832–34**
      Washington, D.C., **834–36**

Ashmun Institute, 89

Association for the Preservation of Civil War Sites (APCWS), **899**

Association for the Relief of Maimed Soldiers, **662**

Atheneum Prison (West Virginia) military prison, 592

Atkinson's Factory (Virginia) military prison, 594

Atlanta, 51, 353, 545

Atlanta campaign (1864), 38, 40, 42, 43, 48, 140, 236, 237, 293, 294, **299–304**, 336–37, 348, 349, 351, 798
   battle maps, *300*, *303*
   Kennesaw Mountain, *301*, **894**

Atlanta (C.S.S./U.S.S.), 528, 533, **553–54,** *554,* 556, 558, **562**
Atlantic Blockading Squadron, 549
Atlantic Monthly, 682, 727, 843, 844
Attorneys general:
  C.S.A., **185–86**
  U.S.A., **177–78**
Atzerodt, George, 232
Augusta, A. T., 679
Augusta Chronicle, 228
Augusta (Georgia) military prison, 592
Augusta Powder Works, *503,* 512
Averasboro/Averasborough, 49, 324
Avery Normal Institute, 797
Ayers and Wade (Richmond, Virginia), **809–10,** 820

Babcock, John C., **456–57**
Bacon, Henry, 835
Bailey, Gamaliel, 727
Bailey, George W., 818
Bailey, Theodorus, 545, 551
Bairstow, Ernest C., 835
Baker, Edward D., 12, 248
Baker, Lafayette C., 454, **457**
Ball, Thomas, 835
Balloons, observation, 346, **362–65,** *363,* 438, 525
Ball's Bluff, Virginia, 12, *248*
Baltimore, 6, 8, 543
Baltimore and Ohio Railroad, 791
Baltimore City Jail (Maryland) military prison, 589
Bancroft, George, 214
Banks/banking, 26, 91, 107
Banks, Nathaniel Prentiss, 38, 264, 281, 296, 298, *378,* 382, 392, 397, **404,** 410, 424, 429, 473, 489, 534, 736, 761
Baptists, 61, 82, 85, 95, 440, 685, 687
Barnard, George N., 295, 812, **813**
Barnburners, 122
Barnes, Joseph K., 653, **654**
Barnum, Phineas T., 746, 816
Barnwell ("Burnwell"), South Carolina, 324
Baron de Kalb (ship), 559

Barrett, Theodore H., 328
Barrett's Factory (Virginia) military prison, 594
Barron, Samuel, 541, 545
Bartlett, Napier, 464
Barton, Clara, 22, **659,** *659,* 660, 706, 746, **890,** 893
Bassett, E. D., *780–81*
Bates, Edward, *171,* **177,** 436
Baton Rouge, Louisiana, 196, 531, 593, 721, 723
Battalion, 375
Battery, 514
Battery Wagner, *see* Fort Wagner
Battle(s), **233–366**
  aftermath (perspective of soldier), **472–74**
  descriptions of significant campaigns/battles (in chronological order), **239–332**
    in 1861, 242–49
    in 1862, 249–74
    in 1863, 274–93
    in 1864, 293–320
    in 1865, 320–32
  major land battles (map), *240–41*
  major naval battles (map), *526–27*
  theaters of war/operation, **236–39**
    definitions, 236
    Eastern Theater, **236–37**
    Lower Seaboard and Gulf Approach, **239**
    map, *238*
    Trans-Mississippi Theater, **237–40**
    Western Theater, **237**
  see also Casualties; specific battle; strategy; Tactics, battle
Battle Cry of Freedom (song), 850
Battlefield(s):
  guides to, **873–74**
  national historic sites, **887–98**
  preservation organizations, **898–900**
Battlefield National Cemetery, Washington D.C., **889**

"Battle Hymn of the Republic" (poem), 843, 849
Baumgarten, Julius, 482
Baxter, Sydney S., 15
Bayonet, 514
Bayou Teche, Louisiana, 531
Bazely (U.S.S.), 536
Beall, Lloyd J., 542
Beardslee telegraphic device, 354
Beatty, John, 447, 468, 479
Beaufort, South Carolina, 543, 751
Beauregard, P.G.T. (Pierre Gustave Toutant), 9, 19, 20, *388,* 390, 399, **404–5,** 566, 624
  battle overviews, 237, 243, 247, 252, 253, 254, 269, 299, 311, 337, 339, 355
Bee, Barnard, 9, 247, 360
Beecher, Catharine Esther, **127**
Beecher, Charles, **128**
Beecher, Edward, **127**
Beecher, Harriet Elizabeth, *see* Stowe, Harriet Beecher
Beecher, Henry Ward, 112–13, **128,** 689
Beecher, Lyman, **127**
Beecher, Thomas Kinnicut, **128**
Bell, Charles H., 544
Bell, John, 66, 121, 126, 127
Belle Isle (Virginia) military prison, 594, **611,** 621
Bellew, Frank, 806
Bellows, Henry Whitney, **654,** 661
Belmont, Missouri, **248–49**
Benét, Stephen Vincent, **845**
Benjamin, Judah P., 36, *179,* 180, **182, 183–84, 185,** 394
Benton (U.S. gunboat), **559**
Benton, Thomas Hart, 109
Benton Barracks (St. Louis) military prison, 589
Bentonville, Arkansas, 49, 255, 324
Berdan Sharpshooters, 494
Berea College, 755
Berkeley, William N., 471
Bermuda Hundred campaign, 38, **299**
Berrien, John M., 544
Berry, Hiram G., 278
Berry, Nathaniel, 198

Bethesda Church, Virginia, 308
Bickerdyke, Mary Ann, **659,** 746
Biddle, Nicholas, 427
Bienville (U.S. ship), 575
Bierce, Ambrose, 838–39
Big Black River Bridge, Mississippi, 30
Bigelow, John, **188**
Bingham, John Armor, 769, 773, **797**
Birney, James G., 61, 122
Black Codes, 218, 738, 754, 756, 765, **766–67,** 777, 793
Blackford, Charles Minor, 21
Blacknall, C. C., 389
Blackshear (Georgia) military prison, 592, 610
Black soldiers, *see* African American(s); African American soldiers
Black Thursday, 326
Blackwell, Elizabeth, 7, 654, 658
Blackwell, Emily, 658
Blackwell, Lucy Stone, 168
Blair, Austin, 198
Blair, Montgomery, *171,* **176,** 188, 711
Blake, George S., 540
Blakely Gun, 514
Blanton Duncan, **810**
Blasdel, Henry Goode, 198
Blelock & Company (New Orleans), **810–11**
Bliss, Alexander, 214
Blockade/blockade running, 51, 143, 153, 172, 176–77, 202, 237, 276, 489, **543–52,** 651, 670, 680
British presence in Naval war, **551–52**
map, *549*
operational organization of, 548–50
squadron commanders, 550–51
Bloody Angle, 307, 308, 342
Blow, Peter, 113, 115
Blue and Gray Education Society, 906
Bluestone Church, 84
Blunt, James G., 271, 382

Bombshell (U.S.S./C.S.S.), 534
Bomefree, Isabella, *see* Truth, Sojourner
Bonds, 26, 672
Bonham, Milledge Luke, 201
Bonnie Blue Flag, The (song), 850
Booth, Edwin, 855
Booth, John Wilkes, 50, 159, 174, 230, *231,* 320, 515, 715, 797, 855, 891
Boreman, Arthur, 199
Boston African American National Historic Site, 889
Boston Yard, 544
Botanico-Medical College (Memphis) military prison, 594
Bounty jumping, 463–64, 478
Bowditch, Henry, 633
Bowser, Mary Elizabeth, 460
Boyd Belle, **457–58,** 703
Bradford, Augustus, 194, 198
Bradford, William F., 37, 298
Brady, Mathew B., 439, 706, 805, 810, 812, **813,** 814, **815,** *815,* 816
Bragg, Braxton, 20, 21, 24, 25, 30, 32, 33, 34, 35, 40, 185, 370, 384, *388,* 392, 399, **405,** 406, 420
battle overviews, 237, 251, 263, 264, 269, 274, 287, 289, 292, 338, 339, 352, 356
Bragg, Thomas, **185–86**
Bramlette, Thomas, 197
Brandy Station, Virginia, 30, 282
Brawner's Farm, Virginia, 264
Breckinridge, John C., 66, 121, 122, 125, 127, **184,** 262, 319, *388,* 394
Breese, Samuel L., 544
Brenisholtz, Samantha French, 354
Brent, Thomas W., 546
Brice's Cross Roads/Station, Mississippi, 41, **310,** 436, **890**
Bridge, Horatio, 539
Bridge Prison, Jackson (Mississippi) military prison, 593
Brigade, **375**
Bristow, Benjamin, 786

Britain, 8, 12, 19, 23, 33, 49, 62, 75, 77, 91, 93, 94, 97, 111, 131, 137, 141, 144, 147, 151, 177, 182, 189, 191, 367, 393, 489, 528, 534, 537, **551–52,** 564, 579, 729; *see also* European powers and American Civil War
Broadsides, 844
Brock Road, Virginia, 304
Brooke, John M., **510,** 542
Brooklyn (U.S.S.), 9
Brooks, Noah, 715
Brooks, Preston S., 64
Brough, John, 167, 199
Brown, George, 532
Brown, Henry ("Box"), 102
Brown, Isaac N., 547
Brown, John, 64, 65–66, 113, **118–19,** *118,* 129, 136, 423, 450, 845, 855, 894; *see also* Harpers Ferry
Brown, Joseph E., 169, 181, 195, 200, 228, 671
Brown, William G., 783
Brown, William Wells, *780–81*
Brown, William Young, 439
Browne, William M., **182**
Brownell, Kady, 445–46
Browning, Orville H., 5
Brownlow, William "Parson," 201, 227, 785, 839
Brownsville, Texas, 239, 330
Bruce, Blanche K., *780–81,* **797**
Bryan, John R., 364–65
Bryant, William Cullen, 746
Buchanan, Franklin, 313, 328, 529, 541, 545, **574–75**
Buchanan, James, 3, 4, 64, 65, 92, 112, 113, 114, 123, 124, 126, **128,** 524, 885
Buck and ball, 514
Buckingham, William Alfred, 192, 197
Buckner, Simon Bolivar, 14, 391, 398, 891
Buell, Don Carlos, 242, 252, 254, 263–64, 338, 384, 397, **405–6**
Buford, John, 31, 496
Bulloch, James Dunwoody, 189, 563, **575**

Bullock, Rufus B., 741, 779
Bull Run (Manassas):
    1861: 9, 10, 12, 37, 146, 233, 235,
        237, 244, **246–47**, *246*, 334,
        337, 352, 355, 363, *472*, 600,
        621, 686, 712, 812
    1862: 181, 237, **264–65**, *265*,
        330, 331, 631
    Manassas National Battlefield
        Park, **895**
Burbridge, Stephen G., 315
Bureau of Colored Troops, 30,
    431
Bureau of Refugees, Freedmen,
    and Abandoned Lands, *see*
    Freedmen's Bureau
Burials (of soldiers), 712–13
Burke, Emily, 54–55
Burns, Anthony, 63
Burns, Ken, 856
Burnside, Ambrose Everett, 26, 28,
    32, 167, 208, 228, *378*, 379,
    384, 397, **406–7**,–436, 457, *472*,
    528, 567
    battle overviews, 236, **251**, 268,
        271, 274, 291–92, 306, 311,
        312
Burton, James H., 485–86, **510–11**
Burton, William, 197
Bushnell, David, 565
Bushnell, Horace, 686
Bushwackers, 17, 237, 271, 289, 450;
    see also Quantrill, William C.
Butler, Andrew P., 64
Butler, Benjamin Franklin, 8,
    18–19, 38, 40, 358, *378*, 385,
    397, **407**, 429, 536, **619**, 659,
    724
    battle overviews, 247, 262, 299,
        321, 364
    nicknames, 407
    prisons/prisoners of war, 596,
        598, 599, 602, 603, **619**, 620
    Reconstruction, 731, 735, 736,
        759, 761, 773, 774
    wartime politics, 144, 146, 148,
        149
Butler, Pierce, 710, 728–29
Butterfield, Daniel, 354, 852
Butternuts, 166

Cabinet members:
    Confederate, *179*
        navy, 185, **394**
        state, **181–82**
        treasury, **182–83**
        war, 183–84, **394**
    United States:
        interior, **177**
        navy, **176–77**, 394
        state, **174**
        treasury, **174**
        war, **175–76**, 394
Cable, George Washington, 262,
    839
Cadwalader, George, 144
Cahaba (Castle Morgan, Alabama)
    military prison, 592, **608**, 618
Cailloux, André, 407–8, 432
Cairo, Illinois, 34, 543, 553
Cairo (U.S.S.), 531, **558**, 559, 568,
    898
Caisson, 514
Calahan, Thomas, 724
Caldwell, Susan Emiline Jeffords,
    704, 705
Caleb Cushing (U.S.S.), 564
Calhoun, A. R., 854
Calhoun, John C., 91, 105, 107,
    109, **128–29**, 133
Caliber, 514
California, 62, 109, 128, 665, 790,
    877
    military prisons in, 587
    wartime governors, 197
Camanche (U.S.S.), 556
Camden Expedition (Arkansas),
    297, 298
Cameron, Simon, 146, *171*, **175**,
    354, 371, 394
Campaigns/battles, significant:
    descriptions, in chronological
        order, **239–332**; *see also*
        specific battle
    in 1861, 242–49
    in 1862, 249–74
    in 1863, 274–93
    in 1864, 293–320
    in 1865, 320–32
    map of major land battles,
        240–41

Camp Asylum (North Carolina)
    military prison, 593
Campbell, Albert H., 347
Campbell, John A., 48, 158, 159
Camp Butler (Illinois) military
    prison, 588
Camp Cass, Virginia, 439
Camp Chase (Ohio) military prison,
    591, **607**, 620
Camp Chase *Gazette*, 904
Camp Davidson (Georgia) military
    prison, 592
Camp Dennison (Ohio) military
    prison, 591
Camp Douglas (Illinois) military
    prison, 588, **605**, *605*, 606
Camp Fisk (Mississippi) military
    prison, 608, 617–18
Camp Ford (Texas) military prison,
    594, 600, **611**
Camp Groce (Texas) military
    prison, 594
Camp Hoffman (Point Lookout,
    Maryland) military prison, 589,
    606
Camp Lawton (Georgia) military
    prison, 592, **610**
Camp Liendo (Texas) military
    prison, 594
Camp Morton (Indiana) military
    prison, 588, **606**, 616, 620
Camp Oglethorpe (Georgia)
    military prison, 593, **610**
Camp Randall (Wisconsin) military
    prison, 592
Camp Sorghum (North Carolina)
    military prison, 593
Camp Sumter (Andersonville,
    Georgia), 36, 585, 593; *see also*
    Andersonville Prison (Georgia)
Camp Van Dorn (Texas) military
    prison, 594
Camp Verde (Texas) military prison,
    594
Canada, 36, 39, 42, 43, 667
Canby, E. R. S., 249, 328, 437
Canister, **509**, 514
Cannon, William, 197
Canonicus class monitors, **557**
Cape Hatteras, North Carolina, 531

Capitation tax clause, 56
Carbines/musketoons, **496–97,** 518
Cardozo, Francis L., 782, **797**
Cardozo, Thomas W., 783
Carnegie, Andrew, 353
Carney, Thomas, 193, 197
Carney, William, 482
Carnifix Ferry, Virginia, 245
Carolina Coast, blockade (1861),
   247–48
Carolinas campaign (1865), 47,
   323–24, *323* (map)
Carondelet (U.S. ironclad), 255, 528,
   529, 558, 561
Carpetbaggers, 737, 779
Carr, Eugene A., 380
Carr, Irving J., 360
Carr, Joseph B., 244
Carriage (gun), 514–15
Carroll, Anna Ella, **726**
Carroll Prison (Washington, D.C.)
   military prison, 588
Carter, Eugene, 472
Carter, Hannibal C., 782
Carter, Henry, 819
Carter, John C., 317
Carter, Jonathan H., 546
Carthage, Missouri, battle of, **244**
Cartoons, *see* Political cartoons/
   cartoonists
Cartridge, 515
Cartwright, Samuel, 105
Cary, Constance, 702
Casco class monitors, **558**
Case shot, **508–9,** 515
Cash, John, 572–73
Castle Godwin (Virginia) military
   prison, 594
Castle Lightning (Virginia)
   military prison, 594
Castle Morgan (Cahaba, Alabama)
   military prison, 592, **608,** 618
Castle Pinckney (South Carolina)
   military prison, 593
Castle San Marcos (Florida)
   military prison, 592
Castle Thunder (Maryland) military
   prison, 589
Castle Thunder (Virginia) military
   prison, 209, 595

Castle Williams (New York)
   military prison, 590
Casualties:
   Confederate battles, 331
   first well-known, 8
   number of deaths (disease *vs.*
      battle), 623
   Union battles, 330
Catawba (U.S.S.), 557
Cater, Douglas J., 471
Cater, Rufus W., 466, 471, 475
Catholics, 82, 85, 87, 88, 440
   immigration, 73, 84–85
   parochial school system
      established, 88
   views against, 120
Catskill (U.S.S.), 556
Cavalry, **342–43,** 438
Cedar Creek, Virginia, 44, **314–15**
Cedar Mountain, Virginia, 264, 279
Celebrations, home front:
   Confederacy, **712–13**
   slaves (emancipation and), **713–14**
   Union, **714–17**
Cemetery Hill (Gettysburg),
   Pennsylvania, 282
Cemetery Ridge (Gettysburg),
   Pennsylvania, 282
Census table (1860), 70–71, 666
Central America, 93, 136
Cevor, Charles, 364
Chain shot, **509,** 515
Chamberlain, Daniel, 787, 795
Chamberlain, Joshua, 481, 841
Chambersburg, Pennsylvania, 24,
   313
Champion Hill, Mississippi, 30, 280
Chancellorsville, Virginia, 29, 146,
   237, 276, **277,** *278,* 282, 330,
   364, 490, 630, 798
Chandler, Zachariah, 146, **188**
Chaney, Josiah, 23
Chaplains, army, **438–41,** *439; see
   also* Religion
Chaplin Hills, Kentucky, 24, 263
Chapman, Conrad Wise, **828**
Charleston, South Carolina, 27, 31,
   46, 47, 48, **243,** 248, **281,** 324,
   355, 376, 532, 533
   Courier, 226

Mercury, 4, 6, 133, 157, 226, 227,
   701, 849
Morris Island, 31, 235, 281,
   506–7, 533, 591; *see also* Fort
   Wagner (Battery Wagner)
navy yard, 545
prisons, 593
Charleston (West Virginia) military
   prison, 592
Charlotte (North Carolina) military
   prison, 593
navy yard, 545
Chase, Mary, 11, 736
Chase, Salmon P., 36, 109, 111, 126,
   149, 155, *171,* **174,** 177, 607,
   672, 885
Chatham Manor, Fredericksburg,
   Virginia, **893**
Chattahoochee River, 302
Chattanooga, Tennessee, 21, 30, 32,
   33, 34–35, 276, 289, 292, 336,
   342, 352, 353, 811
Chattanooga-Ringgold campaign,
   292–93, *292* (map)
Cheatham, Benjamin F., 249, 302,
   304
Cheatham County, Tennessee,
   501
Cheat Mountain, Virginia,
   245–46
Cheeves, Langdon, 364
Cherbourg Harbor, France, 40, 535,
   563
Cherokee Indian National Council,
   26
Chesapeake Bay blockade, **243–44**
Chesney, Charles Cornwallis, 369
Chesnut, James, 3, 726–27
Chesnut, Mary Boykin, 43, 142,
   302, 702, **726–27**
Chester, Thomas Morris, 50, 716,
   727
Chester (Pennsylvania) military
   prison, 591
Chicago Republican, 765
Chicago Tribune, 24, 27, 227
Chichester, Mary, 694
Chickahominy River, 308
Chickamauga (Confederate
   commerce raider), 564

Chickamauga (Georgia), 33, 237, 276, **289–91**, *290*, 292, 330, 338, 352
Chickamauga and Chattanooga National Military Park (Fort Oglethorpe, Georgia), **890**
Chickasaw (U.S.S.), 560
Chickasaw Bluffs, Mississippi, 269, 279
Chicora (Confederate ironclad), 532, **561**
Child, Lydia Maria, 59
Chimborazo (Confederate hospital), 629, 647, 656, 660
Chimborazo Medical Museum, **896**
Chiriqui Improvement Company, 216
Chisolm, John Julian, 638, 640
Choctaw, (U.S.S.), 533
Christadelphians, 83, 696
Christian Commission, U.S., 642, **662**, 686, *706*
Christianity, 15, 83, 440; *see also* Religion
Christian Recorder, 152, 212, 219, 281, 434–35, 700
Chronology of Civil War, *see* Time lines of significant events
Churchill, Thomas J., 889
Cincinnati, 353
   Colored Citizen, 219
   Daily Commercial, 362
   Gazette, 676
   McLean Barracks, 589
   see also Ohio
Cincinnati (Grant's horse), *401*
Cincinnati (river gunboat), 528, 533, 558, 559
Cities, largest (1860), 72
City class ironclads, **558–59**
City of Louisiana (hospital ship), 662
City Point, Virginia, 50
Civil rights:
   Acts, 738, 742, 756, 769, 770, 790, 794, 797–98, 802, 804
   blacks push for, 26, 139, 235, 250, 266, 430, 602, 730, **756–57**
Civil War:
   military, *see* Armies; Battle(s)
   service/pension records of Civil War soldiers/sailors, 900

studying (research and preservation), **859–908**
   artifact/archival collections, **877–87**
   battlefield preservation organizations, **898–900**
   Civil War round tables, **905**
   continuing education programs, **905–8**
   living history (Civil War reenactment), **904–5**
   national historic sites, **887–98**
   organizations for descendants of Civil War veterans, **900–3**
   time line, 1–52
   two primary issues sparking, 52
   United States before, *see* Antebellum America
see Publications about the Civil War, 859–908
Civil War Courier, 904
Civil War Education Association, 906
Civil War Era Center, 906
Civil War Institutes, 906, 907
Civil War Preservation Trust, 899, 907
Civil War Round Table, **905**
Civil War Sites Advisory Commission, 239
Civil War Times, 364
Clarence (C.S.S.) 564, 565
Clark, Charles, 200
Clark, Edward, 201
Clark, Henry Toole, 200
Clay, Cassius M., 397
Clay, Clement C., 42, 67
Clay, Henry, 62, 106, 107, 109, 110, 120, 122, 123, **129**
Clay, Hugh Lawson, 35
Clayton, Powell, 785
Cleburne, Patrick Ronayne, 35, 45, 155, 317, **408–9**, *408*, 494
Clemens, Jeremiah, 839
Clifton (U.S.S.), 533
Clinch Rifles (military unit), 374
Clothing/shoes, 542, **643**, 702–3
Cobb, Howell, 36, 48, **188–89**, 599, 601, 620
Cobb, Thomas R. R., 105, 189

Cobb's Hill, Virginia, *358*
Coburn, Abner, 198
Coffee Mill guns, 488
Coffin, Levi, 95, 102, 841
Coke, Richard, 742
Cold Harbor (Virginia), 39, 304, **308**, *309* (map), 311, 330, 341, 401, **896**
Cold Mountain, 840
Cold Spring Foundry (New York), 506, 511
Colfax, Schuyler, 789
Colfax Massacre (Louisiana), 787, 794, 795
Collingwood, Joseph W., 373
Collins, Napoleon, 536
Colonial National Historical Park (Yorktown National Cemetery), **890**
Colonization for freed slaves, 21, 58, 120, 129, 130, 148, 172, **215–16,** 727
Colored Citizen, The, 724
Colored Orphan Asylum, 720
Colored Troops, *see* African American soldiers
Colt, Samuel, 500
Colt Revolving Rifle, 490
Columbiad, 505, 515
Columbus, Georgia, 545, 670
Columbus, Kentucky, 254, 337, 589
Colyer, Vincent, 16, 725
Commanders in chief, **399–401**
Command of the Army Act, 740
Commerce raiders, 14, 40, 203, 533, 536, 551, **563–65**
Commodore Barney (U.S.S.), 533
Commonwealth v. Aves, 97
Communication, *see* Logistics/communications
Company/battery, **374**
Compromise of 1850, 62, **109–11,** 122, 129, 137
Comstock, Cyrus E., 364
Coney, Samuel, 198
Confederacy:
   agriculture, 674, 675
   aid societies, 701
   capital, 15, 144, 161
   casualties, 331

celebrations in, 712–14
conscientious objectors in, 695–99
constitution, 68, 134, **162–63**, 189
creation of government, 67,
    160–64
economy, 668–72
education in, 679–83
estimated total casualties among
    Confederate forces in later
    battles, 331
flag of, **717**
generals, *388*, **398–99**
government officials, **178–86**
  attorneys general, **185–86**
  governors, 191–201
  navy secretary, **185**
  postal service, 710–11
  postmaster general, **185**
  president, **178–80**
  recruitment of soldiers, 690–95
  refugees in, 721–26
  religion in, 685–88
  riots in, 718–19
  states, secretaries of, **181–82**
  treasury, secretaries of, **182–83**
  vice president, **181**
  war, secretaries of, **183–84**, 370
  women in, 701–5
home front, 665, **666–67**
ironclads, **560–62**
medals, 482
military, *see* Armies of the
    Confederacy
paper money, *668*
Confederate Associated Press, 356
Confederate Bible Society, 686
Confederate Receipt Book, 671
Confederate Roll of Honor, 482
Confederate Spelling Book, 680, *681*
Confederate States Constitution: *see*
    Confederacy, constitution;
    Politics, wartime, constitutions
    compared
*Confederate States Medical and
    Surgical Journal*, 656
Confiscation Acts, 10, 21, 145, 150,
    219, 250, 335, 429, 736, 760
Confiscation of foreign vessels, 173
Congregationalist church, 82, 440;
    see also Religion

Congress (U.S.S.), 529, 574
Congressional Globe, 478, 679
Congressional Reconstruction, 740,
    770–72
Connecticut, 192
  Historical Society, 877
  wartime governors, 197
Connolly, James A., 324
Connor, Jerome, 835
Conrad, 565
Conscience Whigs, 123
Conscientious objection, 15, 156,
    372, **464–65, 695–99**
Conscription/draft, 17, 23, 24, 27,
    31, 32, 40, 148, 151, 155, 192,
    372, 463, 464, 693, 696
  draftees/deserters, 463
  draftee's life *vs.* that of a
    volunteer, 693
  riots, 31, 192, 719–20
  substitutes and, 372
Conservation Fund, 899–900
Conservative Union Party, 783
Constitution (balloon), 364
Constitution, United States, *see*
    United States Constitution
Constitution (U.S.S.), 525
Constitutional Union Party, 66,
    121, 126
Continuing education programs,
    905–8
Contraband Relief Association, 700,
    728
Contrabands (escaped slaves), 8, 11,
    30, 46, 351, 570–71, *674*, 682,
    704, **724–26**, 735, 736
Cook, George Smith, **813**
Cookbook, Confederate, 671
Cooke, James W., 546, 547
Cooke, John Esten, 838
Cooper, Samuel, 399
Copperheads, 20, 27, 28, 33, 39, 43,
    146, **165–67**, 168, 194, 223,
    286, 287, 719, 825
Corbett, Boston, 231
Corbin, Joseph C., 783
Corbin's Bridge, 307
Corinth, Mississippi, 252, **269**, 336,
    624
Cornerstone Speech, 68

Cornish, Dudley, 434
Cornwell, Bernard, 842
Corps, **375**
Corrick's Ford, western, Virginia, 9
Corwin, Thomas, 4
Cotton, 75, 79, 603, 673–74,
    760–61
  "Cotton Is King" speech, 54, 65
  embargo, **204**
Cotton (C.S.S.), 531
Cotton gin, 57, 79, 673
Cotton Whigs, 123
Courage/sacrifice, **481–83**
Cox, Samuel, 719
Cozzens, William, 199
Cracker Line Operation, Tennessee,
    292
Craig's Meeting House, Virginia,
    304
Crampton's Gap, Maryland, 266
Crane, Stephen, 838, 855, 857
Crapo, Henry, 198
Crater, battle of the, 42, **311–12**
Credit Mobilier, 789
Crenshaw, John B., 697
Crew and Pemberton Warehouse
    (Virginia) military prison, 595
Crew's Farm, Virginia, 259
Crimean War, 552, 638
Crittenden, George, 129
Crittenden, John Jordan, 66, **129,**
    145
Crittenden, Thomas, 129
Crittenden Compromise, 66, 129
Crittenden Resolution, 145
Crittendon-Johnson Resolution,
    735
Cross Keys, Virginia, 19, 261
Crowder, John H., 432
Cuba, 92–93, 125, 423
Culver, J., 854
Cumberland (U.S.S.), 529, 544, 574
Cumberland and Tennessee Rivers
    (1862 battle), **251–54**
Cumming, Kate, 24, 32, 46, 51, 276,
    659–60, 692, 702, 805
Cummings v. Missouri, 739
Currier, Nathaniel, 808–9
Currier & Ives (New York), 806,
    808–9, 826, 830

Curtin, Andrew G., 151, 193, 199
Curtis, Benjamin, 773
Curtis, Samuel R., 255, 380, 397
Cushing, Alonzo H., 575
Cushing, William B., 536, 562, **575**
Cushman, Charlotte, 710
Cushman, Pauline, **458,** 707
Custer, Elizabeth Bacon, *409*
Custer, George Armstrong,
  409–10, *409*, 496
Custer, Thomas W., *409*, 410
Cylinder, 515

Daguerre, Louis Jacques Mandé,
  811
Dahlgren, John A. Bernard, 495,
  502, 515, 539, 545, 550,
  575–77, *576*
Dahlgren, Ulric, 296
Dahlgren guns, 515, 528, 552
Dalton (Georgia) military prison,
  593
Dame, William M., 481
Dames of the Loyal Legion, 900,
  901
Dana, Charles A., 30, 132, 228, 433,
  765
Daniel, John Moncure, 718
Daniel, Junius, 308
Danville Prison (Virginia), 595,
  611
Daughters of Union Veterans of the
  Civil War, **901**
Davenport, Alfred, 470
Davenport Daily Gazette (Iowa), 676
"David" (boat), 568
David (C.S.S.), 523, 534, 555, 566
David's Island (New York) military
  prison, 590
Davidson, Hunter, 542
Davies, Henry E., *41*
Davis, Alexander K., 782
Davis, Charles H., 530, 538, 539
Davis, Edmund, 742, 785
Davis, George, **186**
Davis, Henry Winter, 156, 737, 762
Davis, Jefferson Finis, 5, 8, 14, 15,
  24, 26, 29, 33, 34, 35, 36, 40,
  41, 44, 47, 49, 51, 57–68, *143*,
  178–80, *179*, **399–401,** *801*

antebellum, 111, 134
  U.S. Secretary of War, 340, 370
  U.S. Senator, 66, 67, 109, 179
armistice bid, 416
in arts, 810, 831, **833,** 834
assassination plot, 236, 296
Butler (declaring an outlaw), 598,
  619
cabinet, 24, *179*, 180, **181–86,**
  537, 710–11
capture/imprisonment, 51, 159,
  180, 324, 325, 400
cemetery where buried, 832
chaplains, 440
chronology of wartime political
  actions:
  1861, 143–47
  1862, 147–52
  1863, 152–55
  1864, 155–57
  1865, 157–59
commander in chief of
  Confederacy, 370, 394,
  399–401
confederate election of 1863,
  221
Democratic Party and, 164
election/inauguration, 5, 14, 67,
  140, 146, 147, 160–61
England and, 458
establishing Confederate army,
  387
family land set aside for use of
  freedmen, 737
habeas corpus, 15, 148, 208–9, 221
Johnston (J.E.) and, 414, 416
Lee and, 47, 49, 158, 370, 402
Lincoln compared to, 371, 400–1
military strategy/tactics/
  communications, 246, 247,
  263, 337–39, 353, 355, 390,
  393, 399, 414, 449
Negro Soldier Law, 49
officers and, 263, 420, 421
  appointments, 370, 511, 656
  relationship with commanding
    generals, 370
president of Confederacy,
  178–80, *179*
press criticism of, 134, 226

prisoner exchange/treatment,
  430, 431, 596, 597, 598, 602,
  613, 614, 619
proposal about freeing slaves
  purchased for war work, 44
quoted:
  on captured Union officers as
    criminals, 26
  on Chattanooga Union
    occupation, 33
  on Emancipation Proclamation,
    26, 430
  on Johnston (Albert Sidney),
    415
  on lack of foreign recognition,
    207
  on prisoner treatment, 614
  on secession, 143
religion (invoking God in
  speeches), 688
Senate seat once held by, 741, *801*,
  809
Southern governors and, 191
struggle to maintain political and
  financial support for war, 142
support for, 35, 191–92
vetoing office of Confederate
  commanding general, 370
vice president, 68, 181
West Point, 420
wife, *see* Davis, Varina Howell
Davis, Sam, **458**
Davis, Theodore, 636, **821**
Davis, Varina Howell, 178, **187,**
  187, 226, 400
Davis, William C., 908
Davis Bend, Mississippi, 737
Davis Smith Negro Mart (Georgia)
  military prison, 593
Day's Gap, Alabama, 279
De Bow, James Dunwoody
  Brownson, 75, **130**
De Bow's Review, 130, 134
DeBree, John, 542
Declaration of Independence, 95
De Forest, John W., 838
de la Coste, Marie Ravenal, 852,
  702
Delafield, Richard, 395
Delany, Martin R., **130,** 215

Delaware, 67, 142, 793
  military prisons/camps in, 588, 604
  wartime governors, 197
DeLeon, David C., 653
Democratic Party, **121–22, 164–65**
  1860 convention, 66
  1864 platform, 221–22
  disagreement over slavery splits, 66
  division of, 123
  "doughface," 112
Demographics, 69–71, 666–67
Demorest, W. Jennings, 819–20
Dennison, William Morgan, **176,** 199, 353, 711
Dentists, 625
Dependent Pension Act, 745–46
Depression of 1873, 673
Deringer, Henry, 515
Descendants of Civil War veterans, organizations for, **900–3**
Desertion, **477–79**
Devens, Bridget, *446*
Diarrhea/dysentery, **644**
Dickinson, Anna, **189**
"Dictator" mortar, *506,* 507
Dimick, Justin E., 606
Dinsmore, Edgar, 50
Dinwiddie Court House, Virginia, 322
Discrimination/segregation, 104, **218–19, 678–79**
Disease:
  causes of, **638–43**
  deaths from, *vs.* combat, 623–24
  on ships, 635
District of Columbia, *see* Washington, D.C.
Division (military), **375**
Dix, Dorothea Lynde, 9, 658, **660,** 893
Dix, John A., 397, 596, 601, **619**
Dix-Hill cartel, 596, **600–4,** 613, 619, 620, 622
"Dixie" (anthem), 5, 849
Dixie Primer and *Dixie Speller,* 680
Dixon, George, 566
Dixon, Jeremiah, 53

Dixon, Thomas, 854
Doctors, number of, 624–25; *see also* Medical care
Dodge, Grenville, 302, 456, 458
Dodge, Mary Abigail, 709, **727–28**
D'Orleans, Louis Phillippe, **458**
D'Orleans, Robert, **458**
Doughface, 112
Douglas, Stephen A., 62, 65, 66, 109, 110, 111–13, *112,* 115, 121, 122, 123, 124–27, **130–31,** 164, 170, 605
Douglass, Charles, 22
Douglass, Frederick, 13, 21, *22,* 31, 32, 61, 84, 102, 130, **131,** 154, 156, 157, 215, 217, 219, 430, 678–79, 688, 693, 741, 757, 761, *780–81,* 809, 835, 841, **892**
Douglass, Lewis, 22, 31
Douglass' Monthly, 219
Downey, John, 197
Draft, *see* Conscription/draft
Drama (stage/screen/television), **853–57**
Draper, Simon, 395
Drayton, Percival, 248, 539, **577**
Drayton, Thomas Fenwick, 248, 577
Dred Scott case, *see Scott v. Sandford*
Drew, George, 742
Drewry's Bluff, Virginia, 38, 299, 530, 542, 574
Driver, Stephen, 716–17
Drugs and medical supplies, **651–52**
Dubuclet, Antoine, 782
Dun, R. G., 673
Dunkards (Dunker Church), 15, 83, 151, 268, 464, 696, 697, 698
Dunn, Oscar J., 782
Dunnington, John W., 546
Du Pont, Samuel Francis, 12, 27, 248, 281, 525, 529, 532, 544, 550, 555
Durbec, F. W., 814
Durham Station, North Carolina, 50
Dutch Gap Canal, Virginia, 428
Dutch Reformed church, 82
Dyer, Alexander B., 394, 512

Eads, James B., 523, 553
Early, Jubal Anderson, 37, 40, 41, 42, 44, 386, *388,* 398, **410,** 422, 441, 665, 672–73, 821, 832, 843, 889, 895
  battle overviews, 237, 277, 293, 310, **312–13,** 314, 322, 343
Easel art, 826
Eastern Theater, **236–37,** *238* (map)
East Gulf Blockading Squadron (EGBS), 550
Eastman, Mary Henderson, 111
East Point (Georgia) military prison, 593
Eaton, Amos B., 394
Eaton, John, 736, 737
Ebenezer Church, 325
Ebenezer Dodge (whaling ship), 528
Echo, The, 65
Economic conditions/effects, **73–76, 668–73**
  agrarian economy, *see* Agriculture
  antebellum America, **73–76,** 91–92
  Depression of 1873, 673
  economic differences, North and South (antebellum America), 89
  Northern economy, 89, **672–73**
  Panic of 1857, 65
  Southern economy, 89, **668–72**
Edith (blockade runner), 564
E.D.M. Prison (Virginia) military prison, 595
Education programs, continuing (about Civil War), 905–8
Education/schools, **88–90, 679–84,** 703, 707, 725–26, **754–55,** 777–78, 802, 905–8
  antebellum America, **88–90**
  colleges, 683
  compulsory education, 725
  for former slaves, 777–78, 802
  integration, 755
  North, 683–85
  Reconstruction issue, **754–55**
  South, 679–83
  teachers, 703, 707
Edwards, J. D., **814**

Edward's Island (New York) military prison, 590
Edward's Prison (Virginia) military prison, 595
Eggleston, Edward, 837
Einhorn, David, 87
Elder, John Adams, **828**
Elections, **220–24**
  1848, 122
  1852, 123
  1854, 112, 803
  1856, 64, 112, 123
  1858, 131
  1860, 66, 118, **124–27**, 131
  1862, 24, 151–52, **220**
  1863, 33, 154, **220–22**
  1864, 36, 39, 42, 43, 44, 155, 156, 157, **221–24**
    Democrat party platform, **221–22**
    Republican party platform, **222**
  1872, 133, 794
  1876, 742, 795–96
  1877, 798
Electors, three-fifths clause, 56, 769
Elkhorn Tavern (Arkansas), 15, 255, 380, 895
Ellet, Alfred W., 443
Ellet, Charles, Jr., 19, 532, **577**
Ellet, John R., 443
Elliott, J. B., 334
Elliott, Robert B., *780–81*, **797–98**
Elliott, Stephen, **728**
Ellis, John, 200
Ellison, William, 104
Ellsworth, Elmer, 8
Elmira (New York) military prison, 590, **607**
El Paso, Texas, 249
Emancipation:
  compensation for slaveowners, 17
  memorial for, Washington, D.C., **834–35**
Emancipation Proclamation, 21, 23, 26, 150, 151, 152, 154, 172, 175, 192, 207, **210–14**, 219, 227, 235, 276, 333, 336, 430, 585, 602, 682, 688, 693, 713, 729, 759, 760, 761

Emerson, Irene, 113
Emerson, John, 113
Emerson, Ralph Waldo, 86, 92, 689
Emigration, 103–04, 122–23, 132, 215–16, 667; *see also* Immigration
Émile Erlanger and Company, 204
Enfield rifle-musket, 515
England, *see* Britain
Enlistment decision, **462–64**
Eno, Henry C., 811
Enquirer, 225
Enterprise (balloon), 362
Entertainments:
  home front, **700–1**
  soldiers' pastimes:
    sanctioned, **468–69**
    unsanctioned, **469–70**
Entrenchment (defensive tactic), 343
Episcopalians, 82, 95, 440; *see also* Religion
Equal Rights League, **167–68**, 748
Ericsson, John, 523, 558
Erlanger loan, **204–5**
Erysipelas, 644–45
Escapes from military prisons, **616–17**
Espionage, *see* Spies/intelligence gathering
Essex (U.S.S.), **558**, 561
Etheridge, Annie, 446–47
European powers and American Civil War, 141–42, 148, 173, **201–7**; *see also* Britain, France
  cotton embargo, **204**
  CSA quest for recognition, 30, 49, 142, 146, 182, **202–4, 207**, 265–66
  Erlanger loan, **204–5**
  impressment of foreign citizens, **205–6**
  Trent affair, 12, 146, 173, 174, 186, 188, 189, 190, 202–3, 525, 552
European press, 11, 367–68
Evans, Augusta Jane, 838
Evans, Charles M., 364
Evans, Clement, 712

Evans, Nathan G. "Shanks," 248, 360
Evansville (Indiana) military prison, 588
Evarts, William, 773
Everett, Edward, 214
Ewell, Richard Stoddert, 282, 306, *388*, 398, **410–11**, 424
Ewing, Thomas, 32, 43, 289, 773
Exodus/Exodusters, 750
Ex parte Merryman, *see* Merryman, John
Ex parte Milligan, 208, 738
Explosion/accidents (arsenals/ ordnance labs), 27, 702, 705, 834
Ezekiel, Moses Jacob, 836
Ezra Church, Georgia, battle of, 42, 302

Fairbanks, Erastus, 193, 199
Fairfield, John, 102
Fair Oaks, Virginia, battle of, 19, 752
Fanny (U.S.S.), 364, 525
Farms, *see* Agriculture
Farragut, David Glasgow, 18, 42, 261, 262, 313, 321, *378*, 485, 528, 529, 530, 531, 532, 535, 538, *538*, 544, 551, 574, **577–78**, 814, 834
Farrand, Ebenezer, 546
Fasting/prayer days, 712
Faulkner, William, 842
Favill, Josiah Marshall, 20, 271, 480
Faxon, William, 538
Featherstone, Jane, 456
Federal ambulance corps, 631–34
Federal government, *see* United States, wartime government officials
Federal tariffs, 91
Ferrero, Edward, 312, 436
Fessenden, William P., **174–75**
Fifteenth Amendment, 120, 142, 732, 741, 758, 769, **778–79**
Fifth column, 704
Filibustering, 93, 136
Fillmore, Millard, 110–11, 121

Films, **854–57**

Financial system, (antebellum America), 91; *see also* Banks/banking, Economic conditions/effects

Fingal (blockade runner), 553, 562

Finley, Clement A., 170, 653

Finley, Robert, 120

Finney, Charles G., 59, 85, 95

Fire-eaters, 3, 48, 133, 134, 160, 226

First Amendment, 59–60

First ladies, 187, *187*

Fishel, Edwin C., 461

Fisher, Benjamin F., 395

Fisher's Hill, Virginia, **314**

Fitzpatrick, Benjamin, 67

Five Forks, Virginia, 49, **322**, 325

"Flag floppers," 361

Flags, 700, **716–17**

Flanigan, Harris, 196, 200

Flannery, Lot, 834

Fleetwood, Christian Abraham, *435*

Fletcher, Thomas C., 198, 200

Flintlock, 515

Florence (South Carolina) military prison, 593, 599, **610**

Florida:
  during Reconstruction
  military prisons in, 588, 592
  population (1860), 666
  readmittance to Union, 740, 793
  secession, 3, 160
  wartime governors, 200

Florida (C.S.S.), 203, 536, 563, 564, 570, 575

Flying battery, 515

Fogg, Mary Rutledge, 656

Foner, Eric, 784

Food, 27, 30, 281, **470–72**, 712
  disease and, **641–42**

Foote, Andrew Hull, 14, 254, 255, 528, 539, 544, **578**

Foote, Shelby, 842

Forbes, Edwin, 368, 467, 584, **821**

Ford, John S. ("Rest in Peace"), 330

Ford's Theatre, 159, 173, **890–91**

Foreign powers:
  confiscation of foreign vessels, 173

filibustering, 93, 136
  see also European powers and American Civil War

Forest Hall (Washington, D.C.) military prison, 588

Forrest, French, 541, 546

Forrest, Nathan Bedford, 25, 37, 41, 46, 398, **411–12**, *411*, 435, 436, 496, **798**, 890
  battle overviews, 237, 269, 279, 298, **310**, 317, 325, 338
  Ku Klux Klan, 784, 786

Fort Beauregard, South Carolina, 525

Fort Blakely, Alabama, 328, *329*

Fort Clark, South Carolina, 247, 525

Fort Columbus, New York, military prison, 590

Fort Craig (New Mexico Territory) military prison, 249, 590

Fort Darling, Virginia, 299, 530

Fort Davison, Missouri, 43

Fort Delaware (Pea Patch Island, Delaware) prison, 588, **604**, 614, 617

Fort De Russy, Louisiana, 298

Fort Donelson, Tennessee, 14, 251, 252, 331, 337, 384, 420, 490, 528, 600, 606, 721, **891**

Fort Fisher, North Carolina, 46, 146, 294, 319, **321**, 324, 536, 573

Fort Harrison Visitor Center, **897**

Fort Hatteras, North Carolina, 525

Fort Henry, Tennessee, 14, 251, 252, 337, 528, 600; *see also* Fort Donelson, Tennessee

Fort Hill, 533

Fort Hindman, *see* Arkansas Post

Fort Jackson, Louisiana, 261, 529, 545

Fort Jefferson (Florida) military prison, 588

Fort Lafayette (New York) military prison, 590, 600

Fort McHenry, Maryland, 144, 589, 900

Fort McNair, *see* Arsenal Penitentiary

Fort Mifflin (Pennsylvania) military prison, 591

Fort Misner (Columbia, Tennessee) military prison, 594

Fort (Fortress) Monroe, Virginia, 8, 48, 359, 364, 591, 682, 735

Fort Morgan, Alabama, 313

Fort Moultrie, South Carolina, 4, 67, 243, **891**

Fort Myer, Virginia, 360

Fort Norfolk (Virginia) military prison, 591

Fort Pemberton, Mississippi, 279, 532

Fort Pickens, Florida, 5, 6, **243**, 588

Fort Pillow, Tennessee, 37, 146, 255, **298–99**, 435, 559, 602, 798

Fort Pulaski, Georgia, 4, 17, 67, 239, **261**, 336, 588, **891**

Fort Riley (Kansas) military prison, 589

Fort Schuyler (New York) military prison, 590

Fort Scott National Historic Site, **892**

Fort Stedman, Virginia, **322**

Fort Stevens, Washington, D.C., 313, 889

Fort St. Philip, Louisiana, 261, 529

Fort Sumter, South Carolina, 4, 6, 27, 67, 68, 106, 134, 139, 172, 176, 207, 233, 239, 242, **243**, 494, 524, 525, 532, 534, 543, 572, 573, *576*, 666, 675, **892**

Fort Wagner (Battery Wagner), South Carolina, 31, 235, 276, 281, 533

Fort Walker, South Carolina, 525

Fort Warren (Massachusetts) military prison, 589, **606–7**

Fort Wayne (Indiana) military prison, 588

Fort Whipple, Virginia, 360

Fort Wood (Bedloe's Island, New York) military prison, 590

Foster, Charles F., 431

Foster, John G., 384

Fourteenth Amendment, 120, 142, 732, 734–35, 738, 739, 740, 755, 757, 758–59, **767–70**, 794, 799, 802

Fox, Gustavus Vasa, 176, 538, 547, **578**

France, 23, 36, 151, 202, 204, 206

Frank Leslie's Illustrated News, 809, 817, **819**

Franklin, Benjamin, 83

Franklin, Tennessee, 45, **317–19,** 331, 340; *see also* Nashville, Tennessee

Fraser, Trenholm & Co., 183

Fraternal organizations, 83

Frazier, Charles, 840

Frederick County Jail (Virginia) military prison, 595

Fredericksburg, Virginia, 25, 26, 250, 251, **271–74,** 272, 273, 276, 277, 330, 341, 364, 372, 798
National Cemetery, **892–93**
National Military Park, **892**

Free blacks, *see* African American(s)

Freedman's Savings and Trust Company, 48, 737

Freedman's Village, 726

Freedmen, 736, 737, 738, 747–50, 761–2, 775–78
education, 754–56
labor, 753–54
land, 751–52

Freedmen's Aid Bureau, 701

Freedmen's Aid Commission, 135

Freedmen's Bureau, 48, 130, 158, 707, 735, 736, 737, 738, 739, 744, 749, 752, 753, 754–55, **774–78,** 775, 799, 803

Freedom Church, 84

Freedom's Journal, 104, 219

Freeman, Douglas Southall, 902

Freeman, Eugene H., 474

Freeman, Warren H., 16, 29, 37, 250, 367, 473

Freemasons, 83

Freeport Doctrine, 116, 117, 124

Free Soil Party, 62, 63, 96, **122,** 123

Free State Party, 64

Frémont, John C., 10, 11, 64, 112, 123, 145, 146, 156, 176, 188, 210, 245, 396, 410, 662

French, Daniel Chester, 835

French, William H., 293

Frostbite, 641

Fry, James B., 395

Fugitive Slave Clause (U.S. constitution), 56, 97, 99

Fugitive slave laws, 57, 61, 99, 104, 140, 148, 736

Fuller, Margaret, 132

Fullerton, Joseph, 738

Fulton, Robert, 565

Fulton County Jail (Georgia) military prison, 593

Fuse/fuze, 516

Gadsden Purchase, 63

Gag rules, 59–60

Gaines' Mill, Virginia, 256, 896

Gainesville, Virginia, 264

Galena (U.S.S.), **555**

"Galvanized Yankees," 587

Galveston, Texas, **277,** 531, 546, 594

Gamble, Hamilton, 194, 198

Gardner, Alexander, 268, 732, 812, 813, **814,** 815, 816

Gardner, James, 639

Gardner, William H., 545

Garfield, James A., 413, 796, 834

Garland, Augustus, 742

Garnet, Henry Highland, **131–32,** 215, 693, 757, *780–81*

Garnett, Robert S., 9

Garrett, Thomas, 95

Garrison, Ellen Wright, 716

Garrison, William Lloyd, 59, 61, 95, *96*, 119, 122, **132,** 133, 189, 889

Gaston, C. A., 355

Gatling, Richard Jordan, 488, 516

Gatling gun, 488, 516

Gaul, Gilbert, **828**

Gayler, Charles, 853

Generals:
in chief, 158, **401–4**
Confederate, **398–99**
Notable officers, 404–26

Union, **393–97**

Geneva Convention, 587

Geneva Tribunal, 564

George Island (Boston harbor), 606

Georgia, 160, 200, 660, 741, 793
archival/artifact collections, 881
military prisons/camps, 588, 592–93, 608, 621
population (1860: whites/slaves), 666
readmitted, 741, 772, 793
Reconstruction in, 740, 763, 794
secession, 3, 5, 67
Sherman's march to the sea, 45, 46, 47, 316–17, *317*, 357, 387, 610, 713, 799, 890

Georgia (Confederate commerce raider), 565, 579

Georgia Relief and Hospital Association, 663

Gerrish, Theodore, 223

Gerrymandering, 796

Getty, George W., 306

Gettysburg Address, 34, 155, **214–15,** 276, 842, 859

Gettysburg campaign, 30, 31, 33, 34, 205, 237, 276, 281, **282–87,** 338, 340, 341, 342, 354, 368, 376, 532, 665, 714
casualties, 282, 330, 331, 575, 720
maps (first/second/third days), *283, 284, 285*
National Military Park, 827, 830, **893–94**
photographers/artists at, *286*, 811, 816
surgical operation at, 635

Gettysburg Magazine, 876

Gibbs, Jonathan C., 782, 783

Gibson, Ella E., 437

Gibson, George, 394

Gibson, James F., 812, 813, **814**

Gideonites, 682

Gillis, John P., 544

Gillmore, Quincy A., 261

Gilman, Caroline Howard, 242

Gilmer, Jeremy F., 347, 395

Gilmore, James R., 837

Gilmore, Joseph, 198

Gilmore, Patrick S., 852–53

Gist, States Rights, 45, 317
Gladstone, William, 147
Glasson, John J., 544
Gleason's Pictorial Drawing-Room Companion, 816, 817
Gleaves, Richard H., 782
Glendale/Malvern Hill Battlefields Visitor Center, **897**
Globe Tavern, Virginia, 311
Glorieta Pass, New Mexico, 249
Godey's Lady's Book, 689
Gold Rush, 62, 109
Goldsboro/Goldsborough (North Carolina) military prison, 49, 593
Goldsborough, Louis M., 528, 530, 550
Goldsmith, Middleton, 645
Gone with the Wind, 840, 855
Goodwin, Ichabod, 198
Gordon, John Brown, 314
Gordonsville (Virginia) military prison, 595
Goree, Thomas J., 841
Gorgas, Josiah, 35, 46, 47, 294, 320, 332, 394, 395, 486, 490, 491, **511**
Gorgas Report (on Confederate arms/equipment), **491**
Gorman, Willis A., 380
Gosport Naval Yard, Virginia, 6, 525, 546, 547
Gould, Jay, 788
Government, *see* Politics
Governors:
    in the North, 192–94, 196–99
    Reconstruction, 742, 779–84, 786, 787
    in the South, **194–96, 199–200**
    by state, **199–201**
    wartime, 191–201
Granbury, H. B., 317
Grand Army of the Republic (GAR), 900, 903
Grange, 788, 790
Granger, Gordon, 33, 291
Grant, Julia Dent, 893, 898
Grant, Ulysses S., *234, 327, 378*, **401–2,** *401, 818*
    Army of the Tennessee, **382–83**

Belmont, Missouri (1861), 248–49
Chattanooga, 34, 291, 292
Cold Harbor, 39, **308–10,** *401*
Early (Jubal) and, 41, 313
Eaton appointed by, 736
Fort Fisher, 321
Forts Henry and Donelson (Tennessee), 251, 384, 420, 528, 600, 606, 891
general in chief, named, 37, 236, 294, 336, 371, 394
Halleck writing to (quoted), 276
headquarters, 380, 555
historic sites/memorials, 835, 891, **893, 897–98**
intelligence agents for, 456
KKK Act, 786–87
Lee quoted about, 37
Lee's surrender to, 159, 326–28, *327,* 400, 416, 600
literature/arts/photography, 817, *818,* 821, 824, **835**
Mexican War of 1846–1848, 339, 393, 404
military rank, 37, 393, 396, 397
naval forces (combined operations with), 321, 525, 528, 533
nickname (Unconditional Surrender), 251
Overland campaign, *234,* 294, 299, **304–10,** 342, 533
Petersburg, 39, 49, 50, 140, 311, 322, 342, 386
presidency of:
    cabinet/appointments, 188, 422
    elections/campaigns, 740, 741, 785, 787, 791
    scandal involving vice presidents, 789
press lionizing, 14, 17
prisoner exchange/treatment, 47, 249, 436, 598, 599, 603, 619, 621
quoted:
    on art of war, 233
    on Crater battle, 42
    on guerrillas, treatment of captured, 450
    on prisoner exchange, 599, 603

    on pursuing Early "to the death," 41, 313
    on soldier vote (1864), 224
    on strikes, 791
    on surrender terms (message to Lee), 326–27
    on Union conduct of war (1864), 294
    on Vicksburg falling, 31
    on war strategy (1864), 37, 38, 39
Reconstruction, 742, 786, 787, 794
reports/letters to, 314, 470
resources/memorials, 891, 893, 896
Shiloh, 17, **252–54**
Spotsylvania Court House, **307–8**
tactics, 343
Thomas (George) and, 46, 318
Vicksburg (1862), 25, 269–70, 411, 532, 824
Vicksburg (1863), 28, 30, 31, 279–81, 381, 393, 533
Western Theater, **237,** 382
Wilderness, 38, **304–7,** 821
Grant, William, 817
Grant parish, Louisiana, 787
Grant's Factory (Virginia) military prison, 595
Grape shot, **509,** 516
Gratiot Street (Missouri) military prison, 589
Great Awakening, 59, 85, 86
Great/Big Bethel (Bethel Church, Virginia), 244
Greeley, Horace, 22, 42, **132–33,** 151, 226, 235, 678, 746, 791
Green, Paul, 854
Greenbacks, 147
Greene, Theodore P., 544, 551
Greener, R. T., *780–81*
Greenfield, Elizabeth Taylor, 700–701
Greenhow, Robert, 459
Greenhow, Rose O'Neal, 18, **459,** *459,* 703
Gregg, David M., *41*
Grenades, 488, **502–3**
Grierson, Benjamin H., 28, 270, 280

Grierson's Raid (Vicksburg), *270* (map)
Griffen, John, 504
Griffith, D. W., 854
Grimes, Bryan, 18, 293
Grimes, James W., 2, 52
Grimké, Sarah M., 95, **133**
Grimké (Weld), Angelina E., 95, **133**
Grimsley, Mark, 448
Groesbeck, William, 773
Grover, Cuvier, 263
Groveton, 264
Guerin, Jules, 835
Guerrilla Prison (Kansas City), 590
Guerrilla warfare, 32, 39, 44, 51, 234–35, 237, 262, 276, 289, 312, 314, 315, 338, 361, 372, 442, 443, **447–61,** *449,* 723
Gulf Blockading Squadron, 11, 549, 550, 551
Gunpowder production, **501–2**
Guntown, Mississippi, 310
Gurganus, Allan, 842
Gwathmey Warehouse (Virginia) military prison, 595

Habeas corpus, writ of, 15, 36, 143, 144, 145, 148, 153, 172, 192, **207–10,** 221, 225, 726, 739, 786
Hagerstown, Maryland, 312
Hahn, Michael, 37, 200, 736, 737, 762
Haiti, 58, 140, 216
Hale, Sarah Josepha, 689
Hale, William, 502
Hale Rocket Launchers, 502
Haley, Alex, 857
Halifax, North Carolina, Naval yard, 546
Hall, Francis B., 441
Hall, James H., 511
Hall, Normal, *286*
Hall, Willard, 198
Halleck, Henry Wager, 47, 216, 251, 276, 323, 336, 371, 394, 396, **402,** 416, 450, 451, 624, 633
Halstead, Murat, 362
Hamburg, South Carolina, 787
Hamilton, Andrew G., 617

Hamilton, Ed, 836
Hamilton, Gail, 709, 727
Hamlin, Hannibal, 109, **173,** 799
Hammond, James H., 3, 53–54, 65, 204
Hammond, William Alexander, 17, 170, 623, 633, 639, 651, 653, **654–55,** 658
Hampton, Frank Preston, 412
Hampton, Sallie Baxter, 3
Hampton, Wade (III), 39, *388,* 398, **412,** 496, 742, 779, 787, 795, 796, **798**
Hampton, Wade, Jr. (IV), 412
Hampton Roads, Virginia, 15, 364, 529, 536, 549, 552, 553, 580
Hampton Roads Peace Conference, 158, 181
Hancock, Winfield Scott, 306, 339, *378,* 396, **412–13,** 773, 834
Haney, Milton L., 441
Hardee, William Joseph, 302, 340, 377, *388,* 392, 398, **413**
Harper, Fletcher, 819
Harpers Ferry, 6, 64, 65–66, **118–19,** 136, 266, 268, 348, 423, 485, 510, 845, **894;** *see also* Brown, John
Harper's Weekly, 25, 274, 476, 488, 571, 613, 673, 708, 775, 807, 809, 817, **819,** 821, 823, 826, 827
Harriet Lane (U.S.S.), 531, 565
Harris, Clara, 230
Harris, Isham Green, 201
Harris, John, 540
Harrisburg, Mississippi, **310**
Harris Farm, Virginia, 307, 308
Harrison, Burton, 837
Harrison, Constance Cary, 837
Harrison, William Henry, 123
Harrison House, Virginia, 307
Harrison's Landing, Virginia, 530
Hartford (U.S.S.), 261, 313, 530, 532, 544, 577
Hart's Island, New York, military prison, 590
Hartstene, Henry J., 545
Harvey, Louis, 199
Harwood, Andrew A., 539, 545

Harwood's Factory, Virginia, military prison, 595
Hatcher's Run, Virginia (battle of), **322**
Hatteras (U.S.S.), 531
Hatteras Inlet, North Carolina, 11, **247,** 547
Haupt, Herman, 18, 351
Hay, John, 42, 214
Hayes, Rutherford B., 742, 795, 796, 798
Hayne, Henry E., 782
Hayne, Paul Hamilton, **845,** 849
Haynes, Robert Y., 137
Haynes Excelsior grenade, 503
Hays, Alexander, 306
Hays, Charles W., 547
Heartland offensive, Confederate, **263–64**
Heartsill, W. W., 468
Hébert, Paul O., 391
Helper, Hinton Rowan, 66, 89–90
Hempstead (Texas) military prison, 594
Henrico County Jail (Virginia) military prison, 595
Henry, B. Tyler, 516
Henry Rifle, 494, 516
Henson, Josiah, 102
Hepworth, George, 688
Heroes of America (HOA), 27, 169
Herold, David, 231, 232
Herron, Francis J., 271, 382
Heth, Henry, 449
Hewitt, John Hill, 852
Hiatt, James M., 839
Hicks, Thomas, 198
Higginson, Thomas Wentworth, 63, 428
Hill, Ambrose Powell, 31, 268, 306, *388,* 398, **832**
Hill, Daniel Harvey, 266, 392, 596, 601, **619,** 620
Hill, James, 782, 788
Hillard, George Stillman, 684
Hiller Aviation Museum, 364
Hilton Head, South Carolina, 525, 591, 651, 725
Hindman, Thomas C., 271, 391, 451

Hinds, James M., 785
Hines, Thomas C., 36
Hinman, Wilbur F., 837
Historic sites, national, **887–98**
Hitchcock, Ethan Allen, 371, 397, 601, **619**
H.L. Hunley (Confederate submarine), 523, 533, 534, **565–67**
Hobson, Edward H., 289
Hock, Robert D., 854
Hoffman, William, 606, **620**
Hoge, Jane, **655,** 661, 699
Hog Mountain, Alabama, 279
Holbrook, Frederick, 199
Holcombe, James, 42
Holden, Henry, 37
Holden, William W., 33, 154, 169, 195, 226, 228, 719, 741, 765, 786
Hollins, George N., 545, 546
Holly, James, 215
Holly Springs, Mississippi, 25
Hollywood Cemetery (Richmond, Virginia), **832**
Holmes, Emma, 705
Holmes, Oliver Wendell, Jr., 41, 313, 844
Holmes, Theophilus H., 391, 398
Home front, **665–730**
    agriculture, **673–76**
    conscientious objectors, **695–99**
    discrimination in the North, **678–79**
    economic conditions/effects, **668–73**
    education, **679–84**
    flags, **716–17**
    Homestead Act of 1862, **677–78**
    immigration, **676–77**
    notable figures, **726–30**
    patriotic expressions and celebrations, **712–17**
    postal service, **710–11**
    recruitment of soldiers, **690–95**
    refugees and evacuations in the South, **721–26**
    religion, **685–90**
    riots, **718–21**
    slave celebrations and emancipation, **713–14**

volunteer aid societies, **699–701**
    women, **701–10**
Homer, Winslow, 488, 809, **821,** 822, 827
Homestead Act, 19, 126, 149, **677–78**
Homesteads, 752–53
Hood, John Bell, 40, 41, 42, 43, 44, 45, 46, *388,* 392, 398, 399, **413–14,** 417, 422, 424
    battle overviews, 237, 294, 302, 304, 316, 317, 318, 320
Hooker, Joseph, 26, 29, 31, 146, 236, 266, 274, 277, 278, 339, *378,* 379, **414,** 417, 454, 456, 457
Hope, James, **829**
Hope Slater (Maryland) military prison, 589
Hopkins, D. P., 469
Hopkins, Juliet Opie, **656–57**
Hopper, Isaac, 95
Hornets' Nest (Shiloh, Tennessee), 252
Horse Artillery, 515
Hospital(s), 9, 23, 627–29
    field/train/ships, 629–31
    general, 627–29
    hut (development of), 656
Hotchkiss, Jedediah, 37, *260,* 274, 287, 314, 348
Hotchkiss Collection, 348
Hotchkiss projectile, 508
Hotze, Henry, 189
Housatonic (U.S.S.), 534, 566–67, 568
House, Caleb, 489
Houston, Sam, 109, 201
Houston (Texas) military prison, 594
Hovey, Charles, 690
Howard, Charles Eliot, 746
Howard, Oliver Otis, 383, 752, 775, 776, **798–99,** 838
Howard's Factory, Virginia, military prison, 595
Howe, Julia Ward, 709, 843, 849
Howell, Varina, *see* Davis, Varina Howell
Howitzer, 516
Howitzers Monument (Richmond, Virginia), **832**

Howland, Eliza Woolsey, **661**
Hoyer, J. C., 810
Hoyer and Ludwig (Richmond, Virginia), **810**
Huger, Benjamin, **620**
Hull, Joseph B., Jr., 544
Hunley, Horace L., 534, 565, 566
Hunley (H.L.) see H.L. Hunley
Hunson, William L., 544
Hunt, O. E., 507, 508
Hunter, David, 18, 148, 210, 312, 313, 397, 410, 428, 891
Hunter, Robert M. T., 48, 158, **181,** 183–84
Huntington, Collis, 788
Hurlbut, Stephen A., 295
Hyatt, Thaddeus J., 483
Hyndman, William, 224

Illinois, 152
    archival/artifact collections, 881
    military prisons/camps, 588, 604–6
    resolution criticizing Lincoln, 152
    response to Emancipation Proclamation, 152
    State Penitentiary, 604
    wartime governors, 197
Illustrated Daily News, 816
Illustrated journals/newspapers, 806, 819–20
Immigration, **72–73, 676–77**
    Chinese, 72, 790, 797
    European, **72–73,** 676–77, 790
    major countries of immigrants' origin, 677
    number of immigrants to United States, by year (1860 to 1864), 677
    see also emigration
Impressment Act, 153–54
Impressment of foreign citizens, 205–6
Income tax laws, 10, 20, 28, 149
Indiana:
    archival/artifact collections, 881
    military prisons in, 588, 606
    Morgan's Indiana & Ohio Raid, 287, *288,* 289
    wartime governors, 197

Indianola (U.S.S.), 532
Indians, *see* American Indians
Industrial Revolution, 79, 86
Infections, **644–45**
Infirmary corps, Confederate, 633
Inflation, Confederate, 28
Ingraham, Duncan, 542, 545, 546
Insects/vermin (and disease), 641
Intelligence gathering, *see* Spies/ intelligence gathering
Intelligent Whale (U.S. submarine) 544
International law of war, 29
Intrepid (balloon), *363*, 364
Invalid Corps/Veteran Reserve Corp (U.S.), **441–42**
Inventions, 676
Iowa (wartime governors), 197
Ironclad ships, 10, *16*, 204, 510, *522*, **552–62**, 813
  clash of C.S.S. *Atlanta vs.* U.S.S. *Weehawken*, **553–54**
  Monitor and *Merrimack*, 552–53
  notable ironclads, **555–62**
  see also specific ship; Navies/naval events
Ironclad Test Oath, 149, 763
Iron sights, 516
Irving Block (Memphis) military prison, 591
Irwinville, Georgia, 51, 325
Isherwood, Benjamin Franklin, 523, 539
Islam, 83
Iuka, Mississippi, **269**
Ives, James Merritt, 808–9

Jackson, Andrew, 35, 59, 92, 107, 108, 120, 121, 123, 135, 156, 512
Jackson, Claiborne F., 68, 194, 198, 244
Jackson, Mississippi, 30, 233, 280
Jackson, Thomas Jonathan (Stonewall), 9, 15, 16, 18, 19, 29, *260*, *388*, **414–15**, 717
  battle overviews, 237, 247, **259–61**, 264, 266, 277, 278, 279, 314, 348, 360

in literature/art/sculpture, 808, 810–11, 823, 828, 831, **833**, 834, 838, 841, 845
  nickname, 9, 247, 415
  shrine, **893**
  staff/armies, *260*, 348, 382, 398, 404, 410, 423, 454, 457, 466, 489, 625, 633, 687, 703
Jackson (Confederate hospital, Virginia), 629
Jacksonian Democracy, 121
Jackson *Mississippian*, 702
Jacksonville, 47
Jacob Bell (U.S. ship), 564
Jacques, John W., 9, 23, 468
Jakes, John, 857
James, Frank and Jesse, 450
James, Henry, Sr., 689
James River, Virginia, 530, 555
James River Squadron, 536
Japanese warlord, 533
Jay Cooke and Company, 672, 791
Jayhawkers, 237
Jefferson, Thomas, 2, 77, 94, 184
Jefferson (Union hospital, Indiana), 629
Jenkins, Micah, *10*, 307
Jennison, Charles, 450
Jewish religion, 83, 85, 87, 440, 441
Jim Crow laws, 755
John Brown's Body, 845
Johnson, Andrew, 145, 159, 165, **173**, 228, **400**, 737, 738, 739, 740, **764–66**, *765*, **799**
  end of war and, 51, 159, 320, 324, 328
  impeachment and acquittal, 176, 734, 739, 740, **772–74**, 797, 800–2, 804
  Lincoln's death and, 50, 232, 320, 511, 737
  National Historic Site, **888**
  pardons issued by, 232, 511, 737, 765
  Reconstruction policy/actions, 47, 51, 176, 177, 188, 189, 734–35, 737, 738, 743, 752, 756, 758, 763, **764–66**, 776, 802

Tennessee governor/military governor, 196, 201, 736
  vetoes legislation, 739, 769, 770, 771, 803
Johnson, Eastman, **829**
Johnson, Edward, 308
Johnson, Henry, 749
Johnson, Herschel, 125
Johnson, James L., 546
Johnson, L., 681
Johnson, William Henry, 12, 427
Johnson's Island (Ohio) military prison, 591, **607**, 620
Johnston, Albert Sidney, 17, 237, *252*, 253, 337, *388*, 399, 405, **415**
Johnston, Joseph Eggleston, 9, 19, 30, 35, 38, 40, 41, 48, 49, 50, 370, 383, 385, 386, 387, *388*, 390, 392, 393, 399, 400, 405, 412, 413, 414, **415–16**, 422, 424, 574, 580, 600, 712, 816, 834, 894
  battle overviews, 237, 244, 247, 250, 281, 298, 302, 320, 322, 324, 325
Johnston, Mary, 841
Joint Committee on the Conduct of the War, 12, 146, 371–72
Jomini, Antoine-Henri, 402
Jones, Catesby ap R., 545, 546
Jones, Charles, 687
Jones, James S., 541
Jones, John Beauchamp, 671
Jones, John M., 307
Jones, Joseph, **657**
Jonesboro, Georgia, battle of, 302
Josiah Bell (C.S.S.), 531
Juárez, Benito, 36, 206
Julian, George, 752

Kansas, 5, 32, 64, 65, 93, 124, 127, 237, 289
  military prisons in, 589
  Quantrill's raid into (1863), **289**
  wartime governors, 197
  see also Lecompton Constitution
Kansas-Nebraska Act, 63, **111–13**, 115, 116, 123, 131, 132
Kantor, MacKinlay, 839, 841

Kearney, Philip, *378*, 834
Kearsarge (U.S.S.), 38, 40, 339–40, *535*, *535*, 545, 563, 580, 828
Keckley, Elizabeth, 700, **728**
Keen, W. W., 627
Kellogg, William, 794
Kelly, Caroline, 710
Kemble, Frances Ann (Fanny), 710, **728–29**
Keneally, Thomas, 840
Kenner, Duncan F., 49
Kennesaw Mountain, Georgia, 40, *301*, 341, 360, **894**
Kentucky, 11, 57, 263, 333, 617, 666, 748, 755
   archival/artifact collections, 881
   military prisons in, 589
   Union offensive in Eastern, **251**
   wartime governors, 197
   see also Louisville, Kentucky; Perryville, Kentucky
Keokuk (U.S.S.), 534
Kernstown, Virginia, 15, 313
Ketcham hand grenades, 502
Key, David, 796
Key, Francis Scott, 120
Keyes, Wade, **186**
Keystone State (Union vessel), 532
Key West, Florida, 543, 549
Kilpatrick, H. Judson, 296
Kilpatrick-Dahlgren Raid on Richmond, 294, 612
King, John, 817, 819
Kingsport, Tennessee, 319
Kingston (North Carolina) navy yard, 546
Kingville, South Carolina, 357
Kirkwood, Samuel, 192, 193, 197
Knight, William, 827
Knights of the Golden Circle, 20, 167, 453
Knights of the Rising Sun, 784
Knights of the White Camellia, 784
Know-Nothing Party *see* American Party
Knoxville, Tennessee, 33, 34, **292**
   military prison, 591, 594
   Whig, 839
Ku Klux Klan, 735, 738, 741, 755, 778, 784, 785, 786, 798, 854

Ku Klux Klan Act, 741, 786, 787
Kunstler, Mort, 828
Kurz, Louis, 809
Kurz & Allison, Chicago, **809**, 826
   see also Lecompton Constitution

Labor/strikes, 31, 702, 705–6, 720, **753–54**, 791–92
La Crosse Democrat (Wisconsin), 227
Ladies' Freedmen and Soldiers' Relief Association, 700
Ladies' Union Bazaar Association, 701
Lafayette (Indiana) military prison, 588
La Grange, Tennessee, **310**
Laird Rams, 33, 204
Laird Shipyard, 203–4
Lamar, Charles Augustus Lafayette, 65
Lamb, William, 321
Lambert, Louis, 852
La Montain, John, 346, 364, 525
Lancaster (U.S.S.), 532
Lance, 516
Land, abandoned/confiscated, 738, **750–53**
Land battles, major (map), *240–41*
Land forces: general organization, **374–76**
Land grants, 20, 149, 683, 737
Land mines, 488, 512
Landrum, George W., 466
Lane, David, 26, 35, 475, 859
Lane, Henry Smith, 197
Lane, James H., 428
Langston, John Mercer, 167, *780–81*, **799–800**
Lanier, Sidney, 839
Lardner, James Lawrence, 544, 551
Larson, James, 496
Latane, William D., 843
Laundresses, 660, 707
Laurel Hill, 307
Lawley, Francis Charles, 271, 286, 368
Lawson, Thomas, 653
Lawton, Alexander R., 395
Leadbetter, Daniel, 395
Leaves of Grass, 849

Lecompton Constitution, 64, 113, 115, 126, 127
LeConte, Joseph, 652
Ledlie, James H., 312
Lee, Fitzhugh, 296, *388*, 834
Lee, Mary Ann Custis, 836
Lee, Robert Edward, *179*, 327, *388*, **402–3**, *403*, 818
   Antietam, 23, 212, 266, 665
   Appomattox campaign, **325–28**, *326*, *327*
   Arlington, Virginia estate, 726
   Army of Northern Virginia, assuming command of, 19, 20, 250, 251, 259, 390, 416
   black soldiers, 157
   Bull Run (Manassas, second), 22, **264**, 382
   Chancellorsville, Virginia, 29, **277**, 454, *584*
   Cheat Mountain, Western Virginia, 245–46
   Cold Harbor, Virginia, 39, **308–10**
   Dahlgren and, 296
   Davis and, 47, 49, *179*, 180, 370, 413
   in diary entries, 37, 46, 157, 294–95
   faith of Southern people in, 259
   food gathering by troops, 642
   Fredericksburg, Virginia, **271–74**, 723
   general in chief, named, 47, 158, 191, 370, 394, 399
   Harpers Ferry, Virginia (1859), 66, 118
   headquarters, 26
   Hill appointed by, 619
   home state seceding (Virginia), 6
   Hooker, quoted about, 414
   Jackson (Stonewall) and, 259
   in literature/arts/sculpture/ photography, 808, 816, 817, 818, *818*, 826, 828, 831, **832**, 834
   "lost order" of, 266
   mapping and, 346–47
   Mexican War, 339, 404
   Overland campaign, 385

Lee, Robert Edward (*cont.*)
  Pennsylvania/Gettysburg, 30, 31,
    282–87, 403, 411, 417, 419,
    471
  Petersburg, Virginia, 315, 320,
    321–23, 385, 410
  press/newspapers and, 712
  prisoner exchange/treatment,
    599, 600, 603
  quoted:
    anticipating Confederate
      success, 27
    on honor distinctions, 482
    on Hood, 413
    on music, 443
    on Southern refugees from
      Fredericksburg, 723
    on Stonewall Jackson's death,
      415
    on Stuart, 423
    on war strategy/goals, 37, 311
  Richmond, Virginia, 20, 49, 296
  Spotsylvania, Virginia, 38, **307–8**
  strategy/tactics, 30, 31, 37, 259,
    312, **337–339**, 355, 359
  surrender to Grant, 50, 134, 159,
    173, 230, 320, 326, *327*, 328,
    339, 380, 400, 403, 410, 420,
    572, 600, 603, 617, 716, 826,
    888–89
  wife, 836
  Wilderness, Virginia, 38, **304–7**
  Wilmington, North Carolina and,
    321
Lee, Samuel P., 550
Lee, Sidney S., 542, 546
Lee, Stephen D., 310, 398
Lee, Thomas, 759
Leesburg, Virginia, 12
Lefaucheux of Paris, 518
Legal Tender Acts, 15, 147, 672
Leggett, T. B., 817, 819
Lehigh (U.S.S.), *16*, 556
Lemmon v. The People, 63, 97–98
Lenthal, John, 539
Leslie, Frank, 724, 809, 817, 819,
    821, 822, 824, 826
Letcher, John, 195–96, 201, 312, 718
Letterman, Jonathan W., 630,
    631–33, **655**

Levitt, Saul, 854, 856
Lewis, Henry H., 547
Lewis, James T., 199
Lewis, Richard, 9, 13, 33, 477, 480
Lewis, Sinclair, 854
Lexington, Kentucky, **245**, 348, 589
Lexington (U.S.S.), 533
Libby Hill (Richmond, Virginia),
    833
Libby Prison (Richmond, Virginia),
    595, 600, 610, **611–12**, *612*,
    615, 617, 621
Liberalism, 790–91
Liberator, The, 14, 59, 95, 96, 119,
    132, 133, 724
Liberia, 14, 103, 104, 120, 130, 132,
    215, 727
Liberty Party, 61, 96, **122**
Library of Congress, 348, 349,
    877–880
Liddell, St. John R., 328
Lieber, Francis, 29, 90, 450, 597
Lieber Code, 29, 451, 597, 625
Lightning Brigade (Wilder's
    Mounted Brigade, U.S.), 496
Ligon's Warehouse (Virginia)
    military prison, 595
Limber, 516
Lincoln, Abraham, *151*, **170–73**,
    171, *268*, **400–401**, *455*, 707,
    715
  administration/cabinet/staff,
    109–10, *171*, 172, 173,
    174–78, 191, 350, 525, 711
  assassination/death, 50, 158, 159,
    173, 174, 189, **230–32**, *231*,
    320, 457, 545, 717, 737, 744,
    797, 814, 826, 834, 890–91
  assassination plot (prior) foiled,
    454
  Battlefield National Cemetery
    (dedicated by), 889
  black troops, treatment of, 619
  colonization, 216
  as commander in chief, 371, 375,
    394, **400–1**, 407, 525
  commuting sentences, 167, 709,
    721
  critics/opposition to, 42, 133,
    167, 721

  Dahlgren and, 576
  Davis compared to, 371, 399
  debating Douglas (1858), 65,
    115–18, 131
  Douglass (Frederick) and, 21, 32,
    131, 154
  Emancipation Proclamation, 150,
    250, 266, 430, 602, 688; *see
    also* Emancipation
    Proclamation
  field visits:
    Antietam (McClellan), *268*,
      455, 812
    Chatham Manor
      (Fredericksburg), 893
    only time under Confederate
      fire, 41, 313
    Petersburg, 50
    Richmond at end of war, 50,
      159, 536, 716
    Washington Yard, 545, 576
  governors (Northern) and, 191
  Grant and, 294, 401–2
  in literature/art/sculpture/
    photography, 812, 814, 815,
    821, 822, 826, 834, 835, 841,
    846, 847, 848
  McClellan and, 15, 255, 259, *268*,
    269, 375, 403, *455*, 812
  memorials:
    Birthplace, **888**
    Boyhood National Memorial,
      895
    Home National Historic Site,
      895
    Lincoln Memorial, **835**
  political leadership of, 139, 142,
    147, 191
  presidential elections:
    1860 election, 66, 123, 126,
      177, 693
    1861 inauguration, 6, 67, 141,
      141, 821
    1864 election, 36, 39, 43,
      44–45, 140, 141, 157, 165,
      223–24, 228, 236, 294, 302,
      304, 314, 603, 737
    1865 inauguration, 48, 158,
      228–30, 715, 733
  press and, 157, 226–27

prisoner treatment/exchanges and, 600–601, 602, 619
proclamation concerning British citizens, 206
quoted:
    on end of war, 49
    on eye-for-an-eye policy, 31–32
    on freeing slaves, 22, 151
    Gettysburg Address, 34, 276
    on holding men in army, 477
    on liberty, 461
    on racial integration, 216
    on re-election, 42, 155
    on saving the Union, 22, 40, 143
    Second Inaugural Address, 48, **228–30**
    on Stowe (Harriet Beecher), 111
    Thanksgiving proclamation, 689–90
    on Union army/victories, 25, 46, 336
receiving telegraph from balloon *Enterprise*, 362
Reconstruction, 40, 156, 157, 159, 731, 733–34, 737, 744, 750–51, 758, 760, 762, 764, 802, 803, 804
slavery (views on), 2, 139, 171
speeches:
    Cooper Union, 815
    First Inaugural Address, 171
    Gettysburg Address, 34, 155, **214–15**, 276, 842, 859
    invoking God in, 688
    last public address, 159
    Second Inaugural Address, 48, 158, **228–30**, 733
support for, 36, 191, 223–24, 226–28, 726
suspending *habeas corpus*, 143, 144, 209–10, 726
Trent affair and, 203
vice presidents, **173**; *see also* Johnson, Andrew
war strategy, 38, 48, 172, 255, 259, 271, 296, 302, 336, 353, 381, 543, 547

wife, *see* Lincoln, Mary Todd
woman chaplain appointment and, 439
Lincoln, Mary Todd, 170, **187**, *187*, 230, 700, 728
Lincoln University, 89
Lister, Joseph, 623, 627
Literature, *see* Arts/literature, Civil War in
Lithographic prints, 806–11
Little Rock, Arkansas, 33, **291**, 546, 587, 889
Livermore, Mary A., 10, *446*, 476, 655, 661, 699
Living history (Civil War reenactment), 898, **904–5**
Livingston, John W., 544
Lockridge, Ross, 855
Locust Grove, 293
Logan, John A., 304, *378*, 383, 773, 834
Logan's Cross Roads, 251
Logistics/communications, **349–65**
    aeronautics (ballooning), **362–65**
    military railroads, **350–53**
    signal corps/wig-wag signaling, **358–62**
    telegraph, **353–57**
Lombard, Francis O., 495
London *Index*, 189
London Times, 271, 368
Long, Eli, 325
Long, Jefferson, 782
Longfellow, Henry Wadsworth, 119, 746
Longstreet, James, 34, 191, 237, 264, 291, 292, 306, 339, 384, *388*, 398, **416**, *793*, 841
Lookout Mountain, Tennessee, 34
Lorena (song), 851
"Lost Cause," 51, 805, 808
Loughborough, Mary Webster, 702
Louisiana, 37, 38, 156, 196, 452, 663, 736, 761, 763, 767
    archival/artifact collections, 881, 907
    blacks in, 156, 219, 742, 755, 780
    guerrillas, 237, 452
    military prisons in, 589, 593

    population (1860: whites/slaves), 666
    readmitted, 740, 772, 793, 796
    Reconstruction, 736, 739, 742, 755, **761–62**, 767, 782, 791, 794–96
    Republican administration in, 791
    secession, 3, 160
    troops withdrawn from, 742
    wartime governors, 200
    see also New Orleans, Louisiana; Shreveport, Louisiana
Louisiana Hospital, Richmond, 650
Louisiana Native Guards, 408, 432
Louisiana Purchase (1803), 58, 91, 92
Louis Prang & Company, New York, 535, 807, **809**, 830
Louisville (U.S.S.), 558
Louisville, Kentucky, 26, 263, 589, 653; *see also* Kentucky
L'Ouverture, Toussaint, 58
Lovejoy, Elijah P., 60, 96, 127, 133
Lovie, Henri, **821–22**
Low, Frederick, 197
Lowe, Thaddeus S. C., 362, 363, 364, 525, 823
Lowell, James Russell, 848
Lowell, Robert, **845–46**
Lower Seaboard and Gulf Approach, *238*, **239**
Loyall, Benjamin P., 546
Loyal Leagues, 168
Loyalty oaths, 149, 739, 763
Lubbock, Francis, 194, 201
Ludlow, W. H., 601
Ludlow Street Jail (New York) military prison, 590
Ludwig, Charles, 810
Lumley, Arthur, **822–23**
Lumpkin's Jail (Virginia) military prison, 594
Lundy, Benjamin, 132
L'Union, 219
Lynch, James R., 782
Lynch, John, 780
Lynch, William F., 541, 545
Lynchburg, Virginia, 39, 40, 312, 326, 595

Lyon, Nathaniel, 8, 10, 244, 420
Lytle, A. J., **814**

Macarthy, Harry, 850
Mackall, William W., 255
MacMillan Information Now
    Encyclopedia, 674
Macon, Georgia, armory, 511
Madison, James, 55
Maffitt, John Newland, *564*
Maggots, 645
Magoffin, Beriah, 194, 197
Magrath, Andrew, 201
Magruder, George A., 539
Magruder, John B., 277, 343, 356,
    364, 390, 391, 531
Mahan, Dennis Hart, 339, 340
Mahopac (U.S.S.), 557
Mail (in Army camps), **475–76**
Maine, 106–7, 198, 882
Major & Knapp Lithograph
    Company, 327
Malaria, **645–46**
Mallard, Mary, 40
Mallory, Stephen R., 67, *179*, **185**,
    394, 523, 524, 536, 537,
    540–41, 570, **578**, 579, 711
Malone, Mary, 456
Malvern Hill, Virginia, 20, 259,
    530, 896
Manassas (C.S.S.), **560**
Manassas campaign, *see* Bull Run
Manassas National Battlefield Park,
    895; *see also* Bull Run
Manayunk, 557
Manet, Edouard, 827
Manhattan (U.S.S.), **557**
Manifest Destiny, **92–93**, 108, 109
Mansfield, Louisiana, 239, 298, 424
Manumission, 103
Mapping:
    Confederate, **346–47**
    importance of, **345–49**
    on the move, **347–49**
    Union, **345–46**
Maratanza (U.S.S.), 364
Marches, forced, **466–68**
Mare's Island prison, 587
Marietta (Georgia) military prison,
    593

Mariners' Museum, 531, 885
Marines, 442, 534, 540, 542,
    572–74, *573*, *822*
Marion Court House (South
    Carolina) navy yard, 546
Markham, Edwin, **847–48**
Marmaduke, John S., 435
Marshall, John, 135
Marshall, Nichola, 717
Martindale, John H., 40
Martyn, Sarah Towne Smith, 710
Maryland, 44, 145, 331, 666, 748,
    792
    archival/artifact collections, 882
    military prisons in, 589, 606
    wartime governors, 198
    see also Baltimore
Mason, Charles, 53
Mason, Emily V., 825
Mason, James M., 49, 109, 111, 146,
    186, **189**, 202, 525, 552
Mason, John, 102
Mason(s), 83, 85
Mason-Dixon line, 53
Massachusetts:
    education in, 684
    military prisons/camps, 589,
        606–7
    recruitment of black soldiers,
        694–4
    rights for African Americans,
        678
    state arsenal, *708*
    wartime governors, 198
Massachusetts Emigrant Aid
    Company, 122
Massaponax Church, Virginia,
    234
Mathews, Alfred E., 818
Maule, Joshua, 696
Maury, Matthew Fontaine, 541,
    542, **578–79**, *833*, 887
Maximilian, Ferdinand, 36, 206
Maxwell House (Tennessee)
    military prison, 591
Mayo, Joseph, 718
Mayo's Factory (Virginia) military
    prison, 595
Mayre's Heights (Fredericksburg,
    Virginia), 271

Mays, Anna, 830
McCabe, Edward, 750
McCabe, James Dabney, 836, 853
McCallum, Daniel C., 14, 350–51
McCarthy, Carlton, 825
McCauley, Charles S., 544
McClellan, George Brinton, 10, 12,
    13, 15, 17, 18, 19, 20, 23–24,
    31, 43, 45, 140, 146, 147, 157,
    190, *268*, *378* **403**, 454, 495
    aeronauts and, 364
    aides-de-camp, 421, 458
    Antietam, **266**, 406, 812
    Army of the Potomac, 271, 379,
        381–82
    cartoons making fun of, 810
    critics of, 175–76, 188
    dismissal, 268, 406, 455
    Eastern Theater, **236**
    general in chief, 247, 334, 371,
        394
    Hammond (surgeon general) and,
        654
    intelligence gathering for, 454,
        460
    Lincoln and, 268, 405, 406, 455,
        812
    mentioned in press (*National Anti-
        Slavery Standard*), 216
    Mexican War, 339
    nickname, 223
    organizing Union army, 375, 377
    Peninsula campaign, 244, 250,
        255–59, 264, 336, 343, 390,
        409, 412–13, 415, 417, 423,
        529, 600, 695–96, 810
    presidential candidate (election of
        1864), 43, 45, 140, 157, 165,
        190, 223–24, 315
    quoted:
        on field artillery, 503
        on maps, 345
        on religion (respect for the
            Sabbath), 480–81
        on Union, 242
    rank, 396
    sculpture of (Washington, D.C.),
        834
    Western Virginia operations, 245,
        353, 822

McClernand, John A., 381, 397, *455*, 531

McCook, Edward M., 290, 325

McCord, Colonel, 470

McCormick's reapers, 676

McCown, John P., 254, 255

McCulloch, Ben, 244, 255, 420

McCulloch, Hugh, **175**

McCulloch v. Maryland, 91

McCurdy's Warehouse (Virginia) military prison, 595

McDaniel's Jail (Virginia) military prison, 594

McDougal, David Stockton, 533, 545

McDowell, Irvin, 9, 10, 235, 246, 247, 261, 346, *378*, 379, 397, 893

McDowell, Virginia, battle of, 18

McElroy, John, 837

McEnery, John, 794

McGary, Charles P., 547

McGuffey's readers, 680

McGuire, Hunter Holmes, 625, 633, 834

McGuire, Judith, 703

McIntosh, David, 489

McKean, William W., 551

McKee, J. G., 724

McLean, Wilbur, 327

McLean Barracks (Ohio) military prison, 591

McLenan, John, 806

McLeod, M. M., 782

McPherson, James B., 31, 80, 295, 302, 303–4, 382–83, **416–17**, *417*, 834

Meade, George Gordon, *378*, 379, 396, **417**, 456, 494, 598, 834, 885
  battle overviews, *234*, 236, 237, 282, 287, 293, 296, 304, 307, 308, 311, 326, 354

Means, Edward J., 546

Measles, **646**

Medal of Honor, 409, 435, 441, 447, 460, 481, 798
  black soldiers (number awarded to), 435
  first/only woman awarded, 447, 481, 656

musicians, 445
  rescinded, 481
  total number awarded, 481

Medical care, 17, **623–64**
  amputations, 630, 634–35
  for black soldiers, **637–38**
    selected sickness/mortality statistics, 649
  casualties (disease *vs.* battle), 623
  causes of disease, **638–43**
  common diseases/infections (and treatments), **643–51**
  dentists, 625
  doctors (number of), 624–25
  federal ambulance corps, **631–34**
  leaders in Civil War medicine, **654–57**
  medical drug supplies, **651–52**
  medical officers, **652–54**
  naval medical care, 540, 542, **635–37**
  nineteenth century medical care, **625–27**
  nurses, female, **657–61**
  relief organizations, **661–63**
  selected sickness/mortality statistics, 648, 659
  see also Disease, Drugs and medical supplies, Individual diseases, Hospitals

Medill, Joseph, 27

Meigs, John Rodgers, 418, *482*, **836**

Meigs, Montgomery Cunningham, 395, **418**, 495

Melville, Herman, **848**

Memminger, Christopher G., *179*, **182–83**, 668, 669

Memphis, Tennessee, 19, 293, 296, 336, 530, 543, 659, 702, 738, 784; *see also* Tennessee

Mennonites, 15, 83, 151, 464, 465, 696, 697

Mercedita (U.S.S.), 532

Merchant Magazine, 676

Merchant Marine, 564

Mercie, Jean Antoine, 832

Meredith, Sam, 601

Meridian, Mississippi, **295–96**, 593

Meriwether, Elizabeth Avery, 702

Merrill, William E., 348

Merrimack (U.S.S.), 15, 16, 525, 529, 544, 552, 574
  rechristened C.S.S. *Virginia*, 525

Merritt, Wesley, *41*

Merryman, John, 135, 144, 208

Methodist Episcopal Church, 61, 87

Methodists, 61, 82, 85, 87, 95, 440, 685, 687, 748

Mexican War (1846–1848), 61, 62, 92, **108–9**, 122, 132, 161, 178, 334, 339, 367, 381, 393, 401, 405, 413, 415, 416, 422, 452, 572, 579, 580

Mexico, 36, 60, 63, 93, 136, 167, 202, **206–7**, 501, 667

Miantonomoh (U.S.S.), 558

Michigan, 57, 59–60, 167, 198, 882

Middle Creek, Kentucky, 251

Military campaign (defined), 239; *see also* Campaigns/battles, significant

Military department (defined), 239

Military leaders:
  commanders in chief, **399–401**
  Confederate, *388*
  generals (Confederate), **398–99**
  generals (Union), **393–97**
  generals in chief, **401–4**
  high command (Union and Confederate), **394–95**
  medical officers, **652–54**
    Confederate, **653–54**
    U.S.A., **652–53**
  naval organization/staff:
    Confederate, 537, **540–42**
    U.S.A., **537–40**
  notable officers (profiles), **404–26;** *see also specific officer*
  Union, *378*

Military Order of the Loyal Legion of the United States (MOLLUS), **900**, 901–2

Military Order of the Stars & Bars, **902**

Military organization, *see* Armies

Military railroads, *see* Railroad(s)

Military records (service/pension records of Civil War soldiers/sailors), 900

Military schools, South *vs.* North, 369
Militia Act, 250, 432, 720
Milledgeville, 316
Miller, Stephen, 198
Milligan, James F., 360
Milliken's Bend, Mississippi, 30, 235, 276, 533
Mill Springs, Kentucky, 251
Milton, John, 196, 200
Milwaukee class (Union ironclads), **560**
Mine Run, Virginia campaign, **293**
Minié, Claude Etienne, 485, 511
Minie ball/bullet, 179, 435, 485–86, 488, 517
Minnesota, 57, 65, 198, 665
Minnesota (U.S.S.), 529
Minor, George B., 542
Missionary Ridge, 34, 293, 331
Mississippi, 67, 79, 81, 125, 143, 160, 200
  military prisons in, 589, 593
  population (1860), 666
  readmitted, 741, 772, 793
  Reconstruction in, 742, 767
  secession, 3, 4, 67
  see also Vicksburg
Mississippi (C.S.S.), 529
Mississippi (El Monassir), 534
Mississippi (U.S.S.), 532, 826
Mississippi Marine Brigade, **442–43,** 452
Mississippi River, 336, 337, 523, 529, 530, 531, 532, 533, 550
Mississippi Squadron, 531, 534
Mississippi Valley, 736, 762
Missouri, 8, 10, 11, 12, 32, 43, 58, 63–64, 68, 85, 98, 106–7, 127, 144, 145, 161, 194, 210, 222, 333
  debates, 98, 420, 428, 450, 666, 748
  operations to control, 224, **244–45, 315**
  prisons, 589–90
  wartime governors, 198
  see also St. Louis
Missouri Compromise, 2, 58, 63, 64, 103, **106–7,** 112, 129

Missouri Democrat, 227
Missouri Republican, 227
Mitchel, Ormsby M., 397
Mitchell, Barton W., 266
Mitchell, James Billingslea, 462, 474, 476
Mitchell, John K., 542, 546
Mitchell, Margaret, 840, 855
Mitchelville, South Carolina, 725
Mobile, Alabama, 11, 38, 296, 298, 299, 320, **328,** *329* (map), 352, 546, 592, 718
Mobile Bay, Alabama (1864 battle), 42, 49, 239, 261, **313,** 321, 535, 557
Mohr, Charles Theodor, 652
Molly Maguires, 791
Monadnock (U.S.S.), 544, 558
Monadnock class monitors, **557–58**
Monitor (U.S.S.), 14, 15, 16, *522,* 528–29, 530, 531, 532, 545, 552–53, **555,** 574, 580, 821
Monocacy National Battlefield, **895**
Monocacy River, Maryland, 40, 312
Monroe, James, 120, 206
Monroe Doctrine, 206
Montauk, 532, 545, **556,** 580, 813
Montgomery, Alabama, 5, 8, 67, 68, 160–61, 211, 524, 540, 592
  see also Alabama
Montgomery, John B., 544, 545
Montgomery Hill, Indiana, 319
Monument Avenue, Richmond, **832**
Moore, Andrew Barry, 200, 671
Moore, Marinda Branson, 680
Moore, Samuel Preston, 614, 630, 651, 654, **656**
Moore, Thomas O., 196, 200
Morford, Henry, 837
Morgan, Edwin Denison, 199, 397
Morgan, John Hunt, 194, 224, **287–89, 418–19,** *418,* 448, 496, 608, 617, 665
Morgan, Margaret, 99
Morgan, Van Renssalaer, 546
Morgan, William, 85
Mormons, 83
Morning Light (U.S.S.), 531
Morrill, Justin Smith, 683

Morrill Land Grant Acts, 20, 683
Morris, A., 810
Morris, William S., 355–56
Morris Island, Charleston Harbor, South Carolina, 31, 235, 281, 506–7, 533, 591; *see also* Fort Wagner (Battery Wagner)
Morrow, Honoré Willsie, 840
Morse, Charles Fessenden, 25, 294, 473
Morse, Nathaniel, 228
Mortar, 517
Morton, Oliver Perry, 193, 197
Morton, William, 626
Mosby, John Singleton, 17, **419,** 448, 496, 857
Mosby's Rangers, 448
Moses, Franklin J., Jr., 783
Mound City, Illinois, 543
Mound City (naval hospital), 558, 637
Mount Venice Arsenal, 511
Movies, **854–57**
Mower (Union hospital), 629
Moyamensing Penitentiary (Pennsylvania), 591
Moynihan, Frederick, 833
Mudd, Samuel, 232, 855
Mud March, 26
Mule Shoe, 38, 308
Mulligan, James, 245
Munfordville, Kentucky, 263
Munn v. Illinois, 788
Murdoch, James Edward, 843
Murfreesboro, Tennessee, *see* Stones River campaign
Murphy, Isaac, 196, 200
Murrah, Pendleton, 201
Murray, Ellen, 802
Muse, William T., 547
Music/musicians, 25, **443–45,** 806, **849–53**
  as litter bearers, 631
Musket, 517
Musketoons, **496–97,** 517, 518
Muzzle loader, 517
My Cave Life in Vicksburg, 702
Myer, Albert J., 358, 359, 360, 363, 395
Myers, Abraham C., 395

Myrtle Street Prison (St. Louis), 590

Nahant (U.S.S.), 533, 556, 562
Names Index Project, 900
Nantucket (U.S.S.), 556
Napoleon (field artillery piece), 504, 505, 517
Napoleon III of France, 206
Nashville, Tennessee, 15, 45, 46, 237, **317–19**, *318*, 331, 337; *see also* Tennessee and Franklin, Tennessee
Nashville (C.S.S.), 532, 559, 565, 580
Nast, Thomas, *166, 213, 801*, 806, **823**, 827
Nation, The, 744, 773, 791, 796
National Anti-Slavery Standard, 216
National Archives and Records Administration, 880
National Association for Relief of Destitute Colored Women and Children, 700
National Association of Nurses of the Civil War, 901
National Banking Act, 26
National Convention of Colored Citizens of the United States, 157, 756
National Currency Act, 26, 153
National Equal Rights League, 157, **167–68**
National historic sites, **887–98**
National Labor Convention of Colored Men, 741
National Mineral Act (1866), 789
National Museum of Civil War Medicine, 907
National Museum of Health and Medicine, 880
National Park Service, 888, 900
National Union League, **168**
National Union Party, 39, 156, 165
National Woman's Loyal League, **168**
National Woman Suffrage Association, 769
Native Americans, *see* American Indians

Nautilus (submarine), 565
Naval Historical Center, 880
Navies/naval events, 15, 19, **521–81, 635–37**, 736
  artillery, **509**
  blockade/blockade running, 51, 143, 153, 172, 176–77, 202, 237, 276, 489, **543–52**, 651, 670, 680
  British presence in Naval war, **551–52**
  map, *549*
  operational organization of, **548–50**
  squadron commanders, **550–51**
  commerce raiders, **563–65**
  hospitals/medical care, 540, 631, 635–37
  map of battles and notable events (1861-1865), *526–27*
  Marines, 442, 534, 540, 542, **572–74**, *573, 822*
  meals, 569
  Naval Historical Center, 880
  Naval School (Confederate), 542
  notable naval figures, **574–80**
  organization/staff:
    Confederate, 537, **540–42**
    U.S.A., **537–40**
  pay, 568–69
  sailors, **568–72**
  submarines, **565–67**
  theater of operations, 237
  torpedoes (naval mines), **567–68**
  yards/stations:
    Confederate, 543, **545–47**
    Union, 543, **544–45**
  see also Ironclad ships
Navigation, Bureau of, 539–40
Nazarenes, 151, 464, 697
Nebraska, 63, 112
  see Kansas–Nebraska Act
Negro Soldier Act, 49, 158
Nelson, William, 254, 263
Neosho, Missouri, 244
Neosho class (ships), **559**
Nevada, 62, 108, 157, 198
New Albany (Indiana) military prison, 589

New Bern, North Carolina, 251, 419, 446
"New Departure," 792
New England Anti-Slavery Society, 95, 131, 889
New England Emigrant Aid Society/Company, 63, 112, **122–23**
New England Freedmen's Aid Society, 682
New Hampshire, 58, 77, 217
  wartime governors, 198
New Hope Church, Georgia, 302
New Ironsides, 534, 544, **555**
New Jersey, 59, 78, 82, 127, 153, 198, 220, 224
New Madrid, Missouri, **254–55**
New Market, Virginia, 38
New Mexico, 62, 63, 109, 110, **249**, 590
New Orleans:
  African Americans in, 35, 219, 281, 780
  battle of 1815, 35
  capture of (1862), 11, 18, 239, 250, **261–62**, 336, 528, 529, 531, 577
  Lemmon v. The People (1860), 97
  navy yard, 543, 546
  prisoners in, 621
  Reconstruction, 237, 739, 784
  riots, 718, 739, 784
  Slaughterhouse cases (1873), 794
  submarine prototype (*Pioneer*) on display in, 565
  Union base of operations, 237
  Union-occupied, 407, 596, 723, 724, 761, 762; *see also* Butler, Benjamin Franklin; Louisiana, Shreveport
Newport News (Virginia) military prison, 591
Newsom, Ella King, **660**
Newspapers:
  black, **219**
  illustrated, 806, 819–20
  "politics of the press," **224–28**
  popularity of, 817
  role in prison-of-war propaganda, 612–15
  see also individual titles

New York, 32, 33, 63, 78, 83, 97, 121, 122, 167, 174, 187, 217, 220, 223, 544, 661, 673, 676–77, 678, 699, 705–6
  prisons/camps in, 590, **607**
  riots/mob violence, 31, 719–20
  wartime governors, 199
New York Herald, 225
New York Illustrated News, 817, **819–20,** 823, 826, 827
New York Public Library, 883
New York Times, 225, 227, 228, 242, 286, 432, 609, 613, 614, 812
New York Tribune, 132, 151, 226, 235, 773, 791
Nicholls, Francis, 742, 795, 796
Nickless, Sam'l, 844
Nicolay, John, 214
Niepce, Joseph Nicéphore, 811
Nigeria, 104
Nightingale, Florence, 638, 657, 660
Nightingale (slave ship), 6
Nolan, William C., 833
Norfolk, Virginia, 6, 244, 546; *see also* Gosport Naval Yard
Normal schools, 89
Norris, William, 360, 361, 395, 459
North Atlantic Blockading Squadron (N.A.B.S.), 549
North Carolina, 98, 107, 144, 154, 167, 169, 194, 200, 217, 534, 883
  Burnside's expedition (1862), **251**
  Butler's expedition (1864), **319**
  military prisons in, 593, 610
  population (1860), 666
  readmitted, 740, 772, 793
  Reconstruction in, 741, 748, 765
  secession, 6, 146
  see also Raleigh, North Carolina
North Carolina (ship), 534, 562
North Carolina Standard, 33, 154, 169, 226, 228, 719
Northrop, Lucius B., 394
Northwest Ordinance of 1787, 57, 106
Northwest Territory, 92
Norton, Lemuel B., 359
Norton, Oliver Willcox, 320, 477, 852

Nott, Josiah, 105
Novels of the Civil War, **837–42**
Nullification crisis, 59, 91, 92, **107–8,** 128, 129
Nuns as nurses, 658
Nuns of the Battlefield (bronze relief), **835**
Nurses, 9, 655–56, **657–61,** 703, 707, 746

Oberlin College, 89, 683
Observation balloons, 346, **362–65,** *363,* 438, 525
O'Connor House (South Carolina) military prison, 594
"Oertel," 476
Officers, *see* Military leaders
Ogeechee River, 532
Oglesby, Richard, 197
Ohio, 58, 62, 85, 152, 156, 166, 167–68, 193, 194, 199, 884
  military prisons in, 591, 607
  Morgan's raid (1863), **287–89,** *288* (map)
  see also Cincinnati
Oklahoma, 161, 750
O'Laughlin, Michael, 232
Old Capitol Prison (Washington, D.C.) military prison, 588
Olden, Charles S., 198
Old Salem Church, Virginia, **893**
Olmstead, Charles H., 261
Olmsted, Frederick Law, 654, 661, **729**
Oneota (U.S.S.), 557
Onondaga (U.S.S.), **556–57**
Opequon Creek, *see* Winchester
Orchard Knob, Tennessee, 293
Ord, Edward O. C., 385, 386
Order of American Knights, 167
Ordnance, *see* Weaponry
Ordnance Rifle, 504–5, 508
Oregon, 62, 92, 128, 218
Orphanages, 746
Osage (U.S.S.), 559
Osbon, Bradley Sillick, 261, 530
Osborn, James M., **814–16**
Osborne, Wm., 698
Osteomyelitis (bone inflammation), 645

O'Sullivan, Timothy H., 234, 751, 812, 813, **816**
Otey, Lucy, 705
Otsego (U.S.S.), 536
Ould, Robert, 601, **620–21**
Oven Bluff Shipyard, Alabama, 546
Overland campaign (Virginia), 39–40, 234, 294, 299, 302, **304–10,** 342, 368, 695
  Cold Harbor, **308–10,** *309*
  Spotsylvania Court House, **307–8,** *307*
  Wilderness, **304–7,** *305*
Overton's Hill, 319

Pacific Appeal, 219
Pacific Railway Act, 20, 149
Pacifist religious groups, 15, 156, 464, 695–98
Packard, Stephen, 795
Paducah (Kentucky) military prison, 589
Page, Richard L., 545
Paine, Lewis, 231, 232
Paintings/artists of the Civil War, 806, **826–30**
Palmer, Benjamin, 686
Palmer, Flora Bond (Fanny), 830
Palmer, James S., 551
Palmer, William J., 459–60
Palmerston, Lord, 19, 49
Palmetto State (C.S.S.), 532
Palmito Ranch, Texas, 51, 239, 321, **328–30,** 367; *see also* Texas
Pamplin Historical Park, 907
Panic of 1857, 65, 672
Panic/depression of 1873, 673, 791
Parish Prison (New Orleans) military prison, 589
Parker, Joel, 198
Parker, John H., 541
Parker, William H., 542
Parker's Store, Virginia, 304
Parkman, Francis, 790
Parra, John A., 853
Parrott, Robert Parker, 504, **511–12**
Parrott Gun/Rifle, 504–5, 506, 508, 512, 517

Parry, Owen, 840
Partisan rangers, 338, 419, **447–52**
Passaic (U.S.S.), **556**, 577, 813
Pasteur, Louis, 623, 626
Pastimes (Army):
 sanctioned, **468–69**
 unsanctioned, **469–70**
Patapsco (U.S.S.), 556
Patrick, Marsena R., 457
Patrick Henry (C.S.S.), 542
Patriotic expressions, **712–17**
Patrons of Husbandry, 788
Patterson, Robert, 247, 386
Paulding, Hiram, 544
Paxton, Elisha Franklin, 278, 483
Pay, 32, 39, 156, 432, 434, 709
 chaplains, 440–41
 draftees/volunteers, 372
 seamen, 568–69
Payne, George, 713
Payne, Lewis, *see* Paine, Thomas
Peace conventions, 5, 67
Peace Democrats, 27, 28, 30, 36,
 164–65, 168, 223, 286, 294,
 304, 315, 719, 720; *see also*
 Copperheads
Peace negotiations, 42, 47, 48
Peace plank, 157
Peace resolutions, 153
Peace societies/movement, 27, **169,**
 195, 719
Peachtree Creek, Georgia, battle of,
 42, 302
Peake, Mary, 682, 736
Pea Ridge, Arkansas, 15, 239, **255,**
 380, 382, **895;** *see also* Arkansas
Pearson, George, 545
Peck, George W., 838
Pecos National Historical park,
 New Mexico, **896**
"Peculiar institution," 1, 61
Pee Dee Navy Yard, South
 Carolina, 546
Pegram, John, 245, 322
Pekin, Illinois, 20
Pember, Phoebe Yates Levy, **660**
Pemberton, John C., 30, 279, 280,
 281, 339, 393, 398
Pendergast, Garrett J., 544

Peninsula campaign (Virginia), 15,
 16, 17, 181, **255–59,** 334, 336,
 337, 342, 343, 345, 350, 364,
 513, 529, 530, 696, 729, 810,
 812, 821
 Jeb Stuart's ride around
  McClellan (map), *257*
 Seven Days Battles (map), *258*
Pennell, Joseph S., 840
Pennington, James W., 145
Penn School, 802
Pennsylvania, 24, 30, 57, 61, 78, 82,
 95–96, 99, 116, 128, 134, 151,
 152, 168, 199, 591, 884; *see also*
 Gettysburg address,
 Gettysburg campaign,
 Philadelphia
Pennsylvania Railroad, 746–47
Pennypacker, Galusha, 481
Pensacola, Florida, 5, 243, 530, 544,
 546, 550; *see also* Florida
Pensions, 150, **745–47,** 900
Percussion (arm/cap/fuse/shell), 517
Perkins, George Hamilton, 8, 521
Perrin, Abner M., 308
Perry, Madison, 200
Perryville, Kentucky, 24, 263
Persac, A., 810
Pessou and Simon (New Orleans),
 810
Petersburg, Virginia, 15, 39, 42, 49,
 50, 140, 294, 304, 317, 320,
 322, 325, 337, 342, 343, 350,
 487, 536
 campaign (1864), **310–12,** *309*
 campaign (1865), **321–23,** 330,
  358
 military prison, 595
 riot, 718
Petersburg "Dictator" mortar, 507
Petersburg National Battlefield,
 896
Petersen, William, 231
Petersen House, 891
Petigru, James L., 108
Pettus, John, 196, 200
Philadelphia, 679
 Navy Yard, 544
 press, 31, 147, 727, 835
 see also Pennsylvania

Philippi, West Virginia, **245**
Philippoteaux, Paul, 827
Phillips, Eugenia, 703
Phillips, Wendell, 59, 119, **133,**
 738, 770
Photography/photographers,
 811–16
Pickens, Francis, 196, 201
Pickens District, South Carolina,
 501
Picket (duty as), **476–77**
Picket Boat No. 1, 562
Picket Launch No. 1, 536
Pickett, George Edward, 49, 299,
 322, 339, **419–20,** 832
Pickett's Charge (Gettysburg), 282,
 286, 340
Pierce, Franklin, 112, 161, 178, 370,
 399
Pierpont, Francis H., 199
Pillow, Gideon, 596
Pilot Knob, Missouri, 43, 315
Pinchback, Pinckney B. S., 742,
 780–81, 782, 783, **800**
Pine and Palm, 12
Piney Branch Church, 307
Pinfire/rimfire, 515, 517–18
Pinkerton, Allan, 18, 454, *455,*
 456–57, 460–61
Pistols, **498–500,** 518
Pittsburg (U.S.S.), 255, 559
Pittsburg Landing, *see* Shiloh
Planter (steamer), 571–72, *571*
Pleasant Grove; Sabine Cross
 Roads, *see* Mansfield, Louisiana
Pleasant Hill, Louisiana, 38, 298
Pleasanton, Alfred, 30
Pleasants, Henry, 311
Pleasonton, Alfred, 495
Plum Run Bend, Tennessee (battle
 of), 530
Pneumonia, **646–47**
Pocahontas (U.S.S.), 248, 577
Poetry, 315, **843–49**
Poilpot, Theophile, 827
Poindexter's Farm, Virginia, 259
Point Lookout, Maryland, 589, **606,**
 617
Political cartoons/cartoonists, *45,*
 335, 801, 806, 810, 823

Political parties and organizations:
antebellum, **119–24**
Reconstruction, 748–49, 779–84, 792–97
wartime, **164–70**
Politics, *see also* Radical Republicans
antebellum, 54–68
abolition movement, 94–98
compromises, 106–11
1860 election, 122–27
Kansas–Nebraska Act, 111–13
Lincoln–Douglas debates, 115–18
parties and organizations, 121–26
states' rights, 91–93
Reconstruction, 735–72
Congressional Reconstruction, 770–72
1876 election, 795–96
government and business, 789–90
government and labor, 791–92
impeachment of Andrew Johnson, 773–74
redemption by Conservative Democrats, 792–97
reform movement, 790–91
Republican rule in south, 779–84
Union Leagues, 748–49
wartime, 141–232
African American rights, 218–22
conduct of war, and, 235
constitutions (U.S.A. v. C.S.A.), 164–65
creation of Confederate government, 162–66
elections, 222–26
Emancipation Proclamation, 212–16
European powers, 203–9
Gettysburg Address, 216–17
government officials:
Confederate, 180–88
U.S. (Union), 170–78
governors:
Confederate, 200–1
U.S., 196–99

movement to colonize African Americans, 217–18
newspapers' role in, 226–30
notable political figures, 188–93
parties and organizations, 166–72
writ of *habeas corpus*, suspension of, 209–12
see also Habeas corpus, writ of
Polk, James K., 61, 108, 122, 176
Polk, Leonidas, 296, *388*, 398, **420**, 687
Pollard, Edward A., 413, 805
Pomeroy, Samuel C., 155–56, 216
Pomeroy Circular, 36, 155
Pook, Samuel, 553
Pope, John, 17, 254, 264–65, *378*, 380, 381, 382, 397
Pope Gregory XVII, 87
Poplar Grove National Cemetery, Virginia, 896
Popular art, **806–11**
Popular sovereignty, 63, 112, 115, 116, 117, 125, 131
Population/demographics (statistics):
antebellum America, 69–71, 103
free blacks (antebellum America), 103
whites/slaves (in South), by state, 666–67
Porcher, Francis P., 651
Porter, David Dixon, 269, 279–80, 296, 321, *378*, 381, 443, 531, 532, 533, 534, 536, *550*, 578, **579**, 814
Porter, Eliza, 699
Porter, Felicia Grundy, 663, *663*
Porter, Fitz John, 264
Porter, John L., 541, 561
Port Gibson, Mississippi, 30, 280
Port Hudson, Louisiana, 33, 235, 239, 263, 276, **281**, 490, 532, 598
Port Republic, Virginia, 19, 261
Port Royal Relief Committee of Philadelphia, 802
Port Royal Sound, South Carolina, 12, **248**, 525, 543, 550, 674, 736, 760–61

Portsmouth Yard, Maine, 545
Port Walthall Junction, 299
Post, Charles A., 570
Postal service, 176, 185, 707, **710–11**
Potato famine in Ireland, 72, 676
Powell, Lewis, 174
Powhatan (U.S.S.), 579
Prairie Grove (Arkansas) campaign, **271**
Prang, Louis, 809
Prang & Company, New York, 535, 807, **809**, 830
"Prayer of Twenty Millions" (Greeley editorial), 22, 151
Preliminary Emancipation Proclamation, *see* Emancipation Proclamation
Prentiss, Benjamin M., 252–53
Presbyterians, 60, 85, 95, 120, 132, 440, 685, 686
President(s):
C.S.A., **178–80**; *see also* Davis, Jefferson Finis
U.S.A.
wartime, **170–73**; *see also* Adams, Adams (Quincy), Buchanan, Fillmore, Garfield, Grant, Harrison, Hayes, Jackson, Jefferson, Johnson, Lincoln, Madison, Monroe, Pierce, Polk, Taylor, Tyler, Van Buren, Washington
Presidential elections, *see* Elections
Presidential powers (comparison of U.S. and Confederate constitutions), 163
Presidential Reconstruction, **764–66**; *see also* Reconstruction
Press, *see* Newspapers
Preston, William, 36
Price, Joseph, 546
Price, Sterling, 43, 224, 244, 245, 255, 269, 315, 354, 380, 381, *388*, 391, **420–21**
Prigg, Edward, 99
Prigg v. Pennsylvania, 61, 99
Prince Street Jail (Virginia) military prison, 595

Pringle, Cyrus, 465
Pringle, Jane, 721
Prisons/prisoners of war, 21, 29, 36, 37, 47, 146, **583–622**
    escapes, **616–17**
    major prisoner-of-war camps/ military prisons:
        Confederate, **592–96, 608–12**
        map, *586*
        Union, **587–89, 604–7**
    press/published reports, and public opinion, **612–16**
    prisoner exchange and the Dix-Hill cartel, **600–4**
    selected biographies, 619–22
    statistics, 583–84
    Sultana disaster, **617–18**, *618*
Prison Town (Texas) military prison, 594
Prize Cases, 153, 202
Proclamation of Amnesty and Reconstruction, 35, 155, 731, 736, 762–63
Property seizure, 334; *see also* Confiscation Acts, Impressment Act
Proslavery theory, **105–6**
Prospect Hill, 271
Prosser, Gabriel, 58
Prostitutes, 470
Provost marshals, 395, 453, 478
Publications about the Civil War, **859–908**
    African Americans and the Civil War, 867–69
    aftermath/reconstruction, 872–73
    audio and CD-ROM, 876–77
    biographies/autobiographies/ personal narratives, 870–72
    commercial presses, 875
    Confederacy, 864–65
    fiction: notable novels about Civil War, **836–42**
        nineteenth-century, **837–39**
        twentieth-century, **839–42**
    general histories, 862–63
    general reference, 860–62
    guides to battlefields/monuments, 873–74
    Lincoln, 869–70

military subjects, 865–67
    periodicals, 875–76
    specialty presses with Civil War emphasis, 875
    Union, 863–64
    University presses, 874
    women and the civil war, 869
Pulaski, Tennessee, 738, 784
Purvis, Robert, 59

Quaker gun, 518
Quakers, 83, 94–95, 102, 133, 151, 156, 464, 696–99, 855
Quantrill, William C., 17, 32, 51, 271, 289, 449–50
Quartermaster Corps, 362, 395, 495, 631, 632, 633
Queen of the West (U.S.S.), 532, 561

Radford, William, 550
Radical Republicans, 35, 51, 371, 400, 711, 733, 738, 739, 751, 756, 762, 764, 784, 798, 800, 803
Raiders, commerce, **563–64**
Railroad(s), 18, 20, 39, 73–74, 76, 343, **350–53**, 507, 629–31, 740, 783, 794
    antebellum America, 73–74
    hospital trains, 629–31
    military, **350–53**
    Railways and Telegraph Act, 14, 350
Rainey, Joseph H., 741, **780–81**, 782, 786
Rains, Gabriel James, 512, 542
Rains, George Washington, 502, 503, **512**
Raleigh, North Carolina, 33, 593, 718
Raleigh (C.S.S.), **562**
Raleigh Register, 226
Ramrod, 518
Ramsay, George D., 394, 512
Ramsay, Henry A., 545
Ramseur, Stephen Dodson, 44, 641
Ramsey, Alexander, 194, 198
Randall, Alexander William, 199
Randall, James Ryder, 852
Randall (training camp), 620

Randolph, George W., **184**, 333, 352, 394
Randolph, Innes, 851
Randolph, P. B., 739
Randolph, Victor M., 546
Ransier, Alonzo J., 755, 782
Ransom, John L., 36, 615
Raphall, Morris J., 87
Rathbone, Henry, 230, 231
Rattlesnake, (Confederate privateer) 532
Ravenel de la Coste, Márie,-852, 702
Rawlins, John A., 834
Raymond, Henry J., 228
R. B. Hamilton, 568
Read, Thomas Buchanan, 807, 843
Reagan, John H., *179*, **185**, 355, 710–11
Rebellions, slave, 59, 95, **98–103**
Rebel Yell, 9, 247
Reconstruction, 35, 40, 52, 156, 157, **731–804**, 735–42
    Acts, 739, 740, 758, 771, 772
    African Americans during, **747–50**
    Bureau of Refugees, Freedmen, and Abandoned Lands (Freedmen's Bureau), **774–78**; *see also* Freedmen's Bureau
    Congressional, 175, **770–72**
    end of, **792–96**
    impeachment of Johnson, 772–74
    major issues:
        black civil rights, **756–57**
        black suffrage, **757–58**
        confederate disenfranchisement and right to hold office, **758–59**
        education, **754–55**
        labor, **753–54**
        land, **750–53**
    military districts (five) in the south, 770
    North and West during, **788–92**
    notable figures of era of, **797–804**
    Presidential (Johnson's plans), 172, 174, 176, 188, **764–66**

Reconstruction (cont.)
  South and North in aftermath of
    war, 743–44
  Southern governments under
    Republican rule, 779–84
  veterans/pensions, 745–47
  violence in the South, 784–87
  wartime, 759–63
    coastal Georgia and South
      Carolina, 763
    Louisiana and the Mississippi
      Valley, 761–62
    Proclamation of Amnesty and
      Reconstruction (Wade-
      Davis Bill), 762–63
    South Carolina Sea Islands,
      760–61
    see also Black Codes, Thirteenth
      Amendment, Fourteenth
      Amendment, Fifteenth
      Amendment
Recruitment of soldiers, 35, 130,
  335–36, 585–87, 690–95
Rector, Henry, 200
Red Cross, 659
Red River campaign, 38, 296–98,
  297, 532, 534
Red Rover (Union naval hospital),
  636, 637
Red Shirts, 787, 798
Redwood, Allen Christian, 823,
  827
Reed, Charles W., 445, 824
Reenactment organizations, 904–5
Refugees and evacuations in the
  South, 721–26, 722, 805
Regiment, 374–75
Relief groups/organizations, 7, 631,
  661–63, 669–701
Religion:
  army chaplains, 438–41, 439
  on the home front, 685–90
    in the Confederacy, 687–88
    in the North, 688–90
  pacifist groups, 156, 695–98
  pro-slavery arguments based on,
    105
  reform movements and, 81–87,
    95, 112
  soldiers and, 480–81

see also specific religions/
  denominations
Remond, Charles Lenox, 61
Repeater (or repeating rifle),
  494–96, 518
Republican Party, 39, 62, 63, 112,
  115, 123, 131, 132, 165, 222
Republican rule in Reconstruction,
  779–84
Resaca, Georgia, battle of, 302
Revels, Hiram, 741, 782, 800,
  809
Revolvers/pistols, 498–500, 518
Reynolds, John G., 573
Rhett, (Robert) Barnwell, Jr., 226,
  228
Rhett, Robert Barnwell, Sr.,
  133–34, 226
Rhode Island:
  wartime governors, 57, 78, 199,
    217
Rhode Island (U.S.S.), 531
Rice, James C., 308
Richard, James A., 436
Richland County Jail (South
  Carolina) military prison, 594
Richmond, Indiana, military prison,
  589
Richmond, Virginia, 15, 18, 20, 27,
  39, 47, 49, 58, 169, 233, 250,
  264, 274, 294, 310, 320, 325,
  337, 347, 356, 364, 732
  Ambulance Committee, 663
  armory/arsenal, 511, 702
  capital, 233
  Dispatch, 225, 615
  Enquirer, 166, 615, 712, 718
  evacuation of, 536
  explosion, 27
  Kilpatrick-Dahlgren raid on
    (1864 battle), 296
  military actions, 255, 296, 600
  National Battlefield Park, 896
  Navy yard (Rocketts), Virginia,
    546
  prisons, 594–96, 622
  sculpture/memorials, 832–34
  Tredegar Iron Works, 504
  at war's end, 50, 159, 536, 716,
    732

Whig (and Public Advertiser), 44,
  225; see also Virginia
Richmond (C.S.S.), 557, 561
Richmond class casemate rams, 561
Richmond & Danville Railroad,
  326
Richmond & Petersburg Railroad,
  299
Rich Mountain, Western Virginia,
  245
Rifle(s), 374, 486, 490, 492–96, 498,
  504–5, 506, 508, 512, 515, 516,
  517, 518
  Clinch Rifles, 374
  Colt Revolving Rifle, 490
  Enfield rifle-musket, 515
  Henry Rifle, 494, 516
  most commonly used rifles and
    muskets, 492–93
  Ordnance Rifle, 504–5, 508
  Parrott Gun/Rifle, 504–5, 506,
    508, 512, 517
  repeating rifles, 494–96, 518
  Spencer rifles, 494, 495–96, 518
  Springfield rifle-musket, 518
Rifled musket, 518
Rifled weapon/rifling, 261, 340,
  486
Rifle-musket, 486, 518
Riker's Island (New York) military
  prison, 590
Rimfire, 518
Ringgold (Chattanooga-Ringgold
  campaign), 292–93
Riot(s), 27, 701, 718–21, 784, 823
  North, 719–21
  South, 718–19
Riot Act, 718
Ripley, James Wolfe, 394, 495, 512
Riverboat hospital (D.A. January),
  631
River gunboats, armored, 528
River Queen (U.S.S.), 48, 158
Rives, Alfred L., 395
Roanoke (U.S.S.), 556
Roanoke Island, 528
Roanoke River, 534, 536
Robb, Robert G., 546
Robertson, James I., Jr., 908
Robinson, C. H., 698

Robinson, Charles, 123, 197
Robinson, James, 197
Roche, Thomas C., 813
Rock, John, 14, 47, **190**, 216, 218
Rockets, war, **502–3**
Rock Island Prison (Illinois) military prison, 588, **605–6,** 616
Rodgers, John, 533
Rodman, Thomas J., 505–6
Rogerines, 696
Roosevelt, Theodore, 575
Root, George Frederick, 850
Root and Cady, 851
Rootes, Thomas T., 541
Roper Hospital (South Carolina) military prison, 594
Rose, Thomas E., 617
Rosecrans, William Starke, 25, 30, 32, 245, 274, 279, 287, 289, 351, *378*, 380, 381, 383, 397, **421,** 470, 494
Ross's Factory (Virginia) military prison, 595
Round Tables, 905
Rousseau, Lawrence L., 541, 546
Royal Small Arms Manufactory, Enfeld, England, 511
Ruffin, Edmund, 3, **134**
Ruffin, Thomas, 105
Runaway slaves, *see* Contrabands, Fugitive Slave Clause (U.S. Constitution); Fugitive slave laws
Rush's Lancers, 516
Russell, Jerry L., 905
Russell, John, 23
Ruth, Samuel, 456, **460**
Ryan, Abram Joseph, **848–49**

Saber, 518
Sabine Crossroads, Louisiana, 38
Sabine Pass, Texas, 531, 533
SABOT (lead base), 516
Sachem (U.S.S.), 533
Sacramento Daily Union, 715
Saffold Navy Yard, Georgia, 546
Safford, Mary J., *34*
Sailors, **568–72**; *see also* Navies/ naval events

Salado Camp (Texas) military prison, 594
Salem Church, Virginia, 277, 278
Salient or Bloody Angle (Spotsylvania), 307
Salisbury Prison (North Carolina) military prison, 593, **610,** 611, 616, 718
Salomon, Edward, 199
Saltville, Virginia, **315–16,** 319, 602
San Antonio, Texas, 594, 620
Sanford, Edward S., 354, 355
Sanford, John, 113–14
San Francisco Mare Island Naval Shipyard, California, 545
Sangamon (U.S.S.), 556
Sanitary Commission (U.S.), 9, 10, **169–70,** 445, 476, 631, 633, 638–39, *639,* 640, 653, 654, 655, 659, **661–62,** 701, 729, 753
    fairs, 34, 662, 699, 710, 714, 844
    Narrative of the Privations and Sufferings of the United States Officers and Soldiers while Prisoners of War in the Hands of the Rebel Authorities, 614
Sanitation/hygiene, disease and, **638–39**
San Jacinto (U.S.S.), 146, 202, 525, 552
San Pedro Springs (Texas) military prison, 594
Santa Fe, New Mexico, 249
Santa Rosa Island, Florida, 5, 243
Saratoga (U.S.S.), 6
Sarner, Ferdinand L., 440
Sassacus (U.S.S.), 534
Satterlee (Union hospital), 629
Saugus (U.S.S.), 545, **557**
Saunders, C.C., 630
Savannah (C.S.S.), **561**
Savannah, Georgia, 46, 47, 248, 261, **316–17,** *317,* 323, 336, 337, 364, 546, 763
    Sherman's March to the Sea, 45, 46, 47, **316–17,** *317,* 357, 387, 610, 713, 799, 890
    see also Georgia
Saxton, Rufus, 22, 429, 752, 776

Sayler's Creek, Virginia, 50, 326, 331
Scalawags, 779
Scantlon, David, 444
Scharf, J. Thomas, 523
Schell, Frank H., **824**
Schell, Frederick B., **824**
Schimmelfennig, Alexander, 48
Schofield, John M., 317, 382, 384, 385, 774
Schofield Barracks (St. Louis) military prison, 590
Schools, *see* Education/schools
Schurz, Carl, 635, 743
Schuykill Arsenal, Philadelphia, 705
Schwenkfelder Church, 696
Scott, Charlotte, 834
Scott, Dred, *see Scott v. Sandford*
Scott, Evelyn, 842
Scott, Harriet, 113
Scott, Julian, 445, **829**
Scott, Robert K., 783
Scott, Thomas, 788
Scott, Winfield, 8, 12, 123, *171,* 188, 235, 246, 247, 333–34, *335,* 339, 370, 371, 393, 394, 396, 400, **403–4,** 416, 452
Scott's Factory (Virginia) military prison, 596
Scott v. Sandford (Dred Scott case), 48, 56, 64, **113–15,** 117, 126, 128, 132, 135, 176, 711
Sculpture/memorials, **830–36**
    Richmond, Virginia, **832–34**
    Washington, D.C., **834–36**
Seacoast cannon, 505–7
Sea Islands, South Carolina, 12, 714, 737, 760–61, 763, 802
Sea King (ship), 580
Seamstresses, 702, 705–6
Secession Oak, 134
Secret Service network, 18, **452–61**; *see also* Spies/ intelligence gathering
Secret Six, 118
Sectionalism, and Constitutional Convention, 90
Seddon, James A., 24, **184,** 370, 394, 449, 599
Sedgwick, John, 308, *378,* 494

Segregation/discrimination, 104, **218–19,** 427–38, 678–79

Selfridge, Thomas O., Sr., 545

Selma, Alabama, **324–25,** 496, 546, 592; *see also* Alabama

Semi-Weekly Dispatch, 147

Semmes, Raphael, 9, 11, 22, 39, 339–40, *388,* 528, 531, 535, *563,* **579–80,** 828

Semple, James A., 542

Semple, Letitia Tyler, 656

Seneca Falls, New York, 86

Sentinel, 225

Seven Days Battles, 20, *258, 259,* 331, 530; *see also* Peninsula campaign

Seven Pines, battle of, *see* Fair Oak, Virginia, battle of, Peninsula campaign

Seward, William H., 20, 48, 53–54, 55, 109, 110, 111, 126, 150, 158, *171,* **174,** 177, 202, 203, 211, 231, 599

Sewell's Point, Virginia, 244, 346, 364

Seymour, Horatio, 24, 192, 199, 785

Shaara, Michael, 841, 857

Shakers, 83, 464, 696

Sharp, William, 546

Sharpe, George Henry, 454, 456, 457, 460

Sharpsburg, Maryland, 266; *see also* Antietam

Sharps Carbines, 501

Sharpshooters, 445, *488,* **494**

Shaw, H. B., 458

Shaw, Robert Gould, 31, 433–34, 437, *831,* 847, 890

Shelbyville, Tennessee, 274

Shell (artillery), 508, 518

Shenandoah (C.S.S.), 203, 536, 537, 551, 565, 575, 580

Shenandoah Valley campaign (1862; Jackson), 15, 16, 18, 19, **259–60,** *259* (map), 348, 489

Shenandoah Valley campaign (1864–1865; Sheridan), 38, 39, 41, 44, 141, 236, 294, 312, **313–15,** 343, 482

Shepherd College, 906

Shepley, George, 762

Sheppard, Edwin, 810

Sheppard, William Ludwell, **824–25,** 827, 832, 833

Sheridan, Philip Henry, 38, 39, 41, 44, 49, 378, 386, 396, 410, **421–22,** 425, 771, 773, *807,* 825, 834, 843, 894

  battle overviews, 236, 294, 308, 313–15, 322, 326, 343

  horse (Rienzi), 44, 315

Sherman, John, 66, 369

Sherman, Thomas W., 248

Sherman, William Tecumseh, 38, 40, 41, 42, 43, 45, 46, 47, 48, 49, 50, 51, *295,* 378, **422,** 817

  Army of the Mississippi, **381**

  Army of the Tennessee, **382–83**

  Atlanta siege/campaign, 140, **299–304,** 351, 360, 384, 386, 413, 414, 416, 599, 894

  Carolinas campaign, 322, **323–24,** *324,* 386, 715

  Chattanooga-Ringgold campaign, 293

  conciliatory *vs.* hard war policy, 242, 294

  Field Order (Number 15) granting land in Carolinas to black families, 737, 752, 763

  Fort Hindman (Post of Arkansas) memorial, 889

  Johnston's last battles and Army of Tennessee surrender to, 50, 392, 400, 413–14, 416, 424

  Kennesaw Mountain National Battlefield, 894

  March to the Sea, 45, 46, 47, **316–17,** *317,* 357, 387, 610, 713, 799, 890

  mentioned in Gorgas diary, 320

  Meridian campaign, **295–96,** 417

  photos of army, 813

  quoted:

    on civilian resistance, 45

    on evacuation of Atlanta, 43, 721–22

    on feeding an army, 641

    on Forrest, 310, 798

    on slave celebrations encountered, 713

    rank, 396

    statue, Washington, D.C., 834

    Vicksburg campaigns, 269, 280, 532

    Washington (Grand Review, May 1865), 437

    Western theater, **237**

Sherman Publishing Company, 378, 388

Sherman's bummers, 51

Shiloh, Tennessee, 17, 237, **252–54,** *253,* 330, 337, 343, 352, 600, 610, 630, **897;** *see also* Tennessee

Shinn, S. R., 157

Ship(s), *see* Navies/naval events, individual ship names

Ship Island, 11, 543, 550, 589

Shockley, W. S., 373

Shorter, John Gill, 196, 200

Shot, **508–9**

Shotgun, 518

Showalter, John A., 465

Shrady, Henry Merwin, 835

Shrapnel, Henry, 518

Shreveport, Louisiana, 196, 237, 298, 546, 593; *see also* Louisiana

Shy's Hill, Tennessee, 319

Sibley, Ebenezer, 395

Sibley, Henry Hopkins, **249**

Sibley tent, 629

Sickles, Daniel E., *378*

Sickness/mortality statistics, selected, **648;** *see also* Medical care

Sievers, William F., 833

Sigel, Franz, 38, 244, 397

Signal Corps, 353, 354, **358–62,** 395, 445

Simons, Maurice K., 344

Sims, Frederick W., 352

Sinclair, Harold, 855

Sinclair, Upton, 841–42

Singleshot, 518

Singleton, Benjamin "Pap," 750

Sioux Indians, 587, 709; *see also* American Indians

Skeen, William, 449

Slaughterhouse cases, 794

Slaves/Slavery, *see also* Abolition Movement, African Americans, Black codes, Contrabands, Emancipation Proclamation, Freedmen, Thirteenth Amendment

    Clauses in U.S. Constitution concerning, 56–57

    constitutions (U.S. and C.S.A) compared concerning, 163

    distribution of (map), *81*

    education for, 682–83

    Freedmen's Bureau, 775–78

    freeing slaves as war strategy, 213, 733

    history of in America, 77–81

    impressed into war service, 669

    issues in antebellum America, 93–106

        abolition movement, 94–98

        development of proslavery theory, 105–6

        fugitive slaves/Underground Railroad, 99–102

    labor issues and, 674, 753–54

    land issues and, 751–53

    nonslaveholding Southern whites, 79, 667

    "peculiar institution," 1, 61

    population figures, 70–72, 665, 666–67

    reaction to Emancipation Proclamation, 713–14

    recruiting for Confederate army, 694

    as refugees, 724–25

    religion and, 87, 105–6, 687

    rights for former slaves, 734–35

    slave celebrations, 713

    slaveowners, 80

    slave rebellions, 59, 98–103

    Wartime Reconstruction and, 759–62

    women on plantations, 703–4

Slave trade, African, 6–7, **94**, 126

    advertisement (shipboard slave sale), 77

    slave ships, 65, 94

    slave trade clause, 56

Slemmer, Adam G., 5, 243

Slidell, John, 92, 146, 186, **190,** 202, 204, 525, 552

Slocum, Henry W., 386

Slotkin, Richard, 840

Small arms:

    carbines and musketoons, **496–97,** 518

    pistols/revolvers, **498–500**

Smalley's Corn Plow, 676

Smallpox, **647–48**

Smalls, Robert, 571–72, *571*

Smith, A. J., 310, 897

Smith, A. P., 216

Smith, Albert N., 539

Smith, Alvira, 707

Smith, Caleb B., *171*, **177**

Smith, Charles F., 397, 653–54

Smith, Edmund Kirby, 263, 296, 338, *388*, 391, 398, 399, **422–23,** 424, 597

Smith, Gerrit, 122

Smith, Gustavus W., **184,** 394

Smith, J. Gregory, 199

Smith, James Y., 199

Smith, Joseph, 538

Smith, Martin L., 395

Smith, William, 201, 544, 808, 834

Smith, William Mason, 444, 695

Smith, William Sooy, 295

Smith's Factory (Virginia) military prison, 596

Smithsonian Institution, 907

Smith's Plantation, Beaufort, South Carolina, 751

Smoothbore, 518

Snake Creek Gap, Georgia, 299

Soldiers, *see* Army life

Soldiers and Sailors monument, **833**

Solid shot, 518

Somerset v. Stewart, 97

Songs, *see* Music/musicians

Sons & Daughters of United States Colored Troops, **902**

Sons of Confederate Veterans, **902–3**

Sons of Liberty, 39, 167

Sons of Union Veterans of the Civil War (SUVCW), **903,** 904

South Atlantic Blockading Squadron (S.A.B.S.), 549–50

South Carolina, 3, 4, 6, 58, 59, 64, 65, 66, 67, 68, 69, 78, 79, 80, 81, 90, 91, 92, 93, 98, 104, 124, 125, 133–34, 148, 162, 184, 203, 885

    military action in, 27, 31, 47, 233, 235, 243, 247, 248, 276, 281, 323–24, 355, 357, 387, 405, 412, 422, 433, 437, 506

    nullification crisis, 107–8

    population 1860, 666

    prisons, 591, 593–94, 610

    readmitted, 740, 772, 793, 796

    Reconstruction in, 737, 742, 755, 760–61, 767, 782, 795, 796

    Sea Islands, 12, 22, 429, 714, 737, 760–61, 763, 802

    secession, 3, 66–67

    see also Charleston, South Carolina; Fort Sumter, Fort Wagner, individual military campaigns

South Carolina Tract Society, 686

Southern Baptists, 87, 748

Southern Cross, 717

Southern Homestead Act, 738

Southern Illustrated News, 702, 809, 817, **820,** 853

Southern Literary Messenger, 134, 843, 845

Southern Loyalists Convention, 739

Southern Punch, 808

Southern Quarterly Review, 130

Southern Telegraph Company, 355, 357

Southern Women, 705

Southfield, (U.S.S.), 562

South Mountain, battle of, 266

Southwestern Telegraph Company, 355

Spangler, Edmund, 232

Spectator, The, 152

Speed, James, **178**

Spencer, Christopher, 495

Spencer, Lilly Martin, **829–30**

Spencer rifles, 494, 495–96, 518

Spies/intelligence gathering, 16, 18, 36, 361, 372–73, 414, 441, **452–61,** 703, 814

Spinner, Francis, 706
Spotswood, William A. W., 542, 635
Spotsylvania (Spotsylvania Court House) Virginia, 38, 39, 304, **307**, *307*, 311, 330, 331, 494, **892**; *see also* Overland campaign
Sprague, William, 199
Springfield Armory, 488–89, 512
Springfield rifle-musket, 518
St. Charles (Missouri) military prison, 590
St. Francis Academy of Rome (Baltimore), 684
St. Gaudens, Augustus, 437, 831, 847, 890
St. John, Isaac M., 394, 501
St. Louis, Missouri, 13
St. Louis (U.S.S.), 528, 559
St. Marks Naval Station Florida, 547
Stafford, Leroy A., 307
Stager, Anson, 353
Stainless banner, 717
Stanbery, Henry, 771, 773
Standard (newspaper), 228
Stanford, Leland, 197
Stanton, Edwin M., 13, 14, 17, 18, 22, 27, 33, 46, 172, **175–76**, 177, 192, 231, 291, 318, 354, 369, 371, 394, 433, 437
  medical care and, 633, 653, 655
  postwar, 705, 715, 740, 763, 773
  prisons/prisoners of war and, 597, 599, 601, 603, 606, 613, 614
Stanton, Elizabeth Cady, 168, 769
Star of the West, 4, 243
Stars and Bars, 717
Stars and Stripes, 716
Star Spangled Banner, 717
State Journal, 226
States' rights, **90–92**, 145, 163, 189, 193, 756, 765, 769
Stedman, E. C., 845
Steedman, James, 319, 738
Steele, Frederick, 291, *297*, 298, 380
Steele's Bayou Expedition, **279–80**, 532

Stephens, Alexander, 5, 36, 46, 48, 67, 68, *68*, 109, 158, 160–61, *179*, **181**, 607, 766, 834
Stephens, Henry, 806
Steuart, George H., 308
Stevens, Thaddeus, 738, *739*, 773, **800–1**, 804
Stewart, Alexander P., 398
Stewart, Charles, 538
Still, William, 102, **134–35**, 136, 885
Stoddard, R. H., 848
Stone, A. L., 688
Stone, William, 197
Stoneman, George, **319**, 610
Stone Mountain, Georgia, 830–31
Stones River, Tennessee campaign (Murfreesboro), 25, 29, 251, 274, **275**, *275*, 330, 331, **897**
Stonewall (C.S.S.), 575
Storrow, Samuel, 463
Story, Joseph, 99
Stout, Samuel Hollingsworth, **657**
Stowe, Harriet Beecher, 61, 63, 89, **110–11**, *110*, **127–28**, 836, 839, 853, 854
Strader v. Graham, 114
Strahl, O. F., 317
Strategy, 233–36, **332–39**; *see also* Tactics, battle
  Confederate military strategy, **337–39**
  definitions of strategy/military strategy (U.S. Department of Defense), **332**
  national objectives (United States), **332–33**
  Union military strategy, **333–37**
Streight, Abel D., **279**, 448
Streptococcal infection, 645
Stribling, Cornelius K., 544, 551
Strieby, Mary, 158
Strieby, William, 158
Strikes/labor, 31, 702, 705–6, 720, **753–54**, 791
Stringham, Silas H., 247, 538, 544
Strong, George Templeton, 282–83, **729–30**

Stuart, James Ewell Brown (Jeb), 19, 24, 30, 38, 118, *257*, 278, 304, *388*, 409, 419, **423**, 496, 832, **833**, 834, 843
Stubel, Abbie, 354
Sturgis, Samuel D., 310, 890
Submarine(s), evolution of, **565–67**
Substitutes, 35, 148
  for conscientious objectors, 464
  for draftees, 372, 697
Sudley Ford, Virginia, 360
Sultana disaster, 608, **617–18**, *618*
Sumner, Charles, 59, 64, 122, 738, 769, **802**, 804
Sumter, *see* Fort Sumter
Sumter (C.S.S.), 9, 11, 528, 565, 579
Sunken Road, 268
Sunstroke, 641
Supreme Court, 47–48, 61, 64, 113–15, 117, 125, 147–48, 150, 153, 190, 208, 739, 789
  provision in Confederate constitution for, 161
Surgical fevers, 644–45
Surratt, John, 232
Surratt, Mary, 232
"Swamp Angel" (artillery), 506
Swatts, Sargeant, 709
Swift, Henry, 198
Swift Creek, 299
Swim's Jail, Chattanooga, 594
Switzerland (U.S.S.), 532
Swords/sabers, **500–1**

Tacony (C.S.S.), 564, 565
Tactics, battle, **339–45**; *see also* Strategy
  cavalry, use of, 342–43
  infantry, typical movement of, **342**
  portents of modern war, **343–45**
Taggart, John H., 434
Talladega (Alabama) military prison, 592
Tallahassee (C.S.S.), 536, 565
Tallmadge, James, 106
Taney, Roger B., 48, 114–15, **135**, 144, 208
Tappan, Arthur and Lewis, 95, 119

Tariffs, 107, 126
Tate, Captain (District of Columbia Militia), 7
Tattnall, Josiah, 546
Taxes, 10, 20, 28, 56, 149, 672, 675, 792
Taxpayers' Conventions, 792
Taylor, Charles E., 361
Taylor, James E., **825**, 827
Taylor, Joseph T., 394
Taylor, Richard, 298, 345, 392, 398, **423–24**, 465, 597
Taylor, Sarah Knox, 178
Taylor, Susie King, **660**
Taylor, Zachary, 62, 96, 108, 122, 123, 178, 416
Taylor's Factory (Virginia) military prison, 596
Teachers, *see* Education/schools
Teaser (C.S.S.), 365
Tecumseh (U.S.S.), 313, **557**
Telegraph service, 6, 246–47, **353–57**
  Confederate, **355–57**
  Union., **353–54**
Television (notable movies/series/ documentaries), **856–57**
Tennessee, 11, 15, 21, 29, 37, 57, 121
  Johnson appointed governor, 736
  military action in, 14, 17, 25, 30, 32, 34–35, 45, 46, 252, 254, 263, 269, 274, 276, 287, 289–93, 298, 310, 317–19, 337, 338, 351, 352, 381, 383, 384, 392, 402, 406, 411, 414, 416, 417, 418, 421, 423, 424, 450
  population (1860), 666
  prisons, 591, 594
  readmitted, 739, 793
  Reconstruction in, 736, 738, 741
  secession, 9, 144
  see also Chattanooga, Knoxville, Nashville, Memphis, Shiloh
Tennessee (U.S.S.), 313, 553, 558, **562**
Tennessee Plan, 726
Tennessee River, 528

Tenniel, John, 806
Ten Percent Plan, 155
Tenth Amendment, 90
Tenure of Office Act, 739, 740, 804
Terre Haute (Indiana) military prison, 589
Territories, 71, 108, 112, 117
Terry, Alfred H., 321, 385, 536
Tetanus, 644
Texas, 3, 5, 61, 62, 109, 128, 160, 177, 358, 620, 741, 742, 750, 767, 793
  annexation, 92, 108
  archival/artifact collections, 885–86
  military action in, 249, 277, 328
  population (1860), 666
  prisons/prisoners of war, 584–85, 594, 611
  readmitted, 739, 793
  Reconstruction in, 736, 738, 741, 794
  refuge in, 721
  secession, 9, 143
  wartime governors, 201
Texas and Pacific Railroad bill, 796
Textbooks, 680, 681, 684
Thanksgiving, 689–90
Thatcher, Henry K., 328, 551
Thayer, Eli, 63, 112
Theater (stage), 853
Theater(s), military:
  definitions, 236
  of operation, **236–39**
    Eastern Theater, **236–37**
    Lower Seaboard and Gulf Approach, **239**
    map of, *238*
    Trans-Mississippi Theater, **237–40**
    Western Theater, **237**
  of war, **236**
Thirteenth Amendment, 39, 47, 120, 132, 142, 168, 190, 212, 732, 737, 738, **763–64**
Thomas, George Henry, 33, 34–35, 45, 46, 291, 293, 317, 318, 320, 339, *378*, 383, 384, 387, 392, 396, 397, 414, **424**, 834

Thomas, Jesse B., 106
Thomas, Lorenzo, 601, **621**, 737, 773
Thomas, Samuel, 777
Thomason, John W., Jr., 841
Thomasville (Georgia) military prison, 593
Thompson, Ambrose, 216
Thompson, Franklin, 447
Thompson, John Reuben, 843
Thompson, M. Jeff, 255, 449
Thompson, Walter F., 344–45
Thompson, William F., 344
Thomson, M. J., 255, 449
Thornwell, James Henley, 685
Thoroughfare Gap, Virginia, 265
Three-fifths clause, 56, 769
Thulstrup, Thure de, **830**
Tilden, Samuel, 742, 798, 803
Time-fuse, 518
Timrod, Henry, **849**
Tippecanoe (ship), 557
Tishomingo Creek, Mississippi, 310
Tocqueville, Alexis de, 1, 3, 81–82, 85
Tod, David, 194, 199
Todd, Mary, *see* Lincoln, Mary Todd
Todd's Tavern, 304
Tombs Prison (New York) military prison, 590
Tompkins, Sally Louisa, **660–61**
Tonawanda (U.S.S.), 558
Toombs, Robert A., *179*, **181**
Torbert, Alfred T. A., *41*, 386
Torpedo, 313, 488, 518, 531, 536, **567–68**
Torpedo Bureau, 512, 542
Totopotomoy Creek, 308
Totten, Joseph G., 395
Towne, Laura M., **802**
Train(s), *see* Railroad(s)
Training (military), 377, **465–66**, 568
Transcendentalism, 83, 86
Trans-Mississippi: District, Department, and Army (C.S.A.), 391–92

Trans-Mississippi Theater, **237–40**, *238*

Traveler (Lee's horse), 832

Travis, William DeLaney Trimble, 827

Treasury notes, 668

Tredegar Iron Works, 356, 670, **896**

Tree, Joseph B., 357

Trego, William B. T., **830**

Trench warfare, 340–41, 343–44

Trenholm, George A., **183**

Trent affair, 12, 146, 173, 174, 186, 188, 189, 190, 202–3, 525, 552

Trevilian Station (Virginia), 39, 304

Tribune, 219

Trigger guard, 518

Trioni, Don, 828

Tripler, Charles S., 630, 631, 638

Triumph (U.S.S. *Atlanta* renamed), 554

Trumbull, Lyman, **803**

Truth, Sojourner (Isabella Bomefree), 84, **135–36**, 218, 728

Tubman, Harriet, 62, 84, **136**, *136*

Tullahoma, Tennessee, 30, 274, **287**, 289

Tupelo, Mississippi, 41, **310**, 319, **897**

Turner, George B., 377

Turner, Henry McNeal, 213–14, 440, 694, 713, **803**

Turner, Nat, 59, 95, 98–103

Turner, Th. P., 157

Turner, Thomas, 544

Turtle (submarine), 565

Tuscaloosa (C.S.S.), 565

Tuscaloosa (Alabama) military prison, 592, 622

Tweed, "Boss" William, 790

Tweed Ring scandal, 783, 790, 795

Tybee Island, 261

Tyler, John, 108

Tyler, Texas, 594, 600, 611, 723

Typhoid fever, **650**

Typhus, **650**

Uncle Ben (C.S.S.), 531

Uncle Tom's Cabin, 61, 63, 89, **110–11**, 127–28, 836, 839, 853 stage version, *854*

Underground Railroad, 62, 84, 95, **99–102**, *100–1*, 134–35, 136, 885

Union army, *see* Armies of the United States

Union League, 20, 729, 740, 748–49

Union Monitor Club in Norfolk, 748

Union Pacific Railroad Company, 177, 740, 789, 791

Union Party ticket, 173

Union Veterans' Union, 900

Unitarians, 82, 83, 440

United Confederate Veterans (UCV), 900

United Daughters of the Confederacy, 901, **903**

United Sons of Confederate Veterans, 901

United States: *see also* Antebellum America, Elections, Home Front Military campaigns, Politics, Reconstruction

African American rights, 214–15

celebrations, 714–17

constitutional issues, 56, 90–91

differences between North and South, 53–55, 69–90

discrimination and segregation, 218–19

economics, 73–76, 672–73

foreign relations/affairs, 201–7 *Alabama* Claims, 23, 36, 59, 200

France, 23, 36, 58, 202

Great Britain, 23, 36, 62, 201–4

Mexico, 36, 62, 63, 108–9, 206–7

immigration, 72–73, 676–77

largest cities in, 72

map of (in 1861), *69*

population, by state (1860), 70–71

Reconstruction:

Congressional Reconstruction, 770–72

Enforcement acts against Southern violence, 786–88

Federal power over civil rights, 756–57

Federal reluctance to support Republican rule in the South, 795–97

Fifteenth Amendment, 778–79

Fourteenth Amendment, 768

national identity, 743–44

North and west during, 788–92

veterans' pensions, 745–46

Riots, 31, 192, 719–21

Westward expansion:

filibustering, 93, 136

Gadsden Purchase, 63

homesteading, 677–78

Louisiana Purchase, 58

Manifest Destiny, 92–93

Northwest Ordinance, 57

Treaty of Guadalupe Hidalgo, 62

United States Colored Troops (USCT), 585, 902

United States Constitution:

amendments to:

First, 59–60

Tenth, 90

Thirteenth, 39, 47, 120, 132, 142, 168, 190, 212, 732, 737, 738, **763–64**

Fifteenth, 120, 142, 732, 741, 758, 769, 778–79

Fourteenth, 120, 142, 732, 734–35, 738, 739, 740, 755, 757, 758–59, **767–70**, 794, 799, 802

antebellum issues/problems, 55–57

comparison to Confederate constitution, **162–63**

slavery in, 56, 94, 163

states' rights, 163

United States Military Academy, 883

United States Naval Academy, 540

United States Sanitary Commission, *see* Sanitary Commission

Upshur, J. P., 745

Upton, Emory, 325, 342, 402, **424–25**, *425*

Usher, John P., **177**

Utah, 109, 110, 665

Utopian communities, 86

Vairin, A. L. P., 389
Valentine, Edward V., 833
Vallandigham, Clement L., 27, 29, 33, 39, 167, 208, 440, 720–21
Valley Spirit (newspaper), 152
Valverde (New Mexico), 249
Van Alstyne, Lawrence, 34, 464, 471
Van Buren, Martin, 62, 79, 122
Van Buren, W. H., 639
Vance, Zebulon B., 186, 195, 200, 671, 704
Van Dorn, Earl, 25, 255, 262, 269, 338, 380, 391, 420
Van Dorn (C.S.S.), 530
Van Horne, John, 355
Van Horne, Thomas B., 348–49
Van Lew, Elizabeth, 456, **460**, 617, 707
Vannerson, Julian, 403, 805, **816**
Vannerson & Jones, 260
Velocity (U.S.S.), 531
Vent, 518
Vermont, 57, 78, 149, 199, 217, 720
Vesey, Denmark, 58, 98, 103
Veteran(s):
 facing ruined homes and devastated economy, 374
 organizations for descendants of, **900–3**
 pensions, **745–47**
 service/pension records, 900
Veteran Nurses of the Civil War, 900–1
Veteran Reserve Corp (U.S.), **441–42**
Veterans Corps, medical officers of, 652
Vice presidents:
 C.S.A., 173
 U.S.A., 181
 see also Stephens, Alexander; Hamlin, Hannibal; Johnson, Andrew
Vicksburg (Mississippi), 25, 27, 30, 31, 33, 34, 196, 205, 237, 250, 252, 274, 276, 281, 293, 296, 336, 338, 342, 343, 344, 490, 530, 532, 598, 608, 622, 641, 724, 762

 descriptions of campaigns/battles, **262–63, 269,** *270,* **279–81,** *280*
 National Military Park/Cemetery, **898**
 see also Mississippi
Victoria, Queen, 8
Vietnam, 51
Violence, **784–88,** *see also* Guerrilla warfare, Ku Klux Klan, Riots
Virginia, *see also* Harpers Ferry, Petersburg, Richmond, Shenandoah Valley campaigns, West/Western Virginia, Winchester, and individual battles, 3, 8, 11, 15, 18, 27
 in antebellum era, 59, 63, 66, 77–78, 80, 81, 93, 97, 102, 116–17, 119, 134
 military activities in, 9, 12, 14, 17, 19, 20, 26, 29, 30, 38, 39, 40, 42, 44, 49, 50, 233, 243, 245–46, **246–47,** 248, 250, 251, **255–61,** 264–65, **271–74, 277–79,** 293, 294, 296, 299, **304–10,** 310–12, 313–15, 315–16, 319, 321–23, **325–28,** 330, 337, 338, 339, 346, 347, 348, 350, 351, 355, 359, 360, 364, 365, 371, 379, 380, 381–82, 386, 390–91, 402, 403, 404, 407, 409, 410, 415, 419, 424, 436, 437, 449, 460, 488, 489, 511
 politics, 146, 154, 157, 158, 161, 169, 195, 203, 212
 population (1860), 666
 prisons, 591, 594–96, 611–12
 readmitted, 741, 793
 Reconstruction, 735, 748
 secession, 6, 143
 University of (Center for Civil War Studies), 907
Virginia (C.S.S., former U.S.S. *Merrimack*), 15, 510, 522, 525, 529, 530, 533, 544, 545, 552, 553, 555, **560,** 574, 577, 579, 580
Virginia II (C.S.S.), 557
Virginia Military Institute, 38, 312, 887

Visitors (to soldiers), **474–75**
Vizetelly, Frank, **825**
Volck, Adalbert Johann/John, 27, 685, 806, **825**
Volker, Louisa E., 354
Volunteer(s)/volunteer army, 20, 372, 376–78, 389, 397
Volunteer aid societies, 625, **699–701,** 706; *see also* Relief groups/organizations
Voting rights:
 blacks, 35, 37, 87, **217,** 218, 739, 740, **757–58**
 Confederate disenfranchisement, **758–59**

Wachusett (U.S.S.), 536
Waddell, James Iredell, 537, **580**
Wade, Benjamin Franklin, 146, 156, 737, 762, 774, **803–4**
Wade-Davis Bill, 40, 156, 737, 804
Wadley, William M., 352
Wadsworth, James S., 306
Wakeman, Sarah Roseta ("Edwin" or "Lyons"), 447
Walker, David, 59
Walker, Gilbert, 741
Walker, Leroy P., *179,* **183,** 185, 227, 394
Walker, Margaret, 841
Walker, Mary Edwards, 447, **655–56,** 658, 893
Walker, William, 93, **136–37,** 434, 556
Wallace, Lew, 40, 312, 397, 844, 895
Wallace, William, 596
Wanderer, The (slave ship), 65
War Board, 371
War Committee (Union) created, 146
Ward, Cyrenus Osborne, 854
War Democrats, 165, 173
Ward's Island (New York) military prison, 590
Warmouth, Henry, 800
Warner, James H., 545
War of 1812, 91, 334, 512, 601, 834
War of the Rebellion: A Compilation of the Official Records of the Union and Confederate Armies, The, 616

Warren, Edward, 627
Warren, John Collins, 626
Warren, Joseph, 606
Warrenton Turnpike, 264
Wartime politics, *see* Politics
Wartime Reconstruction, **759–63**
Warwick & Barksdale Mill
　(Virginia) military prison, 596
Washburn, Israel, 194, 198
Washington, Booker T., 749
Washington, D.C., 6, 244, 312, 347,
　359
　archival/artifact collections,
　　877–81
　Arsenal, 232, 705, 834
　banning slavery/slave trade in,
　　17, 61, 63, 96, 109, 140, 147,
　　148
　Barracks and Navy Yard, 545,
　　572
　commander (Command of the
　　Army Act) and, 773
　Early's raid on (1864), **312–13,**
　　672–73; *see also* Early, Jubal
　　Anderson
　franchise to blacks, 739, 758
　hospital, 627
　military prisons in, 588
　Morning Chronicle, 152
　National Republican, 453
　streetcar segregation, 679
Washington, George, 83, 147, 393,
　452, 545
Washington, William D., **830**
Washington (balloon), 364
Washington County Jail, 588
Water, disease and, **642–43**
Watertown, Massachusetts, U.S.
　Arsenal, *708*
Water Witch (U.S.S.), 561
Watie, Stand, **426**
Watts, Thomas Hill, **186,** 200
Waud, Alfred R., 271, 273, 286,
　306, 341, 449, 472, 775, 822,
　826
Waud, William, **826**
Waynesborough, Virginia, 315
Weaponry, 336, 340, **485–520**
　accidents in ordnance labs, 27,
　　702, 705, 834

artillery:
　field, **503–7**
　heavy, **505–7**
　light, **504–5**
artillery projectiles, **508–9**
carbines, **496–97**
Gorgas report on Confederate
　arms/equipment, **491**
gunpowder production, **501–2**
minié ball and amputations,
　634
musketoons, **496–97**
muskets, **492–93**
notable figures, **510–12**
ordnance glossary, **512–19**
pistols, **498–500**
repeaters, **494–96,** 498
revolvers, **498–500**
rifles, **492–93,** 498
small arms, **496–500**
swords and sabers, **500–1**
war rockets and hand grenades,
　502–3
Whitworth "sharpshooter,"
　494
women working in ordnance
　plants: South, 702; North,
　705, 834
Webster, Daniel, 109, 111, 120,
　123, **137**
Webster, H. D. L., 851
Webster, Timothy, 18, **460–61**
Weehawken (U.S.S.), 533, **553–54,
　556,** 562, 813
Wehner, William, 827
Welch, Spencer Glasgow, 19, 26,
　44, 249, 251, 475, 479
Weld, Angelina E. Grimké, 95,
　133
Weld, Lewis, 437
Weld, Theodore Dwight, 60, 95
Weldon Railroad operations, **311**
Welles, Gideon, 20–21, 150, *171,*
　176–77, 251, 276, 295, 394,
　525, 537, 547, 570, **580**
West, Jessamyn, 840, 855
West, the American (during
　Reconstruction), **788–92**
Western Freedmen's Aid
　Commission, 724

Western Sanitary Commission, 631,
　662
Western Theater, **237,** *238*
Westfield (U.S.S.), 531
West Gulf Blockading Squadron
　(W.G.B.S.), 550, 635
West Point Foundry, 506
West Point Museum, 883
Westport, Missouri, battle of, 315
West/Western Virginia, 9, 30, 144,
　153, 199, **245–46,** 354, 421,
　449, 485, 592, 735
Wheeler, Joseph, 302, 316, **426,** *426*
Wheeling, West Virginia, 9, 735
Whelan, William, 540, 635
Whig and Public Advertiser, 225
Whig Party, 62, 63, 66, 121, 122,
　123, **124,** 126, 132, 737, 738,
　780, 803
Whipple, Amiel W., 8, 278
Whiskey Ring fraud, 783
White, George H., 796
White Haven, Missouri (Grant
　Memorial), 897
Whitehead, John M., 441
White League, 794
White Line (Mississippi), 784
Whitman, Walt, 32, 716, **846–47,**
　846, 848, 849, 893
Whitney, Eli, 57, 79, 673
Whittier, John Greenleaf, 845
Whittle, William C., 546
Whitworth Guns, 505
Whitworth "sharpshooter," **494**
Wicker, Tom, 842
Wigfall, Louis Trezevant, **191**
Wig-wag signaling, **358–62**
Wilcox's Landing, Virginia, 310
Wilder, C. Douglas, 800
Wilder, John T., 496
Wilderness Virginia battle, 38, 299,
　304–7, *305,* 306, 330, 331, 504
Wilkes, Charles, 146, 202, 203, 552
Wilkeson, Sam, 286
Williams, Ben Ames, 841
Williams, Peter, 104
Williams, Thomas, 773
Williamsburg, Virginia, battle of,
　18
Williamson, William P., 541

Wilmington, North Carolina, 46, 319, **321**, 324, 337, 547, 548, 550; *see also* North Carolina

Wilmington River, 533

Wilmot, David, 62, 109

Wilmot Proviso, 62, 109, 122

Wilson, Henry, 789

Wilson, James H., *41*, 279, **324–25**, 411, 425, 496, 721, 773

Wilson, Theron, 471

Wilson's Creek, Missouri, battle of, 10, 239, **244, 898**

Winchester, Virginia, 261, **314,** 596, 625

Winder, John C., **461**, 599, 620, **621**

Winder (Confederate hospital), 629, 656

Winnebago (U.S.S.), 560

Winslow, John A., 339, 535, 563

Wirz, Henry, 600, 609, **621–22,** 856

Wisconsin, 199, 592, 887

Wise, Henry A., 539

Wise, John, 362–63, 364

Women, **701–10**; *see also* individual women
  African American, during Reconstruction, 749, 767
  in agriculture, 674, 676, 703–4, 707
  attitudes toward enlistment and army service, 692, 694–95
  attitudes toward war, 704–5
  Butler's "Woman's Order," 407
  in education, 88–90, 680–82, 684
  food riots and, 718–19
  "government girls," 706–7
  jobs done by, 702–4, 705, 710
  National Woman Suffrage Association, 769
  nurses, 9, 655–56, **657–61**, 703, 707, 746
  pensions for, 745
  providing Bible education, 687
  as refugees, 721–25
  relief societies and, 7, 654, 658, 661, 663, 699, 701, 714, 903
  rights movement, 86–88, 133, 769–70
    rights during Reconstruction, 780–82
  soldiers/spies, 438, **445–47,** 452–61
  in the West, 709
  writers, 62–63, 110–11, 702, 709–10

Women and the Civil War, Inc., 908

Wood, John Taylor, 536, 541

Wood, Robert C., 653

Wool, John E., 396, 601, 620

Woolsey, Abby, **661**

Woolsey, Georgeanna, **661**

Woolsey, Jane Stuart, 658, **661**

Worden, John Lorimer, 529, 532, **580**

Work, Henry C., 851

Workingwomen's Protective Union, 706

Wormley, James, 795

Wright, Edward N., 465

Wright, Jonathan J., 782

Wyoming (U.S.S.), 533

Yalobusha River, 532

Yates, Richard, 192, 193, 197

Yazoo City, Mississippi (navy yard), 547

Yazoo Pass expedition, **279**, 532

Yazoo River, 530, 531, 532, 559

Yeatman, James, 753

Yellow fever, **651**

Yellow Tavern, Virginia, 38, 304

YMCA, 135, 662

Yorktown, Virginia, 17, 18, 343, 356

Yorktown National Cemetery, 890

Younger, Cole, 450

Yulee, David, 67

Zeilen, Jacob, 540

Zollicoffer, Felix K., 251

Zouave Drill Team, 8